The Legal
Environment
of Business

The Legal Environment of Business

Commerce and Public Policy

Charles R. McGuire
Illinois State University

Charles E. Merrill Publishing Company
A Bell & Howell Company
Columbus Toronto London Sydney

To Joan . . . for everything

Published by Charles E. Merrill Publishing Company
A Bell & Howell Company
Columbus, Ohio 43201

This book was set in Plantin and Helvetica
Production Editor: Gnomi Schrift Gouldin
Cover Design: Cathy Watterson

Library of Congress Catalog Card Number: 85-061330
International Standard Book Number: 0-675-20325-2
Printed in the United States of America
1 2 3 4 5 6 7 8 9 10—93 92 91 90 89 88 87 86

Contents

Preface

Throughout most of the history of western civilization, "the law" was considered a vital subject of instruction for any educated person. In the most famous universities of the world, four subjects were considered essential to the development of a civilized gentleman: religion, mathematics, science, and the law. Even Blackstone, perhaps the best known law teacher of all time, was a lecturer in "the law" at a time when law schools did not exist. The law as a subject of university instruction, like the law as an instrument of social control, is a vehicle for preserving and transmitting the basic notions of civilization.

It is in that spirit that this textbook was written. This book evolved from my conviction that nonprofessional legal education continues to be a vital force in the development of truly educated people and, in fact, a person cannot call himself or herself truly educated or "well-rounded" without some basic understanding of law. A parallel belief is that a citizenry well-schooled in the nature, background, and structure of our legal system is far more capable of performing well in our system of participatory democracy. To put the matter simply, a person who is educated in the law can think more clearly, petition the government more effectively, and vote more intelligently than those who act from ignorance.

In a project of this size, the author's debts are immense. It would be legitimate to thank everyone who had any part in my intellectual development, including every teacher I ever had together with a huge array of lawyers, judges, scholars, and authors who at one time or another made me think. That task is reminiscent of Justice Andrews' statement in *Palsgraf* v. *Long Island Railroad* that, "without each the future would not be the same," but like Justice Andrews, who cut off his search for causation at some arbitrary point, I too must choose some random point to stop thanking people.

Perhaps my largest debt is to my students, particularly those few who had the temerity to ask "why?" I have used many portions of this text in my classes at Illinois State University, and to those students who have wrestled with the book in progress goes my sincere thanks, especially those who have pointed out inconsistencies, errors, omissions, and simple obtuseness.

My colleagues at Illinois State University also deserve thanks, especially Edmund Ficek, Dennis Kruse, Scott Massin, and Carson Varner, who in my mind make up the finest nonprofessional law faculty in the nation. Special thanks must go to Carson Varner, who agreed to use portions of the text in his classes and who put up with rather insistent pestering about "how did it work?" on almost a daily basis. His suggestions and comments have been most helpful.

I must also express my appreciation to Joe W. Fowler, Oklahoma State University; Thomas L. Gossman, Western Michigan University; Elliot I. Klayman, Ohio State University; Nancy Reeves Mansfield, Georgia State University; Leila O. Schroeder, Louisiana State University; and Frank A. Vickory, Florida State University—all of whom read the text or portions of it and provided insightful and helpful comments when I needed it most. In addition, Marilyn Freedman, Gnomi Gouldin, Steve Smith, and Marianne Taflinger of Charles E. Merrill Publishing Company also provided a great deal of assistance and support whenever I needed it.

Finally, my most important debt is to my family. My wife, Joan, and our four sons, Patrick, David, Michael, and Chad, provided far more than the usual moral support during the past two years. The family has been intimately involved from the very beginning in everything from alphabetizing, pagination, and rough editing to emptying my wastebasket and keeping the cat off of my desk. My wife, Joan, has been particularly important to this project by offering her gentle suggestions and just listening as I talked out a difficult area.

While my debts for this project are enormous, the responsibility is simple. I alone am responsible for any errors, omissions, or faulty prose. Perhaps that is why writing is such a lonely chore and why so few textbooks are written by a single author.

Charles R. McGuire
Normal, Illinois

Introduction

Government is itself an art, one of the subtlest of arts. It is the art of making men live together in peace and with reasonable happiness.

Felix Frankfurter

To define the law as an aggregate of rules is to define human thought as an ensemble of the words in the dictionary.

Henri Levy-Ullman

This book will not make the student into a lawyer; only years of concentrated study can do that. Nor will this text fill the need for competent legal advice, either now or later. The old adage that he who represents himself has a fool for a client is generally true, particularly in the complex and ever-changing world of government regulation and public law.

One of the principal purposes of this text and any course in the legal environment of business is to create a healthy fear of the law and of government regulation. Too many students leave the sheltered environment of the university for the business world in naive innocence of just how much, and in what ways, the law regulates our personal and business lives. Such innocence is not merely a regrettable oversight in college curriculums nor an unfortunate omission from the student's overburdened schedule. Such innocence may be dangerous to the student's future, those who employ him or her, and even to society at large.

Upon entering the working world, a business student learns in very short order that all of the beautifully logical theories of accounting, finance, management, and marketing must be considered anew in the harsh glare of the law. If the field is marketing, the student will have to become aware of the limits placed on such activities by the Federal Trade Commission and other government agencies that regulate how products may be sold and advertised. If the field chosen is labor management, the student will spend a great deal of time determining the implications of affirmative action, attempting to comply with National Labor Relations Board regulations, and trying to conform to the rules of the Occupational Safety and Health Administration, the Social Security Administration, and the Internal Revenue Service, to name just a few. Business is no longer economic theory, the psychology of management, and the dictates of the balance sheet. Today's businessperson is just as involved with the problems of environmental impact statements, unfair labor practices, and affirmative action. In the business world, this ignorance is not bliss but may well endanger both the student's own future and that of his or her employer.

To a large extent, the purpose of this text is to point out when the future businessperson should call in an attorney or the firm's legal division. It is an attempt to provide "preventative law." Legal questions are almost always easier to solve before the damage is done. That phone call to a lawyer may well save the employer thousands of dollars and may save the student's job and future career as well. While it is said that a little knowledge is a dangerous thing, a little knowledge of the law may well create concern and respect. In dealing with the law and with government, a little paranoia may well be a healthy thing.

As the legal profession becomes more specialized nonprofessional legal education becomes more important. Each person must, at least to some extent, become his or her own GP, at least sufficiently to know which legal specialist to call. Just as in medicine we learned not to call an orthopedic surgeon if our stomach hurts, we must learn when to call a securities regulation specialist, a tort lawyer, or an estate planner for a particular problem. But we must know enough about the law to know whom to call.

Similarly, the more complex the world becomes, the more important it is that we know a little about the law. Our consumer transactions, our jobs, and our safety all have legal ramifications and impacts, and it is important that we know what they are. After all, as every law instructor has said—at least once a semester—ignorance of the law is no excuse.

Finally, nonprofessional legal studies, particularly in the context of a broad course such as "the legal environment of business," provide perhaps the best opportunity to broaden and truly educate business students. It is often argued with considerable force that business students are too "narrow." The charge that business schools are anti-intellectual (or nonintellectual) is often leveled by those outside the business schools. While we may rail at such biases and attitudes, it is perceived that business students often do not get a solid grounding in political science, history, literature, and philosophy. Business curricula are, and probably ought to be, centered on utilitarian concerns of usefulness and specialization.

On the other hand, a university educator has the responsibility to broaden the horizons and perspectives of his or her students. To graduate a student who is well-schooled in theories of management, accounting, finance, or marketing, but who has no conception of the heritage and history of his or her country, nor any knowledge of Plato, Shakespeare, Locke, Jefferson, or even Roosevelt and Eisenhower, is unfair to the student and business.

The course in legal environment cannot resolve those difficulties by itself. Such an assumption would be at best self-delusive and egocentric. But the course in Legal Environment can go a long way toward resolving some of the problems. The initial chapters in this text expose students to some of the main features of American civilization and culture. Students leaving this course may not be truly sophisticated in the differences between natural rights philosophy and the theories of positivism, nor will they be sound historians in Constitutional and political history, but at least they will be acquainted with the main features of those areas, especially insofar as those areas affect the business community.

This is not to say, of course, that every business graduate will be a tweedy intellectual because of taking this course; it simply means that the graduate will be able to comprehend today's headlines. If, as we hope, the business school graduate will become an important member of society, active in business and civic affairs and of some consequence to society, he or she ought to know a little about how our country and our political and legal systems operate. This book seeks to teach those things, sometimes expressly, but often between the lines. After all, the law is, in the words of Sir Henry Maine, "as extensive as the concerns of mankind."

Finally, every nonprofessional law course seeks to teach the so-called legal method of inquiry and analysis. That method, embodying critical analysis, logic, objectivity, and restraint, cannot tolerate sloppy thinking, the bane of both the businessperson and the lawyer. Exposure to that method of thought and analysis can only bring benefits to both the student and to the society at large.

Topic Selection and the AACSB Standards

The American Association of Collegiate Schools of Business (AACSB), the principal accrediting body for business colleges, has established a requirement that a core course in "the legal environment of business" be taught in such schools. According to the AACSB standard, that course must teach

> (b) a background of the economic and legal environment as it pertains to profit and/
> or non-profit organizations along with ethical considerations and social and political
> influences as they affect such organizations.*

This text has been written with those requirements in mind, and topics have been selected with a view towards meeting those standards. In particular, the following portions of this book expressly speak to the AACSB requirements.

---

*While the author has attempted to aim the text at the AACSB requirement, it should be made clear that there has been no official, or even unofficial, approval of this text by the AACSB or any other organization. This text represents simply, and solely, the author's perception of the AACSB requirement.

A Definition of The Legal Environment

While the AACSB has left the final definition of the term *the legal environment* up to member schools, it seems clear that the term means something more than traditional business law. While this book includes sections on such traditional topics as contracts, agency, business associations, and the U.C.C., this book is based on the idea that the term requires far more than "private law" and includes greater instruction in the intricacies of the legal system and "public law."

In particular, this text attempts to define the legal environment to include *all* the ways in which the law affects business. Chapter 1 contains a broad discussion of the legal environment and defines the term as all laws and regulations that seek to regulate any of the various relationships of the business firm. That definition is in turn used as the basis for the organization of the text, by defining each of those relationships and then devoting a Part of the book to the regulation of each relationship.

The Nonprofit Organization Requirement

This book takes the position that nonprofit organizations, as that term is used in the AACSB standard, means far more than a brief discussion of charitable trusts. Instead, the term means *any actor* in the business environment whose primary purpose is other than the making of a profit.

As a result, the term includes such diverse and important participants in the business world as labor unions, foundations, health care facilities, educational institutions, political parties, and political interest groups. An entire section of Chapter 7 deals with such organizations and the law that controls them. Labor unions are the subject of Chapter 13 and part of Chapter 14, and political organizations are discussed throughout the text, especially in the first three chapters. Other nonprofit actors are discussed in other areas or in the cases.

The Ethical Considerations Requirement

The secondary theme of this text, built into each of the chapters and discussed at length in Chapters 1 and 20, is the tension between "the two great ethics of the 20th century"; that is, the ethic of individualism and the ethic of community. One of the purposes of this text is to describe the various compromises that have been made between individual welfare and social welfare in the legal and political arenas.

In addition, Chapter 20 attempts a discussion of "personal ethics" which tries to avoid the "twin traps" of ethical instruction: "preaching" to students from the author's or instructor's personal viewpoint; and dodging the issue by throwing up one's arms and saying "it's all a matter of opinion." Instead, the chapter tries to stimulate thought about the nature of ethical systems, ethical notions, and ethical dilemmas.

The Social and Political Influences Requirement

This text treats the law as part of the fabric of society, the result of social and political forces and the cause of social and political change. The law cannot be studied in a vacuum, and this text introduces each major topic with a discussion of the social and political history that influenced the creation of the law. That discussion is reinforced by the introductory chapters on philosophy and the American Constitution, the Discussion Questions, and the Pro and Con sections.

Finally, each of the topics chosen for treatment in this text has been chosen with an eye to the nature of the legal environment. The first five chapters (Part I) deal with the "legal matrix" of our society—the philosophy, history, and organization of our judicial system. Chapters 6 and 7 introduce the student to "the common law," including a discussion of the origins of the common law and a consideration of contracts, torts, property, agency, partnerships, and corporations, including a discussion of nonprofit organizations.

The balance of the text, with the exception of Chapter 20, unabashedly considers regulatory topics, including traditional topics such as antitrust, consumer protection, labor law, environmental protection and securities regulation, but also including some topics not ordinarily covered in a legal environment text. Those topics include discrimination (Chapter 16), taxation (Chapter 18), and economic regulation and the concept of deregulation (Chapter 19).

While employment discrimination is a traditional topic in many legal environment courses, the scope of Chapter 16 is much broader and touches on all of the areas in which discrimination is regulated, including public accomodations, housing, voting rights and education as well as the traditional topic of employment. This approach was chosen to illustrate to students the depth of our national committment to eradicate discrimination and the methods chosen by the government to deal with that problem. The chapter also considers at some length the nature of Constitutional equal protection and the problem of defining protected categories.

The chapter on taxation was included for several reasons: first, taxation is one of the most important means by which government regulates, by creating incentives and disincentives for particular activities. Second, taxation is very clearly a part of the legal environment of any business and, in fact, may form one of the most important ways in which a business firm has contact with law and with the government. Finally, it has been the author's experience that students often have a lopsided view of taxation as being concerned solely with the federal income tax. This chapter discusses all of the important types of taxes, together with a consideration of the constitutional and policy limits on government taxing bodies.

Finally, the chapter on economic regulation and the concept of deregulation deals with an important but too often ignored method of regulation, "economic regulation" of government-created monopolies, and the political problems of "deregulation," which began with the economically regulated industries. Since deregulation has been a legal and political football for almost a decade, this topic was thought essential to round out the discussion found in previous chapters.

The Selection of Cases for This Text

Any of tens of thousands of legal decisions could have been used in this book. The choice of which cases to include has been based on three principal criteria: *impor-*

tance, clarity, and *currency,* roughly in that order. In those rare and happy instances in which the most important case is also clear and relatively current, the choice was easy. In all other circumstances, the author was required to balance the three criteria to find the best selection.

The first and in many instances the controlling criterion has been the importance of the decision. Landmark cases are part of the legal culture and heritage of America, and students should be exposed to classic legal literature in the same way they are exposed to the classics in other disciplines. The law is not bare and isolated rules, but a part of the fabric of history in which landmark legal decisions have played a crucial role. To exclude *Marbury* v. *Madison* or *NLRB* v. *Jones and Laughlin Steel* or *U.S.* v. *Brown Shoe* from the legal environment course is like omitting Shakespeare from a course on English literature. Occasionally, a classic case was found to be unclear or obtuse, and a lesser known but more understandable case was chosen to explain the rules found in the classic decision. The third criterion, that of currency, was considered the least important of the three. While it is obviously important that current law be taught the student, mere recency is not enough. It is far more important that students be exposed to a clear exposition of legal ideas, especially through classic or watershed decisions, than that the decision be made within the last few years.

The Pro and Con Sections

Each chapter also carries a section called *Pro and Con,* in which a major issue from the chapter is reconsidered in detail. The issue is defined, then two responsible spokespersons are presented, arguing two different views of the issue. For example, in Chapter 1 the issue is *stare decisis* and the spokespersons are Justices Cardozo and Holmes, who take slightly different views of the problem.

These sections have been added for three principal reasons: first, the very presence of the sections will convince the student that few issues in the law are not debatable and every issue has at least two sides. Second, the sections will expose students to legal literature other than cases, since many of the selections are taken from law review articles and legal periodicals. Finally, the sections permit discussion of controversial topics in a responsible fashion, rather than by expressly or implicitly trying to convince students of the author's point of view. With this device, students are free to make up their own minds.

The Discussion Questions and the Case Problems

At the close of each chapter are *two* sets of questions for students, the Discussion Questions and the Case Problems. In most cases, about ten questions of each type are included.

The Discussion Questions are generally large issues that have arisen within the chapter, often with a political, economic or philosophical bent. These questions have been designed to stir the students' thought and to challenge the assumptions behind the law. They are not review questions in the traditional sense, since those questions are presented in the student guide. These questions are particularly fit for class discussion, bull sessions between students, and essay exams.

The Case Problems are analytical problems based on the law presented in the chapter and are designed to aid the student in learning to apply the concepts learned in the chapter. The majority of these problems are based on real cases, and citations have been supplied so that students and instructors may check out the "right answer" given by the courts if they so desire. In some cases, hypotheticals have been included when actual cases did not suffice.

A Note to Students: Studying Cases

Before you turn many more pages you will find that this book is filled with legal *cases*. It is vitally important that you understand that these cases are not like the "cases" found in other business texts. These cases are not hypothetical examples of material discussed in the text nor are they factual situations in which the student is to apply the concepts learned in the text. The cases in this book are real decisions by real courts in real disputes. Not even the names have been changed, and the words, though edited because of space limitations, are the words used by the courts in deciding the dispute.

It is also vitally important that these cases not be skipped or glossed over. The real "law" found in this book is found in those cases, since, in Justice Holmes' words, "the prophecies of what the courts will do in fact, and nothing more pretentious, are what I mean by the law." The narrative in each chapter is of course important, but a good deal of the meat of this book is found within the cases themselves, and it would be a tragic mistake to skip or speed through those cases. And you should read them with a dictionary by your side, since judicial opinions are written by and for those familiar with legal language.

In a series of lectures to incoming law students at Columbia Law School, Professor Karl Llewellyn tried to point out the necessity of reading the cases carefully.

It is a pity, but you must learn to *read*. To read each word. To understand *each* word. You are outlanders in this country of the law. You do not know the speech. It must be learned. Like any other foreign tongue, it must be learned: by seeing words, by using them until they are familiar; meantime, by constant reference to the dictionary. What, dictionary? Tort, trespass, trover, plea, assumpsit, nisi prius, venire de nova, demurrer, joinder, traverse, abatement, general issue, tender, mandamus, certiorari, adverse possession, dependent relative revocation, and the rest. Law Latin, law French, aye, or law English—what do these strange terms mean to you? Can you rely upon the crumbs of language that remain from school? . . . I fear a dictionary is your only hope—a law dictionary—the one-volume kind you can keep ready on your desk. Can you trust the dictionary, is it accurate, does it give you what you want? Of course not. No dictionary does. The life of words is in the using of them, in the wide network of their long associations, in the intangible something we denominate their feel. But the bare bones to work with, the dictionary offers; and without those bare bones you may be sure the feel will never come.*

This sort of study is sometimes alien to students. It is hard work, but the case system has proven itself by generations of law students, and there is no better way to savor the flavor and texture of the law.

One technique that has proven invaluable to students in legal studies over the years is *case briefing*. Briefing involves writing a synopsis of a case, in your own words. Students who have not been exposed to case briefing before are advised to turn immediately to Appendix A, "Finding and Briefing Cases."

Even a careful reading of the cases may not be enough without some background in the nature of judicial decisions. While Chapter 1 presents a great deal of background on the case system and the nature of *stare decisis* (precedent), Professor Llewellyn has some additional advice for the student.

> You will be looking, in the opinion, or in the preliminary matter plus the opinion, for the following: a statement of the facts the court assumes; a statement of the precise way the question has come before the court—which includes what the plaintiff wanted below, and what the defendant did about it, the judgment below, and what the trial court did that is being complained of; then the outcome on appeal, the judgment; and finally the reasons this court gives for doing what it did. This does not look so bad. But it is much worse than it looks.
>
> For all our cases are decided, all our opinions are written, all our predictions, all our arguments are made, on certain four assumptions. They are the first presuppositions of our study. They must be rutted into you till you can juggle them standing on your head and in your sleep.
>
> (1) *The court must decide the dispute that is before it.* It cannot refuse because the job is hard, or dubious, or dangerous.
>
> (2) *The court can decide only the particular dispute which is before it.* When it speaks to that question it speaks ex cathedra, with authority, with finality, with an almost magic power. When it speaks to the question before it, it announces *law,* and if what it announces is new, it legislates, it *makes* the law. But when it speaks to any other question at all, it says mere words, which no man needs to follow. . . .
>
> (3) *The court can decide the particular dispute only according to a general rule which covers a whole class of like disputes.* Our legal theory does not admit of single decisions standing on their own. If judges are free, are indeed forced, to decide new cases for which there is no rule, they must at least make a new rule as they decide. So far, good. But how wide, or how narrow, is the general rule in this particular case? That is a troublesome matter. The practice of our case-law, however, is I think fairly stated thus: it pays to be suspicious of general rules which look too wide; it pays to go slow in feeling certain that a wide rule has been laid down at all, or that, if seemingly laid down, it will be followed. For there is a fourth accepted canon:
>
> (4) *Everything, everything, everything, big or small, a judge may say in an opinion, is to be read with primary reference to the particular dispute, the particular question before him.* You are not to think that the words mean what they might if they stood alone. You are to have your eye on the case in hand, and learn how to interpret all that has been said *merely* as a reason for deciding *that* case *that* way. At need.**

---

*K. N. Llewellyn, *The Bramble Bush: On Law and Its Study* (New York: Oceana Publications, 1960), p. 41. Copyright, 1960, K. N. Llewellyn.

**K. N. Llewellyn, *The Bramble Bush, ibid.,* p. 42–43.

A part of Llewellyn's meaning is that the study of law cannot be rushed. It is not memorizing great lists of details, nor learning a few basic computations and applying them, nor even reading stacks of books, though it is closer to the latter. At the risk of excessive sentimentality, the study of law is to be slowly savored. Each word in a case must be related to every other word and each sentence related to every other sentence and each paragraph related to every other paragraph and, finally, each case must be related to every other case. It is extremely hard work and, after a while, a great deal of fun.

Another Note to Students: On Pride and Prejudice

Every time we enter a new field of study, we bring with us preconceptions of what we are to learn. Those preconceived notions may be harmless or fatal, depending on the area of study. They may be dispelled by a textbook or a good instructor in the first few hours of study, or they may stay with us for life, constantly interfering with our ability to objectively consider and really learn.

It seems that the areas of law and public regulation of business are especially subject to such preconceptions. Political labels and attitudes, social and economic biases, ancient folk wisdom and cracker-barrel philosophies all seem to interfere with objective study of government and the law and ways in which they regulate business and industry. We seem to see things the way we want to see them, not as they really are.

From the day we first become politically aware, most of us search for a political label in which to wrap ourselves. Whether that label is liberal, conservative, Democrat, Republican, or some other, there is a strong impetus and a strong temptation to adopt that label and wear it proudly. And, that is as it should be, for it is a part of the search for personal identity that can only lead to intellectual maturity.

Virtually every page in this text is pregnant with political controversy. In these pages we discuss or at least allude to almost every social problem and political controversy, including abortion, school prayer, the Equal Rights Amendment, racial discrimination and affirmative action, deregulation, labor-management relations, "shareholder democracy," environmental pollution, regulation of nuclear energy, and much, much more. One of the goals of this text is to show students that such matters can be, and are, considered by the law in a more or less objective and dispassionate manner. It is to that end that the Pro and Con sections have been included.

But, even with these sections, students who have accepted their political identities too quickly and with too much enthusiasm may have a difficult time maintaining their objectivity. Lawyers are often accused of hypocrisy in being able to argue either side of a case. Yet this ability comes from seeing all sides of a question, reserving judgment until all of the evidence is in. In this text, almost every cherished notion of government and politics will be challenged at some point, if not by the author, then surely by the cases and readings. Objective dissection of both the notion and the challenge can only make us intellectually stronger. But blind acceptance or knee-jerk rejection have no benefit at all.

It is also important that we destroy one bit of folk wisdom about the law before we begin. When we speak of "the law," many people think in terms of nice, neat lists of rules set down in writing somewhere. Folk wisdom finds those rules to be immutable, sometimes unjust in their firm application, and written in absolute, black and white terms.

Nothing could be further from the truth. If anything is always true about the law, it is that nothing is always true about the law. The law is definitely not a series of black and white rules. There are no absolutes, no rules without exceptions, even no perfect justice. The law is a vibrant thing, alive with change and controversy and exceptions. If this text teaches no more than that, it will have succeeded.

The Legal Process

An understanding of the legal environment of business requires an understanding of the American legal process—the philosophical, historical, and social input into the law; the nature of the American constitutional system; and the procedures of and restraints on legislatures, courts, and administrative agencies. Those matters will be the subject of the first five chapters.

The law is, first and foremost, a method of social control. Law is meant to restrain behavior into socially acceptable channels. In that sense, the law is the clearest expression of the ethics of society. When society, in the form of its elected representatives, its judges, its juries, and its appointed officers, decides that certain conduct is "wrong," in most instances that conduct will be declared "illegal." Some unethical conduct is not illegal, however, and some illegal conduct is not unethical. But the relationship between law and the ethical norms of society is intimate and vital. As ethics change, so does the law.

The common thread running through the first five chapters is whether the structures of the law—the Constitution, the law-making authorities, the courts and their procedures, and the administrative agencies—are constructed properly to respond to the ethical and moral demands of society. The law can be out of touch with the society it governs, and its prohibitions may have little to do with the needs, values, and ethics of the people. But the law may also be *too* responsive to the ever-changing currents and fads of society. Our question then is how best to structure the law to be both responsive and controlling.

The Cornerstones of Law and Government

Now there are only two subjects of thought—the only two perhaps with the exception of physical science—which are able to give employment to all the powers and capacities which the mind possesses. One of them is Metaphysical Inquiry, which knows no limits so long as the mind is satisfied to work on itself; the other is Law, which is as extensive as the concerns of Mankind.

Sir Henry Maine

The researches of many antiquarians have thrown much darkness on the subject, and it is probable, if they continue, that we shall soon known nothing at all.

Mark Twain

It is a widely held belief that the study of law, and particularly the study of government regulation, involves memorizing long lists of rules and statutes. But those rules and statutes have a habit of changing with the political, social, and economic winds of the moment. The hotly debated and fashionable area of regulation of today may lie completely forgotten tomorrow.

It is far more important that we understand the *reasons* for such statutes and regulations and the *processes* by which they become law. In order to understand such reasons and processes, it is vital that we first understand the philosophical, political, and procedural underpinnings of the law, the sources of government power to regulate, and the formal and informal restrictions on government power. Once we understand those matters, we may then analyze and comprehend the changes in regulation and law that occur long after our studies are complete.

This chapter will consider the philosophical theories of government and law and the nature of "the legal environment of business." Chapters 2 and 3 will deal with the nature of the powers granted to the federal government and the restrictions on the exercise of those powers. Chapter 4 will consider the "nuts and bolts" of court procedure, and Chapter 5 will discuss the source of most of the business regulations in existence, the administrative agency.

The Nature of the Legal Environment of Business

The place of an individual firm in the business world is complex. Every business has relationships with a great number of persons and institutions, and the sum total of those relationships may be defined as the *environment of business.* Businesses have relationships with eight major groups of persons or legal entities: competitors, suppliers, creditors, customers, employees, investors, the anonymous "public," and the various units of government (see Figure 1-1).

"The law" may be viewed as a method of controlling relationships. Every law controls or regulates some relationship because the law-making authority found this control necessary or advisable. For example, the law of labor relations governs the relationship between a firm and its employees; the law of securities regulation governs the relationship between a firm and its investors; and antitrust law governs the relationship between a firm and its competitors and suppliers.

Each of the eight relationships of the business firm has legal implications. In each case, the law steps in at times to limit and control the relationships involved. Those legal limits and controls on the relationships between business and those with whom it deals may be termed the *legal environment of business.*

The relationship of business to government has the greatest impact on the other relationships because it includes the various regulations, statutes, and court decisions

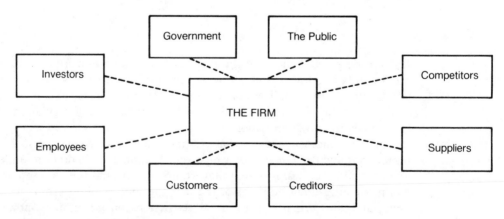

Figure 1-1   The Environment of Business

that regulate the other seven relationships. Those laws not only regulate relationships but in a few cases have *established* relationships where none existed, as in the case of the environmental laws designed to regulate the relationship between business and "the public."

Before we consider each of these relationships in detail, it is important that we discuss the framework of the law, including its philosophical and constitutional bases and the organization and procedures of the courts and administrative agencies. Those matters will be taken up in Chapters 1 through 5. Chapters 6 and 7 will deal with the "basic" law relating to business, including the common law of contracts, torts, and property, and the legal structure of the business firm.

Beginning with Chapter 8, we will examine the various relationships of the business firm. Chapters 8 through 10 will deal with the relationship of the firm to its competitors, and to a lesser extent to its suppliers and customers, in the form of the federal antitrust laws. Chapters 11 and 12 will deal with the relationship of the firm to its customers in the form of various consumer protection statutes and rules, and to its creditors and debtors in the form of the federal bankruptcy law. Chapter 15 will consider the relationship of the firm to its investors in the federal securities laws, and Chapters 16 and 17 will cover some of the firm's duties to the public, in the form of the civil rights, environmental protection, and energy laws. Chapters 18 and 19 will consider other relationships of the firm to government, through the tax laws and through "economic" regulation. Finally, Chapter 20 ponders the problem of business ethics, in both the context of the law and beyond.

Ethics and the Law: A Preview

Business ethics has been a source of concern to businesspeople, lawyers, judges, academics, and the public for a very long time. Simply put, many people believe that unrestrained personal ambition, unbridled by concern for morality, ethics, or the public interest, is extremely dangerous. While we are all taught that ambition is laudable and we should strive to succeed, there must be some checks on that ambition. The first and best check is, of course, self-discipline. But self-discipline may fail for any number of reasons and, as a result, the law must step in to provide limits on ambition and enforce the morality, ethics, and interests of the larger society. In a very large sense the law is the enforced expression of the ethics of society as determined by legislators, judges, and juries.

Societal Ethics and Personal Ethics

The term **ethics** has two principal meanings. First, the term refers to our *personal* set of rules and standards by which we judge our own behavior and the behavior of others. Common personal ethical values include honesty, truthfulness, tolerance, charity, and loyalty. The precise mix of those and other values will vary with each person's upbringing, religion, education, and experience.

It is extremely important to realize that even these honorable values may conflict from time to time. For example, does our loyalty to our family and our concern for their well-being justify "just a little" dishonesty? Can patriotism justify otherwise unethical conduct? Does concern for honesty justify a disregard of our employer's instructions? Questions such as these point out that there is no "pecking order" between the various ethical values. Loyalty to the firm may be used to justify dishonesty, but loyalty is not innately superior to truthfulness, nor is truthfulness superior to loyalty. The choice we make between such conflicting ethical values depends on our personal system of ethical values, and little else. Often, however, the law steps in to resolve such dilemmas by requiring certain kinds of conduct.

The second meaning of the term *ethics* is much broader. **Societal ethics** refers to large groupings of standards and rules adopted by a wide group of people. This group includes all ideologies, such as Communism, Socialism, and Democracy, and all religions, such as Christianity, Islam, and Buddhism. But the term also includes more vague sets of principles that are generally accepted by groups of people. For example, many Americans consciously or subconsciously subscribe to the work ethic or protestant ethic, which places a high value on hard work, sacrifice, and enterprise.

The Two Great Ethics of the 20th Century

Two societal ethics have dominated the 20th century. Since the 18th century, Western culture has been directed by the **individualist ethic.** Individualism in its purest form holds that the individual is supreme and society is merely a means of achieving and maximizing individual welfare. While many of the tenets of individualism are second nature to contemporary America, the idea was a radical heresy in the 18th century, when the dominant philosophy held that the king was all important. Individualism in its most extreme form may be found in **social Darwinism,** which believes that strong individuals *should* win as part of the "survival of the fittest," in **laissez faire** economics, which in its ultimate form holds that government should never interfere in economic matters, and finally may result in political **anarchy,** or the absence of all government.

The **community ethic,** on the other hand, holds that the welfare of society is supreme over the welfare of the individual. In its most extreme form, the doctrine believes that individuals may be used or even destroyed as a means to perfection of society. The ultimate form of the community ethic may be found in the writings of Karl Marx and the various collectivist societies of the world.

We may be tempted, as a kind of "knee-jerk" reaction, to reject all aspects of the community ethic and embrace individualism without thought. But both the ethic of individualism and the community ethic have resulted in major economic, political, and personal miseries, when carried to their extremes. While the community ethic rejects the importance of the individual, individualism may reject all notions of community. While the community ethic in its extreme form results in the evils of communism and totalitarianism, individualism in its extreme form may result in sweat shops, consumer fraud, discrimination, environmental pillage, and even slavery.

There is a middle ground. In fact, most nations on earth have taken that middle ground, although in somewhat different forms. Much of the history of the 20th century, and much of the history of American law and regulation, may be viewed as an attempt to combine the best elements of individualism with the best elements of the community ethic. Our problem is not a stark choice between the individual and the community but a choice of the proper mix of the two ethics.

For example, many of the antidiscrimination statutes of the mid-20th century represent a choice between individualist and community notions. Individualism would hold that each businessperson has the right to sell to whomever he or she desires. Notions of community find that sellers should be prohibited from discriminating against buyers on the basis of race or other irrelevancies.

Throughout much of this text public policy arguments will vacillate between the poles of individualism and community. Usually a compromise is struck, permitting individual freedom within community-oriented "limits." The legal environment of business is fraught with such issues, constantly shifting between the freedom of the individual businessperson and the welfare of the larger society. How those choices have been made, the nature of the compromises that have been reached, and how the courts apply (and sometimes make) those choices is the subject of this text.

Personal Ethics and the Law

Our personal ethical notions of honesty, loyalty, fairness, and so forth will influence to a large extent whether we believe a particular law or regulation to be good or bad. We should also remember that such personal ethical notions also played a very large role in the creation of law. It was, in the first instance, the ideas of honesty and fairness in the minds of judges and legislators that led to the creation of many laws by such lawmakers. In that sense, ethics and morality play a huge role in fashioning the law. They are, in fact, the major "input" into the law.

But personal ethics tend to change over time. While murder and thievery have probably always been wrong and have been outlawed in almost every society, other notions of honesty, fair play and loyalty have changed a great deal over the centuries. Even the legal definition of murder and thievery has changed over time, and laws against sexual misconduct and drunken behavior that made good sense to our Puritan and Victorian ancestors seem curious anachronisms today. Our problem is to create a legal system that will at once reflect the ethics of the larger society and be flexible enough to change as our ethical notions change. The problems of ethics as an input to law will be taken up in greater detail, along with other problems of personal ethics, in the final chapter of this text.

Theories of Law and Government

The study of philosophy is usually not very appealing to today's pragmatic business student. Philosophy seems to be, in the words of Voltaire, "when he who hears doesn't know what he who speaks means, and when he who speaks doesn't know what he himself means." But the study of philosophy is especially central to the study of government and law, particularly in this country. Unlike other systems of government, American institutions are based on a specific philosophy of government and law, the **natural rights theory,** and an understanding of that theory and its competitors is essential to a complete understanding of our entire political, legal, and regulatory system.

Throughout the history of man's thought, philosophers have debated the nature and purpose of government and law. Even the earliest Greek philosophers, including Plato and Aristotle, dealt with issues such as why government must exist, the ideal structure of government, what sort of laws are good or proper, and the overriding problem of defining the term *justice.*

The questions raised by the early Greeks remain a vital part of the law even today. It is fairly common for a contemporary legal opinion to quote Plato or Locke or Jefferson. It is even more common that the ideas of these thinkers are implicit in statutes or judicial decisions. At the very least, philosophy is a major input into the law.

An Introduction to the Philosophy of Law
Roscoe Pound*

For twenty-four hundred years—from the Greek thinkers of the fifth Century B.C. who asked whether right was right by nature or only be enactment and convention, to the social philosophers of today, who seek the ends, the ethical basis and the enduring principles of social control—the philosophy of law has taken a leading role in all study of human institutions.

In all stages of what may be described fairly as legal development philosophy has been a useful servant. But in some it has been a tyrannous servant and in all but form a master. It has been used to break down the authority of outworn tradition, to bend authoritatively imposed rules that admitted of no change to new uses which changed profoundly their practical effect, to bring new elements into the law from without and make new bodies of law from these new materials, to organize and systematize existing legal materials and to fortify established rules and institutions when periods of growth were succeeded by periods of stability and of merely formal reconstruction. Yet all the while its professed aim has been much more ambitious. It has sought to lay down a moral and legal and political chart for all time. It has had faith that it could find the everlasting, unchangeable legal reality in which we might rest, and could enable us to establish a perfect law by which human relations might be ordered forever without uncertainty and freed from need of change.

The questions raised by legal philosophy are perhaps as important as the answers it gives. Traditional legal and political theorists were concerned with the issue of why government exists, and the source of the authority of government. Contemporary analysis of law centers around what function law should play in society and how best to describe the legal process. Implicit in the questions are the issues of what changes should be made in the law, whether the law is fair or just, and the relationship of the public to government. As Pound noted, "ideas of what law is for are so largely implicit in ideas of what law is".

The Beginnings: The Divine Right of Kings

Perhaps the oldest and simplest theory of the origins and nature of government was the doctrine of the **divine right of kings.** This theory justified monarchies from the

---

*(New Haven, Connecticut: Yale University Press, 1922), pp. 1–2. Reprinted by permission.

earliest times through the 16th century on the basis that the authority of the monarch came directly from God. A deity somehow "appointed" the king and authorized him and his descendants to rule. Usually the theory also either expressly or implicitly stated that the actions of the monarch are also directly authorized by God, and in fact God is acting through the king. Therefore, of course, rebellion is impossible and a sin, and only God may punish a wicked king, for "the king can do no wrong."

Beginning in the 17th century, the divine right theory lost its hold. The theory was weakened already by the revival of Greek thought in the Renaissance and the challenge to established authority in the Protestant Reformation. In the late 1600's newer and bolder theories of government began to replace the divine right theory, basing their thought on the primacy of man.

The Theory of Power: Hobbes to Marx

One direction of the new thought was pointed out by Thomas Hobbes (1588–1679). Hobbes believed that the sole basis of government and law was sheer, naked power. His theory began with the assumption that to determine the true source of government we must view man in a "state of nature." In that original society, life must have consisted of a "war of each against all," which meant that life must have necessarily been "poor, nasty, brutish and short."

Thomas Hobbes
Leviathan (1651)

> In such a war nothing is unjust. To this war of every man against every man, this also is consequent: that nothing can be unjust. The notions of right and wrong, justice and injustice, have there no place. Where there is no common power, there is no law; where no law, no injustice. Force and fraud are in war the two cardinal virtues. Justice and injustice are none of the faculties neither of the body nor mind. If they were, they might be in a man that were alone in the world, as well as his senses and passions. They are qualities that relate to men in society, not in solitude. It is consequent also to the same condition that there be no propriety, no dominion, no *mine* or *thine* distinct: but only that to be every man's that he can get, and for so long as he can keep it.

In such a war, the winner is obvious. The strongest must win the struggle, and with it win the right to rule. According to Hobbes, the original source of power of government is then *force.* Hobbes' views were tempered by the belief that enlightened man would give up his individual freedom willingly in order to gain the protection of the stronger and avoid the consequences of the war of each against all.

A special brand of **Hobbesian philosophy** finds some prominence today. The theory of *economic determinism* states simply that wealth is power, and the desire for wealth motivates all men. As a result, the wealthy rule the governments of the world, and governments rule largely for the benefit of the wealthy.

To a large extent economic determinism is an unorganized philosophy, full of cynical folk wisdom. There is an old Spanish proverb that says "laws, like the spider's web, catch the fly and let the hawk go free." Many cynics believe today that the rich are largely untouched by law and government, and government is largely run by the rich for their own benefit. In the words of Anatole France, "The law, in all its majestic equality, forbids all men to sleep under bridges, to beg in the streets, and to steal bread—the rich as well as the poor."

An attempt to build economic determinism into a coherent philosophy of government was made by Karl Marx. Marx believed that capitalists ruled government for their own ends, and that the denial of economic justice would result in worldwide political revolution. Once economic justice was achieved, there would be no need for government at all, and the state would "wither away."

The Theory of Agreement: Natural Rights

A second theory of government came close on the heels of Hobbes. The **natural rights theory,** also known as the *compact theory or social contract theory,* was not new; it may be found in the thought of the early Greek and Roman philosophers. But aside from St. Thomas Aquinas (1225?–1274), the theory lay dormant throughout the Middle Ages. In the 17th century, the theory was reawakened in the thought of John Locke (1632–1704) and his followers.

The natural rights theory would agree that we should look to the state of nature for clues as to the source of government and would also agree that the original state of nature was disorganized and brutal. But here the natural rights theory parts company with Hobbes and states that man is *essentially good.* In order to avoid the conflict of the state of nature, men therefore agreed among themselves to give up their individual freedoms, or a part of them, and appoint some of their number as rulers for the common good and protection. Therefore, while man gave up the right to rule himself, the ruler governed only by the consent of the governed. But the governed only gave up those rights that were necessary for government to exist, and the people retained other rights that could not be transferred, also known as *inalienable rights.* The agreement between ruler and governed was a **contract** or *compact,* and a breach of the agreement gave the injured party a remedy, much as a breach of a private contract gives the innocent party a remedy under law.

John Locke
The Second Treatise on Civil Government (1690), Chapter XVIII

> Wherever law ends, tyranny begins, if the law be transgressed to another's harm; and whosoever in authority exceeds the power given him by the law, and makes use of the force he has under his command to compass that upon the subject which the law allows not, ceases in that to be a magistrate, and acting without authority may be opposed, as any other man who by force invades the right of another.

The theories of Locke, Rousseau, and Montesquieu were quickly adopted by men like Paine, Adams, and Jefferson. Those American philosophers based both their right to revolt against the British king and their concept of how a government ought to be organized directly upon the natural rights theory of government.

The Declaration of Independence
July 4, 1776

> We hold these truths to be self-evident, that all Men are created equal, that they are endowed by their Creator with certain unalienable rights, that among these are Life,

Liberty and the Pursuit of Happiness—That to secure these Rights, Governments are instituted among Men, deriving their just powers from the Consent of the governed, that whenever any Form of Government becomes destructive of these Ends, it is the Right of the People to alter or to abolish it, and to institute new Government, laying its foundation on such principles, and organizing its Powers in such form, as to them shall seem most likely to affect their Safety and Happiness.

Jefferson and his contemporaries were true to their philosophy. Not only did they base the revolution on natural rights principles, but for the first time they made the implicit social contract not only express but written. In a large sense, the American Constitution was merely an expression of the lawyer's adage, "get it in writing."

The philosophical issues raised by Hobbes and the natural rights theorists are still debated today, although on a much more sophisticated basis. Theorists such as Lon Fuller, H. L. A. Hart, Felix Cohen and many others have argued these issues within the contemporary environment, and continue to do so. But the field has recently been invaded by the social scientists, with their own theories and methods of analysis.

Modern Schools of Legal Analysis

Almost every branch of modern social science has advanced its own theory purporting to explain the law. Separate theories of law have developed in the disciplines of history, sociology, and economics, each purporting to give a fairly complete picture of what the law is all about.

The Historical School   The historical view of law holds that the law and legal institutions are the result of historical forces of all kinds that drive the law to its present situation. The study of law cannot be divorced from the study of history and all of the social, political, economic, and even psychological forces that have brought our system of government to its present circumstances.

Lawrence M. Friedman
A History of American Law*

People commonly believe that history and tradition are very strong in American law. There is some basis for this belief. Some parts of the law can be traced back very far—the jury system, the mortgage, the trust, some aspects of land law. But other parts of the law are newborn babies. The living law in a broad social sense, including tax law, traffic codes, and social welfare laws, contains some very recent accessions. While one lawyer is advising his client how to react to a ruling from Washington, issued that very day, another may be telling his client that some plausible course of action is blocked by a statute well known to the lawyers of Henry VIII. . . .

[But] despite a strong dash of history and idiosyncrasy, the strongest ingredient in American law, at any given time, is the present: current emotions, real economic interests, concrete political groups. . . . The history of law has meaning only if we assume that at any given time the vital portion is new and changing, form following function, not

---

*(New York: Simon and Schuster, 1973), pp. 13, 14–15. Copyright © 1973 by Lawrence M. Friedman. Reprinted by permission of Simon & Schuster, Inc.

function following form. History of law is not—or should not be—a search for fossils, but a study of social development, unfolding through time.

The Sociological School Often blending with the historical school, sociology views the law as both an expression and a tool of social forces. The primary difference between the **historical** and **sociological schools** lies in the descriptive nature of the former as opposed to the somewhat more value-oriented approach by the latter. Sociology implies that the law ought to respond to contemporary social forces more closely, while history would merely describe the extent to which it does.

Harry W. Jones
"An Invitation to Jurisprudence"*

A social environment would be intolerable without the existence of efficacious institutions for peace-keeping and dispute settlement, but genuine "social tranquility" has further requirements and overtones. By almost anybody's definition, a good society is, among other things, a society in which creativity is unhobbled by constant apprehensions, diversity flourishes without group or class hostility, and inevitable social change is accepted not as something terrifying but as something to be planned for. We are brought, then, to three other of law's social ends-in-view: (1) the maintenance of a reasonable security of individual expectations, (2) the resolution of conflicting social interests, and (3) the channeling of social change. I am not suggesting for a moment that this is a complete tally of law's tasks in society. . . . Nonetheless, the three go, as Contracts scholars used to say, "to the essence" of law in society and are items that must be taken into account in any serious attempt at evaluation of a questioned legal rule or legal institution.

The Economic School A latecomer to the field of legal analysis, economics teaches that most, if not all, of law may be analyzed according to traditional economic theory. Actors in the legal system are assumed to be rational men, interested in maximizing their welfare. As a result, such actors assess the costs and gains of legal actions in a manner very similar to the way in which consumers buy goods in the marketplace. Such an analysis allows, at least theoretically, some measurement of legal actions and permits a more precise analysis of legal rules and institutions.

Richard A. Posner
"The Economic Approach to Law"**

The basis of an economic approach to law is the assumption that the people involved with the legal system act as rational maximizers of their satisfactions. Suppose the question is asked, when will parties to a legal dispute settle rather than litigate? Since this choice involves uncertainty—the outcome of the litigation is not known for sure in advance—the relevant body of economic theory is that which analyzes decision-making by rational maximizers under conditions of uncertainty. If we are willing to assume, at least provisionally, that litigants behave rationally, then this well-developed branch of

---

economic theory can be applied in a straight-forward fashion to the litigation context to yield predictions with respect to the decision to litigate or settle: we discover, for example, that litigation should be more frequent the greater the stakes in the dispute or the uncertainty of the outcome. These predictions can be, and have been, compared with the actual behavior of litigants in the real world. . . .

Now to some of the major findings of the "new" law and economics research. The first is that participants in the legal process indeed behave as if they were rational maximizers: criminals, contracting parties, automobile drivers, prosecutors and others subject to legal constraints or involved in legal proceedings act in relation to the legal system as intelligent (not omniscient) maximizers of their satisfactions. Like ordinary consumers, they economize by buying less of a good or commodity when its price rises and more when it falls. To be sure, the "good" and the "price" in the economic analysis of law are often unconventional, which is perhaps why it took so long for economists to claim the law as part of economics. The "good" might be crimes to a criminal or trials to an aggrieved plaintiff, and the "price" might be a term of imprisonment discounted by the probability of conviction, or a court queue. . . .

. . . A second important finding emerging from the recent law and economics research is that the legal system itself—its doctrines, procedures, and institutions—has been strongly influenced by a concern . . . with promoting economic efficiency. The rules assigning property rights and determining liability, the procedures for resolving legal disputes, the constraints imposed on law enforcers, methods of computing damages and determining the availability of injunctive relief—these and other important elements of the legal system can best be understood as attempts, though rarely acknowledged as such, to promote an efficient allocation of resources.

. . . .

A third important finding in the law and economics literature is that economic analysis can be helpful in designing reforms of the legal system. . . . For example, while civil procedure reveals many economizing features, the failure to require the losing party to a lawsuit to reimburse the winner for his litigation expense appears to be highly inefficient, and no economic explanation for this settled feature of American procedure has been suggested or is apparent.

Legal Realism (Positivism)   Standing apart somewhat from the traditional philosophies of law and government and the analyses of social science, a final, practical-minded approach to the law is found in the analysis of **legal realism.** This simple school says that all we can be concerned about when we begin to analyze the law is a description of the law itself.

Oliver Wendell Holmes
"The Path of the Law"*

If you want to know the law and nothing else, you must look at it as a bad man, who cares only for the material consequences which such knowledge enables him to predict, not as a good one, who finds his reasons for conduct, whether inside the law or outside of it, in the vaguer sanctions of conscience. . . . Take the fundamental question: What constitutes the law? You will find some text writers telling you that it is something different from what is decided by the courts of Massachusetts or England, that it is a system of reason, that it is a deduction from principles of ethics or admitted axioms or what not, which may or may not coincide with the decisions. But, if we take the view of our friend the bad man, we shall find that he does not care two straws for the axioms or deductions but that he does want to know what the Massachusetts or English courts are

---

*10 *Harvard Law Review* (1897): 809.

likely to do in fact. I am much of his mind. The prophecies of what the courts will do in fact, and nothing more pretentious, are what I mean by the law.

Legal Philosophy and the Choice of Political Systems

While the issues of political and legal philosophy may seem dull and dry to the businesslike and utilitarian student, the choice of philosophy and the issues raised by those competing philosophies have been the cause of wars and revolutions, and even today dictate our choice of government and even the content of statutes in our system of government.

American government is generally considered to be *republican* in form, that is, a government by representatives chosen by the people. In strict terms, a republican form of government is different from a *democracy*, in which the legislative assembly consists of all of the people, as in a New England town meeting where the laws are made at a meeting of all of the citizens. Such forms are necessary if we adopt some form of natural rights theory of government, in which the rulers govern by the consent of the governed.

If our philosophy is closer to some form of divine rights theory, then in all likelihood we would choose a *monarchy* or *aristocracy*, ruled by some king or queen chosen by heredity and, ultimately, by God. Hobbesian thought often logically leads to some form of *authoritarian* or *autocratic* state, such as a *dictatorship*, ruled by one all-powerful ruler, or an *oligarchy*, or government run by a few persons. Such states are also often termed *totalitarian* states, in which there are no limits on governmental authority. The opposite of totalitarianism is *anarchy*, or the complete absence of government. Somewhere in between lie *pluralistic* states, where government exists but is limited. Crises in world history, such as the American and French Revolutions, the English "Glorious Revolution," the Russian Revolution of 1917, and even the Second World War were fundamentally conflicts between competing legal and political philosophies. Such philosophies also determine to a large extent the method by which government is organized, how representatives are chosen, the manner of making laws, and ultimately the issue of whether a government and its laws are considered legitimate by the people it governs.

Origins and Classifications of Law

Philosophical notions aside, lawyers, judges, and scholars have arrived at several classification schemes for law. These classification schemes are important both to describe the law and to analyze it.

"Law" by Its Origins

First, to dispel some cracker-barrel philosophy, the law is *not* a set of nice neat rules found written in a book somewhere. "The law" is found in written form in constitutions, treaties, statutes, case law, and administrative regulations. In the American legal system there is no such thing as an "unwritten law."

Before describing the various origins of law, it is perhaps helpful to remember Holmes' definition previously quoted in "The Path of the Law": "The prophecies of what the courts will do in fact, and nothing more pretentious, are what I mean by the law." In other words, though a law may be written down as a statute, constitutional provision, treaty, or administrative regulation, a great deal depends on how and whether that provision is enforced by the courts. According to that view, an unenforced law is no law at all, and quaint laws forbidding, as one municipal ordinance does, "walking a hippopotamus down a wooden sidewalk after noon on Sundays," are curiosities but not laws.

Perhaps more importantly, it is up to the courts to finally *interpret* the law. Before a judge can enforce a law, he must decide what it means, and it is that interpretation of the written law which finally becomes "the law." All the rest—the constitutions, treaties, statutes, administrative regulations, and even decisions by higher courts—are *guides* to the judges' decisions as to what the law is. Under Holmes' view, it is only what that judge does that is the law. We will consider the nature of judicial interpretation and case precedent further on in this chapter.

The classification of law by its origins then is really a consideration of the various places where one might look to determine what a court will probably do. It is, in Holmes' view, a prediction of the probable outcome of a case. Sometimes that prediction is very easy to make; other times that prediction is extremely difficult and complex.

Constitutions A constitution is a charter of government that expresses both the powers of government and the limits on the exercise of that power. *The Constitution* commonly refers to the federal constitution of 1789 and the 26 amendments enacted since that date. But each state also has its own constitution, which is law in that state.

It is also important to realize that the federal Constitution establishes a pecking order among the various laws. The so-called *supremacy clause* of the Constitution (Article VI, Section 2) provides that "[t]his Constitution . . . shall be the Supreme Law of the Land."

Treaties While not commonly recognized as law, treaties between the United States and foreign governments have the binding force of law and bind the citizens of the United States to live by such agreements as well.

Statutes Legislation duly enacted by either the federal Congress, state legislatures, or even local legislative bodies such as city councils or county boards are clearly law. These enactments are usually set out in list or book form as statutes.

Case Law Judicial decisions written in opinion form and referred to by subsequent courts are "law" just as much as constitutions, treaties, or statutes. These decisions either interpret statutes, treaties, or constitutional provisions, or they state what the law is if there is no statute or constitutional provision. This latter type of decision has created the **common law,** or law by judicial decision. For example, there is usually no statute that provides the elements of a binding contract. Yet for centuries the courts of England and the United States have recognized the elements of a contract, and such recognition and decisions incorporating it are binding upon the citizens of both countries. This judicially created law, whether interpretive or common law, is binding under the principles of **stare decisis,** the ancient rule that states that a judge is bound to follow the written decisions of appellate courts in identical cases (see p. 17).

Administrative Regulations   The newest form of law involves administrative regulations and rules that are created by administrative agencies. Such agencies are created by the legislature through statutes, and the authority to make regulations is delegated to the agency by the legislature. In the strictest sense, such regulations are not considered law but rather are *rules*. But since such rules contain sanctions and are enforceable by the courts, they belong in any list of the origins of law. One form of administrative regulation is the executive order, or a proclamation by the President or executive officer. Such orders are generally given under authority delegated by the legislature to the President or executive officer.

Procedural and Substantive Law

Procedural law tells us the rules of the game. Court rules and procedures including issues of venue, jurisdiction, filing requirements, time limits, and discovery rules make up procedural law. **Substantive law** includes those parts of the law that create, define, and regulate the rights of parties in legal proceedings.

Principal Areas of Substantive Law   Substantive law can be divided into two principal areas: **private law,** which deals with the relations between individuals, including corporations and the government as a private party; and **public law,** which deals with the relations between the individual and the state. The former would include such areas as contracts, agency, torts, corporations, business organizations, bailments, and real property. The latter includes Constitutional law, administrative law, and criminal law. Issues concerning the government's regulation of business generally involve the areas of public law, but the regulations may well affect areas of private law as, for example, a zoning regulation that restricts the use and sale of private real estate.

Legal Remedies

The purpose of any lawsuit, whether civil or criminal, is to redress some grievance. The injured party, which may be an individual or the state or federal government, asks the court to grant some remedy or sanction against the party that allegedly committed some wrong. Often those remedies may seem very inadequate in view of the wrong committed, as in the case of a person claiming a money award for wrongful death or for the loss of a limb, but the law is limited in the types of remedies available to injured parties.

In **civil cases,** or actions between private persons including those in which the government acts as a private person, two basic remedies are available. The first and most common remedy is **damages,** or the payment of a sum of money from the wrongdoer to the injured party. Damages are of three basic forms. **Nominal damages,** or damages in name only, are awarded if the wrongdoer has violated a right of the other party, but caused no injury. For example, if someone walked across your lawn, you would be entitled to nominal damages in the amount of one dollar and court costs for the technical trespass to land. **Compensatory damages** are meant to compensate the injured party for his or her loss. The judge or jury must determine the value of the loss to the injured party and give judgment in that amount. Compensatory damage claims are by far the most common type of lawsuit. **Punitive damages** are damages in excess of the plaintiff's actual loss, granted to punish the wrongdoer for an intentional or malicious act.

The second form of civil remedy is **equitable relief.** Equitable relief takes the form of a court order, requiring a person to do, or not to do, a particular act. A general form of equitable relief is an **injunction,** which forbids a person from doing a certain act, while the more rare **mandatory injunction** requires a person to affirmatively perform an act. Another common form of equitable relief is **specific performance,** which is a court order requiring a person to comply with the exact terms of a contract. Such court orders are enforced through contempt of court proceedings, and the person who violates such an order may be jailed or fined for failure to comply.

Criminal cases are brought by the state or federal government against an individual who has injured the public at large. Criminal cases are very different from civil cases in procedure, burden of proof, and rules of evidence. A person who is found guilty of a criminal offense may be fined, imprisoned or, in a few cases, put to death.

All of the above remedies are sometimes available in cases involving government regulation. For example, the antitrust laws provide criminal penalties against individuals or corporations that violate those statutes, injunctive relief to stop future violations and order changes in corporate structure, and civil damages in favor of injured persons. In fact, those damages may take the form of **treble damages,** a unique form of punitive damages, which give the injured party three times the actual loss. Usually regulatory statutes provide for some type of injunctive relief, but often that relief is known by some other name, such as **cease and desist orders.** More rarely the regulatory statutes permit fines and civil damages. Imprisonment may not be ordered by an administrative agency.

The Doctrine of *Stare Decisis*

American courts generally follow the doctrine of *stare decisis,* which literally means *look to the decided cases.* That doctrine, also known as the rule of **precedent,** means that lower courts are generally required to follow the decisions of higher courts in similar cases. Thus, a trial court in State A is bound to follow the decisions of the State Supreme Court in that state, and is also bound to follow the decisions of the United States Supreme Court when the decisions of that court apply to State A. The only way the decision can be changed is for the appellate court that made the prior decision to change its mind, or for an even higher appellate court to make a contrary decision. The trial court is not bound if the new case is different in its essential facts (distinguishable) from the precedent, nor is the trial court bound by **dicta,** or gratuitous statements in a decision that are unnecessary to the final result of the case.

Judges are bound to follow precedent only by tradition and to some extent by codes of judicial ethics. Judges can, and often do, depart from precedent in proper cases: Judges may depart from precedent if the precedent is old, or if the reasoning of the court that provided the precedent was poor, or if justice would not be served. Sometimes trial judges do so for the conscious purpose of forcing an appeal of a case that is covered by a precedent the court finds singularly bad.

As more fully discussed in Chapter 6, there are no statutes to guide the courts in many areas of the law, including such important areas as contracts, torts, agency, and property. It has been through the slowly evolving law of *stare decisis* that much of the law has been formed over the centuries. That law is generally referred to as the **common law.** The common law is of course just as binding as any statute, since in the final analysis it is what judges do that determines the nature of the law. The following decision illustrates both the concept of *stare decisis* and the nature of the common law.

Flagiello v. The Pennsylvania Hospital

417 Pa. 486, 208 A. 2d 193 (1965)

Mary Flagiello was a paying patient in The Pennsylvania Hospital, a charitable institution. Through the negligence of two employees of the hospital, she was caused to fall and fracture her ankle. That injury in turn caused a longer hospital stay and more hospital expenses. Mrs. Flagiello and her husband (sometimes called **plaintiffs** in the decision) brought suit for their loss against the hospital and the two employees who allegedly caused the injury. The Hospital (sometimes called **defendant** in the decision) claimed that it was not responsible for the injuries on the basis of an ancient common-law doctrine called *charitable immunity*. That doctrine provides that charitable (eleemosynary) institutions are immune from suit for their own negligence or the negligence of their employees. The trial court dismissed the complaint filed by the Flagiellos, and the Flagiellos appealed the decision to the Pennsylvania Supreme Court.

MUSMANNO, Justice

. . . .

The hospital has not denied that its negligence caused Mrs. Flagiello's injuries. It merely announces that it is an eleemosynary institution, and, therefore, owed no duty of care to its patient. It declares in effect that it can do wrong and still not be liable in damages to the person it has wronged. It thus urges a momentous exception to the generic proposition that in law there is no wrong without a remedy. From the earliest days of organized society it became apparent that society could never become a success unless the collectivity of mankind guaranteed to every member of society a remedy for a palpable wrong inflicted on him by another member of that society. In 1844 Justice Storrs of the Supreme Court of Connecticut crystallized into epigrammatic language that wise concept, as follows: "An injury is a wrong; and for the redress of every wrong there is a remedy: a wrong is a violation of one's right; and for the vindication of every right there is a remedy."

. . . .

On what basis then, may a hospital, which expects and receives compensation for its services, demand of the law that it be excused from responding in damages for injuries tortiously inflicted by its employees on paying patients? There is not a person or establishment in all civilization that is not required to meet his or its financial obligations, there is not a person or establishment that is not called upon by the law to render an accounting for harm visited by him or it on innocent victims. By what line of reasoning, then, can any institution, operating commercially, expect the law to insulate it from its debts?

The hospital in this case . . . replies to that question with various answers, some of which are: it is an ancient rule that charitable hospitals have never been required to recompense patients who have been injured through the negligence of their employees; the rule of *stare decisis* forbids that charitable hospitals be held liable . . .; if the rule of charitable immunity is to be discarded, this must be done by the State Legislature; and that since hospitals serve the public, there is involved here a matter of public policy which is not within the jurisdiction of the courts.

. . . .

Whatever Mrs. Flagiello received in the Pennsylvania Hospital was not bestowed on her gratuitously. She paid $24.50 a day for the services she was to receive. And she paid this amount not only for the period she was to remain in the hospital to be cured of the ailment with which she entered the hospital, but she had to continue to pay that rate for the period she was compelled to remain in the hospital as a result of injuries caused by the hospital itself.

. . . .

To say that a person who pays for what he receives is still the object of charity is a self-contradiction in terms. In the early days of public accomodation for the ill and the maimed, charity was exercised in its pure and pristine sense. Many good men and women, liberal in purse and generous in soul, set up houses to heal the poor and homeless victims of disease and injury. The made no charge for this care. . . . The wealthy and the so-called middle class were treated in their homes where usually there could be found better facilities than could be had in the hospitals. . . . Charity in the biblical sense prevailed.

Whatever the law may have been regarding charitable institutions in the past, it does not meet the conditions of today. . . . Hospitals today are growing into mighty edifices in brick, stone, glass and marble. many of them maintain large staffs, they use the best equipment that science can devise, they utilize the most modern methods in devoting themselves to the noblest purpose of man, that of helping one's stricken brother. But they do all this on a business basis, submitting invoices for services rendered—and properly so.

And if a hospital functions as a business institution, by charging and receiving money for what it offers, it must be a business establishment also in meeting obligations it incurs in running that establishment. One of those inescapable obligations is that is must exercise a proper degree of care for its patients, and, to the extent that it fails in that care, it should be liable in damages as any other commercial firm would be liable. . . .

If there was any justification for the charitable immunity doctrine when it was first announced, it has lost that justification today.

. . . .

But, conceding that it could not operate without its paying patients, . . . the defendant still objects to being categorized with business establishments because, it says, the law of charitable immunity is so deeply imbedded in our law and is of such ancient origin that it can only be extirpated by legislative enactment. Leaving aside the fallacy that antiquity *ipso facto* bespeaks correctness or justice, how ancient is the rule of charitable immunity? And how did the rule ever become law in Pennsylvania?

Each court which has upheld the immunity rule has relied for its authority on a previous decision or decisions, scarcely ever placing the subject for study on the table of self-asserting justice. . . . Despite the claims of the supporters of the immunity rule that it is an ancient one, it did not really break through the crust of Pennsylvania's jurisprudence until 1888 in the case of *Fire Insurance Patrol* v. *Boyd*. . . . In that case, Justice Paxson said that the charitable immunity rule "is hoary with antiquity and prevails alike in this country and in England." In support of this assertion he cited the case of *Feoffees of Heriot's Hospital* v. *Ross* . . . decided in 1846, which had rested on *Duncan* v. *Findlater,* decided in 1839. [An English decision.]

. . . .

The appellee [Hospital] . . . insist[s] that if the charity immunity doctrine is to undergo mutation, the only surgeon capable of performing the operation is the Legislature. We have seen, however, that the controverted rule is not the creation of the Legislature. This Court fashioned it, and, what it put together, it can dismantle.

. . . .

Failing to hold back both the overwhelming reasons of rudimentary justice for abolishing the doctrine, and the rising tide of out-of-state repudiation of the doctrine, the defendant Hospital . . . fall[s] back for defense to the bastion of *Stare Decisis*. It is inevitable and proper that they should do so. Without *stare decisis,* there would be no stability in our system of jurisprudence.

Stare decisis channels the law. It erects lighthouses and flys the signals of safety. The ships of jurisprudence must follow that well-defined channel which, over the years, has been proved to be secure and trustworthy. But it would not comport with wisdom to insist that, should the shoals rise in a heretofore safe course and rocks emerge to encumber the passage, the ship should nonetheless pursue the original course, merely because it presented no hazard in the past. The principle of stare decisis does not demand that we follow precedents which shipwreck justice.

Stare decisis is not an iron mold into which every utterance by a Court—regardless of circumstances, parties, economic barometer and sociological climate—must be poured, and, where, like wet concrete, it must acquire an unyielding rigidity which nothing later can change.

. . . .

The history of law through the ages records numerous inequities pronounced by courts because the society of the day sanctioned them. Reason revolts, humanity shudders, and justice recoils before much of what was done in the past under the name of law. Yet, we are urged to retain a forbidden incongruity in the law simply because it is old. That kind of reasoning would have retained prosecution for witchcraft, imprisonment for debt and hanging for minor offenses which today are hardly regarded misdemeanors.

There is nothing in the records of the courts, the biographies of great jurists, or the writings of eminent legal authorities which offers the slightest encouragement to the notion that time petrifies into unchanging jurisprudence a palpable fallacy. As years can give no sturdiness to a decayed tree, so the passing decades can add no convincing flavor to the withered apple of sophistry clinging to the limb of demonstrated wrong. There are, of course, principles and precepts sanctified by age, and no one would think of changing them, but their inviolability derives not from longevity but from their universal appeal to the reason, the conscience and the experience of mankind. No one, for instance, would think of challenging what was written in Magna Charta, the Habeus Corpus Act or the Bill of Rights of the Constitution of the United States. . . .

While age adds venerableness to moral principles and some physical objects, it occasionally becomes necessary, and it is not sacrilegious to do so, to scrape away the moss of the years to study closely the thing which is being accepted as authoritative, inviolable, and untouchable. The Supreme Court of Michigan said sagaciously in the case of *Williams* v. *City of Detroit* . . . that:

> it is the peculiar genius of the common law that no legal rule is mandated by the doctrine of *stare decisis* when that rule was conceived in error or when the times and circumstances have so changed as to render it an instrument of injustice.

The charitable immunity rule proves itself an instrument of injustice and nothing presented by the defendant . . . shows it to be otherwise. . . .

A rule that has become insolvent has no place in the active market of current enterprise. When a rule offends against reason, when it is at odds with every precept of natural justice, and when it cannot be defended on its own merits, but has to depend alone on a discredited geneology, courts not only possess the inherent power to repudiate, but, indeed, it is required, by the very nature of judicial function, to abolish such a rule.

. . . .

Of course, the precedents here recalled do not justify a light and casual treatment of the doctrine of *stare decisis,* but they proclaim unequivocally that where justice demands, reason dictates, equality enjoins and fair play decrees a change in judge-made law, courts will not lack in determination to establish that change.

. . . .

The judgments of the Court below are reversed. . . .*

Statutory Interpretation and *Stare Decisis*

Even when there is a statute, administrative regulation, or constitutional provision directly on point, the courts must often step in to interpret and "flesh out" the meaning of the words in the statute. This need for interpretation is often difficult for laypersons to grasp, especially those who have not had occasion to wrestle with the intricacies of the English language. Words, even commonly used words, often have several meanings, and the precise meaning given to a word or phrase may make a great deal of difference in a crucial case. Various phrases in the U.S. Constitution, such as "freedom of speech," "due process," "Commerce . . . among the several States," and "equal protection of the laws," are particularly subject to interpretation because of their breadth and vagueness. A great many of the cases in this text involve an issue of construction of some statute or constitutional provision.

While the courts have a great deal of latitude in interpreting the words of statutes, constitutional provisions, and administrative regulations, there are a great many "rules of construction," often devised by the courts themselves, to aid the courts in interpreting legislative acts. It is often said that the goal of all statutory construction is to find *"the intent of the legislature,"* or, in the case of the federal Constitution, *"the intent of the Framers,"* and give effect to that intent. Sometimes that intent is easy to determine, particularly if the legislature discloses its intent right in the statute (see, e.g., Section 1b of the National Labor Relations Act, Appendix C), or if the legislative record contains statements of the legislature's intent. But often such help is not available, and the courts must rely on other "rules of construction" to determine the true intent of the legislature.

The so-called golden rule of statutory construction is that the words of a statute should be given their *plain and natural meaning* unless injustice or an absurd result would follow. Other rules require that statutes be construed as *valid and constitutional,* that criminal statutes are to be construed *strictly against the prosecution,* and statutes that *change the common law* are to be interpreted *narrowly.* On the other side of the coin, *remedial statutes* are to be interpreted *liberally.*

Similarly, there are a great many rules for interpreting the specific meaning of particular words or phrases. For example, the principle of *ejusdem generis* holds that the meaning of a general term in a list of terms is taken from the specific terms that precede it. Thus, if a statute lists "deer, bear, wolf, or other large mammal," a whale

---

*Students are invited to turn to *Nolan* v. *Tifereth Israel Synagogue of Mt. Carmel,* p. 109, for developments after *Flagiello* was decided.

might be excluded since the term "other large mammal" takes its meaning from the three specific terms which precede it, and thus would probably be held to mean "four-legged, large, land animal."

When a court interprets a constitutional provision, statute, or administrative regulation, generally that interpretation has the same status in the law as the provision interpreted and, thus, becomes a part of the law. Thus, if the Supreme Court interprets a provision of the U.S. Constitution, the Court's interpretation in effect becomes a part of the Constitution until either the Constitution is amended or the Court changes its mind. If Congress were to pass a statute declaring the Court's interpretation unlawful, that statute would be on no effect, since the Court's decision had the status of the Constitution itself. The statute itself would be subject to judicial interpretation as well, and the courts would have the right to declare that statute unconstitutional under the doctrine of **judicial review.**

The Doctrine of Judicial Review

The source of all governmental authority and power in the United States is the federal Constitution or, more precisely, the people. The Framers of the Constitution, imbued in the theory of natural rights, met as representatives of the people in a Constitutional Convention in 1787. Those representatives then created a federal government, granted that government very specific powers to rule, and placed certain limitations on the privilege of ruling.

The full nature of the American Constitution and its legal impact will be explored in Chapters 2 and 3. Before we begin that discussion, it may be helpful to consider one of the principal "unwritten" provisions of the federal Constitution, the doctrine of **judicial review.** Judicial review is one of our essential tools throughout the rest of this text, and it seems appropriate that we treat it early.

The federal Constitution grants specific powers to all three branches of government—the executive, legislative, and judicial—and provides a variety of well-known "checks and balances" on the authority of each branch. One of the most important limitations on the power of any branch is the concept of **granted powers;** that is, Congress, the President, and the Courts may only do those things which are specifically authorized by the Constitution. The Necessary and Proper Clause (Article I, Section 8, clause 18) provides in addition that Congress may also make laws that are "necessary and proper for carrying into Execution" its granted powers. Those powers, both express and implied through the Necessary and Proper Clause, are limited by the Bill of Rights and other express limitations on power found scattered throughout the Constitution. In other words, the power of the federal government, and of its branches, is *limited,* both by the grants of power and by express limitations found in the Constitution.

It is one thing to make a law, and quite another to enforce it. While the Constitution clearly limits the authority of government to act in many ways, as for example in the entire Bill of Rights, nowhere does the document state what happens if government goes beyond those limits. Some, such as Andrew Jackson, believed that each branch of government should oversee itself, and seemed to believe that no single branch, such as the judiciary, had the right to tell another branch what to do. In Jackson's view, each branch of government was coequal.

For a period of fourteen years after the ratification of the Constitution in 1789, there was no fixed plan to deal with occasions when the government went too far. The Constitution itself was silent on the matter, but in 1803 Chief Justice John Marshall "found" the right of judicial review in the Constitution in the following momentous decision.

Marbury v. Madison

5 U.S. (1 Cranch) 137, 2 L. Ed. 60 (1803)

The election of 1800 was a bitter contest between the Federalist Party, and their incumbent President John Adams, and the upstart Democratic-Republicans and their candidate, Thomas Jefferson. The Federalists lost the election badly, losing the Presidency and control of both Houses of Congress. Adams and the "lame duck" Federalist Congress resolved to retain as much political power as possible during the next few years by appointing as many Federalists as possible to government positions, especially the judiciary. One of these appointments was John Marshall, who, though Jefferson's cousin, was his political arch-rival.

The lame duck Congress also created a large number of new federal judgeships including 42 justices of the peace for the District of Columbia. Adams nominated Federalists, including William Marbury, for these posts, and the Senate was required to advise and consent to the appointments. The appointments were received from the Senate at a late hour, and Adams stayed up much of the night before Jefferson's inauguration signing the appointments. As a result, those appointed were called the *Midnight Judges*. Arguably, the commissions had to be "delivered" to the persons nominated to complete the appointment process, and Chief Justice Marshall's brother James spent much of the night of March 3 travelling the streets of Washington delivering commissions. James Marshall did not finish his task, however, and a few commissions, including that of Marbury, remained undelivered when Jefferson was sworn in.

James Madison, Jefferson's Secretary of State, refused to deliver the rest of the commissions. Under a provision of a federal law passed in 1789, suit could be brought directly in the Supreme Court of the United States to force a public officer to do his duty. Marbury brought suit against Madison directly before the all-Federalist Supreme Court, and Chief Justice Marshall wrote the opinion. The decision surprised both Federalists and Democrat-Republicans. The issue was whether the 1789 law that gave the Supreme Court the power to hear such cases conformed to the mandate of Article III of the Constitution, which set the limits of jurisdiction of the Supreme Court. Marshall decided that it did not, and then the question became whether the Supreme Court had the authority to rule that law unconstitutional and void.

> [T]he following opinion of the court was delivered by the Chief Justice [MARSHALL]. . . .
> The question, whether an act, repugnant to the constitution, can become the law of the land, is a question deeply interesting to the United States; but, happily, not of intricacy proportioned to its interest. It seems only necessary to recognise certain principles, supposed to have been long and well established, to decide it. . . .
> [The] original and supreme will organizes the government and assigns to different departments their respective powers. It may either stop here, or establish certain limits not to be transcended by those departments. The government of the United States is of the latter description. The powers of the legislature are defined and limited; and that those limits may not be mistaken or forgotten, the constitution is written. To what purpose are powers limited, and to what purpose is that limitation committed to writing, if these limits may, at any time, be passed by those intended to be restrained? The dis-

tinction between a government with limited and unlimited powers is abolished, if those limits do not confine the persons on whom they are imposed. . . . It is a proposition too plain to be contested, that the constitution controls any legislative act repugnant to it. . . .

. . . .

Certainly, all those who have framed written constitutions contemplate them as forming the fundamental and paramount law of the nation, and consequently, the theory of every such government must be, that an act of the legislature, repugnant to the constitution, is void. . . .

. . . .

If an act of the legislature, repugnant to the constitution, is void, does it, notwithstanding its invalidity, bind the courts, and oblige them to give it effect? Or, in other words, though it be not law, does it constitute a rule as operative as if it was a law? This would be to overthrow, in fact, what was established in theory; and would seem, at first view, an absurdity too gross to be insisted on. . . .

It is emphatically, the province and duty of the judicial department, to say what the law is. Those who apply the rule to particular cases, must of necessity expound and interpret that rule. If two laws conflict with each other, the courts must decide on the operation of each. So, if a law be in opposition to the constitution; if both the law and the constitution apply to a particular case, so that the court must either decide that case, conformable to the law, disregarding the constitution; or conformable to the constitution, disregarding the law; the court must determine which of these conflicting rules governs the case: this is of the very essence of judicial duty.

. . . .

. . . [T]he peculiar expressions of the constitution of the United States furnish additional arguments in favor of [the proposition]. The judicial power of the United States is extended to all cases arising under the constitution. Could it be the intention of those who gave this power, to say, that in using it, the constitution should not be looked into? That a case arising under the constitution should be decided, without examining the instrument under which it arises? This is too extravagant to be maintained. . . .

There are many other parts of the constitution which serve to illustrate this subject. It is declared, that "no tax or duty shall be laid on articles exported from any state." Suppose, a duty on the export of cotton, or tobacco or of flour; and a suit instituted to recover it. Ought judgment to be rendered in such a case? Ought the judges to close their eyes on the constitution, and only see the law?

. . . .

From these, and many other selections which might be made, it is apparent, that the framers of the constitution contemplated that instrument as a rule for the government of courts, as well as of the legislature. Why otherwise does it direct the judges to take an oath to support it? . . . How immoral to impose it on them, if they were to be used as the instruments, and the knowing instruments, for violating what they swear to support!

. . . If such be the real state of things, this worse than solemn mockery. To prescribe, or to take this oath, becomes equally a crime.

It is also not entirely unworthy of observation, that in declaring what shall be the supreme law of the land, the constitution itself is first mentioned; and not the laws of the United States, generally, but those only which shall be made in pursuance of the constitution, have that rank.

Thus, the particular phraseology of the constitution of the United States confirms and strengthens the principle, supposed to be essential to all written constitutions, that a law repugnant to the constitution is void; and that courts, as well as other departments, are bound by that instrument.

The *Marbury* decision has been called a "legal and logical *tour de force*" since by giving up a little power, the Court assumed a great deal of power. The seemingly pro-Jefferson result gave the Court the right to oversee and void any act of Congress that it considered unconstitutional. The decision has also been called a usurpation of power by the Court, since the branches of government are coequal and the right of judicial review is not found expressly in the Constitution.

Judicial Review of State Court Decisions

But *Marbury* did not end the problems of judicial review. While the decision gave the Court the right to review acts of Congress, it did not speak to the issue of judicial review of state court actions. The problem was whether the United States Supreme Court had the authority to review and void decisions of state courts. State courts jealously guarded their own supremacy, and the issue was a major problem in the developing federalism of the new nation. The issue was not resolved until 1816 in a rather bizarre and provocative case.

Martin v. Hunter's Lessee

14 U.S. (1 Wheat.) 304, 4 L. Ed. 97 (1816)

During and after the Revolutionary War, many states, including Virginia, passed laws forfeiting the title to lands owned by British citizens to the state. Denny Martin (Lord Fairfax) was a British citizen who owned approximately 300,000 acres of prime Virginia land, known as the Northern Neck. That land was ostensibly forfeited by the State of Virginia under one such law, and a portion of the land was granted to David Hunter, who leased the land to another. But, as a result of the peace treaty with Great Britain that ended the revolutionary war in a technical sense in 1783, such forfeitures were barred. Martin filed suit in Virginia state court to have the lessee of the land ejected from the property. The case, which was originally filed in 1781, was delayed by the deaths of various parties, the War of 1812, and a variety of other problems. As might be expected, the Virginia Court of Appeals (state supreme court) held against Martin, and he appealed to the U.S. Supreme Court. Chief Justice Marshall excused himself from the case since he was a principal partner in the syndicate that had purchased much of the land from the State of Virginia. Another noted jurist, Justice Joseph Story, ruled that Virginia's forfeiture statute was in violation of the treaty and therefore void. The case was remanded to the Virginia court, where the court ruled that the U.S. Supreme Court did not have the power to tell them what to do. (In effect, saying that the decision of the U.S. Supreme Court was unconstitutional!) Martin, somewhat at a loss, returned to the Supreme Court. Justice Story wrote a second opinion on the case.

STORY, J., delivered the opinion of the Court.

If . . . it is a duty of Congress to vest the judicial power of the United States, it is a duty to vest the *whole judicial power*. . . .

On the whole, the court are of opinion, that the appellate power of the United States does not extend to cases pending in the state courts. . . . We find no clause in [the Constitution] which limits this power; and we dare not interpose a limitation where the people have not been disposed to create one.

Strong as this conclusion stands upon the general language of the constitution, it may still derive support from other sources. It is an historical fact, that this exposition of the constitution, extending its appellate power to state courts, was, previous to its adoption, uniformly and publicly avowed by its friends, and admitted by its enemies, as the basis of their respective reasonings, both in and out of the state conventions. It is an historical fact, that at the time when the judiciary act was submitted to the deliberations of the first congress, composed, as it was, not only of men of great learning and ability, but of men who had acted a principal part in framing, supporting, or opposing that constitution, the same exposition was explicitly declared and admitted by the friends and by the opponents of that system. It is an historical fact, that the supreme court of the United States have, from time to time, sustained this appellate jurisdiction in a great variety of cases, brought from the tribunals of many of the most important states in the union, and that no state tribunal has ever breathed a judicial doubt on the subject, or declined to obey the mandate of the supreme court, until the present occasion. This weight of contemporaneous exposition by all parties, this acquiescence of enlightened state courts, and these judicial decisions of the supreme court through so long a period, do, as we think, place the doctrine upon a foundation of authority which cannot be shaken, without delivering over the subject to perpetual and irremediable doubts.

Justice Joseph Story's reasoning carried the day, and the Virginia Court decided to follow the decision and mandate of the U.S. Supreme Court. Five years later, the Supreme Court enlarged and expanded upon the reasoning in *Cohens* v. *Virginia*.* It should be noted that the Constitution itself does not grant the Supreme Court any appellate jurisdiction over state court actions. That power comes from a part of the federal Judiciary Act of 1789, which granted the Court the right to hear such cases, though *Martin* v. *Hunter's Lessee* seems to rest on broader constitutional grounds as well.

Judicial Review of Actions of the President

It is generally accepted that the power of the President has grown enormously since 1789. Perhaps the main control over actions of the President is the same power of judicial review that controls actions of Congress and the states. The following decision illustrates the breadth of the doctrine of judicial review in the context of a crisis in both domestic and foreign policy.

Youngstown Sheet & Tube Co. v. Sawyer

342 U.S. 579, 72 S. Ct. 863, 96 L. Ed. 1153 (1952)

In 1951, during the Korean War, a labor dispute arose between the United Steelworkers of America and the steel companies. Federal mediators were called in to no avail, and a strike was set for April 9, 1952. Though President Truman was convinced the strike would harm the war effort immensely, he was unwilling to use the Taft-Hartley Act,** which had been passed over his veto. On April 8, 1952, Truman ordered Secretary of Commerce Sawyer to seize the affected steel mills, which he did. The steel companies filed suit against Sawyer, claiming that the President had acted without constitutional authority. The district court ruled against the President and issued an injunction ordering the President to return the mills to private

---

*19 U.S. (6 Wheat.) 264, 5 L. Ed. 257 (1821). That case involved a state court prosecution of two Virginia citizens for selling District of Columbia lottery tickets in Virginia. Virginia had claimed that the U.S. Supreme Court had no authority to review the conviction. The Supreme Court disagreed on grounds similar to *Martin* v. *Hunter's Lessee.*

**See Chapter 13, p. 480.

control. Through a series of extraordinary maneuvers, the case was heard by the Supreme Court on May 27, only six weeks after the seizure.

    Mr. Justice BLACK delivered the opinion of the Court.
    . . . [I]s the seizure order within the constitutional power of the President?
    . . . .

    The President's power, if any, to issue the order must stem either from an act of Congress or from the Constitution itself. There is no statute that expressly authorizes the President to take possession of property as he did here. Nor is there any act of Congress to which our attention has been directed from which such a power can fairly be implied. . . .

    It is clear that if the President had authority to issue the order he did, it must be found in some provisions of the Constitution. And it is not claimed that express constitutional language grants this power to the President. The contention is that presidential power should be implied from the aggregate of his powers under the Constitution. Particular reliance is placed on provisions in Article II which say that "the executive Power shall be vested in a President. . . ."; that "he shall take Care that the Laws be faithfully executed"; and that he "shall be Commander in Chief of the Army and Navy of the United States."

    The order cannot properly be sustained as an exercise of the President's military power as Commander-in-Chief of the Armed Forces. The Government attempts to do so by citing a number of cases upholding broad powers in military commanders engaged in day-to-day fighting in a theater of war. Such cases need not concern us here. Even though "theater of war" be an expanding concept, we cannot with faithfulness to our constitutional system hold that the Commander-in-Chief of the Armed forces has the ultimate power as such to take possession of private property in order to keep labor disputes from stopping production. This is a job for the Nation's lawmakers, not for its military authorities.

    Nor can the seizure order be sustained because of the several constitutional provisions that grant executive power to the President. In the framework of our Constitution, the President's power to see that the laws are faithfully executed refutes the idea that he is to be a lawmaker. . . .

    The Founders of this Nation entrusted the lawmaking power to the Congress alone in both good and bad times. It would do no good to recall the historical events, the fears of power and the hopes for freedom that lay behind their choice. Such a review would but confirm our holding that this seizure order cannot stand.
    The judgment of the District Court is
    Affirmed

The Secretary of Commerce withdrew his control in compliance with the Court's order. Immediately, a strike began that was to shut down the steel mills for 53 days. President Truman requested authority to act from Congress, which did nothing. Truman continued to refuse to use the Taft-Hartley Act, discussed in Chapter 13, since he felt the imposition of an 80-day "cooling off period" would simply "prolong the agony" without supplying a meaningful solution. Finally, on July 24, Truman called representatives of both sides to the White House, and by the end of the day had personally hammered out a settlement.

    While almost every decision of the Supreme Court involves the doctrine of judicial review, the greatest illustrations of the concept come in so-called *constitutional crises,* when the three branches of government are involved in power struggles of one kind or another. Such a power struggle occured in the early 1970's when the Watergate controversy burst upon the American scene.

U.S. v. Nixon

418 U.S. 683, 94 S. Ct. 3090, 41 L. Ed. 2d 1039 (1974)

During the 1972 presidential election, several men were found inside Democratic National Headquarters at the Watergate complex in Washington late one night. Some of the men had ties with people involved in the campaign to reelect President Nixon, and a thorough investigation was launched. On March 1, 1974, seven men, including the former Attorney General (Mitchell), were indicted by a federal grand jury on charges of obstruction of justice based on the alleged cover-up of the affair.

During Senate hearings the preceding year, information had been received that the President had recorded most or all of the conversations that occurred in the White House. The Special Prosecutor felt those tapes would be most helpful in proving his case against the seven. As a result, he asked federal judge John Sirica to issue a *subpoena duces tecum* to the President for the tapes. (A *subpoena duces tecum* is a court order, requiring an individual to bring physical evidence to court.) The President refused to forward the tapes, and moved to "quash" the subpoena on the grounds of executive privilege. Judge Sirica refused to quash the subpoena, and the President appealed the case to the Supreme Court. Chief Justice Burger, himself a Nixon appointee, delivered the opinion.

Mr. Chief Justice BURGER delivered the opinion of the Court.

[W]e turn to the claim that the subpoena should be quashed because it demands "confidential conversations between a President and his close advisors that it would be inconsistent with the public interest to produce." . . . The first contention is a broad claim that the separation of powers doctrine precludes judicial review of a President's claim of privilege. The second contention is that if he does not prevail on the claim of absolute privilege, the court should hold as a matter of constitutional law that the privilege prevails over the subpoena *duces tecum.*

In the performance of assigned constitutional duties each branch of the Government must initially interpret the Constitution, and the interpretation of its powers by any branch is due great respect from the others. The President's counsel, as we have noted, reads the Constitution as providing an absolute privilege of confidentiality for all presidential communications. Many decisions of this Court, however, have unequivocally reaffirmed the holding of *Marbury* v. *Madison* . . . that "it is emphatically the province and duty of the judicial department to say what the law is . . ."

. . . .

Our system of government "requires that federal courts on occasion interpret the Constitution in a manner at variance with the construction given the document by another branch. . . ." [D]eciding whether a matter has in any measure been committed to another branch of government, or whether the action of that branch exceeds whatever authority has been committed, is itself a delicate exercise in constitutional interpretation, and is a responsibility of the Court as ultimate interpreter of the Constitution.

Notwithstanding the deference each branch must accord the others, the "judicial power of the United States" . . . can no more be shared with the Executive Branch than the Chief Executive, for example, can share with the Judiciary the veto power, or the Congress share with the Judiciary the power to override a presidential veto. Any other conclusion would be contrary to the basic concept of separation of powers and the checks and balances that flow from the scheme of a tripartite government. . . . We therefore reaffirm that it is "emphatically the province and duty" of this Court "to say what the law is" with respect to the claim of privilege presented in this case.

. . . .

In support of his claim of absolute privilege, the President's counsel urges two grounds, one of which is common to all governments and one of which is peculiar to our system of separation of powers. The first ground is the valid need for protection of communications between high government officials and those who advise and assist them in the performance of their manifold duties: the importance of this confidentiality is too plain to require further discussion. Human experience teaches that those who expect public dissemination of their remarks may well temper candor with a concern for appearances and for their own interests to the detriment of the decision-making process. . . .

The second ground asserted by the President's counsel in support of the claim of absolute privilege rests on the doctrine of separation of powers. Here it is argued that the independence of the Executive Branch within its own sphere . . . insulates a president from a judicial subpoena in an ongoing criminal prosecution, and thereby protects confidential presidential communications.

However, neither the doctrine of separation of powers, nor the need for confidentiality of high level communications, without more, can sustain an absolute, unqualified presidential privilege of immunity from judicial process under all circumstances. The President's need for complete candor and objectivity from advisers calls for great deference from the courts. However, when the privilege depends solely on the broad, undifferentiated claim of public interest in the confidentiality of such conversations, a confrontation with other values arises. Absent a claim to protect military, diplomatic or sensitive national security secrets, we find it difficult to accept the argument that even the very important interest in confidentiality of presidential communications is significantly diminished by production of such material for _in camera_ inspection with all the protection that a district court will be obliged to provide.

The impediment that an absolute, unqualified privilege would place in the way of the primary constitutional duty of the Judicial Branch to do justice in criminal prosecutions would plainly conflict with the function of the courts . . . In designing the structure of our Government and dividing and allocating the sovereign power among three coequal branches, the Framers of the Constitution sought to provide a comprehensive system, but the separate powers were not intended to operate with absolute independence.

"While the Constitution diffuses power the better to secure liberty, it also contemplates that practice will integrate the dispersed powers into a workable government. It enjoins upon its branches separateness but interdependence." _Youngstown Sheet and Tube Co._ v. _Sawyer,_ . . . (JACKSON, J., concurring.)

To read the . . . powers of the President as providing an absolute privilege as against a subpoena essential to enforcement of criminal statutes on no more than a generalized claim of the public interest in confidentiality of nonmilitary and nondiplomatic discussions would upset the constitutional balance of "a workable government" and gravely impair the role of the courts. . . .

The court ordered the President to turn over the tapes for an _in camera_ inspection by the trial judge. An _in camera_ inspection is one conducted in private by the judge alone, to see if there are matters of actual privilege in the tapes. The decision was rendered on July 24, 1974. Three days later, before the tapes were all released by the White House, the House Judiciary Committee recommended impeachment of the President, which would require a trial before the Senate. On August 5, 1974, the tapes were released, and those tapes indicated a deep involvement on the part of the President in the cover-up conspiracy. On August 8, President Nixon announced that he would resign effective at noon the following day. A commentator felt that an old Roman aphorism was appropriate to the occasion: _Fiat justitia, ruat coelum,_ which means 'Let Justice be done, though the heavens fall.'*

*Theodore H. White, _Breach of Faith_ (New York: Atheneum, Dell Edition, 1975) p. 13.

The "Styles" of Judicial Review

While almost all would agree that the courts should have the right of judicial review, a substantial disagreement remains over how that right should be exercised. A part of the answer must consider the philosophical and legal thought of the judge—whether he is "liberal" or "conservative," if those terms have any real meaning. But a far more important issue, transcending individual politics, is the judge's view of his function and that of the Constitution. Commentators have generally identified three categories of judicial thought: neutralists, restraintists, and activists.* While no judge consistently fits a single mode, the categories are useful in interpreting judicial opinions and in legal forecasting.

The Neutralist Approach   The neutralist school, sometimes called the absolutist school, finds certain fixed principles of justice embodied in the Constitution. These principles are absolute and unchanging and should be applied to all cases. Judges are treated as mere conduits through which justice and the law speak, never as policymakers or quasi-legislators. Judges of this sort, perhaps best exemplified by Justice Hugo Black, generally rely on the plain meaning of the Constitution. Black, for example, looked at the 1st Amendment guarantee of free speech as such an absolute. The amendment says Congress may make *no law* regarding free speech, and *"no law"* meant exactly what it said. There could be no exceptions, no compromise, no balancing of interests. And this was true regardless of how beneficial the judge might think a particular law might be. Personal politics must be put aside in favor of consistency and the plain language of the Constitution.

The Restraintist Approach   Advocates of judicial restraint find themselves embarrassed by the existence of judicial review and, while they are unwilling to give up the power to review acts of the other two branches, they generally counsel restraint in exercising that power. They generally see the Court as the least powerful branch of government—in Hamilton's terms, "the least dangerous branch"—in that it cannot enforce its decisions on its own, but rather must depend on the good will of the Executive branch. Therefore restraintists generally avoid confrontation with the other, more powerful branches of government except on rare and crucial occasions. Generally, restraintists ask that the Court *avoid* constitutional questions whenever possible. Law is viewed not as a set of immutable principles, but as the history of the resolution of past problems, and the best result is usually found by balancing the interests of the parties to the controversy. Restraintists, like Holmes, Cardozo, and Brandeis, to name a few, feel that law should be "prudently found," not "made" by the Court.

The Activist Approach   The third approach, called the *activist* or the *preferred freedoms* approach, finds the balancing test advocated by the restraintists to be very distasteful, since it usually results in favoring the interests of the stronger members of our society. Judicial activists see a part of the Court's role as an advocate and pro-

---

*The three approaches are defined and explained more fully in Craig R. Ducat and Harold W. Chase, *Constitutional Interpretation* 3d ed. (St. Paul, Minn.: West Publishing Co., 1983), esp. pp. 58–66.

tector of the interests of the weak and disadvantaged groups in our nation. They also seem to make a distinction between economic interests and civil rights and liberties. In the former case, the activists will accept the balancing tests of the restraintists, and therefore the two groups often find themselves allied in those cases. In cases involving civil rights and liberties, the activists find such rights to be fundamental guarantees, or preferred freedoms, and therefore will not permit a balancing of interests to take place. In such cases judicial activists such as Earl Warren and William O. Douglas are often allied with judicial neutralists.

A Note on Judicial Psychology

The foregoing categories, while appealing, are often blurred and inadequate to describe why a particular justice voted in a particular manner. It is true that a prime value of judges is consistency; that is, deciding the same cases the same way. As a result, a neutralist may find himself voting against rather deeply held political beliefs, for example.

Yet it is often said that something strange happens to a person when he or she puts on the black robe. To a large extent that person is no longer governed by the pressures of day-to-day life. Federal judges, for example, are appointed for life, and even their salary cannot be diminished. As a result, they find themselves able to govern their decisions based on conscience and consistency rather than on ideology, ambition, or effect of the decision on their own futures. This pressure results in such judicial anomalies as Chief Justice Earl Warren, an Eisenhower appointee and a former prosecutor who talked an extremely "hard line" on crime. When Warren joined the Court, he quickly became the leader of the judicial activist majority which rendered many of the civil rights and civil liberties decisions of the 1950's and 1960's.

An unknown quantity is just how much the Court bows to public opinion. It is unknown because the Court can, in many instances, refuse to hear cases it does not wish to hear under the doctrine of **certiorari** (see Chapter 4). Obviously, the Court is supposed to be above the pressures of politics because of the variety of safeguards of judicial independence built into the document. Just as obviously the Court must be aware of the feelings of the nation. The extent to which one believes the Court should be influenced by public opinion is determined to a large extent by the nature of one's approach to the concept of judicial review.

Summary and Conclusions

The study of the legal environment of business requires an understanding of the nature of law and the legal process, including the sources of American institutions and the powers of government. American legal and political theory is based on a specific theory of government and law, the theory of natural rights, in which the authority of government is derived from the consent of the governed.

"Law" is best viewed as predictions of what the courts will do. Clues to what the courts may do may be found in the expressions of written law, the Constitutions, statutes, administrative rules, treaties, and judicial decisions. In all cases, the courts interpret those expressions, and the result, in the form of actual decisions, is The Law.

One of the chief checks on the authority of the legislative and executive departments and on the power of the states is found in the doctrine of judicial review. That doctrine holds that if an act of the legislature, the executive, or of the state governments is unconstitutional, the courts, and especially the U.S. Supreme Court, have the power to hold those actions void. The doctrine of judicial review is not found expressly within the Constitution, but was "found" through interpretation of the Constitution in some early cases, particularly *Marbury* v. *Madison*.

PRO AND CON
ISSUE: What Is the Proper Place of Stare Decisis in the Law?

PRO: Stare Decisis is the Starting Point of the Law
Benjamin N. Cardozo*

The work of deciding cases goes on every day in hundreds of courts throughout the land. Any judge, one might suppose, would find it easy to describe the process which he had followed a thousand times and more. Nothing could be farther from the truth. Let some intelligent layman ask him to explain; he will not go very far before taking refuge in the excuse that the language of craftsmen is unintelligible to those untutored in the craft. Such an excuse may cover with a semblance of respectability an otherwise ignominious retreat. It will hardly serve to still the pricks of curiosity and conscience. In moments of introspection, when there is no longer a necessity of putting off with a show of wisdom the uninitiated interlocutor, the troublesome problem will recur, and press for a solution. What is it that I do when I decide a case? To what sources of information do I appeal for guidance? In what proportions ought they to contribute? If a precedent is applicable, when do I refuse to follow it? If no precedent is applicable, how do I reach the rule that will make a precedent for the future? If I am seeking logical consistency, the symmetry of the legal structure, how far shall I seek it? At what point shall the quest be halted by some discrepant custom, by some consideration of social welfare, by my own or the common standards of justice and morals? Into that strange compound which is brewed daily in the caldron of the courts, all these ingredients enter in varying proportions. I am not concerned to inquire whether judges ought to be

allowed to brew such a compound at all. I take judge-made law as one of the existing realities of life. There, before us, is the brew. Not a judge on the bench but has had a hand in the making. The elements have not come together by chance. *Some* principle, however unavowed and inarticulate and subconscious, has regulated the infusion. It may not have been the same principle for all judges at any time, nor the same principle for any judge at all times. But a choice there has been. . . .

Before we can determine the proportions of a blend, we must know the ingredients to be blended. Our first inquiry should therefore be: Where does the judge find the law which he embodies in his judgment? There are times when the source is obvious. The rule that fits the case may be supplied by the constitution or by statute. If that is so, the judge looks no farther. The correspondence ascertained, his duty is to obey. The constitution overrides a statute, but a statute, if consistent with the constitution, overrides the law of judges. In this sense, judge-made law is secondary and subordinate to the law that is made by legislators. It is true that codes and statutes do not render the judge superfluous, nor his work perfunctory and mechanical. There are gaps to be filled. There are doubts and ambiguities to be cleared. There are hardships and wrongs to be mitigated if not avoided. . . .

Sometimes the rule of constitution or of statute is clear, and then the difficulties vanish. . . . We

---

*From his book, *The Nature of the Judicial Process*, (New Haven: Yale University Press, 1921) pp. 9–11, 14, 18–21. Justice Cardozo (1870–1938) served in the New York courts until 1932, when he was appointed to the U.S. Supreme Court, where he served until his death in 1938. Reprinted by permission.

reach the land of mystery when constitution and statute are silent, and the judge must look to the common law for the rule that fits the case. He is the "living oracle of the law" in Blackstone's vivid phrase. Looking at Sir Oracle in action, viewing his work in the dry light of realism, how does he set about his task?

The first thing he does is to compare the case before him with the precedents, whether stored in his mind or hidden in the books. I do not mean that precedents are ultimate sources of the law, supplying the sole equipment that is needed for the legal armory, the sole tools, to borrow Maitland's phrase, "in the legal smithy." Back of precedents are the basic juridical conceptions which are the postulates of judicial reasoning, and farther back are the habits of life, the institutions of society, in which those conceptions had their origin, and which, by a process of interaction, they have modified in turn. None the less, in a system so highly developed as our own, precedents have so covered the ground

that they fix the point of departure from which the labor of the judge begins. Almost invariably, his first step is to examine and compare them. If they are plain and to the point, there may be need of nothing more. *Stare decisis* is at least the everyday working rule of our law. . . . Some judges seldom get beyond that process in any case. Their notion of their duty is to match the colors of the case at hand against the colors of many sample cases spread out upon their desk. The sample nearest in shade supplies the applicable rule. But, of course, no system of living law can be evolved by such a process, and no judge of a high court, worthy of his office, views the function so narrowly. If that were all there was to our calling, there would be little of intellectual interest about it. The man who had the best card index of the cases would also be the wisest judge. It is when the colors do not match, when the references in the index fail, when there is no decisive precedent, that the serious business of the judge begins. . . .

CON: The Life of the Law Has Not Been Logic: It Has Been Experience
Oliver Wendell Holmes*

The object of this book is to present a general view of the Common Law. To accomplish the task, other tools are needed besides logic. It is something to show that the consistency of a system requires a particular result, but it is not all. The life of the law has not been logic: it has been experience. The felt necessities of the time, the prevalent moral and political theories, intuitions of public policy, avowed or unconscious, even the prejudices which judges share with their fellow men, have had a good deal more to do than syllogism in determining the rules by which men should be governed. The law embodies the story of a nation's development through many centuries, and it cannot be dealt with as if it contained only the axioms and corollaries of a book of mathematics. In order to know what it is, we must know what it has been, and what it tends to become. We must alternately consult history and existing theories of legislation. But the most difficult labor will be to understand the combination of the two into new products at every stage. The substance of the law at any given time pretty nearly corresponds, so far as it goes, with what is then understood to be convenient; but its form and

machinery, and the degree to which it is able to work out desired results, depend very much upon its past. . . .

The foregoing history, apart from the purposes for which it has been given, well illustrates the paradox of form and substance in the development of law. In form its growth is logical. The official theory is that each new decision follows syllogistically from existing precedents. But just as the clavicle in the cat only tells of the existence of some earlier creature to which a collar-bone was useful, precedents survive in the law long after the use they once served is at an end and the reason for them has been forgotten. The result of following them must often be failure and confusion from the merely logical point of view.

On the other hand, in substance the growth of the law is legislative. And this in a deeper sense than that what the courts declare to have always been the law is in fact new. It is legislative in its grounds. The very considerations which judges most rarely mention, and always with an apology, are the secret root from which the law draws all the juices of life. I mean, of course, considerations of

---

*From his book *The Common Law* (1881). Justice Holmes (1841–1935) served on the Massachusetts Supreme Court from 1882 to 1902, when he was appointed to the U.S. Supreme Court. He served on that Court until 1933.

what is expedient for the community concerned. Every important principle which is developed by litigation is in fact and at bottom the result of more or less definitely understood views of public policy; most generally, to be sure, under our practice and our traditions, the unconscious result of instinctive preferences and inarticulate convictions, but none the less traceable to views of public policy in the last analysis. And as the law is administered by able and experienced men, who know too much to sacrifice good sense to a syllogism, it will be found that, when ancient rules maintain themselves ... new reasons more fitted to the time have been found for them, and that they gradually receive a new content, and at last a new form, from the grounds to which they have been transplanted.

The truth is, that the law is always approaching, and never reaching, consistency. It is forever adopting new principles from life at one end, and it always retains old ones from history at the other, which have not yet been absorbed or sloughed off. It will be entirely consistent only when it ceases to grow.

However much we may codify the law into a series of seemingly self-sufficient propositions, those propositions will be but a phase in a continuous growth. To understand their scope fully, to know how they will be dealt with by judges trained in the past with the law embodies, we must ourselves know something of the past. The history of what the law has been is necessary to the knowledge of what the law is.

DISCUSSION QUESTIONS

1. Were the laws of Nazi Germany under Adolf Hitler valid? Under which of the philosophies of law would those laws be invalid? Why? Does it make a difference whether we are discussing a traffic law or Hitler's laws concerning the Jewish population?

2. By what right did the Nuremburg Court convict, sentence, and execute Nazi war criminals for committing acts that were perfectly legal under the laws of Germany? What conception of law does this illustrate?

3. An ordinance in a midwestern city makes it illegal for "any person who is disfigured, grotesque, or otherwise obnoxious to public view" to be on the streets after dark. The law has never been enforced and carries no penalty. Is it still a law?

4. Should judges have the right of judicial review? Was Jackson correct in saying that each branch of government should be the sole judge of the constitutionality of its own actions? Should the President veto legislation that he considers unconstitutional? Or should he leave that decision to the Court?

5. Look at the "ammunition" that Justice Marshall used to back up his argument that judicial review must exist: the constitutional provisions he relied on, the logic, and the public policy. Was this interpretation or a mere pretext?

6. Should judges be influenced by public opinion? All judges? If so, why not juries? Should judges be elected?

7. Assume that the Supreme Court orders a state to bus all of its public school students to achieve racial desegregation, and the governor of that state refuses to obey the order. The Supreme Court requests the President to send in U.S. Marshals and federal troops to enforce the order. What happens if the President

refuses? Could it happen? If so, what are the short-term and long-term effects on the rule of law in the United States? Does the Supreme Court have any remedy? Does Congress?

8. It has been said that *Martin* v. *Hunter's Lessee* was not finally resolved until the North won the Civil War. Why?

CASE PROBLEMS

1. How would a neutralist, a restraintist, and an activist decide the following cases? What alliances would you expect?

   a. A Texas statute required all labor organizers to register with the State. Thomas, a union president, defied the law on the grounds it violated his 1st Amendment right to free speech and was arrested and jailed. [*Thomas* v. *Collins,* 323 U.S. 516, 65 S. Ct. 315, 89 L. Ed. 430 (1945).]

   b. A Nebraska statute regulated the weight of loaves of bread to be sold in the state in order to protect buyers from short weights and honest bakers from unfair competition. A baker challenged the statute on 14th Amendment due process grounds. [*Burns Baking Co.* v. *Bryan,* 264 U.S. 504, 44 S. Ct. 412, 68 L. Ed. 813 (1924).]

   c. A West Virginia statute required schoolchildren to salute the flag and say the pledge of allegiance at the beginning of every school day. Barnette and his children held deep religious beliefs that no salute could be given. Barnette's children were expelled, and Barnette sued for deprivation of religious freedom. [*West Virginia* v. *Barnette,* 319 U.S. 624, 63 S. Ct. 1178, 87 L. Ed. 1628 (1943).]

2. McCardle was a newspaper editor in Mississippi following the Civil War. At that time, Mississippi was under military rule, and McCardle was taken into custody by military authorities and charged with publishing libelous and "incendiary" articles. He brought an action for habeus corpus, claiming that the military did not have authority to try him. He appealed the denial of that petition to the U.S. Supreme Court, which began considering the matter. While the matter was pending before the Supreme Court, Congress passed a law which supposedly took away the authority of the Supreme Court to hear appeals of such cases. Must the Supreme Court refuse to hear the case? [*Ex Parte McCardle,* 74 U.S. (7 Wall.) 506, 19 L. Ed. 264 (1869).]

3. In 1896, the U.S. Supreme Court held that state laws that separated the races were permissible if they provided "separate but equal" facilities. Assume you are a federal trial judge in 1953, and you are faced with a case in which a state law *requires* segregation of the races in public facilities. A plaintiff appears before you claiming that he was denied admission to a public restaurant because of his race. *Must* you follow the state law? [See *Plessy* v. *Ferguson,* 163 U.S. 537, 16 S. Ct. 1138,

41 L. Ed. 256 (1896); *Brown* v. *Board of Education,* 347 U.S. 483, 74 U.S. 686, 98 L. Ed. 873 (1954) and infra, Chapter 16.] How may the law be changed?

4. Falstaff had a bad day. He was standing on the sidewalk when he was struck by a car that was owned by Glendower House, a local charitable home for the aged. The car had been driven by Gadshill, one of the residents of the home, who was running an errand for the home. Falstaff survived the accident and was taken to Westmoreland Hospital, a local not-for-profit hospital. Falstaff was indigent and could not pay his bill, but the hospital had a policy of taking all patients regardless of financial condition. While a patient at the hospital, two nurses aides dropped Falstaff, breaking his clavicle. Falstaff filed two lawsuits, one against the Glendower House, and the second against Westmoreland Hospital, charging negligence. How would each case be decided in Pennsylvania after the *Flagiello* case was decided?

SUGGESTED READINGS

Political and Legal Philosophy

Cardozo, Benjamin N. *The Nature of the Judicial Process* (New Haven, Conn.: Yale University Press, 1921).

Frank, Jerome. *Law and the Modern Mind* (New York: Brentano's, 1930).

Fuller, Lon L. *The Morality of Law* (New Haven, Conn.: Yale University Press, 1964).

Hart, H. L. A. *The Concept of Law* (Oxford: Oxford University Press, 1961).

Holmes, Oliver Wendell, Jr. *The Common Law* (Boston: Little, Brown, 1881).

Pound, Roscoe. *An Introduction to the Philosophy of Law* (New Haven, Conn.: Yale University Press, 1922).

Constitutional History

Bickel, Alexander M. *The Least Dangerous Branch* (Indianapolis: Bobbs-Merrill, 1962).

Carr, Robert K. *The Supreme Court and Judicial Review* (New York: Holt, Rinehart & Winston, 1942).

Douglas, William O. *We the Judges* (New York: Doubleday, 1956).

McCloskey, Robert G. *The American Supreme Court* (Chicago: The University of Chicago Press, 1960).

Shapiro, Martin M. *The Supreme Court and Public Policy* (Glenview, Ill.: Scott, Foresman, 1969).

Schwartz, Bernard. *A Commentary on the Constitution of the United States* (New York: Macmillan, 1963), especially volume 1.

The American Constitution: Background, the Commerce Clause, and Economic Liberties

We are under a Constitution, but the Constitution is what the judges say it is, and the judiciary is the safeguard of our liberty and of our property under the Constitution.

Chief Justice Charles Evans Hughes (1907)

Freedom in economic arrangements is itself a component of freedom broadly understood, so economic freedom is an end in itself. . . . Economic freedom is also an indispensable means toward the achievement of political freedom.

Milton Friedman, Capitalism and Freedom *(1962)*

We are inclined to confuse freedom and democracy, which we regard as moral principles, with the way in which these are practiced in America—with capitalism, federalism, and the two party system, which are not moral principles, but simply the accepted practices of the American people.

Senator J. William Fulbright, Senate Speech, March 27, 1964

The source of all government authority in the United States is the people. Under the theory of natural rights, the people join together in a compact, or agreement, for mutual aid and protection. The American Constitution is that agreement, in written form. The agreement was made by representatives of the people who met in a Constitutional Convention in 1787. The representatives formed a federal government out of the states, granted that government very specific powers to rule, and placed certain limits on the privilege of ruling. That document, which is reproduced in full in Appendix B, forms the foundation of all American law.

This chapter will briefly discuss the background and history of the American Constitution and the concept of "granted and implied powers," and will then consider the most important grant of power for business regulation, the Commerce Clause, in substantial detail. The chapter will conclude with a discussion of three potential limitations on the authority of government to regulate commerce, including the Contracts Clause,* the concept of "substantive economic Due Process" under the 14th Amendment, and the economic implications of the Equal Protection Clause, also found in the 14th Amendment. Chapter 3 will then consider the broader implications of the Bill of Rights.

Historical Background of the Constitution

Even before the defeat of the British at Yorktown, the young American nation had begun the business of running its own affairs. The Second Continental Congress had proposed the Articles of Confederation as early as 1777, but those articles, the first attempt at a written constitution, were not ratified or effective until March, 1781. The articles were little more than a treaty or alliance between independent and sovereign nations, and soon proved highly unworkable.

The framers of the Articles of Confederation cannot be blamed for the document's lack of success, since this was the first experiment in constitutional government and they had no model to follow. The articles gave Congress no power to levy taxes, to regulate interstate or foreign commerce, to ensure state compliance with treaties, or even to enforce any of its laws. There was no system of federal courts and no provision for a national executive, or president. Soon state and sectional jealousies gave rise to embargoes of out-of-state goods. The federal government was bankrupt the moment the articles went into effect, since it had no federal authority to tax. It was obvious very soon that the Articles of Confederation would have to be reworked in some way, and quickly, if the new nation was to be successful.

In the summer of 1787, delegates met in Philadelphia for the purpose of amending the Articles of Confederation to make it work. The delegates had been chosen by the legislatures of the states and were a remarkable group of men. The 55 delegates included Washington, Franklin, Hamilton, and Madison, of course, as well as lesser-known but equally brilliant, thoughtful men such as Roger Sherman, James Wilson, and John Dickinson. The delegates were young, with an average age of 42, and 29 of the delegates were lawyers. Conspicuous by his absence was Thomas Jefferson.

We know very little of the internal workings or debates of the Convention. The members immediately pledged themselves to secrecy in order to prevent undue dis-

---

*Article I, Section 10 of the Constitution.

turbance to "the public repose." However, we know that the delegates immediately breached their instructions, which were to amend the Articles of Confederation, by scrapping that document altogether and beginning anew.

On September 17, 1787, the finished document was signed. Not all of the original delegates stayed; in fact, only 39 of the original 55 signed the document. The delegates left the Convention well aware of the political revolution they had begun. Upon leaving the hall, Franklin was stopped by a woman who asked him what sort of government the delegates had given the country. Franklin replied, "A republic, madam, if you can keep it."

The original document contained seven articles. The first three articles created Congress, the Presidency, and the Judiciary and granted specific powers to each of those branches. The organization scheme implicitly created the three branches of government, an arrangement that has proven highly workable both in the United States and abroad. Article IV dealt with federal-state relations, Article V with the method of amending the Constitution, and Article VI contained some miscellaneous provisions that do not fit within the other articles, including the famous Supremacy Clause.* Article VII dealt with the method by which the Constitution would be ratified. That article provided that the Constitution would not be effective until nine states had ratified the document.

The ratification process revived all of the old sectional arguments and added a philosophical dispute about the power of a central government in relation to the states and the people. The fight for ratification was led by the delegates themselves, especially Hamilton, Madison, and John Jay, who wrote a series of essays arguing for ratification, later collected as *The Federalist Papers.* Many of the arguments regarding the "intent of the framers" in contemporary debates on constitutional issues are based upon those essays, particularly since little is known of the actual debates within the Constitutional Convention.

Alexander Hamilton
Federalist Papers, No. 1

After an unequivocal experience of the inefficacy of the subsisting federal government, you are called upon to deliberate on a new Constitution for the United States of America. The subject speaks its own importance; comprehending in its consequences nothing less than the existence of the UNION, the safety and welfare of the parts of which it is composed, the fate of an empire in many respects the most interesting in the world. It has been frequently remarked that it seems to have been reserved to the people of this country, by their conduct and example, to decide the important question, whether societies of men are really capable or not of establishing good government from reflection and choice, or whether they are forever destined to depend for their political constitutions on accident and force. If there be any truth in the remark, the crisis at which we are arrived may with propriety be regarded as the era in which that decision is to be made; and a wrong election of the part we shall act may, in this view, deserve to be considered as the general misfortune of mankind.

---

*Article VI, Section 2. See discussion of preemption, below, pp. 43–45.

By July 26, 1788, eleven states had ratified the Constitution, two more than the Constitution required. In 1789, the first Congress met, and the new nation had begun. Within two years, ten amendments would be made to the original document as a result of substantial pressure from the states and from the public. Those amendments are universally known as *the Bill of Rights.*

The Powers of Government

The federal government received two types of powers under the Constitution. First, each branch received specific **enumerated powers** that are expressly set forth in the Constitution. The rest of the authority to govern is expressly "reserved to the States," both under the theory implicit in the Constitutional idea and expressly under the 10th Amendment. As Chief Justice John Marshall states, "the principle, that [the] government can exercise only the powers granted to it, . . . is now universally admitted."

Second, at least Congress has unspecified, or **implied, powers.** The implied powers of Congress are based upon the Necessary and Proper Clause, Article I, Section 8, clause 18, of the Constitution, which grants Congress the right to "make all laws necessary and proper for carrying into Execution the foregoing [enumerated] Powers. . . ."

The Necessary and Proper Clause was first interpreted by the Supreme Court in a decision that rivals *Marbury* v. *Madison* for its importance:

McCulloch v. Maryland

17 U.S. 316, 4 L. Ed. 579 (1819)

In 1816, Congress created a national bank and located one branch of the bank in Baltimore. The Maryland legislature imposed a tax on all banks not chartered by the state, and the cashier of the national bank refused to pay the tax. The state brought a criminal action against the cashier. A major issue in the case was whether Congress had the authority to establish a bank, since that authority does not exist among the enumerated powers of Article I, Section 8 of the Constitution. Justice Marshall found that Congress indeed had the power, and used the following language in the decision.

> MARSHALL, Chief Justice. . . .
>
> . . . .
>
> If any one proposition could command the universal assent of mankind, we might expect it would be this—that the government of the Union, though limited in its powers, is supreme within its sphere of action. This would seem to result, necessarily, from its nature. It is the government of all; its powers are delegated by all; it represents all, and acts for all. Though any one state may be willing to control its operations, no state is willing to allow others to control them. The nation, on those subjects on which it can act, must necessarily bind its component parts. . . .
>
> Among the enumerated powers, we do not find that of establishing a bank or creating a corporation. But there is no phrase in the instrument which, like the articles of

confederation, excludes incidental or implied powers; and which requires that everything granted shall be expressly and minutely described.

. . . .

But the argument on which most reliance is placed, is drawn from that peculiar language of the [Necessary and Proper] clause. Congress is not empowered by it to make all laws, which may have relation to the powers conferred on the government, but only as may be *"necessary and proper"* for carrying them into execution. The word *"necessary"* is considered as controlling the whole sentence, and as limiting the right to pass laws for the execution of the granted powers, to such as are indispensable, and without which the power would be nugatory. That it excludes the choice of means, and leaves to congress, in each case, that only which is most direct and simple.

Is it true, that this is the sense in which the word "necessary" is always used? Does it always import an absolute physical necessity, so strong, that one thing to which another may be termed necessary, cannot exist without the other? We think it does not. If reference be had to its use, in the common affairs of the world . . ., we find that it frequently imports no more than that one thing is convenient, or useful, or essential to another. . . .

We admit, as all must admit, that the powers of the government are limited, and that its limits are not to be transcended. But we think the sound construction of the constitution must allow to the national legislature that discretion, with respect to the means by which the powers it confers are to be carried into execution, which will enable that body to perform the high duties assigned to it, in the manner most beneficial to the people. Let the end be legitimate, let it be within the scope of the constitution, and all means which are appropriate, which are plainly adapted to that end, which are not prohibited, but consistent with the letter and spirit of the constitution, are constitutional.

Thus, under the Necessary and Proper Clause, Congress has exercised many powers not specifically granted by the Constitution, such as the power to take property under eminent domain for public purposes, create corporations, exclude and deport aliens, and even enact the Federal Criminal Code. It seems that the granted powers are treated as *goals,* and Congress may use any means to reach those goals unless those means are forbidden by the letter or the spirit of the Constitution.

Each of the three branches of government (legislative, executive, and judicial) receives specific enumerated powers within the Constitution (see Figure 2-1). The legislative powers are specifically set forth in Article I, Section 8, while the executive and judicial grants are found in Articles II and III, respectively.

It is, of course, Congress that has the power to "make laws," the so-called legislative power, but only upon those subjects set out in the Constitution. Generally speaking, bills must pass both houses of Congress and be signed by the President or passed over presidential veto before they become law. And that law is subject to scrutiny by the courts under the doctrine of **judicial review,** discussed in Chapter 1.

Compared to the legislative grants of authority, the powers of the President seem quite limited. The President may make certain official appointments, grant reprieves and pardons, make treaties subject to the advice and consent of the Senate, and temporarily fill Congressional vacancies. But, the lack of formal grants of power notwithstanding, the President has become extremely powerful over the years, especially in the last fifty years. If Congress desired continuing federal control over an area, it delegated the authority to make rules to the President or to an administrative agency within the executive branch. Executive orders, actions, and administrative regulations

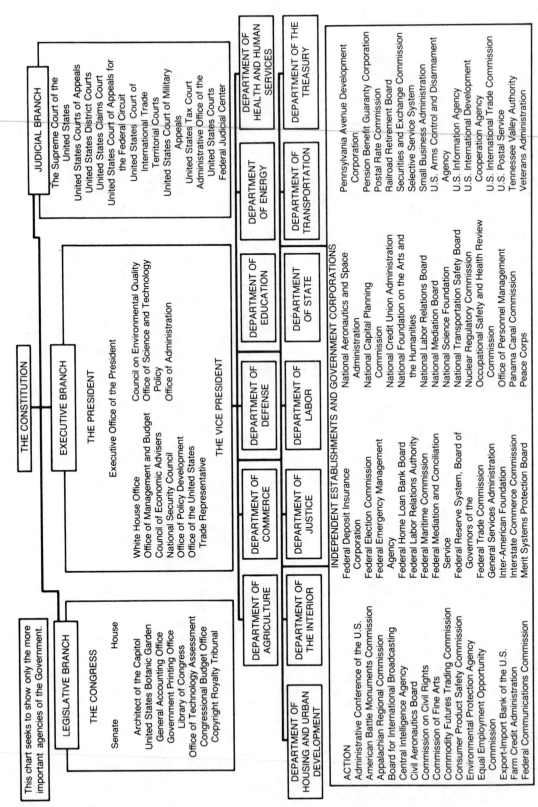

Figure 2-1 The Government of the United States
Source: *U.S. Government Manual, 1984–5* (Washington, D.C.: U.S. Government Printing Office, 1984),
p. 816.

42

require interpretation in the same manner as statutes and are subject to the same judicial review.

The power of the courts is defined in general terms in Article III, but the Constitution is quite vague regarding that power. Congress is given the power to set the size and the organization of the lower federal courts. One of the first actions taken by the first Congress in 1789 was to pass the federal Judiciary Act of that year. That act provided for the formation of lower federal trial courts and the division of the nation into judicial districts. The act also specified what types of cases the federal courts might hear. The Judiciary Act also specified that the Supreme Court should consist of six justices. While much of the Judiciary act has changed over the years, the Act has always existed in one form or another. Two important changes involved enlarging the Supreme Court to nine justices and the creation of "second-tier" appellate courts, called U.S. Courts of Appeals. It is important to remember that Congress may, at any time, change the organization or make-up of the federal courts, remove or enlarge federal court jurisdiction, or alter the size of the Supreme Court.

The Idea of Federalism

One of the more controversial issues throughout American history is the relationship between the states and the federal government. Under the Articles of Confederation, the states were virtually sovereign nations, and the fear of a strong centralized government pervaded the debate over ratification of the Constitution as well. In the debates over the Constitution, Alexander Hamilton favored a "unitary" or centralized government, while the advocates of Jeffersonian Democracy favored dispersing power among several "levels" or "layers" of government. In a way, the Constitution of 1789 was a compromise between these conflicting philosophies, a compromise resulting in massive conflicts that ultimately led to the Civil War. Even in the 20th century that conflict has continued in calls for States' Rights or a New Federalism.

Initially, the reasons for federalism and the existence of multiple levels of government lay in the fear of tyranny. The more points of access to the government, the more the public could hope to influence and limit the excesses of government. Modern arguments favoring more state and local controls that exclude the national government have been based on ideas of efficiency. It is argued that local and state control over various programs involves less waste and a greater degree of responsiveness to local concerns.

Two constitutional provisions are relevant to the continuing debate over the relative roles of the state and federal governments. The 10th Amendment assures that powers not delegated to the federal government are "reserved to the States respectively, or to the people." And the Supremacy Clause (Article VI, Clause 2) provides that the "Constitution and the Laws of the United States which shall be made in Pursuance thereof . . . shall be the supreme Law of the Land. . . ."

The Problem of Preemption

The most common issue of federal-state relations continues to be the authority of the states to govern areas concurrently with the federal government. If a state law and a federal law purport to govern the same problem and the two laws conflict, the state law is **preempted** by the federal law. That means that under the Supremacy Clause, the state law must give way to the federal law. But while the issue may be stated in simple terms, the problem is often very complex. The courts may be asked to determine whether statutes or other laws really do conflict in such situations, which involves a comprehensive analysis of both laws. And, even if the laws do not directly conflict, the problem may be one in which Congress has the exclusive authority to act, in which case the state law is also preempted. And, in some situations, it may have been Congress' intention that no one, including itself, should act in the field.

The following decision illustrates the concept of preemption in a civil case involving well-known facts. Notice that the conflict in this case is between the state "common law" and federal administrative regulations.

Silkwood v. Kerr-McGee Corporation

104 S. Ct. 615 (1984)

Karen Silkwood, a laboratory analyst for Kerr-McGee, was contaminated by plutonium radiation while at work. She was "decontaminated," but tests showed that the contamination had spread into her body. Her apartment was also found to be contaminated, and much of her personal property was destroyed. After tests to determine the extent of physical damage to vital organs, Silkwood returned to work, and was killed "in an unrelated automobile accident." Silkwood's father brought a common-law tort action against Kerr-McGee for the injuries to Silkwood and her property caused by the contamination. The evidence showed that Kerr-McGee did not always comply with safety regulations of the Nuclear Regulatory Commission, the federal administrative agency charged with administering nuclear safety. Kerr-McGee argued that Silkwood had intentionally removed plutonium from the plant to embarrass the company. The jury returned a verdict in favor of Silkwood, finding actual damages of $505,000 and punitive damages of $10,000,000.

Kerr-McGee appealed on the grounds that the common-law tort action filed by Silkwood was preempted by federal law in the form of the Nuclear Regulatory Commission's safety rules. The U.S. Court of Appeals agreed and reversed the portion of the judgment granting punitive damages, since such damages are not provided for by the federal regulations. Silkwood appealed.

Justice WHITE delivered the opinion of the Court.

. . . .

As we recently observed . . . state law can be preempted in either of two general ways. If Congress evidences an intent to occupy a given field, any state law falling within that field is preempted. . . . If Congress has not entirely displaced state regulation over the matter in question, state law is still preempted to the extent it actually conflicts with federal law, that is, when it is impossible to comply with both state and federal law, . . . or where the state law stands as an obstacle to the accomplishment of the full purposes and objectives of Congress. . . .

. . . .

The United States, as *amicus curiae,* contends that the award of punitive damages in this case is preempted because it conflicts with the federal remedial scheme, noting that the NRC is authorized to impose civil penalties on licensees when federal standards have been violated. . . . However, the award of punitive damages in the present case does not conflict with that scheme. Paying both federal fines and state-imposed punitive damages would not appear to be physically impossible. Nor does exposure to punitive damages frustrate any purpose of the federal remedial scheme.

Kerr-McGee contends that the award is preempted because it frustrates Congress' express desire "to encourage widespread participation in the development and utilization of atomic energy for peaceful purposes. . . . [W]e [have] observed that "the promotion of nuclear power is not to be accomplished 'at all costs'" . . . . Congress therefore disclaimed any interest in promoting the development and utilization of atomic energy by means that fail to provide adequate remedies for those who are injured by exposure to hazardous nuclear materials. Thus, the award of punitive damages in this case does not hinder the accomplishment of the [Congressional] purpose. . . .

The judgment of the Court of Appeals with respect of punitive damages is therefore reversed. . . .

Justices POWELL, BURGER, BLACKMUN, and MARSHALL dissented:

The Court's decision, in effect, authorizes lay juries and judges in each of the states to make regulatory judgments as to whether a federally licensed nuclear facility is being operated safely. Such judgments then become the predicate to imposing heavy punitive damages. This authority is approved in this case even though the Nuclear Regulatory Commission (NRC)—the agency authorized by Congress to assure the safety of nuclear facilities—found no relevant violation of its stringent safety requirements worthy of punishment. . . . There is no express authorization in federal law of the authority the Court today finds in a state's common law of torts.

. . . .

Today, the Court opens a wide and inviting door to indirect regulation by juries authorized to impose damages to punish and deter on the basis of inferences even when a plant has taken the utmost precautions provided by law. Not only is this unfair; it also could discourage investment needed to further the acknowledged national need for this alternate source of energy. I would affirm the judgment of the Court of Appeals.

The first issue in most constitutional questions is whether the government has the authority to act. We will consider that question in the context of the regulation of business under the Commerce Clause. Students should be aware that similar bodies of law have grown up around most of the other powers of Congress.

The Commerce Clause: A Case Study in Congressional Power and Constitutional Development

Perhaps the most important change brought about by the Constitutional Convention was the adoption of Article I, Section 8, clause 3, the **Commerce Clause.** This deceptively simple clause gave Congress the authority to "regulate Commerce with foreign Nations, and among the several States, and with the Indian Tribes." These simple words have been called "the fount and origin of vast power," "one of the most prolific sources of national power," and "the direct source of the most important powers which the Federal Government exercises in time of peace." From civil rights to consumer protection, the clause is the source of authority for most of our present regulatory environment.

Yet this was not always so. For the first hundred years of its existence, the clause was a sleeping giant, giving little power and rarely, if ever, used. Beginning with the creation of the Interstate Commerce Commission in 1887, the clause was used affirmatively by Congress as the basis for the creation of regulatory agencies. But even then, it was not until a landmark decision by the Supreme Court in 1937 that Congress possessed any real power to regulate the day-to-day affairs of business. The story of the Commerce Clause is really the constitutional history of business regulation.

The first decision to consider the scope of the Commerce Clause was the famous *Gibbons* v. *Ogden** decision of 1824. The case was partly a preemption problem, dealing with the issue of whether a New York monopoly granted to Robert Fulton to operate his famous steamboat on Lake Erie conflicted with the Commerce Clause. Chief Justice John Marshall's definition of the term *commerce* lives on in decisions today. "Commerce," said Marshall, "undoubtedly is traffic, but it is something more; it is intercourse. It describes the commercial intercourse between nations, and parts of nations, in all its branches." The Court ruled that New York had attempted to regulate commerce in this sense, and therefore had attempted to control something exclusively within federal power.

Commerce Clause questions are commonly centered on one of two issues: first, whether a state regulation has interfered with exclusively federal matters, as in *Gibbons* v. *Ogden;* and, second, whether an action by Congress has gone beyond the scope of the authority granted to it by the Commerce Clause. Early cases tend to be of the first type; later cases tend to be of the second.

State Regulation of Commerce: The Police Power

From 1824 until the 1890's, the vast majority of cases dealt with the issue of whether a state law in some way conflicted with either the latent or exercised federal power over commerce. In one sense this is a preemption question, a conflict between an exercised state power and an unexercised federal power. For much of the 19th century and part of the early 20th century, this meant that state welfare laws and other state statutes were found unconstitutional.

The authority of states to regulate in any field is generally derived from the so-called **police power** of the states. The police power is the power of a state to enact laws for the purposes of health, welfare, safety, and morals. It is one of the reserved powers of the states, under the 10th Amendment, though it is not mentioned specifically there or anywhere else in the Constitution. On many occasions, the courts have held the police power to be an "inherent power of government." Obviously, the police power gives the states ample power to regulate many facets of business. But those regulations may well conflict with federal authority under the Commerce Clause. Generally, a state law regulating commerce may be defective in one of two ways: first, the state law may discriminate against interstate commerce; second, the state law may "unduly burden" interstate commerce.

State Discrimination Against Interstate Commerce   Discrimination against interstate commerce means some form of favoritism of local business over out-of-state business. Such discrimination may take the form of boycotts, embargoes, taxes, or simple discriminatory regulations that affect out-of-state business adversely. Such

---

*22 U.S. (9 Wheat.) 1, 6 L. Ed. 23.

state reguations were a prime moving force in the push for a Constitutional Convention in 1787. The following case illustrates such state discrimination against out-of-state business.

Dean Milk Co. v. City of Madison

340 U.S. 349, 71 S. Ct. 295, 95 L. Ed. 329 (1951)

The facts of the case are found in the court's decision.

Appeal from the Supreme Court of Wisconsin.

Mr. Justice CLARK delivered the opinion of the Court.

This appeal challenges the constitutional validity of two sections of an ordinance of the City of Madison, Wisconsin, regulating the sale of milk and milk products within the municipality's jurisdiction. One section in issue makes it unlawful to sell any milk as pasteurized unless it has been processed and bottled at an approved pasteurization plant within a radius of five miles from the central square of Madison.

. . . .

Appellant is an Illinois corporation engaged in distributing milk and milk products in Illinois and Wisconsin . . . The Supreme Court of Wisconsin upheld the five mile limit on pasteurization. . . .

The City of Madison is the county seat of Dane County. Within the county are some 5,600 dairy farms with total raw milk production in excess of 600,000,000 pounds annually and more than ten times the requirements of Madison. Aside from the milk supplied to Madison, fluid milk produced in the county moves in large quantities to Chicago and more distant consuming areas, and the remainder is used in making cheese, butter and other products. . . .

. . . .

Appellant purchases and gathers milk from approximately 950 farms in northern Illinois and southern Wisconsin, none being within 25 miles of Madison. Its pasteurization plants are located at Chemung and Huntley, Illinois, about 65 and 85 miles respectively from Madison. Appellant was denied a license to sell its products within Madison solely because its pasteurization plants were more than five miles away.

. . . .

This is not an instance in which an enactment falls because of federal legislation. . . . There is no pertinent national regulation by the Congress. . . . Nor can there be objection to the avowed purpose of this enactment. We assume that difficulties in sanitary regulation of milk and milk products originating in remote areas may present a situation in which '' . . . it appears that the matter is one which may appropriately be regulated in the interest of the safety, health and well-being of local communities'' . . .

But this regulation . . . in practical effect excludes from distribution in Madison wholesome milk produced and pasteurized in Illinois. "The importer . . . may keep his milk or drink it, but sell it he may not." . . . In thus erecting an economic barrier protecting a major local industry against competition from without the State, Madison plainly discriminates against interstate commerce. This it cannot do, even in the exercise of its unquestioned power to protect the health and safety of its people, if reasonable nondiscriminatory alternatives, adequate to conserve legitimate local interests, are available.

A different view, that the ordinance is valid simply because it professes to be a health measure, would mean that the Commerce Clause of itself imposes no limitations on state action other than those laid down by the Due Process Clause, save for the rare instance where a state artlessly discloses an avowed purpose to discriminate against interstate goods. . . . Our issue then is whether the discrimination inherent in the Madison ordinance can be justified in view of the character of the local interest and the available methods of protecting them. . . .

It appears that reasonable and adequate alternatives are available. If the City of Madison prefers to rely upon its own officials for inspection of distant milk sources, such inspection is readily open to it without hardship for it could charge the actual and reasonable cost of such inspection to the importing producers and processors.

. . . .

To permit Madison to adopt a regulation not essential for the protection of local health interest and placing a discriminatory burden on interstate commerce would invite a multiplication of preferential trade areas destructive of the very purpose of the Commerce Clause. Under the circumstances here presented, the regulation must yield to the principle that "one state in its dealings with another may not place itself in a position of economic isolation." . . .

For these reasons we conclude that the judgment below sustaining the five-mile provision as to pasteurization must be reversed. . . .

Undue Burdens on Interstate Commerce   Even if a state regulation of commerce is nondiscriminatory, and its effects fall evenly on both intrastate and interstate commerce, the regulation may still be held void under the Commerce Clause if it places an **undue burden on interstate commerce.** Such burdens may take the form of state safety regulations, taxes, licensing fees, or any other rule that is a "clog on interstate commerce." The following case exemplifies such burdens.

Bibb v. Navajo Freight Lines, Inc.

359 U.S. 520, 79 S. Ct. 962, 3 L. Ed. 2d 1003 (1959)

The State of Illinois passed a statute requiring all trucks and trailers operating in the state to be equipped with "contour mud flaps," which fit around the top surface of tires. Forty-five states permitted the use of "straight" mud flaps, and an Arkansas rule required the use of straight mud flaps, which meant that trucks equipped with "contour" mud flaps could not operate in Arkansas. The District Court held the Illinois statute "unduly and unreasonably burdened and obstructed interstate commerce," and found the statute unconstitutional. The state appealed.

Mr. Justice DOUGLAS delivered the opinion of the Court.

. . . .

The power of the State to regulate the use of its highways is broad and pervasive. We have recognized the peculiarly local nature of this subject of safety, and have upheld state statutes applicable alike to interstate and intrastate commerce, despite the fact that they may have an impact on interstate commerce. . . .

These safety measures carry a strong presumption of validity when challenged in court. If there are alternative ways of solving a problem, we do not sit to determine which of them is best suited to achieve a valid state objective. Policy decisions are for the state legislature, absent federal entry into the field. Unless we can conclude on the whole record that "the total effect of the law as a safety measure in reducing accidents and casualties is so slight and problematical as not to outweigh the national interest in keeping interstate commerce free from interferences which seriously impede it" . . . we must uphold the statute.

The court discussed the relative merits of contour and straight mudflaps, including the cost of installation, the hazards associated with straight mudflaps, and the new hazards, including brake drum overheating, associated with the contour mudflaps. The court also discussed the Arkansas regulation that required straight mudflaps and the amount of effort needed to change from straight to contour mudflaps if a truck were to be operated in both states. The court further focused on the practice of "interlining," which involves interchanging complete trailers between trucking companies when the originating carrier does not serve an area served by another carrier.

   The various exercises by the States of their police power stand, however, on an equal footing. All are entitled to the same presumption of validity when challenged. . . . Similarly the various state regulatory statutes are of equal dignity when measured against the Commerce Clause. . . . Like any local law that conflicts with federal regulatory measures. . . , state regulations that run afoul of the policy of free trade reflected in the Commerce Clause must . . . bow.

   This is one of those cases—few in number—where local safety measures that are nondiscriminatory place an unconstitutional burden on interstate commerce. This conclusion is especially underlined by the deleterious effect which the Illinois law will have on the "interline" operation of interstate motor carriers. The conflict between the Arkansas regulation and the Illinois regulation also suggests that this regulation of mudguards is not one of those matters "admitting of diversity of treatment, according to the special requirements of local conditions". . . . A state which insists on a design out of line with the requirements of almost all the other States may sometimes place a great burden of delay and inconvenience on those interstate motor carriers entering or crossing its territory. Such a new safety device—out of line with the requirements of the other States—may be so compelling that the innovating State need not be the one to give way. But the present showing—balanced against the clear burden on commerce—is far too inconclusive to make this mudguard meet that test.

   We deal not with absolutes but with questions of degree. The state legislatures plainly have great leeway in providing safety regulations for all vehicles—interstate as well as local. Our decisions so hold. Yet the heavy burden which the Illinois mudguard law places on the interstate movement of trucks and trailers seems to us to pass the permissible limits even for safety regulations.

   Affirmed.

Federal Regulation Under the Commerce Clause

While the states may regulate commerce under their police powers, albeit in a nondiscriminatory and nonburdensome manner, the federal government may also regulate **interstate commerce.** The term *commerce* generally means interstate commerce. A cursory reading of the Commerce Clause would seem to indicate that federal authority over commerce is **plenary;** that is, total and absolute. And today the Commerce Clause is interpreted to give Congress authority to regulate anything **"in" commerce,** or that **"affects" commerce.** This is to say, in our society of rapid communication and transportation and economic interdependence, that there is very little that Congress could not regulate. As the *Heart of Atlanta Motel* decision (pages 54–55) indicates, if Congress finds a connection with interstate commerce, it may impose regulations for any purpose, including nonbusiness or noncommercial reasons. And the relationship to interstate commerce may be quite remote and indirect as well.

   But this was not always the case. At the beginning of the 20th century, Congressional power was restricted to matters which were "in" interstate commerce, and then only for commercial or business purposes. The story of the changes in the Court's interpretation of the Commerce Clause during the 20th century illustrates the capability of the Supreme Court to change its mind, the impact of political events on the Court, and the impact of the Court's decisions on our nation.

Restricted Powers—the Early Cases   During the late 1800's Congress began to pass statutes designed to help the social welfare of the nation. Congress' concern was with abuses of the common man, such as child labor, sweat shops, protection of female workers, and what it perceived to be the abuses of corporate power. Congress met these problems through the creation of the first regulatory agencies, like the Interstate Commerce Commission, the passage of the first antitrust statutes (such as the Sherman Act of 1890), and the passage of statutes that outlawed the interstate shipment of goods made with child labor. All of these statutes were passed based on the authority of the Commerce Clause. It was not long before the statutes were challenged in the Supreme Court. The Court took an extremely restricted view of these regulations.

Hammer v. Dagenhart

247 U.S. 251, 38 S. Ct. 529, 62 L. Ed. 1101 (1918)

In 1916, Congress passed a statute prohibiting the interstate shipment of goods made with child labor. The statute outlawed the shipment of goods made in mines or quarries that employed persons under the age of 16, and the products of mills, factories or other establishments that employed persons under the age of 14, or that permitted persons 14–16 years of age to work more than eight hours a day, more than six days a week, or between the hours of 7 PM and 6 AM.

Roland and Reuben Dagenhart, both minors, filed an action for an injunction against W. C. Hammer, United States Attorney, seeking to bar the enforcement of the statute. The Dagenhart brothers had been employed in manufacturing prior to the passage of the statute, but had been notified that because of the statute, they would be discharged. The action was based on the argument that Congress had no authority under the Commerce Clause to pass such a statute. The lower court enjoined enforcement of the act and the government appealed.

Mr. Justice DAY delivered the opinion of the Court. . . .

"Commerce consists of intercourse and traffic . . . and includes the transportation of persons and property, as well as the purchase, sale, and exchange of commodities." The making of goods and the mining of coal are not commerce, nor does the fact that these things are to be afterwards shipped, or used in interstate commerce, make their production a part thereof.

Over interstate transportation, or its incidents, the regulatory power of Congress is ample, but the production of articles, intended for interstate commerce, is a matter of local regulation. . . . If it were otherwise, all manufacture intended for interstate shipment would be brought under federal control to the practical exclusion of the authority of the States, a result certainly not contemplated by the framers of the Constitution when they vested in Congress the authority to regulate commerce among the States.
. . . .

The maintenance of the authority of the States over matters purely local is as essential to the preservation of our institutions as is the conservation of the federal power in all matters entrusted to the Nation by the Federal Constitution. . . . To sustain this statute would not be in our judgment a recognition of the lawful exertion of congressional authority over interstate commerce, but would sanction an invasion by the federal power of the control of a matter purely local in its character, and over which no authority has been delegated to Congress in conferring the power to regulate commerce among the states.

We have neither authority nor disposition to question the motives of Congress in enacting this legislation. The purposes intended must be attained consistently with constitutional limitations and not by an invasion of the powers of the states. . . .

. . . .

In our view the necessary effect of this act is, by means of a prohibition against the movement in interstate commerce of ordinary commercial commodities to regulate the hours of labor of children in factories and mines within the States, a purely state authority. Thus the act in a two-fold sense is repugnant to the Constitution. It not only transcends the authority delegated to Congress over commerce but also exerts a power as to a purely local matter to which the federal authority does not extend. The far reaching result of upholding the act cannot be more plainly indicated than by pointing out that if Congress can thus regulate matters entrusted to local authority by prohibition of the movement of commodities in interstate commerce, all freedom of commerce will be at an end, and the power of the State over local matters may be eliminated, and thus our system of government be practically destroyed.

. . . .

Affirmed.

Mr. Justice HOLMES, dissenting.

. . . .

. . . . The objection urged against the power is that the States have exclusive control over their methods of production and that Congress cannot meddle with them, and taking the proposition in the sense of direct intermeddling I agree to it and suppose that no one denies it. But if an act is within the powers specifically conferred upon Congress, it seems to me that it is not made any less constitutional because of the indirect effects that it may have, however obvious it may be that it will have those effects, and that we are not at liberty upon such grounds to hold it void. . . .

The Court-Packing Plan and Enlarged Powers　As a result of the *Hammer* decision and others like it, federal regulation of "purely local" matters, such as manufacturing, was impossible. Federal power over interstate commerce was restricted to the interstate transportation of goods, and regulations could not be imposed that had an impact on such local matters. As *Hammer* indicates, this was especially true if the federal government regulated for some noncommercial purpose.

In 1929, the nation was plunged into the Great Depression. Three years later, Franklin Roosevelt was elected President on his promise to end the economic chaos of that time. He and the Democratic majority in Congress set about enacting various statutes designed to bring economic recovery. Most of those statutes were aimed at regulating manufacturing operations in some manner, but under the authority of the Commerce Clause. Time after time, the Supreme Court held those statutes unconstitutional with reasoning similar to that used in the *Hammer* v. *Dagenhart* decision. Among those statutes was the National Industrial Recovery Act, the Railroad Retirement Act, the Coal Conservation Act, and the Agricultural Adjustment Act.

In 1937, after Roosevelt's reelection, two keystone portions of the New Deal, the National Labor Relations Act* and the Social Security Act,** were up for review before the Supreme Court, along with a major case concerning the right of states to regulate labor†. Frustrated by the prior decisions that he felt emasculated his program

---

NLRB v. *Jones & Laughlin Steel*, p. 52–53.

**Helvering* v. *Davis*, p. 508.

†*West Coast Hotel* v. *Parrish*, p. 59–60.

for recovery and secure in his second term of office, Roosevelt moved against the Court to save the New Deal. On March 9, 1937, Roosevelt proposed an amendment to the Judiciary Act—later termed the **court-packing plan**—in a nationwide radio address.

Franklin D. Roosevelt
Fireside Chat

    .... The American people have learned from the depression. For in the last three national elections an overwhelming majority of them voted a mandate that the Congress and the President begin the task of providing that protection—not after long years of debate, but now.

    The courts, however, have cast doubts on the ability of the elected Congress to protect us against catastrophe by meeting squarely our modern social and economic conditions.

    We have, therefore, reached the point as a Nation where we must take action to save the Constitution from the Court and the Court from itself. We must find a way to take an appeal from the Supreme Court to the Constitution itself. We want a Supreme Court which will do justice under the Constitution, not over it....

    What is my proposal? It is simply this: whenever a judge or justice of any federal court has reached the age of 70 and does not avail himself of the opportunity to retire on a pension, a new member shall be appointed by the President.... This plan will save our National Constitution from hardening of the judicial arteries....

    At the time the plan was proposed, six justices were over the age of 70. Thus, the size of the Supreme Court would have been increased to fifteen members, and Roosevelt could have appointed six new members, more than enough to give him a majority on the Court. Roosevelt's plan was introduced in Congress but encountered heavy resistance, even among members of his own party, and was withdrawn. However, during the Congressional consideration of the plan, the Court considered the National Labor Relations Act (Wagner Act) in the following decision.

National Labor Relations Board v. Jones & Laughlin Steel Co.

301 U.S. 1, 57 S. Ct. 615, 81 L. Ed. 893 (1937)

The National Labor Relations Act outlawed a variety of "unfair labor practices," and gave authority to the National Labor Relations Board to determine whether an action by an employer was an unfair labor practice (see Chapter 13). The NLRB determined that the respondent, Jones & Laughlin Steel, had engaged in such practices and had therefore violated the act. Those practices included discrimination against members of a union with regard to hiring and tenure, coercion and intimidation of employees in order to interfere with their self-organization, and the discharge of employees active in the union. The NLRB ordered Jones & Laughlin to cease and desist from such practices and to reinstate several employees with back pay. Jones & Laughlin refused to comply, and the NLRB petitioned the U.S. Court of Appeals to enforce its order. That court refused, holding that the order of the NLRB was beyond the constitutional grant of authority under the Commerce Clause. The NLRB appealed to the Supreme Court, which granted certiorari.

    Mr. Chief Justice HUGHES delivered the opinion of the Court.

... [T]he respondent argues (1) that the Act is in reality a regulation of labor relations and not of interstate commerce; [and] (2) that the Act can have no application to the respondent's relations with its production employees because they are not subject to regulation by the federal government. ...

The Court described in detail the operations of Jones & Laughlin Steel, which operated mines in Michigan and Minnesota, operated coal mines in West Virginia, operated its own tugboats and towboats on interstate and intrastate waterways, manufactured steel in Pennsylvania, and owned and operated steel fabricating plants in New York.

Summarizing these operations, the Labor Board concluded that the works in Pittsburgh and Aliquippa (Pennsylvania) "might be likened to the heart of a self-contained, highly integrated body. They draw in the raw materials from Michigan, Minnesota, West Virginia, Pennsylvania in part through arteries and by means controlled by the respondent: they transform the materials and then pump them out to all parts of the nation through the vast mechanism which the respondent has elaborated."

....

.... Respondent says that whatever may be said of employees engaged in interstate commerce, the industrial relations and activities in the manufacturing department of respondent's enterprise are not subject to federal regulation. The argument rests upon the proposition that manufacturing in itself is not commerce. ...

The Government. ... urged that these activities constitute a "stream" or "flow" of commerce, of which the Aliquippa manufacturing plant is the focal point, and that industrial strife at that point would cripple the entire movement. ...

... The fundamental principle is that the power to regulate commerce is the power to enact all appropriate legislation for its protection and advancement ... to adopt measures to promote its growth and insure its safety ... to foster, protect, control and restrain. ... That power is plenary and may be exerted to protect interstate commerce, no matter what the source of the dangers which threaten it. ... . Although activities may be intrastate in character when separately considered, if they have such a close and substantial relation to interstate commerce that their control is essential or appropriate to protect that commerce from burdens and obstructions, Congress cannot be denied the power to exercise that control. ... Undoubtedly the scope of this power must be considered in the light of our dual system of government and may not be extended so as to embrace effects upon interstate commerce so indirect and remote that to embrace them, in view of our complex society, would effectually obliterate the distinction between what is national and what is local and create a completely centralized government. ... The question is necessarily one of degree.

....

The close and intimate effect which brings the subject within the reach of federal power may be due to activities in relation to productive industry although the industry when separately viewed is local. ...

....

In view of respondent's far-flung activities, it is idle to say that the effect would be indirect or remote. It is obvious that it would be immediate and might be catastrophic. We are asked to shut our eyes to the plainest facts of national life and to deal with the question of direct and indirect effects in an intellectual vacuum. ... When industries organize themselves on a national scale, making their relation to interstate commerce the dominant factor in their activities, how can it be maintained that their industrial labor relations constitute a forbidden field into which Congress may not enter when it is necessary to protect interstate commerce from the paralyzing consequences of industrial war?

Reversed.

Contemporary Dimensions of the Commerce Power   Following the *Jones &*
Laughlin Steel decision, other decisions refined the federal power until it was clear
that Congress could indeed regulate manufacturing and other local business so long
as they "affected Commerce" in some way. In the years that followed, Congress came
to rely extensively on the Commerce Clause as the source of its authority to enact a
variety of regulatory measures. In 1964 the full scope of the Commerce Power
became evident in the following decision:

Heart of Atlanta Motel v. U.S.

379 U.S. 241, 85 S. Ct. 348, 13 L. Ed. 2d 258 (1964)

In 1964 Congress passed Title II of the Civil Rights Act. That statute provided that "places of
public accomodation," including hotels, motels, restaurants, motion picture theatres, and
sport arenas, could not discriminate against nor segregate patrons on the basis of race, color,
religion, or national origin, if those establishments "affect commerce." The Act specifically
defined *affecting commerce* as serving or offering to serve interstate travellers, or obtaining
food, gasoline, or other products that had moved "in commerce" or presenting films, performances, or athletic teams that had moved "in commerce."

The Heart of Atlanta Motel was a large metropolitan motel in downtown Atlanta, Georgia.
The motel solicited patrons through national advertising and was located near interstate highways. Approximately 75 percent of its patrons came from out of state. Prior to the passage
of the Act, the motel had followed a practice of refusing to rent rooms to black travellers, and
it contended that it intended to do so in the future. The motel filed an action for a declaratory
judgment and for an injunction to restrain the enforcement of the Act. A three-judge panel
sustained the validity of the Act and issued an injunction against the motel, restraining it from
violating the Act. The motel appealed.

Mr. Justice CLARK delivered the opinion of the Court.
. . . .

The appellant contends that Congress in passing this Act exceeded its power to
regulate commerce under Article I, Section 8, clause 3 of the Constitution of the United
States. . . .

The appellees counter that the unavailability to Negroes of adequate accomodations interferes significantly with interstate travel, and that Congress, under the Commerce Clause, has power to remove such obstructions and restraints.
. . . .

. . . [T]he record of [the] passage [of the Act] . . . is replete with evidence of the
burdens that discrimination by race or color places upon interstate commerce. . . . This
testimony included the fact that our people have become increasingly mobile with millions of all races traveling from State to State; that Negroes in particular have been the
subject of discrimination in transient accommodations, having to travel great distances
to secure the same; that often they have been unable to obtain accommodations and
have had to call upon friends to put them overnight. . . . These exclusionary practices
were found to be nationwide, the Under Secretary of Commerce testifying that there is
"no question that this discrimination in the North still exists to a large degree" and in
the West and Midwest as well. . . . This testimony indicated a qualitative as well as
quantitative effect on interstate travel by Negroes. The former was the obvious impair-
ment of the Negro traveller's pleasure and convenience that resulted when he continually was uncertain of finding lodging. As for the latter, there was evidence that this
uncertainty stemming from racial discrimination had the effect of discouraging travel
on the part of a substantial portion of the Negro community. . . .

The power of Congress to deal with these obstructions depends on the meaning
of the Commerce Clause. Its meaning was first enunciated 140 years ago by the great

Chief Justice John Marshall in *Gibbons* v. *Ogden.* . . . In short, the determinative test of the exercise of power by the Congress under the Commerce Clause is simply whether the activity sought to be regulated is "commerce which concerns more than one state" and has a real and substantial relation to the national interest. . . .

. . . .

The same interest in protecting interstate commerce which led Congress to deal with segregation in interstate carriers and the white slave traffic has prompted it to extend the exercise of its power to gambling . . . to criminal enterprises . . . to deceptive practices in the sale of products . . . to fraudulent security transactions . . . to misbranding of drugs . . . to wages and hours . . . to members of labor unions . . . to crop control . . . to discrimination against shippers . . . to the protection of small business from injurious price cutting . . . to resale price maintenance . . . to professional football . . . and to racial discrimination by owners and managers of terminal restaurants. . . .

That Congress was legislating against moral wrongs in many of these areas rendered its enactments no less valid. In framing Title II of this Act Congress was also dealing with what it considered a moral problem. But that fact does not detract from the overwhelming evidence of the disruptive effect that racial discrimination has had on commercial intercourse. It was this burden which empowered Congress to enact appropriate legislation, and given this basis for the exercise of its power, Congress was not restricted by the fact that the particular obstruction to interstate commerce with which it was dealing was also deemed a moral and social wrong.

It is said that the operation of the motel here is of a purely local character. But, assuming this to be true, "if it is interstate commerce that feels the pinch, it does not matter how local the operation that applies the squeeze." . . . Thus the power of Congress to promote interstate commerce also includes the power to regulate the local incidents thereof, including local activities in both the States of origin and destination, which might have a substantial and harmful effect upon that commerce. One need only examine the evidence which we have discussed above to see that Congress may—as it has—prohibit racial discrimination by motels serving travelers, however "local" their operations may appear.

. . . .

We, therefore, conclude that the action of the Congress in the adoption of the Act as applied here to a motel which concededly serves interstate travelers is within the power granted it by the Commerce Clause of the Constitution, as interpreted by this Court for 140 years. It may be argued that Congress could have pursued other methods to eliminate the obstructions it found in interstate commerce caused by racial discrimination. But this is a matter of policy that rests entirely with the Congress and not with the courts. How obstructions in commerce may be removed—what means are to be employed—is within the sound and exclusive discretion of the Congress. It is subject only to one caveat—that the means chosen by it must be reasonably adapted to the end permitted by the Constitution. We cannot say that its choice here was not so adapted. The Constitution requires no more.

Affirmed

Recent cases involving the extent of federal power under the Commerce Clause have followed the lead of the *Heart of Atlanta Motel* decision.* It seems clear that the federal power over commerce allows Congressional regulation of much of American life. The issue of whether regulation is better handled by the states or by the federal government is a matter of policy for Congress, rather than a constitutional issue for

---

*See, e.g., *McLain* v. *Real Estate Board of New Orleans,* 444 U.S. 232, 100 S. Ct. 502, 62 L. Ed. 2d 441 (1980), which held that the activities of local real estate brokers "affected commerce" and were thus subject to federal law and regulations.

the Supreme Court. The Clause is really "the direct source of the most important powers which the Federal Government exercises in time of peace."

The Concepts of Economic Freedom

One of the basic arguments in constitutional affairs has to do with the place of our economic system. It is sometimes argued that a capitalist-style economy is somehow required by the document and that, therefore, various forms of government intervention in the economy or in business affairs is somehow not in keeping with the spirit, if not the letter, of the Constitution. But a search of the document itself discloses very little in the area of economic affairs. Only three provisions remotely touch on the area of economic regulation: the **Contracts Clause** of Article I, Section 10; and the **Due Process** and **Equal Protection** clauses, both of which are found in the 14th Amendment. Thus, while a free-enterprise or "capitalist" economy is probably quite desirable and may well be one of the preconditions to political democracy, such a system is not expressly mandated by the words of the Constitution.

The "Contracts" Clause

Article I, Section 10 of the Constitution provides that "No State shall . . . pass any . . . Law impairing the Obligation of Contracts." Early interpretations of the clause seemed to promise that the clause would be interpreted broadly to prevent state regulation of business and commercial affairs. During the middle and late 19th century, the clause was used to invalidate a variety of state regulations of business.

But the states also have broad "police powers" as indicated previously to regulate for the purposes of health, welfare, safety, and morals; a right not found in any Constitutional grant but is rather "an inherent right of government." At the end of the 19th century, the states began to use that right to regulate a wide variety of business-related activities. The Supreme Court held fairly early that the right of the state to regulate was superior to the Contracts Clause. As early as 1934 the Supreme Court, speaking through Chief Justice Hughes, held that prior decisions "put it beyond question that the prohibition is not an absolute one and is not to be read with literal exactness like a mathematical formula." It thus became clear that regulations which were "in the public interest" would be permitted, even though they may affect contractual obligations in some way.

The Contracts Clause had two other significant problems. First, the clause only prohibited *state* laws that impaired contractual relations and, therefore, had no impact on federal laws. Second, the clause related only to *contracts,* a word that was given a restrictive definition quite early. As a result, business activities which did not involve legal contracts were unaffected.

The Contracts Clause has very little contemporary application. As a result of the difficulties inherent in the clause, most challenges of government regulations were diverted to other areas, such as substantive due process or economic equal protection.

The Idea of Economic Due Process

The first Supreme Court decision to deal with the application of the **Due Process** Clause to business regulation came in 1873.* The Due Process Clause was added to the Constitution with the 14th Amendment in 1868 and stated that no State shall "deprive any person of life, liberty or property, without due process of law". The 1873 case had involved a Louisiana statute aimed at cleaning up the Mississippi River and controlling cholera, which was caused by pollution coming from the slaughterhouses. The state had effectively created a monopoly in one large slaughterhouse and made any other meat processing facilities illegal. The law deprived the owners of their livelihood in the hopes of controlling that one location. The Supreme Court ruled that the law did not violate the *due process* rights of the other owners, however.

But in the next twenty years, the membership of the Court changed and, finally in 1897, the Supreme Court ruled that state regulation of contracts could violate the due process clause. During the next forty years the doctrine of *economic due process* held a majority on the Court, as exemplified by the following decision. Pay particular attention to Justice Holmes' dissent.

Lochner v. New York

198 U.S. 45, 25 S. Ct. 539, 49 L. Ed. 937 (1905)

An 1897 New York statute prohibited employers from allowing employees to work more than 60 hours per week in a bakery. Joseph Lochner was convicted of violating the statute and fined 50 dollars. Two state courts affirmed the conviction, and Lochner appealed to the U.S. Supreme Court.

> Mr. Justice PECKHAM delivered the opinion of the court.
> . . . .
> The statute necessarily interferes with the right of contract between the employer and employees, concerning the number of hours in which the latter may labor in the bakery of the employer. The general right to make a contract in relation to his business is part of the liberty of the individual protected by the 14th Amendment of the Federal Constitution. . . . Under that provision no state can deprive any person of life, liberty, or property without due process of law. The right to purchase or to sell labor is part of the liberty protected by this amendment, unless there are circumstances which exclude the right. There are, however, certain powers, existing in the sovereignty of each state in the Union, somewhat vaguely termed police powers. . . . Those powers, broadly stated . . . relate to the safety, health, morals and general welfare of the public. Both property and liberty are held on such reasonable conditions as may be imposed by the governing power of the state in the exercise of those powers, and with such conditions the 14th Amendment was not designed to interfere. . . .
> The state, therefore, has power to prevent the individual from making certain kinds of contracts, and in regard to them the Federal Constitution offers no protection. . . .
> This court has recognized the existence and upheld the exercise of the police powers of the states in many cases which might fairly be considered as border ones, and it has, in the course of its determination . . . been guided by rules of a very liberal nature. . . .

Butcher's Benevolent Association v. *Crescent City Livestock Landing & Slaughterhouse Co.* (the Slaughterhouse Cases), 83 U.S. 36, 21 L. Ed. 394 (1873).

It must, of course, be conceded that there is a limit to the valid exercise of the police power of the state . . . Otherwise the 14th Amendment would have no efficacy and the legislatures of the states would have unbounded power. . . . In every case that comes before this court, therefore, where legislation of this character is concerned, and where the protection of the Federal Constitution is sought, the question necessarily arises: Is this a fair, reasonable, and appropriate exercise of the police power of the state, or is it an unreasonable, unnecessary, and arbitrary interference with the right of the individual to his personal liberty, or to enter into those contracts in relation to labor which may seem to him appropriate or necessary for the support of himself and his family?. . . .

The question whether this act is valid as a labor law, pure and simple, may be dismissed in a few words. There is no reasonable ground for interfering with the liberty of person or the right of free contract, by determining the hours of labor, in the occupation of a baker. There is no contention that bakers as a class are not equal in intelligence and capacity to men in other trades . . . or that they are not able to assert their rights and care for themselves without the protecting arm of the state. . . .

It is a question of which of two powers or rights shall prevail,—the power of the state to legislate or the right of the individual to liberty of person and freedom of contract. . . .

We think the limit of the police power has been reached and passed in this case. There is, in our judgment, no reasonable foundation for holding this to be necessary or appropriate as a health law to safeguard the public health, or the health of the individuals who are following the trade of baker. . . .

. . . . It seems to us that the real object and purpose were simply to regulate the hours of labor between the master and his employees . . . in a private business, not dangerous in any degree to morals or in any real and substantial degree to the health of the employees. Under such circumstances the freedom of master and employee to contract with each other in relation to their employment, and in defining the same, cannot be prohibited or interfered with, without violating the Federal Constitution.

. . . .

Reversed

Mr. Justice HOLMES, dissenting. . . .

This case is decided upon an economic theory which a large part of the country does not entertain. If it were a question whether I agreed with that theory, I should desire to study it further and long before making up my mind. But I do not conceive that to be my duty, because I strongly believe that my agreement or disagreement has nothing to do with the right of a majority to embody their opinions in law. It is settled by various decisions of this court that state constitutions and state laws may regulate life in many ways which we as legislators might think as injudicious, or if you like as tyrannical, as this, and which equally with this interfere with the liberty to contract. Sunday laws and usury laws are ancient examples. A more modern one is the prohibition of lotteries. . . . The 14th Amendment does not enact Mr. Herbert Spencer's Social Statics . . . Some of these laws embody convictions or prejudices which judges are likely to share. Some may not. But a Constitution is not intended to embody a particular economic theory, whether of paternalism and the organic relation of the citizen to the state or of *laissez faire*. It is made for people of fundamentally differing views, and the accident of our finding certain opinions natural and familiar, or novel, and even shocking, ought not to conclude our judgment upon the question whether statutes embodying them conflict with the Constitution of the United States.

. . . I think that the word ''liberty,'' in the 14th Amendment, is perverted when it is held to prevent the natural outcome of a dominant opinion, unless it can be said that a rational and fair man necessarily would admit that the statute proposed would infringe fundamental principles as they have been understood by the traditions of our people and our law. It does not need research to show that no such sweeping condemnation can be passed upon the statute before us. A reasonable man might think it a proper measure on the score of health. Men whom I certainly could not pronounce unreasonable would uphold it as a first installment of a general regulation of the hours of work. Whether in the latter aspect it would be open to the charge of inequality I think it unnecessary to discuss.

Thus, the basic dispute lay in the tension between the police power of the states and the Due Process Clause of the 14th Amendment. The former, as discussed earlier, gives states the right to regulate for purposes of health, welfare, safety, and morals. The latter provides that property (or property rights) cannot be taken without due process of law. The history of government regulation can be seen in part as the conflict between those two constitutional doctrines, and reaches full flower when the issues underlying the Commerce Clause are considered as well.

The *Lochner* analysis reached its apex in a 1923 decision, *Adkins* v. *Children's Hospital,** which struck down a federal minimum wage law as "a naked, arbitrary exercise of the legislative power." But again the membership of the Court was to change, and the pressures for public regulation of wages and hours took its toll on the Court. Finally, in 1937, following the announcement of the Court-Packing Plan, Holmes' view in *Lochner* was vindicated.

West Coast Hotel v. Parrish

300 U.S. 379, 57 S. Ct. 578, 81 L. Ed. 703 (1937)

A 1913 Washington state statute established a minimum wage for women and minors. The plaintiff was not paid the minimum wage and brought suit to recover the difference between that wage and her actual salary. The trial court ruled against her on the basis of *Lochner* and *Adkins* v. *Children's Hospital,* and she appealed to the State Supreme Court. That court ruled in her favor, and the defendant-employer appealed to the U.S. Supreme Court.

Mr. Chief Justice HUGHES delivered the opinion of the Court.

. . . .

The principle which must control our decision is not in doubt. The constitutional provision invoked is the due process clause of the Fourteenth Amendment. . . . In each case the violation alleged by those attacking minimum wage regulation for women is deprivation of freedom of contract. What is this freedom? The Constitution does not speak of freedom of contract. It speaks of liberty and prohibits the deprivation of liberty without due process of law. In prohibiting that deprivation, the Constitution does not recognize an absolute and uncontrollable liberty. Liberty in each of its phases has its history and connotation. But the liberty safeguarded is liberty in a social organization which requires the protection of law against the evils which menace the health safety, morals and welfare of the people. Liberty under the Constitution is thus necessarily subject to the restraints of due process, and regulation which is reasonable in relation to its subject and is adopted in the interests of the community is due process. . . .

The power under the Constitution to restrict freedom of contract has had many illustrations. That it may be exercised in the public interest with respect to contracts between employer and employee is undeniable. [The Court discussed a vairety of other

---

*261 U.S. 525, 43 S. Ct. 394 (1923).

minimum wage-maximum hours statutes that had been sustained and other regulations
of the contract between employer and employee.]

. . . .

In dealing with the relation of employer and employed, the Legislature has necessarily a wide field of discretion in order that there may be suitable protection of health
and safety, and that peace and good order may be promoted through regulations
designed to insure wholesome conditions of work and freedom from oppression. . . .

We think that the views thus expressed are sound and that the decision in the
Adkins Case was a departure from the true application of the principles governing the
regulation by the state of the relation of employer and employed. . . .

There is an additional and compelling consideration which recent economic experience has brought into a strong light. The exploitation of a class of workers who are in
an unequal position with respect to bargaining power and thus relatively defenseless
against the denial of a living wage is not only detrimental to their health and well being,
but casts a direct burden for their support upon the community. What these workers
lose in wages the taxpayers are called upon to pay. . . .

Our conclusion is that the case of *Adkins* v. *Children's Hospital* . . . should be, and
it is, overruled. The judgment of the Supreme Court of the state of Washington is
affirmed.

Economic Equal Protection

The 14th Amendment also contains the famous Equal Protection Clause which guarantees the "equal protection of the laws" to all persons. The clause has been used by
the courts, although somewhat sparingly, to invalidate laws that discriminate against
one business in favor of another. The application of equal protection principles to
economic regulation came late and did not last long.

Morey v. Doud

354 U.S. 457, 77 S. Ct. 1344, 1 L. Ed. 2d 1485 (1957)

An Illinois statute prohibited currency exchanges from selling money orders in retail establishments, except money orders of the American Express Company. The plaintiff sold money
orders of a competing company and sought an injunction against enforcement of the statute
on the ground that singling out one company for special treatment constituted a violation of
the equal protection clause. A three-judge panel of the District Court enjoined enforcement,
and the state appealed.

Mr. Justice BURTON delivered the opinion of the Court.

. . . .

In determining the constitutionality of the Act's application to appellees in the light
of its exception of American Express money orders, we start with the established proposition that the "prohibition of the Equal Protection Clause goes no further than the
invidious discrimination." . . . . The rules for testing a discrimination have been summarized as follows: "1. The equal protection clause of the Fourteenth Amendment does
not take from the State the power to classify in the adoption of police laws, but admits
of the exercise of a wide scope of discretion in that regard, and avoids what is done
only when it is without any reasonable basis and therefore is purely arbitrary. 2. A classification having some reasonable basis does not offend against that clause merely
because it is not made with mathematical nicety or because in practice it results in
some inequality. 3. When the classification in such a law is called in question, if any
state of facts reasonably can be conceived that would sustain it, the existence of that
state of facts at the time the law was enacted must be assumed. 4. One who assails

the classification in such a law must carry the burden of showing that it does not rest upon any reasonable basis but is essentially arbitrary." . . . To these rules we add the caution that "Discrimination of an unusual character especially suggest careful consideration to determine whether they are obnoxious to the constitutional provision." . . .

The Act creates a statutory class of sellers of money orders. The money orders sold by one company, American Express, are excepted from that class. There is but one "American Express Company." If the exception is to be upheld, it must be on the basis on which it is cast—an exception of a particular business entity and not of a generic category.

The purpose of the Act's licensing and regulatory provisions clearly is to protect the public when dealing with currency exchanges. Because the American Express Company is a world-wide enterprise of unquestioned solvency and high financial standing, the State argues that the legislative classification is reasonable. It contends that the special characteristics of the American Express Company justify excepting its money orders from the requirements of an Act aimed at local companies doing local business, and that appellees are in no position to complain about competitive disadvantages since the Fourteenth Amendment does not protect a business against the hazards of competition. . . .

That the Equal Protection Clause does not require that every state regulatory statute apply to all in the same business is a truism. For example, where size is an index to the evil at which the law is directed, discriminations between the large and the small are permissible. Moreover, we have repeatedly recognized that "reform may take one step at a time, addressing itself to the phase of the problem which seems most acute to the legislative mind." . . . . On the other hand, a statutory discrimination must be based on differences that are reasonably related to the purposes of the Act in which it is found. . . .

The provisions in the Illinois Act, such as those requiring an annual inspection of licensed community currency exchanges . . . make it clear that the statute was intended to afford the public *continuing* protection. The discrimination in favor of the American Express Company does not conform to this purpose. The exception of its money orders apparently rests on the legislative hypothesis that the characteristics of the American Express Company make it unnecessary to regulate their sales. Yet these sales, by virtue of the exception, will continue to be unregulated whether or not the American Express Company retains its present characteristics. On the other hand, sellers of competing money orders are subject to the Act even though their characteristics are, or become, substantially identical with those the American Express Company now has. . . .

The Court affirmed a lower court judgment enjoining enforcement of the Act.

The doctrine of economic equal protection under the *Morey* v. *Doud* decision did not stand for long. The decision seemed to indicate that a state could not discriminate against businesses under almost any circumstances. But, clearly, there are circumstances where the legislature has a sound basis for favoring one business over another. In 1976, the Supreme Court considered a case that, on its face, was a flagrant violation of equal protection principles under the rule of *Morey* v. *Doud.*

City of New Orleans v. Dukes
427 U.S. 297, 96 S. Ct. 2513, 49 L. Ed. 2d 51 (1976)

During the early 1970's there had been a tremendous rise in the number of pushcart food vendors in the French Quarter of New Orleans. In an effort to preserve the ambiance of the French Quarter, the city passed an ordinance prohibiting all pushcarts except those that had been in operation more than eight years. Dukes had operated such a pushcart for two years and, to prevent elimination of his business, he filed suit to challenge the constitutionality of the ordinance. He relied expressly on *Morey* v. *Doud* in his case. The Court of Appeals had held the ordinance unconstitutional under that case, and the city appealed.

PER CURIAM

When local economic regulation is challenged solely as violating the Equal Protection Clause, this Court consistently defers to legislative determinations as to the desirability of particular statutory discriminations. . . . Unless a classification trammels fundamental personal rights or suspect classifications such as race, religion, or alienage, our decisions presume the constitutionality of the statutory discriminations and require only that the classification challenged be rationally related to a legitimate state interest. States are accorded wide latitude in the regulation of their local economies under their police powers, and rational distinctions may be made with substantially less than mathematical exactitude. Legislatures may implement their program step by step . . . in such economic areas, adopting regulations that only partially ameliorate a perceived evil and deferring complete elimination of the evil to future regulations . . . In short, the judiciary may not sit as a superlegislature to judge the wisdom or desirability of legislative policy determinations made in areas that neither affect fundamental rights nor proceed along suspect lines . . . in the local economic sphere, it is only the invidious discrimination, the wholly arbitrary act, which cannot stand consistently with the Fourteenth Amendment. . . .

The Court of Appeals held in this case, however, that the "grandfather provision" failed even the rationality test. We disagree. The city's classification rationally furthers the purpose which the . . . city had identified as its objective . . . that is, as a means "to preserve the appearance and custom valued by the Quarter's residents and attractive to tourists." . . . The legitimacy of that objective is obvious. The City Council plainly could further that objective by making the reasoned judgment that street peddlers and hawkers tend to interfere with the charm and beauty of a historic area and disturb tourists and disrupt their enjoyment of that charm and beauty, and that such vendors in the Vieux Carre, the heart of the city's tourist industry, might thus have a deleterious effect on the economy of the city. They therefore determined that to ensure the economic vitality of that area, such businesses should be substantially curtailed in the Vieux Carre, if not totally banned.

Nevertheless, relying on *Morey* v. *Doud* . . . as its "chief guide," the Court of Appeals held that even though the exemption of the . . . vendors was rationally related to legitimate city interests on the basis of facts extant when the ordinance was amended, the "grandfather clause" still could not stand because "the hypothesis that a present eight year veteran of the pushcart hot dog market in the Vieux Carre will continue to operate in a manner more consistent with the traditions of the Quarter than woud any other operator is without foundation." . . . Actually, the reliance on the statute's potential irrationality in *Morey* v. *Doud* . . . was a needlessly intrusive judicial infringement on the State's legislative powers, and we have concluded that the equal protection analysis employed in that opinion should no longer be followed. *Morey* was the only case in the last half century to invalidate a wholly economic regulation solely on equal protection grounds, and we are now satisfied that the decision was erroneous. *Morey* is . . . essentially indistinguishable from this case, but the decision so far departs from proper equal protection analysis in cases of exclusively economic regulation that it should be, and it is, overruled.

While the *Dukes* case expressly overruled *Morey* v. *Doud,* the whole concept of economic equal protection is not dead. But decisions after *Dukes* make it clear that the courts will uphold a statute against such a claim if there is evidence that the classification scheme is debatable and has a "rational" basis. The simple fact that legislation is "wrong" is not enough.

A Note on Politics

Lawyers, like all professionals, tend to suffer from professional myopia. While legal restrictions found in the Constitution and the concept of judicial review furnish some extremely important checks on possible government overreaching, they are clearly not the only checks on government by any means. The formal checks supplied by our Constitution would be meaningless unless they were widely accepted by our society and our political system. Many of the same provisions found in our Constitution, including our Bill of Rights, are found in the "charters" of many other countries, including some dictatorships and even some Communist nations. The difference appears to be that the American people and their politically elected representatives, for the most part, really believe what the Constitution says.

In that sense, government power is limited by informal and political means as well as by the formal legal restrictions of the Constitution. Public opinion, pressure groups, and political parties all serve as useful channels by which the will of the people is made known to the elected representatives in Congress and the state legislatures. They serve to educate the representatives on the issues before them and to provide a rough "power equation" by which representatives may judge the extent and the intensity of public feeling on an issue.

In that sense, law and politics are intimately intertwined. The final result of the political process is the creation of laws in the form of statutes passed by elected representatives. And that political process is itself in turn "controlled" by the legal process, both in the form of Constitutional limitations and the process of judicial review. Law and politics are in fact two sides of the same coin.

But our political system is based to a very large extent on the concept of majority rule. The electoral process and the method of passing laws in our legislatures are both based on democratic principles, which is to say that whoever or whatever gets the most votes wins. While that concept is essential to democratic government, it raises the specter of "the tyranny of the majority," in which the will of the many may run roughshod over the interest of the few. In the words of Alexis de Tocqueville, an astute French observer of the American scene in the 1830's:

> In my opinion, the main evil of the present democratic institutions of the United States does not arise, as is often asserted in Europe, from their weakness, but from their irresistible strength. I am not so much alarmed at the excessive liberty which reigns in that country as at the inadequate securities which one finds there against tyranny.
>
> When an individual or a party is wronged in the United States, to whom can he apply for redress? If to public opinion, public opinion constitutes the majority; if to the legislature, it represents the majority and implicitly obeys it; if to the executive power, it is appointed by the majority and serves as a passive tool in its hands. The public force consists of the majority under arms; the jury is the majority invested with the right of hearing judicial cases; and in certain states even the judges are elected by the majority. However iniquitous or absurd the measure of which you complain, you must submit to it as well as you can. (*Democracy in America*, 1835).

To some degree the tyranny of the majority is controlled by American sensitivity to the rights of minorities and a possible innate sympathy for the underdog. But the Founding Fathers, and particularly the "public" of the late 18th century, did not trust those informal restrictions. Instead, two years after the ratification of the Constitution, ten amendments were added to the document to act as bulwarks against the authority of the state and the authority of the majority. Those amendments, known as *The Bill of Rights,* are the subject of the next chapter.

Summary and Conclusions

While government has the power to act within the guidelines supplied by the Constitution, there are limits on the exercise of government power. Those limits are supplied, in the first instance, by the grant of power itself, since government can only act within the grant of power, whether express or implied.

What began as an attempt to provide a uniform system of regulation over commerce has become the source of much of the federal authority to regulate commerce. On one hand, the Commerce Clause acts to restrict state authority to discriminate against or unduly burden interstate commerce. On the other hand, the clause has provided the authority for the federal government's authority to regulate such disparate subjects as civil rights, labor, and antitrust.

The concept of economic freedom must be examined within the context of the Constitution itself. Generally the courts have taken a "restraintist," or balancing of interests approach to economic freedom and government regulation of business. This is opposed to the usual "activist" position as taken in the area of civil liberties, an area to be examined in the next chapter.

PRO AND CON

ISSUE: Should the Constitution be Interpreted "Strictly" According to Its Terms or to Reflect the Changing Needs of Society?

PRO: The Constitution Should be Interpreted Strictly
Senator Sam J. Ervin, Jr.*

There is not a syllable in (the Constitution) which gives the Supreme Court any discretionary power to fashion policies based on such considerations as expediency or prudence to guide the course of action of the government of our country. On the contrary, the Constitution provides in plain and positive terms that the role of the Supreme Court is that of an adjudicator, which determines judicially legal controversies. . . .

While (the Founding Fathers) intended the Constitution to endure throughout the ages as the nation's basic instrument of government, the Founding Fathers realized that useful alterations of the Constitution would be suggested by experi-

ence. Consequently they made provision for its amendment in one way, and one way only, i.e., by concurrent action of Congress and the states as set forth in Article V. By so doing, they ordained that "nothing new can be put into the Constitution except through the amendatory process" and "nothing old can be taken out without the same process."

Article III denies the Supreme Court policymaking power in plain and positive terms. It does this by making the Supreme Court a court of law and equity and by granting to it "judicial power" only. . . .

---

*Senator Ervin was a United States Senator and chairman of the Senate Judiciary Committee that investigated the "Watergate" matter. From American Enterprise Institute for Public Policy Research, *Role of the Supreme Court: Policymaker or Adjudicator?* (Washington D.C.: Author, 1970). The debate took place at the Madison Hotel in December 1970. Reprinted with permission of the American Enterprise Institute.

Article III denies the Supreme Court policymaking power in another way. When it is read in conjunction with the supremacy clause . . . Article III obligates Supreme Court Justices to base their decisions in the cases they hear upon the Constitution, the laws, and the treaties of the United States, and thus forbids them to take their personal notions as to what is desirable into account in making their rulings.

The power to interpret the Constitution is an awesome power. This is so because, in truth, constitutional government cannot exist in our land unless this power is exercised aright. . . .

The power to interpret the Constitution, which is alloted to the Supreme Court, and the power to amend the Constitution, which is assigned to Congress and the states acting in conjunction, are quite different. The power to interpret the Constitution is the power to ascertain its meaning, and the power to amend the Constitution is the power to change its meaning.

Since it is a court of law and equity, the Supreme Court acts as the interpreter of the Constitution only in a litigated case whose decision of necessity turns on some provision of that instrument. As a consequence, the function of the Court is simply to ascertain and give effect to the intent of those who framed and ratified the provision in issue. If the provision is plain, the Court must gather the intent solely from its language, but if the provision is ambiguous, the Court must place itself

as nearly as possible in the condition of those who framed and ratified it, and in that way determine the intent the language was used to express. For these reasons, the Supreme Court is duty bound to interpret the Constitution according to its language and history.

Those who champion or seek to justify the activism of the Warren Court assert with glibness that the Constitution is a living document which the Court must interpret with flexibility.

When they say the Constitution is a living document, they really mean that the Constitution is dead, and that activist justices as its executors may dispose of its remains as they please. I submit that if the Constitution is, indeed, a living document, its words are binding on those who pledge themselves by oath or affirmation to support it.

What of the cliche that the Supreme Court should interpret the Constitution with flexibility? If those who employ this cliche mean by it that a provision of the Constitution should be interpreted with liberality to accomplish its intended purpose, they would find me in hearty agreement with them. But they do not employ the cliche to mean this. On the contrary, they use the cliche to mean that the Supreme Court should bend the words of a constitutional provision to one side or the other to accomplish an objective the provision does not sanction. Hence, they use the cliche to thwart what the Founding Fathers had in mind when the fashioned the Constitution.

CON: The Constitution Should be Interpreted to Reflect the Times
Ramsey Clark*

We demean the Constitution of the United States by this endless metaphysical debate over ''strict construction.'' There are real constitutional issues to be faced, perhaps even constitutional crises. They will require all the vision and courage we can muster. The false notion that men who wrote those words 183 years ago—distant age—could foresee the unforeseeable, or that we can look back and in words alone, or from their intent in the context of 1787, divine the author's precise meaning as applied to current facts is contrary to all human experience. Our problems, actual and immense, cannot be solved by such conjury. We are fortunate

that nature spares us from the foresight that would be required to give truth to the doctrine of strict construction, because the only thing worse than such impossibility would be its possibility.

Change is the dominant fact of our times. Populations and technology, the major dynamics, create more change in a decade than centuries witnessed heretofore. Life changes, the meanings of words change, the needs of man change. The Constitution, born in a fundamentally different epoch, must have the durability and wisdom to grow, to encompass essentially new situations, to meet new needs. It can.

---

*Mr. Clark was Attorney General of the United States under President Lyndon Johnson, and is the son of Justice Tom Clark of the U.S. Supreme Court. From American Enterprise Institute for Public Policy Research, *Role of the Supreme Court: Policymaker or Adjudicator?* (Washington, D.C.: Author, 1970). The debate took place at the Madison Hotel in December 1970. Reprinted with permission of the American Enterprise Institute.

To invoke the Founding Fathers against change is to charge them with seeking to deny subsequent generations that to which they were wholly committed for their own. To vest the Supreme Law of the Land with some religious attachment to the status quo is to deny its very meaning and disable the Ship of State in the turbulent seas of change. The purpose behind the doctrine of strict construction as utilized today is not to find specific guidance where none can exist. It is to resist change: to stay where we are, do as we have done and offer no hope. We can no longer afford this.

In 1918, a bare majority of the Supreme Court again showed what strict construction can mean. Reading the Commerce Clause alone, it said the federal government is powerless to prevent interstate shipment of the products of child labor. *Hammer* v. *Dagenhart,* 247 U.S. 251 (1918). The Constitution by that construction—unsupported incidentally in the language of the charter—did not empower the Congress to prevent virtual slave labor of 10 and 12 year old children working in sweatshops 70 hours or more a week for subsistence wages. These men were not deciding issues on the basis of some clear understanding of intentions from 1787. The men in the Hall of Philadelphia could not foresee such questions, much less their answers. They were cruelly used by justices who would decide by fiat what words meant to them, then grace themselves in the mantle of the Founding Fathers. The experience and sympathies of the Court's majority were closer to the cotton mill owners who destroyed children than to justice and humane concerns, and they resisted change. . . .

Strict construction is hardly consistent. Its roots are too shallow to guide its direction. The doctrine is most often grasped by those who find convenient words and prefer to stand on them rather than the constitutional force of their position. In the late 1920s and 1930s the nation faced a constitutional crisis that approached disaster. In a series of cases the Court said in effect—and with no support in the words of the Constitution—that government cannot address itself to new economic problems that overwhelm it. . . .

Strict construction is at best a convenient argument with which to support or attack particular judicial decisions. How many of us are really prepared to have our Constitution construed solely by its words and their intentions when written? There is, after all, not a word in the Constitution about many of our most important protections. The hallowed presumption of innocence, and the requirement that guilt in criminal cases be proven beyond a reasonable doubt are not found in the words of the Constitution. Nor does the Constitution say that state governments may not trample upon freedom of speech or press or religion, that state legislatures must be fairly apportioned, or that any of us have any "right to privacy."

It is hardly surprising that the words of the Constitution, even supplemented by their historical context, do not resolve the great questions of our time. In 1791, when the ink on the Constitution was hardly dry, President Washington, who had chaired the Convention, Thomas Jefferson, and Alexander Hamilton were unable to agree among themselves on whether the "necessary and proper" clause authorized the federal government to charter a national bank. Eventually the matter was resolved not on the basis of some nonexistent "plain meaning" of the constitutional language, but on the best judgment the statesmen of the day could make. . . . The crises which we face today, the great constitutional questions which are put to the Supreme Court for resolution are far more difficult. Mass society, urban poverty, racism, vast industry, huge labor unions, tall skyscrapers, automobiles, jet aircraft, television, nuclear energy, environmental pollution, mass assemblies and protests, the interdependence of nations and individuals create issues undreamed of in the philosophies of the Founding Fathers.

The Constitution guides by general principle—a light that recognizes the existence of change. By its very nature it must embody a whole theory in a quick phrase—to regulate commerce—the general welfare—due process of law—the equal protection of the laws. . . . If it were to be specific, it could not be a Constitution nor hope to maintain a theory and framework of government with general powers and limitations.

DISCUSSION QUESTIONS

1. At the end of *Hammer* v. *Dagenhart,* Mr. Justice Day made some extremely foreboding predictions if Congress ever received the power to regulate production. Congress has now had that power for over 45 years. Were his predictions correct?

2. Was Roosevelt's court packing plan legal? Moral? Ethical? Why or why not? Do you think the Framers of the Constitution intended this result?

3. Does it make sense to refer, in Constitutional issues, to "the intent of the Framers?" How can we determine what that intent was? Even if we can determine the intent, is that intent relevant 200 years later?

4. Under the preemption doctrine and the federal power over commerce, taken together, can you think of anything which Congress could not regulate today?

5. Both Justice Day in *Hammer* v. *Dagenhart* and Justice Clark in *Heart of Atlanta Motel* relied expressly on Justice Marshall's language in *Gibbons* v. *Ogden*. How is that possible? Doesn't one or the other have to be wrong?

6. Should we adopt a constitutional amendment making capitalism the "official" economic system of the United States? Why or why not?

7. As an exercise, try to label the various Supreme Court opinions in this chapter as "neutralist," "restraintist," or "activist." Do you think it is easy to consistently be a "neutralist"? Why do lawyers and judges value consistency so highly?

8. Aren't the judicial activists being very hypocritical by applying one set of standards to economic liberties and another set to civil rights and liberties? Or are civil rights and liberties more important to our system of government?

9. Should a legislator always follow public opinion? If not, under what circumstances shouldn't he do so? When should he listen to lobbyists? Ever?

CASE PROBLEMS

1. An Arizona statute made it illegal to operate a train consisting of more than 14 passenger cars or 70 freight cars in the state for safety reasons. The practical effect of the statute was that trains entering Arizona had to drop off cars at the border, to be picked up by other trains not over the limit. Is the statute constitutional? [*Southern Pacific Co.* v. *Arizona* 325 U.S. 761, 65 S. Ct. 1515, 89 L. Ed. 1915 (1945).]

2. South Carolina prohibited the use of trucks or trailers in the state if their width exceeded 90 inches and their weight exceeded 20,000 pounds. Most trucks were under the limits, but a few trucks, particularly those that travelled "long hauls," exceeded the limits. Is the statute constitutional? [*South Carolina Highway Department* v. *Barnwell Bros.,* 303 U.S. 177, 58 S. Ct. 510, 82 L. Ed. 734 (1938).]

3. An Oklahoma statute made it a crime to ship minnows for sale outside the state. Hughes, a Texas bait dealer, purchased minnows in Oklahoma and was transporting them to his bait shop when he was arrested. May he rely on the Commerce Clause or the preemption doctrine to overturn the statute? [*Hughes* v. *Oklahoma,* 441 U.S. 322, 99 S. Ct. 1727, 60 L. Ed. 2d 250 (1979).]

4. Federal law licenses vessels that sail on the Great Lakes, and a part of the licensing procedure involves federal safety inspection of boilers and engines. A Detroit

ordinance set maximum smoke emission standards. Ships owned by the Huron Portland Cement Company violated the Detroit standards and were fined. Is the Detroit ordinance preempted? Is it an undue burden or discrimination against interstate commerce? [*Huron Portland Cement Co.* v. *City of Detroit,* 362 U.S. 440, 80 S. Ct. 813, 4 L. Ed. 2d 852 (1960).]

5. The Federal Consumer Protection Act makes extortionate debt collection practices a federal crime. Perez loaned money to a local butcher and threatened the butcher and his family when the money was not paid back. Perez was prosecuted under the federal law, and he claimed that the transaction was entirely "local" and therefore beyond federal jurisdiction. What result would you expect and why? [*Perez* v. *U.S.,* 402 U.S. 146, 91 S. Ct. 1357, 28 L. Ed. 2d 686 (1971).]

6. Ollie's Barbeque, a local restaurant in Birmingham, Alabama, refused to serve blacks. There was evidence that few, if any, interstate travelers ate at Ollie's, that Ollie did not advertise at all, and that in fact all of Ollie's supplies were purchased from local distributors. Some of those distributors received their supplies from out-of-state, however. (a.) Is Ollie outside of the scope of the Civil Rights Act of 1964? (b.) Is the application of that Act to Ollie unconstitutional? Why or why not? [*Katzenbach* v. *McClung,* 379 U.S. 294, 85 S. Ct. 377, 13 L. Ed. 2d 290 (1964).]

7. A 1903 Kansas statute prohibited employers from requiring employees to sign "yellow dog" contracts; that is, contracts which require that employees not join or be members of labor unions as a condition of employment. Result in 1915? Result today? [*Coppage* v. *Kansas,* 236 U.S. 1, 35 S. Ct. 240, 59 L. Ed. 441 (1915).]

8. A Michigan statute provided that no woman could obtain a bartender's license unless she was the wife or daughter of the male owner. Result in 1948? Is this a business regulation or a civil liberties problem? [*Goesaert* v. *Cleary,* 335 U.S. 464, 69 S. Ct. 198, 93 L. Ed. 163 (1948).]

9. A New York ordinance made it a crime to advertise anything on a vehicle except identification signs on trucks. Railway Express routinely sold advertising space on its trucks. The purpose of the law was to prevent distractions to people on the street and other drivers. Railway Express was convicted. Result? Are there civil liberties aspects to this case as well? [*Railway Express Agency* v. *New York,* 336 U.S. 106, 69 S. Ct. 463, 93 L. Ed. 533 (1949).]

SUGGESTED READINGS

Alsop, Joseph, and Turner Catledge. *The 168 Days* (New York: Doubleday Doran, 1938).

Baker, Leonard. *Back to Back: The Duel Between FDR and the Supreme Court* (New York: Macmillan, 1967).

Corwin, Edward S. *Liberty Against Government* (Baton Rouge: Louisiana State University Press, 1948).

Needham, Douglas. *The Economics and Politics of Regulation* (Boston: Little, Brown, 1983).

Siegan, Bernard H. *Economic Liberties and the Constitution* (Chicago: The University of Chicago Press, 1980).

Truman, David B. *The Government Process* (New York: Alfred A. Knopf, 1964).

3

The Bill of Rights

It is my belief that there are "absolutes" in our Bill of Rights, and that they were put there on purpose by men who knew what words meant and meant their prohibitions to be "absolutes."

Justice Hugo L. Black

There is danger that, if the Court does not temper its doctrinaire logic with a little practical wisdom, it will convert the constitutional Bill of Rights into a suicide pact.

Justice Robert H. Jackson

The American **Bill of Rights,** consisting of the first ten amendments to the Constitution, is one of the most remarkable legal and political documents in the world. First, it is a statement of things the government may not do. The very idea that a government was in any way restricted in its actions was a revolutionary concept in a time when most nations were ruled by arbitrary monarchs. Second, the Bill of Rights is written in language that is at once both significant and vague. The amendments impose strict limits on government action, but in language sufficiently flexible to adapt to changing historical circumstances. Third, it might be argued that the relatively few words of the first ten amendments contain *all* of the essential preconditions for political liberty and democracy. The 1st Amendment has been called the "heart of political democracy," and it is difficult to envision any other necessary conditions for democratic government aside from those guaranteed by the Bill of Rights. And, finally, Americans and American courts have taken the Bill of Rights seriously. Following the American lead, many other nations have adopted Bills of Rights, some copied almost verbatim from ours. But in many such nations those Bills of Rights lie forgotten and unused.

All this makes it even more curious that the original Constitution contained no Bill of Rights. Federalists had opposed a Bill of Rights during the Constitutional Convention on the grounds that by specifying certain rights, other unspecified rights might go unprotected. Alexander Hamilton also argued that a Bill of Rights might provide a colorable claim that government had powers other than those expressly granted by the Constitution. Hamilton saw no need to prohibit actions that the government had no power to carry out in the first place under the doctrine of enumerated powers, and that by prohibiting those things expressly it provided an argument to those who claimed that the government had powers beyond those specifically granted.

But the nation was unwilling to accept a Constitution without a Bill of Rights. A grass-roots cry arose across the nation demanding a list of protected freedoms. Some states refused to ratify the Constitution unless the framers promised to add a Bill of Rights, and other states made "conditional ratifications" providing that ratification would be revoked unless a Bill of Rights was added. It seemed that the bitter memories of British excesses were too fresh in the minds of the American people.

In the end the supporters of a Bill of Rights had their way. Prominent men throughout the nation made promises that if the Constitution was ratified they would immediately move to add a Bill of Rights by amendment. The body of the Constitution was ratified in 1789 and, on December 15, 1791, the Bill of Rights was formally amended to the Constitution.

The Nature of the Bill of Rights

At the outset we are faced with a problem of definition. Most simple definitions of the Bill of Rights include only the first ten amendments. But if we mean by the term *Bill of Rights* all those parts of the Constitution that protect individual liberty from inappropriate governmental interference, we must include much more. One observer* has counted 63 separate, express guarantees of individual freedom in the Constitution. These include several in the body of the Constitution, such as the Contracts and Supremacy Clauses, all of the specific guarantees in the first ten amendments, and all of the guarantees in later amendments. Many reasonable people argue that the term *Bill of Rights* should include at least the 13th, 14th and 15th Amendments, with their prohibitions of slavery, protection of equal rights, and Due Process clauses. It is that latter definition which we will use in this chapter.

It is impossible to do justice to the Bill of Rights in the space of a single chapter of a textbook. Each amendment, and in fact each phrase in each amendment, has been subjected to close judicial interpretation and judicial evolution. Rather than presenting a superficial survey of all of the amendments, this chapter will consider a few of the major provisions in some depth.

The choice of provisions to discuss is somewhat arbitrary. This chapter discusses the 1st Amendment in some detail, principally because it is so important to our political-legal system and because it has substantial relevance to business in its **commercial**

---

*Irving Brant, *The Bill of Rights* (Indianapolis: Bobbs-Merrill, 1965) pp. 3–15.

speech doctrine. We will also consider the criminal procedure amendments—the 4th, 5th and 6th Amendments—primarily because every educated person should have some knowledge of those provisions and because they also have a business relevance when a business is subjected to administrative or criminal investigation.

The chapter also considers two 14th Amendment provisions, the Due Process and Equal Protection Clauses, because of their overriding significance to many areas discussed later in the text. Consideration of the Due Process Clause involves a discussion of the **selective incorporation** doctrine, under which certain (but not all) provisions of the first ten amendments are made applicable to the states, and of **procedural due process,** especially in its application to administrative agencies. We already met some Equal Protection Clause concepts in our discussion of economic liberties in Chapter 2, and those concepts will again be vital in our consideration of the law of discrimination in Chapter 16.

Finally, we will consider the possibility that rights exist beyond those expressly granted by the Constitution. That possibility has arisen since the judicial creation of the **right of privacy** in the *Griswold* case. The existence of such a broad-based right of privacy has itself enormous significance to both business and the ordinary citizen in a time of computerized information-gathering and advancing technology.

But the concept of "other rights" has a significance that overrides even the development of the right of privacy. That concept underscores and clarifies the basic notion behind the Bill of Rights, namely that the people are the source of government and not the other way around. The rights specified in the Bill of Rights are not *granted* by government, because they are not government's to grant. All rights are *retained* by the people, except those which are expressly granted to government under the enumerated and implied powers. The Bill of Rights, therefore, is merely a formal statement that government has no power to regulate in certain areas or in certain ways, but that formal statement does not mean that other rights, not expressed in the Constitution, are not also retained by the people.

Stare Decisis and Interpretation Revisited

Like any other statute or constitutional provision, the provisions of the Bill may be and must be interpreted by the courts. Those interpretations then, of course, become binding precedent for future court decisions.

Two problems are especially pronounced in interpretations of the Bill of Rights. The first is that there is a special need for interpretation in matters relating to the Bill of Rights, principally because the language used in its provisions is so broad and vague. This does not mean that the amendments are without meaning, however. It is part of the special genius of the American Constitution that it provides both a direction and fixed rules for government and flexibility for future adaptions through judicial construction.

The second issue deals with the status of judicial decisions interpreting the Constitution. Those interpretations have the status of the document itself, and in effect become a part of the Constitution. Those constructions may be changed by later court decisions, or by decisions of higher courts, but until that time they are constitutional law. Thus, the decisions of the U.S. Supreme Court, especially, have the same status as the Constitution and cannot be changed except by a later decision of the Supreme Court or by Constitutional amendment. A Congressional act, for example, that purports to change the effect of a Supreme Court decision interpreting the Constitution would be of no effect.

Finally, before we begin consideration of some selected parts of the Bill of Rights, a word of warning to students seems appropriate: Read the amendment first! The precise language of the Constitution is extremely important to the interpretations by the Court, and a full understanding of the cases is impossible without a knowledge of what the document says. And, even if you are familiar with the Constitution, or think you are, there are likely to be some surprises.

The 1st Amendment

It has been argued that the 1st Amendment is the heart of American political freedom.* That amendment, dealing with freedom of speech, freedom of the press, freedom of religion, freedom of assembly, and the right to petition the government, is based on Thomas Jefferson's **marketplace theory** of public thought. That theory assumes that each person is intelligent and discerning and that all ideas should be permitted into the "marketplace of ideas." Since people are intelligent, they will "buy" the good and true ideas and reject the bad and false ones. But government cannot and should not intervene and tell us which ideas to accept or reject. Later theorists would point to totalitarian dictatorships, where thought control and book-burning are among the first orders of business. The 1st Amendment is sometimes said to protect *freedom of conscience,* since it guarantees the rights of all persons to believe as they wish, to express those beliefs openly, and to attempt to use those beliefs to influence the government. Our discussion will center around freedom of speech, freedom of the press, and freedom of religion, since they seem to be the foundations of the amendment.

Freedom of Speech

The 1st Amendment is written in absolute terms: "Congress shall make *no* law," which on its face indicates that the federal government simply cannot pass a law dealing with speech under any circumstances. But, in at least four areas, the courts have used a "balancing of interests" approach that permits Congress to limit the right of free speech when other social interests predominate. Those areas are (1) advocacy of crime or revolution; (2) **commercial speech;** (3) obscenity; and (4) **defamation (libel** and **slander**). In all four instances the result has been restrictions on the right of individuals to speak. The following case is an example of the balancing test used in the context of the "advocacy of crime or revolution" exception.

---

*For example, Justice William O. Douglas said, "The First Amendment makes confidence in the common sense of our people and in the maturity of their judgment the great postulate of our democracy."

Dennis v. U.S.

341 U.S. 494, 71 S. Ct. 857, 95 L. Ed. 1137 (1951)

Dennis and ten other top ranking officials of the U.S. Communist Party were indicted under the Smith Act, originally enacted in 1940. That act made it a federal crime to "knowingly or willfully advocate, abet, advise, or teach the duty, necessity, desirability, or propriety of overthrowing or destroying any government in the United States by force or violence." The defendants were found guilty by a jury after the evidence showed that they were members of the Communist Party; that the Communist Party advocated worldwide revolution to attain its ends; but that the defendants had not indulged in any act of violence or any other illegal activity. The defendants appealed their conviction.

Mr. Chief Justice VINSON announced the judgment of the Court.

The obvious purpose of the statute is to protect existing Government, not from change by peaceable, lawful and constitutional means, but from change by violence, revolution and terrorism. That it is within the *power* of the Congress to protect the Government of the United States from armed rebellion is a proposition which requires little discussion. Whatever theoretical merit there may be to the argument that there is a "right" to rebellion against dictatorial governments is without force where the existing structure of the government provides for peaceful and orderly change. We reject any principle of governmental helplessness in the face of preparation for revolution, which principle, carried to its logical conclusion, must lead to anarchy.

. . . .

One of the bases for the contention that the means which Congress has employed are invalid takes the form of an attack on the face of the statute on the grounds that by its terms it prohibits academic discussion of the merits of Marxism-Leninism, that it stifles ideas and is contrary to all concepts of a free speech and a free press.

The very language of the Smith Act negates the interpretation which petitioners would have us impose on that Act. It is directed at advocacy, not discussion . . . Congress did not intend to eradicate the free discussion of political theories, to destroy the traditional rights of Americans to discuss and evaluate ideas without fear of governmental sanction. Rather, Congress was concerned with the very kind of activity in which the evidence showed these petitioners engaged.

. . . .

[T]he basis of the First Amendment is the hypothesis that speech can rebut speech, propoganda will answer propoganda, free debate of ideas will result in the wisest governmental policies. It is for this reason that this Court has recognized the inherent value of free discourse. An analysis of the leading cases in this Court . . . however, will demonstrate that . . . this is not an unlimited, unqualified right, but that the societal value of speech must, on occasion, be subordinated to other values and considerations.

. . . .

The rule we deduce . . . is that where an offense is specified by a statute in nonspeech or nonpress terms, a conviction relying upon speech or press as evidence of violation may be sustained only when the speech or publication created a "clear and present danger" of attempting or accomplishing the prohibited crime. . . .

. . . .

Chief Judge Learned Hand . . . interpreted the phrase as follows: "In each case [courts] must ask whether the gravity of the 'evil', discounted by its improbability, justifies such invasion of free speech as is necessary to avoid the danger." . . . We adopt this statement of the rule.

. . . .

The mere fact that from the period 1945 to 1948 petitioners' activities did not result in an attempt to overthrow the Government by force and violence is of course no answer to the fact that there was a group that was ready to make the attempt. The formation by petitioners of such a highly organized conspiracy, with rigidly disciplined members subject to call when the leaders, these petitioners, felt that the time had come for action, coupled with the inflammable nature of world conditions, similar uprisings in other countries, and the touch-and-go nature of our relations with countries with whom petitioners were in the very least ideologically attuned, convince us that their convictions were justified on this score.

. . . .

The judgments of conviction are affirmed.

Mr. Justice BLACK, dissenting.

. . . .

At the outset I want to emphasize what the crime involved in this case is, and what it is not. These petitioners were not charged with an attempt to overthrow the Government. They were not charged with overt acts of any kind designed to overthrow the Government. They were not even charged with saying anything or writing anything designed to overthrow the Government. The charge was that they agreed to assemble and to talk and publish certain ideas at a later date: The indictment is that they conspired to organize the Communist Party and to use speech or newspapers and other publications in the future to teach and advocate the forcible overthrow of the government. No matter how it is worded, this is a virulent form of prior censorship of speech and press, which I believe the First Amendment forbids.

. . . .

Undoubtedly, a governmental policy of unfettered communication of ideas does entail dangers. To the Founders of this Nation, however, the benefits derived from free expression were worth the risk. They embodied this philosophy in the First Amendment's command that ''Congress shall make no law . . . abridging the freedom of speech, or of the press. . . . '' I have always believed that the First Amendment is the keystone of our Government, that the freedoms it guarantees provide the best insurance against destruction of all freedom.

. . . .

So long as this Court exercises the power of judicial review of legislation, I cannot agree that the First Amendment permits us to sustain laws suppressing freedom of speech and press on the basis of Congress' or our own notions of mere ''reasonableness.'' Such a doctrine waters down the First Amendment so that it amounts to little more than an admonition to Congress. The Amendment as so construed is not likely to protect any but those ''safe'' or orthodox views which rarely need its protection.

. . . .

Public opinion being what it now is, few will protest the conviction of these Communist petitioners. There is hope, however, that in calmer times, when present pressures, passions and fears subside, this or some later Court will restore the First Amendment liberties to the high preferred place where they belong in a free society.

Mr. Justice DOUGLAS, dissenting.

If this were a case where those who claimed protection under the First Amendment were teaching the techniques of sabotage, the assassination of the President, the filching of documents from public files, the planting of bombs, the art of street warfare, and the like, I would have no doubts. The freedom to speak is not absolute; the teaching of methods of terror and other seditious conduct should be beyond the pale along with obscenity and immorality. . . . But the fact is that no such evidence was introduced at the trial. There is a statute which makes a seditious conspiracy unlawful. Petitioners, however, were not charged with a ''conspiracy to overthrow'' the Government. They were charged with a conspiracy to form a party and groups and assemblies of people who teach and advocate the overthrow of our Government by force or violence and with a conspiracy to advocate and teach its overthrow. . . . It may well be that indoctrination in the techniques of terror . . . would be indictable under either statute. But the teaching which is condemned here is of a different character.

The *Dennis* case represents a high-water mark for the "advocacy of crime or revolution" doctrine. That case must be considered in the context of its time, which included the Korean War, Stalinism, incipient McCarthyism, and the Cold War. In the years that followed, no decision expressly discredited *Dennis,* but later cases consistently chipped away at its "clear and present danger" test and its rather generous view of what constituted such a danger. Finally, in 1969, the Supreme Court made the following statement.

> These later decisions have fashioned the principle that the constitutional guarantees of free speech and free press do not permit a State to forbid or proscribe advocacy of the use of force or of law violation except where such advocacy is directed to inciting or producing imminent lawless action and is likely to incite or produce such action. (*Brandenburg* v. *Ohio*).*

Later decisions of the court** have followed the lead in *Brandenburg* and held that speech may be punished only if there is a real danger of imminent violence and lawlessness, usually proven by the fact that violence and lawlessness has actually occured. Other decisions have involved issues of what is "speech," including cases of so-called *symbolic speech* of language on T-shirts, marches, and gestures, and whether speech can be more severely limited in certain places at certain times. For example, it is permissible to restrict picketing and marches on army bases, in courtrooms, or near jail facilities.

Commercial Speech: The 1st Amendment and Advertising

A second major exception to the absolute terms of the 1st Amendment's protection of freedom of speech is **commercial speech.** Governmental bodies, such as state and federal legislatures and administrative agencies, often attempt to regulate the nature and content of advertising, and those regulations have been challenged on the basis of the 1st Amendment. Like advocacy of crime or revolution, regulation of advertising has been subjected to a balancing test, weighing the right to advertise against the government's interest in regulating.

The general rule for many years seemed to be that commercial speech, principally advertising, had little to do with the purposes of the 1st Amendment and therefore could be regulated with impunity. As a result, there were few decisions directly on point, and many government agencies undertook to limit or prohibit various types of advertising. Examples of such restrictions include Federal Trade Commission regulations prohibiting "false and misleading" advertising; limits on advertising by certain trades or professions, such as attorneys and public utilities; and prohibition or limitation of certain forms of advertising, such as forbidding the use of outdoor signs in certain locations. Finally, from 1975 to 1980, the Supreme Court decided three

---

*395 U.S. 444, 89 S. Ct. 1827, 23 L. Ed. 2d 430 (1969).

**See, e.g., *NAACP* v. *Claiborne Hardware Co.,* 458 U.S. 886, 102 S. Ct. 3409, (1982).

cases* that provided some protection for advertising as a form of protected speech. The following decision was the second in the series and provides the best theoretical background to the problem.

Virginia State Board of Pharmacy v. Virginia Citizens Consumer Council

425 U.S. 748, 96 S. Ct. 1817, 48 L. Ed. 2d 346 (1976)

A Virginia statute made it a crime for pharmacists to advertise prices on prescription drugs, on the basis that such advertising was unprofessional. The Virginia Citizens Consumer Council brought suit to declare the statute unconstitutional under the 1st Amendment, for the purpose of creating price competition between pharmacists and thereby inducing lower prices for prescription drugs. The District Court struck down the statute, and the State Board appealed.

Mr. Justice BLACKMUN delivered the opinion of the court.

Our pharmacist does not wish to editorialize on any subject, cultural, philosophical, or political. He does not wish to report any particularly newsworthy fact, or to make generalized observation even about commercial matters. The "idea" he wishes to communicate is simply this: "I will sell you the X prescription drug at 'Y' price." Our question, then, is whether this communication is wholly outside the protection of the First Amendment.

We begin with several propositions that already are settled or beyond serious dispute. It is clear, for example, that speech does not lose its First Amendment protection because money is spent to project it, as in a paid advertisement. . . . Speech likewise is protected even though it is carried in a form that is "sold" for profit . . . and even though it may involve a solicitation to purchase or otherwise pay or contribute money. . . .

If there is a kind of commercial speech that lacks all First Amendment protection, therefore, it must be distinguished by its content. Yet the speech whose content deprives it of protection cannot simply be speech on a commercial subject. No one would contend that our pharmacist may be prevented from being heard on the subject of whether, in general, pharmaceutical prices should be regulated, or their advertisement forbidden . . . Purely factual matters of public interest may claim protection.

Our question is whether speech which does "no more than propose a commercial transaction," . . . is so removed from any 'exposition of ideas,' . . . and from 'truth, science, morality, and arts in general, in its diffusion of liberal sentiments on the administration of Government'" that it lacks all protection. Our answer is that it is not.

Focusing first on the individual parties to the transaction that is proposed in the commerical advertisement, we may assume that the advertiser's purpose is a purely economic one. That hardly disqualifies him for protection under the First Amendment. . . .

As to the particular consumer's interest in the free flow of commerical information, that interest may be as keen, if not keener by far, than his interest in the day's most urgent political debate. . . . Those whom the suppression of prescription drug price information hits the hardest are the poor, the sick, and particularly the aged. . . .

Generalizing, society also may have a strong interest in the free flow of commercial information. . . . Advertising, however tasteless and excessive it sometimes may seem, is nonetheless dissemination of information as to who is producing and selling what product, for what reason, and at what price. . . .

Bigelow v. *Virginia*, 421 U.S. 809, 95 S. Ct. 2222, 44 L. Ed. 2d 600 (1975); *Virginia State Board of Pharmacy*, infra; and *Central Hudson Gas & Electric Corp.* v. *Public Service Commission of New York*, infra.

Arrayed against these substantial individual and societal interests are a number of justifications for the advertising ban. These have to do principally with maintaining a high degree of professionalism on the part of licensed pharmacists. . . . Price advertising, it is argued, will place in jeopardy the pharmacist's expertise and, with it, the customer's health. . . .

There is, of course, an alternative to this highly paternalistic approach. That alternative is to assume that this information is not in itself harmful, that people will perceive their own best interests if only they are well enough informed, and that the best means to that end is to open the channels of communication rather than to close them. . . . It is precisely this kind of choice, between the dangers of suppressing information, and the dangers of its misuse if it is freely available, that the First Amendment makes for us.

In concluding that commercial speech, like other varieties, is protected, we of course do not hold that it can never be regulated in any way. Some forms of commercial speech regulation are surely permissible. . . .

The Court listed four permissible regulations of commercial speech: (1) the time, place, and manner of advertising; (2) misleading, deceptive, and false advertising; (3) advertising of transactions that are themselves illegal; and (4) broadcast media regulations.

What is at issue is whether a State may completely suppress the dissemination of concededly truthful information about entirely lawful activity, fearful of that information's effect upon its disseminators and its recipients. Reserving other questions, we conclude that the answer to this one is in the negative.

The judgment of the District Court is affirmed.

The final case in the trilogy explained the doctrine of commercial speech even further, and proposed a four-step analysis in all such cases. The case involved a state utility regulation that banned all advertising promoting the use of electricity by a public utility on the theory that a controlled monopoly need not spend its customers' money on advertising. The Court overturned the regulation on the grounds that the public utility commission had not shown that a less extensive regulation would do as well. In the decision, the Court said that the analysis of commercial speech should involve a specific type of analysis.

In commercial speech cases, then, a four-part analysis has developed. At the outset, we must determine whether the expression is protected by the First Amendment. For commercial speech to come with that provision, it at least must concern lawful activity and not be misleading. Next, we ask whether the asserted governmental interest is substantial. If both inquiries yield positive answers, we must determine whether the regulation directly advances the governmental interest asserted, and whether it is not more extensive than is necessary to serve that interest. (J. POWELL in *Central Hudson Gas & Electric Corp.* v. *Public Service Commission of New York*, 447 U.S. 557, 100 S. Ct. 2343 (1980))

Later cases have applied the commercial speech doctrine in a variety of ways. In 1977, the Court held that a complete ban on For Sale signs on homes was unconstitutional, even though the purpose of the ordinance was to deter "panic selling" by whites fearful of impending racial integration.* A 1981 decision also held a complete

---

Linmark Associates, Inc. v. *Township of Willingboro*, 431 U.S. 85, 97 S. Ct. 1614, 52 L. Ed. 2d 155 (1977).

ban on billboard advertising for aesthetic purposes in violation of the 1st Amendment.* On the other hand, a 1982 decision upheld a ban on all advertising of items used or designed for use with illegal drugs.** Each of the cases used the four-part analysis dictated in the *Central Hudson* case.

Freedom of the Press

Closely tied to the right to speak is the right to publish. In a day of mass media, the right to speak out on issues would be of little value without the right to publish those views to the public. The framers viewed freedom of the press as an essential part of political freedom and the Jeffersonian marketplace concept of freedom of speech.

Like freedom of speech, the Constitutional guarantee of freedom of the press is phrased in absolute terms: "Congress shall make *no law* . . . abridging the freedom . . . of the press." But, like freedom of speech, the Court has carved out various exceptions and limitations on that freedom through various balancing tests. First, the court has generally permitted regulation of the same four areas as in freedom of speech, namely, (1) advocacy of crime or revolution; (2) commercial speech; (3) obscenity; and (4) defamation. Second, the Court has wrestled for years with the conceptual problem of *when* regulations may be imposed, even in those areas. This is the problem of **prior restraint.**

The Prior Restraint Problem   Under British law before the American Revolution and under the 1st Amendment for a major part of its history, the guarantee of freedom of the press meant simply that government could not impose any *prior* restraint on what might be published, but could punish persons for publishing matter *after* it was published. Thus a publisher could not be stopped from publishing an article but could be punished for publishing that article after it appeared.

In 1931, the Supreme Court made major changes in that rule in the case of *Near* v. *Minnesota.*† That case held that prior restraints were indeed permissible in some cases, but also held that freedom of the press also prohibited postpublication punishments in other cases. In the words of Chief Justice Hughes in that case

> the protection . . . as to previous restraint is not absolutely unlimited . . . chiefly because that immunity cannot be deemed to exhaust the conception of the liberty guaranteed by State and Federal Constitutions. . . . The point of criticism has been "that the mere exemption from previous restraints cannot be all that is secured by the constitutional provisions," and that "the liberty of the press might be rendered a mockery and a delusion, and the phrase itself a by-word, if, while every man was at liberty to publish what he pleased, the public authorities might nevertheless punish him for harmless publications."

Metromedia, Inc. v. *City of San Diego,* 453 U.S. 490, 101 S. Ct. 2882, 69 L. Ed. 2d 800 (1981).

**Village of Hoffman Estates* v. *Flipside,* 455 U.S. 489, 102 S. Ct. 1186, 71 L. Ed. 2d 362 (1982).

†283 U.S. 697, 51 S. Ct. 625, 75 L. Ed. 1357 (1931).

Prior restraint is really another name for advance censorship, a problem that has troubled the courts for years. On one hand, if certain material is somehow bad for the public, as is arguably the case in obscenity, it would seem that public authorities should not be limited to postpublication penalties but should be able to protect the public in advance. But granting that right to public authorities opens a whole Pandora's box of issues: Who is to make the decision? How that decision is to be made? What standards are to be applied? The following landmark decision in the law of prior restraint applies to censorship of motion pictures.

Times Film Corp. v. Chicago

365 U.S. 43, 81 S. Ct. 391, 5 L. Ed. 2d 402 (1961)

A Chicago ordinance required that all movies to be shown in the city must be submitted for examination prior to their exhibition. Times Film Corporation owned the rights to the movie *Don Juan* and paid the appropriate license fee but refused to submit the film in advance. The city in turn denied a permit to exhibit the film, and Times Film Corp. brought this action for an injunction. Times Film contended that the ordinance was unconstitutional because it imposed a prior restraint. The federal district court dismissed the complaint, and that decision was affirmed by the U.S. Court of Appeals. Times Film appealed to the Supreme Court, which granted certiorari.

Mr. Justice CLARK delivered the opinion of the Court.

. . . .

. . . Admittedly, the challenged section of the ordinance imposes a previous restraint, and the broad justiciable issue is therefore present as to whether the ambit of constitutional protection includes complete or absolute freedom to exhibit, at least once, any and every kind of motion picture. It is that question alone which we decide. . . . We have concluded that . . . Chicago's ordinance requiring the submission of films prior to their public exhibition is not, on the grounds set forth, void on its face.

. . . .

. . . [T]here is not a word in the record as to the nature and content of *Don Juan*. We are left entirely in the dark in this regard, as were the city officials and the other reviewing courts. Petitioner claims that the nature of the film is irrelevant, and that even if this film contains the basest type of pornography, or incitement to riot, or forceful overthrow of orderly government, it may nonetheless be shown without prior submission for examination. The challenge here is to the censor's basic authority. . . .

. . . .

Petitioner would have us hold that the public exhibition of motion pictures must be allowed under any circumstances. The State's sole remedy, it says, is the invocation of criminal process under the Illinois pornography statute . . . and then only after a transgression. But this position . . . is founded upon the claim of absolute privilege against prior restraint under the First Amendment—a claim without sanction in our cases. . . . Chicago emphasizes here its duty to protect its people against the dangers of obscenity in the public exhibition of motion pictures. To this argument petitioner's only answer is that regardless of the capacity for, or extent of, such an evil, previous restraint cannot be justified. With this we cannot agree. We [have] recognized . . . that "capacity for evil . . . may be relevant in determining the permissible scope of community control," . . . and that motion pictures were not "necessarily subject to the precise rules governing any other particular method of expression." Each method . . . tends to present its own peculiar problems. Certainly petitioner's broadside attack does not warrant, nor could it justify on the record here, our saying that—aside from any consideration of the other "exceptional cases" mentioned in our decisions—the state is stripped of all constitutional power to prevent, in the most effective fashion, the utterance of this class of speech. It is not for this Court to limit the State in its selection of the remedy it deems most effective to cope with such a problem, absent, of course, a showing of unreasonable strictures on individual liberty resulting from its application in particular circumstances.

. . . .

Affirmed.

Mr. Chief Justice WARREN, with whom Mr. Justice BLACK, Mr. Justice DOUGLAS, and Mr. Justice BRENNAN join, dissenting.

I cannot agree either with the conclusion reached by the Court or with the reasons advanced for its support. To me, this case clearly presents the question of our approval of unlimited censorship of motion pictures before exhibition through a system of administrative licensing. Moreover, the decision presents a real danger of eventual censorship for every form of communication, be it newspapers, journals, books, magazines, television, radio, or public speeches. The Court purports to leave these questions for another day, but I am aware of no constitutional principle which permits us to hold that the communication of ideas through one medium may be censored while other media are immune. . . .

The censor performs free from all of the procedural safeguards afforded litigants in a court of law. . . . The likelihood of a fair and impartial trial disappears when the censor is both prosecutor and judge. There is a complete absence of rules of evidence; the fact is that there is usually no evidence at all as the system at bar vividly illustrates. . . .

Shortly after the *Times Film* case the Court imposed limits on such censorship, however.* Those limits (1) placed on the State the burden of proving the film in violation of the established guidelines; (2) afforded the publisher of the film the opportunity to have a judicial determination of the case at some point; and (3) required that the censor's decision be speedy.

Finally, to muddy the waters even more, in 1971, the Supreme Court ruled in the famous "Pentagon Papers" case (*New York Times* v. *U.S.***) that a government suit for an injunction against publication of classified material was unconstitutional as a prior restraint. In a short "Per Curiam" (literally, "by the Court," meaning an opinion of the whole court) decision the justices ruled that

Any system of prior restraints of expression comes to this Court bearing a heavy presumption against its constitutional validity. [See *Near* v. *Minnesota*]. . . . The government thus carries a heavy burden of showing justification for the imposition of such a restraint. . . . The District Court . . . and the Court of Appeals . . . held that the Government had not met that burden. We agree. [Note: the preceding was the *entire* decision.]

That terse opinion was followed by no less than six concurring opinions and two dissenting opinions, each of which took a slightly different view of the problems of prior restraint.

Freedom of Religion

The third "leg" of freedom of conscience is freedom of belief, generally referred to as freedom of religion. The 1st Amendment makes two specific guarantees regarding

---

Freedman v. *Maryland,* 380 U.S. 51, 85 S. Ct. 734, 13 L. Ed. 2d 649 (1965).

**403 U.S. 713, 91 S. Ct. 2140, 29 L. Ed. 2d 822 (1971).

freedom of religion: first, that Congress may not make a law "respecting an establishment of religion"; and, second, that Congress may not make a law "prohibiting the free exercise" of religion. The first guarantee generally prohibits state *support* of religious activities and the second generally prohibits government *interference* with religious activities.

The Establishment Clause The first guarantee against the "establishment of religion" was aimed at preventing state religions and state discrimination against those who fail to adhere to the "official" religion. The problems inherent in that clause have provided many of the major constitutional controversies in our history, including the debate over school prayer and whether evolution and creationism can, must, or should be taught in the public schools. In a business context, the debate has centered around laws that require businesses to close on Sundays, the day of rest for the majority of Americans—but by no means *all* Americans:

McGowan v. Maryland

366 U.S. 420, 81 S. Ct. 1101, 6 L. Ed. 2d 393 (1961)

Maryland, like many other states and municipalities, prohibited "labor, business, and commercial activity on Sundays." The defendant was charged and convicted of selling a three-ring binder, a can of floor wax, a stapler and staples, and a toy submarine in violation of the statute. The defendant appealed to the Supreme Court on the grounds that the statute violated the First Amendment.

Mr. Chief Justice WARREN delivered the opinion of the court.

The essence of appellant's "establishment" argument is that Sunday is the Sabbath day of the predominant Christian sects; that the purpose of the enforced stoppage of labor on that day is to facilitate and encourage church attendance; that the purpose of setting Sunday as a day of universal rest is to induce people with no religion or people with marginal religious beliefs to join the predominant Christian sects; that the purpose of the atmosphere of tranquility created by Sunday closing is to aid the conduct of church services and religious observances of the sacred day. . . .

More recently, further secular justifications have been advanced for making Sunday a day of rest, a day when people may recover from the labors of the week just passed and may physically and mentally prepare for the week's work to come. . . .

We are told that the State has other means at its disposal to accomplish its secular purpose, other courses that would not even remotely or incidentally give state aid to religion. On this basis, we are asked to hold these statutes invalid. . . . It is true that if the State's interest were simply to provide for its citizens a periodic respite from work, a regulation demanding that everyone rest one day in seven, leaving the choice of the day to the individual, would suffice.

However, the State's purpose is not merely to provide a one-day-in-seven work stoppage. In addition to this, the State seeks to set one day apart from all others as a day of rest, repose, recreation and tranquility—a day which all members of the family and community have the opportunity to spend and enjoy together, a day on which there exists relative quiet and disassociation from the everyday intensity of commercial activities, a day on which people may visit friends and relatives who are not available during working days.

Obviously, a State is empowered to determine that a rest-one-day-in-seven statute would not accomplish this purpose; that it would not provide for a general cessation of activities, a special atmosphere of tranquility, a day which all members of the family or friends and relatives might spend together. . . .

Affirmed.

Mr. Justice DOUGLAS dissenting. . . .

The question is not whether one day out of seven can be imposed by a state as a day of rest. The question is not whether Sunday can by force of custom and habit be retained as a day of rest. The question is whether a State can impose criminal sanctions on those who, unlike the Christian majority that makes up our society, worship on a different day or do not share the religious scruples of the majority. . . .

The institutions of our society are founded on the belief that there is an authority higher than the authority of the State; that there is a moral law which the State is powerless to alter; that the individual possesses rights, conferred by the Creator, which government must respect. . . .

But those who fashioned the First Amendment decided that if and when God is to be served, His service will not be motivated by coercive measures of government. . . .

The First Amendment commands government to have no interest in theology or ritual; it admonishes government to be interested in allowing religious freedom to flourish—whether the result is to produce Catholics, Jews, or Protestants, or to turn the people toward the path of Buddha, or to end in a predominantly Moslem nation, or to produce in the long run atheists or agnostics. On matters of this kind government must be neutral. . . .

The courts have also ruled that other religious activities are a part of the American tradition and are therefore permissible. Examples include "In God We Trust" on our coins, opening the Congressional day with prayer, and municipal maintenance of a manger scene during the Christmas season.

The Free Exercise Clause   The second part of freedom of religion has posed somewhat fewer problems. This provision is aimed at preventing government interference with belief. But that clause, like other parts of the 1st Amendment, has been subjected to a balancing test. In a classic case involving door-to-door solicitations by Jehovah's Witnesses in a heavily Catholic neighborhood, the state arrested the solicitors for unlawful solicitation. While the Court held the application of the law to the defendants violated their 1st Amendment rights, it stated in the course of the decision that

> Conduct remains subject to regulation for the protection of society. The freedom to act must have appropriate definition to preserve the enforcement of that protection. In every case the power to regulate must be so exercised as not, in attaining a permissible end, unduly infringe the protected freedom. No one would contest the proposition that a State may not by statute wholly deny the right to preach or to disseminate religious views. . . . It is equally clear that a State may by general and nondiscriminatory legislation regulate the times, the places, and the manner of soliciting upon its streets, and of holding meetings thereon; and may in other respects safeguard the peace, good order and comfort of the community, without unconstitutionally invading the liberties protected. . . . (*Cantwell* v. *Connecticut*)★

As a result, states have constitutionally forbidden bigamous marriages, snake handling, and other practices that invade the "peace, good order, and comfort of the community."

★310 U.S. 296, 60 S. Ct. 900, 84 L. E. 1213 (1940).

The Criminal Procedure Amendments

The 4th, 5th, and 6th Amendments have a great deal to say about the procedures that must be used in criminal arrests and trials in the United States though, clearly, some aspects of those amendments deal with issues other than the criminal law. The founding fathers were quite sensitive about their individual rights in criminal proceedings, since many of the British excesses prior to the Revolution had involved abuses of criminal procedure. Blanket or "sweep" searches of entire cities, arrest without cause, and long-term incommunicado confinement had been principal weapons of the British forces both before and during the American Revolution. It is little wonder that the public insisted upon protections against such government conduct in the Constitution.

On the other hand, a great deal of criticism has been levelled at the courts and the Constitution itself based upon so-called legal technicalities, which supposedly permit guilty persons to go free because of official misconduct. In a large measure those technicalities arose because of the interpretation given those amendments by the Warren Court, during the 1950's and 1960's. Those expansive interpretations have been limited somewhat by later interpretations by the Court.

Business and the Criminal Law

While the traditional view has it that criminal procedure has little relevance to business, that is far from accurate. Many statutes and regulations to be studied further on are actually criminal statutes: the antitrust laws, portions of the Internal Revenue Code, and parts of the Securities Laws, to name a few. Investigations into possible violations of those laws involve the same searches, seizures, interrogations, arrests, and indictments as the investigation of any burglary. Similarly, the protections of the Bill of Rights, including protections against unreasonable searches and self-incrimination, apply with full force to searches of business records, OSHA inspections of business premises, and interrogation by IRS officials.

The second aspect involves business as victim of crime. Businesspeople often find themselves as witnesses in criminal proceedings, from shoplifting to securities frauds. Perhaps the only way to survive the frustrations of such proceedings and the delays inherent in the criminal law is to understand the reasons for the process.

The Exclusionary Rule

Perhaps the largest issue overriding all of the criminal procedure amendments is how those amendments can be enforced. Clearly persons aggrieved by official misconduct may have the right to file civil lawsuits against public officials and governments that abuse their rights, but such lawsuits are often difficult to prove (especially if the plaintiff is a convicted felon) and provide little deterrent against official misconduct. Similarly, some official misconduct, such as some searches and seizures, are themselves violations of the criminal law (e.g., "burglary" and "theft") and the police officers involved could be charged criminally. But, often that option is realistically not available because of the close relationship that must exist between prosecutors and the police. As a result, while the Constitution forbids certain types of police misconduct, there was simply no effective way to enforce those Constitutional prohibitions.

In 1914, the Supreme Court announced* the **exclusionary rule** as an attempt to deter some illegal police conduct. That rule applied only to the federal government from 1914 to 1961. The exclusionary rule provides simply that evidence obtained in violation of any of the provisions of the Constitution cannot be introduced in a court proceeding. Thus, if evidence is seized or found in violation of the 4th Amendment's prohibition of "unreasonable searches and seizures," the 5th Amendment's protection against self-incrimination, or the 6th Amendment's protection of the right to counsel, such evidence cannot be introduced in a later trial. In 1961, that rule was applied to state court proceedings as well in the famous case of *Mapp* v. *Ohio.*** As noted by Mr. Justice Clark,

> There are those who say, as did Justice (then Judge) Cardozo, that under our con-
> stitutional exclusionary doctrine, "[t]he criminal is to go free because the constable has
> blundered." . . . In some cases this will undoubtedly be the result. But . . . "there is
> another consideration—the imperative of judicial integrity." . . . The criminal goes free,
> if he must, but it is the law that sets him free. Nothing can destroy a government more
> quickly than its failure to observe its own laws, or worse, its disregard of the charter of
> its own existence." (*Mapp* v. *Ohio*).

Over time the exclusionary rule developed a number of very technical procedural rules dealing with the nature of search warrants, the scope of interrogation, and
the times when a lawyer must be present. But in the early 1980's the Supreme Court
began rethinking the exclusionary rule and began to chip away at the rule with what
it termed *common sense exceptions.* For example, the Court has said that if a search is
conducted pursuant to a defective search warrant, the evidence seized may still be
introduced if the officer was not responsible for the defect and acted "in good faith."†
Similarly, evidence found illegally may still be introduced if it would have been
"inevitably discovered" through legal means.‡ Thus, while the exclusionary rule is
still the principal means of enforcing the criminal procedure amendments, its effectiveness has been somewhat limited by later decisions.

The 4th Amendment: Unreasonable Searches and Seizures

The 4th Amendment prohibits all "*unreasonable* searches and seizures" and requires
the existence of **probable cause** before a warrant may issue. The amendment does
not require a search warrant in every case, however, and the courts have permitted
warrantless searches in several situations, including searches incident to an arrest (to
protect the officer), to prevent the imminent destruction of evidence, and of items

---

Weeks v. *United States,* 232 U.S. 383, 34 S. Ct. 341, 58 L. Ed. 652 (1914).

**367 U.S. 643, 81 S. Ct. 1684, 6 L. Ed. 2d 1081 (1961).

†*Massachusetts* v. *Sheppard,* _____U.S. _____, 104 S. Ct. 3424, 52 U.S.L.W. 5177 (1984).

‡*Nix* v. *Williams,* _____U.S. _____, 104 S. Ct. 2501, 52 U.S.L.W. 4732 (1984).

"in plain view," since there is really no "search" at all. Similarly, the courts have relaxed the warrant requirement in the case of automobiles because they can be moved quickly. Finally, no warrant is required to inventory the contents of property lawfully in the hands of the police. But aside from those exceptions a warrant is generally required in order to provide an independent judicial analysis of the facts of the case before a search is permitted.

From a business standpoint, perhaps the most important application of the search and seizure doctrines occurs in the context of administrative inspections. A great number of administrative agencies are required by law to conduct various types of inspections. Health department officials must inspect restaurants, building inspectors must inspect construction projects, environmental protection officers must inspect facilities that may pollute, and OSHA inspectors (see Chapter 14) must inspect workplaces. The question inevitably arose whether such inspections are really searches within the meaning of the 4th Amendment. The following case provided an answer.

Camara v. Municipal Court

387 U.S. 523, 87 S. Ct. 1727, 18 L. Ed. 2d 930 (1967)

San Francisco's Housing Code provided that authorized city employees had the right to enter premises to conduct inspections after they had presented their credentials. Camara refused to permit inspectors to enter premises that he leased, and he was charged with a criminal offense for failure to permit such entry. He filed an action in state court for a "writ of prohibition," a type of court order available in some states prohibiting the court from proceeding against him. The trial court refused to issue the writ, and the appellate court sustained the trial court. Camara appealed to the Supreme Court.

Mr. Justice WHITE delivered the opinion of the Court.

. . . .

The Fourth Amendment provides that, "The right of the people to be secure in their persons, houses and effects, against unreasonable searches and seizures, shall not be violated, and no Warrants shall issue, but upon probable cause, supported by Oath or affirmation, and particularly describing the place to be searched, and the persons or things to be seized." The basic purpose of this Amendment, as recognized in countless decisions of this Court, is to safeguard the privacy and security of individuals against arbitrary invasions by governmental officials. The Fourth Amendment thus gives concrete expression to a right of the people which "is basic to a free society." . . .

Though there has been general agreement as to the fundamental purpose of the Fourth Amendment, translation of the abstract prohibition against "unreasonable searches and seizures" into workable guidelines for the decision of particular cases is a difficult task which has for many years divided the members of this Court. Nevertheless, one governing principle, justified by history and by current experience, has consistently been followed: except in certain carefully defined classes of cases, a search of private property without proper consent is "unreasonable" unless it has been authorized by a valid search warrant.

. . . .

We may agree that a routine inspection of the physical condition of private property is a less hostile intrusion than the typical policeman's search for the fruits and instrumentalities of crime . . . But we cannot agree that the Fourth Amendment interests at stake in these inspection cases are merely "peripheral." It is surely anomalous to say that the individual and his private property are fully protected by the Fourth

Amendment only when the individual is suspected of criminal behavior. For instance, even the most law-abiding citizen has a very tangible interest in limiting the circumstances under which the sanctity of his home may be broken by official authority, for the possibility of criminal entry under the guise of official sanction is a serious threat to personal and family security. . . . Like most regulatory laws, fire, health, and housing codes are enforced by criminal process.

. . . .

. . . [W]e hold that administrative searches of the kind at issue here are significant intrusions upon the interests protected by the Fourth Amendment, that such searches when authorized and conducted without a warrant procedure lack the traditional safeguards which the Fourth Amendment guarantees to the individual . . .

. . . .

Since our holding emphasizes the controlling standard of reasonableness, nothing we say today is intended to foreclose prompt inspections, even without a warrant, that the law has traditionally upheld in emergency situations. . . . On the other hand, in the case of most routine area inspections, there is no compelling urgency to inspect at a particular time or on a particular day. Moreover, most citizens allow inspections of their property without a warrant. Thus, as a practical matter and in the light of the Fourth Amendment's requirement that a warrant specify the property to be searched, it seems likely that warrants should normally be sought only after entry is refused unless there has been a citizen complaint or there is other satisfactory reason for securing immediate entry. Similarly, the requirement of a warrant procedure does not suggest any change in what seems to be the prevailing local policy, in most situations, of authorizing entry, but not entry by force, to inspect.

. . . .

Judgment vacated and case remanded.

In a companion case,* the Court ruled that the same rule applied to business and commercial premises. In related decisions, the Court has held that home visits by welfare workers are not searches within the meaning of the 4th Amendment,** and that warrantless inspections of stone quarries by federal mine inspectors are justified since mining is a "closely regulated industry" and because it is one of the most dangerous businesses in the country.† On the other hand, OSHA safety inspections are subject to the warrant requirement.‡

The 5th Amendment: The Privilege Against Self-Incrimination

Certainly the truth is a major consideration in any civil or criminal proceeding. But that truth should only be obtained while the integrity of the individual is protected. If truth were the only consideration, we could shoot the defendant full of truth serum and simply ask him. American law has gone to a great deal of trouble to preserve the dignity of the individual, and a major part of that effort is the right not to convict one's self through compelled testimony.

---

*_See_ v. _Seattle_, 387 U.S. 541, 87 S. Ct. 1737, 18 L. Ed. 2d 943 (1967).

**Wyman v. *James,* 400 U.S. 309, 91 S. Ct. 381, 27 L. Ed. 2d 408 (1971).

†*Donovan* v. *Dewey,* 452 U.S. 594, 101 S. Ct. 2534, 69 L. Ed. 2d 262 (1981).

‡*Marshall* v. *Barlow's, Inc.,* infra, Chapter 5, p. 176.

Like the 4th Amendment, the 5th Amendment is enforced through the exclusionary rule and results in some guilty persons being freed. And, like the 4th Amendment, the right attaches to more than mere police investigations; it has also been applied to administrative investigations. The following landmark decision set the tenor of American 5th Amendment law.

Miranda v. Arizona

384 U.S. 436, 86 S. Ct. 1602, 16 L. Ed. 2d 694 (1966)

Miranda was arrested and charged with rape. At the time of his arrest, he was 23 years old, indigent, and had quit school in the ninth grade. A psychiatrist testified that while Miranda was suffering from a degree of schizophrenia, he was alert, intelligent within normal limits, and competent to stand trial. Miranda was picked out of a line-up by the victim, and two police officers then took Miranda into a separate room for interrogation. Miranda first denied his guilt, but a short time later, after additional questioning, changed his mind and confessed. The confession was used against him in court, and Miranda appealed the resulting conviction.

Mr. Chief Justice WARREN delivered the opinion of the court.

We start here, . . . with the premise that our holding is not an innovation in our jurisprudence, but is an application of principles long recognized and applied in other settings. . . . These precious rights were fixed in our Constitution only after centuries of persecution and struggle. And in the words of Chief Justice Marshall, they were secured "for ages to come, and . . . designed to approach immortality as nearly as human institutions can approach it."

. . . .

Our holding will be spelled out with some specificity in the pages which follow but briefly stated it is this: the prosecution may not use statements, whether exculpatory or inculpatory, stemming from custodial interrogation of the defendant unless it demonstrates the use of procedural safeguards effective to secure the privilege against self-incrimination. By custodial interrogation, we mean questioning initiated by law enforcement officers after a person has been taken into custody or otherwise deprived of his freedom or action in any significant way. As for the procedural safeguards to be employed, unless other fully effective means are devised to inform accused persons of their right of silence and to assure a continuous opportunity to exercise it, the following measures are required. Prior to any questioning, the person must be warned that he has a right to remain silent, that any statement he does make may be used as evidence against him, and that he has a right to the presence of an attorney, either retained or appointed. The defendant may waive these rights, provided the waiver is made voluntarily, knowingly and intelligently. If, however, he indicates in any manner and at any stage of the process that he wishes to consult with an attorney before speaking there can be no questioning. Likewise, if the individual is alone and indicates in any manner that he does not wish to be interrogated, the police may not question him. The mere fact that he may have answered some questions or volunteered some statements on his own does not deprive him of the right to refrain from answering any further inquiries until he has consulted with an attorney and thereafter consents to be questioned.

. . . .

In a series of cases decided by this Court . . . the police resorted to physical brutality—beatings, hanging, whipping—and to sustained and protracted questioning incommunicado in order to extort confessions. The Commission on Civil Rights in 1961 found much evidence to indicate that "some policemen still resort to physical force to obtain confessions."

. . . .

The examples given above are undoubtedly the exception now, but they are sufficiently widespread to be the object of concern. Unless a proper limitation upon custodial interrogation is achieved—such as these decisions will advance—there can be no assurance that practices of this nature will be eradicated in the foreseeable future.

. . . .

[W]e stress that the modern practice of in-custody interrogation is psychologically rather than physically oriented. . . . [T]his Court has recognized that coercion can be mental as well as physical, and that the blood of the accused is not the only hallmark of an unconstitutional inquisition. . . . .

The Court then described at length some of the advised police interrogation procedures aimed at breaking down a subject's will and eliciting a confession, including secrecy, trickery, and the so-called *Mutt and Jeff* or *good-guy–bad-guy* technique.

Even without employing brutality, the "third degree" or the specific stratagems described above, the very fact of custodial interrogation exacts a heavy toll on individual liberty and trades on the weakness of individuals. . . .

[T]he constitutional foundation underlying the privilege . . . is the respect a government—state or federal— must accord to the dignity and integrity of its citizens. To maintain a "fair state-individual balance," to require the government "to shoulder the entire load," . . . to respect the inviolability of the human personality, our accusatory system of criminal justice demands that the government seeking to punish an individual produce the evidence against him by its own independent labors, rather than by the cruel, simple expedient of compelling it from his own mouth. . . . In sum, the privilege is fulfilled only when the person is guaranteed the right "to remain silent unless he chooses to speak in the unfettered exercise of his own will."

. . . .

An individual swept from familiar surroundings into police custody, surrounded by antagonistic forces, and subjected to the techniques of persuasion described above cannot be otherwise than under compulsion to speak. As a practical matter, the compulsion to speak in the isolated setting of the police station may well be greater than in courts or other official investigations, where there are often impartial observers to guard against intimidation or trickery.

. . . .

It is impossible for us to foresee the potential alternatives for protecting the privilege which might be devised by Congress or the States in the exercise of their creative rule-making capacities. Therefore we cannot say that the Constitution requires adherence to any particular solution for the inherent compulsions of the interrogation process as it is presently conducted. Our decision in no way creates a constitutional straitjacket which will handicap solid efforts at reform . . . We encourage Congress and the States to continue their laudable search for increasingly effective ways of protecting the rights of the individual while promoting efficient enforcement of our criminal laws. However, unless we are shown other procedures which are at least as effective in apprising accused persons of their right of silence and in assuring a continuous opportunity to exercise it, the . . . procedures must be observed.

. . . .

A recurrent argument made in these cases is that society's need for interrogation outweighs the privilege. This argument is not unfamiliar to this Court. . . . The whole thrust of our foregoing discussion demonstrates that the Constitution has prescribed the rights of the individual when confronted with the power of government when it provided in the Fifth Amendment that an individual cannot be compelled to be a witness against himself.

. . . .

There is no requirement that police stop a person who enters a police station and states that he wishes to confess to a crime, or a person who calls the police to offer a confession or any other statement he desires to make. Volunteered statements of any kind are not barred by the Fifth Amendment and their admissibility is not affected by our holding today.

[Reversed.]

[Mr. Justice CLARK dissented separately.]

Mr. Justice HARLAN, with whom Mr. Justice STEWART and Mr. Justice WHITE join, dissenting. . . .

I believe the decision of the Court represents poor constitutional law and entails harmful consequences for the country at large. How serious these consequences may prove to be only time can tell.

. . . .

Without at all subscribing to the generally black picture of police conduct painted by the Court, I think it must be frankly recognized at the outset that police questioning allowable under due process precedents may inherently entail some pressure on the suspect and may seek advantage in his ignorance or weaknesses. . . . A confession is wholly and incontestably voluntary only if a guilty person gives himself up to the law and becomes his own accuser. . . . Until today, the role of the Constitution has been only to sift out *undue* pressure, not to assure spontaneous confessions.

. . . .

What the Court largely ignores is that its rules impair, if they will not eventually serve wholly to frustrate, an instrument of law enforcement that has long and quite reasonably been thought worth the price paid for it. There can be little doubt that the Court's new code would markedly decrease the number of confessions. To warn the suspect that he may remain silent and remind him that his confession may be used in court are minor obstructions. To require also an express waiver by the suspect and an end to questioning whenever he demurs must heavily handicap questioning. And to suggest or provide counsel for the suspect simply invites the end of the interrogation.

. . . .

How much harm this decision will inflict on law enforcement cannot fairly be predicted with accuracy. . . . We do know that some crimes cannot be solved without confessions, that ample expert testimony attests to their importance in crime control, and that the Court is taking a real risk with society's welfare in imposing its new regime on the country. The social costs of crime are too great to call the new rules anything but a hazardous experimentation.

. . . .

Nothing in the letter or the spirit of the Constitution or in the precedents squares with the heavy-handed and one-sided action that is so precipitously taken by the Court in the name of fulfilling its constitutional limitations.

The *Miranda* decision has itself been the subject of substantial interpretation, including further definition of **custodial interrogation.** Later decisions, particularly those in the 1980's, have tended to limit the *Miranda* holding. A 1984 decision, for example, holds that *Miranda* warnings need not be given after routine traffic stops, since traffic violators are not in custody.*

The 6th Amendment: The Right to Counsel

The 6th Amendment provides that "In all criminal prosecutions, the accused shall enjoy the right . . . to have the Assistance of Counsel for his defense." While persons accused of crimes in federal court have always enjoyed that right, persons accused in state courts did not receive full protection under the 6th Amendment until 1963, when the Court decided *Gideon* v. *Wainwright* (see p. 91).

Berkemer v. *McCarty*, _____U.S. _____, 104 S. Ct. 3138, 52 U.S.L.W. 5023 (1984).

The right to counsel involves far more than the right to a lawyer at trial. The Supreme Court has noted that the right to counsel is rather illusory if the most "critical stages" of the prosecution have already passed. A defendant may emerge from a secret pretrial interrogation after having made damaging admissions from which no attorney can save him or her. The year after *Gideon* was decided, the Supreme Court held that the right to counsel attached during interrogations,* and the *Miranda* decision can be viewed to simply require informing the defendant of that right. Much of the later law on the issue has dealt with the question of whether particular stages of the proceedings are critical and therefore require the presence of an attorney. For example, the Court has held that a defendant has a right to the presence of an attorney during "line-ups",** but that rule was later limited to line-ups prior to indictment by a grand jury.†

Due Process

One of the murkiest areas of constitutional law deals with the meaning of the phrase "due process" as it is used in both the 5th and 14th Amendments. The term **due process** is itself so general and vague that it conjures up all sorts of differing and conflicting ideas. That vagueness is compounded by the fact that the term appears *twice* in almost identical phrasing, once in the 5th Amendment and again in the 14th. It is probably no overstatement to say that the vast majority of constitutional law cases involve an interpretation of one of the two Due Process Clauses.

Under both the 5th and 14th Amendment, it is traditional to divide due process theory into two broad categories: (1) **"substantive" due process,** involving questions of whether laws are themselves fair; and (2) **"procedural" due process,** involving issues of the fairness of court and administrative procedures. The reason for two Due Process Clauses is found in the nature of substantive due process.

Substantive Due Process and the Selective Incorporation Doctrine

In 1833, the Supreme Court first encountered the argument that the Bill of Rights applied to actions by state governments.‡ In that decision, Chief Justice John Marshall ruled that the Bill of Rights did not apply to state actions. Marshall felt it was obvious from the intent and the wording of the first ten amendments that they were directed against the *federal* government alone, and that citizens were amply protected against state actions by state constitutions. That interpretation, at least technically, remains the law.

---

*Escobedo v. *Illinois,* 378 U.S. 478, 84 S. Ct. 1758, 12 L. Ed. 2d 977 (1964).

**U.S. v. *Wade,* 388 U.S. 218, 87 S. Ct. 1926, 18 L. Ed. 2d 1149 (1967); *Gilbert* v. *California,* 388 U.S. 263, 87 S. Ct. 1951 (1967) (companion cases).

†*Kirby* v. *Illinois,* 406 U.S. 682, 92 S. Ct. 1877 (1972).

‡*Barron* v. *The Mayor and City Council of Baltimore,* 32 U.S. (7 Pet.) 243, 8 L. Ed. 672 (1833).

In 1868, Congress passed the 14th Amendment as the second of the Civil War amendments directed toward slavery. It was thought necessary to include a second Due Process Clause to apply to state actions.

The initial cases to interpret the meaning of due process as applied to the states took the position that the term meant "fundamental fairness," and as long as state laws did not "shock the conscience of the court" the states had met their duty under the 14th Amendment Due Process Clause.* In these early cases, Justice John Harlan stood alone in dissent, arguing that the term *due process* was a shorthand way of applying the standards of the Bill of Rights to the states, effectively arguing that the 14th Amendment totally "incorporated" the first ten amendments and made them applicable to the states.

The Supreme Court has never accepted Justice Harlan's view, but has rather adopted a process of **selective incorporation.** Thus, for example, if a state violates an individual's right of free speech, the Court has held that the concept of free speech is included in the concept of due process. Most of the provisions of the Bill of Rights have been applied to the states through the process of selective incorporation, but the Court has never applied the provisions of the 2nd or 3rd Amendments nor portions of the 7th Amendment to the states.

The process of selective incorporation and the standards to be used have never been defined with a great deal of precision. The following decision, which is also a landmark case in the area of right to counsel, provides some background on that process.

Gideon v. Wainwright

372 U.S. 335, 83 S. Ct. 792, 9 L. Ed. 2d 799 (1963)

Clarence Earl Gideon was charged with breaking and entering with intent to commit theft, a felony, in the Florida state courts. Gideon asked that a lawyer be appointed to represent him, since he did not have enough money to hire one. The trial judge refused, since under Florida law only defendants in capital cases were entitled to a lawyer without charge. Gideon then conducted his own defense, in the words of the Court "about as well as could be expected from a layman." Gideon was convicted and sentenced to serve five years in prison. While in prison, Gideon filed a petition with the Florida Supreme Court, claiming that his 6th Amendment right to counsel had been violated. That petition was denied, and Gideon, without the aid of counsel, appealed that decision to the U.S. Supreme Court. The Supreme Court appointed counsel for Gideon in that Court, and granted certiorari.

There was a major precedent right on point: In *Betts* v. *Brady,*** a 1942 case involving virtually identical facts, the Supreme Court had held that defendants in state courts did not have the right to counsel except in capital cases. That case had held that "refusal to appoint counsel for an indigent defendant charged with a felony did not necessarily violate the Due Process Clause of the 14th Amendment. . . . ''

     Mr. Justice BLACK delivered the opinion of the Court.

     . . . .

     Since the facts and circumstances of the two cases are so nearly indistinguishable, we think the *Betts* v. *Brady* holding if left standing would require us to reject Gid-

---

*Cf., *Hurtado* v. *California,* 110 U.S. 516, 4 S. Ct. 111, 28 L. Ed. 232 (1884).

**316 U.S. 455, 62 S. Ct. 1252, 86 L. Ed 1595 (1942).

eon's claim that the Constitution guarantees him the assistance of counsel. Upon full reconsideration we conclude that *Betts* v. *Brady* should be overruled.

. . . .

We think the Court in *Betts* had ample precedent for acknowledging that those guarantees of the Bill of Rights which are fundamental safeguards of liberty immune from federal abridgment are equally protected against state invasion by the Due Process Clause of the Fourteenth Amendment. This same principle was recognized, explained, and applied in *Powell* v. *Alabama* . . . where the Court held that . . . the Fourteenth Amendment "embraced" those "'fundamental principles of liberty and justice which lie at the base of all our civil and political institutions,'" even though they had been "specifically dealt with in another part of the Federal Constitution". . . . In many cases . . . this Court has looked to the fundamental nature of the original Bill of Rights guarantees to decide whether the Fourteenth Amendment makes them obligatory on the States. Explicitly recognized to be of this "fundamental nature" and therefore made immune from state invasion by the Fourteenth, or some part of it, are the First Amendment's freedoms of speech, press, religion, assembly, association, and petition for redress of grievances. For the same reason, though not always in precisely the same terminology, the Court has made obligatory on the States the Fifth Amendment's command that private property shall not be taken for public use without just compensation, the Fourth Amendment's prohibition of unreasonable searches and seizures, and the Eighth's ban on cruel and unusual punishment. On the other hand, this Court in *Palko* v. *Connecticut* . . . (1937) refused to hold that the Fourteenth Amendment made the double jeopardy provision of the Fifth Amendment obligatory on the States.* In so refusing, however, the Court, speaking through Mr. Justice Cardozo, was careful to emphasize that "immunities that are valid as against the federal government by force of the specific pledges of particular amendments have been found to be implicit in the concept of ordered liberty, and thus, through the Fourteenth Amendment, become valid as against the states" and that guarantees "in their origin . . . effective against the federal government alone" had by prior cases "been taken over from the earlier articles of the Federal Bill of Rights and brought within the Fourteenth Amendment by a process of absorption."

We accept *Betts* v. *Brady's* assumption, based as it was on our prior cases, that a provision of the Bill of Rights which is "fundamental and essential to a fair trial" is made obligatory upon the States by the Fourteenth Amendment. We think the Court in *Betts* was wrong, however, in concluding that the Sixth Amendment's guarantee of counsel is not one of these fundamental rights.

. . . .

Not only these precedents but also reason and reflection require us to recognize that in our adversary system of criminal justice, any person haled into court, who is too poor to hire a lawyer, cannot be assured a fair trial unless counsel is provided for him. This seems to us to be an obvious truth. Governments, both state and federal, quite properly spend vast sums of money to establish machinery to try defendants accused of crime. Lawyers to prosecute are everywhere deemed essential to protect the public's interest in an orderly society. Similarly, there are few defendants charged with crime, few indeed, who fail to hire the best lawyers they can get to prepare and present their defenses. That government hires lawyers to prosecute and defendants who have the money hire lawyers to defend are the strongest indications of the widespread belief that lawyers in criminal courts are necessities, not luxuries. The right of one charged with crime to counsel may not be deemed fundamental and essential to fair trials in some countries, but it is in ours.

. . . .

---

*The specific double jeopardy holding of *Palko* was reversed by the Supreme Court in 1969 in *Benton* v. *Maryland*, 395 U.S. 784, 89 S. Ct. 2056, 23 L. Ed. 2d 707.

The judgment is reversed and the cause is remanded to the Supreme Court of Florida for further action not inconsistent with this opinion.
Reversed.

The case was retried in Florida, and this time Gideon was given a lawyer. At that trial, Gideon was found innocent of all charges by a jury.

Procedural Due Process

A second meaning of due process, both under the 5th and 14th Amendments, is simply *fair procedures.* Whenever a unit of government tries to take away "life, liberty, or property," the persons involved are entitled to procedures such as a hearing, notice of charges, and a right to present one's side of the story. Generally speaking, the more important the interest involved, the more formal the procedures that must be used. Thus, a case involving the death penalty would require extremely formal procedures, but a suspension from high school would involve very informal procedures.

Procedural due process requirements apply to more than the courtroom. Many of the issues of procedural due process will be presented later in the context of administrative agencies in Chapter 5, but any governmental official may deprive an individual of due process rights.

Each procedural due process case is different. The court must first determine that the "protected interest" in the case is in fact "life, liberty, or property" and therefore protected by the Due Process Clause. Once that determination is made, the court must then determine "what process is due," that is, how formal the procedures must be to protect the specific interest involved. Those procedures are then tailored to fit the situation (see *Mathews* v. *Eldridge,* p. 163).

It is important to note that due process does *not* depend on whether the interest involved can be characterized as a right or a privilege. Until 1970, the courts had generally held that if a right was involved, due process procedures attached; but such procedures were not required if all that was involved was a mere privilege. In 1970, the Supreme Court refused to recognize that "wooden distinction" in the case of *Goldberg* v. *Kelly* (p. 161) the famous "welfare rights" case. Due process procedures have been required in cases of suspension or revocation of a driver's license, suspension from school for disciplinary reasons, denial of time off for good behavior in prisons, termination of electrical service by a municipal power company, suspension of welfare payments, dismissal of teachers, police officers, fire fighters, and university professors, and immigration proceedings, among others. But, in each case, the degree of formality of the procedures varied with the importance of the interest being threatened by government action, the risk of an erroneous deprivation of the interest without procedural guarantees, and the value of added procedures.

Of course due process also requires that courtroom procedures also be basically fair. While many of the components of a fair trial are specifically set out in the Constitution—such as the right to trial by jury, the right to counsel, and the right to be free from cruel and unusual punishments—other aspects of fair trial not found in the Constitution have been supplied by interpretation of due process. For example, the courts have held that "mob domination" of trial proceedings, excessive limits on cross-examination by a defendant, the denial of a public trial, and insufficient time to prepare for trial are all denials of due process.

Equal Protection

The concept of equal protection under the 14th Amendment has already been discussed in Chapter 2 in the context of economic liberties. But, obviously, the Equal Protection Clause applies to far more than economic freedoms and, in fact, may apply to any statute that imposes an impermissible classification scheme.

Every statute inevitably classifies—who is to be taxed, who is to be charged with a crime, who must submit to regulation, and the like. Such classification cannot be avoided, but neither may such statutes make **invidious discriminations,** or classifications based on impermissible categories.

The 14th Amendment was enacted in part to prohibit such invidious discrimination, but it did not explain what sorts of classifications were impermissible. Certainly race or color is such a category, and almost as clearly categories such as nationality, religion, wealth, age, and sex are also impermissible, unless the government using such a classification in a statute has a very good reason for adopting such a scheme.

The Reasonable Basis and Strict Scrutiny Tests

The general question in equal protection cases is whether the legislature had a **reasonable basis** (or "rational" basis) for its classification scheme. For example, in *New Orleans* v. *Dukes* in Chapter 2, the Court found that the city council had a *reasonable basis* for treating some pushcart vendors differently from others and, therefore, held that the classification scheme was permissible.

But, if a classification scheme involves **fundamental rights** protected by the Bill of Rights, or a **suspect classification,** such as race, the courts will use a much higher standard—the so-called **strict scrutiny test.** Under that test, the classification will be held to violate the Equal Protection Clause unless the legislature can demonstrate there is no other way to accomplish a valid state objective. The question of whether a particular group belongs in a suspect class depends on three factors: (1) whether membership "carries an obvious badge, such as race or sex do;" (2) whether treatment of members of the group has been historically severe and pervasive; and (3) whether members of the class have been subjected to the "absolute deprivation" of benefits available to nonmembers of the group. If a statute uses a suspect class the courts will apply the strict scrutiny test instead of the reasonable basis test. The following decision illustrates the court's attitude towards a classification scheme based on sex.

Craig v. Boren

429 U.S. 191, 97 S. Ct. 451, 50 L. Ed. 2d 397 (1976)

An Oklahoma statute provided that 3.2% beer might be sold to females over the age of 18 and to males over the age of 21. Craig, a male over the age of 18 but under 21, and Whitener, a seller of 3.2% beer, brought suit to declare the statute unconstitutional under the Equal Protection Clause. A three-judge panel of the district court denied relief, and the plaintiffs appealed to the Supreme Court.

Mr. Justice BRENNAN delivered the opinion of the Court. . . .

Analysis may appropriately begin with the reminder that . . . statutory classifications that distinguish between males and females are "subject to scrutiny under the Equal Protection Clause." . . . To withstand constitutional challenge, previous cases establish that classifications by gender must serve important governmental objectives and must be substantially related to achievement of those objectives. . . .

. . . .

. . . "[A]rchaic and overbroad" generalizations . . . concerning the financial position of servicewomen . . . and working women . . . could not justify the use of a gender line in determining eligibility for certain governmental entitlements. Similarly, increasingly outdated misconceptions concerning the role of females in the home rather than in the "marketplace and world of ideas" were rejected as loose-fitting characterizations incapable of supporting state statutory schemes that were premised on their accuracy. . . . In light of the weak congruence between gender and the characteristic or trait that gender purported to represent, it was necessary that the legislatures choose either to realign their substantive laws in a gender-neutral fashion, or to adopt procedures for identifying those instances where the sex-centered generalization actually comported with the Act. . . .

. . . .

We turn then to the question whether, . . . the difference between males and females with respect to the purchase of 3.2% beer warrants the differential in age drawn by the Oklahoma statute. We conclude that it does not. . . . We accept for purposes of discussion . . . the objective underlying the statute as the enhancement of traffic safety. . . . The appellees introduced a variety of statistical surveys. First, an analysis of arrest statistics . . . demonstrated that 18–20 year old male arrests for "driving under the influence" and "drunkenness" substantially exceeded female arrests for the same age period. Similarly, youths aged 17–21 were found to be overrepresented among those killed or injured in traffic accidents, with males again numerically exceeding females in this regard. Third, a random roadside survey in Oklahoma City revealed that young males were more inclined to drive and drink beer than were their female counterparts. . . .

The Court then criticized the surveys, finding them statistically suspect and unverifiable.

Suffice it to say that the showing offered by the appellees does not satisfy us that sex represents a legitimate, accurate proxy for the regulation of drinking and driving. In fact, when it is further recognized that Oklahoma's statute prohibits only the selling of 3.2% beer to young males and not their drinking the beverage once acquired (even after the purchase by their 18–20 year-old female companions), the relationship between gender and traffic safety becomes far too tenuous. . . .

We hold, therefore, that . . . Oklahoma's 3.2% beer statute invidiously discriminates against males 18–20 years of age. . . .

In the 20th century, the Equal Protection Clause has been used to invalidate laws that required racial discrimination in the schools* and elsewhere, racial restrictions on voting rights, underrepresentation of urban majorities in legislatures (one-man, one-vote) and many others. Perhaps the greatest area of activity in the development of the law surrounding the Equal Protection Clause has been in the context of racial discrimination. That topic will be discussed at length in Chapter 16.

---

*See *Brown* v. *Board of Education*, p. 567.

The Problem of State Action

By its express terms, the 14th Amendment only prohibits "invidious discrimination" on the part of *states*. The amendment has nothing to say about *private* discrimination, as in the case of a landlord who refuses to rent to a person because of race, for example. Clearly, Congress and the states may enact statutes to prohibit various types of private discrimination (See Chapter 16) but if no such statute exists, the 14th Amendment does not prohibit private discrimination.

In *Shelley* v. *Kraemer* (see Chapter 16, p. 565), a 1948 Supreme Court decision, the Court held that judicial enforcement of such private discrimination constituted state action and therefore violated the Equal Protection Clause. In that case, a state court was asked to enforce a discriminatory provision in a real estate deed that prohibited blacks from purchasing property. The Supreme Court held that the court order enforcing that private discrimination was state action and therefore in violation of the Equal Protection Clause.

The Problem of Other Rights

Obviously, the Bill of Rights contains other specific guarantees aside from those discussed so far. Our discussion has not included any mention of the 2nd, 3rd, 7th, 8th, 9th, or 10th Amendments, and it should be clear that a great deal of law surrounds those amendments as well. Our selection of amendments to discuss has reflected a rather arbitrary opinion of which amendments are "more important" and consideration of which "rights" are likely to be most important to the ordinary citizen and businessperson. The law surrounding the 1st Amendment, the criminal procedure amendments, and the 14th Amendment has received more consideration by the Court and, therefore, may be considered more "highly developed."

Even considering that the Constitution contains, by one count, 63 guarantees of individual liberty, it remains at least theoretically possible that there are *other* rights, not specified in the Constitution. That conclusion is bolstered by the somewhat vague and mystical reference in the 9th Amendment to "other rights." Thus, while it seems that the Bill of Rights does a good job of setting out essential civil liberties, it is possible that the founding fathers missed something. This does not mean that the authors of the Bill of Rights were in any way sloppy or lacked intelligence. It may mean only that the times have changed since 1791, and new rights are necessary to protect us from over-zealous government.

The possibility of new rights remained only a theory until 1965, when the following case was decided.

Griswold v. Connecticut

381 U.S. 479, 85 S. Ct. 1678, 14 L. Ed. 2d 510 (1965)

Connecticut law made the use of birth control devices illegal, and also prohibited anyone from giving information on the use of such devices. The executive director and medical director of a planned parenthood association were found guilty of dispensing such information and fined $100 each. They appealed the convictions to the Supreme Court.

Mr. Justice DOUGLAS delivered the opinion of the Court. . . .

We are met with a wide range of questions that implicate the Due Process Clause of the Fourteenth Amendment. . . . We do not sit as a super legislature to determine the wisdom, need, and propriety of laws that touch economic problems, business affairs, or social conditions. The law, however, operates directly on an intimate relation of husband and wife and their physician's role in one aspect of that relation.

The association of people is not mentioned in the Constitution nor in the Bill of Rights. . . .

[Previous] cases suggest that specific guarantees in the Bill of Rights have penumbras, formed by emanations from those guarantees that help give them life and substance. . . . Various guarantees create zones of privacy. The right of association contained in the penumbra of the First Amendment is one. . . . The Third Amendment in its prohibition against the quartering of soldiers "in any house" in time of peace without the consent of the owner is another facet of that privacy. The Fourth Amendment explicitly affirms the "right of the people to be secure in their persons, houses, papers and effects, against unreasonable searches and seizures." The Fifth Amendment in its Self-Incrimination Clause enables the citizen to create a zone of privacy which the government may not force him to surrender to his detriment. The Ninth Amendment provides: "The enumeration in the Constitution, of certain rights, shall not be construed to deny or disparage others retained by the people."

The Fourth and Fifth Amendments were described . . . as protection against all governmental invasions "of the sanctity of a man's home and the privacies of life." We recently referred in *Mapp* v. *Ohio* . . . to the Fourth Amendment as creating a "right to privacy, no less important than any other right carefully and particularly reserved to the people." . . .

We have had many controversies over these penumbral rights of "privacy and repose." . . . . These cases bear witness that the right of privacy which presses for recognition here is a legitimate one.

The present case, then, concerns a relationship lying within the zone of privacy created by several fundamental constitutional guarantees. And it concerns a law which, in forbidding the *use* of contraceptives rather than regulating their manufacture or sale, seeks to achieve its goals by having a maximum destructive impact upon that relationship. Such a law cannot stand. . . . Would we allow the police to search the sacred precincts of marital bedrooms for telltale signs of the use of contraceptives? The very idea is repulsive to the notions of privacy surrounding the marital relationship.

We deal with a right of privacy older than the Bill of Rights—older than our political parties, older than our school system. Marriage is a coming together for better or for worse, hopefully enduring, and intimate to the degree of being sacred. It is an association that promotes a way of life, not causes; a harmony in living, not political faiths; a bilateral loyalty, not commercial or social projects. Yet it is an association for as noble a purpose as any involved in our prior decisions.

Reversed.

While the *Griswold* decision and the right of privacy announced in that case are of comparatively recent origin, the case created a very pervasive right with broad and far-reaching implications. The concept of the "right of privacy" has been applied to hold unconstitutional a variety of state statutes punishing consensual sexual conduct and was the basis of the Supreme Court's decision in *Roe* v. *Wade*,* the controversial

---

*410 U.S. 113, 93 S. Ct. 705, 35 L. Ed. 2d 147 (1973).

case which held state statutes prohibiting abortion unconstitutional. As Mr. Justice Blackmun argued in that case,

> The Constitution does not explicitly mention any right of privacy. In a line of decisions, however. . . . the Court has recognized that a right of personal privacy or a guarantee of certain areas or zones of privacy, does exist under the Constitution. . . . They also make it clear that the right has some extension to activities relating to marriage . . . procreation . . . contraception . . . family relationships. . . . and child rearing and education. . . . This right of privacy . . . is broad enough to encompass a woman's decision whether or not to terminate her pregnancy.

Thus it is clear that new rights may be discovered and applied to the state and federal governments at any time. Following *Griswold* no other new rights have been found so far, but the importance of *Griswold* is that it lays the foundations for the discovery of other rights. That doctrine, perhaps more than any other, makes clear the idea of an ever-changing Bill of Rights, adjusting to social and economic changes and political necessity through judicial interpretation.

Summary and Conclusions

The Bill of Rights, broadly defined to include at least the 14th Amendment, provides the clearest limitations on the powers of government. Many believe that the 1st Amendment contains the basic and essential political rights necessary to any free state. It seems clear that freedom of speech and press are absolutely essential to political democracy, since without them opposition to the government would be impossible. But, while the 1st Amendment is phrased in absolute terms, the courts have permitted some exceptions and allowed governments to regulate advocacy of crime or revolution, obscenity, commercial speech, and defamation.

When read together with freedom of religion, the 1st Amendment seems to protect a general "freedom of conscience." Freedom of religion involves two aspects, freedom from governmental interference with religious beliefs (the Free Exercise Clause) and freedom from governmental support of particular religious bodies or beliefs (the Establishment Clause).

The 4th, 5th, and 6th Amendments, taken together, provide protections against governmental abuse of the criminal process. Those amendments contain, among others, protections against unreasonable searches and seizures, abuses of the privilege against self-incrimination, and guarantees of the right to counsel. However, many of those protections are not limited to criminal prosecutions but include administrative searches, interrogations by taxing and administrative officers, and so forth.

The Due Process Clause of the 14th Amendment operates on two levels: first, it requires that procedures in trials and administrative hearings be "fair"; and, second, it has applied many of the protections of the first ten amendments to the states under the selective incorporation doctrine. The Equal Protection Clause of the 14th Amendment prohibits any state-backed invidious discrimination.

The Bill of Rights may be expanded and stretched. New rights may be "discovered" under the broad phrasing of the 9th and 14th Amendments, and the existing rights under the express amendments may be changed through judicial interpretation of their meaning. In the words of John Marshall, the Constitution was "intended to endure for ages to come, and consequently, to be adapted to the various crises of human affairs." It is the peculiar genius of the American Constitution that it at once erects barriers to government overreaching and makes those barriers flexible enough to account for social, economic, and political necessity.

PRO AND CON
ISSUE: First Amendment Protection of Commercial Speech: Is the Doctrine Justified?

PRO: Commercial Speech Should Be Protected

Daniel A. Farber*

For the past forty years, commercial speech has occupied an awkward position in first amendment theory. Until recently, government was given a free hand in regulating advertising. Although this anomalous gap in first amendment theory was finally closed in 1976, commercial speech stubbornly declines to fit comfortably within our general rules for free speech. The Supreme Court still refuses to give commercial speech the full measure of protection enjoyed by other forms of speech, insisting instead that the "common sense distinction" between commercial speech and other speech justifies a variety of differences in treatment. Nagging questions remain about this treatment of commercial speech. If a political candidate can lie without fear of legal intervention, why can't a used car dealer? Why should a cigarette manufacturer be required to publicize disagreeable facts about his product when a newspaper commentator cannot be penalized for incomplete disclosure?

Once confronted, these questions cannot be easily dismissed because they appeal to the basic first amendment principle of *content neutrality* [emphasis added]. In its purest form, this principle is expressed in the statement that "above all else, the First Amendment means that government has no power to restrict expression because of its message, its ideas, its subject matter, or its content." The content of the advertisement is generally the source of the government's objection, and the commercial subject matter of the advertisement forms the basis of the government's claim to regulatory power.

Can present commercial speech doctrine be justified on the basis of some unique characteristic of commercial speech without impairing the principle of content neutrality? . . .

The natural starting point for analyzing the constitutional status of commercial speech is to ask whether the subject matter of the speech places it outside the boundaries of the first amendment. The subject matter of commercial speech is invariably some commercial product or service about whose existence, price, or qualities the speaker wishes to communicate. If product information were outside the pale of the first amendment, the consumer advocate as well as the commercial speaker would be left unprotected. General Motors could constitutionally enjoin Ralph Nader from revealing unfavorable facts about its cars, and magazines like *Consumer Reports* could be freely suppressed. These results are simply unacceptable.

Suppose that a company publishes an exhaustive and entirely truthful survey of the products of its industry. To make the point clear, assume that the survey was taken by *Consumer Reports* and enjoyed constitutional protection when it was published in that magazine. Distribution by the company could strip the survey of its constitutional protection only if profit motivation were a disqualifying factor. The *Virginia Board* Court was clearly correct in rejecting this approach. Economic motivation could not be made a disqualifying factor without enormous damage to the first amendment. Little

---

*Daniel A. Farber is a professor of law at the University of Illinois. From his article "Commercial Speech and First Amendment Theory," reprinted by special permission of the Northwestern University Law Review, © by Northwestern University School of Law, Vol. 74, No. 3.

purpose would be served by a first amendment which failed to protect newspapers, paid public speakers, political candidates with partially economic motives, and professional authors. Furthermore, the economically motivated speaker is often the most likely to raise important issues, since disinterestedness is less common than apathy.

Eliminating economic motive as a disqualifying factor seems to leave no basis for excluding commercial speech, as a class, from first amendment protection. There may, however, be an argument for denying first amendment protection to certain types of commercial speech. Advertisements frequently contain little information and instead are intended to create irrational product preferences. It might be tenable to treat commercial speech like pornography and require some minimal level of "redeeming social value" as a prerequisite for first amendment protection. Indeed, a social critic might suggest that the analogy is fairly close, that, in a sense, advertising is the pornography of capitalism, intended to arouse desire for objects rather than for persons. Several problems would arise, however, from adopting a requirement of redeeming social value for advertisements, the foremost being that such a scheme has not succeeded in the obscenity area.

Economic motivation and subject matter have already been eliminated as distinguishing factors.

How else does commercial speech differ from noncommercial speech? One obvious distinction is that the commercial speaker not only talks about a product, but also sells it. The sale itself is subject to broad state regulation. May such regulation include the attachment of liability to the use of language in connection with a sales transaction?

To ask this question is very nearly to answer it. Contract law consists almost entirely of rules attaching liability to various uses of language. . . . No first amendment problem exists. . . .

Similar to the language of a written contract, the language in advertising can be seen as constituting part of the seller's commitment to the buyer. . . . So long as a regulation relates to the contractual function of the utterance, the regulation should not be subjected to the intensive scrutiny required . . . [by] the first amendment. . . .

Most traditional consumer protection legislation is based on the contractual nature of the speech. Misrepresentation, duress, overreaching, and unconscionability are well-known contract doctrines. When the state attacks these problems with modern regulatory tools, it can legitimately claim an interest quite distinct from the suppression of free speech.

CON: The "Commercial Speech" Doctrine is Inconsistent
Archibald Cox*

The most venturesome rulings of the Burger Court dealing with freedom of expression have overturned settled law and extended the first amendment to commercial advertising. The key decision is *Virginia State Board of Pharmacy* v. *Virginia Citizens Consumer Council, Inc.,* where the majority held unconstitutional a statute prohibiting pharmacists from advertising the prices at which they would sell prescription drugs.

The opinion underscores the problems of the Burger Court in developing a coherent approach to the first amendment. The Court paid little attention to building a systematic body of law, but instead engaged in particularistic and pragmatic balancing.

The applicable precedents went far to establish that commercial advertising is not protected by the first amendment. In any reconsideration of those rulings, the first question to ask would seem to be whether commercial advertising is enough like other "speech" protected by the first amendment to be given the same protection. If so, the case would be governed by the well-established principle that direct suppression is permissible, if ever, only because of overwhelming public necessity. If not, the advertising would be governed by the principle that a regulatory law is constitutional if it can reasonably be supposed to contribute to the effectuation of some rational view of the public interest.

*Archibald Cox is the Carl M. Loeb University Professor at the Harvard Law School and was solicitor general of the United States, 1961–1965. From *The Harvard Law Review,* "The Supreme Court, 1979 Term", "Forward: Freedom of Expression in the Burger Court." 94 *Harvard Law Review* 1, © 1980, the Harvard Law Review Association. Reprinted by permission.

In the latter event, statutes prohibiting advertising of the price of prescription drugs would surely be upheld. Indeed, such laws had been sustained for decades against attacks under the due process and equal protection clauses.

The interests affected by the statute were overwhelmingly economic. The gist of Justice Blackmun's criticism was that such statutes would interfere with the free operation of the market. . . . It is hardly surprising, therefore, that commentators have taxed the Court with reviving the philosophy of *Lochner* v. *New York* in the guise of first amendment doctrine.

The bench and bar did not have to wait long to witness the consequences of breaking down the category "speech" in order to protect particular communications to which the Court was unwilling to extend full protection. . . . *Young* v. *American Mini Theatres, Inc.* (427 U.S. 50, (1976)) grew out of a challenge to an "anti-skid row" ordinance adopted by Detroit in 1962 which forbade using property for certain businesses if located within 1,000 feet of two other establishments in the same category; included in the list of businesses were dance halls, pool rooms, public lodging houses, shoe shine parlors, bars . . . pawn shops. . . . [and] *adult theaters and adult book stores.* . . . [emphasis added].

In *American Mini Theaters,* however, Justice Stevens . . . made it plain that even though the pictures to be exhibited were within the scope of the first amendment protection, the [court] judged them to belong, like commercial advertising, in the category of second class speech.

[F]ew of us would march our sons and daughters off to war to preserve the citizen's right to see "Specified Sexual Activities" exhibited in the theaters of our choice. Even though the First Amendment protects communication in this area from total suppression, we hold that the State may legitimately use the content of these materials as the basis for placing them in a different classification from other motion pictures.

Few of us would march our sons or daughters off to war to preserve the citizen's right to see pictures of American Nazis marching in uniform in Skokie, Illinois, or to hear advocacy of Stalinist Communism, or to read advertisements stating the price of prescription drugs. That test is both unreasoning and insufficient. . . . [O]ne is bound to wonder where the process of particularization commenced in the *Pharmacists* case will stop.

From the proposition that sexually explicit adult movies are only second-class speech, the [court] proceeded directly to the conclusion that the zoning restriction was sufficiently justified by the city's interest in preserving the character of its neighborhoods.

. . . It is not our function to appraise the wisdom of its decision to require adult theaters to be separated rather than concentrated in the same areas. . . . Moreover, the city must be allowed a reasonable opportunity to experiment with solutions to admittedly serious problems.

Experiment with regulating speech! Surely the words are those of advocates of judicial restraint. . . . The teaching seems to be that in dealing with second-class speech, or, at least, one form of second-class speech, the Court will not make its own findings concerning the relevant social and economic conditions or substitute its own judgment as to the consequences of the challenged law for the judgment of the legislative body.

Why is it a function of the Court to appraise for itself the effects and thus the wisdom of prohibiting price advertisements by pharmacists while it defers as in economic regulation cases to state experimentation with the effects of a zoning ordinance requiring the dispersal of establishments offering "adult" books and theaters? There may be an explanation, but none was offered in the opinions.

DISCUSSION QUESTIONS

1. The framers of the Constitution felt that the Bill of Rights was unnecessary and in Hamilton's terms, even dangerous. Do you think they were correct? Has almost 200 years of history proven Hamilton correct?

2. Many commentators have argued that the 1st Amendment is far more important than any other amendment, especially when it deals with matters of conscience, such as politics and religion. Do you agree?

3. In the 1960's, several courts held that marches by civil rights demonstrators through white areas of cities were protected by the 1st Amendment, as long as the marchers themselves remained peaceful. Should the cities be able to ban such marches if people watching the marchers might become violent? Before you answer, consider that the answer must be the same for those civil rights marchers as for a parade of American Nazis through a Jewish suburb and for a Ku Klux Klan march through an inner city. Should the answer be the same for all three marches? What is the difference?

4. Do you think the exclusionary rule ties the hands of the police? Do you have a better alternative to assure that the police will follow constitutional procedures? Is it a fair criticism of the exclusionary rule to say that it protects the guilty and only very rarely the innocent? Does it protect anyone if the police are not interested in arresting anyone, but merely wish to harass someone?

5. In *Miranda*, the Supreme Court clearly indicated that if a state or federal government could come up with a better alternative than the warnings required by the case, the Court might consider scrapping the warnings. The case is now twenty years old, and no state has taken up the Court's invitation. Can you think of a better alternative? Does it suggest anything to say that no state has tried?

6. Do you think the framers of the Constitution intended that the Bill of Rights apply to the states? Do you think the authors of the 14th Amendment intended the "incorporation doctrine"? Does it matter what those people thought? Do you think the states would all have something like the 1st Amendment in their state constitutions if it was not applied to them by the 14th Amendment?

7. The Equal Rights Amendment says

> Section 1. Equality of rights under the law shall not be denied or abridged by the United States or by any state on account of sex.
>
> Section 2. The Congress shall have the power to enforce by appropriate legislation, the provisions of this article.
>
> Section 3. This amendment shall take effect two years after the date of ratification.

After *Craig* v. *Boren,* is this amendment necessary? Why or why not?

8. By permitting exceptions to the clear language of the Constitution, as in the case of the exceptions to the absolute guarantee of freedom of speech, are we providing precedent for future exceptions and gradually weakening the Constitution? Are such "slippery slide" or "thin edge of the wedge" arguments valid?

9. In a concurring opinion in *Roe* v. *Wade,* Justice Douglas said that he felt there were more "new rights" waiting to be discovered, and gave the following examples.

First is the autonomous control over the development and expression of one's intellect, interests, tastes and personality. . . .

Second is freedom of choice in the basic decisions of one's life respecting marriage, divorce, procreation, contraception, and the education and upbringing of children. . . .

Third is the freedom to care for one's health and person, freedom from bodily restraint or compulsion, freedom to walk, stroll or loaf. . . . "

Should these rights gain the status of constitutionally protected rights? Can you think of any others which Douglas has omitted? Does the fact that you can't think of any mean there are none? Are some of Douglas' rights already secured by the constitution?

CASE PROBLEMS

1. A group of university students gathered at a jail in Florida to protest continuing local policies of racial segregation within the jail. The sheriff ordered the protestors to leave the premises, and when they refused, had them arrested for trespass. The protestors were in an area of the jail restricted from the public. Has the sheriff violated the protesters' right of free speech? [*Adderly* v. *Florida,* 385 U.S. 39, 87 S. Ct. 242, 17 L. Ed. 2d 149 (1967).] Would it make a difference if they were in a public area? [See *Edwards* v. *South Carolina,* 372 U.S. 229, 83 S. Ct. 680, 9 L. Ed. 2d 697 (1963).]

2. Cohen appeared in a Los Angeles courthouse wearing a jacket bearing a common four-letter expletive in reference to the military draft and was promptly arrested for disturbing the peace. The incident took place during the Vietnam War, and Cohen felt (obviously) quite strongly about the war. He defended on the grounds of his 1st Amendment freedom of speech. Is it speech? Is this display protected by the 1st Amendment? [*Cohen* v. *California,* 403 U.S. 15, 91 S. Ct. 1780, 29 L. Ed. 2d 284 (1971).]

3. A Kentucky statute required the posting of a copy of the Ten Commandments in every schoolroom. The copies were purchased with private funds. Does the statute violate the 1st Amendment? [*Stone* v. *Graham,* 449 U.S. 39, 101 S. Ct. 192, 66 L. Ed. 2d 199 (1980).]

4. A state university made its facilities available to all registered student groups, except religious organizations. Does this policy violate the 1st Amendment? [*Widmar* v. *Vincent,* 454 U.S. 263, 102 S. Ct. 269, 70 L. Ed. 2d 440 (1981).]

5. Wisconsin law compelled children to attend school until their sixteenth birthday. The Amish church held that high school education beyond eighth grade was contrary to their beliefs. The Yoder family, devout Amishmen, refused to send its children to school and claimed the law violated their 1st Amendment rights. Result? [*Wisconsin* v. *Yoder,* 406 U.S. 205, 92 S. Ct. 1526, 32 L. Ed. 2d 15 (1972).]

6. Routine warrantless inspections were made by officials of the Occupational Safety and Health Act to assess compliance with federal health standards. Barlow's, Inc., an electrical contractor, contended that such inspections violate the 4th Amendment. Is it a search? Has Barlow's consented to the search by voluntarily entering a business subject to such searches? [*Marshall* v. *Barlow's, Inc.* 436 U.S. 307, 98 S. Ct. 1816, 56 L. Ed. 2d 305 (1978). See also Chapter 5.]

7. Does a defendant have a right to proceed *without* a lawyer if he so desires? [*Faretta* v. *California,* 422 U.S. 806, 95 S. Ct. 2525, 45 L. Ed. 2d 562 (1975).]

8. Schmerber was arrested for driving under the influence of intoxicating liquor, after an accident. At the hospital, despite Schmerber's refusal, and at a police officer's request, a blood sample was taken. The blood sample showed Schmerber was intoxicated, and it was introduced in evidence. Schmerber objected on 5th Amendment grounds, stating that the blood sample amounted to self-incrimination. Result? [*Schmerber* v. *California,* 384 U.S. 757, 86 S. Ct. 1826, 16 L. Ed. 2d 908 (1966).]

9. A Massachusetts statute required that an unmarried minor who is pregnant must obtain the consent of her parents or guardian prior to an abortion. Is this regulation consistent with *Roe* v. *Wade?* [*Bellotti* v. *Baird,* 443 U.S. 622, 99 S. Ct. 3035, 61 L. Ed. 2d 797 (1979).]

10. A New York Statute made it a crime for any person to sell or distribute contraceptives to any person under the age of 16, and also made it illegal to display or advertise contraceptives. Does this statute violate the 1st Amendment or the right of privacy or both? [*Carey* v. *Population Services International,* 431 U.S. 678, 97 S. Ct. 2010, 52 L. Ed. 2d 675 (1977).]

SUGGESTED READINGS

Abernathy, M. Glenn. *Civil Liberties Under the Constitution* 3rd ed. (New York: Dodd, Mead & Co., 1977).

Brandt, Irving. *The Bill of Rights* (Indianapolis: Bobbs-Merrill Company, 1965).

Cox, Archibald, Mark DeWolf Howe, and J. R. Wiggins. *Civil Rights, the Constitution, and the Courts* (Cambridge, Mass.: Harvard University Press, 1977).

Dorsen, Norman, et. al. (Eds). *Emerson, Haber & Dorsen's Political and Civil Rights in the United States* 4th ed. (Boston: Little, Brown & Co., 1979).

Douglas, William O. *A Living Bill of Rights* (Garden City, N.Y.: Doubleday & Co., Inc., 1961).

Ducat, Craig R., and Harold W. Chase. *Constitutional Interpretation* 3rd ed. (St. Paul, Minn.: West Publishing Co., 1983).

Fortas, Abe. *Concerning Dissent and Civil Disobedience* (New York: The World Publishing Co., 1968).

Schwartz, Bernard. *The Bill of Rights: A Documentary History* (New York: Chelsea House Publishers, in association with McGraw-Hill Book Co., 1971).

Schwartz, Bernard. *The Great Rights of Mankind* (New York: Oxford University Press, 1977).

The American Court System

The history of liberty has largely been the history of the observance of procedural safeguards.

Justice Felix Frankfurter in McNabb *v.* U.S., *318 U. S. 332, 63 S. Ct. 608, L. Ed. (1943).*

It is too late in the day and entirely contrary to the spirit of the Federal Rules of Civil Procedure for decisions on the merits to be avoided on the basis of . . . mere technicalities. The Federal Rules reject the approach that pleading is a game of skill in which one misstep by counsel may be decisive to the outcome and accept the principle that the purpose of pleading is to facilitate a proper decision on the merits.

Justice Authur Goldberg in Foman *v.* Davis, *371 U.S. 178, 83 S. Ct. 227, 9 L. Ed. 2d 222 (1962).*

Lawsuit. *n., A machine which you go into as a pig and come out as a sausage.*

Ambrose Bierce, The Devil's Dictionary *(1906)*

An important part of the legal environment of business is the machinery of the court systems that decide many of the cases affecting business. The purpose of this chapter is to describe the nuts and bolts of the American court systems, both federal and state, including how they are organized and some of the rules of the game that apply in those courts.

One way of classifying the law is between procedural and substantive law. **Substantive law** defines, creates, and regulates legal rights and duties, while **procedural law** includes all of the rules by which courts operate. But procedural law is far more than mere technical rules of court. The concept also includes some extremely weighty issues, including the procedural rights of accused persons, the proper role of judges and juries, and threshhold issues of jurisdiction, fair procedure, and the right to bring a case in court. Critical parts of the Bill of Rights also address procedural matters, including the right to counsel, the right to a jury trial, and the whole concept of procedural due process.

This chapter will begin with the authority of courts to rule and proceed to the related concepts of jurisdiction, venue, and organization of the courts. We will then move into a consideration of various procedural doctrines, including problems of federal-state relations, the case or controversy requirement, the rules of standing, or the right to bring a case, and a discussion of some important "special remedies," including class action suits, declaratory judgment actions, and mandamus. Finally, we will trace the course of a civil lawsuit from beginning to end, pausing to compare civil procedures to criminal procedures, and including a discussion of the appellate process.

The Adversary System

Before we begin, it is important to understand that the Anglo-American system of law is based on the **adversary system,** a process with historical roots in trial by combat but that, over the ages, has proven to be a very efficient method of arriving at the truth in judicial proceedings. The adversary system assumes that the truth will emerge from a clash of able and opposing forces. The issues are framed by the lawyers for either side, and issues not raised, objections not made, and points not challenged are all generally waived. The judge sits solely to rule on contested points and usually does not play an active role in the case.

The major competitor to the adversary system in world legal systems is the **inquisitorial system,** used in much of the rest of the world. In such a system, the primary goal of all participants is the truth. Judges tend to take a very active role in such a system. The primary difference is the assumption in the inquisitorial system that the truth can be found by a thorough (and, one hopes, even-handed) search for it, while the adversary system is based on the assumption that truth will be found only through the clash of conflicting interests.

American court procedures are based on the adversary system. Rules of pleading and evidence all assume that each lawyer will use only those procedures that will help his or her client's case. It is then up to the trier of fact (a jury or a judge without a jury) to decide the truth after hearing all sides presented capably and forcefully.

Court Organization: 52 Court Systems

One of the most unique and complicating factors in the American court system is that there are 52 of them. The federal courts are organized by Congress to handle federally related matters and cases that demand federal supervision, and each state had established its own court system to hear cases within its borders. The fifty-second court system is the special set of courts established by Congress to hear cases in the

District of Columbia. Sometimes the American court system is called a *dual* system, referring to the state and federal systems, but that term is misleading since each state maintains its own separate court system. The existence of so many court systems in the United States gives rise to many of the problems we will consider, including many of the issues of jurisdiction and conflicts of law.

Sources of Judicial Organization

The federal Constitution provides almost no guidance for the establishment and organization of the federal courts. Article III only provides for the establishment of "one supreme Court, and ... such inferior Courts as the Congress may ... ordain and establish." The lower federal courts, including the U.S. District Courts and U.S. Courts of Appeals, have all been created by acts of Congress.

Some state constitutions are quite detailed in the types of courts established, while others, like the federal Constitution, are vague and leave much to the state legislature. A common feature is that the salary of judges may not be diminished while the judge is in office. Some states, like the federal government, select judges by appointment of the chief executive (governor) with the advice and consent of the legislature. Others provide for election of judges by popular vote, followed by retention elections, in which the public votes on whether the judge should continue in office after a specified period of time.

The Typical Three-Tiered Court System

The federal courts and a large minority of state courts are organized on a three-tiered basis similar to that shown in Figure 4-1. At the lowest level are the *trial courts.* In the federal system, the trial courts are known as *U.S. District Courts,* and in the state systems they are known by a variety of names, including circuit courts, county courts, courts of general session, courts of common pleas, and superior courts, among others. In the federal system, the nation is divided into districts, at least one in each state, and each district contains a U.S. District Court. Normally, state systems place a separate trial court in each county, though there are variations.

Everything above the trial court level is an appellate court, since almost all cases reach those courts through appeal from decisions of a trial court. The federal system and 23 states have intermediate appellate courts, where most appeals are heard the first time. In the federal system, the nation and its foreign territories are divided into twelve geographic regions, each of which has a U.S. Court of Appeals (see Table 4-1). Because the District of Columbia receives a large volume of cases from federal administrative agencies it has a separate circuit. The thirteenth U.S. Court of Appeals is the U.S. Court of Appeals for the Federal Circuit, a relatively new creation, which hears cases from the district courts involving patents, trademarks, unfair competition, various claims against the government, and appeals from the U.S. Claims Court, the U.S. Court of International Trade, and from certain administrative agencies.

Not all states have intermediate appellate courts. The bare majority of states maintain only a set of trial courts and a state supreme court, and appeals from the trial court proceed directly to the state supreme court. In such states, the state

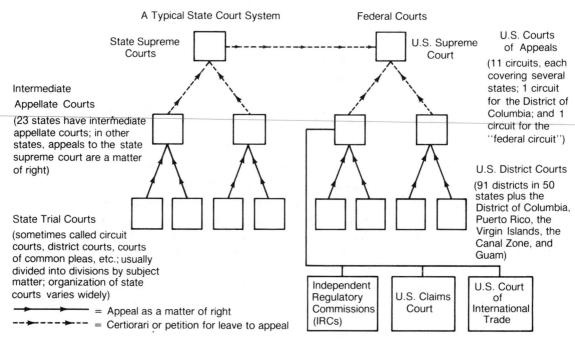

Figure 4-1 The American "Dual" Court System

Table 4-1 Composition of the Thirteen Judicial Court Circuits of the United States

Circuits	Composition
District of Columbia	District of Columbia
First	Maine, Massachusetts, New Hampshire, Puerto Rico, Rhode Island
Second	Connecticut, New York, Vermont
Third	Delaware, New Jersey, Pennsylvania, Virgin Islands
Fourth	Maryland, North Carolina, South Carolina, Virginia, West Virginia
Fifth	District of the Canal Zone, Louisiana, Mississippi, Texas
Sixth	Kentucky, Michigan, Ohio, Tennessee
Seventh	Illinois, Indiana, Wisconsin
Eighth	Arkansas, Iowa, Minnesota, Missouri, Nebraska, North Dakota, South Dakota
Ninth	Alaska, Arizona, California, Idaho, Montana, Nevada, Oregon, Washington, Guam, Hawaii
Tenth	Colorado, Kansas, New Mexico, Oklahoma, Utah, Wyoming
Eleventh	Alabama, Florida, Georgia
Federal	All federal judicial districts

supreme court must hear all appeals directed to it, since the concept of due process means that a litigant has the right to at least one review of his or her case by a higher court.

The Nature of an Appeal

To most Americans weaned on television and movie depictions of the legal process, the appellate process is a mystery. At this level, no trials are held, no witnesses are heard, and lawyers argue the law, not the facts. It is the function of appellate courts to correct errors of law. Appellate courts are generally not concerned with whether the judge in a trial court was mistaken as to the *facts* but whether that judge applied the *law* to the case correctly.

The appellate process is therefore one of intellectual debate, not emotional argument. The attorneys generally submit written arguments, or *briefs,* of their respective positions to be studied by the appellate court. Then, at some designated time, the attorneys will appear to orally argue the case before the judges. If the argument is before an intermediate appellate court, there is usually a panel of three judges, and if the case is before a state or federal supreme court, the entire court considers the case. Sometime in the future—sometimes several months later—the court will issue a written opinion describing its decision and the logic and precedent behind it.

Stare Decisis Revisited

It is now possible to discuss the concept of *stare decisis* in more detail than was allowed in Chapter 1. There, it will be recalled, we considered the idea of precedent as binding on lower courts, and discussed the possibility of changing precedent in the *Flagiello* case (p. 18). But the extent of a particular precedent may not be clear to the lower courts, as shown in the following case.

Nolan v. Tifereth Israel Synagogue of Mt. Carmel

425 Pa. 106, 227 A. 2d 675 (1967) Sup. Ct. of Pennsylvania

Gertrude Nolan fell on the sidewalk in front of the defendant-synagogue's building, resulting in personal injuries. Mrs. Nolan and her husband brought this action against the synagogue, which raised the defense of charitable immunity. The Nolans argued that the *Flagiello* case had overturned the doctrine of charitable immunity in Pennsylvania. The lower court held that the synagogue was a nonprofit religious organization and was exempt from suit under the doctrine of charitable immunity and therefore, dismissed the case. The Nolans appealed to the state supreme court.

O'BRIEN, Justice.

. . . .

The opinion of the court below concludes that our decision in *Flagiello* abrogated the doctrine of charitable immunity only insofar as it related to an action . . . brought by a paying patient in a hospital. This position is also taken by appellee in this appeal. Appellants, on the other hand, contend that *Flagiello* intended to, and did, put an end to the doctrine of charitable immunity in Pennsylvania.

. . . .

To hold that *Flagiello* is limited to the extent found by the court below and contended for by appellee would produce an anomalous situation bordering on the bizarre. We would then be required to say that a paying patient in a hospital could recover for injuries sustained by him as the result of the hospital's negligence, while a nonpaying patient could make no such recovery. We would further be required to say that of all of the charitable institutions in the Commonwealth formerly beneficiaries of the doctrine of charitable immunity, only hospitals had lost the protection and all other charitable institutions retained it. Or, we might be required to say that payment of a fee for service is the criterion upon which a determination of who may recover against a charitable institution in tort is based, if indeed the decision in *Flagiello* is dependent on the circumstance of the plaintiff's having been a paying patient. Were such a conclusion reached, we might be required to hold that in cases such as the one at bar involving a religious institution, that a dues-paying member of the congregation could recover while another person not so situated could not, if indeed the organization were set up on the basis of fixed membership dues, as many religious organizations are.

We cannot conclude that our decision in *Flagiello* did nothing more than remove the protection of the doctrine from hospitals involved in tort litigation with paying patients, and therefore, lest the fact that such a situation was involved in *Flagiello* remain as a source of confusion, we here hold unequivocally that the doctrine of immunity of charitable institutions from liability in tort no longer exists in the Commonwealth of Pennsylvania.

The judgment of the court below is reversed, and the cause remanded for further proceedings consistent herewith.

Thus, while a decision may constitute binding precedent on the lower courts, its decision may also require interpretation. And, the lower courts are not bound by a decision if a new case is different in its essential facts (**distinguishable**) from the precedent. In *Nolan,* the trial court thought that the *Flagiello* decision did not apply to charitable immunity in contexts other than paying patients in hospitals, and thus distinguished the case. But the trial court misinterpreted the *Flagiello* decision.

Secondly, trial courts are not bound by **dicta,** or gratuitous statements in a decision that are not necessary for the final result. For example, many of the statements in the second full paragraph of the *Nolan* decision might be characterized as dicta, and no trial court is bound by such statements.

The organization of the trial and appellate courts presents some tricky problems in applying the rules of *stare decisis.* Assume, for example, that Congress passes a statute prohibiting any person from killing any "deer, bear, wolf, or other large mammal, in federally protected territories." Assume also that John Smith killed a whale in federally protected waters and was charged with a violation of that statute in Federal District Court A in Figure 4-2.

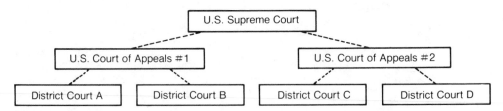

Figure 4-2

Federal District Court A would decide the question of whether a whale was the kind of "large mammal" intended by Congress. Assuming that court convicted Smith, Smith could appeal only to the U.S. Court of Appeals for that Circuit (Court 1). That Court might agree with the lower court and **affirm** Smith's conviction or disagree with the lower court and **reverse** the conviction. If anything further remained to be done in the trial court the appellate court will **remand** the case back to the trial court for further proceedings. The decision becomes precedent for all courts within the circuit served by Court 1. Thus, if Brown were arrested for killing another whale and the case was tried in either Court A or Court B, the judge in either court would be bound by the decision in *U.S.* v. *Smith.*

On the other hand, if Jones were arrested for killing a whale and tried in either Court C or D, the judges in those courts would *not* be bound by the *Smith* decision,* since they are not in Court 1's circuit. The judges in those courts may view the *Smith* case as helpful, or even persuasive, but they are free to disagree and rule differently. Similarly, if Jones were convicted and he appealed to Court 2, that court may also disagree with Court 1. As a result, there is a "split in the appellate courts" created by the *Jones* case, a split which can only be resolved by the Supreme Court. In the meantime, the law is different in two parts of the country.

Finally, to complete the problem, if Black was arrested and tried in any of the District Courts for shooting a walrus, neither the *Smith* nor the *Jones* cases would be binding. The judge might find both cases helpful or persuasive, but since the essential facts (i.e., the character of the mammal) are different, the cases are distinguishable.

Jurisdiction and Venue

The concept of **jurisdiction** means the right of a court to hear a case. It may refer to either **subject matter jurisdiction,** meaning the class of cases a court may hear, or **personal jurisdiction,** also known as *in personam jurisdiction,* which refers to the right of a court to subject a particular person to its judgment.

The subject matter jurisdiction of a court is usually set by statute. Subject matter jurisdiction may be either general or limited, though true general jurisdiction is extremely rare. Most courts, including federal courts, are limited in the types of cases they may hear. Some courts are more limited than others, however, as in the case of the tax court or a state probate court, where the court may only hear tax or probate (wills and estates) matters, respectively. Federal courts are limited to "diversity" and "federal question" jurisdiction (to be discussed more fully), along with a few specific grants of jurisdiction by Congress. Many state courts are referred to as *courts of general jurisdiction,* but that phrase is somewhat misleading since most state courts are divided into specialized areas, such as small claims, criminal, civil, probate, and equity

---

*While this is true in the federal courts and many state court systems, the precedent value of intermediate appellate court decisions in the state courts varies widely, either by statute or court interpretation. Thus *Smith* may, in fact, be binding or may have little value.

courts, none of which have unlimited authority to hear *all* types of cases. Sometimes two or more courts will have overlapping jurisdiction to hear the same case, in which case it is said that the courts have **concurrent jurisdiction.** For example, a federal court may have jurisdiction to hear a case under its diversity jurisdiction, and a state court may have authority to hear the same case as a general civil matter arising within its borders.

Personal jurisdiction, or the right to subject an individual to the judgment of the court, generally depends on the physical availability of the parties within the area served by the court. Originally, in English history, this meant that the sheriff arrested the defendant and physically brought him to court. If the defendant was outside of the area where the sheriff had authority, the defendant could not be brought before the court and therefore no action was possible. In a sense, most of the law of personal jurisdiction is made up of exceptions or clarifications of that rule, though today sheriffs do not physically seize civil defendants except in rare cases. Today, personal jurisdiction is most often obtained by having the sheriff serve a paper on the defendant, ordering him to appear in court or respond in writing to a claim (this "service of process" will be discussed later).

Perhaps the largest group of "exceptions" to the rule of personal presence in the state are the various **long-arm statutes,** originally devised in the latter part of the 19th century. These statutes create a legal fiction, namely that by doing certain acts within a state, a person consents to the jurisdiction of the courts of that state. Thus, by transacting business within a state, by driving on its highways, or by owning property within the state, a person may become subject to the laws and courts of that state, regardless of the person's citizenship or residence.

Uniform Interstate and International Procedure Act
Commissioners on Uniform State Laws (1962)

Section 1.03 *Personal Jurisdiction Based upon Conduct*

(a) A court may exercise personal jurisdiction over a person, who acts directly or by an agent, as to a cause of action or claim for relief arising from the person's

(1) transacting any business in this state;

(2) contracting to supply services or things in this state;

(3) causing tortious injury by an act or omission in this state;

(4) causing tortious injury in this state by an act or omission outside this state if he regularly does or solicits business, or engages in any other persistent course of conduct, or derives substantial revenue from goods used or consumed or services rendered, in this state;

(5) having an interest in, using, or possession real property in this state;

(6) contracting to insure any person, property, or risk located within this state at the time of contracting;

(b) When jurisdiction over a person is based solely upon this section, only a cause of action or claim for relief arising from acts enumerated in this section may be asserted against him.

Each state's long-arm statute varies slightly, though the uniform act covers most of the usual bases of personal jurisdiction. If personal jurisdiction is sought under one of these bases, and the defendant is physically present outside of the state where the suit is filed, the defendant must still be notified by service of process, usually served by the sheriff or other officer in the state where the defendant is present.

It would of course be possible for a state to exercise jurisdiction on the basis of a long-arm statute in a case with only very minimal contacts with the state. That may result in due process objections, as the following case indicates.

World-Wide Volkswagen Corp. v. Woodson

444 U.S. 286, 100 S. Ct. 559, 62 L. Ed. 2d 490 (1980)

Mr. Justice WHITE delivered the opinion of the Court.

The issue before us is whether, consistently with the Due Process Clause of the Fourteenth Amendment, an Oklahoma court may exercise in personam jurisdiction over a nonresident automobile retailer and its wholesale distributor in a products liability action, when the defendant's only connection with Oklahoma is the fact that an automobile sold in New York to New York residents became involved in an accident in Oklahoma.

I

Respondents Harry and Kay Robinson purchased a new Audi automobile from petitioner Seaway Volkswagen, Inc. (Seaway) in Massena, N.Y., in 1976. The following year the Robinson family, who resided in New York, left that state for a new home in Arizona. As they passed through the State of Oklahoma, another car struck their Audi in the rear, causing a fire which severely burned Kay Robinson and her two children.

The Robinsons subsequently brought a products liability action in the District Court for Creek County, Okla., claiming that their injuries resulted from defective design and placement of the Audi's gas tank and fuel system. They joined as defendants the automobile's manufacturer, Audi NSU Auto Union Aktiengesellschaft (Audi); its importer, Volkswagen of America, Inc. (Volkswagen); its regional distributor, petitioner World-Wide Volkswagen Corporation (World-Wide); and its retail dealer, petitioner Seaway. Seaway and World-Wide entered special appearances, claiming that Oklahoma's exercise of jurisdiction over them would offend the limitations on the State's jurisdiction imposed by the Due Process Clause of the Fourteenth Amendment.

The facts presented to the District Court showed that World-Wide is incorporated and has its business office in New York. It distributes vehicles, parts and accessories, under contract with Volkswagen, to retail dealers in New York, New Jersey, and Connecticut. Seaway, one of these retail dealers, is incorporated and has its place of business in New York. Insofar as the record reveals, Seaway and World-Wide are fully independent corporations whose relations with each other and with Volkswagen and Audi are contractual only. Respondents adduced no evidence that either World-Wide or Seaway does any business in Oklahoma, ships or sells any products to or in that state, has an agent to receive process there, or purchases advertisements in any media calculated to reach Oklahoma. In fact, as respondents' counsel conceded at oral argument, there was no showing that any automobile sold by World-Wide or Seaway has ever entered Oklahoma with the single exception of the vehicle involved in the present case.

Despite the apparent paucity of contacts between petitioners and Oklahoma, the District Court rejected their constitutional claim. . . . Petitioners then sought a writ of prohibition in the Supreme Court of Oklahoma to restrain the District Judge, respondent Charles S. Woodson, from exercising in personam jursidiction over them. They renewed their contention that because they had no "minimal contacts," with the State of Oklahoma, the actions of the District Judge were in violation of their rights under the Due Process Clause.

The Supreme Court of Oklahoma denied the writ, holding that personal jurisdiction over petitioners was authorized by Oklahoma's "Long-Arm" Statute. . . .

Oklahoma's long-arm statute contained a provision identical to Section 1.03 (a)(4) of the *Uniform Interstate and International Procedure Act.* The Supreme Court of Oklahoma held that the products sold are so mobile "that petitioners can foresee its possible use in Oklahoma" and that "given the retail value of the automobile, . . . the petitioners derive substantial income from automobiles which from time to time are used in the State of Oklahoma."

II

The Due Process Clause of the Fourteenth Amendment limits the power of a state court to render a valid personal judgment against a nonresident defendant. . . . A judgment rendered in violation of due process is void in the rendering state and is not entitled to full faith and credit elsewhere. . . . Due process requires that the defendant be given adequate notice of the suit. . . . and be subject to the personal jurisdiction of the court. . . . In the present case, it is not contended that notice was inadequate; the only question is whether these particular petitioners were subject to the jurisdiction of the Oklahoma courts.

As has long been settled, and as we reaffirm today, a state court may exercise personal jurisdiction over a nonresident defendant only so long as there exist "minimum contacts" between the defendant and the forum State. . . . The concept of minimum contacts, in turn, can be seen to perform two related, but distinguishable functions. It protects the defendant against the burdens of litigating in a distant or inconvenient forum. And it acts to ensure that the States, through their courts, do not reach out beyond the limits imposed on them by their status as coequal sovereigns in a federal system.

The protection against inconvenient litigation is typically described in terms of "reasonableness" or "fairness." We have said that the defendant's contacts with the forum State must be such that maintenance of the suit "does not offend 'traditional notions of fair play and substantial justice.'" . . . The relationship between the defendant and the forum must be such that it is "reasonable . . . to require the corporation to defend the particular suit which is brought there." Implicit in this emphasis on reasonableness is the understanding that the burden on the defendant, while always a primary concern, will in an appropriate case be considered in light of other relevant factors, including the forum State's interest in adjudicating the dispute . . .; the plaintiff's interest in obtaining convenient and effective relief, . . . at least when that interest is not adequately protected by the plaintiff's power to choose the forum . . .; the interstate judicial system's interest in obtaining the most efficient resolution of controversies; and the shared interest of the several States in furthering fundamental substantive social policies. . . .

The limits imposed on state jurisdiction by the Due Process Clause, in its role as a guarantor against inconvenient litigation, have been substantially relaxed over the years. As we [have] noted . . . this trend is largely attributable to a fundamental transformation in the American economy. . . .

Nevertheless, we have never accepted the proposition that state lines are irrelevant for jurisdictional purposes, nor could we and remain faithful to the principles of interstate federalism embodied in the Constitution. . . .

Thus, the Due Process Clause "does not contemplate that a state may make binding a judgment in personam against an individual or corporate defendant with which the state has no contacts, ties, or relations.". . . . Even if the defendant would suffer minimal or no inconvenience from being forced to litigate before the tribunals of another State; even if the forum State has a strong interest in applying its law to the controversy; even if the forum State is the most convenient location for the litigation, the Due Process Clause, acting as an instrument of interstate federalism, may sometimes act to divest the State of its power to render a valid judgment.

III

Applying these principles to the case at hand, we find in the record before us a total absence of those affiliating circumstances that are a necessary predicate to any exercise of state court jurisdiction. Petitioners carry on no activity whatsoever in Oklahoma. They close no sales and perform no services there. They avail themselves of none of the privileges and benefits of Oklahoma law. They solicit no business there either through salespersons or through advertising reasonably calculated to reach the State. Nor does the record show that they regularly sell cars at wholesale or retail to Oklahoma customers or residents or that they indirectly, through others, serve or seek to serve the Oklahoma market. . . .

It is argued, however, that because an automobile is mobile by its very design and purpose, it was "foreseeable" that the Robinson's Audi would cause injury in Oklahoma. Yet "foreseeability" alone has never been a sufficient benchmark for personal jurisdiction under the Due Process Clause. . . .

If foreseeability were the criterion, a local California tire retailer could be forced to defend in Pennsylvania when a blowout occurs there . . .; a Wisconsin seller of a defective automobile jack could be haled before a distant court for damage caused in New Jersey; or a Florida soft drink concessionaire could be summoned to Alaska to account for injuries happening there. Every seller of chattels would in effect appoint the chattel his agent for service of process. His amenability to suit would travel with the chattel. . . .

This is not to say, of course, that foreseeability is wholly irrelevant. But the foreseeability that is critical to due process analysis is not the mere likelihood that a product will find its way into the forum State. Rather, it is that the defendant's conduct and connection with the forum State are such that he should reasonably anticipate being haled into court there. . . .

When a corporation "purposefully avails itself of the privilege of conducting activities within the forum State," it has clear notice that it is subject to suit there, and can act to alleviate the risk of burdensome litigation by procuring insurance, passing the expected costs on to customers, or, if the risks are too great, severing its connection with the State.

. . . .

Because we find that petitioners have no "contacts, ties, or relations" with the State of Oklahoma, the judgment of the Supreme Court of Oklahoma is reversed.

Venue

Venue is the choice between two courts, each of which has proper jurisdiction over the subject matter and persons involved in a case. Venue is usually set by statute and identifies a convenient court for the parties to litigate a dispute. In the federal system, venue provisions specify the district or districts in which suit may be brought. Thus, although the federal courts may have jurisdiction, there may only be one federal district in which suit may be properly brought. Often that district is where the defendant resides, since it is the defendant who is being forced to defend, where a corporation is incorporated or does business, or where the transaction giving rise to the litigation took place. In state court systems, venue statutes typically establish the proper county where an action may be brought.

Federal Jurisdiction

Federal court jurisdiction is established by an Act of Congress, and thus may be changed at any time by another Act of Congress. There are two major grants of federal jurisdiction—**federal question jurisdiction** and **diversity jurisdiction**—and a series of more *specific grants* of jurisdiction, as in bankruptcy cases, customs litigation, and civil rights actions. Unless a case fits within one of the grants of federal jurisdiction, the federal courts may not hear the case. As a result, the federal courts are often referred to as *courts of limited jurisdiction.*

Federal Question Jurisdiction   Under 28 U.S. Code 1331, the federal courts have the authority to hear cases arising under the federal Constitution or under federal law (see Appendix C). The principal question in such cases is whether the plaintiff's claim is one "arising under" federal law. Simply put, a right or immunity created by federal law must be a basic element of the plaintiff's complaint. Federal jurisdiction is not conferred if the federal issue arises as a defense to the claim, or if the federal law is not the basis of the plaintiff's claim but is merely incidental to the complaint. For many years, federal question jurisdiction also required a showing of a "jurisdictional amount" of $10,000, but that requirement has been removed.

Diversity Jurisdiction   Under 28 U.S. Code 1332, the federal courts have authority to hear cases in which the parties are not residents of the same state and the amount in question exceeds $10,000. The purpose of that jurisdiction is to protect out-of-state parties from potential unfairness in the courts of another state. Diversity jurisdiction extends to citizens of foreign nations as well (see Appendix C).

Mas v. Perry

489 F. 2d 1396 (5th Cir. 1974)

AINSWORTH, J.:

This case presents questions pertaining to federal diversity jurisdiction under 28 U.S.C. 1332, which, pursuant to article III, section II of the Constitution, provides for original jurisdiction in federal district courts of all civil actions that are between, . . . citizens of different States or citizens of a State and citizens of foreign states and in which the amount in controversy is more than $10,000.

Appellees Jean Paul Mas, a citizen of France, and Judy Mas were married at her home in Jackson, Mississippi. Prior to their marriage, Mr. and Mrs. Mas were graduate assistants, pursuing coursework as well as performing teaching duties, for approximately nine months and one year, respectively, at Louisiana State University in Baton Rouge, Louisiana. Shortly after their marriage, they returned to Baton Rouge to resume their duties as graduate assistants at LSU. They remained in Baton Rouge for approximately two more years, after which they moved to Park Ridge, Illinois. At the time of the trial in this case, it was their intention to return to Baton Rouge while Mr. Mas finished his studies for the degree of Doctor of Philosophy. Mr. and Mrs. Mas were undecided as to where they would reside after that.

Upon their return to Baton Rouge after their marriage, appellees rented an apartment from appellant Oliver H. Perry, a citizen of Louisiana. This appeal arises from a final judgment entered on a jury verdict awarding $5,000 to Mr. Mas and $15,000 to Mrs. Mas for damages incurred by them as a result of the discovery that their bedroom and bathroom contained "two-way" mirrors and that they had been watched through them by the appellant during three of the first four months of their marriage.

At the close of the appellees' case at trial, appellant made an oral motion to dismiss for lack of jurisdiction. The motion was denied by the district court. Before this court, appellant challenges the final judgment below solely on jurisdictional grounds, contending that appellees failed to prove diversity of citizenship among the parties and that the requisite jurisdictional amount is lacking with respect to Mr. Mas. Finding no merit to these contentions, we affirm. Under section 1332 (a) (2), the federal judicial power extends to the claim of Mr. Mas, a citizen of France, against the appellant, a citizen of Louisiana. Since we conclude that Mrs. Mas is a citizen of Mississippi for diversity purposes, the district court also properly had jurisdiction under section 1332 (a) (1) of her claim.

It has long been the general rule that complete diversity of parties is required in order that diversity jurisdiction obtain; that is, no party on one side may be a citizen of the same State as any party on the other side. . . . To be a citizen of a State within the meaning of section 1332, a natural person must be both a citizen of the United States and a domiciliary of that State.

For diversity purposes, citizenship means domicile; mere residence in the State is not sufficient. A person's domicile is the place of "his true, fixed, and permanent home and principal establishment, and to which he has the intention of returning whenever he is absent therefrom. . . . " A change in domicile may be effected only by a combination of two elements: (a) taking up residence in a different domicile with (b) the intention to remain there.

It is clear that at the time of her marriage, Mrs. Mas was a domiciliary of the State of Mississippi. . . .

Mrs. Mas' Mississippi domicile was disturbed neither by her year in Louisiana prior to her marriage nor as a result of the time she and her husband spent at LSU after their marriage, since for both periods she was a graduate assistant at LSU. Though she testified that after marriage she had no intention of returning to her parents' home in Mississippi, Mrs. Mas did not effect a change of domicile since she and Mr. Mas were in Louisiana only as students and lacked the requisite intention to remain there. Until she acquires a new domicile she remains a domiciliary, and thus a citizen, of Mississippi. . . .

Thus the power of the federal district court to entertain the claims of appellees in this case stands on two separate legs of diversity jurisdiction: a claim by an alien against a State citizen; and an action between citizens of different States. . . .

Affirmed.

In diversity cases such as the *Mas* decision the plaintiff must allege that he or she has been damaged in an amount in excess of the jurisdictional amount of $10,000. It must appear to the court that there is a probability that the value of the matter in controversy exceeds that amount. It does not matter, as in the *Mas* decision, that the plaintiff ultimately receives less than $10,000, and the federal courts have jurisdiction to award lesser judgments if the evidence does not warrant an amount over $10,000. Courts are reluctant to dismiss actions for lack of the jurisdictional amount unless there is a "legal certainty" that the plaintiff will not recover that amount.

Special Federal Question Jurisdiction

Many federal statutes, such as the antitrust laws, bankruptcy statutes, and others, create a right to sue for violations of the rights or duties established by those laws. While general federal question jurisdiction would provide the right to use the federal courts in those cases in any event, since cases would arise under federal law, those statutes expressly confer federal jurisdiction independent of the general statute. Other examples include the federal securities statutes and the federal labor laws. Sometimes those statutes provide rather unique procedures as well, such as statutes providing that some cases* are to be heard by three-judge panels of the district court with a direct appeal to the U.S. Supreme Court.

Removal to the Federal Courts

Quite often both the state and federal courts have jurisdiction over the same case. In the *Mas* case, for example, Mr. and Mrs. Mas might well have brought their action in the Louisiana state courts, but preferred to bring the action in federal court instead. In such a case, the state and federal courts have **concurrent jurisdiction.** A defendant sued in a state court other than his own state's may petition the federal court for **removal.** If the case could have been filed in the federal court in the first place, removal will be granted under a special federal law (28 U.S. Code 1441) permitting such transfer.

State Law in the Federal Courts

In diversity cases, the question arises as to which law should be applied by the federal courts. Under an old opinion by Justice Story in *Swift* v. *Tyson,*** the federal courts were to ignore state law and apply "general law" in such instances. It thus happened that a "federal common law" began to evolve. A plaintiff might alter the results of a case simply by filing the case in federal courts. The "general law" did not include statutes of the states, which were to be applied by the federal courts, but only judicial decisions. In 1938, all this changed.

Erie R.R. v. Tompkins

304 U.S. 64, 58 S. Ct. 817, 82 L. Ed. 1188 (1938)

Mr. Justice BRANDEIS delivered the opinion of the Court.

. . . .

Tompkins, a citizen of Pennsylvania, was injured on a dark night by a passing freight train of the Erie Railroad Company while walking along its right of way . . . in that state. He claimed that the accident occurred through negligence in the operation, or maintenance, of the train; that he was rightfully on the premises as licensee because [he was] on a commonly used beaten footpath which ran for a short distance alongside the tracks; and that he was struck by something. . . . projecting from one of the moving cars. To enforce that claim he brought an action in the federal court for Southern New York, which had jurisdiction because the company is a corporation of that State. . . .

The Erie insisted that its duty to Tompkins was no greater than that owed to a trespasser. It contended. . . . that its duty to Tompkins . . . should be determined in accordance with the Pennsylvania law; that under the law of Pennsylvania, as declared by the highest court, persons who use pathways along the railroad right of way . . . are to be deemed trespassers, and that the railroad is not liable for injuries to undiscovered

---

*Such cases include injunctions against state regulatory statutes; suits to review some Interstate Commerce Commission orders; government civil antitrust cases, on certificate of importance by the attorney general; suits under some civil rights statutes; and suits challenging the constitutionality of federal statutes.

**16 Pet. 1, 10 L. Ed. 865 (1842).

trespassers resulting from its negligence, unless it be wanton and wilful. Tompkins . . . contended that since there was no statute of the state on the subject, the railroad's duty and liability is to be determined in federal courts as a matter of general law. . . . The Circuit Court of Appeals . . . held . . . that "upon questions of general law the federal courts are free, in the absence of a local statute, to exercise their independent judgment as to what the law is. . . ."

. . . .

First. Swift v. *Tyson* . . . held that federal courts exercising jurisdiction on the ground of diversity of citizenship need not, in matters of general jurisprudence, apply the unwritten law of the State as declared by its highest court; that they are free to exercise an independent judgment as to what the common law of the State is—or should be. . . .

Second. Experience in applying the doctrine of *Swift* v. *Tyson* had revealed its defects, political and social; and the benefits expected to flow from the rule did not accrue. Persistence of state courts in their own opinions on questions of common law prevented uniformity; and the impossibility of discovering a satisfactory line of demarcation between the province of general law and that of local law developed a new well of uncertainties.

On the other hand, the mischievous results of the doctrine had become apparent. Diversity of citizenship jurisdiction was conferred in order to prevent apprehended discrimination in state courts against those not citizens of the State. *Swift* v. *Tyson* introduced grave discrimination by noncitizens against citizens. It made rights enjoyed under the unwritten "general law" vary according to whether enforcement was sought in the state or in the federal court; and the privilege of selecting the court in which the right should be determined was conferred upon the noncitizen. Thus the doctrine rendered impossible equal protection of the law. . . .

Third. Except in matters governed by the Federal Constitution or by Acts of Congress, the law to be applied in any case is the law of the State. And whether the law of the State shall be declared by its Legislature in a statute or by its highest court in a decision is not a matter of federal concern. There is no federal general common law. . . .

As a result of *Erie,* federal courts hearing diversity cases are to apply the law of the state. A later case, *Guaranty Trust Co.* v. *York,** held that in such cases federal procedure would still be used, unless federal procedures would change the outcome of the case (the **outcome determinative test**) in which case state procedures would be used by the federal courts.

The Case or Controversy Requirement and Standing

Section 2 of Article III of the Constitution provides that "The judicial Power shall extend to all Cases . . . [or] Controversies. . . . " The **case or controversy requirement** has resulted in several doctrines that effectively prohibit the federal courts from acting unless an actual dispute is pending. Cases that are *moot,* or already resolved in some fashion, will not be considered, nor will cases where the dispute is not yet *ripe* for judicial action. All of these are generally lumped together under the large catagory of *justiciability.*

---

*326 U.S. 99, 65 S. Ct. 1464, 89 L. Ed. 2079 (1945).

The case or controversy requirement also prohibits the federal courts from giving **advisory opinions.** That means that a legislature or a public officer cannot request the federal courts to rule on the constitutionality of an action before the action is taken. Only one state, Massachusetts, permits its courts to use advisory opinions, though several foreign nations, including Canada, permit the practice.

Standing to Sue

Only injured parties can sue. The concept of legal injury is not as simple as it first appears, however. If your best friend is killed in an auto accident, you cannot sue even though you have suffered a real loss. But his family, from whom he may have been estranged, does have a right to sue for the legal injury they suffered. It is simply a matter of legal recognition of the injury. The family has **standing** to sue, that is, the right to bring the lawsuit, while you do not.

In the federal courts the issue of standing comes up in its most complex form in cases challenging legislation or regulatory activity. Suits filed by public interest groups, political parties, or even private citizens must show that standing exists before the lawsuit may proceed. In other words, each of those groups must show an injury that can be remedied by the law.

One common application of the standing concept is in taxpayer's suits. In theory every American taxpayer is injured when Congress spends tax money for an unconstitutional federal action. As a result each taxpayer in the country would have the right to file a federal lawsuit challenging every federal action he or she felt was unconstitutional. The necessary delays and confusion resulting from such cases was eliminated to a large degree in 1923 in the case of *Frothingham* v. *Mellon,** which was a taxpayer's action to enjoin a federal act that made grants to the states for the aid of mothers. The court permitted local taxpayer suits against municipalities, but refused to permit such actions against the federal government, on the basis that the taxpayer's interest in the use of federal tax money "is shared with millions of others, is comparatively minute and indeterminable, and the effect upon future taxation of any payment out of the funds so remote, fluctuating and uncertain . . . " that standing would not be granted to file such actions. In 1968, in the case of *Flast* v. *Cohen,* the court modified the *Frothingham* result.

Flast v. Cohen

392 U.S. 83, 88 S. Ct. 1942, 20 L. Ed. 2d 947 (1968)

Several taxpayers filed suit to enjoin the expenditure of federal funds under the Elementary and Secondary Education Act of 1965, on the grounds that funds appropriated for that Act had been used to finance instruction in religious schools contrary to the 1st Amendment. The trial court dismissed the case on the basis of *Frothingham* v. *Mellon,* and the taxpayers appealed. The sole injury claimed by the plaintiffs was the expenditure of tax funds.

---

*262 U.S. 447, 43 S. Ct. 597, 67 L. Ed. 1078 (1923).

Mr. Chief Justice WARREN delivered the opinion of the Court.

. . . .

The fundamental aspect of standing is that it focuses on the party seeking to get his complaint before a federal court and not on the issues he wishes to have adjudicated. The "gist of the question of standing" is whether the party seeking relief has "alleged such a personal stake in the outcome of the controversy as to assure that concrete adverseness which sharpens the presentation of issues upon which the court so largely depends for illumination of difficult constitutional questions" *Baker* v. *Carr*, 369 U.S. 186, 204 (1962).

. . . . [W]e find no absolute bar in [the Constitution] to suits by federal taxpayers challenging allegedly unconstitutional federal taxing and spending programs. There remains, however, the problem of determining the circumstances under which a federal taxpayer will be deemed to have the personal stake and interest that imparts the necessary concrete adverseness to such litigation so that standing can be conferred on the taxpayer *qua* taxpayer. . . .

. . . [O]ur decisions establish that, in ruling on standing, it is both appropriate and necessary to look to the substantive issues . . . to determine whether there is a logical nexus between the status asserted and the claim sought to be asserted. . . .

The nexus demanded of federal taxpayers has two aspects to it. First, the taxpayer must establish a logical link between that status and the type of legislative enactment attacked. Thus, a taxpayer will be a proper party to allege the unconstitutionality only of exercises of congressional power under the taxing and spending clause of . . . the Constitution. It will not be sufficient to allege an incidental expenditure of tax funds in the administration of an essentially regulatory statute. . . . Secondly the taxpayer must establish a nexus between that status and the precise nature of the constitutional infringement alleged. Under this requirement the taxpayer must show that the challenged enactment exceeds specific constitutional limitations imposed upon the exercise of the congressional taxing and spending power and not simply that the enactment is generally beyond the powers delegated to Congress. . . . When both nexuses are established, the litigant will have shown a taxpayer's stake in the outcome of the controversy and will be a proper and appropriate party to invoke a federal court's jurisdiction.

The taxpayer-appellants in this case have satisfied both nexuses to support their claim of standing under the test we announce today. Their constitutional challenge is made to an exercise by Congress of its power . . . to spend for the general welfare, and the challenged program involves a substantial expenditure of federal tax funds. In addition, appellants have alleged that the challenged expenditures violate the Establishment and Free Exercise Clauses of the First Amendment. Our history vividly illustrates that one of the specific evils feared by those who drafted the Establishment Clause and fought for its adoption was that the taxing and spending power would be used to favor one religion over another or to support religion in general. . . . The Establishment Clause was designed as a specific bulwark against such potential abuses of governmental power, and that clause of the First Amendment operates as a specific constitutional limitation upon the exercise by Congress of the taxing and spending power. . . .

Reversed

Special Remedies

Unusual cases, particularly those that challenge government actions and regulations, often demand special remedies other than a traditional lawsuit for money damages or for equitable relief. Three such remedies are of special importance to the study of the relationship of government to business. Those remedies are *class action suits, declaratory judgment actions,* and *mandamus.*

Class Actions

Under both the *Federal Rules of Civil Procedure* and state codes of procedure, **class actions** may be brought by representatives of a class of people. Under the Federal Rules, such actions may be brought if (1) the class is so numerous that it would be "impracticable" for each member of the class to appear in person; (2) there is a common question of law or fact; (3) the claims of the representatives are "typical" of the claims of members of the class; and (4) the representatives will "fairly and adequately" protect the interests of the class.

Class actions may be brought by any organized or unorganized group. Cases have been brought on behalf of injured purchasers of a certain product, all members of a race or religion, members of a native American tribe, certain classes of voters or potential voters, taxpayers, to name a few.

The representatives of the class must attempt to notify all members of the class and permit those members to join the lawsuit if they so request. The damages recoverable are the loss to the entire class, and an effort must be made to distribute the damages to all members of the class. Class actions may not be filed without court permission, and courts may dismiss the action if the class is not defined properly.

Declaratory Judgments

Another unusual remedy seems to contradict both the case or controversy and standing requirements. **Declaratory judgment** actions involve neither damages nor injunctive relief but ask the court to declare the rights of the parties under the law. For example, a theater owner who wishes to show a film that might be obscene under a local ordinance may find himself in a difficult situation. If he shows the film he will be prosecuted and risks a finding of guilt. On the other hand, the film may not be obscene, and he would have forgone the profits from the film unnecessarily. The owner who wishes to test the film against the obscenity statute before a criminal prosecution is instituted might file a declaratory judgment action. A judge would "declare the rights" of the parties and determine the film's obscenity before it was exhibited. Obviously, this is close to the sort of hypothetical question not permitted by the case or controversy requirement and, in some cases, the declaratory judgment might be refused if there is no actual controversy. In the example, the prosecutor must have threatened prosecution of the film before a declaratory judgment action would avoid dismissal on the grounds that there was no real dispute. The procedure is also useful in private actions, such as insurance and patent litigation, but is not available in federal tax cases. Jury trials are often available.

Mandamus

A **mandamus** action, resulting in a *writ of mandamus,* orders a public official to perform an act required by law. *Marbury* v. *Madison* involved a mandamus action against the Secretary of State, for example. Such actions may be brought to force regulatory agencies to perform their required duties, but they are not available to force performance of discretionary acts. Mandamus is available only in exceptional circumstances and may be filed against a trial court in certain unusual cases. The Supreme Court has held that it is available against a court only to prevent a judicial "usurpation of power."

The Course of a Lawsuit

The basic rules governing trial court procedures are identical for all kinds of cases, from the simplest collection case to the most complex antitrust action. In the federal courts trial procedure is governed by a statutelike code, the *Federal Rules of Civil Procedure,* a modern code of procedure first adopted in 1937. The federal rules introduced many innovations into civil procedure which have been widely adopted by the states, including "notice pleading" and free discovery. Several states have adopted the federal rules almost in full. The federal rules were adopted by the Supreme Court for use in all federal courts under its general right to supervise those courts.

The Pleadings and Service of Process

The **pleadings** in a lawsuit include the initial papers filed by all of the parties in a case, including **complaints, answers, counterclaims, cross-claims,** and **third-party complaints.** Sometimes, **motions to dismiss** are included in the term as well. **Service of process** refers to the method by which these papers are delivered to the parties to the case.

The Complaint
After an alleged civil wrong has been committed, the wronged party may initiate court action by filing a document called a **complaint** (sometimes called a *petition*) with the clerk of the proper court. The complaint tells the story of the wrong and the resulting injury to the **plaintiff,** or complaining party. Under the federal rules, a complaint must include "(1) a short and plain statement of the grounds upon which the court's jurisdiction depends . . . (2) a short and plain statement of the claim showing the pleader is entitled to relief, and (3) a demand for judgment for the relief to which he deems himself entitled." State rules often demand more complex forms of pleadings.

Complaints may be as short as a half page in simple cases or a hundred pages or more in complex cases. The purpose is to notify the court and the opposing parties of the substance of the claim. The plaintiff will be required to pay a filing fee when the complaint is filed in an amount that often varies with the size of the claim.

Service of Process
After the complaint is filed, the **defendant,** or person sued, must be given notice of the suit in order to defend the case. The procedures for **service of process** depend to a large extent on the requirements of procedural due process, but the idea of service of process is older than the Constitution. Service of process is also related to the idea of personal jurisdiction.

After the complaint is filed, the clerk of the court prepares a document, called a

summons, that tells the defendant that suit has been filed and gives the defendant instructions on what to do now. Usually the defendant must file an answer to the complaint or some other response within a certain time (twenty days in the federal courts), though in some instances the defendant will be required to appear in court personally. That summons and a copy of the complaint must be delivered to the defendant in one of four ways.

1. *Personal service* means physical delivery of the documents to the defendant. The U.S. Marshal, the sheriff, or in some instances a private process server will hand the documents to the defendant. Personal service is the preferred method, since the defendant clearly has actual notice of the suit.

2. *Substituted service* means physical delivery of the documents to some agent of the defendant, such as an attorney, a member of the family, or an employee. Court rules are usually quite specific about which agents may receive service, since the notice is not as good as personal service.

3. *Service by certified mail* is usually possible only in smaller cases under some states' rules. A return receipt signed by the defendant is usually required.

4. *Service by publication* is available in only limited circumstances since it is the worst form of notice. If the defendant has left the state or is in hiding, or in cases involving real estate located in the jurisdiction of the court, many states permit the plaintiff to publish a notice in the "legals" of a newspaper. The notice must usually be published several times, be worded well enough to notify the defendant of the nature of the claim, and appear in a newspaper of general circulation. Often the plaintiff must obtain court approval before publication.

It is vital that a defendant do what the summons instructs him to do. Failure to comply with the instructions on a summons will probably result in a **default judgment** against the defendant, which means that the plaintiff has won the case without a trial. Default judgments may be set aside by the court, but only after a showing that the defendant intended to respond and his failure to respond was not the result of bad faith.

Defendant's Responses to Complaints   Once the defendant has been served, there are several responses that can be made. The two principal responses are **motions to dismiss** and **answers.** In addition, the defendant may also file lawsuits in the form of **counterclaims, cross-claims,** and **third-party complaints.**

Motions to Dismiss: A motion to dismiss is the defendant's statement to the court that the plaintiff's complaint is legally defective and should be dismissed. The dismissal may be without prejudice, which means the plaintiff may amend his complaint or file another lawsuit, or with prejudice, which means that the case is over and the plaintiff must appeal the dismissal in order to proceed.

One of the most common grounds for a motion to dismiss is *failure to state a cause of action.* A **cause of action** is a legally recognized claim, one upon which the courts have granted relief in the past. For example, the courts have never recognized a claim of injury resulting solely from an insult. Therefore, if the plaintiff were to file a complaint stating such a claim, the defendant could move to dismiss based on failure to state a cause of action. For example, the *Nolan* case considered earlier in this chapter involved a motion to dismiss filed on the basis that Pennsylvania did not recognize a claim against a charitable body and, therefore, the plaintiff had not stated a cause of action. Numerous other defects can also be raised by motions to dismiss, including lack of jurisdiction, release or waiver of the claim, bankruptcy, the statute of limitations, and many others. Often the court will dismiss the complaint but give the plaintiff the opportunity to amend the complaint. In some cases, this may happen several times until the plaintiff finally "gets it right." The plaintiff may elect to "stand on his complaint" and appeal if he or she feels that a recognized cause of action cannot be stated.

Similar in form and nature to motions to dismiss are *motions to strike* and *motions for a more definite statement.* A motion to strike asks that certain sentences, paragraphs, or words be stricken from the complaint, usually on grounds that the material is redundant, sham, immaterial, or scandalous. Similarly, a defendant may, through a motion for more definite statement, ask that material in the complaint be clarified, if it is ambiguous, unintelligible, or uncertain. Such motions may not be used as a "fishing expedition" for evidence, however.

Answers: Every complaint that is not dismissed with prejudice must ultimately be answered. The **answer** is a relatively simple document that either admits, denies, or states that a party is without information to answer each allegation of the complaint. Failure to admit an allegation in bad faith may result in an order to pay the expenses of proving the allegation at trial. Sometimes answers contain **affirmative defenses,** which state that the defendant agrees with the allegations of the complaint but has something substantial to add to the story. For example, if the plaintiff sues to collect a debt, the defendant may agree that the debt was made but raise as an affirmative defense the fact that the plaintiff gave the defendant a release. Affirmative defenses, counterclaims, cross-claims, and third-party complaints all must be answered by the opposing party as well.

Counterclaims and Set-Offs: The defendant also has the option of suing the plaintiff in the same case. In an auto accident case, A may sue B, and B, believing that he was in the right, may file a **counterclaim** against the plaintiff. A **set-off** is a credit claimed by the defendant arising from an independent transaction. Thus A, a carpenter, may sue B, a building supply dealer, for failing to provide materials according to a contract. B may claim a set-off from A for amounts due on another contract.

The federal rules provide for two types of counterclaims: *compulsory counterclaims* are those arising from the same occurrence or transaction as the original complaint; and *permissive counterclaims,* roughly equivalent to set-offs, are *any* claims the defendant may have against the plaintiff. Compulsory counterclaims must be filed or will be barred, while defendants *may* file permissive counterclaims, and failure to file them will not bar them in the future in a separate action.

Filing a counterclaim changes the names of the parties somewhat. The defendant becomes the *defendant-counterplaintiff,* and the plaintiff becomes the *plaintiff-counterdefendant.*

Cross-Claims: Suits between parties on the same side of a lawsuit are called **cross-claims.** Thus, if a plaintiff has sued two or more codefendants, one of the codefendants may sue another codefendant by filing a cross-claim. For example, if A was injured by flying glass resulting from a collision between cars driven by B and C, he may sue both in the same case. If B feels the collision was C's fault, he may file a cross-claim against him. The parties become the *cross-plaintiff* and *cross-defendant.*

Third-Party Complaints: A defending party also has the right to bring in new parties to the lawsuit. Under the federal rules, such a **third-party complaint** may be filed by any defending party against any person "who is or may be liable to him for all or part of the plaintiff's claim against him." Plaintiffs may file third-party complaints if a counterclaim has been filed. The party filing such a complaint is the *third-party plaintiff* and the person against whom it is filed is the *third-party defendant.*

Every time a new complaint is filed, including counterclaims, cross-claims, and third-party complaints, the defending party may file a motion to dismiss and ultimately will be required to file an answer. All of these original papers, taken together, are known as the **pleadings,** and until the pleadings are settled, no case may proceed to trial. Often the process takes months. The purpose of the process is to narrow and define the issues in the dispute between the parties and assure the complete resolution of the dispute.

Discovery

Perhaps the most important innovation of the federal rules was the liberalization of the discovery process. At least in the federal courts, the day of the surprise witness and the "bluff" are over. Today, as a result of several discovery procedures available in most courts, a lawyer should know the details of his opponent's case as well as his own when the trial begins. Under the federal rules,

> parties may obtain discovery by one or more of the following methods: depositions . . .; written interrogatories, production of documents or things or permission to enter upon land or other property, for inspection and other purposes; physical and mental examinations; and requests for admission. (Fed. Rules of Civil Procedure, Section 26 (a).)

Following the adoption of the federal rules, many states followed the lead of the federal courts and adopted liberalized discovery rules, usually copying the federal model rather closely. Some states do not go quite as far as the federal rules, but for the most part there has been a national revolution in court procedures centered around the discovery rules.

Depositions   Depositions are meetings between the lawyers, a court reporter, and either a party or a witness in the case. The deponent (the party or witness) is placed under oath and the lawyer who called the deposition may ask questions "reasonably calculated to lead to the discovery of admissible evidence." The questions and answers are transcribed verbatim by the court reporter and a typed transcript of the proceedings is prepared. That transcript may be used to contradict or impeach the testimony of the deponent in the trial or may be introduced if the deponent is dead or otherwise unavailable for trial. In addition, depositions allow the lawyers to see and hear the opposition's witnesses before trial. Witnesses may be compelled to attend a deposition by subpoena, or court order.

Interrogatories   Interrogatories are lists of written questions sent to a party. The questions must be answered under oath within a specific time limit. The interrogatories may also be used to impeach or contradict a party at trial, and failure to answer may result in severe sanctions.

Requests to Produce   A party may request any other party to produce and make available for copying "any designated documents"; or to inspect, copy, or test any tangible thing; or permit entry onto land for the purpose of inspection, measurement, or testing. This rule is "wide open," and the opposing party may be under a continuing duty to send new evidence, documents, or other material to the person requesting it until the trial is over. The only exceptions are the "work product" of an attorney and privileged material.

Special Orders   Other discovery techniques provide for physical or mental examinations of parties and requests for admission. The latter is simply a list of written questions submitted to a party, demanding that the party admit or deny them. If they are admitted, they need not be proven at trial. If denied in bad faith, the court may assess the costs of proving them at trial against the party denying them. Parties may be required to submit lists of witnesses to the opposing party long before trial, and failure to include a name may result in the exclusion of that witness.

Subpoenas and Subpoenas Duces Tecum   While not strictly a discovery device, a **subpoena** or a **subpoena duces tecum** is useful both for discovery purposes and later at the trial. A subpoena is an order from a court to a witness to appear and testify. It is often issued to the witnesses in a trial, but it is also available in the federal system and in most states to force a witness to appear at a deposition. If the witness fails to appear it is a violation of a court order and constitutes a contempt of court, which may be punished by fine or imprisonment.

A subpoena duces tecum is also available at trial and sometimes in the discovery process. That order requires a witness who possesses some document, paper or, in some cases, other evidence to appear and testify, bringing in that evidence. Failure to comply is again a contempt of court.

A subpoena must be distinguished from a summons. A summons is a notification to a defendant that suit has been filed and that he or she must either file an answer or appear in person. Failure to comply with the directions on the summons may result in a default judgment, but does not result in contempt of court or any punishment for failure to appear, aside from the default judgment.

Scope and Purpose of Discovery   Discovery has several purposes. First, discovery shortens trial time considerably, thus saving tax money, since lawyers need not "thrash about" looking for evidence during the trial. Second, discovery lessens the possibility of injustice by assuring an adequate investigation of the facts before trial and eliminating nonverifiable surprises. And, third, discovery encourages settlement by making the parties aware of the strengths and weaknesses of the case.

The federal courts and most state courts view discovery very liberally, holding that almost everything is discoverable.

Federal Rules of Civil Procedure
Rule 26(b)

(b) *Scope of Discovery.* Unless otherwise limited by order of the court in accordance with these rules, the scope of discovery is as follows:

(1) *In General.* Parties may obtain discovery regarding any matter, not privileged, which is relevant to the subject matter involved in the pending action, whether it relates to the claim or defense of the party seeking discovery or to the claim or defense of any other party, including the existence, description, nature, custody, condition and location of any books, documents, or other tangible things and the identity and location of persons having knowledge of any discoverable matter. It is not ground for objection that the information sought will be inadmissible at the trial if the information sought appears reasonably calculated to lead to the discovery of admissible evidence.

Pretrial Motions

After the pleadings are settled, two motions are available to the parties to attempt to dispose of the case: motion for judgment on the pleadings, and motion for summary judgment.

Motion for Judgment on the Pleadings   The motion for **judgment on the pleadings** asks the court to simply look at the pleadings filed to determine whether there is a remaining issue. If not, the court may grant judgment to either party. For example, if a defendant were to admit all of the allegations of a complaint, the plaintiff might file a motion and obtain judgment without the time and expense of trial. The motion is rarely filed and even more rarely granted.

Motion for Summary Judgment   In many controversies, there is no dispute about the facts between the parties. Their dispute centers rather around the legal effect of those facts. In such cases, either party may move for **summary judgment,** and the moving party must show that there is *no material question of fact* in the case. He does so by filing affidavits, depositions, answers to interrogatories and other materials along with the motion. The opposing party may agree that there is no material question of fact, or may file counter-affidavits and materials showing that a dispute actually exists. If the court finds any material question of fact, it must deny the motion. If no such question of fact exists, the court may proceed to decide the case on the remaining legal dispute. A common example would involve a suit on a contract. The parties may agree that the contract was signed and that certain work was performed under the agreement, but they may disagree as to the legal effect of a part of the contract. Either or both parties might file a motion for summary judgment, and the judge would simply decide the legal issue.

Summary judgment has the effect of eliminating unnecessary trials. Even if such a case were to go to jury trial, the trial judge would still have the right to decide the legal issues in the case. Therefore, no party is deprived of his right to trial by jury by the summary judgment procedure.

Pretrial Conferences

In federal cases and under most state procedures, the attorneys and the judge will meet a few weeks prior to trial at a **pretrial conference.**

Federal Rules of Civil Prodcedure
Rule 16

> In any action, the court may in its discretion direct the attorneys for the parties to appear before it for a conference to consider (1) The simplification of issues; (2) The necessity or desirability of amendments to the pleadings; (3) The possibility of obtaining admissions of fact and of documents which will avoid unnecessary proof; (4) The limitation of the number of expert witnesses; (5) The advisability of a preliminary reference of issues to a master for findings to be used as evidence when the trial is to be by jury; (6) Such other matters as may aid in the disposition of the action. . . .

One of the other matters commonly raised by the courts is the possibility of settling the case. Some judges work very hard at the pretrial conference to bring the parties to some compromise.

The pretrial procedures take a great deal of time and occupy much of a trial lawyer's attention. One estimate has said that even the simplest case cannot be ready for trial in less than 90 days from the filing the complaint. The vast majority of all civil lawsuits are settled during the time before trial through the aid of the discovery process and pretrial conferences, however, leaving only a very small number of cases that actually reach trial.

The Trial

Trials may be heard either by a jury or by a judge sitting without a jury. Equity cases, such as actions for an injunction, are heard by a judge alone. While the 7th Amendment guarantees trial by jury in civil cases "at common law," an 1840 Supreme Court decision held that equity cases were not common law cases, since they were heard by a separate court in English procedure. As a result, the right to trial by jury in civil cases only exists if the case is of the kind tried by the ancient English common-law courts. As a tactical matter, even cases where a jury is available may be tried by a judge alone, since it is thought that some complex cases are beyond the comprehension of juries.

Jury Selection   Traditionally, juries were made up of twelve persons (originally twelve male landowners). Recently, courts have experimented with juries of less than twelve, usually six, with some success. The Supreme Court has ruled that a six-person jury is permissible even in criminal trials.*

Jurors should be selected at random from the community. Most jury selection is based upon voter registration lists, though once in a while a story appears about a judge who orders the sheriff into the streets to "draft" jurors when the available panel runs out.

At the very beginning of the trial, the judge and attorneys must select the jury. Prospective jurors are questioned by the court and sometimes by the attorneys** to

---

*Cf., *Williams* v. *Florida,* 399 U.S. 78, 90 S. Ct. 1893, 26 L. Ed. 2d 446 (1970).

**Practice varies a great deal. In many federal courts, attorneys very rarely examine jurors. In some state courts, all examination is conducted by attorneys.

discover any hidden biases or personal relationships with the parties, and the attorneys are permitted to excuse, or challenge, prospective jurors. If the juror discloses any reason why he or she could not act as juror, such as bias or personal relationship to the parties, the juror may be **challenged for cause.** The attorneys are also permitted a varying number of **peremptory challenges** in which no cause need be shown. The initial questioning of the jurors is often called *voir dire examination.*

Opening Statements   Opening statements are brief statements by the attorneys to give the jurors a bird's eye view of the evidence in the case. Defendants sometimes waive opening statements as a tactical matter. Under some state procedures, the plaintiff must describe all of the elements of the case in the opening statements or be subject to dismissal, though this practice is losing ground.

Presentation of Evidence   After the opening statements, the parties proceed to present their proof. All evidence, with exception of **stipulations** (agreed evidence) must be brought in through witnesses. The party having the burden of proof (almost always the plaintiff) has the right to present evidence first and also has the right to close by presenting rebuttal evidence. Throughout all trial procedure, the general rule is that the party who opens has the right to close.

The plaintiff's case may consist of one of more witnesses. The plaintiff will conduct a **direct examination** of each witness, then the defendant has the right to **cross-examine** the witness, and then the plaintiff may conduct a **redirect examination** of that witness. If the plaintiff's redirect brings up new matters not covered in the defendant's cross-examination, the defendant may have a right to a recross-examination, until no new matters have been brought up in the last examination by the opposition. After all of the plaintiff's witnesses have been examined in this manner, the plaintiff will rest. The defense then presents its proof in the same way, but in the defendant's case the defendant presents the direct examination and the plaintiff may cross-examine, and so on. All exhibits must be brought into court through witnesses as well.

Motion to Dismiss at the Close of Plaintiff's Case: After the plaintiff has presented its case, the defendant usually presents a motion to dismiss, arguing that the plaintiff has not proven the required elements of its case. Thus, if the plaintiff failed to prove the existence of a contract in a contract action, the court might dismiss the action before the defendant is forced to put on its defense. It is important that the defendant make that motion even if it seems clear that the plaintiff has indeed proven its case, since the right to appeal on those grounds may be waived if the motion is not made. Similarly, the grounds for appeal on the basis of a lack of evidence would be that the trial judge made an *error of law* in failing to grant the motion. No appeal is possible on the grounds that the jury was simply wrong; the appeal instead is based on the judge's error in permitting the case to proceed on the basis of insufficient evidence. At this point, however, the judge must give all benefits of the doubt to the plaintiff, and if there is any evidence on which a jury might base a verdict for plaintiff, the trial judge must permit the case to go forward and must deny the motion.

The Burden of Proof   As a general rule, the party making an allegation has the burden of proving it. The plaintiff has the burden of proving the allegations of the complaint, and the defendant has no duty to disprove those allegations. Conversely, the defendant has the burden of proving affirmative defenses, and the plaintiff need not disprove them. Just how much proof will be required will depend on the type of case. In criminal cases, it is said that the prosecution must prove their case *beyond a reasonable doubt;* in certain exceptional civil cases, *by clear, strong and convincing evidence;* and in most civil cases, *by a preponderance of the evidence.* There is both a quantitative and qualitative difference.

The usual civil burden of proof of a preponderance of the evidence is generally defined as a search for probabilities. It is proof that leads the jury to find that the existence of a fact is more probable that its nonexistence. This assessment of probability is a recognition that witnesses, jurors, judges, and lawyers are fallible and finding the absolute truth is often impossible. Thus, the jurors may rely on what is more probable and base their verdicts on that assessment. This emphatically does *not* mean a larger number of witnesses or longer testimony or more exhibits. It means simply that a juror believes that a fact is more probably true than not true.

In a very few civil cases, such as charges of fraud, undue influence, and certain types of will contests, the burden is said to be by clear, strong, and convincing evidence. The exact phrasing of this burden varies among the states, from "clear and convincing" in Arizona to "clear, unequivocal, satisfactory and convincing" in Utah, and other formulations in other states. It is generally agreed that that these burdens simply mean that a certain fact is highly probable in light of the evidence.

The famous burden in criminal cases of beyond a reasonable doubt is different in both the amount *(quantum)* of proof that the prosecution must present and the nature of the "belief" that must exist in the minds of the jurors. It is virtually impossible to prove a fact to an absolute certainty, and any search for probabilities contains the possibility of error. In civil cases, a mistake in favor of the plaintiff is no worse than a mistake in favor of the defendant. But in a criminal case the possibility of a mistake in favor of the state is far worse than a mistake in favor of the defendant. As the Supreme Court has noted,

> Where one party has at stake an interest of transcending value—as a criminal defendant his liberty—this margin of error is reduced as to him by the process of placing on the other party the burden . . . of persuading the factfinder at the conclusion of the trial of his guilt beyond a resonable doubt. *Speiser* v. *Randall,* (1958).*

In 1970, the Supreme Court held that proof beyond a reasonable doubt is an essential part of due process.**

One classic definition of reasonable doubt provides some help in defining this troublesome phrase.

> It is that state of the case, which, after the entire comparison and consideration of all the evidence, leaves the minds of jurors in that condition that they cannot say they feel an abiding conviction, to a moral certainty, of the truth of the charge.†

---

*357 U.S. 513, 78 S. Ct. 1332, 2 L. Ed. 2d 1460.

**In re Winship, 397 U.S. 358, 90 S. Ct. 1068, 25 L. Ed. 2d 368 (1970).

†Commonwealth v. Webster, 59 Mass. 295 (1850).

Other definitions emphasize that jurors should not overstress mere possibilities or imaginary doubts. It is axiomatic that a generous and imaginative mind could always find a doubt in any case. But the prosecution must only prove its case beyond a *reasonable* doubt. A great many courts resolve the difficulty of defining reasonable doubt by refusing to define the term for jurors in the court's instructions. Often the term is confused with its blood relative, the presumption of innocence. That means that an accused person is presumed (or assumed) to be innocent unless and until the jury renders a verdict against the defendant. That presumption follows the defendant throughout the trial, and the defendant never has the burden of proving that innocence.

Jury Instructions and Final Argument

After all the evidence has been received, the attorneys will be permitted a final argument, in which the attorneys may summarize the evidence and try to convince the jury that a particular view of the evidence ought to be taken. A century ago, in the "golden age of jury speeches," lawyers like Daniel Webster, William Jennings Bryan, Abraham Lincoln, and later Clarence Darrow often presented ringing and emotional speeches to the jury. Final arguments, delivered by an expert orator, may tug at every human emotion. The following is a classic example.

Clarence Darrow
People v. *Leopold and Loeb*

In 1924, fourteen-year-old Bobby Franks, the son of a wealthy Chicago businessman, was kidnapped and brutally murdered. Some time later two acquaintances of Bobby Franks, eighteen-year-old Nathan Leopold and seventeen-year-old Richard Loeb were charged with the crime. Both Leopold and Loeb were brilliant students (both had already graduated from college) and were themselves the sons of wealthy families. The evidence showed that they had committed the crime merely to see if they could commit "the perfect crime." The families of the youths hired Clarence Darrow, and he astounded the prosecution by pleading the two guilty. Under Illinois law, the judge then had the responsibility to determine the proper sentence in the case. The prosecution demanded the death penalty. Darrow argued for a long term of imprisonment and spoke for several hours. Near the end of his oration he faced the judge directly and said:

> Now, I must say a word more and then I will leave this with you where I should have left it long ago. None of us are unmindful of the public; courts are not, and juries are not. We placed our fate in the hands of a trained court, thinking that he would be more mindful and considerate than a jury. I cannot say how people feel. I have stood here for three months as one might stand at the ocean trying to sweep back the tide. I hope the seas are subsiding and the wind is falling, and I believe they are, but I wish to make no false pretenses to this court. The easy thing and the popular thing to do is to hang my clients. I know it. Men and women who do not think will applaud. The cruel and thoughtless will approve. It will be easy today; but in Chicago, and reaching out over the length and breadth of the land, more and more fathers and mothers, the humane, the kind and the hopeful, who are gaining an understanding and asking questions not only about these poor boys, but about their own—these will join in no acclaim at the death of my clients. They would ask that the shedding of blood be stopped, and the normal feelings of man resume their sway. And as the days and the months and

the years go on, they will ask it more and more. But, Your Honor, what they shall ask may not count. I know the easy way. I know Your Honor stands between the future and the past. I know the future is with me, and what I stand for here; not merely for the lives of these two unfortunate lads, but for all boys and all girls; for all of the young, and, as far as possible, for all of the old. I am pleading for life, understanding, charity, kindness, and the infinite mercy that considers all. I am pleading that we overcome cruelty with kindness, and hatred with love. I know the future is on my side.

Your Honor stands between the past and the future. You may hang these boys; you may hang them by the neck until they are dead. But in doing it you will turn your face toward the past. In doing it you are making it harder for every other boy who, in ignorance and darkness, must grope his way through the mazes which only childhood knows. In doing it you will make it harder for unborn children. You may save them and make it easier for every child that sometime may stand where these boys stand. You will make it easier for every human being with an aspiration and a vision and a hope and a fate.

I am pleading for the future; I am pleading for a time when hatred and cruelty will not control the hearts of men, when we can learn by reason and judgment and understanding and faith that all life is worth saving, and that mercy is the highest attribute of man.

I feel that I should apologize for the length of time I have taken. This case may not be as important as I think it is, and I am sure I do not need to tell this court, or to tell my friends that I would fight just as hard for the poor as for the rich. If I should succeed in saving these boys' lives and do nothing for the progress of the law, I should feel sad, indeed. If I can succeed, my greatest reward and my greatest hope will be that I have done something for the tens of thousands of other boys, for the countless unfortunates who must tread the same road in blind childhood that these poor boys have trod; that I have done something to help human understanding, so temper justice with mercy, to overcome hate with love.

I was reading last night of the Persian poet, Omar Khayyam. It appealed to me as the highest that I can vision. I wish it was in my heart, and I wish it was in the hearts of all.

So I be written in the Book of Love
I do not care about that Book above;
Erase my name or write it as you will
So I be written in the Book of Love.

When Darrow finished, the courtroom was hushed and tears were streaming down the judge's face. The judge later sentenced Leopold and Loeb to life imprisonment. Loeb was later killed in a prison fight. Leopold spent nearly 50 years in prison and was paroled in his old age.

While arguments such as Clarence Darrow's still have a substantial impact, the trend in modern courtrooms is toward closely reasoned and logical statements of the proof. Attorneys are permitted wide latitude in their arguments to the jury.

After final arguments, the jury will be instructed on the law that is to be applied to the case. The judge will usually read previously prepared instructions, which had been discussed and argued by the attorneys during an earlier break in the trial. Many states and the federal courts have prepared books of final instructions that are used in most cases. One of the most common grounds for appeal is that the judge presented an erroneous instruction on the law. Many courts permit the jury to take the typed instructions into the jury room when they consider the verdict. The following is an example of a standard jury instruction (one of many which would be read to the jury) in a negligence case.

Illinois Civil Jury Instructions
Illinois Practice Institute

> *Negligence—Adult—Definition:* When I use the term "negligence" in these instructions, I mean the failure to do something which a reasonably careful person would do or the doing of something which a reasonably careful person would not do, under circumstances similar to those shown by the evidence. The law does not say how a reasonably careful person would act under those circumstances. That is for you to decide.

The jury instructions phase of the trial points out an essential difference between the judge and the jury. The jury is often called the *trier of the facts* or the *fact finder*, while the judge is often called the *trier of the law*. In a jury trial, the jury decides what the facts are, but it is the judge's responsibility to determine the law applicable to the case and tell the jury what that law is. It is also the judge's function to run an orderly trial and rule on questions of procedure and admissibility. An appeal may come only on errors of law, committed by the judge (sometimes called *the court*) and not on the basis that the jury made an error in the facts. In nonjury trials (bench trials), the judge is both fact finder and trier of the law.

Verdict

A civil jury verdict is usually in two parts: the finding of liability, or guilt or innocence, and the amount of **damages,** if any. Sometimes, the court will submit special verdicts to the jury in the form of specific questions for the jury to answer. Depending on the answers to these questions, the judge will decide the case.

Motions Regarding the Verdict Before the verdict is rendered, either party may move for a directed verdict. In such a motion, the court should direct a verdict in favor of the moving party unless there is substantial evidence favoring the other side. Substantial evidence means that there is some evidence on which a jury could rely to base a verdict for the nonmoving party. If the verdict is directed, judgment will be entered for the moving party and the jury will not deliberate.

After the verdict is rendered, two other motions are possible: a *motion for judgment notwithstanding the verdict* (**judgment n.o.v.**) may be made in on the grounds that the jury's verdict was based on insufficient evidence; and a *motion for new trial* may be made if there has been a substantial legal error in the trial. A common basis for appeal is the trial court's refusal to enter a directed verdict, grant a motion for judgment n.o.v., or order a new trial. Usually judgment n.o.v. and new trial motions are made in a single *posttrial motion* and are made in the alternative. Such posttrial motions must be made within ten days of the trial verdict in the federal courts.

Judgment

After all posttrial motions have been argued and denied, the court will enter *judgment on the verdict.* The court's judgment permits the winning party to try to collect the judgment through a variety of collection procedures, including garnishment and attachment of property. In addition, the judgment constitutes a final order that may be appealed. Only on very rare occasions will courts permit **interlocutory appeals,** or appeals prior to a final judment.

Res Judicata

Once a case has been heard and decided by a court, it can never be heard again, under the concept of *res judicata* (literally, "the thing has been decided"). The concept is ancient and is based on the idea that there should be an end to litigation. Thus if A sues B for an auto accident, and the case if finally decided in some way, such as a judgment or a dismissal with prejudice, A may never again sue B on those facts. Likewise, if B did not file a compulsory counterclaim in that action, he may not sue A either. The doctrine even applies to parts of cases under a closely related concept called *collateral estoppel.* Thus, if A sues B on a contract, and the court interprets the contract in a certain way and grants judgment, that interpretation of the court would bind the parties in any future litigation concerning the same contract and must be accepted by the court in the second claim.

A closely related concept applies only to criminal cases, that of **double jeopardy,** which is of constitutional origin. Double jeopardy means that a person cannot be tried twice for the same offense, or for different offenses arising from the same facts. If, for example, a defendant was found not guilty of robbery, the prosecutor could not file assault, battery, and theft charges against the defendant based on the same incident. Only in 1969 did the Supreme Court hold that the protections against double jeopardy were a part of due process under the 14th Amendment, thus imposing the double jeopardy requirements on the states.

Double jeopardy and *res judicata* do not mean that there cannot be more than one trial in a case, however. Appellate courts can and often do order new trials after an appeal, and sometimes trial courts order new trials as well. A criminal defendant may not be retried after an acquittal, however, even if the prosecution attempts to appeal. State appeals in criminal cases are usually restricted to interlocutory matters, such as an appeal of a ruling on evidence, since to do otherwise would constitute double jeopardy.

Criminal Procedure

In many ways, the criminal courts operate identically to the civil courts. The jury selection process, the order of presentation of proof, the order of examining witnesses, the basic rules of evidence, final argument, and the instructions to the jury are all substantially alike with some relatively minor differences. One major difference, the burden of proof, has already been discussed; however, there are some other major differences between civil and criminal cases.

Initiation of Charges

Charges may be filed in criminal cases in two ways: **indictment,** which is a charge made by a grand jury; and **information,** or a complaint filed by the prosecutors. While citizens may begin the process by making a complaint to the prosecutor, the discretion whether to file a charge lies solely in the hands of the prosecutor or grand jury. A common distinction is between **felonies,** which are offenses punishable by death or imprisonment in a penententiary, and **misdemeanors,** which are offenses punished by imprisonment in some other facility than a penententiary (such as a county jail) or by fine only. State classifications vary widely, however.

Prosecutors, also known as *district attorneys* or *state's attorneys* or, in the federal system, *United States attorneys,* have the freedom to charge or not to charge. **Prosecutorial discretion** means the prosecutor is free to file or not to file a charge as he or she sees fit and to dismiss or **plea bargain** the case after it is filed.

Discovery

Discovery in criminal cases is much more limited than in civil cases. The defendant is generally not required to supply much information to the prosecution because of the privilege against self-incrimination. Both the prosecution and the defense may be required to furnish witness lists and their theory of the case, and the prosecution is often required to furnish police reports and records, chemical tests, and other documentary evidence to the defendant. Depositions and interrogatories are sometimes available but are used only in exceptional circumstances, such as to take the testimony of a dying witness.

Pretrial Motions

The defendant often moves for dismissal of the charges on the grounds that the indictment or information is somehow defective. Defects include failure to identify the defendant properly or to state all of the elements of the offense.

Another common pretrial motion is the **motion to suppress** evidence. If evidence is seized illegally, as through an illegal search and seizure, the defendant may move to exclude that evidence in a motion made prior to trial or at a motion during the trial. If granted, the evidence could not be introduced at trial under the exclusionary rule as discussed in Chapter 3. In such motions, the burden of proof is on the prosecution to show that the evidence was seized legally.

Presumption of Innocence

A **presumption** is a rule of law that the court shall draw a particular conclusion until and unless it is disproven. For example, persons are presumed sane until evidence is submitted disproving that fact. Some presumptions are **conclusive,** and may never be disproven, and others are **rebuttable,** meaning that evidence can override the presumption.

Perhaps the most important and famous presumption is the presumption of innocence. Every person is presumed innocent unless and until the prosecution disproves that fact beyond a reasonable doubt. That means that if the evidence is evenly balanced or neutral, the factfinder must find the defendant innocent. Only if the factfinder is convinced of guilt beyond a reasonable doubt may the defendant be found guilty.

Motions Regarding the Verdict

Motions for a directed verdict are available in criminal cases in much the same way that they are available in civil cases. Similarly, motions for a new trial and judgment n.o.v. are also available. A major difference lies in the tests applied to decide those motions in criminal cases, however. Generally speaking, the defendant would argue that the prosecution has not presented sufficient evidence to prove the case beyond a reasonable doubt. Such motions are not available to the prosecution, since the defendant has no burden of proof.

Sentencing

In almost all instances, the sentence imposed on the defendant after a finding of guilt is up to the judge. In a few isolated and rare instances, the jury may recommend a particular sentence, especially in cases involving the death sentence. Statutes provide the available sentences for each offense, including imprisonment, fines, and probation; and, as long as the judge imposes a sentence authorized by the statute, the sentence usually cannot be appealed.

Plea Bargaining

Just as most civil cases are settled before coming to court most criminal cases end in agreed dispositions through the **plea-bargaining** process. Generally, the defendant agrees to plead guilty either to the principal charge, or to a lesser charge, in return for a recommendation by the prosecutor of a specific sentence lighter than the maximum sentence available. Proponents of plea bargaining argue that the process is necessary because of the case load of the courts and prosecutors.

Appellate Procedure

All appellate courts, from the intermediate state appellate courts to the U.S. Supreme Court, operate in much the same way. After the trial court enters a final judgment, any party may begin an appeal by filing a **notice of appeal.** That document simply alerts the court and the opposing parties that an appeal is pending. The notice of appeal must be filed within 30 days of the entry of final judgment in the federal courts. The party appealing is now known as the **appellant** and the opposing party is called the **appellee.**

The appellant must order the **record on appeal,** including all court documents and the transcript of proceedings, within ten days of the filing of the notice of appeal. That record must be sent to the appellate court within 40 days in the federal courts. Forty days after the record is filed, the appellant's **brief** is due. The brief is a written argument, detailing the claims of error in the trial court and arguments of law including citations of cases and statutes dealing with those claims. The appellee must file his brief thirty days later. The appellant has the right to file a reply brief dealing with matters raised by the appellee's brief. Though the process usually ends with the reply brief, if new matters are raised by the appellant's reply brief the appellee may be given an opportunity to respond, and the process continues until no new matter has been raised. Like interrogation of witnesses, the appellant has the right to open and close. The time limits for filing briefs vary in the state courts, and extensions may be granted for good cause. Briefs are sometimes also filed by **amicus curiae,** or friends of the court, who are nonparties interested in the litigation. Any person, corporation, trade association, union, governmental body, or other "legal entity" may request permission to file an amicus curiae brief. For example, if the constitutionality of a federal law is in issue in a private lawsuit, the U.S. attorney general usually appears as amicus curiae to aid the court.

At a later date, the appellate court will order *oral argument.* At that time, the attorneys for the parties will appear before the appellate judges who will decide the case to present their arguments orally. The judges will have read the briefs and record and may interrupt the oral argument at any time to ask questions or make comments. The attorneys receive a set time to argue the case and, ordinarily, the appellant's attorney will open and close the argument.

After the oral argument, the court will usually take the case under advisement while it makes its decision. The court will vote on the case and one of the judges in the majority will write a decision and an opinion, which is later published. The order of the court may **affirm** (agree with) the decision of the lower court, in which case the decision of the lower will stand. Or, the court may **reverse** the decision of the lower court, which means that the appellate court will enter a judgment different from that entered by the lower court. Or, if other matters remain to be done by the lower court, such as holding a new trial or other evidentiary hearings, the appellate court may reverse and **remand** the decision back to the lower court for further proceedings. Following the appellate court's judgment, the parties are free to appeal to an even higher court.

A Note on the Rules of Evidence

Over the centuries the courts, and in a few instances the legislatures, have devised rules of evidence to determine whether particular types of evidence should be permitted to be used. If evidence is allowed, it is admissible; if it is not allowed, it is inadmissible. Some of the most important rules deal with *relevance, prejudicial evidence, hearsay, opinion evidence,* and *privileges.*

Relevant evidence "in some degree advances the inquiry," that is, evidence which helps arrive at the truth regarding one of the issues in the case. Thus, if the issue is whether A killed B, it would be relevant to prove that A was the beneficiary of B's life insurance policy, since motive is an issue in such cases. But it would not be relevant to show that A had a bad driving record (unless B were killed with an automobile) or that A had been convicted of writing bad checks twenty years ago (unless B was blackmailing A).

Prejudicial evidence may in fact be relevant but is inflammatory; that is it could influence the fact finder beyond its relevance. For example, a set of full-color photographs of the injuries caused by an accident prior to their treatment would be relevant, as tending to show the extent of the injuries, but might be so prejudicial that a judge might exclude them regardless of their relevance.

Hearsay statements are statements by a witness in court as to a statement made out of court by a person who is unavailable, introduced to show the truth of the out-of-court statement. For example, in a prosecution of A for the murder of B, if C testifies that D told him (C) that he had witnessed the murder, C's testimony of what D said would be hearsay and inadmissible. The reason for its inadmissibility is that D is not available to be cross-examined by A's lawyer and, as a result, D's statement could not be tested to determine if D could be lying or mistaken.

Some circumstances may make it very likely that D is telling the truth. If D is dying, for example, it is said that D has no good reason to lie and, therefore, is likely to be telling the truth. Or, if D made the statement while still excited, having just witnessed the murder, it is thought that he had not time to make up a lie and was probably telling the truth. As a result, numerous exceptions to the general hearsay rule have been developed, including the dying declarations and spontaneous exclamations *(res gestae)* rules described above.

Opinion evidence is, as a general rule, inadmissible. Witnesses may only testify to *facts* within their knowledge, and not to their *opinions*. Some opinion testimony is permissible, however, if the opinion is based on fact and is within the common experience of laypersons. For example, a person who has driven a car and is familiar with the speed of vehicles may give an opinion as to the speed that another vehicle was travelling. The general rule remains that lay witnesses may only testify as to facts within their knowledge, however, and the opinion of the town gossip as to whether A killed B is inadmissible, both because it is opinion evidence and because it is irrelevant.

"Experts" may give opinion evidence in some cases, however. Such evidence is admissible only if the issue is related to some science, profession, business, or occupation beyond the knowledge of the average layperson, and the witness possesses knowledge or skill in that area which is likely to be of help to the fact finder. Thus, a physicist or accident reconstruction expert might be able to give an opinion regarding the force of impact or speed of vehicles, if that expert had enough facts upon which to base an opinion and the court was satisfied of the person's expertise to venture an opinion. Ordinarily, such opinions are presented in response to hypothetical questions asked by counsel. Usually a great deal of foundation must be laid in previous testimony as well, including all the facts upon which the opinion is based and all of the expert's qualifications.

Privileges have been developed over the centuries to protect certain kinds of relationships. For example, one spouse may not be required to testify against the other because such a requirement would undermine the marital relationship and mitigate against honesty between spouses. Other privileges include the attorney-client privilege, based on the need for total frankness between lawyer and client; the physician-patient privilege, based on the need of doctors to know everything about injuries or illnesses they are treating; and priest-penitent, based on the requirements of some religions that individuals confess their sins. The privilege against self-incrimination is of constitutional origin, as discussed in Chapter 3, and a limited **executive privilege** exists in some circumstances (see *U.S.* v. *Nixon* in Chapter 1). Other potential privileges, including those between accountant and client and news reporter and informant have not been widely accepted by the courts, though there have been cases and legislation dealing with each in some states.

The rules of evidence vary widely between states, and much of the law of evidence is of judicial creation. Some states and the federal courts have adopted statutory rules of evidence, which provide some guidance for the courts. As a general rule, the federal courts will apply federal rules of evidence unless, under the outcome-determinative test in diversity actions, the federal law of evidence affects the outcome of the case, in which case state evidence law is used.

Summary and Conclusions

American courts are organized in a dual system involving both federal and state courts. Both systems include trial, intermediate appellate, and supreme courts. Questions of authority to hear cases are settled by the concepts of jurisdiction and venue. Jurisdiction involves the twin considerations of subject matter jurisdiction and personal jurisdiction. Federal subject matter jurisdiction, which determines the types of cases the federal courts are authorized to hear, is settled by the federal Judiciary Act, which provides for two types of federal jurisdiction: diversity and federal question jurisdiction. There are also special federal statutes providing federal jurisdiction is special types of cases.

The concept of stare decisis meshes with the organization of American courts in that lower courts are bound by the decisions of the higher courts that have jurisdiction over them. The federal courts are bound by the statutes and court decisions of the state courts in diversity cases. Two preconditions to the exercise of jurisdiction are the requirements of standing and the case or controversy doctrine.

Three extraordinary actions are available in certain instances. Class actions, declaratory judgments, and mandamus suits are extremely valuable in contesting government actions. These cases are governed by the same basic trial procedures as other cases.

Trial procedure is dictated in the first instance by the Due Process Clause of the Constitution, which requires fair procedures. Pretrial procedure in civil cases involves the pleadings, discovery, and motions phases of litigation. The trial procedure is generally dictated by the rule that "whoever opens has the right to close." Even after a jury verdict is entered, the trial judge may overturn the verdict. Criminal procedure follows much the same procedure as civil cases, with the exceptions of the method by which charges are brought, the discovery phase, and the burden of proof.

Appellate procedure is generally confined to reviewing the lower court's conduct of the trial to determine whether there was a legal error. Appellate procedure is quite similar in all appellate courts, requiring submission of the record and briefs and oral argument, though minor differences may occur. An appellate court may affirm, reverse, or reverse and remand the decision of the trial court. The opinion of the appellate court then becomes precedent for all trial courts within the appellate court's jurisdiction.

PRO AND CON

ISSUE: Are Major Structural Reforms Necessary to Solve the Workload Problems of the U.S. Supreme Court?

PRO: Procedural Reform Can Help
Erwin N. Griswold*

Discussion about the Supreme Court caseload, and what to do about it, has been proceeding with increasing intensity over the past 10 or 12 years. The problem is a very real one. There can be no doubt about that. Those who say there is no problem seem to me to be largely unaware of its ramifications, and insensitive to its consequences.

There is, however, an aspect of the matter which has not been widely recognized in the discussion to date. This is, as I see it, the fact that the problem is not primarily one relating to the Supreme Court. One of the reasons why we have had difficulty in coming to grips with the issues is that we have been focusing too much of our thought and effort in the wrong place.

I suggest that while the problem of burden on the courts is substantial and serious, the place where it most significantly impinges is on the United States Courts of Appeals. We should focus now on finding ways to cut down on the flow of cases into those courts. . . .

There are some things that can be done about the Supreme Court itself. . . . We have already done a large part of what can be done, for the Court's jurisdiction now is very largely discretionary. The Court has been given the means to protect itself. . . . [I]t need not now undertake to decide any case which does not, first, merit its attention, and, second, fall within the limits of its capacity. . . .

The first step that should be taken is to eliminate the jurisdiction of the federal courts based on diversity of citizenship. Such jurisdiction has now

become an anachronism. It would be pleasant to continue it if we really had the facilities to handle it; and there are certain elements of the bar which value it highly. As things have developed, though, it is a vestige of another day, at least in its domestic application. We can no longer afford the congestion which it produces, and, in my view, the time is well past when it should be repealed. This would reduce the volume of cases in the district courts by 25 percent. . . .

What more can be done? On this, I think, the Supreme Court itself can provide a good deal of help. . . . They are matters of mores and approach, but they are real.

. . . My first point is hard to state, and particularly hard to state in a way which will not be misunderstood. It is presented with deference, and with great respect. . . .

It does not seem to me that the Supreme Court always shows an adequate "institutional" sense. Of course, the justices thoroughly understand the "institution" of the Supreme Court. I am talking about something else, namely, the "institution" of the legal system of the country,. . . If the legal system can be made more intelligible, there will be fewer cases in the lower court, and from this will follow a reduction in the number of cases where review is sought from the Supreme Court.

The importance (within limits) of "correcting errors." . . . We are frequently told that it is not the function of the Supreme Court to correct errors

---

*"The Supreme Court: Does it Need Help?" *Judicature* (August 1983). Reprinted with permission of the author.

which are made in the lower courts. . . . Of course the Supreme Court cannot correct all errors in the lower courts—though the fact that there are uncorrectable errors should give us pause. The point is that outstanding and unreviewed erroneous decisions spawn further litigation. . . . [L]ikely error in a decision . . . is, in my view, a relevant factor in determining whether to grant certiorari. And, as the Supreme Court is able to correct the errors, the volume of litigation in the lower courts will be reduced. . . .

Clarity of decision, without prolixity. . . . Alas, for a number of reasons, decisions of the Supreme Court are often not clear and definitive. Many of them—one might say most of them—are much *too long.* In the second place, there are *too many* opinions. . . .

Activism"—a self-repeating phenomenon. . . . There are situations where the Court should recognize needs for normal development of the law and take steps to provide it. In recent years,

though, the courts have gone very far in this, and have done it frequently. Old doctrines designed to hold down the number of controversies heard by the courts, such as mootness, standing, justiciability, political question, and so on, have been largely swept away. . . . Class actions have been greatly expanded . . . and have been applied to what some would think an absurd extent. All of this adds to the volume of work in the lower courts. . . .

The suggestion that we should have a National Court of Appeals, . . . has not yet met with favor, and I do not advance it here. For many it is too much of a bite all at once. . . .

We should have more courts organized on a topical basis, that is, in accordance with the subject matter of the case. . . . I think it would be better to have a separate Court of Tax Appeals. We could also have courts of appeals with exclusive jurisdiction over labor cases, over commerce, including the Interstate Commerce Commission the Federal Trade Commission, and antitrust.

CON: The Supreme Court Can Solve Its Own Workload Problems
Arthur D. Hellman*

Congress is now giving serious consideration to legislation that would effect the most far-reaching change in the structure of the federal judicial system since the creation of intermediate appellate courts nearly a century ago. Bills introduced by Senator Dole and Congressman Kastenmeier, with the apparent support of Chief Justice Burger, would create an "Intercircuit Tribunal of the United States Courts of Appeals" that would hear and decide cases referred to it by the Supreme Court. Unless overruled or modified by the Supreme Court, decisions of the Tribunal would constitute binding precedents in all other federal courts and, with respect to federal issues, in state courts as well.

Proponents argue that creation of the new court is necessary for two reasons: "to relieve the dramatically increased workload of the Supreme Court" and "provide desperately needed additional decisional capacity for the resolution of disputes where nationwide uniformity is needed." . . .

The premises underlying this proposal raise fundamental questions about the role of the Supreme Court in the American legal system and the extent to which one tribunal of nine justices can

fulfill that role. . . . I conclude that notwithstanding its impressive sponsorship, the legislation should not be enacted. . . . To the extent that it seeks to reduce the workload of the justices, it is unnecessary. To the extent that it seeks to promote uniformity in the law, it rests on assumptions that have not been proved; but even if those assumptions are correct, creation of a temporary tribunal would do little to foster uniformity. . . .

In considering whether the justices are overworked, it is necessary to look separately at the two tasks they perform: selecting the cases they will decide, and deciding them. . . .

With the possible exception of Justice Stevens, no member of the present Court has asserted that the process of screening cases for plenary review has become unmanageable. Nor would such an assertion be persuasive. Admittedly, the number of cases to be examined is much greater than it was two decades ago—4,417 in the 1981 term. But a caseload of that size does not impose nearly the burden that it would, for example, at the court of appeals level.

From Taft onward, the justices have emphasized that the function of the Supreme Court is not

---

*"Caseload, Conflicts, and Decisional Capacity," *Judicature* (July 1983). Reprinted with permission of the author.

to correct errors in the lower courts, but to "secure harmony of decision and the appropriate settlement of questions of general importance. Thus, . . . the purpose of screening is not to determine whether there was error, or even probable error, in the court below. Rather, the Court considers whether the case presents an issue of "wide public importance or governmental interest." . . .

More important, the vast majority of applications clearly do not meet the standard for "certworthiness" that the justices have articulated. . . . Chief Justice Burger—who has been in the forefront of those arguing that the Court is overburdened—has said that two-thirds of the new filings are not only unworthy of review but "utterly frivolous." . . .

The screening process thus constitutes a relatively small part of the justices' total workload. The more time-consuming task is that of reaching decisions and writing opinions in the 140 to 150 cases that do receive plenary consideration each Term. Yet it is far from clear that a calendar of that size truly imposes an intolerable burden on the justices.

Under current conditions, each justice is required to write 15 or 16 majority opinions a term—barely two for each month that the Court is in session. Some of the cases will involve intractable social and political issues warranting extended reflection and research, but not all fit this description. . . .

It might seem intuitively obvious that the justices would write better opinions if they had more time. Nevertheless, the available evidence indicates that the matter is not that simple. In the middle and late 1950s the Court was hearing fewer cases than at any other time in this century; but that was also the era when eminent scholars filled the law reviews with devastating criticisms of the Court's craftsmanship. . . .

In any event, before we can reach any conclusions about the burdens imposed by the plenary docket, we must consider the actions of the justices themselves. . . .

Separate expression or views have proliferated in recent years to an extent never before known. In the 1981 term alone the justices issued more than 175 separate opinions. . . .

. . . [I]t is a necessary first step to find out what the Supreme Court is not doing and how its limited capacity for decisionmaking actually affects people's ability to plan and litigate efficiently. To forego this inquiry is to run the risk of pursuing mischievous "solutions" to problems that exist only in the mind of the beholder.

DISCUSSION QUESTIONS

1. Why are there two sets of courts in the United States? Wouldn't it be more efficient if there was only one set of courts? Is the dual system an anachronism, or are there good and valid reasons for going to all that trouble?

2. Do you think sufficient state bias really exists to give cause for federal diversity jurisdiction? Aren't the federal courts biased as well?

3. Does *stare decisis* eliminate judicial inventiveness and creativity? Some countries get along very nicely without *stare decisis*. Could we? Does *stare decisis* help the ordinary citizen predict the legal outcome of his actions?

4. Under the *Erie* doctrine, what if a federal court finds that a state law is unjust, immoral, or just plain wrong? Must it still apply the law? Should it refuse on ethical grounds to apply such a law?

5. Are advisory opinions advisable? What's wrong with a legislature getting an advance opionion from the state supreme court on whether a piece of pending legislation will be constitutional? Wouldn't such a procedure save a lot of trouble later? Should that court be bound by its advisory opinion when a real controversy comes before it later on?

6. Does a taxpayer actually suffer an injury from the expenditure of tax money for unconstitutional projects? As a matter of public policy, should any and all taxpayers be permitted to sue to enjoin such projects? If we don't permit the taxpayers to sue, who can sue?

7. Are you surprised that a judge may take a case away from a jury through the directed verdict technique, or overturn a verdict through posttrial procedures? Should a court be able to? Isn't this a deprivation of the right of trial by jury?

8. Why may an appellate court only review errors of law and not errors of fact? Do you suppose it might have something to do with the fact that the appellate court did not see the wtinesses testify, but only read the transcript? If trials are videotaped, should this rule be changed?

9. Do trial and appellate procedures guarantee a correct result in a case? Do they help or hurt the search for truth? Which ones help and which ones hurt?

CASE PROBLEMS

1. Finn, a resident of Texas, suffered a fire loss of $25,000 on a building located in that state. He was insured through American Fire & Casualty, a Florida corporation, and Lumbermen's Mutual, an Indiana corporation, and had purchased the insurance through Reiss, a Texas insurance agent. In what courts may Finn sue all of the parties? What courts have venue? [*American Fire & Casualty Co.* v. *Finn*, 341 U.S. 6, 71 S. Ct. 534, 95 L. Ed. 2d 702 (1951).]

2. Cunningham purchased a Ford automobile for $11,221.40 and had nothing but problems. After driving the car for 12,000 miles, he sued Ford under a warranty theory for the entire purchase price. An expert testified that because of the mileage, the car was now worth $1,800 less. Is there federal jurisdiction? [*Cunningham* v. *Ford Motor Co.* 413 F. Supp. 1101 (1976).]

3. Five members of the military reserve, who were also taxpayers, filed a class action suit on behalf of all members of the reserves and as taxpayers against a practice whereby several members of Congress held commissions in the reserves. The claim was that such commissions constituted a conflict of interest, violated Article I, Section 6, clause 2 of the constitution, and opened the door to undue influence by the executive branch. Is this a proper taxpayer action? Do they have standing? [*Schlesinger* v. *Reservists Committee to Stop the War*, 418 U.S. 208, 94 S. Ct. 2925, 41 L. Ed. 2d 706 (1974).]

4. Rush was driving a motorcycle that ran into a hole, throwing her to the ground. She brought suit for damage to the motorcycle against the city, claiming negligence, and won at trial. Later, she filed an action for her personal injuries arising from the same accident, claiming that the trial court's finding of negligence was *res judicata.* The city claimed that the two claims should have been raised in the same case, and she is now barred. Who is right? [*Rush* v. *City of Maple Heights*, 167 Ohio St. 221, 147 N. E. 2d 599 (1958).]

5. Twenty-nine fishermen, wholesalers, and retailers of commercial seafood filed a class action against Allied on behalf of all others "similarly situated" claiming that Allied's discharge of toxic effluents into the Chesapeake Bay was ruining the commercial seafood industry in that area. Allied claimed that the injuries to the parties were different and a class action should not lie since many of the plaintiffs were in direct competition with each other. Result? [*Pruitt* v. *Allied Chemical Corp.,* 85 F.R.D. 100 (E. D. Va., 1980).]

6. The tugboat *J. M. Taylor* sank in the Delaware River, drowning five crewmen. The tug's owners hired a law firm to defend potential lawsuits, and the lawyers took statements from numerous witnesses to the sinking. After suit was filed, an interrogatory was sent to the owners, asking whether such statements were made and requesting the substance of the statements if they existed. Must the tug owner answer? [*Hickman* v. *Taylor,* 329 U.S. 495, 67 S. Ct. 385, 91 L. Ed. 451 (1947).]

7. Curtis filed suit under Title VIII of the federal Civil Rights Act to enjoin discrimination by Loether in rental of housing and for damages caused by Loether's discrimination. Loether demanded a jury trial. Title VIII makes no mention of jury trials, and discrimination actions were unknown at common law. Should Loether get a jury trial? [*Curtis* v. *Loether,* 415 U.S. 189, 94 S. Ct. 1005, 39 L. Ed. 2d 260 (1974).]

8. Olivia, a citizen of Connecticut, is travelling through Missouri on her way to California. Sebastian, a citizen of Montana, is also on the same highway, and has been drinking heavily. Sebastian's auto collides with Olivia's car, and Olivia is injured severely. Olivia is taken to Malvolio Hospital in Missouri for treatment. Unfortunately, she is treated by Dr. Andrew Aguecheek, a citizen of Illinois but also practicing in Missouri, and he botches the operation causing further injury to Olivia. (1) Must Olivia sue Sebastian, Aguecheek, and Malvolio Hospital in the same lawsuit? (2) In what court may she sue all of the parties? (3) Assuming the federal court has jurisdiction over this case, what state's laws would that court apply? (4) In which federal court may the action be brought? (5) If the action were brought in state court, could the defendants ask that the case be transferred to federal court?

9. Page, a citizen of Great Britain and a student at the University of Wisconsin, married a citizen of the United States. Mrs. Page, a resident of Illinois, was working on her master's degree in business administration at the University of Wisconsin at the time, though she continued to maintain her residence at her parents' home in Illinois and voted in that state. The couple had made no plans following their graduation. On a trip back to visit Mrs. Page's parents in Illinois, they were involved in a traffic accident with Ford, a resident of Illinois, and both were injured severely. May they bring an action in federal court?

10. Grey and Erpingham had entered into an employment contract, and Grey alleged that Erpingham owed him money on the deal, which Erpingham denied. Grey filed suit and the summons was delivered to Ely, a deputy sheriff, for service of process. Ely, who was very overworked, threw the summons away and

falsely claimed that he had delivered the summons to Erpingham. When Erpingham failed to appear, Grey moved for a default judgment, which was granted. Some time later Erpingham learned of the judgment and moved to set it aside. Does he have a remedy?

SUGGESTED READINGS

Currie, David P. *Federal Courts* 2nd ed. (St. Paul, Minn.: West Publishing Co., 1975).

Ehrenzweig, Albert A., and David W. Louisell. *Jurisdiction in a Nutshell* (St. Paul, Minn.: West Publishing Co., 1973).

Federal Rules of Appellate Procedure West Law School ed. (St. Paul, Minn.: West Publishing Co., 1983).

Federal Rules of Civil Procedure West Law School ed. (St. Paul Minn.: West Publishing Co., 1983).

Federal Rules of Criminal Procedure West Law School ed. (St. Paul, Minn.: West Publishing Co., 1983).

James, Fielding. *Civil Procedure* (Boston: Little, Brown and Company, 1965).

Kane, Mary Kay. *Civil Procedure in a Nutshell* (St. Paul, Minn.: West Publishing Co., 1979).

Landers, Jonathan M., and James A. Martin. *Civil Procedure* (Boston: Little, Brown and Company, 1981).

Administrative Agencies

The expert should be on tap, but not on top. In this country we have been so anxious to avoid the dangers of having the expert on top that we suffer from a strong reluctance to have him on tap.

Felix Frankfurter, The Public and Its Government *(1930)*

Millions are fascinated by the plan to transform the whole world into a bureau, to make everybody a bureaucrat, and to wipe out any private initiative. The paradise of the future is visualized as an all-embracing bureaucratic apparatus.

Ludwig von Mises, Human Action *(1949)*

The rise of administrative bodies probably has been the most significant legal trend of the last century. . . . They have become a veritable fourth branch of the Government. . . .

Justice Jackson, dissenting, in FTC v. Ruberoid Co., *343 U.S.470 (1952)*

In many ways the study of contemporary American government is the study of administrative agencies. Virtually all domestic policy and some foreign policy is implemented through a huge variety of commissions, boards, bureaus, and agencies, which have the authority to make rules, conduct investigations, and adjudicate claims. A single agency may perform legislative, executive, and judicial funcitons, sometimes in the same case.

Approximately 80,000 persons were employed by the major federal agencies in 1980, and the operating budgets of those agencies exceeded $6 billion. Including the military, approximately 16 percent of the total work force is employed in the public sector, the vast majority, excepting the military, in administrative agencies. It is little wonder that even as early as 1937 a presidential commission on government administration called agencies "the headless fourth branch" of government.

Overview of Agencies

While administrative agencies have few fans and many critics, the growth of agencies has been viewed as a necessary response to the growing complexity of governing a modern nation. Without agencies, Congress would be required to enact every administrative rule into law through its formal processes. This task would be physically impossible and the rules enacted would be of questionable benefit, since such rules would have to be enforced through traditional court procedures. Thus, Congress would have to assign every radio and television channel, set rail and truck routes and rates, specifically describe every type of unfair labor and trade practice, set discount rates for financial institutions, draft specific regulations for each nuclear power plant, and perform a host of functions far beyond its capabilities. And, enforcement of these laws would take place through traditional legal processes in the federal courts.

Since 1887, and some would argue long before that, Congress has passed a simple **enabling act** instead of enacting detailed and complex laws itself. That act creates an agency and delegates the authority to make detailed rules to the agency. The statute also empowers the agency to investigate the facts surrounding its area and to adjudicate conflicts that arise under the rules it makes. The rulemaking, investigative, and adjudicatory roles, discussed later in this chapter, are the three main functions of agencies.

Development of Agencies

Agencies did not, in Justice Frankfurter's terms, "come like a thief in the night," but have been developing for centuries. Experts trace their origins to the powers of the medieval English sheriffs. A rather sophisticated agency was created, complete with enabling act, as early as 1385. Delegations of power to cabinet officers were made by the First Congress in 1789.

Approximately one-third of all agencies were created prior to 1900, and another third were established between 1900 and 1930. A crucial development occurred in 1887 when the Interstate Commerce Commission was created as the first independent regulatory commission (IRC).

Administrative agencies are placed within the organization of government by their status as either a **line agency** or as an **independent regulatory commission** (IRC), see Figure 5-1. Until 1887, all agencies were line agencies, that is, subordinate bureaus of a cabinet office. Line agencies are under the direct control of the President and are usually headed by a single administrator, who serves at the pleasure of the President. For example, the Internal Revenue Service is a subunit of the Treasury Department, and the Commissioner of Internal Revenue is appointed and may be removed by the President. Line agencies may be created by executive order of the President, though authority to make rules, investigate, and adjudicate claims is often delegated to such bodies by Congress.

Independent regulatory commissions (IRC's), on the other hand, were created by Congress to limit the political control of the President. The Interstate Commerce Commission was created as an IRC since that body regulates railroads, and since President Benjamin Harrison had been a railroad lawyer. Typically IRC's are headed by board, rather than by a single head. The members of the board are appointed by the President, but for staggering terms longer than that of the President. Often the membership is required to be bipartisan, i.e., made up of a certain number of members of each political party. Board members cannot be unilaterally removed by the President.

Beginning in 1930, several new agencies wre created to meet the challenges of the depression, including the National Labor Relations Board (NLRB) and the Securities and Exchange Commission (SEC). Three trends that began in that era as well have had a profound effect on the development of administrative agencies: standardization of administrative procedure; concern with administrative efficiency; and a move from purely "economic" regulation towards "social" regulation.

Standardization of Administrative Procedure

Prior to 1947, every agency had its own rules of procedure, which differed from those of every other agency. During the late 1930's, a move toward uniform procedures began, which culminated in 1947 with the unanimous congressional approval of the Administrative Procedure Act (the APA). Much of the discussion of adminsitrative procedures in this chapter will be based upon that Act, since it applies to "each authority of the Government of the United States" except Congress, the courts, and the governments of territories, possessions, and the District of Columbia. Differences in procedure among agencies still persist as a result of different procedures prescribed by the enabling acts but, as a general rule, the APA governs the procedures used in all federal agencies. Many states have adopted similar statutes prescribing uniform procedures for all state agencies.

Concern with Efficiency and Power

Accompanying the rise in power of agencies came criticism of agencies on two bases: first, that agencies were unaccountable to the public and their power must therefore be restrained; and, second, that agencies were often mismanaged and inefficient. In part, the introduction of the APA was a response to the first criticism, as were several citizen access laws discussed later. A second response has been the appointment of several historic presidential commissions to study the management of public agencies. In the late 1970's, the concept of deregulation was introduced to open many economic markets to competition, beginning with natural gas, airlines, financial institutions, and rail and trucking industries. The problems of deregulation will be considered in detail in Chapter 19.

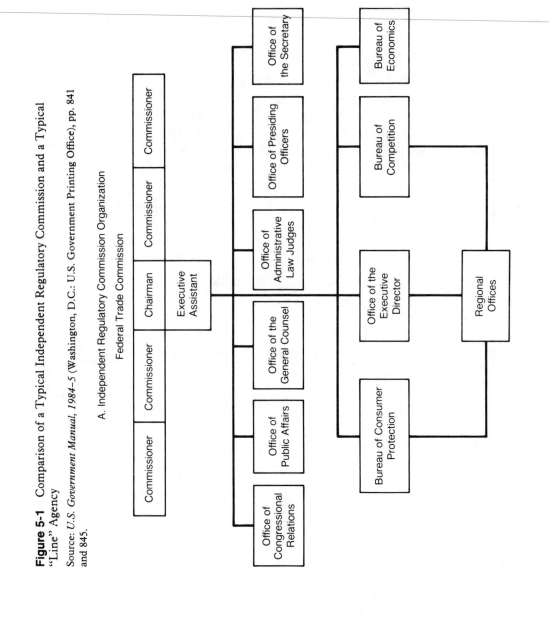

Figure 5-1 Comparison of a Typical Independent Regulatory Commission and a Typical "Line" Agency

Source: *U.S. Government Manual, 1984–5* (Washington, D.C.: U.S. Government Printing Office), pp. 841 and 845.

A. Independent Regulatory Commission Organization

Federal Trade Commission

B. Line Agency Organization
Environmental Protection Agency

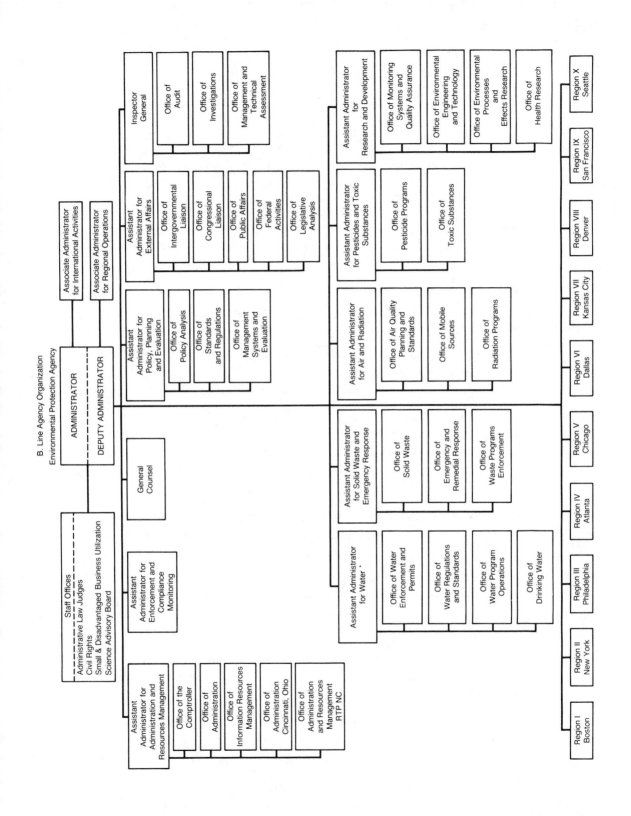

"Economic" versus "Social" Regulation

Until the 1930's, almost all regulation dealt with economic areas, such as regulation of public utilities and markets, rates and routes of various industries, or in the case of the antitrust laws, industry at large. During the 1930's, in partial response to the social dislocation caused by the depression, another type of regulation began to develop, generally categorized as social welfare or mass justice regulation. It generally encompasses such areas as occupational safety and health, consumer product safety, equal opportunity, and environmental protection. Sometimes, those laws are divided into two broad categories: **protective legislation,** which shelters the public from some perceived danger; and **entitlement legislation,** which provides aid for the needy, disabled, or disadvantaged. This division is not inflexible, since many laws, like social security, have both protective and entitlement aspect.

The Delegation of Power

Only the legislature can make a law. Administrative rules are, strictly speaking, not laws but *rules* with the force of law. The difference seems to be a semantic fiction but is crucial to preserve the constitutionality of agencies under the doctrine of the separation of powers. As a result, only Congress can make the law, in the form of the enabling act, and must *delegate authority* to the agency to make rules that fill in the details.

A major question involves how broad the **delegation** of power may be. Must the legislature spell out in detail what sort of rules the agency may make, or may it delegate total authority, without reservation or limitation, to the agency? The problem involves the separation of powers concept since, if the grant is too broad, the legislature will have delegated the authority to "make law" to an agency. On the other hand, if the grant is too specific, Congress will have defeated its own purposes in establishing an agency.

In 1935, the Supreme Court ruled in two cases* that congressional delegations of power in those situations were too broad and violated the concept of separation of powers. The Court held those delegations unconstitutional because Congress had not included a *standard* against which agency action could be measured, and "Congress has declared no policy, has established no standard, has laid down no rule. There is no requirement, no definition of circumstances and conditions. . . ." In the words of Justice Cardozo, "[t]he delegated power of legislation which has found expression [in these cases] is not canalized within banks that keep it from overflowing. It is unconfined and vagrant."

No U.S. Supreme Court case after 1935 has held a delegation of power unconstitutional. In 1944,** the Court seemed to say that enabling acts need no longer set

---

Schechter Poultry Corp. v. *U.S.,* 295 U.S. 495, 55 S. Ct. 837, 79 L. Ed. 1570 (1935); and *Panama Refining Co.* v. *Ryan,* 293 U.S. 388, 55 S. Ct. 241, 79 L. Ed. 446 (1935).

**Yakus* v. *U.S.,* 321 U.S. 414, 64 S. Ct. 660, 88 L. Ed. 834 (1944).

standards for administrative rule-making, but need only establish a congressional *policy* against which the administrative agency's rules might be judged. The difference between policy and standards is probably one of degree, and the failure of the courts to "demand that Congress do its job" has been severely criticized. Such broad delegations of power seem to violate the concept of separation of powers, and complicate the job of the courts in determining whether an agency has overstepped its bounds.

The separation of powers problem seems inevitable due to the split personality of most agencies—part executive, part legislative, and part judicial. In 1983, the court held that the legislature did not have the right to exercise control over administrative actions through the **legislative veto.** Simply put, a legislative veto involves a delegation of authority to an agency but with the provision that administrative action may be overridden by a vote of one or both Houses of Congress. The legislative veto was created during the 1930's and appeared in over 200 major pieces of legislation.

Immigration and Naturalization Service v. Chadha

51 U.S.L.W. 4907 (1983)

Chadha, holder of a British passport, overstayed his nonimmigrant student visa in the United States. The Immigration and Naturalization Service filed an action to deport him, and Chadha filed an application to suspend the deportation with the Attorney General under provisions of the Immigration and Naturalization Act. Under Section 244 of that Act, the Attorney General had the authority to suspend deportation if an alien is of good moral character and if the deportation would result in extreme hardship. According to the Act, if either House of Congress passed a resolution stating that it did not favor the suspension of deportation, the Attorney General was required to deport the alien. The House of Representatives voted to override the Attorney General's suspension in Chadha's case on the grounds that no extreme hardship had been shown. Chadha appealed, first to the Board of Immigration Appeals and then to the U.S. Court of Appeals, which held the legislative veto unconstitutional. The government petitioned for certiorari to the U.S. Supreme Court.

Mr. Chief Justice BURGER delivered the opinion of the Court:

The Court first considered issues of standing, mootness, and other arguments raised by attorneys for the Senate and the House appearing as **amicus curiae** and rejected all of the preliminary arguments. The Immigration and Naturalization Service had agreed with Chadha's argument that the legislative veto was unconstitutional.

We turn now to the question whether action of one House of Congress under §244(c)(2) violates strictures of the Constitution. We begin, of course, with the presumption that the challenged statute is valid. Its wisdom is not the concern of the courts; if a challenged action does not violate the Constitution, it must be sustained. . . .

By the same token, the fact that a given law or procedure is efficient, convenient, and useful in facilitating functions of government, standing alone, will not save it if it is contrary to the Constitution. Convenience and efficiency are not the primary objectives—or the hallmarks— of democratic government and our inquiry is sharpened rather than blunted by the fact that Congressional veto provisions are appearing with increasing frequency in statutes which delegate authority to executive and independent agencies. . . .

JUSTICE WHITE undertakes to make a case for the proposition that one-House veto is a useful "political invention," . . . and we need not challenge that assertion. We can even concede this utilitarian argument although the long range political wisdom of this "invention" is arguable. . . . But policy arguments supporting even useful "political inventions" are subject to the demands of the Constitution. . . .

Explicit and unambiguous provisions of the Constitution prescribe and define the respective functions of the Congress and of the Executive in the legislative process.
. . . .

. . . We have recently noted that "[t]he principle of separation of powers was not simply an abstract generalization in the minds of the Framers: it was woven into the documents that they drafted in Philadelphia in the summer of 1787." . . . [W]e find that purposes underlying the Presentment Clauses, Art. I, §7, cls 2, 3, and the bicameral requirement of Art. I, §1 and §7, cl. 2, guide our resolution of the important question presented in this case. . . .

The records of the Constitutional Convention reveal that the requirement that all legislation be presented to the President before becoming law was uniformly accepted by the Framers. . . .

The bicameral requirement . . . was of scarcely less concern to the Framers than was the Presidential veto and indeed the two concepts are interdependent. By providing that no law could take effect without the concurrence of the prescribed majority of the Members of both Houses, the Framers reemphasized their belief. . . . that legislation should not be enacted unless it has been carefully and fully considered by the Nation's elected officials. . . .

The Constitution sought to divide the delegated powers of the new federal government into three defined categories, legislative, executive and judicial, to assure as nearly as possible that each Branch of government would confine itself to its assigned responsibility. The hydraulic pressure inherent within each of the separate Branches to exceed the outer limits of its power, even to accomplish desirable objectives, must be resisted. . . .

Examination of the action taken here by one House pursuant to §244(c)(2) reveals that it was essentially legislative in purpose and effect. In purporting to exercise power defined in Art. I §8, cl. 4 to "establish an uniform Rule of Naturalization," the House took action that had the purpose and effect of altering the legal rights, duties and relations of persons, including the Attorney General, Executive Branch officials and Chadha, all outside the legislative branch. . . . The one-House veto operated in this case to overrule the Attorney General and mandate Chadha's deportation; absent the House action, Chadha would remain in the United States. Congress has *acted* and its action has altered Chadha's status. . . .

Since it is clear that the action by the House under §244(c)(2) was not within any of the express constitutional exceptions authorizing one House to act alone, and equally clear that it was an exercise of legislative power, that action was subject to the standards prescribed in Article I. The bicameral requirement, the Presentment Clauses, the President's veto, and Congress' power to override a veto were intended to erect enduring checks on each Branch and to protect the people from the improvident exercise of power by mandating certain prescribed steps. To preserve those checks, and maintain the separation of powers, the carefully defined limits on the power of each Branch must not be eroded. To accomplish what has been attempted by one House of Congress in this case requires action in conformity with the express procedures of the Constitution's prescription for legislative action: passage by a majority of both Houses and presentment to the President.

The choices we discern as having been made in the Constitutional Convention impose burdens on governmental processes that often seem clumsy, inefficient, even unworkable, but those hard choices were consciously made by men who had lived under a form of government that permitted arbitrary governmental acts to go unchecked. There is no support in the Constitution or decisions of this Court for the proposition that the cumbersomeness and delays often encountered in complying with explicit Constitutional standards may be avoided, either by the Congress or by the President. See *Youngstown Sheet & Tube Co.* v. *Sawyer*. . . . With all the obvious flaws of delay, untidiness, and potential for abuse, we have not yet found a better way to preserve freedom than by making the exercise of power subject to the carefully crafted restraints spelled out in the Constitution.

We hold that the Congressional veto provision in §244(c)(2) . . . is unconstitutional. . . . Accordingly, the judgment of the Court of Appeals is
Affirmed

JUSTICE WHITE, dissenting.

. . . .

The prominence of the legislative veto mechanism in our contemporary political system and its importance to Congress can hardly be overstated. It has become a central means by which Congress secures the accountability of executive and independent agencies. Without the legislative veto, Congress is faced with a Hobson's choice: either to refrain from delegating the necessary authority, leaving itself with a hopeless task of writing laws with the requisite specificity to cover endless special circumstances across the entire policy landscape, or in the alternative, to abdicate its lawmaking function to the executive branch and independent agencies. To choose the former leaves major national problems unresolved; to opt for the latter risks unaccountable policymaking by those not elected to fill that role. Accordingly, over the past five decades, the legislative veto has been placed in nearly 200 statutes. The device is known in every field of governmental concern: reorganization, budgets, foreign affairs, war powers, and regulation of trade, safety, energy, the environment and the economy.

. . . .

Theoretically, agencies and officials were asked only to "fill up the details," and the rule was that "Congress cannot delegate any part of its legislative power except under a limitation of prescribed conduct." . . . . Chief Justice Taft elaborated the standard . . . : "If Congress shall lay down by legislative act an intelligible principle to which the person or body authorized to fix such rates is directed to conform, such legislative action is not a forbidden delegation of legislative power." In practice, however, restrictions on the scope of the power that could be delegated diminished and all but disappeared. . . .

. . . .

If Congress may delegate lawmaking power to independent and executive agencies, it is most difficult to understand Article I as forbidding Congress from also reserving a check on legislative power for itself. Absent the [legislative] veto, the agencies receiving delegations of legislative or quasi-legislative power may issue regulations having the force of law without bicameral approval and without the President's signature. It is thus not apparent why the reservation of a veto over the exercise of that legislative power must be subject to a more exacting test. . . .

Administrative Rule Making

Once an effective delegation of authority is made to an agency, the agency is empowered to make rules within its grant of authority (see Figure 5-2). At the federal level, these rules become a part of the *Code of Federal Regulations,* a vast compendium of all existing agency rules. The rules have "the force of law." Rules are also made by agencies at the state level with similar effect.

Procedures for Making Rules: "Formal" and "Informal" Rule Making

Under the terms of the APA, certain procedures must be followed before an agency may adopt a new rule. Section 553 of the APA recognizes two forms of rule making: formal and informal.

Figure 5-2 The Development of an Agency and Its Rules

On March 27, 1978, Congress passed the following statute, 42 U.S. Code §2000e-4.

> There is hereby created a Commission to be known as the Equal Opportunity Commission, which shall be composed of five members, not more than three of whom shall be members of the same political party. Members of the Commission shall be appointed by the President by and with the advice and consent of the Senate for a term of five years. . . . The President shall designate one member to serve as Chairman of the Commission. . . . The Chairman shall be responsible on behalf of the Commission for the administrative operations of the Commission, and . . . shall appoint . . . such officers, agents, attorneys, administrative law judges, and employees as he deems necessary to assist it. . . . *Provided,* That assignment, removal, and compensation of administrative law judges shall be in accordance with [the Adminstrative Procedures Act].

The Commission was given the right to make rules and to enforce a large variety of statutes in other parts of the Act. Pursuant to that authority, on April 11, 1980, the following notice was published in the *Federal Register,* Vol. 45, No. 72, p. 25024:

Equal Employment Opportunity Commission

29 CFR part 1604

Discrimination Because of Sex Under Title VII of the Civil Rights Act of 1964, as Amended; Adoption of Interim Interpretive Guidelines

Summary: The Equal Employment Opportunity Commission is amending its Guidelines on Discrimination Because of Sex on an interim basis, in order to clarify its position on the issue of sexual harassment and to invite the public to comment on the issue. . . . These Interim Guidelines are in full effect from the date of their publication; however EEOC will receive comments for 60 days subsequent to the date of publication. After the comment period EEOC will evaluate the comments, make whatever changes to the Interim Guidelines may seem appropriate in light of the comments, and publish the final Guidelines.

Dates: Effective date: April 11, 1980. Comments must be received on or before June 10, 1980.

Supplementary Information: Sexual harassment like harassment on the basis of color, race, religion, or national origin, has long been recognized by EEOC as a violation of . . . the Civil Rights Act of 1964. . . . However, despite the position taken by the Commission, sexual harassment continues to be especially widespread. Because of the continued prevalence of this unlawful practice, the Commission has determined that there is a need for guidelines in this area. . .

The *Federal Register* then discussed each of the proposed guidelines in detail, and set out the proposed guidelines completely. The entire notice ran two full pages, three columns to the page, in the *Register.*

On November 10, 1980, a second notice appeared in the *Federal Register.* That notice said that in the 60 day period set by the initial notice, over 160 letters had been received, and that in light of those comments, several changes were made in the Guidelines. On September 23, 1981, the Commission adopted the following as 29 *Code of Federal Regulation* 1604.

1604.11 *Sexual Harassment.*

(a) Harassment on the basis of sex is a violation of Sec. 703 of Title VII. Unwelcome sexual advances, requests for sexual favors, and other verbal or physical conduct of a sexual nature constitute sexual harassment when (1) submission to such conduct is made either explicitly or implicitly a term or condition of an individual's employment, (2) submission to or rejection of such conduct by an individual is used as the basis for employment decisions affecting such individual, or (3) such conduct has the purpose or effect of unreasonably interfering with an individual's work performance or creating an intimidating, hostile, or offensive working environment.

. . . .

(e) An employer may also be responsible for the acts of non-employees, with respect to sexual harassment of employees in the workplace, where the employer (or its agents or supervisory employees) knows or should have known of the conduct and fails to take immediate and appropriate corrective action. . . .

(f) Prevention is the best tool for the elimination of sexual harrassment. An employer should take all steps necessary to prevent sexual harassment from occurring. . . .

(g) Other related practices: Where employment opportunities or benefits are granted because of an individual's submission to the employer's sexual advances or requests for sexual favors, the employer may be held liable for unlawful sex discrimination against other persons who were qualified for but denied that employment opportunity or benefit.

Formal Rule Making   **Formal rule making** involves a trial-type hearing preceding the adoption of a rule. Section 553 provides simply that if a statute requires that rules be made "on the record," Sections 556 and 557 must be applied. Sections 556 and 557 are the sections that govern formal adjudicatory hearings and require a formal hearing, which is essentially identical to a courtroom trial, including presentation of evidence, the right of cross-examination, and the right of appeal or review.

Formal rule making is only required when a statute requires that rules be made "on the record," and the courts have generally required that those "magic words" actually appear in the statute before requiring formal procedures. Only a very few federal statutes (by one count, only fifteen laws) contain those words and, as a result, formal rule making is the exception rather than the rule. Perhaps the best-known and most important statute requiring formal procedures is the federal Food, Drug and Cosmetic Act of 1938.

Informal Rule Making   Almost all federal rule making takes place under the informal procedures permitted by Section 553 of the APA. **Informal rule making,** sometimes called **notice and comment rule making,** has been called "one of the greatest inventions of modern government"* because of its effective compromise of the needs of governmental efficiency and citizen access to the forums of public affairs.

Section 553 requires that *notice* of any proposed rule making must be published in the *Federal Register,* unless all of the people subject to the rule are somehow personally served or have actual notice of the rule-making proceedings. The notice must

---

*Kenneth Culp Davis, *Administrative Law, Text—Cases—Problems* 6th ed. (St. Paul, Minn.: West Publishing Co., 1975), p. 448.

detail the time, place, and nature of the proceedings, the legal authority under which the rule is proposed, and the terms or substance of the proposed rule. Interested parties must then be given an opportunity to *comment,* either personally or in writing.

The purpose of notice and comment rulemaking is to assure public access to the rule-making process. Agencies need not permit oral comment, but they must at least permit an opportunity for written comments by members of the public. A small number of statutes, such as the Magnuson-Moss Warranty Act, provide that the agency *must* permit oral comment.

Section 553 does not apply to all rule-making proceedings. By its terms, certain types of rules are excluded from the requirements of notice and comment, including rules governing management and personnel matters, and matters that are considered adjudicatory (discussed later). Interpretative rules (that is, rules which interpret statutes or other rules) must be published in the *Federal Register* but are not subject to notice and comment requirements. Various recommendations have been made that such interpretative rules and policy statements be made subject to the notice and comment requirements, however.

Due Process and the Rule-Making Function   Some rule-making procedures involve very substantial personal and individual rights unique to a very small number of individuals. At some point, the distinction between rule making and adjudication begins to blur, and the question arises whether the procedures required by Section 553 are sufficient to protect individual rights. If the case involves adjudication, Section 553 is not sufficient by itself, and the Due Process Clause comes into play.

In two early cases, which were reaffirmed in 1973, the Court explained the difference. A 1908 decision* required due process procedures for a landowner objecting to a *special* assessment on his property, while a 1915 case** held that no such procedures were required for a *general* increase in property tax assessments on all property. The 1973 decision† held that in the former case, a small number of persons "were exceptionally affected, in each case upon individual grounds," and therefore an adjudicatory hearing was required.

The following decision considers whether, even in a rule-making situation, the courts will require more procedural safeguards than mere notice and comment. The case is also important because of its statement of the concept of *judicial deference* to administrative determinations.

Vermont Yankee Nuclear Power Corp. v. Natural Resources Defense Council

435 U.S. 519, 98 S. Ct. 1197, 55 L. Ed. 2d 460 (1978)

The National Environmental Policy Act (NEPA, see Chapter 17) requires that agencies undertaking any major federal action must file an Environmental Impact Statement detailing the

---

Londoner v. *Denver,* 210 U.S. 373, 28 S. Ct. 708, 52 L. Ed. 1103 (1908).

**Bi-Metallic Investment Co.* v. *State Bd.,* 239 U.S. 441, 36 S. Ct. 141, 60 L. Ed. 372, (1915).

†*U.S.* v. *Florida East Coast Ry.,* 410 U.S. 224, 93 S. Ct. 810, 35 L. Ed. 2d 223 (1973).

environmental effect of that action. The Atomic Energy Commission (A.E.C.), later renamed the Nuclear Regulatory Commission (NRC), was required to file such Environmental Impact Statements when it licensed private nuclear power facilities.

The A.E.C. began rule-making proceedings to consider the nature of the Environmental Impact Statement, which it would file for *all* nuclear power facilities (a generic Environmental Impact Statement). A major issue in those proceedings was the nature of the impact of disposing of used nuclear fuel ("spent" fuel) after it was no longer useful for generating power. That nuclear waste was found to be highly toxic to human life, with a life of 250,000 years, and that there were presently no adequate methods of disposing of that waste. On the other hand, the A.E.C. believed that science would ultimately resolve the question of how to dispose of such wastes and that therefore "the environmental effects of the uranium fuel cycle have been shown to be relatively insignificant." Those findings were included in the Environmental Impact Statement, and the A.E.C. assigned an impact of "zero" to the spent fuel cycle. The generic Environmental Impact Statement was then adopted through informal (notice and comment) rule-making procedures.

The Natural Resources Defense Council, an environmental group, challenged the licensing of a nuclear power facility owned by Vermont Yankee Nuclear Power Corporation. In those licensing proceedings, which are adjudicatory in nature, the Defense Council tried to challenge the generic Enviromnental Impact Statement. The A.E.C. granted a license to Vermont Yankee and refused to permit the Defense Council to challenge the Environmental Impact Statement. The Defense Council argued that although the rule-making procedures had satisfied the requirements of Section 553 of the APA, because of the importance of the nuclear disposal problem, procedures should have been used in addition to mere notice and comment. The Defense Council appealed, and the U.S. Court of Appeals for the District of Columbia ruled that both the rule and the licensing proceeding should be reversed, since there was an insufficient factual foundation for the adoption of the generic Environmental Impact Statement. Vermont Yankee appealed to the Supreme Court.

Mr. Justice REHNQUIST delivered the opinion of the Court.

. . . .

In prior opinions we have intimated that even in a rulemaking proceeding when an agency is making a "quasi-judicial" determination by which a very small number of persons are "exceptionally affected, in each case upon individual grounds," in some circumstances additional procedures may be required in order to afford the aggrieved individuals due process. . . . It might also be true, although we do not think the issue is presented in this case . . . that a totally unjustified departure from settled agency procedures of long standing might require judicial correction.

But this much is absolutely clear. Absent constitutional constraints or extremely compelling circumstances, "the administrative agencies should be free to fashion their own rules of procedure and to pursue methods of inquiry capable of permitting them to discharge their multitudinous duties. . . ."

Respondent NRDC argues that section 553 of the Administrative Procedure Act merely establishes lower procedural bounds and that a court may routinely require more than the minimum when an agency's proposed rule addresses complex or technical factual issues or "issues of great public import." . . . We have, however, previously shown that our decisions reject this view.

There are compelling reasons for construing section 553 in this manner. In the first place, if courts continually review agency proceedings to determine whether the agency employed procedures which were, in the Court's opinion, perfectly tailored to reach what the court perceives to be the "best" or "correct" result, judicial review would be totally unpredictable. And the agencies, operating under this vague injunction to employ the "best" procedures and facing the threat of reversal if they did not, would undoubtedly adopt full adjudicatory procedures in every instance. Not only would this totally disrupt the statutory scheme . . . but all the inherent advantages of informal rule-making would be totally lost.

Secondly, it is obvious that the court in this case reviewed the agency's choice of procedures on the basis of the record actually produced at the hearing . . . and not on the basis of the information available to the agency when it made the decision to structure the proceedings in a certain way. This sort of Monday morning quarterbacking not only encourages but almost compels the agency to conduct all rulemaking proceedings with the full panoply of procedural devices normally associated only with adjudicatory hearings.

Finally, and perhaps most importantly, this sort of review fundamentally misconceives the nature of the standard for judicial review of an agency rule. . . . [I]nformal rulemaking need not be based solely on the transcript of a hearing held before an agency. Indeed, the agency need not even hold a formal hearing. . . .

In short, nothing in the APA . . . the circumstances of this case, the nature of the issues being considered, past agency practice, or the statutory mandate under which the Commission operates permitted the court to review and overturn the rule making proceeding on the basis of the procedural devices employed (or not employed) by the Commission so long as the Commission employed at least the statutory *minima,* a matter about which there is no doubt in this case. . . .

All this leads us to make one further observation of some relevance to this case. . . . The proposed plant underwent an incredibly extensive review. The reports filed and reviewed literally fill books. The proceedings took years. The actual hearings themselves over two weeks. To then nullify that effort seven years later because one report refers to other problems . . . borders on the Kafkaesque. Nuclear energy may some day be a cheap, safe source of power or it may not. But Congress has made a choice to at least try nuclear energy, establishing a reasonable review process in which courts are to play only a limited role. The fundamental policy questions appropriately resolved in Congress . . . are *not* subject to reexamination in the federal courts under the guise of judicial review of agency action. Time may prove wrong the decision to develop nuclear energy, but it is Congress or the States within their appropriate agencies which must eventually make that judgment. In the meantime courts should perform their appointed function. . . .

Reversed and remanded.*

As the last paragraph of the *Vermont Yankee* decision indicates, the courts are very hesitant to set aside rules made by administrators acting in the rule-making function, since those actions are generally within the discretion and prerogative of the administrator and the legislature delegating the authority. Under the APA, judicial review of agency determinations made in both the adjudicatory and the rule-making roles of agencies are considered together, and a discussion of all judicial review will take place after the adjudicatory function is discussed.

Administrative Adjudication

Many agencies have as a part of their functions the duty to adjudicate various types of claims in a manner quite analogous to the way in which courts adjudicate claims. For example, part of the function of the National Labor Relations Board is to adju-

---

*For further developments, students are referred to *Baltimore Gas and Electric Co.* v. *Nuclear Regulatory Commission,* p. 621.

dicate claims between employees and employers. Other agencies are required to adjudicate claims of citizens against the agencies themselves, such as citizens' claims for benefits under the Social Security Act, which are heard in the first instance by the Social Security Administration. Examples of adjudicatory hearings before administrative agencies are almost endless, including license applications of various sorts, appeals of tax and zoning decisions at the local level, disciplinary hearings in prisons, and even decisions regarding the expulsion or suspension of a child from school. All of those examples and many more require the administrator to act as a judge. The question then is whether the administrator, acting as a judge, must use the same kinds of procedures used in traditional courtrooms.

Due Process and the Adjudicatory Function

As noted in Chapter 3, the 5th and 14th Amendments provide that no person may be deprived of "life, liberty, or property, without due process of law." Obviously, many administrative procedures do involve potential deprivations of liberty and property. For example, an increase of a real estate tax assessment clearly "deprives" the owner of property by making the tax bill higher;* similarly, if a schoolchild is expelled from school, the Court has held that the child has been deprived of liberty and property rights in education.**

For decades due process rights had to be granted if a person was to be deprived of a *right* but not if the person was to be deprived of a *privilege*. For example, a driver's license was considered a privilege and, therfore, the state could, under the old interpretations, suspend or revoke that license without first giving that person a hearing, an opportunity to present the other side of the case, and notice of the proceedings. In the 1960's this old right-privilege doctrine came under substantial criticism and was finally laid to rest in *Goldberg* v. *Kelly,* the famous "welfare rights" case.

Goldberg v. Kelly

397 U.S. 254, 90 S. Ct. 1011, 25 L.Ed.2d 287 (1970)

Mr. Justice BRENNAN delivered the opinion of the Court.

The question for decision is whether a State that terminates public assistance payments to a particular recipient without affording him the opportunity for an evidentiary hearing prior to termination denies the recipient procedural due process in violation of the Due Process Clause of the Fourteenth Amendment.

This action was brought in the District Court . . . by residents of New York City receiving financial aid under the federally assisted program of Aid to Families with Dependent Children. . . . Their complaint alleged that the New York State and New York City officials administering these programs terminated, or were about to terminate, such aid without prior notice and hearing, thereby denying them due process of law. . . . [The District Court held that a notice prior to termination was required.]

Londoner v. *Denver.*

**Goss* v. *Lopez,* 419 U.S. 565, 95 S. Ct. 729, 42 L. Ed. 2d 725 (1975).

The constitutional issue to be decided, therefore, is the narrow one whether the Due Process Clause requires that the recipient be afforded an evidentiary hearing *before* the termination of benefits. The District Court held that only a pre-termination evidentiary hearing would satisfy the constitutional command, and rejected the argument of the state and city officials that the combination of the post-termination "fair hearing" [which was afforded the plaintiffs] with the informal pre-termination review [by the official in charge of the case] disposed of all due process claims. The court said: "While post-termination review is relevant, there is one overpowering fact which controls here. By hypothesis, a welfare recipient is destitute, without funds or assets. . . . Suffice it to say that to cut off a welfare recipient in the face of . . . 'brutal need' without a prior hearing of some sort is unconscionable, unless overwhelming considerations justify it." . . . The court rejected the argument that the need to protect the public's tax revenues supplied the requisite "overwhelming consideration." . . .

Appellant does not contend that procedural due process is not applicable to the termination of welfare benefits. Such benefits are a matter of statutory entitlement for persons qualified to receive them. Their termination involves state action that adjudicates important rights. The constitutional challenge cannot be answered by an argument that public assistance benefits are "a 'privilege' and not a 'right.'" . . .

It is true, of course, that some governmental benefits may be administratively terminated without affording the recipient a pre-termination evidentiary hearing. But we agree with the District Court that when welfare is discontinued, only a pre-termination evidentiary hearing provides the recipient with procedural due process. . . . Welfare recipients . . . must be given an opportunity to confront and cross-examination witnesses relied on by the department. . . . We do not say that counsel must be provided at the pre-termination hearing, but only that the recipient must be allowed to retain an attorney if he so desires. Counsel can help delineate the issues, present the factual contentions in an orderly manner, conduct cross-examination, and generally safeguard the interests of the recipient. . . . We agree with the District Court that prior involvement in some aspects of a case will not necessarily bar a welfare official from acting as a decision maker. He should not, however, have participated in making the determination under review.

Affirmed

The final rejection of the "wooden disinction" between rights and privileges in *Goldberg* and the cases that came after it does not answer all of the questions. According to a long line of cases following *Goldberg,* procedural due process rights must be accorded whenever a "protected interest" is involved, and such interests have been found in a large variety of situations, from school expulsions and suspensions to parole revocations to termination of welfare and social security benefits. The probable broadness of the rule caused one observer to wonder "whether the government can do anything to a citizen without affording him 'some kind of hearing.'"*

Following *Goldberg* v. *Kelly,* the Supreme Court seemed to back off from broad implications of that case on a case-by-case basis. The Court has not overruled the broad holding of *Goldberg,* but six years after that case was decided the Court ruled in *Mathews* v. *Eldridge* that a pretermination hearing was not required prior to terminating social security benefits, seemingly in direct contradiction of its previous holding in *Goldberg.*

---

*Henry J. Friendly, "Some Kind of Hearing," *University of Pennsylvania Law Review,* 123 (1975): 1267.

Mathews v. Eldridge

424 U.S. 319, 96 S. Ct. 893, 47 L.Ed.2d 18 (1976)

Eldridge, a recipient of worker disability benefits under the Social Security Act, was informed by the Social Security Administration that a determination had been made that his disability had ended and that his benefits would not be continued. The letter to Eldridge also advised him that he could request additional time to submit other relevant information. Eldridge responded by letter, disagreeing with the Administration's determination, but submitting no new information regarding his disability. The agency made a final determination and terminated Eldridge's benefits, but allowed him a hearing *after* the benefits were terminated. Instead of taking advantage of that post-termination hearing, Eldridge filed suit, claiming that the agency's procedures did not afford him due process. The Court of Appeals held for Eldridge, finding that the agency's procedures violated the 5th Amendment due process provision. The administrator of the Social Security Administration appealed the judgment.

Mr. Justice POWELL delivered the opinion of the Court.

The issue in this case is whether the Due Process Clause of the Fifth Amendment requires that prior to the termination of Social Security disability benefit payments the recipient be afforded an opportunity for an evidentiary hearing.

. . . .

Procedural due process imposes constraints on governmental decisions which deprive individuals of "liberty" or "property" within the meaning of the due Process Clause of the Fifth or Fourteenth Amendments. The Secretary [of HEW, the defendant in the case] does not contend that procedural due process is inapplicable to terminations of social security disability benefits. He recognizes, as has been implicit in our prior decisions . . . that the interest of an individual in continued receipt of these benefits is a statutorily created "property" interest protected by the Fifth Amendment. . . . Rather, the Secretary contends that the existing administrative procedures . . . provide all the process that is constitutionally due before a recipient can be deprived of that interest.

This Court consistently has held that some form of hearing is required before an individual is finally deprived of a property interest. . . . The "right to be heard before being condemned to suffer grievous loss of any kind, even though it may not involve the stigma and hardships of criminal conviction, is a principle basic to our society." . . . The fundamental requirement of due process is the opportunity to be heard "at a meaningful time and in a meaningful manner." . . . Eldridge argues that the review procedures available to a claimant before the initial determination of ineligibility becomes final would be adequate if disability benefits were not terminated until after the evidentiary hearing state of the administrative process. The dispute centers upon what process is due prior to the initial termination of benefits, pending review.

In recent years this Court increasingly has had occasion to consider the extent to which due process requires an evidentiary hearing prior to the deprivation of some type of property interest even if such a hearing is provided thereafter. . . .

. . . .

These decisions underscore the truism that "'[d]ue process, unlike some legal rules, is not a technical conception with a fixed content unrelated time, place and circumstances.'". . . . "[D]ue process is flexible and calls for such procedural protections as the particular situation demands." . . . Accordingly, resolution of the issue whether the administrative procedures provided here are constitutionally sufficient requires analysis of the governmental and private interests that are affected. . . . More precisely, our prior decisions indicate that identification of the specific dictates of due process generally requires consideration of three distinct factors: first, the private interest that will be affected by the official action; second, the risk of an erroneous deprivation of such interest through the procedures used, and the probable value, if any, of additional or substitute procedural safeguards; and finally, the government's interest, including the function involved and the fiscal and administrative burdens that the additional or substitute procedural requirement would entail. . . .

. . . .

Since a recipient whose benefits are terminated is awarded full retroactive relief if he ultimately prevails, his sole interest is in the uninterrupted receipt of this source of income pending final administrative decision on his claim. . . .

. . . .

The Secretary concedes that the delay between a request for a hearing before an Administrative Law Judge and a decision on the claim is currently between 10 and 11 months. Since a terminated recipient must first obtain a reconsideration decision as a prerequisite to invoking his right to an evidentiary hearing, the delay between the actual cut-off of benefits and final decision after a hearing exceeds one year.

In view of the torpidity of this administrative review process, . . . and the typically modest resources of the family unit of the physically disabled worker, the hardship imposed upon the erroneously terminated disability recipient may be significant. Still, the disabled worker's need is likely to be less than that of a welfare recipient. In addition to the possibility of access to private resources, other forms of government assistance will become available where the termination of disability benefits places a worker or his family below the subsistence level. . . .

. . . .

By contrast, the decision whether to discontinue disability benefits will turn, in most cases, upon "routine, standard, and unbiased medical reports by physician specialists,". . . . To be sure, credibility and veracity may be a factor in the ultimate disability assessment in some cases. But procedural due process rules are shaped by the risk of error inherent in the truth-finding process as applied to the generality of cases, not the rare exceptions. . . .

. . . .

In striking the appropriate due process balance the final factor to be assessed is the public interest. This includes the administrative burden and other societal costs that would be associated with requiring as, a matter of constitutional right, an evidentiary hearing upon demand in all cases prior to the termination of disability benefits. The most visible burden would be the incremental cost resulting from the increased number of hearings and the expense of providing benefits to ineligible recipients pending decision. No one can predict the extent of the increase, but the fact that full benefits would continue until after such hearings would assure the exhaustion in most cases of this attractive option. . . .

. . . .

But more is implicated in cases of this type than ad hoc weighing of fiscal and administrative burdens against the interests of a particular category of claimants. The ultimate balance involves a determination as to when, under our constitutional system, judicial-type procedures must be imposed upon administrative action to assure fairness. We reiterate the wise admonishment of Mr. Justice Frankfurter that differences in the origin and function of administrative agencies "preclude wholesale transplantation of the rules of procedure, trial and review which have evolved from the history and experience of the courts." . . . The judicial model of an evidentiary hearing is neither a required, nor even the most effective, method of decisionmaking in all circumstances. The essence of due process is the requirement that "a person in jeopardy of serious loss [be given] notice of the case against him and opportunity to meet it." . . . All that is necessary is that the procedures be tailored, in light of the decision to be made, to "the capacities and circumstances of those who are to be heard," . . . to insure that they are given a meaningful opportunity to present their case. In assessing what process is due in this case, substantial weight must be given to the good-faith judgments of the individuals charged by Congress with the administration of the social welfare system that the procedures they have provided assure fair consideration of the entitlement claims of individuals. . . . This is especially so where, as here, the prescribed procedures not only provide the claimant with an effective process for asserting his claim prior to any administrative action, but also assure a right to an evidentiary hearing, as well as to subsequent judicial review, before the denial of his claim becomes final. . . .

We conclude that an evidentiary hearing is not required prior to the termination of disability benefits and that the present administrative procedures fully comport with due process.

The judgment of the Court of Appeals is Reversed.

Mr. Justice BRENNAN, with whom Mr. Justice MARSHALL joins, dissenting:

I would add that the Court's consideration that a discontinuance of disability benefits may cause the recipient to suffer only a limited deprivation is no argument. It is speculative. Moreover, the very legislative determination to provide disability benefits, without any prerequisite determination of need in fact, presumes a need by the recipient which is not this Court's to denigrate. Indeed, in the present case, it is indicated that because disability benefits were terminated there was a foreclosure upon the Eldridge home and the family's furniture was repossessed, forcing Eldridge, his wife and children to sleep in one bed. . . . Finally, it is also no argument that a worker, who has been placed in the untenable position of having been denied disability benefits, may still seek other forms of public assistance.

The *Mathews* "balancing test" has been applied in a variety of situations in cases that followed. The precise nature of the due procedures required in each case depends on the balancing of the three factors mentioned in *Mathews:* (1) the nature of the interest involved; (2) the possibility of erroneous deprivation and whether additional procedures will relieve that possibility; and (3) the nature of the state interest in not providing such additional procedures.

A careful reading of *Goldberg, Mathews,* and the cases that came after them shows ten potential "ingredients" of due process. Which of the ten ingredients will be required depends on the outcome of a balancing test like that used in the *Mathews* decision.* Those potential ingredients of due process include

1. *Notice:* a timely and adequate statement, either oral or written, of the nature of the charges and the time and place of any hearing

2. *Right to confront witnesses:* the right to be present when witnesses contrary to one's position are giving evidence

3. *Oral arguments:* the right to state one's position to the decision maker

4. *Evidence:* the right to present evidence orally, as is done in courtrooms

5. *Cross-examination:* the right to use cross-examination techniques in questioning adverse witnesses

6. *Discovery:* the right to obtain disclosure of evidence by the agency or the adverse party prior to the hearing, if any

7. *Attorney:* the right to have an attorney present and, in some instances, to have an attorney appointed without charge

---

*See Paul Verkuil, "A Study of Informal Adjudicative Procedures," *University of Chicago Law Review,* 43 (1976): 739, 760.

8. *Record:* the right to have the proceedings recorded in some way and to have the decision on the record as well

9. *Decision:* the right to have a statement of the decision maker's reasons for the result and an indication of the evidence relied upon

10. *Decision maker:* the right to an impartial decision maker, rather than one with an obvious bias.

As a very general rule, the more important the interest being protected, the more of these due process "ingredients" that must be afforded. For example, if all that is in issue is a ten-day disciplinary suspension from school, due process only requires an informal conference with the decision maker and the right to present one's side of the case.* On the other hand, in the case of a revocation of parole or of time off for good behavior from a prison term,** a very formal hearing is required, affording all ten of the ingredients of due process in a proceeding that looks very much like a courtroom trial.

Administrative Adjudications Under the APA

The APA provides rather detailed rules for the conduct of adjudicatory hearings in Sections 554 through 559. These sections apply to "every case of adjudication" by agencies, with a few specific exceptions. Those exceptions include employee selection and tenure, military and foreign affairs functions, and the certification of worker representatives (unions) under the National Labor Relations Act. The act provides for many of the ingredients of due process, such as notice (Section 554(b)), oral presentation of arguments and evidence (Section 554(c)), representation by an attorney (Section 555(b)), discovery (Section 555(c) and other sections), and an impartial decision maker (Section 556(b)).

Administrative Law Judges   One of the inherent problems of administrative law is agency bias. There would appear to be a strong potential for conflicts of interest in many agency adjudications, since the prosecutor and the judge are both employees of the same agency. For example, in the *Goldberg* case, the agency was seeking to cut off welfare through the caseworker, and the proceedings were to be held by the caseworker's superior. The Court has held that such *potential* bias is not the same as *actual* bias, and that the courts should not presume bias exists unless it is actually shown that the decision maker is prejudiced.

In federal agencies, the problem of bias has been partially resolved through the appointment of **Administrative Law Judges** (ALJ's). ALJ's are always hired by an agency to act as hearing officers in adjudicatory hearings, but cannot be fired by the agency. The tenure and compensation of ALJs are governed by the Civil Service Act, thereby guaranteeing a fair amount of independence of decision.

---

*See *Goss* v. *Lopez,* 419 U.S. 565, 95 S. Ct. 729, 42 L. Ed. 2d 725 (1975).

***Morrissey* v. *Brewer,* 408 U.S. 471, 92 S. Ct. 2593, 33 L. Ed. 2d 484 (1972).

The Adjudicatory Process   The usual pattern of decision making in the federal system involves the assignment of a case to an ALJ. Prior to a hearing, the ALJ may conduct a prehearing conference, which serves many of the same purposes as pretrial conferences in the courts. A hearing is held later, at which the ALJ administers oaths, issues subpoenas, rules on evidence, and generally regulates the course of the hearing in a manner similar to a courtroom trial. The parties may submit written briefs to the ALJ, who takes the case under advisement for further study. Finally, the ALJ issues his "proposed report," or initial findings of law and fact. That document is then served on the parties and forwarded to the agency. Usually, the ALJ does not make the final decision; that privilege is reserved for the agency itself, but the record and the proposed report by the ALJ form the basis for that decision, and in the great majority of cases the agency will follow the proposed report of the ALJ.

The concept of **institutional decision,** that is, agency decisions based on the reports of ALJs, has strong critics and strong proponents. The critics call attention to the anonymity of the process, the potential for abuse and reliance on external facts, and the frustration of the parties in their inability to deal directly with the decision maker. The proponents rely on the probable correctness of "group" or "committee" decisions, the uniformity of decision, and the probable elimination of individual bias or eccentricity.

Judicial Review of Administrative Actions

One of the oldest controversies in administrative law involves the issue of whether the courts should be permitted to overrule and set aside agency rules or adjudications. On one side of the controversy are those who point to the possibility of agency abuse and arbitrary conduct and who would require that agency actions be subject to review by the courts. On the other side are those who say that the whole point of agencies is to give the responsibility for making a decision to experts in the area and, therefore, the courts are simply not competent to rule.

Some administrative determinations are simply excluded from judicial review by statute. The APA provides that Acts of Congress may simply state that there shall be no judicial review of the actions of an agency, and the courts are deprived of authority to consider acts of that agency. Such **preclusion of review** by statute is fairly rare and is viewed strictly by the courts, but it is totally possible and constitutional. Congress' authority to restrict judicial review is based on its authority to set the jurisdiction of the federal courts under Article III of the Constitution.

Most administrative decisions proceed through some kind of administrative review within the agency itself, from a regional or local board to a national board, or from a lower-level administrative officer to a higher level officer or board. But once the final authority of the agency has spoken, an aggrieved party usually has the right to appeal to the courts.

In the federal arena, this usually means an appeal directly from the agency to the U.S. Courts of Appeals (see Figure 4-1). In some instances, Congress has designated a specific U.S. Court of Appeals to hear cases from a particular agency, in many cases the U.S. Court of Appeals for the District of Columbia or the U.S. Court of Appeals for the Federal Circuit. In other cases, any U.S. Court of Appeals with proper venue may hear the case. The Courts of Appeals hear such cases in much the same manner as appeals from the lower federal courts, based on the record of proceedings before the administrative agency. This is known as a **record review.**

In a few isolated instances, parties have a right to present the evidence again before the courts, under the concept of **review de novo.** Normally, such cases are heard by trial courts rather than appellate courts, and the parties effectively retry the case before the trial courts. The decisions of the trial courts may in turn be appealed to the appellate courts in the usual fashion. Review *de novo* procedures are virtually nonexistent in the federal system and quite rare in state systems, which makes it important to present all of the evidence in effective fashion before the administrative agency, since that is the only opportunity to present evidence if record review procedures are used.

Judicial Review Under the APA

Section 706 of the APA specifies six circumstances in which agency adjudicatory decisions may be reviewed by the courts. Under that section, the courts have the authority to compel an agency to take a particular action, or to set aside a decision by an agency, if the court finds the agency decision to be

(A) arbitrary, capricious, an abuse of discretion, or otherwise not in accordance with law;

(B) contrary to constitutional right, power, privilege, or immunity;

(C) in excess of statutory jurisdiction, authority, or limitations, or short of statutory right;

(D) without observance of procedure required by law;

(E) unsupported by substantial evidence in a case . . . reviewed on the record of an agency hearing . . .; or

(F) unwarranted by the facts to the extent that the facts are subject to trial de novo by the reviewing court. . . .

In addition, the courts have found two other circumstances implied by the terms of Section 706, in which they have authority to review administrative decisions. Those circumstances are questions of law, and interpretation of constitutional, statutory, and administrative terms. While the APA has codified these eight circumstances of review, all eight were recognized by the common law of judicial review of agency actions long before the adoption of the APA.

Judicial Deference to Agency Decisions   As noted in the *Vermont Yankee* decision, above, "[f]undamental policy questions resolved in Congress . . . are *not* subject to reexamination in the federal courts under the guise of judicial review of agency action." This fundamental deference to both Congress and the agencies to which Congress delegates power means that the courts will generally prefer to permit agencies to act within their spheres without judicial interference. As a result, courts are quite reluctant to overturn agency decisions except in strict accordance with the eight reasons found in the APA. Part of this judicial deference is based on the concept of administrative expertise; that is, that the legislature has delegated authority to administrators because they are experts in the particular field, and judges, who are not experts in that field, should not interfere in administrative decisions based on such expertise. Second, judicial deference is also based in part on a separation of powers argument, similar to the idea that judges should not substitute their judgment for that of the legislature (see *New Orleans* v. *Dukes* in Chapter 2), in that judges should also not substitute their judgment for that of the duly authorized agency to whom the legislature has delegated power to make rules.

This judicial deference to agency authority stands behind many of the limitations on judicial review found in Section 706. Our discussion of those limitations on review will be restricted to agency abuse of discretion, under Section 706 (A), the substantial evidence test under Section 706 (E), and the problem of questions of law, which is implied by Section 706. This does not mean that other parts of Section 706 are not important but only that the law seems more fully developed in these areas.

Agency Abuse of Discretion: Section 706(A)   Section 706 (2)(A) of the APA provides that agency actions may be reviewed and set aside if they are "arbitrary, capricious, [or] an abuse of discretion. . . ." At common law, this standard was often expressed as "arbitrary, capricious, or unreasonable," a standard still used in many state courts. Generally, these standards mean that if an agency has been given the authority to act in an area, as long as the agency stays within the boundaries of the discretion granted by the legislature, the courts will not disturb the agency's actions. That is, unless the agency has "abused its discretion," the agency's actions will go untouched. The following decision established much of the current attitude toward matters of "agency discretion."

Citizens to Preserve Overton Park v. Volpe

401 U.S. 402, 91 S. Ct. 814, 28 L. Ed. 2d 136 (1971)

Federal funds were slated to be used to finance the construction of a six-lane interstate highway through a public park in Memphis, Tennessee. The Federal Aid Highway Act of 1968 and the Department of Transportation Act prohibited the Secretary of Transportation from authorizing the use of federal funds to finance construction of highways through public parks if a "feasible and prudent" alternative route exists. If no such route is available, the Secretary may approve construction through parks only if there has been "all possible planning to minimize harm" to the park. The petitioners, private citizens and local and national conservation groups, claimed the Secretary had violated these statutes. The District Court dismissed their claim, and the Court of Appeals affirmed. The petitioners claimed that it was possible to route the highway on either side of the park, or to tunnel under the park, though all of those alternatives were more expensive.

In order to show that the Secretary had not merely rubber-stamped the decision of the Memphis city council and lower administrative officers, the Secretary introduced affidavits in which he swore that he had exercised "independent judgment" and that his findings were supportable. The petitioners claimed that the Secretary should have maintained a record, so that the courts could determine whether he in fact had exercised such judgment and showing the basis of the decision. The District Court and the Court of Appeals held that such formal findings were unnecessary.

Opinion of the Court by Mr. Justice MARSHALL. . . .

We agree that formal findings were not required. But we do not believe that in this case judicial review based solely on litigation affidavits was adequate.

A threshhold question—whether petitioners are entitled to any judicial review—is easily answered. Section 701 of the [APA] . . . provides that the action of "each authority of the Government of the United States," which includes the Department of Transportation, is subject to judicial review except where there is a statutory prohibition on review or where "agency action is committed to agency discretion by law." In this case, there is no indication that Congress sought to prohibit judicial review and there is most certainly no "showing of 'clear and convincing evidence' of a . . . legislative intent" to restrict access to judicial review.

Similarly, the Secretary's decision here does not fall within the exception for action "committed to agency discretion." This is a very narrow exception. . . . The legislative history of the APA indicates that it is applicable in those rare instances where "statutes are drawn in such broad terms that in a given case there is no law to apply." . . .

Section 4(f) of the Department of Transportation Act and §138 of the Federal-Aid Highway Act are clear and specific directives. Both . . . provide that the Secretary "shall not approve any program or project" that requires the use of any public parkland "unless (1) there is no feasible and prudent alternative to the use of such land, and (2) such program includes all possible planning to minimize harm to such park. . . . This language is a plain and explicit bar to the use of federal funds for construction of highways through parks—only the most unusual situations are exempted.

Despite the clarity of the statutory language, respondents (the Secretary of Transportation and others) argue that the Secretary has wide discretion. The recognize that the requirement that there be no "feasible" alternative route admits of little administrative discretion. For this exemption to apply the Secretary must find that as a matter of sound engineering it would not be feasible to build the highway along any other route. Respondents argue, however, that the requirement that there be no other "prudent" route requires the Secretary to engage in a wide-ranging balancing of competing interests. They contend that the Secretary should weigh the detriment resulting from the destruction of parkland against the cost of other routes, safety considerations, and other factors, and determine on the basis of the importance he attaches to these other factors whether, on balance, alternative feasible routes would be "prudent."

But no such wide-ranging endeavor was intended. It is obvious that in most cases considerations of cost, directness of route, and community disruption will indicate that parkland should be used for highway construction whenever possible. Although it may be necessary to transfer funds from one jurisdiction to another, there will always be a smaller outlay required from the public purse when parkland is used since the public already owns the land and there will be no need to pay for right of way.

Congress clearly did not intend that cost and disruption of the community were to be ignored by the Secretary. But the very existence of the statutes indicates that protection of parkland was to be given paramount importance. The few green havens that are public parks were not to be lost unless there were truly unusual factors present in a particular case or the cost or community disruption resulting from alternative routes reached extraordinary magitudes. If the statutes are to have any meaning, the Secretary cannot approve the destruction of parkland unless he finds that alternative routes present unique problems.

. . . The lower courts based their review on the litigation affidavits that were presented. These affidavits were merely *"post hoc"* rationalizations, . . . which have traditionally been found to be an inadequate basis for review. And they clearly do not constitute the "whole record" compiled by the agency: the basis for review required by §706 of the [APA].

Thus it is necessary to remand this case to the District Court for plenary review of the Secretary's decision. That review is to be based on the full administrative record that was before the Secretary at the time he made his decision. But since the bare record may not disclose the factors that were considered or the Secretary's construction of the evidence, it may be necessary for the District Court to require some explanation in order to determine if the Secretary acted within the scope of his authority and if the Secretary's action was justifiable under the applicable standard.

The court may require the administrative officials who participated in the decision to give testimony explaining their action. Of course, such inquiry into the mental processes of administrative decisionmakers is usually to be avoided. . . . And, where there are administrative findings that were made at the same time as the decision, . . . there must be a strong showing of bad faith or improper behavior before such inquiry may be made. But here there are no such formal findings and it may be that the only way there can be effective judicial review is by examining the decisionmakers themselves.

. . . .

Reversed and remanded.

The *Overton Park* case is an unusual result, perhaps dictated by the lack of evidence on which the Court could base a decision that the agency was acting within the scope of its discretion. More often the courts defer to the judgment of the agency as long as the agency has been granted the power to act, as the *Vermont Yankee* case indicates. Generally speaking, more deference is paid to agency rule-making activity than agency adjudication activity, and more respect is given agency findings if they are based on technical expertise of some sort.

The Substantial Evidence Rule   In one sense, administrative agencies are much like juries in that they rule on questions of fact in both rule-making and adjudicatory proceedings. Just as judges are reluctant to go behind a jury's decision on the facts, judges are also quite reluctant to "second guess" an agency's determination of the facts. Section 706 (E) of the APA provides that in adjudicatory and in some rule-making hearings, the courts may set aside an agency finding if it is "unsupported by substantial evidence."

In a classic statement of the rule, Chief Justice Hughes defined substantial evidence as "more than a mere scintilla. It means such relevant evidence as a reasonable mind might accept as adequate to support a conclusion." If that amount of evidence appears on the record, then the courts may not set the agency's decision aside. If that amount of evidence is not present, the court may overturn the result. The courts must search through the entire record, however, and it is not enough that some evidence exists which, standing alone, justifies the result, if other evidence clearly controverts the evidence relied upon.

Questions of Law and Matters of Interpretation   While agencies may be especially competent in their areas of expertise, the courts are by definition expert in determining legal issues. The courts jealously guard their right to determine what the law is and interpret the various constitutional and statutory provisions, including the rules of the agency itself. But there is no clear cut line between law and fact in many instances. As the last paragraph of the *Vermont Yankee* decision implies, the courts are quite hesitant to upset agency determinations of fact or interfere with its discretion. The following decision illustrates the extent of judicial deference, even on questions that look legal on the surface.

NLRB v. Hearst Publications, Inc.

322 U.S. 111, 64 S. Ct. 851, 88 L. Ed. 1170 (1944)

The National Labor Relations Act required employers to bargain with unions representing collective groups of "employees." A union of newsboys desired to bargain under the Act, but the respondent Hearst refused on the grounds that newsboys were not "employees" but were "independent contractors." The NLRB determined that the newsboys were in fact employees, and ordered Hearst to bargain. The U.S. Court of Appeals set aside the NLRB order on the basis that common law standards for determining the meaning of the term *employee* should apply. The NLRB appealed.

Mr. Justice RUTLEDGE delivered the opinion of the Court.

. . . .

The principal question is whether the newsboys are "employees." Because Congress did not explicitly define the term, respondents say its meaning must be determined by reference to common-law standards. In their view, "common law standards" are those the courts have applied in distinguishing between "employees" and "independent contractors" when working out various problems unrelated to the Wagner Act's purposes and provisions.

The argument assumes that there is some simple, uniform and easily applicable test which the courts have used, in dealing with such problems, to determine whether persons doing work for others fall in one class or the other. Unfortunately this is not true. . . . Few problems in the law have given greater variety of application and conflict in results than the cases arising in the borderland between what is clearly an employer-employee relationship and what is clearly one of independent entrepreneurial dealing. . . .

Two possible consequences could follow. One would be to refer the decision of who are employees to local state law. The alternative would be to make it turn on a sort of pervading general essence distilled from state law. Congress obviously did not intend the former result. It would introduce variations into the statute's operation as wide as the differences the forty-eight states and other local jurisdictions make in applying the distinction for wholly different purposes. People who might be "employees" in one state would be "independent contractors" in another. . . . Persons working across state lines might fall in one class or the other, possibly both, depending on whether the Board and the courts would be required to give effect to the law of one state or of the adjoining one, or to that of each in relation to the portion of the work done within its borders.

Both the terms and the purposes of the statute, as well as the legislative history, show that Congress had in mind no such patchwork plan for securing freedom of employees' organization and of collective bargaining. The Wagner Act is federal legislation, administered by a national agency, intended to solve a national problem on a national scale. . . .

. . . .

It is not necessary in this case to make a completely definitive limitation around the term "employee." That task has been assigned primarily to the agency created by Congress to administer the Act. . . . Everyday experience in the administration of the statute gives it familiarity with the circumstances and backgrounds of employment relationships in various industries, with the abilities and needs of the workers for self organization and collective action, and with the adaptability of collective bargaining for the peaceful settlement of their disputes with their employers. The experience thus acquired must be brought frequently to bear on the question who is an employee under the Act. Resolving that question, like determining whether unfair labor practices have been committed, "belongs to the usual administrative routine" of the Board. . . .

. . . [i]n reviewing the Board's ultimate conclusions, it is not the court's function to substitute its own inferences of fact for the Board's, when the latter have support in the record. Undoubtedly questions of statutory interpretation, especially when arising in the first instance in judicial proceedings, are for the courts to resolve, giving appropriate weight to the judgment of those whose special duty is to administer the questioned statute. But where the question is one of specific application of a broad statutory term in a proceeding in which the agency administering the statute must determine it initially, the reviewing court's function is limited. . . . [t]he Board's determination that specified persons are ''employees'' under this Act is to be accepted if it has ''warrant in the record'' and a reasonable basis in law.

In this case the Board found that the designated newsboys work continuously and regularly, rely upon their earnings for the support of themselves and their families, and have their total wages influenced in large measure by the publishers who dictate their buying and selling prices, fix their markets and control their supply of papers. Their hours of work and their efforts on the job are supervised and to some extent prescribed by the publishers or their agents. Much of their sales equipment and advertising materials is furnished by the publishers with the intention that it is be used for the publisher's benefit. Stating that ''the primary consideration in the determination of the applicability of the statutory definition is whether effectuation of the declared policy and purposes of the Act comprehend securing to the individual the rights guaranteed and protection afforded by the Act,'' the Board concluded that the newsboys are employees. The record sustains the Board's findings and there is ample basis in the law for its conclusion. . . .

Reversed and remanded.

The Doctrine of Exhaustion of Remedies

One of the traditional doctrines of administrative law requires a party who is challenging a determination made by an agency to use all of the administrative remedies and procedures available to challenge the decision. The basis for the doctrine is a combination of judicial economy and respect for the decisions of other branches of government. As Chief Justice Burger noted

> Exhaustion of administrative remedies is simply one aspect of allocation of over-taxed judicial resources. . . . The exhaustion principle asks simply that absent compelling circumstances . . . the avenues of relief nearest and simplest should be pursued first.*

But judicial economy is not the only reason for the existence of the rule. The doctrine of separation of powers also dictates that the courts not interfere with administrative determinations, at least until after the administrative agency has finished with the matter. In a classic case, *Myers* v. *Bethlehem Shipbuilding Corp.*,** the National Labor Relations Board brought an action claiming unfair labor practices. The respondent company sued in federal district court to enjoin the proceedings, on the grounds that hearings before the Board would be futile and would result in irreparable damage to the corporation. The Supreme Court ruled that the corporation still must go through all of the administrative steps available before it attempted to obtain court review: "So to hold would, . . . in effect substitute the District Court for the

---

*C. J. Burger, dissenting, in *Moore* v. *East Cleveland,* 431 U.S. 494, 97 S. Ct. (1932), 52 L. Ed., 2d 531 (1977).

**303 U.S. 41, 58 S. Ct. 459, 83 L. Ed. 638 (1938).

Board as the tribunal to hear and determine what Congress declared the Board exclusively should hear and determine." The exhaustion doctrine is an ancient one, with its roots in the theory that an appellate court should only review final decisions. The doctrine is not inflexible, however, as the following case indicates.

McKart v. U.S.

395 U.S. 185, 89 S. Ct. 1657, 23 L. Ed. 2d 194 (1969)

McKart had been reclassified I-A by his local draft board during the Vietnam war, even though he was entitled to be classified IV-A (sole surviving son). He failed to appeal his classification within the Selective Service System and was drafted. He refused to appear for induction and was prosecuted criminally for his failure to appear. At trial McKart tried to raise the fact that he was entitled to a IV-A classification, and the government objected on the grounds that he had failed to exhaust his administrative remedies. The District Court agreed, refused to permit McKart to raise the defense, and McKart was convicted. McKart appealed.

Mr. Justice MARSHALL delivered the opinion of the Court.

. . . .

The doctrine of exhaustion of administrative remedies is well established in the jurisprudence of administrative law. . . . The doctrine provides "that no one is entitled to judicial relief for a supposed or threatened injury until the prescribed administrative remedy has been exhausted." *Myers* v. *Bethlehem Shipbuilding Corp.* The doctrine is applied in a number of different situations and is, like most judicial doctrines, subject to numerous exceptions. Application of the doctrine to specific cases requires an understanding of its purposes and of the particular administrative scheme involved.

Perhaps the most common application of the exhaustion doctrine is in cases where the relevant statute provides that certain administrative procedures shall be exclusive. See *Myers.* The reasons for making such procedures exclusive, and for the judicial application of the exhaustion doctrine in cases where the statutory requirement of exclusivity is not so explicit, are not difficult to understand. A primary purpose is, of course, the avoidance of premature interruption of the administrative process. The agency, like a trial court, is created for the purpose of applying a statute in the first instance. Accordingly it is normally desirable to let the agency develop the necessary factual background upon which decisions should be based. And since agency decisions are frequently of a discretionary nature or frequently require expertise, the agency should be given the first chance to exercise that discretion or to apply that expertise. And of course it is generally more efficient for the administrative process to go forward without interruption than it is to permit the parties to seek aid from the courts at various intermediate stages. The very same reasons lie behind judicial rules sharply limiting interlocutory appeals.

Closely related to the above reasons is a notion peculiar to administrative law. The administrative agency is created as a separate entity and invested with certain powers and duties. The courts ordinarily should not interfere with an agency until it has completed its action, or else has clearly exceed its jurisdiction. . . .

Some of these reasons apply equally to cases like the present one, where the administrative process is at an end and a party seeks judicial review of a decision that was not appealed through the administrative process. Particularly, judicial review may be hindered by the failure of the litigant to allow the agency to make a factual record, or to exercise its discretion or apply its expertise. In addition, other justifications for requiring exhaustion in cases of this sort have nothing to do with the dangers of interruption of the administrative process. Certain very practical notions of judicial efficiency come into play as well. A complaining party may be successful in vindicating his rights in the administrative process. If he is required to pursue his administrative remedies, the courts may never have to intervene. And notions of administrative autonomy require that the agency be given a chance to discover and correct its own errors. Finally, it is possible that frequent and deliberate flouting of administrative processes could weaken the effectiveness of an agency by encouraging people to ignore its procedures.

In Selective Service cases, the exhaustion doctrine must be tailored to fit the peculiarities of the administrative system Congress has created. . . .

. . . We are not here faced with a premature resort to the courts—all administrative remedies are now closed to petitioner. We are asked instead to hold that petitioner's failure to utilize a particular administrative process—an appeal—bars him from defending a criminal prosecution on grounds which could have been raised on that appeal. We cannot agree that application of the exhaustion doctrine would be proper in the circumstances of the present case.

First of all, it is well to remember that use of the exhaustion doctrine in criminal cases can be exceedingly harsh. The defendant is often stripped of his only defense; he must go to jail without having any judicial review of an assertedly invalid order. . . . Such a result should not be tolerated unless the interests underlying the exhaustion rule clearly outweigh the severe burden imposed upon the registrant if he is denied judicial review. . . .

The question of whether petitioner is entitled to exemption as a sole surviving son is . . . solely one of statutory interpretation. The resolution of that issue does not require any particular expertise on the part of the appeal board; the proper interpretation is certainly not a matter of discretion. . . . There is simply no overwhelming need for the court to have the agency finally resolve this question in the first instance. . . .

We are thus left with the Government's argument that failure to require exhaustion in the present case will induce registrants to bypass available administrative remedies. The Government fears an increase in litigation and a consequent danger of thwarting the primary function of the Selective Service System, the rapid mobilization of manpower. . . .

We do not, however, take such a dire view of the likely consequences of today's decision. At the outset, we doubt whether many registrants will be foolhardy enough to deny the Selective Service System the opportunity to correct its own errors by taking their chances with a criminal prosecution and a possibility of five years in jail. . . . And, today's holding does not apply to every registrant who fails to take advantage of the administrative remedies provided by the Selective Service System. For, as we have said, many classifications require exercise of discretion or application of expertise; in these cases, it may be proper to carry his case through the administrative process before he comes into court. . . . In short, we simply do not think that the exhaustion doctrine contributes significantly to the fairly low number of registrants who decide to subject themselves to criminal prosecution for failure to submit to induction. Accordingly, in the present case, where there appears no significant interest to be served in having the System decide the issue before it reaches the courts. . . .

. . . Accordingly, we reverse the judgment of the court below and remand the case for entry of a judgment of acquittal.

As *McKart* indicates, the exhaustion doctrine has been applied in a fairly flexible manner. Generally speaking, the doctrine is not applied in cases challenging the adequacy of the very administrative procedures that the doctrine would require to be exhausted, or where the administrative procedures or remedies are not available as a matter of right, or where, as in *McKart,* the application of the doctrine produces extremely harsh results. Civil rights actions are not subject to the doctrine, though the Court has never explained the exception except to say that the constitutional challenge in such cases is "sufficiently substantial" to justify not imposing the rule. On the other hand, other types of constitutional challenges are subject to the exhaustion doctrine.

Administrative Investigation

In order to fulfill their various quasi-legislative, adjudicatory, and administrative functions, agencies often are required to investigate factual matters. For rule-making purposes, for example, agencies must collect data in order to make informed judgments when enacting a new rule, or in deciding whether a rule is necessary. Likewise, in making decisions on licensing, competing claims of adverse parties, or determination of issues in enforcement actions, agencies need to obtain facts. Finally, and perhaps most controversially, agencies often act as "policemen" to determine whether violations of law have occurred and, therefore, need investigative powers in order to ferret out such violations.

Usually the power to investigate, together with many of the investigative tools, are given to an agency within the enabling act, though some of the powers are implied from the authority to enforce the law. One of the principal investigatory powers is the authority to issue subpoenas requiring an individual to appear before an agency or officer and, perhaps, requiring that certain documents be brought along.

Unlike subpoenas issued by a judge, administrative subpoenas are not **self-executing;** that is, failure to appear before the body in response to a subpoena does not automatically subject the violator to contempt proceedings. In order to enforce the subpoena, the document itself must be issued by a judge, or a judge must issue an order requiring the individual to appear. At that point, if the person still refuses to appear, the court may order him to show cause why he should not be held in contempt of court.

Subpoenas are not the only investigation techniques available to agencies, however. In some instances agency personnel are authorized to conduct searches, much like those by police officers, in order to find evidence of violation of administrative rules. Under such circumstances the issue arises whether the administrative officers must comply with 4th Amendment standards regarding searches and seizures, and whether they must obtain search warrants. The following landmark case dealt with searches to determine compliance with Occupational Safety and Health Administration (OSHA) standards.

Marshall v. Barlow's, Inc.

436 U.S. 307, 98 S. Ct. 1816, 56 L. Ed. 2d 305 (1978)

The Occupational Safety and Health Act empowered agents of the Secretary of Labor to search work areas of any employment facility to find safety hazards and violations of OSHA regulations. No search warrant is required for such inspections under the Act. The respondent refused to permit a search without a warrant, and the Secretary applied for a court order compelling Barlow's to admit the officers. Barlow's requested an injunction against warrantless searches. The district court ruled that a warrant was required and, therefore, the sections of OSHA which permitted searches without a warrant were unconstitutional. The Secretary appealed.

Mr. Justice WHITE delivered the opinion of the Court.

. . . .

The Secretary urges that warrantless inspections to enforce OSHA are reasonable within the meaning of the Fourth Amendment. . . . This Court has already held that warrantless searches are generally unreasonable, and that this rule applies to commercial premises as well as homes. In *Camara* v. *Municipal Court* . . . , we held: "[E]xcept in certain carefully defined classes of cases, a search of private property without proper consent is 'unreasonable' unless it has been authorized by a valid search warrant." . . . [W]e also ruled:". . . . The businessman, like the occupant of a residence, has a constitutional right to go about his business free from unreasonable official entries upon his private commercial property. The businessman, too, has that right placed in jeopardy if the decision to enter and inspect for violation of regulatory laws can be made and enforced by the inspector in the field without official authority evidenced by a warrant." . . . It therefore appears that unless some recognized exception to the warrant requirement applies, . . . a warrant [is required] to conduct the inspection sought in this case.

The Secretary urges that an exception from the search warrant requirement has been recognized for "pervasively regulated businesses," . . . and for "closely regulated" industries "long subject to close supervision and inspection." . . . These cases are indeed exceptions, but they represent responses to relatively unique circumstances. Certain industries have such a history of government oversight that no reasonable expectation of privacy . . . could exist for a proprietor over the stock of such an enterprise. Liquor . . . and firearms . . . are industries of this type; when an entrepreneur embarks upon such a business, he has voluntarily chosen to subject himself to a full arsenal of governmental regulation. . . .

The clear import of our cases is that the closely regulated industry [rule] is the exception. The Secretary would make it the rule. . . .

The Secretary submits that warrantless inspections are essential to the proper enforcement of OSHA because they afford the opportunity to inspect without prior notice and hence preserve the advantages of surprise. . . . To the suggestion that warrants may be issued *ex parte* and executed without delay and without prior notice, thereby preserving the element of surprise, the Secretary expresses concern for the administrative strain that would be experienced by the inspection system, and by the courts. . . .

We are unconvinced, however, that requiring warrants to inspect will impose serious burdens on the inspection system or the courts, will prevent inspections necessary to enforce the statute, or will make them less effective. . . .

Whether the Secretary proceeds to secure a warrant . . . his entitlement will not depend on his demonstrating probable cause to believe that conditions in violation of OSHA exist on the premises. Probable cause in the criminal sense is not required. For purposes of an administrative search such as this, probable cause justifying the issuance of a warrant may be based . . . on a showing that "reasonable legislative or administrative standards for conducting an . . . inspection are satisfied. . . .''

. . . .

We hold that Barlow was entitled to a declaratory judgment that the Act is unconstitutional insofar as it purports to authorize inspections without warrant. . . .

Mr. Justice STEVENS, with whom Mr. Justice BLACKMUN and Mr. Justice REHNQUIST join, dissenting. . . .

Because of the acknowledged importance and reasonableness of routine inspections in the enforcement of federal regulatory statutes such as OSHA, the Court recognizes that requiring full compliance with the Warrant Clause would invalidate all such inspection programs. Yet, rather than simply analyzing such programs under the "reasonableness" clause of the Fourth Amendment, the Court holds the OSHA program invalid under the Warrant Clause and then avoids a blanket prohibition on the all routine, regulatory inspections by relying on the notion that the "probable cause" requirement . . . may be relaxed whenever the Court believes that the governmental need to conduct a category of "searches" outweighs the intrusion on interests protected by the Fourth Amendment. . . .

Fidelity to the original understanding of the Fourth Amendment, therefore, leads to the conclusion that the Warrant Clause has no application to routine, regulatory inspections of commercial premises. . . .

Remedies Against Improper Administrative Acts

If a person is injured as a result of improper actions of an administrative agency, several forms of relief are available. **Injunctions** may be available to order an agency to stop acting, and **declaratory judgments** are sometimes used to declare the rights of the parties in relation to the agency. And, as discussed earlier in this chapter, agency actions may be appealed to the courts directly under most statutes within the concept of **judicial review** of agency actions.

Under some circumstances **civil lawsuits,** claiming money damages, may be filed against the agency itself, against the unit of government of which the agency is a part, or against the individual officer. The primary problem with lawsuits of this kind is the doctrine of **sovereign immunity,** an ancient theory that says simply that the government cannot be sued without its permission. The doctrine is derived from ancient common law and is based on the theory that the the king can do no wrong. Obviously, the doctrine caused some very unfair results and substantial sentiment arose to do away with the doctrine.

Finally, in 1946, Congress passed the Federal Tort Claims Act, which provided in part that "The United States shall be liable . . . relating to tort claims, in the same manner and to the same extent as a private individual under like circumstances." Initial interpretations of the statute were quite restrictive, but later cases seemed to apply the act liberally to most types of common law torts.

The Act contained several exceptions from this wide liability, however, and two of those exceptions are directly applicable to suits against administrative officers. The first exception provides that certain intentional torts, such as libel, slander, misrepresentation, deceit, and others cannot form the basis of a suit against the government. Many of the acts of administrative agencies are "intentional acts" and would therefore fall within this exception. A 1974 amendment reduced the impact of this exception substantially by withdrawing the exemption for suits based on assault, battery, false imprisonment, false arrest, abuse of process, and malicious prosecution by federal investigative or law enforcement officers.

The second exception deals with claims based on the "exercise or performance or the failure to exercise or perform a discretionary function or duty on the part of a federal agency or an employee of the Government." This exception seems to say that if Congress has given an agency the discretion to do an act, the agency may not be sued for performing or not performing the act. The discretionary duty exception extends to the acts of subordinates carrying out orders based on such discretionary matters.

While suit against the government or an agency may not be available, actions may be available against the individual officers who committed the wrong. Generally speaking, such suits may be based on common law principles of liability, various civil rights statutes, or the Constitution itself. Officers may also be cloaked in some form of immunity. Judges have "absolute immunity" from suit while acting in their judicial capacity even though their actions are malicious or undertaken in bad faith. Legislators are immune from suit for their votes and for various activities undertaken in their capacity as legislators, such as speeches before the legislature. Administrators are generally immune from suit if they are acting within their sphere of duties and the acts are performed in good faith and in a reasonable manner.

States have a double protection from civil lawsuits. The common law doctrine of sovereign immunity applies to state governments as well as to the federal government, and states are also protected by the 11th Amendment.* During the 1960's and 1970's many states enacted statutes similar to the Federal Tort Claims Act, with varying degrees of liability.

While sovereign immunity is generally criticized as antiquated and unnecessary, the rule is not without its supporters. The classic defense of the doctrine is found in the following oft-quoted language of Judge Learned Hand.

> It does indeed go without saying that an official, who is in fact guilty of using his powers to vent his spleen upon others, or for any other personal motive not connected with the public good, should not escape liability for the injuries he may so cause; and, if it were possible in practice to confine such complaints to the guilty, it would be monstrous to deny recovery. The justification for doing so is that it is impossible to know whether the claim is well founded until the case has been tried, and that to submit all officials, the innocent as well as the guilty, to the burden of a trial and to the inevitable danger of its outcome, would dampen the ardor of all but the most resolute, or the most irresponsible, in the unflinching discharge of their duties. . . . *Gregoire* v. *Biddle* (1949).**

Public Accessibility to the Administrative Process

During the 1960's and 1970's, a trend seemed to develop toward more citizen access to the administrative process and accountability of officers of agencies to the public they serve. Aspects of that trend include the Freedom of Information Act, the Privacy Act, "government in the sunshine" laws, and "sunset" legislation.

Federal Freedom of Information Act

One concern regarding administrative agencies is the amount and type of records that are kept secret from the public. In 1966, the APA was amended by adding Section 552, known as the Freedom of Information Act. Prior to this amendment, government was only required to release records to "persons properly and directly concerned" with the records, and records could be kept secret if it was "in the public

---

*"The Judicial power of the United States shall not be construed to extend to any suit in law or equity, commenced or prosecuted against any one of the United States by Citizens of another State, or by Citizens or Subjects of any Foreign State."

**177 F. 2d 579, 581 (2d. Cir.).

interest" to do so. The Freedom of Information Act changed that long-standing policy by requiring any agency to make available records requested by "any person." The agency has the burden of proof to show that the records fit within any of the nine exceptions to the Act, such as trade secrets, personnel and medical files, and matters dealing with national security and foreign policy. Requests for records may be directed to the agency, and the agency must respond within ten days. Federal court actions are available to force an agency to produce the records.

Federal Privacy Act

Another concern during the 1970's was the sheer amount of information which the government had collected or might collect in the future about individuals. That concern resulted in 1974 in the Federal Privacy Act, again an amendment to the APA in Section 552a. The Act gives citizens control over the information collected about them by requiring agencies to report the existence of all systems of records maintained on individuals. The Act further requires that the information be accurate, complete, and up-to-date, and provides procedures whereby individuals can inspect records and correct inaccuracies. Agencies cannot share information with other agencies, and must keep an accurate record of all disclosures of information made by the agency. There are exemptions for law enforcement and CIA files, and seven other categories of specific exemptions, including classified documents concerning national defense and foreign policy and government employment matters. Persons dissatisfied with agency action may appeal to higher authorities within the affected agency and may ultimately resort to federal court actions.

Sunshine Statutes

"Sunshine" legislation, also termed *open meeting laws,* has been adopted by the federal government and all fifty states. Such laws require that government meetings be held in public, but the degree of openness and the types of meetings subject to such laws varies considerably.

At the federal level, a 1976 amendment to the APA, found in Section 552b, provides for public meetings of advisory committees, study panels, and **ad hoc** committees within the executive branch, and to congressional committees in the legislative branch, though the principle was applied to Congress through resolutions passed by both Houses of Congress rather than through the APA. Section 552b applies only to multi-headed federal agencies, generally meaning independent regulatory commissions, and not to single-headed bodies. In addition, federal bodies may go into executive session, or closed session, simply by majority vote.

Sunset Legislation

A 1970's innovation in administrative law is so-called **sunset legislation,** which provides for automatic expiration of certain regulatory statutes and certain agency enabling acts. The purpose of such laws is to provide a required legislative review of the law creating an agency from time to time and an affirmative vote of the legislature if the agency is to continue in existence. Without automatic expiration, some agencies might continue to operate indefinitely, even though their purpose is fulfilled or they have ceased to be useful.

Summary and Conclusions

Much of American government policy is made by administrative agencies in their rule-making, adjudicatory, and investigative functions. Such agencies are initially created through a legislative act or executive order, caleld an *enabling act,* which delegates the authority to make rules to the agency. Substantial issues of separation of powers are inherent in the nature of such delegations, and many of those issues are yet unresolved.

The federal Administrative Procedure Act governs the procedures used by agencies at the federal level. That Act provides procedures for making rules, adjudicating claims, and contains the federal Freedom of Information Act, Privacy Act, and Open Meeting Act. In its adjudicatory capacity, an agency is also subject to constitutional restrictions under the Due Process Clauses.

Judicial review of agency decisions is available, but generally the courts defer to the judgment of the agency. The courts will review questions of law and will also review agency decisions if they constitute an abuse of discretion or are not based on substantial evidence, or if the actions are otherwise invalid under the Administrative Procedure Act. Courts will generally refuse to review actions if the party asking the review has failed to exhaust the available administrative remedies.

During the 1960's and 1970's concern with agency accountability and power produced several restrictions on agency authority, including the Freedom of Information, Privacy, and government in the sunshine acts. Similar concerns gave rise to the push towards deregulation of various industries during the same period.

PRO AND CON

ISSUE: Regulatory Reform: Is "Cost-Benefit" Analysis Useful in Assessing Administrative Agencies?

PRO: A Tool for Assessing Social Legislation
Peter H. Schuck*

My perspective on cost-benefit analysis is straight-forward and simple, reflecting my own experience in government. It begins with the premise that many of the public policy issues that regulators face are extremely complex, not technically but as matters of judgment. They are questions of alloca-

*Peter Schuck is a professor of law at Yale University. Excerpted from Timothy B. Clark, Marvin H. Kosters, and James C. Miller, III (Eds.), *Reforming Regulation* (Washington, D.C.: American Enterprise Institute for Public Policy Research, 1979), pp. 117–122. Originally presented as part of a symposium held May 21–22, 1979.

tion of scarce resources among competing social ends. In many respects they resemble what Guido T. Calabresi has referred to as "tragic choices" they require us to sacrifice some things to achieve others. Very rarely are the issues that a regulator confronts simply ones of health and safety, on the one hand, versus profits and dollars on the other. That kind of formulation ignores the fundamental characteristics of the regulatory process and of the most significant regulatory questions. I would like to discuss three of those fundamental characteristics.

The first is the overwhelming uncertainty that attends regulatory decisions. There are uncertainties regarding the causal relationships and the presumed benefits that underlie regulatory decisions. . . . The substantial uncertainties on both the benefit and cost sides are pertinent to the question of what tools the regulatory decision maker should employ.

A second characteristic of the regulatory process . . . is that the decision invariably involves trading off one good thing against another. For example, there is often a trade-off between the health of one group and the health of another. We are concerned not only about the health of people who live near the nuclear power plant at Three Mile Island but also about the health of the group that will mine the substitute for nuclear fuel, that is, coal, and about the health of people living near coal-fired plants who are subject to their pollutants. . . .

. . . It is important to contradict the notion that we are dealing with clear moral decisions in most of the trade-offs we confront. While they clearly do have moral elements, they are fundamentally choices between competing and often compelling moral claims.

A third element of regulatory decisions that pertains to the use of cost-benefit analysis is the tremendous disparity in the intensity of preference of the various people and groups who are affected by a regulation. For some interests, a particular regulation might literally be a matter of life and death—for example, workers employed in very dangerous industries. . . . Other interests, such as consumers benefitted by a product safety regulation, may not even be aware that the regulation exists. . . .

Each of these characteristics—uncertainty, the necessity of trade-offs, and the great disparity in intensity of preferences among affected groups—is exacerbated in the case of social regulation. Here I want to confront an argument that. . . . while cost benefit analysis may be important in economic . . . regulation, it is somehow inap-

propriate in the case of social regulation. I maintain that each of the three elements that I have discussed is, in fact, more troublesome in social regulation and that cost-benefit analysis is at least as justified in the one area as in the other.

The area of social regulation involves relatively great uncertainties because we so seldom possess reliable data on the health, safety and other effects of either the status quo or proposed regulations. . . .

Second, trade-offs are demonstrably more difficult in the area of social regulation because they involve objectives that society values so very highly—health, safety, and human life. The costs of social regulation are highly visible. . . . In comparison, the Interstate Commerce Commission's cartel regulation involves relatively mundane, though certainly important, social and economic values. . . .

Finally, the disparity of intensity of preference is considerably exacerbated in social regulation because of the number of people affected and the diversity of their interests. . . .

I draw several implications from all this. The first is that social regulators need all the help they can get in making these very difficult judgments, these tragic choices. Cost-benefit analysis, even recognizing all its very substantial imperfections, can provide that help. No knowledgeable defender of such analysis would argue that it should be anything more than a tool to inform choice. Anybody who suggests that it should be plugged in mechanically to generate a result that a decision maker must accept is either misinformed or a fool. . . .

The second major conclusion that I draw is implicit in all this. Cost-benefit analysis is at least as appropriate or necessary—indeed, I would argue more necessary—to social regulation as to economic regulation. We do not really need a cost-benefit analysis to tell us that when the ICC restricts entry, it is going to have adverse effects on consumers. We do need some kind of analysis where the decision involves the kinds of uncertainties, consequences, and ramifications in the complex social environment that are entailed in many health and safety regulations.

The third implication is that significant regulatory decisions are ineluctably political, in two important senses. First . . . they require numerous judgments about trade-offs. . . . Second, . . . intensity of preferences ought to receive recognition and weight in the decision-making process. . . . The political process is supposed to weigh those differential impacts and take them into account, . . . Cost benefit analysis, while it cannot make those judgments, can at least illuminate the choices.

. . . I believe that much of the criticism of cost-benefit analysis reflects a denial of the fundamental notion that what regulatory decision makers inevitably do is to make decisions that are ultimately political in the fullest sense of the term. Rather than transform that necessity into a virtue, these critics fall back on an illusionary view of the decision-making process as essentially technical. This enables them to sidestep the most serious need of our system—to require regulators to be made accountable for their decision. . . .

The real question is not whether cost-benefit analysis can be misused—any tool can be misused—but rather whether it will be used to its full potential. . . .

The second question regarding potential use is this: if the regulators are not to use this kind of analysis, or something very much like it, to pose the fundamental questions that they must answer, what criteria *should* they use? . . .

CON: Cost-Benefit Analysis Is a Mirage
Mark J. Green*

Murray Weidenbaum framed the issue best. He proposed that new regulations be limited to those things where total benefits to society exceed total costs. That is, the burden is on those who regulate to show by more than one dollar or one life that the benefits exceed the cost. As a phrase, cost-benefit analysis deserves kudos. It ranks with truth-in-lending and pro-life as an apparently irrefutable slogan. Yet in practice it reminds me of a mirage in the desert—in reality it can turn to sand. This is because there are fundamental conceptual and empirical problems with the use of cost-benefit analysis.

First, we must recognize that regulated businesses always oppose the agency regulating them and, to a large extent, control the available cost data. . . . The automobile industry [for example] is claiming that requiring 27.5 fuel miles as opposed to 26.9 will destroy Western civilization. A community that has a vested interest and a prejudice will always exaggerate the cost of regulation. . . .

Second, benefits obviously can be quite real, although they may not surrender to an economist's yardstick. . . . The Consumer Product Safety Commission estimated a substantial decrease in infant mortality because cribs no longer have the kind of bars that strangle children. It is hard to say how many or what the value of a baby's life is. . . .

The difficulty of valuation of benefits is particularly acute in social regulation. . . . We know there is a value to being able to see across the city or the Grand Canyon, although it is difficult to put a dollar sign on it. . . .

. . . .

As a final exercise, let us take cost-benefit analysis to its logical conclusion. Why not cost-benefit analysis of free speech, separation of church and state, protection of wildlife? In each of those instances, society has made a presumptive judgment that the policy is good. . . . We do not engage in a case-by-case analysis of such policies because basic values are at stake; we cannot prove with numbers the benefit of free speech or separation of church and state. I would argue similarly that there should be a presumption in favor of expert agencies appointed and confirmed by the president and Congress that, after hearing all evidence in due process hearings, arrive at judgment. This judgment, also, is surely subject to checks and oversight: first, there is the process producing the legislative bill; second, due process procedures before the agency; third, inevitable court appeals by unhappy businesses; and fourth, the legislative effort to overrule it.

This is not to be anti-intellectual. Obviously someone has to make the judgment and the trade-offs. The 55-miles-per-hour speed limit is not a perfect judgment. It could be 50 or 30 or 70. It is a trade-off of lives against convenience. That is done on the basis of the evidence brought before the regulatory agency and the judgment of the agency; it is not based on any formalistic, precise computation, which cannot now be made. Before regulators make a decision, they have before them the best estimate of a proposed rule's adverse consequences, if any, to the company and to the consumers generally, as well as the best estimate of its economic and noneconomic benefits. They do not have a precise, numerical cost-benefit calculation. . . . Cost-benefit analysis should be used not as a straitjacket but as a tool to aid regulation, subject to review by the political and judicial processes.

*Mark Green is director of Congress Watch. Excerpted from Timothy B. Clark, Marvin H. Kosters, and James C. Miller, III (Eds.) *Reforming Regulation* (Washington, D.C.: American Enterprise Institute for Public Policy Research, 1979), pp. 113–116. Originally presented as part of a symposium held May 21–22, 1979.

DISCUSSION QUESTIONS

1. Is there is real distinction between the "rules" of an administrative agency and the "laws" made by a legislature? Is the distinction merely semantic and, if so, isn't the whole theory of delegation of responsibility a legal fiction?

2. Is the Court's exclusive reliance on "the intent of the Framers" in the *Chada* case persuasive? Do you thing the Framers had any idea of the importance of administrative agencies in the 20th century?

3. Consider the *Chada, Vermont Yankee, Hearst Publications, Goldberg* and *Mathews* decisions in this chapter. Can you discern any trend in the treatment of administrative agencies by the Supreme Court, particularly in the extent of the deference paid to such agencies?

4. What is the significance of the *Schecter* and *Panama Refining* cases? Are they still "the law," even though, after five decades, no case has followed them?

5. Can you defend the statement that notice and comment rule making is "one of the most creative and important jurisprudential developments of the century?"

6. Should judges defer to the judgment of agencies in their rule-making functions? Always? Under what circumstances should such deference not be paid?

7. Most experts agree that *Matthews* v. *Eldridge* substantially limited *Goldberg* v. *Kelly.* Do you agree? If so, how did it limit the rule of *Goldberg?*

8. Which of the ten ingredients of administrative due process are most important? Which should *always* be accorded?

9. If you had an administrative case for an agency to adjudicate, would you prefer that the final decision be made by the Administrative Law Judge, or by the agency itself under the concept of institutional decision making? Why?

10. Compare the rationales of the *Overton Park* case and the *Vermont Yankee* decision. How do they differ? Which seems more correct? Why?

11. Should all administrative agency meetings be open to the public? Before you answer, recall that the Constitutional Convention of 1787 was held in secret and the reasons for that secrecy.

CASE PROBLEMS

1. A 1970 federal statute gave the President power to "issue such orders and regulations as he may deem appropriate to stabilize prices, rents, wages, and salaries at levels not less than those prevailing on May 25, 1970." The Act permitted the President to further delegate that responsibility to other officers or agencies as

"he may deem appropriate." Using that authority, President Nixon issued an order freezing all prices, rents, wages, and salaries for a period of 90 days. By executive order, the President created the Cost of Living Council, and delegated to that Council all authority to enforce the freeze order. Amalgamated Meat Cutters brought a declaratory judgment action, asking the courts to rule that the delegation by Congress was unconstitutional. Result? [*Amalgamated Meat Cutters* v. *Connally,* 337 F. Supp., 737, (D.C. Cir., 1971).]

2. Several high school students were suspended from school for periods of time exceeding ten days. None of the students was given a hearing prior to the suspension. (1) Have the students been deprived of any protected right (Hint: education is free, public, and mandatory)? (2) If so, what sort of due process "ingredients" apply to such cases? [*Goss* v. *Lopez,* 419 U.S. 565, 95 S. Ct. 729, 42 L. Ed. 2d 725 (1975).]

3. The Civil Aeronautics Board had authority to investigate and determine whether an air carrier was engaged in "unfair or deceptive practices or unfair methods of competition." Ralph Nader had a confirmed reservation on a scheduled flight, but when he arrived he was informed that he and several others had been "bumped" due to overbooking. Nader filed suit for damages on a theory of fraudulent misrepresentation, and a jury awarded him $25,000 in punitive damages. The airline appealed, on the basis that only the agency, and not the courts, have the right to hear the issue of whether the airline was fraudulent. Result? [*Nader* v. *Allegheny Airlines, Inc.* 426 U.S. 290, 96 S. Ct. 1978, 48 L. Ed. 2d 643 (1976).]

4. Agents of the FBI and a local police department burst into plaintiff Norton's home following an anonymous and erroneous tip that Patricia Hearst was hiding on the premises. There was no search warrant nor any consent, but the officers believed the entry was justified under the 4th Amendment. The plaintiff brought suit under the federal Tort Claims Act. Result? [*Norton* v. *United States,* 581, F. 2d 390 (4th Cir., 1978).]

5. James was a recipient of public assistance. A caseworker for the local department that provided the aid insisted on inspecting Ms. James' home to see if there was any change in her circumstances. Ms. James insisted that the agency obtain a search warrant. (1) Must the agency obtain a warrant? (2) May the agency terminate Ms. James public aid if she fails to permit entry without a warrant? [*Wyman* v. *James,* 400 U.S. 309, 91 S. Ct. 381, 27 L. Ed. 2d 408 (1971).]

6. The Internal Revenue Service issued a summons to Euge to give handwriting samples to IRS agents so that those agents could check his signature against those on bank accounts the agents believed Euge held under an assumed name. Euge refused, and the agency requested the court to order Euge to give the samples. Must he do so? [*U.S.* v. *Euge,* 444 U.S. 707, 100 S. Ct. 874, 63 L. Ed. 2d 141 (1980).]

7. Assume the Federal Trade Commission were considering a rule restricting the marketing practices of the buggy whip industry. Assume also that there is only

one producer of buggy whips in the United States, the Scroop Corporation. (1) Is this a rule-making or an adjudicatory function of the FTC? (2) Does the Scroop Corporation have the right to appear, present evidence either orally or in writing, and to cross-examine the witnesses before the Commission? If your answer is that it depends on the rule, what would you like know about the rule?

8. Does the U.S. Department of Agriculture have the right to prevent all citrus products from leaving California without holding a hearing because Mediterranean fruit flies have been seen in California?

9. Rivers wishes to become a real estate broker and, in the state in which Rivers lives, she must be licensed by the State Board of Real Estate. That Board turned Rivers down because of "moral turpitude," since she had been convicted of shoplifting twenty years ago. There is an appeal to the Secretary of State, but the Secretary of State need not hear such cases if he doesn't want to, and in the last twenty years the Secretary of State has never overruled the State Board. May Rivers file suit in court without first applying for an appeal?

10. Hastings served in the U.S. Army, and is now having a difficult time finding a job. He believes that something in his service record is discouraging employers, and he applies to see his full record under Freedom of Information Act. Under what circumstances, if any, may the government refuse to permit Hastings to see his record?

SUGGESTED READINGS

Barry, Donald D. and Howard R. Whitcomb. *The Legal Foundations of Public Administration* (St. Paul, Minn.: West Publishing Co., 1981).

Davis, Kenneth Culp. *Administrative Law and Government* 2nd ed. (St. Paul, Minn.: West Publishing Co., 1975).

Davis, Kenneth Culp. *Administrative Law Treatise* 2nd ed. (St. Paul, Minn.: West Publishing Co., 1978).

Friendly, Henry J. "Some Kind of Hearing," 123 *University of Pensylvania Law Review* (1975): 1267.

Gellhorn, Ernest, and Glen O. Robinson. "Perspectives on Administrative Law," 75 *Columbia Law Review* (1975): 771.

Mashaw, Jerry L. and Richard A. Merrill. *Introduction to the American Public Law System: Cases and Materials* (St. Paul, Minn.: West Publishing Co., 1975).

Verkuil, Paul R. "The Emerging Concept of Administrative Procedure," 78 *Columbia Law Review* (1978): 258.

The Common Law Foundations

Once the proper structures are erected within the law, allowing both flexibility and social control, it is necessary to "flesh out" this skeleton. Given the ethical norms of society, what matters are to be controlled, and in what manner? What should be legally right and what should be legally wrong?

The law reflects the society in which it developed. In the years when the Anglo-American system of law was being formed, certain basic values were almost universally held. Truth, honor and duty were critical values in a society ruled by the Church and by chivalry. The ownership of property came to have almost religious significance and received protection from the law against all claims, even those of individual liberty. With the development of trade, those same values found expression in the developing law of contracts and agency. It was not until individual rights revolted against property that the law of torts began to develop to protect individuals from harm and injury. In other words, as the basic values and ethics of society changed from property to trade to individual rights, the emphasis of the law also changed.

Similarly, the view of business also changed. In the Middle Ages, most trade was considered a sin or, at best, a necessary evil. Money lending at interest (usury) was punishable by the Church, as was reselling any product. This view was reflected in the law by the absence of any real statement about business organizations. But with the growth of trade came the growth of partnership law and, much later, the law of corporations. Again, the ethical framework of society created the legal framework.

Ethical judgments are implicit in much of the private common law. The law of contracts is built upon the assumption that each person should keep his or her promises, and the law of contracts is simply a way of insuring that those promises are kept. The law of torts is built upon the assumption that each person should be responsible for the harm that he or she causes, and tort law is a method of enforcing those values of responsiblity. The law of agency is similarly built upon the assumption that a servant, employee, or agent should be faithful, obedient, and diligent in serving his or her employer. From these ancient and venerable ethical values the modern law of contracts, torts, and business associations was formed.

The Common Law Heritage: Contracts, Torts, and Property

Reason is the life of the law; nay, the common law is nothing else but reason.

Sir Edward Coke

The Common Law. . . . has been laboriously built upon a mythical figure—the figure of "The Reasonable Man."

Sir A. P. Herbert

The Law, wherein, as in a magic mirror, we see reflected not only our own lives, but the lives of all men that have been! When I think on this majestic theme, my eyes dazzle.

Oliver Wendell Holmes, Jr.

Virtually all of American private law is based, either directly or indirectly, on the theories and decisions of the **common law.** Before the new American nation was formed, colonial American law was English law. With independence, it was natural enough for the law of England to form the basis of law in the fledgling states. To make that fact even more clear, many of the new state constitutions expressly adopted the common law of England as the law in those states.

Usually, the term *common law* is applied to the body of law that developed in England. More specifically, the term refers to that body of principles and rules of action derived from the customs and usages of "immemorial antiquity" or from the judgments of courts recognizing and enforcing those customs and usages. In other words, the ancient unwritten law of England is "the common law."

The Common Law and the Legal Environment

However the term *the legal environment of business* is defined, clearly the system of private law in which business operates is a major part of that environment. How contracts are made, what kind of private liability a businessperson may expect for wrongful acts, the nature of property rights, and other aspects of the common law are clearly a major component of the legal atmosphere in which a businessperson must work.

The purpose of this chapter and the one following is to introduce in very broad strokes the major features of the landscape of the common law. Our discussion is analogous to the pilot who banks a jetliner to permit the passengers a ten second view of the Grand Canyon. Students who wish to ride a burro to the bottom of the canyon will have to look elsewhere.

The Development of the Common Law

Ancient English law had several sources. In part, it was based on ancient Roman law, since England was first "civilized" by the Romans in 43 A.D. In part, English law developed from **canon law,** or the law of the Roman Catholic Church. In part, it developed from the customs of the primitive tribes that inhabited the British Isles. In part, it developed from the law of the Normans who invaded and conquered England in 1066 AD. And, in a large part, it developed from the common sense and logic of the ancient English kings and the judges they appointed to keep the peace during England's savage history.

Slowly over the centuries, the kings and judges saw the value of consistency in the law and began to develop the idea of **precedent,** or **stare decisis,** discussed at length in Chapters 1 and 4. Judges made an effort to decide similar cases by similar rules. After judges became literate, some decisions were written down to give judges the benefit of another's reasoning. In this way, the vast amounts of "law" found in the common law was created; law that in many instances is valid and binding today.

For example, the law relating to land ownership is almost entirely of common law origin. Much of the current law of property can be traced back to the earliest decisions of the English courts in the Middle Ages. And, in turn, those decisions rely on customs that developed centuries before those cases were decided. State legislatures may pass statutes that change common law rules, and modern judges may overrule ancient decisions, but that sort of action is relatively rare. A very large part of the contemporary law of property, contracts, torts, agency, bailments, and business associations can be traced directly back hundreds of years to the English courts of the Middle Ages.

The term *common law* has acquired other broader meanings as well. Sometimes the term is applied to all "judge-made" law, even the Supreme Court decision rendered last week. Less commonly, the term is also used to mean the decisions of **civil courts** awarding money damages, as opposed to the decisions of the **equity courts.**

And, sometimes the term is used to mean any civil proceeding, as opposed to criminal cases.

The Early English Courts   During the 1000's and 1100's, the English king and a group of noblemen and officials travelled throughout the country, deciding controversies according to the king's judgment and will. The group of people surrounding the king was known as the king's *court,* and it was probably inevitable that the name would be attached to the judicial process. As the kingdom grew, the king could no longer decide every controversy personally, so he appointed some of the nobles and officials to hear cases. At the same time, a separate set of courts had already grown within the Roman Catholic Church to handle controversies involving church rules, called **canon law.** Medieval history is full of conflicts between the church and the civil authorities regarding jurisdiction over various types of cases.

During the 1200's, the king stopped going into the countryside personally and instead established a system of centralized courts. Judges who represented the king travelled throughout the country and decided cases, but the king retained the right to review the decisions of the judges. The earliest of these courts was the Court of the Exchequer, which collected taxes for the king, followed by the Court of Common Pleas, which heard ordinary civil disputes. Important cases, which were still heard personally by the king, were later referred to the Court of King's Bench, called the Court of Queen's Bench when the monarch was a woman.

After the establishment of Parliament in the form of the House of Lords, that body became the highest court in England. Parliament is still technically known as the High Court of Parliament, and a committee of the House of Lords is really the supreme court of England. It was the law that slowly evolved in these courts, first by oral tradition and later preserved in written decisions, which formed the heart of the common law.

The Development of Equity   Common law rules were often applied so strictly that injustice resulted. The king had the right to review the acts of his judges, and often litigants asked the king to step in and promote fairness, or **equity.** Again, the king quickly became overburdened by these cases, and he delegated the responsibility to hear and determine such cases to one of his officials, the Chancellor. The Chancellor in turn appointed judges to hear those cases. As a result, the equity courts were often called **courts of chancery.**

The equity courts differed a great deal from the traditional law courts. First, equity courts did not permit trial by jury, since the decision was totally within the king's discretion. That rule is still generally followed in the United States. Second, the equity courts had no authority to order the payment of money damages, but only had the authority to prohibit unlawful acts through court orders. Those orders are called **injunctions,** and breach of an injunction will subject the violator to contempt of court proceedings. Injunctions may take one of several different forms: **mandatory injunctions,** which positively order a person to do an act; **specific performance,** which is an order to a person who has made a contract to fulfill it; and **reformation,** which is an order conforming a legal document to the true intent of the parties. Before requesting equitable relief, a party must show the court that he or she has "no adequate remedy at law;" that is, money damages will not totally cure the wrong in the complaint. Equity courts also traditionally pay much less attention to precedent than do the law courts. Equity courts tend to rely more on **equitable maxims,** such as "He who seeks equity must do equity."

In the United States, the historical division between the law courts and the equity courts has generally eroded, and most states now have a single court with the authority to grant both types of relief, often in the same action.

English Common Law Versus "Civil Law" Systems

English law, and by extension American law, stands apart from the legal systems of much of Europe. Most of continental Europe has adopted streamlined legal codes on which civil law is based, often directly traceable to the Justinian Code of the ancient Romans. France, Spain, Germany, and other countries have very detailed codes detailing the duties of contracts, property ownership, and other areas of the law. Judges are called upon to interpret specific statutes, but there is no hazy common law source of the law other than those statutes.

Given the British origins of the United States, it is no surprise that the bulk of American law is based on the English system. One state, Louisiana, bases its law on the French civil law system, specifically the Napoleonic Code in existence when Louisiana was sold to the United States in 1803. Other states with Spanish backgrounds, such as Florida, Texas, California, and much of the Southwest, have adopted some portions of the Spanish civil law system as well. For example, the idea of community property is an invention of the Spanish civil code, and those states with Spanish backgrounds have adopted that rule as a part of the law of property.

The Growth of the Law

The law does not stand still. Common law rules that were quite fitting in 12th century England are clearly out of place in 20th century California. Social, economic, technologic, and political change are often reflected in legal developments, both in specific rules and in sweeping emphasis. And sometimes the law takes a hand at leading such social, economic, and political change as well.

To the society of medieval England, no law was more important than that which defined property rights, particularly rights in land. Ownership of land determined one's social and economic position, one's political power, and even one's military rank to some extent. As one commentator put it,

> Real property meant more than land; the term applied to that cluster of privileges and rights which centered on land, or on the exercise of power which centered on land, or on the exercise of power which had a geographical focus. In medieval England, rights to real property meant jurisdiction as well as ownership. The lord of the manor was a little sovereign as well as an owner of houses, land, and growing crops. Only people with land or land rights really mattered: the gentry, the nobles, the upper clergy; land was the source of their wealth and the source and seat of their power. Well into modern times, power and wealth were concentrated in the hands of great landlords. The social system turned on rights in land.*

---

*Lawrence Friedman, *A History of American Law,* p. 202. Copyright © 1973 by Lawrence M. Friedman. Reprinted by permission of Simon and Schuster, Inc.

Early common law reflected this overriding importance and the relative unimportance of commercial trade, personal safety, and individual worth. Property law grew in infinite detail, specifying in meticulous particularity the rights of property owners, the methods of transfer of land, and every other aspect of land transactions and ownership. The rules of contracts developed almost as an afterthought, as an integral and necessary part of the transfer of land, and the law of torts developed only as it related to land, in the actions for trespass and nuisance.

But as commercial, nonland transactions grew in importance with the development of trade, contract law took on new importance. Merchants found that they were tied to the formalistic contract rules developed for use in relation to land transactions, and soon developed a whole new set of mercantile rules called the *Law Merchant.* These streamlined procedures were enforced in mercantile courts and justice was as fast "as dust can fall from the foot," in Lord Coke's terms. The rules were related to the common law contract rules developed in the property cases, but substantial modifications assured that commercial transactions would be properly accomodated. Slowly, over time, the rules of the Law Merchant were incorporated into the common law.

But still the rules of torts formed only a very small part of the common law, still closely tied to the rights of property owners, and later to the rights of merchants. Some major social and political upheavals were necessary before torts gained the prominence in civil courts that they have today. First came the Enlightenment, as characterized by the American and French Revolutions and the new concern with the rights (and safety) of individuals. And second came the Industrial Revolution and, with it, a collection of dangerous machines. Negligence and the other torts, which had been little more than a footnote in Blackstone's *Commentaries,* rose to overtake the law of property as the most utilized part of the civil law. The invention of the automobile gave tort law an even greater impetus, until today the vast majority of large civil cases filed are for negligence, while property cases are few and far between. And, aside from simple debt collection cases, contract actions are fairly rare as well.

The Americanization of the Common Law

It was simple to import the common law en masse into the new nation, but that common law had to be remolded to fit the unique requirements of the United States. It was not long before all states stripped the common law of all its references to titled nobility and much of the feudal influence. A prime example involved the rights of married women. At common law, a married woman had few, if any rights, as exemplified by an 1818 Connecticut case.

> The husband, by marriage, acquires a right to the use of the real estate of his wife, during her life; and if they have a child born alive, then, if he survives, during his life, as tenant by the curtesy. He acquires an absolute right to her chattels real, and may dispose of them.... He acquires an absolute property in her chattels personal in possession.... As to the property of the wife accruing during coverture, the same rule is applicable. *Griswold* v. *Penniman,* (1818).*

---

*2 Conn. 564.

But colonial law had quickly enlarged the rights of women, and married women's property acts were passed in many states, some as early as 1839,* that gave women, both married and single, much greater freedom in the use of their property.

Property law itself underwent a profound change as soon as it reached American shores. The feudal past and minute detail of the English property law had little place in the broad expanses of Texas or Montana, and soon the pedantic details of English property law lay dormant and forgotten.

Another crucial feature of the American common law experience was that in a sense each state was a separate legal laboratory. What had gone unchallenged for centuries in England's Inns of Court might quickly be challenged in frontier courtrooms in Illinois or South Carolina. And these challenges were not lost upon the other states, which incorporated the best of the rulings of other states in their own decisions. Instead of one common law of almost sacred heritage, there now appeared 50 common laws, changing, adapting and developing.

The Common Law of Property

The Idea of Ownership of Property

To most Americans, the concept of private property is virtually intuitive. It is difficult to imagine living in any society in which private property is not a fundamental concept. Yet, of course, in other politico-economic systems, especially socialism and communism, private property is not nearly so important or is considered contrary to the interests of society. Even some native American tribes found it incomprehensible that a man, a creature of temporary and uncertain tenure, could lay permanent claim to the eternal land. While the concept of private property is not an invention of the common law, the common law clarified and expanded the rights of ownership it received from earlier legal systems.

The term **property** is defined as an aggregate of legal rights that are guaranteed and protected by the government. It is said that the owner of property has a **bundle of rights** in some object or land or intangible thing, and that those rights will be protected by the law. When a government recognizes and enforces certain rights, the possessor becomes the owner and has title to the property.

Generally speaking, the rights of ownership include the right to control, possess, enjoy, and dispose of the property. Those rights may be further broken down to include the rights to use, to sell, to destroy (within limitations), to improve, to profit from, to remove objects from, to transfer by will, and to give away. But to be considered the owner of property not all of those rights need to exist at the same time. For example, the owner of property may not have the right to burn down his house because of criminal prohibitions against arson. Likewise the rights of ownership may be "separated out," as in the case of an owner-landlord who transfers the rights of possession to a tenant.

---

*That law, in Mississippi, dealt primarily with the rights of women to own and deal with slaves. Laws, Mississippi, 1839, ch. 46, as noted in Friedman, *A History of American Law*, ibid., p. 185–186.

The property rights of owners are not absolute. For centuries the courts have recognized that owners of land may not cause injury to the person or property of others, chiefly through the doctrine of **private nuisance** discussed in Chapter 17. Under that doctrine, a property owner may be liable in **tort** (discussed later in this chapter) for emitting too much smoke or gas or noise from his or her property.

One of the backbones of property law is that one who owns property has the right to keep others off that property. But even that right is limited, both by rights of contract and by public policy, as discussed in the following decision.

State v. Shack

58 N.J.297, 277 A. 2d 369 (1971)

A New Jersey statute provided that "[a]ny person who trespasses on any lands . . . after being forbidden so to trespass by the owner . . . is a disorderly person and shall be punished by a fine of not more than $50." The defendant Tejeras was a field worker for the Southwest Citizens Organization for Poverty Elimination (SCOPE), a nonprofit organization funded by the federal government for the purpose of providing for "health services of the migrant farm worker." Defendant Shack was a staff attorney for Camden Regional Legal Services (CRLS), also a nonprofit corporation funded by the federal government to provide legal advice to migrant workers. Tedesco was a farmer who employed migrant workers, and provided a camp for such workers on his property. Tejeras had entered upon Tedesco's property to find a migrant worker who needed medical aid for the removal of 28 sutures, but Tedesco had refused entry. Tejeras sought aid from Shack, and both Tejeras and Shack entered on Tedesco's land. Shack had also intended to go on Tedesco's land for another purpose, that of discussing a legal problem with another worker. Tedesco offered to find both workers and permit consultation in his office and in his presence. Tejeras and Shack insisted that they had the right to see the workers in their living quarters. Tedesco summoned a State Trooper, who refused to remove Tejeras and Shack except on Tedesco's written complaint. Tedesco filed that written complaint, and both Tejeras and Shack were convicted under the New Jersey statute. Tejeras and Shack appealed to the intermediate appellate court, where their convictions were affirmed. They then appealed to the New Jersey Supreme Court.

> The Opinion of the Court was delivered by WEINTRAUB, C.J. . . .
>
> Property rights serve human values. They are recognized to that end and are limited by it. Title to real property cannot include dominion of the destiny of persons the owner permits to come upon the premises. Their well-being must remain the paramount concern of a system of law. Indeed the needs of the occupants may be so imperative and their strength so weak, that the law will deny the occupants the power to contract away what is deemed essential to their health, welfare, or dignity.
>
> . . . .
> A man's right in his real property of course is not absolute. It was a maxim of the common law that one should so use his property as not to injure the rights of others. . . . Although hardly a precise solvent of actual controversies, the maxim does express the inevitable proposition that rights are relative and there must be an accomodation when they meet. Hence it has long been true that necessity, private or public, may justify entry upon the lands of another. . . .
> The subject is not static. As pointed out in 5 Powell, Real Property (Rohan, 1970) § 745, pp. 493–494, while society will protect the owner in his permissible interests in land, yet
>> such an owner must expect to find the absoluteness of his property rights curtailed by the organs of society, for the promotion of the best interests of others for whom these organs also operate as protective agencies. The necessity for

such curtailments is greater in a modern industrialized and urbanized society than it was in the relatively simple American society of fifty, 100, or 200 years ago. The current balance between individualism and dominance of the social interest depends not only upon political and social ideologies, but also upon the physical and social facts of the time and place under discussion.

Professor Powell added in §746, pp. 494–496:

As one looks back along the historic road traversed by the law of land in England and in America, one sees a change from the viewpoint that he who owns may do as he pleases with what he owns, to a position which hesitatingly embodies an ingredient of stewardship; which grudgingly, but steadily, broadens the recognized scope of social interests in the utilization of things.

To one seeing history through the glasses of religion, these changes may seem to evidence increasing embodiment of the golden rule. To one thinking in terms of political and economic ideologies, they are likely to be labeled evidences of "social enlightenment," or of "creeping socialism," or even of "communistic infiltration," according to the individual's assumed definitions and retained or acquired prejudices. With slight attention to words or labels, time marches on toward new adjustments between individuals and the social interests.

. . . .

Thus approaching the case, we find it unthinkable that the farmer-employer can assert a right to isolate the migrant worker in any respect significant for the worker's well-being. The farmer, of course, is entitled to pursue his farming activities without interference, and this defendants readily concede. But we see no legitimate need for a right in the farmer to deny the worker the opportunity for aid available from federal, State, or local services, or from recognized charitable groups seeking to assist him. Hence representatives of these agencies and organizations may enter upon the premises to seek out the worker at his own choice, so long as there is no behavior hurtful to others, and members of the press may not be denied reasonable access to workers who do not object to seeing them.

. . . .

It follows that defendants here invaded no possessory right of the farmer-employer. There conduct was therefore beyond the reach of the trespass statute. The judgments are accordingly reversed and the matters remanded . . . with directions to enter judgments of acquittal.

Types of Property

Property has two broad forms: real property and personal property. **Real property** includes land and everything permanently attached to the land. But the term also includes the airspace above the land and the minerals and other matter found under the land. The attachments to land, such as buildings and fences, are called **fixtures** and are part of the land if they are permanently attached to the property.

Personal property includes both tangible and intangible property. In general, the term means all property that is not real estate. It includes moveable and tangible things, such as a paper clip or a 30-ton crane, and intangible property, such as patents, stocks, and any legal **chose in action,** or legal right to sue.

The law of real property was highly developed by the common law, but the law relating to personal property grew in fits and starts since the beginning of commercial activity. Much of personal property law is governed by modern statutes, enacted in each state, including the Uniform Commercial Code (see Appendix C).

Estates in Land

The early common law categorized the different types of rights and interests in land and referred to such interests as **estates in land.** It was in this area that the common law was most specific and formalistic. Estates in land were in turn classified in many different forms, depending on the interests involved.

Possessory and Nonpossessory Estates   Estates in land may be classified by whether the owner of the estate has the present right to possess the land, or whether that right will only exist in the future. The ancient common law developed a large number of categories of both possessory and future interests to deal with the infinite variety of methods by which persons sought to own land. Possessory estates include, for example, **fee simple** estates, **fee simple determinable** estates, **life estates,** and others. The "greatest" estate in land is considered to be the fee simple estate, or simply the "fee," which encompasses all of the incidents and rights of ownership. At the other end of the spectrum is the life estate, which merely gives the owner the right to use the property during his lifetime. All such ownership interests are called **freehold estates.**

Estates of future possession, or **future interests,** are ownership interests without the right of present possession. For example, in a life estate, the deed may grant the property "to A for life, and then to B." While B has no present right to possess the land, she clearly has an ownership interest in the land. That interest will not become possessory until A's death, however, and is therefore a future interest.

In the Middle Ages and even later, those forms were used as a form of estate planning by landowners and as a method of determining how property would be held long after their deaths. Thus a succession of life estates, for example, might be used to dictate how property would be held for generations yet to come, as in a grant of property "to A for life, and then to A's eldest son for life, and then to A's eldest son's eldest son. . . ." The early common law saw little benefit to such restrictive grants and took action to prevent "the dead hand from the grave" ruling over the future disposition of property.

The common law forms of property ownership have generally survived reasonably intact in contemporary American law, but they are used only rarely. If a property owner wishes to be "creative" in disposing of his property today, it is much more likely that he will use a will and trust device of some sort, devices that are much more flexible than the common law forms of ownership.

Leasehold Estates   Nonownership interests in land are called **leasehold estates.** Such interests generally relate to some temporary possession of property, usually in exchange for a money payment called *rent.* The landlord, or **lessor,** transfers exclusive possession of the property to the tenant, or **lessee,** for some period of time. The common law, and in fact most contemporary doctrine, divides leasehold estates into catagories based on how that time is computed and how the estate may be terminated, such as estates from period to period, which are automatically renewed if neither party terminates, or estates at will, which may be terminated by either party at any time. Estates for a stated term lasted for a specific period of time, and estates by sufferance existed whenever a person lawfully in possession of property "holds over" after the lawful term of possession ends.

Leasehold estates were generally considered both a grant of an estate and a contract. The ancient common law was far more concerned with landlord's rights than those of the tenant, but the move in the United States since the late 19th century has been toward government protection of tenants' interests. Statutes were enacted that forced landlords to give a specific amount of notice before terminating a leasehold or evicting the tenant and, more recently, legislatures and courts have been concerned with the rights of tenants when a landlord fails to provide heat, light, or a decent living environment. Some cities have enacted "rent control" ordinances providing maximum rents for living quarters, and during World War II such rent controls were enforced by the federal government due to the high demand for living quarters in some locations.

Transfer of Property

Ownership of both real and personal property may be transferred in a variety of ways. Such transfer may be either voluntary or involuntary. Involuntary transfer includes condemnation by public authorities under the right of **eminent domain;** foreclosure of a debtor's interest for nonpayment of mortgages, real estate taxes, liens, or judgments; **adverse possession,** in which a private party takes possession of another's property and holds it openly, exclusively, notoriously, and continuously for a period of time set by statute; **escheat** of the land upon death without an heir or will; and finding of lost or mislaid property after satisfaction of procedures for locating the true owner.

Voluntary transfer of property encompasses much of private law, including the law of gifts, sales, contracts, wills, and trusts. Exchanges between living persons, called *inter vivos* transfers, include gifts, sales, contracts, and deeds. Most transfers of real property are made by **deed,** which is a written document that satisfies certain statutory requirements and is delivered by the **grantor,** or person giving the land, to the **grantee,** or recipient.

Transfers upon death are either through **testate** or **intestate succession.** Testate succession refers to a transfer through a will (a written document executed with certain statutory formalities), which disposes of property according to the wishes of the testator, or person making the will. Intestate succession refers to the state **law of descent and distribution,** which provides how property will be distributed in the event a person dies with no will. At common law, surviving spouses were protected by the rights of dower and curtesy, which provided that a surviving spouse would receive a one-third life estate in all real estate owned by the decedent at death. Many states have changed the dower and curtesy rules to provide a forced share of such property, usually a one-third fee-simple ownership interest in all property.

Concurrent Ownership of Property

Both real and personal property may be owned by two or more people at the same time. Again, such concurrent ownership takes several forms, depending on the relative rights of the parties. The two principal forms are **joint tenancy** and **tenancy in**

common, but there are other, more rare forms as well. A tenancy in common simply means that two or more people each own an undivided interest in a single piece of property. The interests may be different or proportional, as in a case where A owns 50 percent of the property, B owns 30 percent and C 20 percent. Upon the death of a party, that party's share is transferred to his heirs.

A joint tenancy is a special, privileged form of concurrent ownership in which, upon the death of one joint tenant, the succeeding joint tenants succeed to his interest. In order to form a joint tenancy, most states require that some very specific words be used in the deed making the conveyance, such as "to A and B in joint tenancy, with the right of survivorship, and not as tenants in common." Failure to use the proper magic words will create a tenancy in common by default. The common law and most states also require compliance with the **four unities** requirement as well; that is, the unities of *time* (all joint tenants must take title at the same time); *title* (all joint tenants must take title through the same document); *interest* (all interests must be identical, such as two joint tenants must each have one-half); and *possession* (all tenants must have an equal right to possess the property). In less than half the states, a special form of joint tenancy, known as a **tenancy by the entirety,** protects marriage partners from the revocation of the survivorship interest without consent. In an ordinary joint tenancy, either party may dispose of his or her interest at any time. But, in a tenancy by the entireties, if the parties are married, neither party may dispose of his or her interest without the consent of the other partner.

Other forms of concurrent ownership include **community property,** generally available in states with a Spanish civil law background, and **partnership property,** a unique form available in business partnerships under the Uniform Partnership Act, which is the law in many states. (See Chapter 7).

The Power of Eminent Domain   The power to take property for public purposes, known as the power of **eminent domain,** was so clear to the founders of the Constitution that it is not even found among the enumerated powers on the theory that it went without saying. What needed saying, however, was that this power could not be abused, and that limitation found its way into the Constitution in the 5th Amendment, which states in part, "nor shall private property be taken for public use without just compensation."

Generally speaking, the rule is that both states (individually or through their municipalities) and the federal government may take property for a *public purpose,* as long as "just compensation" is paid to the owner. This does not mean that the property must be used for a *public use,* however, as shown by the following decision.

Poletown Neighborhood Council v. City of Detroit

410 Mich. 616, 304 N.W. 2d. 455 (1981)

The Detroit Economic Development Corporation planned to acquire a large tract of land in Detroit, encompassing a neighborhood known as Poletown, and convey that property to General Motors as a site for a new assembly plant. The plaintiffs, a neighborhood association, and several individual residents of Poletown, brought suit to challenge the plan, on the grounds that the state's right to acquire property "for public use" under the Michigan statute did not include the right to take property from one private owner to convey to another private owner. The trial court held for the city, and the plaintiffs appealed. The Supreme Court of Michigan permitted the plaintiffs to by-pass the Court of Appeals and appeal directly to the Michigan Supreme Court because of the importance of the case.

PER CURIAM.

. . . .

Does the use of eminent domain in this case constitute a taking of private property for private use and, therefore, contravene [the Michigan Constitution]?

. . . .

We conclude that [this question] must be answered in the negative and affirm the trial court's decision.

This case raises a question of paramount importance to the future welfare of this state and its residents: Can a municipality use the power of eminent domain . . . to condemn property for transfer to a private corporation to build a plant to promote industry and commerce, thereby adding jobs and taxes to the economic base of the municipality and state?

Const. 1963, Art. 10, §2, states in pertinent part that "[p]rivate property shall not be taken for public use without just compensation therefore being first made or secured in a manner prescribed by law." Art. 10 §2 has been interpreted as requiring that the power of eminent domain not be invoked except to further a public use or purpose. Plaintiffs-appellants urge us to distinguish between the terms "use" and "purpose", asserting they are not synonymous and have been distinguished in the law of eminent domain. We are persuaded the terms have been used interchangeably in Michigan statutes and decisions in an effort to describe the protean concept of public benefit. The term "public use" has not received a narrow or inelastic definition by this Court in prior cases. Indeed, this Court has stated that " '[a] public use changes with changing conditions of society' " and that " '[t]he right of the public to receive and enjoy the benefit of the use determines whether the use is public or private.' "

. . . .

What plaintiffs-appellants . . . challenge is the constitutionality of using the power of eminent domain to condemn one person's property to convey it to another private person in order to bolster the economy. They argue that whatever incidental benefit may accrue to the public, assembling land to General Motors' specifications for conveyance to General Motors for its uncontrolled use in profit making is really a taking for private use and not a public use because General Motors is the primary beneficiary of the condemnation.

The defendants-appellees contend, on the other hand, that the controlling public purpose in taking this land is to create an industrial site which will be used to alleviate and prevent conditions of unemployment and fiscal distress. The fact that it will be conveyed to and ultimately used by a private manufacturer does not defeat this predominant public purpose.

There is no dispute about the law. All agree that condemnation for a public use or purpose is permitted. All agree that condemnation for a private use or purpose is forbidden. Similarly, condemnation for a private use cannot be authorized whatever its incidental public benefit and condemnation for a public purpose cannot be forbidden whatever its incidental private gain. The heart of this dispute is whether the proposed condemnation is for the primary benefit of the public or the private user.

The Legislature has determined that governmental action of the type contemplated here meets a public need and serves an essential public purpose.* The Court's

---

*Section 2 of the Economic Development Corporations Act of Michigan gave municipalities the right of eminent domain "to alleviate and prevent conditions of unemployment" and "to encourage the location and expansion of commercial enterprises."

role after such a determination is made is limited. "The determination of what constitutes a public purpose is primarily a legislative function, subject to review by the courts when abused, and the determination of the legislative body of that matter should not be reversed except in instances where such determination is palpably and manifestly arbitrary and incorrect."

. . .

The Legislature has delegated the authority to determine whether a particular project constitutes a public purpose to the governing body of the municipality involved. The plaintiffs concede that this project is the type contemplated by the Legislature and that the procedures set forth in the Economic Development Corporations Act have been followed. This further limits our review.

In the court below, the plaintiffs-appellants challenged the necessity for the taking of the land for the proposed project. In this regard the city presented substantial evidence of the severe economic conditions facing the residents of the city and state, the need for new industrial development to revitalize local industries, the economic boost the proposed project would provide, and the lack of other adequate available sites to implement the project.

As . . . stated over a hundred years ago, "the most important consideration in the case of eminent domain is the necessity of accomplishing some public good which is otherwise impracticable, and . . . the law does not so much regard the means as the need." . . .

When there is such public need, "[t]he abstract right [of an individual] to make use of his own property in his own way is compelled to yield to the general comfort and protection of community, and to a proper regard to relative rights in others." Eminent domain is an inherent power of the sovereign of the same nature as, albeit more severe than, the power to regulate the use of land through zoning or the prohibition of public nuisances.

In the instant case the benefit to be received by the municipality invoking the power of eminent domain is a clear and significant one and is sufficient to satisfy this Court that such a project was an intended and a legitimate object of the Legislature when it allowed municipalities to exercise condemnation powers even though a private party will also, ultimately, receive a benefit as an incident thereto.

. . . .

The decision of the trial court is affirmed.

While local, state, and federal governments have the power to take property for public purposes under eminent domain, the 5th Amendment requires that the owner be paid "just compensation" for that property. The value of the property is generally set at the fair market value of the property just prior to the taking. If a going business is taken, that value generally incudes the business' "goodwill" as well as the value of the real estate.

The power of eminent domain is generally considered a part of the state's "police power" as discussed in Chapter 2. That police power also includes the right to deal with property in a variety of other ways, such as *zoning regulations,* which regulate the manner in which property is used in certain areas, and *building codes,* which regulate the types of construction permitted. Similarly, the federal government has the right to regulate the use of property through the Commerce Clause as shown in Chapter 2.

The Common Law of Property and Some Recent Trends

The importation of English common law to the frontier United States caused a variety of changes in that law. Much of the feudal deadwood was quickly abolished in the American courts. New York, and later other states, enacted statutes that streamlined land law and simplified procedure. In the 20th century much of the emphasis in property law came through refining and establishing the rights of tenants and purchasers of property in relation to landlords and financial institutions.

A new source of government regulation of real property law has been created through sophisticated financing of real estate transactions. Government agencies and institutions that are government-related often impose requirements on financing that act as restrictions on property rights. For example, the Federal Housing Authority (FHA) guarantees mortgage loans, so that in the event an owner-borrower defaults and the property must be sold to pay off the mortgage, the FHA will guarantee that the lender will not lose money on the transaction. This, in turn, benefits the borrower by making it easier to obtain a mortgage in the first place. But the FHA refuses to guarantee mortgages unless the house meets certain property standards and the mortgage is in a certain form. Other federal agencies, such as the Veteran's Administration, the Federal Home Loan Bank Board (FHLBB), the Department of Housing and Urban Development, and several others, also specifically regulate property transactions that come under their jurisdiction.

The Law of Contracts

Accompanying the all-important development of the law of property in the common-law courts was the development of the law of contracts, that great body of law which provides the guidelines for every commercial and private transaction in the English-speaking world. Recent additions to the law of contracts, such as the Uniform Commercial Code and consumer protection statutes, have made minor changes in the effects of some of the doctrines of contract law but, for the most part, transactions in the 1980's are guided by the same doctrines that guided businesspeople in the 1600's and even earlier.

The Necessity of Agreement

First, in order to dispel a common misconception, a **contract** is not a piece of paper. When a person schooled in the law speaks of a contract, he is talking about the intangible *agreement* between the parties. The written document, which often but not always results, is merely *evidence* of the agreement. In point of fact, the vast majority of contracts are oral.

A contract is defined as a promise or set of promises that will be enforced by the courts. Many promises are made, but only a few very specific forms of promises will be enforced by the courts. For example, a promise to make a gift in the future will not be enforced by the courts except in very rare circumstances. But, in those rare circumstances, the enforceable promise is considered to be a contract.

The Elements of a Contract

Contracts generally have four elements: (1) *mutuality* between the parties; (2) *consideration;* (3) *legality of object;* and (4) *capacity of parties.* In addition, some commentators add a fifth element, *compliance with the Statute of Frauds and Perjuries.* Since that is really a negative element, it is best not included in the formal list of elements.

Mutuality The element of mutuality involves a true agreement between the parties to the agreement, sometimes called a *meeting of the minds.* That agreement is in turn created through an **offer** and the **acceptance** of that offer.

An offer is a proposal to make a contract put forth by one party, known as the **offeror.** The offer must be definite, contain all of the essential parts of the proposed contract, and be communicated to the *offeree.* Thus, "I will sell you my car for $400" may be a valid offer, if it is clear which car the offeror has in mind. The offer creates in the offeree the power of acceptance, that is, the right to create a contract by accepting the offer.

Once the offer is outstanding, that offer may be terminated in a variety of ways.

1. *Acceptance:* If the offeree accepts the offer, a contract is completed and the offer terminates.

2. *Rejection and Counteroffer:* If the offeree rejects the offer, the offer terminates. Thus, if the offeree changes his mind, he cannot go back and accept the offer once it has been rejected. Similarly, a counteroffer by the offeree is treated in the same manner as a rejection, and terminates the original offer.

3. *Revocation:* At any time before an offer is accepted, the offeror may change his mind and revoke the offer. The revocation must be actually communicated to the offeree, however.

4. *Lapse of Time:* If the offer contains an express termination date, such as "This offer shall remain in effect until November 24th at 12 noon," the offer will terminate at that time, and cannot be accepted later. If the offer contains no specific termination date, the offer will remain outstanding for a "reasonable time," as determined by the facts and circumstances in each case. Some offers may be terminated in this manner in a matter of hours or even minutes, while others may continue to be outstanding for several months.

5. *Intervening Illegality:* If, while the offer is outstanding, the subject or purpose of the contract becomes illegal, the offer is terminated and cannot be accepted.

6. *Death or Incapacity of a Party:* If, while the offer is outstanding, one of the parties dies or becomes incapable of making a contract, the offer terminates.

7. *Destruction of the Subject Matter:* If, while the offer is outstanding, the property that is the subject of the contract is destroyed, no contract can result, and the offer terminates. Thus, if A offers to purchase B's house and, while B is considering the offer, B's house burns down, B cannot quickly accept the offer and create a contract.

The acceptance is some acknowledgment that the offeree accepts the offer. It must not vary the terms of the original offer in any significant aspect, and it must be communicated to the offeror. Communication to the offeror may take the form of actual communication with the offeror, or the acceptance may be deposited in any authorized means of communication, and becomes effective from the time it is deposited. The following case discusses the nature of an acceptance of a reward offer made to the public.

Glover v. Jewish War Veterans of U.S.

Municipal Court of Appeals, District of Columbia 68 A. 2d 233 (1949)

CLAGETT, Associate Judge. The issue determinative of this appeal is whether a person giving information leading to the arrest of a murderer without any knowledge that a reward has been offered for such information by a non-governmental organization is entitled to collect the reward. The trial court decided the question in the negative and instructed the jury to return a verdict for defendant. Claimant appeals from the judgment on such instructed verdict.

The controversy grows out of the murder on June 5, 1946, of Maurice L. Bernstein, a local pharmacist. The following day, June 6, Post No. 58, Jewish War Veterans of the United States, communicated to the newspapers an offer of a reward of $500 "to the person or persons furnishing information resulting in the apprehension and conviction of the persons guilty of the murder of Maurice L. Bernstein." Notice of the reward was published in the newspaper June 7. A day or so later Jesse James Patton, one of the men suspected of the crime, was arrested and the police received information that the other murderer was Reginald Wheeler and that Wheeler was the "boy friend" of a daughter of Mary Glover, plaintiff and claimant in the present case. On the evening of June 11 the police visited Mary Glover, who in answer to questions informed them that her daughter and Wheeler had left the city on June 5. She told the officers she didn't know exactly where the couple had gone, whereupon the officers asked for names of relatives whom the daughter might be visiting. In response to such questions she gave the names and addresses of several relatives, including one at Ridge Spring, South Carolina, which was the first place visited by the officers and where Wheeler was arrested . . . on June 13. Wheeler and Patton were subsequently convicted of the crime.

Claimant's most significant testimony, in the view that we take of this case, was that she first learned that a reward had been offered on June 12, the day after she had given the police officers the information which enabled them to find Wheeler. . . . We have concluded that the trial court correctly instructed the jury to return a verdict for defendant. . . .

Since it is clear that the question is one of contract law, it follows that, at least so far as private rewards are concerned, there can be no contract unless the claimant when giving the desired information knew of the offer of the reward and acted with the intention of accepting such offer; otherwise the claimant gives the information not in the expectation of receiving a reward but rather out a sense of public duty or other motive unconnected with the reward. "In the nature of the case," according to Professor Williston, "it is impossible for an offeree actually to assent to an offer unless he knows of its existence."

The American Law Institute in its Restatement of the Law of Contracts follows the same rule, thus: "It is impossible that there should be an acceptance unless the offeree knows of the existence of the offer." The Restatement gives the following illustration of the rule just stated: "A offers a reward for information leading to the arrest and conviction of a criminal. B, in ignorance of the offer, gives information leading to his arrest and later, with knowledge of the offer and intent to accept it, gives other information necessary for the conviction. There is no contract."

. . . .
Affirmed.

Consideration   Consideration is the element that sets enforceable contracts apart from unenforceable promises to make a gift. Consideration is the *quid pro quo,* or matters exchanged, within a contract. It is the doing of something for which there is no prior legal duty to do.

For example, in a classic case an uncle promised his nephew that he would give him $5,000 if he would refrain from smoking, drinking, and gambling until his twenty-first birthday. The nephew did so, but in the intervening time the uncle died and the executor of the uncle's estate refused to pay, on the grounds that there was no consideration for the uncle's promise. The court held that while the nephew had a prior legal duty not to drink or gamble, since both were illegal for minors in that state, the minor had a right to smoke. Since he refrained from doing something that he had a legal right to do, there was a valid consideration and therefore a valid contract.★

The courts will generally not inquire into the adequacy of consideration, but only inquire into its existence. Thus, a contract in which A sells his new car to B for $50 is a valid contract, since consideration exists, and the courts refuse to remake bargains for the parties. Consideration may run to some third party other than the contracting party as well. For example, A may promise B $1,000 if B gives his car to C. There is consideration to both A and B in the example.

In fairly rare instances, the courts will enforce promises in which no consideration exists. The usual circumstance is called **promissory estoppel** in which one party makes a promise and, in reliance on that promise, another party changes his position in some way. Thus, if A promises to give $10,000 to his church building fund and, in reliance on that promise, the church makes a contract to build an addition to the church and obligates itself for various goods and services, A might be forced to make that contribution under the doctrine of promissory estoppel; he will be *estopped to deny the promise.* Promissory estoppel is not used often by the courts, however.

Legality of Object   It seems obvious to say that the object and purpose of contracts must be legal. That is, neither the purpose nor the performance of a contract may involve the commission of a crime or a tort or be contrary to public policy. Common examples involve gambling contracts, which are illegal in most states, and contracts in restraint of trade, which violate public policy.

Capacity of Parties   The parties to an agreement must be legally competent to enter into a binding agreement. Problem areas involve the contracts of minors, insane persons, or persons under the influence of drugs or alcohol. Generally speaking, such contracts are *voidable* at the option of the incompetent party, or his legal representative. The following decision considers both the problems of illegality and competence.

★*Hamer v. Sidway,* 124 N.Y. 538, 27 N.E. 256 (1891).

McGinley v. Cleary

2 Alaska 269 (United States District Court for the Territory of Alaska 1904)

WICHERSHAM, District Judge.

On the 29th of last November the plaintiff was, and for some time previous thereto had been, one of the proprietors of that certain two-story log cabin described in the pleadings as the "Fairbanks Hotel,". . . The opening scene discovers him drunk, but engaged on his regular night shift as barkeeper in dispensing whisky by leave of this court on a territorial license to those of his customers who had not been able, through undesire or the benumbing influence of the liquor, to retire to their cabins. The defendant was his present customer. After a social evening session, the evidence is that at about 3 o'clock in the morning of the 30th they were mutually enjoying the hardships of Alaska by pouring into their respective interiors unnumbered four-bit drinks, recklessly expending undug pokes, and blowing in the next spring cleanup. While thus employed, between sticking tabs on the nail and catching their breath for the next glass, they began to tempt the fickle goddess of fortune by shaking plaintiff's dicebox. The defendant testifies that he had a $5 bill, that he laid it on the bar, and that it constituted the visible means of support to the game and transfer of property which followed. That defendant had a $5 bill so late in the evening may excite remark among his acquaintances.

Whether plaintiff and defendant then formed a mental design to gamble around the storm center of this bill is one of the matters in dispute in this case about which they do not agree. The proprietor is plaintively positive on his part that at that moment his brains were so benumbed by the fumes or the force of his own whisky that he was actually non compos mentis; . . . . His customer, on the other hand, stoutly swears that the vigor and strength of his constitution enabled him to retain his memory, and he informed the court from the witness stand that while both were gazing at the bill, the proprietor produced his near-by dicebox, and they began to shake for its temporary ownership. . . .

They were not alone. Tupper Thompson slept bibulously behind the oil tank stove. Whether his mental receiver was likewise so hardened by inebriation as to be incapable of catching impressions will never be certainly known to the court. He testified to a lingering remembrance of drinks which he enjoyed at this time upon the invitation of someone, and is authority for the statement that when he came to the proprietor was so drunk that he hung limply and vine-like to the bar, though he played dice with the defendant, and later signed a bill of sale of the premises in dispute, which Tupper witnessed. Tupper also testified that the defendant was drunk, but according to his standard of intoxication he was not so entirely paralyzed as the proprietor, since he could stand without holding to the bar. . . .

After the dice-shaking had ceased, and the finger-tip bookkeeping had been reduced to round numbers, the defendant testifies that the plaintiff was found to be indebted to him in the sum of $1,800. Whether these dice, which belonged to the bar and seem to have been in frequent use by the proprietor, were in the habit of playing such pranks on the house may well be doubted; nor is it shown that they, too, were loaded. . . .

The plaintiff testifies that during all this time, and until the final act of signing the deed in controversy, he was drunk, and suffering from a total loss of memory and intelligence. The evidence in support of intelligence is vague and unsatisfactory. . . .

The question of consideration is deemed to be an important one in this case. Defendant asserts that it consisted of the $1,800 won at the proprietor's own game of dice, but Tupper Thompson relapses into sobriety long enough to declare that the real consideration promised on the part of the defendant was to give a half interest in his Cleary Creek placer mines for the half interest in the saloon; that defendant said the plaintiff could go out and run the mines while he remained in the saloon and sold hootch to the sour-doughs, or words to that effect. Tupper's evidence lacks some of the earmarks; it is quite evident that he had a rock in his sluice box. . . .

The evidence discloses that about 3 or 4 o'clock p.m. on the evening of the 30th the defendant went to the apartment of the proprietor, and renewed his demand for payment or a transfer of the property in consideration of the gambling debt. After a meal and a shave they . . . appeared, about 5 o'clock, before the commissioner; . . . The bill of sale written by Cleary was presented to the proprietor, who refused to acknowledge it before the commissioner. The commissioner was then requested by Cleary to draw another document to carry out the purpose of their visit there. The reason given for refusing to acknowlege the document . . . was that it conveyed a half interest, whereas the plaintiff refused then to convey more than a quarter interest. The commissioner wrote the document now contained in the record, the plaintiff signed it; it was witnessed, acknowledged, filed for record and recorded in the book of deeds, according to law.

. . . Plaintiff soon after brought this suit to set aside the conveyance upon the ground of fraud (1) because he was so drunk at the time he signed the deed as to be unable to comprehend the nature of the contract, and (2) for want of consideration.

It is currently believed that the Lord cares for and protects idiots and drunken men. A court of equity is supposed to have equal and concurrent jurisdiction, and this case seems to be brought under both branches. . . .

Was McGinley so drunk when he signed the deed in controversy that he was not in his right mind, or capable of transacting any business, or entering into any contract? . . . Who shall guide the court in determining how drunk he was at 3 o'clock in the morning, when the transaction opened? Tupper or the defendant? How much credence must the court give to the testimony of one drunken man who testifies that another was also drunk? . . .

Probably the most satisfactory determination of the matter may be made by coming at once to that point where the deed in question was prepared, signed, and acknowledged. Did the plaintiff exhibit intelligence at that time? He refused to acknowledge a deed which conveyed a half interest, and caused his creditor to procure one . . . which conveyed only a quarter interest; he protected his property to that extent. . . . Upon procuring the paper to read as he desired, he signed it in a public office, before several persons, and acknowledged it to be his act and deed.

. . . .

The evidence in this case raises the single question, will a court of equity set aside a deed made by a keeper of a saloon in payment of a gambling debt contracted by him to one of his customers when no other fraud is shown. By the common law no right of action exists to recover back money which has been paid upon a gambling debt. . . . The general policy of the courts in suits to recover gambling losses is clearly stated. . . . "If notwithstanding the evil tendency of betting . . . parties will engage in it, they must rely upon the honor and good faith of their adversaries, and not look to the courts for relief in the event of its breach."

There are cases where courts will assist in the recovery of money or property lost at gambling, but this is not one of them. The plaintiff was the proprietor of the saloon and the operator of the dice game in which he lost his property. He now asks a court of equity to assist him in recovering it, and this raises the question, may a gambler who runs a game and loses the bank roll come into a court of equity and recover it? He conducted the game in violation of law, conveyed his premises to pay the winner's score, and now demands that the court assist him to regain it. Equity will not become a gambler's insurance company, to stand by while the gamester secures the winnings of the drunken, unsuspecting or weakminded in violation of the law, ready to stretch forth its arm to recapture his losses when another as unscrupulous or more lucky than he wins his money or property. Nor will the court in this case aid the defendant.

The cause will be dismissed. . . .

The Problem of Written Agreements

Since most contracts are in fact oral, some problems may arise in the proof associated with such contracts. There is little to stop a person bent on fraud and perjury from selecting a person at random, bringing suit against the individual alleging that a contract was made orally, and lying in court to prove that contract exists. Since oral contracts are valid and binding, and since "my word against yours" is valid proof in any court, the judge will have to decide the case based on the credibility, or believability, of the parties. This problem was aggravated in the historic English courts by a rule of evidence that prohibited *either* party from testifying in any civil lawsuit. Thus our fraudulent party needed a confederate, which was usually fairly easy to obtain, and the innocent party had to find outside witnesses to prove that he did *not* make a contract, a most difficult task.

The Statute of Frauds and Perjuries   In 1677, Parliament acted to stop these frauds by enacting the Statute Against Frauds and Perjuries. That law has been enacted in virtually every English-speaking jurisdiction in the world since that time and remains essentially effective in most places. The purpose of the Statute of Frauds is to require that a person alleging the existence of a contract have some proof beyond his oral statement that the contract actually existed and of the nature of the agreement. Usually, that proof consists of a written agreement, though other methods of "bringing a contract out of the Statute" exist as well.

Parliament did not require such proof in all contracts, however. Parliament set up six categories of contracts so important to society or so subject to fraud that additional proof was desirable. Those categories were

1. An agreement by an executor or administrator to personally pay the debts of a decedent;
2. An agreement to pay the debts of another;
3. A contract in consideration of marriage;
4. A contract "not to be performed" (impossible to perform) within one year;
5. A contract for the sale of an interest in land; and
6. A contract for the sale of personal property over the value of £20.

All American states have adopted the Statute of Frauds almost verbatim from the original.

Methods of Avoidance of Contracts

The common law permits parties to a contract to avoid their liability under the agreement in several instances. If the contract was entered into as a result of fraud, duress, undue influence, or mutual mistake of fact, the courts found that there was no real "meeting of the minds" and permitted injured parties to obtain relief. Fraud involves a misrepresentation regarding the contract or its subject matter, while duress involves some force or compulsion to enter the contract. Undue influence is unfair persuasion, resulting from some domination or relationship or trust and confidence. And mutual mistake simply means both parties to the agreement were mistaken about the subject matter of the agreement.

Contemporary Developments in Contract Law

Two major trends developed in the middle of the 20th century that have had a vast influence on the law of contracts. The first was the development of uniform statutes regarding contracts, particularly the enactment of the **Uniform Commercial Code.** The UCC was a "model act" suggested by the American Law Institute, an association of lawyers, judges, and legal scholars, to remedy some problems in the common law of contracts, security arrangements, and other commercial transactions. The Code was first suggested in the 1930's, and the first draft was proposed in 1952. By the early 1960's, 49 of 50 states (the sole exception being Louisiana) had adopted the UCC or substantial portions of the act as state law. The Code covers sales of goods, commercial (negotiable) paper, bank deposits and collections, letters of credit, bulk transfers, documents of title, investment securities, and secured transactions. The UCC has little if any effect on real estate transactions but has had a substantial impact on a variety of other contract forms. As a result, the basis of that law is substantially identical in 49 states, though judicial decisions may change the interpretation of the Code somewhat.

The second major trend is the enactment of specific consumer protection statutes, which change common law results. Some of those statutes require affirmative disclosures of matters within an agreement, such as advertising regulations or "truth-in-lending" statutes; others permit an injured purchaser of goods to sue with greater ease; and still others require that goods be safe to use or consume. Those statutes will be discussed at much greater length in Chapters 11 and 12.

The Law of Torts

The term **tort** refers to civil wrongs that are not based on contract. The term is derived from the Latin term for 'twisted' and the term *tort* means simply 'wrong' in French. Scholars have tried for years to arrive at a really satisfactory definition of the term and have been universally unsuccessful, since the term covers so many different types of conduct.

Torts include, among other things, assault, battery, intentional infliction of mental distress, false imprisonment, trespass to land, trespass to personal property, conversion (theft) of personal property, fraud, defamation, libel, slander, malicious prosecution, abuse of court process, intentional interference with another's contracts, nuisance, negligence, recklessness, liability arising from the keeping of dangerous animals, liability from undertaking ultrahazardous activities, products liability, and recently, invasion of privacy. The list is not complete, since new torts may be created at any time through judicial recognition or statute.

Torts and Crimes

Torts are not the same as crimes. While many of the torts listed above are also crimes, and the crimes are called by similar or identical names, the two concepts are entirely separate. If a person strikes another with his fist, the act may well be a crime, and the person may be charged, tried, and punished for the criminal offense of battery. But the injured person also has a totally independent right to sue the person who hit him in a private lawsuit and obtain money damages. Both the criminal and civil actions may be called 'battery,' but the injured person need not wait for the criminal prosecution and, even if the person is found innocent of criminal battery, a civil suit is still possible. And, perhaps obviously, not all crimes involve torts.

The Elements of a Tort

There are four broad requirements in every tort: (1) a legally recognized *duty;* (2) a *breach* of that duty; (3) an injury, or *damages;* and (4) a *causal relation* between the breach of duty and the injury, sometimes called *proximate cause.* It is necessary to prove all four elements in every tort case. If a new set of facts can be brought within the four elements, a new tort may be created by the courts, which happens only rarely.

The Duty   Legal **duties** arise in a large variety of ways. Some duties, such as the duty not to go over the speed limit or not to murder another person, arise from statutes enacted by the legislature. Others arise from the common law, including some of the duties associated with what are otherwise criminal violations, such as the duty not to threaten or strike another. All people are under the duty to conform their conduct to all of the duties imposed upon us and to refrain from doing things that the law, either statutory or common law, tells us not to do.

The Mental Element: While the law may state that a certain action is prohibited, that action must be performed with some specified mental state before it may be considered a breach of the legal duty. For example, the tort of battery requires proof that the defendant *intentionally* struck the plaintiff. Thus, an accidental striking, such as a jostling in a crowd, will not be sufficient to prove battery. Part of the plaintiff's proof in such instances is the defendant's mental state at the time the act occurred.

The law of torts has recognized four basic "mental elements" that may be proven. Torts may be (1) intentional; (2) reckless; (3) negligent; and (4) strict liability, or liability without proof of a mental element.

Intentional Torts: Many of the torts listed above require a showing of "intent" on the part of the defendant, including assault, battery, false imprisonment, fraud, and several others. The intent required is not a hostile intent or malicious intent, however, but an intent to bring about a result that will invade the interests of another. For example, the defendant may be liable even though he meant nothing more than a good-natured practical joke, as in the case of pulling a chair out from under another, or even if he was trying to benefit the plaintiff, as in the case of a person who intervenes in a fight or tries to set someone's broken arm over her protests. The act must be voluntary, as opposed to an act done while unconscious, and intent is not the same as motive. Intent extends also to those results that the actor is substantially certain will follow. For example, a person may fire a gun into a crowd hoping that he will not hit anyone; but since it is virtually impossible *not* to hit someone, the act is intentional.

Negligence: Very broadly, **negligence** is defined as the failure to use that degree of care that a reasonable and prudent person would use under like circumstances. Thus, if road conditions were such that a reasonable and prudent person would drive an automobile at only 30 miles per hour, even though the speed limit might be 45 MPH, driving at 40 or 45 MPH may be negligent under the circumstances and might subject the driver to liability if injury results.

The most common negligent tort action involves automobile accidents, but the standard of care of "a reasonable and prudent person" applies universally. Thus, it may be negligent to fail to clean the floors in a retail store, or to design a hotel so that a floor might collapse, or to leave a crack in a sidewalk unrepaired.

The standard of the reasonable person or in earlier years, the "reasonable man," is an objective standard which none of us live up to at all times. The courts have effectively created a fictional person, an ideal individual against whom our conduct may be compared.

Misleading Cases in the Common Law
Sir A.P. Herbert (1930)

> He is an ideal, a standard, the embodiment of all those qualities which we demand of the good citizen. . . . He is one who invariably looks where he is going, and is careful to examine the immediate foreground before he executes a leap or a bound; who neither star-gazes nor is lost in meditation when approaching trapdoors or the margin of a dock; . . . . who never mounts a moving omnibus and does not alight from any car while the train is in motion. . . . and will inform himself of the history and habits of a dog before administering a caress; . . . . who never drives his ball until those in front of him have definitely vacated the putting-green which is his own objective; who never from one year's end to another makes an excessive demand upon his wife, his neighbors, his servants, his ox, or his ass; . . . . who never swears, gambles or loses his temper; who uses nothing except in moderation, and even while he flogs his child is meditating only on the golden mean. . . .

Procedurally, the jury will hear the evidence in any negligence case and then, during the jury instructions, will be informed that the duty of every citizen is to behave as a "reasonable and prudent person under like circumstances" (see Illinois Pattern Jury Instructions, p. 134). The jury is then effectively asked to compare the conduct of the defendant, whether it be in driving an automobile or cleaning his store's floors or any other conduct, to what the reasonable person would have done. If a reasonable person would have acted in the same manner as the defendant there is no negligence and the defendant is not liable; conversely, if the reasonable person would have acted differently, the defendant may be found guilty of negligence.

Some confusion exists regarding the effect of statutes on the proof of negligence. A traffic law, such as a speed limit, may constitute negligence *per se*, or it may only constitute *evidence* of negligence. In the case of negligence per se, under the law of some states, proof that the defendant violated some statute is enough to prove negligence without more. In other states, proof that the statute was violated is only a *part* of the proof necessary. For example, the defendant who was travelling in his automobile at 55 MPH in a 50 MPH zone would be automatically negligent in the negligence *per se* states; but in "evidence of negligence" states mere proof that he violated the speed limit so slightly is only a *factor* in determining whether it was "reasonable" to do so under the circumstances.

Some people may be held to a higher standard than the reasonable person. A surgeon, for example, would be held to the standard of a reasonable surgeon rather than a reasonable person, since the reasonable person would have no surgical skills. The same is true for all skilled professionals, such as doctors, lawyers, accountants, architects and, even in some cases, for skilled craftsmen, such as carpenters, plumbers, and others. A medical malpractice case, for example, involves allegations that a doctor did not use the same degree of care and skill that a reasonable physician would have used in like circumstances. If the doctor is a specialist, he may be held to an even higher standard of care within the specialty.

Recklessness: Standing between negligence and intentional conduct is a grey area, sometimes characterized as **recklessness,** or gross negligence or aggravated negligence. The catch words in recklessness are "wilful and wanton misconduct." In negligence, the problem was one of a mere unreasonable risk of harm. Recklessness goes farther than negligence, by requiring some conscious indifference to the consequences of an action. It is highly unreasonable conduct, in a situation where the risk is clearly apparent. For example, driving a car at 50 MPH in a 45 MPH zone is probably only negligent, but driving at 90 MPH is probably reckless conduct. However, driving at 30 MPH through a crowded intersection may also be reckless. Much depends on whether the risk of harm is clear, and whether the defendant consciously disregarded that risk. This distinction between negligence and recklessness is important only in those states that grant punitive damages for reckless conduct.

Strict Liability: As a matter of policy, the law has adopted a rule of **strict liability,** or liability without reference to any mental element, in several areas. The first cases dealt with abnormally dangerous activities, such as the use of dynamite and blasting, and with keeping dangerous animals, such as wild bulls. If a person indulged in one of those activities and injury resulted, it did not matter that that person did not intend the act, was not negligent or reckless and, in fact, took every possible precaution that injuries would not occur. As a public policy determination it was felt that such persons ought to be "insurers" of the public's safety.

In the mid-20th century, that rule was extended, in certain circumstances, to manufacturers of products released in commerce. Thus, a manufacturer of a product that is "inherently dangerous " will be liable for the consequences, regardless of the manufacturer's intent or negligence.

The Breach of Duty   Once the legal duty is established, including the required mental element for the specific tort, the plaintiff must also prove that the defendant in some way breached, or failed to live up to, the duty imposed upon him.

Proof of the breach of duty is usually fairly straightforward, involving testimony or other evidence of the facts in the case. But often that proof is difficult to obtain, as in the case of airplane disaster, where there is not objective proof of why the airplane fell from the sky. It is, of course, the plaintiff's burden to prove negligence in all cases, but sometimes that proof is inaccessble to the plaintiff.

One answer is provided in some cases by the doctrine of *res ipsa loquitor.* If a negligence action fulfills three conditions, the burden of proof will shift to the defendant to prove that the accident did *not* result from negligence. Those conditions are (1) the event must be of a kind that ordinarily does not occur without negligence; (2) it must have been caused by an agency or instrumentality within the exclusive control of the defendant; and (3) it must not have been caused by any voluntary act or contribution of the plaintiff. Thus, in an airplane crash, airplanes do not ordinarily fall without somebody's negligence, the plane is of course in the exclusive control of the airline, and a passenger ordinarily does not contribute to the crash. As a result, the burden of proof would shift to the airline to prove that the crash was *not* caused by its negligence. *Res ipsa loquitor* has been successfully applied to cases involving falling elevators, objects falling from the defendant's building, explosions of boilers under the defendant's control, gas main leaks, and many others. The term is itself descriptive, since it is translated 'the thing speaks for itself.'

Proximate Cause   Put simply, the breach of duty must *cause* the injury. That statement is deceptively simple, for causation is often the most difficult of the four elements to prove. Philosophically, all events in the world are interrelated. If a man commits a tort, that tort would not have taken place unless his mother had given birth to him, but it would be silly and senseless to make her liable because she "caused" the tort. The law only considers the "nearest" or **proximate cause.** But the problems do not end by simply requiring the cause to be proximate. Other problems involve whether the defendant should be liable for unforeseeable consequences, and the impact of intervening causes; that is, if some new force of external origin, subsequent to the defendant's conduct, in some way diverted or shifted the chain of events.

The following case is a classic in the law. As an expert in torts noted, "What the *Palsgraf* case actually did was to submit to the nation's then most excellent state court a law professor's dream of an examination question."*

Palsgraf v. Long Island Railroad Co.

248 N.Y.339, 162 N.E.99, (N.Y., 1928)

A passenger was running to board a train operated by the defendant Long Island Railroad Co. One of the defendant's guards negligently tried to help the passenger board the moving train and, in doing so, dislodged a package carried by the passenger. The package fell near the tracks, and sparks from the wheels of the train set the package afire. Inside the package were fireworks, which exploded with some force. The concussion from the explosion overturned a set of scales located some distance away on the loading platform. The scales fell on the plaintiff, Mrs. Palsgraf, and severely injured her. A jury found that the defendant's guard was negligent, but that no harm to the plaintiff could possibly have been anticipated.

CARDOZO, C.J. . . .

The conduct of the defendant's guard, if a wrong in its relation to the holder of the package, was not a wrong in its relation to the plaintiff, standing far away. Relatively to her it was not negligence at all. Nothing in the situation gave notice that the falling package had in it the potency of peril to persons thus removed. Negligence is not

*William L. Prosser, *Law of Torts* 3rd ed. (St. Paul, Minn.: West Publishing Co., 1964) p. 293.

actionable unless it involves the invasion of a legally protected interest, the violation of a right. "Proof of negligence in the air, so to speak, will not do." . . . Negligence is the absence of care, according to the circumstances. . . . The plaintiff as she stood upon the platform of the station, might claim to be protected against intentional invasion of her bodily security. Such invasion is not charged. She might claim to be protected against unintentional invasion by conduct involving in the thought of reasonable men an unreasonable hazard that such invasion would ensue. These, from the point of view of the law, were the bounds of her immunity. . . . If no hazard was apparent to the eye of ordinary vigilance, an act innocent and harmless, at least to outward seeming, with reference to her, did not take to itself the quality of a tort because it happened to be a wrong, though apparently not one involving the risk of bodily insecurity, with reference to some one else. "In every instance, before negligence can be predicated of a given act, back of the act must be sought and found a duty to the individual complaining, the observance of which would have averted or avoided the injury" [citing numerous cases]. . . . The plaintiff sues in her own right for a wrong personal to her, and not as the vicarious beneficiary of a breach of duty to another. . . .

. . . .What the plaintiff must show is "a wrong" to herself; i.e., a violation of her own right, and not merely a wrong to someone else, nor conduct "wrongful" because unso- cial, but not "a wrong" to any one. We are told that one who drives at reckless speed through a crowded city street is guilty of a negligent act and therefore of a wrongful one, irrespective of the consequences. Negligent the act is, and wrongful in the sense that it is unsocial, but wrongful and unsocial in relation to other travelers, only because the eye of vigilance perceives the risk of damage. If the same act were to be committed on a speedway or a race course, it would lose its wrongful quality. . . . This does not mean, of course, that one who launches a destructive force is always relieved of liabil- ity, if the force, though known to be destructive, pursues an unexpected path. . . . Some acts, such as shooting, are so imminently dangerous to any one who may come within reach of the missile however unexpectedly, as to impose a duty of prevision not far from that of an insurer. . . .

The law of causation, remote or proximate, is thus foreign to the case before us. . . . If there is no tort to be redressed, there is no occasion to consider what damage might be recovered if there were a finding of a tort. . . .

The Judgment of the . . . Trial Term should be reversed, and the complaint dismissed.

ANDREWS, J (dissenting). . . . We deal in terms of proximate cause, not of negli- gence. . . . Due care is a duty imposed on each one of us to protect society from unnec- essary danger, not to protect A, B, or C alone. . . .

The proposition is this: Every one owes to the world at large the duty of refraining from those acts that may unreasonably threaten the safety of others. . . . Unreasonable risk being taken, its consequences are not confined to those who might probably be hurt. . . .

. . . .

. . . .What is a cause in a legal sense, still more what is a proximate cause, depend in each case upon many considerations, as does the existence of negligence itself. Any philosophical doctrine of causation does not help us. A boy throws a stone into a pond. The ripples spread. The water level rises. The history of that pond is altered to all eternity. It will be altered by other causes also. Yet it will be forever the resultant of all causes combined. Each one will have an influence. . . . Each cause brings about future events. Without each the future would not be the same. Each is proximate in the sense it is essential. But that is not what we mean by the word. Nor on the other hand do we mean sole cause. There is no such thing. . . .

. . . What we do mean by the word "proximate" is that, because of convenience, of public policy, of a rough sense of justice, the law arbitrarily declines to trace a series of events beyond a certain point. This is not logic. It is practical politics. Take our rule as to fires. Sparks from my burning haystack set on fire my house and my neighbor's.

I may recover from a negligent railroad. He may not. . . . We said the act of the railroad was not the proximate cause of our neighbor's fire. . . . The words we used were simply indicative of our notions of public policy. . . .

. . . A chauffeur negligently collides with another car which is filled with dynamite, although he could not know it. An explosion follows. A, walking on the sidewalk nearby is killed. B, sitting in a window of a building opposite, is cut by flying glass. C, likewise sitting in a window a block away, is similarly injured. And a further illustration: A nurse-maid, ten blocks away, startled by the noise, involuntarily drops a baby from her arms to the walk. We are told that C may not recover while A may. As to B it is a question for court or jury. We will all agree that the baby might not. Because, we are again told, the chauffeur had no reason to believe his conduct involved any risk of injuring either C or the baby. As to them he was not negligent. . . .

. . . The true theory is, it seems to me, that the injury to C, if in truth he is to be denied recovery, and the injury to the baby, is that their several injuries were not the proximate result of the negligence. And here not what the chauffeur had reason to believe would be the result of his conduct, but what the prudent would foresee, may have some bearing—may have some bearing, for the problem of proximate cause is not to be solved by any one consideration. It is all a question of expediency. There are no fixed rules to govern our judgment. There are simply matters of which we may take account. . . . There is in truth little to guide us other than common sense.

There are some hints that may help us. The proximate cause, involved as it may be with other causes, must be, at the least, something without which the event would not happen. The court must ask itself whether there was a natural and continuous sequence between cause and effect. Was the one a substantial factor in producing the other? Was there a direct connection between them, without too many intervening causes? Is the effect of cause on result not too attenuated? Is the cause likely, in the usual judgment of mankind, to produce the result? Or, by the exercise of prudent fore-sight, could the result be foreseen? Is the result too remote from the cause, and here we consider remoteness in time and space. . . . We draw an uncertain and wavering line, but draw it we must as best we can. . . .

[In the present case] Mrs. Palsgraf was standing some distance away. How far cannot be told from the record—apparently 25 or 30 feet, perhaps less. Except for the explosion, she would not have been injured. . . . So the explosion was a substantial factor in producing the result. . . . The only intervening cause was that, instead of blow-ing her to the ground, the concussion smashed the weighing machine which in turn fell upon her. There was no remoteness in time, little in space. . . . [I]njury in some form was most probable.

Under these circumstances I cannot say as a matter of law that the plaintiff's inju-ries were not the proximate result of the negligence. . . . The judgment appealed from should be affirmed. . . .

Defenses

Some defenses are available once the tort has been proven. In intentional torts, it is sometimes a defense to show that the plaintiff consented to the conduct, or that the conduct was privileged, as in self-defense as a defense to battery.

In negligent torts, the two principal defenses are *contributory negligence* and *assumption of risk.* **Contributory negligence** means that the plaintiff in some way con-tributed to the incident. If so, all recovery is blocked and no recovery is possible. Thus, if a jury were to find the defendant was 90 percent of the cause of an accident, while the plaintiff was only 10 percent at fault, the plaintiff would recover nothing.

Assumption of risk means the plaintiff voluntarily assumed a known risk. A plaintiff who walked across a railroad bridge and was injured by a passing train would be unable to recover against the railroad for any negligence on its part, since he knew of the risk and voluntarily assumed it.

Current Trends in Torts

The common law is not dead nor is it static. Many of the doctrines just discussed have been valid law for centuries and will continue to be effective for decades or centuries to come. But changes are constantly occuring. Doctrines are refined by new decisions and influenced by social trends. For example, the whole area of negligence was changed by the introduction of the automobile, causing a refinement of the case law and specific application to the rules of the highway. Some of the current trends and movements in the law of torts include the move toward comparative negligence, the growth of "no-fault" legislation, and the general move towards "risk spreading" across society.

Comparative Negligence   In automobile negligence cases, many people feel that the doctrine of contributory negligence is too harsh. A very small degree of negligence on the part of the plaintiff may block a just recovery entirely. Beginning in the 1960's, several states began to experiment with the doctrine of **comparative negligence,** in which a plaintiff may recover in proportion to his own negligence. Thus, if a plaintiff suffered $10,000 in loss and the jury found that the plaintiff was only 30 percent negligent, the plaintiff could recover 70 percent of his loss, or $7,000. Comparative negligence has been adopted in most states by statute, and the systems of comparative negligence vary widely. The doctrine applies only to automobile cases, and the rule of contributory negligence is still applicable in nonautomobile cases.

"No-Fault" Legislation   Again arising in the automobile context, many observers feel that the fault system has too many variables to permit effective recovery. Proof of negligence is thought to be long and difficult, the lawsuits necessary to recover are lengthy and time consuming, and lawyers tend to charge too much for their services—or so the arguments go. In a few states, "no-fault" legislation has been enacted permitting injured parties to recover directly from their own insurance companies for out-of-pocket expenses, and then to sue for pain and suffering if those expenses go over a specific, and usually high, amount of damages. Perhaps the oldest form of no-fault legislation is worker's compensation, discussed at length in Chapter 14.

Summary and Conclusions

In many ways the history of the United States is the story of the interplay between ancient common law traditions and the unique needs of the changing and growing country. The stagnant and feudal common law, with its origins in English history, was helpful in establishing a system of law that at once fit the culture of the Americans, based as it was on English culture, and that had been fully developed through centuries of trial and error.

But, in other ways, the traditional common law did not fit the new nation. It was not long before American courts and legislatures began to question the sacred doctrines of the common law, retaining those doctrines that worked and boldly discarding those doctrines that had no place in the western hemisphere. Doctrines like primogeniture, which gave only the eldest son rights to his father's property, were quickly discarded, to be replaced by doctrines more in keeping with the philosophical needs of democracy.

Common law was first and foremost property law, since the basis of ancient English society was land. With the rise of mercantile activity, contract law assumed a more important role in the law courts, and much later tort law became of prime importance, illustrating how broad social and economic changes influence the growth of the law. Property law, dealing with ownership and other rights in land, changed drastically upon importation to the United States. Contract law, dealing with enforceable agreements and promises, has been codified in the Uniform Commercial Code insofar as it applies to sales of goods, but other contract law remains based on the common law.

Tort law is perhaps the most important category of civil law today, at least by numbers of cases filed. That law, which attempts to remedy "civil wrongs," affords relief from a variety of "wrongful behavior," including intentional, reckless, and negligent activity. One area of growth appears to be "liability without fault," or strict liability.

Much of government regulation is an effort to soften the touch of the common law. The process of changes and adaptation of the common law to the needs of society has continued, both within the courts and in the state and federal legislatures, constantly accomodating the demands of the law to the society which it attempts to control.

PRO AND CON

ISSUE: Will the Law Continue to Advance Through "Common Law" Case Development?

PRO: Tort Law Will Continue to Develop Through Common Law Means
Thomas F. Lambert, Jr.*

To peer ahead into the mists of the 21st century in the torts field may seem rash, if not downright foolish. There is a worldwide shortage of clairvoyants as well as sages, and great historians remind us that it is only the past that can be predicted with confidence. Not only is the future misty, but the present itself is also plenty murky. As Adam said to Eve as he led her by the hand from the Garden of Eden, "We live, my dear, in a time of transition."

However, our most illustrious constitutional scholar, Professor Paul A. Freund, has taught us that while a transitional period may be painful, "it is apt to be fruitful for the development of principals of social action."

Forecasting the "future of tort law," the bridge from now into a generation hence will arch three areas: an area of stable doctrine; an area of assault upon, possible retreat from, and retrenchment of

*"Tort Law: 2003," Parts 1 and 2, *Trial* (July and August 1983): pp. 90 and 62 et seq. Reprinted by permission from TRIAL magazine, The Monthly Magazine of the Association of Trial Lawyers of America.

existing gains; and the largest sector, steady progress and continued breakthroughs in the area impinging on the liberty and security of the individual.

Stable Tort Doctrine

Not all tort law will be remolded by 2003. Far from it. The bulk of the law relating to intentional torts (assault, battery, false arrest and imprisonment, trespass to land and goods, conversion) will remain fixed, enduring, steadfast. . . .

We hope and predict that, as a legacy from early common-law times to the next generation, tort law will continue to redress the emotional distress that flows from insult, indignity, and shock. . . .

While tort doctrine will continue essentially stable in the field of intentional interference with person or property, it requires no tongue of prophecy to discern that benign expansion of liability will continue in certain yeasty areas of intentional wrongs. Included are the torts of "Outrage" or intentional infliction of emotional distress, retaliatory discharge of at-will employees, damage awards for constitutional torts in the effort to teach government that it must turn square corners when dealing with its citizens, strengthening of the "prima facie tort" remedy, beefing up remedies in the field of misrepresentation, which has always had too many soft spots favoring the knave over the credulous fool, and even the development of "nameless torts" where necessary to prevent injustice.

Throughout the long evolution in which mankind has fought its way up from the cave and savage isolation to cities and a semblance of civilization, one thing has remained fixed and constant. While tort law responds to changes in the physical and social world, our law has always condemned *intentional aggressions* against our legally protected interests more sternly than intrusions that are merely negligent or morally innocent. As Holmes put it once and for all, "Even a dog can distinguish between being stumbled over and being kicked." That insight will hold (and be implemented by awards of punitive damages for flagrant and profligate wrongdoing) as part of the mood, temper, outlook and values of tort law a generation hence.

Considering the large array of toxic torts knowingly inflicted and consciously covered up by public and private industrial malefactors in recent years, ranging from atomic bomb tests to Love Canal, Agent Orange, acid rain, the deadly dust of asbestos fabrications, Thalidomide and MER-29, not to mention the Pinto and Firestone 500 calamities or the celebrated disasters involving Kepone, Vinyl Chloride, DBCP and PBB, we are proud that tort law's capacity to punish corporate malfeasance as well as to compensate for harm remains a secure part of tort law's presuppositions for the future.

Retreat and Retrenchment

The steady progress of tort law since the mid-19th century, reflecting a moving consensus and increased public understanding of the role and mission of tort law, has not been an unbroken advance—all sail and no anchor. . . . Of course there have always been soft spots. . . . Such lapses, however, are sporadic and out of line with basic principles and the general trend of the cases. . . . Two . . . areas are witnessing mounting onslaughts to reduce and undercut consumer rights, namely, so-called legislative reforms in the fields of medical malpractice and products liability. . . .

The modus operandi is the same for both assaults. The industry and its lobbyists fabricate a phony "crisis" and then mount a full-scale, wide-ranging legislative attack. . . . It requires no prophetic gift to foresee that the masked forces of reaction marching under the banner of "reform" will continue their assault, on both federal and state levels, to nullify and reverse the hard-won consumer gains of the last generation. . . .

Tort Law: Future Progress

Notwithstanding the legislative assaults in the latter part of the 1970s upon the remedies of the victims of medical negligence, subsequent dissipation in the crisis atmosphere and constitutional invalidation of a number of the statutory inroads upon patient rights are ushering in a number of developments that, in combination, will help malpractice victims surmount or circumvent the "conspiracy of silence," i.e., the notorious unwillingness of physicians to testify against their colleagues. . . .

Unborn children, prenatal injuries, preconception negligence, wrongful birth, wrongful life, tort liability for improper genetic counseling—this cluster of topics presents a series of anguished questions. . . . Some things are quite clear. Current tort law has uprooted and reversed the old rule disallowing any remedy for prenatal injuries. . . .

Tort law a generation hence will undergird the present majority rule that allows recovery for "loss of enjoyment of life," sometimes termed "loss of amenities of life or "incapacity to live a normal life" or "restriction of recreational activities," i.e., inability of the victim to lead what would have been a normal lifestyle in the absence of injury.

Of one thing I have a robust confidence. Traditional torts is not dead, and the time for its great sunset is not at hand. Because its core consists of all those institutions central to our civilization, one can rejoice to believe that the common law is not fading into slow twilight. In Emerson's phrase, it still has much good work to do and is yet "only at the cockcrowing and the morning star." The common law is not finished, and, with luck, it never will be.

CON: Tort Law Will Be Influenced Substantially by Social Insurance, but the Tort System Will Remain

Orville Richardson*

One hundred lawyers, judges, and laypersons from Missouri met in April, 1980 with speakers of national and regional prominence for a . . . colloquium on "Justice in the Year 2000." . . . Discussion groups followed the speakers, and. . . . among other conclusions were the beliefs:. . . .

2) that we will live in a "global society" by the year 2000. . . .

3) that centralism in government will continue and even transcend national boundaries for handling of some cases;

4) that government will continue its involvement in a wide range of issues, but that there will be a "countervailing trend" toward greater individual or communal economic self-sufficiency, self-government (e.g. voluntary community action . . .)

5) that in terms of lifestyle, we will have a more heterogeneous society overlaid with a "more conservative, traditional attitude. . . ."

6) a computer-based technology. . . .

. . . .

Tort Law

As fewer and fewer lawyers are willing to become legislators, it will become increasingly difficult to effect needed tort law reform by legislation. For the same reason vested interests and insurers will find less opposition to measures they sponsor. . . .

Congress will enact a law modifying substantive and procedural products liability law. Lawyers will learn to live with it. Courts will continue to remove court-created immunities from civil actions. By the beginning of the next century comparative negligence will have almost completely replaced contributory negligence as a defense. Sponsors of remedial legislation will have learned that if it is intended to all civil actions for harms done by violators the statutes should make manifest that legislative intent.

Willard H. Pedrick . . . is one of many who envision the ultimate adoption in America of a universal comprehensive social insurance plan covering medical expenses and wage losses due to sickness or accident. I agree. Pedrick would not be content with that. He assures us that "by the middle of the next century, the future of tort law controlling most physical injury claims is no future at all." Negligence law will disappear and with it claims for pain and suffering. . . .

I disagree. There is no reason that a social insurance system cannot coexist with a private tort law system based on fault. . . . There is no acceptable justification for eliminating damages for the non-economic loss of pain and suffering. The loss is real. The individual should not have to bear it alone, particularly if a careless wrongdoer caused it. The trend is in the opposite direction. . . .

Pedrick assures us that the law of torts will not end and that its future lies with "the protection of relational interests." He concludes that "the focus will not be on claims for physical injuries but on assorted harms to personal dignity, to financial interests, to interests in relationships with the changing family, groups, traders, the community, the political system, and a variety of now unimagined claims to protect the quality and opportunities of life for the individual citizen. . . .

DISCUSSION QUESTIONS

1. Why do we put so much weight on what some ancient, provincial, illiterate judge decided centuries ago? Isn't that carrying tradition a little too far? Or is there more to the common law than mere tradition?

---

*"A Glimpse of Justice to Come," *Trial* (June 1983): p. 36 et seq. Reprinted by permission from TRIAL Magazine, The Monthly Magazine of The Association of Trial Lawyers of America.

2. Which do you prefer, a common law system or an entirely statutory system such as the continental European systems? Why?

3. What has displaced land as the most important commodity in our contemporary society? Money? Political power? Corporate stock? Individual rights? Does the contemporary legal system protect that commodity in the same way, and to the same extent, as medieval law protected property?

4. Assume you are the head of a "normal" family. How do you want the title to your home held as between yourself and your spouse? Why?

5. Why don't we simply enact a federal law of contracts, property, and tort law and eliminate all the problems of having 50 separate "common laws," which often conflict? Why do you suppose the "framers" of the UCC went to all the trouble of approaching 50 separate state legislatures and trying to convince each one that the UCC was a good idea, instead of simply approaching Congress with the same idea?

6. Which is more fair, contributory negligence or comparative negligence? Why?

7. Assume you are in an automobile accident in which you lose your right arm. Your total medical bills are $5,000, and you lose two month's work at $2,000 per month. You are perfectly capable of performing your job with one arm. How much money should the defendant pay you to place you in the same position as you were in prior to the accident?

8. Some commentators have argued that "no-fault" legislation in tort law is eroding the concept of personal responsiblity to the detriment of society. Should we dispense with the concept of "fault" or "guilt" entirely? What does fault or guilt mean *morally?* What do those concepts mean *legally?*

CASE PROBLEMS

1. The New Castle County Board of Assessment assessed pipes buried underground and water storage facilities (tanks) located on land above ground under a state law which permitted counties to tax "real property." The tanks were not fixed to the ground, but were exceptionally large. The water company objected to the characterization and taxation of this property as "real property." Decision? [*Wilmington Suburban Water Corp.* v. *Board of Assessment* 291 A. 2d. 293 (Del., 1972).]

2. A bank was robbed in Eubank, Kentucky, and a reward was offered for the arrest and conviction of the bank robbers. Later that day, the robbers were captured in another county. Employees of the bank furnished information that led to the capture, and the capture was made by county sheriff's deputies from the county in which the bank was located and from the county in which the robbers were found. Who has a right to the reward? [*Denney v. Reppert,* 432 S.W. 2d 647 (Ky. 1968).]

3. Is there causation in the following negligence cases: (1) A parked his taxi negligently, which was struck by another car. A wheel came off the taxi, rolled two blocks, and struck the plaintiff. [*Flores* v. *Sullivan*, 112 S.W. 2d 321(Texas, 1937).] (2) A negligently hung a fire extinguisher on a wall in a horse barn. The extinguisher fell, gave off a hissing sound, which frightened the horses and caused a stampede. The horses injured the plaintiff. [*Kane* v. *Burrillville*, 54 A. 2d 401 (R.I., 1947).] (3) A drove his motorboat too close to B's fishing boat and fouled B's fishing line in the motor. The fishline caught plaintiff's eyeglasses and hurt her eye. [*Dellwo* v. *Pearson*, 107 N.W. 2d 859 (Minn., 1961).] (4) A negligently drove his car into B's car. B, temporarily mentally deranged because of the accident, pulled a gun and shot C, who was walking by on the sidewalk. May C sue A? [*Lynch* v. *Fisher*, 34 So. 2d 513 (La., 1947).]

4. Lee was watching a major league baseball game, and had paid for her ticket in the usual manner. During the game a player fouled a ball into the stands near Lee, and she was injured by a "stampede" of fans eager to get a souvenir. The defendant (in the days of the old National League Milwaukee Braves) hired ushers but never told them to stop such rushes for foul balls. (1) Are the Milwaukee Braves negligent? (2) Did Lee "assume the risk" of injury? [*Lee* v. *National League Baseball Club of Milwaukee*, 4 Wis. 2d 168, 89 N.W. 2d 811 (1958).] What if Lee had simply been hit by the foul ball?

5. Several children darted into the street to meet the afternoon ice cream truck. The truck was parked at the side of the road and several children were milling around the truck when defendant drove his car around the truck. One of the children, intent upon the ice cream, wandered in front of defendant's oncoming car. The children were breaking the law by being in the street and defendant was travelling under the legal speed limit. Is the defendant liable? [*Cf. Mackey* v. *Spradlin*, 397 S.W. 2d 33 (Ky. 1965).]

6. Two Texans agreed, in Texas, that one of them would go to Mexico, purchase a lottery ticket, and split the proceeds if they won. Gambling of any form was illegal in Texas but legal in Mexico. The ticket won, but the Texan holding the ticket refused to split the proceeds. Does the other party have any recourse in the Texas courts? [*Castilleja* v. *Camero*, 414 S.W. 2d 424 (1967).]

7. In 1914, the plaintiff and the defendant made a contract which provided that defendant would furnish 175 quarts of milk each day to plaintiff. During the term of the contract the defendant's cows were quarantined by health inspectors and later killed because they were infected by hoof and mouth disease. Plaintiff sued for damages. The milk was to be delivered at a particular location, and defendant himself was forbidden to leave his farm by law. Does plaintiff have a case? [*Whitman* v. *Anglum*, 92 Conn. 392, 103 A. 114 (1918).]

8. Plaintiff Blatt graduated in the top 10 percent of his law school class. He sued the university and the Order of the Coif (a legal honor society that admits only students in the top 10 percent—but not *all* such students) for denying him Coif membership. He alleged that he had been promised Coif membership in his freshman year if he graduated in the top 10 percent, and it was the practice to

grant membership to all such students at that university. (1) Is there a contract? (2) If there is no contract, is there promissory estoppel? [*Blatt* v. *University of Southern California*, 5 Cal. App. 3d 935, 85 Cal. Rptr. 601 (1970).]

SUGGESTED READINGS

Friedman, Lawrence M. *A History of American Law* (New York: Simon and Schuster, 1973).

Holdsworth, Sir William. *A History of English Law* 12 vols. (London: Methuen & Co., Ltd. and Sweet & Maxwell, Ltd., 1938).

Howard, A. E. Dick. *The Road from Runnymede* (Charlottesville, Va.: University Press of Virginia, 1968).

Jackson, R. M. *The Machinery of Justice in England* 7th ed. (Cambridge: Cambridge University Press, 1977).

Pollock, Sir Frederick, and Frederic Wm. Maitland. *The History of English Law* 2 vols. (Cambridge: Cambridge University Press, 1968).

Prosser, William L. *Law of Torts* (St. Paul, Minn.: West Publishing Co., 1964).

The Legal Structure of Business: Agency, Partnerships and Corporations

Let every eye negotiate for itself
And trust no agent.

William Shakespeare, Much Ado About Nothing, *Act II, Scene i.*

Corporations are invisible, immortal, and have no soul.

Ascribed to Roger Manwood.

Business is often a battle of wits, and some businessmen are unarmed.

Anonymous

Perhaps one of the most striking and least understood phenomenon that grew out of the Industrial Revolution in the 19th century was the "organizational revolution," which began at the same time. Though there had been large business enterprises for centuries, chiefly in the form of the large overseas trading companies, prior to 1850, businesses were generally small and were operated by their owners. But in the next century businesses became far more complex until, by the 1920's, large, sophisticated corporations controlled much of the nation's business.

This chapter is about the different ways in which businesses may organize. At the outset it is necessary to discuss the concept of "agency," an ancient common law doctrine that forms the basis of both the law of business organizations and the law of employment. The chapter will then consider the principal forms of business organization in use today—the sole proprietorship, the partnership, and the corporation—and briefly discuss some of the more exotic business forms as well. Included in that discussion will be a consideration of the major forms of nonprofit associations such as not-for-profit corporations and foundations. The chapter will conclude with a discussion of the various considerations to be taken into account when choosing the proper business form for a particular enterprise.

The Law of Agency

An **agency** relationship involves any relationship in which one person, known as an **agent,** acts for or on behalf of another person, known as the **principal.** In its broadest meaning, the term includes any employment relationship and any other relationship in which a party acts for another, even gratuitously. While a contract may form the basis of an agency, as in the case of an employment contract, a formal agreement is not necessary.

Creation of Agencies

An agency depends on the *grant of authority* from the principal to the agent. That grant of authority may be made *expressly,* through a formal contract or a verbal command, or it may be *implied* from the circumstances. Agencies may even be created unintentionally, under the doctrine of **apparent authority.** That doctrine holds that if A places B in a position in which it appears that B is A's agent, even if B is in fact not A's agent, contracts made by B on A's behalf will be binding on A.

The following decision considers the doctrine of apparent authority and the nature of the duties of third persons dealing with agents.

General Refrigeration & Plumbing Co. v. Goodwill Industries

30 Ill. App. 3d 1081, 333 N.E. 2d 607 (Ill. App. Ct., 1970)

Goodwill Industries leased a building for use as a branch store. During a flood water entered the building and damaged the building's heating equipment. The store's manager, Mrs. Wonnacott, called the plaintiff, General Refrigeration, to repair the damage. General Refrigeration had done work for Goodwill at Mrs. Wonnacott's request previously. After inspecting the damage, General Refrigeration told Mrs. Wonnacott that major repairs were necessary, and that she should phone the main office of Goodwill for authority to proceed with the repairs. Shortly afterwards, Mrs. Wonnacott contacted General Refrigeration and stated that she had the necessary authority, and that General Refrigeration should proceed with the repairs. General Refrigeration completed the repairs, and billed Goodwill $634.59. Goodwill failed to pay, and General Refrigeration sued both Goodwill and Mrs. Wonnacott. The trial court ruled in favor of Goodwill on the grounds that there was no express or apparent authority granted to Mrs. Wonnacott. The plaintiff appealed the judgment of the trial court.

JONES, Presiding Justice: . . .

. . . .[P]laintiff contends that Goodwill Industries should be bound . . . because Mrs. Wonnacott was an agent acting with apparent authority to bind Goodwill Industries. . . .

[W]e feel that General Refrigeration is not entitled to judgment against Goodwill Industries on the basis of the issues brought before the court.

Plaintiff first contends that Mrs. Wonnacott was clothed with apparent authority to bind Goodwill Industries for the services rendered by plaintiff either because she was the general agent of Goodwill Industries or because of an established course of dealing between the parties.

. . . .

Plaintiff asserts that Mrs. Wonnacott, as manager of the Alton Goodwill store, was the general agent of Goodwill Industries and, as such, had apparent authority to bind Goodwill Industries. . . . However, the evidence clearly shows that plaintiff did not in fact believe that Mrs. Wonnacott's authority, as manager of the Alton store, extended to repairs such as are herein involved. . . .

The record in the instant case, . . . clearly shows that General Refrigeration made no efforts to determine whether Mrs. Wonnacott was acting within the scope of her authority as an agent of Goodwill Industries. Instead, General Refrigeration relied exclusively on the statements of Mrs. Wonnacott that she had authority to order the repairs. . . .

General Refrigeration knew that Mrs. Wonnacott did not have authority on her own to order repairs of the type herein involved. A reasonable inquiry by General Refrigeration would have disclosed the true state of Mrs. Wonnacott's powers. However, instead of calling the St. Louis office of Goodwill Industries or making some other effort to determine whether Goodwill Industries would accept responsiblity for payment, General Refrigeration relied totally on the statement of Mrs. Wonnacott that she had authority. Under these circumstances we do not feel that General Refrigeration exercised reasonable diligence and prudence in determining the extent of Mrs. Wonnacott's apparent authority. Goodwill Industries cannot, therefore, be held to have been bound merely on the basis of apparent authority of its agent.

. . . .

For the foregoing reasons, the judgment against General Refrigeration with respect to Goodwill Industries is hereby affirmed.

Closely related to the doctrine of apparent authority is the doctrine of **agency by estoppel.** Under that doctrine, if one person (the principal) leads a third party to believe some fact on which the third party relies to his or her detriment, the law may refuse to permit the principal to deny (estop to deny) that an agency exists. For instance, assume that A steals P's horse and tries to sell it to T. Thinking that the horse resembles P's horse, T calls P and asks him, and P mistakenly denies that it is his horse. If T buys the horse (changes his position to his detriment) in reliance on P's denial of title to the horse, the law would hold that A was P's *agent by estoppel* for the sale of the horse, and P could not recover back the horse from T. On the other hand, if P were to jokingly respond to T's inquiry, "Yes that's my horse, and I sent A to sell it to you," an agency by apparent authority would be created. The difference is that in apparent authority the principal's representation relates to the agency itself, while in estoppel the principal's representation relates to other matters.

Agencies may also be created by **ratification.** That is, even if there is no authority granted to the agent, the principal may be bound if he or she subsequently ratifies an agreement made on his or her behalf. Such ratification may be made expressly, by simply agreeing to the terms of the agreement, or implicitly by conduct, such as by accepting the benefits of the agreement.

Finally, agencies may be created by operation of law. In such cases, the law creates an agency relationship even though there has been no express grant of authority from the principal to the agent. One example is found in many "long-arm" statutes to provide jurisdiction over nonresidential motorists. Under such statutes, any person using the highways of a state automatically appoints the Secretary of State of that state to accept service of process on his or her behalf for cases arising out of the use of that state's highways.

Liability for Contracts Made by Agents

If an agent, with authority from the principal, makes a contract on behalf of the principal with a third person, there is a valid and binding contract between the principal and the third person. The principal may hold the third person liable on the contract, and the third person may hold the principal liable. A principal is also liable for contracts made by agents acting with apparent authority, and for contracts made without authority but which are subsequently ratified by the principal.

As a general rule, agents are not liable on contracts made on behalf of a principal, though that rule has some exceptions. Agents may be liable to third persons if the agent is dealing on behalf of an **undisclosed principal** or a **semi-disclosed** principal. In the former case, the third party does not know that the agent is dealing on behalf of a principal and believes that the agent is acting on his own behalf. In the latter instance, the third party knows that the agent is dealing on behalf of some principal but does not know the identity of the principal. In both cases, the third party must rely on the reliability and credit of the agent to judge whether to enter into the contract. Agents may also be liable for contracts that exceed their authority or if they misrepresent the agency to the third party.

Liability for Torts Committed by Agents: The Doctrine of *Respondeat Superior*

The doctrine of **respondeat superior** (literally, 'let the master answer') provides that a master is liable for the torts of his or her servants committed while the servant was acting within the scope of his or her employment. There is no requirement that the master be negligent or in any way at fault. Thus, if X, a truck driver for the ABC company, negligently injures Y while driving the truck and in the scope of his employment, Y may sue both X and the ABC company, though Y may only recover the total value of his or her loss—in other words, there is no double recovery.

There are two major limitations on the rule of *respondeat superior:* first, the relationship between the employer and employee must be that of **master and servant,** as contrasted to that of employer and **independent contractor.** The distinction is a practical one and not at all clear-cut. An employer has a right to control the activities of a servant, but has no right to control an independent contractor. In the example above, if X supplied his own truck and charged a set rate for hauling goods for the ABC company, he would probably be an independent contractor. But if he drove a company truck and was paid a wage, he would probably be a servant.

Second, the servant must have been acting within the **scope of** his or her **employment** at the time the tort was committed. That means that the tort must be connected in some way to the employment relationship. If the truck driver in the example above was on the authorized route and was simply careless, the act would be in the scope of employment; but if the driver took a detour to visit his sick grandmother and injured Y while he was on such a **frolic and detour,** the employer would not be responsible. Some of the greatest difficulties in applying the scope of employment rule arise in the context of intentional torts committed by employees, as shown in following case.

Ira S. Bushey & Sons, Inc. v. United States

398 F. 2d 167 (2d Cir., 1968)

FRIENDLY, Circuit Judge.

While the United States Coast Guard vessel *Tamaroa* was being overhauled in a floating drydock located in Brooklyn's Gowanus Canal, a seaman returning from shore leave late at night, in the condition for which seamen are famed, turned some wheels on the drydock wall. He thus opened valves that controlled the flooding of the tanks on one side of the drydock. . . . Parts of the drydock sank, and the ship partially did—fortunately without loss of life or personal injury. The drydock owner sought and was granted compensation by the District Court [under the Federal Tort Claims Act—see Chapter 5]; the United States appeals.

. . . .

The Government attacks imposition of liability on the ground that Lane's [the seaman] acts were not within the scope of his employment. It relies heavily on §228(1) of the Restatement of Agency 2d which says that "conduct of a servant is within the scope of employment if, but only if: . . . (c) it is actuated, at least in part, by a purpose to serve the master." Courts have gone to considerable lengths to find such a purpose, as witness a well-known opinion in which Judge Learned Hand concluded that a drunken boatswain who routed the plaintiff out of his bunk with a blow saying "Get up, you big . . . , and turn to," and then continued to fight, might have thought he was acting in the interest of the ship. . . .

It would be going too far to find such a purpose here; while Lane's return to the *Tamaroa* was to serve his employer, no one has suggested how he could have thought turning the wheels to be, even if—which is by no means clear—he was unaware of the consequences.

. . . . It is not at all clear, as the court below suggested, that expansion of liability in the manner here suggested will lead to a more efficient allocation of resources. . . . [A] more efficient allocation can only be expected if there is some reason to believe that imposing a particular cost on the enterprise will lead it to consider whether steps should be taken to prevent a recurrence of the accident. . . . And the suggestion that imposition of liability here will lead to more intensive screening of employees rests on highly questionable premises. . . . It could well be that application of the traditional rule might induce drydock owners, prodded by their insurance companies, to install locks on their valves to avoid similar incidents in the future, while placing the burden on ship-owners is much less likely to lead to accident prevention. It is true, of course, that in many cases the plaintiff will not be in a position to insure, and so expansion of liability will, at the very least, serve *respondeat superior's* loss spreading function. . . . But the fact that defendant is better able to afford damages is not alone sufficient to justify legal responsiblity. . . . and this overarching principle must be taken into account in deciding whether to expand the reach of *respondeat superior.*

A policy analysis thus is not sufficient to justify this proposed expansion of vicarious liability. This is not surprising since *respondeat superior,* even within its traditional limits, rests not so much on policy grounds consistent with the governing princcples of tort law as in a deeply rooted sentiment that a business enterprise cannot justly disclaim responsiblity for accidents which may fairly be said to be characteristic of its activities. It is in this light that the inadequacy of the motive test becomes apparent.

Whatever may have been the case in the past, a doctrine that would create such drastically different consequences for the actions of the drunken boatswain . . . and those of the drunken seaman here reflects a wholly unrealistic attitude toward the risks characteristically attendant upon the operation of a ship.

. . . .

Put another way, Lane's conduct was not so "unforeseeable" as to make it unfair to charge the Government with responsibility. . . .

One can readily think of cases that fall on the other side of the line. If Lane had set fire to the bar where he had been imbibing or had caused an accident on the street while returning to the drydock, the Government would not be liable; the activities of the "enterprise" do not reach into areas where the servant does not create risks different from those attendant on the activities of the community in general. . . .

Affirmed.

Liability of Principals for Crimes of Their Agents

As a general rule, principals are not liable for crimes committed by their agents. This is true because most criminal statutes require a **mental element,** such as intent or knowledge, in order to prove the crime. Thus, if A hired B to drive a cab for him, and B was arrested for reckless driving, B's guilt could not be imputed to A to charge him with the offense as well, since A was not "reckless." A might be found liable in tort, however, if B's driving injured someone.

Some crimes may be imputed to the employer, however. Some criminal statutes provide for such imputed guilt directly, and it is also true that a corporation can only act through its agents. Thus, a statute that prohibits certain actions by a corporation may depend on actions by agents for proof. For example, the antitrust laws prohibit certain actions by corporations, such as price-fixing. If agents of a corporation fix prices, the corporation may be charged with the crime.

The Enforcement of Ethics: The Concept of Fiduciary Duties

Every agent is the **fiduciary** of his or her principal. A fiduciary relationship is a relationship of trust and confidence, in which a person undertakes to act primarily for another's benefit, instead of his or her own benefit. Fiduciary relationships carry certain duties, among them diligence and care, obedience, loyalty or fidelity, and the duties to account for funds or property in the agent's hands and to keep the principal informed, the so-called duty of notice. Fiduciary relationships may be contrasted with ordinary business relationships, sometimes called *arm's length relationships,* in which sharp dealing and a lack of trust is an expected part of the game. As noted by Justice Cardozo

Joint adventurers, like copartners, owe to one another, while the enterprise continues, the duty of finest loyalty. Many forms of conduct permissible in a workaday world for those acting at arm's length are forbidden to those bound by fiduciary ties. A trustee is held to something stricter than the morals of the market place. Not honesty alone, but the punctilio of an honor the most sensitive, is then the standard of behavior.*

At the outset, it is important to note that fiduciary relationships exist in any agency, and agencies exist in some rather unexpected situations. Each partner in a

---

Meinhard v. *Salmon,* 249 N.Y. 458, 164 N.E. 545 (1928).

partnership is the agent of all of the other partners, for example. Similarly, corporate officers are the agents, and therefore the fiduciaries, of the corporations they serve. Attorneys, accountants, and stockbrokers are also considered to be the agents and fiduciaries of their clients.

The Duty of Diligence and Care   An agent is required to act diligently and with reasonable care and skill on behalf of his or her principal and to use any special skill that he or she possesses. The agent must also care for property of the principal's in his or her possession and return it to the principal at the end of the agency. This duty is virtually identical to the duty of care imposed by common law negligence.

The Duty of Obedience   The fiduciary duty of obedience requires that the agent obey all reasonable instructions and directions of the principal regarding the manner of performing the agency, and to refrain from doing things that the principal has not authorized expressly or by implication. The agent may "fill in the gaps" in his or her instructions in emergencies, however, and agent's actions may bind principals in such situations. Thus, if A hired a tow truck to pull the ABC company's truck out of a ditch in an emergency, the ABC company would still be liable to the towing company even if it had not authorized A to make contracts.

The Duty of Loyalty and Fidelity   The duty of loyalty generally means that an agent cannot serve two masters. Fiduciaries cannot work for two parties to the same transaction without full disclosure to each and full, knowledgable consent by both of those parties. Fiduciaries cannot make a "secret profit" in a transaction for the principal, and such secret profits become the property of the principal. Fiduciaries cannot enter into competition with their principals nor involve themselves in any conflict of interest (see *Stern* v. *Lucy Webb Hayes Training School,* p. 256).

The Duty to Account   The duty to account means that the agent is responsible for any property or money belonging to the principal that the agent has in his or her possession. The agent must keep records of those funds or property, and should not **commingle,** or mix, the principal's property with his or her own.

The Duty of Notice   The duty of notice requires that an agent provide the principal with all relevant information regarding the subject matter of the agency. One of the practical reasons for this rule is that the law considers any knowledge or notice of the agent to be knowledge of the principal and holds the principal responsible for such knowledge. For example, if A hires B to sell cars on his behalf, and B learns that a certain car has a major defect but fails to tell A, B's knowledge would be imputed to A. As a result, if A later sells the car to C and fails to tell C of the defect, A might be held liable to C in a later action, even though A did not actually know of the defect.

Duties of Principals to Agents

While the agent has rather substantial duties to the principal, the reverse is not true. The principal has the duty to compensate the agent for the value of his or her services, unless the agent has agreed to serve without compensation. The amount of compensation is either the amount agreed between the parties, or the fair value of the agent's services in the absence of agreement. If there is a contract, the principal has a contractual duty to keep the agent employed for the full term of the contract. The principal must provide the agent with the means to accomplish his or her agency and cannot obstruct the agent in the performance of the agency.

Termination of Agencies

Agencies may be terminated in a variety of ways. Of course, if the agency agreement contains a *time limit,* the agency will terminate at that time. But the parties may terminate the agreement at any time through *mutual assent,* and since an agency is based on the mutual consent of both parties, either party may *withdraw* from the agreement at any time.

The latter method was not always the law, as shown by indentured servant agreements of the 18th and 19th centuries. But the 13th Amendment to the Constitution outlawed involuntary servitude, which made it impossible to hold someone to an agency agreement he or she did not wish to keep. Similarly, an employer or principal could not be required to keep someone in their employ against their wishes. On the other hand, while the employer may have the right to fire and the agent has the right to quit, exercise of those rights may be a violation of an employment contract and may give rise to legal actions for money damages for breach of that agreement. There is a rare exception to that rule if there is an **agency coupled with an interest.** This doctrine holds that if an agent also has a legally protected interest in the subject matter of an agency, the principal may not discharge the agent. For example, if A owes B money, and A tells B to sell some of A's property to satisfy the debt, A has created an agency, but B also has an interest in the subject matter of the agency and, as a result, A may not later withdraw the authority.

Agencies may also terminate by operation of law. The *death* or *insanity* of either party will terminate an agency, since agencies depend on the personal consent of both parties. If either the principal or agent *loses a license or qualification* necessary to the agency, the agency is terminated. And, if the agency becomes *impossible to perform* or *illegal,* the agency is terminated.

Agency Law as the Basis of Business Associations

The broad and ancient rules of agency law have formed the foundations of several other broad areas of law that taken together form the law of business associations. Agency law is the basis of all *partnership law,* since partners are considered to be the agents of each other. Similarly, agency law forms the basis of *corporate law,* since corporate officers are considered the agents of the corporation, and directors are considered the agents of the shareholders. Finally, agency law also forms the basis of all *employment law,* fixing the common-law rights and duties of both employers and employees.

One form of business association only tangentially involves agency law, however—the sole proprietorship. Agency law is only involved insofar as it affects relationships of the proprietor with his or her employees.

Sole Proprietorships

Strictly speaking, a **sole proprietorship** is not a business "organization" at all, since it only involves a single person, the owner. There are no formalities of organization, nothing to file with the state or federal government, and no agreements with others.

There are two possible formalities, however. The businessperson who enters a licensed trade, such as operation of a barbershop or a medical practice, must obtain the necessary state or local licenses. And some businesspersons may wish to operate under some other name than their own, in which case, most states require that the businessperson file a registration statement of that name under state **assumed name statutes,** for the protection of the public.

The law makes no distinction between the businessperson and his or her business. If business debts are incurred, the business creditors may sue the proprietor personally and satisfy their claims from the proprietor's personal assets. Upon the death of the proprietor, the business dies as well, though the proprietor may give the assets of the business to another by a will. Proprietors may sell their businesses, but most states have restrictions preventing sales or transfers of businesses to defeat the claims of creditors or to disinherit spouses and children. The proprietor may, of course, hire employees, who become agents of the owner.

Income and losses from the business must be included on the owner's individual income tax return. Some states and municipalities impose "unincorporated business" taxes however; and, if a license is required, a tax usually accompanies it.

Partnerships

Complexities begin to arise when two or more persons conduct a business together. By definition, and unless some more formal method of organization is chosen, a business operated by more than one co-owner is a **partnership.** A partnership is accorded a specific legal status, unlike a sole proprietorship. There are two distinct forms of partnership: the *general partnership* and the *limited partnership.* Also, some more complex business forms have many of the attributes of partnerships, such as *joint ventures, joint stock associations,* and *business trusts.*

General Partnerships

Forty-eight states have adopted the **Uniform Partnership Act (UPA),** a "model act" established in 1914 by the National Conference of Commissioners on Uniform State Laws. That Act specifies in considerable detail the methods of organizing partnerships, the rights and duties of partners, how property is to be held, the rights and duties of persons dealing with a partnership or with the partners, and how partnerships are terminated. But, it is important to realize that there is also a common law of partnerships that preceded the UPA, and which applies when the UPA is silent. In many ways, the UPA merely codified that preexisting common law.

The UPA defines a partnership as "an association of two or more persons to carry on as co-owners a business for profit." This short definition is important both for what it says and what it does not say. First, it is clear that the UPA only applies in situations of *co-ownership* of a *business* and, second, the Act also only applies to businesses run for the purpose of obtaining a *profit.*

But the UPA does *not* require a formal partnership agreement. It is in fact possible that a partnership might be formed by oral agreement or even by an unexpressed understanding. In fact, it is possible for a partnership to be formed without the intention or even knowledge of the parties. The UPA takes a rather practical view of what constitutes a partnership, and seems to concentrate on whether the parties shared profits. Section 7(4) of the UPA provides

> The receipt by a person of a share of the profits of a business is prima facie evidence that he is a partner in the business, but no such inference shall be drawn if such profits were received in payment:
> (a) As a debt by installments or otherwise,
> (b) As wages of an employee or rent to a landlord,
> (c) As an annuity to a widow or representative of a deceased partner,
> (d) As interest on a loan, though the amount of payment vary with the profits of the business,
> (e) As the consideration for the sale of a good-will of the business or other property by installments or otherwise.

The following case discusses the formation of a partnership "by implication," through the sharing of profits.

Cutler v. Bowen

543 P. 2d 1349 (Utah, 1975)

Bowen leased a building that housed the Havana Club, a tavern in Salt Lake City, and also owned the equipment, furnishings, and inventory in the tavern. He did not work in the club itself, however. In 1968, he made an oral arrangement with Cutler, who had been working for him as a bartender, to take over the management of the club. Cutler was to purchase supplies, pay bills, keep books, and hire and fire employees. Cutler and Bowen were each to take $100 per week from the tavern and split the net proceeds down the middle. In 1972, the Salt Lake City Redevelopment Agency decided to take over the business as part of general redevelopment of a part of the city and paid Bowen $10,000 to relocate the business. A suitable location could not be found and the business was closed down. Cutler filed suit, claiming she was a partner, and asked for half the $10,000. The trial court ruled in her favor.

> CROCKETT, J. . . .
> The dispute giving rise to this lawsuit arose because the defendant [Bowen] contended that he was the sole owner of the entire business; and that the plaintiff's status was merely that of an employee, so defendant was entitled to the whole $10,000. Whereas, plaintiff took the position that, conceding the defendant was the owner of the physical assets of the business . . . insofar as the going concern and goodwill value, as a partner in the business, she was entitled to one-half of the relocation value.
> One of the primary matters to consider in determining whether a partnership exists is the nature of the contribution each party makes to the enterprise. It need not be in the form of tangible assets or capital, but, as is frequently done, one partner may make

such a contribution, and this may be balanced by the other's performance of services and the shouldering of responsibility.

When parties join in an enterprise, it is usually in contemplation of success and making profits, and is often without much concern about who will bear losses. However, when they so engage in a venture for their mutual benefit and profit, that is generally held to be a partnership, in which the law imposes upon them both liability for debts or losses that may occur. . . .

On the question whether profits shared should be regarded simply as wages, it is important to consider the degree to which a party participates in the management of the enterprise and whether the relationship is such that the party shares generally in the potential profits or advantages and thus should be held responsible for losses or liability incurred therein. . . .

It is not shown here that any occasion arose where the plaintiff's responsibility for debts or other liabilities of the business was tested. However, throughout the four years in which she operated and managed the Club, apparently with competence and efficiency, it was her responsibility to see that all bills were paid, including the rental on the lease, employees' salaries, the costs of all purchases, licenses and other expenses of the business. During that time she saw the defendant Bowen only infrequently for the purpose of rendering an accounting and dividing the profits. It is further pertinent that the parties reported their income tax as a partnership.

Under the arrangement as shown and as found by the trial court, a good case can be made out that it was largely through the capability, experience, and efforts of the plaintiff that, in addition to the physical plant, there existed a separate asset in the value of the "going concern and goodwill" of the business, which was being lost by its displacement. On the basis of what has been said we see nothing to persuade us to disagree with the view taken by the trial court: that the plaintiff's involvement in this business was such that she would have been liable for any losses that might have occurred in its operation; and that, concomitantly, she was entitled to participate in any profits or advantages that inured to it. . . .

From the circumstances shown in evidence as discussed herein, there appears to be a reasonable basis for the trial court's view that, except for the physical assets, which belonged to the defendant and to which the plaintiff makes no claim, the further asset of the business: that is, the value of what is called going concern and goodwill, belonged to the two of them as partners in the enterprise; and that when the business could not be relocated, the $10,000 should properly be regarded as compensation for the loss . . . and that the partners having lost their respective equal shares in the going business concern, they should also share equally in the compensation for its loss. . . .

Affirmed.

The UPA provides other rules for determining whether a partnership exists as well. Merely owning property with another does not create a partnership, even if the co-owners share the profits from the property, and similarly sharing the gross returns from property does not create a partnership. The key, it seems, is whether the parties share the profits from a *business,* as defined as a "trade, occupation, or profession," not merely the ownership of property.

Partnerships as Legal Entities

A partnership is not generally considered to be a legal "person" or entity, separate from its individual members. At common law this rule was observed strictly and partnerships had no legal status, but under the UPA partnerships are considered "entities" for a few specific purposes. A partnership may hold property in its own name, partners may make contracts with the partnership, and the assets and liabilities of the firm are considered separate from those of the partners for some purposes. Whether a partnership may sue or be sued in its own name depends on state procedural law, and many states require suits by or against a partnership to be brought in the names of all of the individual partners.

It is clear, however, that the general partnership form provides no protection for the individual partners against liabilities of the partnership. If a general partnership incurs an obligation, whether arising from tort or contract, all of the partners are personally responsible to the creditor for that debt to the full extent of their personal assets and regardless of the amount or type of contribution they have made to the partnership business.

Management, Control and Operation of Partnerships

In the absence of an agreement to the contrary, all general partners have an equal voice in the management and control of a partnership. In the ordinary course of business, most matters are determined by a majority vote of all the partners, but the UPA specifies some extraordinary matters that must be settled by a unanimous vote, such as bringing in a new partner or performing any act in violation of a formal partnership agreement.

A partnership always involves a general, mutual agency among all of the partners. Each partner is the agent of the partnership, and any action by one partner will bind the partnership and all of the partners. The UPA provides a few exceptions to this rule, by providing that a partner may not confess a judgment, submit partnership claims to arbitration, assign partnership property for the benefit of creditors, or dispose of the goodwill of the business without the consent of all of the partners. In all other cases, the partnership is liable for any contract made on its behalf by any of the partners. Because each partner is the agent of the partnership and of all the other partners, the law also implies a fiduciary relationship between the partners.

Partnership Property

The UPA creates a unique type of property, called **partnership property,** which is defined as "all property originally brought into the partnership stock or subsequently acquired by purchase or otherwise, on account of the partnership. . . ." Included in the definition is any property acquired by partnership funds. It does not matter, however, how the property is titled. If John Doe owns a store titled in his name, and "donates" that store to a partnership business, that store may become partnership property. Upon Doe's death, the store may be sold to pay the partnership debts and any surplus remaining after payment of those debts will be distributed to the surviving partners.

Termination of Partnerships

A partnership is one of the most fragile creations of the law. Partnerships are technically dissolved, or terminated, whenever a general partner is removed from or added to the firm. A partner's death, insanity, bankruptcy, withdrawal, or expulsion will cause the partnership to cease to exist, and the affairs of the partnership may be required to be "wound up." The **winding up** procedure involves paying the debts of the partnership and distributing the remaining assets of the partnership to the surviving partners. In many cases, the remaining partners may simply form a new partnership to carry on business, and assume the debts of the former partnership.

A partnership's fragility arises from the doctrine of **delectus personae,** or 'choice of the person.' A partnership is a combination of persons, each bringing unique abilities and credit ratings to the business. Parties dealing with the firm may rely on the joint abilities and credit of the firm's members, and each partner relies on the abilities and credit of his or her partners as well. If a partner leaves the firm for whatever reason, that combination of abilities and credit has been changed. As a result, the remaining partners should be given the opportunity to reassess their relationships with the firm in the light of the changed circumstances.

Liabilities of Partners and the Partnership

One of the principal disadvantages of a general partnership is that the partners have unlimited personal liability for the debts of the partnership. That means that if the assets of the partnership are insufficient to satisfy the claims of creditors, the creditors may proceed against the personal assets of any of the partners, or all of them, in order to satisfy their claims.

On the other hand, a partner's interest in a partnership is also considered a personal asset, and thus the personal creditors of individual partners have a right to proceed against a debtor-partner's interest in a partnership. Creditors may do so through a **charging order,** which is an order from a court against the debtor-partner's partnership interest, and requiring that the partner's profits from the partnership be paid to the creditor. If the partner's profits are insufficient to pay off the creditor, the court may order the partner's interest in the partnership sold, which acts as a termination of the partnership. The partnership is not liable for personal claims against the partners in any other way, however.

In the event there are both partnership creditors and individual creditors, the courts generally follow the **jingle rule,** which provides that partnership creditors will be paid from partnership assets and individual creditors will be paid from individual assets. If partnership assets are insufficient to pay partnership creditors, they must wait until individual creditors have been paid before they proceed against individual assets of the partners. And, if individual assets of a partner are insufficient to pay personal creditors, those creditors must wait until partnership creditors have been paid before they proceed against partnership assets.

Limited Partnerships

A **limited partnership** is entirely a creature of statute, which means that such forms were unknown at common law and exist only under state laws that provide for them. While still a partnership in form, the limited partnership permits some partners to have *limited liability,* instead of the unlimited personal liability found in general partnerships, upon certain conditions specified in the statute. In other words, parties may *invest* in the partnership.

The Uniform Limited Partnership Act (ULPA), also adopted by the National Conference of Commissioners on Uniform State Laws, has been adopted in over 40 states. A firm must follow the requirements of that Act very closely in order to become a limited partnership in the states where it has been adopted. Those requirements include a formal agreement between the partners and registration with some office of the state government.

Assuming the agreement and filing are proper, persons may invest in the firm as limited partners and will only be liable to the extent of their investment for debts and obligations of the partnership. In order to receive that preferred status, limited partners must give up something, however. That something is the right to control or manage the partnership. Limited partners cannot exert any control over the affairs of the partnership and may be held personally liable for obligations of the partnership if they exert such control

Every limited partnership must have at least one general partner, and that general partner must manage the affairs of the partnership. The general partner will be personally liable for all debts of the partnership as well. Limited partners have the right to inspect the books, receive all relevant information, and receive an accounting.

Unlike general partnerships, interests in limited partnerships are transferrable and assignable, though it is necessary to obtain the consent of all partners before a new party is made a partner. Withdrawal of a limited partner will not necessarily dissolve the partnership, but an amendment to the partnership agreement is necessary. Limited partners may withdraw their contributions on six months' notice, or any other time set by the agreement. If there is a full dissolution of a limited partnership, the limited partners will receive their shares and profits before the general partners receive any distribution though, of course, the claims of partnership creditors must be paid first.

Implied Partnerships

The general partnership, as a creature of the common law, is a kind of "base" or "residual" category of business organization. That is, partnerships may be formed by implication by attempting to form some other, more sophisticated arrangement and failing to do so. If parties attempt to form a limited partnership or a corporation and fail to do so, the law may treat the parties as general partners.

Joint Ventures

Like a partnership, a **joint venture** involves a mutual undertaking by two or more persons, and general partnership principles apply in most instances. Joint ventures are usually formed for a specific, limited purpose, however, and often for a very specific duration. Two corporations may form a joint venture, as in the case of the GM-Toyota joint venture to manufacture automobiles. Many speculative undertakings, such as drilling for oil or producing motion pictures, are organized as joint ventures as well.

There are no formalities involved in the creation of a joint venture, though often those agreements are quite formal and detailed. Like a partnership, liability in a joint venture is unlimited. The parties have an equal right to control the affairs of the venture and often establish a "board" to run the affairs of the business.

Joint Stock Associations

A **joint stock association** is in many ways a hybrid form of business organization, somewhere between a partnership and a corporation. Many authorities believe it to be the forerunner of the modern corporation as well. Such associations were fairly prominent in the 19th century as an alternative to incorporation, since at that time incorporation required a special act of the state legislature, but joint stock associations are relatively rare today. There are still a few rather large joint stock associations in existence. Some states, notably New York, maintain rather extensive organizational and regulatory laws for such associations, while other states ignore them completely.

In a joint stock association, potential investors simply "pool" their funds and receive stock certificates that prove their investments. The shareholders then appoint or elect a "board of directors," which manages the affairs of the association. Profits and losses are shared proportionately but each shareholder is personally liable for the debts of the association. Shares are freely transferrable and such associations may have perpetual existence.

Business Trusts

Closely related to the joint stock association is the **business trust,** also called the *Massachusetts Trust.* Business trusts were used in the early part of the 20th century to obtain limited liability without using the corporate form and are still in use today because they provide a degree of confidentiality and secrecy not available in the other business forms.

Any **trust,** busines or otherwise, is based on a division of the rights of property ownership into *legal ownership* and *equitable ownership.* Legal ownership means ownership of the title to property, while equitable ownership means the right to receive the benefits of property. In a trust, the two types of ownership are separated and given to different individuals. Thus, a property owner may give "legal title" to one person, but with the provision that the benefits of the property be given to another. A might transfer her apartment building to "B for the benefit of C." That means that B has legal title, but C has the right to receive rents and profits from the building. A is known as the **settlor** of the trust, B is the **trustee,** and C is the **beneficiary.**

The same theory is used to establish a business trust. Persons wishing to invest in the business give funds or property to a trustee or a board of trustees, who use the funds or property for business purposes. The investors, or beneficiaries, receive the benefits of the trust, namely the profits from the property invested, in the form of dividends. Usually the beneficiaries receive certificates to prove their investments and those certificates are freely transferrable. In almost all business trusts the settlors and the beneficiaries are the same persons.

The sole evidence of participation in the business is the agreement establishing the trust, which is normally a very formal document. Outsiders who wish to discover the identity of persons investing in the business usually must subpoena the business records of the firm, and even then it may not be clear who are the real owners since the certificates are freely transferrable.

Trustees are usually personally liable to third parties but may seek indemnification from the shareholders. The trust document also spells out the duties and compensation of the trustees and also usually provides that the trust will exist indefinitely. A few states also permit a slight variation, in the form of a **land trust,** in which a property owner may place real estate he or she owns in a trust and receive the rents and benefits from the property.

Corporations

By sheer number, most businesses are either sole proprietorships or partnerships, but that number takes into account the huge number of small "mom and pop" ventures in existence. Virtually all large businesses, and a rather large number of smaller ones, are organized as **corporations.** The corporate form provides a great deal of flexibility to a business, both in management and in financing, and is almost essential if a business wishes to encourage wide investment by the public. There may also be tax advantages to the corporate form.

The corporate form was unknown at common law, and therefore all corporate law has its basis in statutes. The earliest corporations were formed by royal charter, granted by the king, to undertake some venture. Until the late 19th century, American corporations were generally formed by a special act of the state legislature or the federal Congress, often with special conditions and privileges. For example, in 1850, the Illinois legislature granted a charter to the Illinois Central Railroad, on condition that it would pay 7 percent of its gross receipts to the state.

Small corporations may sometimes be characterized as **close corporations,** though the term does not depend on size. A close corporation is generally considered to be one in which (1) there is a small number of stockholders; (2) there is no ready market for the stock of the corporation; and (3) the stockholders play a large role in the management and control of the corporation. A few states, notably Delaware, provide a statutory definition of close corporations, including a limit on the number of shareholders (Delaware's limit is 30 shareholders), but generally the term is a practical, vague concept without much legal significance. Control in such corporations is often a major problem, since the firm in fact is an "incorporated partnership." As noted in an Ohio decision

> The old story, so often told, of a prominent Eastern newspaperman's reply to the question of what shares in his company were worth, is very apt: there are 51 shares, he said, that are worth $250,000. There are 49 shares that are not worth a _____.*

The opposite of a close corporation is a publicly owned corporation, in which the shares are widely held and shareholders play very little part in the management and control of the company. The shares of such firms are often traded on one of the national or regional stock exchanges or in the "over-the-counter" market through stock brokers (see Chapter 15).

Corporations may also be classed as *foreign* and *domestic*. A **domestic corporation** is chartered in the state in which it operates, and a **foreign corporation** is chartered in another state. Corporations chartered in other states may do business in any states but often must obtain permission to transact business in foreign states.

A final distinction lies between *business corporations* and *not-for-profit corporations*. Business corporations are, of course, out to make a profit, while not-for-profit corporations are usually organized for some charitable, religious, educational, or other "nonprofit" purpose. Not-for-profit corporations have no shareholders and control is vested in a board of directors usually made up of volunteers.

Creation and Powers of Corporations

A corporation, like a limited partnership, is entirely a creature of statute. Each state maintains a business corporation act, which provides in substantial detail the methods by which a corporation may be formed, the powers of corporations, the organization and structure of corporations, and a great deal more. Those acts vary considerably from state to state, and the differences between those acts provide an incentive for corporate promotors to search out the best state law under which to incorporate. Many states have adopted, in whole or in part, the **Model Business Corporation Act** of the Committee on Corporate Laws of the American Bar Association, though many states have made substantial modifications to that Act. The following discussion is based on that Act.

The Articles of Incorporation   Before a corporation may come into existence, the persons desiring to incorporate (sometimes called *promoters* or *incorporators*) must apply for and receive **articles of incorporation** from the state. The articles, sometimes called the *corporate charter,* are usually issued by the Secretary of State or some administrative agency charged with overseeing corporations. They are the official permission of the state to conduct business as a corporation and establish the corporate name, the powers and purposes of the corporation, the total number of shares of stock that may be issued, and the members of the first board of directors.

The Powers of Corporations   Each corporation has two sets of powers: First, it has authority to do those things that are specifically set out in the articles of incor-

---

Humprys v. *Winous Co.,* 165 Ohio St. 45, 133 N. E. 2d 780 (1956).

poration. Those powers are "applied for" with the application for the articles and are supposed to be rather specific. In practice, most draftsmen prefer to state those powers as broadly as possible. For example, the following purpose clause might be found in the articles of incorporation of a manufacturing firm.

> The corporation shall have the power to: . . .
> manufacture, buy, sell, deal in, and to engage in, conduct, and carry on the business of manufacturing, buying, selling and dealing in, goods, wares and merchandise of every class and description.

Second, corporate powers are derived from the state business corporation act. The Model Act provides seventeen specific powers shared by all corporations, including the right to perpetual existence, the rights to sue and and be sued, to purchase, own and sell real property, to make contracts, to lend money, and many others.

The Doctrine of *Ultra Vires*   While the powers granted to corporations are broadly worded under the Model Act and are usually broadly stated in the articles, the corporation must only do those acts that are within its powers. An action beyond those powers specifically granted to it is said to be **ultra vires** and illegal. At one time the *ultra vires* doctrine was strictly construed in an attempt to restrict the influence and activity of corporations. Two developments have made the doctrine far less influential than it once was, however: first, the articles of incorporation may be amended rather easily to encompass most corporate acts; and second, the doctrine of **implied powers** permits many acts that are not specifically authorized. In the latter case, the Model Act provides that any corporation has the power "to have and exercise all powers necessary and convenient to effect its purposes." The following case discusses *ultra vires*.

Adams v. Smith

275 Ala. 142, 153 So. 2d 221 (Sup. Ct. of Alabama, 1963)

A minority stockholder brought suit to enjoin a corporation from paying sums of money to the widows of a past president and another past officer of the corporation, on the grounds that such payments were not required and were beyond the powers of the corporation. The trial court ruled for the complaining minority stockholders, and the corporation appealed.

> Complainant's right to relief is founded on the proposition that the payment of the corporation's money to the widows, without consideration, is illegal and not within the power of a mere majority of the stockholders over the objection of a single stockholder. As we hereinafter undertake to show, we are of the opinion that complainant's contention is correct, unless there is in the charter of the corporation a provision which confers on the majority the power to give away the corporation's money without consideration.
>   . . . .
> If, in fact, there is no provision in the charter which authorizes the majority stockholders to pay out corporate funds without consideration, then we are of opinion that the bill does have equity. Appellants have devoted many pages of brief . . . to establish the propositions that the alleged payments to the widows are authorized under the so-called "Business Judgment Rule,"* and that the alleged payments may be made law-

*See p. 247.

fully by the directors under their power to manage the internal affairs of the corporation without interference by the courts, or, that if the directors could not do so, then the majority of the stockholders could ratify the alleged acts of the directors, who would not be liable after ratification. We will respond to these contentions.

The directors say . . . that they "do not question the existence or validity of this rule" that "neither the Board of Directors nor the majority stockholders can give away corporate property," and that the rule "is and must be the law of the land."

. . . .

The appellants argue, however, that directors or majority stockholders have power to make bonus or retirement payments to officers and employees of the corporation, and their widows or dependents, because such payments can be and are for the benefit and furtherance of the business of the corporation. We are not disposed to contest the proposition that, in a proper case and under proper procedure, corporations can make bonus and pension payments. That, however, is not the case [here]. The [allegation] is that the payment to the widow was without valid consideration and that the corporation had no contract for the payment of the alleged sums.

. . . .

[In the virtually identical case of *Moore* v. *Keystone Macaroni Mfg. Co.*, 370 Pa. 172, 87 A. 2d 295 (1952), the] Supreme Court of Pennsylvania . . . said:

To further support their argument, [the directors] point to the modern trend in favor of pensions and of permitting corporations to make charitable gifts, and to take other actions which the board of directors are convinced will be for the best interests of the corporation even though no immediate or direct quid pro quo results therefrom. It will be noted, of course, that the payments to [the widow] were not and did not purport to be a pension, nor did they constitute a gift or contribution to a charity or to a community chest as specifically authorized by . . . the Pennsylvania Business Corporation Act. . . .

Moreover, we cannot overlook the fact that to approve the action of this board of directors would result in opening wide the door to a dissipation of the assets of a corporation and to fraud; and it is still the law of Pennsylvania that it is *ultra vires* and illegal for a corporation (unless authorized by statute) to give away, dissipate, waste or divert the corporate assets even though the objective be worthy. This general principal is widely recognized. In Fletcher, *Cyclopedia of Corporations,* Permanent Edition, Vol. 6-a, paragraph 2939, pages 667, 668, the law is thus stated: "It is the general rule that a gift of its property by a corporation not created for charitable purposes is in violation of the rights of its stockholders and is *ultra vires,* however worthy of encouragement or aid the object of the gift may be. It seems to be the rule that a private corporation has no power voluntarily to pay to a former officer or employee a sum of money for past services, which it is under no legal duty to pay, and which would not constitute a legal consideration for a promise to pay." In *Rogers* v. *Hill,* 289 U.S. 582, 591, 53 S. Ct. 731, 735, 77 L. Ed. 1385, the Court . . . said: "If a bonus payment has no relation to the value of services for which it is given, it is in reality a gift in part, and the majority stockholders have no power to give away corporate property against the protest of the minority."

. . .

In the case at bar, we hold that the bill has equity, and that the court did not err. . . .

In earlier times, the doctrine of *ultra vires* was also used as a defense to contract actions against the corporation on the theory that a contract that was beyond the powers of a corporation to make was a nullity, and the corporation could not be held liable. In later years, the courts have tended to discard that theory and hold the corporation liable to the innocent party, especially if the corporation received any of the benefits of the contract. Similarly, a corporation may not escape liability for torts committed in the scope of employment by agents of the corporation on the grounds that such torts were *ultra vires*. In both instances, however, shareholders may be able to hold the individual who made the contract or committed the tort liable to the corporation.

The Entity Theory and Piercing the Corporate Veil   It is traditional to refer to a corporation as a legal "person," who may sue and be sued, hold property, make contracts, lend money, hold the stock of other corporations, go bankrupt, and even be changed with a crime in its own name. Corporations are considered to be persons for the purpose of most statutes and constitutional enactments, unless the statute or constitutional provision obviously refers only to "natural persons." As a result, generally corporations are fully protected by the Constitution against "unreasonable searches and seizures" under the 4th Amendment, against self-incrimination under the 5th Amendment, and against deprivations of "due process' and "equal protection" under the 5th and 14th Amendments.

This separate corporate identity is also the source of **limited liability** for shareholders. Since the corporation is a separate person, it should be liable for its own debts, and the stockholders are only liable to the extent of the funds they have invested in the corporation. But there is also a doctrine, called **piercing the corporate veil,** or **disregarding the corporate fiction,** which permits the courts to impose personal liability on the shareholders of a corporation if the corporate form has been used to defeat the public convenience, justify wrongs, or protect fraud or crime. The following case discusses the doctrine of piercing the corporate veil.

Walkovszky v. Carlton

18 N.Y. 2d 414, 276 N.Y. S. 2d 585, 223 N.E. 2d 6 (Ct. of Appeals of New York, 1966)

FULD, Judge.

This case involves what appears to be a rather common practice in the taxicab industry of vesting the ownership of a taxi fleet in many corporations, each owning only one or two cabs.

The complaint alleges that the plaintiff was severely injured four years ago in New York City when he was run down by a taxicab owned by the defendant Seon Cab Corporation and negligently operated at the time by the defendant Marchese. The individual defendant, Carlton, is claimed to be a stockholder of ten corporations, including Seon, each of which has but two cabs registered in its name, and it is implied that only the minimum automobile liability insurance required by law (in the amount of $10,000) is carried on any one cab.* Although seemingly independent of one another, these corporations are alleged to be "operated . . . as a single entity, unit and enterprise" with regard to financing, supplies, repairs, employees and garaging, and all are named as defendants. The plaintiff asserts that he is also entitled to hold their stockholders personally liable for the damages sought because the multiple corporate structure constitutes an unlawful attempt "to defraud members of the general public" who might be injured by the cabs.

The defendant Carlton has moved . . . to dismiss the complaint on the ground that

---

*As a result, plaintiffs were restricted to recovery of the $10,000 in insurance and the value of the assets of the corporations, namely two taxicabs, even if their damages were much more.

as to him it "fails to state a cause of action." The court . . . granted the motion, but the Appellate Divison . . . reversed, holding that a valid cause of action was sufficiently stated. The defendant Carlton appeals to us. . . .

The law permits the incorporation of a business for the very purpose of enabling its proprietors to escape personal liablity . . . but, manifestly, the privilege is not without its limits. Broadly speaking, the courts will disregard the corporate form, or, to use the accepted terminology, "pierce the corporate veil," whenever necessary "to prevent fraud or to achieve equity.". . . . In determining whether liability should be extended to reach assets beyond those belonging to the corporation, we are guided, as Judge Cardozo noted, by "general rules of agency." . . . In other words, whenever anyone uses control of the corporation to further his own rather than the corporation's business, he will be liable for the corporation's acts "upon the principle of *respondeat superior* applicable even where the agent is a natural person". . . . Such liability, moreover, extends not only to the corporation's commercial dealings . . . but to its negligent acts as well.

In the case before us, the plaintiff has explicitly alleged that none of the corporations "had a separate existence of their own" and . . . all are named as defendants. However, it is one thing to assert that a corporation is a fragment of a larger corporate combine which actually conducts the business. . . . It is quite another to claim that the corporation is a "dummy" for its individual stockholders who are in reality carrying on the business in their personal capacities for purely personal rather than corporate ends. . . . Either circumstance would justify treating the corporation as an agent and piercing the corporate veil to reach the principal but a different result would follow in each case. In the first, only a larger corporate entity would be held financially responsible while, in the other, the stockholder would be personally liable. . . .

 . . . .

The individual defendant is charged with having "organized, managed, dominated and controlled" a fragmented corporate entity but there are no allegations that he was conducting business in his individual capacity. Had the taxicab fleet been owned by a single corporation, it would be readily apparent that the plaintiff would face formidable barriers in attempting to establish personal liability on the part of the corporation's stockholders. The fact that the fleet ownership has been deliberately split up among many corporations does not ease the plaintiff's burden in that respect. The corporate form may not be disregarded merely because the assets of the corporation, together with the mandatory insurance coverage of the vehicle which struck the plaintiff, are insufficient to assure him the recovery sought. . . .

This is not to say that it is impossible for the plaintiff to state a valid cause of action against the defendant Carlton. However, the simple fact is that the plaintiff has just not done so here. While the complaint alleges that the separate corporations were undercapitalized and that their assets have been intermingled, it is barren of any sufficiently particularized statements . . . that the defendant Carlton and his associates are actually doing business in their individual capacities, shuttling their personal funds in and out of the corporations without regard to formality and to suit their immediate convenience. . . . Such a perversion of the privilege to do business in the corporate form . . . would justify imposing personal liability on the individual stockholders. . . . Nothing of the sort has in fact been charged. . . .

 . . . .

The order of the Appellate Division should be reversed. . . .

The doctrine of piercing the corporate veil is not applied very often since, as the *Walkovszky* case indicates, it is perfectly permissible to incorporate for the sole purpose of avoiding liability. The modern trend is to apply the doctrine when the corporate form is used to perpetrate a fraud, where the corporation is undercapitalized, or where the corporation is found to be the "alter ego" of the shareholder, in the sense that the corporation is used as a mere front to conduct private business. In the latter case, the courts often look to see whether the shareholders themselves treated the corporation as a separate entity by actually holding shareholders' and directors' meetings, electing officers, and maintaining separate records and bank accounts.

Corporate Organization and Structure

The organization of all corporations, from the very smallest to the very largest, is set by the state business corporation act and, except in those states that provide for differences for close corporations, that organization is remarkably similar.

The final authority in any corporation is its owners, or **stockholders.** Those shareholders come together annually or at special meetings to determine major policy issues facing the corporation and to elect the board of **directors,** who manage the corporation on behalf of the stockholders. The board of directors in turn appoints the corporate **officers,** usually consisting of the president, vice-president, secretary and treasurer, and sometimes other upper-level management as well (see Figure 7-1). It has been argued that the real power in most large corporations resides in the officers, however, who manage the day-to-day affairs of the corporation and who can in many cases control the board of directors through **proxy** voting and other means. Often the board of directors and the officers are referred to as **management.**

Voting of Shares   Each share of stock is usually entitled to one vote unless the articles of incorporation provide differently. But many articles of incorporation do

Figure 7-1   Traditional Corporate Organization Structure

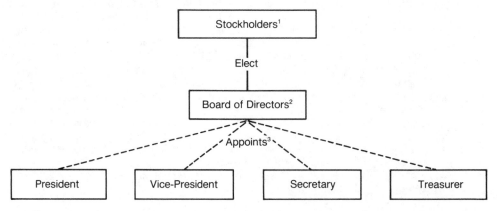

[1]Each share of stock receives one vote. Most states permit a shareholder to vote for every director, or the votes may all be applied to one director under the concept of cumulative voting. In some states, some classes of stock may not have voting rights and, in others, holders of some kinds of debt securities may be given the right to vote.

[2]The number of directors on the board may vary, though there must be at least one. That number is set in the Articles of Incorporation and may be changed by amending the articles. Amendment requires shareholder approval.

[3]The Model Act uses the term *elect,* though it is clear that the officers serve at the pleasure of the Board of Directors. The board also has the authority to appoint other officers and, in many corporations, there is more than one vice-president pursuant to that authority.

provide differently, and voting rights, even in smaller corporations, tend to be quite complex. There are no less than four types of voting rights commonly given shareholders.

Straight voting is the simplest form and means that each share receives one vote for each issue and one vote for each seat on the board of directors. This of course means that minority interests would be outvoted on every issue and for every seat on the board of directors. As a result, some states require **cumulative voting,** which means that shareholders receive one vote for each seat on the board of directors, but they may distribute their votes in any way they see fit. A shareholder may use all of his votes for a single director, spread those votes out among all of the seats, or divide the votes between a few seats. In this way, the owners of any substantial number of shares will be assured of some representation on the board.

The articles may also create **class voting,** also known as *series voting,* in which different classes of stock receive different voting rights. Sometimes the articles go so far as to create different classes of directors and permit voting for one class of directors by one class of shares. Such voting configurations often require a majority of each class to pass certain propositions before the shareholders, rather than a mere majority of all of the shares.

Finally, some corporate articles create **disproportionate voting,** in which one class of shares receives greater voting rights than others. Perhaps the ultimate disproportionate voting is found in nonvoting stock. Most states permit the creation of nonvoting stock as long as at least one class of stock has voting rights. Some stock exchanges have rules prohibiting nonvoting stock and refuse to list such shares, however.

In addition to voting for members of the board of directors, shareholders must vote on any amendment to the articles of incorporation. That means a vote of the shareholders is necessary to change the corporate name, the powers specified in the articles, to change the number of authorized shares, and generally to change any of the relative rights of shareholders or classes of shareholders. Stockholders also have the right to vote on any merger, consolidation, or sale or exchange of all or substantially all of the corporate assets.

Proxy Voting   Usually only those shares whose holders are present at a shareholder's meeting may be voted, though there is a growing tendency to permit voting by mail. Voting rights may be transferred by **proxy,** however, and often management tries to obtain proxies prior to the meeting to permit them to vote the shares and elect directors favorable to management. Sometimes minority shareholders will attempt to obtain proxies as well, and a "proxy contest" results. The federal securities laws and the regulations of the Securities and Exchange Commission provide rules to assure that those contests are run fairly, as more fully described in Chapter 15. Proxies must be given in writing and may be revoked by the shareholder at any time prior to the meeting or if the shareholder attends the meeting in person.

Protection of Shareholders' Rights: Dissenters' Rights

In the event of a merger, consolidation, or sale or exchange of all or substantially all of the assets of a corporation, shareholders may choose to not take part in the corporation any longer. Such moves so thoroughly change the character of a corporation that the Model Act finds it unfair to hold dissenting shareholders in the corporation. As a result the Act (Section 80) provides that dissenters may obtain payment for their shares, but those dissenters must give notice of their decision before a vote on the move is taken and must abstain from voting on the action. (See Chapter 10 for a discussion of mergers, consolidations, and sales of assets.)

Protection of Shareholders' Rights: Direct and Derivative Actions

Shareholders may generally file two types of lawsuits to enforce individual rights or rights of the corporation. A **direct action** is a suit by an individual shareholder to enforce rights as the owner of shares. Suits to recover dividends, to examine corporate books, or to enforce any other individual right of a shareholder may be brought as direct actions against the corporation or its management.

A **derivative action,** on the other hand, is filed by a single shareholder or a group of shareholders to redress an injury to the corporation. The real party in interest in such a case is the corporation itself, though it is filed in the first instance by the shareholders. The action is quite similar to a class action as discussed in Chapter 4 and is often filed in federal court under the federal securities laws. Such actions are usually filed against officers or directors.

Derivative actions have four requirements: (1) the plaintiff must make a good faith effort to convince the corporation to pursue the claim; (2) the plaintiff must make an effort to convince the shareholders to resolve the matter through internal procedures; (3) the plaintiff must have owned shares at the time the corporation suffered the injury; and (4) the plaintiff may be required to post security for the expenses of the case. In addition, the courts must oversee and approve any settlement in order to avoid the **strike suit** phenomenon. A strike suit is filed or threatened, not to redress a corporate grievance, but to obtain a settlement for the individual plaintiffs—a kind of legal blackmail.

The Duties of Management

In most large corporations, shareholders do not take an active role in the management of the corporations in which they hold stock. Shareholders often do not attend shareholders' meetings and generally send the proxies requested by management rather regularly. As a result, management often has the opportunity to operate the corporation relatively free from shareholder direction and control. Management, through its proxies, often can elect the Board of Directors which in turn hire management.

It is important to remember at the outset that corporate managers, including the president, vice-president(s), secretary, and treasurer, are all *employees* of the corporation. The members of the Board of Directors, on the other hand, stand on slightly different footing, since they are elected by the shareholders. The officers of a corporation are considered *agents of the corporation,* while members of the Board of Directors are considered *agents of the shareholders.* In either event, both officers and directors are considered fiduciaries and have fiduciary responsibilities, though they owe those duties to slightly different parties. In fact, the concept of fiduciary responsibilities has reached its fullest flower in the law relating to the duties of corporate officers and directors.

Aside from common-law fiduciary responsibilities, corporate officers and directors are also subject to other contractual and statutory duties. Specifically, those duties arise from the state business corporation act, the articles of incorporation of the corporation, the by-laws adopted by the board of directors, and the individual employment contracts negotiated between the corporation and the individual officers. Other duties may be imposed by federal law or other state laws, including the federal antitrust and federal securities laws, among others.

The Duty of Care   One of the principal fiduciary duties is the duty of care (discussed earlier on p. 229). Corporate officers and directors are of course subject to that duty, as are all fiduciaries. In an early case, the Court of Appeals of New York held that it is the duty of corporate directors to "exercise the same degree of care and prudence that men prompted by self interest generally exercise *in their own affairs*" (emphasis added).* That duty has been further clarified by the Model Act in Section 35 that requires a director to "perform his duties . . . in good faith, in a manner he reasonably believes to be in the best interests of the corporation, and with such care as an ordinary prudent person in a like position would use under similar circumstances."

The Duty of Care and the Business Judgment Rule   The common law and statutory duty of care seem to leave officers and directors of corporations at the mercy of shareholders who disagree with the actions of management, particularly if those actions turn out badly for the corporation. Shareholders could argue that almost any corporate act undertaken by management violates the duty of care if the corporation loses money and, even if such suits are unsuccessful, those actions may be embarrassing and expensive to defend.

The courts generally refuse to grant relief to plaintiffs in such cases if the actions of the officers and directors were within the discretion given them by law. Corporate officers and directors may manage the corporation within the bounds of the powers granted to them by law, and the courts will not interfere with their discretion except in cases of bad faith, fraud, or a dishonest purpose. Other matters are said to rest in the *business judgment* of management, and shareholders may not complain merely because that judgment was erroneous. The following decision illustrates the application of the **business judgment rule.**

Kamin v. American Express Co.

86 Misc. 2d 809, 383 N.Y.S. 2d 807, (N.Y., 1976)

This was a derivative action filed by two minority shareholders of American Express Company. The action alleged that a "dividend in kind" was a waste of corporate assets. American Express had purchased almost 2 million shares of another firm, Donaldson, Lufken and Jen-

---

Hun v. *Cary,* 82 N.Y. 65 (1880).

rette, Inc. (DLJ) for $29.9 million. Three years later, that stock was worth $4.0 million, and the board of directors of American Express decided to distribute the DLJ stock directly to American Express shareholders as a "dividend in kind." The plaintiffs argued that American Express should sell the stock at a loss instead of distributing it to shareholders, since that loss could be used to offset capital gains on the firm's federal income tax. Such a tax strategy would result in a tax savings to the company of $8 million. The company moved to dismiss the complaint on the grounds that such strategic decisions are for the board of directors alone and were within its discretion under the business judgment rule. The opinion is by the trial court, but that opinion was adopted by the appellate court when it affirmed this decision.*

EDWARD J. GREENFIELD, Justice: . . .

Examination of the complaint reveals that there is no claim of fraud or self-dealing, and no contention that there was any bad faith or oppressive conduct. The law is quite clear as to what is necessary to ground a claim for actionable wrongdoing. "In actions by stockholders, which assail the acts of their directors or trustees, courts will not interfere unless the powers have been illegally or unconscientiously executed; or unless it be made to appear that the acts were fraudulent or collusive, and destructive of the rights of the stockholders. Mere errors of judgments are not sufficient as grounds for equity interference, for the powers of those entrusted with corporate management are largely discretionary." . . .

More specifically, the question of whether or not a dividend is to be declared or a distribution of some kind should be made is exclusively a matter of business judgment for the Board of Directors. . . . Courts will not interfere with such discretion unless it be first made to appear that the directors have acted or are about to act in bad faith and for a dishonest purpose. It is for the directors to say, acting in good faith of course, when and to what extent dividends shall be declared. . . .

. . . Courts have more than enough to do in adjudicating legal rights and devising remedies for wrongs. The directors' room rather than the courtroom is the appropriate forum for thrashing out purely business questions which will have an impact on profits, market prices, competitive situations, or tax advantages. As stated by Cardozo, J., ". . . . the substitution of someone else's business business judgment for that of the directors is no business for any court to follow." . . .

. . . The affidavits of the defendants . . . demonstrate that the objections raised by the plaintiffs . . . were carefully considered and unanimously rejected by the Board at a special meeting called precisely for that purpose at the plaintiff's request. . . . [T]hey concluded that there were countervailing considerations primarily with respect to the adverse effect such a sale, realizing a loss of $25 million, would have on the net income figures in the American Express financial statement. Such a reduction of net income would have a serious effect on the market value of the publicly traded American Express stock. . . .

. . . .

All directors have an obligation, using sound business judgment, to maximize income for the benefit of all persons having a stake in the corporate entity. . . . What we have here . . . is . . . a disagreement . . . between two minority stockholders and a unanimous Board of Directors as to the best way to handle a loss already incurred on an investment. The directors are entitled to exercise their honest business judgment on the information before them, and to act within their corporate powers. That they may be mistaken, that other courses of action might have differing consequences, or that their action might benefit some shareholders more than others presents no basis for the superimposition of judicial judgment, so long as it appears that the directors have been acting in good faith. . . . The court will not interfere unless a clear case is made out of fraud, oppression, arbitrary action, or breach of trust.

. . . .

---

*54 A.D. 2d 654, 387 N.Y.S. 2d 993 (1976).

In this case it clearly appears that the plaintiffs have failed as a matter of law to make out an actionable claim. Accordingly, the motion by the defendants . . . for dismissal of the complaint is granted.

The Duty of Loyalty   Corporate officers and directors often find themselves in positions of divided loyalty. Officers and directors sometimes have unique opportunities to make profits for themselves at the expense of their corporation and its stockholders. As early as 1880, the problems of corporate loyalty began to occupy the courts. In that year Mr. Justice Field commented that

> It is among the rudiments of the law that the same person cannot act for himself and at the same time, with respect to the same matter, as agent for another, whose interests are conflicting. . . . The two positions impose different obligations, and their union would at once raise a conflict between interest and duty; and "Constituted as humanity is, in the majority of cases duty would be overborne in the struggle."*

Cases involving the duty of loyalty are generally of one of three types: transactions between a director and his or her corporation *(self-dealing)*; transactions between two corporations in which the director has an interest or a position of authority *(interlocking directorates)*; and situations where the officer or director has taken advantage of a business opportunity that should belong to the corporation *(the corporate opportunity doctrine)*. Also related to the problem of loyalty are the issue of majority oppression of minority shareholders, and the unique questions of special litigation committees.

Self-Dealing: Self-dealing involves any kind of contract or transaction between a corporate director and his or her corporation. The danger in such transactions is potential unfairness to the corporation and its stockholders, since the corporate director is at once both an "adverse" party to the corporation and one of the persons who must make the decision whether to enter into the transaction. Because of that potential unfairness, early corporate law took a strong stand against any self-dealing contract and effectively held that any such contract was voidable at the option of the corporation at any time, regardless of whether or not the transaction was "fair."

But, while self-dealing is certainly suspect, many contracts between corporate directors and their corporations are indeed in the best interests of the corporation. For example, many times the only place a corporation may obtain low interest loans is from its directors. In the early years of the 20th century, the courts began to chip away at the strict common-law rule against such self-dealing.

While the decisions dealing with self-dealing are by no means consistent, several conclusions may be drawn from those cases. First, if a transaction is fair to the corporation, it will be upheld. Second, if the transaction involves fraud, waste of corporate assets, or overreaching on the part of the director, the transaction will be set aside. Third, if transaction is in the "grey area" in between, the courts will uphold the transaction if it was ratified by a disinterested majority of the board of directors

---

*Wardell v. Union Pacific R.R. Co., 103 U.S. 651, 26 L. Ed. 509 (1880).

in which the interested director did not take part or ratified by a majority of the share-holders. In both of the latter circumstances, the interested director must make a full disclosure of all of the relevant facts.

Interlocking Directorates: If an individual sits on the boards of directors of two corporations that deal with each other in some way, there is an opportunity for abuse similar to that found in cases of self-dealing. The common director may "sell out" one corporation in favor of the other. In such cases, as in self-dealing cases, the courts generally look to see whether there is "manifest unfairness" to one company and may set aside transactions if such unfairness exists. The courts also tend to look to the extent of the common director's involvement in the decision-making process in both corporations. If the common director was instrumental in convincing the board of the "losing" corporation to enter into the transaction, the courts will often set the transaction aside.

Of course, **interlocking directorates** may also be used to the benefit of both cor-porations, especially if the corporations are in need of direct links of communication. That use of interlocking directorates is permissible unless the firms are competitors, in which case the interlock between the firms is forbidden under the federal antitrust laws (see Chapter 9, p. 316).

The Corporate Opportunity Doctrine: The knowledge that a director acquires through his or her position can sometimes be turned to personal advantage. One aspect of that problem, the issue of "insider trading" in stock of the corporation, is discussed later in Chapter 15, "Securities Regulation." Another aspect involves direc-tors or officers who "appropriate" corporate business opportunities for their own advantage. The general rule is that a corporate director or officer may not make a secret profit in connection with corporate transactions, compete unfairly with his or her corporation, or take profitable business opportunities that belong to the corpora-tion. Thus, for example, a corporate director who knows that his or her corporation is interested in acquiring certain mining property may not secretly purchase that property in order to resell it to the corporation at a higher price. Sometimes such problems are termed *issues of conflict of interest.*

The first question in such cases is whether an opportunity is indeed a corporate opportunity. Most courts use a "line of business" test, which compares the types of business in which the corporation is engaged to the opportunity. If the opportunity is in the same or a similar line of business, it is considered a corporate opportunity and the directors and officers may not unfairly appropriate it.

This general rule does not preclude officers and directors from taking advantage of such opportunities in all cases, however. If the corporation voluntarily relinquishes the opportunity after full disclosure, the officers and directors may take advantage of the opportunity for their own benefit. Similarly, directors and officers may take advantage of such opportunities if the corporation is unable to take advantage of the opportunity, as in cases where the action would be illegal or *ultra vires* if undertaken by the corporation. The latter doctrine does not include the situation where the cor-poration lacks the funds to undertake an action in many cases, since directors might not exercise their best efforts to obtain funding for a project, though the courts are divided on that issue.

Majority Oppression of Minority Shareholders: Perhaps the most indistinct application of the duty of loyalty deals with the duties of majority stockholders relative to minority interests. As noted by the U.S. Supreme Court,

> The rule of corporation law and of equity invoked is well settled and has been often applied. The majority has the right to control; but when it does so, it occupies a fiduciary relation toward the minority, as much so as the corporation itself or its officers and directors.*

The principal test in dealing with issues of "oppression" of minority stockholders appears to be one of basic fairness, but the situations in which such oppression may take place are so varied that it is difficult to distill a single rule from the cases. Often, these cases involve stock transactions or changes in stock designed to benefit the majority at the expense of the minority, and the courts, perhaps in frustration, tend to rely on the basic fairness test.

> The increasingly complex transactions of the business and financial communities demonstrate the inadequacy of the traditional theories of fiduciary obligation as tests of majority responsibility to the minority. These theories have failed to afford adequate protection to minority shareholders and particularly to those in closely held corporations whose disadvantageous and often precarious position renders them particularly vulnerable to the vagaries of the majority. Although courts have recognized the potential for abuse or unfair advantage when a controlling shareholder sells his shares at a premium over investment value . . . or in a controlling shareholder's use of control to avoid equitable distribution of corporate assets . . . no comprehensive rule has emerged. . . .**

But the lack of a comprehensive rule has not deterred the courts. The courts have, on occasion, set aside both stock transactions by majority shareholders and control devices by majority directors based on the theory of unfairness.†

Derivative Suits Revisited: Oppression and Special Litigation Committees: One of the principal protections against oppression of the minority by the majority is the derivative action, described earlier on page 246. After such suits are filed, the corporation becomes an interested party and has a great deal to say about how such suits are to be prosecuted or settled. But, since the defendants are often members of the board or corporate officers, there is often a strong conflict of interest on such issues. One way of resolving such difficulties is through the formation of special litigation committees, composed of disinterested members of the board of directors, who make decisions regarding the case for the corporation. The courts have generally held that the business judgment rule is applicable to the decisions of such committees. Further protection is afforded minority shareholders by rules that permit the court to review settlements and dismissals of such actions.

---

*Southern Pacific Co. v. Bogert, 250 U.S. 483, 39 S. Ct. 533, 63 L. Ed. 1099 (1919).

**Jones v. H. F. Ahmanson & Co., 1 Cal. 3d 93, 81 Cal. Rptr. 592, 460 P. 2d 464 (S. Ct. of Cal., 1969; opinion by C. Justice Traynor).

†Cf., Zahn v. Transamerica Corporation, 162 F. 2d 36 (3d. Circuit, 1947); Sinclair Oil Corp. v. Levien, 280 A. 2d 717 (S. Ct. of Del., 1971).

Statutory Duties of Officers and Directors

In addition to the fiduciary duties imposed by the common law, state business corporation acts usually impose other duties and liabilities on directors and officers for certain types of transactions. Those provisions often impose personal liability on directors for prohibited acts without regard to bad faith or unfairness. State acts commonly impose such liability for paying dividends in violation of the act, stock repurchases in violation of the act, distributing assets of the corporation to stockholders upon liquidation without first paying corporate creditors, and allowing the corporation to loan money to an officer or director. Directors who wish to avoid such personal liability must vote against such actions.

Corporate Financing

It is doubtful that the huge industrial base of the United States could have been built without the corporate form. The vast amounts of capital necessary to create the giant firms in our economy can only be raised from wide and diverse sources. But the financing methods of the smallest close corporation and the largest public corporation differ only in amounts invested. The basic types of financing remain the same.

Initially, financing for a corporation comes from two sources: investment in the firm, for which shares of stock are issued; and borrowing by the firm, either in the form of direct loans from banks or other institutional lenders or by issuing bonds or other debt instruments. Investment is often termed **equity financing,** while issuance of bonds and other borrowing is often termed **debt financing.**

Initial Funding: Preincorporation Stock Subscriptions   Initially, capital funds of any corporation come from the investments of persons who have "subscribed for shares" prior to incorporation. The promotors of a potential corporation will find persons willing to promise to buy shares if and when the corporation is formed. After the articles of incorporation are issued by the state, the corporation will "accept" those subscriptions and issue the shares when the amount promised is paid. Stock subscriptions are usually revocable until they are accepted by the board of directors at the first meeting.

Authorized, Issued, and Treasury Shares   The articles of incorporation also specify how many shares of stock the corporation is authorized to issue without further state approval, and the classes and relative rights of each class of stock. These are the **authorized shares,** and additional shares may not be issued unless the articles are amended by vote of the shareholders. As a result shareholders have some protection against **dilution** of their proportionate share interests and ownership rights.

The corporation is under no duty to issue all of the authorized shares, however. Those that are issued are called, logically, **issued shares** and, if they remain in the hands of stockholders, may also be called **outstanding shares.** Issued shares that have been reacquired by the corporation are known as **treasury shares.** Treasury shares may not be voted, and state law may require such shares to be restored to the status of unissued shares on the corporate books.

The Nature of Stock Interests Ownership of stock is a three-pronged interest in a corporation. Stockholders may have a right to *earnings* of the corporation, in the form of dividends; a right to *vote* on major issues facing the corporation and for members of the board of directors; and a right to a part of the *assets* of the corporation upon dissolution of the corporation. The term *dissolution* means termination and winding up of corporate affairs.

Not all shares of stock have equal rights regarding earnings, voting, and assets. Stock is often divided into different classes, and those classes may have different configurations of rights regarding earnings, voting, and assets. For example, a rather common configuration establishes two classes of stock, often called **preferred** and **common.** The preferred stock may have the right to receive dividends, often in a pre-established amount, before any dividends are paid to the common stock. But preferred stock may not be able to vote. The common stock may have the right to vote, but must wait until all the holders of preferred stock are paid dividends before it shares in the earnings of the corporation. However, because the amount is pre-established, preferred stock dividends may be lower than those paid on common stock. Preferred shares may be "preferred" as to assets as well as to dividends.

The profits of a corporation may be accumulated within the corporation and used for corporate purposes, or they may be paid out to the shareholders in the form of **dividends.** There are limits imposed by the Internal Revenue Code on how much of the earnings may be held within the corporation without distribution in the form of the **accumulated earnings tax,** however. The decision whether or not to declare and pay a dividend rests, as the *Kamin* case indicates, almost entirely in in the hands of the board of directors. Dividends may be payable in cash, in kind (in property or stock of other corporations), or in stock of the corporation. Most states prohibit giving a dividend if the corporation is insolvent at the time. The term *insolvent* is usually defined as being unable to meet its debts as they come due.

Preferred dividends may be *cumulative, noncumulative,* or *partially cumulative.* If the directors fail to pay dividends in one year, they will be carried forward and paid in later years in the case of **cumulative dividends,** while **noncumulative dividends** are not carried forward if they are not declared. Partially cumulative dividends are usually "cumulative to the extent of earnings," or a first claim on actual earnings only. Preferred stock may also be **participating.** This means that after the preferred dividends are paid, the preferred stockholder also receives the dividend paid to the common stock as well. Typically, preferred stock is nonparticipating, however. Preferred shares may also be convertible into common stock at a specified price or ratio.

Stock **options,** the right to purchase shares in the future, are used to raise capital, provide employee incentives, and sometimes as a control device. Stock subject to those options is not considered issued until the option is exercised. **Warrants** are transferrable options to acquire shares from the corporation at a specific price.

Preemptive Rights By issuing new shares, a corporation may affect the existing financial and voting rights of preexisting shareholders, resulting in **dilution** of existing shareholders' rights. Assume that the XYZ corporation has ten shareholders, each owning ten shares of stock. Obviously each stockholder has a 10 percent interest in dividends, assets, and voting rights. If the company were to issue twenty new shares to the ten existing shareholders equally, each shareholder would have twelve shares, but each would still have a 10 percent ownership interest in dividends, assets, and voting. But if the corporation issued those twenty shares to two new shareholders, the ten preexisting shareholders would no longer have a 10 percent interest but an 8.3 percent interest, resulting in a smaller proportionate share of dividends, assets, and voting rights.

To protect against such dilution of ownership, the common law developed the concept of **preemptive rights.** That concept permits existing shareholders to subscribe for their proportionate shares of new shares to be issued by the corporation. Preemptive rights do not extend to authorized but unissued shares, treasury shares, or shares issued for property or services rather than for cash.

State business corporation acts generally make substantial changes to the common law. Preemptive rights are usually permissive, rather than mandatory, and corporations are permitted to dispense with them entirely in their articles. Such statutes also provide that preemptive rights do not exist between different classes of shares, and that shares issued pursuant to employee incentive plans are not subject to such rights. As a result, the doctrine of preemptive rights is less important than it was under the common law, though the courts may still use the doctrine to protect shareholders from oppressive "freeze outs" by management, designed to limit the stock rights of minority stockholders.

Debt Financing   Corporations may obtain additional funds by borrowing money, usually by issuing debt securities: *bonds, debentures,* and *notes.* A **bond** is secured by some type of mortgage or lien on corporate property, while a **debenture** is an unsecured obligation of the corporation. A note is usually issued for a shorter term than a bond and is made payable to the payee or his order, rather than to "bearer" in the case of many bonds. The term *bond* is often used in a generic sense, to refer to all debt instruments. Debt instruments do not evidence any ownership interest in the corporation, though occasionally debt instruments are given the right to vote as further security for the payment of the debt. Upon dissolution of the corporation the debt instruments must be paid first, prior to any distribution of assets to shareholders.

Corporations usually reserve the right to *redeem* debt instruments, which means the corporation may call in such instruments and pay them, even before they are due. Many debt instruments require the corporation to set aside funds each year to pay off such instruments. Such provisions in the instruments are called *sinking funds.* Some debt securities may be convertible into equity securities, at some predetermined ratio, creating both *convertible bonds* and *convertible debentures.*

Nonprofit Organizations

It is easy for business students (and textbooks written for business students) to become myopic about the relative importance of business and business organizations. But another large group of organizations is extremely important to business and, in fact, transacts business in many areas as well. Those organizations are the nonprofit organizations.

Nonprofit organizations is a term that covers a great deal of ground. Included in the term might be organizations formed for *charitable purposes,* including health, civic, educational, scientific, or religious purposes; *social purposes,* including fraternal groups and other clubs; *trade purposes,* including labor unions, professional organizations, and business groups; and *political purposes,* such as political parties, interest groups, and political action committees. Sometimes nonprofit organizations are divided into two large categories: *public-benefit organizations,* designed to aid the public or others outside of the organization, such as charities; and *mutual-benefit organizations,* formed to aid the group and its members. Regardless of classification, some of the most powerful organizations in America are nonprofit organizations: huge labor unions, giant foundations, political parties, hospitals, and church groups.

Structure of Nonprofit Organizations   Nonprofit organizations are usually organized as *associations, not-for-profit corporations,* or *foundations.* An **association** closely resembles a partnership but is often treated as a corporation for regulatory and tax purposes. They are rarely treated as a separate entity for liability purposes, however, and there seem to be few advantages to this form except simplicity. Associations may or may not have a formal agreement and by-laws establishing the organization. Leadership is often hand-picked by the outgoing leadership.

The most popular form of organization for nonprofit organizations is as a nonprofit or **not-for-profit corporation.** Such corporations, like their business counterparts, are treated as legal entities and must fulfill certain formalities before corporate status is granted by the state. Most states maintain a not-for-profit corporation act to regulate these organizations. If there is a membership, the members usually have the right to select the board of directors or other leadership.

A **foundation** is usually organized as a charitable trust. The settlor of the trust, usually a philanthropist or group of charitable-minded citizens, will establish a board of trustees under a trust document and give a sum of money to that board to be used in accordance with specific directions in the trust document. Some foundations have been established by business corporations, though such a use of corporate funds has been criticized by regulatory bodies and stockholder interests.

Liability of Nonprofit Organizations

The mere fact that an organization is nonprofit does not immunize it from suit. While the common law had generally granted charities immunity from suits for torts, the doctrine of charitable immunity is now in full retreat and no longer exists in many states (see *Flagiello* v. *The Pennsylvania Hospital,* p. 18). Some states have provided specific statutes, immunizing particular types of charities, such as hospitals, from certain kinds of torts. There never was an immunity from suits based on contracts made by charitable organizations, and nonprofit organizations other than charities are generally not immune from any kind of suit.

Perhaps the most important issue in the liability of nonprofit organizations is who is liable. If the organization is an entity, such as a not-for-profit corporation or a trust, the entity is liable in the same manner as business corporations and private trusts. If the organization is an unincorporated association, the common-law rule was that all members of the association were jointly and severally liable for the obligations of the association, much like a business partnership. Some states have provided statutes holding the association primarily liable for such obligations, and permitting suit in the name of the association but, if the assets of the association are insufficient to satisfy the judgment, the plaintiff may proceed against any member of the association for the balance. Such statutes also grant associations the right to sue in their own names, make contracts, and hold property.

Tax Considerations

Nonprofit organizations organized for certain purposes have two distinct advantages under the federal tax laws: first, such organizations pay no taxes themselves; and, second, contributions to such organizations are deductible to the person making the contribution, if the organization is "qualified" and has received a proper letter from the Internal Revenue Service. Deductions are permitted to organizations that are

> organized and operated exclusively for religious, charitable, scientific, literary, or educational purposes or for the prevention of cruelty to children or animals. (Internal Revenue Code, Sec. 501 (c)(3).)

Duties of Officers and Leaders

The leadership of many nonprofit organizations, particularly public-benefit organizations, are "self-chosen." That is, since there is no "membership," the leadership is chosen by invitation by the existing leadership. As a result no one oversees the activities of the leadership, as the stockholders do in a business corporation, and there is very little accountability. Those leaders are still fiduciaries to the organization, but enforcement of those duties is difficult. The following case describes one method of enforcing those duties, with an interesting comparison of duties in a business corporation to those in a nonprofit organization.

Stern v. Lucy Webb Hayes National Training School for Deaconesses and Missionaries

308 F. Supp. 1003 (Dist. of Col., 1974)

The Lucy Webb Hayes School was established in 1891 by a missionary society of the Methodist Church and later constructed Sibley Memorial Hospital, a large urban health care facility in Washington, D.C. In 1906, the group was incorporated as a not-for-profit corporation, managed by a board of trustees that met twice a year. The day-to-day affairs of the corporation were managed by an Executive Committee, and funds received were to be managed by an Investment Committee, made up of members of the board of trustees. In fact, however, the affairs of the hospital were handled by two men, the treasurer and the hospital administrator. Those men dominated the board of trustees, which routinely accepted their recommendations. Evidence showed that the Investment Committee did not even meet for eleven years.

The plaintiffs, who were patients of the hospital, filed a class action alleging that the treasurer routinely deposited all funds in checking accounts that received no interest, and those deposits were made in banks or financial institutions in which other members of the board of trustees were officers or had interests. In 1971, for example, the hospital had over

$4 million available for investment, but almost $1.5 million was held in non-interest-bearing checking accounts. One checking account alone had over $1 million. The plaintiffs alleged that if those funds had been properly invested, health-care costs could have been lowered because of the income to the hospital from the investments. The Court ruled earlier (367 F. Supp. 536) that the class was proper.

GESELL, District Judge.

. . . .

III. Breach of Duty.

Plaintiffs' . . . contention is that . . . the facts . . . reveal serious breaches of duty on the part of the defendant trustees and the knowing acceptance of benefits from those breaches by the defendant banks and savings and loan associations.

A. The Trustees

Basically, the trustees are charged with mismanagement, nonmanagement and self-dealing. The applicable law is unsettled. The charitable corporation is a relatively new legal entity which does not fit neatly into the established common law categories of corporation and trust. . . . [t]he modern trend is to apply corporate rather than trust principles in determining the liability of the directors of charitable corporations, because their functions are virtually indistinguishable from those of their "pure" corporate counterparts.

1. Mismanagement.

Both trustees and corporate directors are liable for losses occasioned by their negligent mismanagement of investments. However the degree of care required appears to differ in many jurisdictions. A trustee is uniformly held to a high standard of care and will be held liable for simple negligence, while a director must often have committed "gross negligence" or otherwise be guilty of more than mere mistakes of judgment. . . .

. . . Since the board members of most large charitable corporations fall within the corporate rather than the trust model, being charged with the operation of ongoing businesses, it has been said that they should only be held to the less stringent corporate standard of care. . . . More specifically, directors of charitable corporations are required to exercise ordinary and reasonable care in the performance of their duties, exhibiting honesty and good faith. . . .

2. Nonmanagement.

Plaintiffs allege that the individual defendants failed to supervise the management of Hospital investments or even to attend meetings of the committees charged with such supervision. . . .

Once again, the rule for charitable corporations is closer to the traditional corporate rule: directors should at least be permitted to delegate investment decisions to a committee of board members, so long as all directors assume the responsibility for supervising such committees by periodically scrutinizing their work. . . .

Total abdication of the supervisory role, however, is improper even under traditional corporate principles. A director who fails to acquire the information necessary to supervise investment policy or consistently fails even to attend the meetings at which such policies are considered has violated his fiduciary duty to the corporation. . . . A director whose failure to supervise permits negligent mismangement by others to go unchecked has committed an independent wrong against the corporation. . . .

3. Self-Dealing.

Under District of Columbia law, neither trustees nor corporate directors are absolutely barred from placing funds under their control into a bank having an interlocking directorship with their own institutions. In both cases, however, such transactions will be subjected to the closest scrutiny to determine whether or not the duty of loyalty has been violated. . . . A deliberate conspiracy among trustees or Board members to enrich the interlocking bank at the expense of the trust or corporation would, for example, constitute such a breach and render the conspirators liable for any losses. . . . Trustees may be found guilty of a breach of trust even for mere negligence in the maintenance of accounts with which they are associated, . . . while directors are generally only required to show "entire fairness" to the corporation and "full disclosure" of the potential conflict of interest to the Board. . . .

. . . .

Applying these standards to the facts in the record, the Court finds that each of the defendant trustees has breached his fiduciary duty to supervise the management of Sibley's investments. . . . [T]hese men have in the past failed to exercise even the most cursory supervision over the handling of Hospital funds. . . .

The management of a non-profit charitable hospital imposes a severe obligation upon its trustees. A hospital such as Sibley is not closely regulated by any public authority, it has no responsibility to file financial reports, and its Board is self-perpetuating. The interests of its patients are funnelled primarily through large group insurers who pay the patients' bills, and the patients lack meaningful participation in the Hospital's affairs. It is obvious that, in due course, new trustees must come to the Board of this Hospital, some of whom will be affiliated with banks, savings and loan associations, and other financial institutions. The tendency of such representatives of such institutions is often to seek business in return for advice and assistance rendered as trustees. It must be made absolutely clear that Board membership carries no right to preferential treatment in the placement or handling of the Hospital's investments and business accounts. The Hospital would be well-advised to restrict membership on its Board to the representatives of financial institutions which have no substantial business relationships with the Hospital. The best way to avoid potential conflicts of interest and to be assured of objective advice is to avoid the possibility of such conflicts at the time new trustees are elected.

The Choice of Business Form

Just as there is no best form of investment, there is no best business form. Which business form is right for a particular business will depend, in all cases, on the specific needs of that business and the desires of the owners of the business. In some cases, the choice will be clear: some types of dangerous enterprise should probably always be incorporated, and businesses that wish to attract a large amount of outside investment should also probably be incorporated. But incorporation may not be worth it for a small, one-owner business because of the formalities involved and the capital tax imposed on corporations. Some of the important considerations when choosing a business form are described in the following sections.

Formalities and Expense

For most businesses, formalities and expense should probably not be a consideration in determining the proper business form. The owner of a small, one-owner business may find incorporation a waste of time and money, but there may be countervailing considerations. For any business in which two parties are involved, some formality is absolutely necessary, if only to formalize the partnership in writing and avoid the almost inevitable conflicts. The corporate registration fees and capital taxes or the fees paid to a competent attorney to draft a partnership agreement or articles of incorporation should probably not be a consideration in light of other benefits.

One word of caution seems advisable: the documents creating a business should always be tailored to that business. "One size fits all" corporation kits and boilerplate forms may indeed work for a particular business, but the forms should be studied very carefully and competent advice sought before they are formally adopted.

Taxation

Corporations are taxed as separate entities with their own tax rates, while proprietorships and partnerships are taxed as extensions of the business owner, at his or her individual tax rate. Thus, there may be a real benefit to incorporating if the individual tax rate is higher than the corporate rate. There is often no detriment to electing the corporate form if the corporate rate is higher than the individual rate, however, since smaller corporations may elect to be taxed as a partnership under **Subchapter S** of the Internal Revenue Code (see, generally, Chapter 18).

Limited Liability

Historically, the limited liability of shareholders of a corporation has often been used to justify incorporation in a great many cases, but the value of incorporation to escape personal liability is probably overstated. In most cases, insurance will be purchased to cover losses and liability regardless of business form. As far as contract obligations are concerned, banks and other lenders are aware of the limited liability of corporate stockholders and will probably require a personal guarantee of any loan to the corporation by the principal stockholders.

Continuity of Existence

While partnerships technically terminate upon the death or resignation of any partner and corporations technically last indefinitely, that difference may be of little practical significance. Partnership agreements may be drafted to provide for smooth transitions, if such events occur, and provide almost as much continuity as the corporate form. It is also important to remember that perhaps the death or retirement of a "key person" *ought* to spell the end of a business.

Management and Control

The corporate form has some important advantages for management and control purposes, especially in the middle-sized business. Large partnerships can be quite unwieldy, since each partner technically has the right to oversee operations in the event there is no formal agreement. Even if there is a formal agreement, all partners have the authority to bind the partnership in dealings with third parties. The corporate form or a limited partnership, with appropriate by-laws and voting rights, may resolve many of these problems.

Transferability of Interests

Again, the surface advantage of free transferability of shares in a corporation can be resolved in a partnership through a formal agreement. It is important to note that in smaller businesses the owners may not desire free transferability, because they may wish to retain some control over the parties in the business. Again, the corporate by-laws and articles may restrict transferability of shares, so that this so-called advantage really makes little difference.

On the other hand, if investment funds are important to a business (and in many cases they are not), the corporate form has some rather substantial advantages. If the owners anticipate that additional capital will be raised by selling interests in the business, the corporate form is usually preferred, though in some cases the same result may be obtained with a limited partnership.

Summary and Conclusions

Much of the law of business associations is based on the common law of agency. That law deals with the creation of authority to deal on behalf of others, and imposes substantial duties on agents in the form of the fiduciary duties. Those duties are imposed on all agents, including partners, corporate officers, and corporate directors.

Partnerships are formed whenever two or more persons conduct a business as co-owners, and may be formed by formal agreement or by implication. All partners are individually liable for partnership obligations unless the firm has become a limited partnership. A variety of more exotic business forms, including joint ventures, joint stock associations, and business trusts are based on partnership law as well.

Corporations are used to limit liability, obtain tax advantages, and encourage public investment. Corporations must be formed according to state law, beginning with an application for articles of incorporation. Corporations only have the power to do those things noted in their articles or permitted by state law.

Corporations are owned by their stockholders, who elect the board of directors. That board in turn appoints the corporate officers. Officers and directors have fiduciary duties to the corporation, which may be enforced by derivative actions filed by shareholders on behalf of the corporation.

Corporations are financed by the sale of stock, known as equity financing, or borrowing money, known as debt financing. Stock may be divided into classes evidencing different claims of shareholders on earnings, assets, or voting rights.

Nonprofit organizations are usually organized as unincorporated associations, not-for-profit corporations, or foundations. Unincorporated associations have more problems of liability than other forms, but those problems have been resolved by recent state statutes. Leaders of such organizations have fiduciary duties as well, though enforcement is difficult.

PRO AND CON

ISSUE: Does Business Have "Social Responsibilities"?

PRO: Businesses Should Step in to Fill Social Needs
Archie B. Carroll*

First, let me give you my views as to what CSR (Corporate Social Responsibilities) means.... In my view CSR involves the conduct of a business so that it is economically profitable, law abiding, ethical, and socially supportive. To be socially responsible, in my view, then means that profitability and obedience to the law are foremost conditions to discussion of the firm's ethics and the extent to which it supports the society in which it exists with contributions of money, time, and talent. Thus, CSR is comprised of four parts: economic, legal, ethical and voluntary or philanthropic.

. . . .

...[S]hould industry respond to the federal government's cutbacks [in social programs] and what should that response look like [?] To be sure this is an ideological question if I ever saw one. Where one stands on this issue depends very heavily on one's broad view of the quality of life the citizenry should expect in the United States and the relative role business versus government should play in delivering this quality of life.

. . . .

In pursuing the question of what business should do, I can't resist posing the two extreme options available, if only to reject them both as overly reactionary. I personally like the way these two extremes were articulated by Stanley Karson, director of the Clearinghouse on Corporate Responsibility in Washington. At one extreme he sees executives misinterpreting the signals of the electorate and withdrawing, even faster than the federal government, from the social arena. The private sector would adopt a business-as-usual posture and continue to pursue higher and higher profits, while the sores that have festered in its communities grow worse. The warning here is that problems ignored become problems enlarged.

At the other extreme we see corporate leaders caught up in the euphoria of a simpatico, pro-business administration and envisioning that they have all the ideas, talents and resources to single-handedly save the nation by solving welfare, public education, and urban development problems. The warning here is that business can no more take over all the functions of government than government can assume the responsibilities of business.

Fortunately, the warnings will be heeded, because concerned business leadership will not take off in either of these extreme directions. Business must assume a moderate, middle-of-the-road role, one that strengthens the country's economic and social system and yet at the same time hacks away at the thickets of social problems—poverty, disease, discrimination, and social unrest—while abiding by the limits of talents and resources that the corporation possesses.

. . . .

When federal outlays for social programs are being scaled back, we must be wary of notions of a slick transfer of responsibility from government to business. The basic approaches of the two institutions are in striking contrast to one another. Government models of helping have been traditionally overly rigid and structured along the lines of a bureaucracy, complete with the typical characteristics of top-heaviness and inefficiency. Activities in the private sector tend to be more localized and varied, sometimes reflecting the specific needs of a particular area or the unique skills that are available there.

. . . .

... [W]e cannot expect business to buy into the same social agenda that has been addressed by federal programs. It is clear that many of these do not warrant private sector support and thus, we have to accept the groping, the experimentation, and the successes and failures that are likely to occur as a refashioned federal role is sought.

Business should do more than it has done in the past. But it could not possibly compensate for federal budget cuts and it should not try.

*Archie Carroll is professor of management at the University of Georgia. From his speech entitled "Corporate Social Responsibility: Will Industry Respond to Cutbacks in Social Program Funding?" delivered at Kent State University, Kent, Ohio, Feb. 28, 1983, and reprinted in *Vital Speeches of the Day*, Vol. 49, no. 9, p. 604. Reprinted by permission.

CON: The Social Responsibility of Business Is to Increase Its Profits
Milton Friedman*

When I hear businessmen speak eloquently about the "social responsibilities of business in a free enterprise system," I am reminded of the wonderful line about the Frenchman who discovered at the age of 70 that he had been speaking prose all his life. The businessmen believe that they are defending free enterprise when they declaim that business is not concerned "merely" with profit but also with promoting desirable "social" ends; that business has a "social conscience" and takes seriously its responsibilities for providing employment, eliminating discrimination, avoiding pollution and whatever else may be the catchwords of the contemporary crop of reformers. In fact they are—or would be if they or anyone else took them seriously—preaching pure and unadulterated socialism. Businessmen who talk this way are unwitting puppets of the intellectual forces that have been undermining the basis of free society these past decades.

. . . .

In a free-enterprise, private-property system, a corporate executive is an employee of the owners of the business. He has a direct responsibility to his employers. That responsibility is to conduct the business in accordance with their desires, which generally will be to make as much money as possible while conforming to the basic rules of the society, both those embodied in law and those embodied in ethical custom. Of course, in some cases his employers may have a different objective. A group of persons might establish a corporation for an eleemosynary purpose—for example, a hospital or a school. The manager of such a corporation will not have money profit as his objective but the rendering of certain services. . . .

What does it mean to say that the corporate executive has a "social responsibility" in his capacity as businessman? If this statement is not pure rhetoric, it must mean that he is to act in some way that is not in the interest of his employers. For example, that he is to refrain from increasing the price of the product in order to contribute to the social objective of preventing inflation, even though a price increase would be in the best interests of the corporation. Or that he is to make expenditures on reducing pollution beyond the amount that is in the best interests of the corporation or that is

required by law in order to contribute to the social objective of improving the environment. Or that, at the expense of corporate profits, he is to hire "hard-core" unemployed instead of better-qualified available workmen to contribute to the social objective of reducing poverty.

In each of these cases, the corporate executive would be spending someone else's money for a general social interest. Insofar as his actions in accord with his "social responsibility" reduce returns to stockholders, he is spending their money. Insofar as his actions raise the price to customers, he is spending the customers' money. Insofar as his actions lower the wages of some employees, he is spending their money.

The stockholders or the customers of the employees could separately spend their own money on the particular action if they wished to do so. The executive is exercising a distinct "social responsibility" rather than serving as an agent of the stockholders or the customers or the employees, only if he spends the money in a different way than they would have spent it.

But if he does this, he is in effect imposing taxes, on the one hand, and deciding how the tax proceeds shall be spent, on the other.

This process raises political questions on two levels: principle and consequences. On the level of political principle, the imposition of taxes and the expenditure of tax proceeds are governmental functions. We have established elaborate constitutional, parliamentary and judicial provisions to control these functions, to assure that taxes are imposed so far as possible in accordance with the preferences and desires of the public—after all, "taxation without representation" was one of the battle cries of the American Revolution. We have a system of checks and balances to separate the legislative function of imposing taxes and enacting expenditures from the executive function of collecting taxes and administering expenditure programs and from the judicial function of mediating disputes and interpreting the law.

Here the businessman—self-selected or appointed directly or indirectly by the stockholders—is to be simultaneously legislator, executive and jurist. He is to decide whom to tax by how

---

much and for what purpose, and he is to spend the proceeds—all this guided only by general exhortations from on high to restrain inflation, improve the environment, fight poverty and so on and on.

The whole justification for permitting the corporate executive to be selected by the stockholders is that the executive is an agent serving the interests of his prinicipal. This justification disappears when the corporate executive imposes taxes and spends the proceeds for "social" purposes. He becomes in effect a public employee, a civil servant, even though he remains in name an employee of a private enterprise. On grounds of political principle, it is intolerable that such civil servants . . . should be selected as they are now. If they are to be civil servants, then they must be selected through a political process. If they are to impose taxes and make expenditures to foster "social" objectives, then political machinery must be set up to guide the assessment of taxes and to determine through a political process the objectives to be served. . . .

DISCUSSION QUESTIONS

1. Why should principals be liable for the torts of their servants? Why shouldn't principals be liable for the torts of their independent contractors?

2. Are the fiduciary duties reasonable? Is it fair to hold agents to a higher moral standard than the rest of society? Why do we do so?

3. Is there a good reason for organizing a business as a joint stock association or business trust?

4. Why should limited partners escape personal liability just because the firm had the forethought to register as a limited partnership with the state? Does registration protect third parties who deal with the partnership?

5. Should, as in the *Walkovszky* case, a business be permitted to incorporate solely to inhibit the claims of members of the public who might be injured as a result of the business' activities? Did Walkovszky choose to be hit by Carleton's cab in the same way parties contracting with Carleton chose to deal with him? Should there be a difference between tort and contract liability?

6. Much of the stock in America's largest corporations is owned by other corporations, particularly so-called institutional investors such as banks, pension plans, and insurance companies. What are the implications of such ownership for the small investor? Who votes that stock?

7. If management solicits proxies from the shareholders for the purpose of electing directors that will retain the present management and pay them high salaries, isn't management violating its fiduciary duties not to indulge in self-dealing?

8. Is there any way to assure that nonprofit organizations will actually do the things they are organized to do, or that directors and trustees of public-benefit organizations will act properly? Who is there to enforce those duties?

9. If a foundation owns shares of stock in a business corporation, who decides how that stock is to be voted?

10. Is there a good reason for a small, single owner business to incorporate aside from tax advantages if they apply? Do you suppose the real reason why many such businesses incorporate is prestige alone? Is that a good reasons?

CASE PROBLEMS

1. Mr. and Mrs. Junkans were building a new home, and Mr. Junkans was doing much of the work himself. He hired a carpenter and his crew to "rough in" the house and also hired a plumber to do much of the plumbing work. Lee, a plumber's helper, fell from scaffolding negligently erected by the carpenter's crew, and was injured. Mr. Junkans had worked directly with the carpenter, though not on the construction of the scaffold, and had given detailed instructions to the carpenter while he was working on the job. Lee sued Mr. and Mrs. Junkans under the theory of *respondeat superior.* Decision as to Mr. Junkans? Mrs. Junkans? [*Lee v. Junkans,* 18 Wis. 2d 56, 117 N.W. 2d 614 (1962).]

2. Pleasant Hills Realty retained salespersons on a purely commission basis to sell real estate and required each salesperson to own a car. The salesmen had little direction except that they received "leads" from Pleasant Hills, and Pleasant Hills did not withhold taxes, furnish a car, or directly oversee the work. Gozdonovic was injured when he was struck by a car driven by a salesperson on the way to show a house. Is Pleasant Hills liable under *respondeat superior?* [*Gozdonovic v. Pleasant Hills Realty Co.,* 357 Pa. 23, 53 A. 2d 73, (1947).]

3. Barrett, an employee of Cook County, accepted bribes for various illegal activities amounting to $180,000. The county filed suit, claiming that the bribes were the property of the county since Barrett was a fiduciary. Result? [*County of Cook v. Barrett,* 36 Ill. App. 3d, 344 N.E. 2d 540 (1975).]

4. Horton and Althouse were in the business of raising potatoes as a partnership. Kaufman and Brown were in the business of distributing potatoes to retailers, also as a partnership. Kaufman and Brown agreed to purchase a 50 percent undivided interest in Horton and Althouse's potato crop for a specified amount of cash. Horton and Althouse were to pay all of the expenses of producing the crop. Upon sale of the crop, Kaufman and Brown were to be paid back the amount they had expended, and the balance of the proceeds from the sale was to be divided among the parties. What kind of business form is involved in the case? [*Kaufman-Brown Potato Co.* v. *Long,* 182 F. 2d 594 (9th Cir., 1950).]

5. In 1903, Henry Ford incorporated the Ford Motor Company. Ford owned 250 shares of stock, and four other men, including Dodge, owned 50 shares each. After 1915, Ford did not declare a dividend, but on several occasions the price

of automobiles was lowered. By 1919, the company was carrying a cash surplus of over $111 million. Ford continued to refuse to issue a dividend, stating that

> My ambition is to employ still more men, to spread the benefits of this industrial system to the greatest possible number, to help them build up their lives and their homes. To do this we are putting the greatest share of our profits back in the business.

Dodge argued that Ford's policy was beyond the corporate powers of a profit-making corporation, and that a dividend should be paid. Result? [*Dodge* v. *Ford Motor Co.*, 204 Mich. 459, 170 N.W. 668 (Michigan Sup. Ct., 1919).]

6. The Seminole Hot Springs Corporation leased and operated a swimming pool for which admission was charged. The corporation had been issued articles of incorporation, and an agreement was signed that three shares of stock were to be issued, one each to Caveney, Kraft, and Wettrick. No shares were ever issued, and the corporation owned no assets. Plaintiff's daughter drowned in the pool, and plaintiff brought suit to "pierce the corporate veil." Result? [*Minton* v. *Caveney*, 15 Cal. Rptr. 641, 364 P. 2d 473, 56 Cal. 2d 576 (1961).]

7. Lovel, a real estate broker, was hired by Morton to sell his farm. Lovel later learned that a geology report showed that there was oil under Morton's farm, a fact which Morton did not know. Lovel then arranged with her brother-in-law, Rivers, to purchase the farm in Rivers' name and then began drilling for oil. If oil is discovered, does Morton have a remedy?

8. Warwick, a member of the board of directors of The Bedford Company, learned that the company was going to begin manufacturing televisions, and that officers of the company were in the midst of negotiating a contract with the Gower Company to purchase television cabinets. Warwick then arranged to purchase a large number of shares in the Gower Company, since the large contract with The Bedford Company would be extremely profitable to Gower. Has Warwick done anything wrong? Has anyone been injured? Does anyone have a remedy against Warwick?

9. Marianna is on the board of trustees of a private university. Her sister, Violenta, is president of a school supplies firm. Marianna convinced the balance of the board of trustees to award a very lucrative contract for various supplies to Violenta's firm. Marianna received no profits from the contract, and Violenta's firm supplied the lowest price for the goods. Has anyone done anything wrong? Who has standing to complain?

10. Which form of business would be best for the following businesses? (1) a part-time direct mail business located in a person's basement; (2) manufacture of fireworks, owned by a single person; (3) two individuals operating a real estate brokerage together; (4) two corporations, three individuals, and a partnership which desire to produce a movie.

SUGGESTED READINGS

Cary, William L., and Melvin A. Eisenberg. *Corporations* 5th ed. (Mineola, N.Y.: The Foundation Press, 1980).

Conrad, Alfred F., Robert L. Knauss, and Stanley Siegel. *Enterprise Organization* (Mineola, N.Y.: The Foundation Press, 1982).

Hamilton, Robert W. *The Law of Corporations in a Nutshell* (St. Paul, Minn.: West Publishing Co., 1980).

Lane, Marc J. *Legal Handbook for Nonprofit Organizations* (New York: AMACOM, a division of American Management Associations, 1980).

Part III

Regulation of the Relationships Between Business, Its Competitors, and Its Suppliers

The first relationships in the environment of business that we will consider are those between the firm and its competitors and suppliers. Part of the ethic of individualism is the economic theories of Adam Smith and his followers, which find that the most efficient economic system is based on competition between firms. This type of "perfect competition" is thought to lead to low prices and high output to the benefit of all of society. But unlimited competition has its dangers and may even tend to destroy itself.

The antitrust laws that are the subject of the next three chapters represent an attempt to *control* competition in order to *preserve* competition and, in the process, regulate the relationship between the firm and its competitors and, to a lesser extent, with the firm's suppliers and customers. They attempt to balance the benefits of competition to the community and the individual freedom of businesses to operate freely. The choice made represents a middle ground between total freedom and total control.

The antitrust laws also represent an effort to enforce some personal ethical standards, particularly in the Federal Trade Commission Act. Those portions of the antitrust laws provide a rather comprehensive "code of ethics" for business, by specifying certain types of unfair business practices. Since most of those types of deception involve the relationship between business and its customers, they will be considered in Part IV.

Antitrust Law: Background, Structures, and the Sherman Act

The basic thesis is not that the system of free private enterprise for profit has failed in this generation, but that it has not yet been tried.

Franklin Delano Roosevelt

Antitrust laws in general, and the Sherman Act in particular, are the Magna Carta of free enterprise. They are as important to the preservation of economic freedom and our free enterprise system as the Bill of Rights is to the protection of our fundamental personal freedoms.

Mr. Justice Marshall in U.S. v. Topco Associates, 405 U.S. 596, (1972)

People of the same trade seldom meet together, even for merriment and diversion, but the conversation ends in a conspiracy against the public, or in some contrivance to raise prices. It is impossible indeed to prevent such meeting by any law which either could be executed, or would be consistent with liberty and justice.

Adam Smith, The Wealth of Nations, *1776*

The term *antitrust* is used to describe a group of four federal statutes that attempt to regulate and control various competitive activities, practices, and market structures in American business. Those laws include the *Sherman Antitrust Act* of 1890, the *Clayton Act* and *Federal Trade Commission Act*, both enacted in 1914, and the *Robinson-Patman Act* of 1936. The laws developed both from ancient common law doctrines that dealt with restraints of trade and from a variety of social, political, and economic factors that arose in the last half of the 19th century.

The term *antitrust* is an anachronism. The laws developed at a time when one of the chief public fears involved a specific form of collusive business arrangement known as a *trust*. That business form is virtually nonexistent today, but the term *antitrust* remains as a legacy.

While the term is antiquated, the antitrust laws themselves remain vital and important. The laws are unique in that they attempt to regulate competitive behavior and structure in a *general* way and as a result continue to be highly controversial almost a century after the first such law was enacted.

This chapter will consider several introductory matters regarding the antitrust statutes, including the various purposes of the laws, the history of the statutes themselves, and the administrative and enforcement agencies of the federal government, together with a consideration of part of the first antitrust statute, the Sherman Act. Subsequent chapters will consider other conduct violations, monopolization, merger problems, and the Federal Trade Commission Act's regulation of advertising.

Students should be cautioned that the antitrust laws are statutory in nature. The main provisions of those laws are included in Appendix C, and students can only understand those laws if they *read the statutes*. It is extremely vital that students become familiar with the statutory language found in these laws, probably more so than in most other areas of the law.

The Purposes and Goals of Antitrust

If statements found in many court decisions are to be believed, the sole purpose of antitrust is a single-minded effort to legislate classical economic theory based on "perfect" competition. Much of the controversy surrounding the antitrust laws involves whether that theory is correct or useful in formulating public policy towards business.

Almost from the very beginning, the antitrust laws involved secondary purposes apart from such traditional economic theory. Those purposes involved the political and social ramifications of big business and various business practices. It also seems obvious that parts of the antitrust laws, particularly the Federal Trade Commission (FTC) Act, were aimed at imposing ethical rules of business behavior.

The Economic Goals of Antitrust Policy

Many observers agree that the main purpose of the antitrust laws is to encourage, as far as possible, "pure" competition. The laws, and the policies underlying the laws, were designed and have been interpreted by the courts to remove the obstacles to "competition" and to prohibit or discourage the effects of "imperfect" competition in the marketplace. As one observer has noted

The American antitrust laws are essentially conservative in nature. Their purpose is to maintain free competition by insuring that such competition is fair. They seek to prevent giant aggregations of economic power from being built unfairly, because the use of such power necessarily stifles the opportunities competitors will have to compete meaningfully. In summary, the antitrust laws seek to prevent conduct which weakens or destroys competition.*

To many laymen the analysis of antitrust as an effort to encourage free competition is contradictory. To such persons antitrust is just another example of government overregulation and interference with the personal affairs of businessmen. Much of the public misunderstanding of the antitrust laws stems from the meaning of the term *competition*. When an economist uses the term, he means something far different from the everyday meaning of the term, that of sharp business practices and rivalry between firms. The economist has in mind a very specific ideal state from which flow very important economic consequences.

The Traditional Theory of Competition   According to Adam Smith, the acknowledged founder of classical economic theory, the ideal economic system is one of "perfect" or "pure" or "atomistic" competition. Markets which are "purely competitive" have several principal characteristics.

1. *A large number of firms.* The number of firms in the market is sufficiently large and the market share of each firm is sufficiently small so that no individual seller has the ability to influence market price.

2. *Perfect knowledge.* Each firm is aware of all of the major market factors affecting its welfare, so that no participant can be exploited because of ignorance.

3. *Homogeneous products.* Each firm's product is identical to the product of every other firm in the market, both in its real characteristics and in the mind of the consumers, so that the products actually compete with one another.

4. *Freedom of entry and exit.* There are no unusual or artificial barriers to entry to the market nor are there restrictions on leaving the market.

5. *Selfish motives.* Each firm is motivated by a desire to maximize its own welfare, usually by making as much "profit" as possible.

Those conditions rarely, if ever, exist in the real world. Perhaps the only industry that approximates the conditions of perfect competition is agriculture, and even there perfect knowledge does not exist, there are substantial barriers to entry in the form of large initial investments, and some participants are motivated by noneconomic factors to continue to farm after profitability declines.

Perfect competition is an ideal or "model" system. Traditional economic theory holds that if such a system did exist, the benefits would be substantial, and the economic results would be ideal or optimal. The two principal benefits of such a system

---

*Earl W. Kintner, *An Antitrust Primer* 2d Ed. (New York: The MacMillan Company, 1973) p. 15.

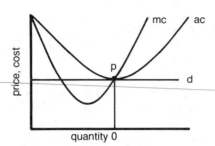

Figure 8-1 Competition Model

are that the prices charged consumers for the product would be the lowest possible, and that the amount of the product supplied would be at its greatest point.

An individual firm in such a market cannot affect price, and therefore faces a perfectly horizontal demand curve, d in Figure 8-1. Each firm can sell any amount it produces at the market price. There is no meaningful pricing decision for that firm since, if it raises its price, it will sell nothing, and there is no incentive to charge less than the market price since its entire output can be sold at the market price. The output of the firm will be determined solely by cost factors. Two types of measurement of costs are possible: *average cost* (ac), that is, the average cost of each unit produced; and **marginal cost** (mc), or the incremental cost of each additional unit produced. In virtually all instances, those costs initially decline because of **economies of scale.** The second unit is generally cheaper to produce than the first because of greater efficiency and utilization of resources. At some point, these economies of scale disappear and each unit becomes more costly to produce than the last because production has passed the point of **diminishing returns.**

In the short run, firms may make excess profits if their costs are lower than other firms in the market. But since access to the market is free, ultimately all firms will be able to produce more cheaply, and the demand curve itself will lower the market price. Similarly, if costs are higher than the price dictated by demand for a single firm, that firm must lower costs or be forced from the market. Adam Smith used the term *the invisible hand* to indicate the forces that tend to produce high efficiency and low cost, lowest possible price, and highest possible output achieved through the processes of perfect competition.

Imperfect Competition The opposite of perfect competition is a pure **monopoly,** in which a single firm is the sole supplier of a product for which there are no close substitutes. The monopolist then faces the demand curve for the entire industry, which by definition is downward sloping as shown by line D in Figure 8-2.

The monopolist does have a pricing decision to make, unlike the firm in the purely competitive market. That is so because he may take advantage of the downward sloping demand curve and vary the price he receives by varying the output he supplies. The price he chooses depends on *two* factors, that of cost and that of **marginal revenue.** Marginal revenue is defined as the increased revenue a producer receives with each additional unit of output. The monopolist, if rational, will choose

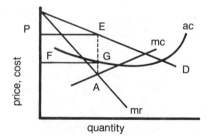

Figure 8-2 Monopoly Model

an ouput where marginal cost equals marginal revenue, shown as point A on Figure 8-2. But that point produces a price at point E on the demand curve, far above the price dictated by cost.

The monopolist then succeeds in doing something that is impossible under perfect competition—charging a price in excess of marginal cost and, perhaps, in excess of long-run average cost. The monopolist also earns profits in excess of price over average cost on each unit sold, as represented by the rectangle FPEG. Such profits tend not to be eroded by the entry of new firms.

Pure monopoly is almost as rare as perfect competition, perhaps existing only in isolated examples (the only general store in a resort town or beer vendors at a ball game, for example) or in government-granted monopolies, such as public utilities. Far more common is the case of **oligopoly,** where there are more than one seller but fewer than the number necessary for perfect competition. Almost all industries reflect this form to a greater or lesser extent.

At first glance, oligopolistic markets seem to be highly competitive and are often marked by bitter price warfare at the outset. But oligopolists soon learn that price warfare hurts all market participants. The end result is often a "shared monopoly," in which several participants coexist and behave as a single monopolist would act. Again, output is lower and prices higher than under the optimum conditions of perfect competition. Those results are obtained by cooperation between the firms, perhaps by outright agreement or by covert conspiracy, or perhaps by **price leadership,** in which all participants simply follow the lead of one firm in determining prices.

Original antitrust theory was based on an attempt to protect and defend perfect competition. The law made competition a goal and removed or made more difficult those business practices that facilitated oligopoly and monopoly or that resulted from such economic markets.

Report of the Attorney General's National Committee to Study the Antitrust Laws
(1955)

Generally speaking, economists support competition for four series of reasons, which are of coordinate importance: (1) because the actual level of prices in competitive markets should in the short run more accurately reflect the influence of demand and of cost, and thus in the long run help guide the flow of capital and other resources toward the most productive possible uses; (2) because the goad of competition provides powerful and pervasive incentives for product innovations and product development, and for long-run cost-reduction, both through improved technology and improved management; these forces make themselves felt in the constant process of product variation, and through the pressures implicit in the fact that competitive conditions offer an open opportunity to new entrants in a particular industry; (3) because competitive conditions in business should lead to an equitable diffusion of the resulting real income among consumers and factors of production; and (4) a view held with somewhat less unanimity than the others, because the more flexible prices of competitive markets should make it easier and cheaper for the economy to adjust to industrial fluctuations, and for the Federal Reserve System and the Government to carry through effective contracyclical programs of stabilization utilizing methods of monetary and fiscal policy.

The graphs and fine points of perfect competition and the imperfections of monopoly and oligopoly are, of course, theory. Many, though not all, argue that Smith's model of perfect competition can never really exist. Certainly the rigorous assumptions are most difficult to fulfill. This use of an ideal system as a basis for public policy is subject to substantial criticism and, to answer such criticism, some economists and policymakers prefer to depend on more practical definitions of competition such as the concept of **workable competition.**

Workable Competition   Beginning in the 1930's, some economists began to speak in terms of "workable" or "effective" competition as a substitute for the precise models of Adam Smith. Generally speaking, the concept of workable competition is a practical one, looking to the effects of market conduct rather than to the precise assumptions of the model. A market is generally considered workably competitive if market forces provide the drive for technological innovation, efficient allocation of resources, and equitable diffusion of income. That is, in a practical sense, the market is more economically advantageous than any other practically attainable alternative.

Modern economists tend to concentrate on three criteria for judging the effectiveness of competition in a market: the *structure* of the market, the *conduct* of firms within the market, and the *performance* of the market in terms of prices, output, and efficiency. Obviously, many of the judgments are subjective, but the emphasis is on practicality. The basic question is not whether Adam Smith's model exists but how well the market works.

Antitrust Policy
Carl Kaysen and Donald F. Turner*

[C]ompetition requires the existence of competitors, in the plural. The vexing question is "how many?" We begin exploring this question by observing that the rigorous model of the perfectly competitive market is the appropriate starting point of any definition, but it cannot be the end of any practically useful one. The model provides us with

---

two important notions: first, a market in which each seller acts as if his own decisions had no influence on any significant market variable—price, supply, the number of other sellers and their sales, etc.; second, a definition of economic efficiency in terms of the relations between costs and prices characteristic of the model. . . . In the model, the first result comes about because sellers are many in number and individually of insignificant size relative to the total market, the product of any seller is a perfect substitute for that of any other, and new sellers enter and old ones leave freely and quickly in response to profits and losses. In real markets—with very few exceptions—these conditions do not hold. The existence of significant economies of scale at both the plant and firm level over some size range means that firms are not generally insignificant in relation to the market. The geography of production and consumption reinforces this result. . . . The outputs of one seller are usually only imperfect substitutes for the outputs of another: product differentiation, advertising, and locational differences among sellers which bring about this result must be taken as permanent features of the economy, answering in some measure to real preferences of consumers. Neither entry nor exit is universally free and speedy. All sorts of barriers to entry, from large capital requirements to high advertising costs and closely held patented technology, are widely characteristic of the economy, though in varying measure in different industries. Frictions, and the influence of uncertainty and risk aversion on business decisions, mean that entry and exit often take place with substantial lags after the changes in profitability which occasion them.

Concentration and Market Power

Nonetheless, though the model of competitive market structure is not usable as such in our definition of competition, other concepts of the model are. Where firms can persistently behave over substantial periods of time in a manner which differs from the behavior that the competitive market would impose on competitive firms facing similar cost and demand conditions, they can be identified as possessing market power. Conversely, where, on the average and viewed over long periods of time, the relations of prices, costs, outputs, capacities, and investments among a group of rivalrous firms are such as would be expected in a competitive model, then it can be inferred that the market does constrain the scope of the individual firm's decisions sufficiently to be called competitive. The existence of such constraints depends on many features of a market. In general, numbers and conditions of entry are the most important of these features. There is also a high correlation between concentration of output in the hands of a small number of large producers and the existence of firms with significant degrees of market power.

The intimate relationship between classical economics and antitrust policy has been criticized from several quarters. Some commentators assert that classical economics is itself a faulty basis for public policy since it is an ideal system. Others claim that the courts have ignored important parts of classical economics in deciding antitrust cases. These critics argue that two principal aspects of economics have been ignored: business efficiency as a "cost" factor, and the influence of foreign competition. Others, such as John Kenneth Galbraith, argue that our basic economic structure has changed so much that classical economic theory is now irrelevant. Regardless, the courts continue to point to the economic rationale of competition as the chief source of antitrust policy.

Political and Social Goals of Antitrust Policy

It is clear from the history of the antitrust movement at the close of the 19th century that antitrust had goals other than the preservation of classical competition. Many of the proponents of antitrust felt that democratic society was being threatened by the accumulation of wealth and by the sheer size of some of the businesses and economic units developed during that time. It was thought that there was a direct relationship between the political power of an individual or group and its wealth. As put by Senator John Sherman, sponsor of the Sherman Antitrust Act, "The popular mind is agitated with ... the inequality of condition, of wealth, and opportunity that has grown within a single generation out of the concentration of capital into vast combinations."

Aside from simple fear of business and wealth and its influence, two other political goals of antitrust policy have been identified. First, it is clear that some of the Congressmen who supported the antitrust statutes did so out of fear of socialism and communism. Their thinking was that if the evils of monopoly became too severe, the public might desert free enterprise and support the various socialist, Marxist, anarchist, and nihilist groups that abounded at the turn of the century.

Second, it has been argued that the alternative to the antitrust laws is inevitably direct government intervention in individual markets. In public utilities, for example, monopolies exist, but they are closely regulated by government at all levels.* If other markets became monopolistic, government might be required to directly intervene and supervise those markets as well. Thus, the broad prohibitions of antitrust were preferable to such close regulation.

Modern courts continue to be influenced by the political purposes of Congress in enacting the various antitrust laws. Courts are generally critical of large business units and generally concerned with the welfare of small units, even when the unit is so small that it cannot make any economic difference to the market. On the other hand, the political desirability of small units is generally treated as subordinate to the competitive goals of the laws, as in cases where restrictive practices that benefit small businesses are found to violate the economic goals of the law.

Ethical Considerations and Goals

It is also true, but often ignored, that the antitrust laws create a code of ethical conduct for businesspersons. The Federal Trade Commission Act in particular prohibits "unfair trade practices" and requires the Federal Trade Commission to make rules that govern various aspects of trade and competition. The Act is aimed at protecting ethical businesspersons from competitive disadvantage suffered because of the actions of unfair competitors and was amended in 1938 to protect customers from being victimized by unscrupulous businesspersons. The Clayton Act and Robinson-Patman Act also contain several sections which prohibit business practices that might be considered unethical or unfair.

The courts seem to follow this ethical goal of the antitrust laws by treating deliberate and knowing conduct more harshly. If a businessperson attempts in good faith to comply with the law and the law still is technically violated, that person may expect more sympathetic treatment from the courts than the businessperson who consciously flouts the law.

---

*See, e.g., the discussion of "economic" regulation in Chapter 19.

It seems clear that the philosophical roots of antitrust may be found in economic theory, political and social fear, and the desire for some kind of ethical code for business. Those goals are important because of the vagueness of the statutes. Courts must flesh out the statutes and their vague terms, and the purposes and goals of a law are always important factors in the interpretation of any law.

The History of Antitrust

Antitrust was not an invention of the 19th century trustbusters. Many of the roots of regulation of competitive activity can be seen in the early common law, while other sources of antitrust are traceable directly to the rapid economic and social changes in the United States following the Civil War. In the 20th century, antitrust continued to grow and change in response to a variety of social and economic factors as well.

Common-Law Regulation of Competition

There were three basic common-law precedents for regulation of competitive activity. First was a series of *criminal offenses* that existed in England for centuries, which prohibited various efforts to "corner" local markets by interfering with distribution processes, especially with regard to the necessities of life. Second was the English *Statute of Monopolies* of 1623, which provided that all monopolies were "contrary to the laws of this realm" and provided that any person injured by a monopoly could recover three times the damages actually sustained. And third was the common law rule against *restrictive covenants* found in various contracts. This rule held that any provision of a private contract which prohibited competition between the parties was totally void. The rule was later relaxed to permit such restrictive covenants if they were reasonable both in time and in geographical space. Such provisions generally find their way into private contracts for the purchase of businesses and in some employment contracts, and the general rule permitting only "reasonable" restraints of trade remains effective today.

The Rise of the Robber Barons

The agricultural nation of the 18th and early 19th century was converted rapidly into an industrial giant through the impetus of the Industrial Revolution and the Civil War. The Industrial Revolution, with its newly developed technology, created the means of production for many new products. The Civil War, often described as an economic struggle between agrarian and industrial economies, produced demand for industrial goods, created a need for quantity production and uniform products, and demonstrated the overwhelming effectiveness of industrial technology.

Soon after the end of the Civil War, a new era of economic organization began that built upon the forces begun by the war itself. New forms of industrial organization were created and the corporation, a rarity before the war, became a popular method of organizing business. At first, intense competition marked various industries, such as railroads, steel, and oil, but the entrepreneurs operating those businesses were quick to see that cooperation, not competition, would better serve their interests. Soon ominous combinations, known as pools and trusts, were formed to facilitate such cooperation.

A **pool** was a voluntary association of competing firms in which the firms would operate together and physically divide the market. The pool procedure was particularly suited to the railroad industry, where firms divided the country geographically into several smaller monopolies, or would confront shippers as a unit, refusing to carry goods unless prices were raised or other concessions granted. Railroads discriminated against shippers in certain areas or among specific firms, thereby creating competitive advantages for certain producers or certain communities. Pools had one troublesome aspect for the parties to the pool, namely that the terms of the pool were unenforceable. Participants could and did violate the terms of agreements between competitors without fear.

In an effort to force compliance with such anticompetitive agreements, the first **trust** was created in 1882 by lawyers for Rockefeller's Standard Oil. In such an arrangement, stockholders of competing companies deposited their stock certificates with a single board of trustees, giving that board the right of management and control and the right to vote the stock, but retaining the right to receive dividends and other benefits. The firms, while nominally independent, were controlled centrally by the board of trustees as if they were a single monopolistic company. By 1887, trusts had been established in several important industries, including oil, lead, cotton, sugar, and even whiskey. Through this device individual business leaders could gain control of an entire industry, set prices, and determine output.

A great deal of hostility quickly developed toward the trusts, and such devices were held illegal in some states as **ultra vires,** or beyond the scope of corporate charters (see Chapter 7). To answer this objection, lawyers developed the **holding company,** in which a parent company acquired the voting stock of other competing corporations and controlled them as subsidiaries. In this way, several major corporations, including Standard Oil of New Jersey, American Telephone and Telegraph, and Federal Steel, the forerunner of U.S. Steel, were all created.

The activities of the pools, trusts, and holding companies and the predatory business practices of others soon created an atmosphere of hostility which resulted in the antitrust laws. Actual monopolies existed in several industries, and the monopolists used their market power to raise prices, withhold supply, and force competitors or potential competitors from the market. Control of supplying industries or transportation facilities also gave the monopolists substantial power in determining who would be given the privilege of competing, if anyone. At that time, the attitude of business leaders toward public criticism of their methods is exemplified by W. H. Vanderbilt's classic phrase, "The public be damned."

Pressure for Reform

The pressure for government control of these corporate giants came from the West and Midwest and from the small farmers and businessmen who had to compete with those companies. An entirely new political party, the Populists, was formed in opposition to such concentrated wealth and influence.

Populist Party Platform, Preamble
July 4, 1892

The conditions which surround us best justify our co-operation; we meet in the midst of a nation brought to verge of moral, political, and material ruin. Corruption dominates the ballot-box, the Legislatures, the Congress, and touches even the ermine of the bench. The people are demoralized; most of the States have been compelled to isolate the voters at the polling places to prevent universal intimidation and bribery. The newspapers are largely subsidized or muzzled, public opinion silenced, business prostrated, homes covered with mortgages, labor impoverished, and the land concentrated in the hands of capitalists. The urban workmen are denied the right to organize for self-protection, imported pauperized labor beats down their wages, a hireling standing army, unrecognized by our laws, is established to shoot them down, and they are rapidly degenerating into European conditions. The fruits of the toil of millions are boldly stolen to build up colossal fortunes for a few, unprecedented in the history of mankind; and the possessors of these, in turn, despise the Republic and endanger liberty. From the same prolific womb of governmental injustice we breed the two great classes—tramps and millionaires.

The first response to the growing public pressure came in 1887 with the creation of the Interstate Commerce Act. That Act attempted to control the excesses of the railroads and further attempted to remove the Interstate Commerce Commission from the influence of politics. In 1889, President Benjamin Harrison called for "prohibiting and even penal legislation" to deal with the corporations themselves which he called "dangerous conspiracies against the public good."

The Sherman Antitrust Act of 1890   In 1890, Senator John Sherman of Ohio introduced the first antitrust legislation at the federal level, later named in his honor. Antimonopoly sentiment was so high that the Act passed both houses of Congress with only one dissenting vote and was signed into law on July 2, 1890. This relatively simple act, which is reprinted in Appendix C, contains two principal sections: Section One prohibited "every contract, combination in the form of trust or otherwise, or conspiracy, in restraint of trade. . . . ;" and Section Two made it a criminal offense to "monopolize" or "attempt to monopolize" any part of interstate commerce.

Initial enforcement of the Act was weak, but continued public pressure for firm enforcement was finally answered by President Theodore Roosevelt. While Roosevelt prosecuted some cases firmly and is known as The Trustbuster, he remains somewhat of an enigma in his personal attitudes towards antitrust. Nevertheless, the Roosevelt Administration instituted some 54 cases under the Sherman Act, to be shortly outdone by his hand-picked successor, President William Howard Taft, who filed 90 cases in little more than half the time.

The Clayton Act and the Federal Trade Commission Act   Despite the pressure of Roosevelt and Taft, antitrust received some setbacks. In 1911, the Supreme Court announced its decision in the *Standard Oil* case, discussed in detail later, in which the Court severely limited the application of the Sherman Act to only *unreasonable restraints of trade.* The Sherman Act was also criticized from many quarters, from businesspeople who felt it was too vague to reformers who felt it did not go far enough.

Finally, in 1914, during the administration of Woodrow Wilson, came the enactment of two remedial statutes: the *Clayton Act,* which amended the Sherman Act and made illegal specific types of business practices, such as certain mergers, tying contracts, and exclusive dealing arrangements; and the *Federal Trade Commission Act,* which generally prohibited "unfair methods" of competition and created an administrative agency, the Federal Trade Commission, to make rules to enforce the antitrust laws and provide for specific definitions of such unfair methods of competition.

The Robinson-Patman Act   A type of conduct specifically prohibited by the Clayton Act was **price discrimination;** that is, charging different prices to different purchasers of the same product. In 1936, Congress passed a very long and technical amendment to the Clayton Act to clarify the policy of the law toward price discrimination in the *Robinson-Patman Act.*

Other Antitrust Statutes   Numerous other minor or amending statutes have been passed over the years. In 1937, Congress passed the *Wheeler-Lea Act,* which amended the FTC Act to include injuries to consumers as a basis for a charge of "unfair trade practices." In 1938, the problem of resale price maintenance (that is, whether a manufacturer may require a retailer to charge a particular retail price) was first considered by Congress. In that year, Congress passed the *Miller-Tydings Act,* which generally permitted the practice as an exception to the Sherman Act. The Miller-Tydings Act was applied to the FTC in the *McGuire Act* but, in 1976, Congress repealed the Miller-Tydings and McGuire Acts, making the practice illegal once again.

In 1950, Congress passed a major amendment to the Clayton Act in the *Cellar-Kefauver Act,* which closed several major "loopholes" in that Act's treatment of mergers and acquisitions. In 1976, Congress again acted in the *Hart-Scott-Rodino Antitrust Improvement Act.* That law dealt principally with mergers and required merging companies over certain sizes to notify the FTC or the Justice Department (**premerger notification**) and provided other procedural changes in the administration of the laws.

Exemptions from the Antitrust Laws   Various types of businesses and other organizations are exempt from the operation of the laws. Most of these businesses are regulated in other ways, either through other federal agencies and specific statutes dealing with the industry or generally by state or local authorities. Those exemptions include agricultural areas, including certain commodities; railroads, trucking, and urban transit; shipping; airlines; pipelines; electricity; telephone and telegraph; radio and television broadcasting; commercial banking; insurance; crude oil; natural gas production; and the anthracite coal industry.

One of the earliest exemptions came in the Clayton Act's Section 6. Early decisions of the courts had indicated that labor unions constituted a "combination . . . in restraint of trade" within the meaning of the Sherman Act, and all labor activity might be illegal. Section 6 of the Clayton Act specifically exempted labor unions from the reach of the antitrust laws.

The courts have also created a variety of exemptions from the antitrust laws. One of the most interesting and questionable decisions was that which exempted major league baseball from the reach of the statutes.*

Antitrust Enforcement Procedures

Antitrust is unique in that two separate agencies of the federal government, the *Department of Justice* and the *Federal Trade Commission,* have overlapping and concurrent jurisdiction to enforce the antitrust laws. In addition, other agencies of government, such as the Interstate Commerce Commission, have authority to enforce some portions of the law or exempt persons or businesses from its application. Recent amendments permit *state attorneys general* to institute federal actions in the name of their citizens (*parens patriae* **actions**). *Private citizens* may bring suits under the laws for injunctive relief and for damages, often in the amount of three times (**treble damages**) the actual loss.

The Department of Justice

Under the Sherman Act, Congress empowered the Department of Justice, as public prosecutor for the federal government, to bring both civil and criminal actions. Later, the Department was also authorized to proceed in cases under the Clayton Act as well, although that authority was shared with the FTC. Civil actions generally take the form of actions for injunctions to stop illegal activity.

The Antitrust Division of the Justice Department is just one of several departments of that cabinet branch. It is headed by an Assistant Attorney General, who is chosen by the Attorney General of the United States. The Attorney General is, of course, a cabinet officer who serves at the pleasure of the President. The result has at least the potential for political control of the department, and of the Antitrust Division, by the President.

The Federal Trade Commission

The FTC has jurisdiction over the Clayton Act and the FTC Act itself. It should be noted that the terms of the FTC Act are so broad that conduct which would violate the Sherman Act, the Clayton Act, or the Robinson-Patman Act may also violate the FTC Act and is, therefore, within the jurisdiction of the FTC.

The FTC was one of the first independent regulatory commissions created by Congress. Five commissioners are appointed by the President for staggered seven-year terms. Only three commissioners may be from the same political party, and one of the commissioners is designated as chairman by the President. The Commission is empowered to make rules that define "unfair or deceptive" trade practices.

Over the years, Congress had delegated responsibility over a wide variety of

Flood v. *Kuhn,* 407 U.S. 258, 92 S. Ct. 2099, 32 L. Ed. 2d 728 (1972).

other, more specific statutes, aside from the FTC and Clayton Act. In all, the FTC has jurisdiction over 27 separate statutes on such diverse topics as Truth-in-Lending, fair packaging and labelling, export trade, trademarks, consumer warranties, fair credit reporting, and cigarette labelling. While the Commission is an independent regulatory commission, as discussed in Chapter 5, it is subject to Congressional control through its budget, which must be approved by Congress.

Federal Antitrust Jurisdiction: The Commerce Clause Revisited

The federal antitrust laws are based on Commerce Clause powers found within the Constitution and discussed in Chapter 2. During the early years of the antitrust experience, the courts took a very restrictive view of antitrust jurisdiction. However, in light of the recent expansive interpretation of the Commerce Clause, it is clear that federal authority reaches most areas of the economy. A 1980 decision held that the activities of local real estate brokers were within antitrust authority based on the interstate nature of real estate financing, for example.*

The Antitrust Remedies

The antitrust laws are extremely flexible, both in the interpretation possible under the broad wording of the statutes and in the administration and enforcement of those statutes. One aspect of that flexibility in administration is the wide variation in remedies available under the antitrust laws, which permits remedies to be crafted to fit the particular circumstances of each case.

Criminal Penalties

Criminal penalties, for the most part, are available only under the Sherman Act. It has generally been the policy of the Department of Justice to ask for criminal sanctions only in cases involving clear-cut **per se** violations of the Act.

The penalties for violation of the Sherman Act are a $1 million dollar fine for corporations and a fine of $100,000 or three years in prison or both for individuals. Those penalties were increased from much lower figures in 1974. Very few persons have served jail time under the antitrust laws, which has caused a great deal of criticism of antitrust enforcement policies. Criminal actions under the antitrust laws are tried as other criminal matters in the federal district courts. One reason for the limited use of criminal sanctions in the antitrust area is the burden of proof, which must be beyond a reasonable doubt as in other criminal cases. The complex proof necessary to prove antitrust violations makes it difficult to meet this burden.

---

*McLain v. *Real Estate Board of New Orleans*, 444 U.S. 232, 100 S. Ct. 502, 62 L. Ed. 2d 441 (1980).

Injunctive Relief

The Justice Department also may go to court to ask for an injunction, or court order, requiring the defendant-corporation to stop its illegal activity. This is the more common method of enforcement by the Justice Department and is used to enforce both the Sherman and Clayton Acts.

The nature of injunctions permits those orders to be carefully crafted to meet the needs of the parties and the case. Perhaps the most complicated decrees come in merger cases under Section 7 of the Clayton Act, in which one of the primary methods of forcing compliance is **divestiture,** a procedure in which a merged company is ordered to divide itself into two or more other companies.

Ford Motor Co. v. U.S.

405 U.S. 562, 92 S. Ct. 1142, 31 L. Ed. 2d 492 (1972)

This merger case involved the acquisition by Ford Motor Company of Autolite Company, a manufacturer of spark plugs. The substantive portions of the case are discussed in detail in Chapter 10. The following excerpt describes the decree of the federal District Court from which the appeal was taken.

> The District Court then held nine days of hearings on the remedy, and, after full consideration, concluded that divestiture and other relief was necessary. . . .
> Accordingly the decree:
> (1) enjoined Ford for 10 years from manufacturing spark plugs;
> (2) ordered Ford for five years to purchase one half of its total annual requirement of spark plugs from the divested plant under the "Autolite" name;
> (3) prohibited Ford for the same period from using its own tradenames on plugs;
> . . . .
> (5) protected employees of the New Fostoria plant by ordering Ford to condition its divestiture sale on the purchaser's assuming the existing wage and pension obligations, and to offer employment to any employee displaced by a transfer of nonplug operations from the divested plant.
>
> . . . .
> A word should be said about the other injunctive provisions. They are designed to give the divested plant an opportunity to establish its competitive position. The divested company needs time so it can obtain a foothold in the industry. The relief ordered should cure the ill effects of the illegal conduct and assure the public freedom from its continuance . . . and it necessarily must fit the exigencies of the particular case. . . . Moreover, it is well settled that once the Government has successfully borne the considerable burden of establishing a violation of law, all doubts as to the remedy are to be resolved in its favor. . . .

Commission Orders

Under the FTC Act, provisions of the Clayton and Robinson-Patman Act, and the various other laws (Truth-in-Lending, etc.) given to the authority of the FTC, that agency has the authority to issue orders after appropriate adjudicatory hearings. An administrative law judge initially hears the case and decides the matter. Appeals may be taken to the full Commission. The Commission has wide discretion to fashion appropriate orders, and violations of Commission orders and rules may result in fines of $10,000 per offense or $10,000 per day in the case of a continuing offense. The Commission may also institute "consumer redress" actions in the courts to obtain rescission or reformation of specific contracts, refunds of money, or payment of appropriate damages for violation of its rules or orders.

The Commission also tries to obtain voluntary compliance with its rules and orders. The Commission may simply request compliance, or it may give confidential advice to individual applicants, publish explanatory guides of its rules, and publish specific rules for particular industries.

Private Suits and Defenses

Private persons may use and enforce the antitrust laws in three ways: injured persons, including competitors, customers, licensees, and suppliers, may bring private lawsuits in federal court for *treble damages,* that is, three times the actual amount lost as a result of violations; such persons may also sue for *injunctive relief* to stop ongoing or threatened violations; and, under certain circumstances, parties sued by violators may raise violations of the antitrust laws *as a defense.*

Parens Patriae Actions

Any state Attorney General may bring a civil action in the name of the state and on behalf of residents to obtain money relief (damages) for such persons. Persons injured may petition for part of that money, in a manner similar to class actions, or the money may be retained by the state as a civil penalty, at the discretion of the trial judge. The federal Attorney General is required to cooperate with the state Attorneys General and must make investigative files available.

Consent Decrees

Both the Justice Department and the FTC make extensive use of **consent decrees,** or negotiated settlements of antitrust cases. Companies that are the subject of antitrust actions by either the Department or the FTC generally prefer such negotiated settlements to full trials for several reasons: antitrust cases are extremely expensive to try in the courts for both sides; a consent decree cannot be used as **prima facie evidence** of violation in a private treble damage action, while a judgment in a criminal or equitable proceeding is evidence in the private suits; and most companies prefer the relative privacy of consent decrees to public airing of their misdeeds in a courtroom.

Section 1 of the Sherman Act

The first and most basic antitrust statute is the Sherman Act of 1890. That statute, enacted in an atmosphere of fear and distrust towards big business, consists of two principal sections. Section 1 deals with specific conduct considered anticompetitive, while Section 2 deals with the vague problems of "monopolization." This chapter deals with some of the more basic problems of Section 1, while the following chapter will discuss some more complex antitrust issues, including the problem of monopolization under Section 2. Chapter 10 will consider the specific area of mergers and acquisitions, and Chapter 11 will consider the FTC Act.

The Problem of "Agreement"

Section 1 of the Sherman Act requires proof of some "contract, combination or conspiracy" between two or more persons; one person acting alone cannot violate Section 1. The terms *"contract, combination or conspiracy"* have generally been used interchangeably by the courts, and often the term *concerted action* is used to refer to the kind of joint activity condemned by Section 1.

Clearly, formal agreements such as contracts are covered by Section 1. Those formal agreements are usually **overt,** which means clear and unconcealed, and are fairly rare. Formal market arrangements, called *cartels,* are even more rare. Such cartel arrangements, such as the OPEC oil cartel of the 1970's and 1980's, generally try to directly set prices or otherwise restrict a market through formal agreements between the parties. Rather obviously all such arrangements violate Section 1. Some formal agreements may be **covert,** or hidden and concealed, but upon discovery those agreements also violate Section 1.

Horizontal and Vertical Agreements   One important categorization of agreements is between horizontal and vertical agreements (see Figure 8-3). Horizontal agreements are between two firms operating at the same level of the distribution process, such as two manufacturers or two distributors or two retailers. Vertical agreements are between firms at different levels of the same process, such as an agreement between a manufacturer and a distributor, or between a distributor and a retailer or between a manufacturer and a retailer.

Whether the agreement is horizontal or vertical may be crucial to the outcome in an antitrust case. For example, horizontal price-fixing agreements, as between competitors to set the prices on their goods, are considered one of the "worst" violations of the Sherman Act and have traditionally been treated very harshly. On the

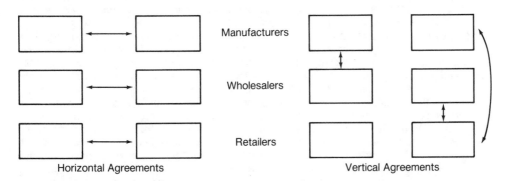

Figure 8-3   Agreements

other hand, vertical price-fixing agreements, such as requirements that a retailer sell products at a price set by the manufacturer, were legal under many circumstances for a long time. Both horizontal and vertical agreements may violate the Sherman Act, but the method of analysis and the legal results may vary sharply between the two forms.

Parallel Action and Price Leadership   Some agreements are never expressed, even in covert conversations between the parties. Such "agreements" are merely tacit understandings that certain practices will be followed, resulting in identical or similar competitive moves at the same time. One example of such **parallel action** is **price leadership,** in which one firm, usually the largest or most powerful in the market, sets its price and all other firms in the market follow its lead. The economic and competitive effect of price leadership is identical to the impact of a pricing cartel, without express agreement. The following case describes the Court's attitude toward parallel action.

Theatre Enterprises, Inc. v. Paramount Film Distributing Corp.

346 U.S. 537, 74 S. Ct. 257, 98 L. Ed. 273 (1954)

The petitioner operated the Crest, a neighborhood movie theatre in an outlying area of Baltimore. The petitioner had sought on numerous occasions to obtain first-run movies for the theatre from various film distributors, but was always refused by the distributors, who uniformly adhered to a policy of restricting first runs to the eight downtown Baltimore theatres. Petitioner brought a private treble damage action under Section 1 of the Sherman Act, claiming a "contract, combination or conspiracy" between the film distributors to deny outlying theatres access to the first-run pictures. A jury returned a verdict for the respondents, who included all of the film distributors involved. The petitioner appealed, arguing that the trial judge should have directed a verdict in its favor on the issue of liability, which would effectively have meant that proof of parallel action was proof of agreement by itself.

Mr. Justice CLARK delivered the opinion of the Court.

. . . .

Admittedly there is no direct evidence of illegal agreement between the respondents and no conspiracy is charged as to the independent exhibitors in Baltimore, who account for 63 percent of first-run exhibitions. The various respondents advanced much the same reasons for denying petitioner's offers. Among other reasons they asserted that . . . first-runs are normally granted only to noncompeting theatres. . . . And even if respondents wished to grant petitioner such a license, no downtown exhibitor would waive his clearance rights over the Crest and agree to a simultaneous showing. As a result, if petitioner were to receive first-runs, the license would have to be an exclusive one. However, an exclusive license would be economically unsound because the Crest is a suburban theatre, located in a small shopping center, and served by limited public transportation facilities; and, with a drawing area of less than one-tenth that of a downtown theatre, it cannot compare with those easily accessible theatres in the power to draw patrons. Hence the downtown theatres offer far greater opportunities for the widespread advertisement and exploitation of newly released features, which is thought necessary to maximize the the overall return from subsequent runs as well as first-runs. . . . Respondents Loews and Warner refused petitioner an exclusive license because they owned the three downtown theatres receiving their first-run product.

The crucial question is whether respondents' conduct toward petitioner stemmed from independent decision or from an agreement, tacit or express. To be sure, business

behavior is admissible circumstantial evidence from which the fact finder may infer agreement. . . . But this Court has never held that proof of parallel business behavior conclusively establishes agreement or, phrased differently, that such behavior itself constitutes a Sherman Act offense. Circumstantial evidence of consciously parallel behavior may have made heavy inroads into the traditional judicial attitude toward conspiracy; but "conscious parallelism" has not yet read conspiracy out of the Sherman Act entirely. . . . Here each of the respondents had denied the existence of any collaboration and in addition had introduced evidence of the local conditions surrounding the Crest operation which, they contended, precluded it from being a successful first-run house. They also attacked the good faith of the guaranteed offers of the petitioner for first-run pictures and attributed uniform action to individual business judgment motivated by the desire for maximum revenue. This evidence, together with other testimony of an explanatory nature, raised fact issues requiring the trial judge to submit the issue of conspiracy to the jury. . . .
Affirmed.

Intraenterprise Conspiracy   A second problem area concerns agreements within a single firm. On one hand, a corporation is a single "person," and a conspiracy or agreement requires two or more persons. On the other hand, a corporation is made up of many individuals, all of whom are capable of agreeing with others involved in the corporation, or perhaps of several corporations with a parent-subsidiary relationship.

The Supreme Court has held that the officers and directors of a corporation may conspire among themselves in violation of Section 1. Shareholders also may conspire with their corporation, since a corporation is considered a separate entity from its shareholders. Corporations may not conspire with their officers and directors, however, since the corporation may only act through those officers and directors. In 1984, the Supreme Court held that an "agreement" could not exist between a parent corporation and its wholly owned subsidiary corporations,* and it has been the law for some time that a corporation cannot "agree" with its unincorporated divisions.

A related problem deals with joint enterprises, which are multi-party business arrangements. An example might be a professional football league, which consists of a number of separately incorporated teams but depends on joint scheduling, similar ticket prices, a common media broadcast policy, and similar contracts with players. Another example, that of newspaper wire services, is considered later in the *Associated Press* decision.

The issue in all such cases is whether the participants in a joint enterprise should be treated as separate parties, and therefore capable of agreement under Section 1, or as a single enterprise. The answer to that question depends on many factors, including the legal nature of the association, the legal and economic desirability of the practices under attack, whether the practices are "predatory" or "coercive," and the practicality of other arrangements to accomplish the otherwise valid objectives of the organization. The courts have not provided any other firm guidelines for such enterprises.

Copperweld Corp. v. *Independence Tube Corp.,* 104 S. Ct. 2731, 52 U.S.L.W. 4821 (1984).

Section 1 and The Rule of Reason

While on its face the Sherman Act prohibits *every* agreement that restrains trade, as a practical matter it is obvious that Congress could not have meant the statute to be applied in so strict and uncompromising a manner. A great many common business practices involve some manner of cooperation and result in some restraint of trade. For example, common business partnership agreements at least restrain trade between the partners. A literal application of Section 1 might make even those innocuous business arrangements unlawful. But it was obvious that such strict application was not intended by Congress when the Sherman Act was passed.

Within a few years after the Sherman Act became law, the Courts retreated from such strict and literal application of the Sherman Act. Lower courts took a more practical view of the Act, and this practical view was adopted by the Supreme Court in 1911, in the landmark case of *U.S.* v. *Standard Oil of New Jersey.** The *Standard Oil* decision has been called "the real starting point of modern antitrust law."**

The *Standard Oil* decision is long, involved, and its language is less than memorable. The end result of the decision was the announcement of the so-called "Rule of Reason," a practical concept that holds that only *unreasonable* restraints of trade would be considered illegal under the Sherman Act. Thus, if a restraint of trade is "reasonable," it is legal and permitted. The courts must decide which restraints of trade are reasonable or unreasonable within the meaning of the Act.

Section 1 and The Per Se Violations

Determining whether a particular restraint of trade is reasonable or not is a long and complex job, generally involving in-depth economic analysis of the industry and markets in the case. But, almost from the beginning, certain kinds of trade restraints were viewed as *always* unreasonable.

> However there are certain agreements or practices which, because of their pernicious effect on competition and lack of any redeeming virtue, are conclusively presumed to be unreasonable and therefore illegal without elaborate inquiry as to the precise harm they have caused or the business excuse for their use. *Northern Pacific Railway Co.* v. *U.S.*†

Those practices always considered unreasonable, termed the **per se categories,** include horizontal price-fixing, geographic division of markets, tying contracts, and group boycotts. Vertical price-fixing, while considered a per se violation, presents a special case due to its legislative history in the context of the fair trade laws. Other types of conduct, such as interlocking corporate directorates, exclusive dealing con-

---

*221 U.S. 1, 31 S. Ct. 502, 56 L. Ed., 619.

**Earl W. Kintner, *An Antitrust Primer* 2d ed. (New York: The MacMillan Co., 1973), p. 18.

†356 U.S. 1, 78 S. Ct. 514, 2 L. Ed. 2d 545 (1958).

tracts, and price-discrimination are sometimes termed *per se categories,* but those types of conduct are made illegal by the Clayton Act and in some cases defenses are available to persons charged with violations of those sections. As a result, such conduct should not be included in a list of strict per se categories.

This is not to say that the per se categories are the only ways in which the Sherman Act may be violated. Other forms of conduct may be illegal under the Act but are subject to the rule of reason, which means that the conduct must be unreasonable. Such cases require the courts to conduct, in the Supreme Court's terms, "incredibly complicated and prolonged economic investigation into the entire history of the industry, as well as related industries," resulting in trials that may last for years. Consequently, antitrust prosecutors and private plaintiffs prefer, if at all possible, to file the more "cut and dried" per se cases.

The following per se catagories were established only after long experience with the practice and substantial economic analysis under the Sherman Act. Even in per se cases the defendant may try to show special industry facts that set the specific case apart from the general per se rule. Thus, the per se catagories are not automatic convictions in every case. The burden of proving such facts is on the defendant and is very heavy, however.

Horizontal Price Fixing

Horizontal price-fixing conspiracies, or agreements between competing firms to set prices, are considered to be perhaps the worst antitrust violation. As noted in an early decision, such agreements have absolutely no economic benefit to the public. The problem in price-fixing cases is not that the prices set are unreasonable, but that the power to fix prices exists at all.

> The aim and result of every price-fixing agreement, if effective, is the elimination of one form of competition. The power to fix prices, whether reasonably exercised or not, involves power to control the market and to fix arbitrary and unreasonable prices. The reasonable price fixed today may through economic and business changes become the unreasonable price of tomorrow. *U.S. v. Trenton Potteries.**

The only thing the government need prove in a price-fixing case is the existence of an agreement to set prices. It need not prove that the prices were too high or that anyone was harmed. The basic problem is proving the existence of an agreement. Compare the following decision to the *Theatre Enterprises* case.

U.S. v. Container Corporation of America

393 U.S. 333, 89 S. Ct. 510, 21 L. Ed. 2d 526 (1969)

Mr. Justice DOUGLAS delivered the opinion of the Court.
This is a civil antitrust action charging a price-fixing agreement in violation of section 1 of the Sherman Act. The District Court dismissed the complaint. . . .
The case as proved is unlike any of other price decisions we have rendered. There was here an exchange of price information but no agreement to adhere to a price schedule. . . .

---

*278 U.S. 392, 47 S. Ct. 377, 71 L. Ed. 700 (1927).

Here all that was done was a request by each defendant from its competitor for information as to the most recent price charged or quoted, whenever it needed such information and whenever it was not available from another source. Each defendant on receiving that request usually furnished the data with the expectation that he would be furnished reciprocal information when he wanted it. That concerted action is of course sufficient to establish the combination or conspiracy, the initial ingredient of a violation of section 1 of the Sherman Act.

. . . .

The defendants account for about 90 percent of the shipment of corrugated containers from plants in the southeastern United States. While containers vary as to dimensions, weight, color, and so on, they are substantially identical, no matter who produces them, when made to particular specifications. The prices paid depend on price alternatives. Suppliers when seeking new or additional business or keeping old customers, do not exceed a competitor's price. It is common for purchasers to buy from two or more suppliers concurrently. A defendant supplying a customer with containers would usually quote the same price on additional orders, unless costs had changed. Yet if a competitor was charging a particular price, a defendant would normally quote the same price or even a lower price.

The exchange of price information seemed to have the effect of keeping prices within a fairly narrow ambit. Capacity has exceeded the demand . . . and the trend of corrugated container prices has been downward. Yet despite this excess capacity and the downward trend of prices, the industry has expanded. . . .

The result of this reciprocal exchange of prices was to stabilize prices though at a downward level. Knowledge of a competitor's price usually meant matching that price. The continuation of some price competition is not fatal to the Government's case. The limitation or reduction of price competition brings the case within the ban, for. . . . interference with the setting of price by free market forces is unlawful *per se*. Price information exchanged in some markets may have no effect on a truly competitive price. But the corrugated container industry is dominated by relatively few sellers. The product is fungible and the competition for sales is price. The demand is inelastic, as buyers place orders only for immediate, short-run needs. The exchange of price data tends toward price uniformity. For a lower price does not mean a larger share of the available business but a sharing of the existing business at a lower return. Stabilizing prices as well as raising them is within the ban of section 1 of the Sherman Act. . . . the inferences are irresistible that the exchange of price information has had an anticompetitive effect in the industry, chilling the vigor of price competition. . . . Price is too critical, too sensitive a control to allow it to be used even in an informal manner to restrain competition.

Reversed.

MARSHALL, J., with whom HARLAN, J., and STEWART, J., join, dissenting.

I agree with the Court's holding that there existed an agreement among the defendants to exchange price information whenever requested. However, I cannot agree that the agreement should be condemned, either as illegal *per se,* or as having had the purpose or effect of restricting price competition in the . . . industry. . . .

. . . .

In this market, we have a few sellers presently controlling a substantial share of the market. We have a large number competing for the remainder of the market, also quite substantial. And total demand is increasing. In such a case, I think it is just as logical to assume that the sellers, especially the smaller and new ones, will desire to capture a larger market share by cutting prices as it is that they will acquiesce in oligopolistic behavior. The likelihood that prices will be cut and that those lower prices will have to be met acts as a deterrent to setting prices at an artificially high level in the first place. Given the uncertainty about the probable effect of an exchange of price information in this context, I would require that the Government prove that the exchange was entered into for the purpose of, or that it had the effect of, restraining price competition.

One of the most common places for horizontal price-fixing to occur is in the activities of trade associations. These voluntary associations of competitors often can result in the type of communication necessary for an agreement under the Act. The Supreme Court has held that meetings between competitors in trade associations, and the gathering and dissemination of statistics about a business by such associations do not, of themselves, constitute a violation of the Sherman Act. But if those associations reach agreements or attempt concerted action respecting the price of their goods, the Act has been violated. Professional organizations, including pharmacist and bar associations, have been held to violate the Act if minimum fee schedules are prescribed for members.

Another potential area of horizontal price-fixing involves bids on government contracts. Since the 1960's, all government agencies have been ordered to report all instances of identical bids received on government contracts over $10,000. This Executive Order was issued by President Kennedy to insure more effective enforcement of the antitrust laws. State and local authorities have often adopted a similar practice of reporting such identical bids to the FTC or the Justice Department.

Group Boycotts: Concerted Refusals to Deal

A seller has the right to choose to whom he sells his goods. This basic doctrine, part of a generally respected "freedom of alienation of property," is one of the fundamental tenets of Anglo-American law. Yet *agreements* to boycott a seller or a buyer are per se violations of the Sherman Act.

Boycotts act as a "clog on competition" by eliminating access to markets or access to supplies needed to compete. In extreme cases, the boycotted firm can be forced out of business, or at least be greatly restricted in its ability to compete with nonboycotted firms. Like all per se violations, there is no excuse for a boycott nor any defense that may be raised.

One common form of group boycott is horizontal in nature, since several competitors agree not to purchase or not to sell to another. One famous case involved an agreement between members of a retail lumber dealer's association to refuse to purchase lumber from lumber wholesalers who also sold lumber to retail customers at wholesale prices. Another case involved an agreement between members of a fashion designer's guild not to sell dresses to retailers who sold "pirated" fashions, copied from designs of guild members. In both cases the group refusal to sell was considered a per se violation of the Sherman Act.

Associated Press v. U.S.

326 U.S. 1, 65 S. Ct. 1416, 89 L. Ed. 2013 (1945)

The publishers of over 1,200 newspapers are members of the Associated Press, a cooperative association incorporated in New York. AP collects, assembles, and distributes news stories to its members. The stories are collected by AP employees or by employees of member newspapers and distributed through various communications media to the members.

The by-laws of the AP prohibited all AP members from selling news to nonmembers, and set up a system by which members of AP could block nonmember competitors from joining the AP. The United States filed a complaint charging these by-laws provisions violated Section 1 of the Sherman Act.

Mr. Justice BLACK delivered the opinion of the Court. . . .

Inability to buy news from the largest news agency, or any one of its multitude of members, can have most serious effects on the publication of competitive newspapers, both those presently published and those which, but for these restrictions, might be published in the future. This is illustrated by the District Court's finding that in 26 cities in the United States, existing newspapers already have contracts with the United Press and International News Service under which new newspapers would be required to pay the contract holders large sums to enter the field. The net effect is seriously to limit the opportunity of any new paper to enter these cities. Trade restraints of this character, aimed at the destruction of competition, tend to block the initiative which brings new-comers into a field of business and to frustrate the free enterprise system which it was the purpose of the Sherman Act to protect.

. . . .

It has been argued that the restrictive bylaws should be treated as beyond the prohibitions of the Sherman Act, since the owner of the property can choose his associates and can, as to that which he has produced by his own enterprise and sagacity, efforts or ingenuity, decide for himself whether and to whom to sell or not to sell. While it is true in a very general sense that one can dispose of his property as he pleases, he cannot "go beyond the exercise of this right, and by contracts or combinations, express or implied, unduly hinder or obstruct the free and natural flow of commerce in the channels of interstate trade." . . . The Sherman Act was specifically intended to prohibit independent businesses from becoming "associates" in a common plan which is bound to reduce their competitor's opportunity to buy or sell the things in which the groups compete. Victory of a member of such a combination over its business rivals achieved by such collective means cannot consistently with the Sherman Act or with practical, everyday knowledge be attributed to individual "enterprise and sagacity;" such hampering of business rivals can only be attributed to that which really makes it possible—the collective power of an unlawful combination. That the object of sale is the creation or product of a man's ingenuity does not alter this principle. . . . It is obviously fallacious to view the bylaws here in issue as instituting a program to encourage and permit full freedom of sale and disposal of property by its owners. Rather these publishers have, by concerted arrangements, pooled their power to acquire, to purchase, and to dispose of news reports through the channels of commerce. They have also pooled their economic and news control power and, in exerting that power, have entered into agreements which the District Court found to be "plainly designed in the interest of preventing competition."

. . . .

Finally, the argument is made that to apply the Sherman Act to this association of publishers constitutes an abridgment of the freedom of the press guaranteed by the First Amendment. . . . It would be strange indeed however if the grave concern for freedom of the press which prompted adoption of the First Amendment should be read as a command that the Government was without power to protect that freedom. The First Amendment, far from providing an argument against application of the Sherman Act, here provides powerful reasons to the contrary. That Amendment rests on the assumption that the widest possible dissemination of information from diverse and antagonistic sources is essential to the welfare of the public, that a free press is a condition of a free society. . . . Freedom to publish means freedom for all, not for some. Freedom to publish is guaranteed by the Constitution, but freedom to combine to keep others from publishing is not. Freedom of the press from governmental interference under the First Amendment does not sanction repression of that freedom by private interests.

[The illegal bylaws were enjoined. Some parts of the membership restrictions were upheld, though the right of city competitors to pass on potential members was barred.]

Affirmed.

A second type of group boycott involves actions by a manufacturer or other supplier to "discipline" its retailers or other subsequent purchasers. If a manufacturer wishes to establish a set retail price for its goods, it may unilaterally refuse to deal with retailers who refuse to charge the set price. But if the manufacturer involves independent wholesalers in such a scheme, the agreement between the manufacturer and the wholesalers constitutes an illegal group boycott.

Horizontal Geographic Market Division

If competitors divide a market into distinct geographic territories, the effect might be the creation of regional monopolies, each with the power to set prices and withhold supply in its assigned territory.

In 1898, one of the earliest antitrust decisions* held that territorial divisions between competitors were illegal under the Sherman Act. The "almost inevitable" result of horizontal territory divisions is the avoidance of price competition, since there is no competition within the territories.

U.S. v. Topco Associates

405 U.S. 596, 92 S. Ct. 1126, 31 L. Ed. 2d 515 (1972)

Topco, a cooperative of 25 small- and medium-sized regional supermarkets, purchased grocery products for its members and distributed them under the Topco brand name owned by the association. Each member of the association operated independently, with no pooling of earnings, capital, profit, management, or advertising. Each Topco member received an exclusive territory, which meant that no other store would be licensed to carry Topco brand products within the area. The government brought this action under Section 1 of the Sherman Act, seeking injunctive relief. The District Court ruled in favor of Topco and the government appealed.

Mr. Justice MARSHALL delivered the opinion of the Court.

. . . .

Topco essentially maintains that it needs territorial divisions to compete with larger chains; that the association could not exist if the territorial divisions were anything but exclusive; and that by restricting competition in the sale of Topco brand goods, the association actually increases competition by enabling its members to compete successfully with larger regional and national chains.

. . . .

The [District] court held that Topco's practices were procompetitive and, therefore, consistent with the purposes of the antitrust laws. But we conclude that the District Court used an improper analysis in reaching its result.

. . . .

U.S. v. *Addystone Pipe & Steel Co.,* 85 Fed. 271 (6th Circ., 1898).

On its face, Section 1 of the Sherman Act appears to bar any combination of entrepreneurs so long as it is "in restraint of trade." . . . Were Section 1 to be read in the narrowest possible way, any commercial contract could be deemed to violate it. . . . The history underlying the formulation of the antitrust laws led this Court to conclude, however, that Congress did not intend to prohibit all contracts, nor even all contracts that might in some insignificant degree or attenuated sense restrain trade or competition. In lieu of the narrowest possible reading of Section 1, the Court adopted a "rule of reason" analysis for determining whether most business combinations or contracts violate the prohibitions of the Sherman Act. . . . An analysis of the reasonableness of particular restraints includes considerations of the facts peculiar to the business in which the restraint is applied, the nature of the restraint and its effects, and the history of the restraint and the reasons for its adoption. . . .

While the Court has utilized the "rule of reason" in evaluating the legality of most restraints alleged to be violative of the Sherman Act, it has also developed the doctrine that certain business relationships are *per se* violations of the Act without regard to a consideration of their reasonableness. . . .

[T]here are certain agreements or practices which because of their pernicious effect on competition and lack of any redeeming virtue are conclusively presumed to be unreasonable and therefore illegal without elaborate inquiry as to the precise harm they have caused or the business excuse for their use. This principle of *per se* unreasonableness not only makes the type of restraints which are proscribed by the Sherman Act more certain to the benefit of everyone concerned, but it also avoids the necessity for an incredibly complicated and prolonged economic investigation into the entire history of the industry involved, as well as related industries, in an effort to determine at large whether a particular restraint has been unreasonable—an inquiry so often wholly fruitless when undertaken. (Citing *Northern Pacific Railway* v. *U.S.,* 356 U.S. 1, 78 S. Ct. 514, 2 L. Ed. 2d 545 (1958).)

It is only after considerable experience with certain business relationships that courts classify them as *per se* violations of the Sherman Act. . . . One of the classic examples of a *per se* violation of section 1 is an agreement between competitors at the same level of the market structure to allocate territories in order to minimize competition. Such concerted action is usually termed a "horizontal" restraint, in contradistinction to combinations of persons at different levels of the market structure, e.g., manufacturers and distributors, which are termed "vertical" restraints. This Court has reiterated time and time again that [h]orizontal territorial limitations . . . are naked restraints of trade with no purpose except stifling of competition." . . . Such limitations are *per se* violations of the Sherman Act. . . .

We think that it is clear that the restraint in this case is a horizontal one, and, therefore, a *per se* violation of Section 1. The District Court failed to make any determination as to whether there were *per se* horizontal territorial restraints in this case and simply applied a rule of reason in reaching its conclusions that the restraints were not illegal. . . .

    . . . .

In applying these rigid rules, the Court has consistently rejected the notion that naked restraints of trade are to be tolerated because they are well-intended or because they are allegedly developed to increase competition. . . .

Antitrust laws in general, and the Sherman Act in particular, are the Magna Carta of free enterprise. They are as important to the preservation of economic freedom and our free enterprise system as the Bill of Rights is to the protection of our fundamental personal freedoms. And the freedom guaranteed each and every business, no matter how small, is the freedom to compete—to assert with vigor, imagination, devotion, and ingenuity whatever economic muscle it can muster. Implicit in such freedom is the notion that it cannot be foreclosed with respect to one sector of the economy because certain private citizens or groups believe that such foreclosure might promote greater competition in a more important sector of the economy. . . .

The District Court determined that by limiting the freedom of its individual members to compete with each other, Topco was doing a greater good by fostering competition between members and other large supermarket chains. But, the fallacy in this is that Topco has no authority under the Sherman Act to determine the respective values of competition in various sectors of the economy. On the contrary, the Sherman Act gives to each Topco member and to each prospective member the right to ascertain for itself whether or not competition with other supermarket chains is more desireable than competition in the sale of Topco brand products. Without territorial restrictions, Topco members may indeed "[c]ut each other's throat." . . . But we have never found this possibility sufficient to warrant condoning horizontal restraints of trade.

. . . .

. . . If a decision is to be made to sacrifice competition in one portion of the economy for greater competition in another portion this . . . is a decision which must be made by Congress and not by private forces or by the courts. Private forces are too keenly aware of their own interests in making such decisions and courts are ill-equipped and ill-situated for such decision-making. . . .

. . . .

We reverse the judgment of the District Court. . . .

Tie-In Contracts

Assume that you are the manufacturer of the world's greatest automobile tire. Through technological breakthroughs, whether patented or not, you are able to produce a tire that will wear for 200,000 miles and that you can produce and sell at a price equal to other tires on the market. Assume also that you produce the world's worst automobile battery, plagued by high prices, constant leakage, and a very short life-span. A most logical marketing strategy under those circumstances would be to refuse to sell tires to wholesalers and retailers who do not purchase the batteries as well. The purchase of the batteries is "tied" to the purchase of the tires. Such **tie-in-sales** (or "tying" sales) are per se illegal under the Sherman Act.

Another similar arrangement involves a "coerced" promise by the purchaser not to deal in the products of a competitor. The tire manufacturer might achieve the same result as a tie-in contract by selling tires only to those retailers who promise not to buy batteries from any of the manufacturer's competitors. In that sense, an **exclusive dealing contract** involves much of the same anticompetitive effect as a tie-in contract.

Because of early judicial reluctance to find people and firms guilty of such offenses under Section 1 of the Sherman Act, Congress passed Section 3 of the Clayton Act in 1914. That Act make it clear that tie-in sales and exclusive dealing contracts were illegal, but added some complex requirements to the proof required of the prosecution.

Jefferson Parish Hospital District No. 2 v. Hyde

104 S Ct. 1551, 52 U.S.L.W. 4385 (1984)

East Jefferson Hospital had a contract with Roux & Associates, a professional corporation, in which Roux & Associates would provide all anesthesiologist services in the hospital. The contract provided that the hospital would provide all necessary space, equipment, maintenance, drugs, supplies, and nursing personnel, and the hospital agreed to "restrict the use of its anesthesia department to Roux & Associates and [that] no other persons, parties or entities shall perform such services within the Hospital for the term of this contract." The contract ran for five years. Any person who elected to have an operation at East Jefferson could not employ any anesthesiologist not associated with Roux, and no anesthesiologist not emplopyed by Roux could practice at East Jefferson.

East Jefferson was located in the New Orleans area, and there were about twenty other hospitals in the area. About 70 percent of the patients living in Jefferson Parish, the area immediately surrounding the hospital go to hospitals other than East Jefferson.

Hyde, a board certified anesthesiologist, applied for admission to the medical staff at East Jefferson, but was refused because of the exclusive contract with Roux. Hyde brought this action for a declaratory judgment and an injunction declaring the contract in violation of the Sherman Act. The District Court found that the Hospital did not possess significant "market power" in the New Orleans "relevant market," and therefore this tying arrangement and exclusive dealing contract was not per se illegal. The Court of Appeals found the relevant market to be Jefferson Parish and found the hospital had market power in that area and reversed the District Court. Hyde appealed.

Justice STEVENS delivered the opinion of the Court.

. . . .

. . . It is far too late in the history of our antitrust jurisprudence to question the proposition that certain tying arrangements pose an unacceptable risk of stifling competition and therefore are unreasonable "per se." The rule was first enunciated in *International Salt Co.* v. *United States,* 332 U.S. 392, 396 (1947) and has been endorsed by this Court many times since. . . .

. . . .

Our cases have concluded that the essential characteristic of an invalid tying arrangement lies in the seller's exploitation of its control over the tying product to force the buyer into the purchase of a tied product that the buyer either did not want at all, or might have preferred to purchase elsewhere on different terms. When such "forcing" is present, competition on the merits in the market for the tied item is restrained and the Sherman Act is violated.

. . . .

Per se condemnation—condemnation without inquiry into actual market conditions—is only appropriate if the existence of forcing is probable. Thus, application of the per se rule focuses on the probability of anticompetitive consequences. Of course, as a threshold matter there must be a substantial potential for impact on competition in order to justify per se condemnation. If only a single purchaser were "forced" with respect to the purchase of a tied item, the resultant impact on competition would not be sufficient to warrant the concern of antitrust law. . . . Similarly, when a purchaser is "forced" to buy a product he would not have otherwise bought even from another seller in the tied product market, there can be no adverse impact on competition because no portion of the market which would otherwise have been available to other sellers has been foreclosed.

Once this threshold is surmounted, per se prohibition is appropriate if anticompetitive forcing is likely. For example, if the government has granted the seller a patent or similar monopoly over a product, it is fair to presume that the inability to buy the product elsewhere gives the seller market power. . . . Any effort to enlarge the scope of the patent monopoly by using the market power it confers to restrain competition in the market for a second product will undermine competition on the merits in that second market. Thus, the sale or lease of a patented item on condition that the buyer make all his purchases of a separate tied product from the patentee is unlawful. . . .

. . . .

In sum, any inquiry into the validity of a tying arrangement must focus on the market in which the two products are sold, for that is where the anticompetitive forcing has its impact. Thus, in this case our analysis of the tying issue must focus on the hospital's sale of services to its patients, rather than its contractual arrangements with the providers of anesthesiological services. In making that analysis, we must consider whether petitioners are selling two separate products that may be tied together, and, if so, whether they have used their market power to force their patients to accept the tying arrangement.

. . . .

Unquestionably, the anesthesiological component of the package offered by the hospital could be provided separately and could be selected either by the individual patient or by one of the patient's doctors if the hospital did not insist on including anesthesiological services in the package it offers to its customers. As a matter of actual practice, anesthesiological services are billed separately from the hospital services petitioners provide. There was ample and uncontroverted testimony that patients or surgeons often request specific anesthesiologists to come to a hospital and provide anesthesia, and that the choice of an individual anesthesiologist separate from the choice of a hospital is particularly frequent in respondent's specialty, obstetric anesthesiology. . . .

. . . .

The question remains whether this arrangement involves the use of market power to force patients to buy services they would not otherwise purchase. Respondent's only basis for invoking the per se rule against tying and thereby avoiding analysis of actual market conditions is by relying on the preference of persons residing in Jefferson Parish to go to East Jefferson, the closest hospital. . . .

Seventy percent of the patients residing in Jefferson Parish enter hospitals other than East Jefferson. . . . Thus East Jefferson's "dominance" over persons residing in Jefferson Parish is far from overwhelming. The fact that a substantial majority of the parish's residents elect not to enter East Jefferson means that the geographic data does not establish the kind of dominant market position that obviates the need for further inquiry into actual competitive conditions. The Court of Appeals acknowledged as much; it recognized that East Jefferson's market share alone was insufficient as a basis to infer market power, and buttressed its conclusion by relying on "market imperfections" that permit petitioners to charge noncompetitive prices for hospital services: the prevalence of third party payment for health care reduces price competition, and a lack of adequate information renders consumers unable to evaluate the quality of the medical care provided by competing hospitals. . . . While these factors may generate "market power" in some abstract sense, they do not generate the kind of market power that justifies condemnation of tying.

. . .

In order to prevail in the absence of per se liability, respondent has the burden of proving that the Roux contract violated the Sherman Act because it unreasonably restrained competition. . . . There is simply no showing here of the kind of restraint on competition that is prohibited by the Sherman Act. Accordingly, the judgment of the Court of Appeals is reversed and the case is remanded to that court for further proceedings consistent with this opinion.

Vertical Price-Fixing: Resale Price Maintenance and the Fair Trade Laws

Vertical price restrictions require that dealers charge prices set by firms higher in the distribution chain. For example, firm A manufactures an item and sells it to firm B, a wholesaler, who resells it to firm C, a retailer. Resale price maintenance might include either a condition imposed by A that B's price to C, or C's price to the consumer, be at or above a certain level.

To the uninitiated, resale price maintenance makes very little sense. It would appear that firm A would wish to sell as much of its product as possible, and supply and demand would seem to indicate that firm A would want its distributors and retailers to sell for as *low* a price as possible. But firm A might wish to impose minimum prices on its products for several very good reasons. Retailers who make more money on a product will probably promote it with more intensity. Greater profitability at the retail level may also permit dealers to increase the number of outlets and, consequently, increase the amount of the product sold. Finally, some products actually sell better at higher prices, so manufacturers may wish to artificially indicate "quality" by forcing higher retail prices. Of course, from the retailer's standpoint, resale price maintenance virtually eliminates price competition for the affected product.

Early cases found that vertical price-fixing to be as evil as horizontal price-fixing, and held those restrictions per se illegal under the Sherman Act. In 1919, a limited exception, termed the *Colgate doctrine,** recognized the right of manufacturers to simply "refuse to deal" with those who failed to charge a price set by the manufacturer. But any activity going beyond a simple refusal to deal, such as enlisting the aid of distributors in enforcing or policing prices, constituted an agreement under the Sherman Act and remained illegal per se.

In 1933, California passed the first **Fair Trade Law,** which applied solely to intrastate commerce. The law simply made resale price maintenance agreements legal within the state, provided that the product was branded or trademarked. A later amendment to the law bound "nonsigners" as well. **Nonsigners clauses** meant that any single resale price maintenance contract between a manufacturer and a single dealer was automatically binding on every other dealer in that product in the state. In 1936, the U.S. Supreme Court upheld the California statute since it affected only intrastate commerce.

Soon other states enacted similar Fair Trade Laws until, by 1938, only three states were without some form of statute permitting resale price maintenance. But since most products are manufactured in one state and sold in other states, the state statutes had little impact. Pressure was put on Congress to amend the antitrust laws to permit resale price maintenance in interstate commerce. The result was the Miller-Tydings Resale Price Maintenance Act of 1937.

The Miller-Tydings Act amended Section 1 of the Sherman Act by permitting resale price maintenance contracts, provided that the product was trademarked or branded and in free and open competition with commodities of the same general class, and providing that such contracts were authorized by state laws. There was no nonsigners provision in the Miller-Tydings Act, but in 1952 Congress passed the *McGuire Act,* which amended Section 5 of the Federal Trade Commission Act, and permitted resale price maintenance agreements that had a nonsigners provision.

In the years following, resale price maintenance encountered severe difficulties. Courts construed the Miller-Tydings Act and the state laws very strictly, and deviations from the strict terms of the laws were dealt with harshly. It was statistically shown in several studies that resale price maintenance resulted in higher consumer prices. Theorists continued to argue that such agreements eliminated horizontal price competition among participating retailers and enhanced the monopoly or oligopoly power of the manufacturers. Finally, actual benefits to both retailers and producers were found to exist only in the short run, since in the long run the higher prices

---

*Because the doctrine originated in *U.S. v. Colgate & Co.,* 250 U.S. 300 (1919).

encouraged new entrants into the markets. As a result, the market shares of the parties to resale price maintenance agreements declined.

As a result of the problems of resale price maintenance, Congress repealed both the Miller-Tydings and McGuire Acts in 1975. Manufacturers have the option of outright refusal to deal under the Colgate doctrine or of providing "suggested retail prices," which are in no way binding upon retailers. In the auto industry, the Automobile Information Disclosure Act of 1958 requires any firm using suggested retail prices on automobiles to post those prices on the cars, and such prices do not violate the antitrust laws if the word *suggested* is clearly displayed.

The Rule of Reason and Franchising

It is tempting to name the per se violations and simply say that everything else is determined by the rule of reason, since *any* business conduct that involves an "agreement" and unreasonably restrains trade is a violation of Section 1. But certain kinds of business conduct commonly come up in the courts and should be discussed. The two most common and controversial are exclusive dealing contracts and vertical territory divisions, particularly in their application to franchising.

Exclusive Dealing Agreements

An **exclusive dealing contract,** like a tie-in contract, may be attacked under either Section 1 of the Sherman Act or Section 3 of the Clayton Act. An exclusive dealing arrangement is generally a vertical agreement between a seller and a subsequent purchaser in which the purchaser agrees not to purchase any products that compete with those purchased from the seller. An automobile manufacturer might require its dealers to purchase only the cars it manufactures, or a cosmetic company may sell its products to a department store on condition that no competing lines of cosmetics are sold, for example.

The major anticompetitive effect of exclusive dealing arrangements is that the market for the product is foreclosed to the seller's competitors. Buyers may, of course, decide on their own to buy only one seller's products, but in such circumstances there is no agreement and therefore no violation. The economic impact of exclusive dealing contracts depends on the number of buyers that enter into such contracts or, alternatively, the market share of the buyers involved. As noted by Justice O'Connor in *Jefferson Hospital District* in her concurring opinion:

> Exclusive dealing arrangements may, in some circumstances, create or extend market power of a supplier or the purchaser party to the exclusive dealing arrangement, and may thus restrain horizontal competition. Exclusive dealing can have adverse economic consequences by allowing one supplier of goods or services unreasonably to deprive other suppliers of a market for their goods, or by allowing one buyer of goods unreasonably to deprive other buyers of a needed source of supply. In determining whether an exclusive dealing contract is unreasonable, the proper focus is on the structure of the market for the products or services in question—the number of sellers and buyers in the market, the volume of their business, and the ease with which buyers and sellers can redirect their

purchases or sales to others. Exclusive dealing is an unreasonable restraint of trade only when a significant fraction of buyers or sellers are frozen out of a market by the exclusive deal. . . . When the sellers of services are numerous and mobile, and the number of buyers is large, exclusive dealing arrangements of narrow scope pose no threat of adverse economic consequences. To the contrary, they may be substantially procompetitive by ensuring stable markets and encouraging long term, mutually advantageous business relationships.

If an exclusive dealing arrangement is to be attacked under Section 3 of the Clayton Act, new requirements are added for a finding of guilt, primarily the necessity of proving that "the effect of such . . . contract for sale . . . may be to substantially lessen competition or tend to create a monopoly in any line of commerce." That language, familiar in other antitrust statutes, provides the requirement of a **relevant market** within which the anticompetitive effect must take place.

The concept of relevant market is considered at length in the context of other antitrust statutes in Chapters 9 and 10. For the purposes of this section, it is sufficient to define it as "the area of effective competition." That is, the exclusive dealing contract must have some substantial anticompetitive effect on some competing product line and in some definable geographic region. The statute also requires proof of the lessening of competition or a tendency to create a monopoly. As a result, Section 3 of the Clayton Act requires what the Sherman Act does not require, at least in per se cases, proof that an anticompetitive effect will probably take place.

Requirements contracts, by which a purchaser agrees to purchase all of its requirements of a certain product from a certain manufacturer, are really nothing more than exclusive dealing contracts and are treated as such. Some courts have treated requirements contracts more leniently than strict exclusive dealing contracts, since there may be more business justification for such agreements. Requirements contracts generally assure supply and lower costs for the buyers in such arrangements and may give protection against rising prices.

A common form of exclusive dealing contract is found in many franchise arrangements. A company that owns a trademark, the main subject of any franchise arrangement, may wish to protect that trademark by restricting the franchise owners from purchasing products elsewhere. Such restrictions may be permissible if the arrangement does not go beyond what is necessary to protect quality control.

Vertical Territory Limitations and the Problem of Franchising

If competitors carve up the territory and create regional monopolies, Section 1 finds a per se violation, as shown earlier in this chapter. But manufacturers and franchise companies often desire to create exclusive territories for their retailers, distributors, and franchisees as well, arguing that imposition of such territorial restrictions ensures maximum sales within an area and those granted exclusive territories will not neglect the home market in favor of greener pastures.

The legal status of vertical territorial divisions was not settled until very late in the history of antitrust and may not yet be settled. In 1963, the Supreme Court ruled that there was simply not enough economic information about the effects of such vertical territorial divisions. In 1967, in a somewhat confusing decision, the Court held in *U.S.* v. *Arnold, Schwinn & Co.** that such divisions were per se illegal. Ten years later that rule was overturned.

Continental T.V., Inc. v. GTE Sylvania, Inc.

433 U.S. 36, 97 S. Ct. 2549, 53 L. Ed. 2d 568 (1977)

GTE Sylvania, a manufacturer of television sets, adopted a "franchised dealer"program for marketing its products. Petitioner Continental GTE was the original franchisee in San Francisco. In 1965, Sylvania decided to license another dealer in the area. At the same time, Continental began plans to expand its services into another area near Sacramento.

The Sylvania marketing strategy did not grant exclusive territories, but a limited number of franchises were granted in a particular area, and franchisees were required to sell only from the locations at which they were franchised. Sylvania retained the right, under the agreement, to increase the number of retailers in an area.

Sylvania denied Continental's request to serve the Sacramento area, but Continental persisted in its plans and began moving television sets to the new location. Sylvania terminated the franchise with Continental and brought an action in the name of the finance company that handled franchise accounts (Maguire) to recover money and merchandise being held by Continental. Continental counterclaimed under Section 1 of the Sherman Act.

A jury brought back a verdict in favor of Continental in the amount of $591,505, which was trebled. Sylvania appealed to the 9th Circuit, which reversed. Continental appealed on the ground that the territorial restrictions imposed by the contract were a per se violation of the Sherman Act under the *Schwinn* case.

Mr. Justice POWELL delivered the opinion of the Court.

. . . .

[In the *Schwinn* decision] the Court proceeded to articulate the following "bright line" *per se* rule of illegality for vertical restrictions: "Under the Sherman Act, it is unreasonable without more for a manufacturer to seek to restrict and confine areas or persons with whom an article may be traded after the manufacturer has parted with dominion over it." . . . But the Court expressly stated that the rule of reason governs when "the manufacturer retains title, dominion, and risk with respect to the product and the position and function of the dealer in question are, in fact, indistinguishable from those of an agent or salesman of the manufacturer." . . .

In the present case, it is undisputed that title to the televisions passed from Sylvania to Continental. Thus, the *Schwinn per se* rule applies unless Sylvania's restriction on locations falls outside *Schwinn's* prohibition against a manufacturer attempting to restrict a "retailer's freedom as to where and to whom it will resell the products." . . .

. . . .

Sylvania argues that if *Schwinn* cannot be distinguished, it should be reconsidered. . . . [W]e are convinced that the need for clarification of the law in this area justifies reconsideration. . . .

. . . . Since the early years of this century a judicial gloss on [Section 1] has established the rule of reason as the prevailing standard of analysis. . . . Under this rule, the factfinder weights all of the circumstances of a case in deciding whether a restrictive practice should be prohibited as imposing an unreasonable restraint on competition. *Per se* rules of illegality are appropriate only when they relate to conduct that is manifestly anticompetitive. . . .

In essence, the issue before us is whether Schwinn's *per se* rule can be justified. . . .

The market impact of vertical restrictions is complex because of their potential for

---

*388 U.S. 350, 87 S. Ct. 1847, 18 L. Ed. 2d 1238 (1967).

a simultaneous reduction of intrabrand competition and stimulation of interbrand competition. . . .

Vertical restrictions reduce intrabrand competition by limiting the number of sellers of a particular product competing for the business of a given group of buyers. Location restrictions have this effect because of practical restraints on the effective marketing area of retail outlets. Although intrabrand competition may be reduced, the ability of retailers to exploit the resulting market may be limited both by the ability of consumers to travel to other franchised locations and perhaps more importantly, to purchase the competing products of other manufacturers. . . .

Vertical restrictions promote interbrand competition by allowing the manufacturer to achieve certain efficiencies in the distribution of his products. These "redeeming virtues" are implicit in every decision sustaining vertical restrictions under the rule of reason. Economists have identified a number of ways in which manufacturers can use such restrictions to compete more effectively against other manufacturers. . . . For example, new manufacturers and manufacturers entering new markets can use the restrictions in order to include competent and aggressive retailers to make the kind of investment of capital and labor that is often required in the distribution of products unknown to the consumer. Established manufacturers can use them to induce retailers to engage in promotional activities or to provide service and repair facilities. . . .

Economists also have argued that manufacturers have an economic interest in maintaining as much intrabrand competition as is consistent with the efficient distribution of their products. . . .

. . . .

[Vertical] restrictions, in varying forms, are widely used in our free market economy. As indicated above, there is substantial scholarly and judicial authority supporting their economic utility. There is relatively little authority to the contrary. Certainly, there has been no showing in this case, either generally or with respect to Sylvania's agreements, that vertical restrictions have or are likely to have a "pernicious effect on competition" or that they "lack . . . any redeeming virtue." Accordingly, we conclude that the *per se* rule stated in *Schwinn* must be overruled. In so holding we do not foreclose the possibility that particular applications of vertical restrictions might justify *per se* prohibition. . . .

In sum, we conclude that the appropriate decision is to return to the rule of reason. . . . When competitive effects are shown to result from particular vertical restrictions they can be adequately policed under the rule of reason. . . .

Affirmed.

Summary and Conclusions

The federal antitrust laws (consisting of the Sherman Act of 1890, the Clayton Act and Federal Trade Commission Act, both of 1914, and the Robinson-Patman Act of 1936) developed during the later years of the 19th century and the early part of the 20th century in response to business activities that threatened the economic, political, and social structure of the country. The primary purpose of those laws is to preserve, so far as possible, the attributes of classical economics, and to bring the economy as close as possible to the requirements of perfect competition.

The antitrust laws are jointly administered by the Department of Justice and the Federal Trade Commission. The Justice Department administers the Sherman Act and portions of the Clayton Act through traditional criminal actions and actions for injunctions in the federal courts. The FTC administers the Clayton, Robinson-Patman, and FTC Acts through administrative proceedings.

Section 1 of the Sherman Act prohibits all "contracts, combinations and conspiracies . . . in restraint of trade." That section has been interpreted to reach all concerted action, but action by a single party is immune.

The rule of reason was announced in 1911 in order to make only unreasonable restraints of trade illegal. Some restraints, such as horizontal and vertical price-fixing, group boycotts, horizontal market divisions, and tie-in sales, have been held to be "so pernicious" that a per se rule will be applied; that is, such restraints are never justifiable except under most unusual circumstances, and the courts are relieved of the burden of conducting a massive inquiry into the reasonableness of the restraint. All other restraints are analyzed under the rule of reason, including exclusive dealing arrangements and vertical territory divisions.

PRO AND CON

ISSUE: Assuming That the Antitrust Laws Are not Meeting Their Objectives, the Reason Is Faulty Administration of the Laws

PRO: Political Pressure and Inadequate Enforcement Have Caused the Failure of Antitrust

Ralph Nader, Mark Green, and Joel Seligman*

. . . [T]he history of federal antimonopoly enforcement has been one of bipartisan support and deficient performance: perhaps the only thing more predictable than the endorsement of competition by Democratic and Republican Administrations was their unwillingness to back up their words with deeds. The gap between antitrust promise and performance remains large, for several reasons:

Resources—"Even if the Antitrust Division and the Federal Trade Commission enjoyed appropriations five times as large as they now have," Professor Edward S. Mason wrote in 1949, "they could not conceivably bring a tenth of the cases it would be possible to bring." It's still true. In 1950, the Antitrust Division had 314 lawyers and staff economists. In 1976, with a real GNP more than double that of 1950, the Division has 427 professional staff. The Federal Trade Commission's antitrust effort has had a comparable incremental growth. But together their approximately $40 million budget still totals one-seventh the budget of the Fish and Wildlife Service and less than one-half the cost of a single B-1 bomber. These few hundred antitrust policemen are simply inadequate to patrol an economy with 203 industrial firms worth over $1 billion; 85,000 with over a million dollars in assets; and 1.8 million firms in all.

An inadequate staff becomes especially glaring when pitted against the army of attorneys corporate defendants can throw into antitrust battle. It has been reported that IBM's legal expenses in its defense against the current Justice Department suit are larger than the entire annual budget of the Antitrust Division. . . .

Politics—With so much potentially at stake for the defendant firm in an antitrust case and with elected officials so dependent on business support, it should hardly be surprising that politics has often compromised antitrust efforts. The problem long predates ITT's clumsy though successful politicking to settle its merger cases in 1971. Members of Congress as powerful as James Eastland, Emanuel Celler, or Everett Dirksen—on behalf of, respectively, Mississippi banks, Schenley Industries, and United Fruit—pressured the Justice Department into favorable settlements. And Attorneys General like Eisenhower's Herbert Brownell or Johnson's Nicholas Katzenbach proved attentive to such importunings. . . .

Penalties—Penalties for antitrust violations are both inadequate and underapplied. Between 1955 and 1974, the maximum penalties were a $50,000 fine and one year in prison. But corporate fines averaged only $13,420 and average individual fines

---

*Reprinted from TAMING THE GIANT CORPORATION by Ralph Nader, Mark Green, and Joel Seligman, by permission of W. W. Norton & Company, Inc. Copyright © 1976 by Ralph Nader.

$3,365—penalties, said one Antitrust Division chief, which were "no more severe than a $3 ticket for overtime parking for a man with a $15,000 income." And, in the Sherman Act's first 82 years, there were only four instances when businessmen actually spent time in jail; sentences were invariably suspended by sympathetic judges. . . .

In 1974 the antitrust law was amended to increase penalties to a maximum of $1 million for corporations and three years in prison for individuals. Given the net income of *Fortune's* 1000 and the historic proclivity of judges, however, the fines imposed will undoubtedly still be a mere cost of doing business to the antitrust violator; and poten-

tially longer jail terms are hardly of consequence when business lawbreakers don't go to jail anyway. . . .

These persistent defects have produced a desultory federal antitrust record. To be sure, if there were no federal antitrust law, economic concentration and anticompetitive behavior would be far worse. "The success of antitrust," said economist Almarin Phillips, with only slight exaggeration, "can only be measured by the hundreds of mergers and price-fixing situations that never happened." But what about all that monopolization that *has* happened?

CON: The Problem of Antitrust Is One of Faulty Economics
Robert H. Bork*

Improbable as the statement may seem, antitrust today is almost an unknown policy. It is ubiquitous: Antitrust constitutes one of the most elaborate deployments of governmental force in areas of life still thought committed primarily to private choice and initiative. It is popular: There is some intellectual but almost no political opposition to its main features. And it is even exportable: This supposedly peculiarly American growth has spread to and taken at least equivocal root in Europe and even in Asia. Yet few people know what the law really commands, how its doctrines have evolved, or the nature of its ultimate impact upon our national well-being. . . .

This state of affairs is curious, and certainly unfortunate, but perhaps it is understandable. Antitrust is a subcategory of ideology, and by the time a once militant ideology triumphs and achieves embodiment in institutional forms, its adherents are likely long since to have left off debating first principles. "The antitrust movement," as Professor Richard Hofstadter remarks, "is one of the faded passions of American reform." But Hofstadter goes on, and probably it is not a paradox—"the antitrust enterprise has more significance in contemporary society than it had in the days of T.R. or Wilson or even in the heyday of Thurman Arnold." . . .

. . . .

We are urged . . . to throw the antitrust book at business in order to improve the quality of American life. One could wish that those who want to throw the book had taken the time to understand

it. . . . Antitrust presents itself as a body of developed knowledge and principle worked out over years of investigation, thought and litigation. That image is misleading. Antitrust is not all of a piece.

Because antitrust's basic premises are mutually incompatible, and because some of them are incorrect, the law has been producing increasingly bizarre results. Certain of its doctrines preserve competition, while others suppress it, resulting in a policy at war with itself. . . .

Given the pace and direction of its development, the overriding need of antitrust today is a general theory of its possibilities and limitations as a tool of rational social policy. Yet there exists among those professionally concerned with antitrust a surprising lack of agreement concerning the most basic questions. The disagreement, though variously phrased, is finally two issues: (1) the goals or values the law may legitimately and profitably implement; and (2) the validity of the law's vision of economic reality. . . . A consideration of the virtues appropriate to law *as* law demonstrates that the only legitimate goal of antitrust is the maximization of consumer welfare. Current law lacks these virtues precisely because the Supreme Court has introduced conflicting goals, the primary one being the survival or comfort of small business.

A consumer oriented law must employ basic economic theory to judge which market structures and practices are harmful and which beneficial. Modern antitrust has performed this task very poorly. Its version of economics is a melange of

---

*From *The Antitrust Paradox* by Robert Bork. Copyright © Basic Books, Inc. Reprinted by permission of the publisher.

valid insights and obviously incorrect—sometimes fantastic—assumptions about the motivations and effects of business behavior. There are many problems here, but perhaps the core of the difficulty is that the courts, and particularly the Supreme Court, have failed to understand and give proper weight to the crucial concept of business efficiency. Since productive efficiency is one of the two opposing forces that determine the degree of consumer well-being (the other being resource misallocation due to monopoly power), this failure has skewed legal doctrine disastrously. Business efficiency necessarily benefits consumers by lowering the costs of goods and services or by increasing the value of the product or service offered; this is true whether the business unit is a competitor. When efficiency is not counted, or when it is seen as a positive evil, it appears that no business structure of behavior has any potential for social good, and there is consequently no reason to uphold its legality if any remote danger can be imagined. The results could not have been worse, and would probably have been better, if the Court had made the opposite mistake and refused to recognize any harm in cartels and monopolies. Yet neither mistake need have been made.

DISCUSSION QUESTIONS

1. Should government policy ever be based on an unsubstantiated theory, even one as generally accepted as Adam Smith's theory of perfect competition? Is Smith's argument still only a theory?

2. Are you surprised by the description of antitrust policy as a *conservative* doctrine? In what ways is it conservative?

3. One of the hallmarks of antitrust is its flexibility, both in the broadness of the statutes and in its administration. Why do you suppose Congress built this type of flexibility into the law? Are they the same, or similar, as reasons that the wording of the Constitution is broad?

4. Are the antitrust penalties and remedies severe enough? Too severe? How would you change them and why? Are there reasons for businesses to comply with the antitrust laws other than to avoid punishment?

5. Part of the reason for the enactment of the Sherman Act was to control the robber barons of the 19th century. Now that there are no more robber barons, is there still a need for the antitrust laws?

6. Is a code of business ethics necessary in today's business climate? If so, should that code be voluntary or enforced in some way? If it is to be enforced in some way, how should it differ—if at all—from the rules of the FTC?

7. Is there a good reason for the concurrent jurisdiction over antitrust between the Justice Department and the FTC? Wouldn't a single superagency work better?

8. Do you suppose our economy is more or less concentrated today than in 1890? If your answer is that it is more concentrated, does that mean antitrust has failed?

9. Is "parallel action" the same thing as "concerted action?" What does the term *agreement* really mean?

10. Do you suppose Congress really intended the rule of reason when it enacted the Sherman Act? Does it mean anything that Congress could have changed the rule of reason by simple statute at any time it desired and, except for the Clayton Act and a few other amendments, has not moved against that rule in almost a century?

11. List the reasons why antitrust cases take years to prepare and try. Can you think of a better way?

CASE PROBLEMS

1. The Goldfarbs contracted to buy a home in Virginia, and the mortgage company which was to lend them the money for the purchase required a title examination before the deal was closed. Only a licensed attorney could conduct such an examination. The Goldfarbs contacted 36 lawyers, and every one indicated that the fee would be the recommended fee for such services as described by the state Bar Association. Habitually charging lower than the recommended fees was grounds for disciplinary action against lawyers. The Goldfarbs sued, claiming a Section 1 violation. Result? [*Goldfarb* v. *Virginia State Bar,* 421 U.S. 773, 95 S. Ct. 2004, 44 L. Ed. 2d 572 (1975).]

2. Klor's, Inc., and Broadway-Hale are two appliance dealers operating stores next door to each other in San Francisco. Both sell the same sort of merchandise, and directly compete in several lines. Broadway-Hale is a chain, however, and Klor's is a small independent shop. None of the large manufacturers of appliances will sell to Klor's, though they sell to many other independents in the San Francisco area. Klor's charges a violation of Section 1. (1) Is there sufficient evidence of an agreement? (2) What type of violation is this? (3) Does it make a difference that Klor's is a small store, whose destruction will not affect the economy? [*Klor's, Inc.* v. *Broadway-Hale Stores, Inc.,* 359 U.S. 207, 79 S. Ct. 705, 3 L. Ed. 2d 741 (1959).]

3. An association of producers of cast iron pipe, used for sewer lines and culverts, adopted a plan in which sales to specified cities would be made by designated members of the association and other sales, outside those cities, would be made through a "bidding" procedure within the association, the winner being the producer who paid the highest "bonus" to the association. Bids in the cities desiring pipe were then rigged so that the successful bidder in the association would also be the low bidder in the city contract-letting procedure. What kind of violation is this? Result? [*U.S.* v. *Addystone Pipe & Steel Co.* 85 F 271 (1898).]

4. Chicken Delight, Inc., licensed Siegel and others under its franchise plan. It charged no franchise or royalty fees, but required Siegel and the other franchisees to purchase a specified amount of cookers and fryers and to purchase packaging supplies and mixes exclusively from Chicken Delight, in return for the right to use the Chicken Delight trademark. Siegel was not given an exclusive territory, but Chicken Delight endeavored to restrict the number of franchises in a given

area. The prices charged by Chicken Delight for its equipment and food materials were substantially higher than those charged by competing suppliers for similar products. Siegel brought a private treble damage action to recover the price difference. Result? [*Siegel* v. *Chicken Delight, Inc.,* 448 F. 2d 43 (9th Cir., 1971).]

5. The Real Estate Board of New Orleans is a trade association of most of the real estate brokers in the New Orleans area, and that association has adopted a rule that all member brokers will charge a 6 percent commission on residential sales. If a member is dropped from the board, that member cannot participate in the multiple listing service through which many sales are made. McLain, a home-buyer, charges that the association has violated Section 1. The board argues that it is beyond the antitrust laws, since all its sales are local and, therefore, beyond the Commerce Clause jurisdiction of the antitrust laws. McLain argues that much of the money to finance real estate purchases comes from out of state, and that many title companies are chartered in other states. Who is right? Is this price-fixing? [*McLain* v. *Real Estate Board of New Orleans,* 444 U.S. 232, 100 S. Ct. 502, 62 L. Ed. 2d 441 (1980).]

6. Owners of musical copyrights, such as composers and music publishers, routinely give nonexclusive rights to the American Society of Composers, Authors and Publishers (ASCAP) or Broadcast Music, Inc. (BMI) to license performances of their works on radio, TV, or in live performances. Both organizations issue "blanket licenses" to broadcasters and others for either a percentage of revenues or a flat fee, in return for which the broadcaster or owner of an establishment performing live music may use any composition of any ASCAP member. A portion of that percentage or flat fee is in turn given to the owner of the copyright. CBS argued that the blanket license is price-fixing. Result? [*ASCAP* v. *CBS,* 441 U.S. 1, 99 S. Ct. 1551, 60 L. Ed. 2d 1 (1979).]

7. Jerrold Electronics manufactured the first community master television antenna for use in communities with poor television reception but sold the system only if the community also entered into a service contract, since they felt only they had the technical expertise to maintain the system. A part of that contract provided that the purchaser would also purchase from Jerrold, "at the then prevailing prices, whatever additional Jerrold Equipment may be necessary. . . . " Communities also agreed not to purchase any other equipment except that provided by Jerrold. Is the contract per se illegal? What kind of contract is it? [*U.S.* v. *Jerrold Electronics Corporation,* 187 F. Supp. 545 (E.D.Pa., 1960), aff'd per curiam, 365 U.S. 567, 81 S. Ct. 755, 5 L. Ed. 2d 806 (1961).]

8. Fortner, a real estate developer, attempted to borrow money from the U.S. Steel Credit Corporation, a wholly owned subsidiary of U.S. Steel. The Credit Corporation refused to loan the money for the purchase of land unless Fortner agreed to construct a U.S. Steel home on each of his lots. Fortner charged that the prefabricated U.S. Steel homes were sold to him at inflated prices and there were inordinate delays in their delivery. He filed suit under Section 1 for treble damages. Result? [*Fortner Enterprises, Inc.* v. *U.S. Steel Corp.,* 394 U.S. 495, 89 S. Ct. 1252, 22 L. Ed. 2d 495 (1969); 429 U.S. 610, 97 S. Ct. 861, 51 L. Ed. 2d 80 (1977).]

9. Albrecht was an independent newspaper carrier, purchasing 1,200 newspapers from the Herald Company each day and selling them on a route he developed. The newspapers carried a suggested retail price, and the contract with Albrecht specified that the contract was subject to termination if this price was not followed. Albrecht determined that he needed to raise the price to make ends meet, but when he did so the Herald Company cancelled his contract, hired another carrier, and told that new carrier that if Albrecht agreed to abide by the suggested price, his contract was cancelled. Albrecht sued under Section 1 instead. Result? [*Albrecht v. The Herald Co.,* 309 U.S. 150, 88 S. Ct. 869, 19 L. Ed. 2d 998 (1968).]

SUGGESTED READINGS

Areeda, Phillip. *Antitrust Analysis* 3rd ed. (Boston: Little, Brown & Co., 1981).

Asch, Peter. *Industrial Organization and Antitrust Policy* (New York: John Wiley & Sons, 1983).

Bork, Robert H. *The Antitrust Paradox* (New York: Basic Books, Inc., 1978).

Galbraith, John Kenneth. *American Capitalism: The Concept of Countervailing Power* (Boston: Houghton-Mifflin Co., 1956).

Kintner, Earl W. *An Antitrust Primer: A Guide to Antitrust and Trade Regulation Laws for the Businessman* 2d ed. (New York: The MacMillan Co., 1973).

Posner, Richard A. *Antitrust* (St. Paul, Minn.: West Publishing Co., 1974).

Schwartz, Louis B. *Free Enterprise and Economic Organization* 2 vols., 3rd ed. (Brooklyn: The Foundation Press, Inc., 1981).

Seplaki, Les. *Antitrust and the Economics of the Market: Text, Readings, Cases* (New York: Harcourt, Brace, Jovanovich, Inc., 1982).

Van Cise, Jerrold G. *The Federal Antitrust Laws* 4th ed. (Washington, D.C.: American Enterprise Institute for Public Policy Research, 1982).

Wilson, James Q. (Ed.). *The Politics of Regulation* (New York: Basic Books, Inc., 1983), particularly Chapters 4 and 5.

Antitrust Law: Price Discrimination, Monopolization, and Legal Monopolies

O, it is excellent to have a giant's strength, but it is tyrannous to use it like a giant.

William Shakespeare, Measure for Measure, *Act 2, Scene 2*

The only argument that has been seriously advanced in favor of private monopoly is that competition involves waste, while monopoly prevents waste and leads to efficiency. This argument is essentially unsound. The wastes of competition are negligible. The economies of monopoly are superficial and delusive. The efficiency of monopoly is at the best temporary.

Louis D. Brandeis

Go directly to jail. Do not pass Go. Do not collect $200.

Chance card. *Parker Brothers'* Monopoly

One of the principal continuing debates is between those who would prosecute anticompetitive *conduct*, such as the behavior punished by Section 1 of the Sherman Act, and those who argue for an attack against the root causes of anticompetitive behavior, striking at business *structure* and *size*. Proponents of the former point of view argue that only objective conduct should be punished, while advocates of the latter point of view argue that only striking at conduct treats the symptoms rather than the disease.

In this chapter, the debate continues. The first section deals with perhaps the most specific antitrust statute, the Robinson-Patman Anti-Price Discrimination Act, aimed at a single form of business conduct in particularized detail. We then briefly consider another conduct violation, that of interlocking corporate directorates. Finally, we move into the area of structure by considering the murky area of monopolization under Section 2 of the Sherman Act. Related to that discussion is the problem of the monopolies legalized by the government through patents, copyrights, and trademark protection. Our discussion of structure regulation continues in Chapter 10 in a discussion of federal regulation of mergers under Section 7 of the Clayton Act.

Price Discrimination and the Robinson-Patman Act

It has been said that "The Robinson-Patman Act is sometimes praised, sometimes abused, much interpreted, little understood, and capable of producing instant arguments of infinite variety."* This Act, which amended the Clayton Act in 1936, is aimed at a variety of price-discrimination techniques and generally prohibits the practice of charging different prices to different purchasers of the same goods.

The Act is sometimes called the *Chain Store Act* because it was aimed at the giant grocery chains that had emerged by the 1930's. Those chains were able to obtain favored prices from suppliers through high-volume purchases. Those price reductions were generally passed on to the consumer, and placed independent grocery stores in an unfavorable competitive position, since the independents could not obtain price concessions from the suppliers.

Pressure from the independents and large-scale public support produced the Robinson-Patman Act in 1936. Section 2(a) of the Act generally prohibits *suppliers* from *granting* price concessions, though Section 2(f) also prohibits *receiving* a discriminatory price as well. The Act provides for some defenses, in the form of cost-justified discrimination and the need to meet competition. Disguised price discrimination, in the form of brokerage fees, commissions, services, and facilities, is also prohibited.

The goals of the Act relate to two different aspects of the market system:

1. To prevent sellers from using discriminatory prices to discipline, injure, or eliminate existing competitors. Thus a firm with monopoly power may use "predatory pricing" in one area to discipline and control its purchasers, and such predatory pricing may be financed by the monopoly profits received in other areas.

2. To prevent powerful buyers from using their economic power to exact discriminatory prices that lowers either the costs of the firm (and thereby raises its profits) or the prices charged by the firm (permitting the firm to obtain a larger market share through such lower prices).

---

*Kintner, *An Antitrust Primer: A Guide to Antitrust and Trade Regulation* 2d ed. (New York: The MacMillan Company, 1973), p. 61.

The Robinson-Patman Act applies by its wording to sellers "engaged in commerce." This is a narrower concept than that found in the Sherman Act, for example, which applies to matters both *in* interstate commerce and which *affect* interstate commerce. Thus, local sales within a state, even those that affect interstate commerce, are not covered by the Act. Many states have laws that cover much of the same ground as the Robinson-Patman Act, however, and that prohibit intrastate price discrimination, which Robinson-Patman does not cover.

Through subsequent judicial interpretation of the Act, the law also requires *two* (or more) *reasonably contemporaneous sales* of a product at different prices. These sales must also obviously be made to two different purchasers. The requirement of two sales is necessary for comparison purposes to prove the discrimination. And the requirement that the sales be reasonably contemporaneous takes into account the effect of time on the price charged for an item. What will be considered "reasonably contemporaneous" must vary with the circumstances of each case. Also, it is important that the transactions are *sales*—a sale to one buyer and an outright refusal to deal with another is not covered by the Act, nor is a sale to one buyer and a consignment or agency transaction with another buyer.

It is also important to note that the law applies to *"commodities of like grade and quality."* First, this phrase means that the law only applies to commodities, not to services. The term *commodities* refers to tangible personal property only, though discrimination in the sale of services may be illegal under Section 5 of the FTC Act as an "unfair method of competition." The requirement that the commodities be of like grade and quality is, of course, satisfied if the products are identical, but may also be satisfied by the sale of the same product under a prominent trademark and under a private label.

Methods of Price Discrimination

Price discrimination may be either *direct* discrimination, as in the obvious case of charging two different prices for the same commodity, or *indirect* discrimination, in which the same price is charged but the terms and conditions of the sale are different for two different purchasers of the same commodity. Sections 2(d) and 2(e) of the Act make it clear that some forms of indirect price discrimination are also illegal.

A seller can favor one customer over another in many ways: advertising and promotional aids, special packaging, payment of transportation expenses, return privileges, display and storage facilities, warehousing facilities and fees for storage, kickbacks and brokerage commissions, to name a few. Congress was well aware of the possibility of such indirect price discriminations and, therefore, provided that such favors be "available on proportionally equal terms to all other customers competing in the distribution of such products or commodities."

The requirement that the favor be available means more than providing the favor on request; the seller must make all competing purchasers *aware* that the favor is available. It is no defense for the seller to say later that the other buyers could have obtained the favor, if they were not aware that it was available. The requirement that it be available to all competing sellers depends on the actual competition between the purchasers. A manufacturer may legally make a favor available to all the purchasers on the East Coast but not to those on the West Coast, if those purchasers do not compete with each other, for example. Similarly, the favor must not be "tailored" to apply only to some firms. For example, if a seller develops a promotional assistance plan which envisions only large-scale aid useful only to huge chains and department stores, the plan is indirect price discrimination if it is not useful to small purchasers of the same product.

The requirement that the favors must be made available on "proportionately equal terms" means that they are available to each according to his worth as a retailer. The Act specifies no single way to obtain "proportional equality." Some plans, based on a percentage of dollar volume of goods purchased or on the quantity of goods purchased over a period of time, are probably valid. Volume discounts based on some sliding scale are especially suspect, however.

The Requirement of Competitive Injury

The Robinson-Patman Act seeks to distinguish those price discrimination schemes with no real competitive effect on commerce from schemes that harm competition in some manner. The principal section of the Act, Section 2(a), requires that proof of a violation include that:

> . . . the effect of such discrimination may be substantially to lessen competition or tend to create a monopoly in any line of commerce, or to injure, destroy or prevent competition with any person who either grants or knowingly receives the benefit of such discrimination, or with customers of either of them. . . .

A careful reading of that wording discloses that three types of anticompetitive effect are illegal under the Act: substantial lessening of competition; a tendency to create a monopoly; or injury to competition by specific persons. The first two types of effect, found throughout the Clayton Act, require an in-depth analysis of the markets and the industries involved. The third form permits proof of injury to specific persons, namely competitors who are harmed by the discriminatory scheme. It is generally said that the antitrust laws protect "competition, not competitors." But in this section, the Robinson-Patman Act does protect at least some competitors. The first two traditional anticompetitive effects take a great deal more effort to prove and, as a result, most of the cases involve specific injuries to competitors under the third type of competitive effect. These cases identify four categories of competitive injury, recognized under the third alternative of proving an anticompetitive effect.

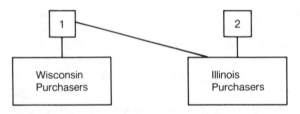

Figure 9-1 Primary-Line Injury

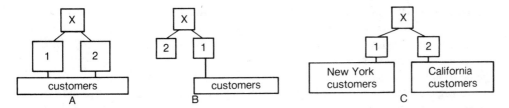

Figure 9-2   Secondary-Line Injuries

Primary-Line Injury to Competition   "Primary-line" injury is nothing more than injury to the *seller's competitors.* Thus, in Figure 9-1, Seller 1 and Seller 2 compete in Illinois, and Seller 1 sells in Wisconsin as well. If Seller 1 were to charge lower prices to Illinois purchasers than to those in Wisconsin in order to obtain more of the market from Seller 2, the result would be a **primary-line injury.**

Primary-line injury usually occurs in cases of geographic or territorial discrimination, but it isn't confined to that form. Primary-line injuries might also arise if a supplier cuts his prices to a competitor's customers while selling at higher prices to his own customers in the same area.

Secondary-Line Injury to Competition   A discrimination scheme that injures *competitors of the buyer* is a **secondary-line injury.** In the Figure 9-2A, Seller X discriminates in price between Buyers 1 and 2. Buyer 2, who does not receive the lowered price, may be less able to compete with Buyer 1 because of the price discrimination. However, discrimination between buyers may not result in competitive injury. In such cases, there is no violation of the Act. Two examples are shown in Figure 9-2B and C.

In Figure 9-2B, Buyer 1 is a retail gasoline dealer and Buyer 2 the owner of a trucking company. If X, a refiner-supplier of gasoline, sells to Buyer 2 at a lower price than to Buyer 1 (or vice-versa) there is no anticompetitive effect. Likewise, in Figure 9-2C, Buyer 1 sells only to retailers in California, while Buyer 2 sells only to retailers in New York. Since they are not competitors, there is no violation. Furthermore, in that case, the New York and California retailers are not in competition either.

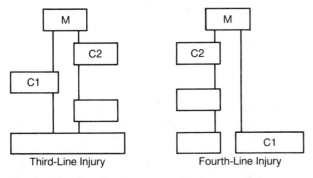

Figure 9-3   Injuries Further Down the Distribution Line

Third-Line and Fourth-Line Injury to Competition   Courts and commentators have also identified competitive injuries that take place even further down the distribution line. **Third-line injury** involves injuries to *customers in competition with customers of the supplier's favored buyer.* **Fourth-line injuries** are suffered by *customers in competition with a customer of a customer of the supplier's favored customer.* As shown in the Figure 9-3, the injury in both instances would be suffered by C1, and the discriminatorily lower price will have been given by M to C2.

In both instances, a lower price is given to C2 because it is a wholesaler or jobber of some sort. But there is no rational reason to favor C2. Thus, to stay within the Robinson-Patman Act, M must charge both C1 and C2 the same price.

Defenses to Charges of Price Discrimination

The Robinson-Patman Act outlines several possible defenses within the law itself. The two principal defenses are cost justified differentials and good faith price moves to meet competition.

Cost Justification   Some buyers are cheaper to sell to than others. A host of factors account for the differences, including savings in shipping costs, reduced sales expenses, and the buyer's purchasing practices. The Robinson-Patman Act permits sellers to pass on such *actual* differences in costs to the purchaser, in the form of price differentials. A mere quantity discount does not meet the standards, however, unless it can be shown that the quantity sold to a particular purchaser resulted in actual cost savings equal to the discount.

Meeting Competition   Lowering one's price to meet a price offered by a competitor is an effective defense to a Robinson-Patman Act claim. The defense is not popular with antitrust enforcers, and legislation has been proposed to abolish it. The defense is difficult to prove as well: it is not available if the competitor's price is unlawful under the Robinson-Patman Act; the price must be a temporary measure to meet competition, not a permanent price schedule resulting in systematically charged discriminatory prices; the price must be given for like quantities as offered by the competitor; the price must *meet,* not *beat,* the competitor's price; and the price must be limited to meeting a specific individual competitor's price to specific individual customers. The following decision considers the **meeting competition** defense.

Great Atlantic and Pacific Tea Co. v. FTC

440 U.S. 69, 99 S. Ct. 925, 59 L.Ed. 2d 153 (1979)

For years the Borden dairy had supplied milk to A & P stores in the Chicago area. In 1965, in order to achieve cost savings, A & P decided to switch from brand-name milk to a private-label milk sold under the A&P label. A & P asked Borden to submit a bid to supply the private-label milk. After prolonged negotiations, Borden offered A & P a discount for switching to private-label milk, provided A & P would accept limited delivery service, an offer Borden claimed would save A & P $410,000 a year. A & P was not satisfied, however, and solicited bids from other dairies. A competitor of Borden's, Bowman dairy, submitted a lower bid. At this point, A & P's Chicago buyer contacted Borden's representative, and told him "I have a bid in my pocket. You [Borden] people are so far out of line it is not even funny. You are not even in the ball park." When the Borden representative asked for more details, he was told nothing except that a $50,000 improvement in Borden's bid "would not be a drop in the bucket." Borden then cut its bid substantially, offering a savings of $820,000 per year. Borden emphasized that the reason for the bid was that it badly needed A & P's business, since it had recently opened a new plant in Illinois and the bid was to meet Bowman's bid. A & P then accepted Borden's bid. The FTC then brought this action under section 2(f) of the Robinson-Patman Act, claiming that by accepting Borden's bid it "knowingly induced or received" an illegal price discrimination. The price bid by Borden was substantially lower than the price charged to other customers.

Mr. Justice STEWART delivered the opinion of the Court.

. . . .

The Robinson-Patman Act was passed in response to the problem perceived in the increased market power and coercive practices of chain stores and other big buyers that threatened the existence of small independent retailers. Notwithstanding this concern with buyers, however, the emphasis of the Act is in § 2(a), which prohibits price discriminations by sellers. Section 2(f), making buyers liable for inducing or receiving price discriminations by sellers provides:

> That it shall be unlawful for any person engaged in commerce, in the course of such commerce, knowingly to induce or receive a discrimination in price *which is prohibited by this section.* [Emphasis added.]

Liability under § 2(f) thus is limited to situations where the price discrimination is one "which is prohibited by this section." . . . Under the plain meaning of § 2(f), therefore, a buyer cannot be liable if a prima facie case could not be established against a seller or if the seller has an affirmative defense. In either situation, there is no price discrimination "prohibited by this section."

The petitioner, relying on this plain meaning of § 2(f) argues that it cannot be liable under § 2(f) if Borden had a valid meeting-competition defense. The respondent, on the other hand, argues that the petitioner may be liable even assuming that Borden had such a defense. The meeting competition defense, the respondent contends, must in these circumstances be judged from the point of view of the buyer. Since A & P knew for a fact that the final Borden bid beat the Bowman bid, it was not entitled to assert the meeting competition defense even though Borden may have honestly believed that it was simply meeting competition.

In a competitive market, uncertainty among sellers will cause them to compete for business by offering buyers lower prices. Because of the evils of collusive action, the Court has held that the exchange of price information by competitors violates the Sherman Act. *United States* v. *Container Corp.* . . . Under the view advanced by the respondent, however, a buyer, to avoid liability, must either refuse a seller's bid or at least inform him that his bid has beaten competition. Such a duty of affirmative disclosure would almost inevitably frustrate competitive bidding and, by reducing uncertainty, lead to price matching and anticompetitive cooperation among sellers.

Accordingly, we hold that a buyer who has done no more than accept the lower of two prices competitively offered does not violate § 2(f) provided the seller has a meeting-competition defense.[5] Borden did in fact have such a defense.

The test for determining when a seller has a valid meeting-competition defense is whether a seller can "show the existence of facts which would lead a reasonable and

---

[5][Court's footnote] In *Kroger Co.* v. *FTC,* the Court of Appeals for the Sixth Circuit held that a buyer who induced price concessions by a seller by making deliberate misrepresentations could be liable under § 2(f) even if the seller has a meeting competition defense.

"This case does not involve a 'lying buyer' situation. . . ."

prudent person to believe that the granting of a lower price would in fact meet the equally low price of a competitor." A good-faith belief, rather than absolute certainty that a price concession is being offered to meet an equally low price offered by a competitor is sufficient to satisfy the 2(b) defense. . . . Since good faith, rather than absolute certainty, is the touchstone of the meeting competition defense, a seller can assert the defense even if it has unknowingly made a bid that in fact not only met but beat his competition. . . .

Since Borden had a meeting competition defense and thus could not be liable under § 2(b), the petitioner who did no more than accept that offer cannot be liable under § 2(f). . . .

Other Defenses   Certain specific types of sales are also exempted from the act. Those exemptions include actual or imminent deterioration of perishable goods; distress sales under court order; obsolescence of seasonal goods; and sales in good faith in the course of discontinuing business in the goods concerned. Generally speaking, those sales are examples of the general defense of "changing conditions affecting the market for or the marketability of the goods concerned," and the statute makes it clear that those four categories are not the only potential exemptions. Other legislation has exempted purchases by schools, colleges, universities, public libraries, churches, hospitals and charitable institutions, and local, state, and federal governments.

Interlocking Directorates

One of the practices outlawed by the Clayton Act in 1914 was **interlocking directorates.** Corporate policy in any firm is made by its board of directors, a group of individuals elected by the shareholders of the corporation. In the early 1900's, the boards of many corporations saw familiar faces at the director's meetings, and those interlocks, in which one person served on several boards, resulted in substantial anticompetitive conduct. In 1913, Louis D. Brandeis wrote a series of articles calling for the restriction of such corporate interlocks. In these articles he described the potential abuse of such practices, admittedly based in part on suppositions.

Louis D. Brandeis
The Endless Chain*

J. P. Morgan (or a partner), a director of the New York, New Haven & Hartford Railroad, causes that company to sell to J. P. Morgan & Co. an issue of bonds. J. P. Morgan & Co. borrow the money with which to pay for the bonds from the Guaranty Trust Co., of which Mr. Morgan (or a partner) is a director. J.P. Morgan & Co. sell the bonds to the Penn Mutual Life Insurance Company, of which Mr. Morgan (or a partner) is a director. The New Haven spends the proceeds of the bonds in purchasing steel rails from the United States Steel Corporation, of which Mr. Morgan (or a partner) is a direc-

---

*Louis D. Brandeis, "The Endless Chain," *Harper's Weekly* (December 6, 1913): 13–14.

tor. The United States Steel Corporation spends the proceeds of the rails in purchasing electrical supplies from the General Electric Company, of which Mr. Morgan (or a partner) is a director. The General Electric sells supplies to the Western Union Telegraph Company, a subsidiary of the American Telephone & Telegraph Company, and in both Mr. Morgan (or a partner) is a director. The telegraph company has a special wire contract with the Reading, of which Mr. Morgan (or a partner) is a director. The Reading buys its passenger cars from the Pullman Company, of which Mr. Morgan (or a partner) is a director. The Pullman Company buys (for local use) locomotives from the Baldwin Locomotive Company, of which Mr. Morgan (or a partner) is a director. The Reading, the General Electric, the steel corporation, and the New Haven, like the Pullman, buy locomotives from the Baldwin Company. The steel corporation, the telephone company, the New Haven, the Reading, the Pullman and the Baldwin companies, like the Western Union, buy electrical supplies from the General Electric. The Baldwin, the Pullman, the Reading, the telephone, the telegraph and the General Electric companies, like the New Haven, buy steel products from the steel corporation. Each and every one of the companies last named markets its securities through J.P. Morgan & Co.; each deposits its funds with J.P. Morgan & Co.; and with these funds of each, the firm enters upon further operations.

The result of Brandeis' articles and other public pressure was Section 8 of the Clayton Act. That statute has specific prohibitions regarding firms in banking, banking associations, and trust companies, and a general prohibition of interlocking directorates if one of the firms has more than $1 million in capital, surplus, and undivided profits. The firms must deal in interstate commerce, and the two firms must compete with each other in some area. The Act does not prohibit other relationships, as in a case where a president or other employee of one corporation serves as a director of another corporation. Actions may be brought against either corporation or the common director, and may result in cease and desist orders. Interlocking directorates may also violate Section 1 of the Sherman Act.

Section Two of the Sherman Act: Monopolization

Perhaps the most vague of the antitrust laws is Section 2 of the Sherman Act, which prohibits **monopolization** and attempts to monopolize. Like the other antitrust statutes, that section has been the subject of a great deal of judicial interpretation. But unlike the other antitrust statutes, the most important interpretation of Section 2 was made by a U.S. Court of Appeals, instead of by the U.S. Supreme Court, in the *Alcoa* case, discussed later in this section.

The Problem of Conduct Versus Structure

One of the most enigmatic parts of Section 2 is the use of the term *monopolize*. The Act does not make possession of a monopoly illegal. Most decisions have held that possession of monopoly power is not enough, and that the monopolist must have *used* this power in some anticompetitive, or **predatory,** fashion. As one of the few Supreme Court decisions dealing with Section 2 noted

> The offense of monopoly under section 2 of the Sherman Act has two elements: (1) the *possession of monopoly power* in the relevant market, and (2) the *wilful acquisition or maintenance of that power* as distinguished from growth or development as a consequence of a superior product, business acumen, or historic accident. *U.S. v. Grinnell Corp.** [Emphasis added].

From the very beginning the courts have required some form of *conduct* along with proof that an industry *structure* was monopolistic. The nature of that conduct, and the amount of "monopoly power" that must be held, have formed the twin issues in every monopolization case.

In early cases, the rule of reason discussed in Chapter 8 was applied to Section 2 as well as Section 1. That rule meant that only *unreasonable* monopolies would be held illegal; that is, monopoly itself was not illegal unless the monopolist behaved unreasonably. In almost all of the early cases, some type of **predatory conduct** was required before a conviction could be obtained. The courts identified several types of predatory conduct.

1. *Predatory pricing*—cutting prices below cost in certain regions or in certain product lines to force competitors out of business, and subsidizing such price cuts with monopoly profits obtained in other areas or from other products

2. *Predatory advertising and promotion*—heavily promoting specific products or brands (sometimes called *fighting brands*) or "bogus independent" firms in order to force competitors out of business, again subsidizing the extra expense by monopoly profits in other lines

3. *Advantages and rebates*—exacting special favors from suppliers or service firms, such as railroads, resulting in cost advantages over competitors unable to exact the same favors

4. *Physical violence*—some firms used actual violence to competitors, their competitors' customers, or their competitors' products

5. *Misuse of patents, copyrights and trademarks*—the use of patents and other "legal monopolies" to exert pressure in other markets

6. *Section 1 Violations*—such tactics as refusals to deal, tie-in sales, and exclusive dealing arrangements.

As noted in a 1920 landmark decision, mere size is not illegal.

> The Corporation is undoubtedly of impressive size. . . . But we must adhere to the law and law does not make mere size an offence or the existence of unexerted power an offence. The law requires overt acts and trusts to its prohibition of them and its power to repress or punish them. It does not compel competition nor require all that is possible. *U.S. v. U.S. Steel***

---

*384 U.S. 563, 86 S. Ct. 1698, 16 L. Ed. 2d 778 (1966).

**251 U.S. 417, 40 S. Ct. 293, 64 L. Ed. 343 (1920).

After the *U.S. Steel* case, prosecutors found it far easier to challenge predatory practices under Section 1 than to file monopolization charges under Section 2. The requirement of proving predatory conduct in order to show monopolization resulted in two decades of dormancy for Section 2.

The Retreat of Predatory Practices: The Alcoa Case

In 1945, a very strange set of procedural facts drove an extremely important Section 2 case into the "hands" of the Second U.S. Circuit Court of Appeals. After a three-year trial, the government's case against the Aluminum Company of America (ALCOA) was dismissed by the trial judge, who relied heavily on the *U.S. Steel* decision. That judge felt that mere size, unaccompanied by predatory practices and abuses, was insufficient to prove a violation of Section 2. On direct appeal, the Supreme Court could not hear the case because four justices had previously participated in the case in some way. The Second Circuit Court of Appeals was designated the court of last resort for the case. A Congressional Act later made the decision of the Second Circuit "binding precedent."

United States v. Aluminum Company of America

148 F. 2d 416 (2d Cir., 1945)

"Before L. HAND, SWAN, and AUGUSTUS N. HAND, Circuit Judges. . . ."
The Aluminum Company of America, known generally as Alcoa, was originally assigned a patent on the process of manufacturing aluminum in 1889 by the inventor of the process. Until that patent and others assigned to Alcoa expired in 1909, Alcoa had either a complete monopoly of the manufacture of aluminum or the process that eliminated all practical competition. During the period when the patents were effective, Alcoa made several contracts, including agreements with the various electric companies serving Alcoa, that prohibited the utilities from selling electricity to any other manufacturer of aluminum. Since electricity is essential in the manufacture of aluminum, these agreements also practically eliminated all competition. Alcoa also entered into four successive cartels with foreign manufacturers by which those foreign manufacturers agreed not to export aluminum to the United States.

Alcoa alone manufactured aluminum from ore. But such "virgin" aluminum had some competition in the form of "secondary" aluminum, that is, aluminum recycled from aluminum already used, such as scraps from plants using aluminum to fabricate items or from used items, such as kitchen utensils. Alcoa also had a wholly owned subsidiary in Canada, which exported aluminum to the United States.

If all aluminum was defined as the market, including secondary aluminum and such foreign aluminum as existed outside of the cartels, Alcoa had only 33 percent of the market. But if the market was defined as only virgin aluminum, Alcoa had 91 percent of the market. The government brought this action under Section 2 of the Sherman Act. The District Court held in favor of Alcoa, and the government appealed.

LEARNED HAND, Circuit Judge:
. . . . It is undisputed that throughout this period "Alcoa" continued to be the single producer of "virgin" ingot in the United States; and the plaintiff argues that this without more was enough to make it an unlawful monopoly. It also takes an alternative position: that in any event during this period "Alcoa" consistently pursued unlawful exclusionary practices, which made its dominant position certainly unlawful, even though it would not have been, had it been retained only by "natural growth." . . . "Alcoa's" position is

that the fact that it alone continued to make "virgin" ingot in this country did not, and does not, give it a monopoly of the market; that it was always subject to the competition of imported "virgin" ingot, and what is called "secondary" ingot and that even if it had not been, its monopoly would not have been retained by unlawful means, but would have been the result of a growth which the Act does not forbid, even when it results in a monopoly. . . .

. . . .

In the case of a monopoly of any commodity which does not disappear in use and which can be salvaged, the supply seeking sale at any moment will be made up of two components: (1) the part which the putative monopolist can immediately produce and sell; and (2) the part which has been, or can be, reclaimed out of what he has produced and sold in the past. By hypothesis, he presently controls the first of these components; the second he has controlled in the past, although he no longer does. . . . Thus, . . . "Alcoa" always knew that the future supply of ingot would be made up in part of what it produced at the time, and if it was as far-sighted as it proclaims itself, that consideration must have had its share in determining how much to produce. How accurately it could forecast the effect of present production upon the future market is another matter. . . . The competition of "secondary" must therefore be disregarded as soon as we consider the position of "Alcoa" over a period of years; it was as much within "Alcoa's" control as was the production of the "virgin" from which it had been derived. . . . We conclude that "Alcoa's" control over the ingot market must be reckoned at over ninety percent; that being the proportion which its production bears to imported "virgin" ingot. . . .

Was this a monopoly within the meaning of § 2? The judge found that over the whole half century of its existence, "Alcoa's" profits upon capital invested . . . had been only about ten percent. . . . [A] profit of ten percent . . . could hardly be considered extortionate.

But the whole issue is irrelevant anyway, for it is no excuse for "monopolizing" a market that the monopoly has not been used to extract from the consumer more than a "fair" profit. The Act has wider purposes. . . . Many people believe that possession of unchallenged economic power deadens initiative, discourages thrift and depresses energy; that immunity from competition is a narcotic, and rivalry is a stimulant, to industrial progress; that the spur of constant stress is necessary to counteract an inevitable disposition to let well enough alone. Such people believe that competitors, versed in the craft as no consumer can be, will be quick to detect opportunities for saving and new shifts in production, and be eager to profit by them. In any event, the mere fact that a producer, having command of the domestic market, has not been able to make more than a "fair" profit, is no evidence that a "fair" profit could not have been made at lower prices. True, it might have been thought adequate to condemn only those monopolies which could not show that they had exercised the highest possible ingenuity, had adopted every possible economy, had anticipated every conceivable improvement, stimulated every possible demand. . . . Be that as it may, that was not the way that Congress chose; it did not condone "good trusts" and condemn "bad" ones; it forbad all. Moreover, in so doing it was not necessarily actuated by economic motives alone. . . .

It is settled, at least as to §1, that there are some contracts restricting competition which are unlawful, no matter how beneficient they may be; no industrial exigency will justify them; they are absolutely forbidden. . . .

Starting with the authoritative premise that all contracts fixing prices are unconditionally prohibited, the only possible difference between them and a monopoly is that while a monopoly necessarily involves an equal, or even greater, power to fix prices, its mere existence might be thought not to constitute an exercise of that power. That distinction is nevertheless purely formal; it would disappear as soon as it began to sell at all—it must sell at some price and the only price at which it could sell is a price which it itself fixed. . . . Indeed it would be absurd to condemn such contracts unconditionally, and not to extend the condemnation to monopolies; for the contracts are only steps toward that entire control which monopoly confers. . . .

. . . .

Throughout the history of these statutes it has been constantly assumed that one of their purposes was to perpetuate and preserve, for its own sake and in spite of possible cost, an organization of industry in small units which can effectively compete with each other. We hold that "Alcoa's" monopoly of ingot was of the kind covered by § 2.

It does not follow because "Alcoa" had such a monopoly, that it "monopolized" the ingot market: it may not have achieved monopoly; monopoly may have been thrust upon it. It is unquestionably true that from the very outset the courts have at least kept in reserve the possibility that the origin of a monopoly may be critical in determining its legality. This notion has usually been expressed by saying that size does not determine guilt; that there must be some "exclusion" of competitors; that the growth must be something else than "natural" or "normal"; that there must be a "wrongful intent," or some other specific intent; or that some "unduly" coercive means must be used. . . . What engendered these compunctions is reasonably plain; persons may unwittingly find themselves in possession of a monopoly, automatically so to say: that is, without having intended either to put an end to existing competition, or to prevent competition from arising when none had existed; they may become monopolists by force of accident. A market may, for example, be so limited that it is impossible to produce at all and meet the cost of production except by a plant large enough to supply the whole demand. Or there may be changes in taste or in cost which drive out all but one purveyor. A single producer may be the survivor out of a group of active competitors, merely by virtue of his superior skill, foresight and industry. In such cases a strong argument can be made that, although, the result may expose the public to the evils of monopoly, the Act does not mean to condemn the resultant of those very forces which it is its prime object to foster. . . . The successful competitor, having been urged to compete, must not be turned upon when he wins. . . . "Alcoa's" size was "magnified" to make it a "monopoly"; indeed, it has never been anything else; and its size, not only offered it an "opportunity for abuse," but it "utilized" its size for "abuse" as can easily be shown.

It would completely misconstrue "Alcoa's" position in 1940 to hold that it was the passive beneficiary of a monopoly, following upon an involuntary elimination of competitors by automatically operative economic forces.

. . . . The only question is whether it falls within the exception established in favor of those who do not seek, but cannot avoid, the control of a market. It seems to us that that question scarcely survives its statement. It was not inevitable that it should always anticipate increases in the demand for ingot and be prepared to supply them. Nothing compelled it to keep doubling and redoubling its capacity before others entered the field. It insists that it never excluded competitors; but we can think of no more effective exclusion than progressively to embrace each new opportunity as it opened, and to face every newcomer with new capacity already geared into a great organization, having the advantage of experience, trade, connections and the elite of personnel. Only in case we interpret "exclusion" as limited to manoeuvres not honestly industrial, but actuated solely by a desire to prevent competition, can such a course, indefatigably pursued, be deemed not "exclusionary." So to limit it would in our judgment emasculate the Act. . . .

We disregard any question of "intent." . . . Although the primary evil was monopoly, the Act also covered preliminary steps, which, if continued, would lead to it. These may do no harm of themselves; but, if they are initial moves in a plan or scheme which, carried out, will result in monopoly, they are dangerous and the law will nip them in the bud. For this reason conduct falling short of monopoly, is not illegal unless it is part of a plan to monopolize, or to gain such other control of a market as is equally forbidden. To make it so, the plaintiff must prove what in the criminal law is known as a "specific intent," an intent which goes beyond the mere intent to do the act. . . .

In order to fall within § 2, the monopolist must have both the power to monopolize, and the intent to monopolize. To read the passage as demanding any "specific" intent, makes nonsense of it, for no monopolist monopolizes unconscious of what he is doing. So here, "Alcoa" meant to keep, and did keep, that complete and exclusive hold upon the ingot market with which it started. That was to "monopolize" that market, however innocently it otherwise proceeded. So far as the judgment held that it was not within § 2, it must be reversed.

The *Alcoa* decision did not do away with the need for some type of conduct to go along with proof of monopoly power, but the decision radically changed the definition of that conduct. No longer would the courts require predatory or abusive conduct, but would rather require proof of a general intent to monopolize, which may be proven, as in *Alcoa,* by proof of *legal* actions taken to maintain or obtain that power.

The *Alcoa* decision has never been reversed by the Supreme Court, but it has never been expressly adopted either. In 1966, the Supreme Court decided *U.S.* v. *Grinnell Corporation,* quoted at the beginning of this section, and seemed to reach similar results in the portion quoted. Some observers believe that *Grinnell* did away with the "thrust upon" defense found in *Alcoa,* since under the quoted language even monopoly lawfully achieved may be maintained unlawfully. The point is not clear.

The Problem of Relevant Market

Section 2 of the Sherman Act requires that the monopolization be of "any part of the trade or commerce among the several States, or with the foreign nations." If a business has a large enough share of a market, it is presumed to have monopoly power over that market. But a central question is the definition of the *market* over which it has such power. This crucial concept of relevant market is a major issue in not only Section 2 monopolization cases, but also in merger cases under Section 7 of the Clayton Act.

The relevant market has been defined as "the area of effective competition," that is, those products and that geographic area within which competition actually takes place. This market breaks down into two subcatagories: the **relevant product market** and the **relevant geographic market.** For example, in the *Alcoa* case, a major issue was whether virgin ingot was "in competition" with secondary ingot. That is another way of asking whether virgin ingot and secondary ingot were in the same relevant product market. If the two types of ingot are in the same market, then Alcoa's share of the total market is proportionately smaller than the market for virgin ingot alone. In many Section 2 cases, the whole issue turns on the proper definition of the relevant markets.

The Product Market   In the product market determination, the issue is whether particular products compete in any meaningful sense. This, in turn, becomes a question of substitutability or, more technically, the **cross-elasticity of demand.** Ultimately, the question of substitutability becomes a question of the ease with which consumers may switch between two similar products. Two types of cola drink may be in competition, for example, and are therefore in the same relevant product market. But does the relevant product market also include orange soda, root beer, coffee, ordinary beer, and imported wine? Are all of those products "in competition" in some meaningful sense? The question would be whether the relevant market should be defined as all beverages, all nonalcoholic beverages, all soda pops, or all colas. Further refinements might take into account diet versus nondiet drinks, caffeinated versus noncaffeinated drinks, and even price differences and types of containers. The ultimate issue would be whether, if the price of one type of beverage goes up, consumers will move quickly and easily to another type of beverage. As the Supreme Court noted

> For every product, substitutes exist. But a relevant market cannot meaningfully encompass that infinite range. The circle must be drawn narrowly to exclude any other product to which, within reasonable variations in price, only a limited number of buyers will turn; in technical terms, products whose "cross-elasticities of demand" are small.*

Some of the factors that may determine the relevant product market include the physical characteristics of the products; the customers for the products; the cross-elasticity of demand for the products; unique production facilities or "supply elasticities;" and industry recognition of differences, even if differences do not actually exist.

The Geographic Market   The geographic market, like the product market, is determined by consumers' ability to switch in the face of price increases, which in turn depends on the proximity and availability of other supply sources. The purchasers of Brand X milk, available only in New York, might be perfectly willing to buy Brand Z milk, available only in Los Angeles. But, in no way can the two brands be considered to be in the same regional market, since the distance between them is so great. As a result, both X and Z might be able to monopolize trade within their respective geographic markets if their power was sufficient. Such geographic markets might be quite small, such as a convenience grocery store located in a resort area where the nearest competitor is twenty miles away, or a hot dog vendor in a ballpark whose customers may not leave the stadium. Other factors, such as legal tariffs and quotas, may exclude foreign competition and thus narrow the geographic market as well.

The Determination of Relevant Market: The DuPont Case   The product market and geographic market determine whether and to what extent a firm may abuse its monopoly power. The degree of abuse is often considered to be how far a firm can raise its price above the price that would be set by competitive markets, and how far a firm might reduce its output below those that would be set by competitive markets. The following "watershed" case considers issues of market.

U.S. v. E.I. DuPont de Nemours & Co.

351 U.S. 377, 76 S. Ct. 994, 100 L.Ed. 1264 (1956)

The government brought this action for injunctive relief under Section 2 of the Sherman Act, charging duPont with monopolization of the cellophane market. DuPont had been licensed

---

Times-Picayune Publishing Co. v. *U.S.*, 345 U.S. 594, 73 S. Ct. 872, 97 L. Ed. 1277 (1953).

under a 1923 agreement to sell cellophane in the United States and, at the time of trial, continued to produce over 75 percent of the cellophane produced in the United States. On the other hand, if all "flexible packaging materials" were considered as the product market, duPont's cellophane accounted for less than 20 percent of the total sales. The government contended that the appropriate relevant market was cellophane, while duPont argued that the market must include all flexible wrappings.

Mr. Justice REED delivered the opinion of the Court.

. . . .

The Government contends that, by so dominating cellophane production, DuPont monopolized a "part of the trade or commerce" in violation of section 2. Respondent agrees that cellophane is a product which constitutes "a 'part' of commerce within the meaning of section 2." But it contends that the prohibition of section 2 against monopolization is not violated because it does not have the power to control the price of cellophane or to exclude competitors from the market. The court below found that the "relevant market for determining the extent of DuPont's market control is the market for flexible packaging materials," and that competition from those other materials prevented DuPont from possessing monopoly power in its sales of cellophane.

. . . .

. . . . Monopoly power is the power to control prices or exclude competition. It seems apparent that DuPont's power to set the price of cellophane has been limited only by the competition afforded by other flexible packaging materials. Moreover, it may be practically impossible for anyone to commence manufacturing cellophane without full access to DuPont's technique. However, DuPont has no power to prevent competition from other wrapping materials. . . . Price and competition are so intimately entwined that any discussion of theory must treat them as one. It is inconceivable that price could be controlled without power over competition or vice-versa. This approach to the determination of monopoly power is strengthened by this Court's conclusion in prior cases that, when an alleged monopolist has power over price and competition, an intention to monopolize may be assumed.

. . . .

Determination of the competitive market for commodities depends on how different from one another are the offered commodities in character or use, how far buyers will go to substitute one commodity for another. For example, one can think of building materials as in commodity competition, but one could hardly say brick competed with steel or wood or cement or stone in the meaning of Sherman Act litigation; the products are too different. This is the interindustry competition emphasized by some economists. . . . On the other hand, there are certain differences in the formulas for soft drinks, but one can hardly say that each one is an illegal monopoly. Whatever the market may be, we hold that control of price or competition establishes the existence of monopoly power under section 2. Section 2 requires the application of a reasonable approach in determining the existence of monopoly power just as surely as did section 1. This, of course, does not mean that there can be a reasonable monopoly. . . .

The Relevant Market

When a product is controlled by one interest, without substitutes available in the market, there is monopoly power. Because most products have possible substitutes, we cannot . . . give "that infinite range" to the definition of substitutes. Nor is it a proper interpretation of the Sherman Act to require that products be fungible to be considered in the relevant market.

. . . .

. . . . [I]llegal monopoly does not exist merely because the product said to be monopolized differs from others. If it were not so, only physically identical products would be part of the market. To accept the Government's argument, we would have to conclude that the manufacturers of plain as well as moistureproof cellophane were monopolists, as so with films such as Pliofilm, foil, glassine, polyethylene, and Saran, for each of these wrapping materials is distinguishable. . . . What is called for is an appraisal of the "cross-elasticity" of demand in the trade. . . . The varying circumstances of each case determine the result. In considering what is the relevant market for determining the control of price and competition, no more definite rule can be declared than that commodities reasonably interchangeable by consumers for the same purposes make up that "part of the trade or commerce," monopolization of which may be illegal. As respects flexible packaging materials, the market geographically is nationwide.

. . . .

But, despite cellophane's advantages, it has to meet competition from other materials in every one of its uses. . . . Food products are the chief outlet, with cigarettes next. . . . Cellophane furnishes less than 7 percent of wrappings for bakery products, 25 percent for candy, 32 percent for snacks, 35 percent for meats and poultry, 27 percent for crackers and biscuits, 47 percent for fresh produce, and 34 percent for frozen foods. Seventy-five to eighty percent of cigarettes are wrapped in cellophane. Thus, cellophane shares the packaging market with others. The overall result is that cellophane accounts for 17.9 percent of flexible wrapping materials measured by the wrapping surface.

. . . .

An element for consideration as to cross-elasticity of demand between products is the responsiveness of the sales of one product to price changes of the other. If a slight decrease in the price of cellophane causes a considerable number of customers of other flexible wrappings to switch to cellophane, it would be an indication that a high cross-elasticity of demand exists between them; that the products compete in the same market. . . .

We conclude that cellophane's interchangeability with the other materials mentioned suffices to make it a part of this flexible packaging material market.

. . . .

The "market" which one must study to determine when a producer has monopoly power will vary with the part of commerce under consideration. The tests are constant. That market is composed of products that have reasonable interchangeability for the purposes for which they are produced—price, use, and qualities considered. While the application of the tests remains uncertain, it seems to us that DuPont should not be found to monopolize cellophane when that product has the competition and interchangeability with other wrappings that this record shows.

On the findings of the District Court, its judgment is affirmed.

WARREN, C. J., with whom BLACK and DOUGLAS, J. J., join, dissenting.

This case, like many under the Sherman Act, turns upon the proper definition of the market. In defining the market in which DuPont's economic power is to be measured, the majority virtually emasculate section 2 of the Sherman Act. They admit that "cellophane combines the desirable elements of transparency, strength, and cheapness more definitely than any of" a host of other packaging materials. Yet they hold that all of those materials are so indistinguishable from cellophane as to warrant their inclusion in the market. We cannot agree that cellophane . . . is "the self-same product as glassine, greaseproof and vegetable parchment papers, waxed papers, sulphite papers, aluminum foil, cellulose acetate, and Pliofilm and other films."

If the conduct of buyers indicated that glassine, waxed and sulphite papers, and aluminum foil were actually "the self-same products" as cellophane, the qualitative differences demonstrated by the comparison of physical properties . . . would not be conclusive. But the record provides convincing proof that businessmen did not so regard these products. During the period covered by the complaint (1923–1947), cellophane enjoyed phenomenal growth. . . . Yet throughout this period, the price of cellophane was far greater than that of glassine, waxed paper, or sulphite paper. . . . We cannot believe that buyers, practical businessmen, would have bought cellophane in increasing amounts over a quarter of a century if close substitutes were available at from one-seventh to one-half cellophane's price. That they did so is testimony to cellophane's distinctiveness. . . .

The Problem of Monopoly Power

After the relevant market has been defined, the next question is whether, within that relevant market, a firm has monopoly power. The term *monopoly power* has been defined in the *DuPont* case, and later in *Grinnell*, as "the power to control prices or exclude competition." The existence of such monopoly power may usually be inferred from the market share of the defendant. A firm need not be the sole occupant of a market, but its market share must be so predominant that it may unilaterally affect prices or exclude competitors. The Supreme Court has not fastened on any clear percentage of the market that would automatically confer market power on a firm.

Most Section 2 cases have involved market shares in excess of 75 percent, but at least one case involved a market share of exactly 50 percent, and several cases have involved shares of 50–75 percent. Judge Learned Hand wrote in the *Alcoa* decision that any percentage over 90 "is enough to constitute a monopoly; it is doubtful whether sixty . . . would be enough; and certainly thirty-three percent is not."

Developments After Alcoa and DuPont

After the *Alcoa* and *DuPont* decisions, the law respecting monopolization did not change to any extent. The *Grinnell* decision, quoted at the beginning of this section, seemed to refine both *Alcoa* and *DuPont,* but little in the basic law of monopolization has changed since 1945.

Few Section 2 cases are filed. Though the language of *Alcoa* would seem to give antitrust prosecutors substantial weapons with which to attack the giants of American industry, those attacks have not come. Part of the reason is that Section 2 cases are among the largest and most complex legal actions in American law. But another reason is the language of *Alcoa* itself, for, as a Court of Appeals decision noted, "the cryptic *Alcoa* opinion is a litigant's wishing well, into which, it sometimes seems, one may peer and find nearly anything he wishes."[*]

One development after *Alcoa,* which met with less than stunning success, was the introduction and failure of statutes that would have made mere size illegal. One such statute, the proposed Industrial Reorganization Act of 1972, would have created a rebuttable presumption of monopoly power if the average rate of return on after-tax net worth of any corporation exceeded 15 percent in any five consecutive years, if there was no substantial price competition for any three consecutive years, or if four or fewer corporations accounted for 50 percent or more of sales in any years. The act did not become law.

---

[*]Kaufman, J., in *Berkey Photo, Inc.* v. *Eastman Kodak Co.,* 603 F. 2d 263 (2d Cir, 1979).

Structure: The Theory of Shared Monopoly   Section 2 also outlaws *conspiracy* to monopolize. In 1945, a Supreme Court decision seemed to apply that portion of the Act to a recent American phenomenon, the oligopolistic industry. The issue is whether Section 2 reaches an industry in which a few giant firms control the industry, and behavior of those firms follows parallel lines in pricing, advertising, and other competitive action.

The 1945 action, *American Tobacco Company* v. *U.S.*,* seemed to indicate that Section 2 could be used to attack oligopolistic industries. In that case, the government charged the three largest tobacco companies with conspiracy to monopolize under Section 2. The evidence showed no agreement between the firms, but rather a "clear course of dealing," the Court's term for parallel action. The Supreme Court affirmed the convictions entered in the lower court, and in doing so stated

> A correct interpretation of the statute and or the authorities makes it the crime of monopolizing, under § 2 of the Sherman Act, for parties, as in these cases, to combine or conspire to acquire or maintain the power to exclude competitors from any part of the trade or commerce . . . provided they also have such a power that they are able, *as a group,* to exclude actual or potential competition from the field and provided that they have the intent and purpose to exercise that power.
>
> It is not the form of the combination or the particular means used but the result to be achieved that the statute condemns. It is not of importance whether the means used to accomplish the unlawful objective are in themselves wholly innocent acts. Yet, if they are part of the sum of the acts which are relied upon to effectuate the conspiracy which the statute forbids, they come within its prohibition. No formal agreement is necessary to constitute an unlawful conspiracy. [Emphasis added.]

Yet in the face of the broad language of the *American Tobacco* case, the decision had little impact. Even though the case contains language, such as that just quoted, which would clearly make most oligopolies illegal if applied to its fullest, the case was simply never followed and was generally ignored as precedent.

During the early 1970's, the Federal Trade Commission brought two cases against the major participants in the oil and cereal industries under the theory of **shared monopoly.** That theory involves possession of massive market shares by a few firms and **parallel action** by the firms in setting prices or other competitive behavior. The oil case was quickly dismissed, but the cereals case lingered until 1982, when the Federal Trade Commission dismissed the action (see the Pro and Con section of this chapter). Even in the light of *American Tobacco* case, shared monopoly remains only a theory.

Conduct: The Nature of Predatory Acts   Following *Alcoa,* and even under the broad language of *Grinnell,* it seemed clear that otherwise legal conduct might be "wrongful" under Section 2, if coupled with sufficient monopoly power. But the 1970's saw, if not a retreat from that position, at least a standstill. Several private actions filed by competitors complaining of allegedly anticompetitive behavior by large firms resulted in similar judgments by several different U.S. Courts of Appeal,

---

*328 U. S. 781, 66 S. Ct. 1125, 90 L. Ed. 1575 (1945).

all of which limited the use of legal actions by monopolists as proof of a violation of Section 2.

The first series of cases were filed by several computer firms complaining of the actions of IBM. Allegedly, IBM had manufactured central computers (CPUs) that were incompatible with peripherals such as disc drives, printers, and tapes, in order to make sure that purchasers of IBM computers would buy peripherals manufactured by IBM as well. At least four separate cases were filed against IBM by manufacturers of peripherals driven from the market, along with an action by the Justice Department. All of the cases resulted in judgments in favor of IBM, with the exception of the Justice Department action, which was simply dismissed by the Department after six years of trial. As one court noted, "[IBM] was under no duty to help [competitors] survive or expand."

The second action bore some striking similarities to the IBM cases. That case involved a private action against Eastman-Kodak Company over introducing a new camera and new film together in such a way that purchasers had to buy the new camera in order to use the new film. The U.S. Circuit Court of Appeals for the Second Circuit held that Kodak's activities did not violate Section 2.

> In sum, although the principles announced by the § 2 cases often appear to conflict, this much is clear. The mere possession of monopoly power does not *ipso facto* condemn a market participant. But, to avoid the proscriptions of § 2, the firm must refrain at all times from conduct directed at smothering competition. This doctrine has two branches. Unlawfully acquired power remains anathema even when kept dormant. And it is no less true that a firm with a legitimately achieved monopoly may not wield the resulting power to tighten its hold on the market.
>
> . . . .
>
> . . . [A]s we have indicated, a large firm does not violate § 2 simply by reaping the competitive rewards attributable to its efficient size, nor does an integrated business offend the Sherman Act whenever one of its departments benefits from association with a division possessing a monopoly in its own market. So long as we allow a firm to compete in several fields, we must expect it to seek the competitive advantages of its broad-based activity—more efficient production, greater ability to develop complementary products, reduced transaction costs, and so forth. These are gains that accrue to any integrated firm, regardless of its market share, and they cannot by themselves be considered uses of monopoly power. *Berkey Photo, Inc.* v. *Eastman Kodak Co.**

Monopolization Through Abuse of the Political Process   One of the knottier problems of monopoly conduct deals with political activity by monopolists. Businesses have long known that government regulations and political action may be used as effective competitive tools. The issue is how far a business, particularly a closely watched monopoly, may use such regulations and procedures.

The complicating factor is the American Constitution. Access to government and to political bodies is guaranteed through the 1st and 14th Amendments to all persons, including corporations and even including monopolists. How then may use of that access constitute illegal conduct under Section 2? Even if such conduct takes the form of obtaining government regulations that harm competitors, or conducting

---

*603 F. 2d 263 (2d Cir., 1979); cert. den., 444 U.S. 1093, 100 S. Ct. 1061, 62 L. Ed. 2d 783 (1980).

press campaigns, ostensibly to influence legislation but with the real effect of inducing public ill-will toward competitors, should such conduct not be privileged under the Constitution?

In *Eastern Railroad Presidents* v. *Noerr Motor Freight,** Justice Black considered a case in which railroads conducted a "vicious, corrupt and fraudulent" campaign to influence passage of state laws dealing with truck weight limits and encourage rigid enforcement of truck weight limits and tax rates.

> We think it equally clear that the Sherman Act does not prohibit two or more persons from associating together in an attempt to persuade the legislature or the executive to take particular action with respect to a law that would produce a restraint or a monopoly. . . .
> In the first place, such a holding would substantially impair the power of government to take actions through its legislature and executive that operate to restrain trade. In a representative democracy such as this, these branches of government act on behalf of the people and, to a very large extent, the whole concept of representation depends upon the ability of the people to make their wishes known to their representatives. Secondly, and of at least equal significance, such a construction of the Sherman Act would raise important constitutional questions. The right of petition is one of the freedoms protected by the Bill of Rights, and we cannot, of course, lightly impute to Congress an intent to invade these freedoms. For these reasons, we think it clear that the Sherman Act does not apply to . . . mere solicitation of governmental action with respect to the passage and enforcement of laws.

But while the use of legislative process is an important aspect of the constitutional system, obviously firms can use governmental procedures to harass consumers and competitors, and obtain anticompetitive effects that would clearly be in violation of the Sherman Act if accomplished by other means. The *Noerr* case held further that if a publicity campaign was a "mere sham to cover what is actually nothing more than an attempt to interfere directly with the business relationships of a competitor" the Sherman Act could be invoked.**

Exemption of Regulated Industries

Many firms are closely regulated by various units of government. Public utilities are regulated by state public utilities commissions, for example, and railroads and airlines are regulated by the Interstate Commerce Commission. On numerous occasions, the courts have been faced with the question whether such close regulation should exempt the regulated industries from the federal antitrust laws. Many of those closely regulated businesses, such as public utilities, are natural monopolies, which caused their close regulation in the first place. It is clear from the following decision that use of the monopoly position by a public utility may cause a Section 2 violation, even in spite of its regulated status.

---

*365 U.S. 127, 81 S. Ct. 523, 5 L. Ed. 2d 464 (1961).

**Cf., *California Motor Transport Co.* v. *Trucking Unlimited,* 404 U.S. 508, 92 S. Ct. 609, 30 L. Ed. 2d 642 (1972).

Otter Tail Power Co. v. U.S.

410 U.S. 366, 93 S. Ct. 1022, 35 L. Ed. 2d 359 (1973)

The U.S. brought this civil antitrust action against the Otter Tail Power Company, an electric utility company serving parts of Minnesota, North Dakota, and South Dakota. Various municipalities within the service area of Otter Tail had voted to establish municipal, or city-owned, power companies rather than rely on Otter Tail. Those municipal power companies had requested (1) that Otter Tail sell power at wholesale to the municipal systems and (2) that Otter Tail "wheel" power over its transmission lines, that is, transmit the power purchased from other power companies over its lines to the municipal power companies. Otter Tail refused both requests and, instead, filed suits designed to prevent or delay the establishment of the municipal power systems. The firm also invoked contracts with other power companies to prevent those companies from selling power to municipal systems. The District Court found that the activities of Otter Tail violated Section 2 of the Sherman Act. The firm appealed on the ground it was "exempt" from the Act.

Mr. Justice DOUGLAS delivered the opinion of the Court.

. . . .

Otter Tail contends that by reason of the Federal Power Act it is not subject to antitrust regulation with respect to its refusal to deal. We disagree with that position.

(1) "Repeals of the antitrust laws by implication from a regulatory statute are strongly disfavored, and have only been found in cases of plain repugnancy between the antitrust and regulatory provisions." Activities which come under the jurisdiction of a regulatory agency nevertheless may be subject to scrutiny under the antitrust laws.

. . .

(2) The District Court below determined that Otter Tail's consistent refusals to wholesale or wheel power to its municipal customers constituted illegal monopolization. Otter Tail maintains here that its refusals to deal should be immune from antitrust prosecution, because the Federal Power Commission has the authority to compel involuntary interconnections of power. . . . Only if a power company refuses to interconnect voluntarily may the Federal Power Commission . . . order the interconnection. The standard which governs its decision is whether such action is "necessary or appropriate in the public interest." Although antitrust considerations may be relevant, they are not determinative.

(3) There is nothing in the legislative history which reveals a purpose to insulate electric power companies from the operation of the antitrust laws. To the contrary, the history of . . . the Federal Power Act indicates an overriding policy of maintaining competition to the maximum extent possible consistent with the public interest. . . .

It is clear, then, that Congress rejected a pervasive regulatory scheme for controlling the interstate distribution of power in favor of voluntary commercial relationships. When these relationships are governed in the first instance by business judgment and not regulatory coercion, courts must be hesitant to conclude that Congress intended to override the fundamental national policies embodied in the antitrust laws. . . .

. . . .

The record makes abundantly clear that Otter Tail used its monopoly power in the cities in its service area to foreclose competition or gain a competitive advantage, or to destroy a competitor, all in violation of the antitrust laws. . . . The District Court determined that Otter Tail has "a strategic dominance in the transmission of power in most of its service area" and that it used this dominance to foreclose potential entrants into the retail arena from obtaining electric power from outside sources of supply. Use of monopoly power "to destroy threatened competition" is a violation of the "attempt to monopolize" clause of section 2 of the Sherman Act. . . .

The District Court found that the litigation sponsored by Otter Tail had the purpose of delaying and preventing the establishment of municipal electric systems "with the expectation that this would preserve its predominant position in the sale and transmission of electric power in the area." [We have] held that the principle of [*Eastern Railroad Conference* v.] *Noerr* may also apply to the use of administrative or judicial processes where the purpose to suppress competition is evidenced by repetitive lawsuits carrying the hallmark of insubstantial claims and thus is within the "mere sham" exception announced in *Noerr*. . . .

Otter Tail argues that, without the weapons which it used, more and more municipalities will turn to public power and Otter Tail will go downhill. The argument is a familiar one. . . . "The promotion of self-interest alone does not invoke the rule of reason to immunize otherwise illegal conduct."

The same may properly be said of § 2 cases under the Sherman Act. That Act assumes that an enterprise will protect itself against loss by operating with superior service, lower costs, and improved efficiency. Otter Tail's theory collided with the Sherman Act as it sought to substitute for competition anticompetitive uses of its dominant economic power.

Affirmed.

The Legal Monopolies

Article I, Section 8, clause 8 of the United States Constitution provides that

> The Congress shall have Power . . . To Promote the Progress of Science and useful Arts, by securing for limited Times to Authors and Inventors the exclusive Right to their respective Writings and Discoveries.

The United States has maintained a patent and copyright system ever since 1790, and, though the system has undergone many changes, the federal government has granted limited monopolies to inventors and authors ever since. The grant to an inventor is known as a **patent;** and the grant to an author, composer, lyricist, illustrator, or photographer is a **copyright.** A related type of exclusive right to use a brand name or advertising symbol is a **trademark.**

It may at first seem contradictory that the federal government at once prosecutes monopolization under the Sherman Act and grants monopolies in the form of patents, coyprights, and trademarks. But in another sense, granting patent rights *protects* competition. Establishing a new product, process, or writing takes a great deal of work and often a large financial investment. Thus, granting a limited monopoly will encourage such work and investment, which means that new products, processes, and writings will enter the marketplace to compete, thus removing a substantial barrier to entry.

Second, no inventor or writer would publicize his or her invention or writing until it was absolutely necessary without the protection of the patent or copyright system, thus slowing "the Progress of Science and the useful Arts." The patent system permits the early disclosure and use of such inventions and, upon the expiration of the patent, its availability to the public, and removes the need for secrecy that would otherwise cloak inventions throughout their lives.

The Patent System

The federal Patent Act grants "for the term of seventeen years . . . the right to exclude others from making, using, or selling the invention throughout the United States."

Once a patent is properly applied for and granted (see below), it becomes a form of intangible personal property, and may be bought, sold, traded, given away, leased, or licensed for the use of others. Typically, patents are assigned to manufacturers or sold outright. Licensees of patents usually pay a royalty to the owner of the patent for the use of the license.

Patentability   Under the Patent Act, "Whoever invents or discovers any new and useful process, machine, manufacture, or composition of matter, or any new and useful improvement thereof, may obtain a patent therefor." The courts have generally found four prerequisites to patentability within that statute: inventiveness, novelty, utility, and subject matter.

The standard of *inventiveness* means that the invention must not be an obvious discovery "to a person having ordinary skill" in the art or science involved, so that merely making a well-known item out of a new material is not inventive nor is putting together two well-known inventions. *Novelty* obviously means that the invention was previously unknown, and *utility* means simply that it is useful.

The *subject-matter* requirement arises from the wording of the statute itself, since it seems to refer only to certain kinds of inventions and not to others. Mathematical formulas, fundamental laws of nature, and managerial techniques, while all highly useful, are not patentable. In *Diamond* v. *Chakrabarty,** the Supreme Court held that a manmade bacteria developed to break down crude oil was patentable and overruled a Patent Office determination that living things are not patentable. The Supreme Court held that the bacteria was a "manufactured" item, not a physical phenomenon or law of nature.

Antitrust Implications of Patents   A valid patent grant is a monopoly sanctioned by public policy and not against the antitrust laws. The Supreme Court has held that "the mere accumulation of patents, no matter how many, is not in and of itself illegal."** Similarly, purchase or license of a patent, by itself, is not illegal. But patents may form a part of an illegal scheme, depending on the ways in which they are used.

Nonuse of a patent is, by itself, not illegal. An invention may not be commercially feasible, or the applicant may have been seeking protection for one part of a larger product which is yet to be developed. But nonuse may be part of a larger scheme to foreclose competitors or may be evidence of intent to monopolize through suppression. Contracts, combinations, or conspiracies for nonuse have been labelled per se violations of the Sherman Act, and nonuse may also be part of the "acquisition or maintenance" proof in a Section 2 monopolization action.

The grant of patent licenses also carries some potential for antitrust violations, especially when "conditions" are attached to the grant of the patent license. Those conditions may become tying contracts or exclusive dealing arrangements or may simply be "unreasonable." The Patent Act permits "reasonable conditions" on the

---

*447 U. S. 303, 100 S. Ct. 2214, 65 L. Ed. 2d 159 (1980).

**Automatic Radio Mfg. Co. Inc.* v. *Hazeltine Research, Inc.,* 339 U.S. 827, 70 S. Ct. 894, 94 L. Ed. 1312 (1950).

grant of a license, but if those conditions are unreasonable they may become a violation of both the Patent Act and the Sherman Act. The "reasonability" of such conditions depends in turn on the patent itself. The patentee may not seek to enlarge his or her rights beyond the patent itself through the use of such conditions.

The Copyright Process

A copyright is a similar to a patent in that it grants an exclusive right to the holder to print, publish, copy, and sell books, periodicals, plays, music, art works, photographs, motion pictures, and other materials. Since 1978, that protection lasts for the life of the creator plus 50 years, and businesses may copyright materials they own for a maximum period of 15 years from the date of publication or 100 years from the date of creation. In order to secure a coypright, the author or publisher must print a coypright notice on the material (see the back side of the title page in this book, for example), produce at least three copies of the piece, and must register the publication with the Copyright Office.

　　If registration has been accomplished properly, the Act authorizes suits against persons who use the copyrighted materials without permission. Such actions are called *infringement actions,* and a person who uses such materials may be liable for damages caused by unauthorized use. The courts may issue an injunction against such use in the future. A major exception is the **fair use doctrine,** which permits the use of copyrighted material without permission for purposes of criticism, comment, news reporting, teaching, scholarship, or research. The following decision considers a major infringement issue, copying television programs using video tape recorders (VTR's).

Sony Corp. v. Universal City Studios (The Betamax Case)
104 S. Ct. 774, 52 U.S.L.W. 4090 (1984)

Sony Corporation manufactures home video tape recorders (VTR's) and markets them through retail establishments. Universal owns the copyrights on some of the television programs that are broadcast on the public airwaves. Universal brought an action in federal district court, claiming the VTR consumers had been recording some of respondent's copyrighted works and thereby infringed its copyrights, and that Sony was liable for such copyright infringement because of their marketing of VTR's. The District Court denied all relief to the petitioners, but the Court of Appeals reversed and held the manufacturer and some retailers of VTR's guilty of "contributory infringement." Sony appealed to the Supreme Court.

　　JUSTICE STEVENS delivered the opinion of the Court:
　　. . . .
　　Copyright protection "subsists . . . in original works of authorship fixed in any tangible medium of expression." . . . This protection has never accorded the copyright owner complete control over all possible uses of his work. Rather, the Copyright Act grants the copyright holder "exclusive" rights to use and to authorize the use of his work . . . including reproduction of the copyrighted work in copies. . . . All reproductions of the work, however, are not within the exclusive domain of the copyright owner; some are in the public domain. Any individual may reproduce a copyrighted work for a "fair use;" . . .
　　. . . .

The Copyright Act provides the owner of a copyright with a potent arsenal of remedies against an infringer of his work, including an injunction to restrain the infringer from violating his rights, the impoundment and destruction of all reproductions of his work made in violation of his rights, a recovery of his actual damages and any additional profits realized by the infringer or a recovery of statutory damages, and attorneys fees.

The two respondents in this case do not seek relief against the Betamax users who have allegedly infringed their coyprights. Moreover, this is not a class action on behalf of all copyright owners who license their works for television broadcast, and respondents have no right to invoke whatever rights other copyright holders may have to bring infringement actions based on Betamax copying of their works. . . . It is . . . the taping of respondents own copyrighted programs that provides them with standing to charge Sony with contributory infringement. To prevail, they have the burden of proving that users of the Betamax have infringed their copyrights and that Sony should be held responsible for that infringement.

. . . .

The Copyright Act does not expressly render anyone liable for infringement committed by another. . . . The absence of such express language in the copyright statute does not preclude the imposition of liability for copyright infringements on certain parties who have not themselves engaged in the infringing activity. For vicarious liability is imposed in virtually all areas of the law. . . .

. . . .

If vicarious liability is to be imposed on petitioners in this case, it must rest on the fact that they have sold equipment with constructive knowledge of the fact that their customers may use that equipment to make unauthorized copies of copyrighted material. . . .

. . . .

The question is thus whether the Betamax is capable of commercially significant noninfringing uses. . . . [O]ne potential use of the Betamax plainly satisfies this standard, however it is understood: private, noncommercial time-shifting in the home. It does so both (A) because respondents have no right to prevent other copyright holders from authorizing it for their programs, and (B) because . . . even the unauthorized home time-shifting of respondents' programs is legitimate fair use.

A. Authorized Time-Shifting

Each of the respondents owns a large inventory of valuable copyrights, but in the total spectrum of television programming their combined market share is small. The exact percentage is not specified, but it is well below 10 percent. . . . No doubt, many other producers share respondents' concern about the possible consequences of unrestricted copying. Nevertheless the findings of the District Court make it clear that time-shifting may enlarge the total viewing audience and that many producers are willing to allow private time-shifting to continue. . . .

B. Unauthorized Time-Shifting

. . . .

. . . [A]lthough every commercial use of copyrighted material is presumptively an unfair exploitation of the monopoly privilege that belongs to the owner of the copyright, noncommercial uses are a different matter. A challenge to a noncommercial use of a copyrighted work requires proof either that the particular use is harmful, or that if it should become widespread, it would adversely affect the potential market for the copyrighted work. Actual present harm need not be shown; such a requirement would leave the copyright holder with no defense against predictable damage. Nor is it necessary to show with certainty that future harm will result. What is necessary is a showing by a preponderance of the evidence that *some* meaningful likelihood of future harm exists.

If the intended use is for commercial gain, that likelihood may be presumed. But if it is for a noncommercial purpose, the likelihood must be demonstrated.

In this case, respondents failed to carry their burden with regard to home time-shifting. . . . [I]n its opinion, the District Court observed: "Most of plaintiffs' predictions of harm hinge on speculation about audience viewing patterns and ratings, . . ."

On the question of potential future harm from time-shifting, the District Court offered a more detailed analysis of the evidence. It rejected respondents' "fear that persons 'watching' the original telecast of a program will not be measured in the live audience and the ratings and revenues will decrease," by observing that current measurement technology allows the Betamax audience to be reflected. . . . It rejected respondents' prediction "that live television or movie audiences will decrease as more people watch Betamax tapes as an alternative," with the observation that "[t]here is no factual basis for [the underlying assumption.]" . . . It rejected respondents' "fear that time-shifting will reduce audiences for telecast reruns," and concluded instead that "given current market practices, this should aid plaintiffs rather than harm them." . . . And it declared that respondents' suggestion "that theater or film rental exhibition of a program will suffer because of time-shift recording of that program" . . . "lacks merit." . . .

. . . .

It may well be that Congress will take a fresh look at this new technology, just as it so often has examined other innovations in the past. But it is not our job to apply laws that have not yet been written. Applying the copyright statute, as it now reads, to the facts as they have been developed in this case, the judgment of the Court of Appeals must be reversed.

Justice Blackmun, with whom Justice Marshall, Justice Powell, and Justice Rehnquist joined, dissented on the grounds that the court defined the concept of "contributory infringement" too narrowly.

Trademark Protection

A trademark or tradename is any distinctive mark, symbol, word, phrase, or picture used to identify a particular corporation or product. The federal *Lanham Act,* first effective in 1947, permits individuals to register trademarks with the Patent Office. Such registration creates no rights, but establishes federal recognition to use the trademark. Tradenames must be registered in each state, on the other hand. Scandalous, obscene, disparaging, or deceptive trademarks may not be registered.

After registration, the user may stop others from using the trademark. Prior to registration, the user must show that he or she was the first to use the trademark. In such cases, the user may sue infringers for damages or for an injunction against future uses. A trademark may be lost by abandonment, that is, by failing to use it on products.

Section 43(a) of the Lanham Act prohibits the use of "any false description or representation" in connection with any goods or services placed in commerce and permits persons likely to be damaged by the false description or representation to bring suit in federal court.

While the point is not totally clear, most federal courts now permit competitors to sue one another for false representations concerning their products, as long as the false representations apply to the defendant's own products. This is considered an expansion of the common law regarding deceptive advertising, as discussed in Chapter 11.

Trademarks may be licensed in much the same manner as patents, and such licensing often forms the basis of franchise agreements. Such agreements may involve tie-in sales, as where the franchisor permits the franchisee to use the trademark of a nationally known firm on condition that the franchisee purchase goods and services from the franchisor. That problem was considered in Chapter 8.

Summary and Conclusions

The Robinson-Patman Act of 1936 makes price-discrimination illegal. This detailed act, which is in fact an amendment to the Clayton Act, makes both discriminating in price and receiving a discriminatory price illegal, and covers both price and nonprice concessions. The Act provides defenses in the form of cost justification and good-faith meeting of competition.

Section 2 of the Sherman Act prohibits monopolization, a word that has given rise to the argument between advocates of structure alone as proof of a violation of the Act and advocates of conduct, who would require some use of monopoly power before a conviction could be obtained. The courts require two elements to prove monopolization: "(1) the possession of monopoly power in the relevant market, and (2) the wilful acquisition or maintenance of that power...." Usually that means a fairly large market share and some conduct to show an "intent to monopolize" by attaining or maintaining monopoly position. Thus, some form of conduct is required for conviction, but that conduct need not be illegal. Traditionally, some form of predatory or abusive conduct has been required.

On the other hand, the federal government also *grants* monopolies, in the form of patents, copyrights, and trademarks. The justifications for such grants include the idea that such monopolies aid firms in entering markets and making them more competitive.

PRO AND CON
ISSUE: Should the Theory of Shared Monopoly Be Enforced as a Part of The Sherman Act?

On January 15, 1982, the Federal Trade Commission formally dismissed a case against the major cereal manufacturers, filed on the theory of "shared" monopoly under Section 5 of the FTC Act (see pp. 280 and 388–389). The Federal Trade Commissioners filed separate statements regarding the dismissal. This Pro and Con section consists of excerpts from two of those statements.

PRO: The Theory of Shared Monopoly Should Have Been Considered on its Merits
Commissioner Michael Pertshuck

The Commission today takes an unprecedented step in refusing to hear the appeal of this matter. This decision raises serious implications for the integrity and propriety of commission adjudicatory procedures. The complaint in this matter was issued in 1972 and it has taken nine years to complete pretrial procedures and the trial itself. The case raises difficult and unanswered legal questions as well as vigorously disputed factual controversies. Legal conclusions about the allegations in the complaint would have important ramifications for the applicability of the antitrust laws to concentrated industries which do not operate competitively. Thus the case is precisely the kind of matter that warrants full-scale review by a responsible Commission, charged by Congress with adjudicatory determinations. . . .

Yet the Commission has precipitously determined that it will not grant full-scale review of this matter, apparently on the grounds that it would be a waste of resources. The resources at stake apparently are the costs of a round of briefs concerning the administrative law judge's opinion, an oral argument, and the preparation of an opinion—not trivial, I grant, but not significant compared to the length, complexity and importance of this matter.

It cannot be ignored that this case has been controversial and that Congress has expressed concern about it. . . . Respondents have . . . engaged in intensive lobbying efforts in Congress to accomplish the premature demise of this case. I do not question their right. . . . I do question, however, the propriety of Congressional intervention in any matter before it has run its course of proper adjudicatory procedures. I also question whether Congress has ever been furnished with a complete analysis of this difficult case and the legal arguments that have been raised in it.

. . . .

The case was argued on the basis of two theories, (1) a conspiracy based on traditional Sherman Act Section 1 principles and (2) a theory of interdependent behavior in a highly structured industry with poor competitive performance and where industry members have engaged in exclusionary conduct, what has come to be known in somewhat misleading shorthand as a "shared monopoly." If the case had been appealed I would, of course, have carefully considered the conspiracy argument. . . . Based upon my tentative review, I am inclined to believe a finding of a traditional conspiracy could not fairly serve as a basis of liability. . . .

. . . .

The shared monopoly theory, as reflected in the Commission's complaint in this matter, was predicated upon an allegation of high concentration as evidenced by a three-firm concentration exceeding 80 percent; poor competitive performance as measured, for example, by sustained high profits and the absence of price competition; and high barriers to entry caused by exclusionary conduct of industry members. . . .

Such a theory is supported by scholarly commentary. . . . Thus it is not the case that "the theory has . . . utterly failed to enter the mainstream of economic thought," as respondents claim. Rather, this case represents a serious, carefully thought out attempt by a no-nonsense Republican-led Commission in 1972 to deal with the problem of a tight oligopoly and poorly performing industry.

Today the Commission turns its back on this attempt, not wishing to deal with the difficult but necessary task of spelling out whether and under what circumstances the antitrust laws reach this problem. Such a step by the Commission is a significant one, with major ramifications for government antitrust policy. We should make no mistake about it: The problem of high concentration—industries operated by a few giant companies with poor competitive performance as indicated by the absence of meaningful price competition and the absence of significant entry of new competitors over a long period—is not going to disappear from our economy in the coming decades. Our economy is now made up of a number of highly concentrated industries without meaningful price competition and, if the merger laws are not to be enforced vigorously, this situation will become more frequent, not less.

I for one believe that Section 5 of the Federal Trade Commission Act *does* reach a situation where an industry is highly concentrated, where the performance of the industry as measured by profit levels, lack of price competition or other factors, is poor, where effective barriers to entry are created by exclusionary conduct on the part of the firms, and where a government-ordered remedy can be shown to be likely to improve competition. . . . But I also conclude that the prospect for some future Commission effectively to apply this theory is highly unlikely. . . . I view today's decision as confirmation of the political inability of a Commission to see such a case through to the end.

As our political system provides, the Commission reflects, to a large extent, the prevailing political attitudes and the economic philosophy of the current administration. And, quite properly, future Commissions will reflect the then-prevailing political philosophy. Unfortunately, an attempt by the inherently lengthy process of litigation to deal with the oligopolistic problem . . . requires a political consensus that an independent commission is legitimate. . . . Today's decision seems to me to tell us that such a consensus is unlikely. Therefore, I believe strongly that Congress . . . should brace itself for the task of spelling out in careful, responsible legislation what the government's role is in dealing with the problem of oligopoly. And I emphasize again that it is a problem which is destined to become more, rather than less, significant for our society.

CON: There Is No Basis for the Theory of Shared Monopoly
Commissioner David Clanton

... After having reviewed the parties most recent submissions ... I cannot find a basis for continuing the case.

. . . .

As to the first theory [of traditional Sherman Act conspiracy] I agree ... that a conspiracy to monopolize was not properly pled. As for the separate shared monopoly theory, I do not believe such a theory, however characterized, can serve as a predicate for the Commission to restructure an industry, at least in the absence of clear predatory behavior, which is not claimed here. . . .

... In issuing the complaint, I think the Commission sought to address a legitimate concern, not about oligopolies *per se,* but rather about oligopolistic behavior that is uniquely anticompetitive. . . .

Even giving the benefit of the doubt to complaint counsel, it is hard to understand why it was necessary to dance-step around the conspiracy issue if the case clearly covered it. After all, the major case now relied upon by complaint counsel, *American Tobacco Co.* v. *United States* ... which was decided twenty-five years before this case was brought, involved an implied conspiracy to monopolize. . . .

Even if a conspiracy ... is not present, that does not end the matter. Complaint counsel alternatively argue that even absent a conspiracy the conduct is sufficiently like one to justify a finding of liability under Section 5 of the FTC Act. It is quite clear ... that Section 5 can reach anticompetitive behavior that is not covered by the Clayton or Sherman Acts. And I believe such authority extends to non-collusive, marketwide behavior that may not involve traditional forms of predation. Presumably, this could include behavior that would not be illegal for a single firm to engage in but, due to the industrywide nature of the practice, could lead to significant anticompetitive effects. . . .

... [U]nder complaint counsel's theory one must recognize the implications of using such an approach to restructure an entire industry. . . . [T]he kind of theory and relief they are seeking require extensive proof of industry structure, performance and conduct. While that kind of analysis is highly commendable, it provides a less than certain guide as to what kinds of conduct or market conditions would be subject to antitrust attack. . . .

Thus absent collusion or clear evidence of predatory behavior, I believe it would be unwise for the Commission to seek dissolution of an industry on the basis of the cumulative effects of multi-firm behavior. That does not mean, however, that such behavior would go unaddressed. Rather, it means that the kind of relief sought [should be] *conduct* remedies. . . .

In this instance, assuming complaint counsel's case were to be established, several practices might be singled out for possible action. For example, a central issue in the case is brand proliferation. . . . A second practice that might be susceptible to correction concerns respondents' shelf-space recommendations to grocery retailers. . . . A third area for possible relief involve the exchange of recent advertising expenditure data among the respondents through the vehicle of a third party reporting service. . . . Another candidate for reform is respondents' fairly consistent refusal to supply private-brand cereals to retailers. . . .

While we might desire a better mix of price and non-price competition in the . . . cereal industry, the potential costs associated with a divestiture order, not to mention the difficulty in getting a court to approve such an exercise of our remedial discretion, lead me to reject this approach. I am also simply not persuaded that the class of cases reflected here is sufficiently large to warrant pursuing this kind of complicated, time-consuming remedial avenue. . . . Accordingly, it is my belief that the Commission should not pursue this case further.

DISCUSSION QUESTIONS

1. It is often said that "economic conservatives" favor enforcement of the conduct portions of the antitrust laws, while "economic liberals" favor enforcement of the structure portions of the laws. Like all generalizations, this statement has many exceptions, but why do you suppose it is true, if it is true?

2. Should simple "business size" be illegal? Do you agree with Mr. Justice Brandeis' observation at the beginning of the chapter that "the economies of monopoly are superficial and delusive?" If you think sheer size should not be illegal, how do you feel about the approach of the Industrial Reorganization Act, which would have made sheer size prima facie proof of monopoly power and permits firms to present defenses? If you think size should be illegal, what size? How would you measure it? Would those limits have to change over time?

3. If part of the purpose behind Section 2 is the political and social fear of size, should conduct play any role? Is a good monopolist any less politically powerful than a bad monopolist?

4. Should only "illegal" conduct (i.e., Section 1 violations) be a basis for a finding of monopolization under Section 2? If so, isn't Section 2 merely a restatement of Section 1, with no purpose? On the other hand, if "legal" conduct may be used to prove a Section 2 violation, what types of conduct would you use to prove a violation? Given the fact that the courts have not established an "automatic" market share which constitutes monopoly power, and therefore a monopolist may not know that he is a monopolist, how is he to know when legal conduct may subject him to Section 2?

5. What do you suppose Senator Sherman had in mind, writing in 1890, when he wrote Section 2 and used the term *monopolization?* Do you think he envisioned the structure versus conduct debate? Why didn't he define his terms, anyway?

6. If the term *conspiracy to monopolize* in Section 2 does not mean the theory of shared monopoly, what does it mean? Is there any economic difference between a single-firm monopoly and a few powerful firms holding most of the market and operating in an identical, or parallel fashion?

7. Who is harmed by price discrimination? Does that depend on what type of price discrimination we are talking about? Shouldn't a firm be permitted to sell its product under its own name and under private labels at different prices?

8. Aren't the patent laws really inconsistent with the antitrust laws? After all, seventeen years is an awfully long time to hold a monopoly, especially when technology is changing as fast as it does now.

CASE PROBLEMS

1. Anheuser-Busch sold beer nationwide. Its product was a so-called "premium beer" and sold for more than its regional competitors in the St. Louis area, Anheuser's home base. In 1953, all national breweries granted a wage increase and put into effect a price increase nationwide. In 1954, however, Anheuser lowered its price by 58¢ in the St. Louis area only, to exactly equal the price charged by regional competitors. Anheuser's share of the market rose from 12.5 percent of the market to 39.3 percent of the market in a year and a half. Anseuser then raised its price by 45¢ a case, which forced its market share back to 21.03 percent.

The FTC brought a price-discrimination action. Result? [*FTC* v. *Anheuser-Busch, Inc.,* 363 U.S. 536, 80 S. Ct. 1267, 4 L. Ed. 2d 1385 (1960).]

2. Morton Salt Company had established a "quantity discount" plan for purchases of its salt. It charged $1.60 per case in less-than-carload purchases, $1.50 per case for carload purchases, $1.40 per case for more than 5,000 cases purchased in twelve months, and $1.35 per case for more then 50,000 cases purchased in twelve months. Only five purchasers, all of whom were large national grocery chains, were able to avail themselves of the lowest price, and those stores were therefore able to sell salt to consumers at prices lower than other retailers. Does Morton's plan violate the Robinson-Patman Act? [*FTC* v. *Morton Salt Co.,* 334 U.S. 37, 68 S. Ct. 822, 92 L. Ed. 1196 (1948).]

3. Grinnell Corporation manufactures plumbing supplies and fire sprinkler systems. It also owns 76 percent of the stock of ADT, which provides burglary and fire protection services, 89 percent of the stock of AFA, which provides only fire protection services, and 100 percent of the stock of Holmes Electric, which provides only burglary protection services. Each offers "central station service," which means that in the event of a fire or break-in, electronic signals are received by the station and guards or fire equipment are dispatched. Central station service is considered the "best" and results in substantial insurance savings.

    ADT, AFA, and Holmes are the three largest firms nationwide: ADT has 73 percent of the business, AFA has 12.5 percent, and Holmes has 2 percent. Each firm has acquired several competitors through mergers. Grinnell argued that the relevant market should include all protective services, such as guard dogs and watchmen, or in the alternative the relevant market should be divided into fire services and burglary services. What result? [*U.S.* v. *Grinnell Corp.,* 384 U.S. 563, 86 S. Ct. 1698, 16 L. Ed. 2d 778 (1966).]

4. Kodak, the nation's largest producer of photographic film, introduced simultaneously a new camera and a new film to fit only that camera. The film was marketed as a revolutionary development, and the camera was described as one of the finest made. To use the film, a consumer had to buy the camera and vice-versa. Berkey, a manufacturer of cameras, brought a private action under Section 2, claiming that Kodak had used its monopoly power in the film market as leverage in the camera market. Result? [*Berkey Photo* v. *Eastman-Kodak Co.,* 603 F. 2d, 263, (2d Cir., 1979).]

5. United Shoe Machinery, a manufacturer of shoemaking equipment and supplies, held 75–85 percent of the market for shoemaking equipment. That equipment is expensive and involves a great deal of expertise to manufacture. United's major patents on those machines expired long ago, but some new patents block some potential competition by leading inventors of new processes to offer their ideas only to United. United does not sell its machines to manufacturers, but since the Civil War has leased machines to shoe manufacturers. Those leases made it more difficult for manufacturers to change from United Machinery to other manufacturers and gave favorable terms to manufacturers who switch to United's machines from those of other manufacturers. Those leases extend for ten years

with rather substantial penalties for early termination, and the lease includes all service on the machines. Does United's scheme violate Section 2 of the Sherman Act? [*U.S.* v. *United Shoe Machinery Corp.* 110 F. Supp. 295 (1953).]

6. Benedick Baking Company has its own brand of bread, Benedick's Best, which is advertised nationally and sold to retailers at 50¢ a loaf. Leonato's Foods, a national grocery chain, makes a contract with Benedick that Benedick will supply bread to Leonato's packaged under Leonato's store brand, Leonato's Loaf, at 35¢ a loaf. The bread in Benedick's Best and Leonato's Loaf is identical. Is there price discrimination? Could Benedick argue that the cost of national advertising is included in the higher price of Benedick's Best?

7. Escalus Root Beer is the only nationwide producer of "keg" root beer sold to drive-ins and restaurants, though there are several producers of canned and bottled root beer. Escalus established its position in the drive-in and restaurant business long ago and maintains an extremely efficient distribution system for root beer. Even though Escalus does not sell root beer at retail, it advertises its brand nationally, and each advertisement features the names of participating chains of drive-ins and restaurants. Froth Root Beer filed a private antitrust action, claiming "monopolization" under Section 2, and alleges that it cannot enter the market because of Escalus' practices. Result?

8. Oberon and Peablossom, Inc., a nationwide department store chain, began marketing the finest stereo equipment on the market at relatively low prices. The only hitch was that to use the stereo equipment purchased from Oberon and Peablossom, consumers had to purchase tapes and records also purchased only from Oberon and Peablossom as well, since the company made sure that no other tapes or records would fit on their stereo equipment. The tapes and records made by Oberon and Peablossom do not work on other stereo equipment, either. Oberon and Peablossom then made contracts with virtually every hard rock and country music star to perform on the O & P record label. In retaliation, Quince and Mustardseed, another department store chain, introduced a line of excellent stereo equipment and made sure that only Q & M tapes and records could be played on its equipment and no other. Quince and Mustardseed then proceeded to line up virtually every "middle of the road," classical, and soft rock star to record for its label. Has there been an antitrust violation or violations? What are they? Who is harmed?

SUGGESTED READINGS

Areeda, Phillip. *Antitrust Analysis* 3d ed. (Boston: Little, Brown & Co., 1981).

Hills, Carla. *Antitrust Advisor* (New York: McGraw Hill Co./Shepard's Citations, Inc., 1971).

Kintner, Earl W. *An Antitrust Primer: A Guide to Antitrust and Trade Regulation Laws for Businessmen* 2d ed. (New York: The MacMillan Co., 1973).

Kintner, Earl W. *A Robinson-Patman Primer* 2d ed. (New York: The MacMillan Co., 1979).

Patman, Wright. *Complete Guide to the Robinson-Patman Act* (Englewood Cliffs, N.J.: Prentice-Hall, 1938, 1963).

Posner, Richard A. *Antitrust* (St. Paul, Minn: West Publishing Co., 1974).

Posner, Richard A. *The Robinson-Patman Act* (Washington, D.C.: American Enterprise Institute for Public Policy Research, 1975).

Sherman, Roger. *Antitrust Policies and Issues* (Reading, Mass.: Addison-Wesley Publishing Co., 1978).

Antitrust: Regulation of Mergers

Competition is the life of trade, but the death of profit.

Anonymous

Great cases, like hard cases, make bad law. For great cases are called great, not by reason of their real importance in shaping the law of the future, but because of some accident of immediate overwhelming interest which appeals to the feelings and distorts the judgment.

Mr. Justice Holmes, dissenting in Northern Securities Co. *v. U.S., 193 U.S. 197 (1904).*

Nobody cheers for Goliath.

attributed to Wilt Chamberlain

One of the principal areas of antitrust concern over the years has been **corporate integration,** which includes mergers, acquisitions of stock or assets, corporate consolidations, and joint ventures. Such corporate integration may be challenged by either the Federal Trade Commission or the Justice Department under the Sherman Act or the Clayton Act. Regulation of mergers and other forms of integration has resulted in bitter debate among experts in the field, within Congress, and among the public.

Almost a century after the passage of the Sherman Act the controversy still rages. A 1981 comment by Attorney General William French Smith that "bigness does not necessarily mean badness" signified a changing view of antitrust among the enforcing authorities, reflecting a judgment that new trends, particularly in international trade, make traditional antitrust regulation of mergers obsolete. On the other hand, concerns about the inefficiency, monopolistic behavior, and political power of large corporations continue to be raised by more traditional analysts.

Why Regulate? The Goals of the Antimerger Statutes

The antimerger provisions of the antitrust laws are clearly based on purposes similar to the other antitrust doctrines already discussed. Mergers can reduce the number of participants in an industry and, thereby, ultimately create a monopolistic or oligopolistic market. Mergers are also clearly related to the "market power" of the firms involved in a merger, which can result in the foreclosure of markets or in radically altered prices in an effort to drive competitors from the market. Both undue market concentration and market power are chief concerns of the antimerger statutes, and both are directly related to the primary economic goal of the antitrust laws, preservation of competition. And, of course, market power is also clearly related to political and social power as well.

Why Merge? The Reasons Why Businesses Integrate

While the result of a merger may be market concentration and power, the real reasons why businesses merge are probably unrelated to such results. The motives of businesspeople in indulging in corporate integration are probably as varied as the number of mergers that take place, each a special situation undertaken for different corporate or even personal goals.

In 1980, the Federal Trade Commission sponsored a study of merger motives in which twelve well-known experts in corporate integration participated. The participants (including attorneys specializing in the field, investment bankers, business consultants and scholars) were separately asked to rank the commonly given reasons for corporate integration according to their relative importance. According to this study, the most important reasons for mergers were found to be as follows, according to the order of their importance:*

1. To take advantage of awareness that a company is undervalued;
2. To achieve growth more rapidly than by internal growth;
3. To satisfy market demand for additional product services;
4. To avoid risks of internal start-ups or expansion;
5. To increase earnings per share;
6. To reduce dependence on a single product or service;
7. To acquire market share or position;
8. To offset seasonal or cyclical fluctuations in the present business;
9. To enhance the power and prestige of the owner, CEO, or management;
10. To make better use of present resources;

   . . . .

28. To achieve economies of scale;
29. To eliminate competition;

---

*Wayne L. Boucher, *The Process of Conglomerate Mergers* (Washington, D.C.: Government Printing Office, 1980), pp. 35–37.

The study is interesting in several respects: first, the traditional merger motives given by both proponents and opponents of government regulation of mergers come in at the very bottom of the list. Economies of scale, the traditional reason for mergers in many texts, is second to last, and elimination of competition, the focus of the antitrust laws themselves, is dead last. Second, the study points out several new reasons for mergers, created by a business environment of wide public ownership and international competition, such as "To increase earnings per share" and "To reduce dependence on a single product or service." Of particular interest is the ninth-ranked item, "To enhance the power and prestige of the owner, CEO, or management." Many persons have argued that one of the most basic reasons for the "merger wave" of the 1980's was the drive of many business managers for power and prestige, and that notion seems to be supported by the relatively high ranking of that reason.

Methods of Corporate Integration

Integrations between business firms can be accomplished in a variety of ways, including true mergers, corporate consolidations, purchases of stock, purchases of assets, and joint ventures. A true **merger** takes place when one firm acquires and absorbs another. The acquired firm ceases to exist and the acquiring firm remains. In a **consolidation,** two firms join together and form a new, third company, and both of the original firms cease to exist.

The same result may be obtained through a purchase of stock or assets. In a **purchase of stock,** one company buys controlling interest in another firm, thereby gaining the right to elect the board of directors of the acquired firm and obtaining operational control of the company. The acquired firm becomes a subsidiary of the acquired firm and has an independent existence only in a technical sense. A **purchase of assets** involves an exchange of cash for the assets of the acquired company. The assets of the acquired firm, including capital, personnel, and market, become a part of the acquiring firm, and the acquired firm consists of only the cash received, which usually must be distributed to shareholders.

The final form of integration is the **joint venture.** That form is a partnership, usually temporary, between two other business entities, for joint participation in an endeavor. Both firms continue to exist, but join forces for the purposes of a transaction. Many oil drilling endeavors and motion pictures are put together as joint ventures of two or more business firms, for example

The most fashionable new form of integration is the **tender offer.** Tender offers are nothing more than a purchase-of-stock acquisition, but usually without the consent and often against the wishes of the acquired firm. In tender offers, the "target" company's stock is usually undervalued on the stock market. The acquiring company makes a public offer to purchase the shares of the target company at a price higher than the trading price on the stock exchange, up to a certain number of shares necessary to obtain control of the target company. Stockholders often sell their shares, control is obtained, and the target company becomes a subsidiary of the acquiring firm. The target company often tries to resist these "take-over bids" in the courts or by a variety of other techniques designed to ensure continued independence. The management of the target company is particularly concerned, since if the take-over is successful, new management will be installed to take their place. A whole new business vocabulary has grown up around such bids, including such terms as *white knight,* which means a competing take-over bid by a firm friendly to management. Cash-rich target companies often move to acquire other firms as a defensive maneuver in order to present a potential antitrust violation by the acquiring company if the take-over is successful. While tender offers began as a somewhat unsavory tactic by business "outsiders" in the 1960's, the technique has been used recently by some of the oldest and most respected firms, such as Pillsbury, W. R. Grace, and Johns-Manville. And target companies may be industrial giants, such as F. W. Woolworth, Del Monte, Carrier Corporation, and Firestone Tire and Rubber.

All such forms of corporate integration are within the theories of the antitrust laws. For ease of reference, all such forms will be referred to as *mergers.*

The Antimerger Statutes

Mergers were first addressed by the antitrust laws under Section 1 of the Sherman Act as "a combination in the form of trust or otherwise." Because of doubts cast on the applicability of the Sherman Act by the 1911 *Standard Oil* decision (see Chapter 8), Congress enacted Section 7 of the Clayton Act in 1914. In order to understand the history of that statute it is important to present the original wording.

> That no corporation engaged in commerce shall acquire, directly or indirectly, the whole or any part of the stock or other share capital of another corporation engaged also in commerce where the effect of such acquisition may be to substantially lessen competition between the corporation whose stock is so acquired and the corporation making the acquisition or to restrain such commerce in any section or community or tend to create a monopoly of any line of commerce.

Over the years, that statute was interpreted by the courts as applying only to "horizontal" mergers, that is, mergers between direct competitors. As a result, other types of mergers were beyond the reach of the Act, as were mergers organized on any basis other than a purchase of stock, such as a purchase of assets. Many merging firms avoided the statute by merging through a purchase-of-assets procedure. In 1950, Congress moved to close these loopholes by enacting the Celler-Kefauver Anti-Merger Act. After that amendment, Section 7 read, and still reads today, as follows:

> That no corporation engaged in commerce shall acquire, directly or indirectly, the whole or any part of the stock or other share capital *and no corporation subject to the jurisdiction of the Federal Trade Commission shall acquire the whole or any part of the assets* of another corporation engaged also in commerce, *where in any line of commerce in any section of the country,* the effect of such acquisition may be *substantially to lessen competition,* or to tend to create a monopoly. (Italicized sections indicate changed wording.)

Obviously the wording of Section 7 is broad and sweeping. Many of the phrases in Section 7 have been the subject of judicial interpretation over the years. Principal areas of interpretation have been the phrases "any line of commerce," which has been interpreted to mean the "relevant product market," "any section of the country" which has been interpreted to mean the "relevant geographic market," and "substantially to lessen competition," which is generally referred to as the "anticompetitive effect."

In 1976, the Clayton Act was amended once again by the Hart-Scott-Rodino Antitrust Improvement Act, which allowed the FTC to adopt a **premerger notification** requirement. If the merging parties reach certain size limitations and the acquisition involves 15 percent or $15 million of assets or stock in the acquired corporation, the parties must notify both the Justice Department and the FTC of the impending merger. Once the firms have notified these agencies, there is a 30 day waiting period before the merger may be consummated. The time limit may be extended, and the Justice Department or the FTC may file injunction actions to stop the merger during this time. Failure to file the appropriate premerger notification may result in a civil fine of up to $10,000 per day.

Actions against mergers may also be filed under either Section 1 or Section 2 of the Sherman Act as well, though most actions are filed under Section 7 of the Clayton Act.

Remedies: Unscrambling the Egg

The same remedies apply to violations of the merger statutes as to the other antitrust statutes, including private civil actions for treble damages, *parens patriae* actions, and actions for injunctions filed by the government. One form of injunctive relief unique to merger problems is **divestiture.** The merging companies may be required, under an order of divestiture, to "unmerge"; that is, to divide into separate companies as best as possible. Court orders of divestiture often order the "acquiring" firm to support the newly re-created firm in a variety of ways. (See excerpt from *Ford Motor Co. v. U.S.,* p. 283.) The order may require the purchase of goods from the new company or other forms of financial support. Because of the extreme complexities of sorting out the assets of the acquired and acquiring firms, divestiture is sometimes called *unscrambling the egg.*

Merger Analysis

For purposes of analyzing mergers under the antitrust statutes, mergers are classified into three general types: *horizontal, vertical,* and *conglomerate. Conglomerate mergers are subdivided into three subtypes: the *market extension, product extension,* and *pure conglomerate* forms.

In order to better understand this analysis, consider a hypothetical industry in the production of aglets, the little plastic tips at the end of shoelaces. Assume that the aglet industry is shared by three manufacturers, companies A, B, and C. Also assume that there are six independent distributors of aglets, firms U, V, W, X, Y, and Z. Those firms purchase aglets from the manufacturers and sell them to the various purchasers of aglets. Let us assume that several purchasers of aglets, including shoestring manufacturers, shoe repair stores, and retail stores, are represented by firms 1–8. The industry might then be charted as in Figure 10-1.

Mergers between any of the firms operating on the same distribution level, such as a merger between firm A with firm C or firm V with firm Y or firm 2 with firm 5, would be a **horizontal merger.** Any merger between firms at different levels of the distribution process is considered to be a **vertical merger,** such as a merger between firm B with firm X or firm Y with firm 7 or firm C with firm 4. Horizontal and vertical

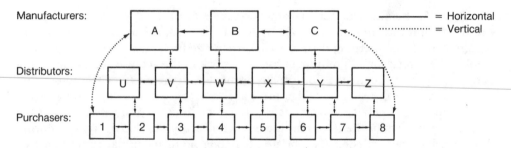

Figure 10-1 The Aglet Industry

mergers involve different effects on competition among the firms and on competition in general and are, therefore, subjected to differing analyses under the antitrust laws.

In order to analyze **conglomerate mergers,** add some facts to our assumptions. If firm X operates exclusively on the West Coast, and firm Z operates solely in New York state, then a merger between the two would not be considered a horizontal merger at all, but a **market extension merger,** since the firms were not "in competition" prior to the merger and such integration would involve somewhat different effects on competition than a traditional horizontal merger. Likewise, if firm B were to merge with a firm that manufactures not aglets but a similar and related product, such as the little plastic or wooden caps used to keep infants' shoes tied, the merger would be viewed as a **product extension merger,** since it has entered a similar and related industry with which it had no prior competition or other relationship.

Finally, if one of the firms merges with a firm in a totally different and unrelated industry, as for example a merger between firm A and a firm that owns popcorn farms, the merger would be a **pure conglomerate.** Pure conglomerate mergers present some of the most difficult and far-reaching issues for the antitrust laws. Much of the recent trend toward merger has been in the pure conglomerate form, perhaps because the courts have yet to rule that a pure conglomerate merger can have anticompetitive effects within the meaning of the antitrust statutes. Some Supreme Court decisions hold that all of the other forms of mergers, including horizontal, vertical, product extension, and market expansion mergers, may violate Section 7.

All of these issues, as raised in the foregoing analysis, are part of the courts' determinations of the "line of commerce" and "section of the country." In part, they are determinations of the issue of the relevant market within which the anticompetitive effect must take place.

Relevant Market—The Line of Commerce

Under Section 7, the anticompetitive effect must take place within a specific "line of commerce," which has been interpreted to mean the **relevant product market.** The question is similar to the relevant product market determination under Section 2 of the Sherman Act, and involves the question of whether the products of the competing firms are reasonably interchangeable. In more sophisticated economic terms, the issue is the **cross-elasticity of demand** for the products, that is, whether an increase in price for one product will shift demand to the other product.

For example, if a merger is proposed between a manufacturer of plastic wrap and a manufacturer of aluminum foil, the courts might determine that the two products are entirely separate; in other words, each product is a separate relevant market. On the other hand, the courts might determine that the appropriate relevant market is flexible wrapping materials, in which case the two products are competing. In the first instance, the merger would be considered as a product extension merger or perhaps even a pure conglomerate. In the second case, the merger would be considered as horizontal.

Relevant Market—The Section of the Country

The anticompetitive effect must also appear in some **relevant geographic market.** That market has been defined as the *area of effective competition,* or the places where the products actually compete. The determination is similar to the determination of relevant geographic market under Section 2 of the Sherman Act. If firms manufacture the same product and actually compete in some location, that location will be the relevant geographic market. If the firms sell the same product in entirely separate locations, a merger would be considered as a market extension merger.

Anticompetitive Effect—The Substantially Lessening of Competition

In order to hold that a merger violates Section 7, the court must find that the acquisition lessens competition within both the product market and the geographic market. Prior to the 1950 Amendment to Section 7, that effect had to be between the acquired and acquiring firms, which effectively meant that only horizontal mergers could be attacked. After that amendment, vertical and conglomerate forms were brought within the statute.

The anticompetitive effect of a merger may take many forms. The only requirements are that the effect be substantial and that it take place within the relevant product and geographic markets. While each case is unique, the courts have focused on some classic anticompetitive effects of each of the forms of merger. Horizontal mergers always involve the removal of a competitor from the market and result in further concentration of the markets involved. Vertical mergers often involve barriers to entry to competitors, such as access to supplies or markets. Market extension and product extension mergers may involve the reduction of potential competition from the acquiring firm, which stands "waiting in the wings" for the market to justify entry through internal expansion or acquisition of a small firm (a toehold entry). Such mergers may also involve reciprocity, or the business practice of purchasing from a subsidiary of a company with which one deals. All forms of merger involve the enhancement of market power through increases in size and the possibility of subsidization of a smaller firm by a larger firm's "deep pocket," thereby enhancing the ability of the smaller firm to compete.

While many mergers involve several different types of corporate integration, as in the *Brown Shoe* decision, p. 352, which had both horizontal and vertical aspects, it is important to focus on each form separately. In each section, the important questions are What is the relevant product market? What is the relevant geographic market? What is the anticompetititive effect?

The Merger Guidelines

Because of the breadth of Section 7 and the vagueness of some of the terms contained in that statute, business people often have a difficult time predicting whether a particular acquisition will be challenged by the Justice Department or the Federal Trade Commission. Even if a firm desires to comply with the law in all respects, it may be difficult to tell if a specific merger has an anticompetitive effect.

In order to remedy the "predictability gap," the Justice Department issued the first *Merger Guidelines* in 1968. Those guidelines had, as their general purpose, "to acquaint the business community, the legal profession, and other interested groups and individuals with the standards currently being applied by the Department of Justice in determining whether to challenge corporate acquisitions and mergers under Section 7. . . ." Specific guidelines were announced for horizontal, vertical, and conglomerate mergers.

In 1982, the Justice Department issued an entirely new set of guidelines and revised them in 1984. The new guidelines eliminated the specific references to conglomerate mergers, any reference to the problems of reciprocity, and introduced the **Herfindahl-Hirschman Index of Industrial Concentration** (see Figure 10-2), a method of determining the concentration of a market based on summing the squares of the percentages of market shares held by each company in a market.

Figure 10-2 Using the Herfindahl-Hirschman Index

Assume a market contains five firms, A, B, C, D, and E. Assume also that firm A has 30 percent of the market, firm B has 25 percent of the market, firms C and D each have 20 percent of the market, and firm E has 5 percent of the market. Under these circumstances the HHI would be figured as follows:

Firm	*Market Share*	*Individual Market Share Squared*
Firm A	30%	900
Firm B	25%	625
Firm C	20%	400
Firm D	20%	400
Firm E	5%	25

Total HHI of the market = 2350

This industry has a premerger HHI of 2350, and thus falls under Section 3.1c of the Merger Guidelines. If firm D were to merge with firm E, the HHI would be recalculated as follows:

Firm	*Market Share*	*Individual Market Share Squared*
Firm A	30%	900
Firm B	25%	625
Firm C	20%	400
Firm D*	25%	625

Total post-merger HHI = 2550

This merger between the two smallest firms in the market creates a change in the HHI of 200 points, and thus under Section 3.1c of the Merger Guidelines, the Department is likely to challenge the merger.

---

*Including firm E's 5 percent of the market.

The Merger Guidelines are not law. In no way are they binding on the courts or even on the Justice Department itself. The 1968 guidelines were ignored by some administrations, and it is likely that the new guidelines will meet a similar fate. Taken together with the premerger notification rules, they may be helpful to business, however.

Horizontal Mergers

By definition, horizontal mergers involve integration of competing firms. While such mergers are not automatically unlawful, they are generally considered the most harmful type of mergers, since they invariably involve the removal of a competitor and increased concentration within the relevant markets.

Merger Guidelines
U.S. Department of Justice (1982, revised 1984)

3. Horizontal Mergers

3.0 Where the merging firms are in the same product and geographic market, the merger is horizontal. In such cases, the Department will focus first on the post-merger concentration of the market and the increase in concentration caused by the merger....

3.1 Concentration and Market Shares

Market concentration is a function of the number of firms in a market and their respective market shares. Other things being equal, concentration affects the likelihood that one firm, or a small group of firms, could successfully exercise market power....

As an aid to the interpretation of market data, the Department will use the Herfindahl-Hirschman Index ("HHI") of market concentration. The HHI is calculated by summing the squares of the individual [percentages of] market shares of all the firms included in the market....

The general standards for horizontal mergers are as follows:

(a) *Post-Merger HHI Below 1000.* ... Because implicit coordination among firms is likely to be difficult and because the prohibitions of section 1 of the Sherman Act are usually an adequate response to any explicit collusion that might occur, the Department will not challenge mergers falling in this region except in extraordinary circumstances.

(b) *Post-Merger HHI Between 1000 and 1800.* Because this region extends from the point at which the competitive concerns associated with concentration are raised to the point at which they become quite serious, generalization is particularly difficult. The Department, however, is unlikely to challenge a merger producing an increase in the HHI of less than 100 points. The Department is *likely* to challenge mergers in this region that produce an increase in the HHI of more than 100 points, unless the Department concludes ... that the merger is not likely substantially to lessen competition.

(c) *Post-Merger HHI Above 1800.* Markets in this region are considered to be highly concentrated. Additional concentration resulting from mergers is a matter of significant competitive concern. The Department is unlikely, however, to challenge mergers producing an increase in the HHI of less than 50 points. The Department is likely to challenge mergers in this region that produce an increase in the HHI of more than 50 points, unless the Department concludes.... that the merger is not likely substantially to lessen competition....

3.12 Leading Firm Proviso

[T]he Department is likely to challenge the merger of any firm with a market share of at least 1 percent with the leading firm in the market, provided the leading firm has a market share that is at least 35 percent. . . .

Court Interpretation of Section 7—Horizontal Mergers

Since there is no per se category in merger cases, every case must involve in-depth analysis of the markets, the industry, and the particular firms involved in the merger. In its original form, the *Brown Shoe* decision was 80 pages long and contained graphs, charts, and in-depth economic analysis of the shoe market at both the retail and manufacturing levels. Because of their complexities, such cases often take years to try and rarely involve jury trials.

Brown Shoe is perhaps the most important merger decision since 1950, since the case was the first to reach the court after the Celler-Kefauver Amendment, and because the case announced far-reaching doctrines regarding relevant product and geographic markets. The case is also complex, since it involved both horizontal and vertical aspects. Both of the merging parties manufactured shoes and both sold shoes at retail, though in much different quantities. The horizontal portion of the case is presented here, and the vertical portion will be presented later.

Brown Shoe Co. v. U.S.

370 U.S. 294, 82 S. Ct. 1502, 8 L. Ed. 2d 510 (1962)

Brown Shoe Company, the nation's fourth largest shoe manufacturer, began acquiring retail outlets in 1951. By 1955, it had acquired 845 such outlets by merging with the parent firms that owned such outlets. In that year, Brown acquired Kinney, the largest family-style shoe retailer in the country, owning over 400 outlets in 270 cities. Kinney also owned some manufacturing facilities, and was the twelfth largest shoe producer in the nation, accounting for 0.5 percent of the nation's shoes. Brown accounted for 4 percent of the nation's shoe production.

The Justice Department brought this action to stop the merger in 1955 as one of the first cases filed under Section 7 as it was amended by the Cellar-Kefauver Act. The trial judge found several trends in the shoe business, including a trend among shoe manufacturers to acquire retail outlets, a trend for the parent-manufacturing firms to supply an ever-increasing percentage of the retail outlets' needs (thereby "drying up" the available outlets for independent shoe manufacturers) and a trend toward a decrease in the number of firms manufacturing shoes. The evidence also showed that while there was a large number of shoe manufacturers, the top four firms, including Brown, accounted for 23 percent of the nation's shoes. In the space of seven years, the number of shoe manufacturers had declined by 10 percent, to 970 firms. The Court also found that Brown was a "moving factor" in these industry trends, through its acquisition of retail outlets and the acquisition of seven other manufacturers through merger. Finally, the evidence showed that although Brown supplied no shoes to Kinney prior to the merger, within two years Brown had become Kinney's largest outside supplier, furnishing 7.9 percent of all of Kinney's needs. The District Court held that the merger violated Section 7 and ordered divestiture. Brown appealed.

Mr. Chief Justice WARREN delivered the opinion of the court.

. . . .

III. Legislative History

This case is one of the first to come before us in which the Government's complaint is based upon allegations that the appellant has violated Section 7 of the Clayton Act, as that section was amended in 1950.

. . . .

The dominant theme pervading congressional consideration of the 1950 amendments was a fear of what was considered to be a rising tide of economic concentration in the American economy. . . . Throughout the recorded discussion may be found examples of Congress' fear not only of accelerated concentration of economic power on economic grounds, but also of the threat to other values a trend toward concentration was thought to pose.

What were some of the factors, relevant to a judgment as to the validity of a given merger, specifically discussed by Congress in redrafting section 7?

First, there is no doubt that Congress did wish to "plug the loophole" and to include within the coverage of the Act the acquisition of assets no less than the acquisition of stock.

Second, by the deletion of the "acquiring-acquired" language in the original text, it hoped to make plain that section 7 applied not only to mergers between actual competitors, but also to vertical and conglomerate mergers whose effect may tend to lessen competition. . . .

Third, it is apparent that a keystone in the erection of a barrier to what Congress saw was the rising tide of economic concentration, was its provision of authority for arresting mergers at a time when the trend to a lessening of competition in a line of commerce was still in its incipiency. Congress saw the process of concentration in American business as a dynamic force; it sought to assure the Federal Trade Commission and the courts the power to brake this force at its outset and before it gathered momentum.

Fourth. . . . Congress rejected, as inappropriate to the problem it sought to remedy, the application of the standards . . . under the Sherman Act. . . .

Fifth, at the same time that it sought to create an effective tool for preventing all mergers having demonstrable anticompetitive effects, Congress recognized the stimulation to competition that might flow from particular mergers. . . . Taken as a whole, the legislative history illuminates congressional concern with the protection of *competition,* not *competitors,* and its desire to restrain mergers only to the extent that such combinations may tend to lessen competition.

Sixth, Congress neither adopted nor rejected specifically any particular tests for measuring the relevant markets, either as defined in terms of product or in terms of geographic locus of competition. . . .

Seventh, . . . Congress indicated plainly that a merger had to be functionally viewed, in the context of its particular industry. . . .

Eighth, Congress used the words "*may be substantially* to lessen competition" (emphasis added), to indicate that its concern was with probabilities, not certainties. Statutes existed for dealing with clear-cut menaces to competition; no statute was sought for dealing with ephemeral possibilities. Mergers with a probable anticompetitive effect were to be proscribed by this Act.

It is against this background that we return to the case before us.

The Court here discussed the vertical aspects of the merger. That section of the case is set out in the section of this chapter dealing with vertical mergers.

V. The Horizontal Aspects of the Merger

An economic arrangement between companies performing similar functions in the production or sale of comparable goods or services is characterized as "horizontal." The effect on competition of such an arrangement depends, of course, upon its character and scope. Thus, its validity in the face of the antitrust laws will depend upon such factors as: the relative size and number of the parties to the arrangement; whether it allocates shares of the market between the parties; whether it fixes prices at which the parties will sell their product; or whether it absorbs or insulates competitors. Where the arrangement effects a horizontal merger between companies occupying the same product and geographic market, whatever competition previously may have existed in that market between the parties to the merger is eliminated. . . .

Thus, again, the proper definition of the market is a "necessary predicate" to an examination of the competition that may be affected by the horizontal merger.

Only the question of the horizontal merger at the *retail* market was before the Court. The following discussion of the relevant product market was included in the vertical merger portion of the decision but was applied to both horizontal and vertical mergers by the Court.

The Product Market

The outer boundaries of a product market are determined by the reasonable interchangeability of use or the cross-elasticity of demand between the product itself and substitutes for it. However, within this broad market, well-defined submarkets may exist which, in themselves, constitute product markets for antitrust purposes. . . . The boundaries of such a submarket may be determined by examining such practical indicia as industry or public recognition of the submarket as a separate economic entity, the product's peculiar characteristics and uses, unique production facilities, distinct customers, distinct prices, sensitivity to price changes, and specialized vendors. . . .

Applying these considerations to the present case, we conclude that the record supports the District Court's finding that the relevant lines of commerce are men's, women's, and children's shoes. These product lines are recognized by the public; each line is manufactured in separate plants; each has characteristics peculiar to itself rendering it generally noncompetitive with the others; and each is, of course, directed toward a distinct class of customers.

Appellant, however, contends that the District Court's definitions fail to recognize sufficiently "price/quality" and "age/sex" distinctions in shoes. Brown argues that the predominantly medium-priced shoes which it manufactures occupy a product market different from the predominantly low-priced shoes which Kinney sells. But agreement with that argument would be equivalent to holding that medium-priced shoes do not compete with low-priced shoes. . . . It would be unrealistic to accept Brown's contention that, for example, men's shoes selling below $8.99 are in a different product market from those selling above $9.00.

This is not to say, however, that "price-quality" differences, where they exist, are unimportant in analyzing a merger; they may be of importance in determining the likely effect of a merger. But the boundaries of the relevant market must be drawn with sufficient breadth to include the competing products of each of the merging companies and to recognize competition where, in fact, competition exists. . . .

The Geographic Market

The criteria to be used in determining the appropriate geographic market are essentially similar to those used to determine the relevant product market . . . Moreover, just as a product submarket may have Section 7 significance as the proper "line of commerce," so may a geographic submarket be considered the appropriate "section of the country." . . . Congress prescribed a pragmatic, factual approach to the definition of the relevant market and not a formal, legalistic one. The geographic market selected must, therefore, both "correspond to the commercial realities" of the industry and be economically significant. Thus, although the geographic market in some instances may encompass the entire Nation, under other circumstances it may be as small as a single metropolitan area. . . .

The District Court found that the effects of this aspect of the merger must be analyzed in every city with a population exceeding 10,000 and its immediate contiguous surrounding territory in which both Brown and Kinney sold shoes at retail. . . . However it is appellant's contention that the areas of effective competition in shoe retailing were improperly defined by the District Court. It claims that such areas should, in some cases, be defined so as to include only the central business districts of large cities, and in others, so as to encompass the "standard metropolitan areas" within which smaller communities are found. . . .

We believe, however, that the record fully supports the District Court's findings that shoe stores in the outskirts of cities compete effectively with stores in central downtown areas, and that while there is undoubtedly some commercial intercourse between smaller communities within a single "standard metropolitan area," the most intense and important competition in retail sales will be confined to stores within the particular communities in such an area and their immediate environs.

We therefore agree that the District Court properly defined the relevant geographic markets in which to analyze this merger. . . . Such markets are large enough to include the downtown shops and suburban shopping centers in areas contiguous to the city, which are the important competitive factors, and yet are small enough to exclude stores beyond the immediate environs of the city, which are of little competitive significance.

The Probable Effect of the Merger

Having delineated the product and geographic markets within which the effects of this merger are to be measured, we turn now to an examination of the District Court's finding that as a result of the merger competition in the retailing of . . . shoes may be lessened substantially in those cities in which both Brown and Kinney stores are located. . . .

The market share which companies may control by merging is one of the most important factors to be considered when determining the probable effects of the combination on effective competition in the relevant market. In an industry as fragmented as shoe retailing, the control of substantial shares of the trade in a city may have important effects on competition. If a merger achieving 5 percent control were now approved, we might be required to approve future merger efforts by Brown's competitors seeking similar market shares. The oligopoly Congress sought to avoid would then be furthered and it would be difficult to dissolve the combinations previously approved. . . .

Other factors to be considered in evaluating the probable effects of a merger in the relevant market lend additional support to the District Court's conclusion that this merger may substantially lessen competition. One such factor is the history of tendency toward concentration in the industry. . . . By the merger in this case, the largest single group of retail stores still independent of one of the large manufacturers was absorbed into an already substantial aggregation of more or less controlled retail outlets. As a result of this merger, Brown moved into second place nationally in terms of retail stores directly owned. Including the stores on its franchise plan, the merger placed under Brown's control almost 1,600 shoe outlets, or about 7.2 percent of the Nation's retail "shoe stores". . . . We cannot avoid the mandate of Congress that tendencies toward concentration in industry are to be curbed in their incipiency, particularly when those tendencies are being accelerated through giant steps striding across a hundred cities at a time. In the light of the trends in this industry we agree with the Government and the court below that this is an appropriate place at which to call a halt.

At the same time appellant has presented no mitigating factors, such as the business failure or the inadequate resources of one of the parties that may have prevented it from maintaining its competitive position, nor a demonstrated need for combination to enable small companies to enter into a more meaningful competition with those dominating the relevant markets. . . .

The judgment is affirmed.

Justices Frankfurter and White did not take part in the decision. Justice Clark concurred in a separate opinion, and Justice Harlan dissented in part and concurred in part.

Over twenty years after *Brown Shoe* was decided, the decision is still controversial. The Court's pioneering efforts in that case in the method of determining the relevant market and the further holdings regarding the vertical aspects of the merger are cited in almost every merger decision as the primary authority. The final paragraph of the decision has been the basis of the principal defenses to merger cases since 1962.

Relevant Market in Horizontal Mergers

Virtually every horizontal merger involves some anticompetitive effect, at least by the substitution of one competitor where two previously existed. As a result, the crucial issue in many horizontal merger cases is the determination of the relevant market. As noted previously, that question involves two separate issues, the determination of the appropriate product market and the appropriate geographic market.

The Relevant Product Market   As in cases under Section 2 of the Sherman Act, the determination of the appropriate "line of commerce" (or relevant product market) under Section 7 depends for the most part on questions of substitutability of products, or more technically, the **cross-elasticities of demand** for the products of the merging firms. In *Brown Shoe,* for example, Brown argued that its medium-priced shoes did not compete with the lower-priced shoes sold by Kinney and, therefore, they were not in the same product market. In later cases, the Supreme Court held that tin cans and glass bottles were in the same relevant product market, since there was a high degree of interchangeability of use of such containers.* In such cases, the defendant will often argue that the relevant product market is either broader or narrower than the market proposed by the government. If the market is found to be broader that that proposed by the government, then the anticompetitive effect is lessened because more firms will be considered as competitors. If the market is found to be narrower than that proposed by the government, the merger is not horizontal at all, but must be analyzed as a **product extension merger,** and such mergers receive much different treatment from the courts.

The Relevant Geographic Market   The question of the relevant geographic market is just as crucial as the determination of the relevant product market. The issue is whether the merging firms competed in some "section of the country." If the firms

---

*U.S. v. *Continental Can Co.,* 378 U.S. 441, 84 S. Ct. 1738, 12 L. Ed. 2d 953 (1964).

operate in different areas, the merger is not a horizontal merger, but will be analyzed as a **market extension merger,** described later in this chapter.

The section of the country need not be a very large area. In *Brown Shoe,* the relevant geographic market was defined as those cities where Kinney and Brown already had competing stores. In later cases, the relevant geographic market was determined to be as small as the city of Los Angeles* or the four-county area surrounding the city of Philadelphia,** for example. Again the defendant may argue that the relevant geographic market is either larger or smaller than the market proposed by the government. If the area is larger, then more firms will be considered as competitors and the effect on competition of the merger will be less. If the area is smaller, the merging firms may not be competitors at all, and the merger will be considered as a market extension merger rather than as a horizontal merger.

Vertical Mergers

Vertical mergers involve integration between firms operating at different levels of the distribution process of the same product. Mergers between a manufacturer and a supplier, a manufacturer and a distributor, or a distributor and a retailer are all examples of vertical mergers. Many of the concerns of horizontal mergers are also matters of importance in vertical mergers, such as relevant product and geographic markets and anticompetitive effect, though the analysis of each is somewhat different in the consideration of vertical mergers. In the consideration of vertical mergers, the anticompetitive effect is likely to be somewhat more remote, though nonetheless powerful. The Department of Justice *Merger Guidelines* contain a separate section regarding such mergers.

Merger Guidelines
U.S. Department of Justice (1982, revised 1984)

4. Horizontal Effect from Non-Horizontal Mergers

4.0 By definition, non-horizontal mergers involve firms that do not operate in the same market. It necessarily follows that such mergers produce no immediate change in the level of concentration in any relevant market. . . . Although non-horizontal mergers are less likely than horizontal mergers to create competitive problems, they are invariably innocuous [sic]. This section describes the principal theories under which the Department is likely to challenge non-horizontal mergers.

. . . .

4.2 Competitive Problems from Vertical Mergers
4.21 Barriers to Entry from Vertical Mergers

In certain circumstances, the vertical integration resulting from vertical mergers could create competitively objectionable barriers to entry. Stated generally, three condi-

---

**U.S.* v. *Von's Grocery Co.,* 384 U.S. 270, 86 S. Ct. 1478 (1966).

***U.S.* v. *Philadelphia National Bank,* 374 U.S. 321, 83 S. Ct. 1715, 10 L. Ed. 2d 915 (1963).

tions are necessary (but not sufficient) for this problem to exist. First, the degree of vertical integration between the two market [sic] must be so extensive that entrants to one market (the "primary market") also would have to enter the other market (the "secondary market") simultaneously. Second, the requirement of entry at the secondary level must make entry at the primary level more difficult and less likely to occur. Finally, the structure and other characteristics of the primary market must be otherwise so conducive to non-competitive performance that the increased difficulty of entry is likely to affect its performance.

. . . .

4.22 Facilitating Collusion Through Vertical Mergers
4.221 Vertical Integration to the Retail Level

A high level of vertical integration by upstream firms into the associated retail market may facilitate collusion in the upstream market by making it easier to monitor price. Retail prices are generally more visible than prices in upstream markets, and vertical mergers may increase the level of vertical integration to the point at which the monitoring effect becomes significant. Adverse competitive consequences are unlikely unless the upstream market is generally conducive to collusion and a large percentage of the products produced there are sold through vertically integrated retail outlets.

The Department is unlikely to challenge a merger on this ground unless (1) overall concentration of the upstream market is above 1800 HHI . . . and (2) a large percentage of the upstream product would be sold through vertically-integrated retail outlets after the merger. . . .

4.222 Elimination of a Disruptive Buyer

The elimination by vertical merger of a particularly disruptive buyer in a downstream market may facilitate collusion in the upstream market. If upstream firms view sales to a particular buyer as sufficiently important, they may deviate from the terms of a collusive agreement in an effort to secure that business, thereby disrupting the operation of the agreement. The merger of such a buyer with an upstream firm may eliminate that rivalry, making it easier for the upstream firms to collude effectively. . . .

The Department is unlikely to challenge a merger on this ground unless (1) overall concentration of the upstream market is 1800 HHI or above . . . and (2) the allegedly disruptive firm differs substantially in volume of purchases or other relevant characteristics from the other firms in its market. . . .

4.23 Evasion of Rate Regulation

Non-horizontal mergers may be used by monopoly public utilities subject to rate regulation as a tool for circumventing that regulation. The clearest example is the acquisition by a regulated utility of a supplier of its fixed or variable inputs. After the merger, the utility would be selling to itself and might be able arbitrarily to inflate the prices of internal transactions. . . . As a result, inflated prices could be passed along to consumers as "legitimate" costs. . . .

Vertical mergers are generally considered to be less anticompetitive than horizontal mergers, all things being equal. Enforcement standards are, therefore, less strict and the burden of showing the anticompetitive effect is heavier. But vertical mergers have been held to violate Section 7 on several occasions. The problems associated with vertical mergers were the impetus behind the adoption of Celler-Kefauver Act of 1950.

The *Brown Shoe* case is also the starting point for any analysis of the problems of vertical mergers. That case was the first, and in many ways the most important, vertical merger case to be heard by the Supreme Court. The Court held that barriers to competitors may create an anticompetitive effect, since competitors of either firm involved in the merger are foreclosed from either the supplies or the markets provided by the other firm in the acquisition.

Brown Shoe Co. v. U.S. (Continued)

IV. The Vertical Aspects of the Merger

Economic arrangements between companies standing in a supplier-customer relationship are characterized as "vertical." The primary vice of a vertical merger or other arrangement tying a customer to a supplier is that, by foreclosing the competitors of either party from a segment of the market otherwise open to them, the arrangement may act as a "clog on competition" . . . which deprives rivals of a fair opportunity to compete. . . . Every extended vertical arrangement by its very nature, for at least a time, denies to competitors of the supplier the opportunity to compete for part or all of the trade of the customer-party to the vertical arrangement. . . .

The Court then determined that the relevant product markets were men's, women's, and children's shoes, and that the relevant geographic market was the entire nation.

The Probable Effect of the Merger

. . . .

Since the diminution of the vigor of competition which may stem from a vertical arrangement results primarily from a foreclosure of a share of the market otherwise open to competition, an important consideration in determining whether the effect of a vertical arrangement . . . is the size of the share of the market foreclosed. If the share of the market foreclosed is so large that it approaches monopoly proportions, the Clayton Act will, of course, have been violated; but the arrangement will also have run afoul of the Sherman Act. . . . On the other hand, foreclosure of a de minimis share of the market will not tend "substantially to lessen competition."

Between these extremes, in cases such as the one before us, in which the foreclosure is neither of monopoly nor de minimis proportions, the percentage of the market foreclosed by the vertical arrangement cannot itself be decisive. In such cases, it becomes necessary to undertake an examination of various economic and historical factors in order to determine whether the arrangement under review is of the type Congress sought to proscribe.

A most important such factor to examine is the very nature and purpose of the arrangement. . . .

Another important factor to consider is the trend toward concentration in the industry. It is true, of course, that the statute prohibits a given merger only if the effect of *that* merger may be substantially to lessen competition. But the very wording of Section 7 requires a prognosis of the probable *future* effect of the merger.

The existence of a trend toward vertical integration . . . is well substantiated by the record. . . .

Moreover, as we have remarked above, not only must we consider the probable effects of the merger upon the economics of the particular markets affected but also we must consider its probable effects upon the economic way of life sought to be preserved by Congress. Congress was desirous of preventing the formation of further oligopolies with their attendant adverse effects upon local control of industry and upon small business. . . .

The Court held that the merger had substantial anticompetitive effects and ordered divestiture.

The foreclosure of competition at another level may take a variety of forms. The following decision was based on such a foreclosure caused by the habits of automobile mechanics. The merger was a classic vertical acquisition of a supplier by a manufacturer. Note also the Court's discussion of the divestiture remedy applied by the lower court.

Ford Motor Co. v. U.S.

405 U.S. 562, 92 S. Ct. 1142, 31 L. Ed. 2d 492 (1972)

Mr. Justice DOUGLAS delivered the opinion of the Court.

This is a direct appeal . . . from a judgment of the District Court . . . holding that Ford Motor Company (Ford) violated section 7 of the Celler-Kefauver Antimerger Act, by acquiring certain assets from Electric Autolite Company (Autolite). The assets included the Autolite trade name, Autolite's only spark plug plant in this country . . . a battery plant, and extensive rights to its nationwide distribution organization for spark plugs and batteries.

In 1961, Ford Motor Company acquired the assets of Autolite, which manufactured spark plugs. Ford's purpose in doing so was to participate in the so-called *aftermarket*. Sparkplug firms generally furnished auto manufacturers with sparkplugs at cost or less, but recovered their losses later when replacement spark plugs were needed for the cars. Auto mechanics usually replaced the sparkplugs with plugs of the same brand as those furnished with a new car. This aftermarket was extremely lucrative, since the cost of manufacturing sparkplugs was less than 6¢ a plug, but those plugs sold at retail for substantially more. The whole process was known as the *OE* (original equipment) *tie,* and retail sale of plugs was known as the *aftermarket*. It was this aftermarket that Ford sought to exploit.

Spark plugs were manufactured by three major firms. General Motors had developed its own brand, AC, and there were two independents, Autolite and Champion. AC had about 30 percent of the market, Champion had about 33 percent of the market, and Autolite had about 15 percent of the market. The remaining share of the market was divided among several small producers. Ford determined that it could establish its own brand of plugs, but that process would take five to eight years. The evidence also showed that at the time 90 percent of the automobiles sold in the United States were manufactured by Ford, General Motors, and Chrysler.

The District Court held that the acquisition of Autolite violated section 7. . . . It gave two reasons for its decision.

First, prior to 1961 when Ford acquired Autolite it had a "pervasive impact on the aftermarket," . . . in that it was a moderating influence on Champion and on other companies. . . .

An interested firm on the outside has a twofold significance. It may someday go in and set the stage for noticeable deconcentration. While it merely stays near the edge, it is a deterrent to current competitors. . . .

. . . .

Second, . . . the acquisition marked "the foreclosure of Ford as a purchaser of about 10 percent of total industry output. . . ."

In short, Ford's entry into the spark plug market by means of the acquisition . . . had the effect of raising the barriers to entry into that market as well as removing one of the existing restraints upon the actions of those in the business of manufacturing spark plugs.

. . . .

We see no answer to that conclusion if the letter and spirit of the Celler-Kefauver Act are to be honored. . . .

It is argued, however, that the acquisition had some beneficial effect in making Autolite a more vigorous and effective competitor . . . than Autolite had been as an independent. But . . . a merger is not saved from illegality under section 7 . . . "because, on some ultimate reckoning of social or economic debits and credits it may be deemed beneficial. A value choice of such magnitude is beyond the ordinary limits of judicial competence, and in any event has been made for us already, by Congress. . . . Congress determined to preserve our traditionally competitive economy. It therefore proscribed anticompetitive mergers, the benign and the malignant alike, fully aware, we must assume, that some price might have to be paid."

II.

The main controversy here has been over the nature and degree of the relief to be afforded.

. . . The District Court . . . concluded that divestiture and other relief was necessary. . . .

The major portions of the lower court's decree were set out in Chapter 8, page 283.

The relief in an antitrust case must be "effective to redress the violations" and "to restore competition." . . . The District Court is clothed with "large discretion" to fit the decree to the special needs of the individual case.

Complete divestiture is particularly appropriate where asset or stock acquisitions violate the antitrust laws.

Divestiture is a start toward restoring the preacquisition situation. Ford once again will then stand as a large industry customer at the edge of the market, with a renewed interest in securing favorable terms for its substantial plug purchases. . . .

Affirmed.

Conglomerate Mergers

Conglomerate mergers, or mergers between firms that are active in industries which are totally unrelated or different geographical markets, are perhaps the most difficult of all merger cases. At first glance, such mergers often seem to have no anticompetitive effect and, therefore, may not fall within the prohibitions of the Clayton Act. Yet on closer analysis some forms of anticompetitive effect may indeed be found, and the courts have held some forms of conglomerate mergers to be in violation of Section 7.

As noted earlier, conglomerate mergers are divided into three basic forms: *product extension mergers,* or mergers between firms dealing in similar but noncompeting products; *market extension mergers,* or mergers between firms dealing in identical products, which would compete, but the firms deal exclusively in different sections of the country; and *pure conglomerate mergers,* which involve firms that are totally unrelated in any way.

The anticompetitive effects of conglomerate mergers center around the *potential competition doctrine, reciprocity,* and the *"deep-pocket" theory.* **Potential competition** deals with the attitude and competitive behavior in a market. Firms which perceive another firm as a potential entrant into the market may modify their competitive behavior on the assumption that if the market becomes too attractive, either through high prices or other factors, the potential entrant will enter the market through internal expansion. If the potential entrant actually enters the market through acquisition, that effect on the attitudes and competitive behavior, sometimes known as the "wings" effect (since the potential entrant is "standing in the wings") is lost.

Reciprocity is a post merger effect that depends on a possible deal, tacit or expressed, between the acquiring firm and other firms in the market. For example, an acquiring firm with monopolistic power in one market may force its suppliers to purchase raw materials from a newly acquired subsidiary. The acquiring firm may thereby exploit its monopolistic power in a market in which it does not have monopoly power.

The **deep pocket theory** refers simply to the benefits that may accrue to the acquired firm because of its ties to a big, rich firm. The big firm may operate a subsidiary in one industry at a loss, for example, and charge lower prices in that industry to undercut the competitors in that market and drive them from the field in an attempt to gain a monopoly position. Once that position is established, the prices would be increased, and the large firm would "subsidize" a similar strategy in another area in which the conglomerate is active. On a somewhat more benign level, the economies of scale may create a competitive advantage for the members of the conglomerate that allows them to compete more effectively.

The potential competition doctrine and reciprocity theory have both been used as a basis to hold conglomerate mergers illegal. The deep pocket doctrine, standing alone, has not yet been so used. That theory raises all of the traditional arguments over the merits and demerits of corporate size, standing alone. In other words, is simple "bigness" bad?

The Potential Competition Doctrine

Whenever an existing firm desires to enter a new market, it may do so in one of three ways: it may build its own facilities and develop its own markets and thereby add a new competitor to the market (**de novo entry**); it may acquire one of the smaller competitors in the market, and help that competitor to become more effective through an infusion of capital (a **toehold acquisition**); or it may acquire through merger one of the larger competitors in the market. It is generally agreed that both de novo entries and toehold acquisitions *aid* competition, since either the number of competitors increases, or the competitive abilities of one of the smaller competitors is increased.

But the very existence of a potential competitor "waiting in the wings" to enter the market may sharply alter the competitive behavior of firms already in a market. Those firms may decide that instead of raising prices so that the market is attractive to the potential competitor, they will keep prices low to discourage the potential competitor. If the potential competitor does in fact enter the market, its effect on the behavior of firms already in the market is lost. If the potential competitor enters the market through de novo entry or a toehold acquisition, there is a net gain in competition, even though the **wings effect** has been lost. But if the potential competitor enters the market by acquiring one of the larger competitors, all that has happened is the substitution of an even larger competitor for one of the market leaders, producing a net decrease in competition.

Merger Guidelines
U.S. Department of Justice (1982, revised 1984)

The factors that the Department will consider [in a potential competition case] are as follows:

4.131 Market Concentration

Barriers to entry are unlikely to affect market performance if the structure of the market is otherwise not conducive to monopolization or collusion. Adverse competitive effects are likely only if overall concentration . . . is high. The Department is unlikely to challenge a potential competition merger unless overall concentration of the acquired firm's market is above 1800 HHI. . . .

4.132 Conditions of Entry Generally

If entry to the market is generally easy, the fact that entry is marginally easier for one or more firms is unlikely to affect the behavior of the firms in the market. The Department is unlikely to challenge a potential competition merger when new entry into the acquired firm's market can be accomplished by firms without any specific entry advantages. . . .

4.133 The Acquiring Firm's Entry Advantage

If more than a few firms have the same or a comparable advantage in entering the acquired firm's market, the elimination of one firm is unlikely to have any adverse competitive effect. The other similarly situated firm(s) would continue to exert a present restraining influence, or, if entry would be profitable, would recognize the opportunity and enter. The Department is unlikely to challenge a potential competition merger if the entry advantage ascribed to the acquiring firm . . . is also possessed by three or more other firms. . . .

4.134 The Market Share of the Acquired Firm

Entry through the acquisition of a relatively small firm in the market may have a competitive effect comparable to new entry. Small firms frequently play peripheral roles in collusive interactions, and the particular advantages of the acquiring firm may convert a fringe firm into a significant factor in the market. The Department is unlikely to challenge a potential competition merger when the acquired firm has a market share of 5 percent or less. . . . The Department is likely to challenge any merger satisfying the other conditions in which the acquired firm has a market share of 20 percent or more.

Potential Competition and Market Extension Mergers   Market extension mergers involve firms dealing in the same product in different geographical areas. The firms are not in horizontal competition since they are in different relevant markets. One effect of such mergers is the loss of potential competition from the acquiring firm. Other firms in the market perceive the acquiring firm as a potential competitor who will enter the market through internal expansion if profits become large. As a result, such firms alter their competitive behavior by keeping prices low. The following decision established the basic law to be applied to market extension mergers.

U.S. v. Falstaff Brewing Corp.

410 U.S. 526, 93 S. Ct. 1096, 35 L. Ed. 2d 475 (1973)

In 1965, Falstaff Brewing Corporation acquired Narragansett Brewing Company. At the time of the acquisition, Falstaff was the fourth largest brewer in the United States, accounting for 5.9 percent of the nation's beer production. Falstaff sold beer in 32 states, but sold none in New England. Narragansett was the largest seller of beer in New England at the time of the acquisition, accounting for approximately 20 percent of the market. The Justice Department brought this action for divestiture under Section 7.

The evidence showed that Falstaff faced significant competition from four other brewers who sold in all 50 states, since national brewers are able to advertise on a nationwide basis, their beers have greater prestige than regional products, and they are less affected by weather and labor problems. The proof also disclosed that while beer sales in New England had increased approximately 9.5 percent in the four years preceding acquisiton, the eight largest sellers had increased their share of the beer market from 74 percent to 81 percent, and that the number of brewers in New England had declined from eleven in 1957 to six in 1964. The evidence also showed that New England had the highest beer consumption of any region of the country. The District Court held for Falstaff, and the government appealed.

Mr. Justice WHITE delivered the opinion of the Court.

. . . .

Before the acquisition was accomplished, the United States brought suit alleging that the acquisition would violate section 7. . . . This contention was based on two grounds: because Falstaff was a potential entrant and because the acquisition eliminated competition that would have existed had Falstaff entered the market *de nova* or by acquisition and expansion of a smaller firm, a so-called "toe-hold" acquisition. . . .

[T]he acquisition by a competitor not competing in the market but so situated as to be a potential competitor and likely to exercise substantial influence on market behavior [is suspect]. Entry through merger by such a company, although its competitive conduct in the market may be the mirror image of the acquired company, may nevertheless violate section 7 because the entry eliminates a potential competitor exercising present influence on the market. . . .

In the case before us, Falstaff was not a competitor in the New England market, nor is it contended that its merger with Narragansett represented an entry by a dominant market force. . . . The District Court, however, relying heavily on testimony of Falstaff officers, concluded that the company had no intent to enter the New England market except through acquisition, and that it therefore could not be considered a potential competitor in that market. Having put aside Falstaff as a potential *de nova* competitor, it followed for the District Court that entry by a merger would not adversely affect competition in New England.

The District Court erred as a matter of law. The error lay in the assumption that because Falstaff, as a matter of fact, would never have entered the market *de nova,* it could in no sense be considered a potential competitor. More specifically, the District Court failed to give separate consideration to whether Falstaff was a potential competitor in the sense that it was so positioned on the edge of the market that it exerted a beneficial influence on competitive conditions in that market.

The specific question with respect to this phase of the case is not what Falstaff's internal company decisions were but whether, given its financial capabilities and conditions in the New England market, it would be reasonable to consider it a potential entrant into that market. . . . This does not mean that the testimony of company officials about actual intentions of the company is irrelevant or is to be looked upon with suspicion; but it does mean that theirs is not necessarily the last word in arriving at a conclusion about how Falstaff should be considered in terms of its status as a potential entrant into the market in issue.

... We leave for another day the question of the applicability of section 7 to a merger that will leave competition in the marketplace exactly as it was, neither hurt nor helped, and that is challengeable under section 7 only on grounds that the company could, but did not, enter *de nova* or through "toe-hold" acquisiton and that there is less competition than there would have been had entry been in such a manner.

Reversed.

Potential Competition and Product Extension Mergers Product extension mergers involve acquisitions between firms that stand at the edge of a product market, in much the same manner that market extension mergers involve firms that stand at the edge of a geographic market. The potential competition doctrine is applicable in product extension mergers in exactly the same way that it applies in a market extension merger.

FTC v. Procter & Gamble Co.

386 U.S. 568, 87 S. Ct. 1224, 18 L. Ed. 2d 303 (1967)

Procter & Gamble, a large, diversified manufacturer of low-price, high turnover household products, acquired the assets of Clorox Chemical Company. Prior to the acquisition, Procter & Gamble did not manufacture household bleach, but it manufactured many other items used in household cleaning and accounted for 54.4 percent of the sales of detergents. Clorox was the leading manufacturer of household bleach, accounting for 48.8 percent of the market. The next largest competitor to Clorox was Purex which accounted for 15.7 percent of the bleach sales. Three other firms accounted for 25 percent of the market, and the balance of the market—approximately 20 percent—was distributed among 200 small producers. Purex did not distribute bleach in the northeast or mid-Atlantic states. The Federal Trade Commission brought this action under Section 7 of the Clayton Act.

The evidence showed that all liquid bleach is chemically identical. As a result, advertising and sales promotion are vital. Clorox had spent $3.7 million on advertising annually and another $1.7 million on other promotional activities. The evidence showed that Procter & Gamble had advertised its products in much the same way that bleach had been advertised, and that Procter was the nation's leading advertiser. The proof also showed that Procter received substantial discounts from the media. The Commission ordered divestiture, and Procter appealed.

Mr. Justice DOUGLAS delivered the opinion of the Court.

. . . .

The anticompetitive effects with which this product-extension merger is fraught can easily be seen: (1) the substitution of the powerful acquiring firm for the smaller, but already dominant, firm may substantially reduce the competitive structure of the industry by raising entry barriers and by dissuading the smaller firms from aggressively competing; (2) the acquisition eliminates the potential competition of the acquiring firm.

The liquid bleach industry was already oligopolistic before the acquisition, and price competition was certainly not as vigorous as it would have been if the industry were competitive. . . . There is every reason to assume that the smaller firms would become more cautious in competing due to their fear of retaliation by Procter. It is probable that Procter would become the price leader and that oligopoly would become more rigid.

The acquisition may also have the tendency of raising the barriers to new entry. The major competitive weapon in the successful marketing of bleach is advertising. . . . Procter would be able to use its volume discounts to advantage in advertising Clorox. Thus, a new entrant would be much more reluctant to face the giant Procter than it would have been to face the smaller Clorox.

. . . .

It is clear that the existence of Procter at the edge of the industry exerted considerable influence on the market. First, the market behavior of the liquid bleach industry was influenced by each firm's predictions of the market behavior of its competitors, actual and potential. Second, the barriers to entry by a firm of Procter's size and with its advantages were not significant. There is no indication that the barriers were so high that the price Procter would have to charge would be above the price that would maximize the profits of the existing firms. Third, the number of potential entrants was not so large that the elimination of one would be insignificant. Few firms would have the temerity to challenge a firm as solidly entrenched as Clorox. Fourth, Procter was found by the Commission to be the most likely entrant. . . .

The judgment of the Court of Appeals is reversed and remanded, with instructions to affirm and enforce the Commission's order.

The Limits of Potential Competition   The "new antitrust majority," formed by the appointments to the Court by Presidents Nixon, Ford, and Reagan, has cast some doubt on the future viability of the potential competition doctrine. There are two forms to the potential entrant theory: **perceived potential entry,** in which it is shown that the competitors in the market perceive the entrant as a possible competitor and thereby alter their behavior; and **actual potential entry,** where the courts are concerned with an actual loss to future competition. The latter theory is severely limited in the following decision, where the court imposes three requirements on the theory: the target market must be concentrated; an alternative method of entry must be available to the acquiring firm; and that method must offer a prospect of competitive improvement.

U.S. v. Marine Bancorporation, Inc.

418 U.S. 602, 94 S. Ct. 2856, 41 L. Ed. 2d 978 (1974)

Mr. Justice POWELL delivered the opinion of the Court.

The United States brought this civil antitrust action under section 7 of the Clayton Act . . . to challenge a proposed merger between two commercial banks. The acquiring bank is a large, nationally chartered bank based in Seattle, Washington, and the acquired bank is a medium-sized, state-chartered bank located at the opposite end of the State in Spokane. The banks are not direct competitors to any significant degree in Spokane or any other part of the State. They have no banking offices in each other's home cities. The merger agreement would substitute the acquiring bank for the acquired bank in Spokane and would permit the former for the first time to operate as a direct participant in the Spokane market.

The proposed merger would have no further effect on the number of banks in Spokane. The United States bases its case exclusively on the potential-competition doctrine under section 7 of the Clayton Act. It contends that if the merger is prohibited, the acquiring bank would find an alternative and more competitive means for entering the Spokane area and that the acquired bank would ultimately develop by internal expansion or mergers with smaller banks into an actual competitor of the acquiring bank and other large banks in sections of the State outside Spokane. The Government further submits that the merger would terminate the alleged procompetitive influence that the acquiring bank presently exerts over Spokane banks due to the potential for its entry into that market.

After a full trial, the District Court held against the Government on all aspects of the case. We affirm that court's judgment. . . .

The acquiring bank, National Bank of Commerce (NBC), is a national banking association with its principal office in Seattle. . . . NBC is a wholly owned subsidiary of a registered bank holding company, Marine Bancorporation, Inc. (Marine), and in terms of assets, deposits, and loans is the second largest banking organization with headquarters in the State of Washington. At the end of 1971, NBC had total assets of $1.8 billion, total deposits of $1.6 billion, and total loans of $881.3 million. . . .

The target bank, Washington Trust Bank (WTB), . . . is a state bank with headquarters in Spokane. . . .

WTB has seven branch offices, . . . [and] is the eighth largest banking organization with headquarters in the State of Washington. . . . At the end of 1971, it had assets of $112 million, total deposits of $95.6 million, and loans of $57.6 million. . . .

As of June 30, 1972, there were 91 national and state banking organizations in Washington. The five largest in the State held 74.3 percent of the State's total commercial bank deposits and operated 61.3 percent of its banking offices. At that time, the two largest in the State, Seattle-First National Bank and NBC held 51.3 percent of total deposits and operated 36.5 percent of the banking offices. . . . There are six banking organizations operating in the Spokane metropolitan area. . . . The target bank held 18.6 percent of total deposits at that time, placing it third in the Spokane area. Taken together (the largest three) hold approximately 92 percent of total deposits in the Spokane area. . . .

The degree of concentration of commercial banking business in Spokane may well reflect the severity of Washington's statutory restraints on *de novo* geographic expansion of its banks. Although Washington permits branching, the restrictions placed on that method of internal growth are stringent.

Washington statutes did not permit branching into any city where there was another bank, except for the county where its home office was located. Another statute provided that no bank might be acquired by another bank for a period of ten years after it was chartered.

. . . .

III. Potential Competition Doctrine

. . . In developing and applying the [potential competition] doctrine, the Court has recognized that a market extension merger may be unlawful if the target market is substantially concentrated, if the acquiring firm has the characteristics, capabilities and economic incentive to render it a perceived potential *de novo* entrant, and if the acquiring firm's premerger presence on the fringe of the target market in fact tempered oligopolistic behavior on the part of existing participants in that market. In other words, the Court has interpreted section 7 as encompassing what is commonly known as the "wings effect"—the probability that the acquiring firm prompted premerger procompetitive effects within the target market by being perceived by the existing firms in that market as likely to enter *de novo*. . . . The elimination of such present procompetitive effects may render a merger unlawful under section 7.

Although the concept of perceived potential entry has been accepted in the Court's prior section 7 cases, the potential-competition theory upon which the Government places principal reliance in the instant case has not. The Court has not previously resolved whether the potential competition doctrine proscribes a market extension merger solely on the ground that such a merger eliminates the prospect for long-term deconcentration of an oligopolistic market that in theory might result if the acquiring firm were forbidden to enter except through a *de novo* undertaking or through the acquisition of a small existing entrant (a so-called foothold or toehold acquisition). *Falstaff* expressly reserved this issue.

In applying the doctrine of potential competition to commercial banking, courts must, as we have noted, take into account the extensive federal and state regulation of banks. Our affirmance . . . in this case rests primarily on state statutory barriers to *de novo* entry and to expansion following entry into a new geographic market. In States where such stringent barriers exist and in the absence of a likelihood of entrenchment, the potential-competition doctrine—grounded as it is on relative freedom of entry on the part of the acquiring firm—will seldom bar a geographic market extension merger by a commercial bank. . . .

Affirmed.

Reciprocity

In its simplest terms, reciprocity means "I'll buy from you if you will buy from me." While reciprocity may be simple good business, the emergence of the giant conglomerates greatly complicates the issue and introduces possible anticompetitive effects to the practice. Such firms often have complex and far-reaching effects in markets not their own. Favored firms may derive advantages from reciprocity without being able to relate such advantages to the merits of the product. If a merger promotes reciprocity or is undertaken expressly to promote reciprocity, the merger may be challenged. The new merger guidelines make little mention of the practice, even though the following decision indicates that the courts frown on reciprocity.

FTC v. Consolidated Foods Corp.

380 U.S. 592, 84 S. Ct. 1220, 14 L. Ed. 2d 95 (1965)

Mr. Justice DOUGLAS delivered the opinion of the Court.

The question presented involves an important construction and application of section 7. . . . Consolidated Foods Corporation—which owns food processing plants and a network of wholesale and retail food stores—acquired Gentry, Inc., in 1951. Gentry manufactures principally dehydrated onion and garlic. The Federal Trade Commission held that the acquisition violated section 7 because it gave respondent the advantage of a mixed threat and lure of reciprocal buying in its competition for business and "the power to foreclose competition from a substantial share of the markets for dehydrated onion and garlic." . . .

We hold at the outset that the "reciprocity" made possible by such an acquisition is one of the congeries of anticompetitive practices at which the antitrust laws are aimed. The practice results in "an irrelevant and alien factor," . . . intruding into the choice among the competing products, creating at the least "a priority on the business at equal prices." . . . Reciprocal trading may ensue not from bludgeoning or coercion, but from more subtle arrangements. A threatened withdrawal of orders if products of an affiliate cease being bought or a conditioning of future purchases on the receipt of orders for products of that affiliate is an anticompetitive practice. . . . Reciprocity in trading as a result of an acquisition violates section 7, if the probability of a lessening of competition is shown. We turn then to that, the principal, aspect of the present case.

Consolidated is a substantial purchaser of the products of food processors who in turn purchase dehydrated onion and garlic for use in preparing and packaging their food. . . .

After the acquisition, Consolidated (though later disclaiming adherence to any policy of reciprocity) did undertake to assist Gentry in selling. An official of Consolidated wrote as follows to its distributing divisions:

> Oftentimes, it is a great advantage to know when you are calling on a prospect, whether or not that prospect is a supplier of someone within your own organization. Everyone believes in reciprocity providing all things are equal.
>
> Attached is a list of prospects for our Gentry products. We would like to have you indicate on the list whether or not you are purchasing any of your supplies from them. If so, indicate whether your purchases are relatively large, small, or insignificant. . . .

Food processors, who sold to Consolidated, stated they would give their onion and garlic business to Gentry for reciprocity reasons if it could meet the price and quality of its competitors' products. Typical is a letter from Armour and Company:

> I can assure you that it is the desire of our people to reciprocate and cooperate with you in any way we can in line with good business practices, and I am sure that if our quality obstacles can be overcome, your quotations will receive favorable consideration. We value our relationship with you very highly and are disappointed that we have been unable lately to reciprocate for your fine cooperation on Armour Pantry Shelf Meats.

> . . . .

> We do not go so far as to say that any acquisition, no matter how small, violates section 7 if there is a probability of reciprocal buying. Sometimes situations may amount only to *de minimus*. But where, as here, the acquisition is of a company that commands a substantial share of a market, a finding of probability of reciprocal buying by the Commission, whose expertise the Congress trusts, should be honored, if there is substantial evidence to support it.

The Court reversed the Court of Appeals ruling which had denied enforcement of the Commission's order.

The Deep Pocket Theory: Is "Bigness" Bad?

No antitrust case has held that simple corporate size of a firm is itself a reason to deny a merger. Mergers must contain some definable anticompetitive effect before the courts will hold them illegal. Removal of a competitor and the exercise of market power in horizontal mergers, foreclosure of markets and barriers to entry in vertical mergers, and foreclosure of potential competition and reciprocity in conglomerate mergers are all specific anticompetitive effects felt in a defineable relevant market.

Many theorists argue that corporate size does have anticompetitive effects, however. The principal effect of size and diversification is the **deep pocket theory,** in which a firm may subsidize one branch of its business with monopoly profits from other branches. The firm may thus undercut the prices of competitors to the subsidized branch and drive those competitors from the market, ultimately achieving a monopoly. Once a monopoly is attained in that branch, the firm may charge monopoly prices for that branch's products and subsidize other branches of the firm's business.

While the deep pocket theory has been argued in academic circles for years, no court has held a pure conglomerate merger unlawful. In 1969, the Justice Department moved against International Telephone & Telegraph (ITT), charging it with a violation of Section 7 because of its acquisitions in various industries: hotels, insurance, finance, rental cars, baking, and many others. The government's case was based on several theories, including reciprocity, foreclosure of competition, and sheer financial power. The trial court ordered divestiture of a few firms where it found reciprocity, but denied full divestiture on the basis of the deep pocket theory. The government had pointed to the degree of economic concentration and the pervasiveness of ITT's influence. The court refused to consider many of these claims.

> The alleged adverse effects of economic concentration brought about by merger activity, especially merger activity by large, diversified corporations such as ITT, arguably may be such that, as a matter of social and economic policy, the standard by which the legality of a merger should be measured under the antitrust laws is the degree to

which it may increase economic concentration—not merely the degree to which it may lessen competition. If the standard is to be changed, however, in the opinion of this court it is fundamental under our system of government that that determination be made by the Congress and not by the courts. . . . Chief Judge Timbers in *U.S.* v. *International Telephone & Telegraph Corp.*, 306 F. Supp. 766 (1969).

Section 7 in the 1980's: Trends and Enforcement Policies

With the election of President Reagan in 1980 came both hopes and fears that enforcement policies under Section 7 would be relaxed. Critics of antitrust enforcement had argued that enforcement of Section 7 emasculated American business in the face of international competition. Even Douglas Fraser, former president of the United Auto Workers, finds that "the problem of monopolistic practices" has become "a completely moot question now in the auto industry because you have the fierce competition with the Japanese. You don't have to break up General Motors; they've got all they can handle from foreign competition. Even if GM would gobble up Chrysler and Ford now, the competition is so stiff from the Japanese that it wouldn't be a tragedy anymore." Fraser finds the mergers between giant firms beneficial if they strengthen companies and save the jobs of workers in the industry (quoted in the *Wall Street Journal*, July 8, 1981). Other critics found merger enforcement old fashioned and outmoded in the new competitive atmosphere.

The critics' hopes and the proponent's fears were justified. Several moves took place in the early 1980's that indicated a relaxed attitude toward mergers among the enforcing authorities. Attorney General William French Smith indicated that to him, "Bigness does not necessarily mean badness." The 1982 merger guidelines eliminated references to reciprocity completely and made only vague references to conglomerate mergers. Funding for FTC enforcement of the antitrust laws was almost eliminated entirely. And the Justice Department permitted, after premerger notification, the largest merger in American history, the acquisition of Conoco Oil, the seventeenth largest American corporation by sales, by the duPont firm, the twenty-first largest company. The two firms together make the seventh largest firm in the nation.

Proponents of antitrust enforcement point to not only the economic power of such large firms in their respective markets, but also to the political and social power of such firms. Such critics point to the bureaucratic hazards of large institutions, complacency toward innovation, and general corporate "arteriosclerosis." Young people entering careers in such corporations have less choice of employers and a much longer climb up the corporate ladder. Such critics also point to probable loss of community responsibility and the ability of such corporate giants to influence both political events through their lobbying efforts and political attitudes through "advocacy advertising."

The relaxed attitude toward mergers may have had a cause and effect relationship to the recent wave of mergers that swept the corporate world in the late 1970's and early 1980's. 1975 saw only 14 mergers in which the purchase price exceeded $100 million; 1980 saw 94 such mergers, almost a sevenfold increase.

Perhaps the largest problem in merger enforcement is the attitude of Americans toward corporate size. As several experts pointed out, the American public is schizophrenic about business size. On the one hand, we admire corporate bigness and those who run such firms. On the other hand, we fear size and the power it brings. Perhaps the antitrust dilemma cannot be resolved until our attitudes toward size are resolved.

Summary and Conclusions

The antitrust laws regulate mergers through Section 7 of the Clayton Act. All types of integration of firms are covered by the statute, including mergers, consolidations, purchases of stock, purchases of assets, and joint ventures. The purpose of the regulation of mergers is to protect competition by outlawing any merger that "substantially lessens competition."

The prohibitions of Section 7 extend to horizontal, vertical, and some types of conglomerate mergers. The prime anticompetitive effect of a horizontal merger is the removal of a competitor from the market. The major impact of vertical mergers is the barriers to entry to the market and the necessary difficulty competitors have to reach the market or source of supplies of the firms involved. The principal anticompetitive effects of conglomerate mergers are reciprocity and the potential competition doctrine.

Every merger case involves a determination of the relevant product market and the relevant geographic market. Relevant product market refers to the line of commerce in which the anticompetitive effect is felt, while the relevant geographic market refers to the physical area in which the impact is felt.

Current debate centers around the proper sphere of conglomerate mergers, particularly the dimensions of the potential competition doctrine and the place of pure size in antitrust theory.

PRO AND CON
ISSUE: Is Business "Bigness" Bad?

PRO: Business Size Should Be Strictly Controlled
Dr. John R. Kuhlman*

I have never been in a lifeboat with an elephant and furthermore, I never *want* to be in a lifeboat with an elephant. In my imagination, anyway, I can see the elephant trying to make himself comfortable. As he moves forward, the aft portion of the boat rises out of the water. As he moves from side to side, I scramble to keep from falling out of the boat. In short, a lifeboat with one very large passenger and one very small passenger has to be an unstable platform and it has to be more unstable than would a lifeboat with the same total amount of weight distributed equally over a large number of passen-

gers. My "ideal society" also consists of a large number of small units. Just as I don't know whether I could co-exist with an elephant in a lifeboat, neither am I sure that I can co-exist with a small number of very large units in the social system. . . .

Let me pose the problems I see here in form of a series of questions, all posed without any promise of answering them. Can the small but equally-efficient independent newspapers and television stations co-exist alongside the giant chains and network-owned stations? Can a system of small and independent farmers co-exist with large corporate

---

*From his article, "In a Lifeboat With an Elephant: The Problem of Corporate 'Bigness,'" 12 *Antitrust Law and Economics Review* 39 (1980):41–42, 51–52, 54. Reprinted by permission.

farms and integrated agribusiness firms? Can we have a system in which small firms go broke on the basis that that is how the system works and then bail out the large firms? . . .

. . . .

Competition has both economic and noneconomic values. As far as the first is concerned, it promotes innovation and stimulates efficiency. If excess returns are being earned, for example, resources will flow toward those higher earnings just as resources will move *away* from areas where the returns are too low. Insofar as the noneconomic values are concerned, competition diffuses power over a large number of economic units rather than concentrating it in a small number of them, all of which is consistent with the political philosophy inherent in our Constitution and in the federal form of government. But competition would be an impossible goal if there were widespread economies of scale present in the economic system. If bigger farms are always more efficient than smaller farms, for example, then the most efficient method of organization would be *one* large farm. Nobody believes this to be the case. There is, however, a rather warm disagreement about how large an automobile company—or a steel company, an airline, or railroad—has to be in order to be efficient. As it stands now, we don't really know how many firms are needed in any given industry if we use *either* efficiency or democratic pluralism as our criteria. Since we have to make policy, however, I would make these sorts of suggestions (remembering that they are only tentative kinds of thoughts).

First, I would prohibit horizontal mergers between all but the very smallest of firms in most

industries. I wouldn't protest, for example, if two small quarries or two local groceries merged but, if two regional groups joined together, I would object.

Second, I would sharply limit vertical mergers—that is, mergers where buyer and seller are joined—if either of the firms is greater than some minimum size. It is much preferable that firms grow through internal expansion rather than merger since industry capacity increases with the former rather than merely changing ownership.

Third, I would simply prohibit growth through mergers for all large companies. I can't really believe that the consumer is better off because Mobil Oil purchased Montgomery Ward or because Exxon purchased Reliance Motor. Conglomerate firms such as ITT probably yield few benefits to the public that would not be equally likely under some other structure. . . .

. . . .

It is very easy to say that the "other fellow" ought to compete. Competition is the accepted national policy—for the other fellow. There are always good reasons why competition should not prevail in medicine, farming, automobiles, insurance, trucking—whatever business *we* are in. Immediate self-interest aside, competition does have some virtues. First, it provides a tremendous stimulus for efficiency, with the result that prices will tend to reflect costs and inefficient producers will tend to be weeded out. Second, it does have certain democratic values. In a competitive system, power is not concentrated and young people have a greater chance to enter business as independent entrepreneurs. And, finally, the competitive markets work in an impersonal manner without the benefit of a bureaucracy, public or private.

CON: Business Size Alone Should Not Be Controlled
J. Fred Weston*

The argument for doing something about conglomerate mergers rests on a few broad areas and arguments. One argument is that a number of anticompetitive behavior patterns might be followed. Among the possible types of behavior objected to are: (1) cross-product subsidization, (2) deep-pocket advantages, (3) business reciprocity, (4) competitive forebearance, (5) increased entry barriers, and (6) entrenched market power. These arguments rest primarily in the area of possibility. Little evidence has been assembled to relate such

possibilities to conglomerate merger activity. Without examining these possibilities in detail their general invalidity may be briefly sketched.

Cross subsidization makes no sense because a firm is better off to drop an unprofitable line rather than to divert returns from profitable activity to make the less profitable segment look better.

The deep-pocket theory makes sense only if there are truly significant capital barriers to entry or expansion. There is considerable evidence that demonstrates that if a firm has investment projects

*From his article, "Section 7 Enforcement: Implementation of Outmoded Theories," 49 *Antitrust Law Journal* 1411 (1982):1432–1435. Reprinted by permission.

that promise favorable returns the capital will be forthcoming. Thus conglomerate firms have no unfair advantage in this regard.

Reciprocity is difficult to carry out in today's business firms in which decentralization is achieved through the use of independent profit centers as the norm. Examples of reciprocity practices are relatively isolated. . . .

Another possibility that has been raised about conglomerate firms is that they may face one another in several industries and work out a pact of mutually avoiding competitive struggles. For this to occur very restrictive assumptions have to be made about the areas of competition among firms such as that they compete only on price. When other variables such as product quality and service are taken into account, competition is seen to take place over many dimensions. . . .

With regard to effects on entry barriers, it has never really been spelled out how conglomerate mergers could possibly increase them. . . .

The second line of attack on conglomerate mergers argues that the continued merger activities of the late 1960's and late 1970's have resulted in either an increase in the aggregate concentration ratio (ACR) or have prevented the occurrence of a decline in the ACR that might otherwise have occurred. The rise in the ACR or its failure to fall is then argued to lead to the possible ability of large firms to increasingly exercise political power and control legislation in the economy.

With regard to movements of the ACR it is sometimes stated that the largest 200 firms now control two-thirds of industrial assets. . . . The data generally refer to manufacturing rather than all industrial assets. When the ratio is calculated for all financial assets the share of the top 200 is about 40 percent. Furthermore, it has been very stable. It was 40.5 percent in 1960, 40.6 percent in 1970, and 39.39 percent in 1975. . . .

Thus we see that no valid basis exists for a case against conglomerate merger activity. In my judgment, the conglomerate merger activity of the late 1960's reflected in part new managerial developments particularly in planning and control. Financial aspects related to the discovery of growth in stock market valuation was also a factor.

The merger activity of the late 1970's has probably been influenced by another set of factors. Of greatest importance has been the substantial discounts on the market values of firms in relation to the current replacement costs of the assets. . . .

Thus if one really wants to strike a blow at the face of merger activity, the way to do it is not by an antimerger law. Rather it would make more sense to deal with the general economic factors that have produced higher capitalization rates and a low ratio of market values to current replacement costs. In other words, if one wishes to alter the pace of merger activity, the fundamental way to do it would be to work on the broader economic policies that have changed the economic climate. . . .

DISCUSSION QUESTIONS

1. Should the political power of huge corporations be an issue in antitrust merger litigation? Does the present wording of Section 7 permit such factors to be considered? How might the wording of Section 7 be changed to permit such factors to be taken into account? Would such changes be constitutional under the 1st Amendment?

2. Legislation has recently been proposed that would prohibit companies with $2.5 billion in sales or $2 billion in assets from merging with one another. The law requires that companies with $350 million in sales or $200 million in assets prove that a merger would encourage competition, and further prohibits companies with $1 billion or more in sales or assets from acquiring any firm with $100 million or more in assets and at least 20 percent of the market. Should the bill be passed? How would such a law affect current antitrust theories?

3. The original *Merger Guidelines,* adopted by the Justice Department in 1968, relied upon set percentages of markets instead of the new Herfindahl-Hirsch-

man Index of market concentration. For example, the Department said that it would challenge a horizontal merger in a market where the market shares of the four largest firms amounted to 75 percent, if the relative market shares of the firms were as follows:

Acquiring Firm	*Acquired Firm*
4%	4% or more
10%	2% or more
15%	1% or more

Is the Herfindahl-Hirschman Index an improvement? Is anything added by the HHI that was not in the old merger guidelines? Is anything left out that ought to be included? How can the Justice Department assert that the guidelines are to help businesspeople predict enforcement of Section 7 if they keep changing the guidelines?

4. Calculate the HHI of the following markets: (1) A four-firm market, with market shares of 30 percent, 30 percent, 20 percent, and 20 percent; (2) A one-firm market with 100 percent of the market; (3) A ten-firm market, each with 10 percent of the market; (4) A ten-firm market, one firm with 55 percent of the market, the rest with 5 percent each; (5) Seventy-one firms, one with 30 percent of the market, the rest with 1 percent of the market each. Rank them in competitiveness.

5. Isn't reciprocity simply good business? How does reciprocity affect classical economic theories of supply and demand?

6. Why should a toehold acquisition be any more beneficial than a merger with one of the larger competitors in a market?

7. Explain the difference between perceived potential entry and actual potential entry. Why is perceived potential entry more important?

8. Compare and contrast the *Falstaff* case with the *Marine Bancorporation* case. Which approach is more realistic? Do you think the Marine Bancorporation acquisition affected competition in the Spokane market? How?

9. Should competition from foreign countries dictate our domestic policy towards business? Always? Aren't the antitrust laws simply an anachronism in the new international business environment? Explain how other countries might have a competitive advantage because of the antitrust laws. Does this end the problems? Aren't there other reasons why the antitrust laws may still be necessary or desirable?

10. Is business concentration inevitable? Is antitrust simply fighting a holding action against the necessary growth in concentration that comes with economic success?

11. Are the remedies under Section 7 appropriate? Isn't divestiture awfully harsh? Can you think of another remedy that might work?

CASE PROBLEMS

1. Von's Grocery Company, the third largest retail grocery chain in Los Angeles, merged with Shopping Bag Food Stores, the sixth largest food chain in the same area. Von's operated 27 stores, while Shopping Bag had 34. The two chains together had 7.5 percent of the retail grocery market in Los Angeles. There were over 3,000 independent grocers in the city, though the number was declining, and 150 other "chains," which were growing. A chain is defined as at least two stores owned by the same firm. What is the relevant geographic market? What impact does this merger have on competition? Does this merger violate Section 7? [*U.S.* v. *Von's Grocery Company,* 384 U.S. 270, 86 S. Ct. 1478, 16 L. Ed. 2d 555 (1966).]

2. The *Star* and the *Citizen* are the only daily newspapers in Tucson, Arizona. While the circulations of the papers were about equal in 1940, the *Star* sold about 50 percent more advertising and made a profit of about $25,000, while the *Citizen* was losing about $23,000 per year. There were no indications that the *Citizen* would be liquidated, however. The *Star* and *Citizen* entered into an operating agreement, whereby each would own stock in another firm, Tucson Newspapers, Inc., and though the papers would be operated separately, the board of directors of Tucson Newspapers, Inc. would set advertising and business policies for both papers. The agreement was to extend for 25 years and was renewed in 1953. In 1964, the Justice Department brought suit under both Section 1 of the Sherman Act and Section 7 of the Clayton Act. What result? [*Citizen Publishing Co.* v. *U.S.,* 394 U.S. 131, 89 S. Ct. 927, 22 L. Ed 2d 148 (1969).]

3. Between 1917 and 1919, DuPont acquired 23 percent of the stock of General Motors Corporation. Over the next 35 years, DuPont exclusively supplied GM with paint and other chemicals and fabrics used in the auto industry. What kind of merger is this? What is the anticompetitive effect? Could the merger have been challenged prior to 1950? After 1950? [*U.S.* v. *E. I. DuPont de Nemours & Co.,* 353 U.S. 586, 77 S. Ct. 872, 1 L. Ed. 2d 1057 (1957).]

4. BOC International, Ltd., is a huge multinational corporation engaged in the manufacture of industrial gases, such as acetylene, carbon dioxide, and helium. BOC is the second largest gas supplier in the world, but did not sell in the United States. BOC acquired controlling interest in Airco, the third largest industrial gas manufacturer in the United States, with approximately 16 percent of the market. Do the antitrust laws apply to BOC? If so, what type of merger is this? Would it matter if BOC could have easily entered the American market *de novo?* [*BOC International* v. *FTC,* 557 F. 2d 24 (2d Cir., 1977).]

5. Pennsalt Chemicals and Olin-Mathieson Chemicals jointly formed a new firm, Penn-Olin, to produce and sell sodium chlorate in the southeastern United States. The chemical is used in the production of paper. Olin had never manufactured sodium chlorate before, and Pennsalt had only done so on the West Coast. Olin owned several valuable patents relevant to the process and Pennsalt was experienced in the manufacture of the chemical. Does this firm have any anticompet-

itive effect? Is this type of business organization within the meaning of Section 7? [*U.S. v. Penn-Olin Chemical Co.,* 378 U.S. 158, 84 S. Ct. 1710, 12 L. Ed. 2d 775 (1964).]

6. Assume that the year following the *Brown Shoe* decision, Montgomery Shoe Company, a manufacturer of shoes, decides to merge with Westmoreland Shoes, a large shoe retailer. Montgomery Shoe is the tenth largest shoe company in the nation, with 4 percent of the nation's production of shoes. Westmoreland is the owner of 75 retail shoe stores, almost all of which are located in shopping malls in the northeastern United States. In that area it is the leading retailer, but sells very few shoes anywhere else in the country. Montgomery has 35 retail outlets in California and none in the Northeast. After *Brown Shoe,* what result?

7. Perdita Wine Company, the manufacturer of the finest and most expensive wines made in America, desires to merge with Dorcas Winery, the manufacturer of $1/gallon "special" wine. What kind of merger is this?

8. Following the *Falstaff* case, assume that Bardolph Brewing Company is acquired by the Falstaff company. Bardolph Brewing is the second largest brewer in New England, after Narraganset, with 12 percent of the market, and has provided stiff competition for Narragansett for years. What result? What if Falstaff were to merge instead with Pym Brewing Company, one of the smallest brewers in the northeast, with only 2 percent of the market?

SUGGESTED READINGS

Bork, Robert. *The Antitrust Paradox* (New York: Basic Books, 1978).

Brooks, John. *The Go-Go Years* (New York: Waybright and Talley, 1973); see especially Chapter 7, "The Conglomerateurs."

Elzinga, Kenneth G., and William Breit. *The Antitrust Penalties: A Study in Law and Economics* (New Haven, Conn.: Yale University Press, 1976).

Kintner, Earl. *An Antitrust Primer* 2d ed. (New York: Macmillan, 1973).

McCarthy, George D. *Acquisitions and Mergers* (New York: The Ronald Press Company, 1963).

Sherman, Roger. *Antitrust Policies and Issues* (Reading, Mass.: Addison Wesley Publishing Co., 1978).

Turner, Donald F. "Conglomerate Mergers and Section 7 of the Clayton Act," *Harvard Law Review,* 78, no. 7 (1965):1313.

U.S. Federal Trade Commission. *Mergers Policy Session* (Washington, D.C.: Government Printing Office, 1980).

U.S. Federal Trade Commission. *Statistical Report on Mergers and Acquisitions* (Washington, D.C.: Government Printing Office, 1980).

U.S. Federal Trade Commission. *The Process of Conglomerate Mergers* (Washington, D.C.: Government Printing Office. 1980).

Van Cise, Jerrold G. *The Federal Antitrust Laws* 3d ed. *(Washington, D.C.: American Enterprise Institute for Public Policy Research, 1975).*

Part IV

Regulation of the Relationship Between Business and Its Customers

To the businessperson, perhaps the most important of the eight relationships is that between the firm and its customers. That relationship ultimately determines whether a business makes a profit or even survives. But obviously that relationship is also subject to a great deal of abuse, including fraud, false advertising, and the sale of shoddy or unsafe products.

Common law protection of consumers has traditionally been quite limited. Beginning in the 1960's, consumers began to organize and approach the various units of government, demanding protection from a variety of selling practices. Many of the specific laws protecting consumers originated during that era of consumerism. But others, including federal regulation of advertising, have been with us for quite some time.

The nature of the customer-business relationship is subject to a unique blend of conflicting ethics. "Individualist" values generally would permit the businessperson virtually total freedom to sell and negotiate with customers. But a variety of more "community" oriented values are allied against such total freedom, including protection from unsafe products and freedom from fraud and deception. Even more basically, notions of such personal ethics as honesty and personal responsibility for harm limit the freedom of sellers.

Once again, the law has stepped in to permit freedom on the part of businesspersons to sell within the limits of safety, responsibility, and honesty. Those limits, both common law and statutory, are the subject of the following two chapters.

Deceptive Advertising and Unfair Competition: The Common Law and the FTC

The codfish lays ten thousand eggs,
The homely hen lays one.
The codfish never cackles
To tell you what she's done.
And so we scorn the codfish,
While the humble hen we prize,
Which only goes to show you
That it pays to advertise.

Anonymous

The world wants to be deceived.

Sebastian Brant, Das Narrenschiff (The Ship of Fools) *(1494).*

We live in an age of advertising. It is probably impossible for any new product to become established, or for any existing product to maintain its market position, without substantial advertising. Critics have argued that product quality is now secondary to advertising in establishing consumer demand for products, and the trend to advertising has now "skewed" all economic analysis of the private sector. Advertising tends to attract some of the most creative people in the business world, who spend lifetimes determining how to best present products to the consumer. New techniques of marketing are constantly in the making, depending on consumer research and the most sophisticated psychological experimentation available.

And yet, as in all businesses, there are people at the fringe of the advertising world who insist on using misleading statements, unethical behavior, and outright lies to sell their products. Unprincipled and unethical advertising gives the entire industry a bad name, and ultimately harms both consumers and competitors. Efforts at controlling such practices have had their primary impetus in the advertising industry itself, but has also involved competitors and consumers.

Controlling unethical advertising has proven to be a very difficult task. Common law attempts have not been fruitful, and federal regulation may have indicted both the innocent and the guilty in order to reach the guilty. This chapter is the story of how the judicial and administrative processes have attempted to deal with deceptive advertising and marketing practices within the general concept of "unfair competition."

Who Is Harmed? Competitors and Consumers

A common thread running through all of the law of unfair and deceptive trade practices is the issue of who the law is trying to protect. On one hand, deception harms consumers, since they may purchase items unable to live up to the claims made for them. On the other hand, deception harms competitors of the unethical advertiser, since business is diverted from honestly presented products. The issue of who the law should protect existed at common law, where competitors seemed to have more protection than consumers. The question pervaded the initial enactment of the FTC Act, which initially protected only competitors, and arose again with the passage of the Wheeler-Lea Act of 1938, which extended the reach of the FTC Act to protect consumers. The question continues to be raised in judicial decisions, sometimes explicitly but often implicitly.

Common Law Protections

The problem of misleading and deceptive marketing and advertising practices arose very early in the history of the common law. Some professions, particularly silversmithing and similar arts, were required by the king to mark their products with distinctive "trade-marks." Craftsmen often took advantage of this requirement and built up substantial trades based on consumer preferences for the products of a particular craftsman, as identified by his trademark. Other, less scrupulous, craftsmen sometimes copied a successful tradesman's mark in order to gain business. The common-law lawsuits that resulted created the basis of our law of trademarks and the common-law tort of trademark infringement, and later the torts of disparagement, "passing off" and product simulation, misappropriation, and malicious competition.

Competitor Torts: Common-Law "Unfair Competition"

The ancient torts are still with us. Even in the light of contemporary regulation by the Federal Trade Commission and the creation of the antitrust laws, the common-law torts that evolved from the law of trademarks remain to protect competitors against unethical conduct by others.

Common-Law Trademark Infringement   The earliest cases simply prohibited craftsmen from exactly duplicating the "mark" of another craftsman in an effort to divert trade. This action was a simple claim that the property was being "passed" as another's work in order to obtain the benefits of his good will and established reputation. Often, the result was a judgment equal to all of the profits received as a result of the infringement and, later, court orders were granted requiring the person infringing another's mark to cease the practice.

The first American trademark law, enacted by Congress in 1845, simply incorporated common-law doctrine. Trademarks were first registered with the federal government in 1870, but the present statute was enacted in 1947. In that year the Lanham Trade-Mark Act became law and protected all marks registered with the Trademark Office. After a trademark is registered with that office, disputes are heard by the Trademark Trial and Appeal Board and, later, by the U.S. Court of Appeals for the Federal Circuit. International trademark protection may also be obtained from further registration and worldwide search procedures, under the *Convention of Paris,* a treaty signed in 1883 in which members agreed to extend the protection of trademarks to citizens of all signing nations. The United States signed that treaty, but many of the "new" nations, especially the communist nations, have not done so.

Disparagement   The common-law tort of **disparagement** is a form of commercial slander, covering all false statements regarding the quality of another merchant's products or services. To be actionable, the statement must be false and must be made with "malice." Courts also require that there be proof of actual loss to the complaining party. One famous example of disparagement involved a car painted with lemons parked in front of a car dealership by a competing dealership. Consumers or others as well as competitors may be sued for disparagement.

"Passing Off" and Product Simulation   Two closely related torts involve efforts to convince the public that a product is actually made by another, more highly regarded, manufacturer. **Passing off** involves some express representation that another manufacturer made the product. Product simulation is an intentional duplication of the physical characteristics of another's product. Thus, duplicating the package design of a product might be product simulation, but actually putting the trade name of another manufacturer on the package would be passing off, sometimes called *palming off.* Both torts are very closely related to trademark infringement.

Misappropriation   The vague tort of **misappropriation** developed in the late 19th century and was fully recognized in a 1918 Supreme Court decision.* The tort is generally described as "reaping what one has not sown," since a product manufactured by another is *passed off* as one's own. It is a type of "product plagiarism," since products of one manufacturer are presented to the public as one's own. (Note that

---

International News Service v. *Associated Press,* 248 U.S. 215, 39 S. Ct. 68, 63 L.Ed. 211 (1918).

passing off is a representation that the product is manufactured by another.) The 1918 case involved real plagiarism: a news service copied or paraphrased uncopyrighted stories written by another news service and presented them as its own work.

Malicious Competition   Perhaps the most indefinite of all of the competitor torts is **malicious competition** or "competing for a predatory purpose." Normal competitive activity is privileged, and it is expected that competitors will "play hardball" in an effort to win customers. But in some instances the courts have held that the activities of a competitor have gone beyond the bounds of expected competitive activity and into the realm of unfairness. One example involved an action by a commercial trapper of wildfowl against a person who discharged guns over his traps in an effort to frighten birds away. The essential element of the tort is **malice,** or evil intent, as discussed in the following case.

Tuttle v. Buck

107 Minn. 145, 119 N.W. 946 (Sup. Ct. of Minn. 1909)

The plaintiff, a barber, had operated a very successful shop in a small town in Minnesota for ten years. The defendant, the local banker, purchased a store and hired barbers to operate the shop. He paid the barbers high wages in some cases, and offered only nominal rents to barbers occupying the shop in other cases, and personally tried to convince many of plaintiff's customers to patronize the new shop. The plaintiff filed a complaint, charging that the defendant's purpose was to drive him out of town, and that all of defendant's activities were done with "malice" due to personal anomosity. The defendant argued that the shop was only an investment and his activities were fair competition. The defendant moved to dismiss the complaint, and the court refused to do so. The defendant appealed this ruling, which was permissible under Minnesota law at the time.

Elliott, J.

. . . .

It has been said that the law deals only with externals, and that a lawful act cannot be made the foundation of an action because it was done with an evil motive.

. . . .

. . . For generations there has been a practical agreement upon the proposition that competition in trade and business is desirable, and this idea has found expression in the decisions of the courts as well as in statutes. But it has led to grievous and manifold wrongs to individuals, and many courts have manifested an earnest desire to protect the individual from the evils which result from unrestrained business competition. The problem has been to adjust matters as to preserve the principle of competition and yet guard against its abuse to the unnecessary injury to the individual. So the principle that a man may use his own property according to his own needs and desires, while true in the abstract, is subject to many limitations in the concrete. Men cannot always, in civilized society, be allowed to use their own property as their interests or desires may dictate without reference to the fact that they have neighbors whose rights are as sacred as their own. The existence and well-being of society requires that each and every person shall conduct himself consistently with the fact that he is a social and reasonable person. The purpose for which a man is using his own property may thus sometimes determine his rights.

. . . To divert to one's self the customers of a business rival by the offer of goods at lower prices is in general a legitimate mode of serving one's own interest, and justifiable as fair competition. But when a man starts an opposition place of business, not for the sake of profit to himself, but regardless of loss to himself, and for the sole purpose of driving his competitor out of business, and with the intention of himself retiring upon the accomplishment of his malevolent purpose, he is guilty of a wanton wrong and an actionable tort. In such a case he would not be exercising his legal right, or doing an act which can be judged separately from the motive which actuated him. To call such conduct competition is a perversion of terms. It is simply the application of force without legal justification, which in its moral quality may be no better than highway robbery. . . .

Affirmed.

Common-Law Consumer Torts

From the very beginning, consumers were not nearly so well protected as competitors from unethical conduct by merchants. Early common-law torts quickly separated into two basic forms: actions for *fraud*, sometimes called *deceit*, and actions for *breach of warranty*. Neither was very effective in protecting the consumer from misleading or deceptive advertising, though warranty protections have been greatly enlarged since the adoption of the Uniform Commercial Code.

Fraud and Deceit   Common-law fraud and deceit actions involve a lawsuit by a consumer who claims that the seller of an item has misrepresented the goods in some way. In order to prove **fraud,** a deceived consumer is required to prove that the seller (1) had misrepresented a material fact about the goods; (2) that the representation was made with knowledge that it was false; (3) that the seller made the misrepresentation intentionally in order to induce the purchaser to buy the item or take some other action; and (4) that the purchaser relied upon the representation in some way.

While it would appear that these elements would be relatively easy to prove in most cases in which a seller lies about the character of his goods, the common-law rule of **caveat emptor** substantially enfeebled the tort of fraud. Caveat emptor, or "let the buyer beware," required each purchaser to examine the goods or obtain expert advice before purchasing a product. If the buyer failed to take that action, the consumer assumed the risks of "sales puffing" and could not recover. The doctrine also meant that consumers must "*reasonably* rely" on the misrepresentation. If the seller's misrepresentation was *too* outrageous, or the consumer did not take sales talk with a sufficient "grain of salt," recovery was simply not permitted on the theory that the purchaser did not reasonably rely on the misrepresentation. Likewise, the requirement that the misrepresentation must be a *fact* permitted the seller to do a great deal of *puffing*, or exaggeration, about the qualities of his products, so long as the exaggeration might be characterized as an opinion rather than a fact. These requirements made fraud most difficult to prove in many cases.

Warranty Claims   **Warranty** claims are essentially contract actions for breach of a promise made when a product is purchased. If a consumer purchases a toaster and, at the time of purchase, the seller says, "This toaster will last for ten years," the seller has effectively promised that the toaster will last that length of time. Warranties may be made orally, as in the example, or in writing, as in written product warranties that often accompany consumer items. Such promises, if not fulfilled, may result in a breach of contract action.

At common law, such claims had a major obstacle in the doctrine of **privity of contract.** That doctrine simply said that a purchaser may sue in contract only those persons with whom he had a contractual relationship. In the usual consumer transaction, the purchaser has no contractual relationship with the manufacturer, since the consumer's contract of purchase is with the retailer. If the manufacturer makes a warranty, the consumer cannot sue since there is no privity of contract with the manufacturer, nor may the consumer sue the retailer since the retailer did not make the promise. Recent court decisions, the Magnuson-Moss Warranty Act, and the Uniform Commercial Code have all changed this result, but at common law it was quite difficult for a consumer to recover under a warranty theory for such "false promises."*

Inadequacies of the Common Law

Both consumers and competitors found it rather difficult to recover for the unethical business practices of business people. The doctrines of caveat emptor and privity of contract resulted in recovery only in unusual cases of consumer fraud, misrepresentation, and false promise. Competitors were somewhat better off, but the difficulties of proving "malice" and actual damages assured that many cases of competitive misbehavior would also go unremedied.

The lack of effective remedies resulted in some very outrageous claims for products, especially during the beginnings of the age of advertising in the latter 19th century. Manufacturers claimed that patent medicines would cure every disease known to man, that corsets charged with electricity would cure both "extreme fatness and leanness" and that products would last "indefinitely." Such claims were made with virtual impunity, since there was simply no remedy.

State Statutes: The Beginnings of Regulation

The first real action against deceptive practices came in 1911, when *Printer's Ink,* a trade publication of the advertising industry, formulated a model state law dealing with the problems of false and deceptive advertising. It is perhaps useful to emphasize that the force behind the regulation of advertising was the advertising industry itself, since the unethical members of that industry had succeeded in giving the trade an extremely bad name. The *Printer's Ink* statute eventually became law in 44 states, though several states modified the language somewhat.

Printer's Ink Model State Statute

Any person, firm, corporation or association who, with intent to sell or in any wise dispose of merchandise, securities, services, or anything offered by such person, firm, corporation or association, directly or indirectly, to the public for sale or distribution, or with intent to increase the consumption thereof, or to induce the public in any manner to enter into any obligation relating thereto, or to acquire title thereto, or an interest therein, makes, publishes, disseminates, circulates, or places before the public, or causes, directly or indirectly, to be made, published, disseminated, circulated, or placed before

*See generally Chapter 12, pages 413–17.

the public, in this State, in a newspaper, bill, circular, pamphlet, or letter, or in any other way, an advertisement of any sort regarding merchandise, securities, service, or anything so offered to the public, which advertising contains any assertion, representation or statement of fact which is untrue, deceptive or misleading, shall be guilty of a misdemeanor.

While the *Printer's Ink* statute is strongly worded, it is only randomly and unevenly enforced by the state courts and prosecutors. Some states have enacted more specific statutes in the intervening years to either augment or replace the original statute.

Federal Regulation: The Federal Trade Commission

As originally enacted in 1914, the Federal Trade Commission Act had nothing to do with the problems of consumer protection and deceptive advertising. Instead the Act was part of a two-pronged effort to improve the enforcement of the antitrust laws, including the FTC Act and the Clayton Act.

In 1911, the Supreme Court announced its decision in the *Standard Oil* case and established the rule of reason, as discussed in Chapter 8. It was felt that the decision substantially weakened the enforcement of the Sherman Act, and Congress acted by specifying certain types of behavior as specifically illegal in the Clayton Act, including merger activities, tying contracts, and interlocking directorates.

But others, especially Louis D. Brandeis, who was later to become a Supreme Court Justice, argued that simply specifying certain conduct as illegal would have little effect, since imaginative businesspeople would quickly find new ways of achieving the same ends.* Brandeis argued for the establishment of an administrative agency with the authority to define and move against other types of conduct that might be considered "unfair."

The result was the FTC Act of 1914, which created the FTC and declared that "Unfair methods of competition in commerce are hereby declared illegal." The FTC was given the authority to make rules defining such unfair methods, and was given the authority to enter orders of restraint, also called **cease and desist orders,** requiring violators to stop the unfair activity.

The Wheeler-Lea Amendments of 1938

While some early decisions held that the FTC Act protected both competitors and consumers from such unfair methods, a 1931 Supreme Court decision held that the term *methods of competition* in the FTC Act required the FTC to prove injury to a *competitor* before the Act was violated. The requirement complicated the proof of violation and increased the cost of proceedings under the Act. But, perhaps more importantly, this requirement made it difficult to prove a violation in those industries

---

*Brandeis' argument was presented in a series of articles in *Harper's Weekly* in late 1913. Those articles are generally credited with producing both the Clayton Act and the FTC Act in 1914. See "The Endless Chain", p. 316 for a small sample.

where it was needed most. If there was no competitor, as in a monopolistic industry, or if every competitor was using unfair methods, there was no competitive injury.

This illogical result caused the FTC itself to approach Congress and request an amendment to the Act. The result was the Wheeler-Lea Act of 1938, which amended section 5 of the Act to declare that "Unfair methods of competition in commerce, *and unfair or deceptive acts or practices in commerce,* are hereby declared unlawful."

The new language in Section 5 of the FTC Act gave the Commission the authority to confront both competitive problems, as an extension of the antitrust laws, and consumer problems. The FTC now finds that it has two missions, that of maintaining competition and that of consumer protection.

Federal Trade Commission
Program Budget, Fiscal Year 1984

The role of the Federal Trade Commission, as defined by Congress, is to enforce the antitrust and consumer protection laws. . . .

Maintaining Competition

The Commission's aim in its Maintaining Competition Mission is to eliminate unlawful impediments to the operation of competitive forces in the markets for goods and services. Specifically, this activity seeks to remove antitrust law violations including collusion, coercion, and other anticompetitive practices and restraints upon independent competitive decisionmaking. . . .

Consumer Protection

The goal of the Commission in its Consumer Protection Mission is to improve market performance so that consumers can make informed purchase choices. The Consumer Protection Mission emphasizes market-oriented remedies for law violations . . .

The Advertising Practices program seeks to reduce unfair or deceptive product claims found in advertising, especially for items that are costly, purchased infrequently, or are difficult to evaluate. . . .

The Credit Practices program, based on the Federal Consumer Credit Protection Act, pursues solutions to problems in the consumer credit market. Activities will continue to deal with unlawful standards for granting credit, protecting the confidentiality of consumer financial data, and preventing economic loss from computer handling of credit and debit transactions.

The Service Industry Practices program will concern itself with potential unfair or deceptive practices affecting the service industry in general. . . . Public and private restrictions on the practice of groups within certain professions can unduly limit competition, inflate prices, or in other ways restrict consumer and practitioner choice. Investigations concerning dentists, denturists, lawyers, and other professionals [are examples]. . . .

. . . .

Under the Marketing Practices program, the Commission will continue to carry out its mandate to eliminate unfair or deceptive acts or practices affecting commerce . . . by investigating companies allegedly using deceptive practices at the point of sale. Practices such as high pressure sales tactics, deceptive product claims, and the failure to provide information critical to the transaction or the product can cause severe economic harm to consumers and small businesses. . . .

In the Warranties program, the Commission must ensure that information about warranty coverage can be understood, is available to consumers prior to sale, and promises made under major consumer warranties are performed. Commission activity in this area is governed by the Magnuson-Moss Warranty Act. . . .

Informal Advice by the FTC: Trade Rules, Guides and Advisory Opinions

The FTC has set out various types of rules and guides to aid business people who wish to follow the law. One form of such rules are the *Trade Practice Rules,* which apply to particular industries. Often these rules are the result of formal requests or conferences within the industry itself. The rules clarify what the law already prevents, and therefore industry members are required to follow the rules.

Another form of informal advice is found in the *FTC Guides.* These guides are general guidelines of what the Commission feels are problem areas. Their purpose is to give the businessperson some idea of what the law requires and must be followed as well. Examples include the *Guides Against Deceptive Pricing, Guides Against Bait Advertising,* and *Guides Against Deceptive Advertising of Guarantees.* Other guides deal with specific types of advertising in particular industries, such as cigarettes and tires.

Guides Against Deceptive Pricing
Federal Trade Commission

Introduction

These Guides are designed to highlight certain problems in the field of price advertising which experience has demonstrated to be especially troublesome to businessmen who in good faith desire to avoid deception of the consuming public. Since the Guides are not intended to serve as comprehensive or precise statements of the law, . . . they will be of no assistance to the unscrupulous few whose aim is to walk as close as possible to the line between legal and illegal conduct. . . .

The basic objective of these Guides is to enable the businessman to advertise his goods honestly. . . . Price advertising is particularly effective because of the universal hope of consumers to find bargains. Truthful price advertising, offering real bargains, is a benefit to all. But the advertiser must shun sales gimmicks which lure consumers into a mistaken belief that they are getting more for their money than is the fact.

Guide I. Former Price Comparisons

One of the most commonly used forms of bargain advertising is to offer a reduction from the advertiser's own former price for an article. If the former price is the actual, *bona fide* price at which the article was offered to the public on a regular basis for a reasonably substantial period of time, it provides a legitimate basis for the advertising of a price comparison. . . . If, on the other hand, the former price being advertised is not bona fide but fictitious—for example, where an artificial, inflated price was established for the purpose of enabling the subsequent offer of a large reduction—the "bargain" being advertised is a false one; the purchaser is not receiving the unusual value he expects. In such a case, the "reduced" price is, in reality, probably just the seller's regular price.

It is often difficult for businesspeople and corporate attorneys to determine whether a particular act is illegal or not under the FTC Act or the various statutes the Commission administers. The Commission will give **advisory opinions** on such points, though it is important to note that the opinions are not binding. The FTC will not give such opinions if (1) the conduct is already being followed; (2) similar action is presently under investigation by the Commission or by another government agency; or (3) the opinion would involve extensive investigation, clinical study, or testing.

The Maintaining Competition Mission of the FTC

The original goal of the FTC was to augment the other, more specific, antitrust statutes, which included the Sherman and Clayton Acts. The primary issue was whether FTC authority extends only to acts already made illegal by the Sherman and Clayton Acts, or whether the FTC Act includes activities "unreachable" under those two statutes. The following decision provides the clearest answer.

FTC v. Sperry & Hutchinson Co.

405 U.S. 233, 92 S. Ct. 898, 31 L. Ed. 2d 170 (1972)

Sperry & Hutchinson Co. (S&H) sold trading stamps to retailers, usually supermarkets and gasoline stations, who then gave the stamps to customers as a bonus upon purchasing the retailer's products, typically at the rate of one stamp for each 10¢ purchased. Consumers pasted the stamps in books of 1,200 and exchanged the books for "gifts" at S&H Redemption Centers.

Consumers began operating stamp exchanges in which collectors of other types of trading stamps traded S&H Green Stamps for the brands collected; some retailers began offering double stamp deals or selling stamps outright to consumers; and some consumers sold their stamps outright for cash. S&H moved against these practices by regulating the maximum rate at which the stamps were dispensed, and moved against the stamp exchanges in a variety of ways, including private lawsuits and refusing to redeem partial books.

The Federal Trade Commission charged that these practices of S&H violated Section 5 of the FTC Act, and issued cease and desist orders following a hearing. S&H appealed to the Court of Appeals, which reversed the Commission. In the lower court's view

> To be the type of practice that the Commission has the power to declare "unfair" the act complained of must fall within one of the following types of violations: (1) a per se violation of antitrust policy; (2) a violation of the letter of either the Sherman, Clayton, or Robinson-Patman Acts; or (3) a violation of the spirit of these Acts as recognized by the Supreme Court. . . .

The Commission appealed to the Supreme Court

Mr. Justice WHITE delivered the opinion of the Court.

. . . .

In reality, the question is a double one: First, does § 5 empower the Commission to define and proscribe an unfair competitive practice, even though the practice does not infringe either the letter or spirit of the antitrust laws? Second, does § 5 empower the Commission to proscribe practices as unfair or deceptive in their effect upon consumers regardless of their nature or quality as competitive practices or their effect on competition? We think the statute, its legislative history, and prior cases compel an affirmative answer to both questions.

When Congress created the Federal Trade Commission in 1914 and charted its power and responsibility under § 5, it explicitly considered, and rejected, the notion that it reduce the ambiguity of the phrase "unfair methods of competition" by tying the concept of unfairness to a common-law or statutory standard or by enumerating the particular practices to which it was intended to apply. . . .

. . . The House Conference Report was . . . explicit. "It is impossible to frame definitions which embrace all unfair practices. There is no limit to human inventiveness in this field. Even if all known unfair practices were specifically defined and prohibited, it would be at once necessary to begin over again. . . .

The 1938 Wheeler-Lea amendment added the phrase "unfair or deceptive acts or practices" to the section's original ban on "unfair methods of competition" and thus made it clear that Congress, through § 5, charged the FTC with protecting consumers as well as competitors. . . .

Thus, legislative and judicial authorities alike convince us that the Federal Trade Commission does not arrogate excessive power to itself if, in measuring a practice against the elusive, but congressionally mandated standard of fairness, it, like a court of equity, considers public values beyond simply those enshrined in the letter or encompassed in the spirit of the antitrust laws. . . .

The Court reversed the judgment of the Court of Appeals and remanded the case to the FTC for further proceedings on other grounds.

As a result of the S&H case, the FTC now has authority to act against unfair competition without reference to the antitrust laws. Clearly the term *unfair competition* is given an expansive definition, encompassing matters made specifically illegal under the specific antitrust laws, but also including conduct not specifically defined in those laws. Elsewhere in the decision, the Court also indicated that Section 5 might also cover acts specifically made legal under state laws and decisions.

The Consumer Protection Mission of the FTC

As indicated in the FTC's 1984 program budget, the "consumer protection mission" of that agency is broad indeed. Congress has given the FTC specific authority to administer 27 different statutes, including such divers topics as cigarette labeling and advertising, fair credit reporting, importation of numismatic (coin collecting) materials, petroleum marketing, electronics funds transfers, and energy related matters. Many of these specific statutes will be considered in subsequent chapters dealing with particular areas of regulation. The balance of this chapter will consider the knotty problem of deceptive advertising under the FTC Act itself and related statutes.

The Basics of Deception

More than almost any other area of the law, FTC handling of the area of deceptive advertising has been on a case-by-case basis. That is, few broad, overriding principles are applicable to every case. The problem is compounded by the very few U.S. Supreme Court decisions in the area. Most of the law has been made by the U.S. Courts of Appeal and by the FTC itself in its orders.

It is possible to make a few generalizations about deceptive advertising, however. The basic question in all cases is whether the advertisement has a *tendency to mislead*. Obviously, an outright lie has such a tendency, but even ads that are literally true may have a tendency to deceive the "ignorant, unthinking and credulous" among us and may, therefore, run afoul of the Commission. An ad must also be literally true, however.

Intent and knowledge are not elements of deception. It does not matter whether the advertiser knew that the advertisment was false or had no intention to deceive consumers. The purpose of the statute is to protect consumers, and therefore the burden is on the advertiser to only disseminate truthful ads that do not mislead. Ads that have ambiguous meanings are interpreted strictly; that is, if the ad has two meanings, one of them legal and the other illegal, the ad will be interpreted to be illegal.

FTC v. Sterling Drug, Inc.

317 F. 2d 669 (2d Circ. 1963)

In 1962, an article appeared in the *Journal of the American Medical Association* in which five pain relievers (Bayer Aspirin, St. Joseph's Aspirin, Bufferin, Anacin, and Excedrin) were studied as to both their pain-relieving effectiveness and their after-effects. The conclusion of the article was that "The data failed to show an any statistically significant difference among any of the drugs." Upon investigating the incidence of stomach upset after administration of the five drugs as well as a placebo on test patients, the researches concluded: "Excedrin and Anacin form a group for which the incidence of upset stomach is significantly greater than is the incidence after Bayer Aspirin, St. Joseph's Aspirin, Bufferin, or the placebo. The rates of upset stomach associated with these last 4 treatments are not significantly different, one from the other." The study was funded by the FTC.

Sterling, the manufacturer of Bayer Aspirin, quickly took out a large advertisement in *LIFE* magazine which read:

> *Government-Supported Medical Team Compares Bayer Aspirin and Four Other Popular Pain Relievers*
>
> Findings reported in the highly authoritative Journal of the American Medical Association reveal that the higher priced combination of ingredients pain relievers upset the stomach with significantly greater frequency than any of the other products tested, while Bayer Aspirin brings relief that is as fast, as strong, and as gentle to the stomach as you can get.
>
> This important new medical study, supported by a grant from the federal government, was undertaken to compare the stomach-upsetting effects, the speed of relief, and the amount of relief offered by five leading pain relievers, including Bayer Aspirin, aspirin with buffering, and combination-of-ingredients products. Here is a summary of the findings.
>
> **Upset Stomach**
>
> According to this report, the higher priced combination of ingredients products upset the stomach with significantly greater frequency than any of the other products tested, while Bayer Aspirin, taken as directed, is as gentle to the stomach as a plain sugar pill.
>
> **Speed and Strength**
>
> The study shows that there is no significant difference among the products tested in rapidity of onset, strength, or duration of relief. Nonetheless, it is interesting to know that within just fifteen minutes, Bayer Aspirin had a somewhat higher pain relief score than any of the other products.

Price

As unreasonable as it may seem, the products which are most likely to upset the stomach—that is, the combination-of-ingredients products—actually cost substantially more than Bayer Aspirin. The fact is that these products, as well as the buffered product, cost up to 75% more than Bayer Aspirin.

The FTC brought an action to prevent the dissemination of this ad on the grounds that it was false and misleading. The trial judge refused to grant an injunction, and the FTC appealed to the U.S. Court of Appeals.

Kaufman, J. . . .

It is not difficult to understand the heartwarming reception [the] article received in the upper echelons of Sterling and its Madison Avenue colleagues; no sooner were the results of the study published . . . when Sterling Drug and its advertising agencies decided to make the most of them. This decision, we may fairly assume, did not surprise Sterling's competitors. The public had long been saturated with various claims proved by the study to be of doubtful validity. One of the products had boasted in its advertisements that it "works twice as fast as aspirin," and "protects you against the stomach distress you can get from aspirin alone"; another, that it "does not upset the stomach" and "is better than aspirin"; and yet another, that it is "50% stronger than aspirin." Believing that the Judgment Day has finally arrived and seeking to counteract the many years of hard-sell by what it now believed to be the hard facts, Sterling and its co-defendants prepared and disseminated [the] advertising. . . .

. . . .

The Commission alleged and sought to prove that the . . . advertising falsely represented, directly and by implication:(a) that the findings . . . were endorsed and approved by the United States Government; (b) that the publication of the article . . . is evidence of endorsement and approval . . . by the medical profession; (c) that . . . Bayer aspirin is not upsetting to the stomach and is as gentle thereto as a sugar pill; (d) that . . . Bayer aspirin . . . affords a higher degree of pain relief than any other product tested. . . .

The legal principles to be applied here are quite clear. The central purpose of the provisions of the Federal Trade Commission Act under discussion is in effect to abolish the rule of *caveat emptor* which traditionally defined rights and responsibilities in the world of commerce. That rule can no longer be relied upon as a means of rewarding fraud and deception. . . . and has been replaced by a rule which gives to the consumer the right to rely upon representations of facts as the truth. . . . In order best to implement the prophylactic purpose of the statute, it has been consistently held that advertising falls within its proscription not only when there is proof of actual deception but also when the representations made have a capacity or tendency to deceive, i.e., when there is a likelihood or fair probability that the reader will be misled. . . . For the same reason, proof of intention to deceive is not requisite to a finding of violation of the statute . . .; since the purpose of the statute is not to punish the wrongdoer but to protect the public, the cardinal factor is the probable effect which the advertiser's handiwork will have upon the eye and mind of the reader. It is therefore necessary in these cases to consider the advertisement in its entirety and not to engage in disputatious dissection. The entire mosaic should be viewed rather than each tile separately. . . .

Unlike that abiding faith which the law has in the "reasonable man," it has very little faith indeed in the intellectual acuity of the "ordinary purchaser" who is the object of the advertising campaign.

The general public has been defined as "that vast multitude which includes the ignorant, and unthinking and the credulous, who, in making purchases, do not stop to analyze but too often are governed by appearances and general impressions." The average purchaser has been variously characterized as not "straight thinking," subject to "impressions," uneducated, and grossly misinformed; he is influenced by prejudice and superstition; and he wishfully believes in miracles, allegedly the result of progress in science. . . . [Callman, *Unfair Competition and Trademarks,* 19.2 (a)(1) at 341–44(1950), and the cases there cited.]

It is well established that advertising need not be literally false in order to fall within the proscription of the act. Gone for the most part, fortunately, are the days when the advertiser was so lacking in subtlety as to represent his nostrum as superlative for "arthritis, rheumatism, neuralgia, sciatica, lumbago, gout, coronary thrombosis, brittle bones, bad teeth, malfunctioning glands, infected tonsils, infected appendix, gallstones, neuritis, underweight, constipation, indigestion, lack of energy, lack of vitality, lack of ambition, and inability to sleep. . . ." See *FTC* v. *National Health Aids, Inc.* . . . (1952). The courts are no longer content to insist simply upon the "most literal truthfulness," . . . for we have increasingly come to recognize that "Advertisements as a whole may be completely misleading although every sentence separately considered is literally true. This may be because things are omitted that should be said, or because advertisements are composed or purposefully printed in such a way as to mislead." . . . There are two obvious methods of employing a true statement so as to convey a false impression: one is the half truth, where the statement is removed from its context and the nondisclosure of its context renders the statement misleading. . . .: a second is the ambiguity, where the statement in context has two or more commonly understood meanings, one of which is deceptive. . . .

The Federal Trade Commission asserts here that the vice of the Bayer advertisement is of these types. It concedes that none of the statements made therein is literally false, but it contends that the half-truths and ambiguities of the advertisement give it "reason to believe" that our hypothetical, sub-intelligent, less-than-careful reader will be misled thereby. Thus we are told that the reference . . . to a "Government-Supported Medical Team" gives the misleading impression that the United States Government endorsed or approved the findings . . . Surely the fact that the word "supported" might have alternative dictionary definitions . . . is not alone sufficient. . . . Most words *do* have alternative dictionary definitions; if that in itself were a sufficient legal criterion, few advertisements would survive. Here, no impression is conveyed that the product itself has its source in or is being endorsed by the Government. . . .

The Commission's third objection deals with. . . . the statement that "Bayer Aspirin, taken as directed, is as gentle to the stomach as a plain sugar pill." "Sugar pill," we are told, is misleading terminology; the advertisement should have used the word "placebo." Again, we are confronted by a simple problem of communication. For how can we expect our hypothetically slow-witted reader to react when he reads that "Bayer Aspirin is as gentle to the stomach as a placebo"! Most likely, he will either read on, completely unaware of the significance of the statement, or impatiently turn the page. Perhaps he will turn to his neighbor, and in response to a request for a definition of the troublesome word be greeted with the plausible query, "A *what?*" (This assumes that the reader will have been able to muster the correct pronunciation of the word.) But, all this aside, the pill used as a control in this case was indeed constituted of milk sugar [and a cornstarch binder] and the use of the term "sugar pill" was neither inaccurate nor misleading.

. . . .

The Commission relies heavily . . . upon *P. Lorillard Co.* v. *FTC.* . . . There, *Reader's Digest* sponsored a scientific study of the major cigarettes. . . . It accompanied its conclusions with a chart which revealed that, although Old Gold cigarettes ranked lowest in [nicotine, tars, and resins], the quantitative differences between the brands were insignificant. . . . The tenor of the study is revealed by the cheery words to the smoker "who need no longer worry as to which cigarette can most effectively nail down his coffin. For one nail is just about as good as another." Old Gold trumpeted its dubious success, claiming that it was found lowest in nicotine, tars and resins. . . . The Court quite properly upheld a cease and desist order. . . . An examination of that case shows that it is completely distinguishable in at least two obvious and significant respects. Although the statements made by Old Gold were at best literally true, they were used in the advertisement to convey an impression diametrically opposed to that intended by the writer of the article. . . . Moreover as to the specifics of brand-comparison, it was found that anyone reading the advertisement would gain "the very definite impression that Old Gold cigarettes were less irritating to the throat and less harmful than other leading brands. . . . The truth was exactly the opposite. . . . In the instant case, Sterling Drug can in no sense be said to have conveyed a misleading impression as to either the spirit or the specifics of the article published in the *Journal of the American Medical Association.*

The Fool's Standard and the Reasonable Person: A Policy Switch

For decades the Federal Trade Commission and the courts refused to apply a "reasonable person" test or other objective criteria to deceptive advertising claims. Under the rule, which was applied consistently since at least the 1930's, the FTC Act was considered to be intended to protect the general public, which includes "the ignorant, the unthinking, and the credulous." It did not matter that most of the consuming public would disbelieve a deceptive ad. As the Supreme Court noted

> There is no duty resting on a citizen to suspect the honesty of those with whom he transacts business. Laws are made to protect the trusting as well as the suspicious. The best element of business has long since decided that honesty should govern competitive enterprises, and that the rule of caveat emptor should not be relied upon to reward fraud and deception.

Thus, the question was not whether the ad would deceive a reasonable person, an intelligent person, or a wise or suspicious person; the question was whether the ad would tend to deceive even the dullest and most trusting member of the public. For this reason, the test has been called **the fool's standard.**

The fool's standard has been severely criticized and may be in retreat before the courts in cases like *Sterling Drug.* The standard also presented problems when sales puffery is involved. Almost every advertisement claims its product is the *best* or is *perfect* or *easy to use* or *safe and simple,* all terms that, if considered objectively and from the standpoint of "the ignorant, the unthinking and the credulous," simply cannot be true. In general, the FTC has permitted such puffing on the grounds that it simply cannot be taken literally. Even such terms may violate the Act if the product cannot possibly fulfill the claims, however. For example, products that are purchased from junk dealers or are worn, dirty, or valueless cannot be "the best in the market."

In a major policy change, the FTC announced a "Policy Statement on Enforcement of Deceptive Acts and Practices," on October 24, 1983, which seems to overturn the old fool's standard. Under the new policy, to be deceptive the representation must be likely to mislead "reasonable consumers under the circumstances." The test is whether the consumer's interpretation of the advertisement is reasonable, and the FTC will look to the effect of the practice on a reasonable number of consumers in the group to whom the advertisement is targeted. The FTC will, under this standard, generally not bring actions based on subjective claims, such as taste, feel, appearance, or smell, or on correctly stated opinion claims. Opinion claims continue to be actionable if they are not honestly held, if they misrepresent the qualifications of the holder or the basis of his opinion, or if the recipient reasonably interprets them as implied statements of fact.

The statement also added the term *materiality* as an element of deception. Some statements are presumptively material: any express claims; omission of information that the seller knows, or should know an ordinary consumer would need to evaluate the product or service; or any false claims. The FTC Statement also considers claims or omissions material if they significantly involve health, safety, or other areas of concern to a reasonable consumer.

While the FTC has changed its policy, at least for the present, the courts have not yet followed the Commission's lead. Before the courts, the fool's standard is still applied, although decisions like *Sterling Drug* cast some doubt on its future viability even there.

Specific Deceptive Advertising Techniques

In the words of the House Conference Report on the Wheeler-Lea Act, "there is no limit to human inventiveness in the field" of deceptive advertising. While the general principles apply to every case, imaginative advertisers have developed unnumbered methods of deceiving the public. The Federal Trade Commission has been confronted with numerous forms of deceptive advertising in the past, and it is impossible to list the methods that have, to this point, been held illegal. A complete list would fill the rest of this textbook and perhaps several more volumes, but it is possible to set out some of the more basic deceptive advertising schemes in broad strokes.

Deceptive Price Claims   Americans love a bargain. One of the most popular forms of advertising claims deals with price representations that appeal to our bargain-hunting instincts. Those claims may violate the FTC Act in many respects.

Comparisons to Former Prices: One of the most common price advertisements compares the present or "bargain" price with a former price for the same item, such as "Was $6.98, now $4.00." Such advertising is perfectly legitimate—if it is truthful. But, too often, the bargain is not really a bargain because the prior price simply never existed or was never offered in good faith.

The *FTC Guides* provide that if the former price is genuine, the ad is permissible. But, if the former price is fictitious, the agency will take action. The former price must be the "actual *bona fide* price at which the article was offered to the public on a regular basis for a reasonably substantial period of time." A retailer could not, for example, first raise the price and then lower the price to seemingly offer an unusual bargain; nor could a retailer compare to a price offered at some remote period in the past, nor use a price only offered for a short time, set simply to be used as a comparison. If the retailer uses the term *sale* without a prior comparison, the amount of reduction must not be so insignificant as to be meaningless. A sale of a $10.00 item for $9.99 would be deceptive, for example.

"Comparable Value" Claims: Another common price advertisement compares the seller's price with prices charged by other retailers, such as "Brand X pens, Price Elsewhere $10, Our Price $7.50." Again, the comparison must be truthful and not misleading. The retailer should be reasonably certain that the higher prices he advertises do not appreciably exceed the price at which substantial sales of the article are being made in the area. If only a few sellers in the area are charging the higher price, the "price elsewhere" is an exception, not the prevailing price, and is deceptive.

A very similar form deals with price comparisons to similar, but not identical goods, such as "Comparable Value $15.00—Our Price, $10.00." The item to which the comparison is made should be essentially similar and the price quoted should again be the prevailing, not the exceptional, price.

"List" and "Suggested Retail" Price Claims: Many manufacturers suggest the appropriate retail prices to be charged for goods, and many consumers believe that the suggested or list retail prices are indeed the actual prevailing prices at which the goods sell. But since the retailer is not required to charge the suggested price, often the price quoted bears little relationship to the actual prevailing price for the item. It is considered deceptive or misleading to quote the suggested retail price if the prevailing price for the item in the community is not the suggested price advertised.

"Special Deals": Retailers are quick to take advantage of any special circumstances which might indicate to the purchaser that a bargain is available. Special purchase, clearance sale, introductory offer, manufacturer's close-out, limited offer, repossession sale, cooperative buying, weaknesses in the market, and innumerable other special circumstances have been and are used to imply that the purchaser is getting some kind of bargain or "special deal." If the event is as the retailer describes it, there is no deception, providing that it does result in a genuine bargain to the consumer. But if the business has been "going out of business" for several years or if no real fire preceded the "fire sale" or if, in any other way, the event did not take place or there is no real bargain or the prices advertised are simply the retailer's customary price, the advertisement is deceptive and misleading.

"Free Goods" and Other Offers: Many advertisements feature such offers as "buy one, get one free," "2-for-1 sale," "half-price sale," "1¢ sale," and "50% Off." Literally, of course, the consumer is not getting anything free, since he must purchase one item in order to get the "free" item. The *FTC Guides* simply state that "No statement . . . of an offer to sell two articles for the price of one . . . should be used unless the sales price for the two articles is the advertiser's usual and customary retail price for the single article in the recent, regular course of his business."

FTC v. Mary Carter Paint Co.

382 U.S. 46, 86 S. Ct. 219, 15 L. Ed. 2d 128 (1965)

Mary Carter Paint distributed paint under its label in 27 states. The basic policy of the company was to sell one gallon of paint at a price comparable to that of the leading national brands and to give the purchaser a second can "free." The leading paint manufacturers had established a consumer preference that equated quality with price, and paint priced below the "quality price" was not considered "quality paint" by the consuming public. Mary Carter paint was in fact of equal quality to any other paint on the market. The advertised price was the only price at which a consumer could purchase Mary Carter paint, and the consumer need not accept the second can. There was no evidence at the hearing of any consumer complaints or of any actual deception of Mary Carter customers. The Commission entered a cease and desist order to prevent Mary Carter from representing that the second can was free. The Court of Appeals reversed the Commission's order, and the Commission appealed.

Mr. Justice BRENNAN delivered the opinion of the Court.

Although there is some ambiguity in the Commission's opinion, we cannot say that its holding constituted a departure from Commission Policy regarding the use of the commercially exploitable word "free." Initial efforts to define the term in decisions were followed by "Guides Against Deceptive Pricing." These informed businessmen that they might advertise an article as "free," even though purchase of another article was required, so long as the terms of the offer were clearly stated, the price of the article required to be purchased was not increased, and its quality and quantity were not diminished. With specific reference to two-for-the-price-of-one offers, the Guides required that either the sales price for the two be "the advertiser's usual and customary retail price for the single article in the recent, regular course of his business," or where the advertiser has not previously sold the article, the price for two be the "usual and customary" price for one in the relevant trade areas. These, of course, were guides, not fixed rules as such, and were designed to inform businessmen of the factors which would guide Commission decision. Although Mary Carter seems to have attempted to tailor its offer to come within their terms, the Commission found that it failed; the offer complied in appearance only. . . .

In sum, the Commission found that Mary Carter had no history of selling single cans of paint; it was marketing twins, and in allocating what is in fact the price of two cans to one can, yet calling one "free," Mary Carter misrepresented. It is true that respondent was not permitted to show that the quality of its paint matched those paints which usually and customarily sell in the $6.98 range, or that purchasers of paint estimate quality by the price they are charged. If both claims were established, it is arguable that any deception was limited to a representation that Mary Carter has a usual and customary price for single cans of paint, when it has no such price. However, it is not for courts to say whether this violates the Act. "[T]he Commission is often in a better position than are the courts to determine when a practice is 'deceptive' within the meaning of the Act." . . . There was substantial evidence in the record to support the Commission's finding; its determination that the practice here was deceptive was neither arbitrary nor clearly wrong. The Court of Appeals should have sustained it. . . .

Judgment . . . reversed. . . .

Mr. Justice HARLAN, dissenting.

In my opinion the basis for the Commission's action is too opaque to justify an upholding of its order in this case. . . .

In administering § 5 in the context of the many elusive questions raised by modern advertising, it is the duty of the Commission to speak and rule clearly so that law-abiding businessmen may know where they stand. In proscribing a practice uncomplained of by the public, effectively harmless to the consumer, allowed by the Commission's long-established policy statement, and only a hair-breadth away from advertising practices that the Commission will continue to permit, I think that the Commission in this instance has fallen far short of what is necessary to entitle its order to enforcement. . . .

Bait and Switch   One of the FTC's prime targets in deceptive advertising is the **bait and switch** technique. This sales device involves advertising of an item at a low, often incredibly modest, price to "bait" the consumer into the store. Upon arrival, the consumer is greeted by a variety of techniques designed to induce him to "switch" to an alternative, higher priced model of the same item. Salespersons will disparage the bait model, or tell the consumer that it is out-of-stock or, in extreme cases, simply refuse to sell the advertised item. Experienced shoppers are familiar with the technique, but less sophisticated buyers are often its victims.

The FTC has been very active in trying to eliminate bait advertising. The *FTC Guides* provide simply that "No advertising containing an offer to sell a product should be published when the offer is not a bona fide effort to sell the advertised product." The Commission has moved against numerous such schemes with a great deal of success.

Bait and switch must be distinguished from a legitimate technique of "trading up." In a trading-up situation, the retailer is willing to sell the advertised item and actually has sufficient stock of the item to fill the demand. The salesperson may extol the virtues of the higher-priced product, but he may not disparage the advertised item.

An interesting practice has developed in response to the Commission's strict attitude toward bait advertising. The **switch after sale** involves an actual sale and delivery of the advertised low-priced item, but the item usually works badly, if at all. When the consumer complains, the consumer is relieved to learn that retailer is willing to accept the malfunctioning item back if the consumer will "trade up" to a better model at a higher price. This technique, which has also been held illegal, should not be confused with legitimate efforts to adjust consumer complaints.

Several states have also enacted criminal statutes directed at both bait and switch and switch after sale techniques, sometimes involving jail terms and substantial fines for violators.

Deceptive Nondisclosure   Failure to tell the consumer something important about the product may be just as deceptive as an outright misrepresentation about the item. While the FTC has never required sellers to tell everything about a product, an advertisement should tell the consumer what he would normally want to know about a product, or would affect the consumer's decision to purchase the item. There are numerous cases in this area, covering many specific categories of matters which ought to be told to the consumer. The following are a few examples.

Product Contents and Construction: The FTC has broad authority to enforce a variety of laws dealing with product labelling in various industries, such as cigarette labelling, wool products labelling, and several others. But also under its broad Section 5 authority, the Commission may require that certain information about product contents and construction be disclosed. If an item is reprocessed, rebuilt, secondhand, repossessed, or otherwise previously used, the FTC generally requires that such facts be told to consumers. Changes in composition of existing products should also be disclosed, as where an ingredient is changed in a product already on the market. If the appearance of a product is deceptively similar to another item, such as a simulated diamond, the fact of simulation must be disclosed. Similarly, condensed and abridged books must be labelled as such.

Product Hazards: The FTC has also been granted substantial authority to deal with product hazards through labelling in a variety of specific statutes, including the Flammable Fabrics Act, the Hazardous Substance Act, and the Cigarette Labelling Act, and the Commission has acted to require specific labels of a variety of products, including the classic warning on cigarette packages.

The FTC also has broad authority to require disclosure under Section 5 in order to prevent deception by silence. If a toy is likely to break and present a hazard, the FTC may act to require a warning to that effect. However, many of those functions have been transferred to the Consumer Product Safety Commission.

Foreign Origin: Americans, it is thought, tend to favor American-made products. As a result, the FTC has a general rule that products manufactured in other countries should be labelled and identified as to their origin. The identification is not necessary if the foreign product has no American-produced competitors. The identification only relates to the product or its package, and advertisements for the foreign product are not required to identify the product as foreign-made.

Endorsements and Testimonials   One of the most effective advertising techniques deals with endorsements and testimonials, by famous people, by "the man on the street," or by governmentally sponsored or prestigious organizations. The *Sterling Drug* case involved problems of governmental endorsement of products, for example. Such endorsements and testimonials must in fact be made, of course, and it would be deceptive and misleading under Section 5 to claim that an endorsement or testimonial existed when in fact it did not.

Implicit Government Endorsement: The U.S. government does not endorse products and any implication that a product is so endorsed is considered misleading or deceptive. In several cases, corporations with names that implied government sponsorship were ordered to change their name, such as the United States Testing Company, which tested products for other companies. Likewise, it is deceptive and misleading to claim or imply endorsement by well-respected private organizations, such as Mayo Brother's Vitamins, which had no connection with the Mayo Clinic; to use the term *M.D.* or *doctor* to falsely suggest that the product has been made by or under the supervision of a doctor; and to use the term *Red Cross* without the notice that "This product has no connection whatsoever with the American National Red Cross."

Solicited and Paid Testimonials: Many testimonials are solicited and paid for by the advertiser. The basic question is whether the solicitation or compensation should be disclosed as part of the advertisement. The rule appears to be that truthful testimonials need not disclose the facts that they were solicited or paid. However, under some state laws and decisions, a person endorsing a product may be liable under either contract or tort theories of warranty or fraud if the the product does not live up to the endorsement made. The advertiser may not imply that payment was *not* made if it in fact was made.

Recommendations by Nonusers: It is clear that testimonials must be based on actual use of the product. One such case involved a testimonial by Olympic star Bruce Jenner that he ate a certain cereal every morning, when in fact he did not. While payment of consideration in such a case need not be disclosed, the testimonial must be the endorser's own views or opinion, based on actual use of the product.

False Testimonials: Several advertisers have attempted to "get around" the prohibitions against false advertising by having the endorser make a false claim for a product, and then simply quote the endorsement in the ad. The courts have held that the use of false testimonials is in fact more obnoxious than a simple false advertisement, since the American public, perhaps illogically, tends to put great stock in such endorsements.

Tests and Surveys   Perhaps the increasing sophistication of the American buying public has led advertisers to make greater use of scientific tests and surveys that in some way "prove" their products' superiority. Clearly, manufacturers are prohibited from falsely advertising that their products have been tested or a survey has taken place. And, the published results of surveys must be clear and not deceptive. Tests must be made in comparison with products readily available to the consumer, not some "straw man" product devised for the purposes of the test. There must be some reference to the standards used in the test; that is, mileage tests must refer to the conditions under which the tests were run. Advertisers may not use incomplete results if complete results would disclose different conclusions.

Consumer and expert surveys are another popular advertising technique, one which is perfectly permissible, if the sampling process is accurate and the advertisement fairly states the results. In order to back up any survey or test results, the advertiser should retain a full file of the test and survey procedures in the event of challenge by the Commission.

Lotteries, Contests and Games   Since 1914, the FTC has been committed to eliminating games of chance as merchandising devices. Thus, in an early decision, the FTC, and later the Supreme Court, held that a scheme in which children were enticed to purchase candy on the chance that one of the wrapped pieces might contain money constituted an "unfair trade practice," even before the Wheeler-Lea Amendments. Similar schemes in which varying sums of money were placed inside containers of coffee were also outlawed in several cases. So popular were such schemes in the 1920's and 1930's that on one day in 1934 the Commission made 48 findings in candy lottery cases. The fact that everyone got something, even if it was only a penny piece of candy, did not detract from the results. The Commission flatly outlawed the sale of devices used in such lottery schemes, such as punchboards and pushcards.

Lotteries are simply illegal, based not so much on their appeal to the gambling instinct in the American consumer but on the fact that the consumers do not get something for nothing. A contest, on the other hand, involves some skill or similar criteria on which the price is awarded. A contest must be a bona fide competition, and the rules must be fully disclosed and truthfully represented. If the contest is so simple that everybody wins and is really a method of procuring customers, it is considered deceptive. Likewise, the prizes must actually exist and their value must be represented accurately.

Games of chance are another popular promotional device. Such games usually have many of the features of a lottery, except that no purchase is necessary. In 1966, the FTC investigated many long-running games in the food and gasoline retailing businesses, and found that many of them were "deceptive" in several ways. Prizes were allocated to the stores or regions in which sales were poor; winners were selected in the early weeks of the game in order to have the greatest impact; large prizes were advertised out of proportion to their availability; and the games were often terminated before the prizes were awarded. Following this investigation, the FTC established rules for such games, requiring that the prizes be awarded randomly, that all of the prizes actually be awarded, and that the game be "secure" against tampering. Most importantly, the rules require complete disclosure of the odds of winning, the length of the games, the number of prizes, and the total number of "game pieces" or entries. Lists of winners must be made available as well.

Pictures and Illustrations   A picture may be worth a thousand words and, in advertising, may be worth millions of dollars. Simply put, photographs and illustrations must accurately portray the product advertised. A photo of one product, showing features not present on the product to be sold, is clearly deceptive.

A much finer point involves *collateral misrepresentation,* in which the presence of a picture implies a fact which is not true. A photo of a man in a white coat with a stethoscope around his neck, holding up a bottle of a pain reliever, could create the impression that the product was endorsed by physicians. Such ads have been considered misrepresentations in some cases. If trick photography, such as superimposition or time-lapse photography, is used, that fact must be disclosed.

Television Advertising   Over the last 30 years, television advertising has become the predominant method of marketing products and, also, the predominant area of FTC concern. Television permits a much wider variety of techniques to the advertiser and, necessarily, involves some broader opportunities for deception. But the limitations of the small screen also present real difficulties for the advertiser who, in good faith, wants to comply with the law and for the FTC, which in good faith, wants to eliminate deception in advertising. As noted in one opinion

> Everyone knows that on television all that glitters is not gold. On a black and white screen white looks grey and blue looks white; the lily must be painted. Coffee looks like mud. Real ice cream melts much more quickly than the firm but false sundae. The plain fact is, except by props and mock-ups, some objects cannot be shown on television as the viewer, in his mind's eye, knows the essence of the object.

Many of the same concerns raised about still pictures may be raised regarding television. The product actually advertised must be pictured and collateral misrepresentation is also controlled. The TV screen lends itself particularly to tests and demonstrations. The problem is that such tests should prove some *meaningfully relevant point about the product.* For example, one ad showed two separate razors, the advertised brand and a "nonsafety" variety, each "shaving" a boxing glove. The nonsafety razor left a long, ugly gash in the glove, while the advertised brand did no damage at all. The FTC said the demonstration was theatrical but proved nothing except that the advertised razor was better at shaving boxing gloves. The following decision considers the problem of television advertising in detail.

FTC v. Colgate-Palmolive Co.

380 U.S. 374, 85 S. Ct. 1035, 13 L. Ed. 2d 904 (1965)

In the Court's words, this case "arises out of an attempt by respondent Colgate-Palmolive Company to prove to the television public that its shaving cream, Rapid Shave, "outshaves them all." At issue were three TV commercials designed to show that Rapid Shave could even shave sandpaper. An announcer told the audience that "To prove RAPID SHAVE'S super-moisturizing power, we put it right from the can onto this tough, dry sandpaper. It was apply—soak—and *off* in one stroke." The camera showed the process while the announcer spoke.

In fact, sandpaper could not be shaved immediately following the application of Rapid Shave, but required 80 minutes of soaking. And, in fact, the substance was not sandpaper at all, but a simulated mock-up consisting of plexiglass to which sand had been applied. The mock-up was used because TV signals would have made real sandpaper look like colored paper. Neither the moistening time nor the mock-up was disclosed to the viewing public. In fact, however, Rapid Shave could shave sandpaper, given sufficient moistening time.

The FTC held that the commercials were deceptive and issued a cease and desist order. The Court of Appeals affirmed, but refused that part of the Commission's order that forbade the future use of undisclosed simulations. The question before the court was the proper use of simulations and mock-ups. The company had not contested the holding that the commercial itself was a misrepresentation of the fact that Rapid Shave could *immediately* shave sandpaper. The FTC appealed.

Mr. Chief Justice WARREN delivered the opinion of the Court.

. . . .

. . . We granted certiorari to consider the Commission's conclusion that even if an advertiser has himself conducted a test, experiment or demonstration which he honestly believes will prove a certain product claim, he may not convey to television viewers the false impression that they are seeing the test, experiment or demonstration for themselves, when they are not because of the undisclosed use of mock-ups.

. . . The parties agree that § 5 prohibits the intentional misrepresentation of any fact which would constitute a material factor in a purchaser's decision whether to buy. They differ, however, in their conception of what "facts" constitute a "material factor" in a purchaser's decision to buy. Respondents submit, in effect, that the material facts are those which deal with the substantive qualities of a product. The Commission, on the other hand, submits that the misrepresentation of *any* fact so long as it materially induces a purchaser's decision to buy is a deception prohibited by § 5.

The Commission's interpretation of what is a deceptive practice seems more in line with the decided cases than that of respondents. This Court said. . . ." [T]he public is entitled to get what it chooses, though the choice may be dictated by caprice or by fashion or perhaps by ignorance." . . .

. . . .

Respondents claim that [prior] cases are irrelevant to our decision because they involve misrepresentations related to the product itself and not merely to the manner in which an advertising message is communicated. This distinction misses the mark for two reasons. In the first place, the present case is not concerned with a mode of communication, but with a misrepresentation that viewers have objective proof of a seller's product claim over and above the seller's word. Secondly, all of the above cases, like the present case, deal with methods designed to get a consumer to purchase a product, not with whether the product, when purchased, will perform up to expectations. . . .

We agree with the Commission, therefore, that the undisclosed use of plexiglass in the present commercials was a material deceptive practice. . . . Respondents claim that it will be impractical to inform the viewing public that it is not seeing an actual test, experiment or demonstration, but we think it inconceivable that the ingenious advertising world will be unable, if it so desires, to conform to the Commission's insistence that the public be not misinformed. If, however, it becomes impossible or impractical to show simulated demonstrations on television in a truthful manner, this indicates that television is not a medium that lends itself to this type of commercial, not that the commercial must survive at all costs. Similarly unpersuasive is respondents' objection that the Commission's decision discriminates against sellers whose product claims cannot be "verified" on television without the use of simulations. All methods of advertising do not equally favor every seller. If the inherent limitations of a method do not permit its use in the way a seller desires, the seller cannot by material misrepresentation compensate for those limitations.

. . . .

. . . The Court of Appeals has criticized the reference in the Commission's order to "test, experiment or demonstration" as not capable of practical interpretation. It could find no difference between the Rapid Shave commercial and a commercial which extolled the goodness of ice cream while giving viewers a picture of a scoop of mashed potatoes appearing to be ice cream. We do not understand this difficulty. In the ice cream case the mashed potato prop is not being used for additional proof of the product claim, while the purpose of the Rapid Shave commercial is to give the viewer objective proof of the claims made. If in the ice cream hypothetical the focus of the commercial becomes the undisclosed potato prop and the viewer is invited, explicitly or by implication, to see for himself the truth of the claims about the ice cream's rich texture and full color, and perhaps compare it to a "rival product," then the commercial has become similar to the one now before us. Clearly, however, a commercial which depicts happy actors delightedly eating ice cream that is in fact mashed potatoes or drinking a product appearing to be coffee but which is in fact some other substance is not covered by the present order.

. . . .

The judgment of the Court of Appeals is reversed. . . .

Federal Trade Commission Remedies for Deceptive Advertising

For most of its history, the FTC was restricted to issuing cease and desist orders to offenders. If the party continued to violate the order, the Commission had to apply to the Attorney General to bring a civil action in federal court to secure a civil penalty of not more than $5,000 per violation. In 1973, the maximum civil penalty was increased to $10,000 per violation. In 1975, the remedies were broadly expanded in the Federal Trade Commission Improvements Act.

Under the FTC Improvements Act, the FTC may now bring an action in its own name to recover penalties from offenders. Perhaps more importantly, the FTC may bring a civil action against any "person, partnership or corporation which violates any rule under this Act respecting unfair or deceptive acts or practices . . . with actual knowledge or knowledge fairly implied on the basis of objective circumstances that such act is unfair or deceptive and is prohibited by such rule." The action may be brought directly in federal court and the penalty for violation is a civil fine of up to $10,000 for each violation.

Retroactive Advertising

Cease and desist orders may be framed in extremely broad terms, and the Supreme Court has approved the broad wording of these orders on the theory that "the Commission is the expert body to determine what remedy is necessary to eliminate the unfair or deceptive trade practice. . . ." One recent technique utilized by the Commission is **retroactive advertising,** which is a cease and desist order that requires the advertiser found guilty of deceptive advertising to "correct" the misimpression left by the misleading scheme. Retroactive, or *corrective,* advertising has become a popular method of remedying deceptive advertising, as described in the following case.

Warner-Lambert Co. v. FTC

562 F. 2d 749 (D.C. Circuit, 1977)

Warner-Lambert, the manufacturer of Listerine mouthwash, advertised that Listerine "kills germs by million on contact" on its label and, in its television ads, claimed that Listerine cured colds. At a hearing, it was shown that Listerine in fact "has no efficacy in the prevention of colds, sore throats or in the amelioration of colds symptoms, including sore throats." Following the hearing, the FTC issued a cease and desist order, which ordered the firm to

(1) cease and desist from representing that Listerine will cure colds or sore throats, prevent colds or sore throats, or that users of Listerine will have fewer colds than non-users;

(2) cease and desist from representing that Listerine is a treatment for, or will lessen the severity of, colds or sore throats; that it will have any significant beneficial effect on symptoms of colds; or that the ability of Listerine to kill germs is of medical significance in the treatment of colds or sore throats or their symptoms;

(3) cease and desist from disseminating any advertisement for Listerine unless it is clearly and conspicuously disclosed in each such advertisment, in the exact language below, that: "Contrary to prior advertising, Listerine will not help prevent colds or sore throats or lessen their severity." This requirement extends only to the next ten million dollars of Listerine advertising.

Warner-Lambert appealed the order to the U.S. Circuit Court of Appeals.

J. SKELLY WRIGHT, Circuit Judge:

. . . .

Petitioner contends that even if its advertising claims in the past were false, the portion of the Commission's order requiring "corrective advertising" exceeds the Commission's statutory power. The argument is based upon a literal reading of Section 5 of the Federal Trade Commission Act, which authorizes the Commission to issue "cease and desist" orders against violators and does not expressly mention any other remedies. The Commission's position, on the other hand, is that the affirmative disclosure that Listerine will not prevent colds or lessen their severity is absolutely necessary to give effect to the prospective cease and desist order; a hundred years of false cold claims have built up a large reservoir of erroneous consumer belief which would persist, unless corrected, long after petitioner ceased making the claims.

. . .[T]he threshold question is whether the Commission has the authority to issue such an order. We hold that it does . . . .

. . . [I]t is clear that the Commission has the power to shape remedies which go beyond the simple cease and desist order. Our next inquiry must be whether a corrective advertising order is for any reason outside the range of permissible remedies. Petitioner . . . argue[s] that it is because (1) legislative history precludes it, (2) it impinges on the First Amendment, and (3) it has never been approved by any court.

A. Legislative History

Petitioner relies on the legislative history of the 1914 Federal Trade Commission Act and the Wheeler-Lea amendments to it in 1938 for the proposition that corrective advertising was not contemplated. In 1914 and in 1938 Congress chose not to authorize such remedies as criminal penalties, treble damages, or civil penalties, but that fact does not dispose of the question of corrective advertising. . . . [P]etitioner's construction of [the statute] runs directly contrary to the congressional intent as expressed in a later subsection: "Nothing in this section shall be construed to affect any authority of the Commission under any other provision of law."

In the next section, the court rejected the claim that corrective advertising was barred by the 1st Amendment. Later, Warner-Lambert raised the issue once again on rehearing, basing its arguments on *Virginia State Board of Pharmacy* v. *Virginia Citizen's Consumer Council,* (see Chapter 3, page 76). The Court found that "Untruthful speech, commercial or otherwise, has never been protected for its own sake" and that, therefore, the FTC could restrict and correct such speech.

C. Precedents

According to petitioner, "The first reference to corrective advertising in Commission decisions occurred in 1970, nearly fifty years and untold numbers of false advertising cases after passage of the Act." In petitioner's view, the late emergence of this "newly discovered" remedy is itself evidence that it is beyond the Commission's authority. This argument fails on two counts. First the fact that an agency has not asserted a power over a period of years is not proof that the agency lacks such power. Second, and more importantly, we are not convinced that the corrective advertising remedy is really such an innovation. The label may be newly coined, but the concept is well established. It is simply that under certain circumstances an advertiser may be required to make affirmative disclosure of unfavorable facts.

One such circumstance is when an advertisement that did not contain the disclosure would be misleading. For example, the Commission has ordered the sellers of treatments for baldness to disclose that the vast majority of cases of thinning hair and baldness are attributable to heredity, age, and endocrine balance (so-called "male pattern baldness") and that their treatment would have no effect whatever on this type of baldness. It has ordered the promoters of a device for stopping bedwetting to disclose that the device would not be of value in cases caused by organic defects or diseases. And it has ordered the makers of Geritol, an iron supplement, to disclose that Geritol will relieve symptoms of tiredness only in persons who suffer from iron deficiency anemia, and that the vast majority of people who experience such symptoms do not have such a deficiency.

. . . .

Having established that the Commission does have the power to order corrective advertising in appropriate cases, it remains to consider whether use of the remedy against Listerine is warranted and equitable. We have concluded that part 3 of the order should be modified to delete the phrase "Contrary to prior advertising." With that modification, we approve the order.

. . . .

The Commission has adopted the following standard for the imposition of corrective advertising:

[I]f a deceptive advertisement has played a substantial role in creating or reinforcing in the public's mind a false and material belief which lives on after the false advertising ceases, there is clear and continuing injury to competition and to the consuming public as consumers continue to make purchasing decisions based on the false belief. Since this injury cannot be averted by merely requiring respondent to cease disseminating the advertisement, we may appropriately order respondent to take affirmative action designed to terminate the otherwise continuing ill effects of the advertisement.

We think this standard is entirely reasonable. It dictates two factual inquiries: (1) did Listerine's advertisements play a substantial role in creating or reinforcing in the public's mind a false belief about the product? and (2) would this belief linger on after the false advertising ceases? It strikes us that if the answer to both questions is not yes, companies everywhere may be wasting their massive advertising budgets. Indeed, it is more than a little peculiar to hear petitioner assert that its commercials really have no effect on consumer belief.

. . . .

We turn next to the specific disclosure required. . . . Petitioner is ordered to include this statement in every future advertisement for Listerine for a defined period. . . .

These specifications are well calculated to assure that the disclosure will reach the public. It will necessarily attract the notice of readers, viewers and listeners, and be plainly conveyed. Given these safeguards, we believe the preamble "Contrary to prior advertising" is not necessary. It can serve only two purposes: either to attract attention that a correction follows or to humiliate the advertiser. The Commission claims only the first purpose for it, and this we think is obviated by the other terms of the order. The second purpose, if it were intended, might be called for in an egregious case of deliberate deception, but this is not one. . . .

Accordingly, the order, as modified, is affirmed.

Summary and Conclusions

Deceptive and misleading advertising is regulated by the common law, state statutes, and the Federal Trade Commission Act. Common-law theories of regulation included fraud and warranty theories, both of which are difficult to prove and less than satisfactory to control misleading advertising. Common-law protections of competition are somewhat more satisfactory, but the torts of trademark infringement, disparagement, passing off and simulation, misappropriation and malicious competition are also difficult to prove.

In the 1914 Federal Trade Commission Act, "unfair methods of competition" were prohibited. A 1938 amendment, the Wheeler-Lea Act, extended the protections of the FTC Act to consumers and enabled the FTC to reach deceptive or misleading advertising.

In considering such misleading or deceptive advertising, the FTC has generally required an act to be literally true, and even a tendency to deceive in a literally truthful advertisement will be considered misleading. The standard applied by the courts is the so-called fool's standard, in which the question is whether the ad would deceive the most ignorant and unthinking consumer. The fool's standard has been abandoned by the FTC, however. The deception need not be intentional nor even made with knowledge of its falsity, and ambiguous ads will be construed to violate the statute.

Under these strict standards, the FTC has developed rules and guidelines covering a large number of specific forms of deception. Generally, the courts have found that a commission determination, if based on the evidence, should stand.

PRO AND CON

ISSUE: Will the Marketplace Regulate Deceptive Advertising?

PRO: There Are Adequate Market Mechanisms to Regulate Deceptive Advertising
Richard N. Posner*

It must be considered whether there are adequate market or legal mechanisms (apart from the type of legal regulation carried on by the Federal Trade Commission) that will deter sellers from making false claims.

There are at least four mechanisms available.

---

*From *Regulation of Advertising by the FTC* (Washington, D.C.: American Enterprise Institute for Public Policy Research, 1973), pp. 4–6, 7–8. Reprinted by permission.

The first is the knowledge and intelligence of the consumer. Many false claims would not be worth making simply because the consumer knows better than to believe them. Rising levels of education have probably reduced the credulity of the average consumer, who, without making a substantial investment in research, can doubtless see through many potential forms of dishonest advertising. This conclusion is especially convincing when one considers products that the consumer inspects or samples before purchasing. . . . Misrepresentations of a cantaloupe's ripeness, the comfort of a pair of shoes, or the glitter of a necklace would rarely be attempted, because they would so rarely succeed. The composition of the shoes or of the necklace might be a different matter.

The second factor that operates to discourage the making of false claims about products is the cost to a seller of developing a reputation for dishonesty. A seller cannot expect a false claim to go undetected indefinitely. If the profitability of his business depends on repeated sales to the same customers, as is true of most established sellers, a policy of false advertising is likely to be short-sighted and therefore bad business. . . .

Conversely, fraud may be attractive to two kinds of sellers. The first is one who sells a product (or service) whose effectiveness is so uncertain that consumers may not detect false claims about its performance even in the long run—as with providers of medical care. The second type of seller is one whose dependence on repeat customers, or on a good reputation generally, is so slight that he is immune to effective retaliation by former customers. . . . An example would be an itinerant peddler.

A third constraint on false advertising is competition. If A's competitor, B, makes a false claim designed to increase B's sales, and the claim is believed by consumers, A will lose sales to B. This will give A an incentive either to rebut B's false claims in an advertising campaign or to sue him. Three qualifications are necessary here, however.

First, A's incentive to rebut the falsity will be limited by the costs of doing so in relation to the gain from recapturing the sales lost to B. That gain may be slight if B's falsehood results in diverting to him a small number of sales from each of many competing firms. . . .

Second, A may do just as well by matching B's falsehood as by attempting to refute it. . . .

Third, if an industry is highly competitive, the costs of entry into and exit from the industry tend to be low. This suggests that the penalty for a firm that develops a reputation for dishonest dealing may be smaller in highly competitive industries.

The monopolization of an industry . . . is conducive to deceptive advertising in two respects. First, the likelihood of effective customer retaliation when the fraud is unmasked is small: the customer has no close substitute to which he can turn . . . Second, the incentive of other sellers to combat false claims is weak. . . .

The fourth deterrent to fraud that we will mention consists of private law remedies. A material misrepresentation in a consumer sale will generally constitute both a breach of contract and a tort. Frequently, to be sure, the cost of enforcing a legal claim will be greater than the value of the product or service involved in the deception. But the emergence of the consumer class action, which permits the pooling of a large number of small consumer claims, has undermined this objection. . . . Moreover, a legal claim or fraud may be quite inexpensive for the consumer to prosecute if the transaction is so arranged that the burden of enforcement falls on the seller (the consumer may be refusing to complete payment under an installment sales contract, claiming that the sale was fraudulent. In some cases, in addition, an individual claim will be so large that it clearly justifies the costs of private suit. . . .

CON: The Case for Government Regulation of Advertising
Robert Pitofsky*

It is occasionally argued that the government has no legitimate role to play in the regulation of advertising, or a very modest role at best, since usually there are adequate market incentives for sellers to provide relevant market information, and to challenge, through their own access to advertising

---

*From "Beyond Nader: Consumer Protection and the Regulation of Advertising," 90 *Harvard Law Review*, 661, 663–670. Copyright © 1977 by the Harvard Law Review Association. Reprinted by permission.

channels, false claims by rivals. In the rare situations where market incentives are inadequate, competitors or consumers may resort to the courts to remedy the effects of false advertising. Finally industry self-regulation may be seen as an alternative to government regulation.

A. Market Failure as a Cause of Consumer Abuse

. . . [T]here . . . remain many areas where key information necessary for consumers to make a sensible choice between rival brands, or to decide whether to buy the product at all, is absent. Until the government intervened and required or induced disclosure, accurate information was not available in the market concerning the durability of light bulbs, octane ratings for gasoline, tar and nicotine content of cigarettes, mileage per gallon for automobiles, or care labeling of textile wearing apparel. At present there continues to be little accurate information available to determine the comparative prices of life insurance policies, funeral services, eyeglasses sold at retail, and legal services;. . . . Moreover, while in many of these product categories there is a record of particular sellers exaggerating the qualities of their own product or service, rarely is there an instance of rivals explicitly challenging those questionable claims.

The causes of such market failures are not particularly difficult to trace. If the seller is a monopolist, it may concentrate promotional efforts on public image advertising. . . . In tight oligopolistic markets, sellers may shy away from disclosures concerning product characteristics for the same reasons they avoid price cutting. . . .

In other product areas, disclosure may rebound to the disadvantage of all sellers. For instance, an intensive advertising campaign stressing low tar and nicotine content as a way of diminishing the health hazards involved in smoking could result in underscoring the health problem and reducing total cigarette sales. . . .

Accumulation and disclosure of accurate product information also might not be undertaken because it would be inordinately expensive—either in absolute terms or because only a relatively small class of consumers would use it. Chemical formulae for over-the-counter drugs, for example, may be incomprehensible to the average consumer. Complexity of disclosed information may also explain the apparent failure of unit pricing data to influence consumers to switch to lower priced brands.

Somewhat different considerations may account for the fact that sellers rarely take advantage of their own media access to challenge claims made by others. In markets with many sellers, counter-advertising may have no appreciable effect. . . . In oligopolistic markets, fear of mutually disadvantageous counter advertising may discourage any firm from initiating such a program. In addition, until recently, explicit counter-advertising on TV was impossible because of network rules preventing advertisers from naming competitive products. . . . Thus most companies prefer to allocate their marketing budget to the accentuation of the affirmative qualities of their own products.

The inability of the free market to generate sufficient incentives for sellers to expose deceptive claims by competitors is indicated by the fact that in scores of proceedings in which the FTC successfully challenged the truth of major advertising themes, there was not a single instance in which rivals used their own access to channels of consumer information to expose deceptions. . . .

B. Alternative Systems of Consumer Protection

Where there are instances of consumer abuse or exploitation as a result of false, misleading or irrelevant advertising, it does not necessarily follow that these need to be remedied by governmental intrusion into the marketplace. It is theoretically possible for consumers' interest to be protected through resort to the courts either by consumers themselves or by those sellers with superior products. . . . In addition, industry self-regulation might overcome problems in the information market more cheaply and promptly than governmental intervention. In practice, however, these alternative approaches have been largely inoperative. Their ineffectiveness is an understandable product of the existing legal system. . . .

Companies occasionally band together to share the expenses of combating "unfair competition". . . . This approach occasionally has had some effect, but is of little general significance. First, industry self-regulation must be carefully designed if problems under the antitrust laws are to be avoided. . . . Second, industry self-regulation schemes can involve considerable expense. . . .

. . . .

Market failure in the dissemination of product information and the ineffectiveness of possible alternative systems for ensuring truthful and relevant advertising indicate that some form of government regulation of the advertising process is warranted. . . .

DISCUSSION QUESTIONS

1. Assume that you purchased a toaster for $15.95 as a result of the seller's fraud, and that, a week later, the toaster stopped working. Assume also that the seller refused to "make good." What is your remedy? Do you file suit for the value of the toaster, if the filing fee is $8.00, the service of process fee is $10.00 (both of which the seller will pay—if you win), and you have to take off a day of work to prosecute the claim? Is this a reason for federal regulation of advertising? Does the class action procedure discussed in Chapter 4 help soften the result?

2. Do the *FTC Guides* really help the average businessperson? How many of the retailers in your hometown do you think have read them? Should the FTC advertise the Guides? How?

3. Should the fool's standard be changed? To what? What level of education would you pick? If you picked the average level of education or intelligence, does that mean it is permissible to deceive half the population? Who are we trying to protect, anyway?

4. Is a photograph of a very macho cowboy in a cigarette ad an example of collateral misrepresentation, conveying the illogical conclusion that smoking X brand of cigarettes will make you manly? How about jeans ads featuring beautiful young starlets in suggestive poses or liquor ads featuring young people frolicking on a beach? Don't these ads convey the same kind of deceptive and illogical conclusion as the man in the white coat holding up a painkiller? Should the FTC or the consumer be concerned?

5. Should ads directed at children be treated differently? In what ways?

6. The FTC may prohibit ads that have only a tendency to deceive the most ignorant and credulous consumer. It need not prove intent or knowledge and now may sue for damages, civil penalties, restitution and order retroactive advertising. Even in the light of the *Virginia Pharmacy* case discussed in Chapter 3, shouldn't all this violate the 1st Amendment?

CASE PROBLEMS

1. The plaintiff manufactured and sold metal safes under several patents. One of the special features of plaintiff's safes was an "explosion chamber" to protect against burglaries. The explosion chamber required the presence of a metal band around the door. Defendant sold safes without an explosion chamber, but with a metal band identical to plaintiff's. What tort, if any, is involved? Result? [*Ely-Norris Safe Co.* v. *Mosler Safe Co.,* 7 F. 2d 603 (2d Cir., 1925).]

2. Clairol hair coloring was advertised as coloring the hair permanently. Obviously, since hair grows, this cannot be the case. Has Clairol violated the FTC Act? [*Gelb* v. *FTC,* 144 F. 2d 580 (2d Cir., 1944).]

3. An inflatable rubber bladder called Swim-Ezy, to be worn under swimming trunks to keep nonswimmers afloat, was advertised as "invisible." Has the manufacturer deceived the public? [*Heinz* v. *Kirchner,* 63 FTC 1282 (1963).]

4. Wonder Bread was advertised with a television sequence that showed a human-looking figure magically "grow" in the background, while an announcer stated that "Wonder Bread builds strong bodies twelve ways," and made other statements which implied that the product was responsible or helpful in the growth of children. The bread did contain extra vitamins, but there was no proof that the bread had any effect on children's growth. Result? Does the result change at all if the commercials are run on a children's cartoon show? [In Re *I.T.T. Continental Baking Co.* 83 FTC 947 (1973).]

5. Louis' Used Cars advertises a 1983 Fitz-Peter Automobile for sale, with only 25,000 miles on the odometer. That much is literally true, but Louis has turned the odometer back from 85,000 miles. Philip, in the market for a Fitz-Peter, is choosing between two virtually identical cars, one sold by Louis and another sold by Gurney. Gurney, also a used car dealer, has not touched the odometer on her car, which reads 45,000 miles. Based solely on the odometer reading, Phillip buys the car from Louis. (1) Of which common law torts is Louis guilty? (2) Who may recover for each?

6. Sly owns a patent medicine company that advertises Sly's Tonic, a concoction of various vitamins, as a cure-all for baldness, gout, debilitation, and the common cold. Petruchio, who is not very bright, believes the ad and purchases the tonic, though virtually no one else believes the representation. Has Sly violated the FTC Act? Would he be prosecuted?

7. Helena, the owner of an appliance store, advertises a Rousillon Electric Range at a price of $350, with the representation that the price is "one-third off of our regular price, $100 under list, and $75 under comparable values in this area." In fact, Helena had never sold Rousillon Ranges before and no one else in 50 miles sold such ranges. The "list" price was indeed $450, but no one ever charged that price. Result?

8. Audrey, a famous author, was asked to endorse Le Beau wine in a magazine advertisement. Audrey was in fact a teetotaler and had never drunk Le Beau wine or any other kind. The money offered for the ad was too good, however, and Audrey took one sip of wine before the ad was published. The ad quoted Audrey as saying Le Beau was "the best wine I ever tasted." Is the ad deceptive?

SUGGESTED READINGS

Henderson, Gerard C. *The Federal Trade Commission: A Study in Administrative Law and Procedure* (New Haven, Conn.: Yale University Press, 1924, repr. 1968).

Kintner, Earl W. *A Primer on the Law of Deceptive Practices: A Guide for the Businessman* (New York: The Macmillan Co., 1971).

Kitch, Edmund, and Harvey S. Perlman. *Legal Regulation of the Competitive Process* (Mineola, N.Y.: The Foundation Press, 1979).

McCall, James R. *Consumer Protection* (St. Paul, Minn.: West Publishing Co., 1977).

McManis, Charles R. *The Law of Unfair Trade Practices in a Nutshell* (St. Paul, Minn.: West Publishing Co., 1983).

12

Consumer Law

I would give all my fame for a pot of ale, and safety.

William Shakespeare, Henry V, *Act III, scene ii*

Consumption is the sole end and purpose of production; and the interest of the producer ought to be attended to only so far as it may be necessary for promotion of that of the consumer.

Adam Smith, The Wealth of Nations *(1776)*

The buyer needs a hundred eyes, the seller not one.

George Herbert, Jacula Prudentum *(1651)*

Consumer movements are by no means new to the American political and legal scene. In many ways, the creation of the Interstate Commerce Commission in 1887, the antitrust laws, various regulations of food and drug purity in the very early 20th century, and the regulation of securities and investments in the 1930's were all a part of a continuing concern with the rights and security of "consumers." That concern has continued for over a century, although it proceeded in somewhat sporadic fashion. From the muckrakers of the turn of the century to the consumer advocates of the 1980's, consumerism has a long heritage in American politics.

In the 1960's and early 1970's, that movement reached a fever pitch and a great number of consumer-oriented changes were made in the legal system. At the same time, related movements took place in environmental protection and worker safety. Among the chief concerns of consumer advocates during that time were product safety and protection of the rights of consumers within a transaction. In many ways, President Kennedy identified the concerns of the movement in a speech to Congress when he stated the four basic rights of consumers: the right to *choose,* the right to *be informed,* the right to *safety,* and the right to *be heard.*

This chapter will deal with several facets of the law of consumer protection, including the common law of products liability, regulation of product warranties, the Consumer Product Safety Act, the Pure Food and Drug Act, the Fair Packaging and Labeling Act, and regulation of consumer transactions, including the Truth-in-Lending Act, the Fair Credit Reporting Act, the Equal Credit Opportunity Act, and others. The chapter will conclude with the ultimate consumer protection—bankruptcy.

Product Quality and Safety

The problems of ensuring product quality and product safety have been considered for centuries by the courts, but in the context of private contract and tort law. When a consumer purchased a product at common law, he entered into a private contract and the rights to quality and to a safe product were determined solely by that contract, with few exceptions. If the product was shoddily made or defective, the consumer had to resort to contract remedies. But consumer remedies were sharply limited by two common-law doctrines: the rules of *caveat emptor* and *privity of contract.*

Caveat Emptor

Caveat Emptor, literally 'let the buyer beware,' was a traditional common-law rule that required a buyer to inspect a product before a purchase was made. If an inspection was not made or if a defect that should have been found was not discovered, the buyer could not later complain that a product was defective. Buyers were also obligated to obtain expert advice on products beyond their expertise. Under this traditional rule, a buyer only had a remedy in cases involving fraud on the part of the seller or if the seller gave a "warranty" on the goods. Caveat emptor remains a general rule of law, but there are so many exceptions and qualifications to that rule, especially in the form of the implied warranties and developments in the field of strict liability, that caveat emptor is considered impotent.

Privity of Contract

The second problem for consumers in recovering for defective products was the rule of **privity of contract.** This rule held that the only duties arising between two parties to a contract were those imposed by the agreement. As a result, a purchaser only had a right to sue those persons with whom he had a contract. Usually this meant that a purchaser could only sue the retailer, the person with whom he had contracted. But most defects arise in the manufacture of the product, and the manufacturer usually does not have a contract with the ultimate purchaser. Retailers defended on the grounds that they did not cause the defect and manufacturers defended on the grounds that they did not have a contract with the consumer, hence no duty to those persons. It was not until a famous decision in 1916 that the doctrine of privity lost its hold (see *MacPherson* v. *Buick Motor Co.,* p. 417).

Even with the problems of caveat emptor and privity of contract, purchasers of defective products and persons injured by dangerous products continued to bring actions against the sellers of such goods. Such consumers had three basic actions in their arsenals: *negligence* theories, *strict liability,* and *breach of warranty.* All three theories were severely limited at the turn of the century. But, by judicial expansion and the adoption of uniform state laws and federal legislation, all three have grown into a vast body of modern law, the law of **products liability.**

Products Liability and Breach of Warranty

A **warranty** is any statement or representation about goods made by the seller having to do with the goods' character, quality, or title. A warranty must be material, in the sense that the representation induces, or tends to induce, the purchaser to buy the goods. Warranties may be express or implied, and may be oral or written. Warranties become a part of the contract of sale of the product, and if the product does not live up to the warranties given, the purchaser may have an action for breach of contract against the seller.

Perhaps the most common form of **express warranty** is the written "guarantee" given with many consumer products. But any express statement or representation by the seller may also be an express warranty, including a salesperson's informal comments about the goods, models, demonstrations, price lists, and advertisements. The statement must be either a promise, an agreement, or a statement about the quality of the goods, however. A mere opinion will not constitute a warranty. Since 1975, express warranties have been closely regulated by the Federal Trade Commission, as will be discussed.

Very early in the history of the law of sales, courts began to enforce not only the express warranties given by a seller but also certain **implied warranties,** which the courts found even without an express statement by the seller. As an 1815 case put it,

> [T]he purchaser has a right to expect a saleable article answering the description in the contract. Without any particular warranty, this is an implied term in every such contract. . . . [T]he intention of both parties must be taken to be, that it shall be saleable in the market. . . . The purchaser cannot be supposed to buy goods to lay them on a dunghill.

An implied warranty is thus a promise by the seller, supplied solely by the law, and existing solely because of the existence of a contract of sale.

Implied Warranties and the Uniform Commercial Code

In the mid-20th century, the concept of implied warranties was substantially broadened with the adoption of the Uniform Commercial Code (UCC) (see Chapter 6). The UCC defines three types of implied warranties: the *implied warranty of title,* the *implied warranty of merchantability,* and the *implied warranty of fitness for a partic-ular purpose.*

The **implied warranty of title** is a promise to the buyer that the seller has the right to transfer the goods, that the title is "good," and that there are no outstanding liens or claims on the goods. Sellers may make express warranties of title as well, and may "disclaim" the implied warranty of title if it is done specifically and clearly.

The **implied warranty of merchantability** is perhaps the buyer's best protection. That warranty is only given by persons who are defined as **merchants** in the code but any person who regularly deals in goods of that kind, claims to be an "expert" in those goods, or who employs a skilled agent in the sale is considered to be a merchant. In those cases, the seller implicitly promises that the goods are *merchantable,* a term given six meanings by the Code:

> U.C.C., 2-314(2). Goods to be merchantable must be at least such as
> (a) pass without objection in the trade under the contract description; and
> (b) in the case of fungible goods, are of fair average quality . . .; and
> (c) are fit for the ordinary purposes for which such goods are used; and
> (d) run, within the variations permitted by the agreement, of even kind, quality and quantity . . .; and
> (e) are adequately contained, packaged and labeled as the agreement may require; and
> (f) conform to the promises or affirmations of fact made on the container or label if any.

A breach of any of those six conditions is treated as a breach of contract and gives the buyer several remedies under the Code.

The **implied warranty of fitness for a particular purpose** is only given under specific circumstances: the seller must know of the buyer's specific requirements for the goods and the buyer must rely on the seller's skill and judgment in choosing the goods. For example, a restaurant owner may wish to buy a toaster for use in her place of business, where it will be used almost continuously. If she simply purchases a toaster from a retailer, she will receive only the implied warranty of merchantability, and if the toaster fails to fulfill her special needs she will be without a remedy. But if she informs the seller of her needs and relies on the seller's expertise to select a "heavy-duty" toaster, the seller will have warranted that the toaster will fulfill those special needs. This warranty is given by both merchants and nonmerchants.

Disclaimer and Modification of Warranties

Either the implied warranty of merchantability or the implied warranty of fitness for a particular purpose may be modified or disclaimed by the seller. The seller must use the correct "magic words" to disclaim a warranty, such as *sold as is,* or *with all faults,* and the term *merchantability* must be specifically mentioned to disclaim that warranty. A disclaimer of the warranty of merchantability may be oral, but a disclaimer of the warranty of fitness for a particular purpose must be written and conspicuous, though general language such as "no implied warranties given" may be used. In some circumstances a disclaimer may be "unconscionable," however (see p. 435).

After some experience with the UCC, sellers began to routinely disclaim the implied warranties. Almost every product came with a little note attached, usually giving the consumer some "limited" warranty, but including a phrase that

> This limited warranty is in lieu of all other warranties, expressed or implied, including warranties of merchantability and fitness for a particular purpose, and excludes all liability. . . .

By the early 1970's, it had become obvious that the warranty provisions of the UCC, first seen as a protection for the consumer, were becoming less valuable as sellers became more sophisticated in the use of such disclaimers.

Federal Regulation of Warranties: The Magnuson-Moss Warranty Act

As a result of FTC hearings in the early 1970's, Congress enacted the Magnuson-Moss Warranty Act (effective January 1, 1975), described by one of its sponsors as "[O]ne of the most important pieces of consumer protection legislation . . . since the Federal Trade Commission Act itself. . . ." The Act was aimed at four major problems: (1) warranties were often written in "legalese," incomprehensible to most laymen; (2) most warranties disclaimed the implied warranties; (3) warranties were often one-sided and unfair; and (4) in some cases, the sellers did not even live up to those one-sided warranties.

The Magnuson-Moss Act did not expand any of the remedies given by the common law or the UCC for breach of warranty. Rather, the Act first required disclosure of the terms of the warranty, established definitions and guidelines for "full" and "limited" warranties, prohibited many disclaimers of warranties, and gave jurisdiction of warranty regulation to the Federal Trade Commission.

Disclosure Provisions The FTC hearings had found that many warranties were virtually incomprehensible to laymen, and did not provide enough information for the consumer to judge the worth of the warranty. To remedy these problems the Act required every written warranty to make thirteen separate disclosures.

1. The clear identification of the names and addresses of the warrantors;

2. The identity of the party or parties to whom the warranty is extended;

3. The product or parts covered;

4. A statement of what the warrantor will do in the event of a defect or malfunction, the expense for such services, if any, and the duration of the warranty;

5. A statement of what the consumer must do and what expenses he must bear;

6. A statement of the exceptions and exclusions from the warranty;

7. The procedures which the consumer must follow in order to obtain performance of the warranty and an identification of the persons authorized to perform services or other obligations under the warranty;

8. A brief description of the legal remedies available to the consumer;

9. If informal dispute resolution procedures are available or are required prior to suit, a description of such procedures;

10. The time at which the warrantor will perform any obligations under the warranty;

11. The period of time within which the warrantor will perform any obligations under the warranty;

12. The characteristics or properties of the products or parts of the product that are not covered by the warranty;

13. The warranty must be stated in words or phrases which would not mislead a reasonable, average consumer as to the nature or scope of the warranty.

Full and Limited Warranties   Under the Act, warranties are classified as either full or limited. If a supplier desires to call his warranty a *full warranty*, the warranty must fulfill several requirements: <u>first</u>, the warrantor must remedy or repair the product within a reasonable time and without charge in the event of a defect, malfunction, or failure of the product to conform to the written warranty; <u>second</u>, the warrantor may not limit the duration of any implied warranties; <u>third</u>, unless the warrantor can remedy the defective product in "a reasonable number of attempts," the consumer has the option of either a refund or a replacement; and <u>fourth</u>, the consumer need only notify the warrantor to obtain repair. Any warranty that does not fulfill these requirements must be designated a *limited warranty*.

Disclaimers of Warranties   Striking at the heart of the problem, the Act prohibited any supplier from disclaiming or modifying any implied warranty if a written warranty is made, or if the supplier and the consumer enter into a service contract covering the product. The implied warranties may be limited in time to the duration of a written warranty, if that length of time is "reasonable." Such a limitation must be "conscionable" and must be set forth in "clear and unmistakable language and prominently displayed on the face of the warranty." Disclaimers and modifications that violate the Act are ineffective for the purposes of state law.

FTC Jurisdiction   Finally, the Act gave the FTC authority to make rules to enforce and administer the law. The Commission was directed to make a rule that written warranties be made available to consumers prior to the purchase of a product and was authorized to make rules specifying the content of written warranties and service contracts.

Remedies   The Act declared that it was the policy of Congress to encourage informal dispute resolution procedures, such as arbitration. The Commission has the authority to prescribe procedures or minimum standards for such procedures. Violation of the Magnuson-Moss Act or the rules is a violation of the FTC Act, and either the FTC or the U.S. Attorney General may sue for an injunction. Individual consumers are given the right to sue as well and class actions are expressly permitted. The Act only applies to consumer products.

Products Liability and Negligence

While many actions concerning defective products are brought under a contract theory of breach of warranty, traditional tort theory has always been an appealing alternative, particularly if the defective product injured the purchaser or some other person. Traditionally, it was almost impossible to recover for personal injuries resulting from a breach of contract. The rules of privity of contract and caveat emptor also stood in the way of such actions.

Every negligence action, as discussed in Chapter 6, requires proof of four elements: a legally recognized *duty;* a breach of that *duty;* an *injury or damages;* and a *proximate causal connection* between the breach of duty and the injury. Early cases grafted certain *contract* duties onto this *tort* doctrine. The doctrine of privity of contract stated that the duties of a seller were established by contract, and therefore, since the manufacturer of a defective product often had no contract with a person injured by the product, the manufacturer had no duty to provide safe products. As a result, the first element of negligence, the existence of a legally recognized duty, was missing.

In 1916, the problem of privity of contract in negligence actions and the nature of the duty of manufacturers and sellers was considered in a landmark case.

MacPherson v. Buick Motor Company

217 N.Y. 382, 111 N.E. 1050 (1916)

The defendant, an automobile manufacturer, sold a car to a retail dealer who, in turn, sold the car to the plaintiff. While the plaintiff was in the car, one of the wooden wheels collapsed, throwing plaintiff from the car and injuring him. Buick Motor Company had purchased the wheel from another firm, but there was evidence that a reasonable inspection of the wheel would have disclosed the defect in the wood that caused the accident. The plaintiff had won in the trial court, and the defendant appealed.

The court began by reviewing a great number of earlier cases in which sellers of certain types of "inherently dangerous" goods, such as poisons, explosives, and firearms, were held liable to any person injured, regardless of whether the injured party had a contract with the seller, if the seller was found "negligent."

> CARDOZO, J. . . .
> . . . .
> We hold, then, that the principle . . . is not limited to poisons, explosives, and things of like nature, to things which in their normal operation are implements of destruction. If the nature of the thing is such that it is reasonably certain to place life and limb in peril when negligently made, it is then a thing of danger. Its nature gives warning of the consequences to be expected. If to the element of danger there is added knowledge that the thing will be used by persons other than the purchaser, and used without new tests, then, irrespective of contract, the manufacturer of this thing of danger is under a duty to make it carefully. . . .
> There is nothing anomalous in a rule which imposes upon A, who has contracted

with B, a duty to C and D and others according as he knows or does not know that the subject matter of the contract is intended for their use. . . .

We think the defendant was not absolved from a duty of inspection because it bought the wheels from a reputable manufacturer. It was not merely a dealer in automobiles. It was a manufacturer of automobiles. It was responsible for the finished product. It was not at liberty to put the finished product on the market without subjecting the component parts to ordinary and simple tests. . . . The obligation to inspect must vary with the nature of the thing to be inspected. The more probable the danger, the greater the need of caution. . . .

The judgment should be affirmed with costs.

The *MacPherson* decision only granted a cause of action to injured purchasers. Later cases extended the rule to a purchaser's employees, family, subsequent purchasers, and even casual bystanders. It seems clear that the question is one of forseeable harm rather than contractual relationship.

The defendant may breach the duty of care in a variety of ways. Cases have held manufacturers or suppliers liable for negligent design, negligent inspection or testing, negligent failure to give proper warnings, negligent failure to provide safety devices, negligent assembly, and negligent manufacture. The duty is an ongoing one and if a defect is discovered after a product is sold, the seller or manufactuer has a duty to seek out and warn the purchaser. The seller is normally not liable for misuse or abuse of the product. Because of differing state rules, there has been pressure for a *federal* products liability statute.

Products that are not "defective" but are dangerous in normal use, or from which the manufacturer can anticipate possible danger, can create liability as well. For example, with oven cleaners so caustic that they may burn skin in normal use, failure to warn the consumer of such a possibility may be negligence. Similarly, a manufacturer ought to anticpate that small children might have access to medicines or chemicals and could be negligent for failure to provide child-proof caps or other safety devices.

Negligence and the Doctrine of *Res Ipsa Loquitor*   The doctrine of privity of contract began to crumble with the *MacPherson* case, and numerous states followed the lead of New York in repudiating the doctrine. But even with the availability of negligence theory in the consumer's arsenal, cases remained difficult to prove and win. Purchasers do not often have access to proof of how the defect came to be in a product, and that proof is essential to the plaintiff's case in any negligence action.

It was not long before consumers began to use an ancient common-law rule of evidence to help prove their cases. The doctrine of *res ipsa loquitor* ('the thing speaks for itself') provides that a plaintiff may satisfy his burden of proof by showing that he has been injured by an instrumentality solely in the possession of the defendant, and that the injury is the sort that ordinarily does not take place in the absence of the defendant's negligence. For example, the doctrine has often been used by plaintiffs in airplane crash cases, since only the defendant airline has possession of the airplane, and airplanes do not ordinarily fall out of the sky without negligence.

The rule of *res ipsa loquitor* has become especially useful in products liability cases. It is extremely difficult for a plaintiff to prove just how a metal defect came to be in an automobile wheel or how a foreign object came to be in a sealed can, for example, but such defects do not ordinarily happen without negligence, and the plaintiff may be able to rely on the doctrine to satisfy his burden of proof.

Under *res ipsa loquitor,* once the plaintiff has shown that the injury resulted from an instrumentality in the sole control of the defendant and that such injuries do not ordinarily occur without negligence, the burden of proof shifts to the defendant to show that he was *not* guilty of negligence.

Products Liability and Strict Liability

Strict liability, or liability without fault, has existed in tort law for centuries in the case of ultrahazardous activities, such as keeping dangerous animals or using dynamite. In the very early 20th century, this theory was extended to sellers of food and drink, followed a national uproar over the problems of impure and unhealthy food. Slowly, the doctrine was extended to other "dangerous" products until, in 1962, the California court decided the following "leading case," which forever changed the face of American tort law.

Greenman v. Yuba Power Products, Inc.

59 Cal. 2d 57, 27 Cal. Rptr. 697, 377 P. 2d 897 (1962)

Greenman's wife purchased a combination power tool, known as a Shopsmith, from a retailer as a Christmas present for her husband in 1955. Greenman did not use the tool for some time, but in 1957, he purchased some attachments for the device and set to work making a large wooden chalice. After working on the project for a time, a piece of wood flew from the machine and struck Greenman in the forehead, injuring him severely.

Enclosed with the machine was an instruction booklet that Greenman had been following. Greenman filed suit on a breach of warranty theory, alleging that the instruction book contained express warranties. A California statute provided that a purchaser of goods had to give notice of a breach of warranty or other promise "within a reasonable time after the buyer knows, or ought to know, of such breach." Greenman gave notice ten and a half months after the accident. The manufacturer defended on the grounds that the plaintiff had not given timely notice. The plaintiff recovered a judgment for $65,000 and the defendant appealed.

TRAYNOR, J. . . .

The notice requirement . . . is not an appropriate one for the court to adopt in actions by injured consumers against manufacturers with whom they have not dealt. . . . As between the immediate parties to the sale [the notice requirement] is a sound commercial rule, designed to protect the seller against unduly delayed claims for damages. As applied to personal injuries, it becomes a booby trap for the unwary. The injured consumer is seldom steeped in the business practice which justifies the rule . . . and at least until he has had legal advice it will not occur to him to give notice to one with whom he has had no dealings. . . . We conclude, therefore, that even if plaintiff did not give timely notice of breach of warranty to the manufacturer, his cause of action based on the representations contained in the brochure was not barred.

Moreover, to impose strict liability on the manufacturer under the circumstances of this case, it was not necessary for plaintiff to establish an express warranty. . . . A manufacturer is strictly liable in tort when an article he places on the market, knowing that it is to be used without inspection for defects, proves to have a defect that causes injury to a human being. Recognized first in the case of unwholesome food products, such liability has now been extended to a variety of other products that create as great or greater hazards if defective. . . .

Although in these cases strict liability has usually been based on the theory of an express or implied warranty running from the manufacturer to the plaintiff, the abandonment of the requirement of a contract between them, the recognition that liability is not assumed by agreement but imposed by law . . ., and the refusal to permit the manufacturer to define the scope of its responsibility for defective products . . . make clear that the liability is not one governed by the law of contract warranties but the law of strict liability in tort. Accordingly, rules defining and governing warranties that were developed to meet the needs of commercial transactions cannot properly be invoked to govern the manufacturer's liability to those injured by their defective products unless those rules also serve the purposes for which such liability is imposed.

We need not recanvass the reasons for imposing strict liability on the manufacturer. . . . The purpose of such liability is to insure that the costs of injuries resulting from defective products are borne by the manufacturers that put such products on the market rather than by the injured persons who are powerless to protect themselves. Sales warranties serve this purpose fitfully at best. . . .

The judgment is affirmed.

Many states followed the *Greenman* decision, resulting in an "explosion" in the law of products liability. Generally speaking, any seller of a product that is in a defective condition and unreasonably dangerous to the user or consumer or his property is liable for any physical harm to the user or consumer of his property. The seller must be in the business of selling such products, and the seller must expect the product to reach the consumer without substantial change. The seller is liable even if he has exercised all possible care in preparing and selling the product, and it does not matter that the consumer did not purchase the product from the seller nor that the consumer and seller were not parties to a contract.

Even in the face of *Greenman* and many other cases like it, some products cases still seemed to show remnants of "fault" theory. Some cases excused liability if the manufacturer did not know of the defect or could not have known of the defect. Others seemed to excuse the manufacturer who did everything possible to prevent injury. A 1970 Illinois case laid those problems to rest in a decision that was followed in many other states.

Cunningham v. MacNeal Memorial Hospital

47 Ill. 2d. 443, 266 N.E. 2d 897 (1970)

The plaintiff, a patient in the defendant-hospital, contracted serum hepatitis from blood transfusions administered while she was a patient. She sued in tort, alleging negligence and strict liability theories. The hospital defended on the grounds that there is no way to tell the presence of serum hepatitis virus in whole blood. The hospital concluded therefore that it was without fault and so not liable.

CULBERTSON, Justice. . . . .

Whatever be the state of the medical sciences in this regard, we disagree with the defendant's conclusion. The Restatement provides in section 402A(2) (a) that "[t]he rule stated in subsection (1) applies although (a) the seller has exercised all possible care in the preparation and sale of his product." To allow a defense to strict liability on the ground that there is no way, either practical or theoretical, for a defendant to ascertain the existence of impurities in his product would be to emasculate the doctrine and in a very real sense would signal a return to a negligence theory. . . .

. . . [I]t is said that strict liability . . ." is strict in the sense that there is no need to prove that the manufacturer was negligent. If the article left the defendant's control in a dangerously unsafe condition . . . the defendant is liable whether or not he was at fault in creating that conditon or in failing to discover and eliminate it. . . . Thus, the test for imposing strict liability is whether the product was unreasonably dangerous, to use the words of the Restatement. . . . It has been suggested that this amounts to characterizing the product rather than the defendant's conduct. This is quite true, but it is easy to rephrase the issue in terms of conduct. Thus, assuming that the defendant had knowledge of the condition of the product, would he then have been acting unreasonably in placing it on the market? This, it would seem, is another way of posing the question of whether the product is reasonably safe or not. And it may well be the most useful way of presenting it.'' . . .

Defendant implicitly raises the *ad terrorem* argument that allowing a strict tort liability theory to obtain in this case will ''open the flood gates'' to disastrous litigation which will utlimately thwart the fulfillment of the hospital's worthy mission by drainage of their funds for purposes other than those intended. Our answer to this contention is that we do not believe in this present day and age, when the operation of eleemosynary hospitals constitutes one of the biggest businesses in this country, that hospital immunity can be justified on the protection-of-the-funds theory. The concept of strict liability in tort logically, and we think, reasonably, dictates that an entity which distributes a defective product for human consumption, whether for profit or not, should legally bear the consequences of injury caused thereby, rather than allowing such loss to fall upon the individual consumer who is entirely without fault.

Soon after the *Cunningham* decision, the Illinois legislature acted to grant immunity from suit to charitable hospitals for blood transfusions.

Several reasons have been advanced for the adoption of strict liability in the products area. First, many argue that consumers ought to be given the maximum possible protection against defective products as a policy matter. Second, only the manufacturer can prevent defective and dangerous products. Third, the theory results in "judicial economy" by preventing numerous and duplicative lawsuits against retailers, distributors, and manufacturers, through permitting the injured party to sue the manufacturer directly. Others argue that the manufacturer gets the benefit from the sale of the product and ought to bear the burdens as well. Finally, others simply argue that the manufacturer is financially better able to bear the burdens of the cost of injuries than are private consumers.

Government Regulation of Product Safety

In addition to common law products liability and federal regulation of warranties, Congress adopted several statutes that regulate product safety. The vast majority of those statutes regulate the safety of specific products, such as food and drugs, firearms, tobacco, motor vehicles, and the like. But one, the Consumer Product Safety Act of 1972, regulates all products in a general fashion.

The Consumer Product Safety Act

The Consumer Product Safety Act of 1972 was the first direct general control of product safety by the federal government. The Act followed a two-year study by the bipartisan National Commission on Product Safety. That Commission estimated that 20 million Americans were injured each year as a result of defective or dangerous products, including 30,000 fatalities and 110,000 permanent injuries, and that those injuries resulted in an annual economic loss of $5.5 billion. The Commission concluded that 20 percent of those injuries were preventable.

The Act regulated only "consumer products" and defined those products to be any article produced or distributed for "personal use, consumption or enjoyment, in a household, in school, or in recreation." The Act specifically excluded food and drugs, cosmetics, motor vehicles, insecticides, and other "heavily regulated" articles.

The Act also created a new independent regulatory commission, the Consumer Product Safety Commission (CPSC), consisting of five members appointed by the President for staggered seven-year terms. The CPSC appoints a fifteen-member Product Safety Advisory Council to aid its determinations. In addition to its grant of authority over consumer products under the Act, the CPSC also was given authority over several existing product safety laws, such as the Federal Hazardous Substances Act, the Flammable Fabrics Act, and the Poison Prevention Packaging Act.

The CPSC is authorized to develop consumer product safety standards. If there is a hazard of injury, illness or death, the CPSC is *required* to issue a standard, which is to be published in the Federal Register, if possible. If the Commission finds an unreasonable risk and no standard will provide adequate protection, the CPSC has the authority to completely ban the product. Interested parties must be afforded an opportunity to be heard, both orally and in writing, and interested persons may petition the CPSC to issue, amend, or revoke a rule. If the CPSC determines that "an imminently hazardous consumer product" is on the market or will be placed on the market, the Commission may petition the federal court for an order to seize the product and call for recall, repair, replacement, or refund.

Manufacturers are required to test and certify that products meet the standards. The CPSC may require warning labels and may prescribe the form of the warnings, and the Commission also has broad authority to inspect products and books. Imported products are subject to the Acts as well. Some acts are made federal crimes, including failure to comply with standards and failure to furnish information. Civil penalties of up to $2,000 per violation may be assessed, and injunctions are available. Private parties also have a right to sue in federal court if their damages exceed the required federal jurisdictional amount, and may recover their attorney's fees. The following decision considers the appropriateness of one of the CPSC's standards.

Aqua Slide 'N' Dive Corp. v. Consumer Product Safety Commission

569 F. 2d 831 (5th Cir., 1978)

In 1973, Aqua Slide 'N' Dive, a corporation that manufactured 95 percent of the swimming pool slides in the United States, requested the Consumer Product Safety Commission to establish a safety standard for swimming pool slides. Aqua Slide's admitted motive in doing so was to prevent a total ban of such products. The CPSC agreed to do so and accepted an offer by the National Swimming Pool Institute, a trade association, to develop the standard. The Institute's proposed rule would have required that slides must impart a low angle of attack into the water, required manufacturers to include warning signs on new slides, and limited installation of large slides to water more than 4 feet deep. The Institute also recommended a ladder chain to warn children to stay off large slides.

The CPSC modified the Institute's proposals in several ways. It rewrote the warning signs to include a specific mention of the danger of paralysis. It also decided it had no jurisdiction to regulate slide installation, and therefore required that slides come with instructions that recommend certain installation depths. The ladder chain provision remained in the standard, however.

Under the Consumer Product Safety Act, a manufacturer or other interested person may ask the courts to review new CPSC standards. The Act provides that CPSC standards must be "reasonably necessary to prevent or reduce an unreasonable risk of injury associated with [a consumer] product." The Act also provides that substantial evidence must appear on the record to support a new standard. Aqua Slide argued that no substantial evidence was present in two respects: first, the warning signs had not been tested and might not work; and, second, the ladder chain may not be effective.

RONEY, Curcuit Judge:

. . . .

The Act does not define the term "reasonably necessary," and apparently Congress intended the Commission and the courts to work out a definition on a case-by-case basis. . . .

In *Forester* v. *Consumer Product Safety Commission,* 559 F. 2d 774 (1977), the D.C. Circuit defined "unreasonable risk" in the Federal Hazardous Substances Act as involving "a balancing test like that familiar in tort law: The regulation may issue if the severity of the injury that may result from the product, factored by the likelihood of the injury, offsets the harm the regulation itself imposes upon manufacturers and consumers." In this case, the legislative history specifies the costs to consumers that are to be considered: increases in price, decreased availability of a product, and also reductions in product usefulness. Implicit in this analysis is an understanding that the regulation is a feasible method of reducing the risk. . . . Also, an important predicate to Commission action is that consumers be unaware of either the severity, frequency, or ways of avoiding the risk. If consumers have accurate information, and still choose to incur the risk, then their judgment may well be reasonable. . . .

. . . The Commission does not have to conduct an elaborate cost-benefit analysis. It does, however, have to shoulder the burden of examining the relevant factors and producing substantial evidence to support its conclusion that they weigh in favor of the standard.

In this case, the severity of the risk is so terrible that virtually any standard which actually promised to reduce it would seem to be "reasonably necessary.". . . After surveying slide accidents, and considering the result of scientific studies of slide dynamics, the Commission identified a risk of "quadriplegia and paraplegia resulting from users (primarily adults using the swimming pool slide for the first time) sliding down the slide in a head first position and striking the bottom of the pool." The risk is greater than an inexperienced "belly slider" would anticipate, because improper head first entry can cause an uncontrollable "snap rotation of the body" that "allows the arms to clear the bottom prior to head impact." Also, a curved slide can disorient persons who are using it for the first time. Without question, paraplegia is a horrible injury.

The risk of paraplegia from swimming pool slides, however, is extremely remote. More than 350,000 slides are in use, yet the Commission could find no more than 11 instances of paraplegia over a six year period. According to Institute figures, the risk, for slide users, is about one in 10 million, less than the risk an average person has of being killed by lightning. . . . Given the severity of the injury, however, . . . it seems likely that a standard which actually promised to reduce the risk without unduly hampering the availability of the slides or decreasing their utility could render this risk "unreasonable." The question then is whether the specific provisions of the standard which Aqua Slide challenges have been shown to accomplish that task.

A. Warning Signs

. . . [T]he record contains only the most ambiguous of indications that the warning signs would actually be heeded by slide users. The Commission did not test the signs.

The only testing was done at the last minute by one Institute committee member, who conducted experiments for two days. The letter describing the tests, although it concluded that the signs "would seem capable of effecting significant risk reduction," also indicated that the test subjects "claimed they understood the belly slide message, but this seemed questionable," the message was "long," few readers "did more than glance" at it, and "[i]t should be cautioned that the signs will not be strong counter-measure to unsafe acts, but of limited effectiveness." . . . Certainly the evidence of actual injuries bespeaks the kind of foolhardiness for which proper instructions would provide no cure. One accident victim had been drinking . . . and had hit a chair floating in the pool. Another dove through a hoop. Still a third went down a slide improperly installed in only three feet of water. Another went down on his knees, a position about which the proposed warning sign is silent. While Congress intended for injuries resulting from foreseeable misuse of a product to be counted in assessing risk, that does not warrant adoption of a standard which has not been shown to prevent misuse. . . . In short, the Commission provided little evidence that the warning signs would benefit consumers.

In this case, the prime disadvantage to which Aqua Slide points is the warning's effect on the availability of slides. . . . The Commission report indicated 20 percent of total sales would be lost over six years. . . .

Certainly, on this record, the economic finding is crucial. . . . We consequently hold that the Commission has failed to provide substantial evidence to demonstrate the reasonable necessity of the warning sign requirement. . . .

B. Ladder Chain

The one aspect of the standard which does promise to reduce the risk of paraplegia is the placement of large slides in deep water. . . . Deep water placement, however, presented the Commission with an increased risk of child drownings. . . .

The Commission took two steps to reduce the risk of drowning associated with deep water slides. It redrew the warning sign to include a drowning figure and it required all such slides to have a ladder chain. That warning sign, however, was never tested for effectiveness. The only tests performed on the ladder chain were done by [an] Institute consultant . . . who tried one out on his neighbors' children at a pool in his own back yard. . . .

This is not the stuff of which substantial evidence is made. . . . Because the Commission failed to produce substantial evidence to show the ladder chain and warning sign would work, its balance collapses and [the standard] must be set aside.

C. Conclusion

. . . The Commission has failed to produce substantial evidence to support the warning sign and ladder chain requirements, and because those requirements are integral parts of the standard's scheme for preventing paralytic injury, [the Commission's standard] must be set aside. . . .

Federal Food and Drug Administration   The Federal Food and Drug Administration (FDA) was created in 1927 and given authority to administer several food and drug laws, including the Federal Pure Food and Drug Act of 1906; the Federal Food, Drug and Cosmetic Act of 1938; the Drug Amendments of 1962; and portions of the Fair Packaging and Labelling Act of 1967. The FDA has authority, under the various statutes, to prevent the sale and transportation of "adulterated" and "misbranded" food, drugs, and cosmetics. The FDA has the power to make rules, order examinations and investigations of the plants and records of food, drug and cosmetic producers, seize and condemn adulterated and misbranded products, and administer "pre-market clearance" of certain products. The following case involves premarket clearance of a controversial cancer treatment.

U.S. v. Rutherford (the Laetrile Case)

442 U.S. 544, 99 S. Ct. 2470, 61 L. Ed. 2d 68 (1979)

Mr. Justice MARSHALL delivered the opinion of the Court.

The question presented in this case is whether the Federal Food, Drug, and Cosmetic Act precludes terminally ill cancer patients from obtaining Laetrile, a drug not recognized as "safe and effective" within the meaning of the Act.

I

Section 505 of the Federal Food, Drug and Cosmetic Act prohibits interstate distribution of any "new drug" unless the Secretary of Health, Education and Welfare [the agency in charge of the FDA] approves an application supported by substantial evidence of the drug's safety and effectiveness. . . .

In 1975, terminally ill cancer patients and their spouses brought this action to enjoin the Government from interfering with the interstate shipment and sale of Laetrile, a drug not approved for distribution under the Act. . . .

On review of the Commissioner's decision, the District Court sustained his determination that Laetrile. . . constituted a new drug. . . . However . . . the District Court ruled that Laetrile was entitled to an exemption from premarketing approval requirements. Alternatively, the court held that by denying cancer patients the right to use a nontoxic substance in connection with their personal health, the Commissioner had infringed constitutionally protected privacy interests.

[T]he Tenth Circuit held that "the safety" and "effectiveness" terms used in the statute have no reasonable application to terminally ill cancer patients. Since those patients, by definition, would "die of cancer regardless of what may be done," the court concluded that there were no realistic standards against which to measure the safety and effectiveness of a drug for that class of individuals. The Court of Appeals therefore approved the District Court's injunction permitting use of Laetrile by cancer patients certified as terminally ill. . . .

II

The Federal Food, Drug and Cosmetic Act makes no special provision for drugs used to treat terminally ill patients. . . . The Act requires premarketing approval for "any new drug" unless it is intended solely for investigative use or is exempt under one of the Act's grandfather provisions. . . .

In the Court of Appeals' view, an implied exemption from the Act was justified because the safety and effectiveness standards . . . could have "no reasonable application" to terminally ill patients. We disagree. . . . Here . . . we have no license to depart from the plain language of the Act, for Congress could reasonably have intended to shield terminal patients from ineffectual or unsafe drugs.

A drug is effective . . . if there is general recognition among experts, founded on substantial evidence, that the drug in fact produces the results claimed for it under prescribed conditions. Contrary to the Court of Appeals' apparent assumption, effectiveness does not necessarily denote capacity to cure. In the treatment of any illness, terminal or otherwise, a drug is effective if it fulfills, by objective indices, its sponsor's claims of prolonged life, improved physical condition, or reduced pain.

So too, the concept of safety . . . is not without meaning for terminal patients. Few if any drugs are completely safe in the sense that they may be taken by all persons in all circumstances without risk. Thus, the Commissioner generally considers a drug safe when the expected therapeutic gain justifies the risk entailed by its use. For the terminally ill, as for anyone else, a drug is unsafe if its potential for inflicting death or physical injury is not offset by the possiblity of therapeutic benefit. . . .

Moreover, there is a special sense in which the relationship between drug effectiveness and safety has meaning in the context of incurable illnesses. An otherwise harmless drug can be dangerous to any patient it if does not produce its purported therapeutic effect. But if an individual suffering from a potentially fatal disease rejects conventional therapy in favor of a drug with no demonstrable curative properties, the consequences can be irreversible. . . .

. . .To accept the proposition that the safety and efficacy standards of the Act have no relevance for terminal patients is to deny the Commissioner's authority over all drugs, however toxic or ineffectual, for such individuals. If history is any guide, this new market would not be long overlooked. Since the turn of the century, resourceful entrepreneurs have advertised a wide variety of purportedly simple and painless cures for cancer, including linaments of turpentine, mustard, oil, eggs and ammonia; peatmoss; arrangements of colored floorlamps; pastes made from glycerin and limburger cheese; mineral tablets; and "Fountain of Youth" mixtures of spices, oil and suet. In citing these examples, we do not, of course, intend to deprecate the sincerity of Laetrile's current proponents, or to imply any opinion on whether that drug may ultimately prove safe and effective for cancer treatment. But this historical experience does suggest why Congress could reasonably have determined to protect the terminally ill, no less than other patients, from the vast range of self-styled panaceas that inventive minds can devise.

We note finally that construing [the Pure Food and Drug Act] to encompass treatments for terminal diseases does not foreclose all resort to experimental cancer drugs by patients for whom conventional therapy is unavailing. The Act exempts from premarketing approval drugs intended solely for investigative use if they satisfy certain preclinical testing and other criteria. An application for clinical testing of Laetrile by the National Cancer Institute is now pending before the Commissioner. That the Act makes explicit provision for carefully regulated use of certain drugs not yet demonstrated safe and effective reinforces our conclusion that no exception for terminal patients may be judicially implied. Whether, as a policy matter, an exemption should be created is a question for legislative judgment, not judicial interference.

The judgment of the Court of Appeals is reversed. . . .

In addition to testing and setting standards for drugs, the FDA also establishes standards for foods. The FDA has the authority to prohibit the sale of "impure" and "adulterated" foods. Since it is often technically or economically impossible to remove all impurities, the FDA has established "maximum standards" for poisons, pesticide residues, additives, filth, and decomposed matter that may be found in foods offered for sale.

In 1958, the Delaney Amendment was added to the Pure Food and Drug Act. That Amendment provided that "no additive shall be deemed to be safe if it is found to induce cancer when ingested by man or animal, or if it is found, after tests . . . to induce cancer in man or animal." That amendment thus established a "zero tolerance" for carcinogens, and has been invoked to ban cyclamates, saccharine, and other additives. The 1973 ban of saccharine caused a public outcry frm diabetics, weight-conscious persons, and others, and resulted in Congress' reconsideration and the passage of a special bill permitting the sale of saccharine with a warning label.

Federal Fair Packaging and Labeling Act

The 1967 Fair Packaging and Labeling Act made it unlawful to distribute any consumer commodity if the packaging or labeling failed to conform to the Act's disclosure requirements. The Act requires labels to disclose the identity of the product; the name of the manufacturer, distributor, or packer; the net quantity of contents expressed by some uniform method; and the net quantity of "servings" by some uniform method. The Act applies to any "consumer commodity," including food, drugs, cosmetics, and "any other article, product or commodity" produced for retail sale, individual use, or individual consumption. Some "heavily regulated" products are exempt.

The FDA is authorized to promulgate regulations dealing with food, drugs, and cosmetics, and the FTC is authorized to make regulations dealing with "any other consumer commodity." Both agencies have made such regulations specifying standards for what may or must be disclosed on labels, including certain advertising representations. Failure to comply is either a violation of the Federal Food, Drug and Cosmetic Act or the Federal Trade Commission Act, depending on the nature of the commodity.

National Traffic and Motor Vehicle Safety Act

The primary purpose of the National Traffic and Motor Vehicle Safety Act of 1966 was to reduce motor vehicle accidents, injuries, and property damage. Administration of the Act was given to the Department of Transportation. Under the Act, manufacturers are required to notify purchasers of motor vehicles containing "a defect which relates to motor vehicle safety." The term *defect* has been defined as follows:

> We find that a vehicle . . . "contains a defect" if it is subject to a significant number of failures in normal operation, including failures either occurring during specified use or resulting from owner abuse (including inadequate maintenance) that is reasonably foreseeable (ordinary abuse), but excluding failures attributable to normal deterioration . . . as a result of age and wear. *U.S.* v. *General Motors.* *

The Act sets minimum informational standards for the recall notices and requires manufacturers to provide repair services without charge. Violation of an order to make a recall may result in injunctions and civil penalties and may be the basis of private lawsuits.

Credit and Collection Practices

The American economy is built on credit. But the extension of credit involves a number of opportunities for abuse of consumers, from the simple ploy of stating interest on a monthly rather than yearly basis to complicated schemes for disguising charges

---

*518 F. 2d 420 (D.C. Cir., 1975).

and "add-ons" in advertisements. As noted by Chief Justice Burger in *Mourning* v. *Family Publications Service**

> From the end of World War II to 1967, the amount of such credit outstanding had increased from $5.6 billion to $95.9 billion, a rate of growth more than 4½ times as great as that of the economy. Yet, as the congressional hearings revealed, consumers remained remarkably ignorant of the nature of their credit obligations and of the cost of deferring payments. Because of the divergent, and at times fraudulent, practices by which consumers were informed of the terms of the credit extended to them, many consumers were prevented from shopping for the best terms available and, at times, were prompted to assume liabilities they could not meet. . . .

The problem was answered in part by passage of the federal Consumer Credit Protection (Truth-in-Lending) Act in 1968. Additional abuses of credit and collection tactics were regulated in subsequent amendments or related acts, including the federal Fair Credit Reporting, Fair Credit Billing, Fair Debt Collection Practices, Real Estate Settlement Procedures, and Equal Credit Opportunity acts, among others, and in some administrative rules adopted by the Board of Governors of the Federal Reserve Board, the Federal Trade Commission, and other agencies.

Truth-in-Lending

The federal Consumer Credit Protection Act, also known as Truth-in-Lending, attempts to provide remedies for credit abuses through disclosure of credit terms to consumers and prospective consumers. The House Committee Report stated that

> By requiring all creditors to disclose credit information in a uniform manner, and by requiring all additional mandatory charges imposed by the creditor as an incident to credit be included in the computation of the applicable percentage rate, the American consumer will be given the information he or she needs to compare the cost of credit and to make the best informed decision on the use of credit.

The Truth-in-Lending Act requires disclosure of a variety of relevant items prior to consummation of a credit transaction and also imposes disclosure requirements on advertisements that contain references to credit terms. Standard terminology is required in both sets of disclosures. The Act applies to any individual or firm that extends or arranges for consumer credit, including financial institutions, stores, credit card issuers, and finance companies, and reaches all extensions "of credit for personal, family, household or agricultural purposes." Personal loans over $25,000, business and commercial loans, transactions involving an SEC-registered securities or commodities broker, and some public utility charges made by regulated companies are excepted. Home mortgages, regardless of amount, are covered by the Act.

Authority to administer the Act was given to the Federal Reserve Board, and in 1969 the Board issued specific regulations, known as *Regulation Z,* to implement the Act. In addition to the Federal Reserve, nine other government agencies administer portions of the Act, including the FTC, which is responsible for all general retailers, consumer finance companies, and all other creditors not regulated by other agencies.

---

*411 U.S. 356, 93 S. Ct. 1652, 36 L. Ed. 2d (1973).

If a credit practice is not covered by the Act, the FTC may still find the practice "deceptive or unfair" under the general provisions of the FTC Act.

Disclosure Requirements   In a typical "closed-end" credit transaction in which only a single transaction is envisioned, such as a consumer loan payable over time, the creditor is required to make eighteen separate disclosures to the consumer before the transaction is consummated. Those disclosures include the amount financed, the "finance charge" as computed under the Act, the annual percentage rate (A.P.R.), the payment schedule, the total of payments, the total sale price (including the finance charge), prepayment options, late payment penalties, security interests, security interest charges, and others. "Open-end" credit, such as revolving charge accounts and credit cards, must make an *initial disclosure* including the finance charge, other charges which may be imposed, security interests, and a statement of the consumer's billing rights. Such plans must also provide a *periodic statement* showing the previous balance, identify all new transactions, show any credits, and disclose the periodic rates, the balance of which finance charges are computed, the amount of the finance charge and other charges, identify the closing date of the billing cycle, and show an address to be used for notice of billing errors. Forms to be used for many of the disclosures are mandated by the regulation.

Advertising of Credit   Regulation Z provides that if an advertisement of credit states that specific terms are available, it shall state only those terms actually available. If an advertisement states a finance charge, it must be stated in terms of the *A.P.R.,* or *annual percentage rate,* which must be stated on an annual basis and include many "hidden" credit charges, such as carrying costs, "points," and loan or assumption fees. If the interest rate may change, the advertisement must disclose that fact.

As a general rule, if an advertisement states *any* figures, it must disclose *all* of the figures.

Advertising of Terms that Require Additional Disclosures
Regulation Z Section 226.4(c)

1. If any of the following terms is set forth in an advertisement, the advertisement shall meet the requirements of paragraph (2) of this section:
    i. The amount or percentage of any down payment.
    ii. The number of payments or period of repayment.
    iii. The amount of any payment.
    iv. The amount of any finance charge.
2. An advertisement stating any of the terms in paragraph (1) of this section shall state the following terms, as applicable:
    i. The amount or percentage of the down payment.
    ii. The terms of repayment.
    iii. The "annual percentage rate," using that term, and, if the rate may be increased after consummation, that fact.

General statements in an advertisement, such as "easy credit," "charge accounts available," "all major credit cards honored," and others do not call for disclosure. But once specific figures are mentioned or statements such as "no money down," "pay only $7 per week," and the like, disclosures are required. And broad statements such as "liberal credit" and "easy credit" may result in charges under the FTC Act, even though they do not require Truth-in-Lending disclosures. Such statements simply must mean what they say.

Right of Rescission   One of the chief concerns of Congress was the fast-talking salesperson who induces a homeowner to make a purchase or loan secured by a second mortgage on the debtor's home. The Act provides a special **right of rescission** in such cases, which gives the debtor the right to void the transaction within three business days. The debtor must be informed in writing of this right, and the three-day period does not start until the written disclosure of the right is made. The consumer must give notice of rescission in writing, but that notice must be already made out and attached to the notice given the debtor. The form of the notice is prescribed by Regulation Z. The right to rescind may be waived in only the most serious emergency situations.

Remedies   Both civil and criminal penalities are provided under the Act. An aggrieved debtor may bring a civil action for double the amount of the finance charge, from a minimum of $100 to a maximum of $1,000, plus attorneys' fees and costs. Criminal penalties for wilful violations include a fine of up to $5,000 or a year in jail or both.

Truth-in-Leasing Act

In 1976, the Consumer Credit Protection Act was amended by adding the Consumer Leasing (Truth-in-Leasing) Act. Congressional concerns in the Act were with the increased trend toward long-term leasing of consumer goods and "that these leases have been offered without adequate cost disclosures." The Act required eleven separate disclosures prior to the consummation of a lease of personal property for a total contract value under $25,000 to be used for personal, family, or household purposes. The Act applied regardless of whether the lessee had an option to purchase the property. The disclosures included a description of the property, the "down payment"; the amount of license fees, taxes, and other official fees; the amount of other charges; the number, amount, and due dates of payments and the total amount of the payments; the cost of the lease on expiration; and statements of warranties and conditions of termination.

Advertisements of leases may not state the amount of any payment, down payment or the number of payments unless the advertisement clearly discloses that the transaction is a lease, the amount of the "down payment, the number, amount, due date and total of payments under the lease, and that the lessee may be liable for the difference between the fair market value and the actual value at the termination of the lease, if the lessee is liable for that amount."

If the lease transaction is through a bank or other financial institution, the Federal Reserve has the authority to administer the law. Virtually all other transactions fall within the authority of the FTC. Remedies include a private civil action for 25 percent of the total of the monthly payments, but not less than $100 nor more than

$1,000, plus costs and attorneys' fees. If an advertisement violates the law, the consumer may sue for his actual damages. Wilful violations may result in criminal penalties of a $5,000 fine, a year in jail, or both.

Federal Fair Credit Reporting Act

In 1970, Congress passed the Fair Credit Reporting Act to remedy some perceived abuses in the credit reporting system, to ensure the accuracy of credit reports, and to secure the consumer's right to privacy. Consumers were given an absolute right to review any file maintained on them by a consumer reporting agency. If a discrepancy was found, consumers were given the right to dispute information, and agencies were required to reinvestigate such disputed information. Subsequent reports were required to show the dispute and if the original information was found to be erroneous, the report had to be corrected. If such a dispute was not resolved, consumers were given the right to file a statement of not more than 100 words regarding the dispute. Those statements must be included either verbatim or accurately summarized in later reports.

If a report is to be used for credit, insurance, or employment purposes, the person who is the subject of the report must be informed that such an investigative report will be prepared or used. If the consumer is denied credit, insurance, or employment because of a report, the user of the report must give the consumer the name and address of the party preparing the report, or at least state that the consumer has a right to such information. The Act contains civil and criminal penalties, imposes civil liability to persons injured, and authorizes administrative enforcement by the FTC.

Federal Fair Credit Billing Act

The Fair Credit Billing Act of 1974, another amendment to the Truth-in-Lending Act, was aimed at the problems of billing errors, the responsibilities of credit card issuers, and the knotty problem of the degree of control that credit card companies may exert over retailers.

All "creditors," which are defined as persons who regularly extend or arrange credit and all credit card issuers, must acknowledge any complaint or inquiry about a billing error within 30 days and must either correct or explain the alleged error within 90 days of the receipt of the complaint. Open-end credit accounts cannot be restricted or closed for failure to pay alleged billing errors until the account has been investigated and explained or corrected. Failure to comply results in forfeiture of the right to collect the disputed amount up to a maximum of $50.

Credit card issuers must credit a consumer's account when notified that a retailer has accepted return of the merchandise or has forgiven payment for any reason. Credit card issuers, which are also banks or savings and loans, may not use funds on deposit to offset credit card indebtedness without a prior written authorization from the consumer, or if the consumer requests that no offset be made during a dispute. Credit card issuers may not prevent sellers from offering "discounts for cash," nor may issuers require "tie-in" purchases as a condition of participating in the credit card plan.

Federal Fair Debt Collection Practices Act

Concern over debt collection tactics resulted in the Fair Debt Collection Practices Act of 1977. The Act applies only to independent collection agencies, not to creditors attempting to collect debts owed to them. Abusive collection techniques are prohibited, including threats of violence, obscene language, publication of the names of debtors, false and misleading representations, and harassment. Collectors may not contact debtors at unusual or inconvenient hours. If a debtor requests that a collector cease contact in writing, the creditor can only contact the debtor to inform him that a specific action will be taken (e.g., filing of a lawsuit) and then only if the action is actually taken. Within five days of the first contact, the debtor must be sent a written notice detailing the debt. The collector may contact others, including employers, but only to find out where the consumer lives or works and may not inform any person of the debt. Generally, other persons may only be contacted once. Collectors may be liable for the actual damages caused by their actions in violation of the Act, plus a civil penalty of up to $1,000, attorneys' fees, and costs. The FTC is charged with administration of the Act.

Electronic Funds Transfer Act

The development of a large variety of electronic funds transfer techniques, including automated tellers, computer funds transfers, and pay-by-phone systems, gave rise to potential consumer problems. These potential problems resulted in passage of the Electronic Funds Transfer Act of 1978. This Act requires that creditors using such systems provide a monthly statement of transactions to the consumer. After the statement is received the consumer has 60 days in which to report an error, after which the creditor has the duty to investigate and report to the consumer within ten days. If an error is discovered it must be corrected, and creditors are liable for all actual damages caused by failure to properly make a transfer.

The Act also limits consumers' liabilities in the event of a lost or stolen credit card to $50 if the issuer is notified within two days after the consumer learns of the loss or theft. After the two-day period, the consumer's liability rises to $500 for the next 60 days. After 60 days, the consumer's liability is unlimited if the issuer can show that prompt notice would have prevented the loss, and the consumer knew or should have known of the theft or loss. The Federal Reserve has provided specific regulations in its Regulation E.

In addition to actual losses, an issuer may be liable for a civil penalty of $100–$1,000, plus attorneys' fees, and costs. Criminal penalties of a $5,000 fine, a year in jail, or both are provided for "knowing" or "wilful" violations.

Real Estate Settlement Procedures Act

The federal Real Estate Settlement Procedures Act of 1974 was aimed at specific abuses in transactions for the purchase of homes. The Act requires disclosure of closing costs prior to the sale of a home or the granting of a mortgage on a home. The Act also prohibits kick-backs between various settlement service providers and requires the use of a standardized settlement form disclosing many hidden costs. All prospective mortgage applicants must be given an information booklet, "Settlement

Costs and You," and all purchasers are given the right to select their own title insurer, attorney, or other service provider. The Act applies to all federally related mortgage transactions.

Federal Equal Credit Opportunity Act

The Equal Credit Opportunity Act of 1974, an amendment to the Consumer Credit Protection Act, prohibits discrimination in giving credit on the basis of race, creed, color, religion, age, national origin, income derived from public assistance, sex, or marital status. Virtually all creditors except individuals are covered, including banks, retailers, and credit card issuers.

The Act gives a credit applicant the right to a decision on the application within 30 days and, in the event of a denial, the creditor must state its reasons in writing, along with the basic provisions of the Act, and the name and address of the federal agency administering compliance. Credit applications may request all information that will permit the creditor to make a reasoned judgment about the applicant's ability to repay, but such applications may not request information regarding the "suspect categories." For example, information regarding marital status is usually irrelevant, unless the spouse will use the property or be liable for the debt, the applicant is relying on income from the spouse to pay the debt, or the property to be purchased may become community property.

An aggrieved applicant may sue for actual damages and punitive damages not to exceed $10,000 plus attorneys' fees and costs. The Act provides for class actions as well, and the FTC is given authority to oversee compliance and make regulations.

Federal Trade Commission Rules

The FTC Act, as discussed in Chapter 11, also authorizes the Federal Trade Commission to make rules regarding "unfair and deceptive trade practices." In addition to the rules already mentioned, the FTC has also imposed a "three-day cooling off period" on door-to-door sales, during which a consumer has a right to rescind transactions over the value of $25, and has regulated mail-order sales.

One of the most far-reaching FTC regulations was adopted in early 1984. That regulation outlaws *confession of judgment clauses,* most *wage assignments,* and some types of *security interests.* In addition, the regulation imposes a disclosure requirement on obligations guaranteed by a *cosigner.*

A **confession of judgment clause** in a credit contract permits a creditor to circumvent most of the procedural protections of the law when a lawsuit is brought. Normally, such clauses permit "any attorney" to confess judgment on behalf of the debtor, which means that the creditor's attorney may simply ask any other lawyer (and in many states even nonlawyers, or "agents") to sign a document that acknowledges the debt and consents to the entry of a legal judgment on behalf of the debtor. Often, confession of judgment clauses also waive service of process and notice of the hearing. As a result, a debtor may not receive notice of the court proceeding until after judgment is entered. Unless the debtor can convince a judge to set the judgment aside, there is no trial and no opportunity to raise a defense. The 1984 regulation (16 C.F.R. 444.2) prohibits all such confession of judgment clauses or any waiver of "notice and the opportunity to be heard."

A **wage assignment** is an agreement by a debtor that the creditor may go directly to the debtor's employer and receive payment of the debt out of the debtor's paycheck. Many states prohibited such clauses or limited the amounts that the creditor could demand from the debtor's paycheck. The FTC regulation outlawed all wage assignments unless the assignment is revocable at will by the debtor or the assignment only applies to wages already earned at the time of the assignment.

A **security interest** is a lien or claim on property, which permits the creditor to repossess the property in the event of default. Some credit contracts included a provision that gave the creditor a security interest in all of the debtor's property, not just the property purchased on credit. Some credit card or "revolving charge" agreements also gave the creditor a security interest in all goods purchased since the account was opened, not just the most recent purchases. The FTC regulation outlaws all security interests in household goods other than purchase money security interests.

Some creditors also may insist on a **cosigner**, or guarantor, of a loan or credit agreement. The cosigner is liable on the debt, even if the creditor does not attempt to collect the debt from the delinquent debtor, but many cosigners do not know this nor even understand the nature of the agreement they are signing. The FTC regulation provides that cosigners must be informed of their obligations under the agreement by providing a printed form as a separate document that states

Notice to Cosigner

You are being asked to guarantee this debt. Think carefully before you do. If the borrower doesn't pay the debt, you will have to. Be sure you can afford to pay if you have to, and that you want to accept this responsibility. You may have to pay up to the full amount of the debt if the borrower does not pay. You may also have to pay late fees or collection costs, which increase this amount. The creditor can collect this debt from you without first trying to collect from the borrower. The creditor can use the same collection method against you that can be used against the borrower, such as suing you, garnishing your wages, etc. If this debt is ever in default, that fact may become a part of *your* credit record.

This notice is not the contract that makes you liable for the debt.

Finally, the regulation also prohibits "pyramiding late charges." That means that a creditor may not assess a late charge on a late charge, if the debtor has made what would otherwise be a full payment.

The full effect of these regulations is not yet clear. It seems likely that those provisions will be available as matters of defense to such actions in the state courts and may be grounds for an injunction in the courts against such practices. Since they are labelled *unfair trade practices,* the FTC may also impose civil penalties against creditors who fail to observe them.

State and Common-Law Consumer Protection

The development of products liability law and federal statutes protecting consumer interests was accompanied by a parallel development in state law. While consumer protection statutes vary widely between the states, four major developments deserve attention: the UCC doctrine of unconscionability, the Uniform Consumer Credit Code (UCCC), state consumer protection agencies, and usury laws.

Unconscionability

One of the most important changes made by the Uniform Commercial Code was found in the new concept of **unconscionability.** Section 2-302 of the UCC provides

> If the court as a matter of law finds the contract or any clause of the contract to have been unconscionable at the time it was made the court may refuse to enforce the contract, or it may enforce the remainder of the contract without the unconscionable clause, or it may so limit the application of any unconscionable clause as to avoid any unconscionable result.

The UCC does not define the term *unconscionability,* even though the rule applies to all sales of goods, including virtually every consumer transaction in personal property. Court decisions have interpreted the term to generally mean grossly unfair, and the courts often require a finding of inequality of bargaining position between the parties to a contract. As one decision stated

> Unconscionability has generally been recognized to include an absence of meaningful choice on the part of one of the parties together with contract terms which are unreasonably favorable to the other party. . . . Did each party to the contract, considering his obvious education or lack of it, have a reasonable opportunity to understand the terms of the contract, or were the important terms hidden in a maze of fine print and minimized by deceptive sales practices? Ordinarily, one who signs an agreement without full knowledge of its terms might be held to assume the risk that he has entered a one-sided bargain. But when a party of little bargaining power, and hence little real choice, signs a commercially unreasonable contract with little or no knowledge of its terms, it is hardly likely that his consent . . . was ever given to all the terms. In such a case the usual rule that the terms of the agreement are not to be questioned should be abandoned and the court should consider whether the terms of the contract are so unfair that enforcement should be withheld. *Williams* v. *Walker-Thomas Furniture Company.* *

The UCC unconscionability doctrine has been adopted in virtually every state and extended by judicial decision to transactions other than those involving the sale of goods in some instances, such as employment contracts and real estate transactions.

Uniform Consumer Credit Code (UCCC)

In 1968, the National Conference of Commissioners on Uniform State Laws approved the final draft of the Uniform Consumer Credit Code (UCCC). Only a few states have totally adopted the law, but many states have used this uniform or "model" act as a guide for state legislation. The UCCC was meant to dovetail with the federal Truth-in-Lending act of the same year. The UCCC requires certain mandatory written notices to the buyer in any credit transaction, similar to those required under Truth-in-Lending, but goes much further by establishing a uniform set of rules governing all aspects of consumer credit. The Act sets maximum interest rates, governs

*350 F. 2d 445 (D.C. Cir., 1965).

door-to-door sales, and extensively regulates the use of credit-line insurance. The Act also prescribes the method of rebating finance charges in the event of prepayment.

Virtually all states have enacted Retail Installment Sales Acts (RISA), however. Such acts are similar in form to the UCCC but relate solely to installment sales of personal property. RISAs generally require advance disclosure and regulate billing practices and may go much farther depending on the state.

State Consumer Protection Agencies

Virtually every state has established some type of consumer protection agency. Those agencies vary considerably in their power and jurisdiction. Some of the state agencies are little more than mediators, taking complaints from consumers and forwarding them to sellers. Others have a great deal of power, including the right to initiate administrative or criminal proceedings.

Usury Statutes

Perhaps the first "government regulation" of business was a **usury statute** that set the maximum rate of permissible interest in ancient Rome. Every state has a usury statute of some sort, though the method of setting the maximum rate of interest and the penalties for violation vary considerably. During the interest rate escalations of the late 1970's many of those laws were "suspended" or preempted by federal regulations, since in many instances the enforcement of the state usury statute would have eliminated any lending whatsoever.

Bankruptcy

Perhaps the ultimate "consumer protection" law is the Federal Bankruptcy Act. Under the Constitution, Article I, Section 8, clause 4, "Congress shall have the power ... to establish ... uniform laws on the subject of bankruptcies throughout the United States." The first bankruptcy act was passed in 1800, though that law applied only to "traders." Such acts were passed and repealed several times in the 19th century, but since 1898 there has been a federal bankruptcy act in continuous existence. The present Act results from substantial amendments to the Act in 1978 and again in 1984.

The purpose of bankruptcy is to permit debtors to make a fresh start. It is possible for anyone to get into financial difficulty through business reverses, marital problems, lawsuits, employment layoffs, and simple overextension in an atmosphere of easy credit. Such problems result in the necessity of fending off creditors, collection agencies, and lawyers at every turn. Bankruptcy gives such debtors a second chance.

Three basic types of bankruptcy are available under the federal law: *liquidation proceedings,* commonly known as "straight" bankruptcy; *adjustment of debts,* or "wage earner plans," for individuals with regular income who wish to pay off their debts over time; and *business reorganizations.*

Liquidation Proceedings: Straight Bankruptcy

The most common and best-known procedure is straight bankruptcy, which is availalbe to any individual, partnership, or corporation. Such cases may be filed by the debtor (a *"voluntary" petition*) or by the creditors of the debtor (an *"involuntary"* *petition*), but less than 1 percent of all cases are initiated by creditors. The law does not require that a debtor be insolvent or unable to pay his or her debts, but only the person filing be a debtor. The case is filed by filing a series of rather complex disclosure forms and a petition asking for a *discharge in bankruptcy*. The petition must list all of the assets, liabilities, and creditors of the debtor, and disclose the location of all assets, books, and records. All creditors are notified and given an opportunity to object to the discharge or make claims against the nonexempt property of the debtor.

After the petition is filed, the U.S. Bankruptcy Court then appoints a trustee to take over the debtor's property and business. The trustee may be elected by the creditors or, as in the usual case, may be appointed by the court. The trustee may sue and be sued on behalf of the debtor and may move to set aside "fraudulent transfers," including transfers of property by the debtor within one year of filing the petition for bankruptcy, if the property was transferred for less than its full value. The bankruptcy court holds a *meeting of creditors* shortly after the petition is filed for the purpose of electing or appointing the trustee and examining the debtor. A date is also set at that meeting for the discharge of the debtor.

Claims of Creditors and Exemptions   The assets of the debtor, less the exemptions permitted by law, are then to be distributed to the creditors who have filed claims, according to their priority as established in the Act. Under the Bankruptcy Act, as amended in 1976 and 1984, the debtor may elect between two different sets of exemptions: the exemptions permitted by the law of the state in which he or she is domiciled, *or* the exemptions permitted by federal law under the Bankruptcy Act. Under the 1984 Amendments, if a husband and wife file a joint bankruptcy petition, they each receive separate exemptions, but both must choose either the state exemptions or the federal exemptions.

Under the Bankruptcy Act, the following property is exempt from the claims of creditors:

1.   The debtor's homestead interest in a residence of up to $7,500;

2.   The debtor's motor vehicle, up to $1,200 in value;

3.   The debtor's interest in household furnishings and other personal property for personal, family, or household use, up to $200 per item up to a maximum of $4,000 of total exemptions;

4.   The debtor's interest in jewelry for personal, family, or household use, totalling $500 in aggregate value;

5.   The debtor's interest in any other property, up to a limit of $400 plus any unused portion of the homestead exemption up to $3,750;

6.   The debtor's interest in tools, professional books, and implements;

7.   Unmatured life insurance policies;

8.   Health aids prescribed by a physician or other health professional;

9.   The debtor's right to receive government benefits, such as social security;

10. The debtor's right to receive certain private payments, such as alimony, child support, and private pensions.

Thus, if all of the debtor's property may be brought within the federal exemptions, or within a list of exemptions permitted by state law, there will be no property to distribute to the creditors. Many cases fall within that category, and are termed *no asset cases,* since there are no assets for distribution.

Even if property technically falls within the list of exempt property, if a creditor has a lien or security interest on the property the creditor is entitled to the property. For example, if debtor A has a home worth $50,000, but has a mortgage of $48,000 on the property, the lending institution or other creditor holding the mortgage would have the right to foreclose the mortgage. The debtor's interest of $2,000 would be claimed under the homestead exemption, and the debtor could claim up to $3,750 of other property under paragraph 5, above. Similarly, if the debtor owned a car worth $5,000 with a $4,500 lien to a lender, the lender would have a right to the car, and if the car were sold for $5,000 the debtor could claim $500 under paragraph 2, above.

Reaffirmation Since secured creditors have a right to their property under any circumstances, debtors often attempt to save property by making a new agreement with the creditor so that they may retain certain property. That means that after the bankruptcy petition is filed, the debtor makes a new agreement with the creditor (or "reaffirms" the debt) to pay certain amounts, in return for the creditor's promise not to take back the goods.

At one time, such reaffirmation agreements could be entered into without court approval, which resulted in a great deal of abuse by both debtors and creditors. Under the 1978 Amendments, the Bankruptcy Court must determine whether such reaffirmations are in "the best interests of the debtor." In addition, the 1984 Amendments provide that the debtor may rescind such agreements at any time up to discharge or within 60 days, whichever is later, and requires that the agreement represent a fully informed and voluntary agreement on the part of the debtor and does not impose an undue hardship on the debtor. The following case, which arose prior to the 1984 Amendments, shows the problems inherent in such reaffirmation agreements.

In Re Jenkins

United States Bankruptcy Court, E.D., Va. 1980 (4 B.R. 651)

HAL J. BONNEY, Jr., Bankruptcy Judge.
Once more into the breach!
Again the Court must express an opinion as to what it considers to be—or not to be—in the best interest of a debtor. Indeed, an awesome thing. Shall the Court interposition itself when both the debtor and the creditor seek approval of an agreement which, in effect, would reaffirm an indebtedness of $792.76 on $200 worth of furniture?
The application for approval of the agreement was filed by the creditor, Carolina Furniture Outlet. At stake are a three piece living room suite and a complete bed.
Faithful to its statutory duty . . . at the appropriate hearing the Court heard the debtor testify to his desire to reaffirm the entire debt since he wished to retain the property. It also heard the creditor recite that the agreed amount was the outstanding balance on the debtor's discharged account, $792.76. But what was the chattel worth? The Court directed an appraisal and this came in for $200.

The issue burns: Is it in the best interest of the debtor to be permitted to become so obligated?

A knowledge of the legislative antecedents of the Bankruptcy Code readily reflects the clear intent of Congress for courts to scrutinize debtor agreements and applications for revival of debts with the utmost care. . . .

The initial draft of the legislation [the 1978 Amendments] prohibited any and all agreements by debtors and creditors to revive pre-bankruptcy debts. There had been such a sordid history of the reaffirmation of debts that the fresh start envisioned by the Congress had been cast away by many bankrupts. The process which would have restored them to the marketplace [society], to their families and to themselves as more useful citizens was thwarted. Indeed, it is clear from this bench that the chief cause of "repeaters" in bankruptcy is reaffirmation of debts.

We can take judicial notice of the fact that in the past many bankrupts almost immediately returned to financial difficulty after discharge because they reaffirmed discharged debts. For some it was a matter of conscience. "I want to repay you as soon as I can." "Good. Sign here." Or the fellow needs a loan and his usual source says, "Sure, sign up again for the old debt and we'll let you have some additional money," knowing that he could not declare straight bankruptcy again for six years.

Some Congressional draftsmen wanted to ban all reaffirmations. Others said there might be, in some cases, genuine *need* to reaffirm. The compromise was close scrutiny by the Court. We are to look them over in an exceedingly fine manner. . . .

The Congress has made a test of that scrutiny. The agreement (i) [must] not impos[e] an[y] undue hardship on the debtor or a dependent of the debtor; and (ii) [it must be] in the best interest of the debtor. . . .

No hardship is anywhere evident.

But what of the debtor's best interest?

The Court notes that the best-interest-of-the-debtor test is largely, though not exclusively, an economic inquiry given a specific factual setting. Simply put, either the debtor is entering into a mutually beneficial agreement or he is not. . . .

It is inconceivable that the debtor could not strike a better bargain than the one presented here. Carolina Furniture makes much of the fact that no interest is accruing over the 25 odd months of the proposed agreement. That is of no moment in light of the incontroverted fact that the parties are applying to the Court for authorization to pay nearly $800 for $200 worth of furniture. What will this furniture be worth in six, twelve, or eighteen months? And should untoward events transpire in the interim, the debtor is bound by a legally enforceable obligation.

The Court will not approve this agreement. It is not in the debtor's best interest to do so.

We find reflected here a factual situation emblematic of the mistakes people make who are likely candidates for bankruptcy. A significant part of the profile is this matter of entering into unfortuitous agreements. In a word, they make poor bargains. And they are prone to take the line of least resistance. "You can keep the stuff if you sign up for it again."

. . . .

What could this debtor have done which would be in his better interest?

(1) He could redeem the furniture for $200.*

(2) He could have sought a better bargain with the creditor for some figure between $200 and $792. It is apparent from the record that no effort at all was directed toward this end.

(3) He could allow the creditor to recover or reclaim the property and then purchase not necessarily new but replacement furniture.

---

*[Section 722 of the Bankruptcy Act empowers debtors to extinguish liens on certain property by paying the holder of the secured claim an amount equal to the value of the encumbered property.]

The post-bankruptcy period is a time for leanness. Debtor Jenkins would be surprised at what he can purchase, on credit, if need be, for two or three hundred dollars.

Debtor Jenkins has previously been in bankruptcy. His schedules reveal recent purchases of such luxuries as a piano, watch and a tape recorder as well as $1,000 cash on his Mastercharge. He apparently has not learned a great deal; perhaps he is not too astute as to what is in his own best interest.

He won't obtain approval of a complete reaffirmation from this Court. Frankly, we do not anticipate that this firm hand on the part of the Court will rehabilitate him, but in this small sphere of influence the Congressional intent shall be followed.

And what of the creditor? Are its rights trampled upon? Naturally, it would like to have its $792.76. However, while it is a "secured creditor," it is secured only to the extent of the value of its collateral. Since this is a no asset case and the debt a dischargeable one, the most it would otherwise receive is what can be realized on its collateral. If it can obtain approval of the proposed agreement—and note that it and not the debtor filed the application—it would realize its unsecured portion, $596.76 in full; the other unsecured creditors will receive nothing.

Under the agreement as proposed, the creditor would receive nearly $600 *more* for allowing the debtor to retain the furniture. This cannot be; it is too high a premium.

. . . Just as we wish people did not become ill or did not become criminals or did not have troubles, we wish people paid their just debts. But they don't always do so. That is the way it is. We wish they didn't need a doctor; we wish they didn't need bankruptcy. Yet through their own hands [extravagance] or through adverse winds that blow over which they have no control [illness, inflation], they require a cure. You must understand that the Congress—and responsible governments throughout history, from Biblical times—is trying to help these people. An effort is being made to restore these people with a fresh start so that they might return to the marketplace as viable, useful citizens. The philosophy of bankruptcy requires no explanation or defense among knowledgeable men and it is not our purpose here to defend it. We have noted over the years, however, that only about five percent, 5%, of the bankrupts-debtors ever return. One could conclude that the vast majority benefit and learn from the process.

The debtor will not be permitted to give nor the creditor receive $800 on $200 of what is now second-hand furniture.

The application for approval of the agreement is hereby denied.

IT IS SO ORDERED.

Discharge

In the vast majority of cases, a discharge is granted. A discharge means that the debtor is relieved from payment of, and released from liability for, all prefiling debts that are properly scheduled. That means that creditors are prevented, both through the nature of a discharge itself and by means of a federal court injunction, from any attempts to collect such debts. Thus, if a debtor is sued on such a debt in state-courts, the defense of discharge in bankruptcy may be asserted, which will act as a complete bar to the action.

Bars to Discharge

There are situations in which the Bankruptcy Court may not grant a discharge, however. Those situations include

1. If the debtor has previously received a discharge in bankruptcy within six years of the filing of the bankruptcy petition;

2. If the debtor has intentionally concealed or transferred assets to evade creditors or has concealed, destroyed, falsified, or failed to keep business records without a reasonable explanation, or has failed to adequately explain any loss of assets;

3. If the debtor has refused to obey an order of the bankruptcy court;

4. If the debtor has made any fraudulent statements or claim in connection with the bankruptcy.

These bars to bankruptcy are not automatic. Some creditor or other person with standing to complain must object to the discharge before the court will refuse to grant the discharge.

Nondischargeable Debts Some types of debts are also nondischargeable. This does not mean that the discharge is barred, but only that those debts will not be discharged. All other dischargeable debts will be discharged. Nondischargeable debts include claims for alimony and child support (both past and current), federal taxes incurred within three years, claims for wilful or malicious torts, and student loans less than seven years old.

The 1984 Amendments added a new and controversial section for consumer debts. That section provided that consumer debts owed to a single creditor for more than $500 worth of "luxury goods or services" incurred within 40 days of discharge are not dischargeable. Similarly, the section also makes cash advances under an open-end credit plan of over $1,000 within 20 days of the discharge are also nondischargeable. The creditor in both instances must ask the court for a determination of dischargeability and, if the court finds that the creditor was not justified in asking for such a determination, the court may order the creditor to pay court costs and attorneys' fees.

The 1984 Amendment also provides that the court may, on its own motion or at the request of a creditor, dismiss a petition for straight bankruptcy filed by an individual debtor if the debts are primarily consumer debts and if the court finds that the discharge would be "a substantial abuse" of the Bankruptcy Act.

Straight Bankruptcy and Employment The 1984 Amendments also made some important changes in the employment relationships of bankrupts and debtors. That Act provides that a private employer may not terminate the employment of, or discriminate against, an individual who is or has been a debtor under any provision of the Bankruptcy Act, or has been associated with such a person. The Act also prohibits employment termination or discrimination if a person is or has been "insolvent" prior to filing under the Act, or has not paid a dischargeable debt that was later discharged under the Act.

Adjustment of Debts: "Wage Earner Plans"

Chapter 13 of the Bankruptcy Act provides a real alternative for debtors who find themselves in financial difficulty but who do not wish to avail themselves of the extreme remedy of straight bankruptcy. Under Chapter 13, any "individual with regular income" and who has less than $100,000 in unsecured debts and less than $350,000 in secured debts may file a Petition for Adjustment of Debts. That petition will contain a "plan" to pay off the debts over a certain period of time. A certain portion of the debtor's income is paid to the trustee on a monthly basis, and the trustee in turn makes payments under the plan to the creditors. Only the debtor may file a petition for Adjustment of Debts, and there is therefore no such thing as an involuntary petition under Chapter 13. Such Chapter 13 petitions are often referred to as *Wage Earner Plans.*

If either the trustee or an unsecured creditor objects to the plan, the court may not approve the plan unless (1) the debt will be fully paid under the plan; or (2) the plan provides that all of the debtor's projected disposable income for the next three years will be applied to make payments on the plan. In the case of secured creditors, the court may not confirm the plan unless one of three things happens: (1) the secured creditor accepts the plan; (2) the proposed payments to the secured creditor have a present value that at least equals the value of the collateral, and the lien remains in place on the collateral; or (3) the collateral is surrendered to the secured party.

A Wage Earner Plan may be converted to a straight bankruptcy at any time, which provides substantial incentive to creditors to accept such plans. After completion of the plan, the debtor receives a discharge. The only debts excepted from the discharge are (1) certain long-term obligations specifically set out in the plan itself; and (2) child support, maintenance, and alimony payments.

Business Reorganizations

Using Chapter 11 of the Bankruptcy Act, businesses may request reorganization, though such petitions may also be filed by creditors. The purpose of such petitions is to continue the business and to pay off the debts of the business over time, in much the same manner as a Wage Earner Plan. Generally, the prior management is retained and continues to run the business (a "debtor in possession"), though a trustee or a committee of creditors may be appointed by the court as well. A plan is filed, either by the debtor or by the creditors, that will pay off the debts over a fixed period of time. The plan is confirmed by majority vote of the creditors, and accepted by two-thirds of the shareholders voting on the plan. Different votes are taken by each *class* of creditors voting on the plan.

Summary and Conclusions

While concern for consumer safety and protection from seller abuse has existed for a century or more, that concern reached a fever pitch in the 1960's and 1970's. Common-law protection for consumers, which had been restricted to the limited rules of warranty, fraud, and tort law, was seen as not sufficient to protect consumers or to ensure safe products. As a result, great numbers of federal and state statutes and regulations came into being.

The common law rules of caveat emptor and privity of contract, which had long prevented recovery in many cases of defective and dangerous products, were eroded by decisions in state courts, and that erosion resulted in an enormous body of law called *products liability.* Negligence theory, strict liability, and warranty theory all contributed to that new body of law.

But even those new protections were seen as insufficient. Federal statutes created new responsibilities in product safety for manufacturers, as in the Consumer Product Safety Act, and in selling practices, as in the Truth-in-Lending Act, and many others.

The final, and ultimate, consumer protection is found in the Federal Bankruptcy Act. That law provides that debtors who become overburdened by debt may receive a discharge from liability under certain conditions, or may arrange to pay them over time under a Wage Earner Plan. Similar provisions are available for overburdened businesses under the business reorganization provisions of the same Act.

PRO AND CON

ISSUE: Does the Emerging Law of Products Liability Benefit Business and Society?

PRO: Products Liability Provides an Incentive and Reason for Business to Produce Safe Products

Thomas F. Lambert, Jr.*

... [O]ne of the most practical measures for cutting down accidents and injuries in the field of product failure is a successful lawsuit against the supplier of the flawed product. Here, as well as elsewhere in Tort Law, immunity breeds irresponsibility while liability induces the taking of preventative vigilence. The best way to make a merchant responsible is to make him accountable for harms caused by his defective products. The responsible merchant is the answerable merchant.

Harm is the tort signature. The primary aim of Tort Law, of the civil liability system, is compensation for harm. Tort law also has a secondary, auxiliary and supportive function—the accident prevention function or prophylactic purpose of tort law—sometimes called the deterrent or admonitory function. Accident prevention, of course, is even better than accident compensation. ..." A Fence at the Top of the Cliff Is Better Than an Ambulance in the Valley Below."

1. Case of the Charcoal Briquets Causing Death from Carbon Monoxide.

Liability was imposed on the manufacturer of charcoal briquets for the carbon monoxide death and injury of young men who used the briquets indoors to heat an unvented mountain cabin. The 10-pound bags read, "Quick to Give Off Heat" and "Ideal for Cooking In or Out of Doors." The manufacturer was guilty of failure to warn of a lethal latent danger.

Any misuse of the product was foreseeable because it was virtually invited. Next time you stop in at the local supermarket or hardware store, glance at the label on the bags of charcoal briquets. In large capital letters you will find the following: "WARNING. DO NOT USE FOR INDOOR HEATING OR COOKING UNLESS VENTILATION IS PROVIDED FOR EXHAUSTING FUMES TO OUTSIDE. TOXIC FUMES MAY ACCUMULATE AND CAUSE DEATH." ...

2. Case of the Exploding Cans of Drano.

When granular Drano is combined with water, its caustic soda interacts with aluminum, another ingredient in its formula, and produces intensive heat, converting any water into steam at a rapid rate. If the mixture is confined, the pressure builds up until an explosion results. The manufacturer's use of a screw-on top in the teeth of such well known hazard was a design for tragedy. ... [A] ... housewife suffered total blindness from the explosion of a Drano can with a screw-on top, eventuating in a $900,000 compensatory and $10,000 punitive award to the wife. ... As a great Torts scholar has said, "Defective products should be scrapped in the factory, not dodged in the home." ...

3. Case of the Tip-Over Steam Vaporizer.

A tip-over steam vaporizer, true to that ominous description, was upset by a little girl who tripped

---

*From his article, "Suing for Safety," © 1983 Association of Trial Lawyers of America. Reprinted with permission from *Trial Magazine,* November, 1983.

over the unit's electric outlet cord on the way to the bathroom in the middle of the night. The sudden spillage of scalding water in the vaporizer's glass jar severely burned the 3-year old girl. . . . The cause of the catastrophe was a loose-lidded top which could have been eliminated by adopting any one of several accessible, safe, practical, available, desirable and feasible design alternatives, such as a screw-on or child-guard top. The truth is that the manufacturer . . . had experienced a dozen prior similar disasters. In the instant case, the little girl recovered a $150,000 judgment. . . . When the manufacturer, with icy indifference to the serious risks to infant users of its household product, refused to take its liability carrier's advice to recall and redesign its loose-lidded vaporizer, persisting in its stubborn refusal when over 100 claims had been filed against it, the carrier balked and refused to continue coverage unless the company would recall and redesign. Then and only then did [the firm] stir itself to redeem and correct the faulty design of its product, thereafter proudly prolcaiming (and I quote), "Cover-lock top protects against sudden spillage if accidentally tipped." Once again Tort Law had to play professor and policeman and teach another manufacturer that safety does not cost: It pays. Under what might be called the Cost-Cost formula, the manufacturer will add safety features when it comes to understand that the cost of accidents is greater than the cost of their prevention. The Tip-Over Steam Vaporizer case is the most graphic example . . . showing that corporate management can be recalled to its social responsibilities by threat of stringent liability. . . .

. . . .

9. Case of the 8-Year Old Boy Who Choked to Death.

. . . This case will indeed rivet the attention . . . of concerned citizens. . . . The present example involves a toymaker whose work is indeed "child's play."

Parker Brothers . . . had big plans for Riveton. This was a toy kit consisting of plastic parts, rubber rivets, and a riveting tool. . . . [O]ne of the . . . Riveton sets . . . ended up under the Christmas tree of an 8-year-old boy. . . . [H]e put one of the quarter-inch long rubber rivets into his mouth and choked to death. Ten months later . . . a second child strangled on a rivet.

. . . As manufacturers, Parker Brothers well knew that they would be held liable to an expert's skill and knowledge in the . . . business of toymaking. . . . When you manufacture for children, you produce for the improvident, the impetuous, the irresponsible. As a seasoned judge put it: " The concept of a prudent child, God forbid, is a grotesque combination." . . . The motto of childhood seems to be "When in doubt, eat it." . . .

Against the marketing milieu and the legal setting sketched above, what should be the proper response of Parker Brothers . . .? Should they have tried to tough it out or luck it out in the well known lottery called "do nothing and wait and see"? The company was sensitive not only to the constraints of the law . . . but also to the imperatives of moral duty and social responsibility, and the commercial value of an untarnished public image. Parker Brothers decided to halt sales and recall the toy. As the company president succinctly stated, "Were we supposed to sit back and wait for death No. 3?"

Business, the Frenchman observed, is a combination of war and sport. Tort law pressures business to realize how profitless it may prove to war against children or to trifle and jest with their safety. The commendable conduct of Parker Brothers in this case is one of the most striking tributes we know to the deterrent value and efficacy of Tort Law and the example would make a splendid case study for the nation's business schools. . . .

CON: The Products Liability System Is Haphazard and Damages Business
Richard A. Epstein*

It is . . . a matter of note when a business bankruptcy . . . that of a company whose current operations are profitable, is the lead story for several days not only in the *Wall Street Journal* but in ordinary newspapers all across the land. Yet just this has happened now that Manville Corp,—known for years under the name Johns-Manville—has sought refuge in a . . . bankruptcy court from an unending onslaught of lawsuits stemming from the use of asbestos.

Manville, long the largest supplier of asbestos, is currently defending itself against about 16,500 asbestos claims, with 500 new ones being brought every month. . . . The discounted cost of all expected claims present and future is by conservative estimates something over $2 billion. The net

*From his article, "Manville: The Bankruptcy of Product Liability Law," *Regulation* 6, no. 5 (September/October 1983): 14 et seq. Reprinted by permission.

worth of the company, the asbestos claims to one side, is just over $1 billion.

The effect of the petition, at least for the moment, is to place the operation of the company's business under the supervision of a bankruptcy judge, and to stay all lawsuits. . . .

One of the obvious questions about the current asbestos litigation is, why did nobody see it coming? Surely even the complexities of corporate structure could not have dulled all instincts to take prudent steps to minimize a loss of this magnitude. . . .

The central element, I believe, with asbestos as with other modern cumulative trauma litigation (DES, Agent Orange, and so on) is the passage of time. It has been conclusively established that there is a period of at least twenty, and often thirty or forty, years between the initial inhalation of asbestos and the manifestation of asbestos related diseases. The exposures to asbestos that were so frequent in the 1930's and 1940's have therefore become the subject of litigation only in very recent times, when the legal environment and medical understanding are vastly different from what they were back then. . . .

. . . .

Now that the battle has moved to the product liability arena, everything has been transformed. Retroactive application of new rules is just one of the problems. There is also a myriad of issues—defect, negligence, assumption of risk, and so forth—that must be litigated in order to determine relative responsibility. As Manville noted in the open announcement of bankruptcy, the tort system is "haphazard" in that different juries hearing the same evidence returned verdicts that ranged from a complete exoneration of Manville to an award of punitive damages against it. The company could have added that all these verdicts are probably consistent with the available evidence. The major source of difficulty is that modern doctrines of product liability law are so loosely formulated (chiefly consisting of a long list of relevant factors with indeterminate "weights") that once any defendant can be proved to have had any knowledge of any possible risk, any verdict, including one for punitive damages, becomes possible—and nonreversible on appeal.

. . . .

Is there, at this late date, any way to take the problem out of the tort system? One suggestion that has been frequently made of late is to establish some kind of comprehensive program, modeled loosely on the black lung disease fund, to which all asbestos victims would be required to apply for compensation.

. . . .

Is there some other way that promises to be both more modest and more successful? Here I think that we should look . . . at the worker's compensation system.

. . . .

One radical way to return to the compensation system is to bar all tort actions against suppliers. While this might seem radical within the American system, it represents the uniform practice in every other industrial country. The likelihood that anyone will adopt this approach in this country is slim for political and perhaps even consititutional reasons.

. . . .

. . . [T]he Manville bankruptcy has shown that even today there is not an endless supply of water at the trough. We must somehow undo the confusion wrought by unsystematic and unthinking judicial activism. Otherwise—as more and more cases work their way through the legal system, and more and more firms take the bankruptcy route—the only doors left will be closed, and marked "No Exit."

DISCUSSION QUESTIONS

1. As a matter of simple economics, do you agree with Adam Smith's statement at the beginning of this chapter? If consumption is not the end of production, what is? Are you surprised that Adam Smith, the "father of capitalism," would make such a statement?

2. As between two morally innocent parties, the seller and the buyer, who should bear the loss if the buyer is injured by a defective or dangerous product? Why? Does either of those parties *in fact* bear the risk of loss? Or is it always passed along to the consumer in the form of higher prices? Should we somehow prevent sellers from passing the cost along? How?

3. Caveat emptor was established as a legal doctrine in a time when the most sophisticated piece of goods that a consumer might buy was a wheelbarrow. In the light of today's sophisticated consumer goods, such as home computers, all sorts of electronic gadgets, and powerful (and dangerous) automobiles, could caveat emptor still work?

4. Some experts claim that we could make a totally safe automobile. The vehicle would weigh several tons, manuever like a tank, and guzzle huge amounts of fuel. Should we require it? Just how safe should products be? Totally safe? "Reasonably" safe? What criteria would you use?

5. A recent estimate placed the number of functionally illiterate American adults at 23 million (!). Do "disclosure" laws such as the Truth-in-Lending Act and RESPA help those people at all? Aren't those persons the very people the law is trying to help? Could the law be drafted differently to protect such persons?

6. Why does the law insist on protecting those who fail to pay their bills? Doesn't the fact that they are "deadbeats" justify any harassment or ill-treatment that a creditor cares to inflict? Or does it?

7. The bankruptcy exemptions have been roundly criticized. Which of the exemptions would you discard or limit, if any? Why?

8. Some critics of the bankruptcy laws have advocated that we only discharge "innocent" debts, that is, debts which were not incurred out of mismanagement of one's finances. Could we draft such a law, and permit discharge only of persons with crushing medical bills, who have lost their jobs, or who suffered other such disasters? List the situations in which you would permit discharge. Might there be others?

9. Another criticism of the consumer legislation passed in the last two decades is that it results in a great deal of unnecessary paperwork. Name all of the consumer legislation that requires such extra paperwork. Is that a good enough reason to do away with the legislation, as some advocate?

10. What do you think has been the overall effect on the price paid for consumer goods from the various consumer laws discussed both in this chapter and the last? Are you willing to pay higher prices for the goods you purchase (if that is the effect you found) in return for the safeguards of these laws?

CASE PROBLEMS

1. Henningsen purchased a Plymouth automobile from Bloomfield Motors, an independent dealer. Chrysler, the manufacturer of the automobile, gave an express warranty but disclaimed "all other warranties, express and implied." The express warranty was printed on the back of the purchase order, along with the disclaimer, in very small print, and no one drew Henningsen's attention to it. Ten days later, while Mrs. Henningsen was driving the car, she heard a loud cracking sound from under the hood, the wheel spun out of her hand, and the car veered into a brick wall. The express warranty specifically excepted personal injuries. Chrysler defended on the basis of caveat emptor, privity of contract,

and disclaimer of warranty. Result? [*Henningsen* v. *Bloomfield Motors,* 32 N.J. 358, 161 A. 2d 69, (1960).]

2. Green, a cigarette smoker, died of lung cancer. Under what theories, if any, may his estate sue the manufacturer of the cigarettes he smoked for forty years? [*Green* v. *American Tobacco Co.,* 409 F. 2d 1166 (5th Cir., 1969.)]

3. Escola was injured when a bottle of Coca-Cola exploded in her hand. She cannot prove why the bottle exploded. How will she prove her case, if at all? [*Escola* v. *Coca Cola Bottling Co.,* 24 Cal. 2d 453, 150 P. 2d 436 (1944).]

4. Smith purchased a new car from Zabriskie Chevrolet, an independent dealer, and paid cash for the car. A few weeks later the plaintiff's wife picked up the car, which had been ordered from the factory. Approximately .7 miles from the showroom, the car refused to move, and could not be driven in "drive." Smith stopped payment on the check, which had not yet cleared his bank, and had the car towed to the defendant's showroom. Zabriskie brought suit against Smith for the purchase price. Result? [*Zabriskie Chevrolet* v. *Smith,* 99 N.J. Super. 441, 240 A. 2d 195 (1968).]

5. Williams maintained a charge account for the purpose of purchasing furniture from the Walker-Thomas Furniture Co. The initial contract for the charge account said that the customer did not own any of the furniture as long as any balance remained on the charge account, and that all payments would be applied pro rata to all purchases. From 1957, when the contract was signed, until 1962, Williams purchased over $1,800 worth of furniture and made payments totalling over $1,400. In 1962, Williams became unable to make payments, since she had been forced to go on public aid and was supporting herself and seven children on $218 per month. Walker-Thomas brought an action to repossess everything Williams had purchased since 1957. Does Williams have a defense? [*Williams* v. *Walker-Thomas Furniture Co.,* 350 F. 2d 445 (D.C. Cir., 1965).]

6. Sheehan purchased a car financed by the Ford Motor Credit Company, then moved several times, and became delinquent in his payments. One of Ford's collection employees phoned Sheehan's mother, identified herself as an employee of a hospital, told her that one of Sheehan's children had been injured in an auto accident and requested that Sheehan call a specific number. Sheehan's mother supplied information regarding Sheehan's home address, business, and home phone numbers as well. The following day Sheehan's car was repossessed. Does Sheehan have a remedy? [*Ford Motor Credit Union* v. *Sheehan,* 373 So. 2d 956 (Fla., 1979).]

7. Martin gave his American Express card to an associate, instructing him orally that only $500 should be charged. Martin later received a bill for $5,300, which he refused to pay. Is he liable? [*Martin* v. *American Express, Inc.,* 361 So. 2d 597 (1978).]

8. Sebastian purchased a new bicycle from Alonso's Bike Shop. At the time of purchase, Sebastian told Alonso that the bicycle would be used in his delivery business and would have to carry heavy loads. Sebastian also informed Alonso that he knew nothing about bicycles and asked Alonso's help in choosing the proper bike. Three days later, the bike frame collapsed under the weight of Sebastian

and 150 pounds of canned goods he was delivering; Sebastian was injured. (1) What warranties did Alonso give Sebastian? (2) What remedies does Sebastian have against Alonso? Against the bicycle manufacturer?

9. Mr. Ford purchased a toaster from Falstaff's Fine Appliances. The toaster was manufactured by the Page Co., which sold the toaster to Evans' Distributing Co., which in turn sold the toaster to Falstaff. When Ford plugged in the toaster, it immediately caught on fire. In the ensuing blaze, Ford's home was destroyed, and high winds blew sparks on the home of his neighbor, Bardolph, which was also destroyed. Ford, Bardolph, Ford's aunt who was staying with him for the summer, and Bardolph's servant, Rugby, were all injured. Who may sue whom? If the toaster was completely destroyed in the fire, what theory or theories might be used to prove the cases? Which suits, if any, would be successful?

10. Mercutio purchased a set of encyclopedias from Tybalt, a door-to-door salesperson. The price of the books was $700, payable at $50 per month. Tybalt forgot to give the "truth-in-lending" statement to Mercutio, so he delivered it six days later. The day after Mercutio received the statement, Mercutio decided that he could not afford the books after all, and sent a letter to Tybalt telling him to cancel the sale. Has the sale been effectively cancelled?

11. Ophelia purchased a television set from Rosencrantz and Guildenstern's Appliances. Ophelia, a semiliterate with a sixth grade education, had never made a credit purchase before. The price of the television was $1,200, almost $800 more than it was really worth, but Rosencrantz and Guildenstern complied with all requirements of "truth-in-lending" and other federal and state consumer protection laws. Ophelia's salary of $75 per week did not cover the payments, and she defaulted. Rosencrantz and Guildenstern sued, repossessed the television, and sold it according to law for $200. They then sued Ophelia for a deficiency judgment of $1,000. Does Ophelia have a defense?

12. Balthazar, an employee of Pedro, purchased furniture from Dogberry's Furniture Store. In the contract was a confession of judgment clause and a wage assignment. (1) If Dogberry attempts to enforce the wage assignment against Pedro, what is Balthazar's remedy? (2) If Dogberry obtains a judgment by confession, what is Balthazar's remedy? (3) How may Dogberry get his money?

SUGGESTED READINGS

Bureau of National Affiars (BNA). *The Consumer Product Safety Act* (Washington, D.C.: Author, 1973).

Epstein, David G. *Consumer Protection in a Nutshell* (St. Paul, Minn.: West Publishing Co., 1976).

Epstein, David G., and Jonathan M. Landers. *Debtors and Creditors* (St. Paul, Minn.: West Publishing Co., 1982).

Hunt, Steven B. *Let the Buyer Beware!* (Skokie, Ill.: National Textbook Co., 1980).

McCall, James R. *Consumer Protection* (St. Paul. Minn.: West Publishing Co., 1977).

McGillian, James J., et al. *Consumer Product Safety Law* (Washington, D.C.: Government Institutes, Inc., 1977).

Warren, William D., and William E. Hogan. *Debtor-Creditor Law* (Mineola, N.Y.: The Foundation Press, 1981).

Part V

Regulation of the Relationship Between Business and Its Employees

Agency law created a large number of duties of employees to their employers but provided very little in the way of duties of employers to employees. The growing industrial revolution of the 19th century also created the incentive and opportunity for abuse by employers of their employees, resulting in sweat shops, unsafe working conditions, meager pay, and a generally uncaring attitude toward the personal fortunes of the employees.

The ethic of individual worth and dignity that began developing in the 18th century and led to our own Declaration of Independence and Bill of Rights also resulted in a major upheaval in the employment relationship. It was, it seemed, a logical extension of that ethic to protect the health, safety, and welfare of employees from the depradations of their employers.

Again the ethic of individualism presents countervailing considerations. Shouldn't an employer have the right to set wages at the lowest at which he can find employees? Doesn't the employer own the business? Isn't the private employment contract just that, an agreement between employer and employee, with no real public effect?

In the area of labor law, the ethic of individualism presents a rather contradictory problem: On the one hand, individualism would protect the right of the businessperson to negotiate the best labor contract possible with individual workers. But another aspect of individualism would protect the right of working people to dignity, safety, and the right to organize for protection. After all, working people are "individuals" as well. These twin concerns of individualism seem to be at odds in the context of the relationship of business and its employees.

Labor Law: Labor-Management Relations

If capital an' labor ever do git t'gether, it's good night fer th' rest of us.

"Abe Martin" (Frank McKinney Hubbard) 1930

There are compelling reasons for the proposition that the actual importance of business monopolies for inflation is quite small compared with that of labor unions.

Gottfried Haberler, Economic Growth and Stability *(1974)*

Labor is prior to, and independent of, capital. Capital is only the fruit of labor, and could never have existed if labor had not first existed. Labor is the superior of capital, and deserves much the higher consideration.

Abraham Lincoln, First Annual Message to Congress (December 3, 1861)

Nearly half the population of the United States is employed. Of that number, 16 percent are members of some trade, craft, or labor union. Almost every major employer in the nation, including units of state and local government, must deal with those unions in the course of ordinary business. Organized labor has become one of the most potent political and economic forces in the nation, revered by many and feared and hated by some.

Yet this was not always so. Employees had no right to even belong to unions in many states until 1935. It took a series of sweeping federal laws to give labor such power, power that grew so quickly that other federal laws were passed to limit its application. In a very large sense, federal law regarding labor is a "power balancer," stabilizing the power of labor and business to produce a rough equilibrium. Much of the controversy over labor law is whether such an equilibrium does in fact exist.

This chapter will provide an overview of federal regulation of labor. After a consideration of the history of the labor movement, we will discuss those laws in broad strokes. The problems of unionization, unfair labor practices, negotiation, enforcement of collective bargaining agreements, and the relationship of members to their own unions will be considered in some detail. The chapter will end with a discussion of the newest area of controversy, unionization of public employees.

The Evolution of the Labor Movement

Labor and management were not always antagonistic. Until the middle of the 19th century employees and employers generally shared a very harmonious and mutually profitable relationship. Though there were glaring exceptions in the cases of slavery and indentured servants and in certain rather isolated instances in other industries, most employers were craftsmen who worked shoulder-to-shoulder with their employees. The New World and the opening frontier within it beckoned to any dissatisfied worker, so labor was in short supply and wages high. Employer and employee often shared the workshop so that working conditions were generally good. Daily contact led to lasting personal relationships. And perhaps most importantly, employers and employees did not consider themselves to be "natural enemies."

Wrenching social and economic changes in the middle of the 19th century destroyed the craft system forever. Factories and assembly lines replaced the workshop. Anonymous corporations replaced individual owners. Businesses grew at a rapid rate, and the number of industrial workers grew proportionately. As costs became a prime concern, working conditions deteriorated and wages fell, to be forced down even further by demands for unskilled labor and by immigration from Europe. The personal relationships of the craft system were replaced by steely animosity and antagonism between employer and employee during the Industrial Revolution.

The Common-Law Employer-Employee Relationship

The legal relationship between employer and employee was determined by the law of agency, the law of contracts, and (in the case of slaves) the law of property. The law of contracts, upon which most employment law was based, assumed that the employment relationship was a mutually negotiated agreement, like any other contract. That assumption in turn depends on equality of bargaining position between the parties. Those assumptions may in fact have been valid under the craft system, but the increasing industrialization of the 19th century produced a "buyer's market" for employers. Unskilled laborers, often illiterate and faced with an oversupply of competing laborers, found employment on a "take it or leave it basis." As noted by the Supreme Court in 1921

A single employee was helpless in dealing with an employer. He was dependent ordinarily on his daily wage for the maintenance of himself and his family. If the employer refused to pay him the wages that he thought fair, he was nevertheless unable to leave the employ and to resist arbitrary and unfair treatment. Union was essential to give laborers an opportunity to deal on equality with their employer. *American Steel Foundries* v. *Tri-City Council*★

The Rise of Unionism

Trade unions had been around for a very long time in the form of guilds and associations of craftsmen for the betterment of the trade and for social functions. Such unions formed the nucleus of the trade union movement, which began in earnest immediately following the Civil War.

Employees quickly recognized that their principal weapon was the **strike,** or work stoppage, and that their goal must be joint negotiation, or **collective bargaining,** of labor contracts. During the late 19th century, many such organizations rose and fell, usually defeated by a combination of efforts by employers and economic depressions. It was not until the creation of the American Federation of Labor (AFL) in 1886 that a lasting labor organization was formed. That organization supported social and labor legislation, but relied on collective bargaining as its principal tool to achieve its objectives. Under the leadership of Samuel Gompers, such agreements were reached in the building trades, stove and glass container industries, and later in the coal mines. By 1903, almost 1.5 million persons claimed membership in the AFL. Perhaps most surprisingly, the AFL seemed able to withstand economic depressions.

Employer Opposition and Tactics

The free-swinging entrepreneurs of the Gilded Age were not about to sit back and permit labor to chip away at profits nor diminish their power to make unilateral decisions. Those men began their own campaign against unions, using a variety of tactics. Generally, the employers' arsenal included various self-help techniques, public opinion, and various legal weapons.

The 19th century capitalists were best able to help themselves. Often they would hire **strikebreakers,** or simply thugs who broke both strikes and strikers. **Scabs** would be hired to take striking laborer's jobs. **Labor spies** would be used to infiltrate labor organizations to determine the leaders, who would soon be fired and placed on a **blacklist,** which was circulated to all employers. Often the employers would simply close a plant in a **lock-out,** a kind of reverse strike designed to starve workers into submission.

While the American labor organizations were developing, some European labor groups were pursuing far more sinister and extreme tactics. Groups like the Irish Molly Maguires and the Wobblies (Industrial Workers of the World) used violence, riots, and even murder to achieve their goals, and succeeded in exporting a small part of their violence to the United States. These groups, taken together with the fearsome

---

★257 U.S. 184, 42 S. Ct. 72, 66 L. Ed. 189 (1921).

call for worldwide revolution by Karl Marx, convinced many Americans that all labor movements were somehow "evil." It was easy for American businessmen and their newspapers to convince the American public that our domestic labor movement should be repudiated as well.

The most potent weapons of businessmen were legal ones. Many labor organizers were jailed under **criminal conspiracy statutes,** which prohibited agreements to strike in many cases. The courts ruled that there was no constitutional right to strike, or even to organize. Many workers were forced to sign **yellow dog contracts,** which required workers to renounce union membership as a condition of employment. And most importantly, businessmen were often able to convince the courts to issue **injunctions** against labor activity. Once an injunction was granted businessmen could seek the aid of the police or even the army to put down labor strikes or organizing activity by force.

The Sherman Act

In 1890, the federal Sherman Act was passed, and a new weapon passed into the hands of employers. By outlawing all "contracts, combinations or conspiracies . . . in restraint of trade," that Act could be applied to labor unions without too much judicial stretching. The theory was that a labor union was nothing more than an agreement between competing workers to set prices and restrain competition for employment. The results were federal court injunctions against labor activity and federal indictments of labor organizers, found proper in the following case.

Loewe v. Lawlor (The Danbury Hatters' Case)

208 U.S. 274, 28 S. Ct. 301, 52 L. Ed. 488 (1908)

The plaintiffs were hat manufacturers in Connecticut who were faced with a threat of unionization. Plaintiffs alleged that the United Hatters of North America, a labor union, had instituted a boycott of the plaintiffs' goods when they failed to recognize the union and requested an injunction against that boycott, claiming the union "conspired intentionally and maliciously to interfere with the plaintiff's production of hats" by inducing a strike. The plaintiffs alleged actual damages of $80,000, and requested a federal injunction against the union and treble damages under the Sherman Act. The District Court dismissed the complaint.

Mr. Chief Justice FULLER delivered the opinion of the Court:

. . . .

In our opinion, the combination described in the declaration is a combination "in restraint of trade or commerce among the several states," in the sense in which those words are used in the act, and the action can be maintained accordingly.

And that conclusion rests on many judgments of this court, to the effect that the act prohibits any combination whatever to secure action which essentially obstructs the free flow of commerce between the states, or restricts, in that regard, the liberty of a trader to engage in business. . . .

In an early case . . . the court, granting the injunction, said:

I think the congressional debates show that the statutes had its origin in the evils of massed capital; but, when the Congress came to formulating the prohibition, . . . [t]he subject has so broadened in the minds of the legislators that the source of the evil was not regarded as material, and the evil in its entirety is dealt with.

They made the interdiction include combinations of labor as well as of capital; in fact, all combinations in restraint of commerce, without reference to the character of the persons who entered into them. . . . [I]t seems to me, its meaning, as far as relates to the sort of combinations to which it is to apply, is manifest, and that it includes combinations which are composed of laborers acting in the interest of laborers. . . .

Judgment reversed and cause remanded. . . .

The Turnabout

Even in the face of employer opposition and staggering legal disadvantages, labor made strong inroads into American public opinion. Bitter and violent strikes and harsh employer responses in the Pullman strike and the anthracite coal confrontation hurt the employers' cause deeply. By the time Woodrow Wilson became President, public sentiment strongly favored federal intervention on the side of workers. Between 1914 and 1935, there came a fairly steady stream of federal labor legislation, first encouraging and later virtually mandating collective bargaining.

Federal Labor Legislation

The Clayton Act

The first major piece of federal labor legislation was the Clayton Act of 1914, already discussed in detail in Chapters 8, 9, and 10. Two sections of the Act were hailed by Samuel Gompers as an "industrial Magna Carta." Section 6 of the Clayton Act provides that "the labor of a human being is not a commodity or article of commerce. Nothing contained in the antitrust laws shall be construed to forbid the existence and operation of labor . . . organizations. . . ." Section 20 of the Clayton Act bars federal injunctions "in any case between an employer and employees" involving a dispute concerning terms and conditions of employment, and specifically prohibits injunctions against activities such as quitting work or persuading others to do so.

But even in the light of these legislative changes, state-court injunctions continued to be issued on the basis of the common law, and the Supreme Court later permitted federal injunctions against labor activity, as long as that activity was not directed against the employees' direct employer, thus limiting the effectiveness of the Clayton Act substantially.

The Railway Labor Act

Because of potential interruptions in service during World War I, the federal government operated the nation's railroads between 1917 and 1920 and, in the process, fostered and encouraged collective bargaining in that industry. When the railroads were transferred back to private hands, Congress created the Railway Labor Board and strengthened its authority greatly, in 1926, by passage of the Railway Labor Act. That Act, signed into law by Calvin Coolidge, emphasized collective bargaining and mediation by a federal board in the event of disputes and declared the right of the parties to designate representatives (unions) without interference, influence, or coercion. The Act was to be used as a model for later, more encompassing federal labor legislation.

The Norris-LaGuardia Anti-Injunction Act

After Section 20 of the Clayton Act had been largely nullified by restrictive court interpretations, labor continued to battle the court injunction in Congress. Finally, in the heart of the Depression and in the year prior to President Roosevelt's inauguration, Congress passed the Norris-LaGuardia Act. That law provided that "yellow-dog" contracts were unenforceable in federal courts and prohibited the issuance of any injunction by a federal court "in a case involving or growing out of a labor dispute." To make sure the courts got the message, the Act included a list of nine very specific situations in which injunctions may not be issued, including court orders which prohibit

   a. Ceasing or refusing to perform any work or to remain in any relation of employment;

   b. Becoming or remaining a member of any labor organization or of any employer organization. . . . ;

   c. Paying or giving to, or withholding from, any person participating or interested in such labor dispute, any strike or unemployment benefits or insurance, or other moneys or things of value;

   d. By all lawful means aiding any person participating or interested in any labor dispute who is being proceeded against in, or in prosecuting, any action or suit in any court of the United States or of any State;

   e. Giving publicity to the existence of, or the facts involved in, any labor dispute, whether by advertising, speaking, patrolling, or by any other method not involving fraud or violence;

   f. Assembling peaceably to act or to organize to act in promotion of their interests in a labor dispute;

   g. Advising or notifying any person of an intention to do any of the acts heretofore specified;

   h. Agreeing with other persons to do or not to do any of the acts heretofore specified; and

   i. Advising, urging, or otherwise causing or inducing without fraud or violence the acts heretofore specified. . . .

Industrial Laissez Faire and the Depression

In a large sense, the Norris-LaGuardia Act simply ushered in an era of industrial **laissez faire.** That is, though the federal government did not take an active role in promoting the interests of labor, it did not actively promote the interests of employers either. Prior to the Act, the federal courts had taken an unabashed pro-employer stand, but the Norris-LaGuardia Act instructed the courts to take a hands-off attitude.

But a hands-off attitude was not enough. The Depression, like all economic downtrends, produced a huge oversupply of labor resulting in a "buyer's market" for employers. Employers could, and did, insist on nonunion employees. State courts continued to be quite adverse to the interests of labor and granted injunctions against organizing, strikes, and other labor activity. The U.S. Supreme Court held both federal and state laws designed to aid labor unconstitutional under the Commerce Clause, the Contracts Clause, or other parts of the document. It was obvious that more positive measures were needed.

At first the "New Deal" Congress tried a form of voluntary compliance in the National Industrial Recovery Act of 1933, which established codes of fair competition in various industries. Those codes were required to contain a recognition of the employees' right to organize and bargain collectively. That Act was held unconstitutional by the Supreme Court in 1935.* It did not seem possible for the federal government to pass any bill relating to general labor conditions under the Supreme Court's interpretation of the Commerce Clause.

The Wagner Act

As recounted in Chapter 2, Congress did pass a sweeping law designed to ameliorate the problems of labor in the National Labor Relations Act (NLRA) of 1935, also known as the Wagner Act. To force the Supreme Court's hand, President Roosevelt announced the famous **court-packing plan** described in Chapter 2. Not long after, the Supreme Court announced its decision in *NLRB* v. *Jones & Laughlin Steel* (Chapter 2, p. 52). That decision not only held the Wagner Act constitutional, but also vastly widened the entire federal authority over interstate commerce and set the stage for many other federal regulations.

The basic policy of the Wagner Act was to first encourage unionization by establishing a right to organize and protecting that right and, second, to encourage collective bargaining between such organizations and employers. The Act promoted those objectives in several ways: it established the *right to organize* and to become a member of labor organizations; it established, at least in general form, a *method* by which employees might choose a union; it created five *unfair labor practices* on the part of employers, generally prohibiting activity which hampered the right to organize, and provided remedies for their violation; and it created a new independent regulatory commission, the *National Labor Relations Board (NLRB)*, with the authority to make rules and with the power to hold elections and to hear unfair labor practice charges. Many of the specific provisions of the NLRA were subsequently amended by the Taft-Hartley Act of 1947 and the Landrum-Griffin Act of 1959, discussed later (see Appendix C).

The National Labor Relations Board (NLRB)   The NLRB is a five-member, independent regulatory commission. The members of the Board are appointed by the President for staggered five-year terms and are assisted by the General Counsel, who is also appointed by the President, but for a four-year term. The NLRB also has established 32 regional offices and a number of field offices, which are under the supervision of the General Counsel.

Schecter Poultry Corp. v. *U.S.*, 295 U.S. 495, 55 S. Ct. 837, 79 L. Ed. 1570 (1935).

The Board has four principle functions under the Act: it may make rules to carry out the provisions of the Act; it must conduct representation elections and certify the results; it must act to prevent "unfair labor practices" as defined in the Act; and it may conduct investigations. The vast majority of the Board's activities involve elections and unfair labor practices.

The NLRA was based on Commerce Clause authority and, thus, all cases must involve activities that "affect commerce." However, as discussed in Chapter 2, Commerce Clause authority is broad indeed, so that virtually any employer save the very smallest, exclusively local business is covered by the Act. The Board established self-imposed limits, however, for exercising its authority. For example, the NLRB will generally not involve itself in disputes involving retail enterprises unless the total annual volume of business is over $500,000, nonretail businesses with under $50,000 per year in direct sales to consumers (outflow), or $50,000 in purchases (inflow), newspapers with under $200,000 in total annual volume of business, or colleges and universities with under $1 million in gross revenues. Under the Act certain types of employees are exempt as well, including agricultural laborers, domestic servants, persons employed by their parents or spouses, independent contractors, supervisors, persons subject to the Railway Labor Act, and government employees at all levels of government.

The term *supervisor* has given substantial problems in interpretation. Under the Act that term includes any person who has the authority to hire, transfer, suspend, lay off, promote, discharge, assign, reward, or discipline another, or who has the authority to direct other employees or adjust grievances, as long as the authority results from independent judgment, and includes persons whose opinion carries substantial weight with management in hiring, firing, and related decisions.

The Taft-Hartley Act

Between 1935 and 1947, organized labor gained vast power. Labor union membership grew from 3 million in 1935 to 15 million in 1947, and two-thirds of all manufacturing employees were covered by labor contracts. This rapid growth, along with a series of crippling strikes in key industries, labor corruption, and heavy-handed tactics by some unions resulted in pressure for reform of the nation's labor laws.

The result of this pressure was the 1947 Taft-Hartley Act, an amendment to the Wagner Act. The Act was passed over the veto of President Truman. It was aimed at a perceived "asymmetry" or imbalance in the prior law, which had been designed solely to protect labor. The new law was designed, at least according to its sponsors, to provide balance between labor and management.

The Act is long and involved, making many technical changes in the Wagner Act along with its substantive provisions. Among its more important sections are (1) the creation of six *union* unfair labor practices; (2) establishment of the right of employers to express their views publicly, as long as there is no threat of reprisal or promise of economic benefit; (3) establishment of the federal **Mediation and Conciliation Service** as an independent agency; (4) creation of some very specific requirements for union elections; (5) creation of a procedure for dealing with strikes during a "national emergency," including a forced "80-day cooling off period"; (6) establish-

ment of the right of an employee *not* to join a union, except in the case of a "union-shop" agreement; and (7) permission to the states to outlaw compulsory union membership (state right-to-work laws will be discussed later, see p. 475).

The Landrum-Griffin Act

During the 1950's, a series of Congressional investigations disclosed that some labor unions had been tainted by corruption and undemocratic procedures. To remedy the situation, Congress passed the Landrum-Griffin Act, also known as the Labor-Management Reporting and Disclosure Act of 1959. That Act required labor unions to register with the Secretary of Labor, adopt constitutions, by-laws and democratic voting procedures, supply annual reports to the Secretary of Labor, and grant their members a list of rights as union members, known as the *Union Member's Bill of Rights*. Embezzlement of union funds was made a federal crime, and the Act added two more union unfair labor practices, dealing with *blackmail picketing* and *hot cargo agreements* (see p. 461).

The Right to Organize

Perhaps the most important part of the Wagner Act is Section 7, which established the rights of employees to organize and join labor unions and to join in concerted action for the purpose of collective bargaining. The Act also provided that employees had the right to refrain from joining unions or engaging in such concerted behavior.

In the relatively few words of Section 7, all of the prior debate over the legality of unions and collective bargaining, the problems of criminal conspiracy laws and the misapplication of the antitrust laws, and the question of the ability of the federal courts to render injunctions against union activity were answered. Section 7, especially when read together with Section 1, established a national policy affirmatively favoring collective bargaining as the principal means of resolving disputes between labor and management.

Establishing a national policy favoring collective bargaining is one thing; enforcing it is quite another. The National Industrial Recovery Act (NIRA) of 1933 had contained a similar expression of policy, but that law was largely unenforceable and was ruled unconstitutional by the Supreme Court. But the Wagner Act was different, because it was held constitutional by the Supreme Court in 1937 in the *Jones and Laughlin Steel* decision (Chapter 2, p. 52), and because the Wagner Act contained real "teeth" in the form of the concept of unfair labor practices.

Unfair Labor Practices

The Wagner Act introduced the concept of "unfair labor practices" by listing five types of conduct by *employers* that were prohibited by the Act. The Taft-Hartley and

Landrum-Griffin Acts later remedied the perceived "imbalance" in the NLRA by listing seven *union* unfair labor practices. Taken together these sections, found in sections 8(a) and 8(b) of the NLRA, provide the principal means of enforcing the Act. The NLRB has jurisdiction to enforce the unfair labor practices provisions. Students should carefully review the statutory language of these sections in Appendix C, since the wording is quite precise and numerous exceptions are permitted.

Section 8(a): "Employer" Unfair Labor Practices

Five "employer" unfair labor practices were established by the Wagner Act.

Section 8(a)(1): Interference, Restraint or Coercion of Employee Rights: This broad section includes any violation of the other four employer unfair labor practices. Examples include threatening employees if they vote for a union, spying, or even questioning employees about union activities (see *NLRB* v. *Exchange Parts*, p. 467).

Section 8(a)(2): Company Dominance or Financial Support of a Union: This section was aimed at the practice of forming "company unions" dominated by the employer, which do not have the same independence or power as unrelated organizations.

Section 8(a)(3): Discrimination Against Employees: This section requires employers to deal even-handedly with both union and nonunion employees. Examples of prohibited conduct include discharge or discipline of union members for union activities or discontinuing an operation at one plant and discharging the employees followed by opening the same operation at another plant with new employees because the employees at the first plant joined a union. Employers may take action for genuine economic reasons and may discriminate against an employee for failure to pay union dues.

Section 8(a)(4): Discrimination for NLRB Activities: This section guards the right of employees to take action under the Act and preserves the integrity of the NLRA by prohibiting action against employees who make use of the Act's provisions.

Section 8(a)(5): Refusal to Bargain in Good Faith: This section, together with section 8(b)(3), imposes a duty to bargain about certain subjects, including "wages, hours and other terms and conditions of employment," on both management and labor. The duty to bargain will be considered in detail later in the chapter.

Section 8(b): "Union" Unfair Labor Practices

Seven union practices were prohibited by the Taft-Hartley and Landrum-Griffin Acts.

Section 8(b)(1): Restraint or Coercion of Employees: This section prohibits unions from forcing persons to join unions or join in union activities. A major exception exists if the employer and the union have formed a "union-shop" agreement, in which all employees must be members of the union. The Section prohibits threats and acts of violence, mass picketing, barring nonstriking employees from entering a plant, and even statements that employees who oppose a union will lose their jobs. Section 8(b)(1)(B) prohibits unions from restraining or coercing *employers* in the selection of a bargaining representative, regardless of whether the union is the choice of the majority of employees.

Section 8(b)(2): Causing or Attempting to Cause Discrimination: Unions may attempt to pressure employers to discriminate against nonunion members. This section prohibits such conduct in the absence of a "union-shop" contract. This section "meshes" with Section 8(a)(3).

Section 8(b)(3): Refusal to Bargain in Good Faith: This section imposes the same duty to bargain on unions as imposed on employers by Section 8(a)(5).

Section 8(b)(4): Prohibited Strikes and Boycotts: This long and complex section prohibits strikes and boycotts to accomplish certain purposes or objects. Those prohibited actions include compelling membership in an employer or labor organization, compelling execution of a **hot cargo agreement,** compelling a **secondary boycott** (discussed later), compelling recognition of an uncertified union, compelling recognition of a union if another union has been certified, and compelling assignment of certain work to certain employees. These prohibitions will be considered later under the Right to Strike.

Section 8(b)(5): Charging Excessive or Discriminatory Membership Fees: The purpose of this section is to prohibit entry barriers to new employees.

Section 8(b)(6): "Featherbedding:" This section prohibits a union from compelling an employer to hire employees that are not needed or paying for work not actually done.

Section 8(b)(7): Organizational and Recognitional Picketing by Noncertified Unions: Picketing by a noncertified union is prohibited if it is done for purposes of obtaining recognition by an employer or obtaining members for the union in three instances: when the employer has already recognized another union and no representation election is possible; when a valid NLRB election has been held within the last twelve months; and when a "representation petition" is not filed within 30 days. **Publicity picketing,** also known as **informational picketing,** is permissible to inform the public that an employer does not employ union members or does not have a contract.

Hot Cargo Agreements

A **hot cargo agreement** is a part of a labor contract which provides that employees are not required to handle or work on goods or materials going to or coming from an employer designated by the union as "unfair." Such agreements were quite common in the construction trades and transportation industries prior to the Landrum-Griffin Act. Strikes or other union action to obtain such agreements are unfair labor practices and entering into such an agreement is an unfair labor practice by both unions and management under Section 8(e) of the Wagner Act.

There are limited exceptions from the "hot cargo" prohibition in the construction and garment industries. In the construction industry, an employer and a union may agree to a provision in a labor contract that restricts the employer from contracting or subcontracting with an employer who has no union contract. Similarly, in the garment industry, an employer and a union may agree that the employer will not subcontract work on goods or other work that is part of "an integrated process of production" in the apparel and clothing industry to an employer which does not have a union contract.

Secondary Boycotts

A **secondary boycott** occurs when a union has a dispute with Company A and causes Company B to cease doing business with Company A to put pressure on Company A. In such a case, Company A is the *primary employer* and Company B is the *secondary employer*. For example, urging employees of a building contractor not to install doors made by a manufacturer with whom a union is having a dispute might be a secondary boycott, and strikes or picketing to obtain such a boycott by the building contractor is an unfair labor practice.

The Act does not protect an employer from the "incidental" effects of union activities against the primary employer, however. As a result, picketing a **common situs,** where both employers do business, is generally not an unfair labor practice, as in the case of picketing a construction site where both the primary and secondary employers are doing business. Picketing at such a common situs is generally limited by the courts to times when the employees of the primary employer are working and when the primary employer is carrying on its normal business, to places where the primary employer is carrying on its business, and must be conducted in such a manner that the signs and conduct of the strikers indicate that the dispute is with the primary employer and not with the secondary employer.

If a company establishes a *reserved gate* to its premises for the exclusive use of a contractor, that gate may not be picketed by employees involved in a dispute with the company. Such picketing would be considered as a secondary boycott, unless the gate was used by both the company and the contractor for whom the gate was reserved.

Enforcement of Unfair Labor Practices

The NLRB has two main functions: to conduct representation elections and certify the results, and to prevent employers and unions from engaging in unfair labor practices. In both cases, the NLRB must be asked to intervene by one of the parties. In the case of unfair labor practices, one of the parties must file a "charge" with the Board. If there is an established grievance procedure, the Board may defer action until the grievance procedure has been carried to completion.

Unfair labor practices are heard initially by an NLRB Administrative Law Judge, who makes findings and recommendations to the Board. Based on those recommendations, the Board may issue an order requiring a party to **cease and desist** from such practices and may order affirmative action, such as reinstatement, or may grant a **bargaining order** requiring the parties to bargain over an issue.

If an employer or a union fails to comply with a Board order, the Board may petition the U.S. Court of Appeals for a court decree enforcing the order of the Board. Likewise, persons aggrieved by a Board order may obtain a review of the order before the Court of Appeals. The Court may enforce the order, remand it to the Board for reconsideration, change it, or set it aside entirely. Failure to comply with the Court order enforcing a Board order is punishable by fine or imprisonment for contempt of court, or even union recognition as in the following case.

NLRB v. Gissel Packing Co.

395 U.S. 575, 89 S. Ct. 1918, 23 L. Ed. 2d 542 (1969)

In three virtually identical cases, a union waged an organizational campaign and succeeded in having a majority of the employees sign **authorization cards.** An authorization card is not a membership card but merely a statement that the employee desires the union to request an election on the question of union representation. Signing an authorization card in no way indicates that the employee will vote for the union once the election is held. All three unions demanded recognition on the basis of the authorization card majority, and all three employers refused to bargain with the unions. Instead, all three employers embarked on vigorous anti-union campaigns, including some actions which gave rise to unfair labor practice charges against the employers.

In the case of one employer (Gissel Packing Co.), the union did not seek an election but filed unfair labor practice charges for refusal to bargain, coercion, and intimidation of employees. In the second case (involving Heck's Inc.), an election was sought but never held because of nearly identical unfair labor practices. And in the third case (involving General Steel Products), an election was won by the employer but later set aside by the NLRB because of unfair labor practices. In each case, the NLRB issued a bargaining order to the employer, requiring the employer to recognize the union, ordered the companies to cease and desist from future unfair labor practices and to offer reinstatement with back pay to employees who had been discriminatorily discharged. The companies appealed and the Court of Appeals rejected the Board's order and refused to enforce the order to bargain.

The Court first considered at length whether an "authorization card majority" was sufficient to impose a duty to bargain on an employer. The Court held that the language of the Taft-Hartley Act provided more than one means of choosing a bargaining representative and, as long as the representative was chosen by the majority of the employees, the employer had a duty to bargain. The Court also found that such authorization cards, while "admittedly inferior" to a secret election, were not so "inherently unreliable indicators of employee desires" that they could not establish a majority and impose a duty to bargain.

Mr. Chief Justice WARREN delivered the opinion of the Court.

. . . .

Remaining before us is the propriety of a bargaining order as a remedy for a §8(a)(5) refusal to bargain where an employer has committed independent unfair labor practices which have made the holding of a fair election unlikely or which have in fact undermined a union's majority and caused an election to be set aside. We have long held that the Board is not limited to a cease-and-desist order in such cases, but has the authority to issue a bargaining order without first requiring the union to show that it has been able to maintain its majority status. . . . And we have held that the Board has the same authority even where it is clear that the union, which once had possession of cards from a majority of the employees, represents only a minority when the bargaining order is entered. . . . We see no reason now to withdraw this authority from the Board. If the Board could enter only a cease-and-desist order and direct an election or a rerun, it would in effect be rewarding the employer and allowing him to "profit from [his] own wrongful refusal to bargain," . . . while at the same time severely curtailing the employees' right freely to determine whether they desire a representative. The employer could continue to delay or disrupt the election processes and put off indefinitely his obligation to bargain; and any election held under these circumstances would not be likely to demonstrate the employees' true, undistorted desires.

The employers argue that the Board has ample remedies, over and above the cease-and-desist order, to control employer misconduct. The Board can, they assert, direct the companies to mail notices to the employees, to read notices to employees during plant time and to give the union access to employees during working time at the plant, or it can seek a court injunctive order . . . as a last resort. In view of the

Board's power, they conclude, the bargaining order is an unnecessarily harsh remedy that needlessly prejudices employees' §7 rights solely for the purpose of punishing or restraining an employer. Such an argument ignores that a bargaining order is designed as much to remedy past election damage as it is to deter future misconduct. If an employer has succeeded in undermining a union's strength and destroying the laboratory conditions necessary for a fair election, he may see no need to violate a cease-and-desist order by further unlawful activity. The damage will have been done. . . . There is, after all, nothing permanent in a bargaining order, and if, after the effects of the employer's acts have worn off, the employees clearly desire to disavow the union, they can do so by filing a representation petition. . . .

We emphasize that under the Board's remedial power there is still a . . . category of minor or less extensive unfair labor practices, which, because of their minimal impact on the election machinery, will not sustain a bargaining order. There is, the Board says, no *per se* rule that the commission of any unfair labor practice will automatically result in a §8(a)(5) violation and the issuance of an order to bargain.

Reversed.

Just what type of unfair labor practices will result in the imposition of a **Gissel-remedy** seems unclear. The remedy is clearly applicable in cases involving the grant of significant benefits to the employees (see *Exchange Parts*, p. 467) and in cases of repeated violations of Section 8(a)(3), such as discharge of employees with union affiliations.

Contemporary Dimensions: The Problem of the "Runaway Shop"

One answer to continuing union pressure is to simply shut down a plant or move operations to a more friendly location, such as a state where unions are less active or to a state with a right-to-work law (see p. 475). But if the move arises from antiunion sentiment, it may be an unfair labor practice.

Textile Workers Union v. Darlington Manufacturing Co.

380 U.S. 263, 85 S. Ct. 994, 13 L. Ed. 2d 827 (1965)

Darlington, a South Carolina corporation, operated a single mill. But a majority of Darlington's stock was held by a New York firm, which in turn was controlled by Roger Milliken. Milliken and his family controlled seventeen different mills, all operated as separate corporations, which marketed their products through another firm controlled by Milliken.

In 1956, the Textile Workers Union began an organizational campaign in the Darlington plant, which the company resisted vigorously. The union won the election on September 6. On September 12, Milliken called a meeting of the Board of Directors, which voted to close the mill and liquidate the corporation. The purpose of the closing was found to be to avoid unionization. The union filed charges with the NLRB on the basis of Sections 8(a)(1), 8(a)(3), and 8(a)(5). The Board found a violation of Section 8(a)(3) and ordered back pay until the employees obtained substantially equivalent work. The Court of Appeals set aside the order and denied enforcement. The union appealed.

Mr. Justice HARLAN delivered the opinion of the Court. . . .

We hold that so far as the National Labor Relations Act is concerned, an employer has the absolute right to terminate his entire business for any reason he pleases, but disagree with the Court of Appeals that such right includes the ability to close part of a business no matter what the reason. . . .

We consider first the argument . . . that an employer may not go completely out of business without running afoul of the Labor Relations Act if such action is prompted by a desire to avoid unionization. Given the Board's findings on the issue of motive, acceptance of this contention would carry the day for the Board's conclusion that the closing of this plant was an unfair labor practice. . . . A proposition that a single businessman cannot choose to go out of business if he wants to would represent such a startling innovation that it should not be entertained without the clearest manifestation of legislative intent or unequivocal judicial precedent so construing the Labor Relations Act. We find neither. . . .

The AFL-CIO suggests in its *amicus* brief that Darlington's action was similar to a discriminatory lockout, which is prohibited "because designed to frustrate organizational efforts, to destroy or undermine bargaining representation, or even the duty to bargain." One of the purposes of the Labor Relations Act is to prohibit the discriminatory use of economic weapons in an effort to obtain future benefits. The discriminatory lockout designed to destroy a union, like a "runaway shop," is a lever which has been used to discourage collective employee activities in the future. But a complete liquidation of a business yields no such future benefit for the employer, if the termination is bona fide. It may be motivated more by spite against the union than by business reasons, but it is not the type of discrimination which is prohibited by the Act. The personal satisfaction that such an employer may derive from standing on his beliefs and the mere possibility that other employers will follow his example are surely too remote to be considered dangers at which the labor statutes were aimed. Although employees may be prohibited from engaging in a strike under certain conditions, no one would consider it a violation of the Act for the same employees to quit their employment en masse, even if motivated by a desire to ruin the employer. The very permanence of such action would negate any future economic benefit to the employees. The employer's right to go out of business is no different.

We are not presented here with the case of a "runaway shop," whereby Darlington would transfer its work to another plant or open a new plant in another locality to replace its closed plant. Nor are we concerned with a shut down where the employees, by renouncing the union, could cause the plant to reopen. Such cases would involve discriminatory employer action for the purpose of obtaining some benefit from the employees in the future. We hold here only that when an employer closes his entire business, even if the liquidation is motivated by vindictiveness toward the union, such action is not an unfair labor practice. . . .

The closing of an entire business, even though discriminatory, ends the employer-employee relationship; the force of such a closing is entirely spent as to that business when termination of the enterprise takes place. On the other hand, a discriminatory partial closing may have repercussions on what remains of the business, affording employer leverage for discouraging the free exercise of §7 rights among remaining employees of much the same kind as that found to exist in the "runaway shop" and "temporary closing" cases. . . . Moreover, a possible remedy open to the Board in such a case, like the remedies available in the "runaway shop" and "temporary closing" cases, is to order the reinstatement of the discharged employees in other parts of the business. No such remedy is available when an entire business has been terminated. . . . [W]e are constrained to hold . . . that a partial closing is an unfair labor practice under §8(a)(3) if motivated by a purpose to chill unionism in any of the remaining plants of the single employer and if the employer may reasonably have foreseen that such closing would likely have that effect.

The Court referred the case back to the NLRB to determine the purpose and effect of the plant closing on employees in other mills operated by Milliken or the New York firm which he controlled.

Two states, Wisconsin and Maine, have enacted statutes requiring firms to give advance notice of impending plant closing. Massachusetts has a "voluntary" notice statute, providing that future grants and tax relief are contingent upon giving such notice, and various notice statutes have been introduced in the legislatures of 38 states.

The Process of Unionization

Most union organizing efforts begin when a group of employees contacts a union, usually because of some deep-rooted dissatisfaction or some unsettling development on the job. The choice of which union to contact is crucial, such as between a very specific "craft" union and a union with a broad jurisdiction, such as the Teamsters. The initial meeting is usually followed by the creation of an "inside" organizing committee, demonstrating local control and providing greater access to the employees. Often the drive is initially kept secret from the employer out of fear of reprisal, but the union may announce its intention right away in order to obtain a list of employee names and address, to which it has a right under NLRB rules.

The National Labor Relations Act requires that *30 percent* of the employees sign **authorization cards** in order to hold an election regarding representation. However, a card *majority* may be used to obtain bargaining rights without an election, or even despite an election loss, if the employer commits unfair labor practices considered by the NLRB to have had a substantial impact on the vote (see *NLRB* v. *Gissel Packing*). When sufficient authorization cards have been signed, the union organizer will write a **recognition letter** to the company president, informing the company that the union has signed up a majority of the employees, offering to prove this to an impartial observer, and requesting that the employer bargain with the union.

While an employer may simply enter into collective bargaining, it may also insist that the union win an election, and the union *must* win an election unless the NLRB finds that the employer's unfair labor practices made a fair result impossible under *Gissell.* Employers usually refuse the demand for recognition.

The union's response is usually to file a petition for an election with the NLRB. The NLRB can only hold such an election if a petition has been filed requesting one. In some circumstances, employers may file such a petition, if more than one labor organization has made a claim for recognition as the exclusive representative of the same group of employees. The Act also provides that **decertification elections** may be held after a petition is filed by employees or someone acting on their behalf to determine whether the current bargaining representative should be retained. Petitions for **union-shop deauthorization elections** may be filed if signed by 30 percent of employees to determine whether to withdraw the authority of their representative to continue a union-shop agreement. Upon receipt of a petition, the NLRB must investigate the petition, hold a hearing if necessary, and direct an election if it finds that a question of representation exists.

The election itself is by secret ballot, and employees are given the choice between one or more bargaining representatives or no representatives at all. To be certified, the organization must receive a majority of all ballots cast. The election may be held by agreement between the parties as to time and place, the choices on the ballot, and the method of determining eligibility to vote. If the parties cannot agree, the NLRB will hold a hearing to determine such matters. To be entitled to vote, an employee must have worked in the unit during the "eligibility period" set by the Board, which is generally set at the employer's payroll period just before the date on which the election was directed. Ordinarily, elections are held 30 days after they are directed, though different dates may be set to obtain fairer representation of employees.

An election may be set aside by the NLRB if the election was accompanied by conduct that the Board feels tended to interfere with the employee's free choice. Threats of loss of jobs or benefits, misstatements of important facts, discharge of employees, incitement of racial or religious prejudice, the use or threat of physical force, or campaign speeches on company time within 24 hours of the election have all resulted in elections being set aside.

The Appropriate Bargaining Unit

One vital issue is the determination of the **appropriate bargaining unit.** The determination of what constitutes such a unit is left to the NLRB, though the Act provides some limits. Any group of two or more employees who share common employment interests and conditions may be a "bargaining unit," but various employees, particularly managerial and supervisory employees, cannot participate. The unit may consist of all employees of a particular employer, all members of a particular craft or trade, or just employees of a particular plant or facility. Often employees of two or more employers constitute an appropriate bargaining unit. The Board is required to consider any history of collective bargaining, the desires of the employees, and the extent to which the employees are already organized.

Unfair Labor Practices in the Organizational Period

Obviously, the organizational period is a crucial time in the employer-union relationship, a period when feelings run high, and the parties are generally not "educated" in labor-management relations and labor law. Many of the unfair labor practice prohibitions are directed specifically at this period, though they may apply at other times as well. The first four of the five employer unfair labor practices have broad application during this time, since there is an obvious temptation to try to sway the votes of employees away from unions. Obviously, physical threats and violence are forbidden, but the purpose of the Act is to guarantee free choice, even when the employer's action takes the form of benefits to employees.

NLRB v. Exchange Parts Co.

375 U.S. 405, 85 S. Ct. 457, 11 L. Ed. 2d 435 (1964)

Exchange Parts Co. rebuilt automobile parts. On November 9, 1959, the International Brotherhood of Boilermakers, Iron Shipbuilders, Blacksmiths, Forgers and Helpers, AFL-CIO, notified the employer that it was conducting an organizational campaign in its shop and had received sufficient authorizations to request an election. On February 19, 1960, the NLRB issued an order directing that an election be held. The election was to be held on March 18, 1960.

Between November and March the Company conferred several new benefits on the workers, including a new floating holiday, a new system for computing overtime that resulted in higher pay for holiday weeks, and a new vacation schedule. A letter to the employees stated that "The Union can't put any of those things in your envelope—only the Company can do that." and "[I]t didn't take a Union to get any of these things and . . . it won't take a Union to get additional improvements in the future."

A complaint was brought against the company, and the NLRB found that the various benefits were conferred with the intention of inducing the employees to vote against the union, and that the conduct violated Section 8(a)(1) of the Act. The Court of Appeals denied enforcement of the Board's order on the grounds that the benefits were unconditional and there was no suggestion that the benefits would be withdrawn if the workers voted for the union. The Board appealed.

Mr. Justice HARLAN delivered the opinion of the Court.

. . . .

. . . We think the Court of Appeals was mistaken in concluding that the conferral of employee benefits while a representation election is pending, for the purpose of inducing employees to vote against the union, does not "interfere with" the protected right to organize.

The broad purpose of Section 8(a)(1) is to establish "the right of employees to organize for mutual aid without employer interference." . . . We have no doubt that it prohibits not only intrusive threats and promises but also conduct immediately favorable to employees which is undertaken with the express purpose of impinging upon their freedom of choice for or against unionization and is reasonably calculated to have that effect. . . . "The action of employees with respect to the choice of their bargaining agents may be induced by favors bestowed by the employer as well as by his threats or domination." Although in that case there was already a designated bargaining agent and the offer of "favors" was in response to a suggestion of the employees that they would leave the union if favors were bestowed, the principles which dictated the result there are fully applicable here. The danger inherent in well-timed increases in benefits is the suggestion of a fist inside the velvet glove. Employees are not likely to miss the inference that the source of benefits now conferred is also the source from which future benefits must flow and which may dry up if it is not obliged. . . .

. . . We cannot agree with the Court of Appeals that enforcement of the Board's order will have the "ironic" result of "discouraging benefits for labor." . . . The beneficence of an employer is likely to be ephemeral if prompted by a threat of unionization which is subsequently removed. Insulating the right of collective organization from calculated good will of this sort deprives employees of little that has lasting value.

Reversed.

Union conduct during an organizational or election campaign may also constitute an unfair labor practice. Unions are also forbidden from using "restraint or coercion" against an employer. Perhaps the most complex area is when a union may strike or picket during initial organizational and election processes.

Strikes and Picketing During the Organizational Process

Section 8(b)(4) provides that strikes, boycotts, and work stoppages are prohibited if their purpose is to compel recognition of an uncertified union where the employees are already represented. Secondary boycotts are also prohibited if their object is to obtain recognition of an uncertified union. Picketing an employer is also prohibited for the purposes of obtaining recognition by an employer or to gain acceptance by employees (1) if the employer has already recognized another union and an election is barred by NLRB rules, (2) if a valid NLRB election has been held in the last 12 months, or (3) if a representation petition is not filed within "a reasonable period of time not to exceed 30 days from the commencement of such picketing." If such picketing does take place, the NLRB may order an expedited election. The period cannot exceed 30 days, and may be considerably shorter if the picketing is accompanied by violence or other indications that the expedited procedure is necessary. But a valid contract for three years or less will bar an election for the period of the contract.

Negotiation of the Collective Bargaining Agreement

Once a labor organization has been certified by the NLRB as the bargaining unit for a particular group of employees, that unit will become the *exclusive* bargaining unit. The employer may not deal with individual employees or any other group for the purpose of setting wages or working conditions, nor may the employer make changes in those areas without first bargaining with the union.

The Duty to Bargain

Both employers and unions are required to bargain collectively under the provisions of Sections 8(a)(5) and 8(b)(3). While the original Wagner Act only required collective bargaining on the part of employers, and did not define the term, the Taft-Hartley Act imposed that obligation on unions as well, and defined the term with more specificity. That Act required bargaining "with respect to wages, hours, and other terms and conditions of employment" and imposed the duty to bargain *in good faith.*

One of the biggest problems in understanding the labor laws is reconciling the seemingly illogical requirement that the parties must bargain, but they need not agree. It is difficult to understand how the law can require the parties to a labor dispute to negotiate, but does not require that the negotiations bear fruit. The idea behind the requirement is that if parties sit down to talk, they will probably find some common ground on which to agree. Even a failure to meet does not necessarily violate the Act if there is a deadlock or impasse and it appears that future discussions would be fruitless. One case even found that a refusal to meet was justified if the individuals on the bargaining team were chosen with the obvious purpose of being disruptive and offensive. One court defined the term *good faith bargaining* as "an obligation . . . to participate actively in the deliberations so as to indicate a present intention to find a basis for agreement." Bad faith has been found from the negotiating tactics of the parties and from refusals to make substantive proposals.

Subjects of Collective Bargaining

The second issue implicit in the duty to bargain is over what subjects must the parties negotiate? As the law developed, there are two categories of collective bargaining subjects: (1) *statutory* or *mandatory* topics, embracing all of the matters specifically set out in the Act, and (2) *permissive* subjects, which by definition are those matters not included expressly in the statute. There are also prohibited topics, such as hot cargo agreements, secondary boycotts, and discrimination against persons who are not union members. **Mandatory bargaining topics** include: wages, including pensions, fringe benefits, profit-sharing and all other forms of compensation; work rules dealing with seniority, work loads, and discipline; union status problems, such as the recognition clause and union-shop problems; and a "grey" area of other problems, generally referred to as "conditions of employment," such as technological change, production volume, and plant location. **Permissive bargaining topics** are all other subjects.

Parties *must* bargain over mandatory subjects, and *may* bargain over permissive topics. But insistence on bargaining on a permissive topic may itself be an unfair labor practice. Failure to bargain over a mandatory subject is a clear violation of either Section 8(a)(5) or Section 8(b)(3). The following case considers whether closing a part of the employer's business is a mandatory bargaining topic.

First National Maintenance Corp. v. NLRB

452 U.S. 666, 101 S. Ct. 2573, 69 L. Ed. 2d 318 (1981)

First National Maintenance (FNM) operated a housekeeping, cleaning, and maintenance business in the New York City area. One of its contracts was with Greenpark Care Center, and the agreement provided for a "cost plus $250 per week" remuneration to FNM. FNM found this to provide too small a profit for an operation in which 35 of its employees were engaged, and notified Greenpark that it intended to terminate the contract unless its remuneration were raised to cost plus $500 per week. Greenpark failed to respond, and FNM gave final notice of termination of the contract effective August 1, 1976.

During FNM's problems with Greenpark, the National Union of Hospital and Health Care Employees, Retail, Wholesale and Department Store Union, AFL-CIO (Union) conducted an organization campaign of FNM's employees. An election was held, and the union won. On July 12, 1976, the president of the union notified FNM that it wished to negotiate a contract.

On July 28, FNM notified all of the employees working in the Greenpark facility that they would be discharged on August 1 because of the termination of the Greenpark contract. The union president requested a delay to negotiate and requested that the parties bargain over the matter. The company refused, and the union filed an unfair labor practice charge, alleging violations of Sections 8(a)(1) and (5). The Board found for the union and the Court of Appeals affirmed. FNM appealed.

Justice BLACKMUN delivered the opinion of the Court. . . .

Must an employer, under its duty to bargain in good faith "with respect to wages, hours, and other terms and conditions of employment," . . . negotiate with the certified representative of its employees over its decision to close a part of its business? . . .

. . . .

. . . Although parties are free to bargain about any legal subject, Congress has limited the mandate or duty to bargain to matters of "wages, hours, and other terms and conditions of employment." . . . Congress deliberately left the words "wages, hours, and other terms and conditions of employment" without further definition, for it did not intend to deprive the Board of the power further to define those terms in light of specific industrial practices.

Nonetheless, in establishing what issues must be submitted to the process of bargaining, Congress had no expectation that the elected union representative would become an equal partner in the running of the business enterprise in which the union's members are employed. . . . In general terms, the limitation includes only issues that settle an aspect of the relationship between the employer and the employees. . . .

Some management decisions, such as choice of advertising and promotion, product type and design, and financing arrangements, have only an indirect and attenuated impact on the employment relationship. . . . Other management decisions, such as the order of succession of layoffs and recalls, production quotas, and work rules, are almost exclusively "an aspect of the relationship" between employer and employee. . . . The present case concerns a third type of management decision, one that had a direct impact on employment, since jobs were inexorably eliminated by the termination, but had as its focus only the economic profitability of the contract with Greenpark, a concern under these facts wholly apart from the employment relationship. This decision, involving a change in the scope and direction of the enterprise, is akin to the decision whether to be in business at all . . . Cf. *Textile Workers* v. *Darlington*. . . . At the same time, this decision touches on a matter of central and pressing concern to the union and its member employees: the possibility of continued employment and the retention of the employees' very jobs. . . .

. . . The concept of mandatory bargaining is premised on the belief that collective discussions backed by the parties' economic weapons will result in decisions that are better for both management and labor and for society as a whole. . . . This will be true, however, only if the subject proposed for discussion is amenable to resolution through the bargaining process. Management must be free from the constraints of the bargaining process to the extent essential for the running of a profitable business. It also must have some degree of certainty beforehand as to when it may proceed to reach decisions without fear of later evaluations labeling its conduct an unfair labor practice. . . . [I]n view of an employer's need for unencumbered decision-making, bargaining over management decisions that have a substantial impact on the continued availability of employment should be required only if the benefit, for labor-management relations and the collective bargaining process, outweighs the burden placed on the conduct of the business. . . .

With this approach in mind, we turn to the specific issue at hand: an economically-motivated decision to shut down part of a business.

. . . .

A union's interest in participating in the decision to close a particular facility or part of an employer's operations springs from its legitimate concern over job security. . . .

. . . .

Management's interest in whether it should discuss a decision of this kind is much more complex and varies with the particular circumstances. If labor costs are an important factor in a failing operation and the decision to close, management will have an incentive to confer voluntarily with the union to seek concessions. . . . At other times, management may have great need for speed, flexibility, and secrecy in meeting business opportunities and exigencies. It may face significant tax or securities consequences that hinge on confidentiality, the timing of a plant closing, or a reorganization of the corporate structure. . . . The employer also may have no feasible alternative to the closing, and even good faith bargaining over it may be both futile and cause the employer additional loss. . . .

. . . .

We conclude that the harm likely to be done to an employer's need to operate freely in deciding whether to shut down part of its business purely for economic reasons outweighs the incremental benefit that might be gained through the union's participation in making the decision, and we hold that the decision itself is *not* part of §8(d)'s "terms and conditions," over which Congress has mandated bargaining.

. . . .

The judgment of the Court of Appeals . . . is reversed. . . .

Justice BRENNAN, with whom Justice MARSHALL joins, dissenting. . . .
As this Court has noted, the words "terms and conditions of employment" plainly

cover termination of employment resulting from a management decision to close an operation. . . . In the exercise of its congressionally-delegated authority and accumulated expertise, the Board has determined that an employer's decision to close part of its operations affects the "terms and conditions of employment" within the meaning of the Act, and is thus a mandatory subject for collective bargaining. . . . Nonetheless, the Court today declines to defer to the Board's decision on this sensitive question of industrial relations, and on the basis of pure speculation reverses the judgment of the Board and of the Court of Appeals. I respectfully dissent.

The Court bases its decision on a balancing test. . . . I cannot agree with this test, because it takes into account only the interests of *management;* it fails to consider the legitimate employment interests of the workers and their union. . . .

In 1983, the NLRB ruled that transfers of operations from union plants to non-union facilities was not a violation of a collective bargaining agreement, unless the contract contained a **work-preservation clause.** The Board ruled that such transfers do not disturb the wages and benefits provisions of the contract, even though the facility may be shut down. Many unions are now insisting on work-preservation clauses as a result of the ruling. Such clauses require bargaining before transfers may be made.

The Right to Strike

Section 7 of the Wagner Act provides in part that "Employees shall have the right . . . to engage in other concerted activities for the purpose of collective bargaining. . . ." Such concerted activities have been defined to include strikes and picketing, the union's chief weapons. Section 13 of the Act also provides that "Nothing in this Act . . . shall be construed so as either to interfere with or impede or diminish in any way the right to strike. . . ."

The lawfulness of a strike may depend on the object or purpose of the strike, however, or on its timing or on the conduct of the strikers. Strikers are put in one of two classes: *economic strikers,* or *unfair labor practice strikers.* Both classes are protected, but unfair labor practice strikers have greater rights of reinstatement to their jobs.

If, as during initial contract negotiations, the object of a strike is to obtain some economic concession from an employer, such as higher pay or better working conditions, the strikers are **economic strikers.** Such strikers cannot be discharged, but they can be replaced and, if the employer has hired bona fide replacements, they are not entitled to reinstatement. But if the strikers do not obtain regular and substantially equivalent employment, they are entitled to be recalled when openings occur if they have made an unconditional request for reinstatment. On the other hand, **unfair labor practice strikers** cannot be discharged or permanently replaced. Such strikers are entitled to their jobs at the end of the strike. In either case, the NLRB may order back pay if the employer unlawfully denies reinstatement.

Limits on Striking and Unlawful Strikes

As noted above, strikes may be illegal if undertaken for illegal objectives, such as imposing secondary boycotts, compelling recognition of the union in certain circumstances, or compelling work assignments to specific workers. Strikes in support of any union unfair labor practice are also prohibited. If a strike is unlawful, employees who participate may be discharged and are not entitled to reinstatement.

No-Strike Clauses   Some collective bargaining agreements contain provisions prohibiting strikes during the contract term. Such agreements usually provide for arbitration of disputes that arise. A strike in violation of such an agreement is called a **wildcat strike** and is illegal. Some "walk-outs" are protected, such as those caused by unsafe working conditions. **No-Strike clauses** are permissible and are found in most collective bargaining agreements, often with a complementary *no lock-out* clause.

Misconduct of Strikers   Both economic and unfair labor practice strikers may lose their protected status if they engage in serious misconduct. Violence, threats, "sit-down" strikes that deprive the owner of the use of his property and attacks on property are all "serious misconduct."

Strikes at the End of the Contract Period   Most strikes occur when the collective bargaining agreement terminates and a new agreement is to be negotiated. The NLRA requires that parties desiring to terminate an existing agreement must notify the other party 60 days prior to the agreement's expiration, and notify the federal Mediation and Conciliation Service within 30 days of the notice to the other party. Any person who engages in a strike before the notice period ends loses the protections of the Act.

Picketing and Refusal to Cross Picket Lines

Like the right to strike, the right to picket is also not absolute. Generally, if a strike is lawful, picketing in support of that strike is also lawful, though the number and placement of those pickets may be restricted by the Board. As noted above, recognitional picketing is unlawful under certain circumstances, though informational or publicity picketing is permissible. And, the employer has the right to try to get its work done by finding someone willing to cross the picket lines.

Refusals to cross picket lines are among the most important weapons of labor. As Judge Learned Hand put it,

> When all the other workmen in a shop make common cause with a fellow workman over his separate grievance, and go out on strike in his support, they engage in a "concerted activity" for "mutual aid or protection," although the aggrieved workman is the only one of them who has any immediate stake in the outcome. The rest know that by their action each one of them assures himself, in case his turn ever comes, of the support of the one whom they are all then helping; and the solidarity so established is "mutual aid" [within the meaning of the Wagner Act] in the most literal sense, as nobody doubts.

The Role of the Federal Mediation and Conciliation Service

The Taft-Hartley Act also established the Federal Mediation and Conciliation Service as an independent agency. The Service is headed by a director, appointed by the President with the advice and consent of the Senate. It is the duty of the Service, "in order to prevent or minimize interruptions of the free flow of commerce growing out of labor disputes, to assist parties to labor disputes . . . to settle such disputes, through conciliation and mediation."

The Service has no authority to impose settlements on parties, but rather offers a neutral third party to present suggestions and attempt to direct the proceedings. The Service may offer mediation upon its own motion or upon the request of either or both of the parties. The Service may be used both in the negotiation of collective bargaining agreements and grievance disputes, but in the latter case "only as a last resort and in exceptional cases." The Service *must* intervene in cases involving a "national emergency" as defined in the Act and declared by the President.

Content and Enforcement of Collective Bargaining Agreements

The ultimate result of collective bargaining is, in most cases, an agreement between the company and the union. In a very few cases, of course, agreement is never reached, and the union stays out on strike indefinitely and the company goes out of business, moves from the community, or hires an entirely new work force. But such changes are drastic and expensive, and the usual result is a **collective bargaining** agreement.

Content of the Collective Bargaining Agreement

While labor contracts will vary a great deal among industries and even among firms in the same industry, some broad generalizations are possible about such agreements. First, it is important to realize that the labor contract is first and foremost a *contract*, establishing enforceable legal rights and duties.

Most labor contracts include a **recognition clause,** in which the company recognizes the union as the exclusive bargaining agent for the employees and promises not to interfere with the rights of the employees to become union members. Often that clause will contain a promise that only union members will be hired, the so-called **union-shop** provision.

Of prime concern are the **wage and benefits** provisions. Such clauses set the wage scales for all covered employees, including cost-of-living adjustments, overtime premiums, and wage increases during the contract term. All benefits, such as insurance, hospitalization, vacations, sick leave, pension plans, personal days, and many others are specifically spelled out. While wage and benefit increases were an accepted way of life for many years, recent trends during economic recessions introduced the idea of company "take-backs" of previous benefits or wages to permit some firms to remain in business.

Two other important provisions set the *hours of work* and *seniority* of laborers. The hours provision generally provides the overtime premium, perhaps a guarantee of a certain number of hours of overtime, and provides for the distribution of overtime among the employees. The seniority provision generally assures that promotional opportunity and job security should increase in proportion to length of service.

It is important to realize that employers almost always retain the right to discharge employees for cause, regardless of seniority, and also may "lay off" workers in the event their services are not needed, usually in order of seniority.

One of the most important provisions sets **grievance procedure.** The purpose of the clause is to set the orderly resolution of differences between employees and employers. Normally, the grievance procedure involves several steps including consultation with the foreman, the superintendent, a consultation with the grievance committee of the union and plant representatives, and ultimately **arbitration.** Arbitration is a binding judgment by a neutral third party.

Suits to Enforce Collective Bargaining Agreements

One of the more important provisions of the Taft-Hartley Act gave both employers and unions the right to sue for violations of contracts, without regard to diversity of citizenship or the jurisdictional amount. Cases have interpreted that section to mean that employers may sue unions, but not individual employees, for damages of violations of collective bargaining agreements. A more difficult question is whether this right includes a right to sue for an injunction. Such actions produce a conflict between the Taft-Hartley and Norris-LaGuardia Anti-Injunction Acts. In 1970, the Supreme Court ruled that injunctions against labor organizations could be granted by the federal courts, even in the face of the Norris-LaGuardia Act, if the collective bargaining agreement contains a no-strike clause and requires arbitration of disputes.

Prohibited Clauses in Labor Agreements

As previously noted, the NLRA prohibits certain clauses in collective bargaining agreements, including featherbedding arrangements and hot cargo agreements. The Act also prohibits nonunion discrimination, which means that a collective bargaining agreement violates the Act if it provides greater benefits for union employees than nonunion employees.

State Right-to-Work Laws

The Taft-Hartley Act provided that states were free to adopt laws prohibiting **union-shop** agreements. Such laws are called **right-to-work laws** and have been adopted in almost half of the states, mostly in the West and South. Those laws are one of the most controversial aspects of modern American labor law. Management interests continue to press for their adoption, and labor unions strenuously resist such efforts.

Union-shop arrangements, in which all employees must join a union as a condition of employment, are considered essential by organized labor. Since employers are prohibited from discriminating against nonunion employees, such employees must receive the same benefits as union employees in an **open shop.** Thus, while the union negotiates the collective bargaining agreement, nonunion employees receive the benefits as **free riders.** There is, therefore, no incentive for an individual employee to join the union and pay the dues. Union membership necessarily declines, and the power to negotiate from a position of strength deteriorates.

Advocates of right-to-work laws respond by stressing the individual's right *not* to join a "voluntary" association. While granting the free rider problem, these advocates would also point to many employees who do not wish to join unions as a matter of principle. Others point to the power of organized labor and assert that the power of labor can only be controlled through such legislation. A final point is that the union shop tends to permit one union to remain in power indefinitely, resulting in stagnation and corruption.

One answer has been permitted in some cases, that of the **agency shop,** in which employees are not required to join the union, but must, as a condition of employment, pay union dues and fees. The agency shop may be prohibited by state law as well. The following decision illustrates some of the problems of the agency shop and the union shop in the context of the Railway Labor Act, which permits both forms of agreement in a manner similar to the Wagner Act.

Ellis v. Brotherhood of Railway, Airline and Steamship Clerks, Freight Handlers, Express and Station Employees

—U.S.—, 104 S. Ct. 1883 52 U.S.L.W. 4499 (1984)

The Railway Labor Act permits union shop agreements. In 1960, the Supreme Court ruled that employees had a right to object to such arrangements and, though such employees still must join the union, the union may not spend an objecting employee's money to support political causes. The defendant union had a union shop agreement with Western Airlines that required all of Western's clerical workers to join the union within 60 days of employment. As the agreement was interpreted, employees need not become formal union members, but must pay an "agency fee" equal to members' dues. The union in turn made a "rebate" to the objecting employees of a pro-rata share of the dues. Certain employees objected to the plan, claiming that some of the union's expenditures left out of the rebate plan and paid for by the objecting employees went for the union's convention, litigation expenses not connected with the negotiation of the collective bargaining agreement, union publications, social activities, death benefits for employees, and general organizing efforts. The District Court found that none of the six categories of activities was a "collective bargaining activity" and held that the objecting employees could not be required to support them. The Court of Appeals reversed, holding that the six activities strengthened the union as a whole and, therefore, benefitted the union's collective bargaining efforts. The objecting employees appealed.

JUSTICE WHITE delivered the opinion of the Court. . . .
In *Machinists* v. *Street,* 367 U.S. 740 (1960), the Court held that the [Railway Labor] Act does not authorize a union to spend an objecting employee's money to support political causes. The use of employee funds for such ends is unrelated to Congress' desire to eliminate "free riders" and the resentment they provoked. . . . The Court did not express a view as to "expenditures for activities in the area between the costs which led directly to the complaint as to 'free riders,' and the expenditures to support union political activities. . . . They do not contest the legality of the union shop as such, nor could they. See *Railway Employees' Department* v. *Hanson,* 351 U.S. 225 (1956). . . . The parties disagree about . . . the legality of burdening objecting employees with six specific union expenses. . . .

. . . .

In *Street,* the Court observed that the purpose of [the statute permitting union shop and agency agreements] was to make it possible to require all members of a bargaining unit to pay their fair share of the costs of performing the function of exclusive bargaining agent. The union shop would eliminate "free riders," employees who obtained the benefit of the union . . . without financially supporting the union. That purpose, the Court held, Congress intended to be achieved without "vesting the unions with unlimited power to spend exacted money." . . . Undoubtedly, the union could collect from all employees what it needed to defray the expenses entailed in negotiating and administering a collective agreement and in adjusting grievances and disputes. . . . But the authority to impose dues and fees was restricted at least to the "extent of denying the union the right, over the employee's objection, to use his money to support political causes which he opposes." . . . even though Congress was well aware that unions had historically expended funds in the support of political candidates and issues.

. . . .

Hence, when employees such as petitioners object to being burdened with particular union expenditures, the test must be whether the challenged expenditures are necessarily or reasonably incurred for the purpose of performing the duties of an exclusive representative of the employees in dealing with the employer on labor-management issues. Under this standard, objecting employees may be compelled to pay their fair share of not only the direct costs of negotiating and administering a collective-bargaining contract and of settling grievances and disputes, but also the expenses of activities or undertakings normally or reasonably employed to implement or effectuate the duties of the union as exclusive representative. . . .

The Court held that the union had a right to collect funds from the objecting employees for the purposes of supporting the union conventions, refreshments at union social activities, union publications, and litigation activities. The Court held that all of those activities implement or effectuate the duties of the union as exclusive representative. The Court found that funds could not be collected for union organizing efforts. The Court of Appeals had held that organizing efforts build a stronger union to the benefit of all employees, but the Supreme Court reversed, saying that Congress did not intend the Act to be "a tool for the expansion of overall union power." The Court did not have to rule on the sixth category, that of union death benefits, because of a procedural ruling in the Court of Appeals. As a result, the Court of Appeals ruling was affirmed in part and reversed in part.

Union shop agreements, sometimes called *union-security agreements*, cannot require that all applicants for employment be members of the union in order to be hired. At most, such agreements may require that all employees in the group covered by the agreement become members of the union within a certain period of time, which cannot be less than 30 days except in the building and construction industries. In those industries a shorter "grace" period of seven full days is permitted. A union security agreement that provides a shorter grace period is invalid, and any employee discharged because of nonmembership is entitled to reinstatement.

Relationship of Union Members to Their Union

One of the more controversial areas of labor law deals with the rights of union members and other employees in relation to their union. During the mid-1950's, a series of Congressional investigations found that some unions had become corrupt and that union leaders were abusing their power in a variety of ways. Since the federal law was in part responsible for the power of these officials, Congress acted by passing the Labor-Management Reporting and Disclosure Act of 1959, known as the Landrum-Griffin Act.

The Landrum-Griffin Requirements

The election of officers is the key to union democracy. But the Congressional hearings had found that many unions had constructed the "rules" of elections so that only a small group of persons was eligible to be elected and provided little or no relief to union members injured or aggrieved by union actions. The Act countered such problems by requiring (1) certain organizational procedures for all unions; (2) disclosure of union affairs to the Secretary of Labor and to the public; (3) the establishment of a union-member's Bill of Rights; and (4) the creation of some new federal crimes, including embezzlement of union funds.

Organizational and Reporting Requirements Under the Act, unions were required to have a constitution and by-laws establishing the rules of election, and those documents were to be filed with the Secretary of Labor. Current information regarding union financial affairs, leadership, and potential areas of conflict of interest must be filed annually. Elections at the local level are required every three years and at the national level at least every five years.

Union Members' Bill of Rights The Act also established certain rights of union members in relation to their own unions. Those rights generally include the right to nominate candidates, vote in elections, attend membership meetings, have a voice in business transactions, vote on dues increases, and sue and testify against the union. Members are also guaranteed the right to free expression in union meetings, and the right to receive a written, specific notice of charges and a fair hearing in union disciplinary actions. Each union member also has the right to a copy of the collective bargaining agreement.

The Duty of Fair Representation

Aside from the protections of the Landrum-Griffin Act, union members also have other rights. Unions stand in a unique position in relation to their members, since they represent the worker at many critical stages of his employment relationship, from general contract negotiations to grievance procedures. From time to time unions may be tempted to represent employees in an uneven-handed manner.

The national labor laws do not expressly require *fair representation* from unions. But, over the years, the courts have inferred that right from the general duties of unions under Section 7 of the Act and the bargaining representative's implied duty of fair representation derived from its status as bargaining representative. As the Supreme Court noted in an early case

> Congress has seen fit to clothe the bargaining representative with powers comparable to those possessed by a legislative body both to create and restrict the rights of those whom it represents. . . . but it has also imposed on the representative a corresponding duty. We hold that the language of the [Railway Labor] Act . . . expresses the aim of Congress to impose on the bargaining representative of a craft or class of employees the

duty to exercise fairly the power conferred upon it in behalf of all those for whom it acts, without hostile discrimination against them. *Steele* v. *Louisville & Nashville R. Co.*★

The duty of fair representation was incorporated from the early Railway Labor Act cases to the NLRA. The duty of fair representation has been used in a variety of contexts, from racial discrimination suits against unions by employees to union action simply based on whim or caprice.

Vaca v. Sipes

386 U.S. 171, 87 S. Ct. 903, 17 L. Ed. 2d 842 (1967)

Owens, an employee of Swift & Company and a member of the National Brotherhood of Packinghouse Workers, suffered from high blood pressure. He became ill and was hospitalized for a long period. He received a doctor's release to go back to work, but the company doctor would not clear him and he was subsequently discharged. He alleged the discharge was in violation of his collective bargaining agreement and requested the union to file a grievance. The company turned down the grievance, and Owens requested the union to take the matter to arbitration. The union refused, and Owens filed a class action against the officers of the union in state court. Owens won in a jury trial, but the trial judge set aside the verdict. The Supreme Court of Missouri reversed and ordered the jury award reinstated. The union officers appealed to the U.S. Supreme Court. During the appeal, Owens died and his administrator was substituted as the plaintiff.

Mr. Justice WHITE delivered the opinion of the Court. . . .

Petitioners challenge the jurisdiction of the Missouri courts on the ground that the alleged conduct of the Union was arguably an unfair labor practice and within the exclusive jurisdiction of the NLRB. . . . For the reasons which follow, we reject this argument.

It is now well established that, as the exclusive bargaining representative of the employees in Owens' bargaining unit, the Union had a statutory duty fairly to represent all of those employees, both in its collective bargaining with Swift . . . and in its enforcement of the resulting collective bargaining agreement. . . . Under this doctrine, the exclusive agent's statutory authority to represent all members of a designated unit includes a statutory obligation to serve the interests of all members without hostility or discrimination toward any, to exercise its discretion with complete good faith and honesty, and to avoid arbitrary conduct. . . . It is obvious that Owens' complaint alleged a breach by the Union of a duty grounded in federal statutes and that federal law therefore governs his case. . .

. . . .

A breach of the statutory duty of fair representation occurs only when a union's conduct toward a member of the collective bargaining unit is arbitrary, discriminatory, or in bad faith. . . . Though we accept the proposition that a union may not arbitrarily ignore a meritorious grievance or process it in perfunctory fashion, we do not agree that the individual employee has an absolute right to have his grievance taken to arbitration regardless of the provisions of the applicable collective bargaining agreement. . . . In providing for a grievance and arbitration procedure which gives the union discretion to supervise the grievance machinery and to invoke arbitration, the employer and the union contemplate that each will endeavor in good faith to settle grievances short of arbitration. Through this settlement process, frivolous grievances are ended prior to the most costly and time-consuming step in the grievance procedures.

. . . .

★323 U.S. 192, 65 S. Ct. 226, 89 L. Ed. 173 (1944).

If the individual employee could compel arbitration of his grievance regardless of its merit, the settlement machinery provided by the contract would be substantially undermined, thus destroying the employer's confidence in the union's authority and returning the individual grievant to the vagaries of independent and unsystematic negotiation. Moreover, under such a rule, a significantly greater number of grievances would proceed to arbitration....

Applying the proper standard of union liability to the facts of this case, we cannot uphold the jury's award, for we conclude that as a matter of federal law the evidence does not support a verdict that the Union breached its duty of fair representation....

In such a case as this, when Owens supplied the Union with medical evidence supporting his position, the Union might well have breached its duty had it ignored Owens' complaint or had it processed the grievance in a perfunctory manner.... But here the Union processed the grievance into the fourth step, attempted to gather sufficient evidence to prove Owens' case, attempted to secure for Owens less vigorous work at the plant, and joined in the employer's efforts to have Owens rehabilitated.... There was no evidence that any Union officer was personally hostile to Owens or that the Union acted at any time other than in good faith.

. . . .

Reversed.

Union Discipline of Its Members

The Landrum-Griffin Act provides that prior to any union discipline of its members, a member is entitled to a "full and fair hearing" and provides certain types of conduct, such as expression of views in a union meeting, that cannot be the subject of union disciplinary proceedings. A union member aggrieved by such discipline may bring suit in federal court, but not before he has "exhausted" all of the internal union remedies. The Act does not set out the type of conduct that may be used to justify discipline, preferring to leave that to the unions themselves.

Unions and the Public Sector

Generally speaking, the national labor laws treat the relationship of labor and management as an essentially private problem in need of rules to prevent disagreements from harming the parties and the public. While labor disputes and collective bargaining agreements may injure the public by stopping the free flow of commerce and by inflating the economy, the laws do not address these problems except to provide methods by which disputes may be settled peacefully and quickly.

Two aspects of labor disputes do have rather severe public consequences, however. First is the problem of strikes in crucial industries during a national emergency, such as a steel strike in the middle of a war. Second is the problem of the unionization of public employees, such as firemen, policemen, and teachers. The first aspect, that of national emergency strikes, is considered by the Taft-Hartley Act; the second, public employee unions, is considered only by state law.

National Emergency Strikes

The President who believes that an actual or threatened strike or lock-out imperils the national health or safety is authorized to appoint a board to inquire into the issues.

Upon receipt of the report of that board, the President may direct the Attorney General to petition a district court for an injunction against the strike or lock-out. If the strike affects an entire industry or a substantial part of an industry engaged in commerce, and if the court finds such peril as well, an injunction *must* issue. The parties to the dispute must "make every effort to adjust and settle their differences. . . ." No party is under a duty to accept any proposal of settlement. A report is compiled by the Mediation and Conciliation Service, and the employees must vote by secret ballot whether to accept the final offer of the employer. At the end of an "80 day cooling off period," the injunction must be dissolved.

In 1959 President Eisenhower used these procedures in a steel strike involving a half-million steelworkers and 97 companies. An injunction was granted, and the unions appealed to the Supreme Court. In a perfunctory opinion, the Court upheld the procedures against a claim that there was no war and the physical well-being of American citizens was not jeopardized. The provisions have been used a few other times in the coal, atomic energy, maritime, and telecommunications industries.

Public Employee Unions

Employees of the various units of government have a vastly different set of laws and considerations with which to contend. Until 1950, unions and collective bargaining agreements between public employees and units of government were extremely rare. Courts initially treated any attempt to organize or bargain as an invasion of governmental sovereignty or a threat to public safety, and usually enjoined such action.

But during the 1960's, the movement to organize public employees and grant them rights similar to employees in the private sector increased. Several reasons existed for this movement. The number of public employees grew rapidly in this period, which increased the number of persons affected and opened a fertile field for union organizers. Public salaries generally could not keep pace with those in the private sector, which was experiencing extraordinary growth, resulting in job dissatisfaction among governmental employees. Public opinion of collective bargaining, which had been limited to wages and hours, became more sophisticated and many persons realized that much more was at issue than those simple concerns, including grievance procedures and job security. And government activities reached into new areas, belying the notion that all government services were crucial or essential. There seemed little difference, for example, between a strike of public school teachers and a strike of private school teachers, or between a strike of employees of a municipally owned utility and those of a privately owned utility.

Public employees remain outside of the protection of the National Labor Relations Act. But many states passed laws, of considerable variation, giving public employees certain rights to collectively bargain and, in a few instances, granted a limited right to strike. Most of those state laws have been copied almost verbatim from the National Labor Relations Act, although most do not grant the right to strike and instead substitute various "impasse resolution" procedures. Many of the laws are limited to certain classes of employees, such as teachers or municipal employees.

The Duty to Bargain

Generally, the state laws are of two types: those requiring **collective negotiation,** and the so-called **meet and confer laws.** The former impose a duty to bargain similar to that imposed by the federal law on the private sector. The latter requires discussions prior to the unilateral adoption of policies by a governmental body—an advisory function, limited sharply by the legislative right to make laws. Many states adopt a model somewhere in between, such as the duty to "meet and confer *in good faith.*" Of course the basic problem with collective bargaining with public bodies is that often the public bodies do not have the final authority over budget matters, and must await an appropriation by a legislature, which may not feel bound by the previous negotiations.

Impasse Resolution Procedures

Instead of a right to strike, most state statutes provide for at least one of four possible **impasse resolution techniques** and often provide more than one: *mediation,* or neutral aid in achieving a solution; *fact-finding,* which involves mediation followed by public airing of the dispute by the mediator if an impasse is not resolved, potentially exposing both sides to bad publicity; *voluntary arbitration,* or a binding decision by a neutral party, entered into by agreement of both parties; or *compulsory arbitration,* or a binding decision by a neutral party that cannot be avoided except by settlement.

Public Employee Strikes

Historically, public employees have not had the right to strike. The theory, of course, was that essential services provided by government, such as fire and police protection, could not be subordinated to the private employee's financial interest in a strike. As noted by President Franklin Roosevelt

> A strike by public employees manifests nothing less than an intent on their part to obstruct the operations of government until their demands are satisfied. Such action looking toward the paralysis of government by those who have sworn to support it is unthinkable.

Most courts and legislatures continue to adopt that view and outlaw all strikes by public employees. A few states have permitted employee strikes if there is no adverse effect on the public health or safety, and there seems to be a trend toward such legislation, though the exact content varies widely.

Yet prohibiting strikes by law and preventing them as a practical matter are two totally separate considerations. "Job actions," "blue flu," and outright strikes have increased dramatically in recent years, even in the face of no-strike legislation. Economic strikes often turn into strikes for amnesty, and as a practical matter government employers must deal with strikers because replacing skilled workers is often impossible.

The courts have held that while there is no constitutional right to strike, there is a constitutionally protected right to join in labor organizations and to express one's opinion under the 1st Amendment. It appears that public-sector labor law will become the legal frontier of labor relations for the foreseeable future.

Summary and Conclusions

In a sense, the federal labor policy may be reviewed as an equalizer or balancer between the conflicting interests of labor and management. With the coming of the Industrial Revolution organized labor was extremely weak and state laws placed labor at a severe disadvantage. An attempt to create a hands-off policy by outlawing injunctions against labor activity in the Norris-LaGuardia Act was not sufficient to give labor any degree of real power.

It was not until Congress passed the Wagner Act in 1935 that labor obtained significant power. That act created the National Labor Relations Board (NLRB), established the right of employees to organize, and outlawed certain employer unfair labor practices. The law did not regulate union activities however, and as a result the strength of labor grew enormously.

In order to counter that power, Congress passed the Taft-Hartley Act in 1947. That Act established certain union unfair labor practices, established detailed procedures for holding union elections, and provided a right *not* to join a labor union. In 1959, in response to charges of corruption in labor unions, the Landrum-Griffin Act was passed to regulate the internal procedures of unions.

The end result of the unionization process is the collective bargaining agreement, a voluntary contract between an employer and its organized employees. While the private purpose of such agreements is to negotiate the best terms possible, the public purpose is to resolve labor disputes quickly and without disruption. To that end, the organization and negotiation process are subject to a variety of regulations in the form of unfair labor practices. The theory behind collective bargaining is, of course, to equalize the bargaining power of the two sides.

Contemporary problems in labor relations involve the continuing debate over right-to-work laws, which are state statutes prohibiting union-shop contracts, and the controversy over the right of public employees to organize, bargain, and strike. Both areas promise to remain in the forefront of the development of American labor-management relations law.

PRO AND CON

ISSUE: Have Unions Outlived Their Usefulness?

PRO: Collective Bargaining Doesn't Do What It Is Supposed To
Daniel Seligman*

What is one to make of organized labor's givebacks—of the avalanche of bargaining concessions at General Motors and Ford, in the steel industry, in rubber, farm equipment, trucking, construction, railroads, airlines and newspaper publishing? The *purpose* of the givebacks is clear enough. They're intended to preserve some jobs and output that were, as the recession dragged on, looking highly endangered. But some other matters are not so clear.

Question: if we tell ourselves that the extraordinary display of collective-bargaining-in-reverse is preserving output and jobs, then shouldn't we also tell ourselves that *ordinary* union behavior destroys them? Related question: what is the economics profession telling us nowadays about the economic

---

*From his article, "Who Needs Unions?" *Fortune* (July 12, 1982): 54, © 1982, *Time,* Inc. All rights reserved. Reprinted by permission.

consequences of unionism? Further question: if unionism does have perverse effects, shouldn't we be reexamining a variety of public policies whose stated purpose is to bolster collective bargaining?

Organized labor is in terrible trouble and there is no compelling reason to think that its long downdrift is nearing an end. Its share of the work force is declining, as is its batting average in collective bargaining elections. . . . Its eternal efforts to "organize the unorganized" go on . . . but it is hard to envision the AFL-CIO suddenly getting hot in the Sunbelt. . . .

. . . .

This is all most peculiar because public policy in the U.S. presumes unionism to be an engine of economic growth. The presumption reflects the ideas of the deflationary Thirties—notably the idea that recovery from the Great Depression required a major shift of resources from capital to labor. The National Labor Relations Act . . . became the foundation on which union power in America was built. The "findings and policy" in . . . the act are a statement of the case for unionism. Collective bargaining is desirable, says the act, because it eliminates the evident "inequality of bargaining power" between the lone employee and the giant corporation. This inequality "tends to aggravate recurrent business depression, by depressing wage rates and . . . purchasing power. . . ."

. . . .

The "findings" built into these laws . . . are hard to reconcile with today's reality. . . . To be sure, economists broadly agree that unions do raise the wages of their working members; on average unionized workers get paid more than they would if they were unorganized. However, there have clearly been some periods, apparently including the late Sixties, in which unionized workers gained less. This could easily happen in any economic environment marked by (a) an unexpectedly strong demand for labor and (b) long-term contracts that left union workers locked in at pay levels below what they could command in a free market.

. . . .

Economists have several rather obvious reasons for reviewing unionism as an impediment to productivity. First, unions impose work rules that sometimes lead to featherbedding and almost always limit flexibility on the job. Second, unions impose rules that overvalue seniority—that make it difficult for managers to pay and promote on the basis of merit. . . . The union emphasis on standard rates also tends to discourage ambitious younger workers from seeking the kind of training that would help them get ahead. Most economists see these deleterious effects as swamping the productivity gains associated with . . . unionized companies.

. . . .

Meanwhile, the case for unionism is being weakened by some interesting new non-economic considerations. . . .

Big government, . . . turns out to be a bit of a competitor for the unions. Do they promise to improve working conditions? So does the Occupational Safety and Health Administration. Do unions promise to raise the wages of low income workers? If so, they're competing with the minimum wage laws. . . . Do unions promise to get better pensions for their members? So does the U.S. Department of Labor, which administers the Employee Retirement Income Security Act of 1974 (ERISA). . . .

The changes in large corporations are harder to evaluate, but to some uncertain extent non-union corporations are manifestly trying harder than they once did to treat employees fairly. Big business takes employee morale seriously these days. Personnel departments are increasingly responding to a "human relations ideology" that labors to take the rough edges off the company's dealings with workers. . . .

The game of excessive wage increases which are then passed on to consumers is coming to an end. This stubborn fact, perhaps more than any large new understanding of what unions do to output and employment, might ultimately lead Americans to reconsider whether public policy should promote collective bargaining.

CON: Collective Bargaining Remains Essential
Lane Kirkland, President, AFL-CIO*

Recently . . . I was asked by a reporter if I had learned anything new. I replied that I have learned nothing new about the world since the Great Depression, Munich, the Molotov-Ribbentrop Pact, and Pearl Harbor.

I was not being facetious, but simply using ver-

---

*From a speech delivered at Dartmouth College, Hanover, N.H., October 4, 1982; printed in *Vital Speeches of the Day* 49, No. 2 (Nov. 1, 1982): 37. Reprinted by permission.

bal shorthand to describe the filters of experience through which I am obliged to view events. If that is a crippling affliction of myself or my generation, be not proud. You will get yours, I pray at a lesser price. . . .

Economic peril is not obsolete. Neither safety nets nor sophisticated computer models render us immune from the prospect faced by the Class of 1930.

Economic mythomania of the kind that has now given voodoo a bad name, that has stripped the public coffers and brought a deficit that will exceed in Reagan's four years that of the previous twenty, may yet exact its full price.

. . . .

Yet none of these unforeseen events and circumstances of our time are accidents of chance or the random whims of fate. They flow from the central, enduring issue of this day and this century: the dilemma and contradiction posed by the dual nature of the State in human affairs.

The State embodies and magnifies the frailties of man and his capacity for good or ill. The State, unchecked and unopposed, is a deadly engine of oppression in its extremes, a vortex sweeping hordes to concentration camps or Gulags. The State, held within democratic bounds by free citizens, is the indispensable instrument of human progress.

. . . .

To suppress and dismantle the benign functions of the latter by raising the specter of the former aspect of the State is the temptation of the political agents of private privilege. That is the apparent thrust of an administration which has taken it as a mission to remove the federal presence from any substantial role save the raising of armies, and overseeing the detaxing, de-regulating and unleashing of private business enterprise.

Business, thus unleashed, has responded with a general collapse, corporate cannibalism, and the fabrication of golden parachutes by and for the executives. . . .

. . . .

The founders of this nation were certainly not immune from the ideas of "academic scribblers of a few years back." They derived from philosophy the notion of the existence of government as a badge of lost innocence and a constant threat to the natural rights of man. They wrote elaborate checks and balances into the Constitution. . . .

. . . .

These safeguards make us free to promote the benign uses of the state as an instrument of constructive ends. That pursuit is just as vital to our future as is constant vigilance against the dark side

of authority. The trade union movement of America is equally committed both to steadfast resistance to the abuse of state power and the vigorous advocacy of democratic solutions to our national problems. . . .

Today, we have an administration devoted to the attrition of the positive and the emphasis of the negative aspect of governance. To avowed aim is to "get government off our backs,". . .

Such a program must rely heavily upon the assumed exhaustion of the nation's collective memory bank, from which the delinquencies of the glorified past need to be from time to time recalled. Enduring free institutions such as trade unions and universities share a duty to maintain that memory bank. . . .

Let me do so briefly now and note what it was really like for many before the New Deal, when the federal presence was remote . . . and when . . . what business wanted, business got.

Old folks were not universally sheltered in the bosom of a warm and loving family. If they couldn't work until they dropped, the county poorhouse awaited. . . .

Regions of the country were stripped of trees and gullied by erosion. . . .

Most roads were unpaved and often impassable. . . .

Farmhouses were isolated and lit by kerosene. . . .

Pellagra, hookworm, malaria, and other diseases were endemic in much of the country. . . .

That list of real national and human problems that were answered only when the federal government got "on our backs" could be extended at tedious length, but let it just be noted that while they profited handsomely from federal action, neither the states nor private industry rose to meet those occasions. . . .

Largely through trade union collective bargaining and legislative endeavors, working hours have been reduced, paid leisure time gained and expanded, family incomes raised, educational opportunities broadened, and earlier pensions gained. As a consequence, the average age of entry into the work force has been delayed significantly and the time of voluntary exit advanced.

The evolution of trade unionism in my lifetime has brought about the democratization of privilege—that is to say, of education, leisure, travel, good health care and housing, and other advantages for centuries reserved to the few—to an extent previously unknown in history. That process, in turn, has created new industries, services, markets and opportunities for enterprise.

Can anyone reasonably hold that these

advances, these revolutions of our time, have impaired rather than enhanced the capacity of man and woman to stand free and independent before the State or any other stronghold of power?

These are no mean achievements. They ought not to be undone.

. . . .

Before I leave you in peace, let me address a canard that has dogged American labor for many years. It has found its way into textbooks, learned papers and baser prose. . . . That is the legend that our founder, Samuel Gompers, when asked what labor wanted, responded simply "More." That has become a synonym for our alleged innocence of ideals, if not unbridled avarice. . . .

A university group . . . recently completed the task of copying and indexing all of Gompers' recorded papers and words. I asked them to find that quote and was informed that it did not exist. The only source from which it could have been derived was an item dated 1893, where Gompers declared:

"What does labor want? . . . We want more schoolhouses and less jails; more books and less arsenals; more learning and less vice; more consultant work and less crime; more leisure and less greed; more justice and less revenge. . . ."

On that, I am willing to stand.

DISCUSSION QUESTIONS

1. Is the balance of power between business and labor equal today? If not, what *specific* changes would you make to equalize the power? Are those changes politically possible?

2. It has been argued that Japanese industry maintains an attitude of cooperation somewhat similar to that which existed in our own "craft" system before the Industrial Revolution, and that our national labor policy aggravates the feeling of "adverseness" between labor and management by treating the parties as having conflicting interests. Do you agree? Are the interests of labor and business really conflicting? Could a different labor policy help reduce the conflict?

3. Is it possible to square the decision in *Textile Workers* v. *Darlington* and *First National Maintenance* and the NLRB rule described after the *First National Maintenance* case? What is the law on runaway shops anyway?

4. Under the *Gissell* doctrine, should employees be told that by signing the authorization card they may be in fact electing a union, rather than simply calling for an election? Do you think a significant number of employees sign the card but vote against the union? Does this result change if more than one union is competing to become the employee's representative?

5. In an agency shop, should the union dues contributed by nonunion members be used for political contributions or purposes, such as campaigning for repeal of right-to-work laws?

6. *Why* are secondary boycotts illegal? What about hot cargo agreements?

7. If you were an employee and, on the eve of a union election, your employer gave you a large pay raise, would you be intimidated or would you consider it to be a

bribe? Does how you consider it make a difference in the *Exchange Parts* decision? Would it cross your mind that the employer might renege on the raise the day after the election?

8. Which is more "critical"—a state university professor or an employee of a private firm that operates a nuclear power plant? In which instance would a strike be more upsetting? Could a state law be designed to permit only certain public employees, the noncritical ones, to strike?

9. Should the impasse procedures used in public employees' bargaining agreements be carried over to the private sector and eliminate the right to strike?

CASE PROBLEMS

1. A union representation election was held among certain employees of Savair Manufacturing Co. Prior to the election, the union circulated "recognition slips" among the employees. An employee who signed the slip before the election became a member of the union and would not have to pay the "initiation fee." If the union was voted in, those who had not signed a recognition slip would have to pay. The employer refused to bargain after the union won the election, and the union filed an unfair labor practices charge against Savair. Result? [*NLRB* v. *Savair Mfg. Co.,* 414 U.S. 270, 94 S. Ct. 495, 39 L. Ed. 2d 495 (1974).]

2. A majority of the employees of Linden Lumber Co. signed authorization cards and the union requested recognition by the company. The company refused to bargain, and the union filed an unfair labor practices charge. There was no allegation that the company had engaged in any unfair labor practice other than the refusal to bargain. (1) Is the company guilty of a refusal to bargain? (2) Does the company or the union have the burden of requesting an election? [*Linden Lumber Div., Summer & Co.* v. *NLRB,* 419 U.S. 301, 95 S. Ct. 429, 42 L. Ed. 2d 465 (1974).]

3. Fiberboard Paper Products decided that it could save a great deal of money by "contracting out" its maintenance work to an independent firm. Fiberboard had a collective bargaining agreement with a union representing its present maintenance employees. At the expiration of the agreement, Fiberboard notified the union that it had made a contract with the independent firm and would not bargain with the union. All present maintenance employees of the firm were discharged. The union filed a series of unfair labor practice charges against the firm. Result? [*Fiberboard Paper Products Corp.* v. *NLRB,* 379 U.S. 203, 85 S. Ct. 398, 13 L. Ed. 2d 233 (1964).]

4. Employees of Boys' Markets were represented by a union that had a no-strike clause in its collective bargaining agreement. The union called a strike in vio-

lation of that provision when supervisory employees began stocking shelves in violation of the collective bargaining agreement. The company requested the federal court to issue an injunction against the strike on the basis of a provision in the Taft-Hartley Act permitting lawsuits against unions. The union argued that injunctions were barred by the Norris-LaGuardia Act. Result? [*Boys' Markets, Inc.* v. *Retail Clerk's Local 770,* 398 U.S. 235, 90 S. Ct. 1583, 26 L. Ed. 2d 199 (1970).]

5. A local of the Fruit and Vegetables Packers union called a strike against fruit packers and warehousemen doing business in Yakima, Washington. The struck packers sold apples to the Safeway grocery chain doing business in Seattle, and the union instituted a consumer boycott against apples in support of the strike. Pickets marched in front of each of the stores and distributed handbills to customers requesting that they refrain from buying Washington apples. The union did not ask store employees to cease work, and no deliveries or pick-ups were obstructed. The union was charged with an unfair labor practice under Section 8(b)(4). Result? [*NLRB* v. *Fruit and Vegetable Packers Local 760,* 377 U.S. 58, 84 S. Ct. 1063, 12 L. Ed 2d 129 (1964).]

6. At most universities, faculty members have responsibilities beyond teaching and research, such as making recommendations regarding tenure, promotion, discharge, and other concerns. Are such full-time faculty members "supervisory and managerial employees" and therefore outside the protection of the NLRA? [*NLRB* v. *Yeshiva University,* 444 U.S. 672, 100 S. Ct. 856, 63 L. Ed. 2d 115 (1980).]

7. The Writers Guild represents writers of motion pictures and television films. A strike was called at the expiration of a collective bargaining agreement with the Association of Motion Picture and Television Producers. Some Guild members performed only executive and supervisory functions, such as producing, directing, and script editing, activities that involve little actual writing. Many such members reported to work during the strike, but did no writing. Guild rules prohibited such conduct as "defeating a strike" and entering struck premises. After the strike was over, the union fined those members for violating union rules, as much as $10,000 in one case and $50,000 in another. Unfair labor practice charges were filed against the Guild under Section 8(b)(1). Result? [*American Broadcasting Companies, Inc.* v. *Writers Guild of America, West, Inc.,* 437 U.S. 411, 98 S. Ct. 2423, 57 L. Ed. 2d 313 (1978).]

8. A provision in the constitution of the United Steelworkers of America limits eligibility for local union office to members who have attended at least one-half of the regular meetings of the local for three years previous to the election, unless prevented by union activities or working hours. The Landrum-Griffin Act provides that all members in good standing may be candidates, subject to "reasonable qualifications." Among the members of Local 3489, 96.5 percent were ineligible under this provision. The Secretary of Labor brought an action to invalidate a union election, claiming the provision in the constitution violated

the Act. Result? [*Local 3489, United Steelworkers of America* v. *Usery,* 429 U.S. 305, 97 S. Ct. 611, 50 L. Ed. 2d 502 (1977).]

9. The XYZ Union had a contract with the ABC Co., which expired. At the first meeting to resolve differences between the company and the union, the union raises the following issues: (1) changes in the company retirement plan; (2) whether employees with seniority should be given preference for overtime work; (3) whether a union representative should sit on the board of directors of the company; (4) changes in the grievance procedures; (5) how much employees will be docked for tardiness; (6) whether certain jobs will be phased out in favor of mechanization; (7) increased vacation time; (8) whether a union-shop agreement will be instituted; (9) whether the company may use a nonunion printer to print materials for the company; and (10) whether the company will close a facility and move part of its operations to another state. The company refused to bargain on each of these issues. How many unfair labor practices has the company committed?

10. Falconbridge Fine Furniture Factory sent around a circular to its unionized employees in an attempt to convince them to de-unionize through the decertification procedure. The union called a strike to protest the circular and, while the union was on strike, Falconbridge hired several nonunion workers to work in the factory. After the strike was settled, Longsword, one of the striking workers, demanded his job back. Falconbridge informed Longsword that Fitz-Peter had been hired to take his place during the strike, but that Longsword would be placed on a waiting list for the first available opening. (1) Is Falconbridge guilty of an unfair labor practice by sending around the circular? (2) Is the union guilty of an unfair labor practice by striking? (3) Does Longsword have a right to his job?

SUGGESTED READINGS

Beal, Edwin F., and James P. Begin. *The Practice of Collective Bargaining* 6th ed. (Homewood, Ill.: Richard D. Irwin, Inc., 1982).

Cox, Archibald, Derek C. Bok, and Robert A. Gorman. *Labor Law, Cases and Materials* 9th ed. (Mineola, N.Y.: Foundation Press, 1981).

Getman, Julius G., and John D. Blackburn. *Labor Relations, Law, Practice and Policy* 2d. ed. (Mineola N.Y.: Foundation Press, 1983).

Goldman, Alvin L. *The Supreme Court and Labor-Management Relations Law* (Lexington, Mass.: D.C. Heath, 1976).

Gould, William B. *A Primer on American Labor Law* (Cambridge, Mass.: The MIT Press, 1982).

Kochan, Thomas A. *Collective Bargaining and Industrial Relations: From Theory to Policy and Practice* (Homewood, Ill.: Richard D. Irwin, Inc., 1980).

Leslie, Douglas L. *Labor Law in a Nutshell* (St. Paul, Minn.: West Publishing Co., 1979).

National Labor Relations Board. *A Guide to Basic Law and Procedures Under the National Labor Relations Act* (Washington, D.C.: U.S. Government Printing Office, 1976).

Schwartz, Bernard, and Robert F. Koretz. *Statutory History of the United States: Labor Organization* (New York: Chelsea House in Association with McGraw-Hill, 1970).

Wilson, Wesley. *The Labor Relations Primer* (Homewood, Ill.: Dow-Jones–Irwin, Inc., 1973).

14

Labor Law: Regulation of Worker Safety, Wages and Security

Pension never enriched [a] young man.

George Herbert, Jacula Prudentum *(1651)*

The government first provides very poor schooling, and then the harm is multiplied by the minimum wage law, which makes it difficult . . . to get on the job training. Without the minimum wage law, the least skilled could offer to work for low wages, which would provide an incentive for employers to hire and train them.

Milton Friedman, Capitalism and Freedom *(1962)*

He that's secure is not safe.

Benjamin Franklin, Poor Richard's Almanac *(1748)*

American labor law can be viewed as two streams running from a single source. The source, of course, is a public concern with the welfare of the individual worker. The first stream, discussed in the preceding chapter, might be called *the market approach,* since it involves a national policy to enhance the bargaining power of workers by legitimizing labor organization and collective bargaining and permitting market forces to protect workers through negotiated labor contracts.

The second stream takes a more direct approach, by identifying and attacking specific "evils" of the workplace. This approach is more truly regulatory, since it involves direct prohibition or regulation of specific problems. Such specific regulations existed long before the NLRA or other collective bargaining laws, and in a sense were the first American labor laws.

While specific regulatory protections vary a great deal, the emphasis of such laws has always been in three areas: (1) protection of workers from unsafe working conditions; (2) protection of employee's security, both from penniless retirement and from unemployment; and (3) protection of workers' pay, chiefly through minimum wage laws. A fourth category, that of protection from employment discrimination, will be discussed in Chapter 16 as part of the general regulation of discriminatory conduct.

Specific regulations of labor have a long and checkered history. Late in the 19th century, several states passed laws dealing with specific abuses of labor, usually in the form of child labor acts, minimum wage laws, and laws prohibiting hiring women for certain dangerous occupations. Because of the restrictive definitions given the Commerce Clause and the broad definitions given the Contracts Clause and the Due Process Clause, such laws were often held beyond the power of both the states and the federal government (see Chapter 2). It was not until the watershed decisions of the Supreme Court in 1937 that the constitutionality of such laws was assured (see especially *West Coast Hotel* v. *Parrish*, p. 59).

Regulation of Worker Safety

One of the prime concerns of American labor law has always been worker safety and decent working conditions. Nineteenth century factories were often extremely hazardous, resulting in large numbers of injured and disabled workers. Such workers found that the law provided little relief for their loss, which resulted in the adoption of state **worker's compensation laws.** Later, similar concerns would result in the adoption of direct regulations of worker safety, including the Occupational Safety and Health Act of 1970 and similar state laws designed to require protection of workers on the job.

Common-Law Remedies for Work-Related Injuries

At common law, work-related injuries were always considered under the tort system, which required the injured worker to prove some type of *fault* on the part of the employer before recovery was permitted. Usually, this meant that the employee had to prove negligence on the part of the employer. The common law imposed certain duties on employers, even at an early date, including the duty to provide a safe place to work, the duty to provide safe appliances, tools, and equipment, the duty to give instructions and warnings to employees regarding unsafe conditions, the duty to provide suitable fellow employees, and the duty to make and enforce suitable rules to make the work safe. These duties were generally found as an implied condition of any employment contract and were used as the basis for civil lawsuits by injured employees.

But even armed with theories of recovery based on such employer duties, employees still found it difficult to recover for work-related injuries. Employers retained three common-law defenses to such claims, which barred recovery in many cases. Those defenses were *assumption of risk, contributory negligence,* and the *fellow-servant rule.*

Assumption of risk is a traditional common-law defense against negligence of all kinds (see Chapter 6, p. 215). The rule holds simply that a person cannot recover for injuries resulting from risks that are voluntarily accepted. Many courts held that workers assumed the risks of employment simply by accepting a job, even though the alternative to accepting that job was either starvation or accepting another equally dangerous job. The doctrine was based on the legal fiction that employees were entirely free to accept or reject employment.

Contributory negligence is another traditional tort defense that had special application to cases against employers (see Chapter 6, p. 215). Any negligence on the part of a workman would act as a complete bar to recovery for injuries caused by the employer's negligence, even if that contributory negligence involved only a momentary lapse of caution during a long work day.

The **fellow-servant rule** was a rule that developed specifically within the context of employer torts. That rule held simply that employees could not recover against his employer for injuries caused by the torts of other employees. Technically, it is an exception to the rule of **respondeat superior,** which imposes liability on the master for the torts of his servants committed in the scope of the servant's employment (see Chapter 7, p. 266). The rule was subject to several exceptions, but generally had the effect of prohibiting recovery in a great many cases.

It is not fair to say that employees were not able to recover against employers for the employer's torts. But the three common-law defenses did prohibit recovery in a great many cases. In addition, judges were generally probusiness and made it very difficult for employees to recover, and attorney's fees and costs often "ate up" much of the proceeds of the few successful lawsuits.

Employees who were severely injured or disabled were no longer able to perform their duties and were often dismissed. Even if a recovery was obtained in the face of the difficulties described, it was often too little and too late to maintain that employee for the rest of his life, or until he obtained other employment. Such employees often became burdens on their family and friends, or sought shelter in the 19th century's version of public welfare, the workhouse.

Worker's Compensation Statutes

The first worker's compensation statutes were passed in Europe in the late 19th century. The first American law was passed in 1902 in Maryland, though that Act was held unconstitutional. The federal government passed a worker's compensation statute in 1908 to cover government workers, and the first state statute to be upheld was passed in Wisconsin in 1911. All states now have some type of worker's compensation statute, though the content of those laws varies widely.

The underlying theory of worker's compensation statutes is that "the cost of the product should bear the blood of the workman." In other words, injuries to workers should be treated as a cost of doing business, like tools that break or goods that are wasted. The financial burden is lifted from the worker's shoulders and shifted to the employer. But the employer is expected to obtain liability insurance to spread the risk of such injuries, and the premiums for that insurance are included in the price of the goods produced. Often liability insurance is made compulsory by state law to assure that such risk-spreading takes place.

Common Worker's Compensation Provisions The typical worker's compensation law is *compulsory,* in that employers and employees have no choice whether to be covered, though a large minority of states permit some employers or some employees to make an election of coverage. Most state laws exempt certain industries or trades, though usually those exemptions are for industries or trades with other forms of protection for injured workers. Commonly, farm workers, domestic servants, and employees of very small businesses are not covered by the laws. Most state laws apply to both *injuries* and *industrial diseases,* but the latter category is often subject to some exceptions.

Arising From Employment Most state statutes are *no fault* in nature. That is, the worker is entitled to compensation regardless of whether he can prove that the employer was "at fault" in causing the injury. Usually, this is accomplished by granting employees a right to recover if the injury "arose from employment." This broad phrasing is generally interpreted to mean that the injury was caused by the employment, with no requirement of proof of fault. Commonly, the traditional tort defenses of assumption of risk, contributory negligence and the fellow-servant rule are expressly disallowed.

As a result, the worker has a very light burden of proof. Even if the injury resulted from the worker's own carelessness, or if the employer was completely blameless in the matter, the injured employee still has a right to recover. The issue is not whether the employer even caused the injury, but whether the employment resulted in the injury.

Decatur-Macon County Fair Association v. Industrial Commission

69 Ill. 2d 262, 371 N.E. 2d 597 (1977)

Morris and his wife were caretakers of the Macon County fairgrounds, hired by the association to live on the grounds in a trailer they owned. They received $20 per month, free ground rent, water, and electricity. The Morris' duties included prevention of vandalism, collection of rents for winter storage of boats housed in the buildings, and keeping some of the association's records. Morris was expected to be on the grounds 24 hours a day. One afternoon a tornado struck the fairgrounds. Morris, who was sitting in his living room in the trailer, was killed. Morris' widow filed a workman's compensation claim for death benefits. An arbitrator awarded compensation, and the association appealed:

> UNDERWOOD, Justice: . . .
> While the courts of this country have not reached uniform conclusions in considering whether injuries resulting from tornadic winds arose "out of and in the course of employment" as that phrase is used in workmen's compensation acts . . . most jurisdictions have recognized that, before compensation can be awarded, there must be

some peculiar or increased risk in the employee's duties which exposes him to special or greater danger from the elements. . . . This court has consistently adhered to that interpretation. . . .

Claimant stresses that petitioner's duties required him to be on the premises 24 hours per day, that when the tornado struck he was seated in the trailer living room where he could view the grandstand, an area in which vandalism frequently occurred, that his employer required him to live in the "flimsy trailer" in an area occupied by buildings of insubstantial construction and that this combination of circumstances indicates his death arose out of and in the course of his employment. We cannot agree.

The trailer was not furnished by the association, nor was decedent "required" by the association to live in it although, admittedly, he may have found it a convenient arrangement since it was necessary that he live on the premises. But, in any event, a not insignificant segment of the general public lives in trailers, and it had been the intention of the Morrises to do so before they became aware of the possibility of employment at the fairgrounds. . . . It is not contended, nor is there in this record any indication, that the area in which the fairground is situated is one abnormally attractive to tornados. In short, the facts of this case do not permit a conclusion that the conditions or duties of decedent's employment increased the risks of this type of injury beyond that to which the general public was exposed unless this court were to adopt the 'positional risk' rationale used by some courts. . . . Under that rationale . . . the fact that an employee's duties required him to be at the place where the tornado struck is sufficient to make the resulting injury compensable.

Absent proof of some increased risk of injury, peculiar to this employment, the award of compensation by the Commission must be held contrary to the manifest weight of the evidence.

DOOLEY, Justice, dissenting:

In my opinion, not only is there substantial evidence to support the finding of the Industrial Commission, but also the majority departs both from the prior opinions of this court and from the majority of other jurisdictions on this issue of the employee's right to compensation when some natural force plays a part in the injury. . . .

. . . .

The general rule seems to be that so long as the employment in any way combines with the elements of nature, the injury is compensable. In *Industrial Comm.* v. *Hampton,* (1931) 123 Ohio St. 500, 176 N.E. 74, decedent, a yardman, was killed while in a warehouse seeking shelter from a storm that destroyed it; in *Many* v. *Bradford* (1935), 266 N.Y. 558, 195 N.E. 199, an employee at a recreation resort, required to be on duty at all times, was struck by lightning while stooping to fasten a tent flap; in *State ex rel. Peoples Coal & Ice Co.* v. *District Court,* (1915), 129 Minn. 502, 153 N.W. 119, the driver of a wagon left his team of horses in a rainstorm and the tree he sought shelter under was struck by lightning resulting in his death; in *Reid* v. *Automatic Electric Washer Co.* (1920), 189 Iowa 964, 179 N.W. 323, a factory worker, while closing windows in the factory, was killed by debris from other parts of the building; and in *Ingram* v. *Bradley* (1969), 183 Neb. 692, 163 N.W. 2d 875, a husband and wife, employed at an outdoor theatre, ran inside a ticket booth to avoid a storm, and were injured when the wind blew over the booth. Each instance was held compensable.

Here, whether there was any such combination between the employment and natural forces causing the death and injury in question was preeminently an issue of fact for the Industrial Commission. . . .

The broad language of the usual worker's compensation statute has given rise to numerous other problems as well. Two of the knottiest areas have involved workers who suffer heart attacks on the job or as a result of the stress of employment, and workers who are injured in traffic accidents commuting to or from work. A final problem area involves workers who contract cancer as a result of prolonged exposure to substances on the job. All three types of cases have resulted in conflicting decisions among the state courts.

Within the Scope of Employment   Some states use language in their statutes to the effect that injuries must arise "within the scope of employment" before they are compensable by worker's compensation. While state court decisions are not consistent, such language seems to indicate a somewhat more narrow view of the kinds of injuries that will be compensated. More specifically, that language seems to indicate that the employee must be actually performing duties related to his or her employment when the injury occurs, while the "arising out of employment" language seems to indicate that there must only be a causal connection between the fact of employment and the injury.

Worker's Compensation Benefits   Benefits available under the state worker's compensation laws and the methods of computing those benefits vary widely. Almost all state acts provide for medical and hospital care on account of the injury, usually for the life of the workman. Most laws also require payment for a part of the worker's lost earnings, both temporarily if he must stop working to recuperate, and permanently if he is disabled. Most states require employers to assist in the rehabilitation program, if any.

Perhaps the most controversial of the worker's compensation benefits are the payments for temporary and permanent disability. Those benefits vary widely between states, causing large differences in the amount of insurance premiums paid by employers to obtain coverage. Thus, in a state where the benefits are high, the insurance premiums are also high. Generally, those rates are highest in the Northeastern and Midwestern industrial states, and some have argued that high insurance premiums in those states have contributed to the exodus of industry to states in which worker's compensation benefits are not high (see Figure 14-1).

Most states also provide some form of death benefit for workers killed on the job. Some states provide for as little as six months' income for widows and orphans, while others provide for many years of support. All states except Oklahoma provide for payment of a portion of the burial expense.

Insurance   Most state laws require employers to maintain insurance to cover losses under the worker's compensation laws, though some states will permit larger employers to become self-insurers, if they can demonstrate financial ability to do so. Some states operate a state fund, either to augment private insurance or to totally replace it. Most states expressly permit employers to "pass through" the costs of such insurance to the consumer in the form of price increases for goods.

Administration and Enforcement   In most states, a special administrative agency, often known as the Industrial Commission or the Worker's Compensation Commission, is charged with the administration of the law. Normally, an injured workman must file a claim with the agency, which is quickly heard by an arbitrator appointed by the agency. Employers are normally required to pay temporary disability after the

Figure 14-1   Example of Worker's Compensation Calculation

Assume that Joe Smith, a carpenter, earns $400 per week on the average. One day Joe fell from scaffolding while erecting a house for his employer, the XYZ Construction Company. Joe broke his arm and was hospitalized for two days. In addition, Joe was off work for a period of six weeks while the arm mended. A physician stated that Joe's arm will always be a little weaker than before, and he may be subject to arthritis in the arm later on.

If this accident happened in Illinois, Joe's benefits would be

1. *Medical costs:* All medical bills resulting from the injury will be paid for the rest of Joe's life.

2. *Temporary Total Disability:* Joe will receive pay for the time he is off work. In order to determine how much, we must determine Joe's *rate.* A worker's rate is found by multiplying the worker's average weekly wage (in this case $400) times ⅔, up to certain maximums and above certain minimums.* Joe's rate will be $400 × ⅔, or $267. Joe will receive $267** per week for the entire time he is temporarily totally disabled, or in this case, $1602.

3. *Permanent Partial Disability:* Joe's arm is permanently injured, though that injury is slight in this case. Statutes provide a certain number of weeks of compensation for each member or part of the human body—for example, in Illinois a leg is worth 200 weeks, a hand is worth 180 weeks, and an arm is worth 235 weeks. Thus in this case Joe's arm is worth 235 weeks times Joe's rate, or $267. Thus, if Joe's arm were 100 percent disabled, it would be worth 235 × $267, or $62,745.

But in this case, the permanent injury to Joe's arm is slight—perhaps 5 to 10 percent. The figure finally selected will either be the result of compromise or imposed by the arbitrator—under Illinois law no physician can testify as to the percentage of disability. Assuming that the arbitrator found a 10 percent disability in Joe's arm, Joe would receive 10 percent × $62,745, or $6,275.

Illinois law also provides for rehabilitation in proper cases, and further provides death benefits.

---

*The maximum rate under the Illinois system is $282.25, payable on all incomes of $423.38 per week and above. The minimum weekly rate is $80.90, payable to single wage earners earning $121.35 per week and below. The minimums change with the marital status and number of children of the wage earner.
**The figures here have been rounded to the nearest dollar.

first week of injury, or even earlier, and must seek Commission approval before terminating those payments. Decisions of the arbitrator may be appealed to the full agency and, ultimately, to the courts, though such decisions are fairly difficult to overturn because of the usual rules governing appeals of administrative determinations as discussed in Chapter 5. Five states still simply permit private lawsuits brought in the state courts instead of utilizing an administrative agency.

Federal Employer's Liability Act (FELA)

An early federal law protecting railroad workers, the Federal Employer's Liability Act, imposes liability on railroads operating in interstate commerce for any injury resulting from a violation of safety rules. The Act virtually eliminates the defenses of assumption of risk and contributory negligence in such actions, and completely eliminates the fellow-servant rule. Contributory negligence will not bar recovery, but will reduce the employee's recovery proportionately. Actions may be brought in any state or federal court having venue. A 1920 Amendment, the Jones Act, extended the same protections to seamen.

The Occupational Safety and Health Act of 1970

Worker's compensation acts and laws like the Federal Employer's Liability Act provide a remedy for injuries after they have occured. But another group of laws, notably the federal Occupational Safety and Health Act (OSHA) take an entirely different approach, that of trying to prevent injuries before they occur. The approach is quite simple: establish safety standards and punish employers who do not meet those standards.

OSHA was not the first preventative safety statute applied to labor. As early as 1877, Massachusetts passed a work safety statute requiring the placement of guards around hazardous machinery. Some rudimentary federal standards appeared in the Walsh-Healey Act of 1936, and the Taft-Hartley Act permitted employees to walk off the job if it was "abnormally dangerous." Specific federal standards were applied to coal mines in 1952, federal work projects in 1969, and railroads in 1970.

In 1969, Congress began holding hearings on injuries in the workplace. The evidence showed that 2.2 million persons were disabled in on-the-job accidents each year, and 14,500 persons were killed in such mishaps. The number of disabling injuries actually was going up, as much as 20 percent higher than it had been twelve years before. The economic waste attributed to such injuries was staggering, amounting to $1.5 billion in lost wages and an annual loss to the GNP of $8 billion.

The result of the hearings was the passage of the Occupational Safety and Health Act of 1970. The Act established a new administrative agency, the Occupational Safety and Health Administration, and gave that agency the authority to make rules and enforce the Act.

Employer Duties The Act provides two principal duties on employers: first, "each employer . . . shall furnish . . . employment and a place of employment which are free from recognized hazards that are causing or are likely to cause death or serious physical harm to his employees." This is the so-called **general duty clause** discussed below. Second, employers must "comply with occupational safety and health standards promulgated under this Act." In addition, the Act imposes some *ancillary duties,* such as maintaining records, reporting injuries, and acquainting employees with their rights under the Act.

The Act sets up four major categories of violations of these duties: *wilful or repeated violations; serious violations,* from which "death or serious physical harm could result . . . unless the employer did not, and could not with the exercise of reasonable diligence, know of the presence of the violation"; *nonserious violations;* and *de minimus violations.* All may be remedied by civil penalties, though criminal penalties may be imposed by the courts for wilful violations that result in death, for false reporting, and for giving advance warning of an inspection. The Secretary of Labor may seek injunctions against dangerous conditions as well; but there is no private right of action for persons injured as a result of OSHA violations.

The Act covers any employer whose work affects commerce—the same criteria used in the *Heart of Atlanta Motel* case (p. 54), which is the broadest assertion of authority by Congress. As a result very few, if any, employers escape coverage under the law.

OSHA Organization   The Occupational Safety and Health Administration is a part of the Department of Labor, headed by an Assistant Secretary of Labor for OSHA. The nation is divided into ten geographical regions, each of which contains several area and district offices and field stations. Each area office is under an Area Director, who is in charge of scheduling and conducting inspections and issuing citations and proposed penalties.

The rule-making function is delegated to the Secretary of Labor and the Secretary of HEW. Originally, the Secretary of Labor was given authority to adopt standards for industry without elaborate rule-making procedures. Those interim standards gave way to formal **notice and comment rule making** in 1973, and such procedures must be followed except in emergency situations in all cases. Such emergency standards may only exist for six months before formal procedures must be followed. Much of the background research behind the standards is done by the National Institute for Occupational Safety and Health (NIOSH). NIOSH has no authority to make standards, but instead conducts research and makes recommendations to the Secretary. A private standards-drafting organization, the American National Standards Institute (ANSI) also works closely with OSHA and with private firms to draft the OSHA standards. The Administrative Procedures Act generally applies to the adoption of OSHA standards.

The judicial function of OSHA is delegated to another administrative agency, the Occupational Safety and Health Review Commission. That body consists of three members appointed by the President for staggered six-year terms. The Review Commission also appoints hearing examiners to hear cases prior to record review by the full Commission. If OSHA issues a citation, the party to whom it is issued may contest the citation before the Commission. A hearing examiner will hear the case and forward a report to the Commission, which either adopts or rejects the examiner's decision. Either party may appeal to the U.S. Courts of Appeal.

OSHA Enforcement   The OSH Administration is required by the Act to inspect workplaces to determine compliance. The Administration has generally adopted a "worst-first" inspections priorities system. The first to be inspected are cases of imminent danger, followed by catastrophe and fatality investigations, employee complaints, and "special emphasis" program inspections. The Act requires that advance notice not be given of any inspection, and provides criminal penalties for persons giving such notice. As noted in *Marshall* v. *Barlow's, Inc.,* p. 176, a search warrant is required for such inspections, but such warrants may be issued on an *ex parte* basis and without a showing of probable cause. Inspectors are known as Compliance Safety and Health Officers, or *COs.* Most of the COs have an engineering background and are required to undergo specialized training before beginning work.

The actual inspection consists of three stages: an *opening conference* in which the inspector discusses the procedures for conducting the inspection, a *walkaround* tour of the facility, and a *closing conference* at which the inspector issues any citations and makes other safety and health suggestions. Employers have a right to know the nature of any employee complaints, but do not have a right to know the name of the complaining employee. Employers may claim certain areas off limits because of trade secrets, but inspectors have a right to ask for a hearing to determine whether or not the claim is justified. Such hearings are held in secret by the Review Commission. At the closing conference, the inspector will issue any citations and propose penalties. If the employer accepts the penalty, there will be no further review. Contests of such penalties take place before the OSH Review Commission.

It was initially argued that OSHA procedure deprived parties of their right to a jury trial and imposed criminallike penalties without due process of law. The following decision considered the first of those contentions and also contains one of the best judicial summaries of OSHA enforcement techniques.

Atlas Roofing Co. v. Occupational Safety and Health Review Commission

430 U.S. 442, 97 S. Ct. 1261, 51 L. Ed. 2d 464 (1977)

Mr. Justice WHITE delivered the opinion of the Court.

The issue in this case is whether, consistent with the Seventh Amendment, Congress may create a new cause of action in the Government for civil penalties enforceable in an administrative agency where there is no jury trial.

I

After extensive investigation, Congress concluded, in 1970, that work-related deaths and injuries had become a "drastic" national problem. Finding the existing state statutory remedies as well as state common law actions for negligence and wrongful death to be inadequate to protect the employee population from death and injury due to unsafe working conditions, Congress enacted the Occupational Safety and Health Act of 1970. . . . The Act created a new statutory duty to avoid maintaining unsafe or unhealthy working conditions, and empowers the Secretary of Labor to promulgate health and safety standards. Two new remedies were provided—permitting the Federal Government, proceeding before an administrative agency, (1) to obtain abatement orders requiring employers to correct unsafe working conditions and (2) to impose civil penalties on any employer maintaining any unsafe working condition. . . .

Under the Act, inspectors, representing the Secretary of Labor, are authorized to conduct reasonable safety and health inspections. . . . If a violation is discovered the inspector, on behalf of the Secretary, issues a citation to the employer fixing a reasonable time for its abatement, and, in his discretion, proposing a civil penalty. . . . Such proposed penalties may range from nothing for de minimus and nonserious violations, to not more than $1,000 for serious violations, to a maximum of $10,000 for willful or repeated violations. . . .

If the employer wishes to contest the penalty or the abatement order, he may do so by notifying the Secretary of Labor within 15 days, in which event the abatement order is automatically stayed. . . . An evidentiary hearing is then held before an administrative law judge of the Occupational Safety and Health Review Commission. The Commission consists of three members, appointed for six-year terms, each of whom is qualified to adjudicate contested citations and assess penalties "by reason of training, education, or experience". . . . At this hearing the burden is on the Secretary to establish the elements of the alleged violation and the propriety of his proposed abatement order and proposed penalty; and the judge is empowered to affirm, modify, or vacate any or all of these items, giving due consideration in his penalty assessment to "the size of the business of the employer . . . the gravity of the violation, the good faith of the employer, and the history of previous violations." The judge's decision becomes the Commission's final and appealable order unless within 30 days a Commissioner directs that it be reviewed by the full Commission.

If review is granted, the Commission's subsequent order directing abatement and the payment of any assessed penalty becomes final unless the employer timely petitions for judicial review in the appropriate court of appeals. . . . The Secretary similarly may seek review of Commission orders . . . but, in either case, "[t]he findings of the Commission with respect to questions of fact, if supported by substantial evidence on the record considered as a whole, shall be conclusive". . . . If the employer fails to pay the assessed penalty, the Secretary may commence a collection action in a federal district court in which neither the fact of the violation nor the propriety of the penalty assessed may be retried. . . . Thus, the penalty may be collected without the employer ever being entitled to a jury determination of the facts constituting the violation.

II

Petitioners were separately cited by the Secretary and ordered immediately to abate pertinent hazards after inspections of their respective work sites conducted in 1972 revealed conditions that assertedly violated a mandatory occupational safety standard. . . . In each case an employee's death had resulted. . . .

III

The Seventh Amendment provides that "in Suits at common law, where the value in controversy shall exceed twenty dollars, the right of trial by jury shall be preserved." The phrase "suits at common law" has been construed to refer to cases tried prior to the adoption of the Seventh Amendment in courts of law in which jury trial was customary as distinguished from courts of equity or admiralty in which jury trial was not . . . Petitioners claim that a suit in federal court by the Government for civil penalties for violation of a statute is a suit for a money judgment which is classically a suit at common law. . . . and that the defendant therefore has a Seventh Amendment right to a jury determination of all issues of fact in such a case. . . . Petitioners then claim that to permit Congress to assign the function of adjudicating the Government's rights to civil penalties for violation of the statute to a different forum—an administrative agency in which no jury is available—would be to permit Congress to deprive a defendant of his Seventh Amendment jury right. We disagree. At least in cases in which "public rights" are being litigated—e.g., cases in which the Government sues in its sovereign capacity to enforce public rights created by statutes within the power of Congress to enact—the Seventh Amendment does not prohibit Congress from assigning the factfinding function and initial adjudicaton to an administrative forum which the jury would be incompatible.

[H]istory and our cases support the proposition that the right to a jury trial turns not solely on the nature of the issue to be resolved, but also on the forum in which it is to be resolved. Congress found the common law and other existing remedies for work injuries resulting from unsafe working conditions to be inadequate to protect the Nation's working men and women. It created a new cause of action, and remedies therefor, unknown to the common law, and placed their enforcement in a tribunal supplying speedy and expert resolutions of the issues involved. The Seventh Amendment is no bar to the creation of new rights or to their enforcement outside the regular courts of law.

The judgments below are affirmed.

Penalty Structure The Act provides for a wide range of penalties, depending on the severity of the offense. The penalty ranges for each of the violations are as follows:

De minimus violations	$0
Nonserious violations	$0–1,000
Serious violations	$1–1,000
Repeated violations	$0–10,000
Wilful violations	$0–10,000
Failure to abate violations	$0–1,000 per day

The amount of the penalty assessed will depend on two principal factors: the *gravity* of the violation and whether the violator was acting in *good faith. Gravity,* in turn, is composed of three factors: (1) the likelihood that an injury would result from the violation; (2) the severity of any resulting injuries; and (3) the extent to which a standard has been violated, e.g., the amount of employee exposure. *Good faith* has likewise been demonstrated by four factors: (1) the employer's overall safety program; (2) actual attempts to comply with the standard; (3) employer cooperation with the CO; and (4) prompt abatement of violations. The Act also provides that the size of a business and the employer's history of compliance also be considered in determining the penalty to be assessed. The Commission retains the authority to either raise or lower the penalty proposed by the CO, but the authority to raise the penalty has been used very sparingly.

Refusal of Employees to Work   While it is clear under the Taft-Hartley Act that an employee may walk-off the job if the work becomes unreasonably hazardous, the issue quickly arose under OSHA whether employees could protect themselves by refusing to work. The following decision resolved the issue.

Whirlpool Corp. v. Marshall

445 U.S. 1, 100 S. Ct. 883, 63 L. Ed. 154 (1980)

Whirlpool manufactured household appliances with the aid of several overhead conveyor systems. In order to protect workers from materials falling from these overhead conveyors, Whirlpool installed a system of wire mesh screens over the plant workers. The safety of that screen had been called into question and it was being replaced by a stronger mesh. Maintenance workers were required to go up on the screen to retrieve objects and clean the screen. A week after a maintenance worker fell through the screen to his death, two other maintenance workers refused to go up on the screen and were disciplined. The Secretary brought this action for an injunction, for back pay, and for expungement of the two worker's records. The trial court held against the Secretary, and the appellate court reversed. Whirlpool appealed.

Mr. Justice STEWART delivered the opinion of the Court.
. . . .
The Occupational Safety and Health Act of 1970 (Act) prohibits an employer from discharging or discriminating against any employee who exercises "any right afforded by" the Act. The Secretary of Labor (Secretary) has promulgated a regulation providing that, among the rights that the Act so protects, is the right of an employee to choose not to perform his assigned task because of a reasonable apprehension of death or serious injury coupled with a reasonable belief that no less drastic alternative is available. The question presented is whether this regulation is consistent with the Act.
. . . .
The regulation clearly conforms to the fundamental objective of the Act—to prevent occupational deaths and serious injuries. . . .
. . . The Act does not wait for an employee to die or become injured. It authorizes

the promulgation of health and safety standards and the issuance of citations in the hope that these will act to prevent deaths or injuries from ever occurring. It would seem anomalous to construe an Act so directed and constructed as prohibiting an employee, with no other reasonable alternative, the freedom to withdraw from a workplace environment that he reasonably believes is highly dangerous.

Moreover, the Secretary's regulation can be viewed as an appropriate aid to the full effectuation of the Act's "general duty" clause. . . . As the legislative history of this provision reflects, it was intended itself to deter the occurrence of occupational deaths and serious injuries by placing on employers a mandatory obligation independent of the specific health and safety standards to be promulgated by the Secretary. Since OSHA inspectors cannot be present around the clock in every workplace, the Secretary's regulation ensures that employees will in all circumstances enjoy the rights afforded them by the "general duty" clause.

The regulation thus on its face appears to further the overriding purpose of the Act, and rationally to complement its remedial scheme. In the absence of some contrary indication in the legislative history, the Secretary's regulation must, therefore, be upheld, particularly when it is remembered that safety legislation is to be liberally construed to effectuate the congressional purpose. . . .

State Enforcement

One of the purposes of the original Act was to encourage the adoption of state standards and procedures to protect worker safety. For that reason, the Act permitted the states to adopt their own standards, and once such standards are adopted and approved, the state governs the area. Those standards must be at least as effective as the federal standards and the enforcement procedures must be "workable". About half the states have adopted such standards and secured the approval of the Secretary of Labor to implement those plans.

Regulation of Wages

The Wagner Act only guaranteed the right to organize and bargain. It provided no protections for the five-sixths of American workers who are not organized. To many unorganized workers, low wages and long hours remained as a fact of life. Those matters continued to go unregulated except by the common law of contracts.

Some states had tried to control wages and hours directly in the late 19th and early 20th centuries, but those laws were often held unconstitutional (see, e.g., *Lochner* v. *New York*, p. 57). After the 1937 *Jones & Laughlin Steel* decision (p. 52) widened the authority of Congress to regulate commerce, Congress passed its own "minimum wage" law: the Federal Fair Labor Standards Act.

The Federal Fair Labor Standards Act

The Federal Fair Labor Standards Act, passed in 1938, set a minimum wage for certain classes of employees and required premium pay, or overtime for all hours over a statutory maximum, usually 40 hours. Contrary to common belief, the law does not permit employees to refuse to work over 40 hours, but only requires the payment of "overtime" for such work. The original minimum wage was 25¢ per hour, but there have been numerous increases until, as of 1985, it stood at $3.35 per hour.

The Fair Labor Standards Act has five principal parts: (1) it requires that employers keep payroll records on all employees; (2) it requires employers to pay men and women "equal pay for equal work;" (3) it requires payment of at least the minimum wage to all covered employees; (4) it requires payment of "overtime," or one and one-half times the ordinary wage, for work over 40 hours in one week; and (5) it prohibited employers from oppressively employing child labor.

Initially, the Act only covered *employees* who were directly engaged in interstate commerce. This restriction resulted in anomalous situations in which two employees, both working for the same employer and doing essentially similar work, might be paid different rates, if one was engaged in interstate commerce and the other was not. In later years, the coverage requirement was changed to *enterprises* engaged in commerce. The Act also initially exempted many categories of employees, but many of those specific exemptions have been removed in recent years. Agricultural workers, domestic servants, and certain government workers have been recently covered, for example.

The creativity of businesses to establish new forms of employer-employee relationships has resulted in many serious questions of coverage under the FLSA. Only "employees" are covered by the Act, and some employers have attempted to create employment relationships that are traditionally treated as some other form by the common law, either to avoid the effect of the FLSA or for other reasons. The following decision considers whether migrant workers are "employees" under the Act.

Hodgson v. Griffin and Brand of McAllen, Inc.

471 F. 2d 235 (5th Cir., 1973)

The defendant owned a large fruit and vegetable packing firm in Texas, and conducted farming operations as well. There was no doubt that its produce ended up in interstate commerce. Many of the laborers for the picking and packing were migrant workers. Griffin and Brand dealt with so-called "crew leaders," who secured the migrant workers and transported them to the work site. The crew leader was paid a weekly sum, from which he paid the migrant workers. An employee of the defendant in turn supervised the crew leaders. The defendant also took it upon itself to withhold social security, since the crew leaders were generally "incapable" of doing the calculations. It was clear that the crew leaders violated the FLSA in several respects, including paying less than the minimum wage, not paying overtime, and hiring children. The Secretary of Labor brought this action under the FLSA, claiming the migrant workers were defendant's "employees". The District Court found that the defendant had violated the Act, and the defendant appealed on the grounds that the employees were not "employees" within the meaning of the Act. The District Court granted an injunction against future violations. The defendant appealed to the U.S. Circuit Court of Appeals.

THORNBERRY, Circuit Judge:

. . . .

The independent contractor status of the crew leaders, if they are independent contractors, does not as a matter of law negate the possibility that Griffin and Brand may be a joint employer of the harvest workers. There may be independent contractors who take part in production or distribution who would alone be responsible for the wages and hours of their own employees, . . . but independent contractor status does not necessarily imply the contractor is solely responsible under the Fair Labor Standards Act. Another employer may be jointly responsible for the contractor's employees. . . .

Whether appellant is an employer of the harvest workers does not depend on technical or isolated factors, but rather on the circumstances of the whole activity. . . . it depends not on the form of the relationship but on the "economic reality." . . . This court has summarized the proper approach to be taken and some important factors to be regarded as follows: "Whether a person or corporation is an employer or joint employer is essentially a question of fact. . . . In considering whether a person or corporation is an 'employer' or 'joint employer,' the total employment situation would be considered with particular regard to the following questions; (1) Whether or not the employment takes place on the premises of the company?; (2) How much control does the company exert over the employees?; (3) Does the company have the power to fire, hire, or modify the employment condition of the employees?; (4) Do the employees perform a 'specialty job' within the production line?; and (5) May the employee refuse to work for the company or work for others?" . . .

We do not think the district court's conclusion in this case that appellant was a joint employer was clearly erroneous; on the contrary, we find that it was amply supported by the evidence. Of course, the work necessarily took place on appellant's premises. The testimony that appellant's field supervisors supervised the harvest work tends to indicate an employment relationship. The fact that appellant effected the supervision by speaking to the crew leaders, who in turn spoke to the harvest workers, rather than speaking directly to the harvest workers does not negate a degree of apparent on-the-job control over the harvest workers. The fact that appellant set the rate of pay of the harvest workers, decided whether crew leaders would pay a piece rate or an hourly rate in a given instance, and handled the social security contributions for the harvest workers also tend to indicate an employment relationship. Viewing the total work arrangement, we agree with the district court that appellant was a joint employer and thus responsible for the violations of the Fair Labor Standards Act.

. . .

Affirmed.

Many states also maintain minimum wage–maximum hours laws, which may be more extensive, either in their coverage or in the required minimum wages. Some employees still remain outside the protections of the Act, including executive, managerial, and professional employees, employees of certain seasonal amusement firms, some small newspapers, casual babysitters and companions to the elderly, and persons in individual or family-owned small businesses.

Child Labor Provisions Both state and federal laws impose restrictions on the employment of children. Most of the federal law regarding child labor is found in the FLSA, but that Act exempts several categories of child labor from the operation of the Act, including newspaper delivery, modeling, acting, nonhazardous farm work when school is not in session, farm work on a farm owned or operated by the child's parent, and any other nonhazardous employment for the child's parent or guardian. Most regulation of child labor problems is done by the states, under state law, however.

The FLSA prohibits children, other than those in an exempt catagory, from working if they are under the age of 14. Children between 14 and 16 may work outside of school hours, provided they work no more than 8 hours a day and 40 hours a week during school vacation periods and 3 hours a day and 18 hours a week while school is in session. Such children may not work between 7 PM and 7 AM (9 PM when school is not in session). In addition, the Secretary of Labor has established certain categories of hazardous employment, in which children cannot be employed. Children between 16 and 18 years of age may work in any nonhazardous employment.

Equal Pay In 1964, the federal Equal Pay Act went into effect as a part of the federal Fair Labor Standards Act. The Act required that "equal work be rewarded with equal wages." Women cannot be paid less than men "for equal work on jobs the performance of which requires equal skill, effort and responsibility, and which are performed under similar working conditions." Different payment is permissible in four instances: a seniority system; a merit system; a system that measures earnings by quantity or quality of production (e.g., piecework); and a differential that measures earnings based on any other factor other than sex. Remedies may include an order to pay back wages to discriminatorily treated workers and injunctions against continued violation. The Secretary of Labor has the authority to file such actions. The problem of sex discrimination in employment is discussed at length in Chapter 16.

Enforcement and Remedies Administrative responsibility for FLSA enforcement is vested in the Wage and Hour Division of the Employment Standards Administration of the Department of Labor. That Division brings compliance actions to force the payment of wages that should have been paid either under the minimum wage or overtime provisions. The bulk of those actions are for small amounts and are settled for the amount due immediately after the inspection that discloses the amount due. The Division may refer the matter to the Solicitor of Labor, a kind of general counsel for the Department of Labor, who may begin litigation in the name of the Secretary. The Solicitor may issue a *subpoena duces tecum* to obtain information and secure records indicating lack of compliance. The Secretary may bring damage actions or may sue for injunctive relief, including mandatory injunctions barring employers from "continuing to withhold unpaid wages." Wilful violations are criminal violations carrying a fine of $10,000. The prosecution is not required to prove an "evil" motive, but only that the violation is deliberate, voluntary, and intentional.

Labor Standards Affecting Federally Related Contracts Aside from the direct regulation of wages and hours under the FLSA, several other federal statutes require payment of higher wages to employees working on federal projects or projects funded by federal dollars in whole or in part. Those four statutes include the Walsh-Healey Public Contracts Act, the McNamara-O'Hara Service Contract Act, the Davis-Bacon Act, and the Contract Work Hours Standards Act. All four laws generally require that employees working on federal projects or on projects funded by federal money must be paid the "prevailing wage" in the area for similar work, but not less than the federal minimum wage. Thus, if a construction worker on a private project would receive $8.00 an hour, a worker on a federal project would receive the same amount. Each Act applies to different types of contracts, and each contains exceptions for smaller contracts of varying amounts. Such laws are generally enforced by private lawsuits to collect the back amounts of such wages. Generally, overtime is also required.

In 1972 Congress passed the Government Employee's Prevailing Rate Systems Act, which requires that federal hourly employees be paid according to the prevailing rate for similar labor in their area. The law does not affect employees under collective bargaining agreements.

Regulation of Employment Security

It is not much of an overstatement to say that in the absence of a contract, employees retain their employment at the discretion of the employer. In the absence of collective bargaining agreements or an individual employment contract, an employee may generally be discharged for any reason or for no reason at all. That basic insecurity of employment has resulted in several attempts by the federal and state governments to provide some basic security for the working people of the nation. That security has taken three important forms: the federal Social Security Act; unemployment compensation laws; and regulation of private pension funds.

The Social Security Act

Almost all workers become less "marketable" as they grow older. Only a very few of us escape the decision whether to retire, and often that decision is made for us by company policy, illness, or physical inability to do the work.

But very few workers make adequate provision for old age. It is tempting to argue that such a lack of foresight, while regrettable, is the workers' "fault," and workers should be left to their own devices. Such a hands-off attitude by government would encourage private savings and private sector involvement and would eliminate a large part of government's activities in providing entitlements to the public.

But such an argument may beg the question. First, those workers who do not provide for their old age would become a burden on family or friends, or would become eligible for some form of public welfare. Second, for most workers it is extremely difficult to set back sufficient amounts of money to adequately care for themselves over an indeterminate period of time. In other words, there may not be enough money available to maintain a reasonable standard of living and set aside such amounts out of the same paycheck. Third, many of the people most in need of help do not have the sophistication necessary to set up such retirement plans. The result of these factors was, in the heart of the Depression, a great number of elderly persons—more than half of those over age 65 in 1935, for example—who were dependent on friends, relatives, or the meager public aid measures of that time. It appears that the choice may not be between Social Security and private systems, but rather between Social Security and other forms of welfare.

Overview and Constitutionality of Social Security

The federal Social Security Act was passed in 1935 to remedy the problems of retiring and elderly persons. The original Act provided one kind of benefit—*old-age insurance*—and covered only a limited number of employees. Employees covered by the Act were required to make contributions out of their pay to the Treasury, which used those contributions as a basis for paying benefits. The plan was never "fully funded," and contributions have never equalled payments. The Act has been amended several times to add other kinds of insurance, notably benefits for some wives, children, and survivors, disabled persons, and self-employed persons and, in 1965, the Medicare amendments were added to provide health insurance for the elderly.

The 1935 Act was challenged in two "companion" cases that reached the Supreme Court in 1937, at about the same time that the *Jones & Laughlin Steel* case came before the Court and while the "court-packing plan" was before Congress (see

Chapter 2). The first case, *Steward Machine* v. *Davis*,* involved the constitutionality of a part of the Act that required an employer's excise tax for the purpose of establishing an unemployment compensation system (discussed later). The Court held the Act's unemployment compensation tax constitutional against a series of claims that it was beyond Congress' authority to tax or regulate for these purposes. The second case involved a much broader claim against the balance of the Act.

Helvering v. Davis

301 U.S. 619, 57 S. Ct. 904, 81 L. Ed. 1307 (1937)

Mr. Justice CARDOZO delivered the opinion of the Court.

The Social Security Act . . . is challenged once again.

. . . In this case Titles VIII and II are the subject of attack. Title VIII lays another excise upon employers. . . . It lays a special income tax upon employees to be deducted from their wages and paid by the employers. Title II provides for the payment of Old Age Benefits, and supplies the motive and occasion, in the view of the assailants of the statute, for the levy of the taxes imposed by Title VIII. The plan of the two titles will now be summarized more fully.

Title VIII, as we have said, lays two different types of tax, an "income tax on employees," and "an excise tax on employers." The income tax on employees is measured by wages paid during the calendar year. . . . The excise tax on the employer is to be paid "with respect to having individuals in his employ," and, like the tax on employees, is measured by wages. . . . The income tax on employees is to be collected by the employer, who is to deduct the amount from the wages "as and when paid." . . . He is indemnified against claims and demands of any person by reason of such payment. . . . The proceeds of both taxes are to be paid into the Treasury like internal revenue taxes generally, and are not earmarked in any way. . . . There are penalties for nonpayment. . . .

Title II has the caption "Federal Old-Age Benefits." The benefits are of two types, first, monthly pensions, and second, lump sum payments, the payments of the second class being relatively few and unimportant.

The first section of this title creates an account in the United States Treasury to be known as the "Old-Age Reserve Account". . . . No present appropriation, however, is made to that account. All that the statute does is to authorize appropriations annually thereafter, beginning with the fiscal year which ends June 30, 1937. . . .

This suit is brought by a shareholder of the Edison Electric Illuminating Company of Boston . . . to restrain the corporation from making the payments and deductions called for by the act which is stated to be void under the Constitution of the United States. The bill tells us that the corporation has decided to obey the statute, that it has reached this decision in the face of the complainant's protests. . . .

The District Court ruled in favor of the government, but the U.S. Court of Appeals reversed, holding that Title II was void as an invasion of powers reserved under the 10th Amendment. A petition for certiorari was filed and granted by the Supreme Court.

. . . . We were asked to determine: (1) "Whether the tax imposed upon employers . . . is within the power of Congress under the Constitution," and (2) "whether the validity of the tax imposed upon employees . . . is properly . . . within the power of Congress under the Constitution." . . .

. . . The scheme of benefits created by the provisions of Title II is not in contravention of the limitations of the Tenth Amendment. . . .

Congress may spend money in aid of the "general welfare." . . . Congress did not improvise a judgment when it found that the award of old age benefits would be con-

---

*301 U.S. 548, 57 S. Ct. 883, 81 L. Ed. 1279 (1937).

ducive to the general welfare. . . . A great mass of evidence was brought together supporting the policy which finds expression in the act. Among the relevant facts are these: The number of persons in the United States 65 years of age or over is increasing proportionately as well as absolutely. What is even more important, the number of such persons unable to take care of themselves is growing at a threatening pace. More and more our population is becoming urban and industrial instead of rural and agricultural. The evidence is impressive that among industrial workers the younger men and women are preferred over the older. In times of retrenchment the older are commonly the first to go, and even if retained, their wages are likely to be lowered. The plight of men and women at so low an age as 40 is hard, almost hopeless, when they are driven to seek for reemployment. . . .

The problem is plainly national in area and dimensions. Moreover, laws of the separate states cannot deal with it effectively. . . . States and local governments are often lacking in the resources that are necessary to finance an adequate program of security for the aged. . . . Apart from the failure of resources, states and local governments are at times reluctant to increase so heavily the burden of taxation to be borne by their residents for fear of placing themselves in a position of economic disadvantage as compared with neighbors or competitors. . . . A system of old-age pensions has special dangers of its own, if put in force in one state and rejected in another. The existence of such a system is a bait to the needy and dependent elsewhere, encouraging them to migrate and seek a haven of repose. Only a power that is national can serve the interests of all.

Whether wisdom or unwisdom resides in the scheme of benefits set forth in Title II, it is not for us to say. The answer to such inquiries must come from Congress, not the courts. Our concern here, as often, is with power, not with wisdom. Counsel for respondent has recalled to us the virtues of self-reliance and frugality. There is a possibility, he says, that aid from a paternal government may sap those sturdy virtues and breed a race of weaklings. If Massachusetts so believes and shapes her laws in that conviction, must her breed of sons be changed, he asks, because some other philosophy of government finds favor in the halls of Congress? But the answer is not doubtful. The issue is a closed one. It was fought out long ago. When money is spent to promote the general welfare, the concept of welfare or the opposite is shaped by Congress, not the states. So the concept be not arbitrary, the locality must yield. Constitution, Art. VI, Par. 2.

Reversed.

Employees Covered   The 1935 Act was fairly restrictive in its coverage of employees, generally sheltering only workers in industry and commerce. A series of amendments since that time has expanded the coverage substantially, generally including three separate categories: (1) any "employee" according to the common law test, namely whether the employer has the right to direct and control the result, details, and means of accomplishing the employee's work; (2) officers of corporations, which may not be covered under the common-law test, are specifically included; and (3) four kinds of "service employees," which may not be covered under the common-law test, including agent drivers and commission drivers, life insurance agents, homeworkers, and travelling salesmen, all of whom generally work on a commission basis.

The Act provides for nineteen specific exempt categories of workers, including some types of agricultural and domestic labor, family employment, ministers, employees of tax-exempt organizations, newspaperboys, employees of colleges, employees of international organizations, sharecroppers, employees of communist governments, and the largest category of all, employees of local, state and federal governments. Some of those employees or employers may voluntarily elect to be covered.

Since 1950, self-employed persons may be covered by social security as well. A tax is levied on *self-employment income,* which is defined as the net earnings from self-employment up to certain maximums. That amount must be paid with the individual's federal income tax, either quarterly or annually.

Insured Status: **Insured status** is required before an individual is eligible to receive benefits of any kind. There are three types of insured status: *fully insured, currently insured,* and *insured for disability benefits.* An individual's status is generally determined by the number of *quarters of eligibility* that he has accumulated. For example, a person is generally considered fully insured after accumulating 40 quarters, or 40 "quarters of a year," under the Social Security system. Currently insured status requires 6 quarters of coverage in the preceding 13 quarters, and disability status requires 20 quarters during the preceding 40 quarters. Each type of benefit requires some form of insured status before payment can be made. Each form is subject to a great number of exceptions and qualifications as well.

Social Security Benefits   The Social Security Act provides four major forms of benefits: *Old-Age Benefits; Survivor's Insurance Benefits; Disability Benefits;* and *Medicare.*

Old Age Benefits: An individual is entitled to social security old-age benefits if he has reached age 62, is fully insured or is under a "transitional exception," and files an application. Benefits generally increase if a worker waits until age 65 to file. Benefits begin the first month the conditions of eligibility are met and end the month preceding his death. The amount of the monthly payment is based on a formula that uses the individual's average monthly wage over a seven-year period. The amount may also be subject to cost of living increases as well. Wives, husbands, and children of such workers are also entitled to benefits, and even divorced spouses of such workers may have a right to social security payments based on the record of the covered employee if they fulfill certain criteria.

Just because someone decides to accept social security does not mean that that person must quit work entirely. The Social Security Administration permits persons receiving Social Security Old Age benefits to work and earn wages up to certain maximums. The Administration uses a "three-tiered" test, which permits persons between the ages of 62 and 65 to earn up to $5,160 per year, and allows persons over the age of 65 to earn up to $6,960 per year while still receiving Social Security benefits. Beyond age 70, earnings do not affect the receipt of Social Security benefits. Of course, these determinations can change at any time.

Survivor's Insurance Benefits: Minor dependent children and in some circumstances the spouses of deceased workers have a right to receive survivor's insurance benefits if a fully insured person dies. Spouses are eligible if they are over 60 (or over 50 and disabled) and are not entitled to receive benefits larger than the deceased spouse's award. The marriage must have taken place at least nine months before the death, or there must have been a child. Parents may also receive benefits under certain circumstances. Children's benefits terminate when a child reaches age 18 or ceases being a full-time student, unless the child is disabled.

Disability Benefits: In order to be eligible for disability benefits, an individual must be under a disability as defined in the Act; file an application; have a "disability insurance status;" complete a five-month waiting period or be exempt; and not have attained the age of 65. The amount of the benefits is equal to the amount that would be received as an old-age beneficiary. Periods on disability are not included in later computations of old-age benefits under the concept of a "disability freeze."

Medicare Benefits: In 1965, Congress passed the Medicare bill, which amended the Social Security Act. The Act provides medical insurance to those entitled to any kind of social security monthly benefits, even if the benefit has been suspended for certain reasons. Amendments in 1972 provided coverage for those disabled persons who have been entitled to disability benefits under the Act for twenty-four consecutive months, and persons insured under social security or their dependents who need kidney dialysis or kidney transplants.

The purpose of the Act is to help pay a major portion of personal health care costs of those covered by the program, but it is *not* intended to pay *all* such expenses. The program is designed to pay the most urgently needed and more expensive health care costs for the majority of those covered.

The Act has two major types of benefits: a hospital insurance plan (called *Part A*) providing coverage essentially for in-patient hospital care and any subsequent posthospital extended care; and a medical insurance program (called *Supplemental Medical Insurance Benefits* or SMIB), which provides for physician services, out-patient care, and many other medical services. Two different trust funds finance the two programs. Part A is generally financed by taxes paid by employees and self-employed persons. SMIB is generally voluntary, and is paid for by insurance premiums, except for persons not covered by Part A and who do not elect to be covered. For such persons SMIB is mandatory. Since Medicare was not intended to be complete, many elderly persons obtain some complementary coverage from a private insurance carrier as well.

Administration and Enforcement of Social Security   The Social Security Administration is a part of the Department of Health, Education and Welfare. Branch offices of the Administration are maintained in major cities across the country. In order to be eligible for any benefit, an individual usually must file a claim with the local office but separate applications need not be filed for Medicare if a person is already eligible for Social Security.

The initial determination of eligibility is made by the local office. Persons dissatisfied with the determination may take the claim through a series of review and appellate steps. An initial determination becomes final unless reconsideration is requested within six months. The final review is a civil action in the United States district court.

Unemployment Compensation

A part of the original Social Security Act provided for a federal tax on employers to finance a system of unemployment compensation. The system was to be state-run, however, and amounts paid to state unemployment compensation systems may be credited against the federal tax. The federal government makes grants to the states to pay the administrative costs of such programs and advances funds to states to pay benefits when state funds run low.

Generally speaking, the states pay the funds directly to unemployed workers for a specific number of weeks, during which the unemployed worker is usually required to look for work. The plans are fairly similar in operation and effect because of the overriding federal requirements attached to the federal grants.

Typical state legislation imposes several eligibility requirements, including (1) that a claimant have worked in covered employment for an appropriate "base period"; (2) that a claimant register for work through the public employment service; and (3) that the claimant be able and available to work. The weekly benefit amount is typically based on the taxable earnings of the claimant during the base period. Every state provides for weekly minimums and maximums, and often provides increments if the claimant has dependents. Usually the maximum number of weeks for which "regular benefits" are payable is 26, though it may be as high as 36. A person who has exhausted the "regular benefits" may be eligible for payments under the Federal-State Extended Unemployment Compensation Program established in 1970, which provides for up to an additional 13 weeks per extension. Most states do not provide benefits if a claimant leaves work voluntarily or is fired for misconduct. The following case considers the question of whether striking workers have the right to unemployment benefits.

New York Telephone Co. v. New York Department of Labor

440 U.S. 519, 99 S. Ct. 1328, 59 L. Ed. 2d 553 (1979)

The Communication Workers of America recommended a nationwide strike of the Bell Telephone Company in 1971. In most places, the strike only lasted a week, but in New York the strike continued for seven months. New York's unemployment insurance law provided no exemption for striking workers, and as a result the 38,000 CWA workers filed for and received unemployment compensation. Those amounts were charged back to the employer, for the most part, under New York's system of establishing employer contributions. The telephone company filed suit, claiming that this part of the New York law had been preempted by the Wagner Act. The District Court granted a declaratory judgment against paying the compensation, but the Court of Appeals reversed. The Company appealed.

Mr. Justice STEVENS announced the judgment of the Court in an opinion in which Mr. Justice WHITE and Mr. Justice REHNQUIST joined.

The question is whether the National Labor Relations Act, as amended, implicitly prohibits the State of New York from paying unemployment compensation to strikers.

. . . .

In this case there is no evidence that the Congress that enacted the National Labor Relations Act in 1935, intended to deny the States the power to provide unemployment benefits for strikers. . . . Far from the compelling congressional direction on which preemption in this case would have to be predicated, the silence of Congress in 1935 actually supports the contrary inference that Congress intended to allow the States to make this policy determination for themselves.

New York was one of five States that had an unemployment insurance law before Congress passed the Social Security and the Wagner Acts in the summer of 1935. Although the New York law did not then assess taxes against employers on the basis of their individual experience, it did authorize the payment of benefits to strikers out of a general fund financed by assessments against all employers in the State. The junior Senator from New York, Robert Wagner, was a principal sponsor of both the National Labor Relations Act and the Social Security Act; the two statutes were considered in Congress simultaneously and enacted into law within five weeks of one another. . . . [I]t is difficult to believe that Senator Wagner and his colleagues were unaware of such a controversial provision, particularly at a time when both unemployment and labor unrest were matters of vital national concern.

Difficulty becomes virtual impossibility when it is considered that the issue of public benefits for strikers became a matter of express congressional concern in 1935 during the hearings and debates on the Social Security Act. . . . [T]he scheme of the Social Security Act has always allowed the States great latitude in fashioning their own programs. From the beginning, however, the Act has contained a few specific requirements for federal approval. One of these provides that a State may not deny compensation to an otherwise qualified applicant because he had refused to accept work as a strikebreaker, or had refused to resign from a union as a condition of employment. By contrast, Congress rejected the suggestions of certain advisory members of the Roosevelt Administration as well as some representatives of citizens and business groups that the States be prohibited from providing benefits to strikers. The drafters of the Act apparently concluded that such proposals should be addressed to the individual state legislatures "without dictation from Washington."

Undeniably, Congress was aware of the possible impact of unemployment compensation on the bargaining process. The omission of any direction concerning payment to strikers in either the National Labor Relations Act or the Social Security Act implies that Congress intended that the States be free to authorize, or to prohibit, such payments.

. . . .

Affirmed.

Under the Trade Act of 1974, Congress sought to ameliorate the problems of workers who had been displaced from their employment as a result of economic dislocations caused by foreign imports. Workers may receive compensation calculated on the basis of their prior weekly wages, employment services, training, a job search allowance, and relocation allowances. The Secretary of Labor must certify that employees are eligible, after a finding that workers are being threatened with total or partial separation of employment.

Regulation of Pension Plans: ERISA

No federal law requires that employers supply a pension plan for their employees. Many employers do supply such plans, of course, some as a result of collective bargaining and others as a method of attracting skilled employees. Federal law is concerned only with how those plans which do exist are administered. On Labor Day, 1974, President Ford signed the Employee Retirement Income Security Act of 1974 (ERISA).

ERISA superceded an earlier 1958 law, the Welfare and Pension Plans Disclosure Act. Generally, the law applies to all plans established by sponsors engaged in interstate commerce, except government plans, church plans, and a few other minor exceptions.

A pension plan is an arrangment whereby an employer can provide for retirement benefits for employees in recognition of their service to the company. The use of such plans grew tremendously between 1940 and 1970, but despite the increase in the use of such plans, some employees who expected to receive benefit payments upon retirement did not receive those benefits. In some cases, employers terminated underfunded plans; in others, plan participants quit or were fired with few or no vested rights. Some plan administrators made bad investments or used assets for their own purposes.

ERISA was aimed at eliminating such abuses. The act includes the establishment of certain *fiduciary duties, participation, vesting* and *funding rules, reporting and disclosure requirements,* and other miscellaneous rules.

Plan Fiduciary Responsibilities   A *fiduciary* is defined in the Act as any person who exercises discretionary control or authority over a plan, gives investment advice for a fee, or has any discretionary responsibility in the administration of the plan. The Act imposes six rules on such fiduciaries. Such fiduciaries must

1. Manage assets solely in the interest of participants and beneficiaries;

2. Act with the care that a prudent person in like circumstances would exercise;

3. Diversify investments in order to minimize the risk of large losses;

4. Invest no more than 10 percent of the fair market value of plan assets in a combination of qualifying employer securities and qualifying employer real property;

5. Transfer assets outside the United States unless specifically permitted by the Secretary of Labor; and

6. Be liable for those acts or omissions of cofiduciaries that constitute breaches of their fiduciary responsibilities.

Participation Requirements   A plan may not require age and service standards for participation by employees stricter than one year of service and the attainment of age 25, or in the alternative age 25 with a three-year waiting period thereafter with 100 percent vesting thereafter. Thus most employees will be eligible for such plans rather quickly after beginning work.

Vesting Requirements   The **vesting** requirements are complex. Those rules are designed to assure employees that they will have a right to the funds in the plan after a set period of time. ERISA provides four alternative vesting rules:

1. Graded vesting of accrued benfits, with at least 25 percent vesting after five years and at least 5 percent each year thereafter for five years, and 10 percent each year thereafter. The whole plan would therefore be vested no later than the fifteenth year.

2. Cliff vesting, or 100 percent vesting after 10 years, with no vesting before the end of the tenth year.

3. Rule of 45 vesting, in which accrued benefits of employees with five or more years of service must be at least 50 percent vested when the sum of his age and years of service equals 45, with 10 percent additional vesting for each year of service thereafter. A participant with ten years of service must be at least 50 percent vested and vest thereafter at a rate not less than 10 percent per year.

4. 40 percent vesting, in which 40 percent must be vested after four years of service and incrementally each year thereafter until the plan is 100 percent vested after eleven years of service. This final category *must* be used unless the employer can demonstrate a rank and file employee turnover rate of less than 6 percent per year.

Funding Requirements   The funding rules require that an employer's contributions include (1) normal cost; (2) interest on unfunded amounts; and (3) a portion of unfunded original past service liability. The purpose of these requirements is to assure a sufficient contribution to fund the plan according to its purposes. Amendments to the Internal Revenue Code that accompanied the enactment of ERISA provide a maximum annual deduction for employer contributions.

Reporting and Disclosure Requirements   ERISA requires that several reports must be made to various government agencies, including a variety of forms that must be submitted to the Internal Revenue Service if the employer is to claim a deduction for the contributions to the plan. The Act also requires disclosure of a great deal of information to participants, including annual reports prepared by independent accountants, and requires that participants receive a full copy of the plan upon request.

Miscellaneous Provisions   ERISA also requires that if a plan provides for a retirement annuity for married participants, it must also provide a joint and survivor annuity for married participants in an amount not less than one-half of the annuity payable to the participant, for the support of surviving spouses. The Act further requires plan administrators to pay annual termination insurance premiums to the Pension Benefits Guaranty Corporation, to provide a guaranty that benefits will be received even if the plan is terminated.

Penalties and Remedies   The Act provides for possible civil actions by plan participants or beneficiaries to recover lost benefits and disqualification of the plan under the tax laws and loss of tax benefits. Excise taxes may be imposed for delinquent contributions. Failure to comply with the reporting and disclosure requirements may lead to fines up to $100,000 and fines of up to $100 per day per participant or beneficiary.

Summary and Conclusions

The second "stream" of American labor law embraces specific regulations of worker safety, wages, and security. Such laws are meant to provide protections to the majority of American workers who are not covered by collective bargaining agreements, though many of the specific protections apply to union workers as well.

Common law protections of worker safety were subject to the employer defenses of assumption of risk, contributory negligence and the fellow-servant doctrine, which resulted in many employee injuries going uncompensated. Around the turn of the century, many states enacted state worker's compensation statutes to provide a remedy for injured workers. Direct regulation of employee safety was not accomplished until 1970 with the Occupational Safety and Health Act (OSHA).

The principal protection of workers' wages is found in the federal Fair Labor Standards Act (FLSA), which requires payment of a minimum wage, provides for overtime, requires payment of equal pay for equal work, and prohibits much child labor. Most states also have similar laws which apply to intrastate businesses.

The future economic security of employees is protected by the federal Social Security Act, unemployment compensation, and the Employees Retirement Income Security Act. Those laws attempt to assure that retirement and unemployment do not become economic catastrophes for most workers.

Many have argued that OSHA and ERISA may in fact be the most important labor laws yet passed, primarily because those laws are so specific yet far-reaching in their application.

PRO AND CON

ISSUE: Can "Voluntary Compliance" Bring About Workplace Safety?

PRO: Voluntary Compliance Will Work Better Than OSHA

Hon. George Hansen, U.S. Representative from Idaho*

The Occupational Safety and Health Administration (OSHA), despite costs of over $25 billion in compliance by American businessmen and over $1 billion to American taxpayers, has failed to achieve a significant positive impact on employee injury and illness rates.

. . . .

. . . Americans can only wonder where is the return on that investment: has OSHA protected workers by significantly decreasing workplace deaths and injuries?

The unfortunate answer: OSHA has not been effective in protecting the American work force. Not only has OSHA failed to reduce serious injuries and fatalities in the workplace, the number and severity of serious injuries and the number of fatalities have sharply increased in recent years despite OSHA's massive regulatory efforts.

. . . .

Since 1971, when OSHA began operations, there have been significant increases in the number of serious injuries and the severity of these injuries, and a more recent upswing in worker fatalities. Conversely, National Safety Council (NSC) statistics for the 8-year period prior to 1971, when industry was handling safety and health concerns itself, show a steady decline in these categories.

. . . .

The disappointing performance of this regulatory nightmare does not warrant providing increased responsibility, but rather it mandates reevaluation and reform.

OSHA's poor performance clearly demonstrates that voluntary safety and health preservation programs through employers' incentives are more certain to protect workers than costly Government regulations geared to rigidity rather than results.

Without the arbitrary and bureaucratic barriers presented by OSHA with its inflexible and nitpicking regulations and exorbitant paperwork and administrative burdens it places on businesses, industry would be able to effect even greater protection for workers through its own efforts. Although industry can be aided by Government encouragement, incentive, and consultation, the ultimate source of worker safety and health must be through the employers themselves with good employee cooperation.

. . . Congress cast the government in a policeman's role establishing a system of crime and punishment for over 4 million workplaces in the United States. Although there may be a valid policeman's role in a limited number of apparent cases of criminal negligence, the vast majority of workplaces should not be subjected to such militant enforcement conditions because they are not hazardous, or at least not criminally so. In short, there is a more reasonable and productive way for the Federal Government to meaningfully participate in improving the occupational safety and health of America's workers.

The better way is for the Government to redirect its policeman's role to functions where it is really needed to deter and correct grave occupational hazards, to provide useful research and information, and to stimulate employer and employee cooperation and initiatives to improve workplace safety and health.

. . . .

---

*From remarks to the U.S. House of Representatives on March 19, 1980.

Basically . . . this new . . . approach provides that workplaces with good safety and health records will be exempt from most OSHA inspections. Thus, OSHA will be forced to direct enforcement activities more efficiently to hazardous firms, and create incentives for businesses to establish a good safety record. . . . Employers with no injuries reported . . . will qualify for the exemption. Bureau of Labor Statistics data happily indicate roughly 85 per cent of all workplaces would qualify through this method . . . without additional paperwork for the employers.

. . . .

I fervently hope that a beleaguered American free-enterprise system will rise up and demand this necessary relief from the burdensome regulations of OSHA so that employers and employees can once again, with increasing safety, provide consumers with the low-cost, high-quality abundance we have been losing. . . .

CON: "Voluntary Compliance" is an Invalid Argument
David Seideman*

Twelve years ago, the Occupational Health and Safety Administration was established to protect Americans from dangers in the workplace, and to ensure that companies . . . save their employees, and themselves, from the exorbitant costs of neglecting worker safety. Today, although industrial injuries around the nation have declined by 13 percent, and in small businesses by as much as 26 percent, OSHA still has a good bit of industrial housekeeping to do. Unfortunately, the Reagan Administration seems to think it is OSHA that is hazardous to our health.

OSHA's director, Thorne Auchter, a 37-year-old former Florida construction executive, has applied formidable political skill to the task of what he calls "lifting unnecessary federal burdens off the American people." He sees worker health and safety standards, by law his prime concern, mostly as a bane to business. Under his leadership, the agency's prime concern has been finding ways to avoid doing its job.

Mr. Auchter has developed three major programs to excuse industries from compliance with OSHA regulations. His "Exemption Plan," . . . would waive the requirement that so-called low-hazard industries keep health and safety records. . . . Mr. Auchter's "Targeting" program would reduce routine safety inspections at many of the more hazardous installations. . . . if a firm's log showed lost workday rate below the national average. The fate of worker protection would rest on the honesty and accuracy of the employer's record-keeping. The "Targeting" program, however, makes no provision for improving or checking such records. (Indeed, the Office of Management and Budget wants OSHA to eliminate the requirement that industry keep logs.) Moreover, a factory could meet the program's single standard and still be a dangerous place to work. Workers could be injured or even killed at a given site, but if the absentee rate were below the national average that year, there would be no inspection.

Mr. Auchter calls his third pilot program, his favorite, "Voluntary Compliance." In order to develop a "less adversarial" relationship with industry, he intends to replace many routine on-site inspections with voluntary compliance agreements. Employers and unions would agree on health and safety standards, and unions would notify the agency in the event of any violation, thus obviating the need for routine inspections.

. . . .

Obviously any program based on the participation of unions requires their approval. Mr. Auchter claims that the reaction of organized labor has been "extremely favorable." This is simply untrue. . . . Because these unions do not possess large staffs with the technical expertise of OSHA's inspection corps, they are worried about a plan that would transfer the responsibility (and the costs) of enforcing the law from the government to unions and ultimately to individual workers, since it is they who would have to initiate any complaint. . . . What Mr. Auchter's projects disregard is that OSHA was created precisely because voluntary compliance had proved to be an oxymoron.

. . . .

Internal OSHA memoranda, in blithe disregard of court rulings and acts of Congress, say that the "traditional labor market" should henceforth be relied upon to protect workers, while OSHA should be concerned with "monetizing wherever possible" and paying careful attention to "cost implementation."

. . . .

Mr. Auchter and his allies in industry protest

*From his article "Occupational Hazard: Three Steps to an Unsafe Workplace," *The New Republic* (December 6, 1982): 11–12. Reprinted by permission.

that all they want to do is to bring some form of cost-benefit analysis to worker health and safety regulation—to take regulation out of the realm of subjectivity and impose upon it the discipline of disinterested scientific truth. It's a specious argument. All regulation—indeed, all decision-making—can be seen as based upon calculations of relative costs and benefits. But neither costs nor benefits can be judged independently of moral or social values. Congress passed the Occupational Health and Safety Act not because it was working from a set of figures different from Mr. Auchter's, but because it was working from a different set of values.

DISCUSSION QUESTIONS

1. Does the "market" approach, as exemplified by the Wagner Act, or the "regulatory" approach, as exemplified by the laws discussed in this chapter, make more sense? Which is more consistent with our economic system? Can we rely on only one approach? Which one? Or are both approaches necessary?

2. It has been argued that the worker's compensation system should be administered by the federal government because a uniform system is necessary. Do you agree? What are the advantages and disadvantages of such a federal system?

3. A few states provide that workers may not recover under worker's compensation for injuries resulting from the worker's reckless conduct or intoxication. Are such qualifications consistent with the purposes of the system? If so, why not prohibit workers from recovering for injuries that result from their own negligence?

4. OSHA is considered by many businesspeople to be the most onerous of all the federal regulations that apply to business and is usually the system of regulation pointed to as an example of government "overreaching" and "overregulation." Why? How would you reform the Act to make it less onerous? Could we do without the Act entirely?

5. Does the OSHA inspection system comply with the requirements of "due process" under the 5th Amendment? Apply the *Mathews* v. *Eldridge* "balancing test" as described in Chapter 3 to the OSHA procedures. What factors are you balancing?

6. Is a minimum wage necessary? Desirable? Is the Friedman quote at the beginning of the chapter correct? Is a minimum wage more necessary in a time of high unemployment or low unemployment? If the minimum wage were abolished, what would be the probable effect on labor union membership? If it were abolished, how would the trainees in Friedman's theory survive *while* they are obtaining their training?

7. Many migrant farm workers are illegal aliens. Does the Fair Labor Standards Act (or any other labor law, for that matter) protect them? Should they be protected?

8. Why do you suppose the federal government insists on "prevailing wage" standards in federally related projects? For federal hourly workers?

9. Is Social Security a "welfare" law? Which would you prefer to receive when you retire, public welfare or social security? Why? Which system permits retiring workers to maintain their dignity? Is dignity an appropriate consideration for a government program?

10. Many argue that Congress made a major error when it enacted the Social Security Act by not insisting that current receipts equal current benefit payments or by not tying an individual's contributions to the amount of benefits he receives. Could it have done so in 1935? What kind of pensions would have been received by those who retired in the late 1930's? How can we rectify the problem today?

11. Would a uniform federal system of unemployment compensation be more desirable? Why do you suppose the system is administered through the states?

12. It has been argued that in the long run OSHA and ERISA may well prove to be the most important federal labor laws. Why? Do you agree?

CASE PROBLEMS

1. Hattaway, an employee of Mississippi State University, reported to work at 7:30 AM and began welding on a water tank. After about five minutes, he went to his supervisor's office and reported that the burning paint had made him nauseated. He rested a short while, then died. A physician testified that he could not explain Hattaway's death. No autopsy was performed. Hattaway's wife and children brought a worker's compensation petition. Did Hattaway's death "arise out of" his employment? [*Mississippi State University* v. *Dependents of Hattaway,* 191 So. 2d 418 (Miss., 1966).]

2. Smith, an employee of National Realty, rode the running board of a frontend loader at a construction site. The loader's engine stalled while going down an earthen ramp and swerved off the ramp. Smith jumped from the loader, but the loader toppled off the ramp and fell on top of him. At the time, no specific OSHA standards related to riding on machinery. An OSHA inspector nevertheless found the company guilty of a "serious violation" and levied a fine of $300. The company appealed. Result? [*National Realty and Construction Company, Inc.* v. *Occupational Safety and Health Review Commission,* 489 F. 2d 1257, (U.S. App. D.C., 1973).]

3. Advance hired Knight, a truck driver, to do work on a project in which Clarkson was the general contractor and Advance a subcontractor of Clarkson. Advance had the authority to control Knight, but Clarkson did not. Knight was driving a truck that had an obstructed rear view. He backed the truck without an observer and without a reverse signal alarm, and killed another employee. An OSHA inspector found a "serious violation" and assessed a fine of $1,000 against Clarkson. Clarkson appealed. Result? [*Clarkson Construction Co.* v. *Occupational Safety and Health Review Commission,* 531 F. 2d. 451 (10th Circ., 1976).]

4. Thomas, a Jehovah's Witness, terminated his employment when he was transferred to a department that produced turrets for military tanks. He claimed his

religious beliefs prevented him from participating in the production of war materials. The Indiana Employment Security Division refused him unemployment
compensation because Indiana law does not permit payment unless an employee
is involuntarily terminated, or terminates voluntarily "with good cause." Result?
[*Thomas* v. *Review Board of the Indiana Employment Security Division,* 450 U.S.
707, 101 S. Ct. 1425, 67 L. Ed. 2d 624 (1981).]

5. Fitzwater, an employee of Willoughby's Welding Works, was welding a piece of
   machinery and burned himself severely with the welding equipment when he
   slipped on a grease spot on the floor. The grease had been negligently dropped
   there by Scroop, another employee. At common law, does Fitzwater have a remedy? What defenses would you expect Willoughby to raise?

6. In the preceding question 5 assume that Fitzwater's salary is $300 per week, and
   that the burns disable Fitzwater's left arm to the extent of 30 percent. Also assume
   that an arm is worth 200 weeks of compensation under the applicable state law.
   How much worker's compensation would Fitzwater receive?

7. Basset is employed in Woodville and Vernon's Machine Shop. Woodville and Vernon have established a pension fund for their employees into which the company
   and the employees both make contributions. Woodville and Vernon have named
   themselves as trustees of the plan. Woodville withdraws the pension fund without
   Vernon's knowledge and absconds to Tierra del Fuego. Does Basset have a remedy or will he be penniless at retirement?

8. Rotheram is an employee of Hastings Foundry Co. One day, Rotheram noticed
   that the belts on the machine on which he was working were old and worn, and
   reported the matter to his foreman. Nothing was done, even though if a belt broke
   it would mean serious injury or death to Rotherham. Finally, out of anger and
   fear, Rotheram walked off the job and refused to work until the belts were fixed.
   Hastings immediately fired Rotheram. Does Rotheram have a remedy?

SUGGESTED READINGS

Abraham, Arthur, and David L. Kopelman. *Federal Social Security* (Philadelphia: American Law Institute,
    1979).

Covington, Robert N., and Alvin L. Goldman. *Legislation Protecting the Individual Employee* (Washington,
    D.C.: The Bureau of National Affairs, Inc., 1982).

Goldman, Alvin L. *Labor Law and Industrial Relations in the United States of America* (Deventer, The
    Netherlands: Kluwer, 1979).

Miller, Glenn W. *Government Policy Toward Labor: An Introduction to Labor Law* (Columbus, Ohio: Grid,
    Inc., 1975).

Rothstein, Mark A. *Occupational Safety and Health Law* (St. Paul, Minn.: West Publishing Co., 1978).

Steinberg, Richard M., and Harold Dankner. *Pensions: An ERISA Accounting and Management Guide* (New
    York: John Wiley & Sons, 1983).

Twomey, David P. *Labor Law and Legislation* 7th ed. (Cincinnati: South-Western Publishing Co., 1985).

Wilson, Wesley M. *The Labor Relations Primer* (Homewood, Ill.: Dow-Jones–Irwin, Inc., 1973).

Part VI

Regulation of the Relationship Between Business and Its Investors

The relationship between a business and its investors is odd indeed. On the one hand, the investors are the owners of the business and, therefore, should control that business. But, on the other hand, investors are often more like customers of a business, buying and selling interests in the business for a profit and sometimes not caring about the control they might exercise.

As a result, the ethic of honesty and truthfulness is quite important, as it is in the business-customer relationship. Businesses and their agents, it is felt, should be truthful to the investing public in presenting facts upon which to form investment decisions. And, to a very large extent, the federal laws that regulate securities trading are designed to foster that kind of truth and honesty.

Because of the status of investors as "owners," the ethic of Individualism has very little to say about the regulation of the relationship between a business and its owners. Here private notions of ethics, such as honesty and loyalty, are generally considered to be more important. It is also sometimes argued that the relationship between investors and the firm is not a relationship at all, since investors are in fact the firm, and that we are really dealing with the relationship between the firm, in the form of the investors, and its managers and agents. As a result, traditional ethical notions of agency, such as obedience, fidelity, and diligence, are appropriately imposed on the managers of the firm.

521

Regulation of Securities and Corporate Structure

Publicity is justly commended as a remedy for social and industrial diseases. Sunlight is said to be the best of disinfectants; electric light the most efficient policeman.

Louis D. Brandeis, Other People's Money *(1932)*

They [corporations] cannot commit treason, nor be outlawed nor excommunicated, for they have no soul.

Sir Edward Coke, Case of Sutton's Hospital *(circa 1625)*

. . . [T]he merchandise of securities is really traffic in the economic and social welfare of our people. Such traffic demands the utmost good faith and fair dealing on the part of those engaged in it. If the country is to flourish, capital must be invested in enterprise. . . . But those who seek to draw upon other people's money must be wholly candid regarding the facts on which the investor's judgment is based.

President Franklin D. Roosevelt, *upon signing the* Securities Exchange Act of 1934

The health of the American economy depends to a very large degree on the ability of business to obtain money from private investors. That money may flow either through the capital markets, such as the various stock exchanges, or through private financing and direct investment of funds in business enterprises. Though the New York Stock Exchange has been in continuous existence since 1792, most capital was invested in business through direct, private investment until well after the Civil War.

During the 1920's, capital flowed into the stock market in ever-increasing amounts until by 1929 over 55 percent of private savings was in the form of investments in securities. The ensuing crash in 1929 impoverished many Americans and gave rise to a demand for control of the stock markets. The result was a system of federal regulation of the securities industry and the creation of the **Securities and Exchange Commission** (SEC), an independent regulatory commission, to regulate the securities markets. State laws regulating securities (**blue sky laws**) are generally older, but less effective, than federal regulation.

State and federal securities laws apply to all **securities,** not just corporate stocks and bonds. The federal laws have been applied to all sorts of investment schemes, including oil and gas drilling programs, whiskey warehouse receipts, real estate cooperatives and investments, and single rows of orange trees. But it is also true that the securities laws are primarily applied to investments in corporations. As a result, much of our attention in this chapter will be devoted to securities problems in public corporations. Students should review the "corporations" section of Chapter 7, particularly the sections on corporate organization and financing, before proceeding further.

The Capital Markets and the Great Depression

The free exchange of both equity and debt securities is vital to the welfare of corporations, since free exchange assures the availability of capital for corporate projects and expansion. If shareholders had to go to a great deal of trouble to buy or sell securities, many potential investors would simply forego investment and deprive firms of needed capital. Two sets of markets for securities have developed to make securities more freely transferable, the *over-the-counter* (OTC) market and the *exchange market.*

The Over-the-Counter Market

The informal **over-the-counter market** has no physical location. It is rather the exchange of securities not listed on any national or regional stock exchange, such as the New York Stock Exchange. Such unlisted securities include stocks or debt securities of small local companies and those of large nationwide firms that have chosen not to list their securities on any of the exchanges. Such stock may be available directly from the company, in the case of smaller firms, or from stockbrokers registered with the SEC. Over 20,000 firms trade their shares in the OTC market.

The Exchange Markets

The **exchange markets** consist of the two national exchanges, the *New York Stock Exchange* (NYSE) and the *American Stock Exchange* (AMEX), and several regional exchanges located in major cities. All of the exchanges have adopted rather strict rules concerning which stocks may be listed and traded on those exchanges. In addition, the **National Association of Securities Dealers** (NASD), a private association of securities dealers, also imposes rules regarding the securities they trade. Together the rules of the exchanges and the NASD form a rather effective system of self-regulation.

The Beginnings of a National Market System

In 1975, Congress instructed the SEC to "facilitate the establishment" of a national market system. As envisioned by the SEC, such a national market system would involve linking the various exchanges and dealer markets conducted over-the-counter. A consolidated system for reporting volume and price information was installed between the NYSE and the AMEX in 1976 and a uniform quotation system for all securities was introduced in 1978. Orders for securities traded on more than one exchange may be routed between the exchange markets for execution as well. The SEC sees the development of a national market system as an evolutionary process, involving both the agency and the securities industry.

The Role of Underwriters

Securities issued by a firm may be sold by the firm directly to the public through private offerings, by direct offerings to existing security holders, or by a direct public offering. A **private offering** simply involves contacting potential investors and soliciting funds in return for securities issued by the firm. A direct **public offering** involves advertising the availability of the investment through public solicitation. Such methods are used primarily by companies with strong track records or by new firms soliciting start-up capital. Existing security holders are an obvious source of new funds, and frequently they are offered new issues of securities before the securities are offered to the public.

An issuer of securities will usually enlist the aid of an **underwriter,** who renders financial advice and serves as manager of the issue. Such underwriters are generally known as **investment bankers,** as distinguished from more traditional commercial bankers. Investment bankers do not accept deposits from the public and generally specialize in the marketing of securities. They are experts in setting the price of securities and exploring the various avenues by which securities may be effectively marketed.

The Role of Securities Professionals

The middlemen in the capital markets are the securities professionals, classified by the federal law as *brokers, dealers,* and *investment advisers.* A **broker** is a person engaged in the business of making transactions in securities for the account of others, while a **dealer** is engaged in the business of buying and selling securities for its own account. Often a single firm or individual will have both such statuses, and be known as a **broker-dealer.** An **investment adviser** is a person who advises others regarding securities for compensation. All three categories must register with the SEC and are subject to regulation.

Customers wishing to purchase securities may first obtain advice from an investment adviser, then purchase stock through a broker-dealer. The stock may be held in the name of the broker-dealer (**street-name**) as a convenience, but the broker-dealer must send written confirmation of the purchase to the customer.

Stock Market Abuses and the Great Depression

The single most influential event in the history of securities law was the stock market crash of 1929 and the ensuing Great Depression of the 1930's. By one estimate, over 55 percent of all personal savings in the late 1920's was invested in corporate stocks, usually through the exchange markets. The aggregate value of all stocks in 1929 was $89 billion, but by 1932 that value had plummeted to $15 billion. The resulting loss of savings, unemployment, and general misery directly caused the election of Franklin Roosevelt as President in 1932, the implementation of the New Deal, and vast political and institutional changes in government. One of those changes was the adoption of a system of federal regulation of securities.

In Senate Hearings in 1932 and 1933, large securities traders and dealers were found to have been involved in a series of stock practices and manipulations that played a principal role in bringing about the crash and the Depression, including market manipulation, insider trading, fraud, excess margin trading, and underwriting practices.

Market Manipulation and Wash Sales   Large traders and dealers may manipulate the price of stock through a variety of techniques. One of the most useful is through **wash sales,** or matched orders. Some investors judge a stock in part by its volume (how many shares are traded during a given length of time) on the assumption that "active" stocks will rise. Large traders can therefore affect the value of a stock by artificially inflating the number of shares traded by buying and selling matched orders of a stock. The price will then go up, and the trader sells his remaining shares in the company at a profit.

Insider Trading and Fraud

Corporate officers and other **insiders** were often able to position themselves to take advantage of developments within their own companies, sometimes by delaying the announcement of oil strikes, research, or financial gains and losses while the "insiders" bought or sold stock in their firm. Officers and large traders and even brokers sometimes indulged in actual fraud to encourage investment in a particular company. One Senate report found that most of the stocks made worthless by the 1929 crash had been sold in transactions marked by actual fraud.

Margin Trading

Many investors entered the market on credit, or on **margin,** during the 1920's. There was no limit to the amount of credit that might be extended by a broker-dealer at that time, and some investors purchased stock with as little as 5 or 10 percent down and sometimes, nothing down. There was no problem as long as the market continued to go up but, if the market went down, the broker would insist on partial payment for the stock, at least to make up the difference between the new lower price and the borrowed amount. If a broker "called the margin," the investor might have to sell other stock to pay the margin. This in turn resulted in price declines and margin calls in other stock, ad infinitum.

Commercial Bank Underwriting and Investing

During the 1920's, many commercial banks (banks that accepted deposits and made loans to the general public) established subsidiary firms specializing in underwriting securities issues. Because those subsidiaries were essentially insiders, they often traded heavily in the shares of their clients and induced the banks with whom they were related to do the same. After the market began to decline in 1929, the banks and their subsidiaries began to lose money on their investments and were unable to meet their depositing customers' demands for their cash. This resulted in either bank closings or demands by the banks on their loan customers for full payment of outstanding loans, including mortgages on homes and farms.* The result was a huge number of foreclosures on the homes and farms of America.

The Call for Regulation

The stock market abuses of the 1920's were not fully known until an investigation of the securities industry by the Senate in 1932 and 1933, and securities regulation was not an integral part of the New Deal until after that investigation. The results of that investigation brought about a call, both inside and outside of the securities industry, for federal regulation. State regulation, which existed in many states prior to the Depression, had proven ineffective. That regulation still exists and must be considered, however.

State Blue Sky Laws

The first state regulation of securities was adopted in Kansas in 1911, to be quickly followed by similar regulations in many other states. State regulation of securities generally follows one of three basic forms: *state brokerage licensing laws; "antifraud" statutes,* forbidding fraud and misrepresentation in the sale or purchase of securities; and *registration and disclosure laws,* which require securities to be listed with the state with certain information about the company and its stock.

Registration and disclosure laws sometimes require some state official or agency to determine whether a particular securities offering is "fair" or "equitable" to the public before it is made. In that sense, those state laws are more strict than federal securities laws, which do not require a determination of fairness. Such laws are generally called **blue sky laws,** since, in the words of an early court decision,** such laws

---

*Most of the mortgages foreclosed were "straight-term" mortgages, which meant they had to be renewed yearly. Banks simply refused to renew and foreclosed.

**Hall v. Geiger-Jones, 242 U.S. 539 (1917).

prohibited "speculative schemes that have no more basis than so many feet of blue sky."

State regulation of securities, while strict on its face, never proved very effective. Some states did not regulate at all, and some of the laws were enforced only sporadically. Persons desiring to sell stocks that would not pass muster in one state had only to move to another state where regulation was lax. Many state laws contained broad exemptions, which removed the teeth from their statutes. Finally, any company that was prosecuted generally offered to pay back the defrauded investors, on condition that charges be dropped.

A **Uniform Securities Act** has now been adopted in several states. That law is intended to "mesh" with the federal securities laws and may simplify state regulation if adopted in more states. The Uniform law has four sections: a broad antifraud provision; broker-dealer licensing provisions; registration and disclosure provisions; and definitions, exemptions, and liability provisions. States are free to adopt any or all of the first three sections and the appropriate parts of the fourth provision. The law has been at least partially adopted in at least 30 states. The law generally imposes civil liability on sellers, broker-dealers, officers, and directors, and any person who "materially aids in the sale" of securities. Such persons may be liable for the purchase price of the security or damages if the security has been sold, subject to the defense of "due diligence."

Federal Regulation of Securities

Federal regulation of securities began after the investigation of the Senate Banking and Currency Committee in 1932. The results of that investigation were the Securities Act of 1933 and the Securities and Exchange Act of 1934, and later resulted in several secondary acts applying to specific industries or practices.

The Securities Act of 1933

The Securities Act of 1933 (the 1933 Act) requires *registration and disclosure* of information, and contains broad *antifraud* prohibitions. It is important to note that the registration and disclosure provisions apply only to *new issues* of securities, while the antifraud provisions apply to *all* sales of securities. The Act does not guarantee the accuracy of the information disclosed, but provides penalties for giving false or misleading information. The Act also in no way guarantees that an issue of securities is "fair." Certain categories of offerings are exempt from registration and disclosure, including **private offerings** and offerings by governmental bodies, but the exemptions do not apply to the antifraud provisions of the Act. Initially, the Federal Trade Commission was given authority to administer the Act but, in 1934, the SEC was created and authority to administer the 1933 Act was shifted to that agency.

The Securities Exchange Act of 1934

The Securities Exchange Act of 1934 (the 1934 Act) performs six major functions: it requires *registration and disclosure* by corporations whose securities are listed on any national securities exchange; it created the *Securities and Exchange Commission* (SEC), an independent regulatory commission with authority to make rules regarding the securities industries; it regulates *solicitation of proxies* (rights to vote stock); it requires *registration of all "national" securities exchanges and all broker-dealers* operating in interstate commerce; it generally prohibits and regulates *insider trading;* and it requires the SEC to conduct *market surveillance* of the securities markets. In 1964, the registration and disclosure provisions were amended to include firms whose securities are traded on the over-the-counter markets, which have assets of over $3 million, and which have over 500 shareholders. Certain types of issuers are exempt from the registration and disclosure provisions, including investment and insurance companies, if they are subject to comparable state regulations.

In addition to these two major acts, the following seven federal statutes are directly applicable to specific areas involving securities.

The Public Utility Holding Company Act of 1935

The Public Utility Holding Company Act of 1935 regulates firms that have no function other than to hold the stock of firms engaged in the business of interstate distribution of electricity or manufactured or natural gas. The Act empowers the SEC to determine whether the corporate structure of such firms may be simplified, and the law permits the SEC to request the courts to dissolve a firm that has no useful purpose (the corporate death sentence provision).

The Trust Indenture Act of 1939

This law provides that debt securities offered for public sale must be issued under a **trust indenture** approved by the SEC. A trust indenture is a underlying contract between the issuing corporation and an independent trustee. The trustee is required to safeguard the interests of the holders of debt securities, enforce the security, and file suit against the corporation, if necessary to obtain payment. Such trustees must be truly independent from the issuing corporation, and the Act requires some form of security for the agreement, usually in the form of mortgages or liens on corporate property.

The Investment Company Act of 1940

An **investment company** is formed for the purpose of investing in the securities of other companies. The Investment Company Act requires such firms to register with the SEC and regulates their selling practices. The law requires "honest and unbiased" management and provides specific regulations of the financial statements and accounting practices of such firms.

The Federal Investment Adviser's Act of 1940

Investment advisers are people who render advice, issue analyses, or prepare reports concerning regulated securities. This law outlaws fraudulent or deceptive practices by such persons, prohibits profit-sharing arrangements with clients, and prevents assignment of "contracts to advise" without the customer's consent.

The Williams Act of 1968

This Act, actually an amendment to the 1934 Act, provides protection for stockholders in firms subject to take-over bids or **tender offers** by other firms. The law provides for disclosure of information to the SEC and to the shareholders of the "target" company whenever more than 5 percent of the stock of the company is purchased by another firm (see Chapter 10 for a discussion of tender offers).

Securities Investor Protection Act of 1970

The purpose of this law is to protect investors in the event they lose cash deposited with a broker-dealer, and it becomes impossible to obtain damages. The law does not apply to ordinary investment losses, however. The Act creates a nonprofit corporation, the Securities Investor Protection Corporation (SIPC), which collects dues from its membership. The membership is made up of all registered broker-dealers. The funds collected are available to pay injured investors, up to a limit of $50,000 per account.

Foreign Corrupt Practices Act of 1977

While strictly not a securities regulation, this law has an impact on the accounting profession similar to that of the securities laws. The law generally prohibits bribery of foreign officials in order to gain contracts or other advantages, but permits small "facilitating" or "grease" payments, such as those to speed goods through foreign customs.

But the law also generally requires all public companies to keep detailed records, which "accurately and fairly" reflect company financial activities, and to devise a system of internal accounting which reasonably assures that transactions are properly authorized and accounted for. These provisions, while intended to strengthen the anti-bribery provisions of the law, apply to *all publicly held corporations,* not just those with foreign operations.

The Definition of Security

It is perhaps a credit to the ingenuity of those involved in the securities and investment businesses that the definition of security under the federal laws is under continual re-examination. Clearly, the term *security* refers to corporate stocks and bonds, but just as clearly the term refers to far more. The 1933 Act defines the term as

> any note, stock, treasury stock, bond, debenture, evidence of indebtedness, certificate of interest or participation in any profit-sharing agreement, collateral-trust certificate, preorganization certificate or subscription, transferable share, investment contract, voting-trust certificate, certificate of deposit for a security, fractional undivided interest in oil, gas, or other mineral rights, or in general, any interest or instrument commonly known as a "security," or any certificate of interest or participation in, temporary or

interim certificate for, receipt for, guarantee of, or warrant or right to subscribe to or puchase, any of the foregoing. (Section 2(1), Securities Act of 1933).

The other federal securities laws and most state blue sky laws contain definitions substantially similar to the definition in the 1933 Act.

While the statutory language is quite specific, some problems of definition remain. The three principal areas of controversy appear to be (1) matters that are called *shares of stock* or some other name specifically used in the statute, but that are issued for noninvestment purposes; (2) financial instruments issued by financial institutions, such as "shares" in a credit union or "certificates" of deposit; and (3) instruments not in the form of traditional stocks or bonds, but which do in fact evidence an investment.

Noninvestment Stock or Notes

Just because something is called a *stock* does not make it one. It is generally a dangerous game to label something by one of the names used in the statute. Generally, "form should be disregarded for substance and the emphasis should be on economic reality," as noted in *United Housing Foundation* v. *Forman.** In the *Forman* case, for example, the court held that "shares of stock" in a cooperative housing project were not "securities" even in spite of their name. The test appears to be whether the investor or lender has contributed "risk capital" to the venture.

Instruments Issued by Financial Institutions

Many of the specialized financial instruments issued by financial institutions, such as certificates of deposit, credit union shares, and others, are specifically exempt from the federal laws. But, if such institutions issue instruments on which the rate of return varies with the profitability of the financial institution or with the profitability of a specific portfolio of securities, the instruments will be considered to be securities under the federal laws. For example, variable annuities have been found to be securities in some cases.

De Facto Securities

The definition of securities in the federal law is broad enough to include a variety of investment schemes that do not fit into any of the traditional meanings of the term *security.* The federal acts clearly cover "investment contracts" and "certificates of interest or participation in any profit-sharing agreement," terms that might cover almost every form of investment that might be devised.

The basic test was established in 1946 in the case of *SEC* v. *W. J. Howey Co.,*** where the court said that the question is whether the investor puts money "in a com-

---

*421 U.S. 837, 95 S. Ct. 2051, 44 L. Ed. 2d 621 (1975).

**328 U.S. 293, 66 S. Ct. 1100, 90 L. Ed. 2d 1244 (1946).

mon enterprise and is led to expect profits from the efforts of the promoter or a third party." That case involved the sale of individual rows of orange trees, together with a service contract in which the seller agreed to cultivate, harvest, and market the crop. The court held the sale to be a security. The following case explained the *Howey* test further.

International Brotherhood of Teamsters, Chauffeurs, Warehousemen and Helpers of America v. Daniel

439 U.S. 551, 99 S. Ct. 790, 58 L. Ed. 2d 808 (1979)

In 1954, Local 705 of the defendant-union negotiated a compulsory and noncontributory (i.e., the employees paid nothing) pension plan with Chicago area trucking firms. Employees had no choice about participating in the plan and could not demand that their employers pay their contribution directly to them. In order to receive a pension, an employee was required to have 20 years of continuous service, including time worked before the start of the plan.

Daniel began working as a truck driver in 1950 and joined Local 705 the following year. When the plan went into effect, he received five years' credit, and he retired in 1973. Daniel was laid off from December 1960 until April 1961, and no contributions were made during that time. In addition, no contributions were made from April 1961 until July of 1961 because of embezzlement by his employer's bookkeeper. Daniel could have made contributions himself during that period, but failed to do so. The administrator of the pension plan determined that Daniel's service was not continuous and refused to grant him a pension. Daniel brought suit in federal court under the securities laws, claiming a violation of Section 10b of the 1934 Act.

Daniel argued that the union, the local, and a trustee of the fund had misrepresented facts about the plan and omitted to tell him other facts about the plan. He argued that those misrepresentations and omissions were a fraud under Section 10b and Rule 10b-5. The District Court held that Daniel's interest in the pension fund was a security under the *Howey* test, since it was, in the court's view, an "investment contract." That determination was based on the view that Daniel voluntarily gave value for his interest in the plan because he had voted on the collective bargaining agreements that chose employer contributions to the plan instead of other wages or benefits. The Court of Appeals affirmed, and the trustees of the pension plan appealed.

Mr. Justice POWELL delivered the opionion of the Court.

. . . .

To determine whether a particular financial relationship constitutes an investment contract, "[t]he test is whether the scheme involves an investment of money in a common enterprise with profits to come solely from the efforts of others." *Howey,* supra, . . . This test is to be applied in light of "the substance—the economic realities of the transaction—rather than the names that may have been employed by the parties." *United Housing Foundation, Inc.,* v. *Forman,* [supra]. . . . Looking separately at each element of the *Howey* test, it is apparent that an employee's participation in a noncontributory, compulsory pension plan such as the Teamster's does not comport with the commonly held understanding of an investment contract.

A. Investment of Money

An employee who participates in a noncontributory, compulsory pension plan by definition makes no payment into the pension fund. He only accepts employment, one of the conditions of which is eligibility for a possible benefit on retirement. Respondent contends, however, that he has "invested" in the Pension Fund by permitting part of his compensation from his employer to take the form of a deferred pension benefit. By allowing his employer to pay money into the Fund, and by contributing his labor to his employer in return for these payments, respondent asserts he has made the kind of investment which the Securities Acts were intended to regulate.

. . . In every decision of this Court recognizing the presence of a "security" under the Securities Acts, the person found to have been an investor chose to give up specific consideration in return for a separable financial interest with the characteristics of a security. . . .

In a pension plan such as this one, by contrast, the purported investment is a relatively insignificant part of an employee's total and individual compensation package. No portion of an employee's compensation other than the potential pension benefits has any of the characteristics of a security, yet these noninvestment interests cannot be segregated from the possible pension benefits. Only in the most abstract sense may it be said that an employee "exchanges" some portion of his labor in return for these possible benefits. He surrenders his labor as a whole, and in return receives a compensation package that is substantially devoid of aspects resembling a security. . . . Looking at the economic realities, it seems clear that an employee is selling his labor primarily to obtain a livelihood, not making an investment.

. . . .

B. Expectation of Profits From a Common Enterprise

[T]he "touchstone" of the *Howey* test is the presence of an investment in a common venture premised on a reasonable expectation of profits to be derived from the entrepreneurial or managerial efforts of others. . . . The Court of Appeals believed that Daniel's expectation of profit derived from the Fund's successful management and investment of its assets. . . .

As in other parts of its analysis, the court below found an expectation of profit in the pension plan only by focusing on one of its less important aspects to the exclusion of its more significant elements. It is true that the Fund, like other holders of large assets, depends to some extent on earnings from its assets. In the case of a pension fund, however, a far larger portion of its income comes from employer contributions, a source in no way dependent on the efforts of the Fund's managers.

. . . .

If any further evidence were needed to demonstrate that pension plans of the type involved are not subject to the Securities Acts, the enactment of ERISA* in 1974 would put the matter to rest. Unlike the Securities Acts, ERISA deals expressly and in detail with pension plans. . . . The existence of this comprehensive legislation governing the use and terms of employee pension plans severely undercuts all arguments for extending the Securities Acts to noncontributory, compulsory pension plans. . . .

We hold that the Securities Acts do not apply to a noncontributory, compulsory pension plan. . . . The judgment below is therefore

Reversed.

Registration and Disclosure Requirements

The initial statutory framework of the 1933 and 1934 Acts provided two separate disclosure systems, one for *new* securities in the 1933 Act, and one for issuers of *existing* securities under the 1934 Act. The dual system resulted in a great deal of inefficiency and duplicaton of effort and, in the 1970's, Congress and the SEC decided to create

*See p. 513.

an *integrated disclosure* system for all registration and disclosure requirements. That system has been evolving for some time and is not yet complete.

The purpose of registration and disclosure is to provide information to would-be investors about the stocks or other securities they may purchase. The SEC does not guarantee that a particular security is "fair" or a "good deal." That is for the individual investor to determine, using the information in the registration and disclosure statements.

Registration and Disclosure Under the 1933 Act: Going Public

The heart of the 1933 Act is Section 5, which provides that before a security may be offered for public sale it must be registered with the SEC. In order to meet that requirement, a firm that desires to issue a security for public sale must file a *registration statement* with the SEC, containing certain required information. In addition, investors must be furnished with a *prospectus,* or selling circular, containing the relevant information from the registration statement. The law does not guarantee the accuracy of the information in those documents, but the Act prohibits false and misleading information under penalty of fine or imprisonment, and provides for a civil action by injured parties against any party providing false or misleading information.

In general, the registration statement must contain: (1) a description of the registering firm's business and property; (2) a description of the security to be offered for sale and its relationship to the registering firm's other securities; (3) information about the management of the registering firm; and (4) financial statements prepared by independent public accountants.

The Registration Process   The SEC staff is available for *prefiling conferences* with firms that have questions about the registration process, though such conferences are not required. After consultation with its attorneys, accountants, and underwriters, the company will prepare the **registration statement.** The accuracy of the statement is the responsibility of the company and its officers, the underwriters, and the independent public accountants who must audit and certify the financial documents. The statement is then delivered to the SEC's main office in Washington, D.C. The SEC has prepared guidelines for accountants for determining whether data is "false or misleading." Those guidelines have had a massive impact on the accounting profession by supplying rules of practice that must be followed in any situation involving a public corporation.

SEC Review and the Effective Date   The statute provides that the *effective date* of the registration statement is twenty days after it is filed, but that date may be delayed by the SEC or accelerated at the request of the registering firm. During that period, the SEC reviews the registration statement and sends a *letter of comments* to the company. Amendments are permitted and, if amendments cannot be made within twenty days, the SEC usually requests a *delaying amendment,* since the letter of comments does not delay the effective date.

If the firm does not amend its original statement, the SEC has three alternatives: it may permit the statement to become *effective though deficient* and advise the company that it may be civilly liable for actions arising from misleading information; it may issue a *refusal order,* and schedule a hearing within ten days after the filing date; or it may issue a *stop order,* either before or after the effective date, which stops further consideraton of the statement before the effective date and stops further trading in the security after the effective date. Such drastic action is rarely needed, since most firms prefer to amend the statement. Because of increasing pressure on the manpower of the SEC, the agency has adopted a policy of *selective review,* concentrating on areas of highest priority.

Waiting Period Activities: Indications of Interest During the **waiting period** between initial filing and the effective date, the company may solicit **indications of interest** from potential investors and dealers. No contract of sale may be executed during the waiting period. An indication of interest does not obligate a party to purchase a security, but potential investors may be lined up during this period.

An indication of interest is usually obtained in one of three ways: *oral communication* with a prospective investor; a *preliminary* or *"red herring" prospectus;* or a *"tombstone ad."*

A **preliminary,** or "red herring" **prospectus** is similar to a final prospectus (see below) but omits information regarding the offering price, dealer commissions, and other price matters. The term *preliminary prospectus* must be stamped in red ink across the front page, and the document must contain a statement that registration is not yet effective and the securities may not yet be sold.

Tombstone ads (Figure 15-1) are circulars or advertisements that list sources from which a prospectus may be obtained and by whom orders will be executed. Such ads commonly appear in major financial publications and must indicate that the announcement is not an offer to sell nor a solicitation of offers to buy.

The Prospectus Requirement The 1933 Act requires every issuer subject to the Act to make a **final** or statutory **prospectus** available not later than the delivery of a security or a confirmation of sale of a security. The *confirmation* is a slip of paper sent to a customer by a broker to confirm the transaction and comply with the "writing" requirement of the Statute of Frauds (see Chapter 6, p. 208). A *prospectus* is defined as any written communication which "offers any security for sale or confirms the sale of any security." The prospectus must contain all of the information generally required in the registration statement, together with the price of the security, information about commissions to be paid by the company relating to the sale of the security, and other information relevant to the price. The following case discusses the prospectus requirement.

SEC v. Manor Nursing Centers, Inc.

458 F. 2d 1082 (2d Cir., 1972)

Manor Nursing Centers made an "all or nothing" offering of shares, which meant the shares were to be sold on condition that if all 450,000 shares were not sold by March 8, 1970, all of the money was to be returned to the investors with interest. The funds were to be held in trust until that date. The stock was not completely sold, but the firm did not return the pro-

June 27, 1984

1,984,730 Shares

JAMES RIVER CORPORATION

OF VIRGINIA

Common Stock

($.10 Par Value)

Price $27.25 per Share

Kidder, Peabody & Co.   Scott & Stringfellow, Inc.   Wheat, First Securities, Inc.
Incorporated

Bear, Stearns & Co.   The First Boston Corporation   Becker Paribas   Alex. Brown & Sons
                                                         Incorporated   Incorporated

Dillon, Read & Co. Inc.   Donaldson, Lufkin & Jenrette   Drexel Burnham Lambert
                            Securities Corporation   Incorporated

Goldman, Sachs & Co.   Hambrecht & Quist   E. F. Hutton & Company Inc.   Lazard Frères & Co.
                       Incorporated

Lehman Brothers   Merrill Lynch Capital Markets   Paine Webber
Shearson Lehman/American Express Inc.   Incorporated

Prudential-Bache   L. F. Rothschild, Unterberg, Towbin   Salomon Brothers Inc
Securities

Smith Barney, Harris Upham & Co.   Wertheim & Co., Inc.   Dean Witter Reynolds Inc.
Incorporated

Atlantic Capital   A. G. Edwards & Sons, Inc.   First Manhattan Co.
Corporation

Montgomery Securities   Moseley, Hallgarten, Estabrook & Weeden Inc.

Oppenheimer & Co., Inc.   Robertson, Colman & Stephens

Swiss Bank Corporation International Securities Inc.   Thomson McKinnon Securities Inc.

William Blair & Company   Dain Bosworth   McDonald & Company
                                 Incorporated   Securities, Inc.

Piper, Jaffray & Hopwood   Prescott, Ball & Turben, Inc.   Bacon Stifel Nicolaus
Incorporated   Stifel, Nicolaus & Company, Incorporated

Robert W. Baird & Co.   Blunt Ellis & Loewi   First of Michigan Corporation
Incorporated   Incorporated

J. J. B. Hilliard, W. L. Lyons, Inc.   Parker/Hunter   Scherck, Stein & Franc, Inc.   Roney & Co.
                                       Incorporated

Figure 15-1   A Typical Tombstone Ad

ceeds; in fact it did not set up the trust as set forth in the prospectus that accompanied the offering. The District Court ruled that the defendants had violated the antifraud and prospectus requirements. Therefore, the court issued an order that enjoined the defendants from further activity with regard to the stock; ordered the firm to "disgorge" the proceeds, profits, and income from the sale; appointed a trustee to receive the funds and distrubute them to investors; and ordered a freeze on the assets of the defendants until the trustee received the proceeds. The company appealed.

TIMBERS, Circuit Judge: . . .

. . . After the registration statement became effective on December 8, 1969, at least four developments occurred which made the prospectus misleading: the public's funds were not returned even though the issue was not fully subscribed; an escrow account for the proceeds of the offering was not established; shares were issued for consideration other than cash; and certain individuals received extra compensation for agreeing to participate in the offering. These developments were not disclosed to the public investors. . . .

In addition to concluding that appellants had violated the antifraud provisions of the federal securities laws, the district court also correctly held that they had violated the prospectus-delivery requirement of . . . the 1933 Act.

Section 5(b) (2) prohibits the delivery of a security for the purpose of sale unless the security is accompanied or preceded by a prospectus which meets the requirements of §10 (a) of the Act. . . . To meet the requirements of § 10(a), a prospectus must contain, with specified excpetions, all "the information contained in the registration statement. . . ." In turn, the registration statement, pursuant to §7 of the 1933 Act must set forth certain information. . . . Among the items of information which [the Act] requires the registration statement, and therefore the prospectus, to contain are the use of proceeds . . . the estimated net proceeds . . . the price at which the security will be offered to the public and any variation therefrom . . . and all commissions or discounts paid to underwriters, directly or indirectly. . . .

The Manor prospectus purported to disclose the information required. . . . The evidence adduced at trial showed, however, that developments subsequent to the effective date of the registration statement made this information false and misleading. Moreover, Manor and its principals did not amend or supplement the prospectus to reflect the changes which had made inaccurate the information which §10 (a) required the prospectus to disclose. We hold that implicit in the statutory provision that the prospectus contain certain information is the requirement that such information be true and correct. . . . A prospectus does not meet the requirements of §10(a), therefore, if information required to be disclosed is materially false or misleading. Appellants violated § 5(b) (2) by delivering Manor securities for sale accompanied by a prospectus which did not meet the requirements of § 10(a) in that the prospectus contained materially false and misleading statements with respect to information required by §10 (a) to be disclosed.

Manor contends, however, that §5(b) (2) does not require that a prospectus be amended to reflect material developments which occur subsequent to the effective date of the registration statement. This contention is premised on the assumptions that the prospectus spoke only as of the effective date of the registration statement and that the prospectus contained no false or misleading statements as of the effective date—December 8, 1969. . . .

In support of their argument . . . appellants cite an administrative decision in which the SEC held that it will not issue a stop order with respect to a registration statement which becomes misleading subsequent to its effective date because of material post-effective events. . . . Assuming that the registration statement does speak as of its effective date and that Manor did not have to amend its registration statement, appellants were obliged to reflect the post-effective developments referred to above in the prospectus. Even those SEC decisions holding that the registration statement need not be amended to reflect post-effective developments recognize that the prospectus must be amended or supplemented in some manner to reflect such changes. . . . Affirmed. . . .

Exemptions   The 1933 Act exempts several categories of issues of securities from registration and disclosure: (1) private offerings, generally to private investors who have access to the kinds of information disclosed in the registration statement and prospectus and who do not intend to redistribute the securities; (2) totally intrastate offerings; (3) securities of municipal, state, and federal governments; (4) offerings not in excess of specified amounts set by the SEC; (5) offerings of "small business investment companies." The "small issues" exemption in (4), sometimes known as a **Regulation A** exemption, exempts issues up to $5 million from the general registration and disclosure requirements, but the SEC does require a simplified **offering circular,** similar to a prospectus, and the filing of a simplified *notification* to the SEC, similar to a registration statement.

Registration and Disclosure Under the 1934 Act: Being Public

While the 1933 Act only requires disclosure and registration of "new issues" of securities, the 1934 Act extended those requirements, for similar reasons, to firms that had already made a public offering of securities. Registration and disclosure are generally required of four types of companies: (1) those which are listed on a national securities exchange; (2) companies whose securities are traded over-the-counter, if the firm's total assets exceed $3 million or if the firm has over 500 shareholders; (3) firms who voluntarily elect to comply with the Act; and (4) firms with over 500 shareholders of a class of securities registered under the 1933 Act.

Annual and *quarterly* reports are required and, if "specified events" take place, a **current report** must be filed as well. Such specified events include changes in control, acquisitions or dispositions of major assets, bankruptcy or receivership, changes in accountants, resignation of directors, and other major "events." There is no prospectus requirement under the 1934 Act, but the "amendment" procedure may apply under the *Manor Nursing Center* case.

The **annual report** must contain audited financial reports for the last two fiscal years; a summary of earnings and management analysis for the past five fiscal years; a brief description of the business; a "line of business" or "product line" report for the last five fiscal years; identification of directors and officers; identification of the principal market(s) in which securities are traded; and the range of market prices and dividends for each quarter of the last two fiscal years. The quarterly report updates the annual report at the close of each quarter, and contains the same information as the annual report, reduced to quarterly segments. Legal proceedings, changes in securities, defaults, and other information must also be included in all reports.

Impact on the Accounting Profession

Obviously, much of the work in preparing disclosure and registration materials under both the 1933 and 1934 Acts is done by accountants. The financial reports must be certified by an independent public accountant, and underwriters and firms issuing securities generally require a **comfort letter** from an independent accountant stating that the reports do not include any "false or misleading" information. If false or misleading information is in fact included, the accountant may be sued in many instances, though subject to the defense of **due diligence,** that is, the required tasks were performed according to generally accepted accounting standards and with proper care. Accountants may also be censured by the SEC.

Under both the 1933 and 1934 Acts, the SEC is given authority to prescribe accounting rules and procedures within the context of the various reports filed with the Commission. Many of those standards have evolved, and continue to evolve, from dialogues between the SEC and professional accounting associations. The SEC standards have, in many instances, influenced general accounting principles and practices.

Antifraud Provisions

Most of the federal securities laws contain provisions prohibiting "fraud or deceit" or "manipulative devices." Perhaps the most important of these provisions is Section 10(b) of the 1934 Act, which provides that it is unlawful

> To use or employ, in connection with the purchase or sale of any security . . . any manipulative or deceptive device or contrivance in contravention of such rules and regulations as the Commission may prescribe. . . .

The Act makes nothing illegal unless the SEC adopts a rule prohibiting a practice. In 1942, the SEC adopted the famous *Rule 10b-5,* which states

> It shall be unlawful for any person, directly or indirectly, by the use of any means or instrumentality of interstate commerce, or of the mails, or of any facility of any national securities exchange (1) to employ any device, scheme, or artifice to defraud, (2) to make any untrue statement of a material fact or to omit to state a material fact necessary in order to make the statements made, in the light of circumstances under which they were made, not misleading, or (3) to engage in any act, practice, or course of business which operates or would operate as a fraud or deceit upon any person, in connection with the purchase or sale of any security.

There are no exemptions in either the rule or the Act, and Rule 10b-5 applies whether or not the securities are registered with the SEC and whether or not there are exemptions from the application of the registration and disclosure rules.

Court decisions have required a further element in the proof of "10b-5" violations, that of scienter. **Scienter** is a criminal law concept meaning "guilty knowledge." The scienter requirement does not mean that alleged violator knew that he or she was violating the law but that the violator intended to defraud or deceive someone. A reckless or negligent act cannot violate the Rule.

Violations of Rule 10b-5 may result in both civil and criminal liability. Private civil actions to recover amounts lost to deceptive schemes are permitted, and the SEC may bring injunctive actions. Criminal violations are possible but are reserved for the most serious cases.

A variety of practices have been held illegal under Rule 10b-5, including *market manipulations, insider* and *tippee trading, misstatements* on registration and disclosure statements or elsewhere, and several types of *corporate mismanagement.*

Market Manipulation   Section 10(b) of the 1934 Act prohibits any "manipulative . . . device." This provision has been used against wash sales or matched orders and similar devices that artifically inflate the price of a stock. Later concerns have dealt with the effect of large block orders by institutional investors. Not all manipulations are illegal, since the SEC is rather sympathetic to "stabilizing" purchases or sales of securities during periods of rapid price changes. Since 1968, the SEC has had the authority to regulate corporate repurchases of stock and prevent fraudulent schemes when corporations are involved in transactions in their own stock.

Insider Trading and Tippees   One of the most common applications of Rule 10b-5 is to trading by persons who have access to "inside information" about a firm. Such persons have a duty to disclose to the persons with whom they deal that they have such information. Similarly, if such persons disclose confidential corporate information to another (a **tippee**), the tippees are subject to the same duty of disclosure as the insider tippers. Thus, the officers of an oil company about to announce the discovery of a new oil field must disclose that fact before they buy stock in their company. The purpose of the rule is to protect persons who deal with insiders or their tippees. The following case discusses the problem of tippees in the famous "Equity Funding" case, but from a slightly different perspective.

Dirks v. SEC

452 U.S. 490, 101 S. Ct. 2478, 69 L. Ed. 2d 185 (1983)

Dirks was an officer of a broker-dealer firm that specialized in investment analysis of insurance company securities for institutional investors. In 1973, he received information from Secrist, a former officer of Equity Funding of America, that the assets of Equity Funding were vastly overstated as the result of fraudulent corporate practices. Secrist urged Dirks to verify the fraud and disclose it publicly. Dirks interviewed several employees of Equity Funding, some of whom corroborated Secrist's allegations. During this time, Dirks openly discussed the allegations with a number of clients and investors. Some of these persons sold their holdings in Equity Funding, including five investment advisers who liquidated holdings of more than $16 million. As a result, the price of Equity Funding stock fell from $26 per share to less than $15 per share. The New York Stock Exchange stopped all trading in Equity Funding securities as a result. Shortly thereafter, California authorities found evidence of fraud. Dirks had also contacted the *Wall Street Journal,* which refused to print any information, and the SEC, which refused to issue a complaint. After the California authorities publicized their findings, the *Journal* printed its story and the SEC filed a complaint against Equity Funding. The SEC also issued a complaint against Dirks, charging "tippee trading."

The SEC found that Dirks had aided and abetted violations of the securities act, concluding that "Where 'tippees'—regardless of their motivation or occupation—come into possession of material 'information that they know is confidential and know or should know came from a corporate insider,' they must either publicly disclose that information or refrain from trading." The SEC recognized that Dirks had played an important role in bringing the Equity Funding fraud to light and imposed only a censure. Dirks appealed to the Court of Appeals, which affirmed the censure. Dirks sought relief from the Supreme Court.

Justice POWELL delivered the opinion of the Court. . . .

In *Chiarella* [v. *United States*, 445 U.S. 222, 100 S. Ct. 1108, 63 L. Ed.2d 348 (1980)] we accepted the two elements . . . for establishing a Rule 10b-5 violation: "(i) the existence of a relationship affording access to inside information intended to be available only for a corporate purpose, and (ii) the unfairness of allowing a corporate insider to take advantage of that information by trading without disclosure." . . . [T]he Court found that there is no general duty to disclose before trading on material nonpublic information, and held that "a duty to disclose under §10(b) does not arise from the mere possession of nonpublic market information". . . . Such a duty arises rather from the existence of a fiduciary relationship. . . .

Not all breaches of fiduciary duty in connection with a securities transaction, however, come within the ambit of Rule 10b-5. . . . There must be "manipulation or deception." . . . In an inside-trading case this fraud derives from the "inherent unfairness involved where one takes advantage" of "information intended to be available only for a corporate purpose and not for the personal benefit of anyone." . . . Thus, an insider will be liable under Rule 10b-5 for inside trading only where he fails to disclose material nonpublic information before trading on it and thus makes "secret profits". . . .

. . . [T]here can be no duty to disclose where the person who had traded on inside information "was not [the corporation's] agent, . . . was not a fiduciary, [or] was not a person in whom the sellers [of the securities] had placed their trust and confidence. . . ." This requirement of a specific relationship between the shareholders and the individual trading on inside information has created analytical difficulties for the SEC and courts in policing tippees who trade on inside information. Unlike insiders who have independent fiduciary duties to both the corporation and its shareholders, the typical tippee has no such relationships. In view of this absence, it has been unclear how a tippee acquires the . . . duty to refrain from trading on inside information.

The SEC's position . . . is that a tippee "inherits" the . . . obligation to shareholders whenever he receives inside information from an insider. . . .

In effect, the SEC's theory of tippee liability . . . appears rooted in the idea that the antifraud provisions require equal information among all traders. This conflicts with the principle set forth in *Chiarella* that only some persons, under some circumstances, will be barred from trading while in the possession of material nonpublic information. . . .

Imposing a duty to disclose or abstain solely because a person knowingly receives material nonpublic information from an insider and trades on it could have an inhibiting influence on the role of market analysts, which the SEC itself recognizes is necessary to the preservation of a healthy market. It is commonplace for analysts to "ferret out and analyze information" . . . and this often is done by meeting with and questioning corporate officers and others who are insiders. And information that the analysts obtain normally may be the basis for judgments as to the market worth of a corporations securities. . . .

The conclusion that recipients of inside information do not invariably acquire a duty to disclose or abstain does not mean that such tippees always are free to trade on the information. The need for a ban on some tippee trading is clear. Not only are insiders forbidden by their fiduciary relationship from personally using undisclosed corporate information to their advantage, but they may not give such information to an outsider for the same improper purpose. . . . Similarly, the transactions of those who knowingly participate with the fiduciary in such a breach are "as forbidden" as transactions "on behalf of the trustee himself." . . . [A] contrary rule "would open up opportunities for devious dealings in the name of the others that the trustee could not conduct in his own." . . . Thus, the tippee's duty to disclose or abstain is derivative from that of the insider's duty. . . .

Thus, some tippees must assume an insider's duty to the shareholders not because they receive inside information, but rather because it has been made available to them *improperly*. . . . Thus, a tippee assumes a fiduciary duty to the shareholders of a corporation not to trade on material nonpublic information only when the insider has breached his fiduciary duty to the shareholders by disclosing the information to the tippee and the tippee knows or should know that there has been a breach. . . .

In determining whether a tippee is under an obligation to disclose or abstain, it thus is necessary to determine whether the insider's "tip" constituted a breach of the insider's fiduciary duty. All disclosures of confidential corporate information are not inconsistent with the duty insiders owe to shareholders. In contrast to the extraordinary facts of this case, the more typical situation in which there will be a question whether disclosure violates the insider's . . . duty is when insiders disclose information to analysts. . . . In some situations, the insider will act consistently with his fiduciary duty to shareholders, and yet release of the information may affect the market. . . . [T]he test is whether the insider personally will benefit, directly or indirectly, from his disclosure. Absent some personal gain, there has been no breach of duty to stockholders. And absent a breach by the insider, there is no derivative breach. . . .

Under the insider-trading and tipping rules set forth above, we find that there was no actionable violation by Dirks. It is undisputed that Dirks himself was a stranger to Equity Funding, with no pre-existing fiduciary duty to its shareholders. He took no action, directly or indirectly, that induced the shareholders or officers of Equity Funding to repose trust or confidence in him. There was no expectation by Dirk's sources that he would keep their information in confidence. Nor did Dirks misappropriate or illegally obtain the information about Equity Funding. Unless the insiders breached their . . . duty to shareholders in disclosing the nonpublic information to Dirks, he breached no duty when he passed it on to investors as well as to the *Wall Street Journal.*

It is clear that neither Secrist nor the other Equity Funding employees violated their . . . duty to the corporation's shareholders by providing information to Dirks. The tippers received no monetary or personal benefit for revealing Equity Funding's secrets, nor was their purpose to make a gift of valuable information to Dirks. As the facts of this case clearly indicate, the tippers were motivated by a desire to expose the fraud. . . . In the absence of a breach of duty to the shareholders by the insiders, there was no derivative breach by Dirks. . . .

Reversed.

Justice BLACKMUN, with whom Justice BRENNAN and Justice MARSHALL join, dissenting:

The Court today takes still another step to limit the protections provided investors by §10(b). . . . The device employed in this case engrafts a special motivational requirement on the fiduciary duty doctrine. This innovation excuses a knowing and intentional violation of an insider's duty to shareholders if the insider does not act from a motive of personal gain. . . .

The fact that the insider himself does not benefit from the breach does not eradicate the shareholder's injury. . . . It makes no difference to the shareholder whether the corporate insider gained or intended to gain personally from the transaction; the shareholder still has lost because of the insider's misuse of nonpublic information. The duty is addressed not to the insider's motives, but to his actions and their consequences on the shareholder. Personal gain is not an element of the breach of this duty.

The obligation to disclose extends beyond corporate directors and officers, however, and includes employees, attorneys, and accountants for the company, and any other person receiving confidential information from a corporate source. The information used must be confidential and material, and the information may not be used until after it is made public and until the news may be circulated. In other words, an investment cannot be made at the instant news is announced. Civil actions by persons dealing with insiders and tippees are permitted, along with actions by the company or stockholders acting on its behalf.

Corporate Misstatements   The provisions of §10(b) and Rule 10b-5 have been applied to any corporate statement, including registration and disclosure statements, prospectuses, press releases, corporate reports, financial statements, or other documents or statements made "in connection with the purchase and sale of securities." Such statements must be "misleading to the reasonable investor." The statements must also be made with "scienter," or "guilty knowledge" that the statements were false or misleading and were made with intent to defraud or deceive.

SEC v. Texas Gulf Sulphur Co.

401 F. 2d 833 (2d Cir., 1968)

This was an action by the SEC for an injunction against Texas Gulf Sulphur (TGS) and several officers, employees, broker-dealers, and others, asking for recission of certain securities transactions. The complaint charged that the individual defendants had used "inside information" to make stock purchases, that others had made "tips" of inside information to others, and that the company had issued a deceptive press release.

TGS' problems began with the discovery by company geologists of a "promising" copper field in Canada. The initial core samples proved better than any the experienced geologists had ever seen, and TGS began a program of land acquisition. During the months from November 1963 to March 1964, when the test drilling was suspended for the land acquisition program, some of the individual defendants gave tips to friends of the possible discovery, and TGS issued stock options to officers and employees, most of whom were aware of the discovery, though the committee issuing the options had no knowledge of the strike.

Drilling resumed on March 31, and the results were even more promising, giving rise to rumors throughout Canada and the United States of a major ore strike. On April 12, TGS issued a statement through its executive vice-president that stated:

> During the past few days, the exploration activities of Texas Gulf Sulpher in the area of Timmins, Ontario, have been widely reported in the press, coupled with rumors of a substantial copper discovery there. These reports exaggerate the scale of operations, and mention plans and statistics of size and grade of ore that are without factual basis and have evidently originated by speculation of people not connected with TGS.
>
> . . . .
>
> Recent drilling on one property near Timmins has led to preliminary indications that more drilling would be required for proper evaluation of this prospect. The drilling done to date has not been conclusive, but the statements made by many outside quarters are unreliable and include information and figures not available to TGS.
>
> The work done to date has not been sufficient to reach definite conclusions and any statement as to size and grade of ore would be premature and possibly misleading. When we have progressed to the point where reasonable and logical conclusions can be made, TGS will issue a definite statement to its stockholders and to the public in order to clarify the Timmins project.

On April 15, a statement was released to the press, which the company expected to be broadcast at 11 PM but which was somehow delayed until 9:40 AM the following day. That statement officially stated there had been a major strike of copper of at least 25 million tons. Several of the individual "insiders" made purchases of stock from midnight on April 15 to 10:20 AM on April 16.

On November 8, 1963, when drilling began, TGS stock sold for 17⅞. By April 10, it had risen to 30⅛, but declined after the announcement of April 12 to 29⅜ by April 15. On April 16 the stock climbed to 36⅜, and had risen to 58¼ by May 15.

WATERMAN, Circuit Judge: . . .

I. The Individual Defendants

. . . .

. . . [T]he Rule [10b-5] is based in policy on the justifiable expectation of the securities marketplace that all investors trading on impersonal exchanges have relatively equal access to material information. The essence of the Rule is that anyone who, trading for his own account in the securities of a corporation has "access, directly or indirectly, to information intended to be available only for a corporate purpose and not for the personal benefit of anyone" may not take "advantage of such information knowing it is unavailable to those with whom he is dealing," i.e., the investing public. Insiders, as directors or management officers are, of course, by this Rule, precluded from so unfairly dealing, but the Rule is also applicable to one possessing the information who may not be strictly termed an "insider" within the meaning of . . . the Act. Thus, anyone in possession of material inside information must either disclose it to the investing public, or, if he is disabled from disclosing it in order to protect a corporate confidence, or he chooses not to do so, must abstain from trading in or recommending the securities concerned while such inside information remains undisclosed. . . .

B. Material Inside Information

An insider is not, of course, always foreclosed from investing in his own company merely because he may be more familiar with company operations than are outside investors. An insider's duty to disclose information or his duty to abstain from dealing in his company's securities arises only in "those situations which are essentially extraordinary in nature and which are reasonably certain to have a substantial effect on the market price of the security. . . ."

We hold, therefore, that all transactions in TGS stock . . . by individuals apprised of the drilling results of the test drilling were made in violation of Rule 10b-5. . . .

C. When May Insiders Act?

Appellant Crawford, who ordered the purchase of TGS stock shortly before the TGS April 16 announcement, and defendant Coates, who placed orders with and communicated the news to his broker immediately after the official announcement was read . . . concede that they were in possession of material information. They contend however, that their purchases were not proscribed purchases for the news had already been effectively disclosed. We disagree. . . . Before insiders may act upon material information, such information must have been effectively disclosed in a manner sufficient to insure its availability to the investing public.

D. Is an Insider's Good Faith a Defense Under 10b-5?

Coates, Crawford and Clayton, who ordered purchases before the news could be deemed disclosed, claim, nevertheless, that they were justified in doing so because they honestly believed that the news of the strike had become public at the time they placed their orders. However . . . proof of a specific *intent* to defraud is unnecessary. In an enforcement proceeding . . . the common law standard of deceptive conduct has been modified in the interests of broader protection for the investing public so that *negligent* insider conduct has become unlawful. A similar standard has been adopted in private actions. . . .

Thus, the beliefs of Coates, Crawford and Clayton that the news of the ore strike was sufficiently public at the time of their purchase orders are to no avail. . . .

E. May Insiders Accept Stock Options Without Disclosing Material Information to the Issuer?

On February 20, 1964, [certain corporate officers] . . . accepted stock options issued to them . . . although not one of them had informed the Stock Option Committee of the Board of Directors or the Board of the results of [the test drilling], which information we have held was then material. [The Court held that the acceptance of the options without disclosure to the issuing party, i.e., the Board of Directors and the Stock Option Committee, was in fact "insider trading."]

II. THE CORPORATE DEFENDANT

At 3:00 PM on April 12, 1964, evidently believing it desirable to comment upon the rumors concerning the Timmins project, TGS issued the press release quoted. . . . The SEC argued . . . and maintains . . . that this release painted a misleading and deceptive picture of the drilling progress at the time of its issuance, and hence violated Rule 10b-5. TGS relies on the holding of the court below that "The issuance of the release produced no unusual market action" and "In the absence of a showing that the purpose of the April 12 press release was to affect the market price of TGS stock to the advantage of TGS or its insiders, the issuance of the press release did not constitute a violation of Section 10(b) or Rule 10b-5 since it was not issued 'in connection with the purchase or sale of any security'" and alternatively, "even if it had been established that the April 12 release was issued in connection with the purchase or sale of any security, the Commission has failed to demonstrate that it was false, misleading or deceptive." . . .

B. The "In Connection With . . ." Requirement

[I]t seems clear from the legislative purpose Congress expressed in the Act, . . . that Congress when it used the phrase "in connection with the purchase or sale of any security" intended only that the device employed, whatever it might be, be of a sort that would cause reasonable investors to rely thereon, and, in connection therewith, so relying, cause them to purchase or sell a corporation's securities. There is no indication that Congress intended that the corporations or persons responsible for the issuance of a misleading statement would not violate the section unless they engaged in related securities transactions or otherwise acted with wrongful motives. . . . Absent a securities transaction by an insider it is almost impossible to prove that a wrongful purpose motivated the issuance of the misleading statement. . . .

. . . [T]he investing public is hurt by exposure to false or deceptive statements irrespective of the purpose underlying their issuance. It does not appear to be unfair to impose upon corporate management a duty to ascertain the truth of any statements the corporation releases to its shareholders or to the investing public at large. Accordingly, we hold that Rule 10b-5 is violated whenever assertions are made, as here, in a manner reasonably calculated to influence the investing public, e.g., by means of the financial media, if such assertions are false or misleading or are so incomplete as to mislead irrespective of whether the issuance of the release was motivated by corporate officials for ulterior purposes. It seems clear, however, that if corporate management demonstrates that it was diligent in ascertaining that the information it published was the whole truth and that such diligently obtained information was disseminated in good faith, Rule 10b-5 would not have been violated.

C. Did the Issuance of the April 12 Release Violate Rule 10b-5?

. . . While we certainly agree with the trial court that "in retrospect, the press release may appear gloomy or incomplete," we cannot, for the present record, by applying the standard Congress intended, definitively conclude that it was deceptive or misleading to the reasonable investor, or that he would have been misled by it. Certain newspaper accounts . . . viewed the release as confirming the existence of preliminary favorable developments. . . . On the other hand, in view of the decline of the market price of TGS stock from . . . April 13 . . . to . . . April 15 . . . it is far from certain that the release was generally interpreted as a highly encouraging report. . . . Accordingly, we remand this issue to the district court . . . for a determination of the character of the release in the light of the facts existing at the time of the release, by applying the standard of whether the reasonable investor, in the exercise of due care, would have been misled by it.

On remand, the District Court held that the company had failed to exercise due diligence in the issuance of the April 12 report. The U.S. Supreme Court refused to grant certiorari. Several civil suits resulted from the action, all of which were settled by a payment of $2.7 million to stockholder-plaintiffs.

Corporate Mismanagement   Management has the opportunity to make transactions in the shares of a company in a variety of ways, including mergers and acquisitions, reorganizations, and the sale of controlling interests. Management may be liable under Rule 10b-5 if such transactions are fraudulent, involve a sale or purchase of stock, and the fraud is "in connection with" the purchase or sale. Many actions under this rule are brought by injured shareholders, or by shareholders on behalf of the corporation. The courts generally require that the person bringing the suit be either a "purchaser" or "seller" however.

Non-10b-5 Regulation

Aside from the general prohibitions found in Section 10(b) of the 1934 Act and Rule 10b-5, several other more specific regulations apply to publicly held corporations, including the *proxy-solicitation rules,* regulation of *tender offers,* and the rules relating to *short-swing profits.*

Proxy-Solicitation Rules   A **proxy** is an authorization by a shareholder to another to vote the shareholder's stock. State corporation acts generally permit shareholders to give proxies to others to vote their shares at stockholders' meetings. Proxies are often solicited by management, but sometimes other groups of stockholder "insurgents" also try to obtain proxies in an attempt to oust the present management, resulting in "proxy fights." Proxies are generally revocable at any time by the shareholders giving them.

The 1934 Act requires that any proxy solicitation, whether by management or by insurgents, be accompanied by a **proxy statement.** That statement is a disclosure to shareholders of all of the material facts regarding matters that will be voted on at the meeting and gives the shareholders the opportunity to register their preference in the proxy. If there is to be a contest for the control of the corporation, the names and interests of all participants in the proxy contest must be disclosed. If securities are registered in a broker's "street name," the parties soliciting the proxies must inquire as to the real owners of the securities, furnish enough copies for each such owner to the broker, and pay the reasonable expenses of distributing the statement.

Proxy statements must be filed with the SEC at least ten days before they are sent to shareholders, and the SEC may require changes in those statements. In an attempt to bring about **shareholder democracy,** the SEC rules also require that proposals by shareholders be included in the proxy statement if they are presented to management a reasonable time before the statements are sent. This rule permits discussion of such items as management compensation, shareholder voting rights, and conduct of the annual meeting—items that management often tries to keep off of the agenda of the annual meeting. Shareholder proposals relating to personal claims or grievances, matters not significantly related to the company's business, and nominations of candidates for the board of directors need not be permitted, and the SEC has the authority to determine whether shareholder proposals must be included in the proxy request.

Tender Offers   As discussed in Chapter 10, a **tender offer** is a general offer to all of the shareholders of a corporation to purchase their shares at a specified price, often subject to a minimum or maximum number of shares that the offeror will accept. Such offers are usually communicated to the shareholders through a newspaper advertisement or through a general mailing to all shareholders. The purpose of the offeror is to obtain enough stock to elect a majority of the board of directors and obtain control of the corporation. Such tender offers are often bitterly contested by the management of the "target" corporation, since they will probably lose their jobs if the bid is successful.

During the conglomerate craze of the 1960's, tender offers were often marked by claims and countercharges on both sides, efforts to manipulate the market, and confusing and sometimes coercive approaches to existing stockholders. In an effort to counter those problems, the Williams Act was passed by Congress in 1968 as an amendment to the 1934 Act. The purpose of the Act was disclosed by Senator Harrison Williams, the sponsor of the Act.

> This legislation will close a significant gap in investor protection under the federal securities laws by requiring the disclosure of pertinent information to stockholders when persons seek to obtain control of a corporation by a cash tender offer or through open market or privately negotiated purchases of securities.*

The Williams Act requires any "person or group" that becomes the owner of 5 percent or more of any class of securities registered under the 1934 Act, or who makes a tender offer to acquire more than 5 percent of such shares, to file a disclosure statement with both the SEC and the issuer of such securities within ten days. That statement must include the background of the persons acquiring the stock, the source of

---

*113 Cong. Rec. 854.

the funds used for the acquisition, the purpose of the acquisition, the total number of shares owned, and any other contracts, arrangements, or understandings relevant to the acquisition.

Shareholders who decide to tender their stock are also protected. Such shareholders may withdraw their shares during the first seven days of the offer and any time after sixty days after the beginning of the offer. If the tender offer is for less than all of the outstanding shares, and more than the requested number of shares are tendered, the offeror must take the shares on a pro-rata basis during the first ten days of the offer to decrease the pressure on shareholders when the offeror makes its offer on a first-come, first-served basis. Finally, if the offered price increases during the course of an offer, all tendering shareholders must receive the additional consideration, even if they tendered their stock before the price increase was announced.

The act also contains a broad antifraud section, making it illegal to make any untrue statement of a material fact or to omit to state any material fact, or to engage in fraudulent, deceptive, or manipulative acts or practices in connection with a tender offer. The Williams Act is enforced by SEC orders, injunctions, and civil actions by injured shareholders (see *Piper* v. *Chris-Craft Industries,* p. 551).

Liability for Short-Swing Profits   In order to provide an additional protection from insider trading, another provision effectively prohibits certain insiders from profiting from short-term gains on the securities of their firms. The provision generally applies to officers, directors, and persons owning more than 10 percent of a class of equity securities registered under the 1934 Act. Such persons must file a report with the SEC when they become officers, directors, or 10 percent shareholders, and must file another report at the end of any month in which they acquire or dispose of any of the company's equity securities. The company, or any shareholder suing on behalf of the company, may obtain from such persons "any profit" realized from the purchase and sale, or sale and purchase, of any equity security within a six-month period.

Regulation of the Securities Business

The 1934 Act also requires brokers and dealers to register with the SEC, and investment advisers are required to register with the Commission under the Investment Advisers Act. The 1934 Act regulates *broker-dealer selling practices,* requires a certain degree of *financial responsibility* on the part of broker-dealers, authorizes the Federal Reserve Board to establish *margin requirements,* and places *restrictions on trading by broker-dealers.*

Broker-Dealer Selling Practices

The 1934 Act and the SEC rules generally regulate broker-dealer selling practices by prohibiting some types of conflicts of interest between the broker-dealer and the customer and by requiring an adequate basis for recommendations by broker-dealers to their customers.

Generally, *conflicts of interest* are controlled under the so-called **shingle theory,** which holds that a securities professional who "hangs out his shingle" represents to the public that he or she is an expert in securities transactions and will act in the general best interests of the customer. This means in part that a securities professional will violate the antifraud provisions of the Act if he or she does not disclose all conflicts of interest prior to a customer's investment decision.

Two of the more important potential conflicts of interest involve **churning** a customer's account by making rapid and unnecessary transactions solely to earn commissions and **scalping,** which means making recommendations to customers to purchase securities in which the broker-dealer has personally invested in order to make the price of the broker-dealer's stock go up.

The SEC has also taken the position that it is a violation of the antifraud provisions for a broker-dealer to recommend the purchase of a security unless the broker-dealer has enough reliable information to form a valid basis for the recommendation.

Broker-Dealer Financial Responsibility

In order to protect customers from the acts of unscrupulous broker-dealers, the securities laws and SEC rules provide three financial responsibility requirements. Since 1972 broker-dealers have been required to keep the *net* cash due to their customers in special accounts, called *special reserve accounts.* A 1975 SEC rule requires broker-dealers to maintain at least $25,000 in net capital, and provides that the aggregate indebtedness of broker-dealers may not exceed 1,500 percent of its net capital. Finally, the Securities Investor Protection Act created the nonprofit Securities Investor Protection Corporation, which maintains a fund from which investors who have suffered cash losses by the acts of broker-dealers may be reimbursed. The Act does not cover ordinary investment losses. The funds are obtained by mandatory contributions from all registered brokers and dealers.

Margin Requirements

The 1934 Act authorized the Federal Reserve Board to limit the amount of credit that may be extended on any security. The Federal Reserve Board has issued several regulations of such credit applying to broker-dealers, banks, and others.

The Federal Reserve's **margin requirements** specify the "maximum loan value" of securities. The Federal Reserve changes those requirements from time to time, in response to changes in the amount of speculative activity and the availability of credit. Thus, if the margin requirement is 50 percent, a customer will have to pay at least half the value of a security before it can be purchased. The Federal Reserve does not require additional margin if the value of stocks declines, but several of the securities exchanges impose such **margin maintenance** rules. The margin rules only apply to equity securities.

Loans by broker-dealers to their customers are specifically exempt from the Truth-in-Lending Act, but the SEC has established disclosure rules for such transactions. Those rules require broker-dealers to disclose the rate and method of computing interest on such indebtedness and the nature of the broker-dealer's interest in the customer's securities.

Broker-Dealer Trading Restrictions

Because broker-dealers can affect the price of a security through their actions, and because broker-dealers have many of the characteristics of insiders, the 1934 Act generally permits the SEC to regulate the trading activities of such persons for their own accounts. The Act generally prohibits any trading by broker-dealers unless the SEC provides an exception, but there are some rather large exceptions to the rule. The primary focus of such regulations is to prohibit manipulations of prices by securities professionals.

Remedies, Sanctions, and Civil Liability

A variety of sanctions and remedies are available under the federal acts, including criminal penalties, civil injunctions, and administrative remedies. In addition, the federal laws may also be used in many instances as the basis for civil lawsuits by injured parties.

Criminal Sanctions

If fraud or other wilful violations of the federal laws are present, the SEC may refer the case to the Justice Department for criminal prosecution. The most usual penalty under the federal laws is a fine of up to $10,000 or five years imprisonment or both. Such action is reserved for the most outrageous cases, however.

SEC Injunction Actions

The SEC may apply to a federal district court for an injunction against practices that violate the federal statutes or the SEC rules. While such injunctions were routinely granted in earlier years, courts have become reluctant to grant injunctions unless the defendant is likely to continue to violate the law or is a "continuing menace" to the public. Courts may order additional or "ancillary" relief in an injunction action, such as requiring a defendant to turn over the profits from an illegal transaction. (See the relief granted the *Manor Nursing* case, p. 535 for example.)

Administrative Remedies

The SEC may, after an investigation and an appropriate hearing, issue orders suspending or expelling members from exchanges or over-the-counter dealer association; denying, suspending, or revoking broker-dealer registrations; or barring individuals from employment with a registered firm, temporarily or permanently. As noted, the Commission may also issue a "stop order," which terminates trading of an issue as well. Such orders are generally reviewable by the U.S. Courts of Appeal. (See the relief granted against Equity Funding in *Dirks* v. *SEC,* p. 540 for example.)

Civil Liability

Perhaps the most important deterrent to violation of the federal securities laws is the possibility of a civil lawsuit. Injured parties, including corporations or shareholders suing on behalf of a corporation, may file lawsuits under two possible theories: *express liability,* which arises under a specific statute granting injured persons the right to sue, and *implied liability,* arising from interpretation of the federal law.

Express Liability   Several sections of the federal laws provide expressly for private civil lawsuits. For example, the 1933 Act gives purchasers of securities sold in violation of the disclosure and registration requirements the right to sue the issuer and the individuals responsible. Similarly, corporations and shareholders suing on behalf of the corporation may sue officers, directors and major shareholders who profit from short-swing profits. The 1934 Act expressly gives persons who purchase or sell securities due to misleading statements a right to sue for their loss.

Implied Liabilities   Some parts of the federal law do not grant an express right to sue, but affect private legal relationships, such as provisions in which contracts in violation of the law are made void. The courts generally grant private civil actions to enforce the rights created by those sections of the securities laws.

Many provisions of the federal law simply make a particular act or transaction unlawful. The courts have generally applied traditional tort principles in such cases and implied a private right of action on behalf of persons injured, if they are in the class of persons the statute was designed to protect. This rule has been applied most extensively in cases involving the general antifraud provisions and the proxy-solicitation rules. It is important that the person suing be in the "protected class," however. The following case considers whether an unsuccessful tender offeror has "standing" to sue.

Piper v. Chris-Craft Industries, Inc.

430 U.S. 1, 97 S. Ct. 926, 51 L. Ed. 2d 124 (1977)

The management of Piper Aircraft Corporation consisted principally of members of the Piper family, who owned 31 percent of Piper's outstanding stock, Chris-Craft Industries, a diversified manufacturer of recreational products, attempted to secure voting control of Piper through a tender offer for Piper common stock. The Piper family enlisted the aid of Bangor Punta Corporation, which made a higher offer for the stock. Bangor Punta issued a general offer for Piper stock and, while that offer was pending, purchased 120,000 shares of Piper stock in privately negotiated off-exchange transactions with three institutional investors. All three purchases were made after the SEC announced a rule that would expressly prohibit a tender offeror from making purchases of the target company's stock while a general tender offer was pending. With the support of the Piper family, the Bangor Punta tender offer was successful.

Chris-Craft brought this action under the Williams Act, charging that Bangor Punta achieved control of Piper as a result of violations of the federal securities laws. The federal securities laws do not grant a right to sue for violation of the Williams Act. A jury awarded Chris-Craft $36 million, and the Court of Appeals affirmed. Piper appealed to the U.S. Supreme Court.

Mr. Chief Justice BURGER delivered the opinion of the Court.

. . . .

III. The Williams Act

We turn first to an examination of the Williams Act, which was adopted in 1968 in response to the growing use of cash tender offers as a means for achieving corporate takeovers. Prior to the 1960's, corporate takeover attempts had typically involved either proxy solicitations, regulated under §14 of the Securities Exchange Act, or exchange offers of securities, subject to the registration requirements of the 1933 Act. The proliferation of cash tender offers, in which publicized requests are made and intensive campaigns conducted for tenders of shares of stock at a fixed price, removed a substantial number of corporate control contests from the reach of existing disclosure requirements of the federal securities laws. . . .

To remedy this gap in federal regulation, Senator Harrison Williams introduced a bill . . . to subject tender offerors to advance disclosure requirements. . . . [T]he legislation requires takeover bidders to file a statement with the Commission indicating, among other things, the ''background and identity'' of the offeror, the source and amount of funds or other consideration to be used in making the purchases, the extent of the offeror's holdings in the target corporation, and the offeror's plans with respect to the target corporation's business or corporate structure. . . .

Besides requiring disclosure . . . the Williams Act also contains a broad antifraud provision, which is the basis of Chris-Craft's claim. Section 14(e) of the Act provides:

> It shall be unlawful for any person to make any untrue statement of a material fact or omit to state any material fact . . . or to engage in any fraudulent, deceptive, or manipulative acts or practices, in connection with any tender offer. . . .

The threshold issue . . . is whether tender offerors, such as Chris-Craft, whose activities are regulated by the Williams Act, have a cause of action for damages against other regulated parties under the statute on a claim that antifraud violations by other parties have frustrated the bidder's efforts to obtain control of the target corporation. . . .

Our analysis begins, of course, with the statute itself. Section 14(e), like §10(b), makes no provision whatever for a private cause of action. . . . This Court has nonetheless held that in some circumstances a private cause of action can be implied with respect to the 1934 Act's antifraud provisions, even though the relevant provisions are silent as to remedies. *J.I. Case Co.* v. *Borak,* 377 U.S. 426, (1964). . . .

The reasoning of these holdings is that, where congressional purposes are likely to be undermined absent private enforcement, private remedies may be implied in favor of the particular class intended to be protected by the statute. For example, in *J.I. Case* v. *Borak,* supra, recognizing an implied right of action in favor of a shareholder complaining of a misleading proxy solicitation, the Court concluded as to such a shareholder's right:

> While [§14(a)] makes no specific reference to a private right of action, among it chief purposes is *''the protection of investors,''* which certainly implies the availability of judicial relief *where necessary to achieve that result.* 377 U.S., at 432 (emphasis supplied [by the Court].)

Indeed, the Court in *Borak* carefully noted that because of practical limitations upon the SEC's enforcement capabilities, "[p]rivate enforcement of the proxy rules provides a *necessary supplement to Commission action."* [Court's emphasis.]

. . . .

The legislative history . . . shows that Congress was intent upon regulating take-over bidders, theretofore operating covertly, in order to protect the shareholders of target companies. That tender offerors were not the intended beneficiaries of the bill was graphically illustrated by the statements of Senator Kuchel, co-sponsor of the legislation, in support of requiring takeover bidders whom he described as "corporate raiders" and "takeover pirates," to disclose their activities.

Today there are those individuals in our financial community who seek to reduce our proudest businesses into nothing but corporate shells. They seize control of the corporation with unknown assets, sell or trade away the best assets, and later split up the remains among themselves. The tragedy of such collusion is that the corporation can be financially raped without management *or shareholders* having any knowledge of the acquisitions. . . . The corporate raider may thus act under a cloak of secrecy while obtaining the shares needed to put him on the road to a successful capture of the company. [Court's emphasis.]

The legislative history . . . shows that the sole purpose of the Williams Act was the protection of investors who are confronted with a tender offer. . . . "The purpose of the Williams Act is to insure that public shareholders who are confronted by a cash tender offer for their stock will not be required to respond without adequate information. . . ." We find no hint in the legislative history . . . that Congress comtemplated a private cause of action for damages by one of several contending offerors against a successful bidder or by a losing contender against the target corporation. . . .

. . .

What we have said thus far suggests that, unlike *J.I. Case* v. *Borak,* supra, judicially creating a damages action in favor of Chris-Craft is unnecessary to ensure the fulfillment of Congress' purposes in adopting the Williams Act. . . .

We therefore conclude that Chris-Craft, as a defeated tender-offeror, has no implied cause of action for damages under §14(e).

Reversed.

Summary and Conclusions

Although the securities markets have been regulated by state laws since 1911, it was not until the stock market crash and the resulting Depression of the 1930's that federal regulation was thought necessary. The state blue sky laws only regulated intrastate offerings of equity and debt securities and were often subject to numerous exemptions and lax enforcement. Stock market abuses during the 1920's, such as market manipulation by large traders, insider trading, excessive margin purchases, and investment by commercial banks and their subsidiaries contributed substantially to the market crash of 1929 and to the pressure for reform and regulation.

Federal securities regulation is found in two major statutes, the Securities Act of 1933 and the Securities Exchange Act of 1934, a series of secondary acts regulating specific transactions or businesses, and the rules of the Securities and Exchange Commission (SEC). The SEC is an independent regulatory commission created by the 1934 Act and has authority to make rules pursuant to both the 1933 and 1934 Acts.

Federal law requires that new issues of securities be registered under the 1933 Act, and disclosure made to prospective investors in a prospectus. The 1934 Act requires registration and disclosure by most publicly traded corporations and others specifically set forth in the Act. The purpose of registration and disclosure is to provide information to prospective investors, who are free to make up their own minds about an investment. Federal law does not guarantee that any investment is "fair" or even a "good deal."

In addition to the registration and disclosure provisions, the federal statutes also include antifraud provisions, prohibiting fraud, deceit, and manipulative practices. The most important such provision is found in SEC Rule 10b-5, through which insider trading, corporate misstatements, and corporate mismanagement are controlled. Other sections of the federal law regulate proxy solicitation and tender offers and prohibit short-swing profits.

The federal laws also regulate the securities business by regulating the selling practices of broker-dealers, imposing financial responsibility on broker-dealers, imposing margin requirements, and restricting the trading practices of broker-dealers.

Remedies for violation of the federal securities laws include criminal penalties, injunctions, and administrative sanctions by the SEC, but perhaps the most important remedy is found in the variety of express and implied civil causes of action found in the federal statutes.

PRO AND CON

ISSUE: Can Corporate Accountability Be Better Served by Strict Enforcement of the Securities Laws or by Voluntary Compliance and Corporate Restructuring?

PRO: Strict Enforcement Is Necessary
John M. Fedders*

In my 81 days at the Commission, I have made an intensive review and assessment of the enforcement program. With recognition that my views have matured for less than a fiscal quarter, I will discuss three topics. First, my approach to enforcement. Second, areas that I believe require renewed vigilance. Finally, I will make several observations about specific aspects of the Commission's enforcement program.

. . . .

The Commission's purpose is to insure that the nation's capital markets operate with an integrity that promotes investor confidence. Our enforcement responsibility is to ferret out those who abuse the market system and who deceive investors. The Division of Enforcement is not in existence to discredit or impair our capital markets.

. . . .

Admittedly, the foregoing is somewhat general. My approach may be understood more fully if I move to a discussion of three areas which I believe require renewed enforcement vigilance. The areas are: First, trading while in possession of material non-public information, or what is often called "insider trading." Second, the manipulation of the securities markets. Third, fraud by reporting companies.

. . . .

All enterprises which have confidential infor-

*John Fedders was director, division of enforcement, SEC. From a speech entitled "The Enforcement of the SEC's Laws: The Integrity of Our Markets Is Essential for Capital Formation," delivered to the Association of General Counsel, Washington, D.C., October 8, 1981, and reprinted in *Vital Speeches of the Day*, Vol. 48, p. 111. Reprinted by permission.

mation in their possession that may affect the securities trading markets have an affirmative obligation to safeguard such information. While no procedures can guarantee that individual employees will not take unfair advantage of their position, enterprises should establish policies and procedures regarding the protection of confidential information and take steps to ensure that all personnel are familiar with those policies, including the serious consequences that may result. . . .

. . . .

Several commentators have suggested that insider trading cannot be effectively prevented. They are wrong. Others argue either that it is not worth preventing or that allowing insiders to trade while in possession of material non-public information will reward them for their entrepreneurial activities. They maintain that such trading leads to efficient markets and that it is not unfair to anyone.

The suggestions are repugnant to the fundamental concept of fairness on which a free market system depends. They deserve no further response.

. . . .

A chief aim of the Securities Exchange Act of 1934 is to eliminate manipulative and other abuses in the securities markets, and to establish markets by the free and honest balancing of investment demand with investment supply. Manipulation threatens the integrity of our capital markets.

. . . .

The practices artificially maintain or increase the price of . . . stock. The artificial price rise often fuels investor demand and causes an upward spiraling effect on both price and demand. These practices detract from an orderly marketplace. They contribute to market activities and prices which are not the result of the natural forces of supply and demand. . . .

The Commission's objective of preserving market integrity and investor confidence will not be achieved unless there is an increase in enforcement presence in market related investigations, and a substantial increase in our capacity to follow up on matters brought to our attention. . . . This is particularly important with respect to trading abuses involving speculative securities and new issues, insider trading, improper selling practices, trading abuses in the securities of foreign issuers, and intermarket manipulative activity. . . .

At the heart of the disclosure requirements . . . is the concept that all material information relating to a company should be fairly and accurately reported. The Commission will continue to devote significant enforcement efforts to the detection and suppression of fraud. . . .

. . . .

Enforcement is an honorable undertaking. The Commission's enforcement efforts must be supported and encouraged because they improve our nation's capital markets and economic stability.

CON: Voluntary Compliance and Corporate Structural Changes Are Important, Too
Harold M. Williams*

My theme [is] that it is vital that corporate structure and governance remain a private sector responsibility. I . . . am most apprehensive of the consequences that would follow from legislation which endeavored to deal directly with how corporations are managed and with the composition and functioning of boards. And yet, I . . . have . . . a high level of confidence that board structure will be one of the central points of attack when next a federal solution is proposed to remedy perceived corporate failures. . . . The next breakdown . . . will be cited as evidence by those who claim that corpo-

rations are concerned only about their own profitability, will do anything to maximize it, and respond only to . . . federal legislation and restriction.

In my view, the burden which the corporate community would need to carry in order to avoid a legislative outcome might prove unsustainable in political terms. Despite a wave of public reaction against government, the polls show that public resistance to more government . . . does not apply to regulation of business.

. . . .

The warning which I am sounding . . . centers

*Harold Williams is chairman, SEC. From a speech entitled "Corporate Accountability—One Year Later," delivered to the Securities Regulation Institute, San Diego, California, January 18, 1979, and reprinted in *Vital Speeches of the Day,* Vol. 45, p. 354. Reprinted by permission.

on the consequences which will follow if we, as businessmen, directors, lawyers, and private citizens, fail to appreciate and act upon the need for meaningful accountability in our corporate system.

. . . .

While our society is increasingly demanding that those who exercise power—corporate or otherwise—be subject to some accompanying mechanism to insure that the resulting societal effects are considered, it cannot depend upon either shareholders or management acting alone to discharge that accountability role in the modern public corporation. The duty must be on the corporate board.

. . . .

If it is accepted that strong and vigorous corporate boards are central to defending against the attack . . . a second question arises. How can the corporate board best structure and operate itself in order to serve as the effective accountability mechanism which, in my view, is the only realistic prophylactic against federal intrusion. . . .

The ultimate determinant of board effectiveness is the quality of the individual directors—their character, integrity, intelligence, and the time, effort, and energy which they are able and willing to bring to the board's work. . . .

The single factor most destructive of the effectiveness of the board and its ability to discharge the accountability function is its members' lack of independence. For this reason, I recommended . . . that, in order to avoid jeopardizing the accountability process, the board should consist exclusively of directors who have no other significant relationship with the corporation: that the corporate chief executive officer be the sole exception to this rule: but that the CEO not serve as chairman of the board.

. . . .

The problem is more extreme when members of management serve on the board. There is an essential conflict between a director's responsibility, as a member of the board, to oversee the stewardship of management, and the responsibility of the members of that same management. To put it conversely, members of management cannot be expected, as a general rule, to assess objectively the performance of the management of which they are a part. . . .

. . . .

My comments about particular potential improvements in board structure could be continued at some length. . . . [I]t is important that consideration of those comments not detract from the objective they serve—to provide a framework within which to tailor corporate structure which promotes meaningful accountability. The board and management must be sensitive to the burden upon the private sector to demonstrate that the exercise of corporate power both is and appears to be accountable to some organ with a broader perspective than either shareholders or management can typically be expected to bring to bear.

Both management and directors also share another, closely related, goal—to develop a board which can bring the best, most informed, and most objective advice available to bear in solving the complex problems which confront the entity. If directors are timid or feel compelled to compromise rather than advocate their views forthrightly—whether because of their personalities, their friendships, or their pocketbooks—then, in the long run, the corporation is the loser. And the officers and directors may be the losers as well, since they may not be able to point to the kind of disinterested decision-making which underlies the Business Judgment Rule.

. . . .

Business leadership, particularly its most politically and socially astute members, must recognize that if we are to safeguard the relative autonomy of American private business and preserve the system, we must assure that it works effectively—more effectively than it does now. We cannot afford the polarization that tends to pit those identified as supporters of the "public interest" against backers of "private interests." If that polarization is permitted to occur, the economic order which prevails in our country today will not survive.

DISCUSSION QUESTIONS

1. Trace the relationship of excessive margin trading, market manipulation, fraud and insider trading, and the involvement of commercial banks in the underwrit-

ing process to the stock market crash of 1929 and the Great Depression of the 1930's. Can another Great Depression occur in the light of federal securities laws, at least one caused by stock market problems?

2. If an investor fails to take advantage of registration and disclosure statements, do the federal securities laws afford him any protection against a "bad deal?" Do you suppose large institutional investors (insurance companies, mutual funds, pension funds, etc.) avail themselves of such information?

3. The federal securities laws have been called "the most successful of all the federal regulations." Do you agree? Why do almost all firms make every effort to comply with the law?

4. If a friend, who happened to be vice-president of a major mining company, mentioned to you that stock in his firm was "an especially good buy," and that it would be a "good idea" to invest before April 16, would you purchase stock in the firm? Would you think your friend had some special information? If you purchased the stock, and it was later disclosed that your friend had made those statements, what would be the likely result? Are your sure you want to invest in the firm?

5. An insider who knows "special information" and desires to purchase stock must disclose that information to the seller before the purchase. (1) How can he or she disclose that information to the unknown public investors from whom the stock is purchased through the exchange markets? (2) If he or she in fact discloses that information without permission from the company, what results would you expect?

6. Assume you are a shareholder of a major manufacturer. Under the concept "shareholder democracy," which of the following proposals could you successfully petition the management to include in a proxy statement: (1) a proposal to cut management salaries by 30 percent; (2) a proposal to invest $10 million in pollution control facilities for the plant; (3) a proposal to pay your brother $20,000 because of an industrial accident at the plant; (4) a proposal to nominate yourself to the board of directors; (5) a proposal to stop manufacturing components for atomic weapons delivery systems? Would you expect management to approve any of the proposals? If not, are you willing to petition the SEC to include those items?

7. If the management of a target company in a tender offer takes action to prevent the tender offer, such as encouraging a tender offer by another, friendly company (a "white knight") or by acquiring a firm in competition with the tender offeror, thereby producing a potential antitrust violation ("shark repellant"), do you, as a shareholder, have any remedy if you *favor* the tender offer?

8. Why do you suppose civil liability has become perhaps the most important of the remedies and sanctions under the federal securities laws?

CASE PROBLEMS

1. Which of the following must be registered under the Securities Act of 1933: (a) shares of limited partnership in a cattle ranch; (b) individual rows of orange trees, with a management contract; (c) a bank certificate of deposit; (d) shares in a mutual fund?

2. Gross advertised for "purchaser-investors" to raise earthworms. Each purchaser would have his or her own "worm ranch," and Gross would supply the initial breeding worms. Gross agreed to repurchase all bait-sized worms for $2.25 a pound, ostensibly for sale as bait, though "ranchers" were free to sell to anyone. Gross represented that the worms bred twenty times per year. In fact, the worms bred eight times per year, and the only market at $2.25 per pound was Gross himself, who used the worms repurchased as "breeders" for new worm ranchers. Smith sued Gross, claiming that the scheme should have registered under the 1933 Act, and claimed a violation of Rule 10b-5. Result? [*Smith* v. *Gross,* 604 F. 2d 292 (9th Circ., 1979).]

3. Smith learns that the ABC Company is going to make a public offering of stock after the SEC clears its registration statement. Smith is a present investor in ABC, and has been very pleased with the performance of ABC stock. Desiring to purchase more such stock, Smith calls his broker and offers to make a contract promising to purchase 1,000 shares of the stock when it is issued. May the broker or the ABC Company accept the offer?

4. Brown is a janitor in the offices of the XYZ firm, which manufactures airplane parts. One evening Brown overhears a conversation between the President and Vice President that the XYZ company has been awarded a big defense contract, which will be announced at noon the following day. At 9 AM, Brown mortgages his home and purchases all of the XYZ stock he can get with the proceeds. Has Brown violated Rule 10b-5? If Brown told his brother-in-law about the deal, and the brother-in-law bought XYZ stock as well, would the brother-in-law violate Rule 10b-5?

5. Sarjem purchased all of the stock of a private corporation that owned two toll bridges across the Delaware River. Sarjem immediately sold the bridges to a local city at twice the price paid for the stock. The city was willing to pay that amount since it was exempt from federal taxation, which meant that the income from the bridge was effectively doubled. Mills, a shareholder who had sold stock to Sarjem, filed suit claiming that Sarjem had a duty to disclose the facts regarding the intended sale of the bridges to prospective sellers of stock. Result? [*Mills* v. *Sarjem Corp.,* 133 F. Supp. 753 (D.C., N.J., 1955).]

6. Accidental Oil Company obtains geologist reports that there may be a large untapped field of oil under the Mojave Desert. Accidental acquires land and begins drilling, but it is impossible to "keep the lid on" the possible discovery and rumors are rampant throughout the industry. There are no firm results from the test wells yet, but Accidental stock begins fluctuating wildly with each suc-

cessive rumor. Is Accidental under a duty to make any statement? What sort of statement should it make?

7. First Securities, a brokerage house, and its President, Nye, had been involved in a scheme to defraud investors for some time. The scheme involving false escrow accounts of customer's money. Ernst & Ernst, an accounting firm, had audited First Securities' books for many years but was unaware of the fraud. Nye committed suicide and left a note confessing all. Customers of First Securities brought an action against Ernst & Ernst, claiming that the firm "should have" discovered the irregularities, and that the firm's failure to do so was a violation of Rule 10b-5. Result? [*Ernst & Ernst* v. *Hochfelder,* 425 U.S. 185, 96 S. Ct. 1375, 47 L. Ed 2d 668 (1976).]

8. Kahn, a broker-dealer, "predicted" to his customers that the stock of Sports Arenas, Inc., would have earnings of $1.18 per share next year. Sports Arenas was in fact a substantial enterprise with 29 bowling alleys which grossed over $5,000,000 and had a net profit of almost $300,000. Its net earnings per share were only 27¢, however. May Kahn be disciplined by the SEC? [*Kahn* v. *SEC,* 297 F. 2d 112 (2d Cir., 1961).]

9. Merrill, Lynch, a broker-dealer, advised Stern, a speculator and long-time customer, not to invest in a particular stock. Stern disregarded the advice and Merrill, Lynch waived the margin requirement in violation of the SEC rules because of the long relationship with Stern. Stern lost a great deal of money on the investment and sued Merrill, Lynch on the theory they should not have waived the margin requirement. Result? [*Stern* v. *Merrill, Lynch, Pierce, Fenner & Smith,* 603 F. 2d 1073 (4th Circ., 1979).]

10. Chiarella was a printer in the offices of an independent firm that prepared financial documents, stock certificates, and other materials dealing with securities. Though the names of firms and participants were kept secret until the last possible moment, Chiarella was able to ascertain that a large tender offer was about to be made, and he and some relatives made large purchases of stock in the company about to be purchased. Is he guilty of "insider trading?" [*Chiarella* v. *U.S.,* 445 U.S. 222, 100 S. Ct. 1108, 63 L. Ed. 2d 348 (1980). Hint: See the references to *Chiarella* in *Dirks* v. *SEC,* p. 540.]

SUGGESTED READINGS

Baruch, Bernard M. *My Own Story* (New York: Henry Holt, 1957).

Douglas, William O. *Go East, Young Man* (New York: Random House, 1974).

Galbraith, John Kenneth. *The Great Crash* (Boston: Houghton-Mifflin, 1954).

Jennings, Richard W., and Harold Marsh. *Securities Regulation* 5th ed. (Mineola, N.Y.: The Foundation Press, 1982).

Karmel, Roberta S. *Regulation by Prosecution: The Securities and Exchange Commission versus Corporate America* (New York: Simon and Schuster, 1982).

Ratner, David L. *Securities Regulation in a Nutshell* (St. Paul, Minn.: West Publishing Co., 1982).

Schlesinger, Arthur M. *The Coming of the New Deal* (Boston: Houghton-Mifflin, 1959).

Skousen, K. Fred. *An Introduction to the SEC* 3rd ed. (Cincinnati: South-Western Publishing Co., 1983).

Wiesen, Jeremy L. *Regulating Transactions in Securities* (St. Paul, Minn.: West Publishing Co., 1975).

Part VII

Regulation of the Relationship Between Business and the Public

Perhaps the newest and most controversial "relationship" of business is that between the firm and the anonymous public. Of course certain public responsibilities of business have been regulated for some time. For example, the antitrust laws are designed to protect not only competitors, but also competition in the abstract, since it is felt that competition is good for society as a whole. For the most part, however, regulation of business has taken place in terms of a real, concrete "relationship," as between a business and its employees or customers or investors.

Does business have responsibilities to others aside from those with whom there is such a firm relationship? In at least two areas, the law says business has such duties. The law of discrimination cuts across several of the areas already discussed, including employment law and the relationship of customer and business, and provides a general statement that irrelevant criteria such as race, sex, religion, and national origin should play no part in business decisions. And perhaps more to the point, environmental law provides that businesses may not dump their waste products on an innocent and unsuspecting public, even though businesses have no direct relationship with those persons.

Discrimination

[I]n view of the Constitution, in the eye of the law, there is in this country no superior, dominant ruling class of citizens. There is no caste here. Our Constitution is color-blind, and neither knows nor tolerates classes among citizens. . . .

> Mr. Justice Harlan, dissenting in Plessy v. Ferguson *(1896)*

I have a dream—that one day on the red hills of Georgia the sons of former slaves and the sons of former slaveowners will be able to sit down together at the table of brotherhood. . . . I have a dream—that my four little children will one day live in a nation where they will not be judged by the color of their skin, but by the content of their character. . . . I have a dream. . . .

> Dr. Martin Luther King, Jr., *Speech at the Civil Rights March on Washington, (August 28, 1963)*

A girl should not expect special privileges because of her sex, but neither should she "adjust" to prejudice and discrimination. She must learn to compete, not as a woman, but as a human being.

> Betty Friedan, The Feminine Mystique *(1963)*

The Declaration of Independence proclaimed to all the world that "all men are created equal," but it is clear that the slaveowners who signed that document did not have their human chattels in mind. This chapter is about the bizarre ability of many Americans since that time to at once defend the cause of freedom and denounce their fellows because of race, sex, age, or a hundred other irrelevancies. On another level, this chapter concerns the often halting and grudging efforts of government to limit discrimination, and the weighty issues and conflicts that infect that effort.

Whenever a legislative body enacts a law, it must inevitably *classify*. A judgment of a legislature about who is to be taxed or who is to receive benefits singles out some groups for special treatment. A threshhold question is then whether the basis of such classifications is permissible under the Consitution, especially under the Equal Protection Clause of the 14th Amendment. That issue was discussed in Chapters 2 and 3, and will be further considered in this chapter.

A knottier problem exists when discrimination results from *private* conduct. Long ago, the Supreme Court held that the 14th Amendment does not prohibit *private* discrimination, but only forbids discriminatory **state action.** A major issue is whether, and under what circumstances, state or federal governments ought to step in to outlaw discrimination by private individuals in employment, housing, public accommodations, or other areas. The largest part of this chapter will consider the instances in which the government has done so.

Discriminatory Classifications

To many Americans, the term *discrimination* automatically conjures up images of racial segregation. And, it is true that a great deal of the political and legal activity in the law of discrimination has taken place in the context of racial discrimination. But other classifications may be illegal as well. The federal civil rights acts passed in the 1960's generally prohibit discrimination on the basis of *race, color, religion, sex,* and *national origin,* and other federal laws deal with discrimination on the basis of *age* and *handicap.*

But even those classifications do not exhaust the possible categories of discrimination. State laws often protect other groups from discriminatory action as well. The Illinois Human Rights Act, for example, prohibits discrimination on the basis of race, color, religion, national origin, ancestry, age, sex, marital status, handicap (either physical or mental), or unfavorable discharge from military service. Political pressures continue for the inclusion of still other groups into the "protected" category. Two of the more controversial pressures, for example, are to include minority language groups and homosexuals in the protected category. Such pressures exist at two levels: first, such groups may simply petition Congress or state legislatures to be included in the various antidiscrimination statutes; and, second, such groups may argue that their rights are being violated under the federal Equal Protection Clause.

Equal Protection Revisited

The Courts have traditionally adopted two tests to determine whether a law violates the Equal Protection Clause. The first, known as the **reasonable basis test,** permits a classification scheme if the legislature had a "reasonable basis" for making the classification. That test was discussed in Chapters 2 and 3.

The second test, sometimes called the **strict scrutiny test,** prohibits a classification scheme unless the legislature can demonstrate that a valid state objective could not be accomplished any other way. The reasonable basis test is used unless the classification scheme involves either **fundamental rights,** such as those protected by the Bill of Rights, or a **suspect classification.** State laws classifying on the basis of race and national origin have generally been subjected to strict scrutiny. Laws classifying on the basis of indigency or age have been subjected to a reasonable basis test. And laws classifying on the basis of sex and illegitimacy have received a mixed reaction from the courts.

The determination of whether a particular group belongs in the suspect class category depends on three factors: (1) whether membership "carries an obvious badge, such as race or sex do;" (2) whether treatment of members of the group has been historically severe and pervasive; and (3) whether members of the class have been subjected to the "absolute deprivation" of benefits available to nonmembers.

The Problem of State Action

Among the earliest cases interpreting the 14th Amendment, the *Civil Rights Cases of 1883** held that the 14th Amendment prohibited discriminatory *state* action but had no effect on discriminatory *private* action. In 1948, the Court again considered the problem of discrimination arising from private action in the following landmark decision.

Shelley v. Kraemer

334 U.S. 1, 68 S. Ct. 836, 92 L. Ed. 1161 (1948)

The creator of a subdivision in St. Louis placed a condition in the deed and other documents relating to the subdivision that lots in the development could not be sold to persons of "the Negro or Mongolian race." Shelley, a black person, purchased one of the lots. Kraemer, a resident of the same subdivision, sued to restrain Shelley from taking possession of the property. The Missouri courts held the condition valid, concluding that it violated no rights guaranteed by the U.S. Constitution, and issued the injunction against Shelley. Shelley argued that the condition violated the Civil Rights Act of 1866, which is quoted in the body of the case. Kraemer contended that the Civil Rights Act of 1866 could not affect "private action" since the 14th Amendment only prohibited discriminatory "state action," and the Civil Rights Act was based on authority given by the 14th Amendment.

Mr. Chief Justice VINSON delivered the opinion of the Court. . . .

Whether the equal protection clause of the Fourteenth Amendment inhibits judicial enforcement by state courts of restrictive covenants based on race or color is a question which this Court has not heretofore been called upon to consider. . . .

It cannot be doubted that among the civil rights intended to be protected from discriminatory state action by the Fourteenth Amendment are the rights to acquire, enjoy, own and dispose of property. Equality in the enjoyment of property rights was regarded by the framers of that Amendment as an essential pre-condition to the realization of other basic civil rights and liberties which the Amendment was intended to guarantee. Thus §1978 [Now §1982] . . . of the Civil Rights Act of 1866 which was enacted by Congress while the Fourteenth Amendment was also under consideration, provides:

**109 U.S. 3, 3 S. Ct. 18, 27 L. Ed. 835 (1883).

All citizens of the United States shall have the same right, in every State and Territory, as is enjoyed by white citizens thereof to inherit, purchase, lease, sell, hold, and convey real and personal property.

It is likewise clear that restrictions on the right of occupancy of the sort sought to be created by the private agreements in these cases could not be squared with the requirements of the Fourteenth Amendment if imposed by state statute or local ordinance. . . .

But the present cases . . . do not involve action by state legislatures or city councils. Here the particular patterns of discrimination and the areas in which the restrictions are to operate, are determined, in the first instance, by the terms of agreements among private individuals. Participation of the State consists in the enforcement of the restrictions so defined. The crucial issue with which we are confronted is whether this distinction removes these cases from the operation of the prohibitory provisions of the Fourteenth Amendment.

. . . .

The short of the matter is that from the time of the adoption of the Fourteenth Amendment until the present, it has been the consistent ruling of this Court that the action of the States to which the Amendment has reference, includes action of state courts and state judicial officials. . . .

We hold that in granting judicial enforcement of the restrictive agreements in these cases, the States have denied petitioners the equal protection of the laws and that, therefore, the action of the state courts cannot stand. We have noted that freedom from discrimination by the States in the enjoyment of property rights was among the basic objectives sought to be effectuated by the framers of the Fourteenth Amendment. That such discrimination has occurred in these cases is clear. . . .

Reversed.

Later decisions held that conviction of black persons under "trespass" ordinances for violating a store policy of segregated lunch counters was also **state action.** But other cases held that the mere fact that a private club possessed a liquor license issued by the state, or that a public utility was closely regulated by state law, were not sufficient "ties" to the state to constitute state action. It appears the state must take some discretionary action to constitute state action.

The Authority of Congress to Regulate Discrimination

Very closely related to the problem of state action is whether Congress has the authority to pass laws designed to end private discrimination. One aspect of that problem was considered in the *Heart of Atlanta Motel* decision, p. 54, where the Court held that Congress had the authority to pass such laws under the authority of the Commerce Clause. Congress may also have such authority under the 13th, 14th, and 15th Amendments, all of which were passed shortly after the close of the Civil War. The 13th Amendment prohibits slavery, and later cases gave Congress the right to legislate against "badges of servitude." In 1968, the Supreme Court held that Congress also had the right to legislate against private discrimination under the 13th Amendment in the landmark decision of *Jones* v. *Alfred H. Mayer Co.*, a decision that involved the same section of the Civil Rights Act of 1866 described in the *Shelley* case.

Negro citizens, North and South, who saw in the Thirteenth Amendment a promise of freedom—freedom to "go and come at pleasure" and to "buy and sell when they please"—would be left with "a mere paper guarantee" if Congress were powerless to assure that a dollar in the hands of a Negro will purchase the same thing as a dollar in the hands of a white man. At the very least, the freedom that Congress is empowered to secure under the Thirteenth Amendment includes the freedom to buy whatever a white man can buy, the right to live wherever a white man can live. If Congress cannot say that being a free man means at least this much, then the Thirteenth Amendment made a promise the Nation cannot keep. (Mr. Justice STEWART in *Jones* v. *Alfred H. Mayer*)*

The 15th Amendment prohibited discrimination in voting rights because of "race, color, or previous condition of servitude." While some voting rights acts were passed during Reconstruction, the first modern federal voting rights act was not passed until 1957 (to be discussed later in this chapter).

The Curious Doctrine: The Rise and Fall of "Separate but Equal"

The 14th Amendment requires that all persons receive the equal protection of the laws. In the latter part of the 19th century, some states tried to evade the spirit of that law by passing laws requiring "equal but separate" treatment of blacks and whites. In 1896, in the notorious decision of *Plessy* v. *Ferguson,*** the Supreme Court approved such statutes, since they required equal facilities for both races. Justice John Marshall Harlan (1833–1911) presented an impassioned dissent calling for a "color-blind" interpretation of the Constitution. Following the Court's decision, the **separate but equal doctrine** was used to justify all sorts of segregationist statutes, including separate (but equal) dual school systems.

Slowly, the Supreme Court began to chip away at the doctrine, usually in the context of segregated educational facilities. In 1954, in the towering decision of *Brown* v. *Board of Education,* the Supreme Court finally overruled the doctrine completely in the context of public schools.

Brown v. Board of Education of Topeka

347 U.S. 483, 74 S. Ct. 686, 98 L. Ed. 873 (1954)

This case arose from common facts in several cases arising in Kansas, South Carolina, Virginia, and Delaware. In each case, the local school board or state statute required that black students attend "black" schools and white students attend "white" schools. In essence in each case there were two separate school systems, one for each race, and students were prohibited from attending the other school system. The school boards attempted to justify the system on the basis of the separate but equal doctrine of *Plessy* v. *Ferguson.* In each case black students sought and were denied admission to the "white" school system.

Mr. Chief Justice WARREN delivered the opinion of the Court. . . .
The plaintiffs contend that segregated public schools are not "equal" and cannot be made "equal," and that hence they are deprived of the equal protection of the laws. . . .
In the first cases in this Court construing the Fourteenth Amendment, decided

*392 U.S. 409, 88 S. Ct. 2186, 20 L. Ed. 2d 1189 (1968).

**163 U.S. 537, 16 S. Ct. 1138, 41 L. Ed. 256 (1896).

shortly after its adoption, the Court interpreted it as proscribing all state-imposed discriminations against the Negro race. The doctrine of "separate but equal" did not make its appearance in this Court until 1896 in the case of *Plessy* v. *Ferguson* . . . involving not education but transportation. American courts have labored with the doctrine for over half a century. . . .

In approaching this problem, we cannot turn the clock back to 1868 when the Amendment was adopted, or even to 1896 when *Plessy* v. *Ferguson* was written. We must consider public education in the light of its full development and its present place in American life throughout the Nation. Only in this way can it be determined if segregation in public schools deprives these plaintiffs of the equal protection of the laws. . . .

We come then to the question presented: Does segregation of children in public schools solely on the basis of race, even though the physical facilities and other "tangible" factors may be equal, deprive the children of the minority group of equal educational opportunities. We believe that it does.

In *Sweatt* v. *Painter* . . . in finding that a segregated law school for Negroes could not provide them equal educational opportunities, this Court relied in large part on "those qualities which are incapable of objective measurement but which make for greatness in a law school." In *McLaurin* v. *Oklahoma State Regents* . . . the Court, in requiring that a Negro admitted to a white graduate school be treated like all other students, again resorted to intangible considerations:" . . . his ability to study, to exchange in discussions and exhange views with other students, and, in general, to learn his profession." Such considerations apply with added force to children in grade and high schools. To separate them from others of similar age and qualifications solely because of their race generates a feeling of inferiority as to their status in the community that may affect their hearts and minds in a way unlikely ever to be undone. The effect of this separation on their educational opportunities was well stated by a finding in the Kansas case by a court which nevertheless felt compelled to rule against the Negro plaintiffs:

> Segregation of white and colored children in public schools has a detrimental effect upon the colored children. The impact is greater when it has the sanction of the law; for the policy of separating the races is usually interpreted as denoting inferiority of the Negro group. A sense of inferiority affects the motivation of a child to learn. Segregation with the sanction of law, therefore, has a tendency to [retard] the educational and mental development of Negro children and to deprive them of some of the benefits they would receive in a racial[ly] integrated school system.

Whatever may have been the extent of psychological knowledge at the time of *Plessy* v. *Ferguson,* this finding is amply supported by modern authority [citing numerous psychological studies]. Any language in *Plessy* v. *Ferguson* contrary to this finding is rejected.

We conclude that in the field of public education the doctrine of "separate but equal" has no place. Separate educational facilities are inherently unequal. Therefore, we hold that the plaintiffs and others similarly situated for whom the actions have been brought are, by reason of the segregation complained of, deprived of the equal protection of the laws guaranteed by the Fourteenth Amendment. . . .

. . . In order that we may have the full assistance of the parties in formulating decrees, the cases will be restored to the docket . . . for reargument. . . .

The following year, the Court announced its decision in *Brown* v. *Board of Education II, (Brown II),* ★ sometimes called the *Implementation Decision.* In that case, the

---

★349 U.S. 294, 75 S. Ct. 753, 99 L. Ed. 1083 (1955).

Court left it to the local school boards to solve the "varied local school problems" with the condition that it should be done "with all deliberate speed." Seventeen years later, the Court found that in many instances local school boards were dragging their feet and held that local federal district courts should supervise desegregation plans under their general equity powers. The same decision held that bussing may be, in appropriate circumstances, a "reasonable, feasible and workable" solution.*

Perhaps the knottiest question yet to be resolved is whether de facto segregation is included within the ban of *Brown* v. *Board*. **De facto segregation** (segregation "in fact") is segregation arising from housing patterns, as contrasted with **de jure segregation,** which is segregation mandated by law, including dual school systems as in *Brown,* gerrymandered school districts, or "private" schools created to replace a closed public school system. Strictly de facto segregation has not been treated by the courts, but any official action encouraging or taking advantage of de facto segregation is strictly prohibited.**

Racial Quotas and Affirmative Action

Brown v. *Board* could easily be read to require only Justice Harlan's color-blind Constitution, outlawing official discrimination but stopping short of any positive steps to "set the record straight." *Brown* appears, on its face, simply to forbid the use of racial criteria.

But racial criteria may be used for benign purposes as well. Such criteria may be used to make up for centuries of racial abuse and intolerance. But such **affirmative action** plans may discriminate against members of the majority race as well.

Regents of the University of California v. Bakke
438 U.S. 265, 98 S. Ct. 2733, 57 L. Ed. 2d 750 (1978)

The University of California Medical School set aside sixteen of one hundred positions in its entering class for disadvantaged and minority students. Students who were found to be disadvantaged or members of specific minorities received special consideration, including waiver of a 2.5 grade point average requirement. The result was that a number of students who did not meet the ordinary criteria for entrance were admitted, and a number of students who did meet the criteria were "bumped" to make room for the disadvantaged and minority students. Bakke had better credentials than any of the minority students admitted under the program, but he was twice denied admission. A state judge found that the special procedures constituted "reverse discrimination" and the state supreme court agreed, ordering Bakke admitted. The University appealed to the U.S. Supreme Court.

Mr. Justice POWELL announced the judgment of the Court. . . .

We have held that in "order to justify the use of a suspect classification, a state must show that its purpose or interest is both constitutionally permissible and substantial, and that its use of the classification is 'necessary . . . to the accomplishment' of its purpose or the safeguarding of its interest." . . . The special admissions program pur-

---

Swann v. *Charlotte-Mecklenburg Board of Education.,* 402 U.S. 1, 91 S. Ct. 1267, 28 L. Ed. 2d 554 (1971).

**See, e.g., discussion of *Milliken* v. *Bradley,* p. 588.

ports to serve the purposes of: (i) "reducing the historic deficit of traditionally disfavored minorities in medical schools and in the medical profession," . . . (ii) countering the effects of societal discrimination; (iii) increasing the number of physicians who will practice in communities currently underserved; and (iv) obtaining the educational benefits that flow from an ethnically diverse student body. It is necessary to decide which, if any, of these purposes is substantial enough to support the use of a suspect classification.

If petitioner's purpose is to assure within its student body some specified percentage of a particular group merely because of its race or ethnic origin, such a preferential purpose must be rejected not as insubstantial but as facially invalid. Preferring members of any one group for no reason other than race or ethnic origin is discrimination for its own sake. This the Constitution forbids. . . .

The State certainly has a legitimate and substantial interest in ameliorating, or eliminating where feasible, the disabling effects of identified discrimination. The line of school desegregation cases, commencing with *Brown,* attests to the importance of this state goal. . . .

We have never approved a classification that aids persons perceived as members of relatively victimized groups at the expense of other innocent individuals in the absence of judicial, legislative, or administrative findings of constitutional or statutory violations. . . .

Hence, the purpose of helping certain groups whom the faculty of the Davis Medical School perceived as victims of "societal discrimination" does not justify a classification that imposes disadvantages upon persons like respondent, who bear no responsibility for whatever harm the beneficiaries of the special admissions program are thought to have suffered. To hold otherwise would be to convert a remedy heretofore reserved for violations of legal rights into a privilege that all institutions throughout the Nation could grant at their pleasure to whatever groups are perceived as victims of societal discrimination. That is a step we have never approved. . . .

. . . Petitioner has not carried its burden of demonstrating that it must prefer members of particular ethnic groups over all other individuals in order to promote better health-care delivery to deprived citizens. Indeed, petitioner has not shown that its preferential classification is likely to have any significant effect on the problem.

The fourth goal asserted by petitioner is the attainment of a diverse student body. This clearly is a constitutionally permissible goal. . . . Ethnic diversity, however, is only one element in a range of factors a university properly may consider in attaining a heterogeneous student body. . . . The diversity that furthers a compelling state interest encompasses a far broader array of qualifications and characteristics of which racial or ethnic origin is but a single though important element. Petitioner's special admissions program, focused *solely* on ethnic diversity, would hinder rather than further attainment of genuine diversity. . . .

In summary, it is evident that the Davis special admissions program involves the use of an explicit racial classification never before countenanced by this Court. It tells applicants who are not Negro, Asian or Chicano that they are totally excluded from a specific percentage of the seats in an entering class. No matter how strong their qualifications, quantitative and extracurricular, including their own potential for contribution to educational diversity, they are never afforded the chance to compete with applicants from the preferred groups for the special admissions seats. At the same time, the preferred applicants have the opportunity to compete for every seat in the class.

The fatal flaw in petitioner's preferential program is its disregard of individual rights as guaranteed by the Fourteenth Amendment. *Shelley* v. *Kraemer.* . . . Such rights are not absolute. But when a State's distribution of benefits or imposition of burdens hinges on ancestry or the color of a person's skin, that individual is entitled to a demonstration that the challenged classification is necessary to promote a substantial state interest. Petitioner has failed to carry this burden. . . .

Opinion of Mr. Justice BRENNAN, Mr. Justice WHITE, Mr. Justice MARSHALL, and Mr. Justice BLACKMUN, concurring in the judgment in part and dissenting in part. . . .

The assertion of human equality is closely associated with the proposition that differences in color or creed, birth or status, are neither significant nor relevant to the way in which persons should be treated. Nonetheless, the position that such factors must be "constitutionally an irrelevance" . . . summed up by the shorthand phrase "[o]ur Constitution is color-blind" . . . has never been adopted by this Court as the proper meaning of the Equal Protection Clause. Indeed, we have expressly rejected this proposition on a number of occasions.

Our cases have always implied that an "overriding statutory purpose" . . . could be found that would justify racial classifications. . . .

We conclude, therefore, that racial classifications are not *per se* invalid under the Fourteenth Amendment. . . .

Unquestionably we have held that a government practice or statute which restricts "fundamental rights" or which contains "suspect classifications" is to be subjected to "strict scrutiny" and can be justified only if it furthers a compelling government purpose, and, even then, only if no less restrictive alternative is available. . . . But no fundamental right is involved here. . . . Nor do whites as a class have any of the "traditional indicia of suspectedness:" the class is not saddled with such disabilities, or subjected to such a history of purposeful and unequal treatment, or relegated to such a position of political powerlessness as to command extraordinary protection from the majoritarian political process. . . .

Accordingly, we would reverse the judgment. . . .

Mr. Justice MARSHALL. . . .

I agree with the judgment of the Court only insofar as it permits a university to consider the race of an applicant in making admissions decisions. I do not agree that petitioner's admissions program violates the Constitution. . . .

Justice Marshall then recounted at length the history of American race relations, from the earliest slave traders to the present.

The position of the Negro today in America is the tragic but inevitable consequence of centuries of unequal treatment. Measured by any benchmark of comfort or achievement, meaningful equality remains a distant dream for the Negro.

A Negro child today has a life expectancy which is shorter by more than five years than that of a white child. The Negro child's mother is over three times more likely to die of complications in childbirth, and the infant mortality rate for Negroes is nearly twice that for whites. The median income of the Negro family is only 60 percent that of the median white family, and the percentage of Negroes who live in families with incomes below the poverty line is nearly four times greater than that of whites.

When the Negro child reaches working age, he finds that America offers him significantly less than it offers his white counterpart. For Negro adults, the unemployment rate is twice that of whites, and the unemployment rate for Negro teenagers is nearly three times that of white teenagers. A Negro male who completes four years of college can expect a median annual income of merely $110 more than a white male who has only a high school diploma. Although Negroes represent 11.5 percent of the population, they are only 1.2 percent of the lawyers and judges, 2 percent of the physicians, 2.3 percent of the dentists, 1.1 percent of the engineers and 2.6 percent of the college and university professors.

The relationship between those figures and the history of unequal treatment afforded to the Negro cannot be denied. At every point from birth to death the impact of the past is reflected in the still disfavored position of the Negro.

In the light of the sorry history of discrimination and its devastating impact on the lives of Negroes, bringing the Negro into the mainstream of American life should be a state interest of the highest order. To fail to do so is to ensure that America will forever remain a divided society.

While I applaud the judgment of the Court that a university may consider race in its admissions process, it is more than a little ironic that, after several hundred years of class-based discrimination against Negroes, the Court is unwilling to hold that a class-based remedy for that discrimination is permissible. In declining to so hold, today's judgment ignores the fact that for several hundred years Negroes have been discriminated against, not as individuals, but rather solely because of the color of their skins. . . . These differences in the experience of the Negro make it difficult for me to accept that Negroes cannot be afforded greater protection under the Fourteenth Amendment where it is necessary to remedy the effects of past discrimination. . . .

It is because of a legacy of unequal treatment that we must permit the institutions of this society to give consideration to race in making decisions about who will hold the positions of influence, affluence, and prestige in America.

The impact of *Bakke* is not clear. First, the decision had *two* plurality opinions. In the first, Justice Powell was joined by four other justices to hold that the special admissions program violated the 14th Amendment. The second plurality, consisting of Justices Powell, Brennan, White, Marshall and Blackmun, held that race might be used as a "plus" in a particular admissions program. Several separate opinions muddy the waters even more.

Second, later cases indicate that *Bakke* might be restricted to the special facts found in that case, specifically, an affirmative action plan required by *state action.* For example, a 1980 decision held that a Congressional Act requiring that 10 percent of federally supported public works contracts go to minority-owned businesses was constitutionally permitted.* Similarly, a 1979 decision held that a private, voluntary, affirmative action program imposed by a collective-bargaining agreement did not violate either the Constitution or the federal Civil Rights Act of 1964.**

Overview of Federal Civil Rights Legislation

The first federal civil rights act was passed in 1866, even before the 14th Amendment was ratified, in response to the so-called Black Codes passed in some states which imposed restrictions on blacks just short of formal slavery. The Act, already discussed in *Shelley* v. *Kraemer,* also provided criminal penalties against depriving persons of their rights "under color of law." Additional civil rights legislation, aimed primarily at the Ku Klux Klan, was passed in 1870, 1871, and 1875, and outlawed threats and intimidation. Both civil and criminal penalties were provided. Most of those laws remain on the books, and the 1866 Act continues to be a prime source of litigation. That Act is simple in form and contains no exceptions, as contrasted with later federal acts.

After the Reconstruction legislation, there was little activity in the area of civil rights until 1957. In that year the federal Voting Rights Act was passed, to be amended in 1960. Another Voting Rights Act was passed in 1965 to expand the rights granted by the earlier laws.

Perhaps the most ambitious federal law was the Civil Rights Act of 1964, an omnibus law that deals with discrimination in employment, public accommodations,

---

Fullilove v. *Klutznick,* 448 U.S. 448, 100 S. Ct. 2758, 65 L. Ed. 2d 902 (1980).

**United Steelworkers of America* v. *Weber,* p. 580.

federally assisted programs, public facilities, and public education. The Act was originally concerned with discrimination on the basis of race, color, religion, or national origin. In 1972, the Equal Employment Opportunity Act amended the Act to add "sex" to the list of prohibited categories. Another ambitious law, the Civil Rights Act of 1968, prohibited discrimination in the sale or rental of housing. The law contained numerous exemptions and, as a result, most housing discrimination cases are brought under the Civil Rights Act of 1866.

In 1963, Congress passed the Equal Pay Act as an amendment to the Fair Labor Standards Act. That law prohibits employers from making sex-based wage differentials for similar work. The Age Discrimination in Employment Act (ADEA) of 1967 prohibits some discrimination based on age, the Rehabilitation Act of 1973 prohibits discrimination in federal projects based on handicap, and the Pregnancy Discrimination Act of 1978 prohibits employment discrimination based on pregnancy.

Federal law generally regulates discrimination in six areas: employment, housing, public accommodations, credit, voting rights, and education.

Discrimination in Employment

The principal legislation dealing with discrimination in employment is found in Title VII of the Civil Rights Act of 1964, as amended by the Equal Employment Opportunity Act of 1972. Additional laws are found in the Equal Pay Act, the Age Discrimination in Employment Act, the Rehabilitation Act, and the Pregnancy Discrimination Act of 1978.

Title VII of the Civil Rights Act of 1964

The 1964 Civil Rights Act devoted an entire section, or "Title" to the problems of discrimination in employment. The Act created the concept of "unlawful employment practices," or categories of prohibited discriminatory acts, and established a new independent regulatory commission, the Equal Employment Opportunity Commission, to administer the Act. The Act also prohibited discrimination in federal employment or in federally related projects.

Coverage of the Act and Exemptions   Title VII covers employers, employment agencies, and labor organizations, all as defined in the Act. An *employer* is defined as a person engaged in an "industry affecting commerce," who has fifteen or more employees for each working day in each of twenty or more calendar weeks in the current or preceding year. An *employment agency* is defined as any person undertaking to procure employees for an employer, as defined in the Act, with or without compensation. A *labor organization* is defined as a labor organization in an industry affecting commerce, organized for the traditional purposes of such labor organizations, such as collective bargaining. The Act does not apply to employers employing aliens outside of the United States, religious groups, religious educational institutions, or religious societies.

Unlawful Employment Practices   The Act prohibits discrimination on the basis of *race, color, religion, sex,* or *national origin,* and specifies six different types of unlawful employment practices:

1. for an *employer* to fail or refuse to hire or to discharge any individual, or to otherwise discriminate in the "compensation, terms, conditions or privileges of employment" on the basis of any of the prohibited categories, or to limit, segregate or classify employees or applicants for employment in any way which would tend to deprive an individual of employment opportunities or "otherwise adversely affect his status as an employee;"

2. for an *employment agency* to fail or refuse to refer for employment, or to otherwise discriminate against individuals because of the prohibited categories;

3. for a *labor organization* to exclude or expel from membership, or to otherwise discriminate against an individual, or to limit, segregate or classify members or applicants, on the basis of any of the prohibited categories;

4. for an *employer, labor organization,* or *joint labor-management committee* to discriminate against any individual in any apprenticeship or training program on the basis of the prohibited categories;

5. for an *employer, labor organization,* or *joint labor-management committee* to discriminate against an individual in any way because the individual has opposed any practice, made an unlawful employment practice, or because the individual has made a charge, testified or assisted in any Title VII proceeding;

6. for an *employer, labor organization,* or *joint labor-management committee* to print or publish any advertisement indicating any preference based on the prohibited categories.

The Act contains several exceptions from these six categories, however. Classification on the basis of *religion, sex* or *national origin* (but not race or color) is permissible if religion, sex, or national origin is a "*bona fide occupational qualification* (bfoq) reasonably necessary to the normal operation of that particular business or enterprise." Schools and universities affiliated with religious groups may restrict hiring to persons of that particular religion. Discrimination against communists and other subversives is permitted, and employers need not shelve "national security" requirements because of the Act. Employers may establish different compensation systems for persons who work in different parts of the country. The Act expressly *permits* affirmative action plans in favor of native Americans, but does not *require* affirmative action or quota plans in any instance.

The Equal Employment Opportunity Commission (EEOC)   Title VII created the Equal Employment Opportunity Commission, a five-member independent regulatory commission. Members are appointed by the President for staggered five-year terms. No more than three members may be from the same political party. The EEOC is charged with enforcement of Title VII, and also may establish guidelines for equal employment (see Figure 5-2).

Charges may be brought before the EEOC by any person, and notice is to be served within ten days on the party charged. The Commission must investigate the charge, and if it finds "reasonable cause" to believe a violation has occurred, it must attempt conciliation of the dispute by informal methods. If such informal methods are unsuccessful, the EEOC may refer the case to the Attorney General, in the case of a charge against a unit of government, or may bring a civil action in federal court in its own name against private parties. The courts have jurisdiction in such cases to issue injunctions, order reinstatement or hiring, order payment of back pay, and may grant any other equitable relief. If the EEOC fails to act within 180 days, private parties may sue in their own names.

The Definitions of Discrimination While Title VII generally makes discrimination in employment illegal, the Act does not define the term *discrimination*. In the relatively short history of Title VII, the courts have supplied two different meanings for the term. The first, called **disparate treatment,** involves overtly different treatment of individuals because of race, color, religion, sex, or national origin. The second, called **disproportionate impact,** involves employment policies which are neutral on their face, but which have a different impact on members of the protected categories.

Disparate Treatment: Discrimination clearly includes employment policies expressly based on race, color, religion, sex, or national origin, such as a company policy refusing to hire members of a particular minority. Most of the controversy in the area of that sort of disparate treatment has involved what the party alleging discrimination must prove. It is clearly not enough simply to prove that an individual is a member of a minority, and that the individual did not get a job. The following case provides some guidelines as to what else must be proved.

Furnco Construction Company v. Waters

438 U.S. 567, 98 S. Ct. 2943, 57 L. Ed. 2d 957 (1978)

Furnco was in the business of relining blast furnaces with "firebrick," a rather delicate and critical job. The company did not maintain a permanent work force, but rather hired a superintendent for a specific job and delegated the task of obtaining a competent work force to the superintendent. In 1971, Furnco made a contract to reline one of Interlake's blast furnaces. The superintendent assigned to the job hired bricklayers whom he knew to be competent or who were referred to him by others in the trade. During the Interlake job, approximately 45 bricklayers were hired at various times, 10 of whom were black. Of the total 1,819 man-days worked on the job, 13.3 percent were worked by black bricklayers. Evidence also showed that 5.7 percent of the qualified bricklayers in the relevant labor force were black.

Three black bricklayers came to the Interlake plant gate requesting employment. They were informed that no hiring was being done at the gate, and were denied employment. One of the three was subsequently hired on the recommendation of someone in the trade, but not until very late in the job. No one, white or black, was hired at the plant gate. The three bricklayers brought this action through the EEOC, charging discrimination on the basis of race under Title VII. The District Court found that the applicants had failed to prove a case of discrimination. The Court of Appeals reversed on the basis of the Supreme Court's decision in *McDonnell Douglas* v. *Green,** which held

---

*411 U.S. 792, 93 S. Ct. 1817, 36 L. Ed. 2d 668 (1973).

The complainant in a Title VII trial must carry the initial burden under the statute of establishing a prima facie case of racial discrimination. This may be done by showing (i) that he belongs to a racial minority; (ii) that he applied and was qualified for a job for which the employer was seeking applicants; (iii) that, despite his qualifications, he was rejected; and (iv) that, after his rejection, the position remained open and the employer continued to seek applicants from persons of complainant's qualifications. . . . The burden then must shift to the employer to articulate some legitimate, nondiscriminatory reason for the employee's rejection. . . . [The applicant must be] afforded a fair opportunity to show that [the employer's] stated reason for . . . rejection was in fact pretext.

The employer appealed, and the Supreme Court granted certiorari.

Mr. Justice REHNQUIST delivered the opinion of the Court. . . .

. . . The Court of Appeals was justified in concluding that as a matter of law respondents made out a prima facie case of discrimination under *McDonnell Douglas*. . . .

We think the Court of Appeals went awry, however, in apparently equating a prima facie showing under *McDonnell Douglas* with an ultimate finding of fact as to discriminatory refusal to hire under Title VII; the two are quite different and that difference has a direct bearing on the proper resolution of this case. The Court of Appeals . . . thought Furnco's hiring procedures not only must be reasonably related to the achievement of some legitimate purpose, but also must be the method which allows the employer to consider the qualifications of the largest number of minority applicants. We think the imposition of that second requirement simply finds no support either in the nature of the prima facie case or the purpose of Title VII.

. . . A prima facie case under *McDonnell Douglas* raises an inference of discrimination. . . . because we presume these acts, if otherwise unexplained, are more likely than not based on the consideration of impermissible factors. And we are willing to presume this largely because we know from our experience that more often than not people do not act in a totally arbitrary manner, without any underlying reasons, especially in a business setting. Thus, when all legitimate reasons for rejecting an applicant have been eliminated as possible reasons for the employer's actions, it is more likely than not the employer, who we generally assume acts only with *some* reason, based his decision on an impermissible consideration such as race.

When the prima facie case is understood in the light of the opinion in *McDonnell Douglas,* it is apparent that the burden which shifts to the employer is merely that of proving that he based his employment decision on a legitimate consideration, and not an illegitimate one such as race. To prove that, he need not prove that he pursued the course which would both enable him to achieve his own business goal *and* allow him to consider the *most* employment applications. Title VII prohibits him from having as a goal a work force selected by any proscribed discriminatory practice, but it does not impose a duty to adopt a hiring procedure that maximizes hiring of minority employees. To dispel the adverse inference from a prima facie showing under *McDonnell Douglas,* the employer need only "articulate some legitimate, nondiscriminatory reason for the employee's rejection." . . .

This is not to say, of course, that proof of a justification which is reasonably related to the achievement of some legitimate goal necessarily ends the inquiry. The plaintiff must be given the opportunity to introduce evidence that the proffered justification is merely a pretext for discrimination. And as we noted in *McDonnell Douglas,* this evidence might take a variety of forms. . . . [T]he employer must be allowed some latitude to introduce evidence which bears on his motive. Proof that his work force was racially balanced or that it contained a disproportionately high percentage of minority employees is not wholly irrelevant on the issue of intent. . . . Thus . . . in this case such proof neither was nor could have been sufficient to *conclusively* demonstrate that Furnco's actions were not discriminatorily motivated, the District Court was entitled to *consider* the racial mix of the work force when trying to make the determination as to motivation. . . .

The judgment of the Court of Appeals is reversed. . . .

A separate opinion by Justice MARSHALL, joined by Justice BRENNAN, concurring in part and dissenting in part, has been omitted.

Later decisions by the Court make it clear that the employer need not *prove* that its reasons for not hiring the applicant were legitimate and nondiscriminatory. The employer need only *articulate* such reasons, and then the burden shifts back to the applicant to show that the reasons were a pretext.

Neutral Employment Policies and Disproportionate Impact: Employment policies which are neutral on their face may have a **disproportionate impact** on certain groups of individuals. For example, a requirement that all employees must have a college education is neutral on its face, but obviously a smaller proportion of many minority groups have a college education than does the white majority. The issue then must become whether the requirement of a college education is related to the employment requirements necessary for the job involved. If so, even though the requirement has a disproportionate impact on minorities, the employment practice is permissible. If not, the practice may be discriminatory. Title VII considers the problems of tests and testing for employment at length.

The Act specifically provides that it is not an unlawful employment practice

> for an employer to give and act upon the results of any professionally developed ability test provided that such test, its administration or action upon the test is not designed, intended or used to discriminate. . . .

Griggs v. Duke Power Co.

401 U.S. 424, 91 S. Ct. 849, 28 L. Ed. 2d 158 (1971)

> Mr. Chief Justice BURGER delivered the opinion of the Court.
>
> We granted the writ in this case to resolve the question of whether an employer is prohibited by the Civil Rights Act of 1964, Title VII, from requiring a high school education or passing of a standardized general intelligence test as a condition of employment in or transfer to jobs when (a) neither standard is shown to be significantly related to successful job performance, (b) both requirements operate to disqualify Negroes at a substantially higher rate than white applicants, and (c) the jobs in question formerly had been filled only by white employees as part of a longstanding practice of giving preference to whites. . . .

Duke Power had previously maintained an openly discriminatory hiring and promotion policy, but in 1955 that policy was rescinded and replaced by a requirement of a high school diploma for all but the lowest paying jobs. On the date that Title VII went into effect in 1965, the company added a requirement that persons for any but the lowest paying jobs must also pass a standardized intelligence test. The company employed 95 persons, 14 of whom were black. All of the black employees worked in the Labor Division, the lowest paid area. None of the standardized tests used was directed or intended to measure the ability to learn a particular job. The District Court and the Court of Appeals ruled against the employees, and they appealed.

> The objective of Congress in the enactment of Title VII . . . was to achieve equality of employment opportunities and remove barriers that have operated in the past to favor an identifiable group of white employees over other employees. Under the Act, practices, procedures, or tests neutral on their face, and even neutral in terms of intent, cannot be maintained if they operate to "freeze" the status quo of prior discriminatory employment practices. . . .

. . . Because they are Negroes, petitioners have long received inferior education in segregated schools . . . . Congress did not intend by Title VII, however, to guarantee a job to every person regardless of qualifications. In short, the Act does not command that any person be hired simply because he was formerly the subject of discrimination, or because he is a member of a minority group. Discriminatory preference for any group, minority or majority, is precisely and only what Congress has proscribed. What is required by Congress is the removal of artificial, arbitrary, and unnecessary barriers to employment when the barriers operate invidiously to discriminate on the basis of racial or other impermissible classification.

. . . The Act proscribes not only overt discrimination but also practices that are fair in form, but discriminatory in operation. The touchstone is business necessity. If an employment practice which operates to exclude Negroes cannot be shown to be related to job performance, the practice is prohibited.

On the record before us, neither the high school completion requirement nor the general intelligence test is shown to bear a demonstrable relationship to successful performance of the jobs for which it was used. Both were adopted . . . without meaningful study of their relationship to job-performance ability. Rather, a vice-president of the Company testified, the requirements were instituted on the Company's judgment that they generally would improve the overall quality of the work force.

The evidence, however, shows that employees who have not completed high school or taken the tests have continued to perform satisfactorily. . . .

The Court of Appeals held that the Company had adopted the diploma and test requirements without any intention to discriminate against Negro employees. . . . [B]ut good intent or absence of discriminatory intent does not redeem employment procedures or testing mechanisms that operate as "built-in headwinds" for minority groups and are unrelated to measuring job capability. . . .

Nothing in the Act precludes the use of testing or measuring procedures; obviously they are useful. What Congress has forbidden is giving these devices and mechanisms controlling force unless they are demonstrably a reasonable measure of job performance. Congress has not commanded that the less qualified be preferred over the better qualified because of minority origins. Far from disparaging job qualifications as such, Congress has made such qualifications the controlling factor, so that race, religion, nationality, and sex become irrelevant. What Congress has commanded is that any tests must measure for the job and not the person in the abstract.

The judgment of the Court of Appeals is . . . reversed.

The Problem of Bona Fide Occupational Qualifications Title VII specifically permits discrimination on the basis of national origin, sex, or religion, if the classification is a "bona fide occupational qualification" or **bfoq.** The Act does *not* provide a bfoq exception in the case of race or color.

It is of course the exceptional situation in which even national origin, sex, or religion is a bfoq. Obviously Catholic priests must be Catholic, rabbis must be Jewish, and ministers must be members of the churches in which they serve. But aside from such obvious situations, the bfoq exception has been very narrowly construed by the Courts.

Dothard v. Rawlinson

433 U.S. 321, 97 S. Ct. 2720, 53 L. Ed. 2d 786 (1977)

Plaintiff, a woman, desired to be considered for a position as a correctional counselor in male maximum-security prisons in Alabama. The Alabama Board of Corrections adopted a rule forbidding women to be employed in "contact" positions, that is, positions requiring close physical proximity to inmates. Ms. Rawlinson filed this action under Title VII, and the District Court held that sex was not a bona fide occupational qualification under the Act. The Court of Appeals affirmed, and the Board appealed.

Mr. Justice STEWART delivered the opinion of the Court. . . .

Unlike . . . statutory height and weight requirements, [the Regulation] explicitly discriminates against women on the basis of their sex. In defense of this overt discrimination, the appellants rely on §703(e) of Title VII which permits sex-based discrimination "in those certain instances where . . . sex . . . is a bona fide occupational qualification reasonably necessary to the normal operation of that particular business or enterprise."

The District Court rejected the bona-fide-occupational-qualification (bfoq) defense, relying on the virtually uniform view of the federal courts that §703(e) provides only the narrowest of exceptions to the general rule requiring equality of employment opportunities. This view has been variously formulated. . . . But whatever the verbal formulation, the federal courts have agreed that it is impermissible under Title VII to refuse to hire an individual woman or man on the basis of stereotyped characterizations of the sexes, and the District Court . . . held that [the regulation] is based on just such stereotypical assumptions.

We are persuaded—by the restrictive language of §703(e), the relevant legislative history, and the consistent interpretation of the Equal Employment Opportunity Commission—that the bfoq exception was in fact meant to be an extremely narrow exception to the general prohibition of discrimination on the basis of sex. In the particular factual circumstances of this case, however, we conclude that the District Court erred in rejecting the State's contention that [the regulation] falls within the narrow ambit of the bfoq exception.

The environment of Alabama's penitentiaries is a peculiarly inhospitable one for human beings of whatever sex. Indeed, a Federal District Court has held that the conditions of confinement in the prisons of the State, characterized by "rampant violence" and a "jungle atmosphere" are constitutionally impermissible. . . . [T]he estimated 20 percent of the male prisoners who are sex offenders are scattered throughout the penitentiaries' dormitory facilities.

In this environment of violence and disorganization, it would be an oversimplification to characterize [the regulation] as an exercise in "romantic paternalism . . . " In the usual case, the argument that a particular job is too dangerous for women may appropriately be met by the rejoinder that it is the purpose of Title VII to allow the individual woman to make the choice for herself. More is at stake in this case, however, than an individual woman's decision to weigh and accept the risks of employment in a "contact" position in a maximum-security male prison.

The essence of a correctional counselor's job is to maintain security. A woman's relative ability to maintain order in a male, maximum security, unclassified penitentiary of the type Alabama now runs could be directly reduced by her womanhood. There is a basis in fact for expecting that sex offenders who have criminally assaulted women in the past would be moved to do so again if access to women were established within the prison. There would also be a real risk that other inmates, deprived of a normal heterosexual environment, would assault women guards because they were women. . . . The likelihood that inmates would assault a woman because she was a woman would pose a real threat not only to the victim of the assault but also to the basic control of the penitentiary and protection of its inmates and the other security personnel. . . .

Reversed.

Mr. Justice MARSHALL, with whom Mr. Justice BRENNAN joins, concurring in part and dissenting in part. . . .

With all respects, this rationale regrettably perpetuates one of the most insidious of the old myths about women—that women, wittingly or not, are seductive sexual objects. . . . The effect of the decision . . . is to punish women because their very presence might provoke sexual assaults. It is women who are made to pay the price in lost job opportunities for the threat of depraved conduct by male prison inmates. Once again, "[t]he pedestal upon which women have been placed has . . . upon closer inspection, been revealed as a cage." . . .

The proper response to inevitable attacks on both female and male guards is not to limit the employment opportunities of law-abiding women who wish to contribute to their community, but to take swift and sure punitive action against the inmate offenders. . . . To deprive women of job opportunities because of the threatened behavior of convicted criminals is to turn our social priorities upside down.

Although I do not countenance the sex discrimination condoned by the majority, it is fortunate that the Court's decision is carefully limited to the facts before it. I trust the lower courts will recognize that the decision was impelled by the shockingly inhuman conditions in the Alabama prisons, and thus that the "extremely narrow [bfoq] exceptions" . . . will not be allowed "to swallow the rule" against sex discrimination. Expansion of today's decision beyond its narrow factual basis would erect a serious roadblock to economic equality for women.

Bakke Revisited: Affirmative Action Under Title VII   The language of Title VII, particularly the words used in Sections 703(a) and (d), seem on their face to prohibit *any* type of discrimination in employment based on race, color, religion, sex, or national origin. Those sections could be construed to also prohibit private, voluntary, affirmative action plans by employers or by employers and unions working together. In 1979, the Supreme Court faced that issue and came to a result contrary to that obtained in the *Bakke* decision of the previous year. In reading the following decision, it is important to remember that *Bakke* involved *state action* by an arm of the California state government.

United Steelworkers of America v. Weber

443 U.S. 193, 99 S. Ct. 2721, 61 L. Ed. 2d 480 (1979)

In 1974, the United Steelworkers of America (USWA) entered into a master collective bargaining agreement with Kaiser Aluminum and Chemical Corp. (Kaiser), covering employment at fifteen Kaiser plants. The agreement contained an affirmative action plan designed to eliminate racial imbalances in Kaiser's then almost exclusively white craftwork labor force. The plan established goals for hiring blacks into the craft trades based on the percentage of blacks in the respective local labor forces. On-the-job training programs for unskilled workers—both black and white—were established to train people for the skilled craft trades, and 50 percent of the spots in such programs were reserved for blacks.

In Kaiser's Gramercy, Louisiana, plant, only 1.83 percent of the skilled craftworkers were black, even though the work force was approximately 39 percent black. In the first year of the plan, thirteen craft trainees were selected from the Gramercy work force. Seven were black and six white, but the most senior black selected for the program had less seniority than several white production workers whose bids for admission were rejected. One of those white workers, Brian Weber, brought this class action in federal court, claiming that the program violated Title VII of the Civil Rights Act of 1964. The District Court held the plan violated Title VII and granted an injunction against Kaiser and the USWA "from denying the plaintiffs, Brian F. Weber and all other members of the class, access to on-the-job training programs on the basis of race." The Court of Appeals affirmed, holding that "all employment preferences based upon race, including those preferences incidental to bona fide affirmative action plans, violated Title VII's prohibition against racial discrimination in employment." Kaiser and the USWA appealed to the Supreme Court.

Mr. Justice BRENNAN delivered the opinion of the Court.

. . . .

We emphasize at the outset the narrowness of our inquiry. Since the Kaiser-USWA plan does not involve state action, this case does not present an alleged violation of the Equal Protection Clause of the Fourteenth Amendment. Further, since the Kaiser-USWA plan was adopted voluntarily, we are not concerned with what Title VII requires or with what a court might order to remedy a past proved violation of the Act. The only question before us is the narrow statutory issue of whether Title VII *forbids* private employers and unions from voluntarily agreeing upon bona fide affirmative action plans that accord racial preferences in the manner and for the purpose provided in the Kaiser-USWA plan. . . .

Respondent argues that Congress intended in Title VII to prohibit all race-conscious affirmative action plans. Respondent's argument rests upon a literal interpretation of §§703(a) and (d) of the Act. Those sections make it unlawful to "discriminate . . . because of . . . race" in hiring and in the selection of apprentices for training programs. . . .

Respondent's argument is not without force. But it overlooks the significance of that fact that the Kaiser-USWA plan is an affirmative action plan voluntarily adopted by private parties to eliminate traditional patterns of racial segregation. In this context respondent's reliance upon a literal construction of §§703(a) and (d) . . . is misplaced. . . . It is a "familiar rule, that a thing may be within the letter of the statute, and yet not within the statute, because not within its spirit, nor within the intention of its makers." . . . The prohibition against racial discrimination in §§703(a) and (d) of Title VII must therefore be read against the background of the legislative history of Title VII and the historical context from which the Act arose. Examination of those sources makes clear that an interpretation of the sections that forbade all race-conscious affirmative action would "bring about an end completely at variance with the purpose of the statute" and must be rejected.

Congress' primary concern in enacting the prohibition against racial discrimination in Title VII of the Civil Rights Act of 1964 was with "the plight of the Negro in our economy." Before 1964, blacks were largely relegated to "unskilled and semi-skilled jobs." Because of automation the number of such jobs was rapidly decreasing. As a consequence, "the relative position of the Negro worker [was] steadily worsening."

Congress feared that the goals of the Civil Rights Act—the integration of blacks into the mainstream of American society—could not be achieved unless this trend was reversed. And Congress recognized that that would not be possible unless blacks were able to secure jobs "which have a future." . . . Accordingly, it was clear to Congress that "[t]he crux of the problem [was] to open employment opportunities for Negroes in occupations which have been traditionally closed to them," and it was to this problem that Title VII's prohibition against racial discrimination in employment was primarily addressed.

. . . .

Given this legislative history, we cannot agree with respondent that Congress intended to prohibit the private sector from taking effective steps to accomplish the goal that Congress designed Title VII to achieve. The very statutory words intended as a spur or catalyst to cause "employers and unions to self-examine and to self-evaluate their employment practices and to endeavor to eliminate, so far as possible, the last vestiges of an unfortunate and ignominious page in this country's history," . . . cannot be interpreted as an absolute prohibition against all private, voluntary, race-conscious affirmative action efforts to hasten the elimination of such vestiges. It would be ironic indeed if a law triggered by a Nation's concern over centuries of racial injustice and intended to improve the lot of those who had "been excluded from the American dream for so long," constituted the first legislative prohibition of all voluntary, private, race-conscious efforts to abolish traditional patterns of racial segregation and hierarchy.

. . . .

We therefore hold that Title VII's prohibition in §§703(a) and (d) against racial discrimination does not condemn all private, voluntary, race-conscious affirmative action plans.

. . . .

Reversed.

Equal Pay Act of 1963

The first modern statute to consider gender-based discrimination was the Equal Pay Act of 1963, which generally prohibited differentials in pay between employees of different sexes performing "equal work." That statute was discussed in Chapter 14.

Age Discrimination in Employment Act

The Age Discrimination in Employment Act (ADEA), passed in 1967 and amended in 1974 and 1978, generally follows the form of Title VII, including its applicability to employers, labor organizations, and employment agencies, and generally prohibits the same types of discrimination as prohibited by Title VII. The prohibitions against discrimination are limited to individuals between the ages of 40 and 70, however. Mandatory retirement before 70 is generally banned, but is permitted at 65 if the individual is employed in a "bona fide executive or a high policy-making position" and will obtain a pension or other deferred compensation benefits of at least $27,000 per year. The Act also contains a bfoq exception identical to that found in Title VII. The Act is administered by the EEOC.

The Rehabilitation Act of 1973

The Rehabilitation Act of 1973 protects handicapped individuals from discrimination in two instances: (1) the Act requires "affirmative action" to hire the handicapped if a firm has a federal contract over $2,500; and (2) the law prohibits discrimination against the handicapped in federal grants and programs. The term *handicapped* includes both physical and mental impairments, but alcoholism and drug abuse are specifically excepted. All remedies provided by Title VII are available.

The Pregnancy Discrimination Act of 1978

In 1978, Congress amended Title VII to further define sex discrimination to include discrimination on account of pregnancy. The amendment provided that "women affected by pregnancy, childbirth, or related medical conditions shall be treated the same for all employment-related purposes, including receipt of benefits under fringe benefit programs, as other persons not so affected but similar in their ability or inability to work. . . . " The total impact of that law has not yet been assessed, particularly in problems relating to abortion, health insurance, and *paternity* leave.

Executive Order 11246

In the unlikely event an employer is not covered by Title VII, the firm may well be covered under Executive Order 11246, issued by President Johnson in 1965. That order requires all employers involved in federal contracts or in any employment situation involving federal funds not to discriminate in employment, to seek out qualified applicants from disadvantaged groups, to provide special training to members of such groups, and to hire preferentially from minority groups if qualifications of applicants are roughly equal. The Order may also apply to firms that deal with firms with government contracts.

Executive Order 4 and Affirmative Action

Executive Order 4, issued by President Nixon in 1971, is the basis of most affirmative action programs in employment. Any firm with a nonconstruction contract with the federal government must file a written affirmative action program with the Office of Federal Contract Compliance. That program must contain a statement of good-faith efforts to achieve equal employment opportunity, an analysis of deficiencies in the use of minorities, and a timetable for correcting such deficiencies. Failure to develop such a program can lead to cancellation of existing contracts and elimination from consideration for future contracts.

Discrimination in Housing

The first American "fair housing act" was the Civil Rights Act of 1866, commonly known as *Section 1982*. Because of the state action doctrine discussed in *Shelley* v. *Kraemer,* Section 1982 was not applied to *private* discrimination in housing after 1883. Finally, in 1968, the Supreme Court reversed that doctrine in *Jones* v. *Alfred H. Mayer,* quoted earlier, and applied Section 1982 to private acts of discrimination in housing.

Because the terms of Section 1982 are extremely broad, and because the Act contains no exceptions and is enforced by private suits brought in federal court, many housing discrimination actions continue to be brought under its terms.

The Civil Rights Act of 1968

Exactly one week after the assassination of Dr. Martin Luther King and only a few weeks before the Supreme Court's decision in *Jones* v. *Mayer,* Congress passed the Civil Rights Act of 1968, also known as the Federal Fair Housing Act. The law became Title VIII of the 1964 Civil Rights Act. The statute is a comprehensive attempt to end private discrimination in housing and related fields.

Unlawful Housing Practices   The Civil Rights Act of 1968 was originally concerned with four of the five "prohibited categories" found in the 1964 Act, those of *race, color, religion,* and *national origin.* The Act was applied to *sex* discrimination in 1974. Illegal practices include

1. Refusal to sell, rent or negotiate, on the basis of the prohibited categories;

2. Discrimination in the terms, conditions, or privileges of sale or rental;

3. Advertising a preference or limitation based on the prohibited categories;

4. Falsely representing that a dwelling is unavailable because of the prohibited categories (sometimes called **steering**);

5. Inducing a person to sell or rent by making representations concerning the entry of persons of a particular race, color, religion, or national origin into an area (called **blockbusting**);

6. Denying loans or discriminating in their terms because of the prohibited categories; and

7. Denying real estate broker's services or membership in broker's organizations because of the prohibited categories.

Exceptions from Coverage   The Act contains several exceptions. Generally, the law does not apply to an owner who sells his or her own home, but that exception does not apply if:

1. The owner owns or has an interest in three or more properties at the time;

2. The owner uses a broker in the transaction;

3. The owner advertises a preference; or

4. The owner does not reside in the home and is not the most recent resident in the home, the exemption may only apply once in a 24-month period.

The Act also does not apply in rental situations if the rental property contains four or fewer units and the owner resides in one unit. Discrimination *in favor* of members of a particular religion is permitted in the case of housing operated by religious organizations.

Enforcement and Remedies   Persons injured by a practice made unlawful under the Act may file a complaint with the Secretary of Housing and Urban Development (HUD). HUD is required to send a copy of the complaint to the person charged and must investigate the charge. After the investigation, HUD may attempt private conciliation or refer the case to the U.S. Attorney General. Legal action must commence within 180 days. If HUD decides not to proceed, the person injured may file a lawsuit within 180 days as well. Courts may grant injunctive relief, award compensatory damages, and grant punitive damages up to $1,000, together with attorney's fees and costs.

Relationship to Section 1982   The relatively complex enforcement procedures and the numerous exemptions found in the 1968 Act are not found in the simple provisions of Section 1982. While Section 1982 only relates to racial discrimination, parties injured by that type of discrimination usually have a choice between Section 1982 and the 1968 Act. As a result, many housing discrimination cases are brought under Section 1982.

State and Local Fair Housing Laws   In addition to Section 1982 and the 1968 Act, many states and some local governments have enacted fair housing statutes or ordinances. Often those statutes parallel the terms of the 1968 Act, but occasionally the terms of those statutes or ordinances are broader and include other categories of discrimination, including marital status, age, and handicap.

Discrimination in Public Accommodations

Title II of the Civil Rights Act of 1964, generally known as the *Public Accommodations* section, generally prohibits discrimination between customers of certain businesses. Title III of the Act also protects "equal utilization of any public facility," such as public parks and beaches. The constitutionality of Title II was established in the *Heart of Atlanta Motel* decision discussed in Chapter 2 (p. 54).

The public accommodations section was probably the most controversial aspect of the Civil Rights Act of 1964. Opponents of the law argued that private businesses ought to be able to sell to whomever they chose as an incident to the right to own private property, that the law was an attempt to legislate morality, and constituted an unwarranted extension of government power. Proponents of the bill argued that racial discrimination is the link between personal prejudice and segregation, that businesses are in business to make money, and that it should make no difference whether that money comes from a black or a white customer. Proponents argued that the right to own property is never absolute and is subject to other restrictions, such as zoning laws or licensing requirements, and that Title II is simply another such restriction.

Forbidden Discrimination and Coverage of the Law

The principal section of Title II provides that

> All persons shall be entitled to the full and equal enjoyment of the goods, services, facilities, privileges, advantages, and accommodations of any place of public accommodation, as defined in this section, without discrimination or segregation on the ground of race, color, religion or national origin.

Four categories of establishments were specifically made "places of public accommodation" under the Act: (1) inns, hotels, motels, or other lodging establishments with more than five rooms for rent; (2) restaurants and gasoline stations; (3) motion picture theaters, concert halls, sports arenas, and stadiums; and (4) any establishment physically located within the premises of any establishment covered by the Act that holds itself out as serving patrons of such covered establishment. All such establishments must "affect commerce" under the Commerce Clause, though under *Heart of Atlanta Motel,* the amount of contact with interstate commerce may be quite minimal. Discrimination supported by state action is also forbidden. The Act expressly exempts action by a "private club or other establishment not in fact open to the public."

Remedies and Enforcement

The Act permits actions for injunctions by either private persons aggrieved by a violation, or by the U.S. Attorney General in the case of persons "engaged in a pattern or practice of resistance to the full enjoyment of any of the rights" established by the Act. Attorneys' fees and costs may be assessed against a violator. The Act does not provide for damages, though damages may be available under state law. Actions under Section 1982 are also possible, and damages are available under that section. The court may refer cases brought under Title II to the *Community Relations Service* to obtain voluntary compliance prior to issuing an injunction. The Community Relations Service was established by the Civil Rights Act as a mediation and conciliation body.

Discrimination in Credit

As noted in Chapter 12, the Equal Credit Opportunity Act of 1974 prohibits discrimination in giving credit on the basis of *race, creed, color, religion, age, national origin, income derived from public assistance, sex,* or *marital status.* In addition, the Civil Rights Act of 1968 prohibits lenders from discriminating in real estate loans because of race, color, religion, or national origin.

Many of the regulatory agencies charged with overseeing the various financial institutions in the country have also adopted rules, guidelines, and regulations requiring equal credit opportunity. For example, the Federal Home Loan Bank Board requires that federally chartered savings and loan associations evaluate "each loan applicant's credit worthiness . . . on an individual basis without reference to presumed characteristics of a group." (38 Fed. Reg. 34653 (1973).) Other regulations were issued to specifically discourage the discounting of a working wife's income. Similar regulations restricting various types of discrimination have been issued by the Federal Housing Authority (FHA), the Veteran's Administration (VA), the Federal Deposit Insurance Corporation (FDIC), the Federal National Mortgage Association (FNMA), the Federal Home Loan Mortgage Corporation (FHLMC), and others.

Several states have also passed statutes prohibiting discrimination in the granting of credit, though the "prohibited categories" vary between states. Many such statutes specifically permit creditors to consider an applicant's ability to repay, but prohibit consideration of other factors.

Discrimination in Voting Rights

The 15th Amendment to the Constitution, adopted in 1868, simply stated that the right to vote may not be denied or abridged "on account of race, color, or previous condition of servitude." The 19th Amendment, adopted in 1920, prohibited the denial or abridgment of the right to vote on account of sex. Both laws provide that Congress may enact legislation to protect those rights.

The 15th Amendment was not popular, as shown by the rapid growth of secret bands of whites bent on dissuading blacks from voting, including the Regulators, the Jayhawkers, the Knights of the White Camelia, and of course the Ku Klux Klan. Some states adopted legislation that effectively disenfranchised blacks as well, such as *literacy requirements* and *poll taxes.* Often such legislation contained exceptions designed to permit poor and illiterate whites to vote, such as "voting grandfather" and "fighting grandfather" clauses.

It was not until 1957 that the first modern legislation protecting voting rights was passed. The Voting Rights Act of that year provided penalties for interference with federal voting rights and created the Civil Rights Commission, a six-member bipartisan independent regulatory commission, to investigate deprivations of voting rights on the basis of race, religion, or national origin. A major amendment in 1960 provided for suits based on *patterns or practices* of discrimination in voting. Another amendment in 1964 required that voter registration standards must be uniformly applied and limited the use of literacy tests.

In 1965, two major developments took place: first, the 24th Amendment was adopted, prohibiting poll taxes; and second, the Voting Rights Act of 1965 was passed by Congress. The latter statute prohibited any "voting qualification or prerequisite to voting, or standard, practice or procedure . . . [which] den[ies] or abridge[s] the right of any citizen . . . to vote on account of race or color." The Act also prohibits the use of literacy tests with very limited exceptions, poll taxes, intimidation and threats, false voting information, destruction of ballots, and conspiracy. Civil and criminal penalties are provided and injuctive relief is available.

Discrimination in Education

As already discussed, *Brown* v. *Board of Education* invalidated the doctrine of "separate but equal" in education and generally held that governmentally sponsored discrimination in education violates the 14th Amendment.

Federal Statutes

Title IV of the Civil Rights Act of 1964 provides that the Attorney General may bring actions in federal court if students are being deprived of the equal protection of the laws or are being denied admission to public colleges or universities by reason of race, color, religion, or national origin. The Act also provides technical assistance in the preparation, adoption, and implementation of desegregation plans for public schools and for training of school personnel in desegregation policies and procedures.

The Higher Education Amendments of 1972 prohibited the use of federal funds for the transportation of students to achieve racial balance and further provided that the Civil Rights Act does not require "assignment or transportation of students or teachers to overcome racial imbalance." That law has been interpreted to mean that bussing cannot be used to overcome de facto segregation, but bussing remains as an alternative to eradicate the remnants of de jure segregation.

Perhaps the most difficult problem in all of discrimination law (and perhaps all of American law) is how to eliminate discrimination in public schools, particularly in large cities. Housing patterns in many cities have created de facto segregation on such a vast scale that simply removing the legal barriers to school integration has little effect. Schools remain essentially one race or another because the area surrounding the schools is racially uniform as well.

The problem is compounded by the fact that inner city schools often do not have a large enough tax base to support good education. The result is that inner city schools often deteriorate, while suburban schools often have a substantial tax base, assuring excellent school facilities. In 1974, the Supreme Court was faced with a challenge to the Detroit school system which argued that the boundaries between the city of Detroit and the suburbs were in fact artificial boundaries and should be ignored when the courts designed a desegregation plan.* The challengers argued that cross-district bussing was the only way to eliminate segregation in the Detroit school system. In a 6–3 decision, the Supreme Court held that unless it could be shown that the suburban school districts had caused the discrimination or contributed to the discrimination in some way, cross-district bussing would not be ordered. Justices Douglas, White, and Marshall dissented. Justice Marshall argued that

> Desegregation is not and was never expected to be an easy task. Racial attitudes ingrained in our Nation's childhood and adolescence are not quickly thrown aside in its middle years. But just as inconvenience of some cannot be allowed to stand in the way of the rights of others, so public opposition, no matter how strident, cannot be permitted to divert this Court from the enforcement of the constitutional principles at issue in this case. Today's holding, I fear, is more a reflection of a perceived public mood that we have gone far enough in enforcing the Constitution's guarantee of equal justice than it is the product of neutral principles of law. In the short run, it may seem the easier course to allow our great metropolitan areas to be divided up each into two cities—one white, the other black—but it is a course, I predict, our people will ultimately regret.

Summary and Conclusions

While the law relating to discrimination grew up in the context of racial segregation, other groups are discriminated against as well, including religious, national, and sexual minorities. The 14th Amendment broadly prohibits state action that deprives individuals of the equal protection of the laws, and the 13th and 15th Amendments are also relevant to a consideration of racial discrimination. The state action requirement has been narrowly interpreted, although for decades the requirement operated to prohibit federal action against private discrimination. Congressional authority to regulate private discrimination was not firmly established until 1968. The 14th Amendment was also interpreted for the first half of the 20th century to permit separate but equal treatment of racial minorities. That curious doctrine was overturned in 1954 in the landmark *Brown* v. *Board* decision.

Milliken v. *Bradley*, 418 U.S. 717, 94 S. Ct. 3112, 41 L. Ed. 2d 1069 (1974).

In the 1960's, Congress passed two major and several minor laws dealing with the problems of discrimination. The Civil Rights Act of 1964 contained separate sections, or *Titles,* dealing with discrimination in public accommodations, public facilities, education, and employment. The Civil Rights Act of 1968 prohibited discrimination in the sale or rental of real estate. Other statutes prohibited discrimination in pay between the sexes for equal work, age discrimination, discrimination against the handicapped, and discrimination on account of pregnancy.

Even in the light of the 1960's legislation, discrimination remains an unresolved problem in contemporary America. Two of the most controversial areas are affirmative action, particularly in the context of claims of reverse discrimination, and the problems of implementing school desegregation in the context of a society that continues to maintain racially segregated housing patterns, not as the result of law, but as a result of past habit and personal bias. Those problems point to the ever-present problem of attempting to legislate the moral feelings of the nation.

PRO AND CON
ISSUE: Is Affirmative Action Necessary?

PRO: Affirmative Action Is Essential Because Discrimination Still Exists
   Vernon E. Jordan, Jr.*

My thesis is a simple one. It can be summed up briefly. Black people have suffered discrimination in the past. They still suffer from the effects of past discrimination combined with continuing discrimination based on negative stereotypes and irrational prejudices. That disadvantage must be overcome through vigorous affirmative action programs.

There can be no doubt that such programs are necessary. There are advocates of the proposition that black progress has been so sweeping that special efforts are no longer necessary. They have met with favor from people who want to hear that message, for it is a message that absolves employers from making costly and inconvenient changes in their operating procedures.

But relatively few blacks have made the kind of progress that should induce complacency. And even among those that have benefitted, the jury is still out. Indeed, there is widespread belief among blacks in managerial positions that there is a firm ceiling on their future prospects, that their white peers will move out of middle management and into the upper levels while they remain behind.

The case for affirmative action does not rest on the few who have made it, but on the many who have not. Blacks as a group remain disproportionately disadvantaged, denied equal social and economic opportunities.

Consider something as basic as income. In this decade, median black family income has declined when measured against median white income. . . .

Consider jobs. Black unemployment is almost two and half times the rate of white unemployment. That's up from less than twice the white rate. In fact, black joblessness in our best years has never been as low as white joblessness in its worst years.

Consider youth. Up to two-thirds of black teenagers are jobless. . . .

. . . .

The rationale for affirmative action was best stated by the late President Lyndon Johnson, when he said:

   To be black in a white society is not to stand on level and equal ground. While the

---

*Vernon Jordan is president of the National Urban League. From a speech entitled "Where is This Black Progress?" delivered at an American Society for Personnel Administration Conference, Milwaukee, Wisconsin, on July 18, 1979, and reprinted in *Vital Speeches of the Day,* vol 45, p. 354. Reprinted by permission.

races may stand side by side, whites stand on history's mountain and blacks stand in history's hollow. Until we overcome unequal history, we cannot overcome unequal opportunity.

. . . .

Thus, affirmative action is the name we give to the attempt to help black people out of "history's hollow." The success of that effort rests partly upon the determination of America's corporate establishment to press forward with effective affirmative action plans.

. . . .

Civil rights laws, more than most, have been indifferently enforced and largely ignored. The new activist enforcement policies are thus to be applauded. They signify that the rule of law, and not the rule of racial discrimination, shall be paramount in our nation.

So the risks of abandoning affirmative action are greater than the risks of continuing strong programs. My message is simple—act right and do right. Press ahead as hard and as fast as possible on affirmative action. Make it a top level priority for your company. And remember that there's only one way to measure its success—and that's by numbers.

. . . .

America's corporations are challenged to overcome the pervasive discrimination of the past and the discriminatory effects of so-called neutral hiring policies of the present. They are challenged to move ahead with affirmative action programs that meet the [Supreme Court's] requirements. . . .

CON: Affirmative Action Violates the Rights of Individuals
Charles Fried*

Anyone who is dogmatic on the subject of quotas doesn't understand it very well. Let me cite my own intuitions. I am very glad that some fifteen years ago I joined in Harvard Law School's efforts to dramatically increase the number of blacks in our student body. Yet I find wrong the argument made in some parts of our educational community that increasing the number of black tenure track professors is far more important than maintaining the standards of academic and scholarly excellence which make the education worth having. . . .

Crucial, I think are the distinctions between public and private, and between rights and aspirations. The power of government should be brought to bear in a coercive way on private institutions and persons primarily to assure that we treat each other justly—and that includes not making discriminations implying the inferior worth and dignity of any person. . . . But it is the essence of a liberal state to allow private persons and private institutions to pursue their own goals, order their own priorities, so long as they do so fairly and decently. Thus the battle over quotas implies several different controversies.

. . . .

. . . [H]ere is the crux of the argument about quotas. If these preferences in reverse discrimination arise from aspirations only and not as a matter of right, then the imposition of quotas, goals, and timetables by government on private institutions represents an assertion of state power with major implications, implications which I believe should be resisted.

. . . .

It is an important feature of our national life that private institutions enjoy a large measure of autonomy. And that autonomy would be no autonomy at all if not enjoyed as a matter of principle. As a matter of principle, the state and public put up with private individuals behaving in ways and pursuing goals which the majority may find silly or even wrong. Every assertion of power by the state, therefore, to fold private institutions into public schemes of public policy raises this major issue of principle. . . .

A similar premise underlies another major thread in this tangled skein: the claim that goals and quotas are a matter of justice and rights after all. The justice, however, is not justice to the individual who happens to benefit. If justice is done it is done not to the individual but to the race. Now we might believe that in our political system all advantages are procured by maneuvers and coalitions and not by appeals to justice anyway, and so for once the fortunate black applicant is part of a successful maneuver, a winning coalition. But that is not the same as justice.

What, then, does justice to a race, not its indi-

---

*Charles Fried is the Carter Professor of General Jurisprudence at the Harvard Law School. From his article, "Questioning Quotas: Individual Rights and Group Wrongs," *The New Republic* (December 26, 1983): 9–11. Reprinted by permission.

vidual members, mean? Once again we are in the presence of a deep controversy about the status of individuals and groups. If an individual is merely an instance of a larger group identity, . . . then the idea of group rights peeping through the veil of individual entitlement has some force. The black vice president holds her job at the bank in the way an ambassador is shown deference at a state cere-mony—as a representative and not in her own person. If this idea appeals to you, you might want to consider some further questions: how do we determine what constitutes a group, who makes that determination, and how do we know who may speak authentically for such a group? Should we perhaps have a legislature constituted on group lines?

DISCUSSION QUESTIONS

1. Is the Constitution color-blind? Should it be color-blind? Are there instances in which the law should take race into account? If so, when?

2. Should any categories be added to the five federally protected classifications of race, color, religion, sex, and national origin? Which ones, and why?

3. Doesn't the separate but equal doctrine also deprive *white* students of the equal protection of the laws? How?

4. Notice that *Brown* and the later cases speak only in terms of desegregation, not integration. What is the difference, and is it significant?

5. Who has the best argument in *Bakke*—Justice Powell, Justice Blackmun, or Justice Marshall? Why? Are you sure your opinion—whatever it is—is not the result of your own biases and economic interests? Can anyone ever be sure? Should the *Bakke* determination be made by Congress, instead of the courts? How do you think Congress would resolve the issue?

6. Aside from the areas of discrimination considered in the chapter—employment, housing, public accommodations, credit, voting, and education—are there other areas of discrimination that ought to be treated by the courts or legislatures?

7. Isn't a high school education a reasonable requirement for every job? If discrimination in education is ever totally ended, would a high school education become a reasonable requirement without running afoul of the disproportionate impact theory?

8. How would you prove that an employer's articulated reasons for not giving you a job were a mere pretext for discrimination? Isn't it awfully easy for an employer to fabricate reasons under the *Furnco* decision?

9. Name five jobs for which sex is a bfoq. Now do the same for religion and national origin. Why do you suppose race or color is not a bfoq? Can you think of any jobs for which race or color might arguably be a bfoq? How narrowly should the courts interpret the exception?

10. Which is more important—the right to own property and do with it as you wish, or the right to be free from discrimination in public accommodations and housing?

11. Can the problem of de facto racial segregation in education be resolved by any other means except bussing and cross-district remedies, as discussed in *Milliken* v. *Bradley?* Isn't de facto segregation largely the result of the existence of separate school districts in the inner cities and the suburbs, because of "white flight" to avoid the inner city schools? If so, is this really a form of de jure segregation?

CASE PROBLEMS

1. New Kent County operates a school system involving a "freedom of choice" plan. There are two elementary schools that serve the entire district, and students and their parents have a choice as to which school they attend. All of the black students attend one school and all white students, by choice, attend the other. Is the system constitutional? [*Green* v. *County School Board of New Kent County,* 391 U.S. 430, 88 S. Ct. 1689, 20 L. Ed. 2d 716 (1968).]

2. Hardison was a member of a church that forbade its members from working on Saturdays. Prior to joining the church, Hardison was employed by Trans-World Airlines as a clerk in a division that must operate year-round and around the clock. After a series of compromises, Hardison was discharged when he did not appear for work on a Saturday. Did Trans-World violate Title VII? [*Trans-World Airlines, Inc.* v. *Hardison,* 432 U.S. 63, 97 S. Ct. 2264, 53 L. Ed. 2d 113 (1977). Compare this case to the *Thomas* decision, Case Problem 4 in Chapter 14.]

3. Wilson and 100 other males applied for positions as flight attendants and ticket agents with Southwest Airlines, but all were turned down. An advertising agency had suggested that Southwest adopt a "sexy" image for its flight attendants and agents in order to attract customers, based on the slogan "At Last There Is Somebody Else Up There Who Loves You." Southwest contended that its requirement that flight attendants and ticket agents be female is a bona fide occupational qualification. Result? [*Wilson* v. *Southwest Airlines Co.* 500 F. Supp., 292 (N.D. Texas, 1981).]

4. Payne worked in McLemore's fertilizer plant during the period preceding the planting season, but was laid off during the off season. After several years of this, Payne, a black, began activities in a local civil rights organization and was actively involved in boycotts against a retail store also owned by McLemore. At the next planting season, McLemore refused to hire Payne. Result? [*Payne* v. *McLemore's Wholesale and Retail Stores,* 654 F. 2d 1130 (5th Cir., 1981).]

5. A nonprofit corporation was organized for the purpose of operating a swimming pool. Funds for the pool were privately raised, and membership was restricted to persons in a three-quarter mile radius. A black who purchased a home in the area was discouraged from membership and, when a white member brought a black guest, the guest policy was changed to limit guests to relatives of members. Are the policies legal? Result under the Civil Rights Act of 1964? Under the Civil Rights Act of 1866? [*Tillman* v. *Wheaton-Haven Recreational Association, Inc.,* 410 U.S. 431, 93 S. Ct. 1190, 35 L. Ed. 2d 403 (1973).]

6. Respondent operated a snack bar in a privately owned recreational facility and sold only to persons on the premises. To be on the premises, one had to be a member of the club, and club membership was restricted to whites. Does the snack bar violate Title II? [*Daniel* v. *Paul*, 395 U.S. 298, 89 S. Ct. 1697, 23 L. Ed. 2d 318 (1969).]

7. Somerset University, a publicly supported institution, designed an affirmative action program in which a point system was established for admission. Points were awarded for a student's high school grade point average, scores on standardized tests, high school activities, and race. Edmund, a white student, and George, a black student, had precisely the same scores for all of the criteria except race. Because George received more "points" for his race, he received the last position to be awarded for admission to Somerset. Does Edmund have a complaint?

8. Hermione wanted to become a fire fighter. In order to do so she had to pass both an intelligence test, a physical stamina test, and had to weigh over 140 pounds and stand 5 feet 6 inches. Hermione was 5 feet 3 inches and weighed 125 pounds. Does she have a remedy? Are the intelligence and physical stamina tests permissible?

9. Martext Manufacturing requires all of its personnel to have at least ten years of schooling and pass a test written in English. Orlando, a recent immigrant from Eastern Europe, had to leave school in the eighth grade because of political developments in his homeland and has only a limited understanding of English. Orlando applied for a job as a janitor in Martext's plant, but was turned down because of his lack of education and his failure on the written test. Does Orlando have a remedy?

10. The Holofernes Company, an American corporation, maintains offices all around the world. Recently, several applicants were turned down for several positions in those offices. Jaquenetta was turned down for a position in a Latin American country because the people in that country would not deal with a woman. Anthony, a black man, was turned down for a position in South Africa because of that nation's racial policies. Henry, who is Jewish, was turned down for a position in Iran because of that nation's policies. And Maria was turned down for a position in the New York office because the manager of that office had a reputation with women and a jealous wife. Which of those people had a valid claim of discrimination?

11. Quince wishes to sell a home he owns, but he is adamant in his refusal to sell to blacks. At this time, Quince owns the home, a vacation retreat in Minnesota, a condominium in Florida, and has a partnership interest in an apartment building. May Quince refuse to sell to blacks?

12. Conrade is the manager of a loan company with ultimate responsibility for determining to whom loans are made. To which of the following persons may he refuse to grant credit? (a) A divorced person; (b) A person who in unemployed; (c) A person who receives welfare; (d) A person newly arrived in the

United States; (e) A person with a low-paying job; (f) A person with a large number of debts.

SUGGESTED READINGS

Babcock, Barbara A., et al. *Sex Discrimination and the Law: Causes and Remedies* (Boston: Little, Brown & Co., 1975).

Bell, Derrick A., Jr. *Race, Racism and American Law* (Boston: Little, Brown & Co., 1973 and 1975 Supplement).

Carothers, Leslie A. *The Public Accommodations Law of 1964: Arguments, Issues and Attitudes in a Legal Debate* (Northampton, Mass.: Smith College, 1968).

Countryman, Vern. *Discrimination and the Law* (Chicago: University of Chicago Press, 1965).

Friedan, Betty. *The Feminine Mystique* (New York: Norton, 1974).

Friedman, Joel Wm., and George M. Strickler, Jr. *The Law of Employment Discrimination* (Mineola, N.Y.: The Foundation Press, 1983).

King, Martin Luther, Jr. *Why We Can't Wait* (New York: Harper & Row, 1963); see especially "Letter from Birmingham Jail."

Livingston, John C. *Fair Game? Inequality and Affirmative Action* (San Francisco: W. H. Freeman & Co., 1979).

Lockard, Duane. *Toward Equal Opportunity: A Study of State and Local Antidiscrimination Laws* (New York: The MacMillan Company, 1968).

Mooney, Christopher F., S. J. *Inequality and the American Conscience: Justice Through the Judicial System* (New York: Paulist Press, 1982).

Myrdal, Gunnar. *An American Dilemma: The Negro Problem and Modern Democracy* (New York: Harper and Brothers, 1944).

Silberman, Charles. *Crisis in Black and White* (New York: Random House, 1964).

Thomas, Claire Sherman. *Sex Discrimination in a Nutshell* (St. Paul, Minn.: West Publishing Co., 1982).

Vieira, Norman. *Civil Rights in a Nutshell* (St. Paul, Minn.: West Publishing Co., 1978).

Woodward, C. Vann. *The Strange Career of Jim Crow* (New York: Oxford University Press, 1957).

Regulation of Energy and the Environment

Universe to each must be
All that is, including me.
Environment in turn must be
All that is, excepting me.

R. Buckminster Fuller, Synergetics 2, sec. 100.12. (1979)

Only to the white man was nature a "wilderness" and only to him was the land "infested"
with "wild" animals and "savage" people. To us it was tame. Earth was bountiful and we
were surrounded with the blessings of the Great Mystery.

Luther Standing Bear, Land of the Spotted Eagle (1933)

We have met the enemy and he is us.

Pogo

Humankind's concern with the environment was not unique to the 1960's and 1970's. Ever since the beginning of the Industrial Revolution people had worried about the effects that dirty air, foul water, and careless disposal of hazardous and toxic chemicals were having on the public health. But in a time when economic "progress" and industrialization were the predominant values of society such concerns were rarely voiced and even more rarely formed the basis for public policy. Environmental pollution and misuse of resources were viewed as unfortunate but necessary costs of industrial development.

Some of the problems of the environment had been addressed by ancient common-law theories of *nuisance, trespass,* and *strict liability,* though not very well. During the 1950's, feeble attempts to control air and water pollution began at the federal level, but those attempts relied on enforcement by the individual states and generally failed to define what was meant by pollution. Such an approach was bound to fail, since each state necessarily must protect its own industries, and since air and water pollution are interstate or even international problems.

Grass-roots pressure for effective laws to protect the environment continued throughout the 1960's and, in 1969, Congress passed the most important of the environmental protection laws, the National Environmental Policy Act (NEPA). That same year, President Nixon issued an Executive Order creating the Environmental Protection Agency (EPA) to centralize authority over environmental matters in one agency. During the 1970's, Congress also passed stronger new laws or amended old weak laws concerning air and water pollution, solid waste disposal, toxic wastes, and preservation of wilderness and wildlife. The same period saw a growing concern with the problems of conserving energy resources and the development of nuclear and other alternative energy sources, resulting in the creation of the Nuclear Regulatory Commission and in a series of statutes designed to encourage energy conservation and development of energy sources.

Ecology and the Environmental Ethic

Ecology studies the interrelationships of all living things and their environment. Biologists had been concerned with those relationships for centuries but, in the 1960's and 1970's, ecology became a matter of public concern and various grass-roots organizations were formed or strengthened to press for environmental legislation. Those groups generally held three basic beliefs: (1) that interrupting any "natural cycle," such as a food chain or other ecological relationship, was dangerous and sometimes deadly; (2) that all matter, including all matter "thrown away" by man, ends up in nature somewhere—that things never "just go away;" and (3) that all things being equal, nature is to be favored, and man-made changes are likely to be detrimental to the natural system.

Common-Law Environmental Protection

Until the creation of some limited environmental remedies in the 1950's, the sole method of dealing with environmental problems was through private lawsuits filed by persons injured by the actions of others, and through the concept of *public nuisance,* a common-law crime. The principal theories by which injured persons might recover are *private nuisance, trespass,* and *strict liability*. All are common-law torts and are enforced by private lawsuits for damages or equitable relief.

Private Nuisance

The tort of **private nuisance** is an ancient and ambiguous doctrine. Nuisance requires proof of an intentional (or sometimes negligent) interference with another's right to use and enjoy the ownership of land. The tort has been applied to smoke or dust settling on a landowner's property, excessive noise, noxious odors, sewage percolating into someone's basement, and a wide variety of other objectionable acts.

Nuisance cases inevitably involve a balancing of interests. Generally, a landowner has the right to use his or her property in any lawful manner, but the doctrine of nuisance says that such use may not interfere with the rights of another landowner to use and enjoy land. The question then becomes *which* landowner's rights are to be protected, as discussed in the following "right to sunlight" case.

Prah v. Maretti

108 Wisc. 2d 223, 321 N.W. 2d 182 (1982)

The plaintiff built the first home in a subdivision and established a solar energy system to partially heat the home. The defendant purchased the lot next to plaintiff's and began construction of his home on the lot. The plaintiff informed the defendant that if the defendant's home were located as originally planned, the plaintiff's solar collectors would be shaded, resulting in inefficiencies in the system and possibly damaging the collectors. The defendant refused to change the location of the house, and the plaintiff (Prah) filed suit, asking for an injunction. The trial court dismissed the complaint and the plaintiff appealed.

ABRAHAMSON, Justice. . . .

We consider first whether the complaint states a claim for relief based on common law private nuisance. This state has long recognized that an owner of land does not have an absolute or unlimited right to use the land in a way which injures the rights of others. The rights of neighboring landowners are relative; the uses by one must not unreasonably impair the uses or enjoyment of the other. . . . When one landowner's use of his or her property unreasonably interferes with another's enjoyment of his or her property, that use is said to be a private nuisance. . . .

The private nuisance doctrine has traditionally been employed in this state to balance the conflicting rights of landowners, and this court has recently adopted the analysis of private nuisance set forth in the Restatement (Second) of Torts. . . . The Restatement defines private nuisance as "a nontrespassory invasion of another's interest in the private use and enjoyment of land" . . .

Although the defendant's obstruction of the plaintiff's access to sunlight appears to fall with the Restatement's broad concept of a private nuisance as a nontrespassory invasion of another's interest in the private use and enjoyment of land, the defendant asserts that he has a right to develop his property in compliance with statutes, ordinances and private covenants without regard to the effect of such development upon the plaintiff's access to sunlight. In essence, the defendant is asking this court to hold that the private nuisance doctrine is not applicable in the instant case and that his right to develop his land is a right which is *per se* superior to his neighbor's interest in access to sunlight. This position is expressed in the maxim "cujus est solum, ejus est usque ad coelum et an infernos," that is, the owner of land owns up to the sky and down to the center of the earth. The rights of the surface owner are, however, not unlimited. . . .

Many jurisdictions in this country have protected a landowner from malicious obstruction of access to light (the spite fence cases) under the common law private nuisance doctrine. If an activity is motivated by malice it lacks utility and the harm it causes others outweighs any social values. . . .

This court's reluctance in the nineteenth and early part of the twentieth century to provide broader protection for a landowner's access to sunlight was premised on three policy considerations. First, the right of landowners to use their property as they wished, as long as they did not cause physical damage to a neighbor, was jealously guarded. . . .

Second, sunlight was valued only for aesthetic enjoyment or as illumination. Since artificial light could be used for illumination, loss of sunlight was at most a personal annoyance which was given little, if any, weight by society.

Third, society had a significant interest in not restricting or impeding land development. . . . This court repeatedly emphasized that in the growth period of the nineteenth and early twentieth centuries change is to be expected and is essential to property and that recognition of a right to sunlight would hinder property development. The court expressed this concept as follows:

> As the city grows, large grounds appurtenant to residences must be cut up to supply more residences. . . . The cistern, the outhouse, the cesspool, and the private drain must disappear in deference to the public waterworks and the sewer; the terrace and the garden, to the need for more complete occupancy. . . . *Miller* v. *Hoeschler* . . . (1905).

. . . .

These three policies are no longer fully accepted or applicable. They reflect factual circumstances and social priorities that are now obsolete.

First, society has increasingly regulated the use of land by the landowner for the general welfare. . . .

Second, access to sunlight has taken on a new significance in recent years. In this case the plaintiff seeks to protect access to sunlight, not for aesthetic reasons or as a source of illumination but as a source of energy. Access to sunlight as an energy source is of significance both to the landowner who invests in solar collectors and to a society which has an interest in developing alternative sources of energy.

Third, the policy of favoring unhindered private development in an expanding economy is no longer in harmony with the realities of our society. . . . The need for easy and rapid development is not as great today as it once was, while our perception of the value of sunlight as a source of energy has increased significantly.

. . . .

Private nuisance law, the law traditionally used to adjudicate conflicts between private landowners, has the flexibility to protect both a landowner's right of access to sunlight and another landowner's right to develop land. . . .

We therefore hold that private nuisance law, that is, the reasonable use doctrine as set forth in the Restatement, is applicable to the instant case. . . .

Reversed.

CALLOW, Justice, dissenting: . . .

The majority believes that the defendant's obstruction of the plaintiff's access to sunlight falls within the broad definition of "use and enjoyment of land." . . . I do not believe the defendant's "obstruction" of the plaintiff's access to sunlight falls within the definition of "invasion" as it applies to the private use and enjoyment of land. Invasion is typically synonymous with "entry," "attack," "penetration," "hostile entrance," "the incoming or spread of something unusually hurtful." . . . Most of the nuisance cases arising under this definition involve noxious odors, smoke, blasting, flooding, or *excessive light* invading the plaintiff's right to the use of enjoyment of his property. . . . Clearly, an owner who merely builds his home in compliance with all . . . regulations is not "invading" anothers right to the use and enjoyment of his property.

The more traditional "smoke and dust" private nuisance cases involved substantial problems of proof for a plaintiff, particularly if there were several persons in the area emitting the same pollutant. Proof of damages may also be difficult.

Public Nuisance

The common-law crime of **public nuisance** has become a part of the criminal statutes in many states. Such laws are generally broadly worded simply to prohibit "maintaining a public nuisance" and have been applied to everything from houses of prostitution to being a "common scold." These laws may also be applied to a variety of environmentally related activities, including smoke, dust, and odors. Often the laws are so broadly worded that they invite challenge on constitutional due process grounds. Persons who are "specially injured" may have the right to bring a private civil lawsuit based on violation of the criminal statute as well. Prosecutors and plaintiffs face similar problems of proof as those found in private nuisance cases.

Trespass

One of the most ancient of all torts is **trespass** to land, which is an unauthorized entry onto land. The common law tort of trespass gave a right of action for all such entries, including intentional, negligent, and even accidental entries. This tort was in fact a strict liability action, since it was not necessary to prove any mental element whatsoever. Since a personal invasion of property is not necessary, the tort may be committed when physical objects are caused to come in contact with another's land. As a result, successful actions have been maintained based on pollutants, such as smoke particles, which settle on the land of another. Again there are substantial difficulties of proof, particularly in showing the extent of damages suffered by such actions. Again both damages and injunctions may be awarded to a successful plaintiff.

Strict Liability

The concept of **strict liability,** or liability without fault, gives a right of action to persons damaged by an ultrahazardous or abnormally dangerous activity which causes an unreasonable risk of harm to others or to the property of others. One of the earliest examples is blasting, and any injury that results from blasting was compensated by the law, even if the person doing the blasting used every conceivable safety precaution. Some modern pollution-generating activities may fall into the requirements of strict liability, such as discharging poisons into a water supply or releasing radioactive materials into the atmosphere.

Limits of the Common Law in Controlling Environmental Damage

The traditional torts of nuisance, trespass, and strict liability proved singularly ineffective in controlling pollution and other environmental damage. Only landowners could recover for nuisance and trespass, reflecting the concern of the ancient common law with the rights of property. But clearly others besides landowners were injured by environmental damage, including the public. Similarly, the common-law torts required that the plaintiff have suffered some "special damage," or injury different or greater than that suffered by the general public. In many cases the damage suffered, though real, was small and difficult to ascertain, resulting in no great incentive to plaintiffs to file such actions, particularly in the face of the amount of money the industrial defendants were willing to spend to defend such cases.

Perhaps most importantly, the common law torts were designed to remedy *individual* injuries, while the damage done by pollution is to the *public as a whole*, or even to *nonhuman elements* of the ecological system. Wildlife, after all, has no standing to bring a lawsuit. The end result was that the remedy afforded by the common law was of little effect in protecting the environment.

Federal Environmental Regulation—NEPA

In retrospect, federal concern with the environment came extremely late, after the nation and its people had been subjected to filthy air, dirty water, and the refuse of industrial society for decades, and after some of the effects of pollution may have become irreversible. But the blissful ignorance of our legislators only mirrored the blissful ignorance of society itself. It was not until refined scientific testing procedures became available in the 1960's that the true extent of environmental damage became known. The ravages of pollution were pointed out to the public in several well-known books, such as Rachel Carson's *Silent Spring**, and a grass-roots movement placed pressure on Congress to take steps to remedy environmental damage. The first and most important result was the National Environmental Policy Act of 1969 (NEPA).

NEPA had three major aspects: (1) it established a national policy of promoting efforts to prevent environmental damage while encouraging "productive and enjoyable harmony between man and his environment;" (2) it established the Council on Environmental Quality (CEQ); and (3) it required the filing of Environmental Impact Statements (EIS) by federal agencies undertaking "major federal actions significantly affecting the quality of the human environment."

The crucial effect of NEPA is on the various federal administrative agencies. The purpose of the requirement of filing Environmental Impact Statements, described later, is to force every federal agency to consider environmental factors in their decision-making processes. In one sense, NEPA is an amendment to every administrative agency's enabling act, requiring each agency to take a hard look at environmental concerns before undertaking agency actions. Prior to NEPA agencies were not required to consider such factors, and many agencies took the position that they *could not* consider such factors under their respective enabling acts. NEPA instead requires "across the board" environmental planning by all federal agencies.

The Council on Environmental Quality (CEQ)

The **Council on Environmental Quality** is a three-member board appointed by the President with the advice and consent of the Senate. The purpose of the CEQ is to coordinate programs and activities that "affect, protect and improve environmental quality" and to assist and advise the President on environmental matters. The CEQ does not enforce laws in the traditional manner of administrative bodies, but acts as a mediator between other agencies of government involved in interagency disputes involving environmental matters. The CEQ may simply mediate such disputes or

---

*Boston: Houghton-Mifflin, 1962.

may pass them on to the President, with its advice, for ultimate resolution. The CEQ also acts as a central filing point for Environmental Impact Statements.

Environmental Impact Statements

Perhaps the most important impact of NEPA, and the most important function of the CEQ, lies in the requirement that **Environmental Impact Statements** (EIS) be filed by federal agencies. An EIS is required "in every recommendation or report on proposals for legislation and other *major Federal actions significantly affecting the quality of the human environment.* . . ." The EIS must contain a detailed statement by the responsible official on

(i) the environmental impact of the proposed action,

(ii) any adverse environmental effects which cannot be avoided should the proposal be implemented,

(iii) alternatives to the proposed action,

(iv) the relationship between local short-term uses of man's environment and the maintenance and enhancement of long-term productivity, and

(v) any irreversible and irretrievable commitments of resources which would be involved in the proposed action should it be implemented. (NEPA, Section 102(2)(c))

NEPA also requires new agency procedures to ensure that environmental factors are taken into account in the decision-making process and to recognize the international and long-range character of environmental problems, though those matters are not specifically required in the EIS. In essence, NEPA requires federal agencies to prepare a detailed explanation of the environmental effects of its actions and to make the report available to Congress, other agencies, and the public.

Use of the EIS   The primary purpose of the EIS is to provide the decision-maker with information. Agencies requesting funds to build a new federal dam will have to prepare an EIS for review by higher level administrators when they decide whether to go through with the project, for example, and other agencies with expertise in the area or whose area is affected by the project are required to comment on the EIS. If there is a dispute between agencies, the agencies involved may refer the matter to the CEQ for resolution by a written "referral" by one agency, and a written "response" by another. The CEQ must act within 25 days and has several options: it may decide that the referral and response have settled the matter; it may act as mediator; it may hold public meetings or hearings; it may decide that the matter lacks national significance; it may publish its findings and recommendations and submit them to the President for action.

NEPA provides no judicial remedies for enforcement of the EIS provisions. It seems clear that NEPA was originally meant to provide an additional administrative hurdle for federal projects which forced agencies to take the environmental effect of their actions into account. But a determined agency with little environmental conscience could, under that view, force an environmentally dangerous project through the decision-making process. Such events would not occur frequently, since public pressure would undoubtedly be brought to bear on such agencies, but it could happen without judicial review and sanctions. The following landmark case established the rule that courts may indeed review agency consideration of an EIS and may hold that an agency has given insufficient consideration to environmental factors in its decision making.

Calvert Cliffs Coordinating Committee v. A.E.C.

449 F. 2d 1109 (D.C. Circ., 1971)

The Atomic Energy Commission (now the Nuclear Regulatory Commission) adopted procedural rules ostensibly to comply with the EIS requirements of NEPA, which included rules which (1) stated that environmental factors need not be considered by the A.E.C. hearing board unless raised by outside parties or staff members; (2) prohibited any party from raising nonradiological environmental issues at any hearing prior to a certain date well after the adoption of NEPA; (3) prohibited the A.E.C. hearing board from considering environmental factors if responsible agencies have already certified that their own environmental standards are satisfied by the proposed action; and (4) prohibited the consideration of environmental factors in nuclear power facility cases until the time of the issuance of the operating license. Petitioners, a private group concerned with nuclear power, brought suit claiming that the A.E.C. rules did not live up to the requirements of NEPA. The A.E.C., on the other hand, claimed that the broadness of NEPA permitted those rules.

J. SKELLY WRIGHT, Circuit Judge:

These cases are only the beginning of what promises to become a flood of new litigation—litigation seeking judicial assistance in protecting our natural environment. Several recently enacted statutes attest to the commitment of the Government to control, at long last, the destructive engine of material "progress." But it remains to be seen whether the promise of this legislation will become a reality. Therein lies the judicial role. In these cases, we must for the first time interpret the broadest and perhaps most important of the recent statutes: the National Environmental Policy Act of 1969 (NEPA). We must assess claims that one of the agencies charged with its administration has failed to live up to the congressional mandate. Our duty, in short, is to see that important legislative purposes, heralded in the halls of Congress, are not lost or misdirected in the vast hallways of the federal bureaucracy.

. . . .

We begin our analysis with an examination of NEPA's structure. . . . The relevant portion of NEPA is Title 1, consisting of five sections. Section 101 sets forth the Act's basic substantive policy: that the federal government "use all practicable means and measures" to protect environmental values. Congress did not establish environmental protection as an exclusive goal; rather, it desired a reordering of priorities, so that environmental costs and benefits will assume their proper place along with other considerations. . . .

. . . .

NEPA . . . makes environmental protection a part of the mandate of every federal agency and department. The Atomic Energy Commission, for example, had continually asserted, prior to NEPA, that it had no statutory authority to concern itself with the adverse environmental effects of its actions. Now, however, its hands are no longer tied. It is not only permitted, but compelled, to take environmental values into account. Perhaps the greatest importance of NEPA is to require the Atomic Energy Commission and other agencies to *consider* environmental issues just as they consider other matters within their mandates. . . .

. . . .

Of course, all of these duties are qualified by the phrase "to the fullest extent possible." We must stress as forcefully as possible that this language does not provide an escape hatch for footdragging agencies; it does not make NEPA's procedural requirements somehow "discretionary." Congress did not intend the Act to be such a paper tiger. Indeed, the requirement of environmental consideration "to the fullest extent possible" sets a high standard for the agencies, a standard which must be rigorously enforced by the reviewing courts. . . .

We conclude, then, that NEPA mandates a particular sort of careful and informed decisionmaking process and creates judicially enforceable duties. The reviewing courts probably cannot reverse a substantive decision on its merits, unless it be shown that the actual balance of costs and benefits that was struck was arbitrary or clearly gave insufficient weight to environmental values. But if the decision was reached procedurally without individualized consideration and balancing of environmental factors—conducted fully and in good faith—it is the responsibility of the courts to reverse. . . .

In the cases before us now, we do not have to review a particular decision by the Atomic Energy Commission granting a construction permit or an operating license. Rather we must review the Commission's recently promulgated rules which govern consideration of environmental values in such individual decisions. The rules were devised strictly in order to comply with the NEPA procedural requirements—but petitioners argue that they fall far short of the congressional mandate. . . .

We believe that the Commission's crabbed interpretation of NEPA makes a mockery of the Act. What possible purpose could there be in the [NEPA] requirement (that the "detailed statement" accompany proposals through agency review processes) if "accompany" means no more than physical proximity—mandating no more than the physical act of passing certain folders and papers, unopened, to reviewing officials along with other folders and papers? What possible purpose could there be in requiring the "detailed statement" to be before hearing boards, if the boards are free to ignore entirely the contents of the statement? NEPA was meant to do more than regulate the flow of papers in the federal bureaucracy. . . . It must, rather, be read to indicate a congressional intent that environmental factors, as compiled in the "detailed statement," be *considered* through agency review processes. . . .

We believe the Commission's rule is in fundamental conflict with the basic purpose of the Act. NEPA mandates a case-by-case balancing judgment on the part of federal agencies. In each individual case, the particular economic and technical benefits of planned action must be assessed and then weighed against the environmental costs; alternatives must be considered which would affect the balance of values. . . . The magnitude of possible benefits and possible costs may lie anywhere on a broad spectrum. Much will depend on the particular magnitudes involved in particular cases. In some cases, the benefits will be great enough to justify a certain quantum of environmental costs; in other cases, they will not be so great and the proposed action may have to be abandoned or significantly altered so as to bring the benefits and costs into a proper balance. . . .

We hold that . . . the Commission must revise its rules governing consideration of environmental issues. . . .

Remanded for proceedings consistent with this opinion.

The Threshold Requirements for an EIS: Major Federal Actions NEPA requires an EIS in the case of any "major federal action significantly affecting the quality of the human environment." In most cases, the "major federal action" requirement is no problem if a federal agency is undertaking or contracting directly for a proposed action. Slightly more difficult problems exist if the agency need only approve or license private action. Generally, if a federal agency has the authority to control the action, it is considered a federal action. It is important to note that it is the *agency's* responsibility to prepare the EIS, and that responsibility cannot be delegated to private individuals or firms involved in the project. The agency may seek the help of such individuals or firms in preparing the EIS, but the ultimate responsibility for preparation of the document is the agency's.

Likewise there is no real problem in determining whether a federal action is major. Any project that involves a substantial commitment of resources or funds is considered major, and the issue has not resulted in much litigation. There is some argument that no project that involves a significant environmental impact could ever be considered anything but "major."

The Threshold Requirements for an EIS: Significant Environmental Effect A somewhat more difficult problem involves whether a proposed federal action "significantly affects the quality of the human environment." To the uninitiated, the term *environment* includes only nature—wild areas, forests, beaches, and the like. But the Act had broader concerns in mind, including the need to preserve cultural and historic areas, enhancing the quality of renewable resources, and achieving a balance between population and resource use.

Metropolitan Edison Co. v. People Against Nuclear Energy

460 U.S. 780, 103 S. Ct. 1556, ——— L. Ed. 2d ——— (1983)

On March 29, 1979, one of the nuclear reactors (TMI-2) owned by Metropolitan Edison at Three Mile Island near Harrisburg, Pennsylvania, suffered a serious accident that damaged the reactor. While no dangerous radiation was released, the accident caused widespread concern and the Governor of Pennsylvania recommended an evacuation of pregnant women and small children. Many area residents left their homes for several days. At the time of the accident, a second reactor (TMI-1) owned by Metropolitan at the same location was not operating, since it had been shut down for refueling.

After the accident, the Nuclear Regulatory Commission ordered Metropolitan to keep TMI-1 shut down until it had an opportunity to determine whether the plant could be operated safely. A citizen's group, People Against Nuclear Energy (PANE), intervened before the NRC, claiming that reopening TMI-1 would cause substantial psychological harm to the people who resided around the Three Mile Island plant, and that the NRC must consider that psychological harm as a "significant environmental effect" under NEPA. The NRC refused to take evidence regarding the psychological impact of restarting TMI-1, and Metropolitan was permitted to restart TMI-1. (TMI-2 was closed completely.) PANE appealed to the Court of Appeals, which held that the NRC improperly failed to consider whether the risk of accident at TMI-1 might cause psychological harm to the residents of the surrounding area. Metropolitan appealed to the Supreme Court.

Justice REHNQUIST delivered the opinion of the Court.

. . . .

All the parties agree that effects on human health can be cognizable under NEPA, and that human health may include psychological health. The Court of Appeals thought these propositions were enough to complete a syllogism that disposes of the case: NEPA requires agencies to consider effects on health. An effect on psychological health is an effect on health. Therefore, NEPA requires agencies to consider the effects on psychological health asserted by PANE. . . . Although these arguments are appealing at first glance, we believe they skip over an essential step in the analysis. They do not consider the closeness of the relationship between the change in the environment and the "effect" at issue. . . .

To paraphrase the statutory language [of NEPA] in light of the facts of this case, where an agency action significantly affects the quality of the human environment, the agency must evaluate the "environmental impact" and any unavoidable adverse environmental affects of its proposal. The theme [of the Act] is sounded by the adjective "environmental": NEPA does not require the agency to assess *every* impact of its proposed action, but only the impact or effect on the environment. If we were to seize the word "environmental" out of its context and give it the broadest possible definition, the words "adverse environmental effects" might embrace virtually any consequence of a governmental action that some one thought "adverse." But we think the context of the statute shows that Congress was talking about the physical environment—the world around us, so to speak. NEPA was designed to promote human welfare by alerting governmental actors to the effect of their proposed actions on the physical environment. . . .

. . . .

Our understanding of the congressional concerns that led to the enactment of NEPA suggests that the terms "environmental effect" and "environmental impact" . . . be read to include a requirement of a reasonably close causal relationship between a change in the physical environment and the effect at issue. This requirement is like the familiar doctrine of proximate cause from tort law. The issue before us, then, is how to give content to this requirement. This is a question of first impression in this Court.

The federal action that affects the environment in this case is permitting renewed operation of TMI-1. The direct effects on the environment of this action include release of low-level radiation, increased fog in the Harrisburg area (caused by operation of the plant's cooling towers), and the release of warm water into the Susquehanna River. The NRC has considered each of these effects in its EIS. . . . Another effect of renewed operation is a risk of a nuclear accident. The NRC has also considered this effect.

PANE argues that the psychological health damage it alleges "will flow directly from the risk of [a nuclear] accident." . . . But a risk of an accident is not an effect on the physical environment. A risk is, by definition, unrealized in the physical world. In a causal chain from renewed operation of TMI-1 to psychological health damage, the element of risk and its perception by PANE's members are necessary middle links. We believe that the element of risk lengthens the causal chain beyond the reach of NEPA. . . .

Time and resources are simply too limited for us to believe that Congress intended to extend NEPA as far as the Court of Appeals has taken it. See *Vermont Yankee Nuclear Power Corp.* v. *NRDC* [see Chapter 5.] . . .

. . . .

We do not mean to denigrate the fears of PANE's members, or to suggest that the psychological health damage they fear could not, in fact, occur. Nonetheless, it is difficult for us to see the differences between someone who dislikes a government decision so much that he suffers similar anxiety and stress, someone who fears the effects of that decision so much that he suffers anxiety and stress, and someone who suffers anxiety and stress that "flow directly" . . . from the risks associated with the same decision. It would be extraordinarily difficult for agencies to differentiate between "genuine" claims of psychological health damage and claims that are grounded solely in disagreement with a democratically adopted policy. . . .

For these reasons, we hold that the NRC need not consider PANE's contentions. . . . The judgment of the Court of Appeals is reversed. . . .

Standing Revisited: Who May Complain?

One of the implicit problems in environmental case is who has **standing** to complain? It will be recalled from the discussion in Chapter 4 that standing means simply the right to bring a lawsuit, and that standing depends on the existence of a legally recognized injury. Many of the environmentally related cases are brought by ad hoc committees of citizens, such as PANE in the above case. The Supreme Court has held that standing in such cases has two requirements: (1) an "injury in fact" and (2) an interest "within the zone of interests to be protected or regulated" by the statute alleged to have been violated. The "injury in fact" may be as simple as an injury to one's aesthetic sensibilities, and the "interest" requirement may be satisfied by showing that the plaintiff has almost any special claim. In one case, for example, the fact that some members of the Sierra Club had hiked a trail in the past, and would be foreclosed from doing so in the future if a proposed resort were built, was enough to confer standing on the Club.* Generally, the standing requirement is liberally construed by the Court, as a recognition that the injury resulting from environmental mischief affects the interests of large numbers of persons in a large and unspecifiable number of ways.

The Environmental Protection Agency

The Environmental Protection Agency (EPA) was created as part of an executive reorganization plan submitted to Congress by President Nixon in 1970. It was given powers originally delegated to fifteen separate agencies or executive departments, such as the Department of Interior, Bureau of Solid Waste Management, and the Department of Agriculture. The EPA is headed by a single Administrator, appointed by the President. The agency is an "independent" agency, but it is not an "independent regulatory commission" in the sense described in Chapter 5, since its administrator generally serves at the pleasure of the President. The EPA is a part of the executive branch.

Congress has, from time to time, delegated additional power to the EPA to enforce new legislation in the environmental area, as in the Clean Air Amendments of 1970. The EPA's enforcement powers vary with the area considered, as in air pollution, water pollution, or solid waste management, for example.

Regulation of Air Pollution

The term *pollution* generally means simply dirt or contamination, and as such is probably far too broad to be used in any law. A basic problem throughout humankind's fight for clean air has been finding some kind of workable definition of air pollution.

A second problem is, of course, that the air is a common sea, and it is extremely difficult to control one small part of that sea without controlling the entire ocean. Pollution in one area clearly affects the quality of the air in all other areas. The same problem makes air pollution extremely dangerous, since we all live in that same sea.

---

*Sierra Club v. Morton, 405 U.S. 727, 92 S. Ct. 1361, 31 L. Ed. 2d 636 (1972).

In 1955, when Congress first attempted to deal with the problems of air pollution in the Air Pollution Control Act, it failed to consider both problems. That Act contained no definition of air pollution, and it also left enforcement of the law up to voluntary efforts by the states. As initially enacted, the law merely provided technical and financial assistance to the states.

Slowly the federal law acquired more teeth. In 1963, federal agencies were authorized to move against interstate air pollution in the Clean Air Act. That Act did not define air pollution either. In 1965, the Act was amended to set standards for emissions by new cars. Throughout this period, the primary emphasis was on state control of air pollution. In 1967, a further amendment required the states to establish air quality standards and to adopt state implementation plans, but the nature of those standards and implementation plans was left up to the states.

Real teeth were finally put in the federal law with the Clean Air Amendments of 1970. Those Amendments generally gave authority over the Act to the EPA, and required or authorized the Administrator of the EPA to make regulations dealing with air quality, but continued to assert that "[E]ach state shall have the primary responsibility for assuring air quality within the entire geographic area comprising such State. . . ."

The Definition of Air Pollution

The 1970 Amendments resolved the problem of defining the term *air pollution* by requiring the Administrator of the EPA to issue a list of *air pollutants* which, "in his judgment has an adverse effect on public health or welfare," and "the presence of which in the ambient air results from numerous or diverse mobile or secondary sources." The term *ambient* means simply "surrounding on all sides." Initially, the Administrator's list included six such pollutants: *sulfur dioxide* (SO_2), *particulates, carbon monoxide* (CO), *photochemical oxidants* (nitrogen oxide and ozone), *hydrocarbons*, and *nitrogen dioxide* (NO_2). In 1977, *lead* was added, and in 1982 hydrocarbons were removed from the list. The Administrator's list contains maximum limits for each of the six pollutants. Those maximum limits are the National Ambient Air Quality Standards, or NAAQS's.

National Ambient Air Quality Standards   For each pollutant, as defined by the Administrator, the Administrator was also required to establish **National Ambient Air Quality Standards (NAAQS's)**. For each such pollutant there are two standards: *primary standards,* which, "allowing an adequate margin of safety, are requisite to protect the public health"; and *secondary standards,* which are "requisite to protect the public welfare from any known or anticipated adverse effects. . . ." The primary standards are generally interpreted to mean those necessary to protect human life and health, while the secondary standards generally mean those necessary to protect non-human elements, such as buildings, animals, and crops. The NAAQS's are generally framed in micrograms per cubic meter over a period of time or, more normally, parts per million over a period of time. The NAAQS's are essentially the maximum limits of pollutants that the air may legally carry.

State Implementation Plans (SIP's)

After the Administrator established the NAAQS's, states were required to establish **State Implementation Plans** (SIP's) to implement, maintain, and enforce the primary standards as "expeditiously as practicable but . . . in no case later than three years from the date of approval of such plan." States were required to meet the secondary standards within a reasonable time specified in the plan itself. The original dates for meeting the primary standards ranged from 1975 to 1977, but nowhere were those goals met. As a result, a series of amendments were passed extending the deadlines. The last such amendment extended the deadline to 1982.

Existing Stationary Souces of Pollution

Emission standards for stationary sources that existed prior to the adoption of the 1970 Amendments are found in the state implementation plans and are often part of state administrative regulations adopted by state environmental protection agencies. In areas in which pollution concentrations exceed the NAAQS's, the Act requires that the state plans impose at least "reasonably available control technology" on such sources. The federal EPA Administrator may amend the state plans to reach those goals. States may adopt implementation plans that exceed the NAAQS's, however. Economic cost and technological feasibility are not to be considered by the administrator in considering and approving a state implementation plan but such issues may be raised before the state agency or in the state courts. Many states have set up a procedure for "hardship variances," which take technological feasibility and economic cost into account.

In 1977, the Clean Air Act was amended when it became obvious that the primary standards would not be met. The 1977 Amendments specified a delayed schedule for general compliance, but also provide specific relief to individual sources unable to meet the NAAQS's, because present facilities are being retired, because of investment in innovative facilities with the promise of better pollution reduction, or due to government orders to convert from cleaner fuels to coal because of the energy crisis. Such sources may obtain *delayed compliance orders,* issued by either state or federal EPAs. Such orders generally contain conditions and compliance schedules that cannot exceed three years after final compliance with requirements specified in the state implementation plan.

State Failure to Attain NAASQ Standards

In the event a state is unable or unwilling to meet the NAAQS standards, the principal sanction is a moratorium on construction and operation of new or modified stationary sources. Another possible remedy is denial of federal grants, including federal grants for highway construction. In 1977, the Clean Air Act was amended to authorize postponement of the date for compliance with the primary standards until 1983, or 1987 in the case of oxidants and carbon monoxide. Early in 1983, the EPA designated over a hundred counties nationwide as "probable noncompliance areas."

New Stationary Sources of Pollution

The Administrator was also required to establish federal standards of performance for *new* sources of pollution. A "new source" is one constructed or modified after the effective date of the permanent regulations, and a "standard of performance" is defined as a limit on emissions of pollutants. Such limits are to be set by taking into account the "best system of emission reduction ... taking into account the cost of achieving such reduction...."*

The issue of cost has been one of the most vehemently litigated questions in air pollution cases. Much of the litigation came up in the context of the cement industry. The Administrator (Ruckleshaus) had established standards of performance by estimating the total capital and operating costs for the necessary control equipment to meet the proposed standards for cement dust, and concluded that such costs were affordable by the industry and could be passed on to customers without substantially affecting competition with manufacturers of construction substitutes, such as steel, asphalt, and aluminum. The Portland Cement Association appealed the standards and argued that the Administrator had not taken cost into account, as required by the statute.

Portland Cement Association v. Ruckleshaus

486 F. 2d 375 (D.C. Cir., 1973)

The Portland Cement Association argued that (1) the standards for cement plants were higher than those imposed on other polluters, including competing building materials plants; and (2) that the Administrator had failed to take "cost" of the control facilities into account. The Administrator had set the standards for cement plants by prescribing a maximum limit of .03 g/scf for particulates, such as cement dust, from newly constructed cement plants and a limit of 10% for the opacity of plumes from the stacks of such plants. Those standards were significantly higher than standards for other industries.

> LEVENTHAL, Circuit Judge. . . .
> Petitioners also challenge the cement standards as unfair in light of lower standards mandated for fossil-fuel-fired steam generating power plants and incinerators. They claim that while the cement standard, as expressed in grains of particulates allowed per standard cubic foot of gas (g/scf) requires a reduction to .03, power plants are permitted to reach .12 and incinerators to be at .10. Also opacity standards differ, with no opacity standard set for incinerators, and with a 20 percent requirement for power plants (with 40 percent opacity permitted for not more than 2 minutes in any hour).
>
> . . . .
> EPA, . . . stated . . . "The difference between the particulate standard for cement plants and those for steam generators and incinerators is attributable to the superior technology available therefor (that is, fabric filter technology has not been applied to coal-fired steam generators or incinerators)."
>
> . . . .
> The core of our response to petitioners is that the Administrator is not required to present affirmative justifications for different standards in different industries. Inter-industry comparisons of this kind are not generally required, or even productive; and

---

*Clean Air Act, Section 111.

they were not contemplated by Congress in this Act. The essential question is whether the mandated standards can be met by a particular industry for which they are set, and this can typically be decided on the basis of information concerning that industry alone. . . . [T]here is no requirement of uniformity of specific standards for all industries. . . .

There is, of course, a significant and proper scope for inter-industry comparison in the case of industries producing substitute or alternative products. This bears on the issue of "economic cost." But this comparison was utilized in arriving at the agency decision, and no contention is raised that such competitive-industry impact was either ignored or assessed invalidly.

. . . .

The objecting companies contend that the Administrator has not complied with the mandate of §111 of the Act, which requires him to "[take] into account the costs" of achieving the emission reductions he prescribes, . . .

The Administrator found in the Background Document that, for a new wet-process plant with a capacity of 2.5 million barrels per year, the total investment for all installed air pollution control equipment will represent approximately 12 percent of the investment for the total facility. He also found that "[a]nnual operating costs for the control equipment will be approximately 7 percent of the total plant operating costs. . . .

Petitioners argue that this analysis is not enough—that the Administrator is required to prepare a quantified cost-benefit analysis, showing the benefit to ambient air conditions as measured against the cost of pollution devices. However desirable in the abstract, such a requirement would conflict with the specific time constraints imposed on the administrator. The difficulty, if not impossibility, of quantifying the benefit to ambient air conditions, further militates against the imposition of such an imperative on the agency. . . .

The EPA contention that economic costs to the industry have been taken into account, derives substantial support from a study prepared for EPA. . . . It concluded that the additional costs of control equipment could be passed on without substantially affecting competition with construction substitutes such as steel, asphalt, and aluminum, because "[d]emand for cement, derived for the most part from public and private construction, is not highly elastic with regard to price and would not be very sensitive to small price changes." . . .

The Court affirmed the lower court judgment on the issue of cost, but remanded the case on the question of whether the specific scientific test for judging plume opacity was sufficiently accurate. The lower court found the test sufficient, and that ruling was later affirmed by the Supreme Court after a second appeal.

In 1977, the Clean Air Act was amended to require the Administrator to prepare an "economic assessment respecting such standard or regulation." The assessment is available to the public, and must analyze the costs of compliance, the potential inflationary or recessionary effects, and the effects on competition, consumer cost, and energy use. These assessments are not to be used to "alter the basis on which a standard or regulation is promulgated," nor do they authorize or permit judicial review of the standards on those bases.

New Motor Vehicle Standards

Under the 1970 Amendments, automobiles beginning with model year 1975 must have reduced their exhaust emissions of hydrocarbons and carbon monoxide by at least 90 percent from the levels permissible in 1970. The Act contained an escape clause, which permitted auto manufacturers to apply for a one-year suspension if technology was not available to achieve timely compliance. International Harvester, Ford, Chrysler, General Motors, and Volvo applied for suspensions in 1972, but the Administrator refused the suspension. The U.S. Court of Appeals for the District of Columbia overruled the Administrator and remanded to the EPA. The Agency reconsidered and granted the suspension. In 1974, Congress amended the Act to delay compliance until 1977, and subsequently the Act was amended once again to delay compliance until model year 1983.

Hazardous Pollutants Other than NAAQS's

There are of course pollutants other than those for which NAAQS's have been established, and the Clean Air Act directs the Administrator to publish a list of "hazardous air pollutants." A hazardous air pollutant is defined as a pollutant for which no NAAQS has been established but which, in the judgment of the Administrator, may cause or contribute to pollution that may result in an increase in mortality or in serious irreversible or incapacitating reversible illness. The Administrator must also prescribe a national emission standard for each such pollutant with "an ample margin of safety to protect the public health."

Offsets and Bubbles

In areas in which the NAAQS standards have not been met (so-called **nonattainment areas**), new sources must obtain permits from the EPA. Permits may be issued only if the total allowable emissions from the new source are less than the total emissions from existing sources under the state implementation plan. In other words, the permit will only be allowed if the new emissions are **offset** by a reduction in old emissions. Thus the owner may have to shut down an old facility in order to open a new one, or by adding new control facilities to old plants. Offsets are permitted because of reductions by others as well, and some owners have gone so far as to pay an owner of a nearby facility to shut down or control an existing facility. Since 1979, the EPA has permitted "banking" of unused emission credits for future offset and the trading and sale of such unused credits. The principal limitation is that the total equation represent "reasonable progress" toward reaching the NAAQS.

There are also offsets permitted within a single source, under the so-called **bubble doctrine.** All of the parts of a single industrial plant are treated as a single source, and offsetting increases and decreases in emission from different parts of the facility are permitted as long as the end result is no net increase in total emissions.

Sanctions and Penalties Against Individual Polluters

Criminal penalties against individual polluters may include fines up to $25,000 per *day* of violation or one year in prison or both for the first offense and fines up to $50,000 per day of violation or two years in prison or both for subsequent offenses. A civil penalty of up to $25,000 per day of violation may also be assessed, and injunctions against continued violations may be issued. Any person may bring a civil lawsuit for violation, and suits are also permitted against the Administrator. If successful, the courts may order the polluter to pay attorney's fees and costs as well as actual damages. In addition, federal agencies may not enter into government contracts with persons convicted of any offense under the Act.

Regulation of Water Pollution

Control of pollution of waters and waterways involves totally different problems and concerns than are involved in air pollution. But, like air pollution concerns, federal water pollution policies began evolving during the 1950's and generally preferred to leave enforcement up to the states. In 1972, federal water pollution policy became effective with major amendments to the Federal Water Pollution Control Act (FWPCA). It is important to briefly consider the major problems facing the nation's water supply before undertaking any examination of that statute, however.

The Nature of Water Pollution

The national water policy focuses on three principal concerns: *aquatic ecology*, or the nature of the relationships between aquatic plants and animals; *recreational and aesthetic concerns*, centering on the inability to use America's waters for fishing, swimming, and boating because of pollutants; and ultimate *contamination of the water supply*.

Water pollutants fall into five major classes: *organic wastes*, principally human sewage; other *nutrients*, such as those found in agricultural fertilizers; *toxic chemicals* and other hazardous substances, such as pesticides, acids, and alkaline substances; *sediment*, or particulate matter that settles to the bottom of lakes and streams; and *heated water*, discharged from industrial sources and nuclear power plants.

One of the most adverse effects of water pollution is *eutrophication*, or the dying of lakes. The natural cycle of fish feeding on algae growing in organic wastes deposited by those fish and dependent on sunlight for growth may be interrupted by the addition of too much organic waste or nutrients from pollution, such as agricultural fertilizers in run-off. The algae grows well—in fact, too well—until the entire top surface of the lake is covered. This reduces the sunlight available for algae growth and soon all the algae dies. The death of the algae means that no food is available for the fish and soon they too die. The entire process is hastened by the addition of warm water, such as that released from a nuclear power plant. Perhaps the prime example is Lake Erie, which was thought to be completely "dead" until the early 1980's.

No less pleasing and probably more dangerous is the damage caused by toxic chemicals and other hazardous substances in the water supply. Pesticides such as DDT and metals like mercury and cadmium may be outright poisons to aquatic life and perhaps ultimately to humans. Excessive acid content and salt may affect aquatic life as well.

Finally, our aesthetic senses are often offended by pollutants as well. Water may smell, become murky and turbid, and may become covered by oil, gasoline, or other pollutants, making it extremely unpleasant in which to swim, boat, or fish, and producing obvious dangers to aquatic life.

Many of the man-made sources of pollutions are controllable, simply because they originate at a single point, and that point may be shut down or limited. Agricultural pollution, generally originating from run-off from farm land, is particularly troublesome since it does not originate from a single point but rather is erosion coupled with pesticides and fertilizers. New farming methods may promise to reduce this sort of pollution, especially "drilled" seeding (also called conservation tillage), which does not involve plowing.

The Federal Water Pollution Control Act (FWPCA)

Prior to 1972, water pollution control was left up to state enforcement in much the same way that air pollution control had been left to the states. The states developed standards applicable to particular segments of a body of water and enforcement did not begin until the quality of the entire segment deteriorated below those standards. Enforcement was difficult, if not impossible, because of the problems of several polluters discharging into the same streams.

In 1972, the FWPCA was amended and a totally different philosophy was adopted. Those amendments established two "goals:" to make the nation's waters *safe for fishing and swimming* by 1983; and to eliminate completely *all pollutant discharges* into navigable waters by 1987. The Act generally imposed a system of gradually increasing strictness, including discharge standards, permits, and enforcement, in order to reach those goals. The Amendment continued to envision enforcement by the states, but federal authorities had the right to enforce the laws as well. Like the Clean Air Act, the FWPCA was again amended in 1977 to permit extensions from the 1983 deadlines on a case-by-case basis, and some of the specific deadlines were generally extended.

Point Source Standards: BPT, BCT, and BAT

The 1972 Amendments required all **point sources** of pollution to reflect the "best practicable technology" (**BPT**) by 1977, and the "best available technology" (**BAT**) by 1983. A point source is defined as "any discernible, confined and discrete conveyance ... from which pollutants are or may be discharged."

Best Practicable Technology   The statute requires, in determining whether a point source is using the "best practicable technology," considerations such as the total cost of applying new technology, the age of equipment, the production process employed, nonwater quality impacts, and such other factors as the Administrator deems appropriate to consider. The courts will not consider the "assimilative ability" of the receiving water, however, so that a source discharging into a large body such as the Pacific Ocean may not claim that the impact of the pollution is small because the size of the receiving body of water is so large.

In balancing the costs in determining whether a point source is using the BPT, EPA need not conduct a full-blown cost-benefit comparison, but only *consider* the cost of pollution control facilities in their analysis. In other words, the EPA has substantial discretion, and is not required to give any particular factor any specific weight. The Supreme Court has held* that the EPA *must* grant variances from the BPT standards to plants that are "fundamentally different" from the norm. Such variances need not be issued to take into account an individual plant's economic inability to sustain the costs. The EPA need only consider costs in relation to the industry as a whole.

In 1977, Congress amended the Act to add a third category, that of "best conventional pollutant control technology" (**BCT**). This category applies only to point sources of "conventional pollutants," as opposed to "toxic" pollutants. BCT standards required achievement by July 1, 1984, and require the EPA to consider the reasonableness of the costs balanced by the benefits of reducing that pollution. In other words, the statute requires a cost-benefit analysis, not applied to toxic or non-conventional pollutants.

Best Available Technology   The point discharges subject to the BAT standards are those that involve either nonconventional or toxic pollutants. The BAT standards set 1984 as a deadline for achieving that level of pollution control. There is no requirement of cost-benefit analysis under the BAT standard, but the EPA may consider the age of equipment, the process employed, engineering aspects, process changes, and the cost of achieving such reductions. Variances are permitted under two conditions: if modified requirements will represent the maximum use of control technology within the economic capacity of the owner; and if the modified requirements will result in reasonable progress toward elimination of the discharges.

Publicly-Owned Sewage Treatment Plants

Sewage treatment is a major problem of water pollution. First, treatment facilities are publicly owned in most instances, and imposition of strict controls on such plants can only result in higher taxes or user fees. The Act provides for control of such facilities but on a somewhat more relaxed schedule than private point discharges and provides for federal assistance in funding plant improvements for pollution control purposes.

The Permit System

The Act also created a permit system, known as the National Pollutant Discharge Elimination System (NPDES). Under that system, *any* point discharge is unlawful unless the polluter has a permit issued by the EPA or by the states acting under the authority of the EPA. Permits must include the applicable limitations and a schedule of compliance to meet the 1977 and 1983 deadlines.

New Sources of Water Pollution

New sources of pollution were held to a higher standard than existing sources. Such sources were held to a BAT standard from the beginning. In determining whether

---

*E. I. duPont de Nemours & Co. v. Train, 430 U.S. 112, 97 S. Ct. 965, 51 L. Ed. 2d 204 (1977).

BAT was being used, the Administrator must view the industry as a whole and may consider the cost of achieving pollution reduction, energy requirements, and non-water quality environmental impact.

Regulation of Toxic Substances and Solid Waste

There is no comprehensive federal statute dealing with the problems of toxic chemicals. Instead, several specific statutes deal with different aspects of the problem: the Federal Insecticide, Fungicide and Rodenticide Act, the Resource Conservation and Recovery Act, and the Toxic Substances Control Act. The general pollution statutes regarding clean air and water may also apply.

Regulation of Pesticides and Other Poisons

The Federal Insecticide, Fungicide and Rodenticide Act (FIFRA), originally enacted in 1947 and substantially amended in 1978, requires "economic poisons" to be registered with the EPA prior to their sale, requires labelling of the product including directions for its use, and, at the request of the Administrator, may require testing of the product. The EPA must approve the registration and may only approve the product if it determines that it will not cause unreasonably adverse effects on the environment. States may certify persons to apply such products as well.

Regulation of Solid Wastes: The Resource Conservation and Recovery Act (RCRA)

The RCRA, with its controversial "superfund," is aimed solid waste disposal, including disposal of toxic substances. The Act classifies solid waste generators, transporters, and disposal sites and gives authority to the EPA to prescribe standards for each. Solid waste generators (i.e., persons or firms "creating" solid waste such as trash, by-products, or liquids) are required to file reports, keep records, label materials, and use appropriate containers. Solid waste transporters must keep accurate records of where they pick up waste and where they dispose of it. Disposal sites must have a permit, and the EPA is given broad inspection powers and the power to issue compliance orders, seek an injunction, or ask for the imposition of criminal penalties. Generally, the federal policy is a cradle to the grave regulation.

In 1980, the Act was amended to include the controversial **superfund** in the Comprehensive Environmental Response, Compensation and Liability Act. That Act authorized the President to require clean up of releases of toxic materials and to establish a national contingency plan to clean up such releases. The Act also makes owners of facilities or contaminated land liable for government clean-up costs but does not include liabilities for injuries to private persons. Finally, the Act creates a fund financed by a tax on the production of toxic chemicals to be used to pay response costs including the expense of the national contingency fund and the government's cost of restoring the natural resources injured by toxic chemicals.

Regulation of Toxic Substances

The Toxic Substances Control Act of 1976 is concerned with the manufacture and processing of toxic substances. The objective of the Act is to keep such substances off the market. The Act applies to any substance that creates an unreasonable risk of danger to health or to the environment and requires manufacturers to test products for their effect on health and the environment. Such manufacturers must give notice to the EPA before manufacturing any new chemical substance and the EPA may apply administrative restrictions or apply for an emergency injunction to stop "imminent hazards."

Protection of Wildlife and Wild Places

While a great deal of environmental law focuses on pollution control, another branch of environmental law seeks to preserve the natural resources and natural beauty of our world. At the outset, this goal of environmental policy is difficult to justify under traditional cost-benefit analysis. While the economic and social costs of pollution may be measured and weighed against the benefits of the industrialization causing such pollution, it is impossible to place a value on having wild places in the world or of maintaining a species of wild animal that, at least for now, is economically useless. Some economists would argue that wildlife and wilderness are public goods, much like fire protection and national defense, which do not fit neatly into cost-benefit analysis. Others argue that wilderness and wild things may acquire value in the future, and thus must be saved in the present. Others simply argue that the world is a better place because of the existence of wilderness and wild things. The end result is that both the public and Congress have chosen a national policy of preserving wilderness areas and wildlife.

The Endangered Species Act

The Endangered Species Act of 1978 imposed planning responsibilities on federal agencies and their licensees and prohibited any commercial trade or activity in endangered species, alive or dead, or in their parts. The Secretary of the Interior, or in some instances the Secretary of Commerce, must prepare a list of those species which are endangered or threatened and must establish regulations protecting the species. The Secretary of the Interior may acquire land to protect the species as well. The Act absolutely prohibits any agency from undertaking *any action* that would jeopardize the continued existence of a listed species or that would result in the destruction or modification of a critical habitat of a listed species.

An agency undertaking an activity that would affect a listed species must do a biological assessment before any construction is done and before contracts are made. Applications for exemptions from the strict wording of the Act may be made to an ad hoc review board, made up of one person named by the Secretary, a resident of the affected state named by the President, and an administrative law judge. The review board makes a report to the Endangered Species Committee, which makes the final decision whether to grant an exemption. That decision is subject to judicial review. In one famous case, the Committee refused an exemption for the Tellico Dam and Reservoir, a $78 million TVA project, on the grounds that it would destroy the habitat of the snail darter, a small fish on the endangered species list which had no known economic purpose. The Supreme Court agreed with the Committee* but Congress later passed a special bill exempting the Tellico Dam from the requirements of the Endangered Species Act.

Both civil and criminal penalties may be used to enforce the Act. The law prohibits violating any of the regulations made pursuant to the Act, taking, killing or selling any species on the endangered list, and prohibits importation or exportation of any such species or products made of such species.

The Wilderness Act of 1964

The Wilderness Act authorizes the establishment of a national wilderness preservation system and requires Congress to formally designate lands which qualify as wilderness. Once land is designated as wilderness, no permanent activity, commercial enterprise, or permanent road may be undertaken in the area. Mining and prospecting could occur until December 31, 1983, but no formal mining claims could be made after that date. Such lands may be used for hydroelectric power projects, including transmission lines, and livestock grazing.

Congress also passed emergency legislation in 1978 in the form of the Endangered American Wilderness Act to immediately declare certain threatened wilderness areas immune from development. Similarly, the Wild and Scenic Rivers Act of 1968 designated certain waterways as immune from development and prohibited even hydroelectric power projects on rivers made a part of the system.

Federal Energy Policies

Like the environment, the existence of an adequate supply of energy was taken for granted by many Americans until the OPEC oil embargo of the mid-1970's. That crisis drove home what many experts had been arguing for years: Energy resources were in fact limited and dependence on foreign energy resources was dangerous and misplaced. Though Congress had shown sporadic concern with energy in the past, the oil crisis was the crucial factor in the creation of the twin energy policies of the federal government. Those policies were (1) conservation of existing resources of traditional fuels, such as oil and coal, and (2) development and control of alternative energy sources, including nuclear power.

Energy and the environment cannot be viewed as isolated categories but must be thought of as intimately interrelated. Operation of new oil refineries and burning high sulfur coal may be important to our national energy policy, but they also result

---

TVA v. *Hill,* 437 U.S. 153, 98 S. Ct. 2279, 57 L. Ed. 2d 117 (1978).

in greater air pollution. Oil pipelines may be necessary to transport fuel cheaply but they leave lasting scars on wilderness areas. Offshore oil development is important but defaces previously pristine coastlines and risks dangerous oil spills. Development of nuclear energy is viewed, at least by many federal authorities, as the ultimate energy solution but results in the release of large amounts of superheated water into reservoirs and runs the risk of radiation release. Everywhere, it seems, concern with the environment must be balanced with concern with energy.

Development and Conservation of Traditional Fuels

Federal policy regarding the traditional fossil fuels, oil and coal, has generally aimed at developing new resources within the United States and conserving the resources already known. Oil policy has been concerned with both *onshore development,* principally in the area of how best to transport oil from the new Alaskan oil fields to refineries in the eastern United States, and with *offshore development,* the development of new oil fields lying under the ocean floor near the continental United States. Federal policy regarding coal has aimed at encouraging the use of coal, which is more plentiful than oil, and finding ways to use high-sulfur coal, despite its greater air pollution than the less plentiful low-sulfur coal.

Liability for Oil Spills

In 1978, the Outer Continental Shelf Lands Act, which mandates oil leases for off-shore drilling, was amended to impose strict liability for clean-up costs and damages on the owner and operator of any offshore oil facility or vessel involved in an oil spill. Liability is limited to $250,000 in the case of a vessel or $35 million plus government removal charges in the case of an offshore facility, but those limits are not applicable if the spill is the result of wilful misconduct, gross negligence, or the violation of a federal safety regulation. Expenses over the amounts paid by the owner and operator are paid by the Oil Spill Pollution Fund, which was created by an amendment to the OCS Lands Act. That fund is financed by a fee of 3¢ per barrel imposed on the owner of oil obtained from offshore drilling.

Several other statutes also impose liability for oil spills. The Clean Water Act makes vessels strictly liable for clean-up costs unless the spill is caused by an act of God, an act of war, an act or omission of third parties, or negligence of the federal government. The Act limits liability to $125,000 for inland oil barges and $250,000 for other vessels. Owners of other facilities, such as offshore wells or refineries, may be liable for clean-up costs of up to $50 million as well. None of the limits apply if the spill is the result of wilful negligence or wilful misconduct. Other statutes imposing liability for oil spills include the Trans-Alaska Pipeline Authorization Act, the Deepwater Port Act, and various state statutes.

Conversion to Coal

Because existing American coal reserves far exceed existing oil reserves, Congress adopted a policy of encouraging the use of coal instead of oil. The National Energy Act requires certain electric power plants and other major fuel-burning installations to switch from gas and oil to coal. The Department of Energy may order individual plants or entire industries to convert to coal or other fuels if it finds that the change is both financially and technologically feasible. The EPA may oppose such changes if they would cause a violation of the NAAQS's, however.

The use of coal instead of oil or gas is not without its environmental effects, however. Strip mining of coal leaves ugly scars on the face of the earth, and large sections of land are unusable once the coal reserves are depleted. Burning coal, particularly the more abundant high-sulfur coal found in the eastern United States, results in higher levels of sulfur oxides, which may fall to earth later in the form of sulfuric acid, known as acid rain. Coal conversions may result in the release of more carbon dioxide, which some scientists claim may result in a global warming trend.

The Surface Mining Control and Reclamation Act of 1977 requires states to adopt policies to protect the environment from strip mining practices, and if states fail to adopt such policies, the Department of Interior may impose a plan on a state. Generally, such plans must require permits for strip mining conditioned on restoration of the land to its original condition and contour, preservation of topsoil, and revegetation.

Air pollution regulations in the Clean Air Act encouraged the use of low-sulfur coal found chiefly in the western states, which in turn posed a threat to the jobs and local economies of the eastern states producing high-sulfur coal. In 1977, the Clean Air Act was amended to permit the EPA to set variable limits on pollution dependent on a percentage reduction in air pollution, rather on than absolute reductions. A 1978 amendment to the Act also permitted the President, on the petition of a state governor, to prohibit major fuel burning installations from using anything but "locally or regionally available coal or coal derivatives" if such action is necessary to "prevent or minimize significant local or regional disruption or unemployment."

Encouragement of Synthetic Fuels

The Synthetic Fuels Corporation Act of 1980 was enacted to encourage the development of manufactured fuels, such as coal gasification and liquefaction programs. A public corporation was established to administer a $20 billion development program, but private corporate interest in the program faded after the oil crisis was over.

Regulation of Nuclear Energy

Perhaps the most controversial form of energy is nuclear power. Originally, the federal government retained a monopoly over nuclear energy and gave control of nuclear power in all forms to the Atomic Energy Commission (AEC) through the Atomic Energy Act of 1946. In 1954, that Act was amended to permit licensing of private nuclear power generating facilities. In 1974, the Atomic Energy Commission was reorganized and renamed the Nuclear Regulatory Commission (NRC).

The NRC is responsible for licensing all private nuclear facilities, including nuclear power plants, and for regulating nuclear health and safety. Under that authority, the NRC develops research in all phases of nuclear energy, inspects nuclear facilities, and investigates accidents. Major controversies exist regarding plant safety and location and in disposal of nuclear waste materials. (See *Silkwood* v. *Kerr-McGee,* Chapter 2, p. 44.)

Plant Licensing: Safety and Location

In the aftermath of the Three Mile Island incident in 1979 and an awakening public concern with the safety of nuclear power plants, the NRC tightened its procedures for licensing and plant safety requirements. (See *Metropolitan Edison Co.* v. *PANE,* p. 604.)

Upon an application for a permit, the NRC conducts a review of the construction plans, safety procedures, and environmental impact of a new nuclear facility. That review includes the preparation of an Environmental Impact Statement under the NEPA requirements, and those documents are usually reviewed by the EPA, state EPA's, and local zoning boards. Under the *Calvert Cliffs* decision, the environmental effects must be considered at every stage of the decision-making process. The NRC makes use of a so-called *generic EIS,* however, to avoid detailed consideration of some environmental decisions. A **generic EIS** is a general statement of the environmental impacts that always accompany construction and operation of a nuclear power facility. The use of a generic EIS was approved by the Supreme Court in 1983 (see *Baltimore Gas & Electric Co.* v. *NRC,* p. 621).

Following the Three Mile Island incident, Congress toughened the procedures relating to licensing and authorized funds for additional federal inspectors. The NRC was ordered to develop a plan for agency response to future accidents and to develop new population limits for the area surrounding a licensed nuclear power plant. The NRC was also directed to develop a plan for improving the technical capabilities of employees in such plants. The agency has also begun including a discussion of the environmental risks of so-called class 9 accidents in the EIS. A class 9 accident, the most serious kind, involves a breach of the reactor and exposure of radiation to the atmosphere. Each violation of NRC regulations carries a civil penalty of up to $100,000.

Under NEPA, consideration of the environmental impact of a plant, including consideration of alternative sites, must *precede* the issuance of a construction permit. The NRC has followed a practice of permitting utility companies to begin site development of the proposed plant before the Commission issues the construction permit. As a result, the site chosen by the utility will often be "superior" to other sites because of the money already spent to develop that site, and other sites will be less favorable since the utility would be required to start over.

Disposal of Nuclear Waste

Operation of a nuclear power facility involves the creation of tons of radioactive waste. Some of that waste can be reprocessed into useable fuel and might constitute a significant energy source, while other waste must be disposed of in some manner. Nuclear waste is generally considered either *low level,* which is generally not considered particularly dangerous and may be incinerated, buried, or deposited at sea, or *high level,* which is extremely dangerous and may remain toxic for 250,000 years. A related problem deals with how to dismantle and dispose of worn-out nuclear power plants, since portions of the plants themselves become radioactive.

The NRC has taken the position that, while science has not yet resolved how to dispose of high-level nuclear waste completely, that problem will be resolved someday, and in the meantime those wastes should be kept at the power plants. The Commission has established Table S-3, which is a part of the generic EIS used for all power plants. That table concludes that "the environmental effects of the uranium fuel cycle have been shown to be relatively insignificant." In *Vermont Yankee Nuclear Power Corp.* v. *NRDC,* Chapter 5, p. 158, the Supreme Court held that the procedures used to adopt Table S-3 conformed to the Administrative Procedures Act. In 1983, the Court again considered the "spent fuel cycle" and Table S-3.

Baltimore Gas and Electric Co. v. Nuclear Regulatory Commission

———— U.S. ————, 103 S. Ct. 2246, ———— L. Ed 2d ———— (1983)

Justice O'CONNOR delivered the opinion of the Court.

... [T]he National Environmental Policy Act ... (NEPA), requires federal agencies to consider the environmental impact of any major federal action. As part of its generic rulemaking proceedings to evaluate the environmental effects of the nuclear fuel cycle for nuclear power plants, the Nuclear Regulatory Commission (Commission) decided that licensing boards should assume, for purposes of NEPA, that the permanent storage of certain nuclear wastes would have no significant environmental impact and thus should not affect the decision whether to license a particular nuclear power plant. We conclude that the Commission complied with NEPA and that its decision is not arbitrary or capricious within the meaning of ... the Administrative Procedure Act. ...

I

. . . .

The Commission first adopted Table S-3 in 1974.... This "original" rule, ... declared that in environmental reports and impact statements for individual licensing proceedings the environmental costs of the fuel cycle "shall be as set forth" in Table S-3 and that "[n]o further discussion of such environmental effects shall be required." ... The original Table S-3 contained no numerical entry for the long-term environmental effects of storing solidified ... high-level wastes, because the Commission staff believed that techology would be developed to isolate the wastes from the environment. The Commission and the parties have later termed this assumption of complete repository integrity as the "zero-release" assumption: the reasonableness of this assumption is at the core of the present controversy.

II

... Much of the debate focuses on whether development of nuclear generation facilities should proceed in the face of uncertainties about their long-term effects on the environment. Resolution of these fundamental policy questions lies, however, with Congress and the agencies to which Congress has delegated authority, as well as with state legislatures and, ultimately, the populace as a whole. Congress has assigned the courts only the limited, albeit important, task of reviewing agency action to determine whether the agency conformed with controlling statutes. As we emphasized in our earlier encounter with these very proceedings, "[a]dministrative decisions should be set aside in this context, as in every other, only for substantial procedural or substantive reasons as mandated by statute . . ., not simply because the court is unhappy with the result reached." *Vermont Yankee*, . . .

. . . Congress in enacting NEPA did not require agencies to elevate environmental concerns over other appropriate considerations. . . . Rather, it required only that the agency take a "hard look" at the environmental consequences before taking a major action. . . . The role of the courts is simply to ensure that the agency has adequately considered and disclosed the enviromental impact of its actions and that its decision is not arbitrary or capricious. See generally *Citizens to Preserve Overton Park* v. *Volpe*. . . .

In its Table S-3 Rule here, the Commission has determined that the probabilities favor the zero-release assumption, because the Nation is likely to develop methods to store the wastes with no leakage to the environment. The NRDC did not challenge. . . . the reasonableness of this determination. . . . and no party seriously challenges it here. The Commission recognized, however, that the geological, chemical, physical and other data it relied on in making this prediction were based, in part, on assumptions which involve substantial uncertainties. Again, no one suggests that the uncertainties are trivial or the potential effects insignificant if time proves the zero-release assumption to have been seriously wrong. After confronting the issue, though, the Commission has determined that the uncertainties concerning the development of nuclear waste storage facilities are not sufficient to affect the outcome of any individual licensing decision.

It is clear that the Commission, in making this determination, has made the careful consideration and disclosure required by NEPA. The sheer volume of proceedings before the Commission is impressive. . . . The [Commission's] Statement summarizes the major uncertainty of long-term storage in bedded-salt repositories, which is that water could infiltrate the repository as a result of such diverse factors as geologic faulting, a meteor strike, or accidental or deliberate intrusion by man. The Commission noted that the probability of intrusion was small, . . . The Commission also found the evidence "tentative but favorable" that an appropriate site could be found. . . . [I]t simply cannot be said that the Commission ignored or failed to disclose the uncertainties surrounding its zero-release assumption.

. . . .

Reversed.

It appears that Congress has adopted the "bedded salt repository" (several hundred meters underground) solution, and all that remains is the choice of location for that repository. Under the Nuclear Waste Policy Act of 1982, the Department of Energy submitted five potential sites to the President by January 1, 1985, and the President must choose one of those sites by March 31, 1987. The "receiving state" must approve that location as well.

State Environmental Protection

All states have adopted some form of environmental protection statute, often based closely on the federal model. State Environmental Protection Agencies, often closely duplicating the federal agency, having authority to enforce many of the federal environmental laws, including the Clean Air and Clean Water Acts, but in addition state legislatures have often gone farther than the federal requirements. Many states include noise pollution and odors in the statutory scheme, along with more traditional concerns of air, water, and wilderness control. In addition, many states impose direct limits on fishing, hunting, and trapping as both a conservation measure and a game management technique.

All states have some kind of *zoning statute,* as well, to regulate the use of land. Often authority to enforce those statutes is delegated to units of local government, which must classify land use and require that uses of land that do not conform to the classifications be terminated. There are numerous types of zoning statutes. Perhaps the most controversial of all land use statutes are the *no-growth ordinances* in place in a few cities. Those cities place a limit on the number of building permits that may be issued, often tying that number to the number of demolition permits, in order to limit the amount of growth of a community.

Summary and Conclusions

A national committment to environmental protection did not arise until the 1960's, when the damage to the environment caused by air and water pollution and disposal of hazardous wastes became clear. The complex and interwoven nature of the environment has resulted in a series of specific statutes, each designed to deal with one phase of the environmental problem. That complex and interwoven nature also creates conflicts between competing environmental and energy policies, since improvement in one area often comes at the expense of another.

The common law provided certain limited remedies to persons injured by actions of others affecting the environment. Those remedies, including the actions of nuisance, trespass, and strict liability, and the common-law crime of public nuisance, are difficult to prove and only provide a remedy under certain stringent conditions. They have proved less than useful in protecting the public interest.

The broadest environmental protection statute is the National Environmental Policy Act of 1969. That Act requires federal agencies to take a "hard look" at environmental considerations before undertaking "major federal actions significantly affecting the quality of the human environment" and requires the filing of Environmental Impact Statements.

Specific federal pollution control statutes include the Clean Air Act, the Federal Water Pollution Control Act, and a variety of laws dealing with toxic substances and solid wastes. Those Acts are all quite detailed and specific in their application to particular problems. Wildlife is also protected under the Endangered Species Act and wilderness is protected by a series of federal statutes.

With the oil crisis of the mid-1970's, Congress began considering the problems of energy and centered on two major policies: (1) conservation of traditional fuels and development of new sources of such fuels, and (2) encouragement of synthetic fuels and nuclear energy. Problems of nuclear energy have centered around plant licensing procedures and disposal of nuclear waste.

State agencies also protect the environment, often by statutes that closely mirror the federal laws. State laws also regulate land use through zoning ordinances and other statutes.

PRO AND CON

ISSUE: America's Natural Resources Should Be Used for Commercial Purposes

PRO: America's Resources May Be Exploited AND Preserved.
John B. Fery*

In the 1970s, we found that our high technology culture is just as dependent on natural resources as any culture in history . . . and perhaps even more vulnerable to sudden imbalances in supply and demand. But nothing can be gained by dwelling on limitations at the expense of developing the possibilities.

I want to explore some of these possibilities with you . . . the opportunities provided by America's forest resource. You should know what this magnificent natural resource could become—if we worked at it. To make this exploration, we will have to move beyond the narrow limits of the official title of my remarks. That title helps define the problem, not the solution. It repeats two frequently voiced options for the future of the resource. America's forest, it says, and then asks: Cash Crop or National Monument?

That pretty well sums up the entrenched positions of many advocates after years of debate over forest land issues in the United States. From either of those positions the choices seem tightly limited and depressing—an unattractive either/or choice. We're told we either can have forests that produce timber crops—or we can have forests that are parks or wilderness.

My thesis is more hopeful: I believe we can have both. . . .

This nation's forests are so abundant . . . so potentially productive that they can meet our domestic needs—and go far beyond that to help satisfy a world demand. And we as a nation can realize this resource opportunity without diminishing our national parks . . . without opening up areas already set aside forever as Wilderness. . . . without disturbing established wildlife refuges and other special use forests.

. . . .

If I could leave you with a single thought today, it would be this: *The United States could be to world wood supply what Saudi Arabia is to world oil supply, only better, because we can grow more wood forever, and they can't grow more oil.*

. . . .

The forests of Europe can't keep up with their own demand. The forests of Japan can't meet national needs there either. So where will the wood come from? Russia's Siberian forests are extensive—but remote from industrial centers and transportation systems. The great tropical forests of the world have an enormous inventory of fast-growing hardwood—but generally don't include the softwood species that are widely used in paper and building products.

The forests of North America offer the best potential for meeting increased demand.

. . . .

In developing a forest resource management program for America, . . . meaningful tax incentives should be considered. . . .

There are also some basic policy questions about the management of Federal forest land. Our national forests, for example, have a huge inventory of old growth timber—trees that are mature and overmature. Much of this older timber is dead or dying and being lost to decay or disease. . . .

Harvesting those trees and planting rapidly growing young forests would do more than yield much-needed wood for building materials and paper products. The proceeds from timber sales could help pay for replanting millions of burned over or poorly stocked acres on Federal government lands, as well as provide funding for recreational and wildlife programs.

. . . .

But economic benefits, as great as they are, do not complete the picture. I said earlier that we could increase productivity of our forests, without diminishing our established parks, wilderness areas or wildlife refuges. And that's quite true. If we managed our nonpark, nonwilderness lands intensively, there simply would be no need to even consider harvesting forests that have been set aside as preserves or primitive areas.

---

*John Fery is chairman of Boise Cascade Corporation. From his speech "America's Forest: Cash Crop or National Monument?" delivered at Gonzaga University, Spokane, Washington, February 17, 1982, reprinted in *Vital Speeches of the Day*, vol. 48, p. 465. Reprinted by permission.

CON: We Must Draw the Line
Brock Evans*

It is . . . important to say this at the outset, so that you will know that we environmentalists recognize many different components of the "national" or "public" interest . . . just as we assume that those of you in the timber or mining or energy business likewise recognize this same fact about values other than those your company may be pursuing at the moment. In this sense, too, we're all in this together.

Well, the topic of this conference is about the new Administration's program for the public lands, and the provocative subtitle is "Access to America's Natural Resources . . ." Like so many other phrases and words these days, "access" has become a buzzword too, usually meaning the presumed right of some commercial interest or other to obtain the resources of interest to them that are located on the public lands.

But I would prefer to use both the word "resource" and the phrase "access to them" in a broader sense—to make us all equal here. To me and to our community, "resources" means not just wood and minerals and oil and gas; but also means wildlife and wildlife habitat, scenic vistas, pure streams, clean air, undisturbed natural places, wild places, national parks, places which maintain the amenities of life as well as the commodities of life. And the phrase "access to them" means the right of those who treasure these resources always to be able to count upon their existence—in substantial measure—on our public lands; because we all know that it is only in the public lands, the lands that belong to the people, that these resources are largely going to be available to our growing population and to future generations. These are basic beliefs of our environmental community, and it is our concern for what is happening to these values, to these resources on public lands, that fuels so much of our alarm. . . .

. . . .

. . . [W]e need to understand a bit about the environmental movement itself: who we are, where we have come from—what is our history?

This is necessary, I think, because to believe some of the rhetoric I sometimes listen to at public hearings, or read in trade association journals, one would think that we're just some johnny-come-late-

lies who just happened on the scene around Earth Day sometime . . . well meaning but confused folks whose knowledge and understanding of the environment is limited to coffee table books and cocktail parties.

We're either "rich elitists" or "long-haired hippies," depending on who is speaking—and I still can't figure out if those two are supposed to go together or not!

. . . .

It's an interesting picture indeed, and as you might imagine, it's not quite how we see ourselves.

First of all, environmentalism is a real, genuine movement; environmentalism, in the sense of commonly accepted goals, beliefs, and values, is widespread and pervasive throughout most of our society, without much distinction between ages, classes, sex, race, or geography. . . . By now I think we have all read about the latest Louis Harris Poll regarding the attitudes of the public about the Clean Air Act. In this widespread sampling, Harris found that about 75–80 percent of the American people, across-the-board: white, black, young, old, liberal, conservative, Republican, Democrat—from all sections of the country, all favored keeping the Clean Air Act as strong as it is or making it stronger.

. . . .

To me, the hard test of whether [there is a large degree of support for environmentalism] or not comes finally in those votes in Congress. . . . How do [Congressmen] believe their constituents feel about these public lands issues?

We look around us now at the whole carefully built structure of public land laws, the whole carefully thought out environmental ethic developed over a century, a philosophy of careful management and protection, of husbanding our resources, or reserving from exploitation some places which have higher values . . . and what do we see?

. . . .

We see everywhere efforts to accelerate exploitation of the outer continental shelf, of coal lands, and of millions of acres of fragile and sensitive lands within either already protected systems or marked for further study so that they might in the

---

*Brock Evans is vice president of the National Audubon Society. From his speech "The Environmental Community: Response to the Reagan Administration Program," delivered at the National Symposium on Public Lands and the Reagan Administration, Denver, Colorado, November 19, 1981, and reprinted in *Vital Speeches of the Day*, vol. 48, p. 235. Reprinted by permission.

future be protected, and to eliminate the necessary environmental controls on them. . . . We see efforts to open up Wilderness Areas and National Parks to incompatible, damaging uses. . . . and other efforts to transfer lands out of the National Wildlife Refuge System entirely.

From the Wilderness Act to the Forest Management Act, from the Land and Water Conservation Fund Act to the Surface Mine Act, from the Endangered Species Act to the Outer Continental Shelf Act—the pattern is overwhelmingly the same:

cut or eliminate the budget for the protective, planning and enforcement functions of the laws—and increase the funds for the exploitive parts . . . get those logs out, and get those minerals and oil and gas out faster—and remove or weaken the laws and regulations designed to protect the environment in the process.

. . . .

. . . [W]e are fighting back, there is no recourse left to us . . . we will continue to fight back until at last we can have peace. . . .

DISCUSSION QUESTIONS

1. Clearly pollution is an economic "cost of production" and therefore, in any rational economic system, the firm or individual profiting from the production ought to bear those costs. Do the federal pollution laws impose those costs on the proper persons? Is there a better way?

2. Doesn't each property owner have the right to use his or her property in any way he or she sees fit? Aren't the environmental protection laws a substantial interference with the rights of private property? Then again, aren't laws prohibiting operating gambling houses or "houses of ill repute" also substantial invasions of private property rights? Is there a difference?

3. Why do you suppose NEPA only deals with *government* actions? Why don't we require an EIS in cases of major *private* actions significantly affecting the human environment? Could we do so? Should we do so?

4. Have we been too lax in permitting exemptions or granting extensions to the stated goals of the pollution laws, such as the "fishable and swimmable waters" goal of the FWPCA or the automobile emission standards? Do you suppose industry is purposely "dragging its feet" in meeting such standards? If so, is it a responsible thing for industry to do—for its stockholders, its management, or the public?

5. One argument holds that since there is a limited amount of wilderness available, if we continue to grant exceptions to wilderness preservation statutes "just one more time," ultimately there will be no wilderness left. Is the argument sound? Of what possible use is wilderness, anyway?

6. Which is more important—the habitat of the snail darter, or a $78 million dam, the jobs it produces, and the electricity it generates? The argument has been made that future technology may find economic uses for endangered species, and such future uses justify preservation of such species at all costs. For example, what if we discovered that a cure for cancer could have been produced in the spleen of the snail darter (and *only* in the spleen of the snail darter) after they have become extinct? Is the Tellico Dam worth it? Is the argument sound?

7. Who should pay to clean up oil and toxic chemical spills? Should corporations be permitted to pass those costs on to their customers? How would you stop them from passing such costs on to customers? Should shareholders bear these costs?

8. Which is more important—clean air or cheap and abundant energy from high-sulfur coal?

9. What if the NRC's assumption—that we will ultimately find a safe way to dispose of nuclear waste—is wrong? Should federal policies be built on such faith in American technology? Is such faith justified?

CASE PROBLEMS

1. Abergavenny's home is in a rather exclusive subdivision. Unfortunately, he has some rather interesting hobbies that his neighbors find objectionable. Those hobbies include (1) blacksmithing, which requires a rather large, smoky forge; (2) taxidermy, which requires that he dry smelly pelts and animal parts in the sun; (3) playing the bagpipes on his patio on summer evenings. Assuming that Abergavenny's hobbies violate no local criminal laws, do his neighbors have a remedy?

2. Cornwall Construction Company has several projects on the drawing board at the moment, including (1) building a new office building for a private investor; (2) building a new post-office on the outskirts of town; (3) repairing a federal highway; (4) building a new federal highway; (5) remodeling the interior of an existing federal courthouse. For which of the projects is an Environmental Impact Statement required?

3. The Kent Company has been in business for many years, and has been introducing smoke and gases from burning high-sulphur coal into the environment since its creation. In addition, the profit margin of the company is so slim that using any other fuel will force it to operate at a loss. The total pollution in the area of the Kent plant is higher than the NAAQS's for all types of pollution. The state implementation plan requires all plants in the area to reduce pollutant emissions by 25 percent by 1986. To do so will put Kent out of business. Does Kent have a remedy?

4. The Mowbray Company has been discharging waste materials into the Mississippi River for years. It manufactures various plastic products using a production process entirely different than other plastic companies, since it was established just before pollution controls were instituted, and its machinery is relatively new. In order to comply with pollution controls, it would have to retool the entire plant, despite the years of useful life left in its equipment. While retooling would not put the Mowbray Company out of business, the profit margin on the company would be cut substantially by such a requirement. Must Mowbray retool?

5. Blanche owned a home near the Three Mile Island plant during its "accident" in 1979. After the incident, she found herself so fearful of future incidents that she moved to another state. Now a utility company is considering construction of

a nuclear power plant three miles from Blanche's new home. Does she have any recourse?

6. Falconbridge Power Company has requested a license to construct a nuclear power plant. It filed an Environmental Impact Statement that assumes that there will never be a release of radiation and that spent fuel will be stored "temporarily" on the site. Is its EIS proper?

7. Bianca recently purchased a lot in Florida on which she intended to build a home after her retirement as a schoolteacher in Massachusetts. The land was previously owned by Curtis Development Company, a real estate developer. A year after Bianca purchased the property, Curtis went out of business. Unknown to Bianca, the Sly Chemical Company had been secretly using the lot for years to dump polychlorinated biphenyls (PCB's), a toxic contaminant, and continued to do so for the first year or two Bianca owned the property. Sly also went out of business, Bianca received a bill in the mail for $218,000, the estimated cost of the clean-up of her property from the federal government. Must she pay?

8. The Northern Tier Pipeline is designed to move oil and gas from the Alaskan Oil Pipeline across the states of Washington, Idaho, Montana, North Dakota, and Minnesota to refineries in the eastern United States. There is evidence that the construction of that pipeline will disrupt the grazing patterns of the American elk, and the grizzly bear will have less food, in the form of elk, during the winter. The grizzly bear is on the "endangered species list." May the federal government fund the Northern Tier Pipeline?

SUGGESTED READINGS

Findley, Roger W., and Daniel A. Farber. *Environmental Law in a Nutshell* (St. Paul, Minn.: West Publishing Co., 1983).

Hanks, Eva M., A. Dan Tarlock, and John L. Hanks. *Environmental Law and Policy* (St. Paul, Minn.: West Publishing Co., 1975).

Liroff, Richard A. *A National Policy for the Environment* (Bloomington, Ind.: Indiana University Press, 1976).

Murphy, Earl F. *Nature, Bureaucracy and the Rules of Property* (New York: North-Holland Publishing Co., 1977).

Rodgers, William H., Jr. *Environmental Law* (St. Paul, Minn.: West Publishing Co., 1977).

Shaw, Bill. *Environmental Law: People, Pollution and Land Use* (St. Paul, Minn.: West Publishing Co., 1976).

Sive, Mary Robinson. *Environmental Legislation: A Sourcebook* (New York: Praeger, 1978).

Skillern, Frank F. *Environmental Protection: The Legal Framework* (New York: Shepard/McGraw-Hill, 1981).

Vig, Norman J., and Michael E. Kraft (Eds.). *Environmental Policy in the 1980s: Reagan's New Agenda* (Washington, D.C.: The CQ Press, a division of Congressional Quarterly, Inc., 1984).

Part VIII

Other Relationships of Business and Government

The past ten chapters discussed a variety of specific regulations imposed on businesses by government, providing a sound grounding in the methods by which government regulates business. However, two relationships between government and business remain that must be discussed to complete the picture.

Businesses and the individuals that comprise them are all taxed in some way. Those taxes form a major part of the "regulation" of business, by providing incentives or disincentives for certain kinds of activities. Two countervailing "ethics" are involved in taxation: the Biblical injunction "Render unto Caesar that which is Caesar's" and our own Revolutionary battle-cry of "No taxation without representation."

The ethics of taxation presents one of the muddiest puzzles of all. Sometimes it seems that we are involved in a "catch me if you can" game with the government, in which "everybody cheats on their taxes." That game is made possible by the present "self-assessment" method of imposing taxes, in which each person determines his or her own tax liability. Yet a nagging bit of conscience must impose itself on every tax cheater, based on personal values of honesty and truth. Cheating and deception can be rationalized by dozens of other values—duty to family, disagreement with government policies funded by taxes, and others—but our personal value systems continue to tell us that cheating is wrong. Perhaps, that is why compliance with the tax laws continues to be quite high.

Finally, an old and important method of regulation remains to be discussed. In "economic" regulation, prices and output are set directly by the government, rather than by the workings of the marketplace. Though it is perhaps the oldest form of government regulation, it is probably the clearest example we have of the community ethic in which businesses are run for the public good rather than the private benefit of the owners.

There is perhaps no better example of the conflicts between various public and private ethics than the controversy surrounding the various types of "deregulation." Deregulation renews old arguments about the ethical nature of various regulations and revives old disputes about the proper "mix" of individualism and community in any of the regulations discussed. At the same time, deregulation of some areas revives old arguments regarding whether government ought to be enforcing personal ethical values, such as honesty and tolerance.

13

Taxation

The power to tax involves the power to destroy.

  Chief Justice John Marshall in McCulloch v. Maryland, *4 Wheat. 316, 407 (1819)*

The power to tax is not the power to destroy while this Court sits.

  Mr. Justice Holmes in Panhandle Oil Co. v. Knox, *277 U.S. 223 (1928)*

When there is an income tax, the just man will pay more and the unjust less on the same amount of income.

  Plato, The Republic (*circa 360* B.C.)

Taxes are what we pay for civilized society.

  Mr. Justice Holmes in Compania de Tabacos v. U.S., *275 U.S. 87, 100 (1904)*

It is generally assumed that the purpose of taxes is to raise money to pay for government activities. But *revenue* is not the sole purpose of taxation. It is clear that taxes perform two other functions as well: taxes may be used as a means of *regulation,* since a tax is a negative incentive; and taxes may be used, along with government spending, as a means of controlling the economy through government *fiscal policy.*

It is not the purpose of this chapter to go into detail about the federal income tax or any other specific tax. The purpose is rather to provide a background in the legal principles that underlie all taxation and to provide a brief overview of the basic principles of all of the common methods of taxation. A secondary goal of the chapter is to make the student aware of the "tax angle" inherent in all business and even personal activity. It is perhaps only a mild overstatement to say that "everything comes back to taxes."

Classifications of Taxes

Taxes are imposed at every level of government in the United States. Therefore, one of the principal classifications of taxes is among *federal, state,* and *local* taxation. The term *taxation* automatically conjures up images of the federal income tax, but it is important to realize that there are other federal taxes in the form of *estate, gift,* and *excise taxes,* and rather substantial *state income, sales and use,* and *excise taxes.* And in considering the "tax angle," the most important consideration may well be hefty *local property taxes.* But taxes may be classified in other ways as well.

Excise, Property and Poll Taxes

An **excise tax** is a tax on a privilege. Such taxes are usually measured by the amount of business done, the amount of income received, or the extent to which a particular privilege may have been enjoyed by the taxpayer. Excise taxes are often flat rate taxes upon the sale of a particular item, such as federal excise taxes on liquor or gasoline, which are levied on a per gallon basis. *License fees* on certain activities or businesses are also considered excise taxes.

A *property tax,* on the other hand, is a tax on the right to own property levied on the basis of the value of the property. Local real estate taxes are an annual charge based on the value of the property owned, for example. Some states also impose personal property taxes on certain classes of personal property.

Poll taxes are specific sums levied on each person in the taxing jurisdiction, and were often limited in the past to persons of a particular class, such as males or voters. The 24th Amendment limits the application of such poll taxes to voters, and the Equal Protection Clause further restricts the classifications used in such taxes. Such taxes are virtually nonexistent today.

Income taxes do not fit neatly into any of the three general categories. Some courts hold that income taxes are excise taxes, since they are levied on the privilege or right to follow an occupation or make an income. Other courts hold that an income tax is a property tax, since they are based on the value of the income earned in a specific period.

General and Special Taxes

A **general tax** is levied on all persons in a widely defined class and has no relationship to the benefits received by the taxpayers. A **special tax** is levied on particular taxpayers to pay for specific benefits received by the taxpayers. While all persons who pay federal income taxes receive benefits from those taxes in the form of national defense and a wide variety of other government activities, the tax itself bears no relationship to, and is not dependent upon, the benefits received. Therefore, the federal income tax is a general tax. On the other hand, a fishing license is a special tax since it is levied only on fishermen, and generally only fishermen receive the benefits from that tax in the form of conservation activities.

Ad Valorem and Specific Taxes

Various taxes on property may be either *ad valorem* or *specific.* An **ad valorem tax** is based upon the value of the property, usually on a percentage of value, while **specific taxes** are flat rate taxes. Real estate taxes are ad valorem taxes since they are based on a percentage of the value of property, while federal excise taxes on cigarettes or telephones are specific taxes based on the number of packs or instruments.

Direct and Indirect Taxes

Most taxes are *direct* in the sense that they are levied on the persons whom the government desires to pay them. Some taxes, such as state sales taxes, are imposed on one group of persons with the full expectation that they will be passed on to others through increased prices or other means.

Classification by the Matter Taxed

The most common method of classifying taxes is by the matter taxed, such as *income* taxes, *sales* taxes, *property* taxes and the like. *License* fees are imposed on certain activities or occupations. Most states and the federal government impose *death* taxes, in the form of *estate* and *inheritance* taxes, and *gift* taxes to make sure that death taxes are not avoided by gifts prior to death. *Franchise* or *capital* taxes are imposed on corporations, and *excise* taxes are imposed on certain goods sold, such as tires or cigarettes. *Customs duties* are imposed on certain imported goods by the federal government.

Federal Taxation

Until the Civil War, the revenue needs of the federal government were met almost totally by customs duties and income from the sale of public lands. During the Civil War, those receipts were insufficient to carry the load and Congress levied an income tax of .5 percent on incomes from $5,000 to $10,000, and 10 percent on incomes over $10,000. The Confederacy also imposed an income tax.

After the Civil War, the tax was repealed, but labor and agrarian groups continued to call for reductions in the tariff and for a revival of the income tax throughout the 1870's and 1880's. Such a tax was resisted by eastern business interests as "communism" and "confiscation." In 1893, a federal income tax was again passed as part of the same Populist movement that brought about the Sherman Act and the Interstate Commerce Commission Act. A flat 2 percent tax on incomes over $4,000 was imposed.

The Problem of Constitutionality

The Constitution imposed three requirements on federal taxes. **Direct taxes** cannot be levied, unless *in proportion to the census,* under Article I, Section 9; they must be *apportioned* among the states under Article I, Section 2; and Article I, Section 8 requires that duties, imposts, and excises must be *uniform.* Direct taxes are, of course, those demanded from the persons whom the government intends to pay them. An early construction of the clauses by Mr. Justice Chase stated the rule: "Congress . . . must impose direct taxes by the rule of apportionment, and indirect taxes by the rule of uniformity."*

Apportionment of Direct Taxes   The requirement of **apportionment** means that direct taxes must be divided among the states in proportion to their respective populations. Apportionment was required in order to prevent the federal government from improperly burdening some states to the advantage of others. Thus any direct tax must be assessed proportionately, based on population, among the states.

Shortly after the 1893 federal income tax went into effect, it was challenged on the basis that it was an unapportioned direct tax. A previous decision had held the Civil War income tax constitutional under a similar challenge. But, in 1895, in *Pollock v. Farmer's Loan and Trust Co.***, the Court held that the income tax was in fact a direct tax, at least insofar as it taxed the rents received on real estate and was invalid since it was not apportioned. It was impossible to apportion an income tax, since income varied widely between states, and apportionment would mean that a resident of a high-income state would pay a lower percentage of income as tax than a resident of a low-income state.

But pressure for an income tax continued. Advocates of such a tax then turned their attention to a Constitutional amendment, and in 1913 the 16th Amendment was adopted. That Amendment permitted Congress to enact a tax on incomes "from whatever source derived, without apportionment . . . and without regard to any census or enumeration." Shortly after adoption of the Amendment, Congress passed the Revenue Act of 1913, which imposed a tax of 1 percent on incomes, with a progressive surtax of 1–6 percent on incomes over $20,000. The income tax has been in continuous existence since that time.

Uniformity of Indirect Taxes   It has long been settled that the requirement of uniformity means only *geographical* uniformity. Whenever some method of taxation is used somewhere in the United States, the same method must be used throughout the country.

Due Process   The procedures used in imposing, assessing, and collecting taxes must, of course, conform to the requirements of procedural due process. But in many instances Congress has passed laws that taxed income earned prior to the enactment

---

License Tax Cases, 72 U.S. 462, 471 (1866).

**157 U.S. 429, 15 S. Ct. 673 (1895).

of the taxing statute, and the courts found such retroactive taxes did not violate either the Due Process Clause or the ex post facto prohibition. Taxes must not be "arbitrary or capricious" and, in a few instances, the courts have found that a tax was not really a tax but a confiscation of property and, therefore, in violation of the 5th Amendment.

Federal Taxing Policies

Every tax has an inescapable regulatory effect. The mere imposition of a tax on an activity will provide a negative incentive for that activity, and some people will decide not to undertake the taxed activity. Similarly, exemptions or deductions from tax will generally provide positive incentives for such activity. Thus, a great deal of tax policy on all levels depends on political decisions regarding what kinds of activities are to be favored or not favored by the government. The 1982 "targeted jobs credit" was not a revenue matter at all, for example, but a recognition of the need for employment of certain groups and encouraged employment of such persons through a federal income tax credit for employers. Such policies are often temporary and reflect the shifting winds of politics rather than long-term revenue policies. But certain broad, long-term policies do exist.

Progression   The principle of *progression* states simply that higher incomes will be taxed at higher marginal rates. A person earning $10,000 per year will pay a lower percentage of his income as tax than a person earning $25,000. The opposite of progression is *regression,* or taxes that burden lower incomes more than higher ones. A flat-rate excise tax on cigarettes may be regressive, since every taxpayer pays the same amount, and since the value of the money paid as tax by the lower-income taxpayers is greater than the value of the same amount of money to a higher-income taxpayer. Real estate taxes are often criticized as regressive, since their impact is often greater on low-income retired persons.

A number of arguments have been advanced for progressive taxes: it is less painful for higher-income taxpayers to relinquish a single dollar than for lower-income taxpayers; higher-income taxpayers simply have a greater ability to pay; and higher-income taxpayers receive more protection and benefits from government and ought to pay more.

While the principle of progression is widely adopted and accepted and is reflected in progressive tax rates at both the state and federal levels, the presence of deductions and exemptions clearly make some taxes less progressive. A great deal of political rhetoric is spent on such "loopholes" and proposals for alternative taxing systems.

Tax Incidence   Taxes can obviously be shifted among taxpayers. Sales taxes, while paid by sellers of goods, may be shifted to customers either directly or through price increases. While the owner of rental property pays the real estate tax on that property, obviously the rent on such property paid by the owner's tenants will be increased to shift the tax to the renters. For a long time it was assumed that income taxes on wages could not be shifted, but it has become clear that at least in the long run those taxes may be shifted through labor's insistence on higher wages, and that those wage increases are in turn shifted to the consumer. The whole problem of **incidence of tax** involves questions of who ultimately bears the real burden of the tax.

Economic Incentives   It is often argued that the income tax undermines the incentive to work or invest, and a whole host of exemptions and deductions have developed to provide incentives the tax supposedly took away. The relationship between the income tax and the incentive to work is not clear, since some persons work harder under a heavy tax burden, others lose their incentive under a fairly light burden, and still others are unaffected. It is often puzzling, for example, to hear of persons of great wealth who refuse to retire, until one realizes that money is only one of the many reasons for working.

The effect of taxes on savings and consumption is a little more clear than its effect on the incentive to work. The usual view is that a tax deprives low-income taxpayers of funds that would be used to purchase consumer goods and services, while high-income groups would use the "taxed away" funds for savings or investment. Thus, a highly progressive tax with a high incidence on higher-income groups reduces savings and investments, while a regressive tax reduces consumption and demand for goods and services.

It is also clear that the precise make-up of the taxing statutes at any given time will affect the types of investments made. For example the current tax make-up encourages investment in municipal bonds rather than corporate securities. The precise effect will depend on the nature of the taxing laws, which in turn depends on political matters.

Fiscal Policies   In the time since 1930, the taxing laws have become less of a revenue-generating device than a tool to control inflation and depression in the economy. At the risk of monumental oversimplification, and all things being equal (the favorite refuge of the economist), a rise in taxes reduces the amount of money in the economy, and thus might be used to "cool off" an inflationary economy. Likewise, a reduction in taxes increases the amount of money in the economy and thus might be used to "heat up" a depressed economy. Normally, such policies are undertaken with an accompanying decrease in government spending (to cool off an inflation) or increase in government spending (to heat up a depressed economy). These *contra-cyclical* efforts are known as **fiscal policy.**

Of course, where those tax cuts or increases are made makes a substantial difference. Conventional wisdom holds that changes at lower-income levels have a greater impact, since most of the income of low-income taxpayers is devoted to consumption. That conventional wisdom has been challenged by those who assert that tax changes for higher income taxpayers will ultimately "trickle down" throughout the economy through changes in investment and savings.

Sources of Federal Tax Law

The basic source of all federal tax law is the *Internal Revenue Code of 1954* as amended (the Code). The Code contains all of the federal taxes imposed by Congress and creates the Internal Revenue Service (IRS), a line agency of the Treasury Department.

The Secretary of the Treasury is given authority by the Code to make rules for the enforcement of the Code. Under this authority, the Secretary has established the *Treasury Regulations* (the Regs), which interpret the Code and establish some substantive rules. In response to specific inquiries regarding tax liability, the IRS may issue *Revenue Rulings,* which are published and act as precedent for decisions by local IRS officers. While the *Revenue Rulings* do not have the force or effect of the Regs, they do reflect current IRS policies. The majority of *Revenue Rulings* relate to individual cases and are not published, however. There are also judicial decisions by the various courts with jurisdiction over tax matters, and the published opinions of those courts may act as precedent as well. The following case considers the constitutionality of such a regulation against a 1st Amendment claim.

Bob Jones University v. United States

———— U.S. ————, 103 S. Ct. 2017, ———— L. Ed. 2d ————
(1983)

Bob Jones University is a nonprofit corporation that operates a school taking students from kindergarten through graduate school. Though it is not affiliated with any particular church or denomination, its purpose is "to conduct an institution of learning . . . giving special emphasis to the Christian religion and the ethics revealed in the Holy Scriptures." Entering students are screened as to their religious beliefs, and their private and public conduct is strictly regulated. One of the rules of the school read as follows:

There is to be no interracial dating
1. Students who are partners in an interracial marriage will be expelled.
2. Students who are members of or affiliated with any group or organization which holds as one of its goals or advocates interracial marriage will be expelled.
3. Students who date outside their own race will be expelled.
4. Students who espouse, promote, or encourage others to violate the University's dating rules and regulations will be expelled.

Until 1970, the IRS extended tax exempt status to the university under Section 501(c)(3) of the Internal Revenue Code and therefore contributions to the university were tax deductible to the contributors, and the university itself was exempt from tax. In that year, the IRS notified private schools that it could "no longer legally justify allowing tax-exempt status . . . to private schools which practice racial discrimination," and that it would no longer treat "gifts to such schools as charitable deductions for income tax purposes." Several private schools, including the petitioner, challenged the IRS ruling. It was determined that Bob Jones University owed the government $21.00 in taxes, which it paid, and then it filed suit for a refund. The District Court held that the IRS ruling went too far and ordered a refund. The government appealed and the Court of Appeals reversed. The University appealed.

Chief Justice BURGER delivered the opinion of the Court.

. . . .

In Revenue Ruling 71-447, the IRS formalized the policy first announced in 1970, that . . . §501(c)(3) embrace[s] the common law "charity" concept. Under that view, to qualify for a tax exemption . . . an institution must show, . . . that its activity is not contrary to settled public policy.

Section 501(c)(3) provides that "[c]orporations . . . organized and operated exclusively for religious, charitable . . . or educational purposes" are entitled to tax exemption. The petitioners argue that the plain language of the statute guarantees them tax-exempt status.

. . . .

Tax exemptions for certain institutions thought beneficial to the social order of the country as a whole, or to a particular community, are deeply rooted in our history. . . .

More than a century ago, this Court announced the caveat that is critical in this case:

> [I]t has now become an established principle of American law, that courts of chancery will sustain and protect . . . a gift . . . to public charitable uses, *provided the same is consistent with local laws and public policy.* . . .

. . . .

When the Government grants exemptions or allows deductions all taxpayers are affected; the very fact of the exemption or deduction for the donor means that other taxpayers can be said to be indirect and vicarious "donors." Charitable exemptions are justified on the basis that the exempt entity confers a public benefit—a benefit which the society or the community may not itself choose or be able to provide, or which supplements and advances the work of public institutions already supported by tax revenues. History buttresses logic to make clear that, to warrant exemption under §501(c)(3), an institution must fall within a category specified in that section and must demonstrably serve and be in harmony with the public interest. The institution's purpose must not be so at odds with the common community conscience as to undermine any public benefit that might otherwise be conferred.

. . . .

. . . [T]here can no longer be any doubt that racial discrimination in education violates deeply and widely accepted views of elementary justice. . . . Over the past quarter of a century, every pronouncement of this Court and myriad Acts of Congress and Executive Orders attest a firm national policy to prohibit racial segregation and discrimination in public education.

. . . .

Few social or political issues in our history have been more vigorously debated and more extensively ventilated than the issue of racial discrimination, particularly in education. Given the stress and anguish of the history of efforts to escape from the shackles of the "separate but equal" doctrine . . . it cannot be said that educational institutions that, for whatever reasons, practice racial discrimination, are institutions exercising "beneficial and stabilizing influences in community life," . . . or should be encouraged by having all taxpayers share in their support by way of special tax status.

. . . .

Petitioners contend that, regardless of whether the IRS properly concludes that racially discriminatory private schools violate public policy, only Congress can alter the scope of . . . §501(c)(3). Petitioners accordingly argue that the IRS overstepped its bounds in issuing its 1970 and 1971 rulings.

Yet ever since the inception of the tax code, Congress has seen fit to vest in those administering the tax laws very broad authority to interpret those laws. In an area as complex as the tax system, the agency Congress vests with administrative responsibility must be able to exercise its authority to meet changing conditions and new problems. Indeed, as early as 1918, Congress expressly authorized the Commissioner "to make all needful rules and regulations for the enforcement" of the tax laws. . . .

Congress, the source of IRS authority, can modify IRS rulings it considers improper; and courts exercise review over IRS actions. In the first instance, however, the responsibility for construing the Code falls to the IRS. Since Congress cannot be expected to anticipate every conceivable problem . . . it relies on the administrators and on the courts to implement the legislative will. . . .

. . . .

The actions of Congress since 1970 leave no doubt that the IRS reached the correct conclusion in exercising its authority. It is, of course, not unknown for independent agencies of the Executive Branch to misconstrue the intent of a statute; Congress can and often does correct such misconceptions, if the courts have not done so. Yet for a dozen years Congress has been made aware—acutely aware—of the IRS rulings of

1970 and 1971. . . . Failure of Congress to modify the IRS rulings . . . and Congress' awareness of the denial of tax-exempt status for racially discriminatory schools when enacting other and related legislation make out an unusually strong case of legislative acquiescence in and ratification by implication of the 1970 and 1971 rulings. . . .

. . . .

Petitioners contend that, even if the Commissioner's policy is valid as to nonreligious private schools, that policy cannot constitutionally be applied to schools that engage in racial discrimination on the basis of sincerely held religious beliefs. As to such schools, it is argued that the IRS construction . . . violates their free exercise rights under the Religion Clauses of the First Amendment. . . .

This Court has long held the Free Exercise Clause of the First Amendment an absolute prohibition against governmental regulation of religious beliefs. . . . However, "[n]ot all burdens on religion are unconstitutional. . . . The state may justify a limitation on religious liberty by showing that it is essential to accomplish an overriding governmental interest". . . .

The governmental interest at stake here is compelling. As discussed . . . the Government has a fundamental, overriding interest in eradicating racial discrimination in education—discrimination that prevailed, with official approval, for the first 165 years of this Nation's history. That governmental interest substantially outweighs whatever burden denial of tax benefits places on petitioner's exercise of their religious beliefs. . . .

Affirmed.

Justice POWELL, concurring in part and concurring in the judgment.

I join the Court's judgment . . . holding that denial of tax exemptions does not violate the First Amendment. I write separately because I am troubled by the broader implications of the Court's opinion with respect to the authority of the Internal Revenue Service. . . .

The Federal Income Tax

The Concept of Income

The Code imposes a federal income tax on **taxable income,** which is defined as *adjusted gross income* less *personal deductions* and *exemptions.* **Adjusted gross income** is in turn defined as *gross income* less *business deductions.* For example, if a taxpayer had $50,000 in gross income from his business, but had business expenses of $15,000, his adjusted gross income would be $35,000. If that same taxpayer had $8,000 in personal deductions and claimed two exemptions at $1,000 each (see below), his taxable income would be $25,000.

The term **gross income** is defined in the Code as "all income from whatever source derived." The meaning of that term has been the source of a great deal of litigation, and the meaning is still not clear. It is clear that income does not mean the same to the IRS as it does to economists. The term has received a broad interpretation by the courts, to include such items as stock dividends, punitive damages received in a lawsuit, money or property found on the street, and even illegal income. Loans are clearly not income. One Supreme Court decision defined gross income as "undeniable accessions to wealth, clearly realized, and over which the taxpayers have complete dominion." Another case held that income was "the gain derived from capital, from labor, or from both combined, provided it be understood to include profit gained through a sale or conversion of capital assets."

The Code provides fifteen specific types of income as examples, including wages, business income, interest, rents, royalties, and dividends. The Act also provides several exclusions from income, including the proceeds of life insurance, bequests, gifts, compensatory damages, and benefits from health and accident insurance, though many of those exclusions are themselves subject to exceptions. The following landmark case established the general definition of "income" in income tax cases.

Eisner v. Macomber

252 U.S. 189, 40 S. Ct. 189, 64 L. Ed. 521 (1920)

Mr. Justice PITNEY delivered the opinion of the Court.

This case presents the question whether, by virtue of the Sixteenth Amendment, Congress has the power to tax, as income of the stockholder and without apportionment, a stock dividend. . . .

A stock dividend is a payment of a dividend to shareholders in the form of additional shares of stock in the company, as contrasted to an ordinary cash dividend. See Chapter 7.

Defendant in error, being the owner of 2,200 shares of the old stock, received certificates for 1,100 additional shares, of which 18.07 percent, or 198.77 shares, par value $19,877, were treated as representing surplus earned. . . . She . . . paid a tax based upon a supposed income of $19,877 . . . [and sued for a refund]. In her complaint she alleged . . . that in imposing such a tax the Revenue Act . . . violated Article I, Sec. 2, Cl. 3 and Article I, Sec. 9, Cl. 4 of the Constitution . . . and that the stock dividend was not income within the meaning of the Sixteenth Amendment.

. . . .

In order, therefore, that the clauses cited from Article I of the Constitution may have proper force and effect, save only as modified by the amendment, and that the latter also may have proper effect, it becomes essential to distinguish between what is and what is not "income," as the term is there used, . . .

The fundamental relation of "capital" to "income" has been much discussed by economists, the former being likened to the tree or the land, the latter to the fruit or the crop; the former depicted as a reservoir supplied from springs, the latter as the outlet stream, to be measured by its flow during a period of time. . . . Income may be defined as the gain derived from capital, from labor, or from both, combined, provided it be understood to include profit gained through a sale or conversion of capital assets. . . .

Can a stock dividend, considering its essential character, be brought within the definition? . . .

A "stock dividend" shows that the company's accumulated profits have been capitalized, instead of distributed to the stockholders or retained as surplus available for distribution. . . . Far from being a realization of profits of the stockholder, it tends rather to postpone such realization, in that the fund represented by the new stock has been transferred from surplus to capital, and is no longer available for actual distribution.

The essential and controlling fact is that the stockholder has received nothing out of the company's assets for his separate use and benefit. . . . Having regard to the very truth of the matter, to substance and not to form, he has received nothing that answers the definition of income within the meaning of the Sixteenth Amendment. . . .

It is said that a stockholder may sell the new shares acquired in the stock dividend; and so he may, if he can find a buyer. It is equally true that if he does sell, and in doing so realizes a profit, such profit, like any other, is income, and so far as it may have arisen since the Sixteenth Amendment is taxable by Congress without apportionment. . . .

The court ruled in favor of the taxpayer, holding the stock dividend was not "income."

Mr. Justice HOLMES, dissenting. . . . I think that the word "income" in the Sixteenth Amendment should be read in "a sense most obvious to the common understanding at the time of its adoption." . . . For it was for public adoption that it was proposed. . . . The known purpose of this Amendment was to get rid of nice questions as to what might be direct taxes, and I cannot doubt that most people not lawyers would suppose when they voted for it that they put a question like the present to rest. . . .

Mr. Justice BRANDEIS, dissenting. . . . Financiers, with the aid of lawyers, devised long ago two different methods by which a corporation can, without increasing its indebtedness, keep for corporate purposes accumulated profits, and yet, in effect, distribute these profits, among its shareholders. One method is a simple one. The capital stock is increased; the new stock is paid up with accumulated profits; and the new shares of paid-up stock are then distributed among the shareholders pro rata as a dividend. . . . The other method is slightly more complicated. Arrangements are made for an increase of stock to be offered to stockholders . . . and at the same time, for the payment of a cash dividend equal to the amount which the stockholder will be required to pay to the company if he avails himself of the right to subscribe for his pro rata of the new stock. . . . In order to ensure that all the new stock so offered will be taken, the price at which it is offered is fixed far below . . . its market value. . . .

It is conceded that if the stock dividend paid to Mrs. Macomber had been made by the more complicated method . . . [it] would have been taxable. . . . But it is contended that, because the simple method was adopted . . ., the new stock is not to be deemed income. . . . If such a different result can flow merely from the difference in the method pursued, it must be because Congress is without power to tax as income . . . the stock received . . .: for Congress has, by the provisions in the Revenue Act . . . expressly declared its purpose to make stock dividends, by whichever method paid, taxable as income. . . .

The specific problems of stock dividends, as described in *Eisner* v. *Macomber*, have had a checkered history, and the doctrine is now subject to a number of exceptions and limitations following the Tax Reform Act of 1969 and other statutes. The general rule, requiring **realization** of income before it may be taxed, is still in effect. That rule means simply that unrealized gain in property values is not taxed until those gains are actually received.

The Individual Taxpayer

Most taxpayers are individual citizens whose sole sources of income are wages from employment, interest on a bank account, and perhaps some dividends. The Code does not treat individuals engaged in business differently than individuals not so engaged, though the determination of adjusted gross income is more complex if the taxpayer is engaged in business. *Adjusted gross income* is defined as *gross income* minus *business deductions*. A taxpayer not engaged in business may have no business deductions, and therefore gross income and adjusted gross income will be the same. Employees may have certain business expenses as well, including union or association dues, business travel, employment agency fees, moving expenses, and the cost of some college courses. From adjusted gross income, the Code permits subtraction of certain *personal deductions* and *personal exemptions* to determine *taxable income*.

In defining *gross income* for the individual taxpayer, some specific exclusions from income are important: gifts, bequests, or other property acquired through inheritance; certain prizes and awards including scholarships and fellowships; the proceeds of life insurance policies; compensation for personal injuries or sickness; certain annuity payments; and interest on most state and municipal obligations.

Personal Deductions   Only taxable income, not gross income, is taxed under the Code. Taxable income is determined by subtracting those deductions and exemptions permitted by the Code from adjusted gross income. Deductions and exemptions are allowable only when specifically authorized by the Code and are strictly construed *against* the taxpayer. Business deductions, which are subtracted from gross income rather than adjusted gross income, will be discussed later in the context of the business taxpayer.

The Code provides generally that "no deduction shall be allowed for personal living or family expenses," but then goes on to provide several exceptions to that general rule. The usual deductions under the Code are for (1) extraordinary *medical expenses,* subject to exclusions; (2) *charitable contributions* to eligible donees; (3) *alimony expenses* (but not property settlements or child support); (4) *interest* on the taxpayer's indebtedness; (5) *taxes* paid to other government units; and (6) *casualty losses.* All of the deductions are subject to limitations and exceptions.

One of the most common questions regarding personal deductions is why these particular "personal living or family expenses" should be deductible and others, such as food, clothing, and shelter, are not deductible. There seems to be no simple answer, since each deduction has its own political history and justification in the Congressional deliberations on the Code. A part of the answer may also be that the allowable deductions are all relatively easy to verify.

Individual Retirement Accounts (IRA's)   Employer contributions to deferred compensation plans, such as pension or profit-sharing plans, are not taxed to the employee until such compensation is actually received, usually after retirement and therefore at much lower tax rates. But for a long time, if a self-employed person established a retirement program for himself and paid amounts into the plan, the amounts paid in were taxed as they were received. So-called Keogh or H.R.10 plans were initiated to permit self-employed persons to deposit sums for their own retirement and those sums were not taxed until withdrawn. In effect, the taxpayer was permitted to deduct the amount deposited from his adjusted gross income, subject to limitations.

The Employment Retirement Income Security Act (ERISA) discussed in Chapter 14 permitted employed persons to establish similar accounts, called **Individual Retirement Accounts,** for their benefit as well. The rules for such accounts were liberalized in the Tax Act of 1981. Employees may deposit $2,000 per year ($4,000 for married taxpayers) in a qualified IRA plan and deduct those amounts from their adjusted gross incomes in the year of deposit. Such amounts will be taxed upon withdrawal at the tax rates then applicable to the taxpayer. Interest that accumulates on the account is also not taxed until withdrawal.

The Zero-Bracket Amount   Taxpayers must elect to take deductions. In lieu of the deductions, the Code provides a *zero-bracket amount,* or a deduction allowable to all taxpayers. In 1985 that amount was $3,400 for married taxpayers filing jointly and $1,700 for single taxpayers. The zero-bracket amount replaced the old "standard deduction." Taxpayers have a choice between simply using the zero-bracket amount and itemizing deductions. The zero-bracket amount is "built in" to the tax tables, which require that it be subtracted from the itemized deductions.

Exemptions   In addition to the specific itemized deductions, the Code grants each taxpayer a $1,000 personal exemption. Married taxpayers filing jointly may each claim a $1,000 exemption. An additional exemption of $1,000 is permitted if the taxpayer is blind or over 65. Each qualified dependent of a taxpayer also receives a $1,000 exemption. To be qualified, a dependent must (1) be related to the taxpayer by marriage, blood, or adoption; (2) derive at least one-half of his or her support from the taxpayer; and (3) have a gross income of less than $1,000, unless the dependent is a full-time student.

Determination of the Tax   The tax is assessed on the taxable income of the taxpayer, as defined above. Tax rates are progressive, running from 0 percent on taxable incomes under $2,300 to 50 percent on taxable incomes over $55,300 (single taxpayers) or over $109,400 (married taxpayers filing jointly). Tax tables are provided by the Secretary of the Treasury.

Credits Against Tax   Once the tax is found, it may be reduced by certain **credits against tax,** including credits for the elderly, foreign taxes paid, investments, small political gifts, energy conservation measures,* and creation of certain new jobs. Such credits are further reflections of Congressional policies favoring certain activities. For example, the *investment tax credit* was added in 1962 to provide incentive to encourage new investment in business equipment and machinery. The law permits taxpayers to deduct from their tax bill 10 percent of the cost of property with a useful life of seven years or more and used in manufacturing, mining, transportation, or certain other businesses. The investment tax credit was the forerunner of a large variety of other credits designed to provide incentives for certain activities.

The Business Taxpayer

The Code does not treat business and individual taxpayers differently, though it is convenient to treat them so. Perhaps the most striking difference lies in the ability of all taxpayers to elect between the *cash* and *accrual methods* of accounting, though individual taxpayers rarely choose the accrual method. The **cash method** simply means that receipts and expenses are counted as they are actually received or paid, while the **accrual method** means that income is reported as customers are billed for goods or services and expenses are deducted as they are incurred rather than as they are paid. The accrual method must be used if the inventory of a business is significant.

As noted, business deductions are subtracted from gross income to find adjusted gross income. However, the Code treats business deductions somewhat differently than personal deductions.

Business Deductions   Personal deductions are allowed only if the Code expressly and specifically permits a deduction, while the expenses and losses connected with

*Until January 1, 1986.

earning an income are generally fully deductible. The Code permits three types of business deductions: (1) all ordinary and necessary *expenses* involved in carrying on any trade or business; (2) all ordinary and necessary *expenses* involved in producing or collecting income, or for the management, conservation or maintenance of income-producing property; and (3) any uncompensated *losses.* Specific types of deductions may be subject to exceptions or limitations imposed by Congress, however. The following case established the basic rules of deductibility for business expenses.

Welch v. Helvering

290 U.S. 111, 54 S. Ct. 8, 78 L. Ed. 212 (1933)

Petitioner (Welch) was a "commission agent" for a company that had gone bankrupt (Welch Co.). He then became an agent for another firm. In order to reestablish his credibility with the persons he dealt with, he decided to pay the debts of the bankrupt corporation as far as he was able. Over five years, he paid approximately $38,000 of the bankrupt corporation's debts and made approximately $108,000 in commissions. The Commissioner of Internal Revenue ruled that the payments on behalf of his former employer were not deductible as business expenses, and Court of Appeals affirmed.

Mr. Justice CARDOZO delivered the opinion of the Court. . . .

In computing net income there shall be allowed as deductions . . . all the ordinary and necessary expenses paid or incurred during the taxable year in carrying on any trade or business." Revenue Act of 1924. . . .

We may assume that the payments to creditors of the Welch Company were necessary for the development of the petitioner's business, at least in the sense that they were appropriate and helpful. . . . He certainly thought they were, and we should be slow to override his judgment. But the problem is not solved when the payments are characterized as necessary. . . . There is need to determine whether they are both necessary and ordinary. . . . Ordinary in this context does not mean that the payments must be habitual or normal in the sense that the same taxpayer will have to make them often. A lawsuit affecting the safety of a business may happen once in a lifetime. The counsel fees may be so heavy that repetition is unlikely. None the less, the expense is an ordinary one because we know from experience that payments for such a purpose, whether the amount is large or small, are the common and accepted means of defense against attack. . . . The situation is unique in the life of the individual affected, but not in the life of the group, the community, of which he is a part. . . .

The line of demarcation is now visible between the case that is here and the one supposed for illustration. . . . Men do at times pay the debts of others without legal obligation or the lighter obligation imposed by the usages of trade or by neighborly amenities, but they do not do so ordinarily, not even though the result might be to heighten their reputation for generosity and opulence. Indeed, if language is to be read in its natural and common meaning. . . . we should have to say that payment in such circumstances, instead of being ordinary is in a high degree extraordinary. . . . One struggles in vain for any verbal formula that will supply a ready touchstone. The standard set up by the statute is not a rule of law; it is rather a way of life. Life in all its fullness must supply the answer to the riddle.

The Commissioner of Internal Revenue resorted to that standard in assessing the petitioner's income, and found that the payments in controversy . . . [were not] ordinary and necessary expenses in the operation of a business. His ruling has the support of a presumption of correctness, and the petitioner has the burden of proving it wrong. . . .

Many cases in the federal courts deal with phases of the problem presented in the case at bar. To attempt to harmonize them would be a futile task. They involve the appreciation of particular situations, at times with borderline conclusions. Typical illustrations are cited in the margin.[1]

The decree should be affirmed.

Many of the specific situations described in *Welch* are now covered by specific statutes or regulations, but the general rule regarding "ordinary" business deductions remains in effect.

Determination of Tax   After subtraction of business deductions from gross income from business, that figure is then added to other income, if any, to form adjusted gross income on the individual tax return.

The Corporate Taxpayer

Corporations are treated as separate taxpayers. Even though corporate assets are indirectly owned by the shareholders and profits and losses are shared by the shareholders, corporate income is subjected to double taxation. Such income is taxed once as income to the corporation, and again as income to the shareholders when dividends are paid. The sole exception to this rule, the Subchapter S corporation, is discussed below.

All deductions available to individuals are available to corporations, though obviously many such deductions have little applicability to such firms. Corporations may elect the *accrual method* and often elect a *fiscal year* different from the calendar year.

Corporate tax rates, while progressive, are far less complex than those imposed on individuals. There are only five corporate tax brackets:

$0–$25,000	16%
$25,000–$50,000	18%
$50,000–$75,000	30%
$75,000–$100,000	40%
Over $100,000	46%

Since the highest corporate tax rate is lower than the highest individual tax rate (50 percent) some corporations may have an incentive not to pay dividends but to

---

[1]*Ordinary expenses:* . . . expenses incurred in the defense of a criminal charge growing out of the business of the taxpayer; . . . contributions to a civic improvement fund by a corporation employing half of the wage earning population of the city, the payments being made, not for charity, but to add to the skill and productivity of the workmen; . . . donations to a hospital by a corporation whose employees with their dependents made up two thirds of the population of the city; . . . payments of debts discharged in bankruptcy, but subject to be revived by force of a new promise; . . . where additional compensation, reasonable in amount, was allowed to the officers of a corporation for services previously rendered.

Not ordinary expenses: . . . payments by the taxpayer for the repair of fire damage, such payments being distinguished from those for wear and tear; . . . counsel fees incurred by the taxpayer, the president of a corporation, in prosecuting a slander suit to protect his reputation and that of this business; . . . gratuitous payments to stockholders in settlement of disputes between them, or to assume the expense of a lawsuit in which they had been made defendants; . . . payments in settlement of a lawsuit against a member of a partnership, the effect being to enable him to devote his undivided efforts to the partnership business and also to protect its credit.

[The Court's citations have been deleted.]

accumulate funds in the corporate treasury. To counter that option, Congress has also imposed a substantial **accumulated earnings tax** on corporations, an extra tax on accumulations over a specified figure. Since corporate relationships can be quite complex, most of the tax statutes dealing with corporations are extremely detailed and specific.

Tax Treatment of Partnerships

Business partnerships are not taxed as separate entities. Partnerships are required to file **informational returns** detailing the income received and expenses paid by the partnership and the amounts of income and expense attributable to each partner. The individual partners must then add the income from the partnership to their individual gross income and may deduct their portion of partnership expenses as well, even if the income from the partnership has not been distributed.

Subchapter S Corporations

Corporations are formed for a variety of reasons, including protection from individual liability and flexibility. Since incorporation may subject a firm to higher taxes than a partnership or sole proprietorship, smaller corporations, known as **close corporations,** may be deterred from using the corporate form. Congress has permitted such close corporations to elect to be taxed as a partnership under Subchapter S of the Code, if the corporation has less than 25 shareholders. There is no asset or income limitation on such an election. The corporation may have only one class of stock. After such an election, all income and expenses are allocated to the shareholders in the same manner as a partnership, and shareholders are taxed at their individual rates.

Capital Gains and Losses

Almost from the beginning, the federal income tax laws have treated gains and losses from capital assets differently than other income. A capital asset is defined as property that is not a part of the owner's stock in trade and that is not ordinarily offered for sale, such as machinery or shares of stock in a corporation. Such assets may increase or decrease in value during the time they are held by the owner. While such increases are clearly income and decreases are clearly losses, those gains and losses are not realized until the property is ultimately sold. If A purchased a share of stock for $100 in 1982 and sold it for $200 in 1987, he will have had "income" of $100. The tax laws could tax such increases as they occur and before they are realized (but see *Eisner* v. *Macomber*), such as by taxing $20 per year as income, but the law prefers to wait until 1987 to include the entire $100 in A's income for that year.

Two basic policies underlie the treatment of capital gains and losses: (1) such gains and losses should not be taxed or deducted until they are realized; and (2) such gains and losses should receive favorable treatment through lower tax rates. Favorable treatment is thought necessary to provide an incentive for prompt realization and to stimulate investment. Assets held for more than one year (*long-term capital gains or losses*) receive more favorable treatment than those held for less than one year (*short-term capital gains or losses*). Favorable tax treatment is accorded only *net capital gain,* which is defined as the excess of net long-term capital gain for the taxable year over the net short-term capital loss for such year. The deduction permitted is 60 percent of the taxpayer's net capital gain.

Federal Income Tax Procedure

The vast majority of income tax returns are due by April 15 of each year, though firms that have adopted a different fiscal year will have different due dates. In addition, persons not subject to withholding, such as self-employed persons or business-owners, usually are required to make quarterly deposits of taxes based on *estimates* of their tax liability.

Everybody makes mathematical errors, and the Code permits summary correction of those errors by the IRS. The tax system is also known as a **self-assessment** or *quasi-voluntary* **system,** since each taxpayer initially determines his or her own tax. Controversies over tax liability occur in two ways: (1) *tax audits,* followed by an assertion by IRS that more is owed; or (2) *claims for refund* by taxpayers.

The Tax Audit System   The government keeps taxpayers in the dark as to how returns are selected for audit, doubtlessly on an *in terrorem* principal analogous to the unmarked patrol car. Tax officials have a great deal of authority to inquire into matters affecting tax liability, including subpoenas and seizure of business records. Two responses to an audit are possible: a *no change letter,* or *30-day letter.* The dreaded latter alternative states proposed adjustments and is accompanied by the examining agent's report. Taxpayers have 30 days in which to request an *administrative review.* The administrative review is not a precondition to a suit by the taxpayer, but does cut down the number of cases brought to court. Administrative review is conducted by the Appeals offices in each of the seven regions of the IRS. Taxpayers need not go through the administrative process, and may file suit at any time.

The Refund System   Taxpayers may discover mistakes in their returns after they are filed, and the Code permits *amended returns* claiming a refund. Refund claims may also arise after a taxpayer has paid a deficiency after an audit. In either case, filing an amended return begins administrative procedures similar to those found in audit cases.

Tax Litigation   Deficiency cases are tried in the U.S. Tax Court, while claims for refunds are made to the U.S. Court of Claims, because of a quirk in the Tax Court's jurisdiction, though the Tax Court may also order a refund in the context of deficiency proceedings. Claims for refund may also be brought in the Federal District Court. The losing party may appeal to the U.S. Court of Appeals, and the losing party in the Court of Appeals may petition for certiorari to the U.S. Supreme Court (see *Bob Jones University* v. *U.S.*). Injunctions and declaratory judgment procedures are not available in tax controversies.

Tax Collection   Not surprisingly, the government has methods of collecting taxes far beyond those ordinarily given other creditors. Conventional collection suits are possible, but IRS may simply use *levy and distraint procedures,* permitting the government to simply seize the taxpayer's property and sell it to satisfy the obligation, without judicial help. Unpaid federal taxes become a **lien** on the taxpayer's property. Such a lien means that even if the taxpayer has transferred the property to another, IRS may still seize the property and sell it.

Tax Fraud and Penalties

The Code provides that any person who "wilfully attempts . . . to evade or defeat any tax . . . or the payment thereof" is guilty of a felony and may be punished by a $100,000 fine, five years imprisonment, or both. Corporations may receive a $1 million fine. That section generally requires a substantial understatement of taxable income for conviction. Another section makes it a misdemeanor to wilfully fail to file returns, keep required records, pay the tax, or supply required information, and conviction of that section may carry a penalty of a $25,000 fine, one year imprisonment, or both. Other parts of the Code punish false statements, bribery, conspiracy, and perjury.

In addition, several penalties may be assessed on a return. Failure to file on time may carry up to a 5 percent per month penalty, up to 25 percent, unless the failure "is due to reasonable cause and not due to wilful neglect." Failure to pay the tax shown on the return carries a penalty of .5 percent per month. Normal interest is also charged, however. If any part of an underpayment is due to negligence or intentional disregard of rules or regulations, but not due to fraud, the taxpayer may be liable for an additional 5 percent of the underpayment. If any part of an underpayment is due to fraud, a civil fraud penalty of 50 percent of the underpayment may be assessed, even if the taxpayer is prosecuted criminally.

Federal Estate and Gift Taxes

The first federal tax on transfers of property at death was employed in 1862, but that tax was subsequently repealed. A Federal Estate Tax was again enacted in 1916 and has been in continuous existence ever since. To avoid the tax, some persons transferred property before their death, and to counter that tax avoidance technique the Federal Gift Tax was enacted in 1924. The estate and gift taxes were both overhauled in 1976 and again in 1981. The policy behind the laws is twofold: first, to raise money for government operations; and, second, to attempt to break up large concentrations of wealth.

For purposes of the estate tax, the Code provides that the gross estate be defined as "the value at the time of . . . death of all property, real or personal, tangible or intangible, wherever situated," and includes some property transferred before death, some trusts created and controlled by the decedent, some life insurance proceeds and annuity payments, and other property not usually considered as "owned" by an individual. After the gross estate is determined, *deductions* are permitted for funeral and administrative expenses, claims against the state, unpaid mortgages, state and foreign death taxes, transfers to religious and charitable organizations, uncompensated casualty losses during estate administration, and for all transfers to a spouse (the *marital deduction*). Taxes are imposed at progressive rates on the remaining *taxable estate*.

The Federal Gift Tax is imposed on "the transfer of property by gift," and includes transfers of real, personal, tangible, and intangible property. Every *donor,* or person making such gifts, is permitted an *annual exclusion* of $10,000 per *donee,* or recipient of such gifts, and an unlimited exclusion of gifts to charitable, educational, and health care institutions. An unlimited exclusion for all gifts between spouses is also allowed. The gift tax is cumulative over the lifetime of the donor, and progressive rates apply.

The Tax Reform Act of 1976 provided a *unified credit system,* tying the estate and gift taxes together, and the credits were increased by the Tax Act of 1981. Every donor is given a lifetime credit to apply against both gifts and the donor's estate upon death. The amount of that credit is $121,800 for 1985, $155,800 for 1986, and $192,800 for 1987 and thereafter. No gift tax is owed until the total of gifts over the donor's lifetime, less exclusions and credits, exceeds that amount. Whatever portion of that amount that has not been used is applied to the estate tax upon the donor's death.

Other Federal Taxes

Aside from the income tax and the estate and gift taxes, there are lesser-known but no less important federal taxes. Those taxes include a variety of excise taxes on alcoholic beverages, cigarettes, gasoline, tires, and a variety of other goods, the Federal Unemployment Tax, noted in Chapter 14, airport and airway taxes, telephone excise taxes, and customs duties, among many others.

State and Local Taxation

The power of the states to tax is an inherent right of government. In the words of Chief Justice John Marshall,

> It is admitted that the power of taxing the people and their property is essential to the very existence of government, and may be legitimately exercised on the objects to which it is applicable, to the utmost extent to which the government may choose to carry it. The only security against the abuse of this power, is found in the structure of the government itself. In imposing a tax the legislature acts upon its constituents. This is in general a sufficient security against erroneous and oppressive taxation. *McCulloch* v. *Maryland.**

The Constitution does impose certain limitations on the power to tax, however. State taxes may not unduly burden interstate commerce nor discriminate against interstate commerce, as discussed in Chapter 2. Likewise the Due Process Clause of the 14th Amendment provides procedural guarantees for the taxing process, as discussed in Chapter 3.

The problem of state taxation of interstate commerce is, in Justice Clark's words, a "tangled underbrush of past cases." The complex make-up of most state taxing

*4 Wheat. 316 (1819). See p. 40.

statutes, the incredible complexity of interstate commerce itself, and the less than sterling clarity of most court opinions in the area make it impossible to state any but the most basic rules and doctrines with any confidence.

It is clear, however, that states may only tax persons, firms, or property that have a **nexus** with the taxing state. That means that such persons, firms, or property are connected in some way with the taxing state, either by residence in the state, physical presence in the state, or utilization of state facilities in some way.

It is also clear that state taxes cannot be imposed on activities of an individual or firm that take place outside of the taxing state. If a firm is incorporated in State X, but transacts business nationwide, State X cannot impose a tax on all of the income of the firm. The states must instead *apportion* their taxes and apply them only to the aspects of the firm arising in that state.

Finally, it is clear that the states may not tax the property of other units of government, such as federal property or that of other states, under the doctrine of federal supremacy and the "full faith and credit" clause of the Constitution. It is also clear that the property or income of religious bodies cannot be taxed, since to do so poses the potential of a limitation on the "free exercise" of religion under the 1st Amendment.

State Income Taxes

Most state income taxes are based in some way on the federal income tax, usually by using federal adjusted gross income or taxable income as the figure upon which the tax is imposed. Often some figures have to be added to the federal income figure, such as state income taxes or interest on state and municipal obligations. Some deductions are also different, such as interest on federal obligations that cannot be taxed.

State Sales and Use Taxes

Sales and use taxes, first introduced in the 1930's, are complementary taxes on the purchase or use of property. A **sales tax** is imposed only on sales within the taxing state, while a **use tax** is a tax on property purchased in another state and is used to prevent circumvention of the sales tax.

For example, assume the sales tax in State X is 5 percent and the sales tax in State Y is 3 percent. If a company in State X were to purchase a $100,000 piece of equipment, it could save $2,000 by purchasing the item in State Y. In such a case, State X would impose a use tax on items stored or used in State X in an amount equal to the difference between the sales tax of the two states—in this example, 2 percent. Any higher use tax would discriminate against interstate commerce, and any lower use tax leaves an incentive for persons to purchase goods out-of-state.

There are five basic kinds of sales taxes: (1) *retail sales* taxes, imposed on retail sales alone; (2) *general sales* taxes, imposed on all sales including retail sales; (3) *gross proceeds* taxes based on both sales and services; (4) *gross receipts* taxes on all receipts of businesses; and (5) *selective sales* taxes on particular items, such as alcohol, tobacco, and gasoline. Gross receipts taxes tax the total sales of businesses and are not usually separately stated to consumers, but the other forms are separately charged and passed on directly to the purchaser. Vendors are ordinarily required to collect the tax and forward it to the taxing body. Most states exclude from taxation sales to selected parties, such as the U.S. government (exempt in all cases), the state itself, educational organizations, or religious bodies. Casual or isolated sales are also usually excluded. Items purchased for resale are usually exempt as well, since all of such taxes would be bunched and passed on to the ultimate consumers. Some types of goods are also excluded or taxed at lower rates in some states, such as food and drugs.

State Franchise or Capital Taxes

The **franchise tax** is a tax on the value of the capital of a corporation, though some states measure the tax based on the income of the corporation, and is, in that sense, a tax on the privilege of using the corporate form. Such taxes have existed at least as early as 1805. Such taxes were initially imposed only on **domestic corporations,** or corporations formed under the laws of the taxing state. Later forms extended the tax to all firms qualified to do business in the state even though they were incorporated elsewhere. The tax is usually a fairly small percentage of the corporation's capital, normally under 8 percent and often much less. A yearly report must also be submitted to the state with payment of the tax. Failure to pay the tax or submit the report may result in civil penalties or dissolution of the firm.

Value-Added Taxes (VAT's)

Though **value-added taxes** have existed in Europe since the end of World War II, they have not been widely adopted in the United States. Michigan became the first state to do so in 1976 with the adoption of its "Single Business Tax." Other states are studying the tax for possible adoption.

A VAT is a tax imposed on the value added to a product by the producer or vendor. The tax is meant as a substitute for both the income tax and the franchise tax. Thus, if a firm purchases goods for $10,000, and sells them for $17,000, a tax will be imposed on the $7,000 of value added to the products. That $7,000 may consist of $3,000 in costs incurred in making changes to the product and $4,000 in profits, but both figures are included as "value." If another firm buys those products for $17,000 and resells them for $23,000, that firm will in turn have added $6,000 to the value of the products, and will be taxed on that amount. The taxes are of course passed on to the consumer.

VAT's have several advantages over income and franchise taxes. VAT's do not discriminate between capital-intensive and labor intensive industries and do not penalize efficient firms by taxing only profits or income. It is also thought that VAT's do not influence business decision making, since neither the size of the business nor the amount of debt or equity financing affects the tax burden. All businesses pay a tax proportional to the economic size of the business. When Michigan adopted its VAT, it was able to repeal eight other taxes, including the corporate income tax, the business portion of the state income tax, and the corporate franchise tax.

State License Fees

All states impose a variety of *license fees* on various activities and occupations, such as driving or registering a car, fishing, owning a liquor store, or becoming a real estate broker. Often the purpose of the license fee is simply to offset the expense of regulating those activities as opposed to raising revenue. Nonpayment of the fee may result in revocation of the license.

State Death Taxes

Some states impose an inheritance or death tax similar in form to the Federal Estate Tax. While the Federal Estate Tax is imposed on *giving* property at death and is payable by the estate of the decedent, many state inheritance taxes are imposed on *receiving* property from a decedent and are paid by the heirs of the decedent. Often the state taxes dovetail with the federal tax for ease of administration.

Property Taxes

The large majority of local government activities is supported through the property tax, an **ad valorem** charge on real estate, personal property, or both. Some personal property taxes are levied by the states instead of by local governments. Most property taxes are imposed on real estate alone.

While the authority to tax originates with the state government, the assessment of tax is done at the local level, and tax rates may vary between counties or even within a country. The tax rate is set by each unit of local government, such as cities, counties, school districts, fire protection districts, and a host of others, and each such unit imposes a separate tax. Each unit determines its tax rate based on the following formula:

$$\text{Tax Rate} = \frac{\text{Revenue needed by the taxing unit}}{\text{Assessed value of all taxable property within the taxing unit}}$$

Thus, if a school district needs $4 million to finance its operations, and there is $120 million in property in the district, the tax rate would be 3.3 percent. Normally each taxing unit will forward its tax rate to the county assessor who will total the tax rates applicable to each piece of property in the county. Thus, if a homeowner resides in each of the following districts, the county assessor will send a single bill for 5.0659 percent, composed of the following taxes:

County	.5952
Town	.1180
Road and Bridge	.1968
Village	.7338
Library	.0995
Fire District	.0464
Park District	.0508
Junior College	.2254
School District	3.0000
Total Tax Rate =	5.0659%, or 5.0659 dollars per hundred

The tax rate is then applied to the *assessed value* of the property. The assessed value is some percentage of *market value* of the property, varying from 25 percent to

100 percent. If state law assessed property at 33⅓ percent of market value, a home worth $60,000 would be assessed at $20,000. Applying the tax rate of 5.0659 percent to that figure, the tax on such a home would be $1,013.18.

Property taxes are payable annually and property is reassessed periodically. Often, states place upper limits on the tax rates that may be assessed or require that taxing units seek the approval of voters to tax increases over a certain amount by referendum. Failure to pay the tax may result in a tax sale of the property. All states exempt certain property from taxation, such as property owned by units of government or religious organizations, and may provide exemptions or credits to some groups of people, such as disabled veterans or the elderly. Local governments sometimes also provide reduced property taxes to new businesses as an incentive for them to locate in the area.

Special assessments are special taxes on real property to pay for specific local improvements. For example, if a local government decides to put a sidewalk in front of all the property on a particular block, the public is of course benefitted, but the property owners will benefit specially by the improvement. The cost of the sidewalk will then be apportioned between the public and the property owners receiving the benefit. The public portion will be paid by general revenues, and the owner's shares will be paid directly by the owners in the form of a special assessment.

Revenue Sharing

Federal **revenue sharing** is a method of allocating federal tax revenues to the state or local governments for their use. Such aid has existed since 1911, and began on a large scale in 1914. Proponents of the idea assert that local and state governments can better provide the services needed in their areas, that power is more desirable if it is dispersed, and that it is highly inefficient for the federal government to provide local programs. Opponents point to the traditional inability of states to resolve some difficult questions and the possibility that minority groups might be discriminated against by state-run programs.

Most revenue sharing is in the form of *grants-in-aid,* or cash grants involving population and income formulas and matching requirements. Perhaps the best known example is in the federal highway system. If a state decides to build a federal highway, the federal government will provide the lion's share of the money to do so. That system has been in operation since 1916. General revenue sharing, in which a fixed portion of federal tax dollars is distributed to the states without restrictions on its use, has been in existence since 1972.

Summary and Conclusions

Taxes have three main functions; the revenue, regulatory, and fiscal policy purposes. Taxes may also be classified by whether they are imposed by federal, state, or local governments; by the subject matter taxed; and by various other distinctions.

The federal government imposes income, estate, gift, and various excise taxes. Constitutional problems made it necessary to pass the 16th Amendment before the federal income tax could be imposed. The federal government now imposes a comprehensive, progressive income tax on individuals and corporations. The tax is only imposed on income that is "realized." All business expenses and losses may be deducted from gross income to find the adjusted gross income, and a variety of personal deductions and exemptions may be subtracted from adjusted gross income to find the taxable income. Progressive tax rates are applied to taxable income and some credits are permitted.

State governments impose a variety of taxes which differ widely among states. The most usual types of taxes are the state income taxes, sales and use taxes, death taxes, corporate franchise tax, and license fees. Experimentation with a value-added tax is continuing.

Local governments receive most of their income from ad valorem property taxes. Federal revenue sharing has now lightened the property tax burden, however.

PRO AND CON
ISSUE: What *Kind* of Tax Reform?

PRO: We Need a Tax System That Makes Sense and Maintains Incentives
Duane R. Kullberg*

If we have a [tax policy], it seems to me to be one of knee-jerkism. When a problem taps us in the right spot—whether economic, social or whatever—we respond by a jerk in the tax system. As a result, we have a tax system burdened with appalling complexities and tarnished by distrust. It is perceived by those who bear its burden as unfair. It punishes, rather than rewards, those who would work and save.

. . . .

In facing political realities, we . . . must understand that theoretical dimension of the budget process known as "tax expenditures." The Budget Act defines "tax expenditures" as "those revenue losses attributable to provisions of the Federal tax laws which allow a special exclusion, exemption or deduction from gross income, or which provide a special credit, a preferential tax rate or a deferral of tax liability." On its face, the term sounds relatively neutral, since we all know that our tax code is rife with special rules, exceptions, exclusions, preferences, incentives or what have you. And each of us benefits, directly or indirectly, from one or more of these.

What is distressing about the concept of "tax expenditure" is its use as a policy-making tool. . . . The Joint Committee [on Taxation] estimates that, for fiscal 1984, the total "tax expenditure budget" will be almost $330 billion and that it will exceed $490 billion by fiscal 1988. During that same period, deficits will remain at about $200 billion and spending will range between $800 and $900 billion. . . . [T]he tax committees will be tempted to raise the required funds by selecting items from the so-called "tax expenditure budget." Experience tells us that such selection will be based solely on the revenues they will provide, and not on the basis of sound tax policy.

. . . .

Any new tax system must meet several basic tests. Thus, it must be fair, it must be simple and it must encourage work and saving.

What kind of tax system will give us that? I am convinced that it cannot be a system that is so simple that it will allow, as some suggest, compliance on a postcard. It would be just as difficult to explain to taxpayers why they have suddenly lost all of their deductions, exemptions and credits as it is now to

*Duane Kullberg is managing partner and CEO of Arthur Andersen and Company. From his speech, "Our Tax and Spending Policies: A Call for Change," delivered at the Regional Meeting of the Tax Foundation, Inc., Stamford, Conn., May 19, 1983, and reprinted in *Vital Speeches of the Day*, vol. 49, p. 627. Reprinted by permission.

explain the complexities of our present law. The concept of sudden tax simplification is seductive; but its reality is virtually sure to cause distortions, inequities and further taxpayer distrust. This can be avoided only by a carefully planned transition period.

Basic changes in our tax system will require some crucial decisions. The threshold issue is whether any new tax scheme should replace the income tax, in whole or in part, or merely supplement it. . . . Let's examine the alternatives.

In the last few months, considerable attention has been given to various so-called flat rate tax proposals. . . . But the term "flat tax" does not always mean the same thing; it has become a shorthand for a broad range of proposals. . . .

Although the various flat rate tax proposals differ to some degree, they are all alike in their essentials. They contemplate substantial broadening of the income tax base by eliminating all or many of the deductions, credits and exclusions that are presently allowed and applying to that broadened base either a single tax rate, or a series of graduated rates. Obviously, with a broadened tax base, a lower rate structure can be applied to generate the same revenues now required. . . .

The Joint Committee on Taxation has estimated that a 16 percent flat rate, . . . would generate the revenues that our government requires for fiscal 1984. In all likelihood, however, this type of simple system would shift a significant part of the tax burden from taxpayers with incomes of $50,000 or more to those with incomes at lower levels, par-

ticularly below $30,000. From a political standpoint, this would be hard to sell.

. . . .

Major changes in the income tax system like these would cause major disruptions in our economy—particularly if such common deductions such as charitable contributions and home-owner interest and taxes are eliminated. Were that to happen, values of residential real estate could be adversely affected and the funds now being directed from the private sector to hospitals, schools and churches could be significantly reduced. . . .

. . . .

Meaningful tax reform cannot be accomplished without coming to grips with tax expenditures. This will require some selfless appraisals of tax expenditures by each of us who presently enjoys their benefits.

Many critics of the tax system say that the special rules and preferences that give rise to tax expenditures have eroded the tax base. I cannot completely disagree with that. . . .

Each of those so-called expenditures became a part of our tax policy with good reason—to encourage investment in productive assets, to encourage exploration for natural resources and for other reasons.

But true tax reform requires some soul-searching when it comes to excluding any part of the revenue base. . . . This will require a careful and honest review of each expenditure or preference. None should be exempt from scrutiny. . . .

CON: Ill-Conceived Tax Incentives Distort and Hurt Our Economy
Arthur Burck*

America's sputtering economy is on the brink of crisis. Countless businesses are obsolete or crippled. That is why we have double digit unemployment, and the end is nowhere in sight since we continue to lose manufacturing jobs faster than our ability to create new employers.

The causes are many, but one is pervasive: obsolescence has overtaken the giant corporation as the mainstay of our industrial structure.

Through most of this century our giants prospered, especially in concentrated industries, because of relative insulation from foreign competition. . . . Thus our economy became structured

primarily around gigantic corporations burdened by burgeoning bureaucracies. . . .

Things are likely to get worse. The reason is that most of the goodies of government aid go to the obsolete Goliaths—the Davids don't even get cut-rate slingshots, and indeed the entrepreneurial companies that are the future of America are in the "third world" in terms of government neglect and comparative wealth.

Mesmerized by the former success of the corporate giants and the great wealth that they have accumulated, the federal government for several decades has fostered a vast array of subsidies and

---

*Arthur Burck is president of Arthur Burck and Company. From his speech, "Ill-Conceived Tax Incentives Distort and Hurt Our Economy: Helping the Goliaths," delivered to Rotary International, West Palm Beach, Fla., May 10, 1983, and reprinted in *Vital Speeches of the Day*, vol. 49, p. 537. Reprinted by permission.

tax breaks that are now wasted more often than not on the stagnating giants. These subsidies take a wide variety of forms: fast depreciation, depletion, import quotas, tax credits, loan guarantees, increased tariffs, subsidized loans, "voluntary" export limitations, tax credits on foreign earnings, taxpayer bailouts of huge companies (Lockheed, Chrysler), prolongation of tax carry-back periods, and last but not least the "sale" of tax credits whereby prospering corporations reduce their taxes by acquiring credits, usually from the huge dinosaur companies that are unable to use these tax credits themselves.

As a result, today's somewhat shocking statistic is that corporate taxes are now only 5.9 percent of federal revenues, in contrast to the 25 percent that prevailed during the 1950s and 1960s, the "Golden Age" of American prosperity. . . . This means that most large companies today pay negligible taxes—because of the array of tax breaks they enjoy. On the other hand, it has been my experience that most small and medium sized corporations pay close to the maximum rates. . . . Smaller companies have nowhere to hide.

. . . .

Pro-bigness" tax policies are more pernicious than appears on the surface. The face of business America has been irrevocably altered—for the worse—by the tax-induced merger mania that during the past three decades has meant the loss of independence to over 50,000 once-prospering American businesses. Most of these acquisitions were made by big companies. Following are some of the disastrous effects upon our economy:

—The big became bigger. This has meant concentration of our business assets in fewer and fewer hands.

—We now know that most of these acquisitions did not work out. Perhaps the majority of companies acquired by giants were ruined, damaged or weakened. Since the giants for decades have been beating the bushes to find and acquire the most promising growth companies, we have lost a generation of our best companies. . . .

—The main reason for the failure of most acquisitions is the inability of the bureaucracy of the giants to mesh with fragile entreprenuerial smaller companies.

. . . .

Now it is ironic that taxpayers have been subsidizing the merger activity that has been so deleterious to our economy. I estimate that four out of five of the huge takeovers depend on tax breaks: (1) the tax-free exchange of stock, and (2) the deductibility of interest on the huge loans that float these deals.

Even though our economy burns, legislators have been ignoring what is happening, not unlike Nero. That is hardly surprising since when issues collide with the power and the "deep pockets" of the corporate giants, can one blame any legislator for tempering valor with discretion? . . . What else can we expect so long as most legislators must cater to big business in order to raise the massive sums needed for reelection?

And so it is highly unlikely that government will rearrange the incentives and disincentives that have contributed to the sorry current state of the nation's industry. To be sure, there is understandable nostalgia for big business. We all grew up with the idea that bigness is as much a part of America as is apple pie. Trying to question bigness in America is almost like questioning motherhood. But we've got to change our thinking away from helping the Goliaths. Their day is gone.

DISCUSSION QUESTIONS

1. Should taxes be used for purposes other than raising revenue? Is it possible to *avoid* the regulatory effect of taxation? Is it possible to *avoid* the fiscal policy effect of the federal income tax?

2. Why do you suppose the income tax was so important to the American Populists at the turn of the century? Do those same reasons exist today?

3. Why were the Founding Fathers so concerned with direct taxes and the problems of apportionment and uniformity? Do those same concerns exist today?

4. Review each of the taxes discussed in the chapter. Which of the taxes is the

fairest? Which of the taxes are progressive or regressive? What is the incidence of each tax?

5. Under what constitutional authority does the federal government undertake fiscal policy? What would be the long-term and short-term effects on fiscal policy of a Constitutional amendment requiring a balanced federal budget?

6. Why aren't the proceeds of life insurance, health and accident insurance benefits, and compensatory damages considered income under the Internal Revenue Code? Why are punitive damages considered income?

7. Why do you suppose only *specific* personal and living expenses are deductible, while *all* (or almost all) business expenses and losses may be deducted?

8. Why shouldn't capital gains be taxed as they occur, rather than when they are realized? What would be the economic impact if they were taxed as they occurred?

9. Is "breaking up large concentrations of wealth" a valid reason for imposing an estate tax? Was it a valid reason in 1916? Could the same rationale be used as a basis for very high income tax rates on very large incomes?

10. Could a state sales tax exist without a complementary use tax?

11. Is a value-added tax progressive or regressive? What is the true incidence of the tax? Who would benefit from such a tax if it were enacted in your state? Could it be enacted at the federal level?

12. Is the property tax an efficient means of providing revenue for local government? Determine its true incidence for renters and landlords, retail store owners, and industrial facilities. Does the tax bear any relationship to the benefits derived from local government by property owners?

CASE PROBLEMS

1. Duberstein and Berman were personal friends and presidents of competing firms. For years, Berman had a working relationship in which Duberstein would tell Berman of potential customers with whom Duberstein's firm was not interested in dealing. Berman gave Duberstein a Cadillac because the information had proven helpful, though Duberstein had never requested anything in return for the information. Berman's firm deducted the value of the Cadillac as a business expense on the corporate tax return. Is the Cadillac "income" to Duberstein? [*Commissioner* v. *Duberstein,* 363 U.S. 278, 80 S. Ct. 1190, 4 L. Ed. 2d 1218 (1960).]

2. Rosenspan was a travelling salesman in the jewelry business who travelled over 300 days a year. Five or six times a year he would return to his employer's home office, but maintained no permanent residence anywhere. He resided in hotels and motels almost all the time, except for a very few days he spent with his brother. May he deduct his hotel and motel bills? [*Rosenspan* v. *U.S.,* 438 F. 2d 905 (2d Cir., 1971).]

3. Olivia owns a home with a market value of $60,000. In the state where the home is located, property is assessed at 33⅓ percent of market value for real estate tax purposes. The tax rate in Olivia's county is 6.8 percent. How much tax does Olivia owe each year?

4. The sales tax in State A is 6 percent and in State B is 4 percent. Ariel, a resident of State A, purchased an automobile in State B for $8,000, and paid the applicable sales tax. How much use tax will Ariel have to pay?

5. Firm A buys iron ore for $300 and makes it into steel worth $1,000, which it sells to Firm B. Firm B fashions that steel into automobiles worth $4,000, which it sells to Dealer C. Dealer C resells the car for $7,000. Assume State X imposes a 4 percent value-added tax. How much would each firm pay? Would the state obtain more money through a straight 4 percent sales tax? What would be the incidence of each tax?

6. Wessex County School District No. 1 needs $4,650,000 to operate next year. The total market value of all the property in the school district is $380 million, and property in the state in which the school district is located is assessed at 50 percent of market value by law. What tax rate should the school district impose?

7. Surrey College is a private university for men only. It depends on contributions from the public and from alumni to supplement the tuition paid by its students. The Internal Revenue Service asserts that Surrey must admit women or lose its "exempt" status. Must Surrey comply?

SUGGESTED READINGS

Bittker, Boris I., and Lawrence M. Stone. *Federal Income Taxation* (Boston: Little, Brown and Co., 1980).

Chommie, John C. *Federal Income Taxation* (St. Paul, Minn.: West Publishing Co., 1968).

Freeland, James J., Stephen A. Lind, and Richard B. Stephens. *Fundamentals of Federal Income Taxation* (Mineola, N.Y.: The Foundation Press, 1982).

Gaa, Charles J. *Contemporary Thought on Federal Income Taxation* (Belmont, Cal.: Dickenson Publishing Co., 1969).

Hoffman, William H., and Eugene Willis (Eds). *West's Federal Taxation: Comprehensive Volume* 1984 annual edition (St. Paul, Minn.: West Publishing Co., 1983).

McIntyre, Michael J., Frank E. Sander, and David Westfall (Eds.). *Readings in Federal Taxation* 2d ed. (Mineola, N.Y.: The Foundation Press, 1983).

McNulty, John K. *Federal Income Taxation of Individuals in a Nutshell* (St. Paul, Minn.: West Publishing Co., 1983).

Sobeloff, Jonathan. *Federal Income Taxation of Corporations and Stockholders in a Nutshell* (St. Paul, Minn.: West Publishing Co., 1978).

Surrey, Stanley C., William C. Warren, Paul R. McDaniel, and Hugh J. Ault. *Federal Income Taxation* vols. I and II (Mineola, N.Y.: The Foundation Press, 1973).

Wolfman, Bernard, and James P. Holden. *Ethical Problems in Federal Tax Practice* (Charlottesville, Va.: Michie-Bobbs Merrill, 1981).

Economic Regulation and the Concept of "Deregulation"

Every man holds his property subject to the general right of the community to regulate its use to whatever degree the public welfare may require it.

Theodore Roosevelt, Speech (August 31, 1910)

Reader, suppose you were an idiot. And suppose you were a member of Congress. But I repeat myself. . . .

Mark Twain

To every action there is always opposed an equal reaction. . . .

Sir Isaac Newton, Laws of Motion (1687)

It may appear from the large number and diversity of government regulations that every move of the businessperson is directly controlled from Washington, the state capitol, or the local city hall. But, by and large, businesspeople have a great deal of freedom, to buy and sell, to hire and fire, to succeed and fail. The antitrust laws and the "specific evils" regulations of the preceding chapters merely set limits beyond which business cannot go. Within those limits businesspeople have a great deal of discretion and will ultimately succeed or fail based upon the rules of economics, not the rules of government.

While the American economy is not a totally free market in the sense that all decisions are made by the economic marketplace, neither is it a totally controlled market in the sense that exists in the communist and some socialist countries. Generally, speaking, the limits placed on businesses are intended to remedy specific evils that our legislators see as unfortunate results of total market freedom. **Laissez faire** capitalism will not, at least in the short run, protect consumers from deceptive advertising or shoddy products, or protect workers from unhealthy, dangerous, or discriminatory treatment, or protect the environment from irresponsible use. Congress and the state legislatures have seen fit to impose limits to protect consumers, competitors, workers, and the environment from such specific evils through legislation. And, whether one agrees with the wisdom of any particular specific evil statute, at least it is clear that at some time our elected representatives had enough concern about the problems to enact a law designed to cure it.

But there is another, far more pervasive form of regulation that is applied to a few industries. **Economic regulation,** defined as the detailed regulation of prices, price schedules, routes, and output, has been historically applied to the transportation, communication, energy transmission, and public utility industries. In those industries, an administrative agency makes the basic business decisions of price, output, and routes, which other industries make based on principles of supply and demand. Traditionally, the industries subject to economic regulation have been considered to be "natural monopolies" or, more controversially, were marked by "ruinous competition" requiring government intervention.

The Move to Deregulation

Beginning in the 1970's, economists and policy makers began to question many of the bases of economic regulation. It was argued that such direct, specific regulation was unnecessary in the first place or that conditions in particular industries had changed over the years to make such regulation unnecessary. The result was a move in several areas, including motor and air transportation and natural gas pipelines, to *deregulate* the industries and permit supply and demand to set prices and routes.

It was not long before the term *deregulation* became political gold. There has always been a feeling, at least among those regulated, that government regulates too much and that the requirements of all of the government regulations imposed to remedy specific evils were costing business too much, were contributing to inflation, and constituted unwarranted interference in private business affairs. It was not a long step from pressure for deregulation of the economically regulated industries to pressure to deregulate many other areas by repeal or loosening of the specific evil legislation that had developed since the 19th century.

While the term *deregulation* seems to have joined apple pie, motherhood, and the flag in our national litany of sacred terms, it is important to realize that the term has several very distinct meanings. It originally meant the removal of some of the direct economic regulations applied to the regulated industries. It was later applied to a general weeding out of specific evil legislation, such as OSHA and Consumer Product Safety Act regulations. It has been applied to the use of cost-benefit analysis to all new regulations, and even to reductions in the budgets of some administrative agencies. The term has been used to justify reorganization of some agencies and to simplification of procedures in others. Perhaps most dubious of all is the use of the term as a justification for lax enforcement of the antitrust laws.

The Regulatory Tangle

In any discussion of regulation and deregulation, it is important to consider the full impact of any change in regulatory policy. Every change in government policy involves trade-offs and impacts that reverberate throughout society and the economy, whether that change in policy is called *regulation* or *deregulation.* It is probably not an overstatement to say that every regulation helps someone and hurts someone else, and that there is no such thing as a totally beneficial regulation.

For example, deregulation of air transportation may result in lower fares and better service on many routes, particularly long-distance flights and service to larger cities. But smaller cities may find themselves without service, some support businesses may be forced into bankruptcy, and short-haul fares may be higher. Similarly, deregulation of telephone communications may result, as many consumers have noted, in higher local service charges, but also may result in lower long-distance charges and lower prices for telephone instruments. Deregulation of OSHA regulations may result in lower costs for industry, but may cost the lives of workers. To paraphrase Sir Isaac Newton, to every political action, there is an equal and opposite political reaction.

This chapter will consider first the origin of economic regulation and the various justifications usually advanced for such regulation. Next, the chapter will consider in more detail the concept of deregulation, both as applied to the regulated industries and in other contexts. Finally, the chapter will consider the four principal industries in which economic regulation has taken place and the nature of deregulation in those industries.

The Nature of Economic Regulation

"Close" or "economic" regulation is perhaps the oldest form of government regulation of business, dating back at least to the first "public" utilities in the middle of the 19th century. It soon became obvious that only one water, sewer, gas, or electric company could economically serve an area. Sometimes, such services were provided by the local governments themselves but, more often, the service was provided by a private firm under a **franchise** or grant of authority from the local government. The local city council gave the firm a monopoly on such services, but required the firm to follow certain rules and often imposed the price to be charged for the service. Later, the states would follow a similar pattern in regulating railroads.

But the grant of such franchises and their regulation was uniquely subject to political pressure and corruption. As a result, many state and local governments moved to the creation of independent regulatory commissions (IRC's) as discussed in Chapter 5, which were more removed from political pressure. The IRC's set rates, routes, and outputs for such firms based on "expertise" rather than on political considerations. In 1887, Congress formally adopted the IRC scheme when it first decided to regulate the rates and routes of railroads through the Interstate Commerce Commission (ICC). The IRC system has been adopted in a wide variety of other contexts, aside from economic regulation.

The Reasons for Economic Regulation

There are both economic and political reasons why specific industries have been subjected to economic regulation. The three principal reasons are (1) such firms may be "natural monopolies"; (2) the industries may be subject to "ruinous competition"; and (3) some of the regulated firms *requested* to be regulated.

Some industries, such as public utilities, are thought to be natural monopolies. That is, the business is such that only one firm can efficiently supply the product, and the existence of more than one firm would mean that the prices would in fact go up. Such industries are usually marked by very large capital investments, such as power plants, transmission lines, or pipelines, so that the more of a product produced the lower is the cost per unit sold. As a result, the lowest price is charged by a single large firm. But since such firms are monopolies, they may charge monopoly prices for their services or cut back output to obtain even higher prices unless they are regulated.

Other industries are said to be subject to ruinous competition. That means that entry costs are so low that virtually anyone may enter the field, thus reducing the profits for all. For example, during the Depression, many unemployed workers bought a truck and entered the trucking field, compressing profits for the older, more "responsible" firms. Many economists view any argument that there is *too much* competition with some distaste and, instead, argue that trucking firms and others who insist on regulation to overcome ruinous competition are merely seeking government protection from the rigors of the market.

Finally, and related to the rationale of ruinous competition, is the argument that many regulated industries have actually *sought* regulation to protect themselves from competition or to regulate competitors. For example, it is clear that the railroads actively sought regulation by the ICC to stop cutthroat competition among themselves, and it is also clear that railroads sought regulation of the new trucking industry to protect themselves from motor carrier competition.

Once it is determined that a particular industry should be subject to economic regulation and an appropriate agency is established to regulate the industry, the agency's activities are usually divided into two main categories: (1) *licensing* or *certification,* and (2) *rate-making.*

Licensing and Certification   Simply put, the licensing and certification activities of economic regulatory agencies involve a determination of who gets the business. Such issues are highly political and often involve judgements of "who is the best." For example, broadcast licenses of radio and television stations are originally issued after a determination that a particular licensee would best serve the public "interest, convenience and necessity." Such licenses are often renewable, and public comment is solicited during the recertification process to determine whether the firm is conducting the business properly.

Rate-Making   Once an industry is made subject to economic regulation, prices are no longer set by the open market but imposed by the regulatory agency. Theoretically, those prices should be set at the rate that would evolve in a competitive market, but that figure is nonexistent. Instead, the administrative body views two somewhat opposing considerations: prices should be set as *low* as possible to satisfy consumers' interests yet they must be *high* enough to cover all of the costs of the regulated firm. Those "costs" should include all of the firm's out-of-pocket costs, so it could continue to operate and supply the service to the public, and also provide a fair return for investors in the firm so investment funds will continue to be available to the firm.

On a superficial analysis, out-of-pocket costs should be relatively easy to determine by simply adding up the expenses of the firm. But such costs can often be controlled by the regulated firm, as in the case of management salaries. A related problem is whether regulated firms, particularly public utilities, should be permitted to advertise and include such expenses as costs in determination of the proper rate to charge.

A far more difficult question is the determination of the proper fair return to be allowed to investors in the regulated firm. Most regulatory agencies use the firm's assets as a guide in determining the proper rate of return on the assumption that the value of the assets is related to investment return. The value of the assets is known as the **rate base,** and a great deal of the controversy within agencies deals with how to most effectively value those assets.

Regardless of the method used, agency administrators assume the rate base is the amount invested by the firm. Regulators then look at the rate of return earned by investments in similar private sector industries, and apply that rate of return to the rate base to determine the overall return for the firm. For example, if the rate base is determined to be $100 million, and investors in similar industries in the private sector receive a 12 percent return on their investment, the agency would allow 12 percent of $100 million, or $12 million, plus all out-of-pocket expenses, as the *overall return* of the regulated firm.

But the regulators' work is not finished when the overall return is computed. Most regulated industries do not charge a single price for their products, but rather maintain a range of prices for their products and services. That range, called the **rate structure,** often results from differences in the cost of supplying service at particular times or in the amount of demand for particular services. For example, telephone companies often charge business customers a higher rate than residential customers, on the assumption that a residence can do without a telephone while a business cannot. Regulatory agencies often are required to either set the rate structure within the context of the overall return or at least to approve the rate structure as set by the firm.

Some regulatory agencies do not set the price precisely but set a range of prices or maximum or minimum prices beyond which firms may not go. Agencies also permit firms to establish rules for the conduct of their business or establish those rules themselves. The detailed rate structures and rules applicable to a firm are sometimes called **tariffs.**

The Constitutionality of Economic Regulation While one would perhaps expect that the Supreme Court, in its earlier years, might have held economic regulation to violate concepts of "economic due process" and "economic equal protection," in fact the opposite is the case. As early as 1877* the Supreme Court held that economic regulation was constitutional if the business to be regulated was "clothed with a pub-

---

*Munn v. Illinois, 94 U.S. 113, 24 L. Ed. 77 (1877).

lic interest." There was little argument, even during the 1920's and 1930's, that economic regulation was constitutionally impermissible. The following decision reaffirmed the constitutionality of economic regulation.

Nebbia v. New York

291 U.S. 502, 54 S. Ct. 505, 78 L. Ed. 940 (1934)

During the Depression, dairy farmers found that the prices received in the retail markets were insufficient to cover the costs of production and transportation. As a result, many such farmers refused to produce or even "dumped" their milk, and milk became difficult to obtain. The State of New York passed a statute which forbade any retailer from selling milk lower than the price set by the state's Milk Control Board (9¢ a quart). Nebbia was convicted of selling two quarts of milk and a 5¢ cent loaf of bread for 18¢. He challenged the statute as a violation of 5th and 14th Amendment Due Process.

Mr. Justice ROBERTS delivered the opinion of the Court. . . .

The Fifth Amendment, in the field of federal activity, and the Fourteenth, as respects state action, do not prohibit governmental regulation for the public welfare. They merely condition the exertion of the admitted power, by securing that the end shall be accomplished by methods consistent with due process. And the guaranty of due process, as has often been held, demands only that the law shall not be unreasonable, arbitrary or capricious, and that the means selected shall have a real and substantial relation to the object sought to be attained. . . .

. . . .

But we are told that because the law essays to control prices it denied due process. Notwithstanding the admitted power to correct existing economic ills by appropriate regulation of business, . . . the appellant urges that the direct fixation of prices is a type of regulation absolutely forbidden. . . .

. . . .

But if, as must be conceded, the industry is subject to regulation in the public interest, what constitutional principle bars the state from correcting existing maladjustments by legislation touching prices? We think there is no such principle. The due process clause makes no mention of sales or of prices any more than it speaks of business or contracts or buildings or other incidents of property. The thought seems nevertheless to have persisted that there is something peculiarly sacrosanct about the price one may charge for what he makes or sells, and that, however able to regulate other elements of manufacture or trade, with incidental effect upon price, the state is incapable of directly controlling the price itself. This view was negatived many years ago. *Munn* v. *Illinois.* . . . The appellant's claim is, however, that this court, in there sustaining a statutory prescription of charges for storage by the proprietors of a grain elevator, limited permissible legislation of that type to businesses affected with a public interest, and he says no business is so affected except it have one or more of the characteristics he enumerates [primarily businesses that are public utilities or monopolies]. But this is a misconception. . . . It is true that the [*Munn*] court cited a statement . . . that when private property is "affected with a public interest, it ceases to be [purely private property] only", but the court proceeded at once to define what it understood by the expression, saying: "Property does become clothed with a public interest when used in a manner to make it of public consequence, and affect the community at large". . . . Thus understood, "affected with a public interest" is the equivalent of "subject to the exercise of the police power"; and it is plain that nothing more was intended by the expression. . . .

It is clear that there is no closed class or category of businesses affected with a public interest, and the function of the courts in the application of the Fifth and Fourteenth Amendments is to determine in each case whether circumstances vindicate the challenged regulation as a reasonable exertion of governmental authority or condemn it as arbitrary or discriminatory. . . . The phrase "affected with a public interest" can, in the nature of things, mean no more than that an industry, for adequate reason, is subject to control for the public good. . . . There can be no doubt that upon proper occasion and by appropriate measures the state may regulate a business in any of its aspects, including the prices to be charged for the products or commodities it sells.

So far as the requirement of due process is concerned, and in the absence of other constitutional restriction, a state is free to adopt whatever economic policy may reasonably be deemed to promote public welfare, and to enforce that policy by legislation adapted to its purpose. . . . Price control, like any other form of regulation, is unconstitutional only if arbitrary, discriminatory, or demonstrably irrelevant to the policy the legislature is free to adopt, and hence an unnecessary and unwarranted interference with individual liberty. . . .

The judgment is affirmed.

The *Nebbia* case thus brought "economic" regulation into the same category as any other type of state regulation, to be tested solely by the question of whether the state has the authority to regulate the business under its police power. The *Nebbia* case is often read together with the *West Coast Hotel* v. *Parrish* decision (Chapter 2, p. 59) to establish the scope of state regulatory power.

Deregulation

As noted in the beginning of this chapter, the term *deregulation* has a variety of meanings. In its strictest sense, the term applies to repeal or loosening of detailed economic regulation of those industries that have historically been closely regulated. This was the original, and perhaps most accurate, meaning of the term. But the term has been expanded to cover a general relaxation of all government regulation, usually on the grounds that there is too much regulation, and has even been used to justify lenient enforcement of the federal antitrust laws. The term has, it seems, become synonymous with a general reform of all regulation.

Pressure for reform of regulation has always existed. The same pressure for reform created the first independent regulatory commissions in the 19th century, the Administrative Procedures Act in 1946, and a variety of more specific changes, commission reports, and advisory opinions, spread over the nation's century-long employment of administrative agencies.

In the 1970's, the pressure for regulatory reform had become enormous. Attacks on "red tape" and "excessive paper work" seemed to join with philosophical and economic objections to "government intervention" to produce solid political pressure for regulatory reform. Both Presidents Carter and Reagan were elected, at least in part, on their pledges to reform the federal bureaucracy. And, in the period after 1976, a great many government regulations were repealed, amended, or rewritten.

Classical Deregulation

Originally, deregulation was applied to the removal of direct economic regulation of certain specific industries, such as transportation, communications, and energy transmission. Actually the term *deregulation* is misleading, since in all instances the government retains some control over those industries, though clearly the *extent* of regulation has been lessened in many cases.

Economic regulation of those industries had been criticized for many years. In some instances the original justification for regulation was challenged. In the trucking industry, for example, regulation was initially imposed on the theory that the industry would be subject to ruinous competition in the absence of governmentally controlled entry barriers. But the theory of ruinous competition had been viewed by economists as merely an attempt to avoid the consequences of the competitive marketplace.

In other instances, the original justification for regulation had changed over the years and no longer existed. Federal regulations designed to protect the fledgling commercial airlines were no longer necessary in the competitive struggles of the giant air carriers, for example.

Finally, the industries most subject to economic regulation are also essential services, such as transportation, communications, and energy. Thus, inefficiencies in those industries are most likely to be passed on to the consumer and, as a result, are most likely to contribute to inflation and the inability of American industries to compete worldwide. Many observers felt that a healthy dose of competition might make those industries more efficient, and, thus, reduce inflation and aid in international competition.

Deregulation to Counter Overregulation

Soon the term *deregulation* acquired a much different and broader meaning. The creation of dozens of new administrative agencies in the 1930's and from 1950–1975 resulted in a great number of regulations aimed at specific evils, such as those issued by the OSHA, CPSC, NLRB, FTC, EEOC, and FDA. It was easy to find a general feeling (particularly among those regulated) that our nation was "overregulated."

Critics used a variety of arguments to assert that the sheer number and extent of those specific evil regulations ought to be reduced. First, it was argued, overregulation makes the economy less productive, since resources must be shifted from research and other productive activities to compliance activities and "form filling." As a result, it was argued, American business is less productive and less competitive with international firms not subject to the same restrictions. Second, the same critics argued that the price of those regulations often outweighed the benefits of regulation. OSHA regulations imposing detailed requirements for toilet seats might save an occasional injury, for example, but at a very high price for industry. Third, some critics asserted that some regulations were simply not cost-effective; that is, cheaper and better methods of obtaining the same result were available. For example, detailed economic regulation of airlines was not necessary to guarantee safety when the same result could be obtained by specific evil regulations of the Federal Aviation Administration (FAA) at much lower cost. Finally, some critics argued that some government regulations actually work at cross-purposes to other government regulations. For example, while EPA regulations require high air quality standards, federal energy policy encourages the use of high-sulfur coal, even though high-sulfur coal produces more pollution than low-sulfur coal.

While there appears to be somewhat of a consensus regarding the need to deregulate some parts of the industries traditionally subject to economic regulation, no such consensus is clear regarding deregulation efforts in the specific evils area. Conventional reformers may see a need for improved adminstrative procedures and efficiency but also advocate the need for regulation to protect the public from "predatory" business activities. Others, following the "Jeffersonian" political tradition, tend to agree that "that government which governs least governs best." Such Jeffersonians argue from philosophical and economic grounds that any government intervention is a restriction on human freedom and ought to be made to prove itself before it is adopted. Finally, a large and diverse group, deriving their arguments from the Populist philosophy of the 19th century, seems to distrust any regulation that benefits corporate power or results from corporate influence. All of the conflicting strands of American politics seem to tug at the administrative process, creating differing results in different areas.

Cost-Benefit Analysis*   The largest single change in the administrative process dealing with the control of overregulation has been the adoption of **cost-benefit analysis.** That analysis was first used by the Defense Department in the 1960's to evaluate different weapons systems and was required by President Ford in 1974, when he issued an Executive Order requiring agencies to evaluate the effects of their actions on inflation. President Carter refined the process in the creation of the Regulatory Analysis Review Group, which reviewed all regulations that had potential costs over $100 million. President Reagan continued the process by requiring the Office of Management and Budget (OMB) to review all regulations and conduct cost-benefit analyses when preparing the budget of the executive branch.

Simply put, cost-benefit anaysis requires that the costs of a new regulation, including both the government's cost of administering the regulation and industries' costs of compliance, must be weighed against the probable benefits of the regulation. But while cost-benefit analysis seems simple on its face, it is highly controversial.

Perhaps the greatest difficulty with cost-benefit analysis is putting a dollar value on "untraded goods," such as clean air, wilderness, freedom from discrimination, or human life. For example, if an OSHA regulation were to cost $10 million to put into effect, but the regulation could be shown statistically to save five lives per year, it is necessary to put a value on those five lives. Of course, it is possible to put such a value on human life: actuarial tables exist and juries are asked to compute the value of human life and injury every day. That determination will be extremely value-laden, however; that is, the value placed on human life will depend to a very large extent on the subjective values of the person making the analysis. If that person values human life dearly, the benefits will outweigh the costs, and vice-versa. Even more complex questions exist in valuing such nontraded goods such as wilderness, scenic beauty, discrimination, and competition in the abstract.

A second problem of cost-benefit analysis is that the analysis itself involves costs. The collection of information on costs and benefits may itself be very costly and the review of such regulations inevitably involves substantial amounts of time. It has also been argued that the creation of a "review" body, such as the Office of Management and Budget, permits persons opposed to a particular regulation to make an "end run"

---

*See, generally, Pro and Con, Chapter 5, pp. 181–183.

around an agency charged with regulating a particular area. By obtaining the ear of officials of the OMB, a group or firm may defeat the intent of parts of the Administrative Procedures Act and the whole notion behind the creation of independent regulatory commissions.

But, while cost-benefit analysis has its problems, that kind of analysis can be highly useful, at least in those cases in which the dollar costs and benefits can be accurately foretold. Advocates of cost-benefit analysis also argue that *every* decision made really involves an informal and often subconscious weighing of costs and benefits. The Occupational Safety and Health Administration, if it should enact a particular regulation, has already made an informal determination that the benefits of the regulation outweigh the costs. Advocates argue that formal cost-benefit analysis merely makes that process explicit and open and requires a standard measure of economic costs. Opponents argue that use of economic costs and benefits inevitably favors those whose loss or gain can be measured in dollars, and, therefore, inevitably favors business and industry over those whose gain or loss, though real, is not readily measured in dollars.

Deregulation and the Antitrust Laws

As part of the general move towards deregulation, the Reagan Administration took a new tack towards antitrust enforcement. As noted in the chapters on antitrust, the Reagan Justice Department dropped several major antitrust actions including the IBM case. The FTC also dropped its suit against the cereal manufacturers. It is argued that the Justice Department "Merger Guidelines" of 1982 (revised in 1984) are clearly less restrictive than previous ones, particularly in their lack of mention of conglomerate mergers and treatment of vertical mergers and the "potential competition" doctrine. Most important, however, has been Administration approval of several extremely large mergers, including the largest mergers to take place in American history. All of this has taken place in an administration that alleges "bigness is not necessarily badness" and that has vowed to "get government off of our backs."

Some observers question the inclusion of lax enforcement of the antitrust laws as a part of deregulation and, in fact, would argue that strict antitrust enforcement is consistent with economic deregulation and deregulation for the purpose of countering overregulation. Those observers would argue that one of the principal purposes of the antitrust laws was to *avoid* specific, direct economic regulation of business. If a business becomes a monopoly, almost inevitably government must step in and control that business closely, as in the case of public utilities and other industries. By protecting competition as an abstract goal, the antitrust laws make such direct economic control unnecessary and, conversely, when such direct controls are removed, antitrust laws are absolutely essential to protect competition from the possible predatory conduct and "evils" of the uncontrolled monopoly or oligopolistic industry.

Methods of Deregulation

Most deregulation is obtained either through direct repeal by Congress or by administrative decisions to deregulate. Since many laws *require* agencies to regulate, much of the deregulation has come about through Congressional action. In a few instances, as in the determination by the Federal Communications Commission that FM radio need not be regulated as closely as it had been, administrative agencies themselves took the initiative to change existing regulations. And, in the case of AT&T, deregulation came about as a result of an antitrust settlement that made close regulation unnecessary by requiring competition.

Students should be careful in using the term *deregulation,* since it can mean so many different things. Clearly, it can mean direct repeal of all laws relating to a specific industry. But such complete repeals are very rare, perhaps only in the abolition of the Civil Aeronautics Board. More usually deregulation means the relaxation of certain aspects of regulation, while other aspects continue under government supervision. In a few cases, it might be argued that Congress or agencies have merely substituted one system of rules for another under the guise of deregulation, as in the 1980 banking deregulation act. Deregulation may simply be one of those political catch words with much sentiment and little real meaning.

Regulation of Transportation

Federal regulation of transportation began with the creation of the Interstate Commerce Commission (ICC) in 1887. The ICC was given authority to set railroad routes and rates. Its authority was extended to interstate trucks in the Motor Carrier Act of 1935 and to inland and coastal waterway common carriers in 1940. The ICC's authority over interstate trucking was substantially reduced in the Motor Carrier Act of 1980.

Similarly, authority to regulate airlines was initially given to the ICC, but was transferred to the newly created Civil Aeronautics Board (CAB) in 1938. In 1958, authority to regulate airline safety was transferred to the Federal Aviation Administration (FAA). In 1978, Congress abolished the CAB effective in 1985 in the Airline Deregulation Act.

The ebb and flow of transportation regulation provides a case study of many of the conflicting policies inherent in virtually every area of economic regulation. Real or perceived abuses in the industries created a demand for regulation and the enactment of a variety of regulatory statutes. During the mid-19th century, railroads had been involved in real abuses, including rate extortion and discrimination, price-fixing, and market division, and intense popular feeling arose for regulation. The result was the creation of the Interstate Commerce Commission, with the authority to fix rates at equitable and nondiscriminatory levels. Initial ICC regulation was ineffective, since the Commission did not have the power to set individual maximum rates, but could only declare specific rates unlawful after they were set by a railroad. That loophole was plugged in 1906 by the Hepburn Act, which gave the ICC the power to set maximum lawful rates. That Act also gave the ICC power over interstate pipelines.

The main purpose for ICC regulation of motor, air, and inland water carriers was substantially different. Those industries did not involve large capital expenditures, which discouraged new entrants in the railroad industry. Instead, anyone with enough money to buy an airplane, truck, or boat could enter the industry and compete. Those industries were, and are, very competitive, and regulation was deemed necessary to stabilize the industry and eliminate irresponsible competitors. In addition, it seems clear that the railroads pressed for regulation of those carriers as soon as they posed a competitive threat.

In all of the transportation industries, regulation followed a similar pattern. Entry into the business was controlled through the issuance of **certificates of public convenience and necessity,** maximum permissible rates were assigned in rather complex rate structures, routes were assigned to specific carriers, and specific and detailed rules were enforced. Enforcement generally came through **cease and desist orders** enforceable in federal court. As noted, regulation of air carriers was shifted from the ICC to the CAB in 1938, though enforcement patterns remained the same.

Control of Entry and the Problem of Intermodal Competition

Both the ICC and the CAB historically have had the right to issue certificates of public convenience and necessity to limit the number of competitors in a given industry. Generally, once such a certificate was granted, existing firms were permitted to retain those routes, and in fact were *required* to serve those routes even after they became unprofitable. Existing carriers often opposed new entrants or extensions of service by other carriers. The certificates were quite detailed, specifying the exact routes and commodities that must be carried.

The assignment of routes and service made the ICC, and for a time the CAB, the final arbiter of the fates of transportation businesses. Granting a particularly lucrative route to one carrier over another meant high profits for one and lean times or bankruptcy for the other. In some cases, the ICC was called upon to determine the comparative prices of two competing "modes" of competition and, therefore, to determine which of the two modes would be successful.

Deregulation of Transportation

During the late 1970's, the Carter Administration proposed substantial changes in the regulation of all three major types of carriers. The overall objective in all three cases was the reintroduction of competition as the primary "controller," rather than administrative regulation.

Airlines   In 1978, Congress passed the Airline Deregulation Act, which introduced gradually less strict controls until 1985, when the CAB was to be abolished. That Act came about as a result of an investigation by the CAB into domestic passenger fares, which concluded that airline fares should be based solely upon the costs of service. Within a year of the beginning of deregulation, the CAB found that the relaxation of government control of market entry and the easing of fare restrictions had produced real price competition, which resulted in lower prices in the long-haul markets. Similarly, average service levels had increased, though some smaller communities lost service. The CAB concluded that service was increasing at the points that had the greatest demand.

One of the principal concerns of airline deregulation was that airline safety would suffer. The theory was that if true competition was introduced into the airline industry, airlines would find it beneficial to cut costs, perhaps at the expense of safety standards. New, smaller carriers, which were permitted to enter the market, might also not maintain the same safety levels under conditions of pure competition. The Federal Aviation Administration (FAA), which has ultimate responsibility for airline safety, was unaffected by deregulation and continues to issue guidelines and standards for air traffic safety. The ultimate impact on safety is not yet clear.

Motor Carriers   Deregulation in the trucking industry has been less extensive than in the airlines, though the Motor Carrier Act of 1980 relaxes regulation substantially. Even before the Act was passed, the ICC had eased a number of regulations as well. Entry into the field was eased substantially, and existing carriers must prove that a new carrier would *not* benefit the public, rather than requiring new carriers to prove that new service *will* be in the public interest. The areas in which trucks may operate without ICC regulation was expanded, and private carriers (trucks owned by the shipper) may haul products of other firms on return trips (backhauls). Motor carriers may also raise or lower rates by 10 percent, rather than charge the precise rate mandated by the Commission.

Railroads   The least deregulation has occurred in the railroad industry. The Railroad Revitalization and Reform Act of 1976 gave the railroads the right to increase or decrease their rates by 7 percent in any one year without ICC approval, and the Staggers Railroad Act of 1980 gave even more rate flexibility. The Staggers Act also eased a series of specified railroad regulations dealing with contract rate agreements with shippers. ICC regulations have also relaxed restrictions on particular commodities and on "piggyback" services.

Regulation of Communications

Regulation of communications originally began in 1910, when radio frequencies were first assigned by the Department of Commerce. Later, regulation of interstate telephone and telegraph communications was given to the ICC. In 1934, Congress passed the Communications Act, which established the Federal Communications Commission, with general authority over all means of communications.

The FCC is an independent regulatory commission composed of five commissioners appointed by the President for staggered seven-year terms. Not more than three Commissioners may come from the same political party. The Commission has three major bureaus to deal with each of its major areas of authority: the *Mass Media Bureau* deals with commercial broadcasting, including radio, television, and cable systems; the *Common Carrier Bureau* regulates telephone, telegraph, telephoto, and satellite transmissions; and the *Private Radio Bureau* handles all other radio uses, such as citizens' band, police and fire bands, and industrial uses. The Commission is required to carry out its mission in a manner consistent with "the public interest, convenience and necessity," a standard that has been broadly interpreted by the courts to give the agency a great deal of discretion.

FCC Regulation of Broadcasting

Because of the limited number of broadcast frequencies available on which to broadcast, one of the principal broadcast functions of the FCC is to license broadcasters and assign frequencies. That authority extends to AM and FM radio and television. Frequencies are assigned and licenses are issued based on the "public interest, convenience and necessity" standard, and applicants must show financial and technical ability to use the frequency, along with basic requirements of citizenship and good character. Licenses are renewable every three years, and the public is permitted to comment on license renewal applications.

An additional factor that the FCC considers is diversity of media ownership. It will be recalled that the 1st Amendment is premised on a marketplace concept, in which differing and divergent views are available to the public in the marketplace of ideas, and the public "buys" those ideas it finds worthwhile. The FCC diversity rules attempt to further that goal by limiting ownership of broadcast media and requiring many different owners.

FCC v. National Citizens Committee for Broadcasting

436 U.S. 775, 98 S. Ct. 2096, 56 L. Ed. 2d 697 (1978)

Mr. Justice MARSHALL delivered the opinion of the Court.

At issue in the cases are Federal Communications Commission regulations governing the permissibility of common ownership of a radio or television broadcast station and a daily newspaper located in the same community. The regulations, adopted after a lengthy rule-making proceeding, prospectively bar formation or transfer of co-located newspaper-broadcast combinations. Existing combinations are generally permitted to continue in operation. However, in communities in which there is common ownership of the only daily newspaper and the only broadcast station, or (where there is more than one broadcast station) of the only daily newspaper and the only television station, divestiture of either the newspaper or the broadcast station is required within five years, unless grounds for waiver are demonstrated.

The questions for decision are whether these regulations either exceed the Commission's authority under the Communications Act of 1934, or violate the First or Fifth Amendment rights of newspaper owners. . . .

I

. . . .

In setting its licensing policies, the Commission has long acted on the theory that diversification of mass media ownership serves the public interest by promoting diversity of program and service viewpoints, as well as by preventing undue concentration of economic power. This perception of the public interest has been implemented over the years by a series of regulations imposing increasingly stringent restrictions on multiple ownership. . . .

. . . .

Various parties—including the National Citizens Committee for Broadcasting (NCCB), the National Association of Broadcasters (NAB), the American Newspaper Publishers Association (ANPA), and several licensees subject to the divestiture requirement—petitioned for review of the regulations. . . .

. . . [T]he Court of Appeals affirmed the prospective ban on new licensing of co-located newspaper-broadcast combinations. . . .

II

. . . .

Section 303(r) of the Communications Act, provides that "the Commission from time to time, as public convenience, interest, or necessity requires, shall . . . [m]ake such rules and regulations and prescribe such restrictions and conditions, . . . as may be necessary to carry out the provisions of [the Act]. . . . [I]t is now well established that this general rulemaking authority supplies a statutory basis for the Commission to enact regulations codifying its view of the public interest licensing standard, so long as that view is based on consideration of permissible factors and is otherwise reasonable. . . .

. . . .

Our past decisions have recognized, moreover, that the First Amendment and antitrust values underlying the Commission's diversification policy may properly be considered by the Commission in determining where the public interest lies. . . . And, while the Commission does not have power to enforce the antitrust laws as such, it is permitted to take antitrust policies into account in making licensing decisions. . . .

Petitioners NAB and ANPA also argue that the regulations, though designed to further the First Amendment goal of achieving "the widest possible dissemination of information from diverse and antagonistic sources," nevertheless violate the First Amendment rights of newspaper owners. We cannot agree, for this argument ignores the fundamental proposition that there is no "unbridgeable First Amendment right to broadcast comparable to the right of every individual to speak, write or publish."

The physical limitations of the broadcast spectrum are well known. Because of problems of interference between broadcast signals, a finite number of frequencies can be used productively; this number is far exceeded by the number of persons wishing to broadcast to the public. In light of this physical scarcity, government allocation and regulation of broadcast frequencies are essential, as we have often recognized. No one here questions the need for such allocation and regulation, and, given that need, we see nothing in the First Amendment to prevent the Commission from allocating licenses so as to promote the "public interest" in diversification of the mass communications media.

. . . .

In the instant case, far from seeking to limit the flow of information, the Commission has acted, in the Court of Appeals' words, "to enhance the diversity of information heard by the public without ongoing governmental surveillance of the content of speech." The regulations are a reasonable means of promoting the public interest in diversified mass communications; thus they do not violate the First Amendment rights of those who will be denied braodcast licenses pursuant to them. Being forced to "choose among applicants for the same facilities," the Commission has chosen on a "sensible basis," one designed to further, rather than contravene "the system of freedom of expression."

The judgment of the Court of Appeals is affirmed. . . .

FCC Supervision of Broadcasting and Self-Deregulation

While the FCC is specifically forbidden to censor broadcast material, clearly the FCC plays a role in the content of programming. That role is most evident in political broadcasting, particularly in the "equal time" requirement and the so-called "fairness doctrine." The former requires that equal use be granted to all legally qualified candidates at equal rates. The latter requires that opportunities be granted to persons opposing viewpoints expressed by the broadcaster. The FCC also regulates obscenity, lotteries, prime-time programming, and a vague area of family programming, involving sexually stimulating or drug-related topics.

In 1979, the FCC began to back off from some of its content-related program requirements, especially those which limited the amount of time that might be devoted to commercials and rules designed to require a certain amount of news and public service programming. The Commission made those changes as a result of studies which showed that listener preferences would force broadcasters to limit commercials and provide news service even in the absence of regulation.

FCC Regulation of Telephone Transmissions: The AT&T Story

The FCC also regulates other forms of communications including telephone and telegraph transmissions. Historically, FCC regulation of telephone transmissions has been directed at only one company, AT&T, simply because that firm maintained a monopoly on most aspects of that business for many years. Regulation of AT&T ultimately resulted in a federal court antitrust settlement requiring AT&T to "break up," or divest itself of many parts of its business, and a total restructuring of the telephone industry in the United States. That divestiture and resulting deregulation has produced perhaps more controversy than any other aspect of regulatory reform.

The AT&T decision results from the complex history of AT&T itself, from certain challenges by competitors or possible competitors of AT&T, and from a series of decisions by the FCC that made the antitrust challenge almost inevitable. Because of the controversial nature and importance of the AT&T divestiture, it is necessary to trace the history of telephone regulation in outline form.

Early History and Regulation   AT&T was incorporated in 1885 to take advantage of Alexander Graham Bell's patent for the telephone and, until the early 1900's, AT&T was the sole provider of telephone service in the nation. But when Bell's patent expired, large numbers of independent telephone companies were set up, usually to provide regional or local service. Determined to maintain its previously dominant position in the industry, AT&T began a program of acquiring such independents or, if the independents could not be purchased, of refusing to connect independent firms' lines into the nationwide long-distance system run by AT&T.

Some of the independents fought back under state and federal antitrust laws, and, after an investigation by the Interstate Commerce Commission in 1913, AT&T agreed to permit the independents to connect to the AT&T long-distance lines. AT&T also agreed in those proceedings not to acquire any directly competing independents. Congress later adopted legislation which undercut that agreement by permitting AT&T to acquire independents after approval by the ICC, however.

In 1934, Congress created the Federal Communications Commission (FCC) and transferred authority over telephone and telegraph communications from the ICC to the FCC. By that time, AT&T had again become the dominant force in the telephone industry and was a genuine monopoly in many parts of the country. It owned virtually all long-distance facilities, most local telephone companies, and the only producer of telephone equipment in the nation, Western Electric. One of the means by which it maintained control was a company rule, or **tariff,** that only equipment approved by AT&T could be connected to telephone lines.

In spite of its regulated status, AT&T was vulnerable to antitrust challenges. In

1949 the government brought a "monopolization" case against the firm, asking divestiture of Western Electric and Bell Telephone Laboratories, the research unit of the firm. The case was finally settled by consent decree in 1956, though both Western Electric and Bell Laboratories remained a part of AT&T.

The Beginnings of the Break-up: Hush-a-Phone, Carterfone, and MCI

AT&T's downfall began shortly after the 1956 consent decree and developed from a most unlikely chain of events. AT&T, in an attempt to police its tariff against connection of any unapproved device, requested the FCC to rule that a small plastic cup, called a *Hush-A-Phone,* could not be attached to the mouthpiece of telephone instruments. The device, intended to provide privacy for people talking on the phone in a crowded room, was manufactured by an independent firm. The FCC ruled that the device could not be attached, but the U.S. Court of Appeals reversed the ruling by holding that the device did no harm to telephone equipment.* In its opinion, the Court ruled that AT&T could not interfere with the right of telephone subscribers to use their equipment "in ways which are privately beneficial without being publicly detrimental."

While the *Hush-A-Phone* decision did not involve momentous issues at the time, the decision sparked a whole new industry of telephone attachments. Independent firms began manufacturing all sorts of devices that could be connected to telephone equipment, and those devices became more and more sophisticated. Meanwhile AT&T continued its policy of policing the tariff through the FCC.

In 1968, the FCC reconsidered the "attachments" tariff in the context of a case dealing with a rather sophisticated independent mobile radio service in the *Carterfone* decision, 13 F.C.C. 420. That decision marked a change in FCC policy in which the FCC began to aggressively encourage competition in some phases of telecommunications.

> [A] customer desiring to use an interconnecting device to improve the utility to him of both the telephone system and a private radio system should be able to do so, so long as the interconnection does not adversely affect the telephone company's operations or the telephone system's utility for others. A tariff which prevents this is unreasonable; it is also unduly discriminatory when, as here, the telephone company's own interconnecting equipment is approved for use. The vice of the present tariff, here as in *Hush-A-Phone,* is that it prohibits the use of harmless as well as harmful devices.**

The next year, AT&T's position was weakened even more. One of the reasons for regulation of AT&T was that its long-distance communications system, involving hundreds of thousands of miles of wire, was thought to be a natural monopoly. But much of that wire had been replaced by microwave transmission, and such installations are less costly than wire. In 1969, the F.C.C. considered the first application to compete with AT&T in long-distance service.

Hush-A-Phone Corp. v. *U.S.,* 238 F. 2d 266 (U.S. App. D.C., 1956).

**In the Matter of Use of the Carterfone Device,* 13 F.C.C. 420 (1968).

In Re the Application of Microwave Communications, Inc. (MCI)

18 F.C.C. 953 (1969)

Commissioner BARTLEY for the Commission:

This proceeding involves applications filed by Microwave Communications, Inc. (MCI) for construction permits for new facilities in the Domestic Point-to-Point Service at Chicago, Ill., St. Louis, Mo., and nine intermediate points. MCI proposes to offer its subscribers a limited common carrier microwave radio service, designed to meet the interoffice and interplant communications needs of small business. . . .

MCI contends that it will offer its subscribers substantially lower rates than those charged for similar services by the established carriers and that subscribers with less than full-time communication needs will be able to achieve additional savings through the channel-sharing and half-time use provisions of its proposed tariff. . . .

MCI's applications are opposed by Western Union Telegraph Co. (Western Union), General Telephone Co. of Illinois (General), and the Associated Bell System Cos., American Telephone & Telegraph Co., Illinois Bell Telephone Co., and Southwestern Bell Telephone Co. (Bell), which presently provide microwave services to the geographical area which MCI proposes to serve.

The evidentiary hearings commenced on February 13, 1967. . . . Hearing Examiner Herbert Sharfman recommended the grant of MCI's applications. . . . [H]e concluded that MCI's lower rates and more flexible use would enable it to serve a market whose needs are unfulfilled by the available common carrier services; that consequently there would be no unnecessary or wasteful duplication; and that the public interest would be served by authorizing MCI's proposed microwave system. . . . Except as modified below . . . we adopt the hearing examiner's findings and conclusions.

The principal contentions advanced by Bell, General, and Western Union against the grant of MCI's applications are: (1) that MCI is not financially qualified to construct and operate the proposed facilities; (2) that no need has been shown for the common carrier services proposed; (3) that MCI will be unable to provide a reliable communications service; (4) that the proposal represents an inefficient utilization of the frequency spectrum; and (5) that the proposal is not technically feasible. Each of these contentions will be considered below.

MCI's Financial Qualifications

The examiner found that MCI's estimate of its construction costs at $564,000 is reasonable, and that there is consumer interest in, and a market for, a communications service with the features MCI proposes. . . . We conclude that MCI is financially qualified to construct and to operate its proposed microwave system. . . .

Need for MCI's Proposals

. . . .

The record . . . establishes that there are members of the public who require the microwave communications service proposed by MCI; that there exists, at the very least, a reasonable expectancy that one or more of such persons will avail themselves of the said facilities if they are authorized, and we conclude that MCI has demonstrated a need for the common carrier communications service which it proposes.

The carriers argue that even if lower rates for MCI communications services have been shown, that factor may not be properly considered in resolving the issue of need. They assert that they are required by the Commission to serve both high-density high-profit and low-density low-profit areas and in order to maintain rates which are relatively uniform, all rates are based on a cost averaging principle. Claiming that MCI is "cream skimming," i.e., proposing to operate solely on high density routes where lower fixed costs per channel permit lower rates with higher profits, the carriers state that in order to compete with MCI they will be forced to abandon their cost averaging policies with a resultant increase in rates for subscribers on lightly used routes.

MCI is offering a service intended primarily for interplant and interoffice communications with unique and specialized characteristics. In these circumstances we cannot perceive how a grant of the authorizations requested would pose any serious threat to the established carrier's price averaging policies. . . . It may be, as the telephone companies and Western Union argue, that some business will be diverted from the existing carriers . . . but that fact provides no sufficient basis for depriving a segment of the public of the benefits of a new and different service.

Reliability of Service

. . . .

No specific standards have been enunciated by the Commission as to what constitutes a minimum degree of reliability which is acceptable for a common carrier communications service. . . . On the basis of the evidence before us, however, we find that the MCI proposal may reasonably be expected to achieve a degree of reliability which, while not matching the high degree of reliability claimed by the major carriers, will provide an acceptable and a marketable common carrier service. . . .

Efficient Utilization of the Frequency Spectrum

We recognize, as the carriers argue, that MCI will not make the fullest possible use of the frequencies which it seeks. . . . We have found that by reason of its low-cost, sharing, and part-time use provisions, MCI can reasonably be expected to furnish an economical microwave communications service to a segment of the public which presently cannot avail itself of such a service. . . . When frequencies are used to meet a significant unfulfilled communications need, we do not believe that such use may be considered as "inefficient."

The Feasibility of Loop Service*

We are not unmindful of the fact that the carriers maintain that loop service is not technically feasible and there is no provision for such service in their tariffs. However, insufficient evidence is contained in this record to support a conclusion that the proposed interconnection is not feasible. . . . What seems a more likely obstacle to interconnection is . . . the carriers' intransigence. . . . In these circumstances, the carriers are not in a position to argue that consideration of the interconnection question is premature. Since they have indicated that they will not voluntarily provide loop service we shall retain jurisdiction of this proceeding in order to enable MCI to obtain from the Commission a prompt determination on the matter of interconnection. Thus, at such time as MCI has customers and the facts and details of the customers' requirements are known, MCI may come directly to the Commission with a request for an order of interconnection. We have already concluded that a grant of MCI's proposal is in the public interest. We likewise conclude that, absent a significant showing that interconnection is not technically feasible, the issuance of an order requiring the existing carriers to provide loop service is in the public interest. . . .

Following the *Carterfone* and *MCI* decisions, a number of new competitors to the existing AT&T organization sprang up, and AT&T responded by making it very difficult for such new firms to interconnect with the existing telephone system. Those competitors fought back through the FCC and through private antitrust actions. Finally, in 1974, the Justice Department filed an antitrust action against AT&T, Western Electric, and Bell Telephone Laboratories. That suit charged monopoliza-

---

*"Loop Service" is the interconnection between the subscriber's facilities and MCI's transmission lines. That service must be supplied by other carriers, presumably the local telephone company.

tion under Section 2 of the Sherman Act, and asked divestiture of Western Electric and many of the local telephone companies.

Breaking up Is Hard to Do: The Divestiture Decree The antitrust case took six years to get to trial, and began about a week before President Reagan took office. The trial itself was an "on-again, off-again" affair, finally terminating on January 8, 1982, when the parties announced they had reached a settlement subject to the approval of the court. Since the trial judge has the authority to approve or disapprove such settlements, the consent decree was changed considerably under pressure from the trial judge prior to final approval.

Under the terms of the consent decree, the "competitive" aspects of AT&T are separated from aspects of the business that are still monopolistic. AT&T retains its "long-lines" department, its equipment manufacturer (Western Electric) and Bell Telephone Laboratories, all of which have substantial competition from independent firms. AT&T was required to divest itself of its 22 local telephone companies, which were reorganized into 7 regional phone companies.

The newly created local firms were barred from marketing "customer premises equipment"—in other words, telephones and other equipment—unless they were manufactured by some other firm. Those firms were also required to permit any long distance firm, including AT&T and all of the new competing long distance companies, to have access to the local lines, as long as those carriers are equal "in type, quality and price" to that provided by AT&T. AT&T was barred from using the Bell name and trademark, and several of the regional phone companies have adopted that name and trademark for their facilities. AT&T was barred from engaging in "electronic publishing" over its transmission lines. The decree also limited the amount of debt which AT&T could transfer to the regional firms.

FCC Implementation Decisions The antitrust decree changed the rules of the game for the FCC, and that Commission has issued new rules to deal with the new state of affairs. For years, local service was often subsidized by long-distance charges, particularly in sparsely populated areas. After the break-up of AT&T the smaller local phone companies no longer had the long-distance subsidy and as a result higher local charges were necessary. In July 1983, the FCC approved a plan by the regional companies that imposed a gradually increasing "user access fee" on local service, which will be reevaluated at a later date. Another decision requires the long distance companies to provide some support for local companies until 1988.

The Impact of Divestiture The long-range impact of the AT&T divestiture is not yet clear and may not be clarified for several years. It does seem clear, however, that intense competition in long-distance communication and in the sale and lease of telephone equipment has developed, and most economists expect that competition to result in lower prices in those fields. Subsidization of local service by long-distance charges is at an end, which will probably result in higher local phone charges. Finally, the FCC continues to have jurisdiction over telephone communication, though the nature of FCC regulation is being altered drastically as a result of the divestiture.

Deregulation has occured in the telephone industry, not because of legislative acts or even administrative decisions, but because of application of the federal anti-trust laws, and has resulted in a competitive telephone industry, at least in many of its important aspects. Since the industry is now competitive, close regulation may now be relaxed, and the FCC is in the process of modifying many previous rules to accommodate the new, competitive industry.

Regulation of Energy Transmission

The third industry to be subjected to close economic regulation is the transmission of energy resources, including regulation of the production of energy resources. Much of the federal policy toward energy was discussed in Chapter 17, but an additional factor in that policy has been the direct regulation of prices of natural gas and oil. Much of that regulation is undertaken by the Department of Energy (DOE), though the Reagan Administration has proposed to abolish the Department of Energy and scatter its duties to several other agencies.

The DOE regulates the "wellhead" price for natural gas through a nationwide pricing system. The price of oil was first regulated in 1970 when President Nixon used the authority granted under the Economic Stabilization Act of that year to impose a general 90 day wage, rent, and price freeze. Oil prices continued to be regulated until 1981, when the authority to regulate those prices expired. There are no present regulations on the price of oil, though it is clear that Congress could impose those controls once again if the international situation or domestic inflation demand regulation.

The federal government also regulates hydroelectric power, or electric power generated by turbines turned by falling water. The Federal Water Power Act permits the Federal Energy Regulatory Commission (FERC) to issue licenses to citizens, corporations, or state or municipal governments to construct, operate, and maintain hydroelectric dams over any navigable waterway. Many of the original licenses issued in the Depression are now expiring, and the FERC is presently considering many renewal applications.

Regulation of Public Utilities

Public utilities, such as local electric, natural gas, and sometimes water and sewer companies, have traditionally been regulated at the state or local level. Water and sewer facilities are usually municipally owned, though occasionally a locality has granted a "franchise" to a private firm. Local electric and natural gas utilities are commonly private firms regulated by a state or sometimes a local agency. That agency usually is required to establish rates and other regulations for such facilities, usually under the guidelines as discussed in the introduction to this chapter.

Until 1978, the federal government had stayed out of the rate-making process for local public utilities. In that year, Congress passed the Public Utilities Regulatory Policies Act as part of its overall concern with energy conservation and demonstrated Congressional concern with rates and conservation measures adopted by state public utility commissions. The Act generally requires state utility commissions to reexamine rate-making and operating practices and creates federal standards regarding rates, the rate structure, and certain conservation measures. Those standards need not be adopted but must be considered, and inducements in the form of federal grants are created.

Summary and Conclusions

"Economic" regulation exists in several major industries, including transportation, communication, transmission of energy, and public utilities. Those industries usually do not fit the classical form of competition; they are natural monopolies, because of factors inherent in the industry which make competition difficult or because the industry is subject to "ruinous" competition. The ruinous competition justification for economic regulation is not unanimously endorsed.

Economic regulation generally involves licensing or certification by an administrative agency and rate making by the administrative body. Rate making sets prices for the products or services of the regulated industry, usually through some cost-based system taking into account a fair return for investors. Such rate making also involves setting a rate structure for the full range of products and services sold by the regulated industry.

Substantial questions have arisen about the efficiency of economic regulation and, in many areas, notably natural gas and airlines, substantial deregulation has taken place. Such deregulation usually involves permitting market forces to set prices or determine routes and output, though usually some residual regulation remains to govern some of the specific evils inherent in the industry. For example, while airline rates and routes are deregulated, airline safety is still governed.

The term *deregulation* has acquired meanings aside from the simple removal of economic regulation, however. The term is also applied to a general cut-back in the number and scope of federal regulations dealing with specific evils, usually through some type of cost-benefit analysis, and to lax enforcement of the antitrust laws. Some observers argue that antitrust laws should be more strictly enforced in a climate of deregulation, however, since it is a primary purpose of those laws to assure that the competitive marketplace exists and will determine prices and output properly.

There seems little doubt that the mood of the country generally favors deregulation, in the sense of getting government "off of the backs" of the people. It is important to remember, however, that every political and legal action benefits one group and injures another. Regulation benefitted some and injured others, and deregulation, of whatever form, must have the same effect. The regulatory system must be viewed as a web, in which a change in one strand affects all of the other strands, positively or negatively.

PRO AND CON

ISSUE: How Should Business Respond to Deregulation?

PRO: Business Must Use Its New Freedom Responsibly

Wes Poriotis*

Business, it would seem, is about to enter a new era of less regulation. The wraps of restraint are coming off. And it's all being done in the interest of unleashing that indomitable tendency of Americans to be one of the most inventive people in the world when left to their own resources.

. . . .

Deregulation is not, in any way shape or form, going to make the life of this nation's chief executives any easier. Deregulation has not simplified life for the executive management of this country's banking institutions. Deregulation has not eased the strain of those who manage the airline companies. And deregulation has, most assuredly, not made the phone company's existence less trying. In fact, the decontrol of the private sector is certain to make the running of your businesses vastly more complicated than it ever was in the days of increased federal and state regulation.

The reason this is so for companies is the same as the reason it is so for individual human beings. It is onerous, dislocating, dispiriting to lead a life governed at every turn by this rule and that law. Rules inhibit discovery, imagination, and innovation. Rules breed cautious people and cautious institutions. And yet it does not conversely follow that the lighter the rules and regulations, the easier the living. In fact, the greater our freedom the more complex things become. Because with freedom, the individual and the institution will be guided not by the dictates of external authority but by the good sense and perception of the individual or the institution. The self-responsible individual, in other words, has a harder time of it than the automaton who does not have to bother figuring things out for himself.

And so it will be for the self-responsible company. Instead of determining whether it is in conformity with the law, the job of today's business leadership will be to know whether business is in conformity with the emerging public will. . . .

And this raises, in my mind at least, the question as to precisely what kind of PR counsel will

best serve the needs of business leaders in the 1980s. . . .

I would want my PR counsel . . . to remind the management of my company that deregulation can in no way lessen the commitment to equal opportunity. The sheer weight of labor market demographics makes it abundantly clear that women want and will fight for their rightful place in the job market, and in your companies. . . .

. . . I would expect the head of my public relations department to understand that the challenge of intelligently responding to the consumer movement will be no less great in the 1980's than it was in the 1970's. In spite of less regulation, the American consumer will go on holding American business legally accountable for high quality products and services. This is inbred in the character of our nation.

I'd want my PR officer to remember what the great French political observer, Tocqueville, noticed about Americans way back in the 1840's. "Those Americans," he said, "everytime they think there is an injustice, they solve it with a new law." Deregulation or not, the fact is that we Americans abhor legal vacuums. New laws will come just as surely as night follows day if the American people believe business is not socially responsible. . . .

I'd want a PR professional who understands, as well, that though we unquestionably are in a period of less control of our lives, it still remains a fact that the essential purpose of all societies is to protect the citizen from harm. However much you and I may yearn for reduced rules and regulations, you and I know that it takes but one perilous mistake to revive public demand for tighter controls. . . .

Some say we are witnessing a resurgence of political conservatism in our nation today. Perhaps this is so. Some say further that conservatives have a natural affinity for the business ethos. . . .

The conservative conscience can be more severe when the public weal is ignored than the most burning liberal ever was. The conservative,

---

*Wes Poriotis is president of Wesley-Brown Enterprises, Ltd. From his speech, "Corporate Public Relations in a Deregulated Economy: Now Comes the Hard Part," delivered to the Virginia State Chamber of Commerce and Industry, Charlottesville, Va., April 13, 1981, reprinted in *Vital Speeches of the Day,* vol. 47, p. 482. Reprinted by permission.

the true conservative, believes in the inherent perfectability of mankind. The true conservative expects individuals and institutions to act responsibly. The true conservative is not unyieldingly pro-business. The true conservative is unyielding pro-individual.

I'd expect my PR executive not to misread the will of conservatism in our nation today.

CON: Business Should Reject Some Deregulation

Ralph M. Baruch*

... [G]overnment has spread its roots and it has grown. It has grown as fast or faster than private enterprise ever has or ever could. Perhaps, not surprisingly, no facet of government expanded more than regulatory agencies. First they multiplied like flies, then they grew like Topsy. There were two regulatory agencies in 1930, and by 1980 we were approaching the 50 mark,. . . .

The cumbersomeness of compliance seems to choke entire industries and it even began to choke on itself. When you add the cost structure to the regulatory impulse, the point really bangs home. For example: General Motors estimates that the paperwork alone involved with compliance reached nearly $1,000 per vehicle. On a more personal basis, it reaches all of us: Federal regulatory costs are more than $400 a year for every man, woman and child in America.

. . . .

I believe that the public often perceives its interests as having been ignored by government. The theme of Jimmy Carter's "bring an outsider to Washington" campaign was the promise of a new broom to sweep aside inefficiencies in government; the themes became "deregulation" and a "lessening of bureaucratic thinking."

To some degree, Carter was successful. In his administration came the first rumblings of "sunset legislation". . . .

And now, with the election of Ronald Reagan, the Jimmy Carter broom was exchanged for a vacuum cleaner. The Carter move to "sunset regulation" was trampled in the crush to deregulate entirely. But deregulation should be based on two important, crucial and vital factors: (1) the ease of entry into the marketplace, and (2) the ease to compete in that marketplace.

How can we deregulate a business and talk about an open marketplace when that marketplace offers no opportunity of entry?

Take the airline industry—it does offer opportunity of entry and competition. It was substantially deregulated and today, city after city receives less service than it did prior to deregulation.

True enough, you can fly from coast to coast for less than ever before, but, I ask you, is it in the public interest to have the traveller between Houston and Miami pay more than it costs to fly from coast to coast?

You know and I know that it may not be fair. We know the traveller in other corridors is subsidizing the coast-to-coast bargains. But that's business—"You's take your chances" and you compete or you stay out of the hot kitchen.

When Mr. Reagan appointed some members of the Federal Communications Commission, the term "deregulation" instantly became something between a buzz-word and a buzz-saw. Then it was said "why not deregulate broadcasting?" Now wait just a minute—broadcasting is an animal of a different color. . . .

Deregulation in the television industry is a delicate and multifacted proposition and should be treated prudently. . . .

Under the guise of deregulation, the FCC is in the process of deciding whether networks should again be allowed to obtain a financial interest in the programs which they broadcast and be entitled to re-enter the syndication market from which they were barred. . . .

The inability of networks to control programming or be engaged in selling network reruns by virtue of FCC regulation, has given many producers, including my company, the opportunity to harvest the fruits of our labor. . . .

. . . .

As a result of this rule, new sales organizations have sprung up: competition has increased substantially, and isn't this the real justification of good regulation—to stimulate competition?

We believe that if this rule were to be stricken, a compression of the marketplace would take place, competition would *decrease*—which is certainly something which both our president and our legislators, as well as our regulators, don't intend to happen and want to avoid.

. . . .

---

*Ralph Baruch is chairman and CEO of Viacom International, Inc. From his speech, "The Dangers of the Hasty Heart: Deregulation of the Public Interest," delivered to the Houston Rotary Club, Houston, Texas, August 19, 1982, and reprinted in *Vital Speeches of the Day*, vol. 48, p. 765. Reprinted by permission.

DISCUSSION QUESTIONS

1. What factors influence whether a particular industry is a natural monopoly? Do you think telephone communications was a natural monopoly *before* the development of long-distance microwave transmissions? *After* that development? Are local phone companies still natural monopolies? Are railroads? Pipelines? Airlines?

2. Why do economists have such problems with the theory of ruinous competition? Who would you suppose would assert that competition was ruinous?

3. If the rates to be charged by regulated industries are to be set by administrative bodies on the basis of costs, should those industries have the right to set the salaries of management at whatever level they desire? Should such industries, particularly public utilities, be permitted to advertise? Why would they want to?

4. Does the same pressure for deregulation exist in an industry that is a natural monopoly as in one in which regulation is justified because of ruinous competiton? Is it significant that most deregulation has taken place in the trucking and airline industries, and very little deregulation has taken place in the railroad and public utility industries?

5. Does cost-benefit analysis make any sense in social legislation? For example, the "costs" of school desegregation might be accurately assessed, as the total of the price of busses, new schools, redistricting, and various other factors, and would presumably be quite high. Now, what is the dollar value of the *benefits* of school desegregation? And finally, do the *benefits* outweigh the costs? Do you suppose it depends on who is making the assessment?

6. Should any prosecutor be permitted to pick and choose the laws he wishes to enforce? Should the Justice Department be permitted to refuse to enforce portions of the antitrust laws?

7. Is the Office of Management and Budget substituting its judgment for that of administrative agencies by imposing cost-benefit analysis on all regulations? Isn't the purpose of agencies to delegate responsibility to *expert* administrators? Is OMB "usurping" power granted by Congress to the agencies?

8. Which is more important: (a) low air fares and heavy competition in big cities or service to smaller cities and short-haul flights? (b) preservation of diversity of views on the airwaves or efficient, integrated businesses under a single owner? (c) low long-distance phone rates or low local-service charges?

CASE PROBLEMS

1. Carlisle operates a gasoline station. In order to counter massive price increases by oil suppliers, Congress passed an Act permitting the President to establish maximum prices on petroleum products. The President in turn established a maxi-

mum retail price for gasoline. Carlisle can prove that he would make 30 percent more profit if the price were uncontrolled. May he argue that the action taken by Congress or the President is unconstitutional?

2. Gloster Airlines has been serving the city of Fitzwater for twenty years and is the only airlines to do so. The route makes a small profit, but Gloster realizes that it could make a larger profit if it were to use the aircraft used in the Fitzwater routes on other routes. The airline is the only way the citizens of Fitzwater have to get to Salisbury, a larger city 80 miles away. If Gloster abandons its route to Fitzwater, several jobs will be lost and many people will be forced to move closer to Salisbury. May Gloster abandon its route?

3. Montgomery Trucking Company wishes to serve certain businesses in the community of Exeter and applies to the ICC for permission to do so. Northumberland Trucking already serves that community and is afraid that Montgomery will cut into its business. Who has the burden of proof at the ICC hearing, and what must that company prove?

4. Pembroke Broadcasting wishes to air a very violent movie, featuring some rather explicit scenes of dismemberment. The movie contains no nudity or obscenity, however. May the movie be aired?

5. Northumberland Power Company is under the jurisdiction of the State Utilities Board. The sum of all of the assets of Northumberland is $150 million, based on the reproduction cost of those assets today. Similar private sector investments obtain a rate of return on capital of 9 percent, and the out-of-pocket costs to the firm are $8 million dollars per year. Northumberland produced 300 million kilowatt hours of electricity last year. Assuming the State Utilities Commission sets the rate of return based on those facts, and assuming there is a totally uniform rate structure, how much should each kilowatt-hour of electricity cost consumers? If Pierce uses 750 kilowatt hours in October, how much will his electric bill be, exclusive of taxes?

6. If the federal government were to decide that the railroads ought be operated as a monopoly, purchased all of the existing railroads, then sold all of the assets purchased to a single new corporation that was subject to close federal economic regulation, would the action be Constitutional?

SUGGESTED READINGS

Needham, Douglas. *The Economics and Politics of Regulation: A Behavioral Approach* (Boston: Little, Brown and Company, 1983).

Schnitzer, Martin. *Contemporary Government and Business Relations* 2d ed. (Boston: Houghton Mifflin Company, 1983).

Shooshan, Harry M., III (Ed.). *Disconnecting Bell: The Impact of the AT&T Divestiture* (New York: Pergamon Press, 1984).

Stone, Alan. *Regulation and Its Alternatives* (Washington, D.C.: CQ Press, a division of Congressional Quarterly, Inc., 1982).

Weiss, Leonard W., and Allyn D. Strickland. *Regulation: A Case Approach* (New York: McGraw-Hill, 1982).

Part IX

Beyond the Law: The Social and Ethical Responsibilities of Business

In one sense, this entire book is about the "social and ethical responsibilities of business." It should be quite clear by this time that "ethics" and "the law" are intimately related. Virtually, every legal theory and even every government regulation found in this text has its ethical side, either in the sense that the general ethics of society created pressure for the law or that the law influenced our perception of what is right and wrong. But it should also be quite clear that not everything that may be called *unethical* is also illegal, nor is everything illegal also unethical.

Much of our discussion to this point has centered around the tension between the two great ethics of the 20th century: the ethic of Individualism and the ethic of Community. Most of the laws we studied have been an attempt to find a middle ground between those two societal ethics, to permit freedom of individual action while restricting the excesses of Individualism.

It is now time to speak more directly of the relationships between the law and personal ethics. We must round out our discussion by considering the full relationship of ethics to the law, and by considering whether business has ethical and social duties beyond those required by the law. In other words, is the law all there is, or is law merely the "ethical foundation," upon which other ethical notions can and must be constructed?

Ethics and the Law

Man is an animal with primary instincts of survival. Consequently his ingenuity has developed first and his soul afterwards. Thus the progress of science is far ahead of man's ethical behavior.

Charlie Chaplin, My Autobiography *(1964)*

I have gained this by philosophy: that I do without being commanded what others do only from fear of the law.

Aristotle, Diogenes Laertius *(circa 350* B.C.*)*

Laws are sand, customs are rock. Laws can be evaded and punishment escaped, but an openly transgressed custom brings sure punishment.

Mark Twain, The Gorky Incident *(1906)*

The study of "ethics," particularly "business ethics," seems to be experiencing a revival in the United States. Entire courses in business ethics are taught in some schools. Businesspeople openly call for a "renewal" of business ethics and corporate responsibility, sometimes as a matter of conscience and sometimes as a method to forestall further government regulation. Spokespersons for consumer, environmental, and civil rights groups point to the failure of business ethics as a rationale for further government regulation. We have even seen the creation of entire foundations and nonprofit associations for the propagation of business ethics. And, it is a rare trade association that has not adopted some code of ethics for its members.

It is perhaps important to note at the outset that ethics is perhaps *best* studied in conjunction with a study of the law. Ethics is intimately related to the law in a number of ways. Perhaps most importantly, ethics is an *input* to the law, in the sense that ethical notions of right and wrong are often incorporated into a nation's laws. And, conversely, the law acts as an input to society's ethics as well, since by making an act illegal we often also make it ethically wrong.

There seems to be a great deal of disagreement about the place and nature of ethical instruction in the classroom. Some argue that such instruction belongs in the home and the church and has no place in a university class. Others insist that it is simply not proper for a collegiate instructor to "preach" to his students. And indeed there are two common traps for ethical instruction of those from diverse cultural and religious backgrounds. First, instructors and textbooks may end up preaching about ethics from the personal viewpoint of the teacher or the author. Second, instructors and textbooks may merely proclaim that "it's all a matter of opinion" and simply admonish students to "let your conscience be your guide." Neither approach is satisfactory, and this chapter tries to avoid both.

Ethics are indeed highly personal matters, and it is quite inappropriate, particularly in an academic setting, to try to convince someone that a particular ethical system is "correct." But that does not mean that instruction in ethics is impossible. It means rather that instruction in ethics should encourage students to *think about* their personal ethical systems, to work on them logically and consistently, so that when real ethical dilemmas arise the student will have the intellectual tools with which to face them. This chapter merely aims at developing those intellectual tools.

For far too many people, the term *ethics* means simply honesty or fair play, without much consideration of what those terms mean. Such simplistic, illogical, and incomplete ethical systems are simply insufficient when a real ethical dilemma appears. It is the purpose of this chapter to encourage you to consider and work on your personal ethical system. This chapter has very little to say about what *is* right and wrong; but it is my hope that it has some things to say about *how to think about* what is right and wrong, particularly in relation to the law.

Some Definitions of Ethics: Personal Ethics and Societal Ethics

For most of us, the term *ethics* means a set of rules of behavior by which we judge our own behavior and the behavior of others. Those sets of rules are usually personal, in that each of us establishes our own notions of right and wrong. But we are vastly influenced by **societal ethics,** which are systems of ethical beliefs held by groups of people. Examples might include the "work ethic," the "materialist ethic," and the two principal ethical systems of the 20th century: the **Individualist ethic** and the **Community ethic.** Thus, a person who grew up in the 20th century, like the law of the 20th century, would be profoundly influenced by those two great ethics. Similarly, the ethical systems of the world's religions are also societal ethics, and the adherents of a particular religion would be profoundly influenced by the ethics of their religion.

Throughout this text we have used the two great ethics of Individualism and Community as a springboard for discussion. Individualism, it will be remembered, places primary emphasis on the individual, to the exclusion of society; while Community places primary importance on the group, sometimes justifying the sacrifice of individual rights for the benefit of the larger society. We have seen that much of the public law of the United States is an effort to compromise the rights of individuals with the needs of the greater society, and that much of the political and legal controversy of our time is about precisely how those compromises are to be made.

While the ethics of Individualism and Community are of overriding importance in any discussion of how and why *public* issues are decided in a particular way, they are of only limited importance in deciding how and why *personal* ethical issues are decided in a particular fashion. Notions of Individualism and Community are simply not very relevant in deciding questions of honesty, fairness, and loyalty.

The emphasis of this chapter will be on personal ethics and their relationship to the law. We will begin with a description of one of the more helpful frameworks for discussing personal ethics, the theory of the two ethics (not to be confused with the two great ethics discussed above). Then, as a reference source, we will briefly consider some of the great ethical systems of the world. Using the theory of the two ethics, we will consider the nature of "ethical dilemmas," the various ways in which ethics and the law are related, and the ethics of the legal system. Finally, we will consider whether ethics and "ethical codes" are a reasonable substitute for government regulation.

The Theory of the Two Ethics

Many great philosophers have concluded that each of us has within us *two* ethical systems, and a great deal of our ethical and moral difficulty is caused by our failure to recognize the existence and difference between these two systems. While the names of the two systems vary, we may call them the *ethics of duty* and the *ethics of excellence.* *

The ethics of duty include those fundamental rules necessary for an organized society. Those ethics include most of the Thou Shalt Nots of our culture, including our *moral* prohibitions of murder, violence, theft, lying, and cheating. Though we are often bound by the law not to violate these standards, we are also bound by moral and ethical standards to comply. Many social scientists conclude that such duties are essential to civilized society and find remarkable uniformity in such standards from culture to culture. Almost every society forbids murder for example, and it is undoubtedly true that a society that freely permits murder would soon drown in its own blood.

The ethics of excellence, on the other hand, contain our ideals of perfection and the good life. These are the "shoulds" and "oughts" of our society, including both our personal aspirations and our personal standards of perfect conduct. Most particularly, they contain our views of what a "good life" consists. For perhaps too many,

---

*Perhaps the clearest expression of this theory is Lon Fuller's book, *The Morality of Law* (New Haven, Conn.: Yale University Press, 1964), pp. 13–33, though he uses the terms *morality of duty* and *morality of aspiration* to describe the two ethics. Many others have established similar formulations.

a good life means only personal wealth; for others it means physical pleasure, personal beauty, wisdom, virtue, or holiness. The ethics of excellence also contains our ideals of perfection in ethical matters, such as *total* honesty, *perfect* justice, and *complete* loyalty.

Adam Smith, a philosopher turned economist, used an analogy that may prove helpful in telling the difference between the two types of ethics. The ethics of duty may be compared to the basic rules of grammar, while the ethics of excellence may be compared to "the rules which critics lay down for the attainment of what is sublime and elegant" in writing. If we fail to follow the rules of grammar, our writing is automatically "bad"; but merely following the rules of grammar does not make our writing "good." We may be blamed for failing to follow the rules of grammar, but not for failing to write elegantly and with style. And, in Smith's words, the principles of perfection in ethics and in writing are both "loose, vague, and indeterminate, and present us rather with a general idea of the perfection we ought to aim at, than afford us any certain and infallible directions of acquiring it."

Smith's analogy points out a rather surefire test for determining the difference between an ethic of duty and an ethic of excellence. We tend to *blame* people for failing to live up to an ethic of duty, but we do not blame them for not living up to the ethics of excellence. On the other hand, we tend to *praise* people for reaching, or even almost reaching or trying to reach, the ethics of excellence, but we do not praise people for "merely" living up to the ethics of duty. We do not praise people for *not* murdering or *not* stealing, for example.

There is, of course, a rather substantial grey area in between the two sets of ethics. For example, it is probably a universal ethic of duty to refrain from telling deliberate lies for selfish purposes. On the other hand, total honesty, frankness, and candor at all times is a laudable but perhaps unreachable goal. In between those ideas are "white" lies, silence when one should speak, and speaking the literal truth while implying something else by tone of voice, gesture, and expression.

In the following selection, Professor Fuller uses the term *morality of duty* to represent what we have called the *ethics of duty,* and the term *morality of aspiration* to describe what we have called the *ethics of excellence.*

The Moral Scale*
Lon L. Fuller

As we consider the whole range of moral issues, we may conveniently imagine a kind of scale or yardstick which begins at the bottom with the most obvious demands of social living and extends upward to the highest reaches of human aspiration. Somewhere along this scale there is an invisible pointer that marks the dividing line where the pressure of duty leaves off and the challenge of excellence begins. The whole field of moral argument is dominated by a great undeclared war over the location of this pointer. There are those who struggle to push it upward; others work to pull it down. Those whom we regard as being unpleasantly—or at least, inconveniently—moralistic are forever trying to

---

*From *The Morality of Law* (New Haven, Conn.: Yale University Press, 1964), pp. 9–10, 27–28. Reprinted by permission.

inch the pointer upward so as to expand the area of duty. Instead of inviting us to join them in realizing a pattern of life they consider worthy of human nature, they try to bludgeon us into a belief we are duty bound to embrace this pattern. All of us have probably been subjected to some variation of this technique at one time or another. Too long an exposure to it may leave in the victim a lifelong distaste for the whole notion of moral duty.

. . . .

This line of division [or pointer] serves as an essential bulwark between the two moralities. If the morality of duty reaches upward beyond its proper sphere the iron hand of imposed obligation may stifle experiment, inspiration, and spontaneity. If the morality of aspiration invades the province of duty, men may begin to weigh and qualify their obligations by standards of their own and we may end with the poet tossing his wife into the river in the belief—perhaps quite justified—that he will be able to write better poetry in her absence.

The Conflict of Ideals and Ethics

Many contemporary observers have pointed to the "lack of values," "aimlessness," and "lack of commitment" of society. These issues are essentially problems of the ethics of excellence. At one time in human history, there was no such confusion, since the ideals of perfection and excellence were provided by the church, which had both religious and secular authority. But as the authority of the church declined people began to choose their own ideals, often with very little to guide their choice. Personal ideals often became contradictory, confused, and even petty. Sometimes those searches ended in despair and "dropping out" in drugs and alcohol. A major school of philosophy, called *existentialism*, developed on the theory that there were *no* ideals, and that the search for them was "absurd."

The great ordered system of the church produced *consistency* in ethics. The relationship between the ethics of duty and the ethics of excellence made sense and was very clear. The ethics of excellence required the ethics of duty, and the ethics of duty led to the ethics of excellence. While certainly ethical conflicts arose, those matters could be settled through the authority of the church. The system was complete and totally ordered.

But as humankind began to choose its own ideals, sometimes the ethics of duty could not be related to the ethics of excellence, and sometimes they came into direct conflict. To a person who chose power or wealth as the ideal and goal, the duty not to murder or not to steal might interfere with that quest. If personal beauty or physical pleasure was one's ideal, the obligations imposed by the ethics of duty might be at best irrelevant and might also directly conflict. People had to *choose* between their ideals and their duties, producing conflicts, contradictions and sometimes unethical conduct.

The Law and the Ethical Scale

At least in the United States, the law is chiefly concerned with the ethics of duty and has little influence on the ethics of excellence. That is not necessarily the case in other nations, where the law may be intimately involved in enforcing the ethics of excellence. In theocratic (church-based) states, for example, the law imposes religious duties, while in the Soviet Union the whole purpose of the system, at least as espoused in theory, is to create a "perfect" society and ultimately to create Soviet Man, an idealized perfect person. In both cases Professor Fuller might say that the "iron hand of imposed obligation may stifle experiment, inspiration, and spontaneity."

But American political and legal tradition tends to restrict the law's emphasis to the sphere of the ethics of duty. There remains, of course, a major question just where the "moral pointer" on the ethical scale should be placed. It could be argued that the two great ethics of the 20th century, Individualism and Community, are actually conflicting pressures on the moral pointer. The ethic of Community seems to be pressing the pointer upwards, ever enlarging the duties of humankind towards each other and toward the community. Individualism, on the other hand, seems to be pressing the pointer downwards so that people may be free to decide their duties by their own personal standards. Thus a businessperson whose ideals are wealth and power might feel that laws against fraudulent and deceptive practices are restrictions of his right to pursue his notions of the good life.

Are Ethics All a Matter of Opinion?

Thoughtful students everywhere are now shutting this book with the statement "That may be true, but it's all relative: everybody has his or her own opinion of what is right and what is wrong." To an extent that is true, since morals and ethics are learned and developed through personal experience. Your right and wrong and my right and wrong may be very different if we were brought up differently, or if we went to different churches or read different books.

Yet, there seems to be an amazing amount of agreement about ethical values, at least in the ethics of duty range. Most cultures have evolved very similar standards of basic behavior, probably as a means of ensuring the survival of society and civilization. Violence, deception, theft, incest, rape, and a great many other types of behavior are forbidden in almost every culture, including many of the most "uncivilized" tribes of the world. Societies differ on close questions and exceptions, but basic duties seem startlingly consistent.

Within a single culture, there is even more agreement on what is right and wrong. Members of that culture may not be able to explain *why* a certain action is unethical, but their judgments will be very similar on many issues. Like good art and music, we may not understand "ethics" but we know it when we see it. Again we may differ on close cases and exceptions. But, it could be argued, we have spent far too much time arguing the close cases and not enough time solidifying the areas of clear agreement.

There is substantially less agreement over conduct relating to the ethics of excellence. Our ideas differ widely over the meaning of excellence and a good life. Even the meanings of such terms as *totally honest* and *completely loyal* are disputed, and the "fit" goals and aspirations of human life are as varied as human interests and personalities.

The fact that there is any agreement on ethics at all probably reflects the cultural ties of morality and ethics. In other words, we *learn* our ethical values from our earliest human contacts and continue to learn and clarify them every day of our lives.

The culture from which we learn notions of right and wrong has a long and rich ethical heritage of religion, philosophy, logic, and experience, and that long heritage has permeated the culture around us. We are all exposed to similar teachings, similar family lives, and the same books, television programs, movies, and music. Those similar experiences affect us daily and result in similar ethical development for most members of society.

This does not mean that there cannot be nor should not be disagreements over values and ethics. Some ethical notions may simply be wrong, such as "the only good Indian is a dead Indian," and others may have outworn their usefulness as society grew and developed. During the 1960's, many people began rethinking some of the traditional values and ethics that had been accepted for generations. Much of that rethinking took place within the ethics of excellence, but some of the traditional ethics of duty were challenged as well. The result was an upheaval of values and the discarding of many outworn notions. Many of those involved in the rethinking suffered a great deal, however, both as a result of the pressure of society and as a result of personal struggles to find appropriate ideals.

Basic Ethical Systems

Almost every philosophy and religion has its own ethical system, and some of those systems, particularly those found in some religions, are extremely detailed and rigid. Philosophy is generally broken down into two major branches: *metaphysics,* which deals with the ultimate nonphysical nature of being and the universe, natural and supernatural; and *ethics,* which deals with the nature of human relationships. For many philosophers and for all religions, the two questions are intimately related.

Philosophy has developed over the centuries, but not in the same way that science or mathematics has developed. It is not accurate to say that the older philosophers were "incorrect" or "crude" simply because they are older. It is quite possible to believe that Plato and Aristotle were correct and all that followed is misguided or merely variations on their themes. A great many people believe in the teachings of Moses or St. Augustine and totally reject the teachings of more modern philosophers such as Nietzsche or Marx, for example.

Greek Philosophy

The word *ethics* was coined by Aristotle as a part of the title of his book *Nicomachean Ethics.* All of the Greek philosophers, including Plato and Aristotle, spent most of their time discussing the ideals of the ethics of excellence to determine the object of man's existence and "the Good." Aristotle argued that all men seek "happiness," a point from which many other philosophers begin. Aristotle said that man could reach happiness only by practicing the virtues of courage, temperance, liberality, justice, good temper, and the intellectual virtues of prudence (good sense) and wisdom. The ultimate good life to Aristotle consisted of a contemplative use of the mind, and man can only be free to use his mind in that way if he is practicing the virtues. Therefore, only through the virtues can we arrive at the state of happiness we all so greatly desire.

Nicomachean Ethics
Aristotle

> There are then three dispositions, two being vices, excess and deficiency, and one virtue, which is the mean between them; and they are all in a sense mutually opposed. The extremes are opposed both to the mean and to each other, and the mean is opposed to the extremes. . . . Thus the brave man appears foolhardy compared with the coward, but cowardly compared with the foolhardy. Similarly, the temperate man appears licentious compared with the insensible man but insensible compared with the licentious; and the liberal man appears extravagant compared with the stingy man but stingy compared with the spendthrift. The result is that the extremes each denounce the mean as belonging to the other extreme; the coward calls the brave man foolhardy, and the foolhardy man calls him cowardly; and so on in other cases. . . .
>
> That is why it is so hard to be good; for it is always hard to find the mean in anything; it is not everyone but only a man of science who can find the mean or center of a circle. So too anybody can get angry—that is easy—and anybody can give or spend money, but to give it to the right person, to give the right amount away, at the right time, for the right cause and in the right way, this is not what anybody can do, nor is it easy. That is why goodness is rare and praiseworthy and noble.

Other Greek philosophers built upon Aristotle's definition of "the Good" as happiness. The *Epicureans* disagreed with Aristotle's result, and found that the way to happiness was through "pleasure," though they included both physical and mental pleasures in the definition, and found that pleasures of the mind, especially wisdom, were more important. An offshoot of Epicureanism, known as *Hedonism*, found pleasures of the body were all that mattered, but that philosophy is generally regarded as a misuse of the Epicurean terms. The *Stoics*, on the other hand, found the greatest good in contentment and unruffled peace of mind in the face of any adversity and concentrated on the virtues that brought grace under pressure.

The influence of the Greeks cannot be overestimated. Greek philosophy had a major impact on later Christian thought, and much later had a massive effect on all of western culture when it was revived during the Renaissance of the 15th century.

Judeo-Christian Thought

Perhaps the best known and most widely accepted statement of ethical conduct is found in the Ten Commandments (Exodus 20:2–17). The Hebrew ethics of the Old Testament, sometimes called simply *The Law*, state the ethical duties of human beings in substantial detail, especially in the so-called *Covenant Code* (Exodus 21–23). One important aspect of the Hebrew law was that it was written in the form of a "contract" or "covenant" between man and God, in which man promised to live by God's rules, and God promised to bless the Hebrew people. Much of the Old Testament is concerned with the ethics of duty, with substantially less attention paid to the ethics of excellence. The God of the Old Testament is generally characterized as stern, forbidding, and vengeful. Many of the stories in the Old Testament are "case histories" of moral and ethical problems resolved by reference to the law of God.

As compared to the detailed rules of conduct spelled out in the Old Testament, the New Testament adds very little to the ethics of duty with the exception of the so-called *Eleventh Commandment,* (John 15:12) "that you love one another." The New Testament, in fact, proclaims that "merely" following the duties of the Hebrew law is not the way to perfection. In other words, the ethics of duty are not enough. Instead, the New Testament spends a great deal of time on the ethics of excellence, and even provides a model of perfection in the figure of Jesus. Christian doctrine even presents a reversal of sorts, by repudiating the idea that following the duties of The Law will lead to perfection; rather, that doctrine holds that faith will lead us to God and God will help us to follow The Law. In other words, being virtuous will not lead to perfection; rather perfection, in the form of faith and love, will permit us to be virtuous.

For a great many, the search for ethics stops here. Western culture is a joint creation of Greek thought and the Judeo-Christian heritage. Greek culture found its way into the thought of many of the early Christian thinkers, and later rose again during the Renaissance. Our present ethical structure is in a very large measure the combination of those two streams of thought, with some additions and changes along the way.

Other World Religions

In our ever-shrinking world, the influence of other religions on our ethical structure is growing. Eastern religions have placed an important role in the thought of many western philosophers and some people have found those religions to be more acceptable than the Judeo-Christian heritage. At the very least, we must give consideration to the impact of those religions when we deal with businesspersons from other cultures.

Perhaps the most specific ethical duties are established in the holy book of *Islam,* the *Koran.* That book specifies the ethics of duty in tremendous detail, providing God-given requirements for almost every incident of daily living.

The Koran

Surely this Koran guides to the way that is the straightest and gives good tidings to the believers who do deeds of righteousness.... Thy Lord has decreed you shall not serve any but Him, and to be good to parents.... And give the kinsman his right.... and never squander.... And keep not thy hand chained to thy neck, nor outspread it widespread altogether, or thou wilt sit reproached and denuded.... And approach not fornication; surely it is an indecency, and evil as a way. And slay not the soul God has forbidden.... And fill up the measure when you measure, and weigh with a straight balance.... And walk not in the earth exultantly; certainly thou wilt never tear the earth open, nor attain the mountains in height. (Sura XVII, 9, 23–27).

Hinduism, on the other hand, has very little to say about personal ethics, since Hindus stress the soul's release from this world. That religion requires a detachment from the affairs of this world, though the teachings of holy men require charity, gentleness, and kindness as a way of securing release from the cares of worldly existence.

The oriental religions of *Buddhism* and *Confucianism* have a great deal to say about personal ethics. In fact, Confucianism is not really a religion at all but a moral and ethical philosophy. Both streams of thought emphasize kindness, gentleness, temperance, and nonviolence, and encourage personal ethical reflection.

Analects

(records of conversations with Confucius by his followers)

Tzu Yu asked about filial piety. Confucius said, "Nowadays a filial son is just a man who keeps his parents in food. But even dogs or horses are given food. If there is no feeling of reverence, wherein lies the difference?" . . .

Tzu Yu asked about the worship of ghosts and spirits. Confucius said: "We don't know yet how to serve men, how can we know about serving the spirits?"

"What about death?" was the next question. Confucius said: "We don't know yet about life, how can we know about death?"

Fan Ch'ih asked about wisdom. Confucius said: "Devote yourself to the proper demands of the people, respect the ghosts and spirits but keep them at a distance—this may be called wisdom."

Tzu Kung asked: "Is there any one word that can serve as a principle for the conduct of life?" Confucius said: "Perhaps . . . 'reciprocity'; Do not do to others what you would not want others to do to you."

Someone inquired: "What do you think of 'requiting injury with kindness'?" Confucius said: "How will you then requite kindness? Requite injury with justice, and kindness with kindness."

Tzu Kung asked about the gentleman. Confucius said: "The gentleman first practices what he preaches and then preaches what he practices."

Confucius said: "The young are to be respected. How do we know that the next generation will not measure up to the present one? But if a man has reached forty or fifty and nothing has been heard of him, then I grant that he is not worthy of respect."

Because of the gentleness of oriental philosophy, many persons were attracted to those religions during the ethical upheavals of the 1960's and 1970's. The influence of Hindu and oriental nonviolence also provided a great deal of the tactics of civil disobedience during the civil rights and antiwar demonstrations of that period. It is clear that the philosophy and tactics of Gandhi in India strongly influenced the thought and tactics of Rev. Martin Luther King, Jr., for example.

Rationalism

Once the authority of the Catholic Church had been cracked by Martin Luther and other religious reformers, philosophers began building the courage to attack and dispute the religious dogmas that had ruled Europe for a thousand years. The interest of philosophers shifted from the supernatural to the natural and tried to extend the teachings of science and mathematics into the area of philosophy. Human reason, rather than divine inspiration, became the sole source of moral authority. The *rationalists* believed that man could logically deduce ethical values and arrive at a moral system through reasoning.

The rationalist philosophies led to a large number of other philosophies, including the different varieties of *humanism,* which stressed the importance of human experience and developed philosophies independent of theology and religion. While most humanists would say simply that we cannot know about the supernatural, some, such as Marx, repudiated the existence of God and the supernatural entirely. Humanism teaches that all people have dignity and worth and should command the respect of their fellow humans. That philosophy was embraced by the American humanists of the American Revolution, including Jefferson, Franklin, and Thomas Paine.

Humanism has remained the dominant philosophy throughout the 19th and 20th centuries, though there have been hundreds of variations. Two of those variations, *Individualism* and *Community,* have formed the framework for much of this text. A third, *Utilitarianism,* has had a major impact on political and economic thought in the last century.

Utilitarianism

Utilitarianism originated in the thought of three English philosophers, Jeremy Bentham, James Mill, and his son, John Stuart Mill, and found its fullest expression in John Stuart Mill's little book, *On Liberty.* Utilitarianism is an immensely practical philosophy with deep economic overtones.

Utilitarianism begins with Aristotle's premise that happiness is the greatest good. Therefore, Mill continues, human action should aim at creating, maintaining, and increasing human happiness. A "good society" is therefore one in which the greatest possible number of persons enjoy the greatest possible amount of happiness. Individual actions may be classed as "good" or "bad" by the amount to which they contribute or detract from total human happiness.

Mill was concerned with excellence and perfection of society, a part of the ethics of excellence. The way to assure an excellent society, Mill wrote, was not to force excellence upon men, but to permit each individual the greatest possible amount of freedom. In that sense, Mill's philosophy was very reminiscent of Aristotle's. But Mill made a stronger protest against external authority, aimed at groups, governments, and institutions that would "raise the moral pointer" too far. Mill did not defend personal *irresponsibility,* however, but only presented a plea to permit people to take more responsibility for their own actions.

On Liberty
John Stuart Mill

There is a limit to the legitimate interference of collective opinion with individual independence: and to find that limit, and maintain it against encroachment, is as indispensable to a good condition of human affairs, as protection against political despotism.

But though this proposition is not likely to be contested in general terms, the practical question, where to place the limit—how to make the fitting adjustment between individual independence and social control—is a subject on which nearly everything remains to be done. All that makes existence valuable to any one, depends on the enforcement of restraints upon the actions of other people. Some rules of conduct, therefore, must be imposed, by law in the first place, and by opinion on many things which are not fit subjects for the operation of law. What these rules should be, is the principal question in human affairs; but if we except a few of the most obvious cases, it is one of those which least progress has been made in resolving. No two ages, and scarcely any two countries, have decided it alike; and the decision of one age or country is a wonder to another.

. . . .

The object of this Essay is to assert one very simple principle, as entitled to govern absolutely the dealings of society with the individual in the way of compulsion and control, whether the means used be physical force in the form of legal penalties, or the moral coercion of public opinion. That principle is, that the sole end for which mankind are warranted, individually or collectively, in interfering with the liberty of action of any of their number, is self-protection. That the only purpose for which power can be rightfully exercised over any member of a civilized community, against his will, is to prevent harm to others. His own good, either physical or moral, is not a sufficient warrant. He cannot rightfully be compelled to do or forbear because it will be better for him to do so, because it will make him happier, because, in the opinions of others, to do so would be wise, or even right. These are good reasons for remonstrating with him, or reasoning with him, or persuading him, or entreating him, but not for compelling him, or visiting him with any evil in case he do otherwise. . . . Over himself, over his own body and mind, the individual is sovereign.

. . . .

I regard utility as the ultimate appeal on all ethical questions; but it must be utility in the largest sense, grounded on the permanent interests of man as a progressive being. Those interests, I contend, authorize the subjection of individual spontaneity to external control, only in respect to those actions of each, which concern the interest of other people.

To Mill and to many others who followed, the principle at work in Utilitarianism is similar to "marginal utility" economics. If an action by an individual produces more total utility and contributes more toward the total amount of happiness in the world, then that action should be undertaken. If it reduces utility and total happiness, it should not be undertaken. The former act is laudable and "good," the latter conduct punishable and "bad."

The Nature of Ethical Dilemmas

Most problems of ethics center around ethical dilemmas, the so-called *close questions* which were referred to earlier. While breaches of strongly held ethical notions with no countervailing circumstances are rather easily recognized, the "ethical world" is not one of "blacks and whites" and easy answers in many situations.

An ethical dilemma involves conflicting moral duties, each of which pushes an individual in a different direction. For example, consider the following set of facts.

A's child is dying of a rare blood disease. B, a chemist, has discovered a substance which may cure that disease. The cure costs $100 to manufacture, but B realizes that he may charge a great deal more for the treatment. A, a poor person, tries to raise the money but succeeds in raising only $300 of the $1,000 asked by B. A gives the $300 to B as a "down payment" and is unsuccessful in raising the balance. Finally, in desperation, A begs B to let him have the cure on credit, but B refuses.

Variation 1: A burglarizes B's offices and steals the cure.

Variation 2: A robs C's store, obtains the money, and buys the cure from B.

There are numerous ethical conflicts in the example. In the example, A is clearly guilty of illegal and probably immoral conduct when he committed burglary or robbery. But the ethical duty not to steal conflicts with the ethical duty to save one's child's life. While the conduct was "illegal," whether it was "morally wrong" will depend on whether one finds that the duty to obey the law or the duty to save a child's life is more important.

Hidden in the example is another ethical dilemma. B's talent and work led to the cure in the first place, and, by most ethical standards, B ought to be able to profit from that talent and work. Similarly, if B permitted A to buy the cure for less than the "going rate," he would set a precedent for future occurrences and reductions. But B's conduct obviously conflicts with widely held moral beliefs about the importance of human life and the nature of charity. B, like A, may be both "right" and "wrong," depending on which ethical values are considered more important.

The example also points out two other important considerations in many ethical questions. First, a person's *motivation* and *state of mind* are extremely important in determining moral "rightness" or "wrongness." In the example, A was acting out of concern for a child, and therefore we may find his conduct less objectionable than if he had stolen the cure for resale on the black market. On the other hand, B was acting out of self-interest and ambition, and we may find his conduct more objectionable than A's.

Secondly, Variation 2 points out that the *relationship between the parties* has a great deal of importance in framing moral judgments. A was dealing directly with B, and it may seem only "fair" that A burglarized his premises. On the other hand, C is a stranger to the transaction—an innocent victim—and therefore A's conduct in robbing him may be quite objectionable.

Finally, our point of view may be very important. A would consider B's conduct immoral and B would consider A's conduct immoral. Both A and B consider their own conduct right. And C might consider both A and B to be wrong. An outside objective observer, such as a judge or a jury, might come to a totally different conclusion. Members of A's family, other drug manufacturers, "businesspersons" in general, and the consuming public might also arrive at differing conclusions, based on their respective interests and their conceptions of which ethical values are more important.

It would be impossible to discuss every ethical conflict that could arise, even if we restricted our inquiry to "business" ethical dilemmas. It is possible to consider some of the basic ethical considerations inherent in such dilemmas, however. Those basic issues involve (1) the overriding considerations of motivation and the relationship of the parties, and particularly the legal expression of those considerations; (2) the nature of some of the more common ethical norms, including honesty, loyalty, fairness, and community responsibility; and (3) whether there is in any sense a hierarchy of ethical values, that is, is honesty more important than loyalty, for example.

Motivation and State of Mind in Ethical Dilemmas

It is quite clear that in many instances the state of mind and motivation of a person is extremely important in determining the moral rightness of his or her actions. Even Aristotle held that moral acts must be both voluntary and flow from a noble motive. And the law supports that judgment by condemning only voluntary acts and by requiring as an element of almost every tort and crime a mental element, such as intent, knowledge, or recklessness.

Voluntariness is the basic mental state required by both the law and morality as a basis for guilt. We do not condemn or hold a person morally guilty for any act performed involuntarily. Acts performed while unconscious, insane, or while under compulsion fall into this category and are generally not blamed on the individual. The key seems to be *individual choice*. If the individual may choose to perform or not to perform a morally wrongful act and chooses to perform it, that person is generally considered more guilty than a person who has no choice but to perform the same act.

It is also clear that we do maintain a rough sort of hierarchy of voluntariness, depending on the amount of choice we have in the matter. Assume for example the same physical act of D shooting E. If D is unconscious at the time and the shooting results from an involuntary twitch of a finger, we would probably totally excuse D and call it an unfortunate accident, since D had no choice whatsoever. If D is insane, we would also tend to excuse his conduct, but chances are there would be "more" guilt attached, or at the least we would be more suspicious. If D was intoxicated at the time, we would find him morally guilty, but perhaps less so than a person who had a clear mind at the time. It seems that the more choice a person has, the more he or she may be held morally or ethically responsible for his or her actions.

The law generally follows our ethical notions of responsibility, particularly in the law of crimes and the law of torts. Almost every criminal statute has a mental element which must be proven by the prosecutor before the defendant may be convicted of the offense. The prosecutor may be required to show that the defendant did the act intentionally or knowingly or with some specific intent, such as "with intent to kill" or "with intent to defraud." If the statute only requires proof of an intent to commit the act the statute prohibits, the statute is said to be a **general intent** crime; but if it requires proof of some other intent, such as assault "with intent to kill" or writing bad checks "with intent to defraud," the crime is known as a **specific intent** statute.

State of mind may also be used as an aggravating or mitigating circumstance. Assault, which only requires proof of "intent to assault," is less aggravated than "assault with intent to kill," for example. Thus, it seems, the more voluntary an act is, the more both our ethical standards and our legal standards impose moral and legal guilt.

Motive on the other hand may be defined as the purpose for which an act is performed. That motive has a great deal to do with the amount of moral guilt attached to an act, but substantially less to do with the amount of legal guilt assessed. In our introductory example, A's conduct was perhaps excusable because his motive was to save another's life. The same conduct undertaken to obtain some personal benefit, such as to sell the cure on the black market, would have been much more guilty.

It thus seems that there is also some rough hierarchy of motives to which we attach greater or lesser moral guilt. Perhaps the most important distinction is between "selfless" and "selfish" motives. An act performed out of selfless or altruistic motives is generally far less guilty than an act performed out of totally selfish motives.

The law does not very often excuse behavior on the basis of "good motives." In our introductory example, A would very likely be found guilty of a crime in either of the two variations, regardless of his motive of saving his child's life. His motives might be taken into account by the judge when it came time to impose a sentence as a matter of "aggravation and mitigation." Similarly, our ethical notions might not permit us to excuse A completely, but might permit us to understand his crime.

Personal Relationships and Ethical Guilt

It is also clear that our relationships with the persons with whom we are dealing are vitally important to our ethical conclusions. The complex web of human relationships establishes a similarly complex web of ethical standards with finely graded differences. It is as if the moral pointer moves up and down for each person with whom we deal.

For our purposes, two separate sets of widely recognized ethical standards are applied to two groups of people. We use one set of standards to apply to family, friends, and neighbors, which we may call *intimate ethics.* Generally, we hold ourselves and others to a higher set of standards when dealing with such persons—a greater degree of honesty, more loyalty, and so on.

On the other hand, we maintain a different set of ethical standards when we are dealing with people in a business relationship, which we may call *marketplace ethics.* We deal with such persons on an "arm's length" basis and expect the same from them. This generally means a lower degree of trust, honesty, and the like. In other words, everyone expects businesspeople who deal with them to use a "sharp pencil" as part of the game of business—unless that person happens to be a friend, relative, or neighbor.

There are, of course, finely graded differences within both intimate ethics and marketplace ethics. Within intimate ethics, we tend to treat close relatives with higher standards than distant relatives. If a relative has breached his own intimate ethics in his treatment of us, we feel more free to treat him in a similar fashion. Some business relationships are of such closeness and long duration that they become subject to an intimate ethics all their own. And relatives or friends may announce to each other that "this is business," which warns the parties that intimate ethics are suspended and marketplace ethics will be used for a particular transaction, at least temporarily.

The law recognizes the differences between marketplace ethics and intimate ethics in a variety of ways. One way to look at the fiduciary duties, discussed in Chapter 7, is as an extension of a form of intimate ethics to places where one would not expect to find them. The relationship between employer and employee or between corporate officer or director and the corporation is, after all, business, and one would ordinarily expect marketplace ethics to be used in any business relationship. But the law insists that a form of intimate ethics be used in any agency relationship.

One of the reasons for the distinction between intimate and marketplace ethics is *power,* or the possibility that power will be abused. We tend to expect intimate ethics in certain relationships because the parties are vulnerable to each other, and high ethical standards are a way of guaranteeing that such vulnerability will not be exploited. Friends and family members are vulnerable to each other because of the emotional commitment the parties have to each other. A "false friend" might exploit that emotional commitment and gain an unfair advantage. Our society tries to guard against such abuse by imposing very high ethical standards on such relationships. Similarly, an agent has the power to bind his or her principal to contracts or make the principal liable for torts. As a result, the law tries to insulate the principal from abuses of power by imposing the fiduciary duties.

Marketplace ethics have traditionally assumed some rough equality of power between the parties. That equality of power permits the parties to protect themselves against potential abuses, at least to some extent. At the very least, persons in a business relationship are forewarned that a different set of ethical standards applies. The law may not recognize those distinctions, however.

Eaton v. Sontag

387 A. 2d 33 (Supreme Court of Maine, 1978)

Mr. and Mrs. Sontag and Mr. and Mrs. Eaton had been good friends for over fifteen years. The Eatons were in the process of developing a campground in Maine and were looking for a purchaser. During numerous social visits the Eatons "sounded out" the Sontags about purchasing the campground, and finally the Sontags agreed. The Sontags agreed to pay $80,000 for the property; $26,000 down and the balance over three years.

The first summer the camp grossed $400, and the Sontags wrote the Eatons complaining that they had been overcharged by at least $25,000 and claimed that the Eatons had misrepresented the earning potential of the camp. Finally, the Sontags stopped making payments, and the Eatons brought an action seeking payment of the overdue installments. The Sontags counterclaimed, asking rescission of the contract and a refund of all of the money owed. The Eatons replied that the doctrine of *caveat emptor* ("let the buyer beware") applied to the case. The jury found for the Eatons, and the Sontags appealed.

DUFRESNE, Active Retired Justice. . . .
The charge of fraud which the defendants set out to prove against the plaintiffs . . . was that the Eatons misrepresented to them that the campsite was a gold mine; they had taken in fifteen hundred dollars in five weeks of their first season of operation; there was city water on the premises; the Sontags could live on the premises year-round; also they failed to disclose that the value . . . of the campground did not reflect the true value of the property. . . .
The defendants argue on appeal that the past association of the parties as social friends for the period of fifteen years raised their relationship in connection with any business transaction between them to one of a confidential nature, and, under such circumstances, the rule of caveat emptor did not apply, but rather, there existed a duty on the part of the plaintiff vendors to disclose to the defendant vendees the plaintiff's financial embarrassment by reason of the campground development instead of representing the operation as a gold mine opportunity. We disagree.
We agree . . . that the "fiduciary or confidential relation" concept when used in connection with improper influence affecting the validity of some transaction was one of broad application and that it embraced not only technical fiduciary relations such as may exist between parent and child, guardian and ward, attorney and client, etc., but may also encompass relationships wherein confidence is actually reposed in another by reason of their social ties. . . .
[We have held that] "[t]he salient elements of a confidential relation are the actual placing of trust and confidence in fact by one party in another *and a great disparity of position and influence* between the parties to the relation." . . . [Court's emphasis.]
[M]ere kinship itself . . . does not establish a confidential relation; *often relatives*

are hostile to each other or deal at arm's length and act independently and so are held not to have been a confidential relation. (Court's emphasis) [sic].

[E]ven where specific facts tend to show intimate dealings, as between family members or friends, the existence of a confidential relationship remains a question of fact and need not be imposed by law. If the parties to a transaction are of mature years and in full possession of their faculties, their continuing lifelong relation as [relatives] and friends will not give rise to a confidential relation as a matter of law unless there is evidence of superior intellect or will on the part of the one or the other, or of trust reposed or confidence abused.

. . . .

The evidence here fails to disclose any particular dependence of one party upon the other's judgment for business transactions during their acquaintanceship of fifteen years. That one had developed a reliance on the other in a business way does not appear in this case. . . . That the parties believed in their mutual honesty, sincerity and truthfulness on account of their social intercourse is not sufficient to constitute a confidential relationship as the term implies in the law. . . .

. . . .

The assertion that the campsite operation is a gold mine was, and should have been understood to be . . . "seller's talk," i.e., "that picturesque and laudatory style affected by nearly every trader in setting forth the attractive qualities of the goods he offers for sale," and this even among friends. But such is not actionable. . . . The law recognizes the fact that sellers may naturally overstate the value and quality of the articles or property which they have to sell. Everybody knows this, and a buyer has no right to rely upon such statements. . . .

. . . .

Furthermore, it is not fraud for one party to say nothing respecting any particular aspect of the subject property for sale where no confidential or fiduciary relation exists and where no false statement or acts to mislead the other are made, as was the case here. . . .

Every man has the right to ask any price he sees fit for the wares or lands he has to sell and the matter of fixing the price, even for friends who might be interested in their purchase, may be predicated upon divers bases, one of which may be what he thinks he can get for it from a prospective purchaser. To seek a price commensurate with one's investment in the property would not only be non-fraudulent in itself, but mere good business acumen.

. . . .

Appeal denied.

But marketplace ethics present some real problems. Some persons are naively unaware of the two sets of standards, and others are aware of those standards but are simply unable to protect themselves because of great differences in power. In such cases the law has stepped in, either to restrict the power of one side or to "balance the power equation" on one side. In dealing with consumers, who may not be aware of differing standards and who may not be able to deal from a position of strength, businesses are subject to a variety of consumer protection statutes. In dealing with labor, businesses traditionally had the better of the "power equation," so government stepped in to balance the equation through the national labor laws. In dealing with shareholders, who simply did not have enough individual power to protect their own interests, the national securities laws stepped in to restrict the power of management and stock sellers. In all cases the effect has been to "soften" the rigors of marketplace ethics with some of aspects of intimate ethics and to raise the "moral pointer."

Some Common Ethical Notions

We tend to express our ethical values in terms of a few overriding notions, such as "honesty," "loyalty," "fairness," and "community responsibility." It is important at the outset to recognize that these terms are all generalizations. Each refers to a *set* of ethical notions that may be related, but that also often conflict. Many persons tend to generalize all ethics as *honesty,* for example, but it is clear that what they mean by honesty is far more than mere truth-telling and includes elements of loyalty, fairness, and diligence.

It is also important to realize that in the case of each ethical notion there is a range of duties, stretching from the most basic notions of the ethics of duty to the farthest reaches of the ethics of excellence. Honesty, for example, may mean only not telling outright lies, all the way to total frankness and candor. Our problem in each case is to locate our personal moral pointer somewhere on that scale, with due consideration for our state of mind and motivation and with regard to the specific human relationship involved.

Honesty   The term *honesty* may mean a great many things and may, in fact, make up the entire idea of ethics to many people. It may also mean trustworthiness, truth-telling, fairness, reliability, sincerity, impartiality, or total candor, each of which might be a separate ethical standard of itself.

At the ethics-of-duty level, we have a basic duty not to tell outright lies, quite analogous to our legal duty not to indulge in fraudulent practices or perjure ourselves. Somewhere in the far reaches of the ethics of excellence, we may set standards of total frankness and candor and may, in fact, require "truth in all circumstances." But such total honesty is dangerous and may not be a virtue, as in the case of telling a lie to a murderer to protect his victim. Those who "always tell the truth" probably have few friends. Deciding the proper location of the moral pointer is not an easy task.

The law does not require total frankness and candor in every situation, as shown by the *Eaton* case. The law does require us to avoid fraud, and extends that doctrine under some circumstances. In the fiduciary relationship, the law requires full disclosure, something very similar to the ethics of excellence requirement of total candor. Similarly, the doctrine of unconscionability carries that duty farther then merely avoiding fraud if there is a difference in power between the parties. FTC regulation of deceptive advertising is another case where law has stepped in to require duties higher than the duty to refrain from fraud, by creating a new relationship of advertiser-consumer and requiring virtual total honesty in advertising.

Loyalty   The term *loyalty* implies the existence of some relationship and requires one party to the relationship to give allegiance and fidelity to the other. This term, like honesty, has a variety of related meanings as well, such as reliability, dependability, and trustworthiness.

At the ethics-of-duty level, loyalty merely requires what the agreement between the parties requires. In its ethics-of-excellence aspects, loyalty would require perfect fidelity, perhaps merging into a kind of fanatical allegiance and "other-centeredness." It has been argued that modern cynicism and self-centeredness has chipped away at the traditional notions of loyalty, with some rather unfortunate effects.

Mr. Justice Harlan Stone
Address (June 15, 1934)

> I venture to assert that when the history of the financial era which has just drawn to a close comes to be written, most of its mistakes and its major faults will be ascribed to the failure to observe the fiduciary principle, the precept as old as holy writ, that "a man cannot serve two masters." . . . No thinking man can believe that an economy built upon a business foundation can permanently endure without some loyalty to that principle. The separation of ownership from management, the development of the corporate structure so as to vest in small groups control over the resources of great numbers of small and uninformed investors, make imperative a fresh and active devotion to that principle if the modern world of business is to perform its proper function. Yet those who serve nominally as trustees, but relieved, by clever legal devices, from the obligation to protect those whose interests they purport to represent, corporate officers and directors who award to themselves huge bonuses from corporate funds without the assent or even the knowledge of their stockholders, reorganization committees created to serve interests of others than those whose securities they control, financial institutions which, in the infinite variety of their operations, consider only last, if at all, the interests of those whose funds they command, suggest how far we have ignored the necessary implications of that principle. The loss and suffering inflicted on individuals, the harm done to a social order founded upon business and dependent upon its integrity are incalculable.

Abstract loyalty presents some rather large problems however. First, it is necessary to decide, Loyalty to whom? A corporate manager may feel duties of loyalty to the firm itself, to its stockholders, to its customers, to the other members of management, to the board of directors, or to its employees; and those loyalties may directly conflict.

Second, loyalty often conflicts with other ethical notions. A firm may insist that its employees lie to customers, for example, in which case the employees' duty of loyalty directly conflicts with the duty of honesty. In fact, the duty of loyalty seems to occupy a central place in many of the most serious conflicts of ethics.

Fairness and Lack of Oppression   One of the most ambiguous ethical notions is fairness or justice. Aristotle thought, for example, that "Justice . . . is not a part of virtue but the whole of virtue; its opposite, injustice, is not a part of vice but the whole of vice." Again the term *fairness* may have many meanings, including honesty, lack of bias or prejudice, equity, and reasonableness.

One meaning of the term *fairness* has particular significance for business. The term may also mean lack of oppression or, as sometimes stated, "not taking advantage of others." In marketplace ethics, one is always looking for an advantage to press; in intimate ethics one is constrained from pressing those advantages. Our problem is again just how far intimate ethics intrude upon the marketplace.

Oppression is intimately related to power. In fact, the whole notion of oppression assumes that one party to a transaction has power over another and uses that power "too much." Thus, an employer who takes advantage of an employee's lack of bargaining power by offering low wages may be said to be guilty of oppression or unfairness. Similarly, a firm that takes advantage of a monopoly position to raise prices or a seller who takes advantage of consumer's lack of bargaining skills or lack of knowledge may be said to be oppressing others.

In a very large sense, many of the government regulations studied in this text are an attempt to limit this kind of unfair advantage. Perhaps the clearest example are the national labor laws, which try to act as a "balancer" in the power equation between labor and management. But consumer protection statutes, securities regulations, antitrust laws, and even civil rights statutes are in a sense efforts to even out differences in power between business and other groups that society views as being oppressed.

Obedience to Law   A rather strongly held ethical notion is that we should obey the law. "Respect for the law" has been built into our political traditions so much that it has become an ethical duty, probably grouped among the most basic ethics of duty. That is so perhaps because of some instinctive recognition that our society cannot function without law, and the law cannot function without willing obedience on the part of the great majority of society.

The ethics of duty require us to obey, at least, the letter of the law. It should be clear by now that even obeying the letter of the law may not be an easy task, given the huge number of laws and regulations and the occasional difficulty of determining just what the letter of the law actually requires. It is also clear that when the law makes illegal an act that is immoral as well, our ethics of duty make such lawbreakers doubly guilty; first for performing an immoral or unethical act, and second for breaking the law. But if the law merely prohibits an act that is "morally neutral," such as crossing the street against a red light or violating a building code, our ethical system still imposes moral guilt for simply violating the law itself. But in the latter case the party is not as morally guilty as in the first case. The criminal law sometimes makes a distinction between such laws, by distinguishing between **malum in se** (evil of itself) and **malum prohibitum** (evil only because it is prohibited) offenses.

The ethics of excellence may get us into substantial ethical difficulty with regard to obedience to law. First, it is not at all clear what the ethics of excellence require with regard to obedience to law. "Perfect" obedience to law may require total obedience to every law of any sort, or it may also require obedience to not only the *letter* of the law but the *spirit* of the law as well. Such obedience is generally laudatory, but runs the risk of blind obedience and unquestioning subservice, two of the essential preconditions to totalitarianism.

Second, the ethics of excellence may encounter substantial difficulties when faced with a bad law. It should be clear by now that not all laws are "good," and some, like "Jim Crow" segregation statutes, may conflict with some very basic ethical notions. The notion that we should obey all laws conflicts directly with some very basic ethical beliefs in such cases.

Letter from Birmingham Jail*
Rev. Martin Luther King, Jr.

My Dear Fellow Clergymen;
 . . . .
You express a great deal of anxiety over our willingness to break laws. This is certainly a legitimate concern. Since we so diligently urge people to obey the Supreme

---

*From *Why We Can't Wait,* copyright © 1963 by Martin Luther King, Jr. Reprinted by permission of Harper & Row, Publishers, Inc.

Court's decision of 1954 outlawing segregation in the public schools, at first glance it may seem rather paradoxical for us consciously to break laws. One may well ask: "How can you advocate breaking some laws and obeying others?" The answer lies in the fact that there are two types of laws: just and unjust. I would be the first to advocate obeying just laws. One has not only a legal but a moral responsibility to obey just laws. Conversely, one has a moral responsibility to disobey unjust laws. I would agree with St. Augustine that "an unjust law is no law at all."

Now, what is the difference between the two? How does one determine whether a law is just or unjust. A just law is a man-made code that squares with the moral law or the law of God. An unjust law is a code that is out of harmony with the moral law. To put it in the terms of St. Thomas Aquinas: An unjust law is a human law that is not rooted in eternal law and natural law. Any law that uplifts human personality is just. Any law that degrades human personality is unjust. All segregation statutes are unjust because segregation distorts the soul and damages the personality. It gives the segregator a false sense of superiority and the segregated a false sense of inferiority. . . . Hence segregation is not only politically, economically, and sociologically unsound, it is morally wrong and sinful. . . . Thus it is that I can urge men to obey the 1954 decision of the Supreme Court, for it is morally right; and I can urge them to disobey segregation ordinances, for they are morally wrong.

. . . .

I hope you are able to see the distinction I am trying to point out. In no sense do I advocate evading or defying the law, as would the rabid segregationist. That would lead to anarchy. One who breaks an unjust law must do so openly, lovingly, and with a willingness to accept the penalty. I submit that an individual who breaks a law that conscience tells him is unjust, and who willingly accepts the penalty of imprisonment in order to arouse the conscience of the community over its injustice, is in reality expressing the highest respect for law.

. . . .

We should never forget that everything Adolf Hitler did in Germany was "legal" and everything the Hungarian freedom fighters did in Hungary was "illegal." It was "illegal" to aid and comfort a Jew in Hitler's Germany. Even so, I am sure that, had I lived in Germany at the time, I would have aided and comforted my Jewish brothers. If today I lived in a Communist country where certain principles dear to the Christian faith are suppressed, I would openly advocate disobeying that country's anti-religious laws.

Community Responsibility   Perhaps the newest and perhaps the most ambiguous of all of the principal ethical notions is something called *community responsibility*. In fact the term is not an ethical duty at all, but a new relationship that may involve new duties. The term simply means that there is an interdependence and relationship between individual businesses and the communities of which they are a part. It was not always clear, and may not yet be clear, that such a relationship actually exists, as evidenced by Vanderbilt's "the public be damned" comment. But, in the mid-20th century, it began to become obvious that business did have a connection to the community of which it was a part, and business and social theorists began speaking of the "community responsibilities of business."

But just to state that business has a connection to the community does not identify what are the responsibilities of business. For some, those responsibilities consist of grudging and miserly contributions to charity, while for others it means businesses operated primarily for the public benefit. The exact nature of those responsibilities are only now being "filled in" by the public, by social and business thinkers, and to some extent by the courts.

The Politicalization of the Corporation
Phillip A. Blumberg*

. . . .

Business is already doing much, and must do much more, toward the solution of the major social and environmental problems of the times and in the struggle to deal with urban problems, poverty, race relations, product safety and environmental abuse. The following four examples are illustrations of the priority areas for management.

A. Increase in Philanthropic Support

. . . [T]he extent of corporate expenditures in the social sphere—as distinct from the environmental area—is essentially limited by competitive factors. Only a few companies devote amounts that approach the . . . [limit] that the Internal Revenue Code permits corporations to deduct for philanthropic contributions to qualified tax-exempt organizations. Contributions of this nature enable business to support the entire spectrum of agencies that are dealing with social needs, as well as traditional areas such as higher education.

In view of the magnitude of the problems of society, the campaign to raise corporate contributions . . . is one of the great challenges facing business leadership. It is a matter of the general attitude of business with respect to what constitutes an acceptable level of social costs. If enough courageous businessmen will take the lead to obtain acceptance within their industries of progressively higher levels of support, business will be demonstrating its concern for social betterment in unmistakable terms. Such action will provide it with a considerably stronger position from which to respond to the social reformers who would seek to alter the structure of business itself.

. . . .

B. Minority-Group Representation

In the area of race relations, the absence of blacks and other minority-group members on the boards of directors of all but a few major American corporations presents a serious social problem. . . .

. . . [T]he large American corporation is a quasi-political organization and . . . its executive circle, like that of government itself, should include representatives of all sectors of society. This view is a long-overdue recognition of the legitimate aspirations of deprived groups of Americans to participate in the important decision-making centers of power in American society. It is a conservative effort to widen the stake of deprived groups in the existing order. Business must respond to retain the confidence of the society.

It is gratifying to note that leading corporations are responding, and that the pattern of American corporate life is changing; major American business is beginning to correct the injustices of the past. It is, however, obvious that the process has just commenced. The strength of the pressures for corporate reform will vary with the degree of business response.

C. The Role of "Outside" Directors

. . .[A] significant number of the social reform proposals relate to the organic structure of the corporation. They include such suggestions as shareholder committees for corporate responsibility, inclusion of competing slates of directors in the corporate proxy solicitation, and election of directors nominated by, or representing, employees, suppliers, consumers and dealers.

[It has been pointed out] that specialized board representation presents many serious problems. Nevertheless, such proposals do highlight the importance of the "outside" director on the board, and the ultimate strength of such proposals will undoubtedly depend on the extent to which so-called "outside" directors introduce a different perspective into board deliberations and decisions, and in practice, as well as theory, truly function as public directors. Where "outside" directors are not truly independent of management, such as in the case of corporate counsel, investment bankers or commercial bankers, all of whom are vitally interested in preserving business opportunities for their own firms, and are, therefore, not in a position to tangle with management, they are not free to represent the public—either the limited public of the shareholders or the wider public of the community generally.

Business must recognize these wider responsibilities and have genuine "outside" directors, free to represent public attitudes and expectations. If it fails to do so, it may face increasing pressure for "outside" directors who would represent not the interest of public shareholders or the general public, but the specialized interest of employees, consumers, suppliers or dealers or similar groups.

D. The Environment

In the environmental field, the intensity of public demand for corrective action has reached such overwhelming proportions that business has lost much of its freedom of choice. It must respond vigorously.... [B]usiness cannot only prevail in the battle for public opinion, but can achieve favorable recognition, provided that, in the words of President George Weyerhauser [of the Weyerhauser Company] both management and shareholders are prepared to sacrifice "short-term gain for long-term appreciation."

Conclusion

Business can only prosper by being part of a healthy society, and can only preserve its present degree of independence from public control by participation in the solution of social and environmental problems in accordance with public expectations and demands. This can be accomplished by joining in the battle for social justice: the struggle against poverty, race and sex discrimination, environmental abuse, urban blight, and by having a significant number of independent directors reflecting public attitudes on its boards. Business has no alternative but to respond to the public demand. It must operate in the light of the realities of the times. In short, it is in part a political institution. The only question that remains is how far politicalization will proceed.

. . . .

An extensive degree of politicalization of the corporation has already occurred. The pressures for further politicalization will continue to increase and may ultimately change the structures and objectives of American corporate enterprise, unless business has the wisdom and strength to respond to the moral imperatives of our times and to display . . . an "unprecedented order of leadership in helping to solve the social problems of our time." The response of business management to the challenge will be the major factor in determining whether the American corporation will survive in its present form.

Conflicts of Ethics

There is an entire body of law, called conflicts of laws, that determines which of two conflicting statutes will govern. There is, perhaps unfortunately, no such doctrine to tell us which of two conflicting ethical notions should govern when ethics conflict.

Even the most detailed and rigid religious system is of little help when two ethical duties collide.

And ethical notions do conflict, as shown by our introductory example. Honesty may conflict with loyalty to the firm if the firm insists that its employees lie. Loyalty to the firm may conflict with community responsibility, if the firm insits that its employees pollute or design cheap but dangerous products. It seems there is no "hierarchy" of ethical values to tell us when honesty is more important than loyalty or what to do in hundreds of other potential conflicts between ethical values. Some ethical systems attempt to construct a sort of hierarchy, but such hierarchies tend to be extremely general and vague. For example, Aristotle's system places justice above all other virtues, but his definition of justice includes all of those virtues and is therefore not very helpful.

It is tempting at this point to simply advise "Let your conscience be your guide" and drop the whole matter. Such decisions between conflicting ethical values ultimately must depend on personal convictions of the relative importance of the conflicting values, and any attempt to impose a hierarchy of values would constitute an unjustified invasion of the student's personal values.

But two comments seem appropriate and potentially helpful: first, it may be advantageous to spend some time thinking about the ethical values we have already discussed and others as well. As already noted, some people's ethical systems are quite unsophisticated and consist of "gut feelings" of honesty alone. Considering the various ethical concepts and notions and their differences and possible exceptions may well forearm us against the day when we are faced with a real ethical conflict.

Second, some ethical conflicts have been resolved for us by the law. In fact, much of the law may be characterized as case-by-case resolution of such ethical collisions. The study of law is, in many ways, the study of enforced ethical notions. Thus, the further study of the law may well prepare us for future inevitable ethical problems.

The law is helpful in another way. Very often the law coincides with the ethics of duty, and outlaws that which society considers immoral. Thus, when one is faced with the possibility of violating an ethic of duty, one really is faced with violating *two* ethical notions. For example, if a company requires its employees to indulge in fraud, the employee must violate two notions: (1) the duty not to lie; and (2) the duty not to break the law. When weighed against one's loyalty to the firm, which may also be an ethic of duty, one may be forced to the conclusion that breaching one ethical notion is better than breaching two. And, since the law is rarely internally inconsistent, merely following the law may resolve many ethical conflicts.

The Relationship of Ethics to the Law

Ethics as an Input to Law

It is probably quite obvious by now that the ethical beliefs of a society can easily become embodied in the law. If the mass of human beings believe that an act is wrong, it is but a short step for the legislature to outlaw the act and provide a legal punishment for its commission. Theft, murder, rape, and other "base" conduct is not only illegal, it is highly unethical according to the norms of almost every civilized society and quite a few uncivilized ones.

Our problem is, in Fuller's terms, where to place the pointer between matters that should be the subject of the law and matters in which the law has no business. Mill provided one possible answer, namely when the activities of one person hurt another. Mill's pointer would be placed quite low on the yardstick, it would seem. But even using Mill's theory, it would seem that virtually every regulation we have studied acts to prevent harm to others. Discrimination laws prevent harm to the persons discriminated against; worker safety regulations prevent injuries to employees; antitrust laws prevent harm to competitors, customers, suppliers, and the general public; and so on. It seems that injuries abound, and Mill provides a clear justification for undoing or preventing those injuries by legal action.

In a democratic or representative government, it is logical that ethics would play a larger role in determining the nature of law than in autocratic or totalitarian states. Yet that is not entirely true. The ethics of the masses will of course play a larger role, but since those ethics are conflicting and contradictory, the legislators must usually find the "lowest common denominator" among the ethics of society. In a totalitarian society, the personal ethics of the leader or cadre will be the sole determining factor in the law. Thus we see the facially contradictory result of totalitarian systems with rather priggish legal orders. In other words, in democratic states the moral pointer will usually be lower on the scale than in totalitarian states, at least insofar as ethics are incorporated into the law.

The Law as a Creator of Ethics

The relationship between law and ethics is not a one-way street. While ethics are obviously an "input" into the law, the law also may create ethical values. Since there is a recognized duty to obey the law, once the law makes an act illegal we tend to view that act as immoral or unethical as well. For example, there is nothing innately immoral about crossing the street against a red light. But because the law has made that act illegal, we tend to view it as somehow wrong as well. For that reason we sit at stoplights when there is no one, including a policeman, anywhere in sight and suffer pangs of guilt when we gather the courage to go through that light anyway.

Similarly, the publicity given to acts by the process of making them illegal may stir our moral consciousness and "create" new ethical norms. It is doubtful that many people considered price discrimination immoral prior to the passage of the Robinson-Patman Act or gave much thought to price discrimination at all, for that matter. But with the passage of that Act, many more individuals gave some thought to the matter until now it is widely considered to be an unethical practice.

The Ethics of the Legal Profession

Lawyers are fiduciaries of their clients. That says a great deal about the nature of the ethical duties of lawyers. But, in addition, like many other groups of professionals, lawyers have adopted a variety of codes of ethics to further explain and detail the duties of attorneys. Most of those codes are administered state by state, but are often based on the Code of Professional Responsibility of the American Bar Association (excerpted in Figure 20-1).

It is important to realize that the codes of ethics are enforceable by the state Bar Associations and ultimately by the state supreme courts. Lawyers may be disbarred, suspended, or reprimanded for violating those rules. The Codes are then far different from the codes of ethics of other business associations, which are often voluntary statements which are not binding or not enforceable.

Figure 20-1 American Bar Association's Model Rules of Professional Conduct (Adopted 1983)

Preamble

A lawyer is a representative of clients, an officer of the legal system and a public citizen having special responsibility for the quality of justice.

As a representative of clients, a lawyer performs various functions. As advisor, a lawyer provides a client with an informed understanding of the client's legal rights and obligations and explains their practical implications. As advocate, a lawyer zealously asserts the client's position under the rules of the adversary system. As negotiator, a lawyer seeks a result advantageous to the client but consistent with requirements of honest dealing with others. As intermediary between clients, a lawyer seeks to reconcile their divergent interests as an advisor and, to a limited extent, as spokesman for each client. A lawyer acts as evaluator by examining a client's legal affairs and reporting about them to the client or to others.

. . . .

As a public citizen, a lawyer should seek improvement of the law, the administration of the law, the administration of justice and the quality of service rendered by the legal profession. As a member of a learned profession, a lawyer should cultivate knowledge of the law beyond its use for clients, employ that knowledge in reform of the law and work to strengthen legal education. A lawyer should be mindful of deficiencies in the administration of justice and of the fact that the poor, and sometimes persons who are not poor, cannot afford adequate legal assistance, and should therefore devote professional time and civic influence in their behalf. A lawyer should aid the legal profession in pursuing these objectives and should help the bar regulate itself in the public interest.

. . . .

Rule 1.1 Competence. A lawyer should provide competent representation to a client. Competent representation requires the legal knowledge, skill, thoroughness and preparation reasonably necessary for the representation.

. . . .

Rule 1.6 Confidentiality of Information. (a) A lawyer shall not reveal information relating to representation of a client unless the client consents after consultation, except for disclosures that are impliedly authorized in order to carry out the representation, and except as stated in paragraph (b)

(b) A lawyer may reveal such information to the extent the lawyer reasonably believes necessary: (1) to prevent the client from committing a criminal act that the lawyer reasonably believes is likely to result in imminent death or substantial bodily harm; or (2) to establish a claim or defense on behalf of the lawyer in a controversy between the lawyer and the client, to establish a defense to a criminal charge or civil claim against the lawyer based upon conduct in which the client was involved, or to respond to allegations in any proceeding concerning the lawyer's representation of the client.

Rule 1.7 Conflict of Interest: General Rule. (a) A lawyer shall not represent a client if the representation of that client will be directly adverse to another client, unless:

(1) the lawyer reasonably believes the representation will not adversely affect the relationship with the other client; and (2) each client consents after consultation.

. . . .

Rule 2.1 Advisor. In representing a client, a lawyer shall exercise independent judgment and render candid advice. In rendering advice, a lawyer may refer not only to law, but to other considerations, such as moral, economic, social and political factors, that may be relevant to the client's situation. . . .

Rule 3.1 Meritorious Claims and Contentions. A lawyer shall not bring or defend a proceeding, or assert or controvert an issue therein, unless there is a basis for doing so that is not frivolous, which includes a good faith argument for an extension, modification, or reversal of existing law. A lawyer for the defendant in a criminal proceeding, or the respondent in a proceeding that could result in incarceration, may nevertheless so defend the proceeding as to require that every element of the case be established.

. . . .

Rule 3.5 Impartiality and Decorum of the Tribunal. A lawyer shall not: (a) seek to influence a judge, juror, prospective juror or other official by means prohibited by law; (b) communicate ex parte with such person except as permitted by law; or (c) engage in conduct intended to disrupt a tribunal.

. . . .

Rule 4.1 Truthfulness in Statements to Others. In the course of representing a client a lawyer shall not knowingly: (a) make a false statement of material fact or law to a third person; or (b) fail to disclose a material fact to a third person when disclosure is necessary to avoid assisting a criminal or fraudulent act by a client, unless disclosure is prohibited by Rule 1.6.

. . . .

Rule 8.4 Misconduct. It is professional misconduct for a lawyer to:
(a) violate or attempt to violate the Rules of Professional Conduct. . . .
(b) commit a criminal act that reflects adversely on the lawyer's honesty, trustworthiness, or fitness as a lawyer in other respects;
(c) engage in conduct involving dishonesty, fraud, deceit or misrepresentation;
(d) engage in conduct that is prejudicial to the administration of justice;
(e) state or imply an ability to influence improperly a government agency or official;
(f) knowingly assist a judge or judicial officer in conduct that is a violation of applicable rules of judicial conduct or other law.

Columbus Bar Association v. Grelle

14 Ohio St. 2d 208, 237 N.E. 2d 298 (1968)

Grelle, an attorney of long-standing and high reputation, filed a personal injury action on behalf of Lloyd I. Perine in 1963. Three months later, Perine and his wife agreed to separate, agreed on all of the terms of the separation privately, and obtained the help of Grelle in preparing the separation papers. Later, Mrs. Perine requested Grelle to help her get a divorce. There was some conflict in the evidence as to whether Grelle initially declined the case, but ultimately he filed the divorce petition on behalf of Mrs. Perine. Part of the divorce settlement was that Mrs. Perine (who ten weeks later became Mrs. Pinto) was to obtain a part of the proceeds of the personal injury action. In February 1965, the personal injury action was settled, and Grelle paid over the total proceeds to Mr. Perine. Mrs. Pinto brought an action for a money judgment for her share of the proceeds, which Grelle successfully defended on behalf of Mr. Perine. Mrs. Pinto then brought the facts to the attention of the Columbus Bar Association, which brought this action against Grelle in the Supreme Court of Ohio. A Board of

Commissioners on Grievances and Discipline concluded that Grelle had violated his oath of office and parts of the Canons of Ethics, and recommended that he be suspended for an indefinite period.

Per Curiam.

One of the major objections of respondent pertains to the conclusion of the board that his conduct violated Canon 6 of the Canons of Professional Ethics. Canon 6 reads as follows:

Adverse Influences and Conflicting Interests.

It is the duty of a lawyer at the time of retainer to disclose to the client all the circumstances of his relations to the parties, and any interest in or connection with the controversy, which might influence the client in the selection of counsel.

It is unprofessional to represent conflicting interests, except by express consent of all concerned given a full disclosure of the facts. Within the meaning of this canon, a lawyer represents conflicting interests when, in behalf of one client, it is his duty to contend for that which duty to another client requires him to oppose.

The obligation to represent the client with undivided fidelity and not to divulge his secrets or confidences forbids also the subsequent acceptance of retainers or employment from others in matters adversely affecting any interest of the client with respect to which confidence has been reposed.

Respondent notes that there was no finding that he did not disclose to each of the Perines his representation of the other, and he argues that the evidence shows that there was, in fact, full disclosure of this mutual representation. We agree with respondent on this point. Dorothy Pinto testified at the hearing that when she went to the respondent's office it was with full knowledge and approval of her husband, Lloyd Perine. She also testified that she had previously agreed with Lloyd Perine that he would pay for any divorce received.

There was no misrepresentation by the respondent as to his position with respect to either of the parties. It appears that with respect to the separation agreement and the divorce appearance he was not primarily protecting anyone or advising anyone, but was rather carrying out the mutual wishes of the parties. Conflicting interests arose out of the separation agreement, but not until over a year after the divorce was final. Any representation of the wife by the respondent had long since ceased.

The agreement between the parties which had reference to a division of the net proceeds of the contemplated settlement of Mr. Perine's claim for damages contained no promise by the respondent to protect the rights assigned to Mrs. Perine at the time of distribution. There is no claim that there was any representation that attorney Grelle would represent her or protect her interest in that fund upon distribution. It is understandable, however, that Mrs. Perine might have concluded that this was to be one of Mr. Grelle's functions. The fact that such misunderstandings are likely to occur under such circumstances must lead to the conclusion that only in the clearest cases should counsel hazard to represent interests which are or may become adverse, even after disclosing his dual representation.

In retrospect, this was not such a case. Too many experienced lawyers have accepted such employment in separation or divorce matters under such circumstances, only to ultimately abandon the interest of one or the other of their clients. In such instances of dual representation, a party disappointed in the financial results, as was Mrs. Pinto, may validly argue after the fact that the dual representation brought about the omission from the agreement of specific language protecting her upon distribution of the anticipated settlement fund.

At all events, when Mrs. Pinto filed her motion to reduce to judgment that part of the agreement drawn by respondent which gave her a one-third interest in the proceeds of the personal injury settlement, Mr. Grelle should have withdrawn from the matter. His failing promptly to disclose to Mrs. Perine the fact that a settlement had occurred and that distribution to Perine had been made, and his ardent advocacy of the husband's adverse interest to the agreement violated the second paragraph of Canon No. 6, and was unprofessional conduct which justifies a reprimand.

We find, however, in view of all the facts in this case, including his full disclosure to the parties of this position and their consent to that position, that Mr. Grelle did not violate his oath of office. In view of the previously unblemished record of the respondent the reprimand which we here impose is judged to be suitable disciplinary action.

Judgment Accordingly.

Ethics as an Alternative to Regulation

To many, including possibly many of those who have found their way through the preceding nineteen chapters, business in particular and American society in general is "overregulated." A common answer to those who say that business still needs controls is that business can regulate itself through individual notions of ethics and through codes of ethics similar to those that regulate the conduct of lawyers, doctors, and other professionals. And, in fact, many industries and professions have adopted codes of ethics that detail the ethical duties of members of the profession or trade. The theory is, perhaps, that such Codes of Ethics might take the place of enforced government regulation through law.

That position has several problems: (1) most codes of ethics, unlike those of attorneys, doctors and other professionals, are voluntary in nature and are unenforceable; (2) such codes of ethics may in fact be anticompetitive in nature or otherwise hurtful to the public welfare; (3) such codes will undoubtedly subordinate the will of some of the members of the industry to other members of the industry, but they will rarely subordinate the interests of the entire industry to the interests of the public.

Enforceability

The argument that lawyers, doctors, and other professionals govern themselves admirably through codes of ethics and, therefore, other trades and industries might adopt the same policy and avert government regulation has some problems. Law, medicine, and those other professions are *licensed* trades; in order to practice those professions one must obtain permission from the state, in the form of a license, to do so, and that license may be withdrawn. Thus the codes of ethics are not voluntary in any sense, and in fact are an *adjunct of* government regulation, not a *replacement for* such regulation.

Actual Harm

While codes of ethics generally have a positive effect on an industry, their use may in fact involve harm to the public. Those codes may be little more than efforts to restrain trade between members of the profession or trade.

Goldfarb, et ux. v. Virginia State Bar

421 U.S. 773, 95 S. Ct. 2004, 44 L. Ed. 2 572 (1975)

In 1971, Mr. and Mrs. Goldfarb made a contract to purchase a home in Virginia. The institution financing their purchase required them to secure title insurance, and title insurance required an examination of the title to the real estate. Only a member of the Virginia State Bar could legally perform a title examination.

The Goldfarbs contacted 37 lawyers, all of whom quoted precisely the same fee. The county bar association published a "recommended" fee schedule. Membership in the county bar association is voluntary, but the Virginia State Bar, an administrative agency of the Virginia Supreme Court, had issued ethical opinions that stated that fee schedules could not be ignored. No lawyer nad ever been formally disciplined for failure to conform to the fee schedules, however. Membership in the State Bar is required to practice law in Virginia.

The Goldfarbs brought an action under Section 1 of the Sherman Act, claiming price fixing. The District Court held for the Goldfarbs, but the Court of Appeals held that the fee schedule was outside of the scope of the antitrust laws because law is a learned profession and therefore was not "trade or commerce" within the meaning of the Act. The Goldfarbs appealed.

MR. CHIEF JUSTICE BURGER delivered the opinion of the Court.

. . . .

The County Bar argues that because the fee schedule is merely advisory, the schedule and its enforcement mechanism do not constitute price fixing. Its purpose, the argument continues, is only to provide legitimate information to aid member lawyers in complying with Virginia professional regulations. . . .

A purely advisory fee schedule issued to provide guidelines, or an exchange of price information without a showing of an actual restraint on trade, would present us with a different question . . . Here a fixed, rigid price floor arose from respondents' activities: every lawyer who responded to petitioners' inquiries adhered to the fee schedule, and no lawyer asked for additional information in order to set an individualized fee. The price information disseminated did not concern past standards, . . . but rather minimum fees to be charged in future transactions, and those minimum rates were increased over time. The fee schedule was enforced through the prospect of professional discipline from the State Bar, and the desire of attorneys to comply with announced professional norms . . . ; the motivation to conform was reinforced by the assurance that other lawyers would not compete by underbidding. This was not merely a case of an agreement that may be inferred from an exchange of price information . . . for here a naked agreement was clearly shown, and the effect on prices is plain. . . .

. . . The County Bar makes much of the fact that it is a voluntary organization; however, the ethical opinions issued by the State Bar provide that any lawyer, whether or not a member of his county bar association, may be disciplined for "*habitually* charg[ing] less than the suggested minimum fee schedule adopted by his local bar [sic] Association. . . ." On this record respondents' activities constitute a classic illustration of price fixing.

The Court found that the activities of attorneys did indeed "affect interstate commerce" since mortgage financing and title insurance are "interstate businesses." The Court's discussion paralleled *McLain* v. *Real Estate Board of New Orleans,* 444 U.S. 232, 100 S. Ct. 502, 62 L.Ed.2d 441 (1980), a later case which held the activities of local real estate brokers to be subject to the antitrust laws for similar reasons. That case also involved price-fixing by "ethical code."

c

   The County Bar argues that Congress never intended to include the learned professions within the terms "trade or commerce" in §1 of the Sherman Act, and therefore the sale of professional services is exempt from the Act. No explicit exemption or legislative history is provided to support this contention; rather, the existence of state regulation seems to be its primary basis. Also, the County Bar maintains that competition is inconsistent with the practice of a profession because enhancing profit is not the goal of professional activities; the goal is to provide services necessary to the community.[3] That, indeed, is the classic basis traditionally advanced to distinguish professions from trades, businesses, and other occupations, but it loses some of its force when used to support the fee control activities involved here.

. . . .

   The language of §1 of the Sherman Act, of course, contains no exceptions. . . . And our cases have repeatedly established that there is a heavy presumption against implicit exemptions. . . . Indeed, our cases have specifically included the sale of services within §1. . . . Whatever else it may be, the examination of a land title is a service; the exchange of such a service for money is "commerce" in the most common usage of that word. It is no disparagement of the practice of law as a profession to acknowledge that it has this business aspect. . . . In the modern world it cannot be denied that the activities of lawyers play an important part in commercial intercourse, and that anticompetitive activities by lawyers may exert a restraint on commerce.

. . . .

   Reversed and Remanded.

Differing Interests

Closely related to the problem of actual harm that may be caused by ethical codes is that ethical codes can only regulate activities *within* a profession or trade and can have little impact on relations of the industry to other industries or to the society as a whole. It is one thing, for example, to regulate the activities of lawyers or stockbrokers or accountants that adversely affect individuals within those industries. It is a totally different problem to adopt and enforce ethical duties that subordinate the entire business of law, investment advice, or accountancy to the interests of the larger society or economy. It is doubtful that any trade association could adopt rules of that sort and, even if they were adopted, it is highly doubtful that they would or could be enforced. It is far more likely that such associations will "build up" the industry they regulate, even when such building up adversely affects other groups or interests.

   These considerations do not mean, of course, that codes of ethics are useless nor that they should not be adopted. Trade associations and professional organizations have done a great deal of good through their adoption of codes of ethics by way of defining and refining the ethical duties of members of their respective trades and

---

[3]The reason for adopting the fee schedule does not appear to have been wholly altruistic. The first sentence in respondent State Bar's 1962 Minimum Fee Schedule Report states: "The lawyers have slowly, but surely, been committing economic suicide as a profession." [Court's footnote.]

professions. It just means that codes of ethics are very limited in their ability to replace government regulation as a control technique.

Summary and Conclusions

The relationship between ethics and the law is intimate. Ethics, or standards and rules of conduct of human relations, are the learned duties of people towards other people. Many of those ethical duties have, over time, become embodied and sanctioned by the law.

One way to look at ethics is as two distinct systems, the ethics of duty and the ethics of excellence. The ethics of duty provide basic rules essential for the survival of society and civilization, while the ethics of excellence provide our goals, aspirations, and standards of perfection. The law is generally concerned, at least in democratic societies, with the ethics of duty. There seems to be rather strong agreement about the ethics of duty, but opinions regarding the ethics of excellence vary widely.

Common ethical duties include honesty, loyalty, fairness, obedience to law, and community responsibility. Each of those duties has a variety of meanings and those meanings may conflict. Those duties may conflict as well, and the resolution of those conflicts must be a matter of personal decision, though reflection on ethical matters and reference to the law may be of some help.

Ethics is an "input" to the law, but law is also an input to ethics. The two systems, legal and ethical, are often parallel. As ethics change, the law also must change through the courts and legislatures. And sometimes, as the law changes ethics also change because of our social values of obedience and respect for the law.

Ethical codes are sometimes viewed as an alternative to government regulation, but they are of limited usefulness. Such codes are often unenforceable, may create actual harm, and can have limited effect on professional activities that are in the interest of the group enacting the code.

PRO AND CON

ISSUE: Are Business Ethics Different from Other Ethical Notions?

PRO: Business Must Set Standards Others Will Follow
Ivan Hill*

I am here to discuss ethics. I have chosen the special topic Compromise and Conviction because these factors constitute a continuously recurrent ethical dilemma.

Today, much of the popular discussion of ethics is about "business ethics." . . . Although the term "business ethics" is frequently used, I do not believe there is any such thing as business ethics,

*Ivan Hill is president emeritus of the Ethics Resource Center. From his speech, "Compromise and Conviction: The Ethical Dilemma," delivered to the Associated General Contractors, Houston, Texas, March 15, 1982, and reprinted in *Vital Speeches of the Day*, vol. 48, no. 14, p. 434. Reprinted by permission.

per se. I do not believe there is a merchant's ethics, or an educator's ethics or a politician's ethics. There is only ethics, no matter what your vocation or profession happens to be.

. . . .

The interest of business in ethics is not philosophical but highly pragmatic. Business' interest in ethics did not originate in theories so much as in headlines. A free market economy and a democratic form of government both rest on a strong underpinning of ethics, upon public trust in the institutions of society and in its leaders. Both conditions require a high degree of honesty and individual responsibility at every level. And both are now endangered by irresponsible, unethical actions that have undermined public confidence and trust. . . .

What do we mean by ethics? . . . [T]he Ethics Resource Center conducted a survey to determine what ethics means to the general public. . . . We found that the public understands very well what ethics means. More than 86 percent of people interviewed associated ethics with standards and rules of conduct, morals, right and wrong, values and honesty. The public also understood that if ethics appeared in the headlines, the story would tell about the *lack* of ethics—the doing of wrong as opposed to right.

. . . .

We view ethics as character that manifests itself in action. . . . One cannot do good by doing nothing. How do you arrive at what your convictions are? First, one should be confident enough of his own convictions as to be able and willing to defend them in open discussion. Convictions are . . . strengthened and . . . illuminated by discussions and observations. Real growth comes from finally learning which convictions to hold—those that have passed the test of evaluation by others and yourself—and which convictions to modify or change or selectively apply.

. . . .

Convictions are developed from deeply held beliefs and the . . . values of the culture, but these factors alone, however powerful their imprintation, are not capable of crystalizing convictions. . . . The conscience is where the ethical and the real unite to become one force. . . .

. . . .

Any social system operates on at least a few common convictions and shared understandings. One of the serious problems facing the United States right now is that we have too few common denominators of convictions, too few commonly shared beliefs, that serve to make us a cohesive nation where traditional values and tested principles can be applied to this new and complex world. America has always been a pluralistic nation, not only politically but culturally. . . .

Often we think that to compromise is to be weak or bad. Lord Morley states that we should "admit the necessity of a measure of accommodation in the very interest of truth itself." Indeed, compromise may be the scientific approach to problem solving—the synthesis of opinions and observations as to what might be realizable objectives. . . .

But how does one know when one is compromising out of his best wisdom or compromising from expediency and personal greed? As Morley says some folks are "cautious not so much lest it should not pay." . . . Yet, at some point one should draw the line and say, "Here is my territory of principle and personal conviction and I shall protect it and not open the gate to compromise."

. . . .

Compromise that is laced with intentional ambiguities and reservations is not compromise, it is dishonesty. No one should be so dishonest as to enter a discussion or negotiation having been given prior instructions to consider no contrary opinion nor should one determine ahead of time to place blinders on his mind or soul to restrict his vision of alternatives. Dishonesty corrupts communication, destroys trust and defeats the purpose of compromise which is the highly ethical attempt to find the shared interest and the common cause that permits cooperation and progress—the very conditions for civilized society.

. . . .

The irony of all the criticism of business, especially big business, is that with rare exception every business that is continuously profitable has probably never needed to engage in any dishonesty or corrupting compromise. That they didn't need to does not mean they did not, however. Even today, with all the criticism of business from the public and many special groups, most businesses could open their doors to all their operations and methods and still come up 99 and nine-tenths percent clean. But, as any good chemist knows, a one-tenth of one percent alloy can ruin a whole warehouse full of the purest product. Business must strive for a "pure" product, for the highest degree of honesty and ethics possible. It must understand the ethical principles that are the basis of private enterprise, honesty, mutual trust, individual and institutional responsibility. And it must understand that these principles cannot be compromised without endangering the private enterprise system itself.

CON: Business Ethics Reflect Society's Ethics
Patrick M. Boarman*

It would be difficult to find an American business-man of repute today who, charged by his critics with failure to recognize and live up to the ethical imperatives of his position . . . would reply with the once self-evident . . . dictum: "The business of business is business." On the contrary, our busi-nessman is more likely than not to acquiesce in the premise that business, especially big business, has indeed quite special ethical obligations, which it behooves him to discover, to analyze, and to pro-claim. And lest there should be any faltering in busi-nessmen's commitment in their ethical mission, phalanxes of Naderites move in periodically to stage moral extravaganzas featuring the "crimes" of business from Lockheed bribery to the Equity Funding Fraud, to the environmental desecrations of such as U.S. Steel or Dow Chemical—all assid-uously reported by the print and electronic media.

For those on the left, it is a truism that busi-nessmen are bastards, that profits are obscene . . . and that capitalism subsists and flourishes in a moral vacuum, a state of affairs that, allegedly, only socialism can fix. Even on the right, surprisingly, the image of the predatory, morally obtuse, grasp-ing capitalist is sometimes offered as a reality to be accepted, if not admired, only with the proviso that the discipline of the free market can be counted on to keep the bastard in line.

. . . .

Can it be that morally repugnant behavior somehow inheres in the market economy? What is the ethical content of the market mechanism, if any? Does the market nurture and exploit merely simple self-interest, as Adam Smith long ago asserted, or does it incorporate a quite profound and hitherto unsuspected ethical dimension, even a sort of altruism, in which entrepreneurs can be viewed as givers rather than takers . . . ? And finally: can one talk about business ethics as if it were a separate, unique, perhaps more exalted set of rules for the corporation than for the individual? Or is there, in fact, one set of standards for right behavior applicable to all alike?

. . . .

To begin with the last question first: Is there a special ethics for business which expects and demands from businessmen a higher, more rigor-ous code of conduct than from the rest of us? Apparently so. . . . The key point . . . is that in respect to momentous moral issues there was [traditionally] one standard of right conduct—in a given culture and time—for the individual and for the organization. But the business ethics now fash-ionable in some quarters in the United States would have it differently. For it asserts that acts that are not unethical or wrong if done by the man in the street . . . are indeed unethical or immoral if done by business.

No one, observes [Peter] Drucker, has ever had a good word to say for extortion. "But if you and I are found to have paid extortion money under threat of physical or material harm, we are not con-sidered to have behaved immorally or illegally." If, however, an American businessman yields to the solicitations of a foreign customer for sweetners to close the deal . . . he is considered under current business ethics . . . to have acted unethically.

. . . .

The fact is that a relativist business ethics, in which the moral rules that apply to individuals differ from those which apply to business, is not ethics at all. What it is, says Drucker . . . is casuistry.

Casuistry, a 17th century doctrine . . . declares that the ethics of a given act can be determined only on a *case by case* basis. . . . Ethics . . . is instead a cost-benefit calculation involving the demands of individual conscience and the demands of position—and that means that some are exempt from the demands of ethics, if only their behavior can be argued to confer benefits on other people. And this, of course, can only mean the defeat of ethics in the traditional sense. . . .

. . . .

The casuist approach to ethical questions is, ironically, enjoying something of a renaissance in Schools of Business. In some of these schools, stu-dents are instructed in "situational ethics," that is, the ability to resolve the array of moral dilemmas that arise in business, not on moral grounds, but

---

*From his speech "Business and Ethics: Contemporary Capitalism," delivered to the California Council for the Humanities, Seminar on Humanities and Business, National University, March 19, 1982, and reprinted in *Vital Speeches of the Day*, vol. 48, p. 532. Reprinted by permission.

pragmatically, with the objective being to survive in business. . . .

. . . .

Fortunately, there are two extremely powerful mechanisms or structures which the market-oriented society has at its disposal to ensure a convergence of business behavior with the received notions . . . of traditional ethics. The first is, quite simply, the market itself, and the second is the moral and cultural framework within which the market operates.

. . . .

The great disciplinarian of the market, the market policeman if you will, is competition: for it compels the reciprocity . . . which is the ethical justification for the exchange process. Hence, the overweening concern of most economists with the need to defend and preserve competition through such institutional arrangements as the antitrust laws, for example.

. . . .

It is also the framework of the economic system, especially its moral and cultural components, that we must look for the second great influence on and, indeed, the ultimate sanction of business behavior. No special business ethic is . . . conceivable or desirable. The ethics of the businessman are or should be those of the society of which he is a part. If there is a moral failure in the society, if truth, decency, courage, prudence, loyalty, and honor are deficient, then the mores of businessmen, as of government officials, as of university professors, as of us all, will reflect this. By the same token, a moral renaissance, in business or elsewhere, will only be possible if there is a renewed commitment to ethical precepts. . . .

DISCUSSION QUESTIONS

1. Does everyone have a set of ethical standards—even criminals? How do those standards become "misguided"?

2. Make up your own list of ethics of duty, and make it as complete as possible. Compare that list with that of a friend. Now make up a list of your ethics of excellence and compare that to the same friend. Do they coincide?

3. Can you think of an instance where the law enforces an ethic of excellence? Why is it more difficult for democratic societies to embed ethics of excellence in the law than it is for totalitarian societies? Shouldn't we be trying to make our society the best it can possibly be? What's wrong with using the law to enforce the ethics of excellence?

4. How is it possible that both the ethic of Individualism and the ethic of Community evolved from the same sources of philosphical Humanism?

5. Do you think it is possible to construct an *economic* theory of ethics, based on the theory of Utilitarianism? How would you do so?

6. Should state of mind, motivation, and relationship play a part in our ethical judgments? Why or why not?

7. Why do you suppose we make a distinction between marketplace ethics and intimate ethics? Is business just a game with different rules? Should it have different rules? Shouldn't we just apply the same high standards of intimate ethics to all our dealings?

8. Consider whether "loyalty" isn't the chief culprit in most ethical dilemmas. In other words, wouldn't it be much easier to be honest, obey the law, be fair, and be responsible to the community without loyalty? What is loyalty anyway?

9. Can you add any other notions to Blumberg's list of areas of community responsibility? Notice the article was written in 1971; have things changed since then? Is it significant that Blumberg's reasons for imposing community responsibility is to avoid further "politicalization" and regulation of the corporation?

10. If ethical codes are not much use in avoiding regulation, of what use are they?

CASE PROBLEMS

1. As an ambitious business graduate, you are rapidly climbing the corporate ladder. Your immediate superior, who is also ambitious, asks you to negotiate a contract and directly instructs you to lie to the other party to the contract. You have three choices: (a) violate your superior's instructions and tell the truth, and hope the contract goes through anyway; (b) inform your superior's boss of the instruction to lie and ask for guidance; and (c) go ahead and lie. What do you do, and why?

2. The company for which you work is under investigation for violations of the antitrust laws, laws with which you vehemently disagree on grounds of principle. The Department of Justice has directly subpoenaed all records in your possession. In those records you know there is evidence of price-fixing, which will probably result in indictment and conviction of your company. There is a strong possibility that if the company is convicted, the adverse publicity will put the company out of business and put you out of a job. Failure to turn over the evidence or destruction of the evidence is a federal offense as well, but probably no one will ever know. What do you do, and why?

3. You are in desperate need of cash to finance your final semester in college. You also own an old car. Recently a mechanic told you that while the car still sounds and runs quite well, it is actually in need of a major motor overhaul that will cost $700, and that the car could "quit" at any time. The retail value of the car, if it is in good condition, is $1,800. You decide to sell the car, and you have three offers—from your roommate, your brother, and a total stranger. How much do you tell each of them about the engine defect? If there was a difference, why?

4. After graduation, you begin working in your father's chemical business. One lunchtime you decide to take a stroll along the river running next to the plant and you notice a pipe with a slimy substance discharging into the river from the plant. You ask your father about it, and he admits it is waste products from the plant. He also tells you that the expense of disposing of such materials properly

is very high. That afternoon an EPA inspector stops by and directly asks you if you know of any pollution from the plant. What do you say and why?

5. Your first job is as a sales manager in an appliance store. You learn rather quickly that while the store stays within the letter of the law, the store specializes in selling shoddy merchandise at high prices to people who cannot afford the goods. In fact, most of the goods are later repossessed and resold, and the purchasers are sued for deficiency judgments. Do you keep the job? Why or why not?

6. After graduation you become a real estate salesperson working on a "straight commission" basis. In that job you often hold deposits on property for clients. One Friday you are holding $4,000 in deposit money on behalf of a client. The following Tuesday you will "close" a sale and receive a $3,000 commission. The $4,000 deposited with you is for another sale, and no one will call for that money for at least three weeks. You are flat broke and the rent is due. What do you do and why?

7. Your employer is involved in a large contract dispute with another company that results in a lawsuit against your firm. From your classes in Business Law, you know that if your company can prove that the other firm, or its representatives, agreed to take certain products back that were sold to your firm, your firm will win the case. You are friendly with the sales manager of the other firm, and you met with him for lunch and played tennis on several occasions. He never agreed to take those products back, however. You also know it is your word against his, and that if your testimony wins the case, you can expect a sizable raise. What do you do and why?

8. A close friend, who happens to be an employee of a major oil company, calls you one evening and tells you that his firm has made a major "strike," which will be announced at noon the next day. The stock exchange opens at 9 AM. You also know that "tippee trading" is illegal. What do you do and why?

9. Because of your expertise in the legal relationships of government and business, you are assigned to your firm's Washington office, which primarily deals in lobbying. A crucial piece of legislation is coming up for a vote, and the vote is likely to be very close. You also know that Congressman X faces a crucial election in his home state (not your own) and is in desperate need of campaign funds. You also know that Congressman X has a history of being "grateful" for such campaign contributions. What do you do and why?

10. You are assigned as foreign sales manager for your firm in another nation. After several unsuccessful attempts to sell your products, you learn that it is the custom in that country to pay bribes to purchasing agents. Such bribes are illegal in both that nation and in the U.S., but in that nation the enforcement authorities receive 10 percent of the bribe and look the other way. Your competitors have been bribing purchasing agents for years. Do you pay a bribe? Why or why not?

Suggested Readings

Braybrooke, David. *Ethics in the World of Business* (Totowa, N.J.: Rowman & Allanheld, 1983).

Fuller, Lon L. *The Morality of Law* (New Haven, Conn.: Yale University Press, 1963).

Kuperberg, Mark, and Charles Beitz. *Law, Economics and Philosophy* (Totowa, N.J.: Rowman & Allanheld, 1983).

Pound, Roscoe. *An Introduction to the Philosophy of Law* (New Haven, Conn.: Yale University Press, 1922).

Appendix A
Finding and Briefing Cases

All of the cases found in this text, including many of the cases found in the Case Problems sections at the end of each chapter, are taken from actual court decisions. Most college libraries contain a law collection in which most, if not all, of these decisions may be found. While actual legal research is not necessary in most legal environment courses, it is often helpful to be able to locate cases in the law library.

FINDING CASES

While actual legal research may not be necessary for this course, it is helpful to be able to locate cases in the law library. In order to locate a case, first look at the citation to the case. The citation will always include some numbers, some initials, and some more numbers. For example, the citation to *Hammer v. Dagenhart* on p. 50 is "247 U.S. 251." *U.S.* refers to a set of lawbooks, the *United States Reports,* which includes all of the decisions of the United States Supreme Court. The first set of numbers, 247, refers to the volume of the *United States Reports* in which the case may be found. The second set of numbers, 251, refers to the page in that volume. Thus, *Hammer v. Dagenhart* may be found in volume 247 of the *United States Reports* beginning on page 251.

All citations follow much the same form. Citations to state court decisions will carry abbreviations of the state name as the set of books, such as *Ill.* or *Wash.,* which refers to the *Illinois Reports* or the *Washington Reports.* Decisions from the U.S. Court of Appeals will use the designation *Fed.* which means *Federal Reporter,* or *F.2d,* which means *Federal Reporter, Second Series.* Often sets of books have gone into a second series, since the number of cases has been so substantial. Decisions from the U.S. District Court use the designation *F. Supp.,* meaning *Federal Supplement.*

Even law review articles and textbooks use the same method of citation. For example, the article by Posner in Chapter 1 is cited as 53 *Texas Law Review* 757, and a set of commentaries might be cited as 1 Schwartz, *A Commentary on the Constitution of the United States* 281.

A great number of the cases in this text are opinions of the U.S. Supreme Court. Those cases have *three* citations following the case title, together with a date. That means that those cases may be found in three different sets of books. For example, the citation to *U.S. v. Nixon* in Chapter 1 is 418 U.S. 683, 94 S. Ct. 3090, 41 L. Ed. 2d 1039. The first citation, *U.S.* (reporter), is to the official publication of the U.S. government and is really the official citation to the case. The *S. Ct.* citation is to the *Supreme Court Reporter,* published by West Publishing Company. The *L. Ed.* citation is to the *Lawyer's Edition,* a publication of the Lawyer's Cooperative Publishing Company, which contains not only the decision of the court, but also abstracts of the briefs of the lawyers in the case. All three volumes contain all of the cases decided by the court. In addition, very recent decisions of the Court may be found in *U.S. Law Week* (sometimes cited *U.S.L.W.*), published by the Bureau of National Affairs. Since it takes time for the actual decisions to be printed in the other sets, often *U.S. Law Week* is the only source for very recent Supreme Court decisions.

READING CASES

Students who are accustomed to "speed reading" through their texts in other courses often have a rude awakening in legal studies. The law is, above all, words. And the exact placement, choice, and definition of those words may be crucial to the meaning of the case. Semantic distinctions may well be vital to a full understanding of the case, and those distinctions are usually not obvious on a fast "once over" of the decision. The case must be read and reread, carefully analyzing the language used and comparing and contrasting those words with the language of other cases.

For example, Chapter 2 presents a progression of three Commerce Clause cases. A quick reading of *Hammer* v. *Dagenhart* and *NLRB* v. *Jones and Laughlin Steel* does not show a great deal of difference. But, if the words are analyzed, the problems thought through, and the facts of the cases compared, it soon becomes clear that *NLRB* v. *Jones and Laughlin Steel* represents a major turning point in the law.

A recent student remarked with considerable accuracy that the law must be read in the same way one would read poetry. The care with which the student reads the cases will bear a direct relationship to how much he or she will get out of the case. A very wise old trial lawyer once observed that "the law is the only profession which allows you to work while staring out the window." Usually the work going on at that time is reflection upon the meaning of cases, the relationships between cases, and their effects.

BRIEFING CASES

A tried and true method of studying cases in law schools and in law practice may be of help to the legal environment student. "Briefing" a case involves little more than a formalized system of notetaking and analysis, which forces the reader to identify issues and problems in the case. Students are often required to prepare briefs and, even if the practice is not required, many students find briefing to be very helpful.

Above all, a brief should be written in the student's own words. Briefs generally contain four major sections: facts, issue(s), judgment, and reasons.

Facts The facts include the names of the parties, who is suing whom and for what (the requested relief), and the *relevant* facts of the case. The relevant facts would be those facts which are important to the case and its outcome. All facts that do not make a difference, i.e., are irrelevant, are omitted. Usually the "procedural" facts are included as well, such as what happened in the lower courts and why the appellate court from which the appeal is taken ruled as it did.

A brief of *Hammer* v. *Dagenhart* might appear as follows.

Hammer v. Dagenhart
247 U.S. 251 (1918) (Citation and date should be included)

FACTS: The Dagenhart brothers, both minors, were discharged from their jobs because of a federal statute which prohibited interstate shipment of goods made with child labor. They brought suit against Hammer, the U.S. Attorney, to enjoin enforcement of the statute. The brothers claimed that the statute was beyond the authority of Congress to enact under the Commerce Clause, since it regulated "production" which they argued was an essentially local matter. The lower court enjoined enforcement of the statute, and the government appealed.

Notice that several nonessential facts have been omitted, such as the first names of the parties, the specific provisions of the statute, and similar matters. The usual rule of thumb is, When in doubt, throw it in.

Issue In many ways the issue, or question that the case attempts to answer, is the most important part of the case brief. The purpose is to recognize problems from the facts. The facts as presented in the brief should lead the reader to the issue. In *Hammer,* for example, the issue could be framed as follows.

> ISSUE: Does Congress have the authority, under the Commerce Clause, to regulate child labor, since child labor is a part of "production?"

Often there is more than one issue in a case. In such cases, all of the issues must be stated, and answers and reasons given for each. In many cases the court sets out the issue itself. Often this is helpful, but students should critically analyze whether the court's statement of the issue is accurate, or is a "red herring" stated to divert the reader's attention from the real problem of the case.

Judgment Normally, the judgment will be a one word answer to the question posed by the issue. Some students prefer to use procedural terms, such as *affirmed* or *reversed.* If that is the case, the student should be careful to frame the facts and issue so that the answer to the issue makes sense. In *Hammer,* the judgment would be a simple "No."

Reasons This section sets out the court's stated reasons why it answered the issue in the manner in which it did. Usually, this will be the longest portion of the brief. Again, the reasons should be stated in the student's own words, though quotes from the opinion may be used sparingly. In *Hammer* the reasons might be stated as follows.

> REASONS: The Court relied on the definition of Commerce as the transportation of goods and the "purchase, sale and exchange" of goods. The Court stated that while production of such goods affected commerce, it was not "Commerce" and therefore was beyond the power of Congress. Such production was found to be a "purely local" matter, fit for the states to regulate only, and attempted regulation of production would be an invasion of the rights of states to regulate.

Students often find it helpful to add a fifth section, a critique of the decision, where the case is criticized for its reasoning, compared to other decisions, and analyzed for its impact on society.

Theoretically, when the brief is finished the student should not have to look at the case in the text again. In class and at exam time, the brief should be used for study, rather than rereading the entire case. Notes may be made on the brief when cases are discussed in class, and those notes and the brief itself should be enough to give the student plenty of material to study.

Appendix B
The Constitution of the United States (Unabridged)

PREAMBLE

We the People of the United States, in Order to form a more perfect Union, establish Justice, insure domestic Tranquility, provide for the common defence, promote the general Welfare, and secure the Blessings of Liberty to ourselves and our Posterity, do ordain and establish this Constitution for the United States of America.

Article I

Section 1. All legislative Powers herein granted shall be vested in a Congress of the United States, which shall consist of a Senate and House of Representatives.

Section 2. (1) The House of Representatives shall be composed of Members chosen every second Year by the People of the several States, and the Electors in each State shall have the Qualifications requisite for Electors of the most numerous Branch of the State Legislature.

(2) No Person shall be a Representative who shall not have attained to the Age of twenty five Years, and have been seven Years a Citizen of the United States, and who shall not, when elected, by an Inhabitant of that State in which he shall be chosen.

(3) Representatives and direct Taxes shall be apportioned among the several States which may be included within this Union, according to their respective Numbers, which shall be determined by adding to the whole Number of free Persons, including those bound to Service for Term of Years, and excluding Indians not taxed, three fifths of all other Persons. The actual Enumeration shall be made within three Years after the first Meeting of the Congress of the United States, and within every subsequent Term of ten Years, in such manner as they shall by Law direct. The Number of Representatives shall not exceed one for every thirty Thousand, but each State shall have at Least one Representative; and until such enumeration shall be made, the State of New Hampshire shall be entitled to choose three, Massachusetts eight, Rhode Island and Providence Plantations one, Connecticut five, New York six, New Jersey four, Pennsylvania eight, Delaware one, Maryland six, Virginia ten, North Carolina five, South Carolina five, and Georgia three.

(4) When vacancies happen in the Representation from any State, the Executive Authority thereof shall issue Writs of Election to fill such Vacancies.

(5) The House of Representatives shall choose their Speaker and other Officers; and shall have the sole Power of Impeachment.

Section 3. (1) The Senate of the United States shall be composed of two Senators from each State, chosen by the Legislature thereof, for six Years; and each Senator shall have one Vote.

(2) Immediately after they shall be assembled in Consequence of the first Election, they shall be divided as

equally as may be into three Classes. The Seats of the Senators of the first Class shall be vacated at the Expiration of the Second Year, of the second Class at the Expiration of the fourth Year, and of the third Class at the Expiration of the sixth Year, so that one third may be chosen every second Year; and if Vacancies happen by Resignation, or otherwise, during the Recess of the Legislature of any State, the Executive thereof may make temporary Appointments until the next Meeting of the Legislature, which shall then fill such Vacancies.

(3) No Person shall be a Senator who shall not have attained to the Age of thirty Years, and been nine Years a Citizen of the United States, and who shall not, when elected, be an Inhabitant of that State for which he shall be chosen.

(4) The Vice President of the United States shall be President of the Senate, but shall have not Vote, unless they be equally divided.

(5) The Senate shall choose their other Officers, and also a President pro tempore, in the Absence of the Vice President, or when he shall exercise the Office of President of the United States.

(6) The Senate shall have the sole Power to try all Impeachments. When sitting for that Purpose, they shall be on Oath or Affirmation. When the President of the United States is tried, the Chief Justice shall preside: And no Person shall be convicted without the Concurrence of two thirds of the Members present.

(7) Judgment in Cases of Impeachment shall not extend further than to removal from Office, and disqualification to hold and enjoy any Office of honor, Trust or Profit under the United States: but the Party convicted shall nevertheless be liable and subject to Indictment, Trial, Judgment, and Punishment, according to Law.

Section 4. (1) The Times, Places and Manner of holding Elections for Senators and Representatives, shall be prescribed in each State by the Legislature thereof; but the Congress may at any time by Law make or alter such Regulations, except as to the Places of choosing Senators.

(2) The Congress shall assemble at least once in every Year, and such Meeting shall be on the first Monday in December, unless they shall by Law appoint a different day.

Section 5. (1) Each House shall be the Judge of the Elections, Returns, and Qualifications of its own Members, and a Majority of each shall constitute a Quorum to do Business; but a smaller Number may adjourn from day to day, and may be authorized to compel the Attendance of absent Members, in such Manner, and under such Penalties as each House may provide.

(2) Each House may determine the Rules of its Proceedings, punish its Members for disorderly Behavior, and, with the Concurrence of two thirds, expel a Member.

(3) Each House shall keep a Journal of its Proceedings, and from time to time publish the same, excepting such Parts as may in their Judgment require Secrecy; and the Yeas and Nays of the Members of either House on any

question shall, at the desire of one fifth of those Present, be entered on the Journal.

(4) Neither House, during the Session of Congress, shall, without the Consent of the other, adjourn for more than three days, nor to any other Place than that in which the two Houses shall be sitting.

Section 6. (1) The Senators and Representatives shall receive a Compensation for their Services, to be ascertained by Law, and paid out of the Treasury of the United States. They shall in all Cases, except Treason, Felony and Breach of the Peace, be privileged from Arrest during their Attendance at the Session of their respective Houses, and in going to and returning from the same; and for any Speech or Debate in either House, they shall not be questioned in any other Place.

(2) No Senator or Representative shall, during the Time for which he was elected, be appointed to any civil Office under the Authority of the United States, which shall have been created, or the Emoluments whereof shall have been increased during such time; and no Person holding any Office under the United States, shall be a Member of either House during his Continuance in Office.

Section 7. (1) All Bills for raising Revenue shall originate in the House of Representatives; but the Senate may propose or concur with Amendments as on other bills.

(2) Every Bill which shall have passed the House of Representatives and the Senate, shall, before it becomes a Law, be presented to the President of the United States; If he approve he shall sign it, but if not he shall return it, with his Objections to the House in which it shall have originated, who shall enter the Objections at large on their Journal, and proceed to reconsider it. If after such Reconsideration two thirds of that House shall agree to pass the bill, it shall be sent together with the Objections, to the other House, by which it shall likewise be reconsidered, and if approved by two thirds of that House, it shall become a Law. But in all such Cases the Votes of Both Houses shall be determined by yeas and Nays, and the Names of the Persons voting for and against the Bill shall be entered on the Journal of each House respectively. If any Bill shall not be returned by the President within ten Days (Sundays excepted) after it shall have been presented to him, the Same shall be a Law, in like Manner as if he had signed it, unless the Congress by their Adjournment prevent its Return in which Case it shall not be a Law.

(3) Every Order, Resolution, or Vote, to Which the Concurrence of the Senate and House of Representatives may be necessary (except on a question of Adjournment) shall be presented to the President of the United States; and before the Same shall take Effect, shall be approved by him, or being disapproved by him, shall be repassed by two thirds of the Senate and House of Representatives, according to the Rules and Limitations prescribed in the Case of a Bill.

Section 8. (1) The Congress shall have Power To lay and collect Taxes, Duties, Imposts and Excises, to pay the Debts and provide for the common Defence and general

Welfare of the United States; but all Duties, Imposts and Excises shall be uniform throughout the United States;

(2) To borrow money on the credit of the United States;

(3) To regulate Commerce with foreign Nations, and among the several States, and with the Indian Tribes;

(4) To establish an uniform Rule of Naturalization, and uniform Laws on the subject of Bankruptcies throughout the United States;

(5) To coin money, regulate the Value thereof, and of foreign Coin, and fix the Standard of Weights and Measures;

(6) To provide for the Punishment of counterfeiting the Securities and current Coin of the United States;

(7) To Establish Post Offices and Post Roads;

(8) To promote the Progress of Science and useful Arts, by securing for limited Times to Authors and Inventors the Exclusive Right to their respective Writings and Discoveries;

(9) To constitute Tribunals inferior to the supreme Court;

(10) To define and punish Piracies and Felonies committed on the high Seas, and Offenses against the Law of Nations;

(11) To declare War, grant Letters of Marque and Reprisal, and make Rules concerning Captures on Land and Water;

(12) To raise and support Armies, but no Appropriation of Money to that Use shall be for a longer Term than two Years;

(13) To provide and maintain a Navy;

(14) To make Rules for the Government and Regulation of the land and naval forces;

(15) To provide for calling forth the Militia to execute the Laws of the Union, suppress Insurrections and repel Invasions;

(16) To provide for organizing, arming, and disciplining the Militia, and for governing such Part of them as may be employed in the Service of the United States, reserving to the States respectively, the Appointment of the Officers, and the Authority of training the Militia according to the discipline prescribed by Congress;

(17) To exercise exclusive Legislation in all Cases whatsoever, over such District (not exceeding ten Miles square) as may, by Cession of particular States, and the Acceptance of Congress, become the Seat of the Government of the United States, and to exercise like Authority over all Places purchased by the Consent of the Legislature of the State in which the Same shall be, for the Erection of Forts, Magazines, Arsenals, dock-Yards, and other needful Buildings;—And

(18) To make all Laws which shall be necessary and proper for carrying into Execution the foregoing Powers, and all other Powers vested by this Constitution in the Government of the United States, or in any Department or Officer thereof.

Section 9. (1) The Migration or Importation of Such Persons as any of the States now existing shall think proper to admit, shall not be prohibited by the Congress prior to the Year one thousand eight hundred and eight, but a Tax or duty may be imposed on such Importation, not exceeding ten dollars for each person.

(2) The privilege of the Writ of Habeus Corpus shall not be suspended, unless when in Cases of Rebellion or Invasion the public Safety may require it.

(3) No Bill of Attainder or ex post facto Law shall be passed.

(4) No Capitation, or other direct, Tax shall be laid, unless in Proportion to the Census or Enumeration herein before directed to be taken.

(5) No Tax or Duty shall be laid on Articles exported from any State.

(6) No Preference shall be given by any Regulation of Commerce or Revenue to the Ports of one State over those of another; nor shall Vessels bound to, or from, one State be obliged to enter, clear, or pay Duties in another.

(7) No money shall be drawn from the Treasury, but in Consequence of Appropriations made by Law; and a regular Statement and Account of the Receipts and Expenditures of all public Money shall be published from time to time.

(8) No Title of Nobility shall be granted by the United States: And no Person holding any Office of Profit or Trust under them, shall, without the Consent of Congress, accept any present, Emolument, Office, or Title, of any kind whatever, from any King, Prince, or foreign State.

Section 10. (1) No State shall enter into any Treaty, Alliance, or Confederation; grant Letters of Marque and Reprisal; coin Money; emit Bills of Credit; make any Thing but gold and silver Coin a Tender in payment of Debts; pass any Bill of Attainder, ex post facto Law, or Law impairing the Obligation of Contracts, or grant any Title of Nobility.

(2) No State shall, without the Consent of the Congress, lay any Imposts or Duties on Imports or Exports, except what may be absolutely necessary for executing it's inspection laws: and the net Produce of all Duties and Imposts, laid by any State on Imports or Exports, shall be for the Use of the Treasury of the United States; and all such Laws shall be subject to the Revision and Controul of the Congress.

(3) No State shall, without the Consent of Congress, lay any Duty of Tonnage, keep Troops, or Ships of War in time of Peace, enter into any Agreement or Compact with another State, or with a foreign Power, or engage in War, unless actually invaded, or in such imminent Danger as will not Admit of Delay.

Article II

Section 1. (1) The executive Power shall be vested in a President of the United States of America. He shall hold his Office during the Term of four Years, and, together with the Vice President, chosen for the same Term, be elected, as follows:

(2) Each State shall appoint, in such Manner as the Legislature thereof may direct, a Number of Electors, equal to the whole Number of Senators and Representatives to which the State may be entitled in the Congress; but no Senator or Representative, or Person holding an Office of Trust or Profit under the United States, shall be appointed an Elector.

(3) The Electors shall meet in their respective States, and vote by Ballot for two Persons, of whom one at least shall not be an Inhabitant of the same State with themselves. And they shall make a List of all the Persons voted for, and of the Number of Votes for each; which List they shall sign and certify, and transmit sealed to the Seat of the Government of the United States, directed to the President of the Senate. The President of the Senate shall, in the Presence of the Senate and House of Representatives, open all the Certificates, and the Votes shall then be counted. The Person having the greatest Number of Votes shall be the President, if such a Number be a Majority of the whole Number of Electors appointed; and if there be more than one who have such Majority, and have an equal Number of Votes, then the House of Representatives shall immediately choose by Ballot one of them for President; and if no Person have a Majority, then from the five highest on the List the said House shall in like Manner choose the President. But in choosing the President, the Votes shall be taken by States the Representation from each State having one Vote; A quorum for this Purpose shall consist of a Member or Members from two thirds of the States, and a Majority of all the States shall be necessary to a Choice. In every Case, after the Choice of the President, the Person having the greater Number of Votes of the Electors shall be the Vice President. But if there should remain two or more who have equal Votes, the Senate shall choose from them by Ballot the Vice President.

(4) The Congress may determine the Time of choosing the Electors, and the Day on which they shall give their Votes; which Day shall be the same throughout the United States.

(5) No person except a natural born Citizen, or a Citizen of the United States, at the time of the Adoption of this Constitution, shall be eligible to the Office of President; neither shall any Person be eligible to that Office who shall not have attained to the Age of thirty-five Years, and been fourteen Years a Resident within the United States.

(6) In case of the removal of the President from Office, or of his Death, Resignation or Inability to discharge the Powers and Duties of the said Office, the Same shall devolve on the Vice President , and the Congress may by Law provide for the Case of Removal, Death, Resignation or Inability, both of the President and Vice President, declaring what Officer shall then act as President, and such Officer shall act accordingly, until the Disability be removed, or a President shall be elected.

(7) The President shall, at stated Times, receive for his Services, a Compensation, which shall neither be increased nor diminished during the period for which he shall have been elected, and he shall not receive within that Period any other Emolument from the United States, or any of them.

(8) Before he enter on the Execution of his Office, he shall take the following Oath or Affirmation: "I do solemnly swear (or affirm) that I will faithfully execute the Office of President of the United States, and will to the best of my Ability, preserve, protect, and defend the Constitution of the United States."

Section 2. (1) The President shall be Commander in Chief of the Army and Navy of the United States, and of the militia of the several States, when called into the actual Service of the United States; he may require the Opinion, in writing, of the principal Officer in each of the Executive Departments, upon any Subject relating to the Duties of their respective Offices, and he shall have Power to grant Reprieves and Pardons for Offenses against the United States, except in Cases of Impeachment.

(2) He shall have Power, by and with the Advice and Consent of the Senate to make Treaties, provided two thirds of the Senators present concur; and he shall nominate, and by and with the Advice and Consent of the Senate, shall appoint Ambassadors, other public Ministers and Consuls, Judges of the supreme Court, and all other Officers of the United States, whose Appointments are not herein otherwise provided for, and which shall be established by Law; but the Congress may by Law vest the Appointment of such inferior Officers, as they think proper, in the President alone, in the Courts of Law, or in the Heads of Departments.

(3) The President shall have power to fill up Vacancies that may happen during the Recess of the Senate, by granting Commissions which shall expire at the End of their next Session.

Section 3. He shall from time to time give to the Congress Information of the State of the Union, and recommend to their Consideration such Measures as he shall judge necessary and expedient; he may, on extraordinary Occasions, convene both Houses, or either of them, and in Case of Disagreement between them, with Respect to the Time of Adjournment, he may adjourn them to such Time as he shall think proper; he shall receive Ambassadors and other public Ministers; he shall take Care that the Laws be faithfully executed, and shall Commission all the Officers of the United states.

Section 4. The President, Vice President and all civil Officers of the United States, shall be removed from Office on Impeachment for, and Conviction of, Treason, Bribery, or other high Crimes and Misdemeanors.

Article III

Section 1. The judicial Power of the United States, shall be vested in one supreme Court, and in such inferior Courts as the Congress may from time to time ordain and establish. The Judges, both of the supreme and inferior Courts, shall hold their offices during good Behaviour, and shall, at stated Times, receive for their Services a Compensation, which shall not be diminished during their Continuance in Office.

Section 2. (1) The judicial Power shall extend to all Cases, in Law and Equity, arising under this Constitution, the Laws of the United States, and Treaties made, or which shall be made, under their Authority;—to all Cases affecting Ambassadors, other public Ministers and Consuls;—to Controversies to which the United States shall be a Party;—to Controversies between two or more States;—between a State and Citizens of another State;—between Citizens of different States;—between Citizens of the same State claiming Lands under the Grants of different States, and between a State, or the Citizens thereof, and foreign States, Citizens or Subjects.

(2) In all Cases affecting Ambassadors, other public Ministers and Consuls, and those in which a State shall be a Party, the supreme Court shall have original Jurisdiction. In all the other Cases before mentioned, the supreme Court shall have appellate Jurisdiction, both as to Law and Fact, with such Exceptions, and under such Regulations as the Congress shall make.

(3) The trial of all Crimes, except in Cases of Impeachment, shall be by Jury; and such Trial shall be held in the State where the said Crimes shall have been committed; but when not committed within any State, the Trial shall be at such Place or Places as the Congress may by Law have directed.

Section 3. (1) Treason against the United States, shall consist only in levying War against them, or, in adhering to their Enemies, giving them Aid and Comfort. No Person shall be convicted of Treason unless on the Testimony of two Witnesses to the same overt Act, or on Confession in open Court.

(2) The Congress shall have Power to declare the Punishment of Treason, but no Attainder of Treason shall work Corruption of Blood, or Forfeiture except during the Life of the Person attainted.

Article IV

Section 1. Full Faith and Credit shall be given in each State to the public Acts, Records, and judicial Proceedings of every other State. And the Congress may by general Laws prescribe the Manner in which such Acts, Records and Proceedings shall be proven, and the Effect thereof.

Section 2. (1) The Citizens of each State shall be entitled to all Privileges and Immunities of Citizens in the several States.

(2) A Person charged in any State with Treason, Felony, or other Crime, who shall flee from Justice, and be found in another State, shall on demand of the executive Authority of the State from which he fled, be delivered up, to be removed to the State having Jurisdiction of the Crime.

(3) No Person held to Service or Labour in one State, under the Laws thereof, escaping into another, shall, in Consequence of any Law or Regulation therein, be discharged from such Service or Labour, but shall be delivered up on Claim of the Party to whom such Service or Labour may be due.

Section 3. (1) New States may be admitted by the Congress into this Union; but no new State shall be formed or erected within the Jurisdiction of any other State; nor any State be formed by the Junction of two or more States, or Parts of States, without the Consent of the Legislatures of the States concerned as well as of the Congress.

(2) The Congress shall have Power to dispose of and make all needful Rules and Regulations respecting the Territory or other Property belonging to the United States; and nothing in this Constitution shall be so construed as to Prejudice any Claims of the United States, or of any particular State.

Section 4. The United States shall guarantee to every State in this Union a Republican Form of Government, and shall protect each of them against Invasion; and on Application of the Legislature, or of the Executive (when the Legislature cannot be convened) against domestic Violence.

Article V

The Congress, whenever two thirds of both Houses shall deem it necessary, shall propose Amendments to this Constitution, or, on the Application of the Legislatures of two thirds of the several States, shall call a Convention for proposing Amendments, which, in either Case, shall be valid to all Intents and Purposes, as part of this Constitution, when ratified by the Legislatures of three fourths of the several States, or by Conventions in three fourths thereof, as the one or the other Mode of Ratification may be proposed by the Congress; Provided that no Amendment which may be made prior to the Year One thousand eight hundred and eight shall in any Manner affect the first and fourth Clauses in the Ninth Section of the first Article; and that no State, without its Consent, shall be deprived of its equal Suffrage in the Senate.

Article VI

(1) All Debts contracted and Engagements entered into, before the Adoption of this Constitution shall be as valid against the United States under this Constitution, as under the Confederation.

(2) This Constitution, and the Laws of the United States which shall be made in Pursuance thereof; and all Treaties made, or which shall be made, under the Authority of the United States, shall be the supreme Law of the Land; and the Judges in every State shall be bound

thereby, any Thing in the Constitution or Laws of any State to the Contrary notwithstanding.

(3) The Senators and Representatives before mentioned, and the Members of the several State Legislatures, and all executive and judicial Officers, both of the United States and of the several States, shall be bound by Oath or Affirmation, to support this Constitution, but no religious Test shall ever be required as a Qualification to any Office or public Trust under the United States.

Article VII

The Ratification of the Conventions of nine States shall be sufficient for the Establishment of this Constitution between the States so ratifying the Same.

AMENDMENTS

Amendent I (1791)

Congress shall make no law respecting an establishment of religion, or prohibiting the free exercise thereof; or abridging the freedom of speech, or of the press; or the right of the people peaceably to assemble, and to petition the Government for a redress of grievances.

Amendment II (1791)

A well regulated Militia, being necessary to the security of a free State, the right of the people to keep and bear Arms, shall not be infringed.

Amendment III (1791)

No soldier shall, in time of peace be quartered in any house, without the consent of the Owner, nor in time of war, but in a manner to be prescribed by law.

Amendment IV (1791)

The right of the people to be secure in their persons, houses, papers, and effects, against unreasonable searches and seizures, shall not be violated, and no Warrants shall issue, but upon probable cause, supported by Oath or affirmation, and particularly describing the place to be searched, and the persons or things to be seized.

Amendment V (1791)

No person shall be held to answer for a capital, or otherwise infamous crime, unless on a presentment or indictment of a Grand Jury, except in cases arising in the land

or naval forces, or in the Militia, when in actual service in time of War or public danger; nor shall any person be subject for the same offence to be twice put in jeopardy of life or limb; nor shall be compelled in any criminal case to be a witness against himself, nor be deprived of life, liberty, or property, without due process of law; nor shall private property be taken for public use, without just compensation.

Amendment VI (1791)

In all criminal prosecutions, the accused shall enjoy the right to a speedy and public trail, by an impartial jury of the State and district wherein the crime shall have been committed, which district shall have been previously ascertained by law, and to be informed of the nature and cause of the accusation; to be confronted with the witnesses against him; to have compulsory process for obtaining witnesses in his favor, and to have the Assistance of Counsel for his defence.

Amendment VII (1791)

In Suits at common law, where the value in controversy shall exceed twenty dollars, the right of trial by jury shall be preserved, and no fact tried by jury, shall be otherwise re-examined in any Court of the United States, than according to the rules of the common law.

Amendment VIII (1791)

Excessive bail shall not be required, nor excessive fines imposed, nor cruel and unusual punishments inflicted.

Amendment IX (1791)

The enumeration in the Constitution, of certain rights, shall not be construed to deny or disparage others retained by the people.

Amendment X (1791)

The powers not delegated to the United States by the Constitution, nor prohibited by it to the States, are reserved to the States respectively, or to the people.

Amendment XI (1798)

The Judicial power of the United States shall not be construed to extend to any suit in law or equity, commenced or prosecuted against one of the United States by Citizens of another State, or by Citizens or Subjects of any Foreign State.

Amendment XII (1804)

The Electors shall meet in their respective states and vote by ballot for President and Vice-President, one of whom, at least, shall not be an inhabitant of the same state with themselves; they shall name in their ballots the person voted for as President, and in distinct ballots the person voted for as Vice-President, and they shall make distinct lists of all persons voted for as President, and of all persons voted for as Vice-President, and of the number of votes for each, which lists they shall sign and certify, and transmit sealed to the seat of government of the United States, directed to the President of the Senate;—the President of the Senate shall, in the presence of the Senate and House of Representatives, open all the certificates and the votes shall then be counted;—The person having the greatest number of votes for President, shall be the President, if such number be a majority of the whole number of Electors appointed; and if no person have such majority, then from the persons having the highest numbers not exceeding three on the list of those voted for as President, the House of Representatives shall choose immediately, by ballot, the President. But in choosing the President, the votes shall be taken by states, the representation from each state having one vote; a quorum for this purpose shall consist of a member or members from two-thirds of the states, and a majority of all the states shall be necessary to a choice. And if the House of Representatives shall not choose a President whenever the right of choice shall devolve upon them before the fourth day of March next following, the Vice-President shall act as President, as in the case of the death or other constitutional disability of the President.—The person having the greatest number of votes as Vice-President, shall be the Vice-President, if such number be a majority of the whole number of Electors appointed, and if no person have a majority, then from the two highest numbers on the list, the Senate shall choose the Vice-President; a quorum for the purpose shall consist of two thirds of the whole number of Senators, and a majority of the whole number shall be necessary to a choice. But no person constitutionally ineligible to the office of President shall be eligible to that of Vice President of the United States.

Amendment XIII (1865)

Section 1. Neither slavery nor involuntary servitude, except as punishment for a crime whereof the party shall have been duly convicted, shall exist within the United States, or any place subject to their jurisdiction.

Section 2. Congress shall have power to enforce this article by appropriate legislation.

Amendment XIV (1868)

Section 1. All persons born or naturalized in the United States, and subject to the jurisdiction thereof, are citizens of the United States and of the State wherein they reside. No State shall make or enforce any law which shall abridge the privileges or immunities of citizens of the United States; nor shall any State deprive any person of life, liberty, or property, without due process of law; nor deny to any person within its jurisdiction the equal protection of the laws.

Section 2. Representatives shall be apportioned among the several States according to their respective numbers, counting the whole number of persons in each state, excluding Indians not taxed. But when the right to vote at any election for the choice of electors for President and Vice President of the United States, Representatives in Congress, the Executive and Judicial officers of a State, or the members of the Legislature thereof, is denied to any of the male inhabitants of such State, being twenty-one years of age, and citizens of the United States, or in any way abridged, except for participation in rebellion, or other crime, the basis of representation therein shall be reduced in the proportion which the number of such male citizens shall bear to the whole number of male citizens twenty-one years of age in such State.

Section 3. No person shall be a Senator or Representative in Congress, or elector of President and Vice President, or hold any office, civil or military, under the United States, or under any State, who having previously taken an oath, as a member of Congress, or as an officer of the United States, or as a member of any State legislature, or as an executive or judicial officer of any State, to support the Constitution of the United States, shall have engaged in insurrection or rebellion against the same, or given aid or comfort to the enemies thereof. But Congress may by a vote of two-thirds of each House, remove such disability.

Section 4. The validity of the public debt of the United States, authorized by law, including debts incurred for payment of pensions and bounties for services in suppressing insurrection or rebellion, shall not be questioned. But neither the United States nor any State shall assume or pay debt or obligation incurred in aid of insurrection or rebellion against the United States, or any claim for the loss or emancipation of any slave; but all such debts, obligations and claims shall be held illegal and void.

Section 5. The Congress shall have power to enforce, by appropriate legislation, the provisions of this article.

Amendment XV (1870)

Section 1. The right of citizens of the United States to vote shall not be denied or abridged by the United States or by any State on account of race, color, or previous condition of servitude.

Section 2. The Congress shall have power to enforce this article by appropriate legislation.

Amendment XVI (1913)

The Congress shall have power to lay and collect taxes on incomes, from whatever source derived, without apportionment among the several States, and without regard to any census or enumeration.

Amendment XVII (1913)

(1) The Senate of the United States shall be composed of two Senators from each State, elected by the people thereof, for six years; and each Senator shall have one vote. The electors in each State shall have the qualifications requisite for electors of the most numerous branch of the State legislatures.

(2) When vacancies happen in the representation of any State in the Senate, the executive authority of such State shall issue writs of election to fill such vacancies: Provided, That the legislature of any State may empower the executive thereof to make temporary appointments until the people fill the vacancies by election as the legislature may direct.

(3) This amendment shall not be so construed as to affect the election or term of any Senator chosen before it becomes valid as part of the Constitution.

Amendment XVIII (1919)

Section 1. After one year from the ratification of this article, the manufacture, sale, or transportation of intoxicating liquors within, the importation thereof into, or the exportation thereof from the United States and all territory subject to the jurisdiction thereof for beverage purposes is hereby prohibited.

Section 2. The Congress and the several States shall have concurrent power to enforce this article by appropriate legislation.

Section 3. This article shall be inoperative unless it shall have been ratified as an amendment to the Constitution by the legislatures of the several States, as provided in the Constitution, within seven years from the date of the submission hereof to the States by the Congress.

Amendment XIX (1920)

[1] The right of citizens of the United States to vote shall not be denied or abridged by the United States or any State on account of sex.

[2] Congress shall have power to enforce this article by appropriate legislation.

Amendment XX (1933)

Section 1. The terms of the President and Vice President shall end at noon on the 20th day of January, and the terms of Senators and Representatives at noon on the 3d day of January, of the years in which such terms would have ended if this article had not been ratified; and the terms of their successors shall then begin.

Section 2. The Congress shall assemble at least once in every year, and such meeting shall begin at noon on the 3d day of January, unless they shall by law appoint a different day.

Section 3. If, at the time fixed for the beginning of the term of the President, the President elect shall have died, the Vice President elect shall become President. If the President shall not have been chosen before the time fixed for the beginning of this term, or if the President elect shall have failed to qualify, then the Vice President elect shall act as President until a President shall have qualified; and the Congress may by law provide for the case wherein neither a President elect nor a Vice President elect shall have qualified, declaring who shall then act as President, or the manner in which one who is to act shall be selected, and such person shall act accordingly until a President or Vice President shall have qualified.

Section 4. The Congress may by law provide for the case of the death of any of the persons from whom the House of Representatives may choose a President whenever the right of choice shall have devolved upon them, and for the case of the death of any of the persons from whom the Senate may choose a Vice President whenever the right of choice shall have devolved upon them.

Section 5. Sections 1 and 2 shall take effect on the 15th day of October following the ratification of this article.

Section 6. This article shall be inoperative unless it shall have been ratified as an amendment to the Constitution by the legislatures of three-fourths of the several States within seven years from the date of its submission.

Amendment XXI (1933)

Section 1. The eighteenth article of amendment to the Constitution of the United States is hereby repealed.

Section 2. The transportation or importation into any State, Territory, or possession of the United States for delivery or use therein of intoxicating liquors, in violation of the laws thereof, is hereby prohibited.

Section 3. This article shall be inoperative unless it shall have been ratified as an amendment to the Constitution by conventions in the several States, as provided in the Constitution, within seven years from the date of the submission hereof to the States by the Congress.

Amendment XXII (1951)

Section 1. No person shall be elected to the office of the President more than twice, and no person who has held the office of President, or acted as President, for more than two years of a term to which some other person was elected President shall be elected to the office of President more than once. But this Article shall not apply to any person holding the office of President when this Article was proposed by the Congress, and shall not prevent any person who may be holding the office of President, or acting as President, during the term within which this Article becomes operative from holding the office of President or acting as President during the remainder of such term.

Section 2. This article shall be inoperative unless it shall have been ratified as an amendment to the Constitution by the legislatures of three-fourths of the several States within seven years from the date of its submission to the States by the Congress.

Amendment XXIII (1961)

Section 1. The District constituting the seat of Government of the United States shall appoint in such manner as the Congress may direct:

A number of electors of President and Vice President equal to the whole number of Senators and Representatives in Congress to which the District would be entitled if it were a State, but in no event more than the least populous state; they shall be in addition to those appointed by the states, but they shall be considered, for the purposes of the election of President and Vice President, to be electors appointed by a state; and they shall meet in the District and perform such duties as provided by the twelfth article of amendment.

Section 2. The Congress shall have power to enforce this article by appropriate legislation.

Amendment XXIV (1964)

Section 1. The right of citizens of the United States to vote in any primary or other election for President or Vice President, for electors for President or Vice President, or for Senator or Representatives in Congress, shall not be denied or abridged by the United States, or any State by reason of failure to pay any poll tax or other tax.

Section 2. The Congress shall have power to enforce this article by appropriate legislation.

Amendment XXV (1967)

Section 1. In case of the removal of the President from office or of his death or resignation, the Vice President shall become President.

Section 2. Whenever there is a vacancy in the office of the Vice President, the President shall nominate a Vice President who shall take office upon confirmation by a majority vote of both Houses of Congress.

Section 3. Whenever the President transmits to the President pro tempore of the Senate and the Speaker of the House of Representatives his written declaration that he is unable to discharge the power and duties of his office, and until he transmits to them a written declaration to the contrary, such powers and duties shall be discharged by the Vice President as Acting President.

Section 4. Whenever the Vice President and a majority of either the principal officers of the executive departments or of such other body as Congress may by law provide, transmit to the President pro tempore of the Senate and the House of Representatives their written declaration that the President is unable to discharge the powers and duties of his office, the Vice President shall immediately assume the powers and duties of the office as Acting President.

Thereafter, when the President transmits to the President pro tempore of the Senate and the Speaker of the House of Representatives his written declaration that no inability exists, he shall resume the power and duties of his office unless the Vice President and a majority of either the principal officers of the executive department or of such other body as Congress may by law provide, transmit within four days to the President pro tempore of the Senate and the Speaker of the House of Representatives their written declaration and the President is unable to discharge the powers and duties of his office. Thereupon Congress shall decide the issue, assembling within forty-eight hours for that purpose if not in session. If the Congress, within twenty-one days after receipt of the latter written declaration, or, if Congress is not in session, within twenty-one days after Congress is required to assemble, determines by two-thirds vote of both Houses that the President is unable to discharge the powers and duties of his office, the Vice President shall continue to discharge the same as Acting President; otherwise the President shall resume the powers and duties of his office.

Amendment XXVI (1971)

Section 1. The right of citizens of the United States, who are eighteen years of age or older, to vote shall not be denied or abridged by the United States or by any State on account of age.

Section 2. The Congress shall have power to enforce this article by appropriate legislation.

Proposed Consitutional Amendment*

Section 1. For purposes of representation in Congress, election of the President and Vice President, and Article V of this Constitution, the District constituting the seat of government of the United States shall be treated as though it were a State.

Section 2. The exercise of the rights and powers conferred under this article shall be by the people of the District constituting the seat of government and shall be as provided by Congress.

Section 3. The twenty-third Amendment to the Constitution is hereby repealed.

Section 4. This article shall be inoperative, unless it shall have been ratified as an amendment to the Constitution by the legislatures of three-fourths of the several States within seven years from the date of its submission.

Proposed Constitutional Amendment (The Equal Rights Amendment):

Section 1. Equality of rights under the law shall not be denied or abridged by United States or by any state on account of sex.

Section 2. The Congress shall have the power to enforce by appropriate legislation the provisions of this article.

Section 3. This amendment shall take effect two years after the date of ratification.

---

*Congress submitted this proposed amendment to the states for ratification in August of 1978.

Appendix C
Selected Statutes

Note to Students: The following important federal statutes have been excerpted and edited as an aid to study. Often important portions of these laws have been omitted because of lack of relevance to the matters studied in the text.

FEDERAL JURISDICTION (28 U.S. CODE)

Section 1331. Federal Question Jurisdiction. The district courts shall have original jurisdiction of all civil actions arising under the Constitution, laws, or treaties of the United States.

Section 1332. Diversity of Citizenship; Amount in Controversy; Costs.

(a) The district courts shall have original jurisdiction of all civil actions where the matter in controversy exceeds the sum or value of $10,000, exclusive of interest and costs, and is between—

(1) citizens of different States;

(2) citizens of a State and citizens or subjects of a foreign state;

(3) citizens of different States and in which citizens or subjects of a foreign state are additional parties; and

(4) a foreign state . . . as plaintiff and citizens of a State or of different States.

(b) . . . where the plaintiff who files the case originally in the Federal courts is finally adjudged to be entitled to recover less than the sum or value of $10,000, . . . the district court may deny costs to the plaintiff and, in addition, may impose costs on the plaintiff.

. . . .

THE ADMINISTRATIVE PROCEDURE ACT

Section 551. Definitions. For the purpose of this subchapter—

(1) "agency" means each authority of the Government of the United States, whether or not it is within or subject to review by another agency, but does not include (A) the Congress; (B) the courts of the United States; (C) the governments of the territories or possessions of the United States. . . .

(4) "rule" means the whole or a part of an agency statement of general or particular applicability and future effect designed to implement, interpret, or prescribe law or policy or describing the organization, procedure, or practice requirements of an agency and includes the approval or prescription for the future of rates, wages, corporate or financial structures or reorganizations thereof, prices, facilities, appliances, services or allowances therefor or of valuations, costs, or accounting, or practices bearing on any of the foregoing;

(5) "rule making" means agency process for formulating, amending, or repealing a rule;

(6) "order" means the whole or a part of a final disposition, whether affirmative, negative, injunctive, or declaratory in form, of an agency in a matter other than rule making but including licensing;

(7) "adjudication" means agency process for the formulation of an order;

(8) "license" includes the whole or a part of an agency permit, certificate, approval, registration, charter, membership, statutory exemption, or other form of permission;

(9) "licensing" includes agency process respecting the grant, renewal, denial, revocation, suspension, annulment, withdrawal, limitation, amendment, modification, or conditioning of a license;

. . . .

(12) "agency proceeding" means an agency process as defined in paragraphs (5), (7), and (9) of this section;

. . . .

Section 552. Public Information; Agency Rules, Opinions, Orders, Records and Proceedings (The Freedom of Information Act)

(a) Each agency shall make available to the public information as follows:

(1) Each agency shall separately state and currently publish in the Federal Register for the guidance of the public—

(A) descriptions of its central and field organization and the established places at which, the employees . . . from whom, and the methods whereby, the public may obtain information, make submittals or requests, or obtain decisions;

(B) statements of the general course and method by which its functions are channelled and determined, including the nature and requirements of all formal and informal procedures available;

(C) rules of procedure, descriptions of forms . . . and instructions. . . .

(D) substantive rules of general applicability . . . and statements of general policy or interpretations of general applicability. . . .

(E) each amendment, revision or repeal of the foregoing.

Except to the extent that a person has actual and timely notice of the terms thereof, a person may not in any manner be required to resort to, or be adversely affected by, a matter required to be published in the Federal Register and not so published. . . .

(2) Each agency, in accordance with published rules, shall make available for public inspection and copying—

(A) final opinions . . . made in the adjudication of cases;

(B) those statements of policy and interpretations which have been adopted . . . and not published in the Federal Register; and

(C) administrative staff manuals and instructions . . . that affect a member of the public;

unless the materials are promptly published and copies offered for sale. To the extent required to prevent a clearly unwarranted invasion of personal privacy, an agency may delete identifying details when it makes available or publishes an opinion, statement of policy, interpretation, or staff manual or instruction. . . .

. . . .

(4) (B) On complaint, the district court of the United States . . . has jurisdiction to enjoin the agency from withholding agency records and to order the production of any agency records improperly withheld from the complainant. In such a case the court shall determine the matter de novo, and may examine the contents of such agency records in camera to determine whether such records or any part thereof shall be withheld under any of the exemptions set forth in subsection (b) of this section, and the burden is on the agency to sustain the action.

. . . .

(6) (A) Each agency, upon any request for records made under paragraph (1), (2), or (3) of this subsection, shall—

(i) determine within ten days . . . after the receipt of any such request whether to comply with such request and shall immediately notify the person making such request of such determination and the reasons therefor, and of the right of such person to appeal to the head of the agency any adverse determination; and

(ii) make a determination with respect to any appeal within twenty days. . . .

(b) This section does not apply to matters that are—

(1) (A) specifically authorized under criteria established by an Executive order to be kept secret in the interest of national defense or foreign policy and (B) are in fact properly classified pursuant to such Executive order;

(2) related solely to the internal personnel rules and practices of an agency;

(3) specifically exempted from disclosure by statute. . . .

(4) trade secrets and commercial or financial information obtained from a person and privileged or confidential;

(5) inter-agency or intra-agency memorandums or letters which would not be available by law to a party other than an agency in litigation with the agency;

(6) personnel and medical files and similar files the disclosure of which would constitute a clearly unwarranted invasion of personal privacy;

(7) investigatory records compiled for law enforcement purposes. . . .

(8) contained in or related to examination, operating or condition reports prepared by, on behalf of, or for the use of an agency responsible for the regulation or supervision of financial institutions; or

(9) geological and geophysical information and data, including maps, concerning wells.

. . .

552(b) Open Meetings. Members shall not jointly conduct or dispose of agency business other than in accordance with this section. Except as provided in subsection (c), every portion of every meeting of an agency shall be open to public observation.

(c) Except in a case where the agency finds that the public interest requires otherwise, the second sentence of subsection (b) shall not apply to any portion of an agency meeting, and the requirements of subsections (d) and (e) shall not apply to any information pertaining to such meeting otherwise required by this section to be disclosed to the public, where the agency properly determines that such portion or portions of its meeting or the disclosure of such information is likely to—

(1) disclose matters that are (A) specifically authorized under criteria established by an Executive order to be kept secret in the interests of national defense or foreign policy and (B) in fact properly classified pursuant to such Executive order;

(2) relate solely to the internal personnel rules and practices of an agency;

(3) disclose matters specifically exempted from disclosure by statute. . . .

(4) disclose trade secrets and commercial or financial information obtained from a person and privileged or confidential;

(5) involve accusing any person of a crime, or formally censuring any person;

(6) disclose information of a personal nature where disclosure would constitute a clearly unwarranted invasion of personal privacy;

(7) disclose investigatory records compiled for law enforcement purposes. . . .

(8) disclose information contained in or related to examination, operating, or condition reports prepared by, on behalf of, or for the use of an agency responsible for the regulation or supervision of financial institutions;

(9) disclose information the premature disclosure of which would—

(A) in the case of an agency which regulates currencies, securities, commodities, or financial institutions, be likely to (i) lead to significant financial speculation . . . or (ii) significantly endanger the stability of any financial institution; or

(B) in the case of any agency, be likely to significantly frustrate implementation of a proposed agency action.

. . . .

(1) specifically concern the agency's issuance of a subpoena, or the agency's participation in a civil action. . . .

(d) (1) Action under subsection (c) shall be taken only when a majority of the entire membership of the agency . . . votes to take such action. . . .

(e) (1) In the case of each meeting, the agency shall make public announcement, at least one week before the meeting, of the time, place, and subject matter of the meeting, whether it is to be open or closed to the public. . . . Such announcement shall be made unless a majority of the members of the agency determines . . . that agency business requires that such meeting be called at an earlier date, in which case the agency shall make public announcement . . . at the earliest practicable time.

. . . .

Section 553. Rulemaking. (a) This section applies, according to the provisions thereof, except to the extent that there is involved—

(1) a military or foreign affairs function of the United States; or

(2) a matter relating to agency management or personnel or to public property, loans, grants, benefits or contracts.

(b) General notice of proposed rule making shall be published in the Federal Register, unless persons subject thereto are named and either personally served or otherwise have actual notice thereof in accordance with law. The notice shall include—

(1) a statement of the time, place, and nature of public rule making proceedings;

(2) reference to the legal authority under which the rule is proposed; and

(3) either the terms or substance of the proposed rule or a description of the subjects and issues involved.
Except when notice or hearing is required by statute, this subsection does not apply—

(A) to interpretative rules, general statements of policy, or rules of agency organization, procedure, or practice; or

(B) when the agency for good cause finds . . . that notice and public procedure thereon are impracticable, unnecessary, or contrary to the public interest.

(c) After notice required by this section, the agency shall give interested persons an opportunity to participate in the rule making through submission of written data, views, or arguments with or without opportunity for oral presentation. After consideration of the relevant matter presented, the agency shall incorporate in the rules a concise general statement of their basis and purpose.

(d) The required publication or service of a substantive rule shall be made not less than 30 days before its effective date. . . .

(e) Each agency shall give an interested person the right to petition for the issuance, amendment, or repeal of a rule.

Section 554. Adjudication. (a) This section applies, according to the provisions thereof, in every case of adjudication required by statute to be determined on the record after opportunity for an agency hearing, except to the extent that there is involved—

(1) a matter subject to a subsequent trial of the law and the facts de novo in a court;

(2) the selection or tenure of an employee, except an administrative law judge . . .

(3) proceeding in which decisions rest solely on inspections, tests, or elections;

(4) the conduct of military or foreign affairs functions;

(5) cases in which an agency is acting as an agent for a court; or

(6) the certification of worker representatives.

(b) Persons entitled to notice of an agency hearing shall be timely informed of—

(1) the time, place, and nature of the hearing;

(2) the legal authority and jurisdiction under which the hearing is to be held; and

(3) the matters of fact and law asserted.

. . . .

(c) The agency shall give all interested parties the opportunity for—

(1) the submission and consideration of facts, arguments, offers of settlement, or proposals of adjustment when time, the nature of the proceeding, and the public interest permit; and

(2) to the extent that the parties are unable so to determine a controversy by consent, hearing and decision on notice. . . .

. . . .

Section 702. Right of Review. A person suffering legal wrong because of agency action, or adversely affected or aggrieved by agency action within the meaning of a relevant statute, is entitled to judicial review thereof. An action in a court of the United States seeking relief other than money damages and stating a claim that an agency or an officer or employee thereof acted or failed to act in an official capacity or under color of legal authority shall not be dismissed nor relief therein be denied on the ground that it is against the United States or that the United States is an indispensable party. The United States may be named as a defendant in any such action, and a judgment or decree may be entered against the United States: Provided, That any mandatory or injunctive decree shall specify the Federal officer or officers (by name or title), and their successors in office, personally responsible for compliance. Nothing herein (1) affects other limitations on judicial review or the power or duty of the court to dismiss any action or deny relief on any other appropriate legal or equitable ground; or (2) confers authority to grant relief if any other statute that grants consent to suit expressly or impliedly forbids the relief which is sought.

. . . .

Section 704. Actions Reviewable. Agency action made reviewable by statute and final agency action for which there is no other adequate remedy in a court are subject to judicial review. A preliminary, procedural, or intermediate agency action or ruling not directly reviewable is subject to review on the review of the final agency action. Except as otherwise expressly required by statute, agency action otherwise final is final for the purposes of this section whether or not there has been presented or determined an application for a declaratory order, for any form of reconsideration, or, unless the agency otherwise requires by rule and provides that the action meanwhile is inoperative, for an appeal to superior agency authority.

Section 705. Relief Pending Review. When an agency finds that justice so requires, it may postpone the effective date of action taken by it, pending judicial review. On such conditions as may be required and to the extent necessary to prevent irreparable injury, the reviewing court, including the court to which a case may be taken on appeal from or on application for certiorari or other writ to a reviewing court, may issue all necessary and appropriate process to postpone the effective date of an agency action or to preserve status or rights pending conclusion of the review proceedings.

Section 706. Scope of Review. To the extent necessary to decision and when presented, the reviewing court shall decide all relevant questions of law, interpret constitutional and statutory provisions, and determine the meaning or applicability of the terms of an agency action. The reviewing court shall—

(1) compel agency action unlawfully withheld or unreasonably delayed; and

(2) hold unlawful and set aside agency action, findings, and conclusions found to be—

(A) arbitrary, capricious, an abuse of discretion, or otherwise not in accordance with law;

(B) contrary to constitutional right, power, privilege, or immunity;

(C) in excess of statutory jurisdiction, authority, or limitations, or short of statutory right;

(D) without observance of procedure required by law;

(E) unsupported by substantial evidence. . . .

(F) unwarranted by the facts to the extent that the facts are subject to trial de novo by the reviewing court.

In making the foregoing determinations, the court shall review the whole record or those parts of it cited by a party, and due account shall be taken of the rule of prejudicial error.

THE FEDERAL ANTITRUST LAWS

The Sherman Antitrust Act (July 2, 1890, as amended)

Section 1. Every contract, combination in the form of trust or otherwise, or conspiracy, in restraint of trade or commerce among the several States, or with foreign nations, is hereby declared to be illegal. Every person who shall make any such contract or engage in any such combination or conspiracy shall be deemed guilty of a felony, and, on conviction thereof, shall be punished by fine not exceeding one million dollars if a corporation, or, if any other person, one hundred thousand dollars or by imprisonment not exceeding three years, or by both said punishments in the discretion of the court.

Section 2. Every person who shall monopolize, or attempt to monopolize, or conspire with any other person or persons, to monopolize any part of the trade or commerce among the several States, or with foreign nations, shall be deemed guilty of a felony, and, on conviction thereof, shall be punished by fine not exceeding one million dollars if a corporation, or, if any other person, one hundred thousand dollars or by imprisonment not exceeding three years, or by both said punishments, in the discretion of the court.

The Clayton Act as Amended by the Robinson-Patman Act (Oct. 15, 1914, amended June 19, 1936)

Section 2. This section is also known as the Robinson-Patman amendment to Section 2 of the Clayton Act. (a) That it shall be unlawful for any person engaged in commerce, in the course of such commerce, either directly or indirectly, to discriminate in price between different purchasers of commodities of like grade and quality, where such ... commodities are sold for use, consumption, or resale within the United States or any Territory thereof ... and where the effect of such discrimination may be substantially to lessen competition or tend to create a monopoly in any line of commerce, or to injure, destroy, or prevent competition with any person who either grants or knowingly receives the benefit of such discrimination, or with customers of either of them: Provided, That nothing herein contained shall prevent differentials which make only due allowance for differences in the cost of manufacture, sale, or delivery resulting from the differing methods or quantities in which such commodities are to such purchasers sold or delivered: Provided, however, That the Federal Trade Commission may, after due investigation and hearing ... fix and establish quantity limits, ... as to particular commodities or classes of commodities, where it finds that available purchasers in greater quantities are so few as to render differentials on account thereof unjustly discriminatory or promotive of monopoly in any line of commerce; and the foregoing shall then not be construed to permit differentials based on differences in quantities greater than those so fixed and established: And provided further, That nothing herein contained shall prevent persons engaged in selling goods, wares, or merchandise in commerce from selecting their own customers in *bona fide* transactions and not in restraint of trade: And provided further, That nothing herein contained shall prevent price changes from time to time where in response to changing conditions affecting the market for or the marketability of the goods concerned, such as but not limited to actual or imminent deterioration of perishable goods, obsolescence of seasonal goods, distress sales under court process, or sales in good faith in discontinuance of business in the goods concerned.

(b) Upon proof being made, at any hearing on a complaint under this section, that there has been discrimination in price or services or facilities furnished, the burden of rebutting the *prima facie* case thus made by showing justification shall be upon the person charged with a violation of this section, and unless justification shall be affirmatively shown, the Commission is authorized to issue an order terminating the discrimination: Provided, however, That nothing herein contained shall prevent a seller rebutting the *prima facie* case thus made by showing that his lower price or the furnishing of services or facilities to any purchaser or purchasers was made in good faith to meet an equally low price of a competitor, or the services or facilities furnished by a competitor.

(c) That it shall be unlawful for any person engaged in commerce, in the course of such commerce, to pay or grant, or to receive or accept, anything of value as a commission, brokerage, or other compensation, or any allowance or discount in lieu thereof, except for services rendered in connection with the sale of purchase of goods, wares, or merchandise, either to the other party to such transactions or to an agent, representative, or other intermediary therein where such intermediary is acting in fact for or in behalf, or is subject to the direct or indirect control, of any party to such transaction other than the person by whom such compensation is granted or paid.

(d) That it shall be unlawful for any person engaged in commerce to pay or contract for the payment of anything of value to or for the benefit of a customer of such person in the course of such commerce as compensation or in consideration for any services or facilities furnished by or through such customer in connection with the processing, handling, sale, or offering for sale of any products or commodities manufactured, sold, or offered for sale by such person, unless such payment or consideration is available on proportionally equal terms to all other customers competing in the distribution of such products or commodities.

(e) That it shall be unlawful for any person to discriminate in favor of one purchaser against another purchaser or purchasers of a commodity bought for resale, with or without processing, by contracting to furnish or furnishing, or by contributing to the furnishing of, any services or facilities connected with the processing, handling, sale, or offering for sale of such commodity so purchased upon terms not accorded to all purchasers on proportionally equal terms.

(f) That it shall be unlawful for any person engaged in commerce, in the course of such commerce, knowingly to induce or receive a discrimination in price which is prohibited by this section.

Section 3. That it shall be unlawful for any person engaged in commerce, in the course of such commerce, to lease or make a sale or contract for sale of goods, wares, merchandise, machinery, supplies, or other commodities, whether patented or unpatented, for use, consumption, or resale within the United States or ... other place under the jurisdiction of the United States, or fix a price charged therefor, or discount from, or rebate upon, such price, on the condition, agreement, or understanding that the lessee or purchaser thereof shall not use or deal in the goods, wares, merchandise, machinery, supplies, or other commodities of a competitor or competitors of the lessor or seller, where the effect of such lease, sale, or contract for sale or such condition, agreement, or understanding may be to substantially lessen competition to tend to create a monopoly in any line of commerce.

Section 4. That any person who shall be injured in his business or property by reason of anything forbidden in the antitrust laws may sue therefor . . . without respect to the amount in controversy, and shall recover threefold the damages by him sustained, and the cost of suit, including a reasonable attorney's fee.

. . . .

Section 4C. (a) (1) Any attorney general of a State may bring a civil action in the name of such State, as *parens patriae* on behalf of natural persons residing in such State . . . to secure monetary relief . . . for injury sustained by such natural persons to their property by reason of any violation of [the Sherman Act.]

. . . .

Section 6. That the labor of a human being is not a commodity or article of commerce. Nothing contained in the antitrust laws shall be construed to forbid the existence and operation of labor, agricultural or horticultural organizations, instituted for the purposes of mutual help, and not having capital stock or conducted for profit, or to forbid or restrain individual members of such organizations from lawfully carrying out the legitimate objects thereof; nor shall such organizations or the members thereof, be held or construed to be illegal combinations or conspiracies in restraint of trade, under the antitrust laws.

Section 7. That no corporation engaged in commerce shall acquire, directly or indirectly, the whole or any part of the stock or other share capital and no corporation subject to the jurisdiction of the Federal Trade Commission shall acquire the whole or any part of the assets of another corporation engaged also in commerce, where in any line of commerce in any section of the country, the effect of such acquisition may be substantially to lessen competition, or to tend to create a monopoly.

No corporation shall acquire, directly or indirectly, the whole or any part of the stock or other share capital and no corporation subject to the jurisdiction of the Federal Trade Commission shall acquire the whole or any part of the assets of one or more corporations engaged in commerce, where in any line of commerce in any section of the country, the effect of such acquisition, of such stocks or assets, or of the use of such stock by the voting or granting of proxies or otherwise, may be substantially to lessen competition, or to tend to create a monopoly.

This section shall not apply to corporations purchasing such stock solely for investment and not using the same by voting or otherwise to bring about, or in attempting to bring about, the substantial lessening of competition. Nor shall anything contained in this section prevent a corpo-

ration engaged in commerce from causing the formation of subsidiary corporations for the actual carrying on of their immediate lawful business, or the natural and legitimate branches or extensions thereof, or from owning and holding all or a part of the stock of such subsidiary corporations, when the effect of such formation is not to substantially lessen competition.

. . . .

Nothing contained in this secton shall apply to transactions duly consummated pursuant to authority given by the Civil Aeronautics Board, Federal Communications Commission, Federal Power Commission, Interstate Commerce Commission, the Securities and Exchange Commission. . . .

Section 8. . . . No person at the same time shall be a director in any two or more corporations any one of which has capital, surplus, and undivided profits aggregating more than $1,000,000 engaged in whole or in part in commerce, . . . if such corporations are or shall have been theretofore, by virtue of their business and location of operation, competitors, so that the elimination of competition by agreement between them would constitute a violation of any of the provisions of the antitrust laws. . . .

The Federal Trade Commission Act (1914)

Section 5. (a) (1) Unfair methods of competition in or affecting commerce, and unfair or deceptive acts or practices in or affecting commerce, are hereby declared unlawful.

(2) The Commission is hereby empowered and directed to prevent persons, partnerships, or corporations . . . from using unfair methods of competition in or affecting commerce and unfair or deceptive acts or practices in or affecting commerce.

The Federal Labor Laws

The National Labor Relations Act, As Amended

Section 1. . . . (b) Industrial strife which interferes with the normal flow of commerce and with the full production of articles and commodities for commerce, can be avoided or substantially minimized if employers, employees, and labor organizations each recognize under law one another's legitimate rights in their relations with each other, and above all recognize under law that neither party has any right in its relations with any other to engage in acts or practices which jeopardize the public health, safety, or interest.

It is the purpose and policy of this Act, in order to promote the full flow of commerce, to prescribe the legitimate rights of both employees and employers in their relations affecting commerce, to provide orderly and peaceful procedures for preventing the interference by either with the legitimate rights of the other, to protect the rights of individual employees in their relations with labor organizations whose activities affect commerce, to define and proscribe practices on the part of labor and management which affect commerce and are inimical to the general welfare, and to protect the rights of the public in connection with labor disputes affecting commerce.

Section 2. Definitions.   When used in this Act—

(1) The term "person" includes one or more individuals, labor organizations, partnerships, associations, corporations, legal representatives, trustees, trustees in bankruptcy, or receivers.

. . . .

(5) The term "labor organization" means any organization of any kind, or any agency or employee representation committee or plan, in which employees participate and which exists for the purpose, in whole or in part, of dealing with employers concerning grievances, labor disputes, wages, rates of pay, hours of employment, or conditions of work.

. . . .

(11) The term "supervisor" means any individual having authority, in the interest of the employer, to hire, transfer, suspend, lay off, recall, promote, discharge, assign, reward, or discipline other employees, or responsibly to direct them, or to adjust their grievances, or effectively to recommend such action, if in connection with the foregoing the exercise of such authority is not of a merely routine or clerical nature, but requires the use of independent judgment.

(12) The term "professional employee" means—

(a) any employee engaged in work (i) predominately intellectual and varied in character as opposed to routine mental, manual, mechanical, or physical work; (ii) involving the consistent exercise of discretion and judgment in its performance; (iii) of such a character that the output produced or the result accomplished cannot be standardized in relation to a given period of time; (iv) requiring knowledge of an advanced type in a field of science or learning customarily acquired by a prolonged course of specialized intellectual instruction and study. . . .

(b) any employee, who (i) has completed the courses of specialized intellectual instruction and study described in clause (iv) of paragraph (a) and (ii) is performing related work under the supervision of a professional person to qualify himself to become a professional employee as defined in paragraph (a).

. . . .

Section 3. National Labor Relations Board.   (a) The National Labor Relations Board (hereinafter called the "Board") . . . as an agency of the United States, shall consist of five . . . members, appointed by the President by and with the advice and consent of the Senate . . . for terms of five years each,. . . . The President shall designate one member to serve as Chairman of the Board. Any member of the Board may be removed by the President, upon notice and hearing, for neglect of duty or malfeasance in office, but for no other cause.

. . . .

Section 6.   The Board shall have authority from time to time to make, amend, and rescind, in the manner prescribed by the Administrative Procedure Act, such rules and regulations as may be necessary to carry out the provisions of this Act.

Section 7. Rights of Employees.   Employees shall have the right to self-organization, to form, join, or assist labor organizations, to bargain collectively through representatives of their own choosing, and to engage in other concerted activities for the purpose of collective bargaining or other mutual aid or protection, and shall also have the right to refrain from any or all of such activities except to the extent that such right may be affected by an agreement requiring membership in a labor organization as a condition of employment as authorized in section 8(a) (3).

Section 8. Unfair Labor Practices.   (a) It shall be an unfair labor practice for an employer—

(1) to interfere with, restrain, or coerce employees in the exercise of the rights guaranteed in section 7;

(2) to dominate or interfere with the formation or administration of any labor organization or contribute financial or other support to it: Provide, that subject to rules and regulations made and published by the Board pursuant to section 6, an employer shall not be prohibited from permitting employees to confer with him during working hours without loss of time or pay;

(3) by discrimination in regard to hire or tenure of employment or any term or condition of employment to encourage or discourage membership in any labor organization: Provide, that nothing in this Act . . . shall preclude an employer from making an agreement with a labor organization . . . to require as a condition of employment membership therein. . . . Provided further, that no employer shall justify any discrimination against an employee for nonmembership in a labor organization (A) if he has reasonable grounds for believing that such membership was not available to the employee on the same terms and conditions generally applicable to other members, or (B) if he has reasonable grounds for believing that membership was denied or terminated for reasons other than the failure of the employee to tender periodic dues and initiation fees uniformly required as a condition of acquiring or retaining membership;

(4) to discharge or otherwise discriminate against an employee because he has filed charges or given testimony under this Act;

(5) to refuse to bargain collectively with the representatives of his employees, subject to the provisions of section 9(a).

(b) It shall be an unfair labor practice for a labor organization or its agents—

(1) to restrain or coerce (A) employees in the exercise of the rights guaranteed in section 7: Provided, that this

paragraph shall not impair the right of a labor organization to prescribe its own rules with respect to the acquisition or retention of membership therein; or (B) an employer in the selection of his representatives for the purposes of collective bargaining or the adjustment of grievances;

(2) to cause or attempt to cause an employer to discriminate against an employee in violation of subsection (a) (3) or to discriminate against an employee with respect to whom membership in such organization has been denied or terminated on some ground other than his failure to tender the periodic dues and the initiation fees uniformly required as a condition of acquiring or retaining membership;

(3) to refuse to bargain collectively with an employer, provided it is the representative of his employees subject to the provisions of section 9 (a).

(4) (i) to engage in, or to induce or encourage any individual employed by any person engaged in commerce or in an industry affecting commerce to engage in, a strike or a refusal in the course of his employment to use, manufacture, process, transport, or otherwise handle or work on any goods, articles, materials, or commodities or to perform any services; or, (ii) to threaten, coerce, or restrain any person engaged in commerce or in an industry affecting commerce, where in either case an object thereof is:

(A) forcing or requiring any employer or self-employed person to join any labor or employer organization or to enter into any agreement which is prohibited by section 8 (e);

(B) forcing or requiring any person to cease using, selling, handling, transporting, or otherwise dealing in the products of any other producer, processor, or manufacturer, or to cease doing business with any other person, or forcing or requiring any other employer to recognize or bargain with a labor organization as the representative of his employees unless such labor organization has been certified as the representative of such employees.... Provided, that nothing contained in this clause (B) shall be construed to make unlawful, where not otherwise unlawful, any primary strike or primary picketing;

(C) forcing or requiring any employer to recognize or bargain with a particular labor organization as the representative of his employees if another labor organization has been certified as the representative of such employees....

(D) forcing or requiring any employer to assign particular work to employees in a particular labor organization or in a particular trade, craft, or class....

Provided, that nothing contained in this subsection (b) shall be construed to make unlawful a refusal by any person to enter upon the premises of any employer (other than his own employer), if the employees of such employer are engaged in a strike ratified or approved by a representative of such employees whom such employer is required to recognize under this Act: Provided further, that for the purposes of this paragraph (4) only, nothing contained in such paragraph shall be construed to prohibit publicity, other than picketing, for the purpose of truthfully advising the public, including consumers and members of a labor orga-

nization, that a product or products are produced by an employer with whom the labor organization has a primary dispute and are distributed by another employer, as long as such publicity does not have an effect of inducing any individual employed by any person other than the primary employer in the course of his employment to pick up, deliver, or transport any goods, or not to perform any services, at the establishment of the employer engaged in such distribution;

(5) to require of employees covered by an agreement authorized under subsection (a) (3) the payment, as a condition precedent to becoming a member of such organization, of a fee in an amount which the Board finds excessive or discriminatory....

(6) to cause or attempt to cause an employer to pay or deliver or agree to pay or deliver any money or other thing of value, in the nature of an exaction, for services which are not performed or not to be performed; and

(7) to picket or cause to be picketed, or threaten to picket or cause to be picketed, any employer where an object thereof is forcing or requiring an employer to recognize or bargain with a labor organization as the representative of his employees, or forcing or requiring the employees of an employer to accept or select such labor organization as their collective bargaining representative, unless such labor organization is currently certified as the representative of such employees:

(A) where the employer has lawfully recognized in accordance with this Act any other labor organization and a question concerning representation may not appropriately be raised under section 9(c) of this Act.

(B) where within the preceding 12 months a valid election under section 9(c) of this Act has been conducted, or

(C) where such picketing has been conducted without a petition under section 9(c) being filed within a reasonable period of time not to exceed 30 days from the commencement of such picketing: Provided, that when such a petition has been filed the Board shall forthwith, without regard to the provisions of section 9(c) (1) or the absence of a showing of a substantial interest on the part of the labor organization, direct an election in such units as the Board finds to be appropriate and shall certify the results thereof: Provided further, that nothing in this subparagraph (C) shall be construed to prohibit any picketing or other publicity for the purpose of truthfully advising the public (including consumers) that an employer does not employ members of, or have a contract with, a labor organization, unless an effect of such picketing is to induce any individual employed by any other person in the course of his employment, not to pick up, deliver or transport any goods or not to perform any services.

Nothing in this paragraph (7) shall be construed to permit any act which would otherwise be an unfair labor practice under this section 8(b).

(c) The expressing of any views, argument, or opinion, or the dissemination thereof, whether in written, printed, graphic, or visual form, shall not constitute or be evidence of an unfair labor practice under any of the provisions of this Act, if such expression contains no threat of reprisal or force or promise of benefit.

(d) For the purposes of this section, to bargain collectively is the performance of the mutual obligation of the employer and the representative of the employees to meet at reasonable times and confer in good faith with respect to wages, hours, and other terms and conditions of employment, or the negotiation of an agreement, or any question arising thereunder, and the execution of a written contract incorporating any agreement reached if requested by either party, but such obligation does not compel either party to agree to a proposal or require the making of a concession: Provided, that where there is in effect a collective bargaining contract covering employees in an industry affecting commerce, the duty to bargain collectively shall also mean that no party to such contract shall terminate or modify such contract, unless the party desiring such termination or modification—

(1) serves a written notice upon the other party to the contract of the proposed termination or modification 60 days prior to the expiration date thereof, or in the event such contract contains no expiration date, 60 days prior to the time it is proposed to make such termination or modification;

(2) offers to meet and confer with the other party for the purpose of negotiating a new contract or a contract containing the proposed modifications;

(3) notifies the Federal Mediation and Conciliation Service within 30 days after such notice of the existence of a dispute. . . .

(4) continues in full force and effect, without resorting to strike or lockout, all the terms and conditions of the existing contract for a period of 60 days after such notice is given or until the expiration date of such contract, whichever occurs later.

. . . .

(e) it shall be an unfair labor practice for any labor organization and any employer to enter into any contract or agreement, express or implied, whereby such employer ceases or refrains or agrees to cease or refrain from handling, using, selling, transporting, or otherwise dealing in any of the products of any other employer, or to cease doing business with any other person, . . . Provided, that nothing in this subsection (e) shall apply to an agreement between a labor organization and an employer in the construction industry relating to the contracting or subcontracting of work to be done at the site. . . .

Section 9. Representatives and Elections. (a) Representatives designated or selected for the purposes of collective bargaining by the majority of the employees in a unit appropriate for such purposes, shall be the exclusive representatives of all the employees in such unit for the purposes of collective bargaining in respect to rates of pay, wages, hours of employment, or other conditions of employment: Provided, that any individual employee or a group of employees shall have the right at any time to present grievances to their employer and to have such grievances adjusted, without the intervention of the bargaining representative, as long as the adjustment is not inconsistent with the terms of a collective bargaining contract or agreement then in effect: Provided further, that the bargaining representative has been given opportunity to be present at such adjustment.

(b) The Board shall decide in each case whether, in order to assure to employees the fullest freedom in exercising the rights guaranteed by this Act, the unit appropriate for the purposes of collective bargaining shall be the employer unit, craft unit, plant unit, or subdivision thereof: Provided, that the Board shall not (1) decide that any unit is appropriate for such purposes if such unit includes both professional employees and employees who are not professional employees unless a majority of such professional employees vote for inclusion in such unit; or (2) decide that any craft unit is inappropriate for such purposes on the ground that a different unit has been established by a prior Board determination, unless a majority of the employees in the proposed craft unit vote against separate representation or (3) decide that any unit is appropriate for such purposes, if it includes, together with other employees, any individual employed as a guard to enforce against employees and other persons, rules to protect property of the employer or to protect the safety of persons on the employer's premises; but no labor organization shall be certified as the representative of employees in a bargaining unit of guards if such organization admits to membership, or is affiliated directly or indirectly with an organization which admits to membership, employees other than guards.

(c) (1) Wherever a petition shall have been filed, in accordance with such regulations as may be prescribed by the Board—

(A) by an employee or group of employees or any individual or labor organization acting in their behalf alleging that a substantial number of employees (i) wish to be represented for collective bargaining and that their employer declines to recognize their representative as the representative defined in section 9(a), or (ii) assert that the individual or labor organization, which has been certified or is being currently recognized by their employer as the bargaining representative as defined in section 9(a); or

(B) by an employer, alleging that one or more individuals or labor organizations have presented to him a claim to be recognized as the representative defined in section 9(a);

the Board shall investigate such petition and if it has reasonable cause to believe that a question of representation affecting commerce exists shall provide for an appropriate hearing upon due notice. Such hearing may be conducted by an officer or employee of the regional office, who shall not make any recommendations with respect thereto. If the Board finds upon the record of such hearing that such a question of representative exists, it shall direct an election by secret ballot and shall certify the results thereof.

. . . .

(3) No election shall be directed in any bargaining unit or any subdivision within which, in the preceding 12-month period, a valid election shall have been held. Employees engaged in an economic strike who are not entitled to reinstatement shall be eligible to vote under such regulations as the Board shall find are consistent with the purposes and provisions of this Act in any election conducted within 12 months after the commencement of the strike. In any election where none of the choices on the ballot receives a majority, a runoff shall be conducted, the ballot providing for a selection between the two choices receiving the largest and second largest number of valid votes cast in the election.

(4) Nothing in this section shall be construed to prohibit the waiver of hearings by stipulation for the purposes of a consent election in conformity with regulations and rules of decision of the Board.

(5) In determining whether a unit is appropriate for the purpose specified in subsection (b) the extent to which the employees have organized shall not be controlling.

. . . .

(e) (1) Upon the filing with the Board, by 30 per centum or more of the employees in a bargaining unit covered by an agreement between their employer and a labor organization made pursuant to section 8(a) (3), of a petition alleging they desire that such authority be rescinded, the Board shall take a secret ballot of the employees in such unit and certify the results thereof to such labor organization and to the employer.

(2) No election shall be conducted pursuant to this subsection in any bargaining unit or any subdivision within which, in the preceding 12-month period, a valid election shall have been held.

Section 10. Prevention of Unfair Labor Practices. (a) The Board is empowered, as hereinafter provided, to prevent any person from engaging in any unfair labor practice affecting commerce. This power shall not be affected by any other means of adjustment or prevention that has been or may be established by any other means of adjustment or prevention that has been or may be established by agreement, law, or otherwise. . . .

(b) Whenever it is charged that any person has engaged in or is engaging in any such unfair labor practice, the Board . . . shall have power to issue and cause to be served upon such person a complaint stating the charges in that respect, and containing a notice of hearing before the Board or a member thereof, or before a designated agent or agency, at a place therein fixed, not less than five days after the serving of said complaint. . . . The person so complained of shall have the right to file an answer to the . . . complaint and to appear in person or otherwise and give testimony. . . .

(c) The testimony taken by such member, agent, or agency or the Board shall be reduced to writing and filed with the Board. Thereafter, in its discretion, the Board

upon notice may take further testimony or hear argument. If upon the preponderance of the testimony taken the Board shall be of the opinion that any person named in the complaint has engaged in or is engaging in any such unfair labor practice, then the Board shall state its findings of fact and shall issue and cause to be served on such person an order requiring such person to cease and desist from such unfair labor practice, and to take such affirmative action including reinstatement of employees with or without back pay, as will effectuate the policies of this Act. . . . If upon the preponderance of the testimony taken the Board shall not be of the opinion that the person named in the complaint has engaged in or is engaging in any such unfair labor practice, then the Board shall state its findings of fact and shall issue an order dismissing the said complaint. No order of the Board shall require the reinstatement of any individual as an employee who has been suspended or discharged, or the payment to him of any back pay, if such individual was suspended or discharged for cause.

. . . .

(e) The Board shall have power to petition any court of appeals of the United States, . . . for the enforcement of such order and for appropriate temporary relief or restraining order, and shall file in the court the record in the proceedings. . . . Upon the filing of such petition, the court shall cause notice thereof to be served upon such person, and thereupon shall have jurisdiction of the proceeding and of the question determined therein, and shall have power to grant such temporary relief or restraining order as it deems just and proper, and to make and enter a decree enforcing, modifying, and enforcing as so modified, or setting aside in whole or in part the order of the Board.

. . . .

(j) The Board shall have power, upon issuance of a complaint as provided in subsection (b) charging that any person has engaged in or is engaging in an unfair labor practice, to petition any district court of the United States. . . . for appropriate temporary relief or restraining order. . . .

. . . .

Section 13. Limitations. Nothing in this Act, except as specifically provided for herein, shall be construed so as to interfere with or impede or diminish in any way the right to strike, or to affect the limitations or qualifications on that right.

Section 14. (a) Nothing herein shall prohibit any individual employed as a supervisor from becoming or remaining a member of labor organization, but no employer subject to this Act shall be compelled to deem individuals defined herein as supervisors as employees for the purpose of any law, either national or local, relating to collective bargaining.

(b) Nothing in this Act shall be construed as authorizing the execution or application of agreements requiring membership in a labor organization as a condition of employment in any State or Territory in which such execution or application is prohibited by State or Territorial law.

. . . .

Section 19. Individuals with Religious Convictions.

Any employee who is a member of and adheres to established and traditional tenets or teachings of a bona fide religion, body, or sect which has historically held conscientious objections to joining or financially supporting labor organizations shall not be required to join or financially support any labor organization as a condition of employment; except that such employee may be required in a contract between such employee's employer and a labor organization in lieu of periodic dues and initiation fees, to pay sums equal to such dues and initiation fees to a nonreligious, nonlabor organization chartiable fund exempt from taxation under section 501(c) (3) of title 26 of the Internal Revenue Code. . . .

. . . .

Section 206. National Emergencies.

Whenever in the opinion of the President of the United States, a threatened or actual strike or lockout affecting an entire industry or a substantial part thereof engaged in trade, commerce, transportation, transmission, or communication among the several States or with foreign nations, or engaged in the production of goods for commerce, will, if permitted to occur or continue, imperil the national health or safety, he may appoint a board of inquiry into the issues involved in the dispute and to make a written report to him within such time as he shall prescribe. Such report shall include a statement of the facts with respect to the dispute and to make a written report to him within such time as he shall prescribe. Such report shall include a statement of the facts with respect to the dispute, including each party's statement of its position but shall not contain any recommendations. The President shall file a copy of such report with the [Federal Mediation and Conciliation] Service and shall make its contents available to the public.

. . . .

Section 208.

(a) Upon receiving a report from a board of inquiry the President may direct the Attorney General to petition any district court of the United States having jurisdiction of the parties to enjoin such strike or lockout or the continuing thereof, and if the court finds that such threatened or actual strike or lockout—

(i) affects an entire industry or a substantial part thereof engaged in trade, commerce, transportation, transmission, or communication among the several States or with foreign nations, or engaged in the production of goods for commerce; and

(ii) if permitted to occur or to continue, will imperil the national health or safety, it shall have jurisdiction to enjoin any such strike or lockout, or the continuing thereof, and to make such other orders as may be appropriate.

. . . .

Section 209.

(a) Whenever a district court has issued an order under section 208 enjoining acts or practices which imperil or threaten to imperil the national health or safety, it shall be the duty of the parties to the labor dispute giving rise to such order to make every effort to adjust and settle their differences, with the assistance of the [Federal Mediation and Conciliation] Service created by this Act. Neither party shall be under any duty to accept, in whole or in part, any proposal of settlement made by the Service.

(b) Upon the issuance of such order, the President shall reconvene the board of inquiry which has previously reported with respect to the dispute. At the end of a 60 day period (unless the dispute has been settled by that time), the board of inquiry shall report to the President the current position of the parties. . . . The President shall make such report available to the public. The National Labor Relations Board, within the succeeding 15 days, shall take a secret ballot of the employees of each employer involved in the dispute on the question of whether they wish to accept the final offer of settlement made by their employer as stated by him and shall certify the results thereof to the Attorney General within 5 days thereafter.

Section 210.

Upon certification of the results of such ballot or upon a settlement being reached, whichever happens sooner, the Attorney General shall move the court to discharge the injunction, which motion shall then be granted and the injunction discharged. . . .

THE FEDERAL CIVIL RIGHTS LAWS

42 U.S. Code, Section 1982. (1866)

All persons within the jurisdiction of the United States shall have the same right in every State and Territory and the District of Columbia to make and enforce contracts, to sue, be parties, give evidence, and to the full and equal benefit of all laws and proceedings for the security of persons and property as is enjoyed by white citizens, and shall be subject to like punishment, pains, penalities, taxes, licenses and exactions of every kind, and no other.

42 U.S. Code, Section 1982. (1866)

All citizens of the United States shall have the same right, in every State and Territory, as is enjoyed by white citizens thereof to inherit, purchase, lease, sell, hold and convey real and personal property.

42 U.S. Code, Section 1983. (1871)

Every person who, under color of any statute, ordinance, regulation, custom, or usage, of any State or Territory, subjects, or causes to be subjected, any citizen of the United States or other person within the jurisdiction thereof to the deprivation of any rights, privileges, or immunities secured by the Constitution and laws, shall be liable to the party injured in an action at law, suit in equity, or other proper proceeding.

Title II of the Civil Rights Act of 1964—The Public Accomodations Section

Section 201. (a) All persons shall be entitled to the full and equal enjoyment of the goods, services, facilities, privileges, advantages, and accomodations of any place of public accomodation, as defined in this section, without discrimination on the ground of race, color, religion, or national origin.

(b) Each of the following establishments which serves the public is a place of public accomodation within the meaning of this title if its operations affect commerce, or if discrimination or segregation by it is supported by State action:

(1) any inn, hotel, motel, or other establishment which provides lodging to transient guests, other than an establishment located within a building which contains not more than five rooms for rent or hire and which is actually occupied by the proprietor of such establishment as his residence;

(2) any restaurant, cafeteria, lunchroom, lunch counter, soda fountain. . . .

(3) any motion picture house, theater, concert hall, sports arena, stadium. . . .

(4) any establishment (A) (i) which is physically located within the premises of any establishment otherwise covered by this subsection, or (ii) within the premises of which is physically located any such covered establishment, and (B) which holds itself out as serving patrons of such covered establishment.

(c) The operations of an establishment affect commerce within the meaning of this title if (1) it is one of the establishments described in paragraph (1) of subsection (b); (2) in the case of an establishments described in paragraph (2) of subsection (b), it serves or offers to serve interstate travelers or a substantial portion of the food which it serves, or gasoline or other products which it sells, has moved in commerce; (3) in the case of an establishment described in paragraph (3) of subsection (b), it customarily presents films, performances, athletic teams, exhibitions, or other sources of entertainment which move in commerce; and (4) in the case of an establishment described in paragraph (4) of subsection (b), it is physically located within the premises of, or there is physically located within its premises, an establishment the operations of which affect commerce within the meaning of this subsection. For purposes of this section, "commerce" means travel, trade, traffic, commerce, transportation, or communication among the several States, or between the District of Columbia and any State, or between any foreign country or any territory or possession and any State or the District of Columbia, or between points in the same State but through any other State or the District of Columbia or a foreign country.

Section 202. All persons shall be entitled to be free, at any establishment or place, from discrimination or segregation of any kind on the ground of race, color, religion, or national origin, if such discrimination or segregation is or purports to be required by any law, statute, ordinance, regulation, rule, or order of a State or any agency or political subdivision thereof.

Section 203. No person shall (a) withhold, deny, or attempt to withhold or deny, or deprive or attempt to deprive, any person of any right or privilege secured by section 201 or 202, or (b) intimidate, threaten, or coerce, or attempt to intimidate, threaten, or coerce any person with the purpose of interfering with any right or privilege secured by section 201 or 202, or (c) punish or attempt to punish any person for exercising or attempting to exercise any right or privilege secured by section 201 or 202.

. . . .

Title VII of the Civil Rights Act of 1964—The Employment Discrimination Section

Section 703. Unlawful Employment Practices. (a) It shall be an unlawful employment practice for an employer—

(1) to fail or refuse to hire or to discharge any individual, or otherwise to discriminate against any individual with respect to his compensation, terms, conditions, or privileges or employment, because of such individual's race, color, religion, sex, or national origin; or

(2) to limit, segregate, or classify his employees or applicants for employment in any way which would deprive or tend to deprive any individual of employment opportunities or otherwise adversely affect his status as an employee, because of such individual's race, color, religion, sex, or national origin.

(b) It shall be an unlawful employment practice for an employment agency to fail or refuse to refer for employment, or otherwise to discriminate against, any individual because of his race, color, religion, sex, or national origin, or to classify or refer for employment any individual on the basis or his race, color, religion, sex, or national origin.

(c) It shall be an unlawful employment practice for a labor organization—

(1) to exclude or to expel from its membership, or otherwise to discriminate against, any individual because of his race, color, religion, sex, or national origin;

(2) to limit, segregate, or classify its membership or applicants for membership, or to classify or fail or refuse to refer for employment any individual, in any way which would deprive or tend to deprive any individual of employment opportunities, or would limit such employment opportunities or otherwise adversely affect his status as an employee or as an applicant for employment, because of such individual's race, color, religion, sex, or national origin; or

(3) to cause or attempt to cause an employer to discriminate against an individual in violation of this section.

(d) It shall be an unlawful employment practice for any employer, labor organization, or joint labor-management committee controlling apprenticeship or other training or retraining, including on-the-job training programs to discriminate against any individual because of his race, color, religion, sex, or national origin in admission to, or employment in, any program established to provide apprenticeship or other training.

(e) Nothwithstanding any other provision of this subchapter,

(1) it shall not be an unlawful employment practice for an employer to hire and employ employees, for an employment agency to classify, or refer for employment any individual, for a labor organization to classify its membership or to classify or refer for employment any individual, or for an employer, labor organization, or joint labor-management committee controlling apprenticeship or other training or retraining programs to admit or employ any individual in any such program, on the basis of his religion, sex, or national origin in those certain instances where religion, sex, or national origin is a bona fide occupational qualification reasonably necessary to the normal operation of that particular business or enterprise, and

(2) it shall not be an unlawful employment practice for a school, college, university, or other educational institution or institution of learning to hire and employ employees of a particular religion if such school, college, university, or other educational institution or institution of learning is, in whole or in substantial part, owned, supported, controlled, or managed by a particular religion or by a particular religious corporation, association, or society, or if the curriculum of such school, college, university, or other educational institution or institution of learning is directed toward the propagation of a particular religion.

(f) As used in this subchapter, the phrase "unlawful employment practice" shall not be deemed to include any action or measure taken by an employer, labor organization, joint labor-management committee, or employment agency with respect to an individual who is a member of the Communist Party of the United States or of any other organization required to register as a Communist-action or Communist-front organization. . . .

(g) Notwithstanding any other provision of this subchapter, it shall not be an unlawful employment practice for an employer to fail or refuse to hire and employ any individual for any position, for an employer to discharge any individual from any position, or for an employment agency to fail or refuse to refer any individual for employment in any position, or for a labor organization to fail or refuse to refer any individual for employment in any position, if—

(1) the occupancy of such position, or access to the premises in or upon which any part of the duties of such position is performed or is to be performed, is subject to any requirement imposed in the interest of the national security of the United States . . . and

(2) such individual has not fulfilled or has ceased to fulfill that requirement.

(h) Notwithstanding any other provision of this sub-chapter, it shall not be an unlawful employment practice for an employer to apply different standards of compensation, or different terms, conditions, or privileges of employment pursuant to a bona fide seniority or merit system, or a system which measures earnings by quantity or quality of production or to employees who work in different locations, provided that such differences are not the result of an intention to discriminate because of race, color, religion, sex, or national origin, nor shall it be an unlawful employment practice for an employer to give and act upon the results of any professionally developed ability test provided that such test, its administration or action upon the results is not designed, intended or used to discriminate because of race, color, religion, sex, or national origin. . . .

(j) Nothing contained in this subchapter shall be interpreted to require any employer, employment agency, labor organization, or joint labor-management committee subject to this subchapter to grant preferential treatment to any individual or to any group because of the race, color, religion, sex, or national origin of such individual or group on account of an imbalance which may exist with respect to the total number of percentage of persons of any race, color, religion, sex, or national origin employed by any employer, referred or classified for employment by any employment agency or labor organization, or admitted to, or employed in, any apprenticeship or other training program, in comparison with the total number or percentage of persons of such race, color, religion, sex, or national origin in any community, State, section, or other area, or in the available work force in any community, State, section, or other area.

. . . .

Section 704. Other Unlawful Employment Practices. (a) It shall be an unlawful employment practice for an employer to discriminate against any of his employees or applicants for employment, for an employment agency, or joint labor-management committee controlling apprenticeship or other training or retraining, including on-the-job training programs, to discriminate against any individual, or for a labor organization to discriminate against any member thereof or applicant for membership, because he has opposed any practice made an unlawful employment practice by this subchapter, or because he has made a charge, testified, assisted, or participated in any manner in an investigation, proceeding, or hearing under this subchapter.

(b) It shall be an unlawful employment practice for an employer, labor organization, employment agency, or joint labor-management committee controlling apprenticeship or other training or retraining, including on-the-job training programs, to print or publish or cause to be printed or published any notice or advertisement relating to employment by such an employer or membership or any classification or referral for employment by such a labor organization, or relating to any classification or referral for employment by such an employment agency, or relating to admission to, or employment in, any program established to provide apprenticeship or other training by such a joint-labor-management committee, indicating any preference, limitation, specification, or discrimination, based on race, color, religion, sex, or national origin, except that such a notice or advertisement may indicate a preference, limitation, specification, or discrimination based on religion, sex or national origin when religion, sex, or national origin is a bona fide occupational qualification for employment.

The Federal Civil Rights Act of 1968

Section 803. (a) Subject to the provisions of subsection (b) and section 807, the prohibitions against discrimination in the sale or rental of housing set forth in section 804 shall apply:

(1) . . . to (A) dwellings owned or operated by the Federal Government; (B) dwellings provided in whole or in part with the aid of loans, advances, grants, or contributions made by the Federal Government. . . . (C) dwellings provided in whole or in part by loans insured, guaranteed, or otherwise secured by the credit of the Federal Government. . . . (D) dwellings provided by the development of real property purchased, rented, or otherwise obtained from a State or local public agency receiving Federal financial assistance for slum clearance or urban renewal. . . .

(2) . . . to all dwellings covered by paragraph (1) and to all other dwellings except as exempted by subsection (b).

(b) Nothing in section 804 . . . shall apply to—

(1) any single-family house sold or rented by an owner: Provided, That such private individual owner does not own more than three such single-family houses at any one time: Provided further, That in the case of the sale of any such single-family house by a private individual owner not residing in such house at the time of such sale or who was not the most recent resident of such house prior to such sale, the exemption granted by this subsection shall apply only with respect to one such sale within any twenty-four month period: Provided further, That such bona fide private individual owner does not own any interest in, nor is there owned or reserved on his behalf, under any express or voluntary agreement, title to any right to all or a portion of the proceeds from the sale or rental of, more than three such single-family houses at any one time: Provided further, That . . . the sale or rental of any such single-family house shall be excepted from the application of this Title only if such house is sold or rented (A) without the use in any manner of the sales or rental facilities or the sales or rental services of any real estate broker, agent, or salesman, or of such facilities or services of any person in the business of selling or renting dwellings, or of any employee or agent of any such broker, agent, or salesman, or person and (B) without the publication, posting, mailing, after notice, of any advertisement or written notice in violation of section 804(c) of this title; . . . or

(2) rooms or units in dwellings containing living quarters occupied or intended to be occupied by no more than four families living independently of each other, if the owner actually maintains and occupies one of such living quarters for his residence.

(c) for the purposes of subsection (b), a person shall be deemed to be in the business of selling or renting dwellings if—

(1) he has, within the preceding twelve months, participated as principal in three or more transactions involving the sale or rental of any dwelling. . . .

(2) he has, within the preceding twelve months, participated as agent . . . in two or more transactions involving the sale or rental of any dwelling. . . .

(3) he is the owner of any dwelling designed or intended for occupancy by, or occupied by, five or more families.

Section 804. Discrimination in the Sale or Rental of Housing. As made applicable by section 803 and except as exempted by sections 803(b) and 807, it shall be unlawful—

(a) to refuse to sell or rent after the making of a bona fide offer, or to refuse to negotiate for the sale or rental of, or otherwise make unavailable or deny, a dwelling to any person because of race, color, religion, sex, or national origin.

(b) To discriminate against any person in the terms, conditions, or privileges of sale or rental of a dwelling, or in the provision of services or facilities in connection therewith, because of race, color, religion, sex, or national origin.

(c) To make, print or publish, . . . any notice, statement, or advertisement, with respect to the sale or rental of a dwelling that indicates any preference, limitation, or discrimination based on race, color, religion, sex, or national origin, or an intention to make any such preference, limitation, or discrimination.

(d) To represent to any person because of race, color, religion, sex, or national origin that any dwelling is not available for inspection, sale, or rental when such dwelling is in fact so available.

(e) For profit, to induce or attempt to induce any person to sell or rent any dwelling by representations regarding the entry or prospective entry into the neighborhood of a person or persons of a particular race, color, religion, sex, or national origin.

Section 807. Nothing in this title shall prohibit a religious organization, association, or society, or any nonprofit institution or organization operated, supervised, or controlled by or in conjunction with a religious organization, association or society, from limiting the sale, rental or occupancy of dwellings which it owns or operates for other than a commercial purpose to persons of the same religion, or from giving preference to such persons, unless membership in such religion is restricted on account of race, color, sex, or national origin. Nor shall anything in this title prohibit a private club not in fact open to the public, which as an incident to its primary purpose or purposes provides lodging which it owns or operates for other than a commercial purpose, from limiting the rental or occupancy of such lodgings to its members or from giving preference to its members.

. . . .

UNIFORM COMMERCIAL CODE (SELECTED PROVISIONS)

Section 2-302. Unconscionable Contract or Clause.

(1) If the court as a matter of law finds the contract or any clause of the contract to have been unconscionable at the time it was made the court may refuse to enforce the contract, or it may so limit the application of any unconscionable clause as to avoid any unconscionable result.

(2) When it is claimed or appears to the court that the contract or any clause thereof may be unconscionable the parties shall be afforded a reasonable opportunity to present evidence as to its commercial setting, purpose and effect to aid the court in making the determination.

Section 2-313. Express Warranties by Affirmation, Promise, Description, Sample.

(1) Express warranties by the seller are created as follows:

(a) Any affirmation of fact or promise made by the seller to the buyer which relates to the goods and becomes a part of the basis of the bargain creates an express warranty that the goods shall conform to the affirmation or promise.

(b) Any description of the goods which is made part of the basis of the bargain creates an express that the goods shall conform to the description.

(c) Any sample or model which is made part of the basis of the bargain creates an express warranty that the whole of the goods shall conform to the sample or model.

(2) It is not necessary to the creation of an express warranty that the seller use formal words such as "warrant" or "guarantee" or that he have a specific intention to make a warranty, but an affirmation merely of the value of the goods or a statement purporting to be merely the seller's opinion or commendation of the goods does not create a warranty.

Section 2-314. Implied Warranty: Merchantability; Usage of Trade.

(1) Unless excluded or modified (Section 2-316), a warranty that the goods shall be merchantable is implied in a contract for their sale if the seller is a merchant with respect to goods of that kind. Under this section the serving for value of food or drink to be consumed either on the premises or elsewhere is a sale.

(2) Goods to be merchantable must be at least such as

(a) pass without objection in the trade under the contract description; and

(b) in the case of fungible goods, are of fair average quality within the description; and

(c) are fit for the ordinary purposes for which such goods are used; and

(d) run, within the variations permitted by the agreement, of even kind, quality and quantity within each unit and among all units involved; and

(e) are adequately contained, packaged, and labeled as the agreement may require; and

(f) conform to the promises or affirmations of fact made on the container or label if any.

(3) Unless excluded or modified (Section 2-316) other implied warranties may arise from course of dealing or usage of trade.

Section 2-315. Implied Warranty: Fitness for Particular Purpose.

Where the seller at the time of contracting has reason to know any particular purpose for which the goods are required and that the buyer is relying on the seller's skill or judgment to select or furnish suitable goods, there is unless excluded or modified under the next section an implied warranty that the goods shall be fit for such purposes.

Section 2-316. Exclusion or Modification of Warranties.

(1) Words or conduct relevant to the creation of an express warranty and words or conduct tending to negate or limit warranty shall be construed wherever reasonable as consistent with each other; but subject to the provisions of this Article . . . negation or limitation is inoperative to the extent that such construction is unreasonable.

(2) Subject to subsection (3), to exclude or modify the implied warranty of merchantability or any part of it in the language must mention merchantability and in case of a writing must be conspicuous, and to exclude or modify any implied warranty of fitness the exclusion must be by a writing and conspicuous. Language to exclude all implied warranties of fitness is sufficient if it states, for example, that "There are no warranties which extend beyond the description on the face hereof."

(3) Notwithstanding subsection (2)

(a) unless the circumstances indicate otherwise, all implied warranties are excluded by expressions like "as is," "with all faults," or other language which in common understanding calls the buyer's attention to the exclusion of warranties and makes plain that there is no implied warranty; and

(b) when the buyer before entering into the contract has examined the goods or the sample or model as fully as he desired or has refused to examine the goods there is no implied warranty with regard to defects which an examination ought in the circumstances to have revealed to him; and

(c) an implied warranty can also be excluded or modified by course of dealing or course of performance or usage of trade.

(4) Remedies for breach of warranty can be limited in accordance with the provisions of this Article on liquidation or limitation of damages and on contractual modification of remedy. . . .

Section 2-318. Third-Party Beneficiaries of Warranties Express or Implied.

Alternative A A seller's warranty whether express or implied extends to any natural person who is in the family or household of his buyer or who is a guest in his home if it is reasonable to expect that such person may use, consume or be affected by the goods and who is injured in person by breach of the warranty. A seller may not exclude or limit the operation of this section.

Alternative B A seller's warranty whether express or implied extends to any natural person who may reasonably be expected to use, consume or be affected by the goods and who is injured in person by breach of the warranty. A seller may not exclude or limit the operation of this section.

Alternative C A seller's warranty whether express or implied, extends to any person who may reasonably be expected to use, consume or be affected by the goods and who is injured by breach of the warranty. A seller may not exclude or limit the operation of this section with respect to injury to the person of an individual to whom the warranty extends.

Section 2-714. Buyer's Damages for Breach in Regard to Accepted Goods.

(1). . . .

(2) The measure of damages for breach of warranty is the difference at the time and place of acceptance between the value of the goods accepted and the value they would have had if they had been as warranted, unless special circumstances show proximate damages of a different amount.

(3) In a proper case any incidental and consequential damages under the next section may also be recovered.

Section 2-715. Buyer's Incidental and Consequential Damages.

(1) Incidental damages resulting from the seller's breach include expenses reasonably incurred in inspection, receipt, transportation and care and custody of goods rightfully rejected, any commerically reasonable charges, expenses or commissions in connection with effecting cover and any other reasonable expense incident to the delay or other breach.

(2) Consequential damages resulting from the seller's breach include

(a) any loss resulting from general or particular requirements and needs of which the seller at the time of contracting had reason to know and which could not reasonably be prevented by cover or otherwise; and

(b) injury to person or property proximately resulting from any breach of warranty.

Section 2-719. Contractual Modification of Limitation of Remedy.

(1) Subject to the provisions of subsections (2) and (3) of this section and of the preceding section on liquidation and limitation of damages,

(a) the agreement may provide for remedies in addition to or in substitution for those provided in this Article and may limit or alter the measure of damages recoverable under this Article, as by limiting the buyer's remedies to return of the goods and repayment of the price or to repair and replacement of non-conforming goods or parts; and

(b) resort to a remedy as provided is optional unless the remedy is expressly agreed to be exclusive, in which case it is the sole remedy.

(2) Where circumstances cause an exclusive or limited remedy to fail of its essential purpose, remedy may be had as provided in this Act.

(3) Consequential damages may be limited or excluded unless the limitation or exclusion is unconscionable. Limitation of consequential damages for injury of the person in the case of consumer goods is prima facie unconscionable but limitation of damages where the loss is commercial is not.

Glossary

The list of terms in this glossary is not meant as a substitute for a good law dictionary. Students should also be aware that various terms have "shades" of meaning, which can only be derived from the context of a case or a particular discussion. The definitions provided are merely the most useful definition of the term for the purposes of this text.

Words in italics are defined elsewhere in this glossary. It may be necessary to look those words up in order to be sure of a full definition. Definitions also often refer to other terms which are related in some way.

acceptance   (contract law) agreement or acquiescence to the terms of an offer; compliance by an offeree with the terms and conditions of the terms of an offer.

accrual method   (taxation) a method of figuring income and expenses for the federal income tax based on claiming income as it becomes due to the taxpayer and charging expenses as they are incurred, as opposed to when such income is actually received and such expenses are actually paid (see *cash method*).

accumulated earnings tax   (taxation) a tax imposed by the federal government on the earnings of a corporation, over a specified amount, which are not either used within the corporation or distributed to shareholders as dividends.

Activists   judges who see the courts' role as advocate and protector of the interests of the weak and disadvantaged (see *Restraintists; Neutralists*).

actual potential competition   (antitrust law) a possible anticompetitive effect of a *product extension* or *market extension merger*, in which the courts are concerned with the actual loss to potential competition, as opposed to the loss of *perceived potential competition*. The courts generally do not accept actual potential competition as an anticompetitive effect under Section 7 of the Clayton Act unless (1) the target market is concentrated, (2) there is an alternative method of entry into the market, and (3) the alternative method offers a prospect of competitive improvement.

ad hoc   for this purpose only; on a case-by-case basis.

adjudicatory function   (administrative law) the function of administrative agencies in deciding cases that arise under their authority.

adjusted gross income   (taxation) for federal income tax purposes, *gross income* less *business deductions.*

administrative agency   (1.) any *independent regulatory commission* or *line agency;* (2) for purposes of the *Due Process* clause, any governmentally related entity or person.

Administrative Law Judge (ALJ)   an officer who hears administrative cases before *administrative agencies.* While these judges are attached to a particular agency, they are hired under the Civil Service system and have a measure of independence from the agency they serve.

administrative regulations   rules enacted by administrative agencies pursuant to a delegation of authority to make such rules by a legislative body. While such regulations are not law, they have the force of law.

ad valorem   (taxation) literally 'by value.'

adversary system   the system of law in the United States, Great Britain, and the British Commonwealth. In the adversary system, lawyers for opposing sides present their cases, and the judge acts as a neutral decision-maker. The assumption is that the truth will surface from the conflict of opposing forces (see *inquisitorial system*).

adverse possession   a method of acquistion of title to property. Possession must be actual, notorious, open, and hostile for a statutorily specified period of time. That period may often be shortened by payment of real estate taxes and "color of title," that is, some legal claim to the property.

advisory opinions   opinions issued by a court or other authority based upon a hypothetical question rather than a real case involving adversary interests.

affecting commerce   having an impact on goods or people moving between states.

affirm   to confirm a former judgment, usually of a lower court judgment by a higher appellate court.

affirmative action   policies attempting to remedy historic segregation through racial quotas or advantages to minorities, especially in employment and public education.

affirmative defense   a portion of an *answer* to a *complaint* that agrees that the plaintiff's complaint is accurate, but that there is more to the story. The defendant usually has the burden of proving affirmative defenses.

agency   (1) a legal relationship in which one person (the *agent*) acts for and on behalf of another person (the *principal*); (2) short for *administrative agency.*

agency by estoppel   an *agency* (definition 1) created by operation of law, and established by proof of such acts of the principal as reasonably lead others to conclude that the agency exists.

agency coupled with an interest   an irrevocable *agency;* an agency in which the agent has both the authority to act and an interest in the subject matter of the agency.

agency shop   (labor law) a form of *open shop agreement* in a labor contract in which employees are not required to join a union but are required to pay a portion of the union dues attributable to collective bargaining activities (see *union shop*).

agent   one who acts for and on behalf of another (see *agency*).

amicus curiae   literally 'friend of the court'; a person or group not directly involved in a lawsuit but permitted to make an argument in the case.

anarchy   the complete absence of government.

annual report   (securities regulation) a yearly report filed with the Securities and Exchange Commission by all corporations subject to the 1934 Securities and Exchange Act.

answer   a responsive *pleading* in a lawsuit, filed by the *defendant* or other party in response to a *complaint* filed against that party, denying, admitting, or stating that the defendant is without information to answer, the allegations of the complaint.

antifraud provisions   (securities regulation) provisions of the securities laws outlawing specific practices in dealing with securities such as fraud, market manipulation, and corporate mismanagement.

apparent authority   a method of creation of agency relationships in which the *principal* places another in a position in which it reasonably appears to third persons that the *agent* has authority to deal on behalf of the principal.

appellant   the person filing an appeal; the appealing party.

appellate jurisdiction   the power to hear a case at the appellate level; the right to review a case decided by a lower court or an administrative agency.

appellee the person against whom an appeal is filed; the party defending the judgment of the lower court.

apportionment (taxation) a constitutional requirement that *direct taxes* be divided among the states according to their population. Apportionment was eliminated as a constitutional requirement by the 16th Amendment.

appropriate bargaining unit (labor law) the proper unit, whether shop, company, trade, or other, that is to elect a union representative, as determined by the National Labor Relations Board.

arbitration submitting a dispute for final and binding settlement to a third person (the arbitrator), outside of the judicial process. If such submission is required by law, it is compulsory arbitration.

Articles of Confederation the first attempt at a written constitution in America. The Articles were proposed in 1777 and ratified in 1781, but were little more than a treaty or alliance between the states with little power in the central government.

articles of incorporation the grant of authority from the state to a *corporation* to act in the corporate form and defining the specific powers of the corporation.

assessed value (taxation) the amount of value placed on property to be taxed under some *ad valorem* property tax.

association any group of persons joined together for a particular purpose, but especially any *partnership* or other business form taxed as a corporation but that has not organized as a corporation.

assumed name statutes state laws requiring that businesses which operate under some name other than the name(s) of the owner must register the business name with state or local government officials.

assumption of risk a *tort* doctrine in which a person who assumes the consequences of injury occurring through the fault of another may not recover for such injuries; a voluntary exposure to a known risk.

authorization cards cards signed by workers authorizing a union to request an election. Such cards are not membership cards.

authorized shares the number of shares of stock a corporation is permitted to issue by virtue of its articles of incorporation, as amended.

bait and switch a deceptive sales device wherein the seller offers a product at a low price and then convinces the consumer to switch to a higher priced version of the product.

bargaining order an order from the NLRB requiring the employer and the union to bargain over a particular issue.

BAT standards Best Available Technology for dealing with water pollution from a point source, which must be in place by 1984. BAT standards do not take cost into account.

BCT standards Best Conventional Technology for point sources of conventional water pollutants (as opposed to toxic pollutants), which must be in place by July 1, 1984, and which require a consideration of the costs of such technology.

beneficiary a person who is to receive the benefits from something, especially of a *trust,* insurance policy, or an estate.

bfoq see *bona fide occupational qualification.*

Bill of Rights commonly understood to be the first ten amendments to the U. S. Constitution, but often defined to include the 13th, 14th, and 15th Amendments; those portions of the U.S. Constitution that protect individual liberties.

blacklist a list of employees active in union affairs or the labor movement that is circulated to employers, who then refuse to hire such individuals.

blackmail picketing an *unfair labor practice* by unions in which a union or employees picket in order to gain representation or obtain union members, if certain conditions are present: (1) when the employer has already recognized another union; (2) when an NLRB election has been held in the last twelve months; or (3) if a representation petition is not filed within 30 days of the onset of picketing.

blockbusting inducing a person to sell or rent by making representations about the prospective entry of persons of a particular race or other prohibited category into a neighborhood; inducing panic-selling.

blue sky laws state statutes regulating the sale of securities or requiring registration of securities brokers or dealers, and usually containing *antifraud* provisions.

bona fide occupational qualification   an exception to the general prohibition of discrimination in employment, permitting classification on the basis of religion, sex, or national origin (but not race or color) if such classification is "reasonably necessary to the normal operation of that particular business or enterprise."

bond   (1) a debt security of a corporation secured by a pledge or mortgage on corporate property; (2) all debt securities (improper, but common usage).

BPT standards   Best Practicable Technology for dealing with water pollution from point sources, which had to be in place by 1977. BPT standards take the cost of such technology into account.

breach of duty   one of the elements of any *tort;* violation or omission of some legally recognized duty.

brief   a written or printed document, prepared by counsel, which serves as the basis for argument before a court. Briefs are almost always filed in appellate cases and are sometimes used to present arguments in trial courts as well.

broker   (securities regulation) a person engaged in the business of making transactions in securities for the account of others. (see *dealer; broker-dealer*).

broker-dealer   (securities regulation) a person who has both the status of *broker* and the status of *dealer* under the federal securities laws.

bubble doctrine   the theory that all parts of a single industrial plant should be treated as a single pollution source, and that offsetting increases and decreases in pollution from parts of the same plant should be permitted.

bundle of rights theory   the concept of ownership of *property* as a group of rights enabling the holder of those rights to deal with the property in certain ways.

burden of proof   the duty or necessity of affirmatively proving a fact or facts in dispute by a certain level of evidence. In most civil cases that level is by a "preponderance of the evidence," but in criminal cases it is "beyond a reasonable doubt." Some types of civil cases require a higher level, such as by "clear and convincing evidences."

business deductions   (taxation) for federal income tax purposes, all expenses and losses connected with operating a business that may be deducted from gross income.

business judgment rule   the rule that corporate officers and directors may manage the corporation within the bounds of the discretion granted to them by law, the *articles of incorporation,* and the corporate *by-laws,* all without interference by the courts.

business trust   a form of business organization in which investors give money or property to a board of trustees, which then uses that money or property for business purposes for the benefit of the investor-beneficiaries.

by-laws   rules adopted by a corporation, through its board of directors, for the operation of corporate affairs.

canon law   the law of the Roman Catholic Church that was incorporated in or influenced the development of secular *common law.*

capacity   (contracts) the legal ability of a person to contract.

capital gains   (taxation) for purposes of the federal income tax, appreciation of property, while income, is treated differently and taxed at lower rates than ordinary income.

case law   judicial decisions in written form that act as precedent for future cases (see *stare decisis*).

case or controversy requirement   a Constitutional requirement that the federal courts cannot act and have no *jurisdiction* unless there is an actual, adverse case between parties.

cash method   an accounting method in which income and expenses are counted only as they are actually received or actually paid. (See *accrual method*).

cause of action   a legally recognized basis for a lawsuit.

caveat emptor   literally 'let the buyer beware'; the general rule that a purchaser must examine a product before it is purchased and, in the event of defect, the buyer must bear the loss.

cease and desist orders   orders from an administrative agency to stop a certain act or practice; especially, an order of the NLRB to an employer or union.

CEQ   see *Council on Environmental Quality.*

certificate of public convenience and necessity   an operating license for a business subject to economic regulation by a unit of government.

certiorari   a petition to an appellate court, especially the U.S. Supreme Court, for leave to file an appeal to that court.

C.F.R.   See *Code of Federal Regulations.*

challenge for cause   an objection to a juror's serving on a case for some reason, such as potential bias or prejudice (see *peremptory challenge*).

charging order   an order by a court requiring a *partnership* to pay over a partner's income from a partnership to a personal creditor of the partner.

charitable contributions   (taxation) for purposes of the federal income tax, contributions to qualified charities or other qualified nonprofit organizations that may be deducted from adjusted gross income prior to taxation.

chose in action   a personal right to sue; a right of property not in possession.

churning   an unlawful practice by securities *brokers* involving making numerous unnecessary transactions in a customer's account in order to obtain the commission on those transactions.

civil cases   lawsuits between two or more private persons, including cases in which the government acts as a private party, usually asking for *damages* or *equitable relief.*

class action   suits filed on behalf of a group or class of individuals who are injured in the same way by the same or similar acts of the same defendant.

classical deregulation   the removal or alleviation of direct *economic regulation.*

class voting   a method of voting in a corporation in which each class of stock has different voting rights; also known as series voting.

close corporation   a small corporation; a corporation managed by its shareholders and often family-owned.

Code of Federal Regulations (C.F.R.)   the comprehensive compilation of all federal administrative regulations.

collective bargaining   negotiations on behalf of a group of employees for a common employment contract, usually through a labor union.

collective negotiation laws   state statutes requiring negotiation between public employee unions and their employers. Such laws usually do not require agreement, but do require the parties to negotiate.

comfort letter   a written statement by independent public accountants that reports filed with the SEC do not contain any false or misleading information, written for the protection of the issuer and the underwriter of stock issues, and which imposes liability on the accountants if false or misleading information is present unless the accountant used *due diligence.*

Commerce Clause   Article 1, Section 8, Clause 3 of the U.S. Constitution, which provides much of the authority by which Congress regulates matters which are either *in commerce* or *affecting commerce.*

commercial speech   one of the exceptions to the 1st Amendment rule that Congress may not make laws limiting freedom of speech. Commercial speech, such as advertising, may be limited by both federal and state governments in most cases.

commingle   to mix; to mix one's own property with the property of another.

common law   (1) that body of law which developed in England, as distinguished from civil law systems which developed on the European continent; (2) that body of law which is derived from the customs and usages of history or from the judgments of courts recognizing such customs and usages; (3) all of the positive law of any state or nation.

common situs   a common employment site, such as a construction site, where several employers are at work at the same time.

common stock   one of the types of shares in a corporation, usually granting voting rights but receiving dividends after dividends are paid to preferred shares (see *preferred stock; participating preferred stock; equity financing*).

Community Ethic   the *societal ethic* that places primary emphasis on society and often justifying the sacrifice of individual rights for the greater good. At its extreme, this ethic corresponds to Marxism and totalitarianism, while in its more moderate aspects reflects a simple concern for the good of the community.

Community Relations Service   a federal agency created by the Public Accommodations section of the Civil Rights Act of 1964 for the purpose of obtaining voluntary compliance with those sections of the Act.

compact theory   see *natural rights theory*

company dominated unions   unions that are dependent on the employer for their existence or support; company unions.

comparative negligence   the doctrine accepted in many states that weighs the fault in *negligence* cases and permits a pro-rata recovery based on the differences in guilt of the parties to the case, as opposed to *contributory negligence.*

compensatory damages   money awarded to the *plaintiff* in a civil action to make good or replace the loss caused by the injury and to put the plaintiff in the same position as prior to the injury.

complaint   the first *pleading* on the part of a *plaintiff* in a lawsuit, setting forth facts and allegations on which his or her claim for relief is based; sometimes called a petition in some types of cases or in some courts.

Compliance Safety and Health Officers (CO's)   inspectors who conduct investigations and inspections regarding violations of OSHA.

concentration   (antitrust law) the degree to which an industry is gathered into one or a few hands, as in the case of *monopoly* or *oligopoly.*

conclusive presumption   a presumption that cannot be overcome by evidence, as opposed to a *rebuttable presumption,* which can be overcome by evidence.

concurrent jurisdiction   two or more courts with the power to hear the same subjects or cases.

confession of judgment clause   a clause in a contract or promissory note permitting the creditor to sue and obtain *judgment* against the debtor without notice, and that waives the right to notice, *summons,* and trial.

conflicts of laws   legal rules used to choose between the law of two or more states or nations that may apply to the same case.

conglomerate merger   (antitrust law) *corporate integration* between firms that are not related horizontally or vertically as competitors, buyers, or suppliers (see *product extension merger; market extension merger; pure conglomerate merger*).

consent decree   (antitrust law) negotiated settlements of government antitrust cases, which cannot be used as *prima facie proof* of violations in subsequent civil antitrust cases.

consideration   (contract law) the inducement to a contract; the cause, motive, price, or impelling influence that induces a party to enter into a contract; an act, forebearance, or promise of an act or forebearance, which is offered by one party to an agreement and accepted by another; the quid pro quo of the agreement.

consolidation   a method of *corporate integration* in which two firms join together to form a new third firm and both of the pre-existing firms cease to exist.

constitution   a charter of government that expresses both the powers of government and limitations on those powers.

contract   an agreement between two or more persons that creates, modifies, or destroys a legal relationship.

Contracts Clause   a part of Article 1, Section 10 of the U.S. Constitution that prohibits the states from passing laws which impair the obligation of contracts. The clause is rarely used, since States may pass laws within their *police powers,* even though they affect private contracts.

contributory negligence   (tort law) the rule that if one party was in any way *negligent* that party may not recover for injuries suffered as a result of another's negligence (see *comparative negligence*).

copyright   the grant of a limited *monopoly* to the author of a work.

corporate charter   see *articles of incorporation.*

corporate integration   any method by which two firms join together.

corporate mismanagement   (securities regulation) a requirement of Rule 10b-5 of the SEC that corporate officers may not make fraudulent or misleading statements in transactions in the shares of their own company.

corporation   a business form which is created by the state and granted limited legal liability to the owners, or shareholders, and is treated as a separate legal entity for most purposes (see *not-for-profit corporations; articles of incorporation*).

corrective advertising   see *retroactive advertising*.

cosigner   a guarantor of a debt; a person who agrees to pay a debt on behalf of another, and who is liable for the debt if the debtor defaults.

cost-benefit analysis   a balancing of the costs of an activity versus the benefits of that activity, usually measured in dollars.

Council on Environmental Quality (CEQ)   (environmental law) a three-member board appointed by the president to coordinate environmental programs and advise and assist the President on environmental matters.

counterclaim   a case filed by the *defendant* in a civil case against the *plaintiff* in the same case. Counterclaims may be mandatory, in the sense that they arise from the same transaction and therefore must be filed, or permissive, which arise from other transactions or occurrences between the parties and which are not lost if not filed as a counterclaim.

counteroffer   (contracts) a response to an initial offer that materially or substantially changes the initial *offer*. Counteroffers are treated in the same way as a *rejection* of the initial offer and create a power of acceptance in the initial offeror.

Court-Packing Plan   a plan proposed to Congress by President Franklin Roosevelt in 1937 to increase the number of judges on the Supreme Court by one new judge for each existing judge over the age of 70. The plan was proposed because of the Supreme Court's resistance to New Deal programs and was withdrawn after the Court's decision in *NLRB* v. *Jones & Laughlin Steel* and resistance to the plan by Congress.

Courts of Chancery   the equity courts originally set up in England to mitigate the harsh results sometimes obtained in the law courts. Judges in such courts were called chancellors (see *equity*, definition 2).

covert conspiracy   a hidden or concealed conspiracy.

credits against tax   (taxation) for purposes of the federal income tax, certain payments may be directly subtracted from the tax owed.

criminal conspiracy statutes   (labor law) state laws that forbade organization of labor unions.

criminal law   law that punishes individuals for injuring the public at large.

cross-claim   an action filed by a *defendant* against a codefendant arising from the same transaction as the *plaintiff's* complaint.

cross-elasticity of demand   an economic concept that determines the interchangeability of goods; whether, given a price increase in one product, consumers will readily shift to another product; the principle of substitutability. The concept is used in antitrust law in determining the *relevant product market*.

cross-examination   the questioning of an opposing witness; the first examination of an adverse witness.

cumulative dividends   corporate stock dividends that accumulate if they are not paid from year to year.

cumulative voting   a method of voting in a corporation in which a a shareholder receives a number of votes equal to the number of shares of stock owned times the number of directors to be elected, permitting the shareholder to apply those vote in any way he or she sees fit.

current report   a report filed with the SEC by any firm subject to the 1934 Securities and Exchange Act if certain events take place, and which is filed in addition to *annual* and *quarterly reports*.

custodial interrogation   one of the requirements of the *Miranda* decision. Warnings must be given when a suspect is "in custody" and being interrogated.

customs duties   a tax on imported items.

damages   money paid to a person who has suffered loss, detriment, or injury to person, property, or rights, as a result of actions of another and under the *judgment* of a court (see *nominal damages; compensatory damages; punitive damages*).

dealer   for purposes of the federal securities laws, a person engaged in the business of buying and selling securities for his or her own account (see *broker; broker-dealer*).

deauthorization elections   (labor law) elections held by the NLRB to determine whether to withdraw the authority of a union representative to continue a union shop agreement (see *decertification elections*).

debenture   a form of corporate debt unsecured by corporate property or mortgages on corporate proberty.

debt financing   financing a corporation through borrowed money (see *equity financing; bond; debenture*).

deceptive nondisclosure   failure to tell consumers some important fact about a product, such as its foreign origin, product hazards, or important matters regarding its contents or construction.

decertification elections   (labor law) elections held by the NLRB to determine whether to retain the current bargaining representative (see *deauthorization elections*).

declaratory judgment   an action of a court that states the rights of parties to a case, but does not result in *damages* or *equitable relief.*

deed   a written document, signed by the *grantor* of *real property,* in which *title* to or interests in real property are transferred from the grantor to the *grantee.*

deep pocket theory   (1) (agency or tort law) the theory of *respondeat superior,* based on the idea that the employer is better able to bear the risk of loss because of greater financial resources; (2) (antitrust law) in *conglomerate mergers,* the theory that one part of an integrated firm may subsidize another part of the same firm to drive competitors from the market and thereby obtain a greater market share. The theory has not been accepted as an "anticompetitive effect" in dealing with conglomerate mergers.

de facto   literally 'in fact'; actual, a situation that actually exists.

de facto segregation   separation that exists in fact, as opposed to separation by mandate of law (see *de jure segregation*).

defamation   *libel* and *slander;* intentional falsehoods written or spoken about a living person, bringing injury to that person's reputation.

default judgment   a judgment entered against a defendant because he or she failed to answer a *summons.*

defendant   the person against whom a lawsuit, civil or criminal, is filed.

de jure   by law; by right; legitimate, whether or not true in actual fact (see *de facto*).

de jure segregation   separation required by law, as opposed to that resulting from custom or social forces (see *de facto segregation*).

delectus personae   literally "the choice of the person"; the doctrine in partnership law that changing the combination of partners in a *partnership* destroys the previous relationship and terminates the partnership.

delegation   (1) (administrative law) the grant, from the legislative branch to an administrative agency, of authority to make rules and regulations; (2) (contract law) the transfer of a contract duty to another; (3) (agency law) the transfer of authority from the principal to an agent.

de minimus   small; unimportant; trifling.

de minimus violations   unimportant violations of OSHA for which no penalty is imposed.

de novo entry   entry into a market by creation of new facilities, as opposed to entry through acquisition or merger.

democratic government   a government of all of the people, governing themselves (see *republican government*).

depletion   (taxation) a deduction against gross income for the value of depleted natural resources, applied similarly to *depreciation.*

deposition   a part of *discovery;* the written record of a witness' sworn testimony taken outside of court.

depreciation   (taxation) a deduction permitted for the decline in value of income-producing assets.

derivative action   a form of lawsuit brought by corporate stockholders on behalf of the corporation to enforce rights of the corporation.

dicta   statements in a judicial opinion that are not essential to the case and are unnecessary to reach the result in the case; statements in a judicial opinion that are not binding as *precedent* (see *stare decisis*).

dilution of shares   any change in the corporate stock relationships that changes the relative proportion of ownership of corporate assets that a share represents.

diminishing returns   the economic doctrine that teaches that after a business reaches a certain optimal size, *economies of scale* no longer take place and each unit of output becomes increasingly more expensive to produce.

direct action   a form of lawsuit by a shareholder to enforce his or her individual rights as a shareholder (see *derivative action*).

direct examination   the first questioning of one's own witnesses in a trial or other hearing (see *cross-examination*).

directors   persons elected by the shareholders of a corporation to manage the affairs of the corporation; also, the persons elected or appointed to manage the affairs of a not-for-profit corporation.

direct tax   a tax levied on the persons ultimately expected to pay them.

disability benefits   benefits payable under Social Security to injured or disabled workers who are eligible under the Social Security Act.

disclaimer of warranties   a statement or attempt to limit or foreclose *warranties* implied by law.

discovery   the exchange of information between the sides in a lawsuit, generally through *interrogatories, depositions, requests to produce,* and special motions.

discrimination against interstate commerce   treating the goods and other commerce of other states differently than the goods and commerce of the "home" state.

disparagement   false statements regarding the goods or services of another; commercial *libel* or *slander.*

disparate treatment   overtly different treatment of persons in employment because of race, color, religion, national origin, or sex, under the Civil Rights Act of 1964, as amended (see *disproportionate impact*).

disproportionate impact   employment policies that are apparently neutral but that have a different effect on employees because of race, color, religion, national orgin, or sex, under the Civil Rights Act of 1964 (see *disparate treatment*).

disproportionate voting   voting in a corporation in which one class of shares receives greater voting rights than other shares. (see *class voting*).

disregarding the corporate fiction   see *piercing the corporate veil.*

dissenters' rights   the rights of shareholders of a corporation to sell their stock to the corporation if a *merger, consolidation,* or sale or exchange of all or a substantial part of the assets is proposed. Such rights must be exercised before the shareholders of the corporation vote on the move.

distinguish   to point out differences between cases, usually based on distinctions between the facts of two cases.

diversity jurisdiction   the authority of the federal courts to hear cases between citizens of more than one state, if the amount in controversy between them is more than $10,000.

divestiture   (antitrust law) the remedy under Section 7 of the Clayton Act that forces improperly merged firms to undo the *merger* and become separate firms once again.

dividends   distribution of earnings of a corporation to shareholders. Dividends may take the form of money, property, or shares of stock.

divine right of kings   the philosophy that kings rule by a grant from God and, therefore, the king can do no wrong.

domestic corporation   a corporation created under the laws of the state in question (see *foreign corporation*).

double jeopardy   the requirement under the 5th Amendment to the U.S. Constitution that no person may be tried twice for the same offense; not to be confused with *res judicata.*

due diligence   (securities regulation) the requirement that accountants who certify reports filed with the SEC use proper care in reviewing those reports and in obtaining information about the material in those reports.

Due Process   a part of a clause found in both the 5th and 14th Amendments to to U.S. Constitution. The clause generally requires both fair procedures (*procedural due process*) and fair laws (*substantive due process*).

duty   a human action required by law. Duty is the correlative of right, in that if one person has a right, there must rest upon some other person a corresponding duty; that which is due from a person.

duty of fair representation   the duty of a union to exercise its right to represent workers fairly and without discrimination.

duty to bargain   the requirement under the National Labor Relations Act that both the union and management bargain with each other on certain topics. There is no requirement that they agree, however.

economic regulation   licensing, certification, and direct economic supervision of certain industries, such as government-granted monopolies, public utilities, and certain other industries; "close" regulation.

economic school of jurisprudence   the philosophy that the law is the expression of economic forces, in which each actor assesses the costs and gains of every action including the legal costs and gains.

economic strikers   persons who strike to gain some economic concession from the employer.

economies of scale   the economic doctrine that as more is produced, each unit of output becomes less expensive to produce, up to a certain point (see *diminishing returns*).

eminent domain   the power of the government to take private property for a public use or purpose, subject to the government's duty to pay just compensation for that property.

enabling act   a legislative act that creates an *administrative agency* and grants it authority to make rules by the *delegation* of authority. Some enabling acts grant additional authority to already existing agencies.

entitlement legislation   laws creating rights to particular types of public welfare or other benefits, such as Social Security or Veterans' Benefits; social welfare legislation.

entity theory   the doctrine that certain business firms, such as corporations, are separate legal "persons" under the law.

enumerated powers   the *granted powers* of the federal government; those powers expressly set out in the Constitution.

Environmental Impact Statement (EIS)   a report of the effects of any federal project that "significantly affects the quality of the human environment" filed by the federal agency involved in the project and filed with the *Council on Environmental Quality,* as required by the National Environmental Policy Act.

equalization   (taxation) for purposes of many state property taxes, a process to make taxes fairer between regions or counties and to change the tax burden caused by differences in assessment by different assessors.

Equal Protection Clause   a part of the 14th Amendment that prohibits various forms of discriminatory *state action.* Under the Amendment, any classification scheme must have a *reasonable basis,* unless it involves *fundamental rights* or a protected category such as race, in which case the courts will subject the classification to the *strict scrutiny test.*

equitable maxims   a general statement of law universally admitted or applied in *equity* cases; an aphorism of law. Such maxims may take the place of decided cases in equity cases.

equitable relief   relief granted by a court of *equity;* usually in the form of a court order, such as an *injunction* or *specific performance,* but not including *damages.*

equity   (1) the spirit of fairness, justice, and fair dealing; (2) a system of jurisprudence administered by special courts, which was developed to mitigate the harsh results of the Law Courts through direct recourse to the King and which gives types of relief, such as *injunctions* and *specific performance,* that the law courts are incompetent to give (see *common law,* definition 2); (3) the difference between the value of property and the amount of the mortgages and liens on that property; the net value of property.

equity financing   financing through investment and ownership in a corporation through stock or shares (see *stockholder; debt financing; common stock; preferred stock*).

escheat   the reversion of property to the state or other unit of government in the event no person is competent to inherit the property upon the owner's death.

estates in land   any interest in land; any property interest in land, including both *freehold estates* and *leasehold estates.*

Establishment Clause   one of two parts of freedom of religion under the 1st Amendment to the U.S. Constitution that generally forbids government from establishing, supporting, or favoring a particular religion or sect (see *Free Exercise Clause*).

ethical dilemma   a clash between two or more ethical notions; a situation in which an individual cannot fulfill his or her personal ethics completely, but must choose between two or more ethical notions.

ethics (1) the set of rules, norms, and values by which each person judges the actions of others and of himself or herself; (2) the set of commonly held beliefs, rules, norms, and values of a particular group or society (see *societal ethics*); (3) a branch of philosophy that studies the actions of human beings and their relationships, as opposed to metaphysics, which studies the relationship of human beings to the universe, natural and supernatural.

exchange markets (securities law) the two national stock exchanges and the several regional stock exchanges.

excise tax a tax on a privilege, such as on the sale of a particular item or on carrying on a certain activity.

exclusionary rule a rule adopted by the courts to enforce the various criminal procedure requirements of the Constitution under the 4th, 5th, and 6th Amendments. The rule generally states that evidence seized in violation of those Amendments may not be introduced into evidence.

exclusive dealing arrangements (antitrust law) business contracts in which a purchaser agrees to deal only with a certain supplier (see *requirements contracts*) or a supplier agrees to deal only with a certain purchaser. Such arrangements may be illegal under either the Sherman or Clayton Acts.

executive privilege the doctrine that the executive branch need not turn over certain types of evidence to the legislative or judicial branches of government.

exemptions (taxation) for purpose of the federal income tax, subtractions from gross income for dependents, age, or blindness.

exhaustion of remedies (administrative law) the rule that before one may appeal an administrative judgment to the courts, all of the existing administrative procedures for review of that judgment must be used. The doctrine has many exemptions.

ex parte with only one side present; without participation by all of the parties.

express liability (securities law) express statements in the securities laws providing for civil actions to redress grievances for violations of those laws (see *implied liability*).

express warranty an explicit promise regarding a *contract* or the subject of the contract, made either orally or in writing.

fact-finding (labor law) mediation of a labor dispute, particularly those in the public sector, followed by a public airing of the dispute and the positions of the parties by the mediator if an impasse is not resolved.

Fair Trade laws state statutes that permitted *resale price maintenance* under the Miller-Tydings Act.

fair use doctrine the rule that permits the use of copyrighted material without permission for purposes of criticism, comment, news reporting, teaching, scholarship, or research.

featherbedding clauses in union-management contracts that require the employer to hire workers who are not needed.

Federalist Papers a set of essays written by Alexander Hamilton, John Jay, and James Madison that argued for the ratification of the Constitution. Much of our knowledge of the "intent of the Framers" comes from those essays.

Federal Register an official publication of the U.S. government that contains, among other things, notice of proposed administrative rules, in order to fulfill the "notice" requirement of *notice and comment rule making.*

federal question jurisdiction the authority of the federal courts to hear cases arising under the federal Constitution or federal law.

Federal Trade Commission (FTC) an *independent regulatory commission* created in 1914 and given authority over all "unfair and deceptive trade practices" together with a wide variety of other federal regulations of commerce.

fee simple (property law) an *estate in land* given to a person and his or her heirs absolutely, without condition or limitation; total ownership; the greatest interest in land that one may own (see *fee simple determinable; life estate*).

fee simple determinable (property law) also known as a fee simple conditional, base fee, or qualified fee; a *fee simple* subject to termination upon the happening of a certain condition, e.g., "to A and his heirs forever, unless the property is used for the sale of alcoholic beverages."

fellow-servant rule (tort law) the doctrine that one employee cannot recover *damages* from his or her employer for injuries caused by the *negligence* of another employee of the same employer; an exception to the doctrine of *respondeat superior.*

felony a serious crime, usually punishable by imprisonment in a state facility rather than a county jail, or by death.

fiduciary a person who stands in a relationship of trust and confidence to another.

fiduciary duties the duties imposed on any *fiduciary* by the law, including the duties of care, obedience, to account, loyalty, and notice.

final judgment the last action by a court from which appeals may be taken to a higher court.

final prospectus (securities law) any written communication that offers a security for sale or confirms the sale of a security. The final prospectus must contain much of the information required to be in the *registration statement.*

fiscal policy the theory that the economy can be controlled through taxing and spending policies.

fixtures a piece of personal property permanently affixed to real estate, thus becoming a part of the real estate.

fool's standard the FTC and judicial standard that the FTC advertising rules protect all consumers, not just the "reasonable person," and include the "ignorant, the unthinking, and the credulous."

foreign corporation a corporation formed under the law of some state other than the state in question (see *domestic corporation*).

formal rule making a procedure for making rules in an *administrative agency* that involves a trial-type hearing prior to the adoption of a new rule; required only if the *enabling act* requires the rule-making procedure to be "on the record."

forum non conveniens literally 'the court is not convenient'; the doctrine that provides that if two or more courts have proper *venue,* the court may determine which of those courts should hear the case based on fairness and convenience to the parties.

foundation a form of nonprofit organization, usually organized as a charitable *trust.*

fourth-line competition (injury to) (antitrust law) injury to customers in competition with a customer of a customer of the supplier's favored customer, caused by price discrimination.

four unities (property law) one of the basic requirements to create a *joint tenancy.* In order to create a joint tenancy with the right of survivorship, the property must be acquired by the owners (1) at the same time, (2) under the same title, (3) with the same proportionate interest, and (4) with equal rights of possession (see *joint tenancy; tenancy in common*).

franchise (1) a business arrangement in which an individual or firm buys the right to sell the products and services of a company and to use that company's name or trademark to do business; (2) a grant of a special privilege by a unit of government, such as the right to provide water or utility service to a community; (3) a grant of the privilege to incorporate by the government, usually by special act of the legislature; (4) any grant of a special privilege.

francise tax a tax paid by corporations for the privilege of being incorporated, usually paid annually and varying with the net worth or some other financial variable of the company.

fraud a misrepresentation of a material fact that induces another to take some action to his or her detriment.

Free Exercise Clause one of two parts of freedom of religion under the 1st Amendment to the Constitution that generally forbids government from interfering with personal religious beliefs (see *Establishment Clause*).

freehold estate an ownership interest in land, as distinguished from a *leasehold estate,* which grants only temporary rights of possession by lease. The term also includes all *future interests.*

free riders nonunion employees in an *open shop* who receive the benefits of a union contract but who do not join the union or pay union dues.

frolic and detour (tort law) the exception to the doctrine of *respondeat superior* that a master is not responsible for the torts of his or her servants if the tort was committed while the servant was not acting within the scope of employment but for personal purposes.

FTC see *Federal Trade Commission.*

FTC Guides   general guidelines of the Federal Trade Commission regarding certain problem areas, particularly deceptive trade practices and advertising, and providing information about what the law and FTC rules require.

full warranty   under the Magnuson-Moss Act, any warranty in which the warrantor agrees to remedy or repair a defect within a reasonable time, which does not limit the duration of the *implied warranties,* in which the warrantor agrees to replace the product if the defect cannot be remedied in a reasonable number of attempts and in which the consumer need only notify the warrantor to remedy the defect. Any other warranty must be designated as a *limited warranty.*

fundamental rights   those rights secured by the *Bill of Rights;* those rights which, if impaired, will cause the courts to apply the *strict scrutiny test* as opposed to the *reasonable basis test* in questions involving the *Equal Protection Clause.*

fungible   interchangeable goods; goods easily replaced by others that are identical. Fungible goods are usually sold by weight or volume, such as flour or wheat.

future interest   interests in lands or other things in which the right of possession and enjoyment is delayed until the future. Such interests may be *vested,* in which case the holder of the future interest will take possession at some future time, or contingent, in which case the holder may take possession if certain events take place.

general duty clause   the clause under the Occupational Safety and Health Act that requires employers to provide their employees with a workplace free from recognized hazards of employment.

general intent   the intent to perform a specific act, as the intent to pull the trigger on a gun, as opposed to the *specific intent,* to shoot someone with intent to obtain a specific result, e.g., to kill or injure.

general jurisdiction   the authority of a court to hear any type of case arising within the geographical area that court serves.

general partnership   a partnership in which all of the partners have a right to manage the affairs of the partnership equally and in which all of the partners are personally liable for the debts of the partnership (see *partnership; limited partnership*).

general tax   a tax levied on all persons in a widely defined class and bearing no relationship to the benefits received by the taxpayers (see *special tax*).

generic EIS (Environmental Impact Statement)   an *Environmental Impact Statement* used in relation to nuclear reactors, which contains a "boilerplate" or form statement of the environmental impact that will obtain in every case.

geographic market division   see *market division.*

Gissel remedy   an order by the National Labor Relations Board that, because unfair labor practices by an employer have so tainted a union election, a fair election cannot be held and, therefore, no election is required. The union is automatically considered to be the bargaining representative, even though no election is held and even if the union lost the election.

government in the sunshine statutes   open meetings laws; laws that require meetings of government bodies to be open to the public.

granted powers   the doctrine that the federal government and its branches have only those powers expressly granted to it by the Constitution (see *implied powers*).

grantee   the person receiving property by *deed.*

grantor   the person conveying property by *deed.*

grievance procedure   the portions of a labor contract that spell out how differences between employees and the employer are to be resolved.

gross income   (taxation) all income, from whatever source derived.

group boycotts   agreements between two or more persons that they will not purchase goods from another firm, or that they will not sell goods to another firm; a *per se* violation of the Sherman Act.

hazardous air pollutant   a pollutant for which no *National Ambient Air Quality Standard* has been established, but which may contribute to mortality or serious illness.

hearsay   repetition in court of a statement made by some person outside of court that is admitted to prove the truth of the out-of-court statement.

Herfindahl-Hirschman Index (HHI)   a numerical index of *concentration* of industries used in the Justice Department's *Merger Guidelines*. The percentage of market share of each firm is squared, and the squares of all of the firms are added together to find the HHI of the industry.

HHI   see *Herfindahl-Hirschman Index*.

historical school of jurisprudence   the philosophy of law that teaches that all law and legal institutions are the result of historical forces.

Hobbesian philosophy   the philosophy of Thomas Hobbes (1588–1679), which teaches that power gives right, based on the natural outcome of a "war of each against all," and that the stronger is the legitimate ruler, at least until someone still stronger appears.

holding company   a company whose sole purpose is holding stocks or securities in other companies.

horizontal agreements   agreements between competitors; agreements between firms or individuals at the same level of the distribution process of the same good or service (see *vertical agreements*).

horizontal geographic market division   see *market division*.

horizontal mergers   mergers or other corporate integration between competing firms.

hot cargo agreements   a part of a labor contract providing that employees are not required to handle or work on goods or materials going to or coming from an employer the union designates as "unfair."

impasse resolution techniques   methods of resolving disputes in public sector labor conflicts, instead of striking; *mediation, fact-finding,* voluntary *arbitration,* and compulsory *arbitration.*

implied liability   (securities regulation) liabilities imposed by the courts in the absence of an express statement in those laws permitting private civil actions to redress violation of the securities laws.

implied partnership   partnership found by the acts of the parties, rather than by express agreement of the partners; a failed attempt to form a corporation or a limited partnership may create an implied general partnership, for example.

implied powers   the powers of the federal government not expressly granted to the branches of government but "necessary and proper" to the execution of the *granted powers.*

implied warranties   warranties imposed by law, as opposed to *express warranties,* which are made by agreement of the parties.

implied warranty of fitness for a particular purpose   the *implied warranty* that a product will serve a consumer's special needs. The warranty is found if (1) the seller knows of the buyer's specific requirements for the product, (2) the buyer relies on the seller's skill and judgment in choosing the item. The warranty is given by both *merchants* and nonmerchant sellers.

implied warranty of merchantability   an *implied warranty* given by *merchants* that goods are fit to be sold, under six specific definitions of the term found in the Uniform Commercial Code.

implied warranty of title   a promise that the seller has the right to transfer goods, that the title to the goods is satisfactory, and that there are no outstanding *liens* or claims on the goods.

incidence of tax   the persons who actually pay a tax, after all shifting of the tax burden among taxpayers is completed.

in commerce   goods or commerce actually moving between states, as opposed to *affecting commerce,* in which goods are not moving between states but have an impact on *interstate commerce.*

independent contractor   one who acts for another (an *agent*) on an independent basis without being subject to the control of the *principal* (see *master-servant relationship; respondeat superior*).

independent regulatory commission (IRC)   administrative agencies that are somewhat independent from the executive branch, in that the members of the commission are appointed for overlapping terms longer than that of the President and who generally cannot be fired from their position without the consent of Congress (see *line agency*).

indication of interest   (securities regulation) a statement by a potential investor that he or she may purchase a stock or other security once it is available for sale after SEC review of the issue (see *waiting period; preliminary prospectus; tombstone ad*).

indictment   a formal accusation of a crime made by a grand jury (see *information*).

indirect tax   a tax levied on one person with the full understanding that it will be shifted to another (see *incidence of tax; direct tax*).

Individualist ethic the *societal ethic* that teaches that the individual is supreme and the interests of the community must submit to those of the individual. At its extreme, this ethic becomes anarchism and social Darwinism, while in its more moderate aspects simply holds that the interests of the individual must be protected against undue limitation (see *community ethic*).

Individual Retirement Account (IRA) a self-established retirement program in which a person makes a yearly contribution to a fund and which in turn is not taxed until the retiree withdraws those amounts from the account, usually at lower tax rates.

informal rule making see *notice and comment rule making.*

information a formal accusation of a crime made by a prosecutor or other public official, often on oath, but not presented to a grand jury (see *indictment*).

informational picketing picketing for the purpose of informing the public rather than for forcing some action on the part of the employer.

informational return (taxation) a tax return filed by partnerships or other entities not taxed simply informing the government of the amounts received and expended.

inheritance tax a tax imposed by many states on receiving money from a decedent or from an estate.

injunction an order issued by a court of *equity* directing a person not to do a certain act or stopping the continuance of that act. See *mandatory injunction.*

inquisitorial system the system of law in most of the world aside from the United States and Great Britain. In the inquisitorial system, all parties, including the judge, actively seek evidence to arrive at the truth. The judge usually represents the state's interest in the trial, and searches for evidence independent of the parties (see *adversary system*).

insider (securities regulation) a person who has access to nonpublic information about a corporation by way of a position within the corporation.

insider trading (securities regulation) trading of securities of a corporation by *insiders* (see *tippee*).

institutional decisions (administrative law) a method of administrative decision-making in *adjudicatory* proceedings in which a hearing officer or *Administrative Law Judge* takes the evidence on the record and then forwards the record to the agency's board, which makes the final decision based on that record.

insured status (Social Security law) the status of an employee necessary to be covered by the Social Security Act. There are three forms: (1) fully insured, (2) currently insured, and (3) insured for disability benefits. The insured status is determined by quarters of eligibility, i.e., the number of three-month segments a person has worked under the Social Security Act.

interlocking directorates (antitrust law) when one or more persons serve on the boards of directors of two or more corporations; a violation of the Clayton Act if the corporations are competing, though some businesses are exempt from this provision.

interlocutory appeals an appeal of something other than a *final judgment,* such as appeal of an order of discovery or a pretrial motion. Interlocutory appeals are permitted in only exceptional circumstances.

interrogatories a part of *discovery;* a list of written questions submitted to a party to a lawsuit by another party, which must be answered under oath and in writing (see *deposition*).

interstate commerce commerce moving between two or more states (see *intrastate commerce; in commerce; affecting commerce*).

intestate succession a succession to property owned by a person who had no will or whose will is void, as determined by state statutes that determine who shall inherit property (see *testate succession; law of descent and distribution*).

intraenterprise conspiracy (antitrust law) an agreement or conspiracy between individuals or firms that are a part of the same firm, e.g., agreements between a parent company and its subsidiaries or between the officers of the same firm.

intrastate commerce commerce totally within one state (see *interstate commerce; in commerce; affecting commerce*).

investigative function the function of *agencies* to collect data to aid in their *rule-making* and *adjudicatory* functions.

investment advisors (securities regulation) persons who advise others regarding *securities* for compensation.

investment bankers bankers who specialize in marketing securities, often acting as *underwriters* for issues of stock or securities.

investment company a corporation formed for the purpose of investing in the stock of another company.

invidious discrimination objectionable discrimination; in a legislative act, discrimination or classification based on impermissible categories, such as race.

IRA see *Individual Retirement Account.*

issued shares *authorized shares* that have in fact been issued to shareholders.

jingle rule a rule of priority between personal creditors of partners and partnership creditors. Individual creditors must proceed against individual assets of partners, partnership creditors must proceed against partnership assets, and each must stand behind the other if assets are insufficient.

joint stock association an unincorporated business form in which investors pool their funds and receive stock certificates in return, and which is managed by a board of directors elected or appointed by the shareholders.

joint tenancy (property law) ownership of *property* by two or more persons whereby at the death of one of the joint tenants, the surviving joint tenants automatically and as a matter of law take the deceased joint tenant's share (see *four unities*). State statutes usually prescribe strict rules for the formation of joint tenancies, including the use of certain specific language in a deed creating the joint tenancy (see *tenancy in common*).

joint venture a *partnership,* usually temporary, between two or more business entities, for joint participation in an endeavor.

judgment the official and final decision of a court on the rights and claims of the parties to a lawsuit; the law's last word on a controversy.

judgment n.o.v. literally, 'judgment notwithstanding the verdict'; a motion filed by a party after an adverse *verdict,* asking that the court enter *judgment* contrary to the verdict.

judgment on the pleadings a motion made by a party asserting that there is no issue to resolve after the pleadings are filed and asking judgment without further proceedings.

judicial review the doctrine that the courts, particularly the U.S. Supreme Court, have the right to hold acts of the executive and legislative branches unconstitutional and void.

jurisdiction (1) the power and authority to hear a case; (2) the geographical area a court serves; (3) the persons and subject matter over which a court has authority to hear cases and make decisions (see *venue*).

jurisprudence the study of philosophy of law; the study of law itself.

jury instructions oral or written instructions to the jury from the judge regarding the law that the jury is to apply in a case.

labor spies (labor law) persons employed by management to infiltrate labor organizations to determine the plans and leadership of such organizations.

laissez faire literally 'let the people do as they choose'; the doctrine of opposition to governmental interference, particularly in economic affairs.

land trust (property law) a form of ownership of land in *trust,* in which the owner of property *deeds* the property to a *trustee,* and the land is to be used by the trustee for the benefit of some other person.

law courts courts that give legal remedies, or money *damages,* instead of equitable remedies (see *equity,* definition 2).

law of descent and distribution a statute in each state providing how property is to be distributed in the event a person dies without a will (see *interstate succession*).

Law Merchant the system of rules, customs, and usages used by traders in England and later incorporated into the common law to regulate contracts and transactions in goods.

leasehold estates (property law) an *estate in land* under a lease; an estate for a fixed term or a period of time, sometimes renewable or at will; an estate of temporary possession of land.

legal fiction an assumption or statement of the law that is not true but is given effect by the law, e.g., that a corporation is a "person."

legality   (contract law) one of the elements of a *contract*, which requires that an agreement, in order to be considered a valid contract, must be legal both in its object and in the means by which it is to be accomplished.

legal realism   the school of legal philosophy that teaches that all we can be concerned about in any analysis of the law is a description of the law itself; also called legal positivism.

legislative veto   the retention in an *enabling act* of the right of the legislature to override the actions of the *administrative agency* to which power was delegated, usually by legislative actions involving less formality than formal law making activity, e.g., by the vote of one house of Congress.

lessee   one who holds property under a lease; a tenant.

lessor   one who grants possession of land to another under a lease; a landlord.

libel   a written *defamation* (see *slander*).

lien   a claim on *property* that is allowed by law, which usually receives priority over other claims based merely on contract or other grounds.

life estate   (property law) a *freehold estate* in which *property* is granted to another for his or her lifetime only, as in a grant "to A for life, then to B." A common variant is a life estate pur autrie vie (for the life of another) in which the measuring life is some other person than the holder of the life estate, as in "to A for the life of C, then to B."

limited jurisdiction   the power and authority of a court to hear a case that is somehow less than *general jurisdiction* (see *jurisdiction*).

limited liability   the concept that business investors may only be liable to the extent of their investment, and creditors of the business may not attack personal assets of investors to satisfy business debts (see *corporation; limited partnership*).

limited partnership   a form of partnership available under statute in which certain partners may invest in the partnership and be liable only to the extent of the funds invested for partnership debts; such limited partners may not take part in the management of the partnership, and there must be at least one general partner (see *partnership; general partnership*).

limited warranties   any warranty that does not fulfill the requirements of a *full warranty,* under the Magnuson-Moss Warranty Act.

line agency   (administrative law) an *administrative agency* directly responsible to the executive and usually headed by a single administrator, who serves at the pleasure of the executive (see *independent regulatory commissions*).

line of commerce   part of the language of Section 7 of the Clayton Act, which requires that an anticompetitive effect of a *merger* must take place in a particular *relevant product market.*

lock-outs   (labor law) plant closings by employers to force employees to submit to employer demands.

long-arm statutes   state statutes that permit the courts of a state to exercise *jurisdiction* over persons or property outside of that state.

malice   ill will or bad motive; having no moral or legal justification.

malicious competition   a common law *tort* forbidding competing for a predatory purpose.

malum in se   literally, 'evil of itself'; crimes that are also morally wrong in the eyes of most people, such as murder or robbery (see *malum prohibitum*).

malum prohibitum   literally, 'evil because it is prohibited'; crimes that are crimes only because the law makes them so, rather than because the acts are morally wrong, such as traffic laws (see *malum in se*).

management   a general term indicating those who actually run a business; in the corporate form the term refers to the board of directors and the *officers.*

mandamus   a court order requiring a public official to perform his or her duties.

mandatory bargaining topics   (labor law) issues over which labor and management must bargain, such as wages, work rules, union status, and conditions of work.

mandatory injunction   a court order issued by an equity court ordering a person to affirmatively perform an act, as distinguished from an *injunction,* which orders a person not to perform an act.

margin   (securities regulation) purchasing stock on credit; the margin is the amount of credit extended (see *margin maintenance rules; margin requirements*).

marginal cost   the incremental cost of each additional unit produced.

marginal revenue   the increased revenue a producer receives with each additional unit produced.

margin maintenance rules   (securities regulation) rules imposed by many securities exchanges requiring the payment of additional margin if the value of stocks purchased on credit declines (see *margin; margin requirements*).

margin requirements   (securities regulation) rules of the Federal Reserve Board specifying the maximum amount of credit that may be given by brokers on the sale of stock and further specifying how much of a "down payment" is required (see *margin; margin maintenance requirements*).

market divison   (antitrust law) also known as horizontal geographic market division, the concept involves agreements between competing firms to divide up a market geographically and create regional monopolies; a *per se* violation of the Sherman Act.

market extension merger   (antitrust law) a merger between firms that produce identical products but sell them in different regions.

market manipulation   (securities regulation) trading in shares that, of itself, affects the price of the shares for the benefit of the person trading (see *wash sales*).

marketplace theory of speech   the idea that all ideas should be allowed to enter the "marketplace of ideas," since the public will only accept those ideas that are valid and good, and will refuse to "buy" those that are invalid or untrue; one of the principal justifications for the 1st Amendment to the Constitution.

Massachusetts trust   see *business trust.*

master   an employer (see *master-servant relationship; respondeat superior*).

master-servant relationship   (agency law) a type of *agency* relationship, distinguished from that involving an *independent contractor,* whereby the master has the right to control the work of the *servant.* The distinction is factual and based on the degree to which the principal may control the activities of the agent (see *respondeat superior*).

mediation   a dispute settlement technique in which an outside third party (a mediator) tries to settle a dispute through persuasion. The mediator has no power to force a settlement (see *arbitration*).

Mediation and Conciliation Service   (labor law) an independent federal agency that offers a neutral third party to mediate labor disputes, either on its own motion or at the request of either party (see *mediation*).

Medicare   (Social Security law) a 1965 amendment to the Social Security Act, which provides medical insurance to those otherwise eligible for any form of Social Security.

meet and confer laws   (labor law) in public employee labor negotiations, statutes that require the union and the employer to meet and discuss issues prior to the adoption of policies by the employer-government (see *impasse resolution techniques*).

meeting competition defense   (antitrust law) a defense to a charge of *price discrimination* under the Robinson-Patman Act, based on lowering one's price to a specific purchaser to meet (but not beat) a competitor's price to that customer.

mental element   a part of the proof required in many criminal statutes of a particular mental state or intention on the part of the defendant, such as "knowingly," or "intentionally" or "recklessly."

merchant   a special status accorded or imposed by the Uniform Commercial Code on persons who regularly deal in goods of the kind sold, or who hold themselves out as having knowledge or skill peculiar to the goods sold, or who deal through *agents* who hold themselves out as having such special knowledge or skill.

merger   (1) a method of *corporate integration* in which one firm acquires and absorbs another, causing the acquired firm to cease to exist; (2) sometimes used to refer to all methods of corporate integration, somewhat improperly.

Merger Guidelines   (antitrust law) a set of guides established by the U.S. Department of Justice, first in 1968, substantially amended in 1982, and re-amended in 1984, which provides guidelines for business regarding which *mergers* or other *corporate integrations* will be prosecuted by the Department. The Guidelines are not binding on the Department or on the courts.

misappropriation   a common law *tort* forbidding asserting that another's product is one's own.

misdeameanor   a less serious criminal offense, usually punishable by imprisonment in a facility other than the state penitentiary, or by fine.

Model Business Corporation Act   a model act specifying most of the law relating to *corporations* and adopted in whole or in part in many states.

monopolization   (antitrust law) an offense under Section 2 of the Sherman Act, consisting of (1) possession of *monopoly* power in the *relevant market;* and (2) wilful acquisition or maintenance of that power.

monopoly   total *concentration* of an industry in the hands of one person or firm.

motion to dismiss   a motion filed at the outset of a case, claiming that a *complaint* is deficient in some way and should be dismissed, either with or without prejudice to filing an amended complaint.

motion to suppress   the legal procedure used to obtain exclusion of evidence from trial under the *exclusionary rule.*

mutuality   (contract law) sometimes considered an element of a *contract,* in that both parties are mutually bound to the agreement, and no party is bound unless all are bound.

NAAQS   see *National Ambient Air Quality Standards.*

NASD   see *National Association of Securities Dealers.*

National Ambient Air Quality Standards (NAAQS)   (environmental law) standards for air quality, established by the EPA (see *primary standards; secondary standards*).

National Association of Securities Dealers (NASD)   (securities regulation) a private association of securities *dealers* and *brokers* which has established rules regarding *securities.*

National Institute for Occupational Safety and Health (NIOSH)   a research body established by OSHA to aid in the formulation of health and safety standards for the Secretary of Labor.

National Labor Relations Board (NLRB)   a federal *independent regulatory commission* established by the Wagner Act with authority to make rules, to hold elections on labor matters, and to hold hearings on *unfair labor practice* charges.

natural rights theory   the doctrine that government arose out of a *contract* (compact) between human beings, in which each person gave up the right to rule himself in return for the protection of government, and therefore government ruled by the consent of the governed; the basis of the American Declaration of Independence.

negligence   the failure to do that which an ordinary and prudent person would do under like circumstances.

Neutralists   judges who find certain fixed principles of justice in the Constitution, and apply the "plain meaning" of the words in the Constitution. Such judges think of themselves as "mere conduits" through which the Constitution speaks (see *Activists; Restraintists*).

nexus   a connection; for purposes of state taxation, a state may only tax if the object taxed has a connection, or nexus, with that state.

NIOSH   see *National Institute of Occupational Safety and Health.*

NLRB   see *National Labor Relations Board.*

no change letter   (taxation) a letter sent by the IRS following an audit stating that there is no additional amount owing.

nominal damages   damages in name only; money, usually one dollar plus costs of suit awarded to a plaintiff who has suffered some injury to a right, but no other loss compensable in money (see *damages; compensatory damages; punitive damages*).

nonattainment areas   (environmental law) areas in which the National Ambient Air Quality Standards have not been met.

noncumulative dividends   *dividends* that do not accumulate from year to year if they are not paid.

nonparticipating preferred shares   *preferred stock* that receives its own *dividends* prior to *common stock* but that does not receive a dividend with the common stock, as in the case of *participating preferred shares.*

nonsigner's clause   (antitrust law) clauses in a *resale price maintenance* agreement between a manufacturer and a retailer that bind all other sellers of that product to the agreement, regardless of whether they are parties to the agreement.

no-strike clauses   (labor law) provisions of a labor contract prohibiting strikes during the contract period (see *wildcat strike*).

not-for-profit corporation   a special form of organization permitting *limited liability* for participants and specifying organization and structure of nonprofit or charitable organizations.

notice and comment rule making   (administrative law) a method of administrative *rule making* wherein the *agency* is required by the Administrative Procedure Act to give advance notice to the public of a proposed rule and provide an opportunity to the public to comment on that rule before the rule becomes effective.

notice of appeal   the first paper filed in an appeal, usually setting out in general terms the fact that an appeal is intended and the general nature of the appeal, and required to be filed within a specific time of the final *judgment* of the lower court.

Nuclear Regulatory Commission (NRC)   the federal agency (previously the Atomic Energy Commission) responsible for licensing of nuclear power plants, research in atomic energy, and inspection of nuclear facilities.

nuisance   something or some activity that annoys or disturbs unreasonably (see *private nuisance; public nuisance*).

Occupational Safety and Health Administration   a part of the Department of Labor established by the Occupational Safety and Health Act to enforce the provisions of the Act and the rules established by the Secretary of Labor for workplace safety.

offer   (contract law) an act on the part of one person giving to another the legal power to create a contract; a proposal to make a contract.

offeree   (contract law) the person to whom an *offer* is made.

offering circular   (securities regulation) a document, similar to a *prospectus,* that gives information about a stock issue and a corporation not subject to the prospectus requirement because the issue is under $5 million (see *Regulation A exception*).

offeror   (contract law) the person making an *offer.*

officers   the persons elected or appointed by the board of directors to manage the day-to-day affairs of a corporation; usually the president, vice-president, secretary, and treasurer.

offset   (environmental law) in *nonattainment areas,* polluters may obtain permits to build new pollution sources only if they shut down existing ones, thus creating an offset.

old-age benefits   (Social Security law) benefits payable in the form of a pension to workers who have reached a certain age and are otherwise eligible to receive Social Security benefits.

oligopoly   concentration of an industry in a few hands.

open meetings acts   see *government in the sunshine statutes.*

open shop agreements   (labor law) union contracts that permit employees to either join or not join the labor union that is the bargaining representative of the employees (see *union shop; Right-to-Work laws*).

option   (contract law) an irrevocable *offer;* an offer in which the *offeree* has given consideration for the offer to remain open for a period of time.

original jurisdiction   the power of a court to try a case, as opposed to *appellate jurisdiction.*

OSHA   see *Occupational Safety and Health Administration;* also stands for Occupational Safety and Health Act.

outcome determinative test   the test used in federal courts to determine whether state federal procedures will be used in diversity jurisdiction cases. If the use of federal procedures will change or affect the outcome of the case, the federal courts will use state procedures (see *diversity jurisdiction*).

outstanding shares   *issued shares* that remain in the hands of stockholders, as opposed to *treasury shares,* which are issued shares that have been reacquired by the corporation.

overt conspiracy   an open conspiracy; one made publicly or without attempt at concealment.

over-the-counter market (OTC market)   (securities regulation) the market in which securities not listed on any national or regional stock exchange are traded. This "market" has no physical location (see *exchange market*).

parallel action   similar action by two or more parties without express agreement or communication, as in *price leadership*.

parens patriae action   (antitrust) a remedy that permits state attorneys general to sue under the federal antitrust laws on behalf of the citizens of their states.

participating preferred shares   *preferred stock* that receives its own preferred *dividend* and also receives a dividend with the common shares (see *nonparticipating preferred shares*).

partnership   under the *Uniform Partnership Act,* an association of two or more persons to carry on as co-owners a business for profit (see *general partnership; limited partnership*).

partnership property   a form of *property* ownership created by the *Uniform Partnership Act,* which consists of "all property originally brought into a partnership or subsequently acquired by purchase or otherwise, on account of the partnership."

passing off   common law *tort* that forbids asserting that one's product was made by another (see *product simulation*).

patent   (1) the grant of a limited *monopoly* to the inventor of a product; (2) the original grant of title to land from the government to a private individual; the first grant of private ownership.

permissive bargaining topics   (labor law) all topics over which labor and management may bargain; all bargaining topics except those designated as *mandatory bargaining topics* by the National Labor Relations Act.

perceived potential competition   (antitrust law) a doctrine used to show the anticompetitive effect of *product extension* and *market extension mergers* by showing that persons in a market changed their competitive behavior based on their perception that a particular firm might enter the market; the "wings" effect (see *potential competition; actual potential competition*).

per curiam   literally 'by the court'; a decision of the whole court; a unanimous decision, often without written opinion.

peremptory challenge   an objection to a juror's serving on a case for no expressed reason. Usually attorneys receive a set number of peremptory challenges in a case, and may excuse jurors until that number runs out, unless there is a reason for excusing the juror sufficient to provide grounds for a *challenge for cause.*

perfect competition   an ideal economic state of small buyers and a small sellers, none of which can affect price, and creating optimal economic benefits of low price and high output and efficiency.

per se rules   (antitrust) literally 'of itself' exceptions to the *Rule of Reason,* which provide that in-depth analysis of whether a particular restraint of trade is unreasonable or unnecessary; situations in which the courts hold that a restraint of trade always occurs.

personal deductions   (taxation) specific items that may be subtracted from *adjusted gross income* in order to find *taxable income.*

personal ethics   individually held notions of right and wrong; an individual's moral code, by which he or she judges the actions of others and of himself or herself.

personal jurisdiction   *jurisdiction* over an individual, obtained through *service of process.*

personal property   all property not considered a *freehold estate* or an interest in land; movable property, including both tangible and intangible property.

piercing the corporate veil   imposing personal liability on shareholders for actions of the corporation in instances where the corporation is a "mere shell" and the shareholders have treated the corporation as an "alter ego" of themselves; disregarding the corporate fiction.

plaintiff   the party who files a lawsuit; the injured party seeking relief from the court.

plea bargaining   a process in criminal cases in which the defendant and prosecutor agree that the defendant will plead guilty to certain charges, and the prosecutor will either dismiss other charges or recommend a certain sentence or punishment (see *prosecutorial discretion*).

pleadings   the formal, written statements filed by the parties to a lawsuit, consisting of the *complaint, answer(s), cross-claims, counterclaims, third-party complaints,* and the *answers* to them, and sometimes including *motions to dismiss.*

plenary power   full, complete or unqualified power.

pluralism   any form of government in which the government's authority is limited in some way.

point source   (environmental law) a single source of water pollution, such as a pipe or drainage tile.

police power   the inherent power of the states to regulate for purposes of health, welfare, safety, and morals.

poll tax   a tax on the right to vote, or on all persons within a specific jurisdiction of a particular class, such as on all males, or all voters.

pool   a voluntary association of competing firms, operating together and physically dividing a market between them.

Populists   an American political third party that existed in the late 1800's centered in the agricultural Midwest, and that favored regulation of railroads and banks, strict antitrust enforcement, and a graduated income tax.

Positivism   see *legal realism.*

potential competition   (antitrust law) the doctrine that firms in a market change their competitive behavior based on the threat of entry into the market by other firms; the "wings" effect (see *actual potential competition; perceived potential competition*).

precedent   see *stare decisis.*

preclusion of review   (administrative law) a statement in a statute which provides that courts may not review the actions of an *administrative agency.*

predatory conduct   (antitrust law) some conduct, legal or illegal, evidencing an intent to obtain a larger market share by anticompetitive means.

preemption   the doctrine that state laws in conflict with legitimate federal laws or administrative regulations are void under the Supremacy Clause (Article VI, Section 2) of the U.S. Constitution.

preemptive rights   the doctrine that shareholders should have the right of first refusal of stock that may dilute their ownership interests.

preferred stock   stock that gets special rights, usually to *dividends* or assets, over other shares; often the preferred stock must give up voting rights in order to receive rights to dividends or assets (see *common stock; participating* and *nonparticipating preferred shares*).

preliminary prospectus   (securities regulation) also known as a "red herring" prospectus; a document used to solicit *indications of interest* during the *waiting period* of SEC review of a stock issue. (see *final prospectus*).

premerger notification   (antitrust law) the requirement under the Hart-Scott-Rodino Antitrust Improvements Act of 1976 that firms over certain thresholds must notify the Justice Department and the FTC prior to actually merging.

presumption   an inference as to the existence of some fact not yet proven, drawn from the existence of some other fact already proven.

pretrial conference   a meeting prior to trial between the attorneys for all sides and the judge, at which the *pleadings* are settled, *discovery* finalized, and settlement discussed.

price discrimination   (antitrust law) charging different prices to different customers for goods of the same type in two reasonable contemporaneous sales.

price fixing   (antitrust law) an agreement between two or more persons to set the price of a product or service. *Horizontal* price fixing involves agreements between competitors to set the price of a good or service, while *vertical* price fixing is an agreement between a supplier and a purchaser that the purchaser's resale price will be set at a certain level. Both forms are *per se* illegal.

price leadership   a form of *parallel action* in which competitors follow the lead of one firm in setting prices.

prima facie proof   evidence that suffices for the proof of a particular fact until overcome or contradicted by other evidence.

primary line competition (injury to)   (antitrust law) injury caused by *price discrimination* to the seller's competitors.

primary standards   (environmental law) air quality standards which are necessary to protect the public health (see *National Ambient Air Quality Standards*).

principal   one on whose behalf an *agent* acts (see *agency,* definition 1).

Printer's Ink Model Statute   a "uniform act" first proposed by the advertising trade journal *Printer's Ink* and adopted by many states, which outlaws deceptive advertising.

prior restraint   regulation of speech or press before the speech or printed word is disseminated; prior censorship, as opposed to punishment after dissemination.

private law   law that regulates the relationships between private individuals, including the law of *contracts, torts, agency, partnerships, corporations,* and *property* (see *public law*).

private nuisance   a *tort* involving special harm to the plaintiff arising from some unreasonable use of property (see *public nuisance*).

private offering   (securities regulation) an offering for sale of a security to a single individual or group of individuals, rather than to the public as a whole.

privileges   the right or duty of certain persons to withhold evidence under certain circumstances, e.g., spousal privilege, attorney-client privilege, doctor-patient privilege, or priest-penitent privilege. Others may exist by statute in some states.

privity of contract   the doctrine that only the parties to a *contract* may sue for breaches of the contract.

probable cause   one of the requirements for a valid search and seizure under the 4th Amendment; it generally means "reasonable cause" or "reasonable ground for belief," which must exist before a warrant may issue or a search may be made.

procedural due process   fair procedures, both in the courtroom and in administrative hearings, requiring at least notice of the proceedings and a right to be heard.

procedural law   the legal machinery for carrying on a lawsuit, as distinguished from *substantive law* such as contracts, torts, etc.

product extension merger   (antitrust law) a *corporate integration* between firms involved in a similar but noncompeting products.

product simulation   intentional duplication of the physical characteristics of a competitor's product (see *passing off*).

products liability   that field of *tort* and *contract* law which imposes liability on sellers or others for injuries or damages resulting from the sale of defective or unsafe products.

progressive tax   a tax that taxes higher incomes at higher marginal rates and lower incomes at lower marginal rates (see *regressive tax*).

promissory estoppel   (contract law) a promise that the promisor should reasonably expect to induce action or forebearance of the promisee; a promise on which another relies, to his or her detriment.

property   an aggregate of rights protected by the government; a *bundle of rights* in some tangible or intangible thing.

proprietorship   see *sole proprietorship.*

prosecutorial discretion   the right of prosecutors to run cases in the way they see fit, including the right to dismiss or refuse to dismiss and the right to *plea bargain.*

prospectus   see *final prospectus; preliminary prospectus.*

protective legislation   laws that protect the public from some perceived danger.

proximate cause   that which, in a natural and continuous sequence, and unbroken by any intervening cause, produces an injury; that without which the result would not have occured; the immediate, direct cause.

proxy   voting by representation in a *corporation;* the statement by which a shareholder gives another the right to vote stock.

proxy solicitation rules   (securities regulation) restrictions on obtaining and soliciting *proxies.*

proxy statement   (securities regulation) a statement filed with the SEC when *proxies* are solicited, disclosing all of the material facts regarding the matters to be voted upon at the meeting for which the proxy is solicited; one of the *proxy solicitation rules.*

public law   the law regulating the relationship between the government and individuals, including Constitutional law, criminal law, and administrative law (see *private law*).

public nuisance   a crime involving injury to the public arising from an unreasonable use of land (see *private nuisance*).

public offering   (securities regulation) a solicitation to sell securities made to the general public (see *private offering*).

publicity picketing   see *informational picketing*.

punitive damages   money damages over and above *compensatory damages* awarded to the *plaintiff* to punish the *defendant* for a malicious or intentional (and in a few states, reckless) act; exemplary damages (see *damages; nominal damages*).

purchase of assets   a form of *corporate integration* in which one firm pays cash to another firm in return for all of the assets of that firm. The acquired firm usually must liquidate since all of its assets are in the form of cash.

purchase of stock   a form of *corporate integration* in which one firm purchases all or a controlling portion of the stock of another corporation (see *tender offer*).

pure conglomerate merger   a merger between firms involved in the production, sale, or distribution of totally unrelated products or services (see *conglomerate merger; product extension merger; market extension merger*).

quarterly report   a report filed quarterly with the SEC by firms subject to the 1934 Securities and Exchange Act (see *annual report* and *current report*).

rate base   the value of the assets of a firm subject to *economic regulation* upon which the rate of return to investors in such firm is determined.

rate making   the administrative process in *economic regulation* of establishing prices for firms subject to such regulation.

rate structure   the various prices set by an administrative agency involved in *rate making* for an economically regulated firm.

ratification   to approve after the fact; as when a *principal* approves an action taken on his or her behalf by an *agent* without authority.

realization   (taxation) for purposes of the federal income tax, the principle that income must be actually received or available for use before it is taxed.

real property   (property) land and all things permanently affixed to the land, and including all interests in land.

reasonable basis test   the test to determine whether a classification system in a statute violates the *Equal Protection Clause* of the 14th Amendment, if the classification scheme is not based on a *suspect classification* or does not involve *fundamental rights*. The issue in such cases is whether the legislature had a "reasonable basis" for making the classification (see *strict scrutiny test*).

rebuttable presumption   a *presumption* that may be overcome by evidence, as distinguished from a *conclusive presumption*, which cannot be overcome by evidence.

reciprocity   (antitrust law) an agreement or requirement that one firm will sell to or buy from another firm on condition that the second firm will sell to or buy from a subsidiary or parent of the first firm.

recklessness   carelessness, heedlessness, inattention or indifference to consequences; wilful and wanton disregard of known circumstances.

recognition clause   (labor law) a clause in a labor contract in which the employer recognizes the union as the exclusive bargaining agent of the employees.

recognition letter   (labor law) a letter from a union to management requesting recognition of the union as the bargaining representative of the employees based on an *authorization card* majority.

record on appeal   the formal, written account of a case, consisting of all of the papers filed with the court and either a transcript of the proceedings or a summary of the evidence as agreed to by the parties and the judge.

record review   (administrative law) a review of an administrative decision by a court based on the record before the agency; no new evidence may be presented before the court (see *review de novo*).

redirect examination   the second examination of one's own witnesses, following the opponent's *cross-examination* (see *direct examination*).

reformation   (contract law) a remedy granted by a court of *equity* to the parties to a written instrument, which reforms the instrument to conform to the real intent of the parties.

registration statement   (securities regulation) a form filed with the SEC by any issuer of new securities, with certain exceptions, disclosing a description of the issuing firm's business, a description of the security, information about the management of the firm, and financial statements prepared by independent accountants.

regressive tax   (taxation) a tax that taxes lower incomes at the same or a higher marginal rate than higher incomes (see *progressive tax*).

Regulation A exception   (securities regulation) an exemption from the registration requirements of the 1933 Securities Act covering small issues of securities; an *offering circular* is required, however.

rejection   refusal to accept the terms of an *offer* to make a *contract*, expressed to the *offeror*.

relevant evidence   evidence that bears upon and has a tendency to prove a fact in issue.

relevant geographic market   (antitrust law) the geographic area within which two or more firms effectively compete.

relevant product market   (antitrust law) the products that effectively compete with each other.

remand   to send a case back to a lower court for further proceedings, usually in conjunction with a reversal of that court's judgment, when there is something more to be done by the lower court, such as take additional evidence or retry the case (see *reverse; affirm*).

removal   the transfer of a case from one court to another, particularly the transfer of a case from the state courts to the federal courts.

republican government   a government by representatives chosen by the people (see *democratic government*).

request to produce   a letter or other document, from one side of a case to another, requesting that evidence be turned over for inspection and copying; a part of *discovery*.

requirements contracts   an agreement by a purchaser that it will purchase all of its requirements of a particular good or service from a particular supplier.

resale price maintenance   (antitrust law) a vertical *price-fixing* agreement; agreement between buyer and seller that the buyer will charge a certain price for the products purchased upon resale.

rescission   to cancel out a *contract* and return the parties to their original position.

res ipsa loquitor   literally 'the thing speaks for itself'; the *tort* doctrine that shifts the burden to the defendant to prove that he or she was not responsible for an injury, if the plaintiff proves that the injury was caused by an instrumentality in the exclusive control of the defendant, and the incident is of a type not ordinarily caused except by *negligence.*

res judicata   literally 'the thing has been adjudicated'; the rule that once a court has decided a case or an issue, that case or issue cannot be adjudged again, and the prior decision must be accepted unless it is overturned on appeal; not to be confused with the Constitutional doctrine of *double jeopardy.*

respondeat superior   literally 'let the superior respond'; a *tort* and *agency* doctrine in which an employer *(master)* is liable for the torts of his or her employees *(servants)* if the tort is committed in the scope of the employee's employment; the master is not liable for the torts of *independent contractors,* however.

Restraintists   judges who counsel restraint in dealing with Constitutional matters and who avoid Constitutional confrontations whenever possible. Such judges typically use a "balancing of interests" approach to such controversies (see *Activists; Neutralists*).

restrictive covenants   *contracts* that involve a condition that one party will not enter into competition with another party, usually found in contracts for the sale of a business or employment contracts. Such contracts may be valid if they are reasonable, both in their duration and in the geographic areas in which a party is restricted from competing.

retroactive advertising   a judicial remedy for deceptive or misleading advertising in which the court orders the guilty party to advertise, at its own expense, corrections of past deceptions; corrective advertising.

Revenue Rulings   rulings of the Internal Revenue Service on individual tax cases which are available as guidelines and limited precedents for other taxpayers.

revenue sharing   federal sharing of tax revenues with the states in the form of grants.

reverse   to vacate or set aside a prior judgment, usually of a lower court (see *remand; affirm*).

review de novo   (administrative law) a review of the actions of the *administrative agency* by the courts in which the court permits evidence to be presented, usually by retrying the entire case (see *record review*).

revocation   (contract law) the recall or withdrawal of an *offer* by an *offeror.*

right of privacy   a Constitutional right found by interpretation of several parts of the Constitution, generally prohibiting government interference with those aspects of a person's life the courts consider private.

right of rescission   the right given to consumers under some federal laws and regulations to terminate a *contract* within a certain period of time; the consumer must return whatever he or she received under the contract, and the seller must return the money paid and void the contract.

Right-to-Work laws   (labor law) state statutes that outlaw *union shop* contracts.

rule making   (administrative law) the function of *administrative agencies* in making rules and regulations pursuant to a *delegation* of authority from the legislature (see *enabling act*).

Rule of Reason   (antitrust) the doctrine that, even though the Sherman act prohibits "every contract, combination . . . or conspiracy . . . in restraint of trade . . .", the legislators really intended that only unreasonable restraints be prohibited. The doctrine requires a full-scale economic analysis in each case, unless a *per se rule* applies.

runaway shop   (labor law) shutting down or moving a plant to avoid unionization or union pressure.

sales tax   (taxation) a tax on the sale of a good, usually computed as a percentage of the sales price.

scabs   persons hired to take the place of striking workers; also, workers who refuse to strike.

scalping   (securities regulation) an illegal practice of securities *brokers* who make recommendations to customers to purchase securities in which the broker has personally invested, in order to make the value of the broker's stock go up.

scienter   knowingly or with guilty knowledge; with intent to defraud or deceive.

scope of employment doctrine   the rule that a *master* is only liable for the torts of his or her servants that are committed while in the limits of the employment authority (see *respondeat superior*).

SEC   see *Securities and Exchange Commission.*

secondary boycotts   (labor law) union pressure on one employer to not deal with another employer or with the goods of another employer.

secondary line competition (injury to)   (antitrust law) injury to competitors of the buyer caused by the seller's *price discrimination.*

secondary standards   (environmental law) air quality standards necessary to protect nonhuman elements, such as buildings, animals, and crops (see *primary standards; National Ambient Air Quality Standards*).

section of the country   (antitrust) a part of the statutory language of Section 7 of the Clayton Act, which has been interpreted to require proof in *merger* cases of an anticompetitive effect in some *relevant geographic market.*

Securities and Exchange Commission (SEC)   the federal independent regulatory commission created in 1934 to regulate the sale of securities and related matters.

security   (1) (securities regulation) any investment of money or property in a common enterprise for profit; (2) (contract law) any *lien,* mortgage, collateral, or other device used to assure a creditor of repayment.

security interest   a *lien* or claim on property given to secure payment of a debt, and that may be foreclosed, resulting in the sale of the property to pay the debt.

selective incorporation doctrine   the idea that the 14th Amendment *Due Process* Clause applies certain portions of the Bill of Rights to the states, notably those parts that are *fundamental rights* or are "essential to the concept of ordered liberty;" a part of the 14th Amendment *substantive due process.*

self-assessment   (taxation) the system of federal income taxation, which is based on each taxpayer's assessing his or her own taxes, at least in the first instance.

self-executing subpoena   a *subpoena* that is a court order and, therefore, the violation of which is itself a contempt of court and punishable as such.

semi-disclosed agency   an *agency* in which a third party knows that an *agent* is working for some *principal,* but the identity of the principal is not known (see *undisclosed agency*).

separate but equal doctrine   the historic doctrine that the *Equal Protection Clause* was satisfied by providing equal but segregated facilities. The doctrine was repudiated in *Brown* v. *Board of Education* in 1954.

series voting   see *class voting.*

servant   (agency law) an *agent* over whom a *principal* has the right of control; an ordinary employee (see *master; master-servant relationship; independent contractor; respondeat superior*).

service of process   the delivery of a *summons* by an authorized person to the *defendant* or other party in a lawsuit, thereby conferring *personal jurisdiction* over the person served.

settlor   the person who creates a *trust* by transferring property to a *trustee* for the benefit of the *beneficiary.* The settlor may also be the trustee or beneficiary.

set-off   a claim by a *defendant* against a *plaintiff* that the defendant wishes to have credited against the claim by the plaintiff against the defendant, usually arising from some transaction other than that which formed the basis of the plaintiff's original complaint.

shared monopoly   (antitrust law) the theory that in certain markets a highly concentrated *oligopoly* will behave like a *monopoly,* and is therefore subject to a charge of "monopolization" under Section 2 of the Sherman Act. The theory has not been accepted by the courts.

shareholder democracy   a concept of actual control of corporations by their shareholders, in which shareholders have real power as opposed to control by *management.*

shingle theory   the theory under the securities laws that holding one's self out as a security *investment advisor, broker,* or *dealer* ("hanging out a shingle") is equivalent to a representation that one has expertise in securities.

short-swing profit   (securities regulation) a profit on a *security* of a corporation made by an *officer,* director, or owner of more than 10 percent of the shares, made within a six-month period.

SIP's   see *State Implementation Plans.*

slander   an oral *defamation.*

small issues exception   see *Regulation A exception.*

social contract theory   see *natural rights theory.*

social Darwinism   the social philosophy that holds that the "fittest" should survive and the less fit should not, even in a social and economic context.

societal ethics   widely held beliefs of right and wrong, including all religions and political ideologies; systems on belief held by groups of people (see *personal ethics*).

sociological school of jurisprudence   the philosophy that the law and legal institutions are the expression and tool of social forces.

sole proprietorship   an unincorporated business owned by one person.

sovereign immunity   the immunity of government from suit.

special assessment   (taxation) a system of property taxation to pay for public projects that specially benefit particular property owners and in which those property owners pay for that special benefit.

special tax   (taxation) a tax levied on specific taxpayers to pay for special benefits received by them, as in a *special assessment* (see *general tax*).

specific intent   the intent to obtain a specific result. Many criminal statutes require proof of a specific intent, such as assault with intent to kill, in which case the prosecution must prove the defendant commited the act while maintaining that specific type of intent (see *general intent*).

specific performance   a remedy afforded by a court of *equity* ordering a party to a contract to comply with the terms of the contract and to perform the acts required by the agreement.

specific tax   (taxation) a flat rate tax, as opposed to an *ad valorem* tax.

standing   the doctrine that a person must have a legally protected private interest before he or she may bring an action in federal court; the right to sue; the interest upon which suit may be based (see *case or controversy requirement*).

stare decisis   literally 'look to the decided cases'; the doctrine of precedent; the rule that lower courts will follow the previously decided cases of the appellate courts having *jurisdiction* over those lower courts (see *case law*).

state action   the doctrine that the Equal Protection clause of the 14th Amendment only prohibits discrimination that has as its source or is aided by the authority of state governments. Private discrimination is not prohibited by the Equal Protection Clause unless it is aided by state action.

State Implementation Plans (SIP's)   (environmental law) state plans to reach the goals set by the EPA administrator in the *National Ambient Air Quality Standards.*

stationary sources   (environmental law) sources of air pollution that do not move, as opposed to automobiles, for example.

Statute of Frauds   (contracts) a statute originally passed by Parliament and adopted in every English-speaking jurisdiction in the world. The statute makes unenforceable certain types of oral agreements, and requires some additional proof of those agreements other than a mere oral statement by one of the parties that they exist.

statutes   rules and laws enacted by legislatures, including the federal Congress, state legislatures, and local legislative bodies such as city councils.

statutory prospectus   see *final prospectus.*

steering   falsely representing that a dwelling is unavailable in order to encourage or maintain racially segregated housing.

stipulation   an agreed piece of evidence.

stockholder   a person who owns shares in a *corporation;* an investor, as opposed to a lender (see *equity financing*).

stock options   rights to purchase stock at a previously agreed price, at some time in the future.

stock subscriptions   the initial agreement to purchase stock in a *corporation* when it is formed, revocable at any time by the subscriber prior to acceptance by the corporation.

straight bankruptcy   a bankruptcy proceeding in which the debtor is relieved of payment of his or her debts (see *Wage Earner Plans*).

straight voting   a method of voting in *corporations* in which each shareholder receives one vote per share for each director to be elected, and which requires those votes to be used for a specific director's seat (see *cumulative voting*).

street name   (securities regulation) a security *broker's* name; many securities are held for customers in the name of the broker for convenience and ease of sale.

strict liability   liability without fault; liability without proof of a mental element, such as negligence, recklessness, or intention.

strict scrutiny test   the test to determine whether a classification scheme in a statute violates the Equal Protection Clause of the 14th Amendment if the classification scheme involves *fundamental rights* or a *suspect classification* (see *reasonable basis test*).

strike   a work stoppage by employees.

strikebreakers   (labor law) thugs hired by employers to force employees to go back to work during a strike through violence.

strike suit   a legal action filed against a *corporation,* its officers or directors to force a settlement with the plaintiffs rather than to force payment to the stockholders of the corporation in a *derivative action.*

Subchapter S corporation   a *corporation* taxed essentially as a *partnership,* thereby avoiding double taxation of corporate income, and permitted by the Internal Revenue Code if the corporation fulfills certain requirements.

subject-matter jurisdiction   the authority of the courts to hear particular kinds of cases (see *jurisdiction*).

subpoena   a court order requiring a person to appear in court and give evidence, and punishable by contempt of court proceedings for failure to appear (see *subpoena duces tecum*).

subpoena duces tecum   a court order requiring a person to appear in court and bring along certain documents or articles specified in the *subpoena.* Like a simple subpoena, a *subpoena duces tecum* is punishable by contempt of court proceedings for failure to appear

subsidization   see *deep pocket theory,* definition 2.

substantial evidence test (administrative law) the rule that a court will not overturn a decision by an *administrative agency* if there is substantial evidence on which that decision was based.

substantive due process the requirement under the 5th and 14th Amendments that laws not be unreasonable, arbitrary, or capricious and that the means bear a reasonable relationship to the ends of the law (see also *selective incorporation doctrine*).

substantive law that part of the law which creates, defines, and regulates legal rights and duties.

summary judgment the process by which cases may be decided without trial if there is no material fact in issue between the parties; summary judgment may be rendered on parts of cases as well; "trial by affidavit."

summary procedures (administrative law) action by an administrative agency with no due process procedures prior to the action, generally taken only in emergency situations, and requiring a hearing after the action is taken.

summons a paper delivered by the sheriff or other officer notifying a person of the existence of a lawsuit filed against that person, and requiring the person to file an answer or appear in court or face a *default judgment.*

sunset legislation automatic termination of administrative agencies or other laws, requiring an affirmative act on the part of the legislature to extend or continue the operation of the law beyond a specific date.

superfund (environmental law) a fund financed by a tax on the production of toxic chemicals to be used to clean up toxic waste sites, and created by the Comprehensive Environmental Response, Compensation and Liability Act of 1980.

survivor's insurance benefits (Social Security Law) benefits payable under Social Security to minor dependent children and sometimes spouses of deceased workers who are eligible under the Social Security Act.

suspect classification a classification by group, in which (1) membership in the group carries some "obvious badge" such as race or sex, (2) treatment of the members of the group has been historically pervasive and severe, and (3) members have been subjected to absolute deprivation of benefits available to nonmembers (see *strict scrutiny test*).

switch after sale a variant of *bait and switch,* in which the bait is actually sold to the consumer but which is somehow unsatisfactory, and upon the consumer's complaint, the seller agrees to "trade up" to a more expensive product.

tariff a public list of services, rates, charges, and rules of a company subject to *economic regulation.*

taxable income (taxation) the *gross income* less *business deductions* less *personal deductions* and *exemptions,* which is subject to tax.

taxpayer suits suits filed by taxpayers, alleging that a certain use of public funds is illegal, and basing their *standing* to sue on their status as taxpayers.

tenancy by the entireties (property law) a form of *joint tenancy,* with the right of survivorship, which cannot be broken by a single party acting alone and without the consent of the other party. This form exists only in marital situations and exists only in a few states.

tenancy in common (property law) a form of concurrent ownership of property, to be distinguished from *joint tenancy* and *tenancy by the entireties.* No right of survivorship is involved, and if one tenant in common dies, his or her interest passes on to his or her heirs rather than to the surviving tenants. Proportionate interests are permitted, and the *four unities* are not required for its creation.

tender offer a public offer by one corporation to purchase outstanding stock of another corporation in a sufficient amount to obtain control over the corporation.

testate succession transfer of *property* by will. (see *intestate succession*).

third-line competition (injury to) (antitrust law) injury to customers in competition with customers of the supplier's favored buyer, caused by *price discrimination.*

third-party complaints suits filed by existing parties in a lawsuit against new parties to the case.

tie-in contracts (antitrust law) also called "tying contracts"; agreements or conditions wherein a seller of two goods or services will not provide one without the other. Such contracts are *per se* illegal, though only if the seller has market power in the tying product.

tippee (securities regulation) a person who receives information from a corporate *insider* (see *insider trading*).

toehold acquisition entry into a market through *merger* with one of the smaller competitors already in the market.

tombstone ad (securities regulation) an advertisement stating that a *security* will be available for sale; used to attract *indications of interest*.

tort a private wrong or injury; a wrong not based on *contract*. The four elements of every tort are (1) a legal duty not depending on contract, (2) a breach of that duty, (3) an injury, and (4) proximate causal relationship between the breach of duty and the injury (see *proximate cause*).

totalitarianism a form of government in which there is no limit on the government's authority.

trademark a distinctive mark, symbol, word, phrase, or picture used to identify a particular firm or product.

Treasury Regulations (taxation) published regulations of the Secretary of the Treasury, having the force of any administrative regulation.

treasury shares *issued shares* that have been reacquired by the corporation, as opposed to *outstanding shares,* which remain in the hands of stockholders.

treble damage actions (antitrust law) a remedy in private antitrust actions whereby the injured party may collect three times its actual *damages;* a type of *punitive damages.*

trespass (1) doing a wrongful act to the injury of another's person or property; (2) unlawful entry or presence upon the land of another.

trust (1) a right of property held by one party (the *trustee*) for the benefit of another party (the *beneficiary*); (2) (antitrust) a form of agreement in which the voting rights of the stock in competing corporations is assigned to a board of trustees, who then operate all of the competing firms as one firm in an anticompetitive manner (see also *business trust*).

trustee a person who holds property under a *trust* for the benefit of another.

trust indenture an agreement between a *corporation* issuing *bonds* and an independent *trustee* to secure payment of those bonds, usually containing a mortgage or pledge of corporate property as *security* for repayment (definition 2).

tying contract see *tie-in contract.*

ultra vires actions of a corporation that are beyond the powers granted to it by law or in its *articles of incorporation.*

unconscionability gross unfairness; particularly sales practices so unfair that a court will not permit them, as established by the Uniform Commercial Code.

underwriter a person or firm specializing in giving financial advice, management, and marketing of issues of securities.

undisclosed agency an *agency* in which a third party dealing with an *agent* does not know that the agent is representing someone else.

undue burdens on interstate commerce an even-handed, nondiscriminatory but "too heavy" burden on *interstate commerce* imposed by a state.

unemployment compensation state systems providing benefits to unemployed workers, financed in part by the federal government.

unfair labor practices (labor law) practices by either unions or employers that are illegal under the National Labor Relations Act or its amendments.

unfair labor practice strikers (labor law) employees striking because of some employer *unfair labor practice* (see *economic strikers*).

Uniform Commercial Code (UCC) a "model" act consisting of ten articles dealing with various subjects of commercial law, e.g., sales, negotiable instruments, investment securities, and others, and adopted in whole or in part in every state.

Uniform Consumer Credit Code (UCCC) a "model" act adopted in several states dealing with credit practices and generally requiring full disclosure in a manner similar to federal Truth in Lending.

Uniform Partnership Act (UPA) a "model" act governing *general partnerships,* adopted in many states.

Uniform Securities Act   a "model" act regulating sales of securities at the state level.

uniform tax   (taxation) a tax that is the same throughout the United States.

Union Members Bill of Rights   (labor law) a statement of the rights of union members in relation to their own unions as found in the Landrum-Griffin Act of 1959.

union shop   (labor law) a labor contract which provides that all employees in the bargaining unit must become union members as a condition of employment (see *open shop; Right-to-Work laws*).

unlawful employment practices   discriminatory practices in employment as defined by the Civil Rights Act of 1964.

unlawful housing practices   discriminatory practices in the sale or rental of housing made illegal by the Civil Rights Act of 1968.

use tax   (taxation) a tax complementary to the *sales tax* imposed on items purchased out of state but used within a state, in an amount equal to the difference between the sales tax of the two states, imposed to remove the incentive for purchasing goods out of state.

usury statutes   state laws limiting the amount of interest that may be charged on loans or credit purchases; sometimes called "loan shark acts."

value-added tax (VAT)   a tax imposed on the value added to a product by the producer or vendor, used as a substitute for both the income and franchise tax.

venue   the courts of a particular county, city or other geographical region that hear a case; not to be confused with *jurisdiction;* venue refers to which of the courts with jurisdiction should hear the case.

verdict   the decision of a jury; not to be confused with *judgment;* judges sitting without a jury may render a verdict as well, to be followed later by a judgment.

vertical agreements   (antitrust law) agreements between parties involved at different levels of the distribution process of the same good or service, e.g., an agreement between a supplier and a retailer of the same product (see *horizontal agreements*).

vertical merger   (antitrust law) a *corporate integration* between two firms which stand in the relationship of buyer and seller or could potentially stand in that relationship.

vertical territory limitations   (antitrust law) limitations imposed by a seller on a buyer on the area within which the buyer may operate.

vesting   absolute; with a fixed right; a right that cannot be taken away.

vicarious liability   liability for an act committed by another, e.g., the liability of the *master* under the doctrine of *respondeat superior.*

wage and benefit provisions   (labor law) parts of a labor contract spelling out the financial parts of the labor agreement.

wage assignment   a clause in a contract or promissory note that requires the debtor's employer to pay the debtor's salary directly to the creditor upon demand.

Wage Earner Plans   (bankruptcy law) a procedure under the federal Bankruptcy Act in which a debtor pays off his or her debts but obtains a delay in payment in accordance with a "plan" filed with the court.

waiting period   (securities regulation) the time between the filing of the registration documents with the SEC of a new issue of stock and the approval by the SEC of that issue (see *indications of interest; preliminary prospectus; tombstone ads*).

warrants   options to buy stock.

warranty   a promise, either contained in a *contract,* or implied by law (see various forms of *implied warranty; limited warranty; full warranty*).

wash sales   (securities regulation) also known as "matched orders"; a technique of inflating the price of stock by placing large orders to buy and sell the same stock, thus increasing volume and indicating to unsophisticated investors that there is activity in the stock, thereby raising the price of the stock (see *market manipulation*).

watering of shares   see *dilution of shares.*

wildcat strikes   (labor law) a strike in violation of a *no-strike clause* in a labor contract.

winding up (partnership law) the process of terminating a *partnership*, including gathering of assets, payment of debts, and distribution of remaining assets to the partners.

wings effect see *perceived potential competition.*

workable competition (antitrust law) a compromise of classical competition (the theories of Adam Smith), which holds that while "perfect competition" cannot be attained, government policy should be aimed at achieving the best possible competitive conditions.

worker's compensation statutes (labor law) state laws that provide benefits to employees whose injuries arose out of their employment and that assess those benefits directly against their employers.

work preservation clause an agreement by an employer in a *collective bargaining* agreement that it will not close the plant without prior opportunity to negotiate by the union or, alternatively, an agreement not to close the plant under any circumstances.

writ of prohibition a procedure available in some state courts, in which a superior court orders a lower court to cease the prosecution of a case.

yellow dog contracts (labor law) employment contracts that required employees never to join a labor union and provided that any employee who joined such a union would automatically lose the job.

zoning state laws or local ordinances that regulate the uses to which land may be put.

Index of Cases

The principal cases are in italic type. Cases cited or discussed are in roman type.

Index